To my family—DAF

To my father, Jean-Jacques Ponce —JP

COMPUTER VISION
A MODERN APPROACH

SECOND EDITION

DAVID A. FORSYTH

University of Illinois at Urbana-Champaign

JEAN PONCE

Ecole Normale Supérieure

International Edition contributions by

SOUMEN MUKHERJEE

RCC Institute of Information Technology

ARUP KUMAR BHATTACHARJEE

RCC Institute of Information Technology

PEARSON

Boston Columbus Indianapolis New York San Francisco Upper Saddle River
Amsterdam Cape Town Dubai London Madrid Milan Munich Paris Montreal Toronto
Delhi Mexico City Sao Paulo Sydney Hong Kong Seoul Singapore Taipei Tokyo

Vice President and Editorial Director, ECS:
   Marcia Horton
Editor in Chief: Michael Hirsch
Acquisitions Editor: Tracy Dunkelberger
Editorial Project Manager: Carole Snyder
Vice President Marketing: Patrice Jones
Marketing Manager: Yez Alayan
Marketing Coordinator: Kathryn Ferranti
Marketing Assistant: Emma Snider
Vice President and Director of Production:
   Vince O'Brien
Managing Editor: Jeff Holcomb
Senior Production Project Manager: Marilyn Lloyd
Publisher, International Edition: Angshuman Chakraborty
Acquisitions Editor, International Edition:
   Somnath Basu

Publishing Assistant, International Edition:
   Shokhi Shah
Print and Media Editor, International Edition:
   Ashwitha Jayakumar
Project Editor, International Edition:
   Jayashree Arunachalam
Senior Operations Supervisor: Alan Fischer
Operations Specialist: Lisa McDowell
Art Director, Cover: Jayne Conte
Text Permissions: Dana Weightman/RightsHouse, Inc.
   and Jen Roach/PreMediaGlobal
Cover Image: © Maxppp/ZUMAPRESS.com
Media Editor: Dan Sandin
Cover Printer: Lehigh-Phoenix Color

Pearson Education Limited
Edinburgh Gate
Harlow
Essex CM20 2JE
England

and Associated Companies throughout the world

Visit us on the World Wide Web at:

www.pearsoninternationaleditions.com

Authorized adaptation from the United States edition, entitled Computer Vision, A Modern Approach, 2nd edition, *ISBN 978-0-13-608592-8 by David A. Forsyth and Jean Ponce published by Pearson Education © 2012.*

ISBN 10: 0-273-76414-4
ISBN 13: 978-0-273-76414-4

British Library Cataloguing-in-Publication Data
A catalogue record for this book is available from the British Library

10 9 8 7 6 5 4 3 2 1
14 13 12

Typeset in CMR10 by David Forsyth
Printed and bound by Edwards Brothers in The United States of America

The publisher's policy is to use paper manufactured from sustainable forests.

Credits and acknowledgments borrowed from other sources and reproduced, with permission, in this textbook appear on the appropriate page within text.

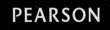

Contents

Preface

Computer vision as a field is an intellectual frontier. Like any frontier, it is exciting and disorganized, and there is often no reliable authority to appeal to. Many useful ideas have no theoretical grounding, and some theories are useless in practice; developed areas are widely scattered, and often one looks completely inaccessible from the other. Nevertheless, we have attempted in this book to present a fairly orderly picture of the field.

We see computer vision—or just "vision"; apologies to those who study human or animal vision—as an enterprise that uses statistical methods to disentangle data using models constructed with the aid of geometry, physics, and learning theory. Thus, in our view, vision relies on a solid understanding of cameras and of the physical process of image formation (Part I of this book) to obtain simple inferences from individual pixel values (Part II), combine the information available in multiple images into a coherent whole (Part III), impose some order on groups of pixels to separate them from each other or infer shape information (Part IV), and recognize objects using geometric information or probabilistic techniques (Part V). Computer vision has a wide variety of applications, both old (e.g., mobile robot navigation, industrial inspection, and military intelligence) and new (e.g., human computer interaction, image retrieval in digital libraries, medical image analysis, and the realistic rendering of synthetic scenes in computer graphics). We discuss some of these applications in part VII.

IN THE SECOND EDITION

We have made a variety of changes since the first edition, which we hope have improved the usefulness of this book. Perhaps the most important change follows a big change in the discipline since the last edition. Code and data are now widely published over the Internet. It is now quite usual to build systems out of other people's published code, at least in the first instance, and to evaluate them on other people's datasets. In the chapters, we have provided guides to experimental resources available online. As is the nature of the Internet, not all of these URL's will work all the time; we have tried to give enough information so that searching Google with the authors' names or the name of the dataset or codes will get the right result.

Other changes include:

- We have **simplified.** We give a simpler, clearer treatment of mathematical topics. We have particularly simplified our treatment of cameras (Chapter 1), shading (Chapter 2), and reconstruction from two views (Chapter 7) and from multiple views (Chapter 8)

- We describe a **broad range of applications**, including image-based modelling and rendering (Chapter 19), image search (Chapter 22), building image mosaics (Section 12.1), medical image registration (Section 12.3), interpreting range data (Chapter 14), and understanding human activity (Chapter 21).

- We have written a comprehensive treatment of the **modern features**, particularly HOG and SIFT (both in Chapter 5), that drive applications ranging from building image mosaics to object recognition.

- We give a detailed treatment of **modern image editing techniques**, including removing shadows (Section 3.5), filling holes in images (Section 6.3), noise removal (Section 6.4), and interactive image segmentation (Section 9.2).

- We give a comprehensive treatment of **modern object recognition techniques**. We start with a practical discussion of classifiers (Chapter 15); we then describe standard methods for image classification techniques (Chapter 16), and object detection (Chapter 17). Finally, Chapter 18 reviews a wide range of recent topics in object recognition.

- Finally, this book has a very detailed index, and a bibliography that is as comprehensive and up-to-date as we could make it.

WHY STUDY VISION?

Computer vision's great trick is extracting descriptions of the world from pictures or sequences of pictures. This is unequivocally useful. Taking pictures is usually nondestructive and sometimes discreet. It is also easy and (now) cheap. The descriptions that users seek can differ widely between applications. For example, a technique known as structure from motion makes it possible to extract a representation of what is depicted and how the camera moved from a series of pictures. People in the entertainment industry use these techniques to build three-dimensional (3D) computer models of buildings, typically keeping the structure and throwing away the motion. These models are used where real buildings cannot be; they are set fire to, blown up, etc. Good, simple, accurate, and convincing models can be built from quite small sets of photographs. People who wish to control mobile robots usually keep the motion and throw away the structure. This is because they generally know something about the area where the robot is working, but usually don't know the precise robot location in that area. They can determine it from information about how a camera bolted to the robot is moving.

There are a number of other, important applications of computer vision. One is in medical imaging: one builds software systems that can enhance imagery, or identify important phenomena or events, or visualize information obtained by imaging. Another is in inspection: one takes pictures of objects to determine whether they are within specification. A third is in interpreting satellite images, both for military purposes (a program might be required to determine what militarily interesting phenomena have occurred in a given region recently; or what damage was caused by a bombing) and for civilian purposes (what will this year's maize crop be? How much rainforest is left?) A fourth is in organizing and structuring collections of pictures. We know how to search and browse text libraries (though this is a subject that still has difficult open questions) but don't really know what to do with image or video libraries.

Computer vision is at an extraordinary point in its development. The subject itself has been around since the 1960s, but only recently has it been possible to build useful computer systems using ideas from computer vision. This flourishing has been driven by several trends: Computers and imaging systems have become very cheap. Not all that long ago, it took tens of thousands of dollars to get good digital color images; now it takes a few hundred at most. Not all that long ago, a color printer was something one found in few, if any, research labs; now they are in many homes. This means it is easier to do research. It also means that there are many people with problems to which the methods of computer vision apply. For example, people would like to organize their collections of photographs, make 3D models of the world around them, and manage and edit collections of videos. Our understanding of the basic geometry and physics underlying vision and, more important, what to do about it, has improved significantly. We are beginning to be able to solve problems that lots of people care about, but none of the hard problems have been solved, and there are plenty of easy ones that have not been solved either (to keep one intellectually fit while trying to solve hard problems). It is a great time to be studying this subject.

What Is in this Book

This book covers what we feel a computer vision professional ought to know. However, it is addressed to a wider audience. We hope that those engaged in computational geometry, computer graphics, image processing, imaging in general, and robotics will find it an informative reference. We have tried to make the book accessible to senior undergraduates or graduate students with a passing interest in vision. Each chapter covers a different part of the subject, and, as a glance at Table 1 will confirm, chapters are relatively independent. This means that one can dip into the book as well as read it from cover to cover. Generally, we have tried to make chapters run from easy material at the start to more arcane matters at the end. Each chapter has brief notes at the end, containing historical material and assorted opinions. We have tried to produce a book that describes ideas that are useful, or likely to be so in the future. We have put emphasis on understanding the basic geometry and physics of imaging, but have tried to link this with actual applications. In general, this book reflects the enormous recent influence of geometry and various forms of applied statistics on computer vision.

Reading this Book

A reader who goes from cover to cover will hopefully be well informed, if exhausted; there is too much in this book to cover in a one-semester class. Of course, prospective (or active) computer vision professionals should read every word, do all the exercises, and report any bugs found for the third edition (of which it is probably a good idea to plan on buying a copy!). Although the study of computer vision does not require deep mathematics, it does require facility with a lot of different mathematical ideas. We have tried to make the book self-contained, in the sense that readers with the level of mathematical sophistication of an engineering senior should be comfortable with the material of the book and should not need to refer to other texts. We have also tried to keep the mathematics to the necessary minimum—after all, this book is about computer vision, not applied mathematics—and have chosen to insert what mathematics we have kept in the main chapter bodies instead of a separate appendix.

TABLE 1: Dependencies between chapters: It will be difficult to read a chapter if you don't have a good grasp of the material in the chapters it "requires." If you have not read the chapters labeled "helpful," you might need to look up one or two things.

Part		Chapter	Requires	Helpful
I	1:	Geometric Camera Models		
	2:	Light and Shading		
	3:	Color	2	
II	4:	Linear Filters		
	5:	Local Image Features	4	
	6:	Texture	5, 4	2
III	7:	Stereopsis	1	22
	8:	Structure from Motion	1, 7	22
IV	9:	Segmentation by Clustering		2, 3, 4, 5, 6, 22
	10:	Grouping and Model Fitting		9
	11:	Tracking		2, 5, 22
V	12:	Registration	1	14
	13:	Smooth Surfaces and Their Outlines	1	
	14:	Range Data		12
	15:	Learning to Classify		22
	16:	Classifying Images	15, 5	
	17:	Detecting Objects in Images	16, 15, 5	
	18:	Topics in Object Recognition	17, 16, 15, 5	
VI	19:	Image-Based Modeling and Rendering	1, 2, 7, 8	
	20:	Looking at People		17, 16, 15, 11, 5
	21:	Image Search and Retrieval		17, 16, 15, 11, 5
VII	22:	Optimization Techniques		

Generally, we have tried to reduce the interdependence between chapters, so that readers interested in particular topics can avoid wading through the whole book. It is not possible to make each chapter entirely self-contained, however, and Table 1 indicates the dependencies between chapters.

We have tried to make the index comprehensive, so that if you encounter a new term, you are likely to find it in the book by looking it up in the index. Computer vision is now fortunate in having a rich range of intellectual resources. Software and datasets are widely shared, and we have given pointers to useful datasets and software in relevant chapters; you can also look in the index, under "software" and under "datasets," or under the general topic.

We have tried to make the bibliography comprehensive, without being overwhelming. However, we have not been able to give complete bibliographic references for any topic, because the literature is so large.

What Is Not in this Book

The computer vision literature is vast, and it was not easy to produce a book about computer vision that could be lifted by ordinary mortals. To do so, we had to cut material, ignore topics, and so on.

We left out some topics because of personal taste, or because we became exhausted and stopped writing about a particular area, or because we learned about them too late to put them in, or because we had to shorten some chapter, or because we didn't understand them, or any of hundreds of other reasons. We have tended to omit detailed discussions of material that is mainly of historical interest, and offer instead some historical remarks at the end of each chapter.

We have tried to be both generous and careful in attributing ideas, but neither of us claims to be a fluent intellectual archaeologist, and computer vision is a very big topic indeed. This means that some ideas may have deeper histories than we have indicated, and that we may have omitted citations.

There are several recent textbooks on computer vision. Szeliski (2010) deals with the whole of vision. Parker (2010) deals specifically with algorithms. Davies (2005) and Steger *et al.* (2008) deal with practical applications, particularly registration. Bradski and Kaehler (2008) is an introduction to OpenCV, an important open-source package of computer vision routines.

There are numerous more specialized references. Hartley and Zisserman (2000a) is a comprehensive account of what is known about multiple view geometry and estimation of multiple view parameters. Ma *et al.* (2003b) deals with 3D reconstruction methods. Cyganek and Siebert (2009) covers 3D reconstruction and matching. Paragios *et al.* (2010) deals with mathematical models in computer vision. Blake *et al.* (2011) is a recent summary of what is known about Markov random field models in computer vision. Li and Jain (2005) is a comprehensive account of face recognition. Moeslund *et al.* (2011), which is in press at time of writing, promises to be a comprehensive account of computer vision methods for watching people. Dickinson *et al.* (2009) is a collection of recent summaries of the state of the art in object recognition. Radke (2012) is a forthcoming account of computer vision methods applied to special effects.

Much of computer vision literature appears in the proceedings of various conferences. The three main conferences are: the IEEE Conference on Computer Vision and Pattern Recognition (CVPR); the IEEE International Conference on Computer Vision (ICCV); and the European Conference on Computer Vision. A significant fraction of the literature appears in regional conferences, particularly the Asian Conference on Computer Vision (ACCV) and the British Machine Vision Conference (BMVC). A high percentage of published papers are available on the web, and can be found with search engines; while some papers are confined to pay-libraries, to which many universities provide access, most can be found without cost.

ACKNOWLEDGMENTS

In preparing this book, we have accumulated a significant set of debts. A number of anonymous reviewers read several drafts of the book for both first and second edition and made extremely helpful contributions. We are grateful to them for their time and efforts.

Our editor for the first edition, Alan Apt, organized these reviews with the help of Jake Warde. We thank them both. Leslie Galen, Joe Albrecht, and Dianne Parish, of Integre Technical Publishing, helped us overcome numerous issues with proofreading and illustrations in the first edition.

Our editor for the second edition, Tracy Dunkelberger, organized reviews with the help of Carole Snyder. We thank them both. We thank Marilyn Lloyd for helping us get over various production problems.

Both the overall coverage of topics and several chapters were reviewed by various colleagues, who made valuable and detailed suggestions for their revision. We thank Narendra Ahuja, Francis Bach, Kobus Barnard, Margaret Fleck, Martial Hebert, Julia Hockenmaier, Derek Hoiem, David Kriegman, Jitendra Malik, and Andrew Zisserman.

A number of people contributed suggestions, ideas for figures, proofreading comments, and other valuable material, while they were our students. We thank Okan Arikan, Louise Benoît, Tamara Berg, Sébastien Blind, Y-Lan Boureau, Liang-Liang Cao, Martha Cepeda, Stephen Chenney, Frank Cho, Florent Couzinie-Devy, Olivier Duchenne, Pinar Duygulu, Ian Endres, Ali Farhadi, Yasutaka Furukawa, Yakup Genc, John Haddon, Varsha Hedau, Nazli Ikizler-Cinbis, Leslie Ikemoto, Sergey Ioffe, Armand Joulin, Kevin Karsch, Svetlana Lazebnik, Cathy Lee, Binbin Liao, Nicolas Loeff, Julien Mairal, Sung-il Pae, David Parks, Deva Ramanan, Fred Rothganger, Amin Sadeghi, Alex Sorokin, Attawith Sudsang, Du Tran, Duan Tran, Gang Wang, Yang Wang, Ryan White, and the students in several offerings of our vision classes at UIUC, U.C. Berkeley and ENS.

We have been very lucky to have colleagues at various universities use (often rough) drafts of our book in their vision classes. Institutions whose students suffered through these drafts include, in addition to ours, Carnegie-Mellon University, Stanford University, the University of Wisconsin at Madison, the University of California at Santa Barbara and the University of Southern California; there may be others we are not aware of. We are grateful for all the helpful comments from adopters, in particular Chris Bregler, Chuck Dyer, Martial Hebert, David Kriegman, B.S. Manjunath, and Ram Nevatia, who sent us many detailed and helpful comments and corrections.

The book has also benefitted from comments and corrections from Karteek Alahari, Aydin Alaylioglu, Srinivas Akella, Francis Bach, Marie Banich, Serge Belongie, Tamara Berg, Ajit M. Chaudhari, Navneet Dalal, Jennifer Evans, Yasutaka Furukawa, Richard Hartley, Glenn Healey, Mike Heath, Martial Hebert, Janne Heikkilä, Hayley Iben, Stéphanie Jonquières, Ivan Laptev, Christine Laubenberger, Svetlana Lazebnik, Yann LeCun, Tony Lewis, Benson Limketkai, Julien Mairal, Simon Maskell, Brian Milch, Roger Mohr, Deva Ramanan, Guillermo Sapiro, Cordelia Schmid, Brigitte Serlin, Gerry Serlin, Ilan Shimshoni, Jamie Shotton, Josef Sivic, Eric de Sturler, Camillo J. Taylor, Jeff Thompson, Claire Vallat, Daniel S. Wilkerson, Jinghan Yu, Hao Zhang, Zhengyou Zhang, and Andrew Zisserman.

In the first edition, we said

> If you find an apparent typographic error, please email DAF... with the details, using the phrase "book typo" in your email; we will try to credit the first finder of each typo in the second edition.

which turns out to have been a mistake. DAF's ability to manage and preserve email logs was just not up to this challenge. We thank all finders of typographic errors; we have tried to fix the errors and have made efforts to credit all the people who have helped us.

We also thank P. Besl, B. Boufama, J. Costeira, P. Debevec, O. Faugeras, Y. Genc, M. Hebert, D. Huber, K. Ikeuchi, A.E. Johnson, T. Kanade, K. Kutulakos, M. Levoy, Y. LeCun, S. Mahamud, R. Mohr, H. Moravec, H. Murase, Y. Ohta, M. Okutami, M. Pollefeys, H. Saito, C. Schmid, J. Shotton, S. Sullivan, C. Tomasi, and M. Turk for providing the originals of some of the figures shown in this book.

DAF acknowledges ongoing research support from the National Science Foundation. Awards that have directly contributed to the writing of this book are IIS-0803603, IIS-1029035, and IIS-0916014; other awards have shaped the view described here. DAF acknowledges ongoing research support from the Office of Naval Research, under awards N00014-01-1-0890 and N00014-10-1-0934, which are part of the MURI program. Any opinions, findings and conclusions or recommendations expressed in this material are those of the authors and do not necessarily reflect those of NSF or ONR.

DAF acknowledges a wide range of intellectual debts, starting at kindergarten. Important figures in the very long list of his creditors include Gerald Alanthwaite, Mike Brady, Tom Fair, Margaret Fleck, Jitendra Malik, Joe Mundy, Mike Rodd, Charlie Rothwell, and Andrew Zisserman. JP cannot even remember kindergarten, but acknowledges his debts to Olivier Faugeras, Mike Brady, and Tom Binford. He also wishes to thank Sharon Collins for her help. Without her, this book, like most of his work, probably would have never been finished. Both authors would also like to acknowledge the profound influence of Jan Koenderink's writings on their work at large and on this book in particular.

Figures: Some images used herein were obtained from IMSI's Master Photos Collection, 1895 Francisco Blvd. East, San Rafael, CA 94901-5506, USA. We have made extensive use of figures from the published literature; these figures are credited in their captions. We thank the copyright holders for extending permission to use these figures.

Bibliography: In preparing the bibliography, we have made extensive use of Keith Price's excellent computer vision bibliography, which can be found at http://iris.usc.edu/Vision-Notes/bibliography/contents.html.

TABLE 2: A one-semester introductory class in computer vision for seniors or first-year graduate students in computer science, electrical engineering, or other engineering or science disciplines.

Week	Chapter	Sections	Key topics
1	1, 2	1.1, 2.1, 2.2.x	pinhole cameras, pixel shading models, one inference from shading example
2	3	3.1–3.5	human color perception, color physics, color spaces, image color model
3	4	all	linear filters
4	5	all	building local features
5	6	6.1, 6.2	texture representations from filters, from vector quantization
6	7	7.1, 7.2	binocular geometry, stereopsis
7	8	8.1	structure from motion with perspective cameras
8	9	9.1–9.3	segmentation ideas, applications, segmentation by clustering pixels
9	10	10.1–10.4	Hough transform, fitting lines, robustness, RANSAC,
10	11	11.1-11.3	simple tracking strategies, tracking by matching, Kalman filters, data association
11	12	all	registration
12	15	all	classification
13	16	all	classifying images
14	17	all	detection
15	choice	all	one of chapters 14, 19, 20, 21 (application topics)

SAMPLE SYLLABUSES

The whole book can be covered in two (rather intense) semesters, by starting at the first page and plunging on. Ideally, one would cover one application chapter— probably the chapter on image-based rendering—in the first semester, and the other one in the second. Few departments will experience heavy demand for such a detailed sequence of courses. We have tried to structure this book so that instructors can choose areas according to taste. Sample syllabuses for busy 15-week semesters appear in Tables 2 to 6, structured according to needs that can reasonably be expected. We would encourage (and expect!) instructors to rearrange these according to taste.

Table 2 contains a suggested syllabus for a one-semester introductory class in computer vision for seniors or first-year graduate students in computer science, electrical engineering, or other engineering or science disciplines. The students receive a broad presentation of the field, including application areas such as digital libraries and image-based rendering. Although the hardest theoretical material is omitted, there is a thorough treatment of the basic geometry and physics of image formation. We assume that students will have a wide range of backgrounds, and can be assigned background readings in probability. We have put off the application chapters to the end, but many may prefer to cover them earlier.

Table 3 contains a syllabus for students of computer graphics who want to know the elements of vision that are relevant to their topic. We have emphasized methods that make it possible to recover object models from image information;

TABLE 3: A syllabus for students of computer graphics who want to know the elements of vision that are relevant to their topic.

Week	Chapter	Sections	Key topics
1	1, 2	1.1, 2.1, 2.2.4	pinhole cameras, pixel shading models, photometric stereo
2	3	3.1–3.5	human color perception, color physics, color spaces, image color model
3	4	all	linear filters
4	5	all	building local features
5	6	6.3, 6.4	texture synthesis, image denoising
6	7	7.1, 7.2	binocular geometry, stereopsis
7	7	7.4, 7.5	advanced stereo methods
8	8	8.1	structure from motion with perspective cameras
9	10	10.1–10.4	Hough transform, fitting lines, robustness, RANSAC,
10	9	9.1–9.3	segmentation ideas, applications, segmentation by clustering pixels
11	11	11.1-11.3	simple tracking strategies, tracking by matching, Kalman filters, data association
12	12	all	registration
13	14	all	range data
14	19	all	image-based modeling and rendering
15	13	all	surfaces and outlines

understanding these topics needs a working knowledge of cameras and filters. Tracking is becoming useful in the graphics world, where it is particularly important for motion capture. We assume that students will have a wide range of backgrounds, and have some exposure to probability.

Table 4 shows a syllabus for students who are primarily interested in the applications of computer vision. We cover material of most immediate practical interest. We assume that students will have a wide range of backgrounds, and can be assigned background reading.

Table 5 is a suggested syllabus for students of cognitive science or artificial intelligence who want a basic outline of the important notions of computer vision. This syllabus is less aggressively paced, and assumes less mathematical experience.

Our experience of teaching computer vision is that no single idea presents any particular conceptual difficulties, though some are harder than others. Difficulties are caused by the tremendous number of new ideas required by the subject. Each subproblem seems to require its own way of thinking, and new tools to cope with it. This makes learning the subject rather daunting. Table 6 shows a sample syllabus for students who are really not bothered by these difficulties. They would need to have quite a strong interest in applied mathematics, electrical engineering or physics, and be very good at picking things up as they go along. This syllabus sets a furious pace, and assumes that students can cope with a lot of new material.

NOTATION

We use the following notation throughout the book: Points, lines, and planes are denoted by Roman or Greek letters in italic font (e.g., P, Δ, or Π). Vectors are

TABLE 4: A syllabus for students who are primarily interested in the applications of computer vision.

Week	Chapter	Sections	Key topics
1	1, 2	1.1, 2.1, 2.2.4	pinhole cameras, pixel shading models, photometric stereo
2	3	3.1–3.5	human color perception, color physics, color spaces, image color model
3	4	all	linear filters
4	5	all	building local features
5	6	6.3, 6.4	texture synthesis, image denoising
6	7	7.1, 7.2	binocular geometry, stereopsis
7	7	7.4, 7.5	advanced stereo methods
8	8, 9	8.1, 9.1–9.2	structure from motion with perspective cameras, segmentation ideas, applications
9	10	10.1–10.4	Hough transform, fitting lines, robustness, RANSAC,
10	12	all	registration
11	14	all	range data
12	16	all	classifying images
13	19	all	image based modeling and rendering
14	20	all	looking at people
15	21	all	image search and retrieval

usually denoted by Roman or Greek bold-italic letters (e.g., $\boldsymbol{v}$, $\boldsymbol{P}$, or $\boldsymbol{\xi}$), but the vector joining two points P and Q is often denoted by $\overrightarrow{PQ}$. Lower-case letters are normally used to denote geometric figures in the image plane (e.g., p, $\boldsymbol{p}$, δ), and upper-case letters are used for scene objects (e.g., P, Π). Matrices are denoted by Roman letters in calligraphic font (e.g., $\mathcal{U}$).

The familiar three-dimensional Euclidean space is denoted by $\mathbb{E}^3$, and the vector space formed by n-tuples of real numbers with the usual laws of addition and multiplication by a scalar is denoted by $\mathbb{R}^n$, with $\boldsymbol{0}$ being used to denote the zero vector. Likewise, the vector space formed by $m \times n$ matrices with real entries is denoted by $\mathbb{R}^{m \times n}$. When $m = n$, Id is used to denote the identity matrix— that is, the $n \times n$ matrix whose diagonal entries are equal to 1 and nondiagonal entries are equal to 0. The transpose of the $m \times n$ matrix $\mathcal{U}$ with coefficients u_{ij} is the $n \times m$ matrix denoted by $\mathcal{U}^T$ with coefficients u_{ji}. Elements of $\mathbb{R}^n$ are often identified with column vectors or $n \times 1$ matrices, for example, $\boldsymbol{a} = (a_1, a_2, a_3)^T$ is the transpose of a 1×3 matrix (or *row vector*), i.e., an 3×1 matrix (or *column vector*), or equivalently an element of $\mathbb{R}^3$.

The *dot product* (or *inner product*) of two vectors $\boldsymbol{a} = (a_1, \ldots, a_n)^T$ and $\boldsymbol{b} = (b_1, \ldots, b_n)^T$ in $\mathbb{R}^n$ is defined by

$$\boldsymbol{a} \cdot \boldsymbol{b} = a_1 b_1 + \cdots + a_n b_n,$$

and it can also be written as a matrix product, i.e., $\boldsymbol{a} \cdot \boldsymbol{b} = \boldsymbol{a}^T \boldsymbol{b} = \boldsymbol{b}^T \boldsymbol{a}$. We denote by $|\boldsymbol{a}|^2 = \boldsymbol{a} \cdot \boldsymbol{a}$ the square of the Euclidean norm of the vector $\boldsymbol{a}$ and denote by d the distance function induced by the Euclidean norm in $\mathbb{E}^n$, i.e., $d(P, Q) = |\overrightarrow{PQ}|$. Given a matrix $\mathcal{U}$ in $\mathbb{R}^{m \times n}$, we generally use $|U|$ to denote its *Frobenius norm*, i.e., the square root of the sum of its squared entries.

TABLE 5: For students of cognitive science or artificial intelligence who want a basic outline of the important notions of computer vision.

Week	Chapter	Sections	Key topics
1	1, 2	1.1, 2.1, 2.2.x	pinhole cameras, pixel shading models, one inference from shading example
2	3	3.1–3.5	human color perception, color physics, color spaces, image color model
3	4	all	linear filters
4	5	all	building local features
5	6	6.1, 6.2	texture representations from filters, from vector quantization
6	7	7.1, 7.2	binocular geometry, stereopsis
8	9	9.1–9.3	segmentation ideas, applications, segmentation by clustering pixels
9	11	11.1, 11.2	simple tracking strategies, tracking using matching, optical flow
10	15	all	classification
11	16	all	classifying images
12	20	all	looking at people
13	21	all	image search and retrieval
14	17	all	detection
15	18	all	topics in object recognition

When the vector a has unit norm, the dot product $a \cdot b$ is equal to the (signed) length of the projection of b onto a. More generally,

$$a \cdot b = |a|\,|b|\,\cos\theta,$$

where θ is the angle between the two vectors, which shows that a necessary and sufficient condition for two vectors to be orthogonal is that their dot product be zero.

The *cross product* (or *outer product*) of two vectors $a = (a_1, a_2, a_3)^T$ and $b = (b_1, b_2, b_3)^T$ in $\mathbb{R}^3$ is the vector

$$a \times b \stackrel{\text{def}}{=} \begin{pmatrix} a_2 b_3 - a_3 b_2 \\ a_3 b_1 - a_1 b_3 \\ a_1 b_2 - a_2 b_1 \end{pmatrix}.$$

Note that $a \times b = [a_\times]b$, where

$$[a_\times] \stackrel{\text{def}}{=} \begin{pmatrix} 0 & -a_3 & a_2 \\ a_3 & 0 & -a_1 \\ -a_2 & a_1 & 0 \end{pmatrix}.$$

The cross product of two vectors a and b in $\mathbb{R}^3$ is orthogonal to these two vectors, and a necessary and sufficient condition for a and b to have the same direction is that $a \times b = 0$. If θ denotes as before the angle between the vectors a and b, it can be shown that

$$|a \times b| = |a|\,|b|\,|\sin\theta|.$$

TABLE 6: A syllabus for students who have a strong interest in applied mathematics, electrical engineering, or physics.

Week	Chapter	Sections	Key topics
1	1, 2	all; 2.1–2.4	cameras, shading
2	3	all	color
3	4	all	linear filters
4	5	all	building local features
5	6	all	texture
6	7	all	stereopsis
7	8	all	structure from motion with perspective cameras
8	9	all	segmentation by clustering pixels
9	10	all	fitting models
10	11	11.1–11.3	simple tracking strategies, tracking by matching, Kalman filters, data association
11	12	all	registration
12	15	all	classification
13	16	all	classifying images
14	17	all	detection
15	choice	all	one of chapters 14, 19, 20, 21

PROGRAMMING ASSIGNMENTS AND RESOURCES

The programming assignments given throughout this book sometimes require routines for numerical linear algebra, singular value decomposition, and linear and nonlinear least squares. An extensive set of such routines is available in MATLAB as well as in public-domain libraries such as LINPACK, LAPACK, and MINPACK, which can be downloaded from the Netlib repository (http://www.netlib.org/). In the text, we offer extensive pointers to software published on the Web and to datasets published on the Web. OpenCV is an important open-source package of computer vision routines (see Bradski and Kaehler (2008)).

ABOUT THE AUTHORS

David Forsyth received a B.Sc. (Elec. Eng.) from the University of the Witwatersrand, Johannesburg in 1984, an M.Sc. (Elec. Eng.) from that university in 1986, and a D.Phil. from Balliol College, Oxford in 1989. He spent three years on the faculty at the University of Iowa, ten years on the faculty at the University of California at Berkeley, and then moved to the University of Illinois. He served as program co-chair for IEEE Computer Vision and Pattern Recognition in 2000 and in 2011, general co-chair for CVPR 2006, and program co-chair for the European Conference on Computer Vision 2008, and is a regular member of the program committee of all major international conferences on computer vision. He has served five terms on the SIGGRAPH program committee. In 2006, he received an IEEE technical achievement award, and in 2009 he was named an IEEE Fellow.

Jean Ponce received the Doctorat de Troisieme Cycle and Doctorat d' État degrees in Computer Science from the University of Paris Orsay in 1983 and 1988. He has held Research Scientist positions at the Institut National de la Recherche en Informatique et Automatique, the MIT Artificial Intelligence Laboratory, and the Stanford University Robotics Laboratory, and served on the faculty of the Dept. of Computer Science at the University of Illinois at Urbana-Champaign from 1990 to 2005. Since 2005, he has been a Professor at Ecole Normale Superieure in Paris, France. Dr. Ponce has served on the editorial boards of Computer Vision and Image Understanding, Foundations and Trends in Computer Graphics and Vision, the IEEE Transactions on Robotics and Automation, the International Journal of Computer Vision (for which he served as Editor-in-Chief from 2003 to 2008), and the SIAM Journal on Imaging Sciences. He was Program Chair of the 1997 IEEE Conference on Computer Vision and Pattern Recognition and served as General Chair of the year 2000 edition of this conference. He also served as General Chair of the 2008 European Conference on Computer Vision. In 2003, he was named an IEEE Fellow for his contributions to Computer Vision, and he received a US patent for the development of a robotic parts feeder.

PART ONE

IMAGE FORMATION

CHAPTER 1

Geometric Camera Models

There are many types of imaging devices, from animal eyes to video cameras and radio telescopes, and they may or may not be equipped with lenses. For example, the first models of the *camera obscura* (literally, dark chamber) invented in the sixteenth century did not have lenses, but instead used a *pinhole* to focus light rays onto a wall or translucent plate and demonstrate the laws of perspective discovered a century earlier by Brunelleschi. Pinholes were replaced by more and more sophisticated lenses as early as 1550, and the modern photographic or digital camera is essentially a camera obscura capable of recording the amount of light striking every small area of its backplane (Figure 1.1).

FIGURE 1.1: Image formation on the backplate of a photographic camera. *Figure from US NAVY MANUAL OF BASIC OPTICS AND OPTICAL INSTRUMENTS, prepared by the Bureau of Naval Personnel, reprinted by Dover Publications, Inc. (1969).*

The imaging surface of a camera is in general a rectangle, but the shape of the human retina is much closer to a spherical surface, and panoramic cameras may be equipped with cylindrical retinas. Imaging sensors have other characteristics. They may record a spatially discrete picture (like our eyes with their rods and cones, 35mm cameras with their grain, and digital cameras with their rectangular picture elements, or pixels), or a continuous one (in the case of old-fashioned TV tubes, for example). The signal that an imaging sensor records at a point on its retina may itself be discrete or continuous, and it may consist of a single number (as for a black-and-white camera), a few values (e.g., the RGB intensities for a color camera or the responses of the three types of cones for the human eye), many numbers (e.g., the responses of hyperspectral sensors), or even a continuous function of wavelength (which is essentially the case for spectrometers). Chapter 2 considers cameras as *radiometric* devices for measuring light energy, brightness, and color. Here, we focus instead on purely geometric camera characteristics. After introducing several models of image formation in Section 1.1—including a brief description of this process in the human eye in Section 1.1.4—we define the *intrinsic* and *extrinsic* geometric parameters characterizing a camera in Section 1.2, and finally show how to estimate these parameters from image data—a process known as *geometric camera calibration*—in Section 1.3.

1.1   IMAGE FORMATION

1.1.1   Pinhole Perspective

Imagine taking a box, using a pin to prick a small hole in the center of one of its sides, and then replacing the opposite side with a translucent plate. If you hold that box in front of you in a dimly lit room, with the pinhole facing some light source, say a candle, an inverted image of the candle will appear on the translucent plate (Figure 1.2). This image is formed by light rays issued from the scene facing the box. If the pinhole were really reduced to a point (which is physically impossible, of course), exactly one light ray would pass through each point in the plane of the plate (or *image plane*), the pinhole, and some scene point.

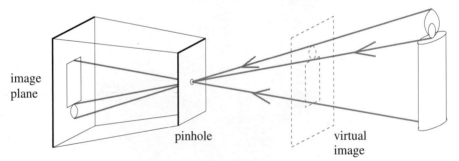

FIGURE 1.2: The pinhole imaging model.

In reality, the pinhole will have a finite (albeit small) size, and each point in the image plane will collect light from a cone of rays subtending a finite solid angle, so this idealized and extremely simple model of the imaging geometry will not strictly apply. In addition, real cameras are normally equipped with lenses, which further complicates things. Still, the *pinhole perspective* (also called *central perspective*) projection model, first proposed by Brunelleschi at the beginning of the fifteenth century, is mathematically convenient and, despite its simplicity, it often provides an acceptable approximation of the imaging process. Perspective projection creates inverted images, and it is sometimes convenient to consider instead a *virtual image* associated with a plane lying *in front* of the pinhole, at the same distance from it as the actual image plane (Figure 1.2). This virtual image is not inverted but is otherwise strictly equivalent to the actual one. Depending on the context, it may be more convenient to think about one or the other. Figure 1.3 (a) illustrates an obvious effect of perspective projection: the apparent size of objects depends on their distance. For example, the images b and c of the posts B and C have the same height, but A and C are really half the size of B. Figure 1.3 (b) illustrates another well-known effect: the projections of two parallel lines lying in some plane Φ appear to converge on a horizon line h formed by the intersection of the image plane Π with the plane parallel to Φ and passing through the pinhole. Note that the line L parallel to Π in Φ has no image at all.

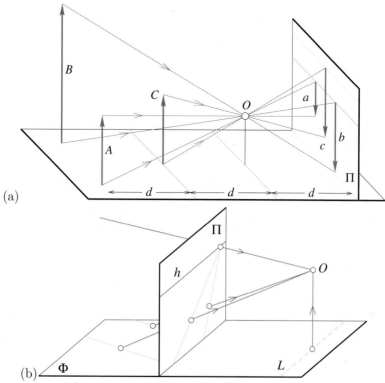

FIGURE 1.3: Perspective effects: (a) far objects appear smaller than close ones: The distance d from the pinhole O to the plane containing C is half the distance from O to the plane containing A and B; (b) the images of parallel lines intersect at the horizon (after Hilbert and Cohn-Vossen, 1952, Figure 127). Note that the image plane Π is *behind* the pinhole in (a) (physical retina), and *in front* of it in (b) (virtual image plane). Most of the diagrams in this chapter and in the rest of this book will feature the physical image plane, but a virtual one will also be used when appropriate, as in (b).

These properties are easy to prove in a purely geometric fashion. As usual, however, it is often convenient (if not quite as elegant) to reason in terms of reference frames, coordinates, and equations. Consider, for example, a coordinate system $(O, \boldsymbol{i}, \boldsymbol{j}, \boldsymbol{k})$ attached to a pinhole camera, whose origin O coincides with the pinhole, and vectors $\boldsymbol{i}$ and $\boldsymbol{j}$ form a basis for a vector plane parallel to the image plane Π, itself located at a positive distance d from the pinhole along the vector $\boldsymbol{k}$ (Figure 1.4). The line perpendicular to Π and passing through the pinhole is called the optical axis, and the point c where it pierces Π is called the *image center*. This point can be used as the origin of an image plane coordinate frame, and it plays an important role in camera calibration procedures.

Let P denote a scene point with coordinates (X, Y, Z) and p denote its image

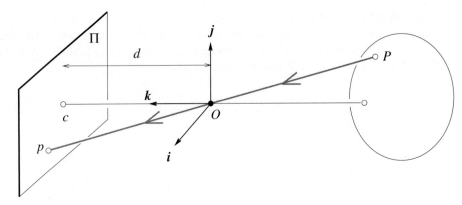

FIGURE 1.4: The perspective projection equations are derived in this section from the collinearity of the point P, its image p, and the pinhole O.

with coordinates (x, y, z). (Throughout this chapter, we will use uppercase letters to denotes points in space, and lowercase letters to denote their image projections.) Since p lies in the image plane, we have $z = d$. Since the three points P, O, and p are collinear, we have $\overrightarrow{Op} = \lambda \overrightarrow{OP}$ for some number λ, so

$$\begin{cases} x = \lambda X \\ y = \lambda Y \\ d = \lambda Z \end{cases} \iff \lambda = \frac{x}{X} = \frac{y}{Y} = \frac{d}{Z},$$

and therefore

$$\begin{cases} x = d\dfrac{X}{Z}, \\ y = d\dfrac{Y}{Z}. \end{cases} \tag{1.1}$$

1.1.2 Weak Perspective

As noted in the previous section, pinhole perspective is only an approximation of the geometry of the imaging process. This section discusses a coarser approximation, called *weak perspective*, which is also useful on occasion.

Consider the *fronto-parallel plane* Π_0 defined by $Z = Z_0$ (Figure 1.5). For any point P in Π_0 we can rewrite Eq. (1.1) as

$$\begin{cases} x = -mX, \\ y = -mY, \end{cases} \quad \text{where} \quad m = -\frac{d}{Z_0}. \tag{1.2}$$

Physical constraints impose that Z_0 be negative (the plane must be in front of the pinhole), so the *magnification* m associated with the plane Π_0 is positive. This name is justified by the following remark: consider two points P and Q in Π_0 and their images p and q (Figure 1.5); obviously, the vectors $\overrightarrow{PQ}$ and $\overrightarrow{pq}$ are parallel, and we have $||\overrightarrow{pq}|| = m||\overrightarrow{PQ}||$. This is the dependence of image size on object distance noted earlier.

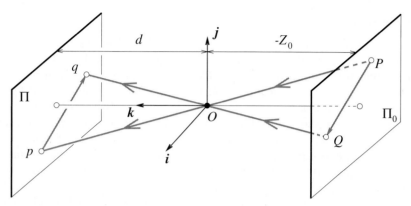

FIGURE 1.5: Weak-perspective projection. All line segments in the plane Π_0 are projected with the same magnification.

When a scene's relief is small relative to its average distance from the camera, the magnification can be taken to be constant. This projection model is called *weak perspective*, or *scaled orthography*.

When it is a priori known that the camera will always remain at a roughly constant distance from the scene, we can go further and normalize the image coordinates so that $m = -1$. This is *orthographic projection*, defined by

$$\begin{cases} x = X, \\ y = Y, \end{cases} \tag{1.3}$$

with all light rays parallel to the $\boldsymbol{k}$ axis and orthogonal to the image plane π (Figure 1.6). Although weak-perspective projection is an acceptable model for many imaging conditions, assuming pure orthographic projection is usually unrealistic.

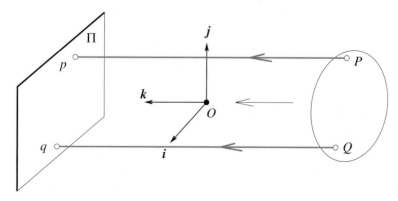

FIGURE 1.6: Orthographic projection. Unlike other geometric models of the image formation process, orthographic projection does not involve a reversal of image features. Accordingly, the magnification is taken to be negative, which is a bit unnatural but simplifies the projection equations.

1.1.3 Cameras with Lenses

Most real cameras are equipped with lenses. There are two main reasons for this: The first one is to gather light, because a single ray of light would otherwise reach each point in the image plane under ideal pinhole projection. Real pinholes have a finite size, of course, so each point in the image plane is illuminated by a cone of light rays subtending a finite solid angle. The larger the hole, the wider the cone and the brighter the image, but a large pinhole gives blurry pictures. Shrinking the pinhole produces sharper images but reduces the amount of light reaching the image plane, and may introduce *diffraction* effects. Keeping the picture in sharp focus while gathering light from a large area is the second main reason for using a lens.

Ignoring diffraction, interferences, and other physical optics phenomena, the behavior of lenses is dictated by the laws of geometric optics (Figure 1.7): (1) light travels in straight lines (*light rays*) in homogeneous media; (2) when a ray is reflected from a surface, this ray, its reflection, and the surface normal are coplanar, and the angles between the normal and the two rays are complementary; and (3) when a ray passes from one medium to another, it is *refracted*, i.e., its direction changes. According to Snell's law, if r_1 is the ray incident to the interface between two transparent materials with indices of refraction n_1 and n_2, and r_2 is the refracted ray, then r_1, r_2, and the normal to the interface are coplanar, and the angles α_1 and α_2 between the normal and the two rays are related by

$$n_1 \sin \alpha_1 = n_2 \sin \alpha_2. \tag{1.4}$$

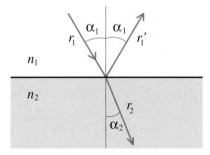

FIGURE 1.7: Reflection and refraction at the interface between two homogeneous media with indices of refraction n_1 and n_2.

In this chapter, we will only consider the effects of refraction and ignore those of reflection. In other words, we will concentrate on lenses as opposed to *catadioptric optical systems* (e.g., telescopes) that may include both reflective (mirrors) and refractive elements. Tracing light rays as they travel through a lens is simpler when the angles between these rays and the refracting surfaces of the lens are assumed to be small, which is the domain of *paraxial* (or *first-order*) geometric optics, and Snell's law becomes $n_1\alpha_1 \approx n_2\alpha_2$. Let us also assume that the lens is rotationally symmetric about a straight line, called its *optical axis*, and that all refractive surfaces are spherical. The symmetry of this setup allows us to determine

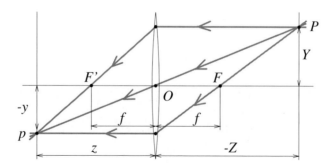

FIGURE 1.8: A thin lens. Rays passing through O are not refracted. Rays parallel to the optical axis are focused on the focal point F'.

the projection geometry by considering lenses with circular boundaries lying in a plane that contains the optical axis. In particular, consider a lens with two spherical surfaces of radius R and index of refraction n. We will assume that this lens is surrounded by vacuum (or, to an excellent approximation, by air), with an index of refraction equal to 1, and that it is *thin*, i.e., that a ray entering the lens and refracted at its right boundary is immediately refracted again at the left boundary.

Consider a point P located at (negative) depth Z off the optical axis, and denote by (PO) the ray passing through this point and the center O of the lens (Figure 1.8). It easily follows from the paraxial form of Snell's law that (PO) is not refracted, and that all the other rays passing through P are focused by the thin lens on the point p with depth z along (PO) such that

$$\frac{1}{z} - \frac{1}{Z} = \frac{1}{f},$$

(1.5)

where $f = \frac{R}{2(n-1)}$ is the *focal length* of the lens.

Note that the equations relating the positions of P and p are exactly the same as under pinhole perspective projection if we take $d = z$ since P and p lie on a ray passing through the center of the lens, but that points located at a distance $-Z$ from O will be in sharp focus only when the image plane is located at a distance z from O on the other side of the lens that satisfies Eq. (1.5), the *thin lens equation*. Letting $Z \to -\infty$ shows that f is the distance between the center of the lens and the plane where objects such as stars (that are effectively located at $Z = -\infty$) focus. The two points F and F' located at distance f from the lens center on the optical axis are called the *focal points* of the lens. In practice, objects within some range of distances (called *depth of field* or *depth of focus*) will be in acceptable focus. As shown in the problems at the end of this chapter, the depth of field increases with the *f-number* of the lens, i.e., the ratio between the focal length of the lens and its diameter.

Note that the *field of view* of a camera, i.e., the portion of scene space that actually projects onto the retina of the camera, is not defined by the focal length alone but also depends on the effective area of the retina (e.g., the area of film that can be exposed in a photographic camera, or the area of the sensor in a digital camera; see Figure 1.9).

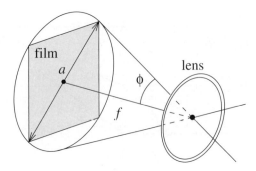

FIGURE 1.9: The field of view of a camera. It can be defined as 2ϕ, where $\phi \stackrel{\text{def}}{=} \arctan \frac{a}{2f}$, a is the diameter of the sensor (film, CCD, or CMOS chip), and f is the focal length of the camera.

A more realistic model of simple optical systems is the *thick lens*. The equations describing its behavior are easily derived from the paraxial refraction equation, and they are the same as the pinhole perspective and thin lens projection equations, except for an offset (Figure 1.10). If H and H' denote the *principal points* of the lens, then Eq. (1.5) holds when $-Z$ (resp. z) is the distance between P (resp. p) and the plane perpendicular to the optical axis and passing through H (resp. H'). In this case, the only undeflected ray is along the optical axis.

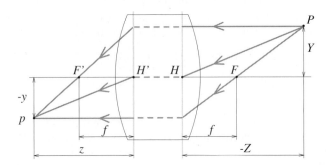

FIGURE 1.10: A simple thick lens with two spherical surfaces.

Simple lenses suffer from a number of *aberrations*. To understand why, let us remember that the paraxial refraction model is only an approximation, valid when the angle α between each ray along the optical path and the optical axis of the length is small and $\sin \alpha \approx \alpha$. This corresponds to a first-order Taylor expansion of the sine function. For larger angles, additional terms yield a better approximation, and it is easy to show that rays striking the interface farther from the optical axis are focused closer to the interface. The same phenomenon occurs for a lens, and it is the source of two types of *spherical aberrations* (Figure 1.11 [a]): Consider a point P on the optical axis and its paraxial image p. The distance between p and the intersection of the optical axis with a ray issued from P and refracted by the lens is called the longitudinal spherical aberration of that ray. Note that if an image plane Π were erected in P, the ray would intersect this plane at some distance from the axis, called the transverse spherical aberration of that ray. Together, all rays passing through P and refracted by the lens form a circle of confusion centered in P as they intersect Π. The size of that circle will change if we move Π along the optical axis. The circle with minimum diameter is called the *circle of least confusion*, and its center does not coincide (in general) with p.

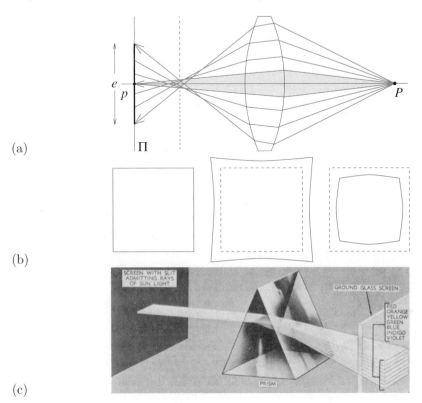

(a)

(b)

(c)

FIGURE 1.11: Aberrations. (a) Spherical aberration: The gray region is the paraxial zone where the rays issued from P intersect at its paraxial image p. If an image plane π were erected in p, the image of p in that plane would form a circle of confusion of diameter e. The focus plane yielding the circle of least confusion is indicated by a dashed line. (b) Distortion: From left to right, the nominal image of a fronto-parallel square, pincushion distortion, and barrel distortion. (c) Chromatic aberration: The index of refraction of a transparent medium depends on the wavelength (or color) of the incident light rays. Here, a prism decomposes white light into a palette of colors. *Figure from US NAVY MANUAL OF BASIC OPTICS AND OPTICAL INSTRUMENTS, prepared by the Bureau of Naval Personnel, reprinted by Dover Publications, Inc. (1969).*

Besides spherical aberration, there are four other types of *primary aberrations* caused by the differences between first- and third-order optics, namely *coma, astigmatism, field curvature,* and *distortion*. A precise definition of these aberrations is beyond the scope of this book. Suffice to say that, like a spherical aberration, the first three degrade the image by blurring the picture of every object point. Distortion, on the other hand, plays a different role and changes the shape of the image

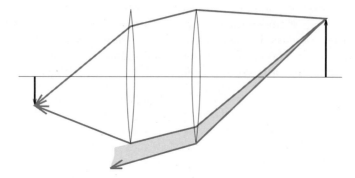

FIGURE 1.12: Vignetting effect in a two-lens system. The shaded part of the beam never reaches the second lens. Additional apertures and stops in a lens further contribute to vignetting.

as a whole (Figure 1.11 [b]). This effect is due to the fact that different areas of a lens have slightly different focal lengths. The aberrations mentioned so far are monochromatic, i.e., they are independent of the response of the lens to various wavelengths. However, the index of refraction of a transparent medium depends on wavelength (Figure 1.11 [c]), and it follows from the thin lens equation (Eq. [1.5]) that the focal length depends on wavelength as well. This causes the phenomenon of *chromatic aberration*: refracted rays corresponding to different wavelengths will intersect the optical axis at different points (longitudinal chromatic aberration) and form different circles of confusion in the same image plane (transverse chromatic aberration).

Aberrations can be minimized by aligning several simple lenses with well-chosen shapes and refraction indices, separated by appropriate stops. These *compound lenses* can still be modeled by the thick lens equations, but they suffer from one more defect relevant to machine vision: light beams emanating from object points located off-axis are partially blocked by the various apertures (including the individual lens components themselves) positioned inside the lens to limit aberrations (Figure 1.12). This phenomenon, called *vignetting*, causes the image brightness to drop in the image periphery. Vignetting may pose problems to automated image analysis programs, but it is not quite as important in photography, thanks to the human eye's remarkable insensitivity to smooth brightness gradients. Speaking of which, it is time to have a look at this extraordinary organ.

1.1.4   The Human Eye

Here we give a (brief) overview of the anatomical structure of the eye. It is largely based on the presentation in Wandell (1995), and the interested reader is invited to read this excellent book for more details. Figure 1.13 (left) is a sketch of the section of an eyeball through its vertical plane of symmetry, showing the main elements of the eye: the *iris* and the *pupil*, which control the amount of light penetrating the eyeball; the *cornea* and the crystalline *lens*, which together refract the light to create the retinal image; and finally the *retina*, where the image is formed. Despite its globular shape, the human eyeball is functionally similar to a camera with a field of view covering a 160° (width) × 135° (height) area. Like any other optical system, it suffers from various types of geometric and chromatic aberrations. Several models of the eye obeying the laws of first-order geometric optics have been proposed, and Figure 1.13 (right) shows one of them, *Helmoltz's schematic eye*. There are only three refractive surfaces, with an infinitely thin cornea and a homogeneous lens. The constants given in Figure 1.13 are for the eye focusing at infinity (*unaccommodated eye*). This model is of course only an approximation of the real optical characteristics of the eye.

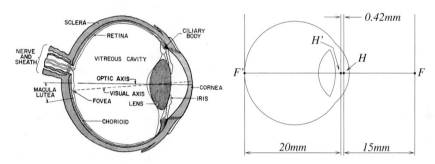

FIGURE 1.13: Left: the main components of the human eye. *Reproduced with permission, the American Society for Photogrammetry and Remote Sensing. A.L. Nowicki, "Stereoscopy." MANUAL OF PHOTOGRAMMETRY, edited by M.M. Thompson, R.C. Eller, W.A. Radlinski, and J.L. Speert, third edition, pp. 515–536. Bethesda: American Society of Photogrammetry, (1966).* Right: Helmoltz's schematic eye as modified by Laurance (after Driscoll and Vaughan, 1978). The distance between the pole of the cornea and the anterior principal plane is 1.96 mm, and the radii of the cornea, anterior, and posterior surfaces of the lens are respectively 8 mm, 10 mm, and 6 mm.

Let us have a second look at the components of the eye one layer at a time. The cornea is a transparent, highly curved, refractive window through which light enters the eye before being partially blocked by the colored and opaque surface of the iris. The pupil is an opening at the center of the iris whose diameter varies from about 1 to 8 mm in response to illumination changes, dilating in low light to increase the amount of energy that reaches the retina and contracting in normal lighting conditions to limit the amount of image blurring due to spherical aberration in the eye. The refracting power (reciprocal of the focal length) of the eye is, in large part, an effect of refraction at the the air–cornea interface, and it is fine-tuned by deformations of the crystalline lens that accommodates to bring objects into sharp focus. In healthy adults, it varies between 60 (unaccommodated case) and 68 diopters (1 diopter = 1 m^{-1}), corresponding to a range of focal lengths between 15 and 17 mm.

The retina itself is a thin, layered membrane populated by two types of photoreceptors—*rods* and *cones*. There are about 100 million rods and 5 million cones in a human eye. Their spatial distribution varies across the retina: The *macula lutea* is a region in the center of the retina where the concentration of cones is particularly high and images are sharply focused whenever the eye fixes its attention on an object (Figure 1.13). The highest concentration of cones occurs in the *fovea*, a depression in the middle of the macula lutea where it peaks at $1.6 \times 10^5/\text{mm}^2$, with the centers of two neighboring cones separated by only half a minute of visual angle. Conversely, there are no rods in the center of the fovea, but the rod density increases toward the periphery of the visual field. There is also a *blind spot* on the retina, where the ganglion cell axons exit the retina and form the optic nerve.

The rods are extremely sensitive photoreceptors, capable of responding to a single photon, but they yield relatively poor spatial detail despite their high number because many rods converge to the same neuron within the retina. In contrast, cones become active at higher light levels, but the signal output by each cone in the fovea is encoded by several neurons, yielding a high resolution in that area. As discussed further in Chapter 3, there are three types of cones with different spectral sensitivities, and these play a key role in the perception of color. Much more could (and should) be said about the human eye—for example how our two eyes verge and fixate on targets, and how they cooperate in stereo vision, an issue briefly discussed in Chapter 7.

1.2   INTRINSIC AND EXTRINSIC PARAMETERS

Digital images, like animal retinas, are spatially discrete, and divided into (usually) rectangular picture elements, or *pixels*. This is an aspect of the image formation process that we have neglected so far, assuming instead that the image domain is spatially continuous. Likewise, the perspective equation derived in the previous section is valid only when all distances are measured in the camera's reference frame, and when image coordinates have their origin at the image center where the axis of symmetry of the camera pierces its retina. In practice, the world and camera coordinate systems are related by a set of physical parameters, such as the focal length of the lens, the size of the pixels, the position of the image center, and the position and orientation of the camera. This section identifies these parameters. We will distinguish the *intrinsic* parameters, which relate the camera's coordinate system to the idealized coordinate system used in Section 1.1, from the *extrinsic* parameters, which relate the camera's coordinate system to a fixed world coordinate system and specify its position and orientation in space.

We ignore in the rest of this section the fact that, for cameras equipped with a lens, a point will be in focus only when its depth and the distance between the optical center of the camera and its image plane obey Eq. (1.5). In particular, we assume that the camera is focused at infinity, so $d = f$. Likewise, the nonlinear aberrations associated with real lenses are not taken into account by Eq. (1.1). We neglect these aberrations in this section, but revisit radial distortion in Section 1.3 when we address the problem of estimating the intrinsic and extrinsic parameters of a camera (a process known as *geometric camera calibration*).

1.2.1   Rigid Transformations and Homogeneous Coordinates

This section features our first use of *homogeneous* coordinates to represent the position of points in two or three dimensions. Consider a point P whose position in some coordinate frame $(F) = (O, \boldsymbol{i}, \boldsymbol{j}, \boldsymbol{k})$ is given by

$$\overrightarrow{OP} = X\boldsymbol{i} + Y\boldsymbol{j} + Z\boldsymbol{k}.$$

We define the usual (nonhomogeneous) coordinate vector of P to be the vector $(X, Y, Z)^T$ in $\mathbb{R}^3$ and its homogeneous coordinate vector as the vector $(X, Y, Z, 1)^T$ in $\mathbb{R}^4$. We use bold letters to denote (homogeneous and nonhomogeneous) coordinate vectors in this book, and always state which type of coordinates we use when it is not obvious from the context. We also use a superscript *on the left side of* coordinate vectors when necessary to indicate which coordinate frame a position is expressed in. For example, $^F\boldsymbol{P}$ stands for the coordinate vector of the point P in the frame (F). Homogeneous coordinates are a convenient device for representing various geometric transformations by matrix products. For example, the change of coordinates between two Euclidean coordinate systems (A) and (B) may be represented by a 3×3 rotation matrix $\mathcal{R}$ and a translation vector $\boldsymbol{t}$ in $\mathbb{R}^3$, and the corresponding *rigid transformation* can be written in nonhomogeneous coordinates as

$$^A\boldsymbol{P} = \mathcal{R}\,^B\boldsymbol{P} + \boldsymbol{t}, \tag{1.6}$$

where $^A\boldsymbol{P}$ and $^B\boldsymbol{P}$ are elements of $\mathbb{R}^3$. In homogeneous coordinates, we write instead

$$^A\boldsymbol{P} = \mathcal{T}\,^B\boldsymbol{P}, \quad \text{where} \quad \mathcal{T} = \begin{pmatrix} \mathcal{R} & \boldsymbol{t} \\ \boldsymbol{0}^T & 1 \end{pmatrix}, \tag{1.7}$$

and $^A\boldsymbol{P}$ and $^B\boldsymbol{P}$ are this time elements of $\mathbb{R}^4$.

Before going further, let us recall a few facts about rotations. Rotation matrices form a mulitplicative group. From an analytical viewpoint, they are characterized by the facts that (1) the inverse of a rotation matrix is equal to its transpose, and (2) its determinant is equal to one. It can also be shown that any rotation matrix can be parameterized by three *Euler angles*, or written as the product of three elementary rotations about the $\boldsymbol{i}$, $\boldsymbol{j}$, and $\boldsymbol{k}$ vectors of some coordinate system. As shown in Chapters 7 and 14, other parameterizations—by exponentials of antisymmetric matrices or quaternions for example—may prove useful as well. Geometrically, the matrix $\mathcal{R}$ in Eq. (1.6) also represents the basis vectors $(\boldsymbol{i}_B, \boldsymbol{j}_B, \boldsymbol{k}_B)$ of (B) in the coordinate frame (A)—that is, the matrix $\mathcal{R}$ in Eq. (1.6) is given by:

$$\mathcal{R} \stackrel{\text{def}}{=} \left(^A\boldsymbol{i}_B, {}^A\boldsymbol{j}_B, {}^A\boldsymbol{k}_B\right) = \begin{pmatrix} \boldsymbol{i}_A \cdot \boldsymbol{i}_B & \boldsymbol{j}_A \cdot \boldsymbol{i}_B & \boldsymbol{k}_A \cdot \boldsymbol{i}_B \\ \boldsymbol{i}_A \cdot \boldsymbol{j}_B & \boldsymbol{j}_A \cdot \boldsymbol{j}_B & \boldsymbol{k}_A \cdot \boldsymbol{j}_B \\ \boldsymbol{i}_A \cdot \boldsymbol{k}_B & \boldsymbol{j}_A \cdot \boldsymbol{k}_B & \boldsymbol{k}_A \cdot \boldsymbol{k}_B \end{pmatrix}, \tag{1.8}$$

and, as shown in the problems at the end of this chapter, Eq. (1.6) easily follows from this definition. By definition, the columns of a rotation matrix form a right-handed orthonormal coordinate system of $\mathbb{R}^3$. It follows from properties (1) and (2) that their rows also form such a coordinate system. One may wonder what happens when $\mathcal{R}$ is replaced in Eq. (1.7) by some arbitrary nonsingular 3×3 matrix, or when the matrix $\mathcal{T}$ itself is replaced by some arbitrary nonsingular 4×4 matrix. As further discussed in Chapter 8, the coordinate frames (A) and (B) are no longer separated by rigid transformations in this case, but by *affine* and *projective transformations* respectively.

As will be shown in the rest of this section, homogeneous coordinates also provide an algebraic representation of the perspective projection process in the form of a 3×4 matrix $\mathcal{M}$, so that the coordinate vector $\boldsymbol{P} = (X, Y, Z, 1)^T$ of a point P in some fixed world coordinate system and the coordinate vector $\boldsymbol{p} = (x, y, 1)^T$ of

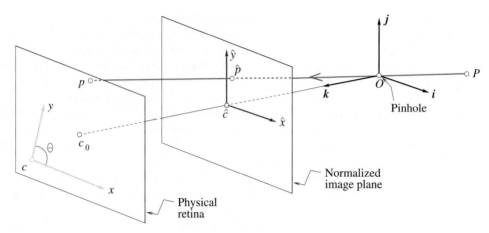

FIGURE 1.14: Physical and normalized image coordinate systems.

its image p in the camera's reference frame are related by the *perspective projection equation*

$$p = \frac{1}{Z}\mathcal{M}P. \tag{1.9}$$

1.2.2 Intrinsic Parameters

It is possible to associate with a camera a *normalized image plane* parallel to its physical retina but located at a unit distance from the pinhole. We attach to this plane its own coordinate system with an origin located at the point $\hat{c}$ where the optical axis pierces it (Figure 1.14). Equation (1.1) can be written in this normalized coordinate system as

$$\begin{cases} \hat{x} = \dfrac{X}{Z} \\[2mm] \hat{y} = \dfrac{Y}{Z} \end{cases} \Longleftrightarrow \hat{p} = \frac{1}{Z}\begin{pmatrix} \text{Id} & \mathbf{0} \end{pmatrix}P, \tag{1.10}$$

where $\hat{p} \stackrel{\text{def}}{=} (\hat{x}, \hat{y}, 1)^T$ is the vector of homogeneous coordinates of the projection $\hat{p}$ of the point P into the normalized image plane, and P is as before the homogeneous coordinate vector of P in the world coordinate frame.

The physical retina of the camera is in general different (Figure 1.14): It is located at a distance $f \neq 1$ from the pinhole (remember that we assume that the camera is focused at infinity, so the distance between the pinhole and the image plane is equal to the focal length), and the coordinates (x, y) of the image point p are usually expressed in pixel units (instead of, say, meters). In addition, pixels may be rectangular instead of square, so the camera has two additional scale parameters

k and l, and

$$\begin{cases} x = kf\dfrac{X}{Z} = kf\hat{x}, \\[2mm] y = lf\dfrac{Y}{Z} = lf\hat{y}. \end{cases} \tag{1.11}$$

Let us talk units for a second: f is a distance, expressed in meters, for example, and a pixel will have dimensions $\frac{1}{k} \times \frac{1}{l}$, where k and l are expressed in pixel $\times \mathrm{m}^{-1}$. The parameters k, l, and f are not independent, and they can be replaced by the magnifications $\alpha = kf$ and $\beta = lf$ expressed in pixel units.

Now, in general, the actual origin of the camera coordinate system is at a corner c of the retina (in the case depicted in Figure 1.14, the lower-left corner, or sometimes the upper-left corner, when the image coordinates are the row and column indices of a pixel) and not at its center, and the center of the CCD matrix usually does not coincide with the image center c_0. This adds two parameters x_0 and y_0 that define the position (in pixel units) of c_0 in the retinal coordinate system. Thus, Eq. (1.11) is replaced by

$$\begin{cases} x = \alpha\hat{x} + x_0, \\ y = \beta\hat{y} + y_0. \end{cases} \tag{1.12}$$

Finally, the camera coordinate system might also be skewed, due to some manufacturing error, so the angle θ between the two image axes is not equal to (but of course not very different from) 90 degrees. In this case, it is easy to show that Eq. (1.12) transforms into

$$\begin{cases} x = \alpha\hat{x} - \alpha\cot\theta\,\hat{y} + x_0, \\[2mm] y = \dfrac{\beta}{\sin\theta}\hat{y} + y_0. \end{cases} \tag{1.13}$$

This can be written in matrix form as

$$\boldsymbol{p} = \mathcal{K}\hat{\boldsymbol{p}}, \quad \text{where} \quad \boldsymbol{p} = \begin{pmatrix} x \\ y \\ 1 \end{pmatrix} \quad \text{and} \quad \mathcal{K} \overset{\text{def}}{=} \begin{pmatrix} \alpha & -\alpha\cot\theta & x_0 \\ 0 & \dfrac{\beta}{\sin\theta} & y_0 \\ 0 & 0 & 1 \end{pmatrix}. \tag{1.14}$$

The 3×3 matrix $\mathcal{K}$ is called the (internal) *calibration matrix* of the camera. Putting Eqs. (1.10) and (1.14) together, we obtain

$$\boldsymbol{p} = \frac{1}{Z}\mathcal{K}\begin{pmatrix} \mathrm{Id} & \mathbf{0} \end{pmatrix}\boldsymbol{P} = \frac{1}{Z}\mathcal{M}\boldsymbol{P}, \quad \text{where} \quad \mathcal{M} \overset{\text{def}}{=} \begin{pmatrix} \mathcal{K} & \mathbf{0} \end{pmatrix}, \tag{1.15}$$

which is indeed an instance of Eq. (1.9). The five parameters α, β, θ, x_0, and y_0 are called the *intrinsic parameters* of the camera.

Several of these parameters, such as the focal length, or the physical size of the pixels, are often available in the *EXIF tags* attached to the JPEG images recorded by digital cameras (this information might not be available, of course, as in the case of stock film footage). For zoom lenses, the focal length may vary with time, along with the image center when the optical axis of the lens is not exactly perpendicular to the image plane. Simply changing the focus of the camera will also affect the magnification because it will change the lens-to-retina distance, but we will continue to assume that the camera is focused at infinity and ignore this effect in the rest of this chapter.

1.2.3   Extrinsic Parameters

Equation (1.15) is written in a coordinate frame (C) attached to the camera. Let us now consider the case where this frame is distinct from the world coordinate system (W). To emphasize this, we rewrite Eq. (1.15) as $\boldsymbol{p} = \frac{1}{Z}\mathcal{M}\,{}^{C}\boldsymbol{P}$, where ${}^{C}\boldsymbol{P}$ denotes the vector of homogeneous coordinates of the point P expressed in (C). The change of coordinates between (C) and (W) is a rigid transformation, and it can be written as

$$
{}^{C}\boldsymbol{P} = \begin{pmatrix} \mathcal{R} & \boldsymbol{t} \\ \boldsymbol{0}^{T} & 1 \end{pmatrix} {}^{W}\boldsymbol{P},
$$

where ${}^{W}\boldsymbol{P}$ is the vector of homogeneous coordinates of the point P in the coordinate frame (W). Taking $\boldsymbol{P} = {}^{W}\boldsymbol{P}$ and substituting in Eq. (1.15) finally yields

$$
\boldsymbol{p} = \frac{1}{Z}\mathcal{M}\boldsymbol{P}, \quad \text{where} \quad \mathcal{M} = \mathcal{K}\begin{pmatrix} \mathcal{R} & \boldsymbol{t} \end{pmatrix}. \tag{1.16}
$$

This is the most general form of the perspective projection equation, and indeed an instance of Eq. (1.9). Knowing $\mathcal{M}$ determines the position of the camera's optical center in the coordinate frame (W)—that is, its homogeneous coordinate vector $\boldsymbol{O} = {}^{W}\boldsymbol{O}$. Indeed, as shown in the problems at the end of this chapter, $\mathcal{M}\boldsymbol{O} = \boldsymbol{0}$.

As mentioned earlier, a rotation matrix such as $\mathcal{R}$ is defined by three independent parameters (for example, Euler angles). Adding to these the three coordinates of the vector $\boldsymbol{t}$, we obtain a set of six *extrinsic parameters* that define the position and orientation of the camera relative to the world coordinate frame.

It is very important to understand that the depth Z in Eq. (1.16) is *not* independent of $\mathcal{M}$ and $\boldsymbol{P}$, because if $\boldsymbol{m}_1^{T}$, $\boldsymbol{m}_2^{T}$ and $\boldsymbol{m}_3^{T}$ denote the three rows of $\mathcal{M}$, it follows directly from Eq. (1.16) that $Z = \boldsymbol{m}_3 \cdot \boldsymbol{P}$. In fact, it is sometimes convenient to rewrite Eq. (1.16) in the equivalent form:

$$
\begin{cases} x = \dfrac{\boldsymbol{m}_1 \cdot \boldsymbol{P}}{\boldsymbol{m}_3 \cdot \boldsymbol{P}}, \\[2mm] y = \dfrac{\boldsymbol{m}_2 \cdot \boldsymbol{P}}{\boldsymbol{m}_3 \cdot \boldsymbol{P}}. \end{cases} \tag{1.17}
$$

A perspective projection matrix can be written explicitly as a function of its five intrinsic parameters, the three rows $\boldsymbol{r}_1^{T}$, $\boldsymbol{r}_2^{T}$, and $\boldsymbol{r}_3^{T}$ of the matrix $\mathcal{R}$, and the three coordinates t_1, t_2, and t_3 of the vector $\boldsymbol{t}$, namely:

$$
\mathcal{M} = \begin{pmatrix} \alpha \boldsymbol{r}_1^{T} - \alpha \cot\theta\, \boldsymbol{r}_2^{T} + x_0 \boldsymbol{r}_3^{T} & \alpha t_1 - \alpha \cot\theta\, t_2 + x_0 t_3 \\[2mm] \dfrac{\beta}{\sin\theta} \boldsymbol{r}_2^{T} + y_0 \boldsymbol{r}_3^{T} & \dfrac{\beta}{\sin\theta} t_2 + y_0 t_3 \\[2mm] \boldsymbol{r}_3^{T} & t_3 \end{pmatrix}. \tag{1.18}
$$

When $\mathcal{R}$ is written as the product of three elementary rotations, the vectors r_i ($i = 1, 2, 3$) can of course be written in terms of the corresponding three angles, and Eq. (1.18) gives an explicit parameterization of $\mathcal{M}$ in terms of all 11 camera parameters.

1.2.4 Perspective Projection Matrices

This section examines the conditions under which a 3×4 matrix $\mathcal{M}$ can be written in the form given by Eq. (1.18). Let us write without loss of generality $\mathcal{M} = \begin{pmatrix} \mathcal{A} & b \end{pmatrix}$, where $\mathcal{A}$ is a 3×3 matrix and b is an element of $\mathbb{R}^3$, and let us denote by a_3^T the third row of $\mathcal{A}$. Clearly, if $\mathcal{M}$ is an instance of Eq. (1.18), then a_3^T must be a unit vector since it is equal to r_3^T, the last row of a rotation matrix. Note, however, that replacing $\mathcal{M}$ by $\lambda\mathcal{M}$ in Eq. (1.17) for some arbitrary $\lambda \neq 0$ does not change the corresponding image coordinates. This will lead us in the rest of this book to consider projection matrices as *homogeneous objects*, only defined up to scale, whose canonical form, as expressed by Eq. (1.18), can be obtained by choosing a scale factor such that $||a_3|| = 1$. Note that the parameter Z in Eq. (1.16) can only rightly be interpreted as the depth of the point P when $\mathcal{M}$ is written in this canonical form. Note also that the number of intrinsic and extrinsic parameters of a camera matches the 11 free parameters of the (homogeneous) matrix $\mathcal{M}$.

We say that a 3×4 matrix that can be written (up to scale) as Eq. (1.18) for some set of intrinsic and extrinsic parameters is a *perspective projection matrix*. It is of practical interest to put some restrictions on the intrinsic parameters of a camera because, as noted earlier, some of these parameters will be fixed and might be known. In particular, we will say that a 3×4 matrix is a *zero-skew perspective projection matrix* when it can be rewritten (up to scale) as Eq. (1.18) with $\theta = \pi/2$, and that it is a *perspective projection matrix with zero skew and unit aspect-ratio* when it can be rewritten (up to scale) as Eq. (1.18) with $\theta = \pi/2$ and $\alpha = \beta$. A camera with *known* nonzero skew and nonunit aspect-ratio can be transformed into a camera with zero skew and unit aspect-ratio by an appropriate change of image coordinates. Are arbitrary 3×4 matrices perspective projection matrices? The following theorem answers this question.

Theorem 1. Let $\mathcal{M} = \begin{pmatrix} \mathcal{A} & b \end{pmatrix}$ be a 3×4 matrix, and let a_i^T ($i = 1, 2, 3$) denote the rows of the matrix $\mathcal{A}$ formed by the three leftmost columns of $\mathcal{M}$.

- A necessary and sufficient condition for $\mathcal{M}$ to be a perspective projection matrix is that $\mathrm{Det}(\mathcal{A}) \neq 0$.

- A necessary and sufficient condition for $\mathcal{M}$ to be a zero-skew perspective projection matrix is that $\mathrm{Det}(\mathcal{A}) \neq 0$ and

$$(a_1 \times a_3) \cdot (a_2 \times a_3) = 0.$$

- A necessary and sufficient condition for $\mathcal{M}$ to be a perspective projection matrix with zero skew and unit aspect-ratio is that $\mathrm{Det}(\mathcal{A}) \neq 0$ and

$$\begin{cases} (a_1 \times a_3) \cdot (a_2 \times a_3) = 0, \\ (a_1 \times a_3) \cdot (a_1 \times a_3) = (a_2 \times a_3) \cdot (a_2 \times a_3). \end{cases}$$

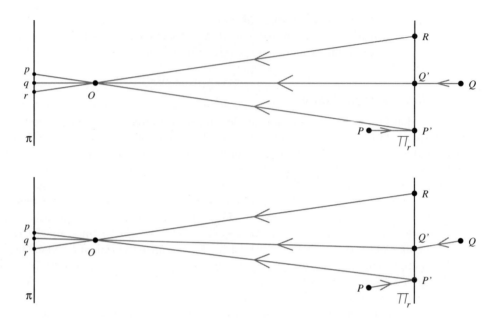

FIGURE 1.15: Affine projection models: (top) weak-perspective and (bottom) paraperspective projections.

The conditions of the theorem are clearly necessary: By definition, given some perspective projection matrix $\mathcal{A}$, we can always write $\rho\mathcal{A} = \mathcal{KR}$ for some nonzero scalar ρ, calibration matrix $\mathcal{K}$, rotation matrix $\mathcal{R}$, and vector $\boldsymbol{t}$. In particular, $\rho^3\text{Det}(\mathcal{A}) = \text{Det}(\mathcal{K}) \neq 0$ since calibration matrices are nonsingular by construction, so $\mathcal{A}$ is nonsingular. Further, a simple calculation shows that the rows of the matrix $\frac{1}{\rho}\mathcal{KR}$ satisfy the conditions of the theorem under the various assumptions imposed by its statement. These conditions are proven to also be sufficient in Faugeras (1993).

1.2.5 Weak-Perspective Projection Matrices

As noted in Section 1.1.2, when a scene's relief is small compared to the overall distance separating it from the camera observing it, a weak-perspective projection model can be used to approximate the imaging process (Figure 1.15, top). Let O denote the optical center of the camera, and let R denote a scene reference point. The weak-perspective projection of a scene point P is constructed in two steps: the point P is first projected orthogonally onto a point P' of the plane Π_r parallel to the image plane Π and passing through R; perspective projection is then used to map the point P' onto the image point p. Since π_r is a fronto-parallel plane, the net effect of the second projection step is a scaling of the image coordinates.

As shown in this section, the weak-perspective projection process can be represented in terms of a 2×4 matrix $\mathcal{M}$, so that the *homogeneous* coordinate vector $\boldsymbol{P} = (X, Y, Z, 1)^T$ of a point P in some fixed world coordinate system and the *nonhomogeneous* coordinate vector $\boldsymbol{p} = (x, y)^T$ of its image p in the camera's reference frame are related by the *affine projection equation*

$$\boldsymbol{p} = \mathcal{M}\boldsymbol{P}. \tag{1.19}$$

It turns out that this general model accomodates various other approximations of the perspective projection process. These include the orthographic projection model discussed earlier, as well as the *parallel projection* model, which subsumes the orthographic one, and takes into account the fact that the objects of interest may lie off the optical axis of the camera. In this model, the viewing rays are parallel to each other but not necessarily perpendicular to the image plane. Paraperspective is another affine projection model that takes into account both the distortions associated with a reference point that is off the optical axis of the camera and possible variations in depth (Figure 1.15, bottom). Using the same notation as before, and denoting by Δ the line joining the optical center O to the reference point R, parallel projection in the direction of Δ is first used to map P onto a point P' of the plane Π_r; perspective projection is then used to map the point P' onto the image point p.

We will focus on weak perspective in the rest of this section. Let us derive the corresponding projection equation. If Z_r denotes the depth of the reference point R, the two elementary projection stages $P \to P' \to p$ can be written in the normalized coordinate system attached to the camera as

$$\begin{pmatrix} X \\ Y \\ Z \end{pmatrix} \longrightarrow \begin{pmatrix} Z \\ Y \\ Z_r \end{pmatrix} \longrightarrow \begin{pmatrix} \hat{x} \\ \hat{y} \\ 1 \end{pmatrix} = \begin{pmatrix} X/Z_r \\ Y/Z_r \\ 1 \end{pmatrix},$$

or, in matrix form,

$$\begin{pmatrix} \hat{x} \\ \hat{y} \\ 1 \end{pmatrix} = \frac{1}{Z_r} \begin{pmatrix} 1 & 0 & 0 & 0 \\ 0 & 1 & 0 & 0 \\ 0 & 0 & 0 & Z_r \end{pmatrix} \begin{pmatrix} X \\ Y \\ Z \\ 1 \end{pmatrix}.$$

Introducing the calibration matrix $\mathcal{K}$ of the camera and its extrinsic parameters $\mathcal{R}$ and $\boldsymbol{t}$ gives the general form of the projection equation, i.e.,

$$\boldsymbol{p} = \frac{1}{Z_r} \mathcal{K} \begin{pmatrix} 1 & 0 & 0 & 0 \\ 0 & 1 & 0 & 0 \\ 0 & 0 & 0 & Z_r \end{pmatrix} \begin{pmatrix} \mathcal{R} & \boldsymbol{t} \\ \mathbf{0}^T & 1 \end{pmatrix} \boldsymbol{P}, \tag{1.20}$$

where $\boldsymbol{P}$ and $\boldsymbol{p}$ denote as before the homogeneous coordinate vector of the point P in the world reference frame, and the homogeneous coordinate vector of its projection p in the camera's coordinate system. Finally, noting that Z_r is a constant and writing

$$\mathcal{K} = \begin{pmatrix} \mathcal{K}_2 & \boldsymbol{p}_0 \\ \mathbf{0}^T & 1 \end{pmatrix}, \quad \text{where} \quad \mathcal{K}_2 \stackrel{\text{def}}{=} \begin{pmatrix} \alpha & -\alpha \cot\theta \\ 0 & \dfrac{\beta}{\sin\theta} \end{pmatrix} \quad \text{and} \quad \boldsymbol{p}_0 \stackrel{\text{def}}{=} \begin{pmatrix} x_0 \\ y_0 \end{pmatrix},$$

allows us to rewrite Eq. (1.20) as

$$\boldsymbol{p} = \mathcal{M}\boldsymbol{P}, \quad \text{where} \quad \mathcal{M} = \begin{pmatrix} \mathcal{A} & \boldsymbol{b} \end{pmatrix}, \tag{1.21}$$

where $\boldsymbol{p}$ is, this time, the *nonhomogeneous* coordinate vector of the point p, and $\mathcal{M}$ is a 2×4 projection matrix (compare to the general perspective case of Eq. [1.16]). In this expression, the 2×3 matrix $\mathcal{A}$ and the 2-vector $\boldsymbol{b}$ are respectively defined by

$$\mathcal{A} = \frac{1}{Z_r}\mathcal{K}_2\mathcal{R}_2 \quad \text{and} \quad \boldsymbol{b} = \frac{1}{Z_r}\mathcal{K}_2\boldsymbol{t}_2 + \boldsymbol{p}_0,$$

where $\mathcal{R}_2$ denotes the 2×3 matrix formed by the first two rows of $\mathcal{R}$, and $\boldsymbol{t}_2$ denotes the 2-vector formed by the first two coordinates of $\boldsymbol{t}$.

Note that t_3 does not appear in the expression of $\mathcal{M}$, and that $\boldsymbol{t}_2$ and $\boldsymbol{p}_0$ are coupled in this expression: the projection matrix does not change when $\boldsymbol{t}_2$ is replaced by $\boldsymbol{t}_2 + \boldsymbol{a}$ and $\boldsymbol{p}_0$ is replaced by $\boldsymbol{p}_0 - \frac{1}{Z_r}\mathcal{K}_2\boldsymbol{a}$. This redundancy allows us to arbitrarily choose $x_0 = y_0 = 0$. In other words, the position of the center of the image is immaterial for weak-perspective projection. Note that the values of Z_r, α, and β are also coupled in the expression of $\mathcal{M}$, and that the value of Z_r is a priori unknown in most applications. This allows us to write

$$\mathcal{M} = \frac{1}{Z_r}\begin{pmatrix} k & s \\ 0 & 1 \end{pmatrix}\begin{pmatrix} \mathcal{R}_2 & \boldsymbol{t}_2 \end{pmatrix}, \tag{1.22}$$

where k and s denote the aspect ratio and the skew of the camera, respectively. In particular, a weak-perspective projection matrix is defined by two intrinsic parameters (k and s), five extrinsic parameters (the three angles defining $\mathcal{R}_2$ and the two coordinates of $\boldsymbol{t}_2$), and one scene-dependent *structure* parameter Z_r.

A 2×4 matrix $\mathcal{M} = \begin{pmatrix} \mathcal{A} & \boldsymbol{b} \end{pmatrix}$ where $\mathcal{A}$ is an arbitrary rank-2 2×3 matrix and $\boldsymbol{b}$ is an arbitrary vector in $\mathbb{R}^2$ is called an *affine projection matrix*. Both weak-perspective and general affine projection matrices are defined by eight independent parameters. Weak-perspective projection matrices are affine ones of course. Conversely, a simple parameter-counting argument suggests that it should be possible to write an arbitrary affine projection matrix as a weak-perspective one. This is confirmed by the following theorem.

Theorem 2. An affine projection matrix can be written uniquely (up to a sign ambiguity) as a general weak-perspective projection matrix as defined by Eq. (1.22).

This theorem is proven in Faugeras *et al.* (2001, Propositions 4.26 and 4.27) and the problems.

1.3   GEOMETRIC CAMERA CALIBRATION

This section addresses the problem of estimating the intrinsic and extrinsic parameters of a camera from the image positions of scene features such as points of lines, whose positions are known in some fixed world coordinate system (Figure 1.16). In this context, camera calibration can be modeled as an optimization process, where the discrepancy between the observed image features and their theoretical positions is minimized with respect to the camera's intrinsic and extrinsic parameters.

Specifically, we assume that the image positions (x_i, y_i) of n fiducial points P_i $(i = 1, \ldots, n)$ with known homogeneous coordinate vectors $\boldsymbol{P}_i$ have been found

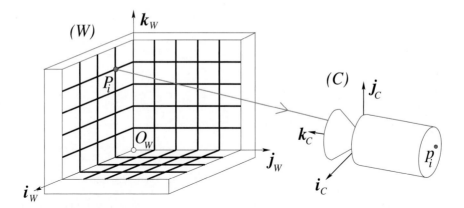

FIGURE 1.16: Camera calibration setup: In this example, the calibration rig is formed by three grids drawn in orthogonal planes. Other patterns could be used as well, and they may involve lines or other geometric figures.

in a picture of a calibration rig, either automatically or by hand. In the absence of modeling and measurement errors, geometric camera calibration amounts to finding the intrinsic and extrinsic parameters $\boldsymbol{\xi}$ such that

$$
\begin{cases}
x_i = \dfrac{\boldsymbol{m}_1(\boldsymbol{\xi}) \cdot \boldsymbol{P}_i}{\boldsymbol{m}_3(\boldsymbol{\xi}) \cdot \boldsymbol{P}_i}, \\[2ex]
y_i = \dfrac{\boldsymbol{m}_2(\boldsymbol{\xi}) \cdot \boldsymbol{P}_i}{\boldsymbol{m}_3(\boldsymbol{\xi}) \cdot \boldsymbol{P}_i},
\end{cases}
\tag{1.23}
$$

where $\boldsymbol{m}_i^T(\boldsymbol{\xi})$ denotes the ith row of the projection matrix $\mathcal{M}$, explicitly parameterized in this equation by the camera parameters. In the typical case where there are more measurements than unknowns (at least six points for 11 intrinsic and extrinsic parameters), Eq. (1.23) does not admit an exact solution, and an approximate one has to be found as the solution of a *least-squares* minimization problem (see Chapter 22). We present two least-squares formulations of the calibration problem in the rest of this section. The corresponding algorithms are illustrated with the calibration data shown in Figure 1.17.

1.3.1 A Linear Approach to Camera Calibration

We decompose the calibration process into (1) the computation of the perspective projection matrix $\mathcal{M}$ associated with the camera, followed by (2) the estimation of the intrinsic and extrinsic parameters of the camera from this matrix.

Estimation of the Projection Matrix. Let us assume that our camera has nonzero skew. According to Theorem 1, the matrix $\mathcal{M}$ is not singular, but otherwise arbitrary. Clearing the denominators in Eq. (1.23) yields two *linear* equations in $\boldsymbol{m}_1$, $\boldsymbol{m}_2$, and $\boldsymbol{m}_3$ (we omit the parameters $\boldsymbol{\xi}$ from now on for the sake of con-

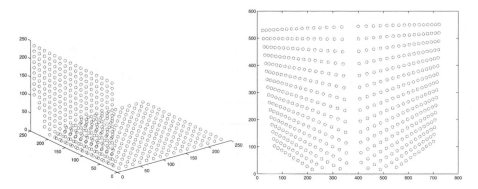

FIGURE 1.17: Camera calibration data. Left: A rendering of 491 3D fiducial points measured on a calibration rig. Right: The corresponding image points. Data courtesy of Janne Heikkilä; data copyright ©2000 University of Oulu.

ciseness), namely

$$\begin{cases} (\boldsymbol{m}_1 - x_i \boldsymbol{m}_3) \cdot \boldsymbol{P}_i &= \boldsymbol{P}_i^T \boldsymbol{m}_1 + \boldsymbol{0}^T \boldsymbol{m}_2 - x_i \boldsymbol{P}_i^T \boldsymbol{m}_3 &= 0, \\ (\boldsymbol{m}_2 - y_i \boldsymbol{m}_3) \cdot \boldsymbol{P}_i &= \boldsymbol{0}^T \boldsymbol{m}_1 + \boldsymbol{P}_i^T \boldsymbol{m}_2 - y_i \boldsymbol{P}_i^T \boldsymbol{m}_3 &= 0. \end{cases}$$

Collecting the constraints associated with all points yields a system of $2n$ homogeneous linear equations in the 12 coefficients of the matrix $\mathcal{M}$, namely,

$$\mathcal{P}\boldsymbol{m} = 0, \tag{1.24}$$

where

$$\mathcal{P} \overset{\text{def}}{=} \begin{pmatrix} \boldsymbol{P}_1^T & \boldsymbol{0}^T & -x_1 \boldsymbol{P}_1^T \\ \boldsymbol{0}^T & \boldsymbol{P}_1^T & -y_1 \boldsymbol{P}_1^T \\ \dots & \dots & \dots \\ \boldsymbol{P}_n^T & \boldsymbol{0}^T & -x_n \boldsymbol{P}_n^T \\ \boldsymbol{0}^T & \boldsymbol{P}_n^T & -y_n \boldsymbol{P}_n^T \end{pmatrix} \quad \text{and} \quad \boldsymbol{m} \overset{\text{def}}{=} \begin{pmatrix} \boldsymbol{m}_1 \\ \boldsymbol{m}_2 \\ \boldsymbol{m}_3 \end{pmatrix} = 0.$$

When $n \geq 6$, homogeneous linear least-squares can be used to compute the value of the unit vector $\boldsymbol{m}$ (hence the matrix $\mathcal{M}$) that minimizes $||\mathcal{P}\boldsymbol{m}||^2$ as the eigenvector of the 12×12 matrix $\mathcal{P}^T \mathcal{P}$ associated with its smallest eigenvalue (see Chapter 22). Note that any nonzero multiple of the vector $\boldsymbol{m}$ would have done just as well, reflecting the fact that $\mathcal{M}$ is defined by only 11 independent parameters.

Degenerate Point Configurations. Before showing how to recover the intrinsic and extrinsic parameters of the camera, let us pause to examine the *degenerate configurations* of the points P_i $(i = 1, \dots, n)$ that may cause the failure of the camera calibration process. We focus on the (ideal) case where the positions $\boldsymbol{p}_i$ $(i = 1, \dots, n)$ of the image points can be measured with zero error, and identify the *nullspace* of the matrix $\mathcal{P}$ (i.e., the subspace of $\mathbb{R}^{12}$ formed by the vectors $\boldsymbol{l}$ such that $\mathcal{P}\boldsymbol{l} = \boldsymbol{0}$).

Let $\boldsymbol{l}$ be such a vector. Introducing the vectors formed by successive quadruples of its coordinates—that is, $\boldsymbol{\lambda} = (l_1, l_2, l_3, l_4)^T$, $\boldsymbol{\mu} = (l_5, l_6, l_7, l_8)^T$, and

$\boldsymbol{\nu} = (l_9, l_{10}, l_{11}, l_{12})^T$—allows us to write

$$
\mathbf{0} = \mathcal{P}l = \begin{pmatrix} \boldsymbol{P}_1^T & \mathbf{0}^T & -x_1\boldsymbol{P}_1^T \\ \mathbf{0}^T & \boldsymbol{P}_1^T & -y_1\boldsymbol{P}_1^T \\ \dots & \dots & \dots \\ \boldsymbol{P}_n^T & \mathbf{0}^T & -x_n\boldsymbol{P}_n^T \\ \mathbf{0}^T & \boldsymbol{P}_n^T & -y_n\boldsymbol{P}_n^T \end{pmatrix} \begin{pmatrix} \boldsymbol{\lambda} \\ \boldsymbol{\mu} \\ \boldsymbol{\nu} \end{pmatrix} = \begin{pmatrix} \boldsymbol{P}_1^T\boldsymbol{\lambda} - x_1\boldsymbol{P}_1^T\boldsymbol{\nu} \\ \boldsymbol{P}_1^T\boldsymbol{\mu} - y_1\boldsymbol{P}_1^T\boldsymbol{\nu} \\ \dots \\ \boldsymbol{P}_n^T\boldsymbol{\lambda} - x_n\boldsymbol{P}_n^T\boldsymbol{\nu} \\ \boldsymbol{P}_n^T\boldsymbol{\mu} - y_n\boldsymbol{P}_n^T\boldsymbol{\nu} \end{pmatrix}. \tag{1.25}
$$

Combining Eq. (1.23) with Eq. (1.25) yields

$$
\begin{cases} \boldsymbol{P}_i^T\boldsymbol{\lambda} - \dfrac{\boldsymbol{m}_1^T\boldsymbol{P}_i}{\boldsymbol{m}_3^T\boldsymbol{P}_i}\boldsymbol{P}_i^T\boldsymbol{\nu} = 0, \\[3mm] \boldsymbol{P}_i^T\boldsymbol{\mu} - \dfrac{\boldsymbol{m}_2^T\boldsymbol{P}_i}{\boldsymbol{m}_3^T\boldsymbol{P}_i}\boldsymbol{P}_i^T\boldsymbol{\nu} = 0, \end{cases} \quad \text{for} \quad i = 1, \dots, n.
$$

Thus, after clearing the denominators and rearranging the terms, we finally obtain:

$$
\begin{cases} \boldsymbol{P}_i^T(\boldsymbol{\lambda}\boldsymbol{m}_3^T - \boldsymbol{m}_1\boldsymbol{\nu}^T)\boldsymbol{P}_i = 0, \\ \boldsymbol{P}_i^T(\boldsymbol{\mu}\boldsymbol{m}_3^T - \boldsymbol{m}_2\boldsymbol{\nu}^T)\boldsymbol{P}_i = 0, \end{cases} \quad \text{for} \quad i = 1, \dots, n. \tag{1.26}
$$

As expected, the vector l associated with $\boldsymbol{\lambda} = \boldsymbol{m}_1$, $\boldsymbol{\mu} = \boldsymbol{m}_2$, and $\boldsymbol{\nu} = \boldsymbol{m}_3$ is a solution of these equations. Are there other solutions?

Let us first consider the case where the points P_i $(i = 1, \dots, n)$ all lie in some plane Π, so $\boldsymbol{P}_i \cdot \boldsymbol{\Pi} = 0$ for some 4-vector $\boldsymbol{\Pi}$. Clearly, choosing $(\boldsymbol{\lambda}, \boldsymbol{\mu}, \boldsymbol{\nu})$ equal to $(\boldsymbol{\Pi}, \mathbf{0}, \mathbf{0})$, $(\mathbf{0}, \boldsymbol{\Pi}, \mathbf{0})$, $(\mathbf{0}, \mathbf{0}, \boldsymbol{\Pi})$, or any linear combination of these vectors will yield a solution of Eq. (1.26). In other words, the nullspace of $\mathcal{P}$ contains the four-dimensional vector space spanned by these vectors and $\boldsymbol{m}$. In practice, this means that the fiducial points P_i should not all lie in the same plane.

In general, for a given nonzero value of the vector l, the points P_i that satisfy Eq. (1.26) must lie on the curve where the two quadric surfaces defined by the corresponding equations intersect. A closer look at Eq. (1.26) reveals that the straight line where the planes defined by $\boldsymbol{m}_3 \cdot \boldsymbol{P} = 0$ and $\boldsymbol{\nu} \cdot \boldsymbol{P} = 0$ intersect lies on both quadrics. It can be shown that the intersection curve of these two surfaces consists of this line and of a *twisted cubic* curve Γ passing through the origin. A twisted cubic is determined entirely by six points lying on it, and it follows that seven points chosen at random will not fall on Γ. In addition, since this curve passes through the origin, choosing $n \geq 6$ random points will in general guarantee that the matrix $\mathcal{P}$ has rank 11 and that the projection matrix can be recovered in a unique fashion.

Estimation of the Intrinsic and Extrinsic Parameters.   Once the projection matrix $\mathcal{M}$ has been estimated, its expression in terms of the camera's intrinsic and extrinsic parameters (Eq. [1.18]) can be used to recover these parameters as follows: We write as before $\mathcal{M} = \begin{pmatrix} \mathcal{A} & \boldsymbol{b} \end{pmatrix}$, with $\boldsymbol{a}_1^T$, $\boldsymbol{a}_2^T$, and $\boldsymbol{a}_3^T$ denoting the rows of $\mathcal{A}$, and obtain

$$
\rho\begin{pmatrix} \mathcal{A} & \boldsymbol{b} \end{pmatrix} = \mathcal{K}\begin{pmatrix} \mathcal{R} & \boldsymbol{t} \end{pmatrix} \Longleftrightarrow \rho\begin{pmatrix} \boldsymbol{a}_1^T \\ \boldsymbol{a}_2^T \\ \boldsymbol{a}_3^T \end{pmatrix} = \begin{pmatrix} \alpha\boldsymbol{r}_1^T - \alpha\cot\theta\,\boldsymbol{r}_2^T + x_0\boldsymbol{r}_3^T \\ \dfrac{\beta}{\sin\theta}\boldsymbol{r}_2^T + y_0\boldsymbol{r}_3^T \\ \boldsymbol{r}_3^T \end{pmatrix},
$$

where ρ is an unknown scale factor, introduced here to account for the fact that the recovered matrix $\mathcal{M}$ has unit Frobenius form since $||\mathcal{M}||_F = ||\boldsymbol{m}|| = 1$.

In particular, using the fact that the rows of a rotation matrix have unit length and are perpendicular to each other yields immediately

$$\begin{cases} \rho = \varepsilon/||\boldsymbol{a}_3||, \\ \boldsymbol{r}_3 = \rho\boldsymbol{a}_3, \\ x_0 = \rho^2(\boldsymbol{a}_1 \cdot \boldsymbol{a}_3), \\ y_0 = \rho^2(\boldsymbol{a}_2 \cdot \boldsymbol{a}_3), \end{cases} \tag{1.27}$$

where $\varepsilon = \mp 1$.

Since θ is always in the neighborhood of $\pi/2$ with a positive sine, we have

$$\begin{cases} \rho^2(\boldsymbol{a}_1 \times \boldsymbol{a}_3) = -\alpha\boldsymbol{r}_2 - \alpha\cot\theta\boldsymbol{r}_1, \\ \rho^2(\boldsymbol{a}_2 \times \boldsymbol{a}_3) = \dfrac{\beta}{\sin\theta}\boldsymbol{r}_1, \end{cases} \quad \text{and} \quad \begin{cases} \rho^2||\boldsymbol{a}_1 \times \boldsymbol{a}_3|| = \dfrac{|\alpha|}{\sin\theta}, \\ \rho^2||\boldsymbol{a}_2 \times \boldsymbol{a}_3|| = \dfrac{|\beta|}{\sin\theta}, \end{cases} \tag{1.28}$$

thus:

$$\begin{cases} \cos\theta = -\dfrac{(\boldsymbol{a}_1 \times \boldsymbol{a}_3) \cdot (\boldsymbol{a}_2 \times \boldsymbol{a}_3)}{||\boldsymbol{a}_1 \times \boldsymbol{a}_3||\,||\boldsymbol{a}_2 \times \boldsymbol{a}_3||}, \\ \alpha = \rho^2||\boldsymbol{a}_1 \times \boldsymbol{a}_3||\sin\theta, \\ \beta = \rho^2||\boldsymbol{a}_2 \times \boldsymbol{a}_3||\sin\theta, \end{cases} \tag{1.29}$$

since the sign of the magnification parameters α and β is normally known in advance and can be taken to be positive.

We can now compute $\boldsymbol{r}_1$ and $\boldsymbol{r}_2$ from the second equation in Eq. (1.28) as

$$\begin{cases} \boldsymbol{r}_1 = \dfrac{\rho^2\sin\theta}{\beta}(\boldsymbol{a}_2 \times \boldsymbol{a}_3) = \dfrac{1}{||\boldsymbol{a}_2 \times \boldsymbol{a}_3||}(\boldsymbol{a}_2 \times \boldsymbol{a}_3), \\ \boldsymbol{r}_2 = \boldsymbol{r}_3 \times \boldsymbol{r}_1. \end{cases} \tag{1.30}$$

Note that there are two possible choices for the matrix $\mathcal{R}$, depending on the value of ε. The translation parameters can now be recovered by writing $\mathcal{K}\boldsymbol{t} = \rho\boldsymbol{b}$, and hence $\boldsymbol{t} = \rho\mathcal{K}^{-1}\boldsymbol{b}$. In practical situations, the sign of t_3 is often known in advance (this corresponds to knowing whether the origin of the world coordinate system is in front of or behind the camera), which allows the choice of a unique solution for the calibration parameters.

Figure 1.18 shows the results of an experiment with the dataset from Figure 1.17. The recovered calibration matrix is

$$\mathcal{K} = \begin{pmatrix} 970.2841 & 0.0986 & 372.0050 \\ 0 & 963.3466 & 299.2921 \\ 0 & 0 & 1 \end{pmatrix}$$

for this 768×576 camera, with estimated values of 1.0072 for the aspect ratio, and 0.0058 degree for the skew angle $|\theta - \pi/2|$.[1] The recovered image center is located about 15 pixels away from the center of the image array.

---

[1] In this book, an $m \times n$ matrix normally has m rows and n columns. Digital images and camera retinas are the only exceptions, and we follow the tradition by assuming that an $m \times n$ picture has m columns and n rows. For example, the camera used in this experiment has 768 columns and 576 rows.

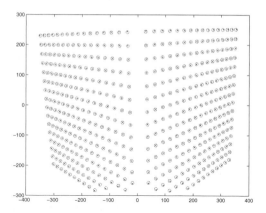

FIGURE 1.18: Results of camera calibration on the dataset shown in Figure 1.17. The original data points (circles) are overlaid with the reprojected 3D points (dots). The root-mean-squared error is 0.96 pixel for this 768×576 image.

1.3.2   A Nonlinear Approach to Camera Calibration

The method presented in the previous section ignores some of the constraints associated with the calibration process. For example, the camera skew was assumed to be arbitrary instead of (very close to) zero in Section 1.3.1. We present in this section a nonlinear approach to camera calibration that takes into account *all* the relevant constraints.

This approach is borrowed from *photogrammetry*, an engineering field whose aim is to recover quantitative geometric information from one or several pictures, with applications in cartography, military intelligence, city planning, etc. For many years, photogrammetry relied on a combination of geometric, optical, and mechanical methods to recover three-dimensional information from pictures, but the advent of computers in the 1950s has made a purely computational approach to this problem feasible. This is the domain of *analytical photogrammetry*, where the intrinsic parameters of a camera define its *interior orientation*, and the extrinsic parameters define its *exterior orientation*.

In this setting, we assume once again that we observe n fiducial points P_i ($i = 1, \ldots, n$) whose positions in some world coordinate system are known, and minimize the mean-squared distance between the measured positions of their images and those predicted by the perspective projection equation with respect to a vector of camera parameters $\boldsymbol{\xi}$ in $\mathbb{R}^{11+q}$, where $q \geq 0$, which might include various distortion coefficients in addition to the usual intrinsic and extrinsic parameters. (This assumes that the aspect-ratio and skew are unknown. When they are known, fewer parameters are necessary.) In particular, let us see how to account for *radial distortion*, a type of aberration that depends on the distance separating the optical axis from the point of interest. We model the projection process by

$$\boldsymbol{p} = \frac{1}{Z} \begin{pmatrix} 1/\lambda & 0 & 0 \\ 0 & 1/\lambda & 0 \\ 0 & 0 & 1 \end{pmatrix} \mathcal{M} \boldsymbol{P}, \qquad (1.31)$$

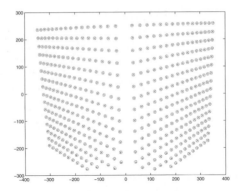

FIGURE 1.19: Results of nonlinear camera calibration on the dataset shown in Figure 1.17. The original data points (circles) are overlaid with the reprojected 3D points (dots). The root-mean-squared error is 0.39 pixel for this 768×576 image. Three radial distortion parameters were used in this case.

where λ is a polynomial function of the squared distance between the image center and the image point p in normalized image coordinates, or:

$$d^2 = \hat{x}^2 + \hat{y}^2 = ||\mathcal{K}^{-1}\boldsymbol{p}||^2 - 1. \tag{1.32}$$

In most applications, it is sufficient to use a low-degree polynomial (e.g., $\lambda = 1 + \sum_{p=1}^{q} \kappa_p d^{2p}$, with $q \le 3$) and the *distortion coefficients* κ_p ($p = 1, \dots, q$) are normally assumed to be small.

Using Eq. (1.32) to write λ as an explicit function of $\boldsymbol{p}$ in Eq. (1.31) yields highly nonlinear constraints on the $11 + q$ camera parameters. The least-squares error can be written as

$$E(\boldsymbol{\xi}) = \sum_{i=1}^{2n} f_i^2(\boldsymbol{\xi}), \text{ where } \begin{cases} f_{2j-1}(\boldsymbol{\xi}) & = x_j - \dfrac{\boldsymbol{m}_1(\boldsymbol{\xi}) \cdot \boldsymbol{P}_j}{\boldsymbol{m}_3(\boldsymbol{\xi}) \cdot \boldsymbol{P}_j}, \\ f_{2j}(\boldsymbol{\xi}) & = y_j - \dfrac{\boldsymbol{m}_2(\boldsymbol{\xi}) \cdot \boldsymbol{P}_j}{\boldsymbol{m}_3(\boldsymbol{\xi}) \cdot \boldsymbol{P}_j}, \end{cases} \text{ for } j = 1, \dots, n.$$

$$\tag{1.33}$$

Contrary to the cases studied so far, the dependency of each error term $f_i(\boldsymbol{\xi})$ on the unknown parameters $\boldsymbol{\xi}$ is not linear. Instead, it involves a combination of polynomial and trigonometric functions, and minimizing the overall error measure involves the use of the nonlinear least-squares algorithms discussed in Chapter 22. These algorithms require computing the Jacobian of the vector function $\boldsymbol{f}(\boldsymbol{\xi}) = (f_1[\boldsymbol{\xi}], \dots, f_{2n}[\boldsymbol{\xi}])^T$ with respect to the vector $\boldsymbol{\xi}$ of unknown parameters, which is easily done analytically (see problems).

Figure 1.19 shows the results of an experiment with the dataset from Figure 1.17 using three radial distortion coefficients. The recovered calibration matrix is

$$\mathcal{K} = \begin{pmatrix} 1014.0 & 0.0001 & 371.8 \\ 0 & 1008.9 & 292.3 \\ 0 & 0 & 1 \end{pmatrix}$$

Perspective projection	$\begin{cases} x = d\dfrac{X}{Z} \\ y = d\dfrac{Y}{Z} \end{cases}$	$X, Y, Z:$ world coordinates $(Z < 0)$ $x, y:$ image coordinates $d:$ pinhole-to-retina distance
Weak-perspective projection	$\begin{cases} x' = -mX \\ y' = -mY \\ m = -\dfrac{d}{Z_0} \end{cases}$	$X, Y:$ world coordinates $x, y:$ image coordinates $d:$ pinhole-to-retina distance $Z_0:$ reference-point depth (< 0) $m:$ magnification (> 0)
Orthographic projection	$\begin{cases} x = X \\ y = Y \end{cases}$	$X, Y:$ world coordinates $x, y:$ image coordinates
Thin lens equation	$\dfrac{1}{z} - \dfrac{1}{Z} = \dfrac{1}{f}$	$Z:$ object-point depth (< 0) $z:$ image-point depth (> 0) $f:$ focal length

TABLE 1.1: Reference card: Projection models.

for this 768×576 camera, with estimated values of 1.0051 for the aspect ratio, and less than 10^{-5} degree for the skew angle. The recovered image center is located about 9 pixels away from the center of the image array. The three radial distortion coefficients are -0.1183, -0.3657, and 1.9112 in this case.

1.4 NOTES

The classical textbook by Hecht (1987) is an excellent introduction to geometric optics, paraxial refraction, thin and thick lenses, and their aberrations, as briefly discussed in Section 1.1. Vignetting is discussed in Horn (1986). Wandell (1995) gives an excellent treatment of image formation in the human visual system. Thorough presentations of the geometric camera models discussed in Section 1.2 can be found in Faugeras (1993), Hartley and Zisserman (2000b), and Faugeras *et al.* (2001). The paraperspective projection model was introduced in computer vision by Ohta, Maenobu, and Sakai (1981), and its properties have been studied by Aloimonos (1990).

The linear calibration technique described in Section 1.3.1 is detailed in Faugeras (1993). Its variant that takes radial distortion into account is adapted from Tsai (1987). The book of Haralick and Shapiro (1992) presents a concise introduction to analytical photogrammetry. The *Manual of Photogrammetry* is of course the gold standard, and newcomers to this field (like the authors of this book) will probably find the ingenious mechanisms and rigorous methods described in the various editions of this book fascinating (Thompson *et al.* 1966; Slama *et al.* 1980). We will come back to photogrammetry in the context of structure from motion in Chapter 8. The linear and nonlinear least-squares techniques used in the approaches to camera calibration discussed in the present chapter are presented in some detail in Chapter 22. An excellent survey and discussion of these methods in the context of analytical photogrammetry can be found in Triggs *et al.* (2000).

We have assumed in this chapter that a 3D calibration rig is available. This is

Perspective projection equation (homogeneous)	$p = \dfrac{1}{Z}\mathcal{M}P$
Matrix of intrinsic parameters	$\mathcal{K} = \begin{pmatrix} \alpha & -\alpha\cot\theta & x_0 \\ 0 & \beta/\sin\theta & y_0 \\ 0 & 0 & 1 \end{pmatrix}$
Perspective projection matrix	$\mathcal{M} = \mathcal{K}\begin{pmatrix} \mathcal{R} & t \end{pmatrix}$
Affine projection equation (nonhomogeneous)	$p = \mathcal{M}\begin{pmatrix} P \\ 1 \end{pmatrix} = \mathcal{A}P + b$
Weak-perspective projection matrix	$\mathcal{M} = \begin{pmatrix} \mathcal{A} & b \end{pmatrix} = \dfrac{1}{Z_r}\begin{pmatrix} k & s \\ 0 & 1 \end{pmatrix}\begin{pmatrix} \mathcal{R}_2 & t_2 \end{pmatrix}$

TABLE 1.2: Reference card: Geometric camera models.

the setting used in (Faig 1975; Tsai 1987; Faugeras 1993; Heikkilä 2000) for example. However, it is difficult to build such a rig accurately—see Lavest, Viala, and Dhome (1998) for a discussion of this problem and an ingenious solution—and many authors prefer using multiple checkerboards or similar planar patterns (Devy, Garric & Orteu 1997; Zhang 2000). This includes the widely used C implementation of J.-Y. Bouguet's algorithm, distributed as part of *OpenCV*, an open-source library of computer vision routines, available at `http://opencv.willowgarage.com/wiki/`. A MATLAB version is also freely available at his web site; see: `http://www.vision.caltech.edu/bouguetj/calib_doc/`.

Given the fundamental importance of the notions introduced in this chapter, the main equations derived in its course have been collected in Tables 1.1 and 1.2 for reference.

PROBLEMS

1.1. Derive the perspective equation projections for a virtual image located at a distance d *in front* of the pinhole.

1.2. Prove geometrically that the projections of two parallel lines lying in some plane Φ appear to converge on a horizon line h formed by the intersection of the image plane Π with the plane parallel to Φ and passing through the pinhole.

1.3. Equation 1.23 gives the expression for the image position (x_i, y_i) of a scene point whose homogeneous coordinates are P_i, assuming this point is viewed by a camera with intrinsic and extrinsic parameters ξ; derive this equation.

1.4. Consider a camera equipped with a thin lens, with its image plane at position z and the plane of scene points in focus at position Z. Now suppose that the image plane is moved to $\hat{z}$. Show that the diameter of the corresponding blur circle is

$$a\frac{|z - \hat{z}|}{z},$$

where a is the lens diameter. Use this result to show that the depth of field (i.e., the distance between the near and far planes that will keep the diameter of the blur circles below some threshold ε) is given by

$$D = 2\varepsilon f Z(Z + f)\frac{a}{f^2 a^2 - \varepsilon^2 Z^2},$$

and conclude that, for a *fixed* focal length, the depth of field increases as the lens diameter decreases, and thus the f number f/a increases.

Hint: Solve for the depth $\hat{Z}$ of a point whose image is focused on the image plane at position $\hat{z}$, considering both the case where $\hat{z}$ is larger than z and the case where it is smaller.

1.5. Why do cameras have lenses?

1.6. Show that equations 1.6 and 1.7 describe the same transformation. What properties must the matrix $\mathcal{R}$ have for this to be a rigid transformation?

1.7. Using equations 1.7 and 1.14, derive equation 1.18.

1.8. Prove the conditions stated in Theorem 1 are necessary, that is, that any perspective projection matrix (respectively, zero skew perspective projection matrix, and zero skew perspective projection matrix with unit aspect-ration) must satisfy these conditions.

1.9. Let O denote the *homogeneous* coordinate vector of the optical center of a camera in some reference frame, and let $\mathcal{M}$ denote the corresponding perspective projection matrix. Show that $\mathcal{M}O = 0$. Explain why this intuitively makes sense.

1.10. Show that the conditions of Theorem 1 are necessary.

1.11. Show that any affine projection matrix $\mathcal{M} = \begin{pmatrix} \mathcal{A} & b \end{pmatrix}$ can be written as a general weak-perspective projection matrix as defined by Eq. (1.22), i.e.,

$$\mathcal{M} = \frac{1}{Z_r}\begin{pmatrix} k & s \\ 0 & 1 \end{pmatrix}\begin{pmatrix} \mathcal{R}_2 & t_2 \end{pmatrix}.$$

1.12. Give an analytical expression for the Jacobian of the vector function $f(\xi) = (f_1[\xi], \ldots, f_{2n}[\xi])^T$ featured in Eq. (1.33) with respect to the vector ξ of unknown parameters.

PROGRAMMING EXERCISES

1.13. Implement the linear calibration algorithm presented in Section 1.3.1.

1.14. Implement the nonlinear calibration algorithm from Section 1.3.2.

CHAPTER 2

Light and Shading

The brightness of a pixel in the image is a function of the brightness of the surface patch in the scene that projects to the pixel. In turn, the brightness of the patch depends on how much incident light arrives at the patch and on the fraction of the incident light that gets reflected (Models in Section 2.1).

This means that the brightness of a pixel is profoundly ambiguous. Surprisingly, people can disentangle these effects quite accurately. Often, but not always, people can tell whether objects are in bright light or in shadow, and do not perceive objects in shadow as having dark surfaces. People can usually tell whether changes of brightness are caused by changes in reflection or by shading (cinemas wouldn't work if we got it right all the time, however). Typically, people can tell that shading comes from the geometry of the object, but sometimes get shading and markings mixed up. For example, a streak of dark makeup under a cheekbone will often look like a shading effect, making the face look thinner. Quite simple models of shading (Section 2.1) support a range of inference procedures (Section 2.2). More complex models are needed to explain some important effects (Section 2.1.4), but make inference very difficult indeed (Section 2.4).

2.1 MODELLING PIXEL BRIGHTNESS

Three major phenomena determine the brightness of a pixel: the response of the camera to light, the fraction of light reflected from the surface to the camera, and the amount of light falling on the surface. Each can be dealt with quite straightforwardly.

Camera response: Modern cameras respond linearly to middling intensities of light, but have pronounced nonlinearities for darker and brighter illumination. This allows the camera to reproduce the very wide dynamic range of natural light without saturating. For most purposes, it is enough to assume that the camera response is linearly related to the intensity of the surface patch. Write $\boldsymbol{X}$ for a point in space that projects to $\boldsymbol{x}$ in the image, $I_{patch}(\boldsymbol{X})$ for the intensity of the surface patch at $\boldsymbol{X}$, and $I_{camera}(\boldsymbol{x})$ for the camera response at $\boldsymbol{x}$. Then our model is:

$$I_{camera}(\boldsymbol{x}) = kI_{patch}(\boldsymbol{x}),$$

where k is some constant to be determined by calibration. Generally, we assume that this model applies and that k is known if needed. Under some circumstances, a more complex model is appropriate; we discuss how to recover such models in Section 2.2.1.

Surface reflection: Different points on a surface may reflect more or less of the light that is arriving. Darker surfaces reflect less light, and lighter surfaces reflect more. There is a rich set of possible physical effects, but most can be ignored. Section 2.1.1 describes the relatively simple model that is sufficient for almost all

FIGURE 2.1: The two most important reflection modes for computer vision are diffuse reflection (**left**), where incident light is spread evenly over the whole hemisphere of outgoing directions, and specular reflection (**right**), where reflected light is concentrated in a single direction. The specular direction S is coplanar with the normal and the source direction (L), and has the same angle to the normal that the source direction does. Most surfaces display both diffuse and specular reflection components. In most cases, the specular component is not precisely mirror like, but is concentrated around a range of directions close to the specular direction (**lower right**). This causes specularities, where one sees a mirror like reflection of the light source. Specularities, when they occur, tend to be small and bright. In the photograph, they appear on the metal spoon and on the plate. Large specularities can appear on flat metal surfaces (arrows). Most curved surfaces (such as the plate) show smaller specularities. Most of the reflection here is diffuse; some cases are indicated by arrows. *Martin Brigdale © Dorling Kindersley, used with permission.*

purposes in computer vision.

Illumination: The amount of light a patch receives depends on the overall intensity of the light, and on the geometry. The overall intensity could change because some *luminaires* (the formal term for light sources) might be shadowed, or might have strong directional components. Geometry affects the amount of light arriving at a patch because surface patches facing the light collect more radiation and so are brighter than surface patches tilted away from the light, an effect known as *shading*. Section 2.1.2 describes the most important model used in computer vision; Section 2.3 describes a much more complex model that is necessary to explain some important practical difficulties in shading inference.

2.1.1   Reflection at Surfaces

Most surfaces reflect light by a process of *diffuse reflection*. Diffuse reflection scatters light evenly across the directions leaving a surface, so the brightness of a diffuse surface doesn't depend on the viewing direction. Examples are easy to identify with this test: most cloth has this property, as do most paints, rough wooden surfaces, most vegetation, and rough stone or concrete. The only parameter required to describe a surface of this type is its *albedo*, the fraction of the light arriving at the surface that is reflected. This does not depend on the direction in which the light arrives or the direction in which the light leaves. Surfaces with very high or very low albedo are difficult to make. For practical surfaces, albedo lies in the range $0.05 - 0.90$ (see Brelstaff and Blake (1988b), who argue the dynamic range is closer to 10 than the 18 implied by these numbers). Mirrors are not diffuse, because what you see depends on the direction in which you look at the mirror. The behavior of a perfect mirror is known as *specular reflection*. For an ideal mirror, light arriving along a particular direction can leave only along the *specular direction*, obtained by reflecting the direction of incoming radiation about the surface normal (Figure 2.1). Usually some fraction of incoming radiation is absorbed; on an ideal specular surface, this fraction does not depend on the incident direction.

If a surface behaves like an ideal specular reflector, you could use it as a mirror, and based on this test, relatively few surfaces actually behave like ideal specular reflectors. Imagine a near perfect mirror made of polished metal; if this surface suffers slight damage at a small scale, then around each point there will be a set of small facets, pointing in a range of directions. In turn, this means that light arriving in one direction will leave in several different directions because it strikes several facets, and so the specular reflections will be blurred. As the surface becomes less flat, these distortions will become more pronounced; eventually, the only specular reflection that is bright enough to see will come from the light source. This mechanism means that, in most shiny paint, plastic, wet, or brushed metal surfaces, one sees a bright blob—often called a *specularity*—along the specular direction from light sources, but few other specular effects. Specularities are easy to identify, because they are small and very bright (Figure 2.1; Brelstaff and Blake (1988b)). Most surfaces reflect only some of the incoming light in a specular component, and we can represent the percentage of light that is specularly reflected with a *specular albedo*. Although the diffuse albedo is an important material property that we will try to estimate from images, the specular albedo is largely seen as a nuisance and usually is not estimated.

2.1.2   Sources and Their Effects

The main source of illumination outdoors is the sun, whose rays all travel parallel to one another in a known direction because it is so far away. We model this behavior with a *distant point light source*. This is the most important model of lighting (because it is like the sun and because it is easy to use), and can be quite effective for indoor scenes as well as outdoor scenes. Because the rays are parallel to one another, a surface that faces the source cuts more rays (and so collects more light) than one oriented along the direction in which the rays travel. The amount of light collected by a surface patch in this model is proportional to the cosine of the angle θ between the illumination direction and the normal (Figure 2.2). The figure yields *Lambert's cosine law*, which states the brightness of a diffuse patch illuminated by a distant point light source is given by

$$I = \rho I_0 \cos \theta,$$

FIGURE 2.2: The orientation of a surface patch with respect to the light affects how much light the patch gathers. We model surface patches as illuminated by a distant point source, whose rays are shown as light arrowheads. Patch A is tilted away from the source (θ is close to 90^0) and collects less energy, because it cuts fewer light rays per unit surface area. Patch B, facing the source (θ is close to 0^0), collects more energy, and so is brighter. Shadows occur when a patch cannot see a source. The shadows are not dead black, because the surface can see interreflected light from other surfaces. These effects are shown in the photograph. The darker surfaces are turned away from the illumination direction. *Martin Brigdale © Dorling Kindersley, used with permission.*

where I_0 is the intensity of the light source, θ is the angle between the light source direction and the surface normal, and ρ is the diffuse albedo. This law predicts that bright image pixels come from surface patches that face the light directly and dark pixels come from patches that see the light only tangentially, so that the shading on a surface provides some shape information. We explore this cue in Section 2.4.

If the surface cannot see the source, then it is in *shadow*. Since we assume that light arrives at our patch only from the distant point light source, our model suggests that shadows are deep black; in practice, they very seldom are, because the shadowed surface usually receives light from other sources. Outdoors, the most important such source is the sky, which is quite bright. Indoors, light reflected from other surfaces illuminates shadowed patches. This means that, for example, we tend to see few shadows in rooms with white walls, because any shadowed patch receives a lot of light from the walls. These *interreflections* also can have a significant effect on the brightness surfaces that are not in shadow. Interreflection effects are sometimes modelled by adding a constant *ambient illumination* term to the predicted intensity. The ambient term ensures that shadows are not too dark, but this is not a particularly successful model of the spatial properties of interreflections. More detailed models require some familiarity with radiometric terminology, but they are important in some applications; we have confined this topic to Section 2.3.

2.1.3   The Lambertian+Specular Model

For almost all purposes, it is enough to model all surfaces as being diffuse with specularities. This is the *lambertian+specular model*. Specularities are relatively seldom used in inference (Section 2.2.2 sketches two methods), and so there is no need for a formal model of their structure. Because specularities are small and bright, they are relatively easy to identify and remove with straightforward methods (find small bright spots, and replace them by smoothing the local pixel values). More sophisticated specularity finders use color information (Section 3.5.1). Thus, to apply the lambertian+specular model, we find and remove specularities, and then use Lambert's law (Section 2.1.2) to model image intensity.

We must choose which source effects to model. In the simplest case, a *local shading model*, we assume that shading is caused only by light that comes from the luminaire (i.e., that there are no interreflections).

Now assume that the luminaire is an infinitely distant source. For this case, write $N(x)$ for the unit surface normal at x, S for a vector pointing from x toward the source with length I_o (the source intensity), $\rho(x)$ for the albedo at x, and $Vis(S, x)$ for a function that is 1 when x can see the source and zero otherwise. Then, the intensity at x is

$$I(x) \quad = \quad \rho(x)\,(N \cdot S)\,\mathrm{Vis}(S,\, x) \quad + \quad \rho(x)A \quad + \qquad M$$

$$\begin{array}{lcl} \text{Image} \\ \text{intensity} \end{array} \; = \; \begin{array}{c} \text{Diffuse} \\ \text{term} \end{array} \; + \; \begin{array}{c} \text{Ambient} \\ \text{term} \end{array} \; + \; \begin{array}{c} \text{Specular (mirror-like)} \\ \text{term} \end{array}$$

This model can still be used for a more complex source (for example, an area source), but in that case it is more difficult to determine an appropriate $S(x)$.

2.1.4   Area Sources

An *area source* is an area that radiates light. Area sources occur quite commonly in natural scenes—an overcast sky is a good example—and in synthetic environments—for example, the fluorescent light boxes found in many industrial ceilings. Area sources are common in illumination engineering, because they tend not to cast strong shadows and because the illumination due to the source does not fall off significantly as a function of the distance to the source. Detailed models of area sources are complex (Section 2.3), but a simple model is useful to understand shadows. Shadows from area sources are very different from shadows cast by point sources. One seldom sees dark shadows with crisp boundaries indoors. Instead, one could see no visible shadows, or shadows that are rather fuzzy diffuse blobs, or sometimes fuzzy blobs with a dark core (Figure 2.3). These effects occur because rooms tend to have light walls and diffuse ceiling fixtures, which act as area sources. As a result, the shadows one sees are area source shadows.

To compute the intensity at a surface patch illuminated by an area source, we can break the source up into infinitesimal source elements, then sum effects from each element. If there is an occluder, then some surface patches may see none of the source elements. Such patches will be dark, and lie in the *umbra* (a Latin word meaning "shadow"). Other surface patches may see some, but not all, of the source elements. Such patches may be quite bright (if they see most of the elements), or

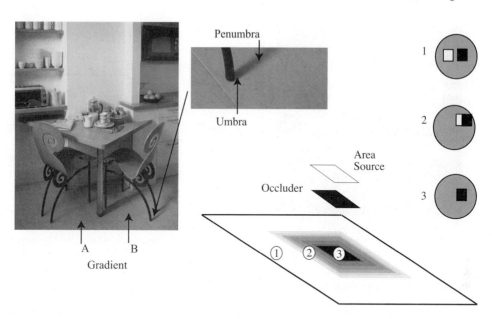

FIGURE 2.3: Area sources generate complex shadows with smooth boundaries, because from the point of view of a surface patch, the source disappears slowly behind the occluder. **Left:** a photograph, showing characteristic area source shadow effects. Notice that A is much darker than B; there must be some shadowing effect here, but there is no clear shadow boundary. Instead, there is a fairly smooth gradient. The chair leg casts a complex shadow, with two distinct regions. There is a core of darkness (the *umbra*— where the source cannot be seen at all) surrounded by a partial shadow (*penumbra*— where the source can be seen partially). A good model of the geometry, illustrated **right**, is to imagine lying with your back to the surface looking at the world above. At point 1, you can see all of the source; at point 2, you can see some of it; and at point 3, you can see none of it. *Peter Anderson © Dorling Kindersley, used with permission.*

relatively dark (if they see few elements), and lie in the *penumbra* (a compound of Latin words meaning "almost shadow"). One way to build intuition is to think of a tiny observer looking up from the surface patch. At umbral points, this observer will not see the area source at all whereas at penumbral points, the observer will see some, but not all, of the area source. An observer moving from outside the shadow, through the penumbra and into the umbra will see something that looks like an eclipse of the moon (Figure 2.3). The penumbra can be large, and can change quite slowly from light to dark. There might even be no umbral points at all, and, if the occluder is sufficiently far away from the surface, the penumbra could be very large and almost indistinguishable in brightness from the unshadowed patches. This is why many objects in rooms appear to cast no shadow at all (Figure 2.4).

2.2 INFERENCE FROM SHADING

Shading can be used to infer a variety of properties of the visual world. Successful inference often requires that we calibrated the camera radiometrically, so that we know how pixel values map to radiometric values (Section 2.2.1). As Figure 2.1

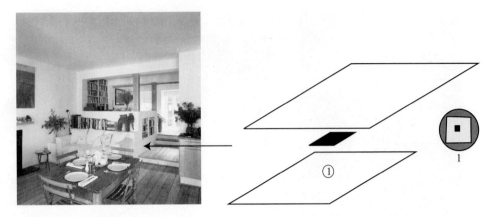

FIGURE 2.4: The photograph on the **left** shows a room interior. Notice the lighting has some directional component (the vertical face indicated by the arrow is dark, because it does not face the main direction of lighting), but there are few visible shadows (for example, the chairs do not cast a shadow on the floor). On the **right**, a drawing to show why; here there is a small occluder and a large area source. The occluder is some way away from the shaded surface. Generally, at points on the shaded surface the incoming hemisphere looks like that at point 1. The occluder blocks out some small percentage of the area source, but the amount of light lost is too small to notice (compare figure 2.3). *Jake Fitzjones © Dorling Kindersley, used with permission.*

suggests, specularities are a source of information about the shape of a surface, and Section 2.2.2 shows how this information can be interpreted. Section 2.2.3 shows how to recover the albedoes of surfaces from images. Finally, Section 2.2.4 shows how multiple shaded images can be used to recover surface shape.

2.2.1 Radiometric Calibration and High Dynamic Range Images

Real scenes often display a much larger range of intensities than cameras can cope with. Film and charge-coupled devices respond to energy. A property called *reciprocity* means that, if a scene patch casts intensity E onto the film, and if the shutter is open for time Δt, the response is a function of $E\Delta t$ alone. In particular, we will get the same outcome if we image one patch of intensity E for time Δt and another patch of intensity E/k for time $k\Delta t$. The actual response that the film produces is a function of $E\Delta t$; this function might depend on the imaging system, but is typically somewhat linear over some range, and sharply non-linear near the top and bottom of this range, so that the image can capture very dark and very light patches without saturation. It is usually monotonically increasing.

There are a variety of applications where it would be useful to know the actual radiance (equivalently, the intensity) arriving at the imaging device. For example, we might want to compare renderings of a scene with pictures of the scene, and to do that we need to work in real radiometric units. We might want to use pictures of a scene to estimate the lighting in that scene so we can postrender new objects into the scene, which would need to be lit correctly. To infer radiance, we must determine the film response, a procedure known as *radiometric calibration*. As we shall see, doing this will require more than one image of a scene, each obtained at different exposure settings. Imagine we are looking at a scene of a stained glass window lit from behind in a church. At one exposure setting, we would be able to resolve detail in the dark corners, but not on the stained glass, which would be saturated. At another setting, we would be able to resolve detail on the glass, but the interior would be too dark. If we have both settings, we may as well try to recover radiance with a very large dynamic range—producing a *high dynamic range image*.

Now assume we have multiple registered images, each obtained using a different exposure time. At the i, j'th pixel, we know the image intensity value $I_{ij}^{(k)}$ for the k'th exposure time, we know the value of the k'th exposure time Δt_k, and we know that the intensity of the corresponding surface patch E_{ij} is the same for each exposure, but we do not know the value of E_{ij}. Write the camera response function f, so that

$$I_{ij}^{(k)} = f(E_{ij}\Delta t_k).$$

There are now several possible approaches to solve for f. We could assume a parametric form—say, polynomial—then solve using least squares. Notice that we must solve not only for the parameters of f, but also for E_{ij}. For a color camera, we solve for calibration of each channel separately. Mitsunaga and Nayar (1999) have studied the polynomial case in detail. Though the solution is not unique, ambiguous solutions are strongly different from one another, and most cases are easily ruled out. Furthermore, one does not need to know exposure times with exact accuracy to estimate a solution, as long as there are sufficient pixel values; instead, one estimates f from a fixed set of exposure times, then estimates the exposure times from f, and then re-estimates. This procedure is stable.

Alternatively, because the camera response is monotonic, we can work with its inverse $g = f^{-1}$, take logs, and write

$$\log g(I_{ij}^{(k)}) = \log E_{ij} + \log \Delta t_k.$$

We can now estimate the values that g takes at each point and the E_{ij} by placing a smoothness penalty on g. In particular, we minimize

$$\sum_{i,j,k} (\log g(I_{ij}^{(k)}) - (\log E_{ij} + \log \Delta t_k))^2 + \text{smoothness penalty on } g$$

by choice of g. Debevec and Malik (1997) penalize the second derivative of g. Once we have a radiometrically calibrated camera, estimating a high dynamic range image is relatively straightforward. We have a set of registered images, and at each pixel location, we seek the estimate of radiance that predicts the registered image values best. In particular, we assume we know f. We seek an E_{ij} such that

$$\sum_k w(I_{ij})(I_{ij}^{(k)} - f(E_{ij}\Delta t_k))^2$$

is minimized. Notice the weights because our estimate of f is more reliable when I_{ij} is in the middle of the available range of values than when it is at larger or smaller values.

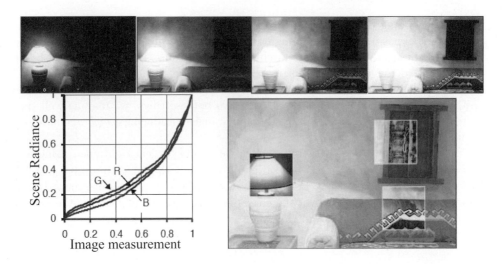

FIGURE 2.5: It is possible to calibrate the radiometric response of a camera from multiple images obtained at different exposures. The **top** row shows four different exposures of the same scene, ranging from darker (shorter shutter time) to lighter (longer shutter time). Note how, in the dark frames, the lighter part of the image shows detail, and in the light frames, the darker part of the image shows detail; this is the result of non-linearities in the camera response. On the **bottom left**, we show the inferred calibration curves for each of the R, G, and B camera channels. On the **bottom right**, a composite image illustrates the results. The dynamic range of this image is far too large to print; instead, the main image is normalized to the print range. Overlaid on this image are boxes where the radiances in the box have also been normalized to the print range; these show how much information is packed into the high dynamic range image. *This figure was originally published as Figure 7 of "Radiometric Self Calibration," by T. Mitsunaga and S. Nayar, Proc. IEEE CVPR 1999, © IEEE, 1999.*

2.2.2   The Shape of Specularities

Specularities are informative. They offer hints about the color of illumination (see Chapter 3) and offer cues to the local geometry of a surface. Understanding these cues is a useful exercise in differential geometry. We consider a smooth specular surface and assume that the brightness reflected in the direction V is a function of $V \cdot P$, where P is the specular direction. We expect the specularity to be small and isolated, so we can assume that the source direction S and the viewing direction V are constant over its extent. Let us further assume that the specularity can be defined by a threshold on the specular energy, i.e., $V \cdot P \geq 1 - \varepsilon$ for some constant ε, denote by N the unit surface normal, and define the *half-angle direction* as $H = (S + V)/2$ (Figure 2.6(left)). Using the fact that the vectors S, V and P have unit length and a whit of plane geometry, it can easily be shown that the boundary of the specularity is defined by (see exercises)

$$1 - \varepsilon = V \cdot P = 2\frac{(H \cdot N)^2}{(H \cdot H)} - 1. \tag{2.1}$$

Because the specularity is small, the second-order structure of the surface

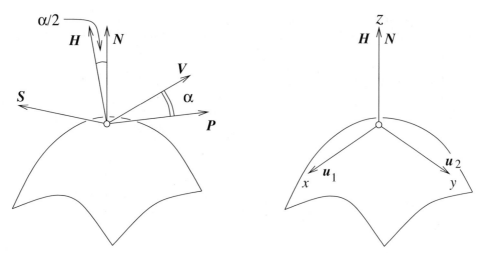

FIGURE 2.6: A specular surface viewed by a distant observer. We establish a coordinate system at the brightest point of the specularity (where the half-angle direction is equal to the normal) and orient the system using the normal and principal directions.

will allow us to characterize the shape of its boundary as follows: there is some point on the surface inside the specularity (in fact, the brightest point) where $\boldsymbol{H}$ is parallel to $\boldsymbol{N}$. We set up a coordinate system at this point, oriented so that the z-axis lies along $\boldsymbol{N}$ and the x- and y-axes lie along the principal directions $\boldsymbol{u}_1$ and $\boldsymbol{u}_2$ (Figure 2.6(right)). As noted earlier, the surface can be represented up to second order as $z = -1/2(\kappa_1 x^2 + \kappa_2 y^2)$ in this frame, where κ_1 and κ_2 are the principal curvatures. Now, let us define a *parametric surface* as a differentiable mapping $\boldsymbol{x} : U \subset \mathbb{R}^2 \to \mathbb{R}^3$ associating with any couple $(u, v) \in U$ the coordinate vector $(x, y, z)^T$ of a point in some fixed coordinate system. It is easily shown (see exercises) that the normal to a parametric surface is along the vector $\frac{\partial}{\partial u}\boldsymbol{x} \times \frac{\partial}{\partial v}\boldsymbol{x}$. Our second-order surface model is a parametric surface parameterized by x and y, thus its unit surface normal is defined in the corresponding frame by

$$\boldsymbol{N}(x, y) = \frac{1}{\sqrt{1 + \kappa_1^2 x^2 + \kappa_2^2 y^2}} \begin{pmatrix} \kappa_1 x \\ \kappa_2 y \\ 1 \end{pmatrix},$$

and $\boldsymbol{H} = (0, 0, 1)^T$. Because $\boldsymbol{H}$ is a constant, we can rewrite Eq. (2.1) as $\kappa_1^2 x^2 + \kappa_2^2 y^2 = \zeta$, where ζ is a constant depending on ε. In particular, the shape of the specularity on the surface contains information about the second fundamental form. The specularity will be an ellipse, with major and minor axes oriented along the principal directions, and an eccentricity equal to the ratio of the principal curvatures. Unfortunately, the shape of the specularity on the surface is not, in general, directly observable, so this property can be exploited only when a fair amount about the viewing and illumination setup is known (Healey and Binford 1986).

Although we cannot get much out of the shape of the specularity in the image, it is possible to tell a convex surface from a concave one by watching how a specularity moves as the view changes (you can convince yourself of this with the aid of a spoon).[1] Let us consider a point source at infinity and assume that the specular lobe is very narrow, so the viewing direction and the specular direction coincide. Initially, the specular direction is $\mathbf{V}$, and the specularity is at the surface point P; after a small eye motion, $\mathbf{V}$ changes to $\mathbf{V'}$, while the specularity moves to the close-by point P' (Figure 2.7).

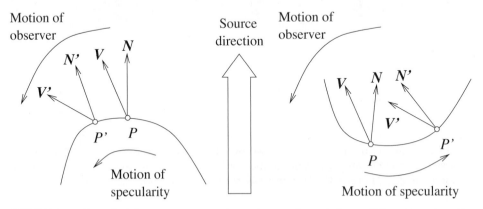

FIGURE 2.7: Specularities on convex and concave surfaces behave differently when the view changes. With an appropriate choice of source direction and motion, this could be used to obtain the signs of the principal curvatures.

The quantity of interest is $\delta a = (\mathbf{V'} - \mathbf{V}) \cdot \mathbf{t}$, where $\mathbf{t} = \frac{1}{\delta s}\overrightarrow{PP'}$ is tangent to the surface, and δs is the (small) distance between P and P': if δa is positive, then the specularity moves in the direction of the view (back of the spoon), and if it is negative, the specularity moves against the direction of the view (bowl of the spoon). By construction, we have $\mathbf{V} = 2(\mathbf{S} \cdot \mathbf{N})\mathbf{N} - \mathbf{S}$, and

$$
\begin{aligned}
\mathbf{V'} &= 2(\mathbf{S} \cdot \mathbf{N'})\mathbf{N'} - \mathbf{S} = 2(\mathbf{S} \cdot (\mathbf{N} + \delta\mathbf{N}))(\mathbf{N} + \delta\mathbf{N}) - \mathbf{S} \\
&= \mathbf{V} + 2(\mathbf{S} \cdot \delta\mathbf{N})\mathbf{N} + 2(\mathbf{S} \cdot \mathbf{N})\delta\mathbf{N} + 2(\mathbf{S} \cdot \delta\mathbf{N})\delta\mathbf{N},
\end{aligned}
$$

where $\delta\mathbf{N} \stackrel{\text{def}}{=} \mathbf{N'} - \mathbf{N} = \delta s\, d\mathbf{N}(\mathbf{t})$. Because $\mathbf{t}$ is tangent to the surface in P, ignoring second-order terms yields

$$
\delta a = (\mathbf{V} - \mathbf{V'}) \cdot \mathbf{t} = 2(\mathbf{S} \cdot \mathbf{N})(\delta\mathbf{N} \cdot \mathbf{t}) = 2(\mathbf{S} \cdot \mathbf{N})(\delta s)(\mathrm{II}(\mathbf{t}, \mathbf{t})).
$$

Thus, for a concave surface, the specularity always moves against the view, and for a convex surface, it always moves with the view. Things are more complex with hyperbolic surfaces; the specularity may move with the view, against the view, or perpendicular to the view (when $\mathbf{t}$ is an asymptotic direction).

---

[1] Of course, there is a simpler way to distinguish (by sight) the concave bowl of a spoon from its convex back: it is just the side where your reflection is upside down. This property of concave mirrors was demonstrated to one of the authors by one of his friends at a dinner party, causing much consternation since the author in question was at the time bragging about differential geometry, and his friend, who does not pretend to know anything about mathematics, just looked at herself in the spoon.

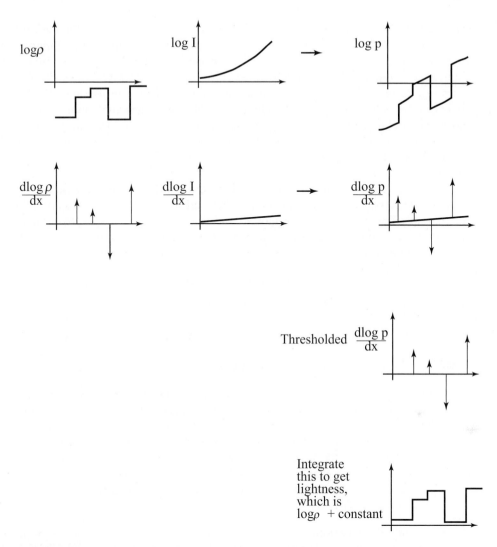

FIGURE 2.8: The lightness algorithm is easiest to illustrate for a 1D image. In the **top row**, the graph on the **left** shows $\log \rho(x)$, that in the **center** $\log I(x)$, and that on the **right** their sum, which is $\log C$. The log of image intensity has large derivatives at changes in surface reflectance and small derivatives when the only change is due to illumination gradients. Lightness is recovered by differentiating the log intensity, thresholding to dispose of small derivatives, and integrating at the cost of a missing constant of integration.

2.2.3   Inferring Lightness and Illumination

If we could estimate the albedo of a surface from an image, then we would know a property of the surface itself, rather than a property of a picture of the surface. Such properties are often called *intrinsic representations*. They are worth estimating, because they do not change when the imaging circumstances change. It might seem that albedo is difficult to estimate, because there is an ambiguity linking albedo and illumination; for example, a high albedo viewed under middling illumination will give the same brightness as a low albedo viewed under bright light. However, humans can report whether a surface is white, gray, or black (the *lightness* of the surface), despite changes in the intensity of illumination (the *brightness*). This skill is known as *lightness constancy*. There is a lot of evidence that human lightness constancy involves two processes: one process compares the brightness of various image patches and uses this comparison to determine which patches are lighter and which darker; the second establishes some form of absolute standard to which these comparisons can be referred (e.g. Gilchrist *et al.* (1999)).

Current lightness algorithms were developed in the context of simple scenes. In particular, we assume that the scene is flat and frontal; that surfaces are diffuse, or that specularities have been removed; and that the camera responds linearly. In this case, the camera response C at a point x is the product of an illumination term, an albedo term, and a constant that comes from the camera gain:

$$C(\boldsymbol{x}) = k_c I(\boldsymbol{x}) \rho(\boldsymbol{x}).$$

If we take logarithms, we get

$$\log C(\boldsymbol{x}) = \log k_c + \log I(\boldsymbol{x}) + \log \rho(\boldsymbol{x}).$$

We now make a second set of assumptions:

- First, we assume that albedoes change only quickly over space. This means that a typical set of albedoes will look like a collage of papers of different grays. This assumption is quite easily justified: There are relatively few continuous changes of albedo in the world (the best example occurs in ripening fruit), and changes of albedo often occur when one object occludes another (so we would expect the change to be fast). This means that spatial derivatives of the term $\log \rho(\boldsymbol{x})$ are either zero (where the albedo is constant) or large (at a change of albedo).

- Second, illumination changes only slowly over space. This assumption is somewhat realistic. For example, the illumination due to a point source will change relatively slowly unless the source is very close, so the sun is a particularly good source for this method, as long as there are no shadows. As another example, illumination inside rooms tends to change very slowly because the white walls of the room act as area sources. This assumption fails dramatically at shadow boundaries, however. We have to see these as a special case and assume that either there are no shadow boundaries or that we know where they are.

We can now build algorithms that use our model. The earliest algorithm is the Retinex algorithm of Land and McCann (1971); this took several forms, most of which have fallen into disuse. The key insight of Retinex is that small gradients are changes in illumination, and large gradients are changes in lightness. We can use this by differentiating the log transform, throwing away small gradients, and integrating the results (Horn 1974); these days, this procedure is widely known as

Retinex. There is a constant of integration missing, so lightness ratios are available, but absolute lightness measurements are not. Figure 2.8 illustrates the process for a one-dimensional example, where differentiation and integration are easy.

This approach can be extended to two dimensions as well. Differentiating and thresholding is easy: at each point, we estimate the magnitude of the gradient; if the magnitude is less than some threshold, we set the gradient vector to zero; otherwise, we leave it alone. The difficulty is in integrating these gradients to get the log albedo map. The thresholded gradients may not be the gradients of an image because the mixed second partials may not be equal (integrability again; compare with Section 2.2.4).

Form the gradient of the log of the image
At each pixel, if the gradient magnitude is below
  a threshold, replace that gradient with zero
Reconstruct the log-albedo by solving the minimization
  problem described in the text
Obtain a constant of integration
Add the constant to the log-albedo, and exponentiate

Algorithm 2.1: Determining the Lightness of Image Patches.

The problem can be rephrased as a minimization problem: choose the log albedo map whose gradient is most like the thresholded gradient. This is a relatively simple problem because computing the gradient of an image is a linear operation. The x-component of the thresholded gradient is scanned into a vector $\boldsymbol{p}$, and the y-component is scanned into a vector $\boldsymbol{q}$. We write the vector representing log-albedo as $\boldsymbol{l}$. Now the process of forming the x derivative is linear, and so there is some matrix $\mathcal{M}_x$, such that $\mathcal{M}_x\boldsymbol{l}$ is the x derivative; for the y derivative, we write the corresponding matrix $\mathcal{M}_y$.

The problem becomes finding the vector $\boldsymbol{l}$ that minimizes

$$| \mathcal{M}_x\boldsymbol{l} - \boldsymbol{p} |^2 + | \mathcal{M}_y\boldsymbol{l} - \boldsymbol{q} |^2 \, .$$

This is a quadratic minimization problem, and the answer can be found by a linear process. Some special tricks are required because adding a constant vector to $\boldsymbol{l}$ cannot change the derivatives, so the problem does not have a unique solution. We explore the minimization problem in the exercises.

The constant of integration needs to be obtained from some other assumption. There are two obvious possibilities:

- we can assume that the *brightest patch is white*;

- we can assume that the *average lightness is constant*.

We explore the consequences of these models in the exercises.

More sophisticated algorithms are now available, but there were no quantitative studies of performance until recently. Grosse *et al.* built a dataset for

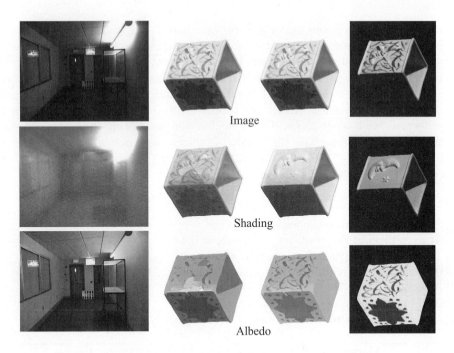

FIGURE 2.9: Retinex remains a strong algorithm for recovering albedo from images. Here we show results from the version of Retinex described in the text applied to an image of a room (**left**) and an image from a collection of test images due to Grosse *et al.* (2009). The **center-left** column shows results from Retinex for this image, and the **center-right** column shows results from a variant of the algorithm that uses color reasoning to improve the classification of edges into albedo versus shading. Finally, the **right** column shows the correct answer, known by clever experimental methods used when taking the pictures. This problem is very hard; you can see that the albedo images still contain some illumination signal. *Part of this figure courtesy Kevin Karsch, U. Illinois. Part of this figure was originally published as Figure 3 of "Ground truth dataset and baseline evaluations for intrinsic image algorithms," by R. Grosse, M. Johnson, E. Adelson, and W. Freeman, Proc. IEEE ICCV 2009, © IEEE, 2009.*

evaluating lightness algorithms, and show that a version of the procedure we describe performs extremely well compared to more sophisticated algorithms (2009). The major difficulty with all these approaches is caused by shadow boundaries, which we discuss in Section 3.5.2.

2.2.4 Photometric Stereo: Shape from Multiple Shaded Images

It is possible to reconstruct a patch of surface from a series of pictures of that surface taken under different illuminants. First, we need a camera model. For simplicity, we choose a camera situated so that the point (x, y, z) in space is imaged to the point (x, y) in the camera (the method we describe works for the other camera models described in Chapter 1).

In this case, to measure the shape of the surface, we need to obtain the depth to the surface. This suggests representing the surface as $(x, y, f(x, y))$—a representation known as a *Monge patch* after the French military engineer who first used it (Figure 2.10). This representation is attractive because we can determine a unique point on the surface by giving the image coordinates. Notice that to obtain a measurement of a solid object, we would need to reconstruct more than one patch because we need to observe the back of the object.

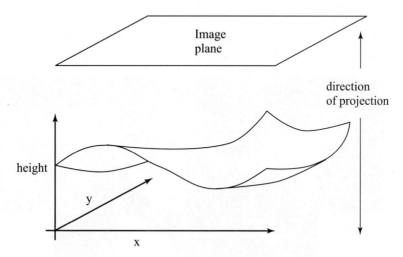

FIGURE 2.10: A Monge patch is a representation of a piece of surface as a height function. For the photometric stereo example, we assume that an orthographic camera—one that maps (x, y, z) in space to (x, y) in the camera—is viewing a Monge patch. This means that the shape of the surface can be represented as a function of position in the image.

Photometric stereo is a method for recovering a representation of the Monge patch from image data. The method involves reasoning about the image intensity values for several different images of a surface in a fixed view illuminated by different sources. This method recovers the height of the surface at points corresponding to each pixel; in computer vision circles, the resulting representation is often known as a *height map, depth map*, or *dense depth map*.

Fix the camera and the surface in position, and illuminate the surface using a point source that is far away compared with the size of the surface. We adopt a local shading model and assume that there is no ambient illumination (more about this later) so that the brightness at a point $\boldsymbol{x}$ on the surface is

$$B(\boldsymbol{x}) = \rho(\boldsymbol{x})\boldsymbol{N}(\boldsymbol{x}) \cdot \boldsymbol{S}_1,$$

where $\boldsymbol{N}$ is the unit surface normal and $\boldsymbol{S}_1$ is the source vector. We can write $B(x, y)$ for the radiosity of a point on the surface because there is only one point on the surface corresponding to the point (x, y) in the camera. Now we assume that the response of the camera is linear in the surface radiosity, and so have that the value of a pixel at (x, y) is

$$\begin{aligned}
I(x, y) &= kB(\boldsymbol{x}) \\
&= kB(x, y) \\
&= k\rho(x, y)\boldsymbol{N}(x, y) \cdot \boldsymbol{S}_1 \\
&= \boldsymbol{g}(x, y) \cdot \boldsymbol{V}_1,
\end{aligned}$$

where $\boldsymbol{g}(x, y) = \rho(x, y)\boldsymbol{N}(x, y)$ and $\boldsymbol{V}_1 = k\boldsymbol{S}_1$, where k is the constant connecting the camera response to the input radiance.

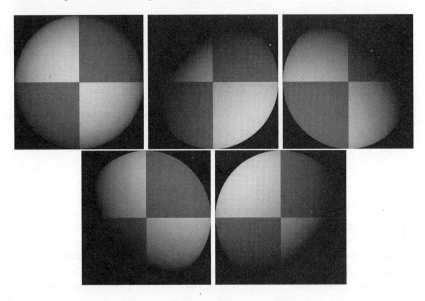

FIGURE 2.11: Five synthetic images of a sphere, all obtained in an orthographic view from the same viewing position. These images are shaded using a local shading model and a distant point source. This is a convex object, so the only view where there is no visible shadow occurs when the source direction is parallel to the viewing direction. The variations in brightness occuring under different sources code the shape of the surface.

In these equations, $\boldsymbol{g}(x, y)$ describes the surface, and $\boldsymbol{V}_1$ is a property of the illumination and of the camera. We have a dot product between a vector field $\boldsymbol{g}(x, y)$ and a vector $\boldsymbol{V}_1$, which could be measured; with enough of these dot products, we could reconstruct $\boldsymbol{g}$ and so the surface.

Now if we have n sources, for each of which $\boldsymbol{V}_i$ is known, we stack each of these $\boldsymbol{V}_i$ into a known matrix $\mathcal{V}$, where

$$\mathcal{V} = \begin{pmatrix} \boldsymbol{V}_1^T \\ \boldsymbol{V}_2^T \\ \ldots \\ \boldsymbol{V}_n^T \end{pmatrix}.$$

For each image point, we stack the measurements into a vector

$$\boldsymbol{i}(x, y) = \{I_1(x, y), I_2(x, y), \ldots, I_n(x, y)\}^T.$$

Notice that we have one vector per image point; each vector contains all the image brightnesses observed at that point for different sources. Now we have

$$i(x, y) = \mathcal{V}g(x, y),$$

and g is obtained by solving this linear system—or rather, one linear system per point in the image. Typically, $n > 3$, so that a least-squares solution is appropriate. This has the advantage that the residual error in the solution provides a check on our measurements.

Substantial regions of the surface might be in shadow for one or the other light (see Figure 2.11). We assume that all shadowed regions are known, and deal only with points that are not in shadow for any illuminant. More sophisticated strategies can infer shadowing because shadowed points are darker than the local geometry predicts.

We can extract the albedo from a measurement of g because N is the unit normal. This means that $|g(x, y)| = \rho(x, y)$. This provides a check on our measurements as well. Because the albedo is in the range zero to one, any pixels where $|g|$ is greater than one are suspect—either the pixel is not working or $\mathcal{V}$ is incorrect. Figure 2.12 shows albedo recovered using this method for the images shown in Figure 2.11.

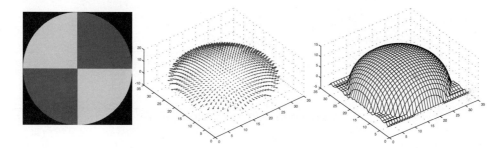

FIGURE 2.12: The image on the **left** shows the magnitude of the vector field $g(x, y)$ recovered from the input data of Figure 2.11 represented as an image—this is the reflectance of the surface. The **center** figure shows the normal field, and the **right** figure shows the height field.

We can extract the surface normal from g because the normal is a unit vector

$$N(x, y) = \frac{g(x, y)}{|g(x, y)|}.$$

Figure 2.12 shows normal values recovered for the images of Figure 2.11.

The surface is $(x, y, f(x, y))$, so the normal as a function of (x, y) is

$$N(x, y) = \frac{1}{\sqrt{1 + \frac{\partial f}{\partial x}^2 + \frac{\partial f}{\partial y}^2}} \left\{ \frac{\partial f}{\partial x}, \frac{\partial f}{\partial y}, 1 \right\}^T.$$

To recover the depth map, we need to determine $f(x, y)$ from measured values of the unit normal.

Obtain many images in a fixed view under different illuminants
Determine the matrix $\mathcal{V}$ from source and camera information

Inferring albedo and normal:
For each point in the image array that is not shadowed
    Stack image values into a vector $\boldsymbol{i}$
    Solve $\mathcal{V}\boldsymbol{g} = \boldsymbol{i}$ to obtain $\boldsymbol{g}$ for this point
    Albedo at this point is $|\boldsymbol{g}|$
    Normal at this point is $\frac{\boldsymbol{g}}{|\boldsymbol{g}|}$
    p at this point is $\frac{N_1}{N_3}$
    q at this point is $\frac{N_2}{N_3}$
end
Check: is $(\frac{\partial p}{\partial y} - \frac{\partial q}{\partial x})^2$ small everywhere?

Integration:
Top left corner of height map is zero
For each pixel in the left column of height map
    height value = previous height value + corresponding q value
end
For each row
    For each element of the row except for leftmost
        height value = previous height value + corresponding p value
    end
end

Algorithm 2.2: Photometric Stereo.

Assume that the measured value of the unit normal at some point (x, y) is $(a(x, y), b(x, y), c(x, y))$. Then

$$\frac{\partial f}{\partial x} = \frac{a(x, y)}{c(x, y)} \text{ and } \frac{\partial f}{\partial y} = \frac{b(x, y)}{c(x, y)}.$$

We have another check on our data set, because

$$\frac{\partial^2 f}{\partial x \partial y} = \frac{\partial^2 f}{\partial y \partial x},$$

so we expect that

$$\frac{\partial \left(\frac{a(x,y)}{c(x,y)} \right)}{\partial y} - \frac{\partial \left(\frac{b(x,y)}{c(x,y)} \right)}{\partial x}$$

should be small at each point. In principle it should be zero, but we would have to estimate these partial derivatives numerically and so should be willing to accept small values. This test is known as a test of *integrability*, which in vision applications always boils down to checking that mixed second partials are equal.

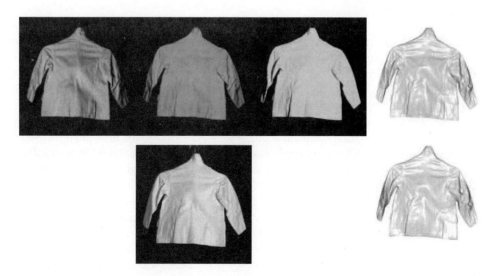

FIGURE 2.13: Photometric stereo could become the method of choice to capture complex deformable surfaces. On the **top**, three images of a garment, lit from different directions, which produce the reconstruction shown on the **top right**. A natural way to obtain three different images at the same time is to use a color camera; if one has a red light, a green light, and a blue light, then a single color image frame can be treated as three images under three separate lights. On the **bottom**, an image of the garment captured in this way, which results in the photometric stereo reconstruction on the **bottom right**. *This figure was originally published as Figure 6 of "Video Normals from Colored Lights," G. J. Brostow, C. Hernández, G. Vogiatzis, B. Stenger, and R. Cipolla, IEEE Transactions on Pattern Analysis and Machine Intelligence, 2011 © IEEE, 2011.*

Assuming that the partial derivatives pass this sanity test, we can reconstruct the surface up to some constant depth error. The partial derivative gives the change in surface height with a small step in either the x or the y direction. This means we can get the surface by summing these changes in height along some path. In particular, we have

$$f(x, y) = \oint_C \left(\frac{\partial f}{\partial x}, \frac{\partial f}{\partial y} \right) \cdot d\boldsymbol{l} + c,$$

where C is a curve starting at some fixed point and ending at (x, y), and c is a constant of integration, which represents the (unknown) height of the surface at the start point. The recovered surface does not depend on the choice of curve (exercises). Another approach to recovering shape is to choose the function $f(x, y)$ whose partial derivatives most look like the measured partial derivatives. Figure 2.12 shows the reconstruction obtained for the data shown in Figure 2.11.

Current reconstruction work tends to emphasize geometric methods that reconstruct from multiple views. These methods are very important, but often require feature matching, as we shall see in Chapters 7 and 8. This tends to mean that it is hard to get very high spatial resolution, because some pixels are consumed in resolving features. Recall that resolution (which corresponds roughly to the spatial frequencies that can be reconstructed accurately) is not the same as accuracy (which involves a method providing the right answers for the properties it estimates). Feature-based methods are capable of spectacularly accurate reconstructions. Because photometric cues have such spatial high resolution, they are a topic of considerable current interest. One way to use photometric cues is to try and match pixels with the same brightness across different cameras; this is difficult, but produces impressive reconstructions. Another is to use photometric stereo ideas. For some applications, photometric stereo is particularly atractive because one can get reconstructions from a single view direction—this is important, because we cannot always set up multiple cameras. In fact, with a trick, it is possible to get reconstructions from a single frame. A natural way to obtain three different images at the same time is to use a color camera; if one has a red light, a green light and a blue light, then a single color image frame can be treated as three images under three separate lights, and photometric stereo methods apply. In turn, this means that photometric stereo methods could be used to recover high-resolution reconstructions of deforming surfaces in a relatively straightforward way. This is particularly useful when it is difficult to get many cameras to view the object. Figure 2.13 shows one application to reconstructing cloth in video (from Brostow *et al.* (2011)), where multiple view reconstruction is complicated by the need to synchronize frames (alternatives are explored in, for example, White *et al.* (2007) or Bradley *et al.* (2008*b*)).

2.3   MODELLING INTERREFLECTION

The difficulty with a local shading model is that it doesn't account for all light. The alternative is a *global shading model*, where we account for light arriving from other surfaces as well as from the luminaire. As we shall see, such models are tricky to work with. In such models, each surface patch receives power from all the radiating surfaces it can see. These surfaces might radiate power that they generate internally because they are luminaires, or they might simply reflect power. The general form of the model will be:

$$\left(\begin{array}{c} \text{Power leaving} \\ \text{a patch} \end{array} \right) = \left(\begin{array}{c} \text{Power generated} \\ \text{by that patch} \end{array} \right) + \left(\begin{array}{c} \text{Power received from} \\ \text{other patches and reflected} \end{array} \right)$$

This means we need to be able to model the power received from other patches and reflected. We will develop a model assuming that all surfaces are diffuse. This leads to a somewhat simpler model, and describes all effects that are currently of interest to vision (it is complicated, but not difficult, to build more elaborate models). We will also need some radiometric terminology.

2.3.1   The Illumination at a Patch Due to an Area Source

The appropriate unit for illumination is **radiance**, defined as

> the power (amount of energy per unit time) traveling at some point in a specified direction, per unit area *perpendicular to the direction of travel,* per unit solid angle.

The units of radiance are watts per square meter per steradian ($Wm^{-2}sr^{-1}$). The definition of radiance might look strange, but it is consistent with the most basic phenomenon in radiometry: the amount of energy a patch collects from a source depends both on how large the source looks from the patch *and* on how large the patch looks from the source.

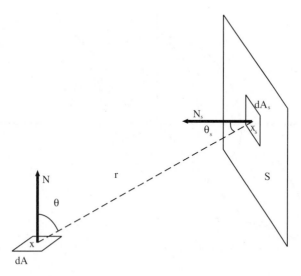

FIGURE 2.14: A patch with area dA views an area source S. We compute the power received by the patch by summing the contributions of each element on S, using the notation indicated in this figure.

It is important to remember that the square meters in the units for radiance are *foreshortened* (i.e., perpendicular to the direction of travel) to account for this phenomenon. Assume we have two elements, one at $\boldsymbol{x}$ with area dA and the other at $\boldsymbol{x}_s$ with area dA_s. Write the angular direction from $\boldsymbol{x}$ to $\boldsymbol{x}_s$ as $\boldsymbol{x} \to \boldsymbol{x}_s$, and define the angles θ and θ_s as in Figure 2.14. Then the solid angle subtended by element 2 at element 1 is

$$d\omega_{2(1)} = \frac{\cos\theta_s dA_s}{r^2},$$

so the power leaving $\boldsymbol{x}$ toward $\boldsymbol{x}_s$ is

$$\begin{aligned}
d^2 P_{1\to 2} &= \text{(radiance)(foreshortened area)(solid angle)} \\
&= L(\boldsymbol{x}, \boldsymbol{x} \to \boldsymbol{x}_s)(\cos\theta dA)(d\omega_{2(1)}) \\
&= L(\boldsymbol{x}, \boldsymbol{x} \to \boldsymbol{x}_s)\left(\frac{\cos\theta \cos\theta_s}{r^2}\right) dA_s dA.
\end{aligned}$$

By a similar argument, the same expression yields the power arriving at $\boldsymbol{x}$ from $\boldsymbol{x}_2$; this means that, in a vacuum, *radiance is constant along (unoccluded) straight lines*.

We can now compute the power that an element dA collects from an area source, by summing the contributions of elements over that source. Using the notation of Figure 2.14, we get

$$dP_{S\to dA} = \left(\int_S L(\boldsymbol{x}_s, \boldsymbol{x}_s \to \boldsymbol{x})\left(\frac{\cos\theta_s \cos\theta}{r^2}\right) dA_s\right) dA.$$

To get a more useful area source model, we need further units.

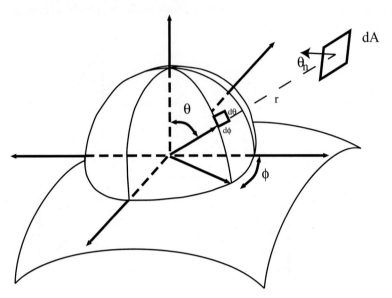

FIGURE 2.15: A hemisphere on a patch of surface, to show our angular coordinates for computing radiometric quantities. The coordinate axes are there to help you see the drawing as a 3D surface. An infinitesimal patch of surface with area dA which is distance r away is projected onto the unit hemisphere centered at the relevant point; the resulting area is the solid angle of the patch, marked as $d\theta d\phi$. In this case, the patch is small so that the area and hence the solid angle is $(1/r^2)dA\cos\theta_n$, where θ_n is the angle of inclination of the patch.

2.3.2   Radiosity and Exitance

We are dealing with diffuse surfaces, and our definition of a diffuse surface is that the intensity (formally, the radiance) leaving the surface is independent of the direction in which it leaves. There is no point in describing the intensity of such a surface with radiance (which explicitly depends on direction). The appropriate unit is *radiosity*, defined as

the total power leaving a point on a surface per unit area on the surface.

Radiosity, which is usually written as $B(x)$, has units watts per square meter (Wm^{-2}). To obtain the radiosity of a surface at a point, we can sum the radiance leaving the surface at that point over the whole exit hemisphere. Thus, if x is a point on a surface emitting radiance $L(x, \theta, \phi)$, the radiosity at that point is

$$B(x) = \int_\Omega L(x, \theta, \phi) \cos\theta d\omega,$$

where Ω is the exit hemisphere, $d\omega$ is unit solid angle, and the term $\cos\theta$ turns foreshortened area into area (look at the definitions of radiance and of radiosity again). We could substitute $d\omega = \sin\theta d\theta d\phi$, using the units of Figure 2.15.

Consider a surface element as in Figure 2.14. We have computed how much power it receives from the source as a function of the source's radiance. The surface element is diffuse, and its albedo is $\rho(\boldsymbol{x})$. The albedo is the fraction of incoming power that the surface radiates, so the radiosity due to power received from the area source is

$$B(\boldsymbol{x}) = \frac{dP_{S \to dA}}{dA} = \rho(\boldsymbol{x}) \left(\int_S L(\boldsymbol{x}_s, \boldsymbol{x}_s \to \boldsymbol{x}) \left(\frac{\cos\theta_s \cos\theta}{r^2} \right) dA_s \right).$$

Now if a point $\boldsymbol{u}$ on a surface has radiosity $B(\boldsymbol{u})$, what is the radiance leaving the surface in some direction? We write L for the radiance, which is independent of angle, and we must have

$$B(\boldsymbol{u}) = \int_\Omega L(\boldsymbol{x}, \theta, \phi) \cos\theta d\omega = L(\boldsymbol{u}) \int_\Omega \cos\theta d\omega = L(\boldsymbol{u})\pi.$$

This means that if the area source has radiosity $B(\boldsymbol{x}_s)$, then the radiosity at the element *due to the power received from the area source* is

$$\begin{aligned} B(\boldsymbol{x}) &= \rho \left(\int_S L(\boldsymbol{x}_s, \boldsymbol{x}_s \to \boldsymbol{x}) \left(\frac{\cos\theta_s \cos\theta}{r^2} \right) dA_s \right) \\ &= \rho \left(\int_S \frac{B(\boldsymbol{x})}{\pi} \left(\frac{\cos\theta_s \cos\theta}{r^2} \right) dA_s \right) \\ &= \frac{\rho}{\pi} \left(\int_S B(\boldsymbol{x}) \left(\frac{\cos\theta_s \cos\theta}{r^2} \right) dA_s \right). \end{aligned}$$

Our final step is to model illumination generated internally in a surface—light generated by a luminaire, rather than reflected from a surface. We assume there are no directional effects in the luminaire and that power is uniformly distributed across outgoing directions (this is the least plausible component of the model, but is usually tolerable). We use the unit *exitance*, which is defined as

the total power internally generated power leaving a point on a surface per unit area on the surface.

2.3.3 An Interreflection Model

We can now write a formal model of interreflections for diffuse surfaces by substituting terms into the original expression. Recall that radiosity is power per unit area, write $E(\boldsymbol{x})$ for exitance at the point $\boldsymbol{x}$, write $\boldsymbol{x}_s$ for a coordinate that runs over all surface patches, S for the set of all surfaces, dA for the element of area at $\boldsymbol{x}$, $V(\boldsymbol{x}, \boldsymbol{x}_s)$ for a function that is one if the two points can see each other and zero otherwise, and $\cos\theta$, $\cos\theta_s$, r, as in Figure 2.14. We obtain

$$\begin{array}{ccccc} \text{Power leaving} & = & \text{Power generated} & + & \text{Power received from} \\ \text{a patch} & & \text{by that patch} & & \text{other patches and reflected} \end{array}$$

$$B(\boldsymbol{x})dA \quad = \quad E(\boldsymbol{x})dA \quad + \quad \frac{\rho(\boldsymbol{x})}{\pi} \int_S \left[\begin{array}{c} \frac{\cos\theta \cos\theta_s}{r^2} \\ \times \\ V(\boldsymbol{x}, \boldsymbol{x}_s) \end{array} \right] B(\boldsymbol{x}_s) dA_s dA$$

and so, dividing by area, we have

$$B(\boldsymbol{x}) \quad = \quad E(\boldsymbol{x}) \quad + \quad \tfrac{\rho(\boldsymbol{x})}{\pi} \int_{\mathcal{S}} \left[\tfrac{\cos\theta\cos\theta_s}{r^2} \mathrm{Vis}(\boldsymbol{x},\boldsymbol{x}_s) \right] B(\boldsymbol{x}_s) dA_s.$$

It is usual to write

$$K(\boldsymbol{x},\boldsymbol{x}_s) = \frac{\cos\theta\cos\theta_s}{\pi r^2}$$

and refer to K as the interreflection kernel. Substituting gives

$$B(\boldsymbol{x}) = E(\boldsymbol{x}) + \rho(\boldsymbol{x}) \int_{\mathcal{S}} K(\boldsymbol{x},\boldsymbol{x}_s)\mathrm{Vis}(\boldsymbol{x},\boldsymbol{x}_s)B(\boldsymbol{x}_s)dA_{\boldsymbol{x}_s}$$

an equation where the solution appears inside the integral. Equations of this form are known as Fredholm integral equations of the second kind. This particular equation is a fairly nasty sample of the type because the interreflection kernel generally is not continuous and may have singularities. Solutions of this equation can yield quite good models of the appearance of diffuse surfaces, and the topic supports a substantial industry in the computer graphics community (good places to start for this topic are Cohen and Wallace (1993) or Sillion (1994)). The model produces good predictions of observed effects (Figure 2.16).

2.3.4 Qualitative Properties of Interreflections

Interreflections are a problem, because they are difficult to account for in our illumination model. For example, photometric stereo as we described it uses the model that light at a surface patch comes only from a distant light source. One could refine the method to take into account nearby light sources, but it is much more difficult to deal with interreflections. Once one accounts for interreflections, the brightness of each surface patch could be affected by the configuration of every other surface patch, making a very nasty global inference problem. While there have been attempts to build methods that can infer shape in the presence of interreflections (Nayar *et al.* 1991*a*), the problem is extremely difficult. One source of difficulties is that one may need to account for every radiating surface in the solution, even distant surfaces one cannot see.

An alternative strategy to straightforward physical inference is to understand the qualitative properties of interreflected shading. By doing so, we may be able to identify cases that are easy to handle, the main types of effect, and so on. The effects can be quite large. For example, Figure 2.17 shows views of the interior of two rooms. One room has black walls and contains black objects. The other has white walls and contains white objects. Each is illuminated (approximately!) by a distant point source. Given that the intensity of the source is adjusted appropriately, the local shading model predicts that these pictures would be indistinguishable. In fact, the black room has much darker shadows and crisper boundaries at the creases of the polyhedra than the white room. This is because surfaces in the black room reflect less light onto other surfaces (they are darker), whereas in the white room other surfaces are significant sources of radiation. The sections of the camera response to the radiosity (these are proportional to radiosity for diffuse surfaces) shown in the figure are hugely different qualitatively. In the black room, the radiosity is constant in patches, as a local shading model would predict, whereas in the white room slow

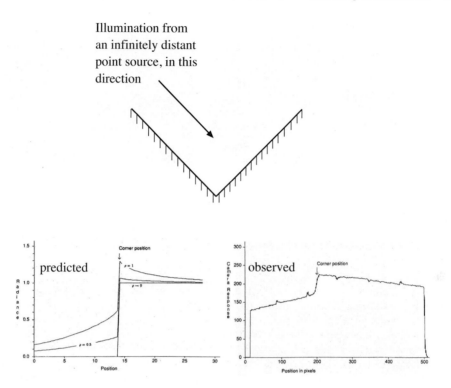

FIGURE 2.16: The model described in the text produces quite accurate qualitative predictions for interreflections. The **top** figure shows a concave right-angled groove illuminated by a point source at infinity where the source direction is parallel to the one face. On the **left** of the bottom row is a series of predictions of the radiosity for this configuration. These predictions have been scaled to lie on top of one another; the case $\rho \to 0$ corresponds to the local shading model. On the **right**, an observed image intensity for an image of this form for a corner made of white paper, showing the roof-like gradient in radiosity associated with the edge. A local shading model predicts a step. *This figure was originally published as Figures 5 and 7 of "Mutual Illumination," by D.A. Forsyth and A.P. Zisserman, Proc. IEEE CVPR, 1989, © IEEE, 1989.*

image gradients are quite common; these occur in concave corners, where object faces reflect light onto one another.

First, interreflections have a characteristic smoothing effect. This is most obviously seen when one tries to interpret a stained glass window by looking at the pattern it casts on the floor; this pattern is almost always a set of indistinct colored blobs. The effect is seen most easily with the crude model illustrated in Figure 2.18. The geometry consists of a patch with a frontal view of an infinite plane, which is a unit distance away and carries a radiosity $\sin \omega x$. There is no reason to vary the distance of the patch from the plane, because interreflection problems have scale invariant solutions, which means that the solution for a patch two units away can be obtained by reading our graph at 2ω. The patch is small enough that its contribution to the plane's radiosity can be ignored. If the patch is

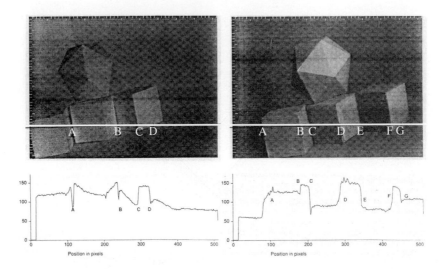

FIGURE 2.17: The column on the **left** shows data from a room with matte black walls and containing a collection of matte black polyhedral objects; that on the **right** shows data from a white room containing white objects. The images are qualitatively different, with darker shadows and crisper boundaries in the black room and bright reflexes in the concave corners in the white room. The graphs show sections of the image intensity along the corresponding lines in the images. *This figure was originally published as Figures 17, 18, 19, and 20 of "Mutual Illumination," by D.A. Forsyth and A.P. Zisserman, Proc. IEEE CVPR, 1989, © IEEE, 1989.*

slanted by σ with respect to the plane, it carries radiosity that is nearly periodic, with spatial frequency $\omega \cos \sigma$. We refer to the amplitude of the component at this frequency as the gain of the patch and plot the gain in Figure 2.18. The important property of this graph is that high spatial frequencies have a difficult time jumping the gap from the plane to the patch. This means that shading effects with high spatial frequency and high amplitude generally cannot come from distant surfaces (unless they are abnormally bright).

The extremely fast fall-off in amplitude with spatial frequency of terms due to distant surfaces means that, if one observes a high-amplitude term at a high spatial frequency, *it is very unlikely to have resulted from the effects of distant, passive radiators* (because these effects die away quickly). There is a convention, which we see in Section 2.2.3, that classifies effects in shading as due to reflectance if they are fast ("edges") and the dynamic range is relatively low and due to illumination otherwise. We can expand this convention. There is a mid range of spatial frequencies that are largely unaffected by mutual illumination from distant surfaces because the gain is small. Spatial frequencies in this range cannot be transmitted by distant passive radiators unless these radiators have improbably high radiosity. As a result, spatial frequencies in this range can be thought of as *regional properties*, which can result only from interreflection effects within a region.

The most notable regional properties are probably *reflexes*— small bright patches that appear mainly in concave regions (illustrated in Figure 2.19). A second

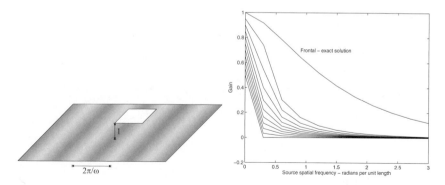

FIGURE 2.18: A small patch views a plane with sinusoidal radiosity of unit amplitude. This patch has a (roughly) sinusoidal radiosity due to the effects of the plane. We refer to the amplitude of this component as the *gain of the patch*. The graph shows numerical estimates of the gain for patches at 10 equal steps in slant angle, from 0 to $\pi/2$, as a function of spatial frequency *on the plane*. The gain falls extremely fast, meaning that large terms at high spatial frequencies must be regional effects, rather than the result of distant radiators. This is why it is hard to determine the pattern in a stained glass window by looking at the floor at the foot of the window. *This figure was originally published as Figures 1 and 2 from "Shading Primitives: Finding Folds and Shallow Grooves," J. Haddon and D.A. Forsyth, Proc. IEEE ICCV, 1998 © IEEE, 1998.*

important effect is *color bleeding*, where a colored surface reflects light onto another colored surface. This is a common effect that people tend not to notice unless they are consciously looking for it. It is quite often reproduced by painters.

2.4 SHAPE FROM ONE SHADED IMAGE

There is good evidence that people get some perception of shape from the shading pattern in a single image, though the details are uncertain and quite complicated (see the notes for a brief summary). You can see this evidence in practice: whenever you display a reconstruction of a surface obtained from images, it is a good idea to shade that reconstruction using image pixels, because it always looks more accurate. In fact, quite bad reconstructions can be made to look good with this method. White and Forsyth (2006) use this trick to replace surface albedos in movies; for example, they can change the pattern on a plastic bag in a movie. Their method builds and tracks very coarse geometric reconstructions, uses a form of regression to recover the original shading pattern of the object, and then shades the coarse geometric reconstruction using the original shading pattern (Figure 2.20). In this figure, the pictures look plausible, not because the reconstruction is good (it isn't), but because the shading pattern masks the errors in geometric reconstruction.

The cue to shape must come from the fact that a surface patch that faces the light source is brighter than one that faces away from the source. But going from this observation to a working algorithm remains an open question. The key seems to be an appropriate use of the *image irradiance equation*. Assume we have a surface in the form $(x, y, f(x, y))$ viewed orthographically along the z-axis. Assume that the surface is diffuse, and its albedo is uniform and known. Assume also that

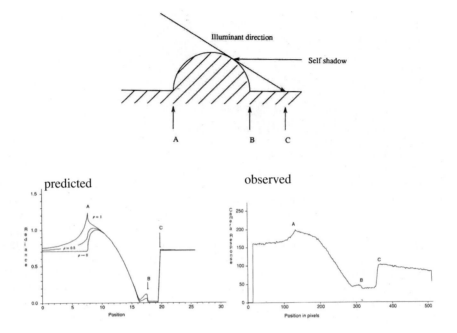

FIGURE 2.19: Reflexes occur quite widely; they are usually caused by a favorable view of a large reflecting surface. In the geometry shown on the **top**, the shadowed region of the cylindrical bump sees the plane background at a fairly favorable angle: if the background is large enough, nearly half the hemisphere of the patch at the base of the bump is a view of the plane. This means there will be a reflex with a large value attached to the edge of the bump and inside the cast shadow region (which a local model predicts as black). There is another reflex on the other side, too, as the series of solutions (again normalized for easy comparison) on the **left** show. On the **right**, an observation of this effect in a real scene. *This figure was originally published as Figures 24 and 26 of "Mutual Illumination," by D.A. Forsyth and A.P. Zisserman, Proc. IEEE CVPR, 1989, © IEEE, 1989.*

the model of Section 2.1.3 applies, so that the shading at a point with normal N is given by some function $R(N)$ (the function of our model is $R(N) = N \cdot S$, but others could be used). Now the normal of our surface is a function of the two first partial derivatives

$$p = \frac{\partial f}{\partial x}, \; q = \frac{\partial f}{\partial y}$$

so we can write $R(p, q)$. Assume that the camera is radiometrically calibrated, so we can proceed from image values to intensity values. Write the intensity at x, y as $I(x, y)$. Then we have

$$R(p, q) = I(x, y).$$

This is a first order partial differential equation, because p and q are partial derivatives of f. In principle, we could set up some boundary conditions and solve this equation. Doing so reliably and accurately for general images remains outside our competence, 40 years after the problem was originally posed by Horn (1970a).

FIGURE 2.20: On the **left**, an original frame from a movie sequence of a deforming plastic bag. On the **right**, two frames where the original texture has been replaced by another. The method used is a form of regression; its crucial property is that it has a very weak geometric model, but is capable of preserving the original shading field of the image. If you look closely at the *albedo* (i.e., the black pattern) of the bag, you may notice that it is inconsistent with the wrinkles on the bag, but because the shading has been preserved, the figures look quite good. This is indirect evidence that shading is a valuable cue to humans. Little is known about how this cue is to be exploited, however. *This figure was originally published as Figure 10 of "Retexturing single views using texture and shading," by R. White and D.A. Forsyth, Proc. European Conference on Computer Vision. Springer Lecture Notes in Computer Science, Volume 3954, 2006 © Springer 2006.*

There are a variety of difficulties here. The physical model is a poor model of what actually happens at surfaces because any particular patch is illuminated by other surface patches, as well as by the source. We expect to see a rich variety of geometric constraints on the surface we reconstruct, and it is quite difficult to formulate shape from shading in a way that accomodates these constraints and still has a solution. Shading is a worthwhile cue to exploit, because we can observe shading at extremely high spatial resolutions, but this means we must work with very high dimensional models to reconstruct. Some schemes for shading reconstruction can be unstable, but there appears to be no theory to guide us to stable schemes. We very seldom actually see isolated surfaces of known albedo, and there are no methods that are competent to infer both shading and albedo, though there is some reason to hope that such methods can be built. We have no theory that is capable of predicting the errors in shading-based reconstructions from first principles. All this makes shape inference from shading in a single image one of the most frustrating open questions in computer vision.

2.5 NOTES

Horn started the systematic study of shading in computer vision, with important papers on recovering shape from a local shading model using a point source (in (Horn 1970*b*), (Horn 1975)), with a more recent account in Horn (1990).

FIGURE 2.21: This picture shows two important mechanisms by which it might be possible to infer surface shape from single images. First, patches that face away from the light (like A, on the **left**) are darker than those that face the light (B). Second, shadows pick out relief—for example, small dents in a surface (more easily seen in the detail patch on the **right**), have a bright face facing the light and a dark face which is in shadow. *Peter Wilson © Dorling Kindersley, used with permission.*

Models of Shading

The first edition of this book contained more formal radiometry, which was widely disliked (and for good reason; making the subject exciting is beyond our skills). We've cut this down, and tried to avoid using the ideas, but point those who really want to know more toward that earlier edition. We strongly recommend François Sillion's excellent book (Sillion 1994) for its clear account of radiometric calculations. There are a variety of more detailed publications for reference (Nayar *et al.* 1991*c*). Our discussion of reflection is thoroughly superficial. The specular plus diffuse model appears to be originally due to Cook, Torrance, and Sparrow (Torrance and Sparrow 1967, Cook and Torrance 1987). A variety of modifications of this model appear in computer vision and computer graphics. Reflection models can be derived by combining a statistical description of surface roughness with electromagnetic considerations (e.g., Beckmann and Spizzichino (1987)) or by adopting scattering models (as in the work of Torrance and Sparrow (1967) and of Cook and Torrance (1987)).

It is commonly believed that rough surfaces are Lambertian. This belief has a substantial component of wishful thinking because rough surfaces often have local shadowing effects that make the radiance reflected quite strongly dependent on the illumination angle. For example, a stucco wall illuminated at a near grazing angle shows a clear pattern of light and dark regions where facets of the surface face toward the light or are shadowed. If the same wall is illuminated along the normal, this pattern largely disappears. Similar effects at a finer scale are averaged to endow rough surfaces with measurable departures from a Lambertian model (for details, see Koenderink *et al.* (1999), Nayar and Oren (1993), (1995), Oren and Nayar (1995), and Wolff *et al.* (1998)).

Inference from Shading

Registered images are not essential for radiometric calibration. For example, it is sufficient to have two images where we believe the histogram of E_{ij} values is the same (Grossberg and Nayar 2002). This occurs, for example, when the images are of the same scene, but are not precisely registered. Patterns of intensity around edges also can reveal calibration (Lin *et al.* 2004).

There has not been much recent study of lightness constancy algorithms. The basic idea is due to Land and McCann (1971). Their work was formalized for the computer vision community by Horn (1974). A variation on Horn's algorithm was constructed by Blake (1985). This is the lightness algorithm we describe. It appeared originally in a slightly different form, where it was called the *Retinex* algorithm (Land and McCann 1971). Retinex was originally intended as a color constancy algorithm. It is surprisingly difficult to analyze (Brainard and Wandell 1986).

Retinex estimates the log-illumination term by subtracting the log-albedo from the log-intensity. This has the disadvantage that we do not impose any structural constraints on illumination. This point has largely been ignored, because the main focus has been on albedo estimates. However, albedo estimates are likely to be improved by balancing violations of albedo constraints with those of illumination constraints.

Lightness techniques are not as widely used as they should be, particularly given that there is some evidence that they produce useful information on real images (Brelstaff and Blake 1987). Classifying illumination versus albedo simply by looking at the magnitude of the gradient is crude, and ignores important cues. Sharp shading changes occur at shadow boundaries or normal discontinuities, but using chromaticity (Funt *et al.* 1992) or multiple images under different lighting conditions (Weiss 2001) yields improved estimates. One can learn to distinguish illumination from albedo (Freeman *et al.* 2000). Discriminative methods to classify edges into albedo or shading help (Tappen *et al.* 2006*b*) and chromaticity cues can contribute (Farenzena and Fusiello 2007). Shading and albedo are sometimes known as *intrinsic images*. Tappen *et al.* (2006*a*) regress local intrinsic image patches against the image, exploiting the constraint that patches join up. When more than one image is available, recent methods can recover quite complex surface properties (Romeiro *et al.* 2008). When geometry is available, Yu *et al.* (1999) showed significant improvements in lightness recovery are possible.

In its original form, photometric stereo is due to Woodham. There are a number of variants of this useful idea (Horn *et al.* (1978), Woodham (1979), (1980), (1989), (1994), Woodham *et al.* (1991)). Current methods for photometric stereo require at least two unshadowed views; see Hernandez *et al.* (2008) which describes methods to cope in this case. There are a variety of variations on photometric stereo. Color photometric stereo seems to date to Petrov (1987), with a variant in Petrov (1991).

Photometric stereo depends only on adopting a local shading model. This model need not be a Lambertian surface illuminated by a distant point source. If the brightness of the surface is a known function of the surface normal satisfying a small number of constraints, photometric stereo is still possible. This is because the intensity of a pixel in a single view determines the normal up to a one-parameter family. This means that two views determine the normal. The simplest example of this case occurs for a surface of known albedo illuminated by a distant point source.

In fact, if the radiosity of the surface is a k-parameter function of the surface normal, photometric stereo is still possible. The intensity of the pixel in a single view determines the normal up to a $k+1$ parameter family, and $k+1$ views give the normal. For this approach to work, the brightness needs to be given by a function for which our arithmetic works (e.g., if the brightness of the surface is a constant function of the surface normal, it isn't possible to infer any constraint on the normal from the brightness). One can then recover shape and reflectance maps simultaneously (Garcia-Bermejo *et al.* (1996); Mukawa (1990); Nayar *et al.* (1990); Tagare and de Figueiredo (1992); (1993)).

A converse to photometric stereo might be as follows: Assume we have a diffuse sphere, immersed in an environment where illumination depends only on direction. What can we determine about the illumination field from the surface brightness? The answer is very little, because diffuse surfaces engage in a form of averaging that heavily smoothes the illumination field (Ramamoorthi and Hanrahan 2001). This is valuable because it suggests that complex representations of the directional properties illumination aren't required in a diffuse world. For example, this result allowed Jacobs (1981) to produce a form of photometric stereo that requires no illuminant information, using sufficient images.

Interreflections

The effects of global shading are often ignored in the shading literature, which causes a reflex response of hostility in one of the authors. The reason to ignore interreflections is that they are extremely hard to analyze, particularly from the perspective of inferring object properties given the output of a global shading model. If interreflection effects do not change the output of a method much, then it is probably all right to ignore them. Unfortunately, this line of reasoning is seldom pursued because it is quite difficult to show that a method is stable under interreflections. The discussion of spatial frequency issues follows Haddon and Forsyth (1998a), after an idea of Koenderink and van Doorn (1983). Apart from this, there is not much knowledge about the overall properties of interreflected shading, which is an important gap in our knowledge. An alternative strategy is to iteratively reestimate shape using a rendering model (Nayar *et al.* 1991*b*).

Horn is also the first author to indicate the significance of global shading effects (Horn 1977). Koenderink and van Doorn (1983) noted that the radiosity under a global model is obtained by taking the radiosity under a local model, and applying a linear operator. One then studies that operator; in some cases, its eigenfunctions (often called *geometrical modes*) are informative. Forsyth and Zisserman (1989, 1990, 1991) then demonstrated a variety of the qualitative effects due to interreflections.

Shape from One Shaded Image

Shape from shading is an important puzzle. Comprehensive surveys include (Horn and Brooks (1989); Zhang *et al.* (1999); Durou *et al.* (2008*b*)). In practice, despite the ongoing demand for high-resolution shape reconstructions, shape-from-shading has been a disappointment. This may be because, as currently formulated, it solves a problem that doesn't commonly occur. Image irradiance equation methods are formulated to produce reconstructions when there is very little geometric data, but it is much more common to want to improve the resolution of a method that already produces quite rich geometric data.

Methods are either too fragile or the reconstructions too poor for the method to be useful. Some of this may be due to the effects of interreflections. Another source of difficulty could be the compromises that need to be made to obtain a solution in the presence of existence difficulties. Most reconstructions shown in the literature are poor. In a comparative review, Zhang *et al.* (2002) summarize: "All the SFS algorithms produce generally poor results when given synthetic data . . . Results are even worse on real images, and . . . [r]esults on synthetic data are not generally predictive of results on real data." More recently, Tankus *et al.* (2005) showed good looking reconstructions of various body structures from endoscopic images, but cannot compare with veridical information. Prados and Faugeras show a good-looking reconstruction of a face, but cannot compare with veridical information (Prados and Faugeras (2005*a*); (2005*b*)). Durou *et al.* (2008*a*), in a recent comparative review, show some fair reconstructions on both synthetic and real data. However, on quite simple shapes methods still produce reconstructions with profound eccentricities.

These problems have driven a search for methods that do not require a reconstruction. Some local features of a shading field—*shading primitives*—are revealing because some geometric structures generate about the same shading pattern whatever the illumination. For example, a pit in a surface will always be dark; grooves and folds tend to appear as a thin, light band next to a thin, dark band; and the shading on a cylinder is usually either a dark band next to a light band, or a light band with dark band on either side. This idea originates with Koenderink and Doorn (1983), and is expounded in (Haddon and Forsyth 1997, Haddon and Forsyth 1998*b*, Han and Zhu 2005, Han and Zhu 2007). On a larger spatial scale, the family of shading patterns that can be produced by a particular object—the *illumination cone*—is smaller than one might expect (Basri and Jacobs 2003, Belhumeur and Kriegman 1998, Georghiades *et al.* 2001), allowing illumination invariant detection by detecting elements of such cones or by matching with an image distance that discounts changes in illumination (Chen *et al.* 2000, Jacobs *et al.* 1998).

PROBLEMS

2.1. We see a diffuse sphere centered at the origin, with radius one and albedo ρ, in an orthographic camera, looking down the z-axis. This sphere is illuminated by a distant point light source whose source direction is $(0,0,1)$. There is no other illumination. Show that the shading field in the camera is

$$\rho\sqrt{1-x^2-y^2}$$

2.2. Why are area sources common in illumination engineering?

2.3. We have a square area source and a square occluder, both parallel to a plane. The source is the same size as the occluder, and they are vertically above one another with their centers aligned.

(a) What is the shape of the umbra?

(b) What is the shape of the outside boundary of the penumbra?

2.4. Horn started the systematic study of shading in computer vision, with important papers on recovering shape from a local shading model using a point source.

(a) What is the difficulty with a local shading model?

(b) How can this difficulty be overcome?

2.5. Give the name of the units defined as follows:

(a) The total power leaving a point on a surface per unit area on the surface.

(b) The total power internally generated power leaving a point on a surface per unit area on the surface.

2.6. What is reciprocity? How is reciprocity related to energy and power?

2.7. Explain why the common belief that rough surfaces are Lambertian is reasonably accurate.

2.8. As in Figure 2.18, a small patch views an infinite plane at unit distance. The patch is sufficiently small that it reflects a trivial quantity of light onto the plane. The plane has radiosity $B(x,y) = 1 + \sin ax$. The patch and the plane are parallel to one another. We move the patch around parallel to the plane, and consider its radiosity at various points.

(a) Show that if one translates the patch, its radiosity varies periodically with its position in x.

(b) Fix the patch's center at $(0,0)$; determine a *closed form* expression for the radiosity of the patch at this point as a function of a. You'll need a table of integrals for this (if you don't, you're entitled to feel very pleased with yourself).

2.9. If one looks across a large bay in the daytime, it is often hard to distinguish the mountains on the opposite side; near sunset, they are clearly visible. This phenomenon has to do with scattering of light by air—a large volume of air is actually a source. Explain what is happening. We have modeled air as a vacuum and asserted that no energy is lost along a straight line in a vacuum. Use your explanation to give an estimate of the kind of scales over which that model is acceptable.

2.10. Read the book *Introduction to Color Imaging Science*, by Hsien-Che Lee, published by Cambridge University Press, 2005

PROGRAMMING EXERCISES

2.11. An area source can be approximated as a grid of point sources. The weakness of this approximation is that the penumbra contains quantization errors, which can be quite offensive to the eye.

  (a) Explain.

  (b) Render this effect for a square source and a single occluder casting a shadow onto an infinite plane. For a fixed geometry, you should find that as the number of point sources goes up, the quantization error goes down.

  (c) This approximation has the unpleasant property that it is possible to produce arbitrarily large quantization errors with any finite grid by changing the geometry. This is because there are configurations of source and occluder that produce large penumbrae. Use a square source and a single occluder, casting a shadow onto an infinite plane, to explain this effect.

2.12. Make a world of colored objects with colored lights (colored paper, colored lights and spray-paint are useful here) and observe the effects of interreflection. Can you come up with a criterion that reliably identifies colored interreflections *from an image*? (If you can, publish it; the problem looks easy, but isn't.)

2.13. (This exercise requires some knowledge of numerical analysis.) Do the numerical integrals required to reproduce Figure 2.18. These integrals aren't particularly easy: if one uses coordinates on the infinite plane, the size of the domain is a nuisance; if one converts to coordinates on the view hemisphere of the patch, the frequency of the radiance becomes infinite at the boundary of the hemisphere. The best way to estimate these integrals is using a Monte Carlo method on the hemisphere. You should use importance sampling because the boundary contributes rather less to the integral than the top does.

2.14. Set up and solve the linear equations for an interreflection solution for the interior of a cube with a small square source in the center of the ceiling.

2.15. Implement a photometric stereo system.

  (a) How accurate are its measurements (i.e., how well do they compare with known shape information)? Do interreflections affect the accuracy?

  (b) How repeatable are its measurements (i.e., if you obtain another set of images, perhaps under different illuminants, and recover shape from those, how does the new shape compare with the old)?

  (c) Compare the minimization approach to reconstruction with the integration approach; which is more accurate or more repeatable and why? Does this difference appear in experiment?

  (d) One possible way to improve the integration approach is to obtain depths by integrating over many different paths and then average these depths (you need to be a little careful about constants here). Does this improve the accuracy or repeatability of the method?

CHAPTER 3

Color

The light receptors in cameras and in the eye respond more or less strongly to different wavelengths of light. Most cameras and most eyes have several different types of receptor, whose sensitivity to different wavelengths varies. Comparing the response of several types of sensor yields information about the distribution of energy with wavelength for the incoming light; this is color information. Color information can be used to identify specularities in images and to remove shadows. The color of an object seen in an image depends on how the object was lit, but there are algorithms that can correct for this effect.

3.1 HUMAN COLOR PERCEPTION

The light coming out of sources or reflected from surfaces has more or less energy at different wavelengths, depending on the processes that produced the light. This distribution of energy with wavelength is sometimes called a *spectral energy density*; Figure 3.1 shows spectral energy densities for sunlight measured under a variety of different conditions. The visual system responds to light in a range of wavelengths from approximately 400nm to approximately 700nm. Light containing energy at just one wavelength looks deeply colored (these colors are known as *spectral colors*). The colors seen at different wavelengths have a set of conventional names, which originate with Isaac Newton (the sequence from 700nm to 400nm goes Red Orange Yellow Green Blue Indigo Violet, or **R**ichard **of Y**ork **g**ot **b**listers **in V**enice, although indigo is now frowned upon as a name because people typically cannot distinguish indigo from blue or violet). If the intensity is relatively uniform across the wavelengths, the light will look white.

Different kinds of color receptor in the human eye respond more or less strongly to light at different wavelengths, producing a signal that is interpreted as color by the human vision system. The precise interpretation of a particular light is a complex function of context; illumination, memory, object identity, and emotion can all play a part. The simplest question is to understand which spectral energy densities produce the same response from people under simple viewing conditions (Section 3.1.1). This yields a simple, linear theory of color matching that is accurate and extremely useful for describing colors. We sketch the mechanisms underlying the transduction of color in Section 3.1.2.

3.1.1 Color Matching

The simplest case of color perception is obtained when only two colors are in view on a black background. In a typical experiment, a subject sees a colored light—the *test light*—in one half of a split field (Figure 3.2). The subject can then adjust a mixture of lights in the other half to get it to match. The adjustments involve changing the intensity of some fixed number of *primaries* in the mixture. In this

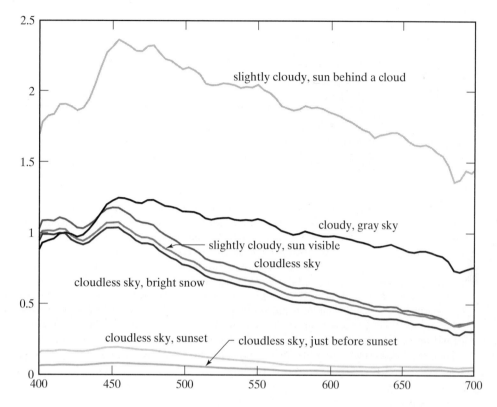

FIGURE 3.1: Daylight has different amounts of power at different wavelengths. These plots show the spectral energy density of daylight measured at different times of day and under different conditions. The figure plots relative power against wavelength for wavelengths from 400 nm to 700 nm for a series of seven different daylight measurements, made by Jussi Parkkinen and Pertti Silfsten, of daylight illuminating a sample of barium sulphate (which gives a high reflectance white surface). At the foot of the plot, we show the names used for spectral colors of the relevant wavelengths. Plot from data obtainable at http://www.it.lut.fi/ip/research/color/database/database.html.

form, a large number of lights may be required to obtain a match, but many different adjustments may yield a match.

Write T for the test light, an equals sign for a match, the weights—which are non-negative—as w_i, and the primaries P_i. A match can then be written in an algebraic form as

$$T = w_1 P_1 + w_2 P_2 + \dots,$$

meaning that test light T matches the particular mixture of primaries given by $(w_1, w_2, \dots)$. The situation is simplified if *subtractive matching* is allowed. In subtractive matching, the viewer can add some amount of some primaries to the *test light* instead of to the match. This can be written in algebraic form by allowing the weights in the expression above to be negative.

Under these conditions, most observers require only three primaries to match a test light. This phenomenon is known as the principle of *trichromacy*. However,

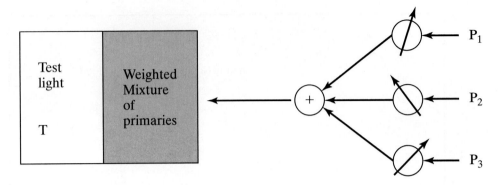

FIGURE 3.2: Human perception of color can be studied by asking observers to mix colored lights to match a test light shown in a split field. The drawing shows the outline of such an experiment. The observer sees a test light T and can adjust the amount of each of three primaries in a mixture displayed next to the test light. The observer is asked to adjust the amounts so that the mixture looks the same as the test light. The mixture of primaries can be written as $w_1 P_1 + w_2 P_2 + w_3 P_3$; if the mixture matches the test light, then we write $T = w_1 P_1 + w_2 P_2 + w_3 P_3$. It is a remarkable fact that for most people three primaries are sufficient to achieve a match for many colors, and three primaries are sufficient for all colors if we allow subtractive matching (i.e., some amount of some of the primaries is mixed with the test light to achieve a match). Some people require fewer primaries. Furthermore, most people choose the same mixture weights to match a given test light.

there are some caveats. First, subtractive matching must be allowed; second, the primaries must be independent, meaning that no mixture of two of the primaries may match a third. There is now clear evidence that trichromacy occurs because there are three distinct types of color transducer in the eye (Nathans *et al.* 1986*a*, Nathans *et al.* 1986*b*). Given the same primaries and test light, most observers select the *same* mixture of primaries to match that test light, because most people have the same types of color receptor.

Matching is (to an accurate approximation) linear. This yields *Grassman's laws*. First, if we mix two test lights, then mixing the matches will match the result—that is, if

$$T_a = w_{a1} P_1 + w_{a2} P_2 + w_{a3} P_3$$

and

$$T_b = w_{b1} P_1 + w_{b2} P_2 + w_{b3} P_3,$$

then

$$T_a + T_b = (w_{a1} + w_{b1})P_1 + (w_{a2} + w_{b2})P_2 + (w_{a3} + w_{b3})P_3.$$

Second, if two test lights can be matched with the same set of weights, then they will match each other—that is, if

$$T_a = w_1 P_1 + w_2 P_2 + w_3 P_3$$

and

$$T_b = w_1 P_1 + w_2 P_2 + w_3 P_3,$$

then

$$T_a = T_b.$$

Finally, matching is linear: if

$$T_a = w_1 P_1 + w_2 P_2 + w_3 P_3,$$

then

$$kT_a = (kw_1)P_1 + (kw_2)P_2 + (kw_3)P_3$$

for non-negative k.

Given the same test light and set of primaries, most people use the same set of weights to match the test light. This, trichromacy, and Grassman's laws are about as true as any law covering biological systems can be. The exceptions include the following:

- people with too few kinds of color receptor as a result of genetic ill fortune (who may be able to match everything with fewer primaries);

- people with neural problems (who may display all sorts of effects, including a complete absence of the sensation of color);

- some elderly people (whose choice of weights differ from the norm because of the development of macular pigment in the eye);

- very bright lights (whose hue and saturation look different from less bright versions of the same light);

- and very dark conditions (where the mechanism of color transduction is somewhat different than in brighter conditions).

3.1.2 Color Receptors

Trichromacy occurs because there are (usually!) three distinct types of receptor in the eye that mediate color perception. Each of these receptors turns incident light into neural signals. The *principle of univariance* states that the activity of these receptors is of one kind (i.e., they respond strongly or weakly, but do not signal the wavelength of the light falling on them). Experimental evidence can be obtained by carefully dissecting light-sensitive cells and measuring their responses to light at different wavelengths or by reasoning backward from color matches. Univariance is a powerful idea because it gives us a good and simple model of human reaction to colored light: two lights will match if they produce the same receptor responses, *whatever their spectral energy densities.*

Because the system of matching is linear, the receptors must be linear. Write p_k for the response of the kth type of receptor, $\sigma_k(\lambda)$ for its sensitivity, $E(\lambda)$ for the light arriving at the receptor, and Λ for the range of visible wavelengths. We can obtain the overall response of a receptor by adding up the response to each separate wavelength in the incoming spectrum so that

$$p_k = \int_\Lambda \sigma_k(\lambda)E(\lambda)d\lambda.$$

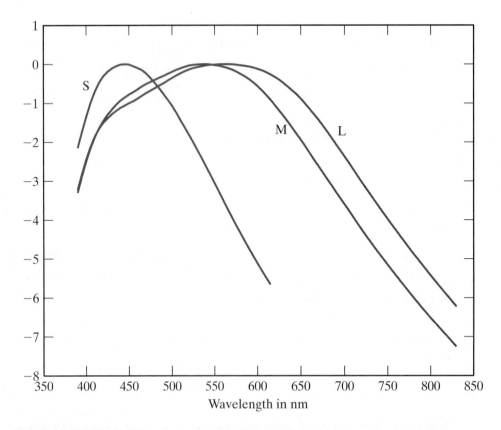

FIGURE 3.3: There are three types of color receptor in the human eye, usually called *cones*. These receptors respond to all photons in the same way, but in different amounts. The figure shows the log of the relative spectral sensitivities of the three kinds of color receptor in the human eye, plotted against wavelength. On the wavelength axis, we have shown the color name usually associated with lights which contain energy only at that wavelength. The first two receptors—properly named the *long-* and *medium-wavelength* receptors— have peak sensitivities at quite similar wavelengths. The third receptor (*short-wavelength* receptor) has a different peak sensitivity. The response of a receptor to incoming light can be obtained by summing the product of the sensitivity and the spectral energy density of the light over all wavelengths. Notice that each receptor responds to quite a broad range of wavelengths. This means that human observers must perceive color by comparing the response of the receptors to one another, and that there must be many spectral energy densities that cannot be distinguished by humans. *Figures plotted from data disseminated by the Color and Vision Research Laboratories database, compiled by Andrew Stockman and Lindsey Sharpe, and available at* `http://www.cvrl.org/`.

Anatomical investigation of the retina shows two types of cell that are sensitive to light, differentiated by their shape. The light-sensitive region of a *cone* has a roughly conical shape, whereas that in a *rod* is roughly cylindrical. Cones largely dominate color vision and completely dominate the fovea. Cones are somewhat less sensitive to light than rods are, meaning that in low light, color vision is poor and it is impossible to read (one doesn't have sufficient spatial precision, because the fovea isn't working).

The sensitivities of the three different kinds of receptor to different wavelengths can be obtained by comparing color matching data for normal observers with color matching data for observers lacking one type of cone. Sensitivities obtained in this fashion are shown in Figure 3.3. The three types of cone are properly called *S cones*, *M cones*, and *L cones* (for their peak sensitivity being to short-, medium-, and long-wavelength light, respectively). They are occasionally called blue, green, and red cones; however, this is bad practice, because the sensation of red is definitely not caused by the stimulation of red cones, and so on.

3.2   THE PHYSICS OF COLOR

Several different mechanisms result in colored light. First, light sources can produce different amounts of light at different wavelengths. This is what makes incandescent lights look orange or yellow, and fluorescent lights look bluish. Second, for most diffuse surfaces, albedo depends on wavelength, so that some wavelengths may be largely absorbed and others largely reflected. This means that most surfaces will look colored when lit by a white light. The light reflected from a colored surface is affected by both the color of the light falling on the surface, and by the surface, and so is profoundly ambiguous. For example, a white surface lit by red light will reflect red light, and a red surface lit by white light will also reflect red light.

3.2.1   The Color of Light Sources

The most important natural light source is the sun. The sun is usually modeled as a distant, bright point. Light from the sun is scattered by the air. In particular, light can leave the sun, be scattered by the air, strike a surface, and be reflected into the camera or the eye. This means the sky is an important natural light source. A crude geometrical model of the sky has it as a source consisting of a hemisphere with constant exitance. The assumption that exitance is constant is poor, however, because the sky is substantially brighter at the horizon than at the zenith. A natural model of the sky is to assume that air emits a constant amount of light per unit volume; this means that the sky is brighter on the horizon than at the zenith because a viewing ray along the horizon passes through more sky.

A patch of surface outdoors during the day is illuminated both by light that comes directly from the sun—usually called *daylight*—and by light from the sun that has been scattered by the air (sometimes called *skylight* or *airlight*; the presence of clouds or snow can add other, important, phenomena). The color of daylight varies with time of day (Figure 3.1) and time of year.

For clear air, the intensity of radiation scattered by a unit volume depends on the fourth power of the frequency; this means that light of a long wavelength can travel much farther before being scattered than light of a short wavelength (this is known as *Rayleigh scattering*). This means that, when the sun is high in the sky, blue light is scattered out of the ray from the sun to the earth—meaning that the sun looks yellow—and can scatter from the sky into the eye—meaning that the sky looks blue. There are standard models of the spectral energy density of the sky at different times of day and latitude, too. Surprising effects occur when there are fine particles of dust in the sky (the larger particles cause much more complex scattering

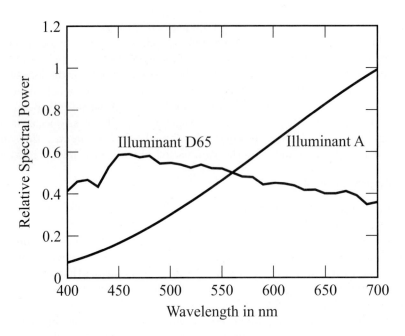

FIGURE 3.4: There is a variety of illuminant models; the graph shows the relative spectral power distribution of two standard CIE models, illuminant A—which models the light from a 100W Tungsten filament light bulb, with color temperature 2800K—and illuminant D-65—which models daylight. *Figure plotted from data available at* `http://www.cvrl.org/`.

effects, usually modeled rather roughly by the *Mie scattering* model, described in Lynch and Livingston (2001) or in Minnaert (1993)) One author remembers vivid sunsets in Johannesburg caused by dust in the air from mine dumps, and there are records of blue and even green moons caused by volcanic dust in the air.

Artificial Illumination

Typical artificial light sources are commonly of a small number of types:

- An *incandescent light* contains a metal filament that is heated to a high temperature. The spectrum roughly follows the black-body law (Section 3.2.1), but the melting temperature of the element limits the color temperature of the light source, so the light has a reddish tinge.

- A *fluorescent light* works by generating high-speed electrons that strike gas within the bulb. The gas releases ultraviolet radiation, which causes phosphors coating the inside of the bulb to fluoresce. Typically the coating consists of three or four phosphors, which fluoresce in quite narrow ranges of wavelengths. Most fluorescent bulbs generate light with a bluish tinge, but some bulbs mimic natural daylight (Figure 3.5).

- In some bulbs, an arc is struck in an atmosphere consisting of gaseous metals and inert gases. Light is produced by electrons in metal atoms dropping from an excited state to a lower energy state. Typical of such lamps is strong radiation at a small number of wavelengths, which correspond to particular state transitions. The most common cases are *sodium arc lamps* and *mercury arc lamps*. Sodium arc lamps produce a yellow-orange light extremely efficiently and are quite commonly used for freeway lighting. Mercury arc lamps produce a blue-white light and are often used for security lighting.

Figure 3.5 shows a sample of spectra from different light bulbs.

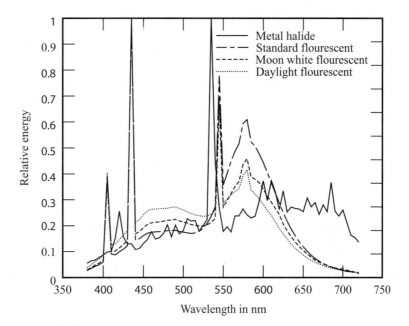

FIGURE 3.5: The relative spectral power distribution of four different lamps from the Mitsubishi Electric Corporation. Note the bright, narrow bands that come from the flourescing phosphors in the fluorescent lamp. *The figure was plotted from data made available by the Coloring Info Pages at* `http://www.colorpro.com/info/data/lamps.html`; *the data was measured by Hiroaki Sugiura.*

Black Body Radiators

One useful abstraction is the *black body*, a body that reflects no light. A heated black body emits electromagnetic radiation. It is a remarkable fact that the spectral power distribution of this radiation depends only on the temperature of the body. If we write T for the temperature of the body in Kelvins, h for Planck's constant, k for Boltzmann's constant, c for the speed of light, and λ for the wavelength, we have

$$E(\lambda) \propto \frac{1}{\lambda^5} \frac{1}{(\exp(hc/k\lambda T) - 1)}.$$

This means that there is one parameter family of light colors corresponding to black body radiators—the parameter being the temperature—and so we can talk about the *color temperature* of a light source. This is the temperature of the black body that looks most similar. At relatively low temperatures, black bodies are red, passing through orange to a pale yellow-white to white as the temperature increases (Figure 3.12 shows this locus). When $hc \gg k\lambda T$, we have $1/(\exp(hc/k\lambda T) - 1) \approx \exp(-hc/k\lambda T)$, so

$$E(\lambda; T) = C\frac{\exp(-hc/k\lambda T)}{\lambda^5}$$

where C is the constant of proportionality; this model is somewhat easier to use than the exact model (Section 3.5.2).

3.2.2 The Color of Surfaces

The color of surfaces is a result of a large variety of mechanisms, including differential absorbtion at different wavelengths, refraction, diffraction, and bulk scattering (for more details, see, for example Lamb and Bourriau (1995), Lynch and Livingston (2001), Minnaert (1993), or Williamson and Cummins (1983)). If we ignore the physical effects that give rise to the color, we can model surfaces as having a diffuse and a specular component. Each component has a wavelength-dependent albedo. The wavelength-dependent diffuse albedo is sometimes referred to as the *spectral reflectance* (sometimes abbreviated to *reflectance* or, less commonly, *spectral albedo*). Figures 3.6 and 3.7 show examples of spectral reflectances for a number of different natural objects.

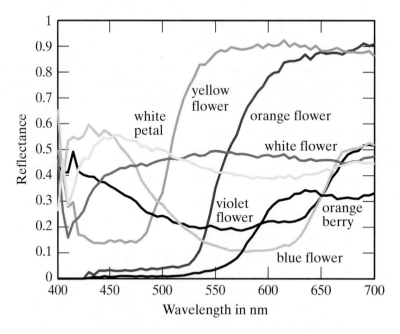

FIGURE 3.6: Spectral albedoes for a variety of natural surfaces measured by Esa Koivisto, Department of Physics, University of Kuopio, Finland, plotted against wavelength in nanometers. *These figures were plotted from data available at* `http://www.it.lut.fi/ip/research/color/database/database.html`.

There are two color regimes for specular reflection. If the surface is dielectric (i.e., does not conduct electricity), specularly reflected light tends to take the color of the light source. If the surface is a conductor, the specular albedo may depend quite strongly on wavelength, so that white light may result in colored specularities.

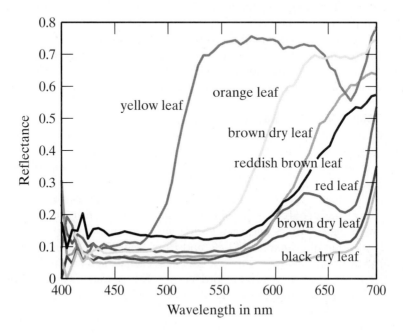

FIGURE 3.7: Spectral albedoes for a variety of natural surfaces measured by Esa Koivisto, Department of Physics, University of Kuopio, Finland, plotted against wavelength in nanometers. *These figures were plotted from data available at* http://www.it.lut.fi/ip/research/color/database/database.html.

3.3 REPRESENTING COLOR

Describing colors accurately is a matter of great commercial importance. Many products are closely associated with specific colors—for example, the golden arches, the color of various popular computers, and the color of photographic film boxes—and manufacturers are willing to go to a great deal of trouble to ensure that different batches have the same color. This requires a standard system for talking about color. Simple names are insufficient because relatively few people know many color names, and most people are willing to associate a large variety of colors with a given name.

3.3.1 Linear Color Spaces

There is a natural mechanism for representing color: agree on a standard set of primaries, and then describe any colored light by the three values of weights that people would use to match the light using those primaries. In principle, this is easy to use. To describe a color, we set up and perform the matching experiment and transmit the match weights. Of course, this approach extends to give a representation for surface colors as well if we use a standard light for illuminating the surface (and if the surfaces are equally clean, etc.).

Performing a matching experiment each time we wish to describe a color can be practical. For example, this is the technique used by paint stores; you take in a flake of paint, and they mix paint, adjusting the mixture until a color match is obtained. Paint stores do this because complicated scattering effects within paints mean that predicting the color of a mixture can be quite difficult. However, Grassman's laws mean that mixtures of colored lights—at least those seen in a simple display—mix *linearly*, which means that a much simpler procedure is available.

Color Matching Functions

When colors mix linearly, we can construct a simple algorithm to determine which weights would be used to match a source of some known spectral energy density given a fixed set of primaries. The spectral energy density of the source can be thought of as a weighted sum of single wavelength sources. Because color matching is linear, the combination of primaries that matches a weighted sum of single wavelength sources is obtained by matching the primaries to each of the single wavelength sources and then adding up these match weights.

For any set of primaries, P_1, P_2, and P_3, we can obtain a set of *color matching functions* by experiment. We tune the weight of each primary to match a unit energy source at every wavelength, and record a table of these weights against wavelengths. These tables are the color matching functions, which we write as $f_1(\lambda)$, $f_2(\lambda)$, and $f_3(\lambda)$. Now for some wavelength λ_0, we have

$$U(\lambda_0) = f_1(\lambda_0)P_1 + f_2(\lambda_0)P_2 + f_3(\lambda_0)P_3$$

(i.e., f_1, f_2, and f_3 give the weights required to match a unit energy source at that wavelength).

We wish to choose the weights to match a source $S(\lambda)$. This source is a sum of a vast number of single wavelength sources, each with a different intensity. We now match the primaries to each of the single wavelength sources and then add up these match weights, obtaining

$$S(\lambda) = w_1 P_1 + w_2 P_2 + w_3 P_3$$
$$= \left\{ \int_\Lambda f_1(\lambda)S(\lambda)d\lambda \right\} P_1 + \left\{ \int_\Lambda f_2(\lambda)S(\lambda)d\lambda \right\} P_2 + \left\{ \int_\Lambda f_3(\lambda)S(\lambda)d\lambda \right\} P_3.$$

General Issues for Linear Color Spaces

Linear color naming systems can be obtained by specifying primaries, which imply color matching functions, or by specifying color matching functions, which imply primaries. It is an inconvenient fact of life that, if the primaries are real lights, at least one of the color matching functions is negative for some wavelengths. This is not a violation of natural law; it just implies that subtractive matching is required to match some lights, whatever set of primaries is used. It is a nuisance, though.

One way to avoid this problem is to specify color matching functions that are everywhere positive (which guarantees that the primaries are imaginary because for some wavelengths their spectral energy density is negative). Although this looks like

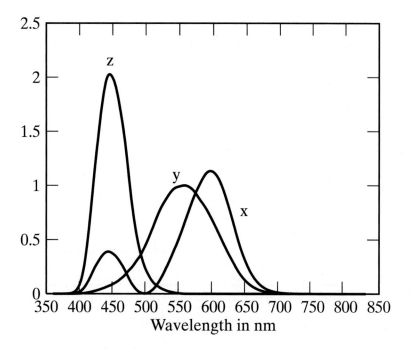

FIGURE 3.8: Color matching functions for the CIE X, Y, and Z primaries; the color matching functions are everywhere positive, so no subtractive matching is required, but the primaries are not real. *Figures plotted from data disseminated by the Color and Vision Research Laboratories database, compiled by Andrew Stockman and Lindsey Sharpe, and available at* http://www.cvrl.org/.

a problem—how would one create a real color with imaginary primaries?—it isn't, because color naming systems are hardly ever used that way. Usually, we would simply compare weights to tell whether colors are similar, and for that purpose it is enough to know the color matching functions. A variety of different systems have been standardized by the CIE (the *commission international d'éclairage,* which exists to create standards for such things).

Important Linear Color Spaces

The *CIE XYZ color space* is one quite popular standard. The color matching functions were chosen to be everywhere positive (Figure 3.8), so that the coordinates of any real light are always positive. It is not possible to obtain CIE X, Y, or Z primaries because for some wavelengths the value of their pectral energy density is negative. However, given color matching functions alone, one can specify the XYZ coordinates of a color and hence describe it. Linear color spaces allow a number of useful graphical constructions that are more difficult to draw in three dimensions than in two, so it is common to intersect the XYZ space with the plane $X + Y + Z = 1$ (as shown in Figure 3.10) and draw the resulting figure using coordinates

$$(x, y) = \left(\frac{X}{X + Y + Z}, \frac{Y}{X + Y + Z} \right).$$

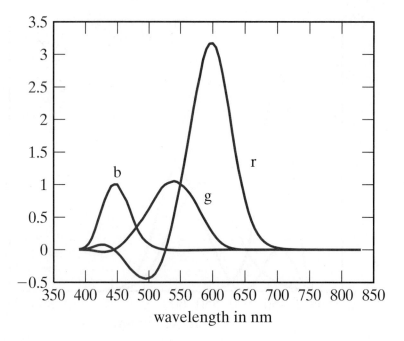

FIGURE 3.9: Color matching functions for the primaries for the RGB system. The negative values mean that subtractive matching is required to match lights at that wavelength with the RGB primaries. *Figures plotted from data disseminated by the Color and Vision Research Laboratories database, compiled by Andrew Stockman and Lindsey Sharpe, and available at* http://www.cvrl.org/.

This space, which is often referred to as the *CIE xy color space* is shown in Figure 3.12. CIE xy is widely used in vision and graphics textbooks and in some applications, but is usually regarded by professional colorimetrists as out of date.

The *RGB color space* is a linear color space that formally uses single wavelength primaries (645.16 nm for R, 526.32 nm for G, and 444.44 nm for B; see Figure 3.9). Informally, RGB uses whatever phosphors a monitor has as primaries. Available colors are usually represented as a unit cube—usually called the *RGB cube*—whose edges represent the R, G, and B weights. The cube is drawn in Figure 3.13.

The *opponent color space* is a linear color space derived from RGB. There is evidence that there are three kinds of color system in primates (e.g., see Mollon (1982); Hurvich and Jameson (1957)). The oldest responds to intensity (i.e., light-dark comparisons). A more recent, but still old, color system compares blue with yellow. The most recent color system compares red with green. In some applications, it is useful to use a comparable representation. This can be obtained from RGB coordinates using $I = (R + G + B)/3$ for intensity, $(B - (R + G)/2)/I$ for the blue-yellow comparison (sometimes called B-Y), and $(R - G)/I$ for the red-green comparison (sometimes called R-G). Notice that B-Y (resp. R-G) is positive for strongly blue (resp. red) colors and negative for strongly yellow (resp. green)

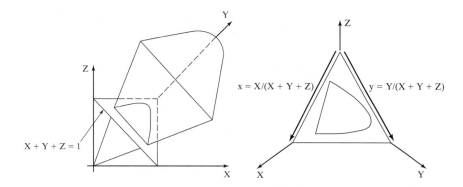

FIGURE 3.10: The volume of all visible colors in the CIE XYZ coordinate space is a cone whose vertex is at the origin. Usually it is easier to suppress the brightness of a color, which we can do because, to a good approximation, perception of color is linear, and we do this by intersecting the cone with the plane $X + Y + Z = 1$ to get the CIE xy space shown in Figure 3.12.

colors, and is intensity independent.

There are two useful constructions that work in linear color spaces, but are most commonly applied in CIE xy. First, because the color spaces are linear, and color matching is linear, all colors that can be obtained by mixing two primaries A and B lie on the line segment joining them plotted on the color space. Second, all colors that can be obtained by mixing three primaries A, B, and C lie in the triangle formed by the three primaries plotted on the color space. Typically, we use this construction to determine the set of colors (or *gamut*) that a set of monitor phosphors can display.

Subtractive Mixing and Inks

Intuition from one's finger-painting days suggests that the primary colors should be red, yellow, and blue, and that yellow and blue mix to make green. The reason this intuition doesn't apply to monitors is that paints involve pigments—which mix subtractively—rather than lights. Pigments can behave in quite complex ways, but the simplest model is that pigments remove color from incident light, which is reflected from paper. Thus, red ink is really a dye that absorbs green and blue light—incident red light passes through this dye and is reflected from the paper. In this case, mixing is subtractive.

Color spaces for this kind of mixing can be quite complicated. In the simplest case, mixing is linear (or reasonably close to linear), and the *CMY space* applies. In this space, there are three primaries: *cyan* (a blue-green color), *magenta* (a purplish color), and *yellow*. These primaries should be thought of as subtracting a light primary from white light; cyan is $W - R$ (white − red); magenta is $W - G$ (white − green), and yellow is $W - B$ (white − blue). Now the appearance of mixtures can be evaluated by reference to the RGB color space. For example, cyan

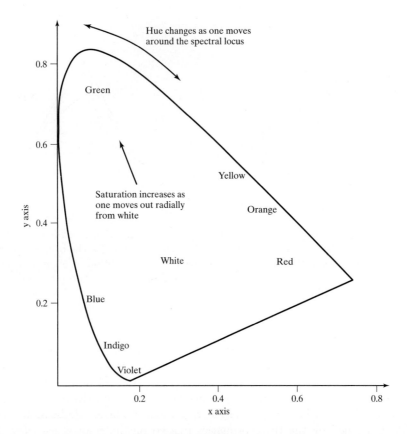

FIGURE 3.11: The figure shows a constant brightness section of the standard 1931 standard CIE xy color space, with color names marked on the diagram. Generally, colors that lie farther away from the neutral point are more saturated—the difference between deep red and pale pink—and hue—the difference between green and red—as one moves around the neutral point.

and magenta mixed give

$$(W - R) + (W - G) = R + G + B - R - G = B,$$

that is, blue. Notice that $W + W = W$ because we assume that ink cannot cause paper to reflect more light than it does when uninked. Practical printing devices use at least four inks (cyan, magenta, yellow, and black) because mixing color inks leads to a poor black, it is difficult to ensure good enough registration between the three color inks to avoid colored haloes around text, and color inks tend to be more expensive than black inks. Getting really good results from a color printing process is still difficult: different inks have significantly different spectral properties, different papers also have different spectral properties, and inks can mix non-linearly.

One reason that fingerpainting is hard is that the color resulting from mixing paints can be quite hard to predict. This is because the outcome depends very strongly on details such as the specific pigment in the paint, the size of pigment particles, the medium in which the pigment is suspended, the care put into stirring

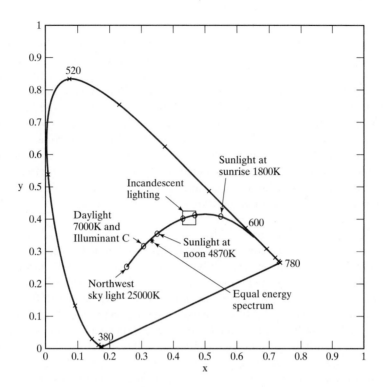

FIGURE 3.12: The figure shows a constant brightness section of the standard 1931 standard CIE xy color space. This space has two coordinate axes. The curved boundary of the figure is often known as the *spectral locus*; it represents the colors experienced when lights of a single wavelength are viewed. The figure shows a locus of colors due to black-body radiators at different temperatures and a locus of different sky colors. Near the center of the diagram is the neutral point, the color whose weights are equal for all three primaries. CIE selected the primaries so that this light appears achromatic. Generally, colors that lie farther away from the neutral point are more saturated—the difference between deep red and pale pink—and hue—the difference between green and red—as one moves around the neutral point.

the mixture, and similar parameters; usually, we do not have enough detailed information to use a full physical model of these effects. A useful study of this difficult topic is (Berns 2000).

3.3.2   Non-linear Color Spaces

The coordinates of a color in a linear space may not necessarily encode properties that are common in language or are important in applications. Useful color terms include: *hue*, the property of a color that varies in passing from red to green; *saturation*, the property of a color that varies in passing from red to pink; and *brightness* (sometimes called *lightness* or *value*, the property that varies in passing from black to white. For example, if we are interested in checking whether a color lies in a particular range of reds, we might wish to encode the hue of the color directly.

Another difficulty with linear color spaces is that the individual coordinates do not capture human intuitions about the topology of colors; it is a common intuition that hues form a circle, in the sense that hue changes from red through orange to yellow, and then green, and from there to cyan, blue, purple, and then red again. Another way to think of this is to picture local hue relations: red is next to purple and orange; orange is next to red and yellow; yellow is next to orange and green; green is next to yellow and cyan; cyan is next to green and blue; blue is next to cyan and purple; and purple is next to blue and red. Each of these local relations works, and globally they can be modeled by laying hues out in a circle. This means that no individual coordinate of a linear color space can model hue, because that coordinate has a maximum value that is far away from the minimum value.

Hue, Saturation, and Value

A standard method for dealing with this problem is to construct a color space that reflects these relations by applying a non-linear transformation to the RGB space. There are many such spaces. One, called *HSV space* (for hue, saturation, and value), is obtained by looking down the center axis of the RGB cube. Because RGB is a linear space, brightness—called *value* in HSV—varies with scale out from the origin. We can flatten the RGB cube to get a 2D space of constant value and for neatness deform it to be a hexagon. This gets the structure shown in Figure 3.13, where hue is given by an angle that changes as one goes round the neutral point and saturation changes as one moves away from the neutral point.

There are a variety of other possible changes of coordinate from linear color space to linear color space, or from linear to non-linear color spaces (Fairchild (1998) is a good reference). There is no obvious advantage to using one set of coordinates over another (particularly if the difference between coordinate systems is just a one–one transformation) unless one is concerned with coding, bit rates, and the like, or with perceptual uniformity.

Uniform Color Spaces

Usually one cannot reproduce colors exactly. This means it is important to know whether a color difference would be noticeable to a human viewer. It is generally useful to compare the significance of small color differences, but it is usually dangerous to try and compare large color differences; consider trying to answer the question, "Is the blue patch more different from the yellow patch than the red patch is from the green patch?".

One can determine *just noticeable differences* by modifying a color shown to observers until they can only just tell it has changed in a comparison with the original color. When these differences are plotted on a color space, they form the boundary of a region of colors that are indistinguishable from the original colors. Usually ellipses are fitted to the just noticeable differences. It turns out that in CIE xy space these ellipses depend quite strongly on where in the space the difference occurs, as the MacAdam ellipses in Figure 3.14 illustrate.

This means that the size of a difference in (x, y) coordinates, given by $((\Delta x)^2 + (\Delta y)^2)^{(1/2)}$, is a poor indicator of the significance of a difference in color (if it were a good indicator, the ellipses representing indistinguishable colors would be circles).

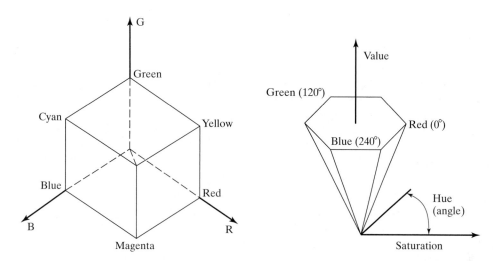

FIGURE 3.13: On the **left**, we see the RGB cube; this is the space of all colors that can be obtained by combining three primaries (R, G, and B—usually defined by the color response of a monitor) with weights between zero and one. It is common to view this cube along its neutral axis—the axis from the origin to the point (1, 1, 1)—to see a hexagon. This hexagon codes hue (the property that changes as a color is changed from green to red) as an angle, which is intuitively satisfying. On the **right**, we see a cone obtained from this cross-section, where the distance along a generator of the cone gives the value (or brightness) of the color, the angle around the cone gives the hue, and the distance out gives the saturation of the color.

A *uniform color space* is one in which the distance in coordinate space is a fair guide to the significance of the difference between two colors—in such a space, if the distance in coordinate space were below some threshold, a human observer would not be able to tell the colors apart.

A more uniform space can be obtained from CIE XYZ by using a projective transformation to skew the ellipses; this yields the *CIE u׳v׳ space CIE u'v' space*, illustrated in Figure 3.15. The coordinates are:

$$(u', v') = \left(\frac{4X}{X + 15Y + 3Z}, \frac{9Y}{X + 15Y + 3Z} \right).$$

Generally, the distance between coordinates in u׳, v׳ space is a fair indicator of the significance of the difference between two colors. Of course, this omits differences in brightness. *CIE LAB* is now almost universally the most popular uniform color space. Coordinates of a color in LAB are obtained as a non-linear mapping

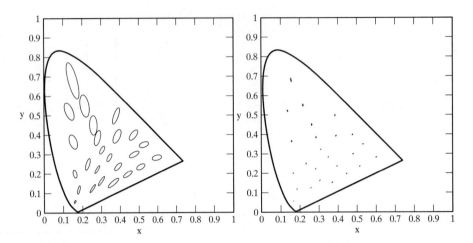

FIGURE 3.14: This figure shows variations in color matches on a CIE xy space. At the center of the ellipse is the color of a test light; the size of the ellipse represents the scatter of lights that the human observers tested would match to the test color; the boundary shows where the just noticeable difference is. The ellipses in the figure on the **left** have been magnified 10x for clarity; on the **right** they are plotted to scale, with color names on the CIE diagram as a reference. The ellipses are known as MacAdam ellipses after their inventor. Notice that the ellipses at the top are larger than those at the bottom of the figure, and that they rotate as they move up. This means that the magnitude of the difference in x, y coordinates is a poor guide to the difference in color. Ellipses are plotted using data from MacAdam (1942).

of the XYZ coordinates:

$$L^* = 116 \left(\frac{Y}{Y_n} \right)^{\frac{1}{3}} - 16$$

$$a^* = 500 \left[\left(\frac{X}{X_n} \right)^{\frac{1}{3}} - \left(\frac{Y}{Y_n} \right)^{\frac{1}{3}} \right]$$

$$b^* = 200 \left[\left(\frac{Y}{Y_n} \right)^{\frac{1}{3}} - \left(\frac{Z}{Z_n} \right)^{\frac{1}{3}} \right]$$

Here X_n, Y_n, and Z_n are the X, Y, and Z coordinates of a reference white patch. The reason to care about the LAB space is that it is substantially uniform. In some problems, it is important to understand how different two colors will look *to a human observer*, and differences in LAB coordinates give a good guide.

3.4   A MODEL OF IMAGE COLOR

Assume that an image pixel is the image of some surface patch. Many phenomena affect the color of this pixel. The main effects are: the camera response to illumination (which might not be linear); the choice of camera receptors; the amount of light that arrives at the surface; the color of light arriving at the surface; the dependence of the diffuse albedo on wavelength; and specular components. A quite

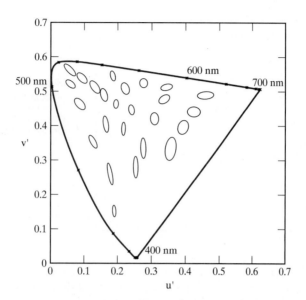

FIGURE 3.15: This figure shows the CIE 1976 $u\prime$, $v\prime$ space, which is obtained by a projective transformation of CIE x, y space. The intention is to make the MacAdam ellipses (from Figure 3.14) uniformly circles. This would yield a uniform color space. A variety of non-linear transforms can be used to make the space more uniform (see Fairchild (1998) for details).

simple model can be used to separate some of these effects.

Generally, it is easier to model linear cameras. CCDs are intrinsically linear devices. However, most users are used to film, which tends to compress the incoming dynamic range (brightness differences at the top end of the range are reduced, as are those at the bottom end of the range). The output of a linear device tends to look too harsh (the darks are too dark and the lights are too light), so that manufacturers apply various forms of compression to the output. We assume that the camera response has been calibrated, perhaps using the methods of Section 2.2.1, so that it is linear.

Assume that the surfaces that we are dealing with can be described by the diffuse+specular model. Write $\boldsymbol{x}$ for a point, λ for wavelength, $E(\boldsymbol{x}, \lambda)$ for the spectral energy density of the light leaving a surface, $\rho(\boldsymbol{x}, \lambda)$ for the albedo of a surface as a function of wavelength and position, $S_d(\boldsymbol{x}, \lambda)$ for the spectral energy density of the light source (which may vary with position; for example, the intensity might change), and $S_i(\boldsymbol{x}, \lambda)$ for the spectral energy density of interreflected light. Then we have that:

$$
\begin{aligned}
E(\boldsymbol{x}, \lambda) &= [\text{diffuse term}] + (\text{specular term}) \\
&= [(\text{direct term}) + (\text{interreflected term})] + (\text{specular term}) \\
&= (\rho(\boldsymbol{x}, \lambda)(\text{geometric term}))[(S_d(\boldsymbol{x}, \lambda) + S_i(\boldsymbol{x}, \lambda))] + (\text{specular term}).
\end{aligned}
$$

The geometric terms represent how intensity is affected by surface normal. Notice that the diffuse term is affected both by the color of the surface and by the color

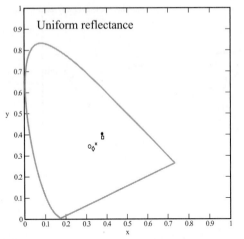

FIGURE 3.16: Light sources can have quite widely varying colors. This figure shows the color of the four light sources of Figure 3.5, compared with the color of a uniform spectral power distribution, plotted in CIE x, y coordinates.

of the light (examples in Figures 3.16 and 3.17).

Because the camera is linear, the pixel value at $\boldsymbol{x}$ is a sum of terms corresponding to each of the terms in $E(\vec{x}, \lambda)$. Write $\boldsymbol{d}(\boldsymbol{x})$ for the color taken by a flat patch facing the light source at $\boldsymbol{x}$ with the same albedo as the actual patch there, $g(\boldsymbol{x})$ for a geometric term (explained below), $\boldsymbol{i}(\boldsymbol{x})$ for the contribution of the interreflected term, $\boldsymbol{s}(\boldsymbol{x})$ for the unit intensity color of the specular term, and $g_s(\boldsymbol{x})$ for a geometric term (explained below). Then we have:

$$
\begin{aligned}
\boldsymbol{C}(\boldsymbol{x}) &= [(\text{direct term}) + (\text{interreflected term})] + (\text{specular term}) \\
&= g_d(\boldsymbol{x})\boldsymbol{d}(\boldsymbol{x}) + \boldsymbol{i}(\boldsymbol{x}) + g_s(\boldsymbol{x})\boldsymbol{s}(\boldsymbol{x}).
\end{aligned}
$$

Generally, to work with this model, we ignore $\boldsymbol{i}(\boldsymbol{x})$; we identify and remove specularities, using the methods of Section 3.5.1, and so assume that $\boldsymbol{C}(\boldsymbol{x}) = g_d(\boldsymbol{x})\boldsymbol{d}(\boldsymbol{x})$.

3.4.1   The Diffuse Term

There are two diffuse components. One, $\boldsymbol{i}(\boldsymbol{x})$, is due to interreflections. Interreflections can be a significant source of colored light. If a large colored surface reflects light onto another surface, that surface's color can change quite substantially. This is an effect that people find hard to see, but which is usually fairly easy to spot in photographs. There are no successful models for removing these color shifts, most likely because they can be very hard to predict. This is because many different surface reflectances can have the same color, so that two surfaces with the same color (but different reflectances) can have quite differently colored interreflections. The interreflection term is often small, and usually is simply ignored.

Ignoring the interreflected component, the diffuse term is

$$
g_d(\boldsymbol{x})\boldsymbol{d}(\boldsymbol{x}).
$$

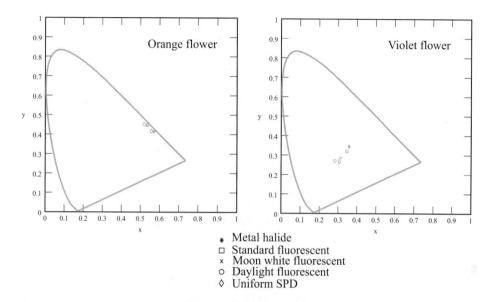

* Metal halide
□ Standard fluorescent
× Moon white fluorescent
○ Daylight fluorescent
◇ Uniform SPD

FIGURE 3.17: The color of a light source affects the color of surfaces lit by the source. The different colors obtained by lighting the violet flower of Figure 3.6 (**left**) and the orange flower of Figure 3.6 (**right**) with the four light sources of Figure 3.5.

Here $d(x)$ is the *image* color of an equivalent *flat* surface facing the light source and viewed under the same light. The geometric term, $g_d(x)$, varies relatively slowly over space and accounts for the change in brightness due to the orientation of the surface.

We can model the dependence of $d(x)$ on the light and on the surface by assuming we are viewing flat, diffuse surfaces, illuminated from infinitely far behind the camera. In this case, there will be no effects due to specularities or to surface orientation. The color of light arriving at the camera will be determined by two factors: first, the wavelength-dependent albedo of the surface that the light is leaving; and second, the wavelength-dependent intensity of the light falling on that surface. If a patch of perfectly diffuse surface with diffuse albedo $\rho(\lambda)$ is illuminated by a light whose spectrum is $S(\lambda)$, the spectrum of the reflected light is $\rho(\lambda)S(\lambda)$. Assume the camera has linear photoreceptors, and the k'th type of photoreceptor has sensitivity $\sigma_k(\lambda)$. If a linear photoreceptor of the kth type sees this surface patch, its response is:

$$p_k = \int_\Lambda \sigma_k(\lambda)\rho(\lambda)S(\lambda)d\lambda,$$

where Λ is the range of all relevant wavelengths.

The main engineering parameter here is the photoreceptor sensitivities $\sigma_k(\lambda)$. For some applications such as shadow removal (Section 3.5.2), it can be quite helpful to have photoreceptor sensitivities that are "narrow-band" (i.e., the photoreceptors respond to only one wavelength). Usually, the only practical methods to change the photoreceptor sensitivities are to either put colored filters in front of the camera or to use a different camera. Using a different camera doesn't work particularly

well, because manufacturers try to have sensitivities that are reasonably compatible with human receptor sensitivities. They do this so that cameras give about
the same responses to colored lights that people do; as a result, cameras tend to
have quite similar receptor sensitivities. There are three ways to proceed: install
narrow-band filters in front of the lens (difficult to do and seldom justified); apply a
transformation to the receptor outputs that makes them behave more like narrow-
band receptors (often helpful, if the necessary data are available, Finlayson *et al.*
(1994*b*);Barnard *et al.* (2001*a*)); or assume that they are narrow-band receptors
and tolerate any errors that result (generally quite successful).

3.4.2   The Specular Term

The specular component will have a characteristic color, and its intensity will change
with position. We can model the specular component as

$$g_s(\boldsymbol{x})\boldsymbol{s}(\boldsymbol{x}),$$

where $\boldsymbol{s}(\boldsymbol{x})$ is the unit intensity *image* color of the specular reflection at that pixel,
and $g_s(\boldsymbol{x})$ is a term that varies from pixel to pixel, and models the amount of energy
specularly reflected. We expect $g_s(\boldsymbol{x})$ to be zero at most points, and large at some
points.

The color $\boldsymbol{s}(\boldsymbol{x})$ of the specular component depends on the material. Generally,
metal surfaces have a specular component that is wavelength dependent and so
takes on a characteristic color that depends on the metal (gold is yellow, copper
is orange, platinum is white, and osmium is blue or purple). Surfaces that do
not conduct—*dielectric surfaces*— have a specular component that is independent
of wavelength (e.g., the specularities on a shiny plastic object are the color of the
light). Section 3.5.1 describes how these properties can be used to find specularities,
and to find image regions corresponding to metal or plastic objects.

3.5   INFERENCE FROM COLOR

Our color model supports a variety of inferences. It can be used to find specularities (Section 3.5.1); to remove shadows (Section 3.5.2); and to infer surface color
(Section 3.5.3).

3.5.1   Finding Specularities Using Color

Specular reflections can have strong effects on an object's appearance. Typically,
they appear as small, bright patches, called *highlights* or *specularities*. Highlights
have a substantial effect on human perception of a surface properties; the addition
of small, highlight-like patches to a figure makes the object depicted look glossy
or shiny. Specularities are often bright enough to saturate the camera, so that the
color of a specularity can be hard to measure. However, because the appearance of
a specularity is quite strongly constrained, there are a number of effective schemes
for marking them, and the results can be used as a shape cue.

The dynamic range of practically available albedoes is relatively small. Surfaces with very high or very low albedo are difficult to make. Uniform illumination
is common too, and most cameras are reasonably close to linear within their operating range. This means that very bright patches cannot be due to diffuse reflection;

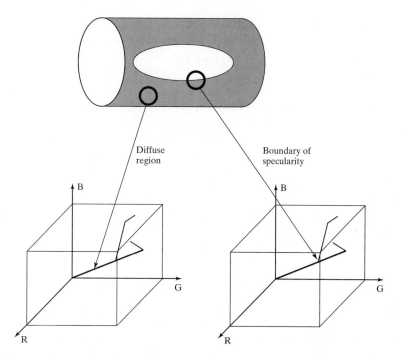

FIGURE 3.18: The linear clusters produced by specularities on plastic objects can be found by reasoning about windows of image pixels. In a world of plastic objects on a black background, a background window produces a region of pixels that are point-like in color space—all pixels have the same color. A window that lies along the body produces a line-like cluster of points in color space, because the intensity varies, but the color does not. At the boundary of a specularity, windows produce plane-like clusters because points are a weighted combination of two different colors (the specular and the body color). Finally, at the interior of a specular region, the windows can produce volume-like clusters, because the camera saturates, and the extent of the window can include both the boundary-style window and saturated points. Whether a region is line-like, plane-like, or volume-like can be determined easily by looking at the eigenvalues of the covariance of the pixels.

they must be either sources (of one form or another—perhaps a stained glass window with the light behind it) or specularities. Furthermore, specularities tend to be small. Thus, looking for small, bright patches can be an effective way to find specularities (Brelstaff and Blake 1988a).

   An alternative is to use image color. From our model, the color of specularities on dielectric objects is the color of the light source. Assume we can ignore the interreflection term, either because we have an isolated object or because the term doesn't change much over the object we are viewing. Our model gives the image color as a sum of a diffuse term and a specular term. Now consider a patch of surface around a specularity. We expect that this patch is small, because we expect specularities to be small (this will be true on curved surfaces; the approach we are describing might not work for flat surfaces). Because the patch is small, we expect that $d(x)$ does not change in the patch; we do not expect to be unlucky, and have a specularity on an albedo boundary. We expect that $s(x)$ does not change within the patch, because the color of the specularity will be the color of the light source, and this will not change within a small patch.

On a dielectric object, as we move from a patch with no specular reflection to one with a specular component, the image color will change, because the size of the specular component changes. We can write the image color as

$$g_d(x)d + g_s(x)s,$$

where s is the color of the source and d is the color of the diffuse reflected light, $g_d(x)$ is the geometric term that depends on the orientation of the surface, and $g_s(x)$ is a term that gives the extent of the specular reflection.

If the object is curved, then $g_s(x)$ is small over much of the surface and large only around specularities; $g_d(x)$ varies more slowly with the orientation of the surface. We now map the colors produced by this surface in receptor response space and look at the structures that appear there.

The term $g_d(x)d$ produces a line that should extend to pass through the origin because it represents the same vector of receptor responses multiplied by a constant that varies over space. If there is a specularity, then we expect to see a second line due to $g_s(x)s$. This does not, in general, pass through the origin (because of the diffuse term). This is a line, rather than a planar region, because $g_s(x)$ is large over only a small range of surface normals. We expect that, because the surface is curved, this corresponds to a small region of surface. The term $g_d(x)$ should be approximately constant in this region. We expect a line, rather than an isolated pixel value, because we expect surfaces to have (possibly narrow) specular lobes, meaning that the specular coefficient has a range of values. This second line might collide with a face of the color cube and get clipped.

The resulting dog-leg pattern leads pretty much immediately to a specularity marking algorithm: find the pattern and then find the specular line. All the pixels on this line are specular pixels, and the specular and diffuse components can be estimated easily. For the approach to work effectively, we need to be confident that only one object is represented in the collection of pixels. This is helped by using local image windows, as illustrated by Figure 3.18. The observations underlying the method hold even if the surface is not monochrome—a coffee mug with a picture on it, for example—but finding the resulting structures in the color space now becomes something of a nuisance and, to our knowledge, has not been demonstrated.

3.5.2   Shadow Removal Using Color

Lightness methods make the assumption that "fast" edges in images are due to changes in albedo (Section 2.2.3). This assumption is usable, but fails badly at shadows, particularly shadows in sunlight outdoors (Figure 3.20), where there can be a large and fast change of image brightness. People usually are not fooled into believing that a shadow is a patch of dark surface, so must have some method to identify shadow edges. Home users often like editing and improving photographs, and programs that could remove shadows from images would be valuable. A shadow removal program would work something like a lightness method: find all edges, identify the shadow edges, remove those, and then integrate to get the picture back.

There are some cues for finding shadow edges that seem natural, but don't work well. One might assume that shadow edges have very large dynamic range (which albedo edges can't have; see Section 2.1.1), but this is not always the case. One might assume that, at a shadow edge, there was a change in brightness but not in color. It turns out that this is not the case for outdoor shadows, because the lit region is illuminated by yellowish sunlight, and the shadowed region is illuminated by bluish light from the sky, or sometimes by interreflected light from buildings, and so on. However, a really useful cue can be obtained by modelling the different light sources.

We assume that light sources are black bodies, so that their spectral energy density is a function of temperature. We assume that surfaces are diffuse. We use the simplified black-body model of Section 3.2.1, where, writing T for the temperature of the body in Kelvins, h for Planck's constant, k for Boltzmann's constant, c for the speed of light, and λ for the wavelength, we have

$$E(\lambda; T) = C \frac{\exp(-hc/k\lambda T)}{\lambda^5}$$

(C is some constant of proportionality). Now assume that the color receptors each respond only at one wavelength, which we write λ_k for the k'th receptor, so that $\sigma_k(\lambda) = \delta(\lambda - \lambda_k)$. If we view a surface with spectral albedo $\rho(\lambda)$ illuminated by one of these sources at temperature T, the response of the j'th receptor will be

$$r_j = \int \sigma_j(\lambda)\rho(\lambda)K \frac{\exp(-hc/k\lambda T)}{\lambda^5} d\lambda = K\rho(\lambda_j) \frac{\exp(-hc/k\lambda_j T)}{\lambda_j^5}.$$

We can form a color space that is very well behaved by taking $c_1 = \log(r_1/r_3)$, $c_2 = \log(r_2/r_3)$, because

$$\begin{pmatrix} c_1 \\ c_2 \end{pmatrix} = \begin{pmatrix} a_1 \\ a_2 \end{pmatrix} + \frac{1}{T} \begin{pmatrix} b_1 \\ b_2 \end{pmatrix}$$

where $a_1 = \log \rho(\lambda_1) - \log \rho(\lambda_3) + 5 \log \lambda_3 - 5 \log \lambda_1$ and $b_1 = (hc/k)(1/\lambda_3 - 1/\lambda_1)$ (and a_2, b_2 follow). Notice that, when one changes the color temperature of the source, the (c_1, c_2) coordinates move along a straight line. The direction of the line depends on the sensor, *but not on the surface*. Call this direction the **color temperature direction**. The intercept of the line depends on the surface.

Now consider a world of colored surfaces, and map the image colors to this space. There is a family of parallel lines in this space, whose direction is the color temperature direction. Different surfaces may map to different lines. If we change the color temperature of the illuminant, then each color in this space will move along the color temperature direction, but colors will not move from line to line. We now represent a surface color by its line. For example, we could construct a line through the origin that is perpendicular to color temperature direction, then represent a surface color by distance along this line (Figure 3.19). We can represent each pixel in the image in this space, and in this representation the color image becomes a gray-level image, *where the gray level does not change inside shadows* (because a shadow region just has a different color temperature to the non-shadowed

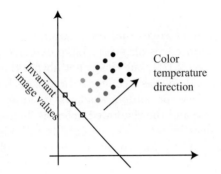 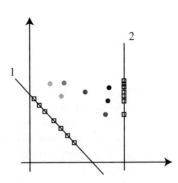

FIGURE 3.19: Changing the color temperature of the light under which a surface is viewed moves the (c_1, c_2) coordinates of that surface along the color temperature direction (**left**; the different gray patches represent the same surface under different lights). If we now project the coordinates along the (c_1, c_2) direction onto some line, we obtain a value that doesn't change when the illuminant color temperature changes. This is the invariant value for that pixel. Generally, we do not know enough about the imaging system to estimate the color temperature direction. However, we expect to see many different surfaces in each scene; this suggests that the right choice of color temperature direction on the **right** is 1 (where there are many different types of surface) rather than 2 (where the range of invariant values is small).

region). Finlayson (1996) calls this the *invariant image*. Any edge that appears in the image but not in the invariant image is a shadow edge, so we can now apply our original formula: find all edges, identify the shadow edges, remove those, and then integrate to get the picture back.

Of course, under practical circumstances, usually we do not know enough about the sensors to evaluate the as and bs that define this family of lines, so we cannot get the invariant image directly. However, we can infer a direction in (c_1, c_2) space that is a good estimate by a form of entropy reasoning. We must choose a color temperature direction. Assume the world is rich in differently colored surfaces. Now consider two surfaces S_1 and S_2. If $\boldsymbol{c}_1$ (the (c_1, c_2) values for S_1) and $\boldsymbol{c}_2$ are such that $\boldsymbol{c}_1 - \boldsymbol{c}_2$ is parallel to the color temperature direction, we can choose T_1 and T_2 so that S_1 viewed under light with color temperature T_1 will look the same as S_2 viewed under light with color temperature T_2. We expect this to be uncommon, because surfaces tend not to mimic one another in this way. This means we expect that colors will tend to spread out when we project along a good estimate of the color temperature direction. A reasonable measure of this spreading out is the *entropy* of the histogram of projected colors. We can now estimate the invariant image, without knowing anything about the sensor. We search directions in (c_1, c_2) space, projecting all the image colors along that direction; our estimate of the color temperature direction is the one where this projection yields the largest entropy. From this we can compute the invariant image, and so apply our shadow removal strategy above. In practice, the method works well, though great care is required with the integration procedure to get the best results (Figure 3.20).

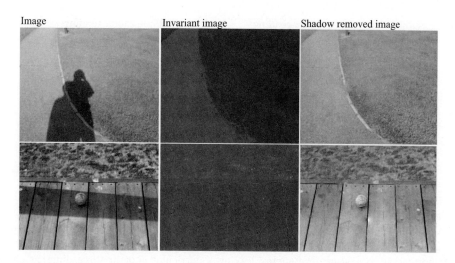

FIGURE 3.20: The invariant of the text and of Figure 3.19 does not change value when a surface is shadowed. Finlayson *et al.* use this to build a shadow removal system that works by (a) taking image edges; (b) forming an invariant image; then (c) using that invariant image to identify shadow edges; and finally (d) integrating only non-shadow edges to form the result. The results are quite convincing. *This figure was originally published as Figures 2 and 4 of "On the Removal of Shadows From Images," G. Finlayson, S. Hordley, C. Lu and M. Drew, IEEE Transactions on Pattern Analysis and Machine Intelligence, 2006 © IEEE, 2006.*

3.5.3 Color Constancy: Surface Color from Image Color

In our model, the image color depends on both light color and on surface color. If we light a green surface with white light, we get a green image; if we light a white surface with a green light, we also get a green image. This makes it difficult to name surface colors from pictures. We would like to have an algorithm that can take an image, discount the effect of the light, and report the actual color of the surface being viewed.

This process is called *color constancy*. Humans have some form of color constancy algorithm. People are often unaware of this, and inexperienced photographers are sometimes surprised that a scene photographed indoors under fluorescent lights has a blue cast, whereas the same scene photographed outdoors may have a warm orange cast. The simple linear models of Section 3.3 can predict the color an observer will perceive when shown an isolated spot of light of a given power spectral distribution. But if this spot is part of a larger, more complex scene, these models can give wildly inaccurate predictions. This is because the human color constancy algorithm uses various forms of scene information to decide what color to report. Demonstrations by Land and McCann (1971), which are illustrated in Figure 3.21, give convincing examples of this effect. It is surprisingly difficult to predict what colors a human will see in a complex scene (Fairchild (1998); Helson (1938a); (1938b); (1934); (1940)). This is one of the many difficulties that make it hard to produce really good color reproduction systems.

Human color constancy is not perfectly accurate, and people can choose to

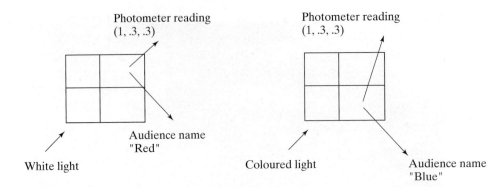

FIGURE 3.21: Land showed an audience a quilt of rectangles of flat colored papers—since known as a Mondrian for a purported resemblance to the work of that artist—illuminated using three slide projectors, casting red, green and blue light respectively. He used a photometer to measure the energy leaving a particular spot in three different channels, corresponding to the three classes of receptor in the eye. He recorded the measurement, and asked the audience to name the patch. Assume the answer was "red" (on the **left**). Land then adjusted the slide projectors so that some other patch reflected light that gave the same photometer measurements, and asked the audience to name that patch. The reply would describe the patch's color in white light—if the patch looked blue in white light, the answer would be "blue" (on the **right**). In later versions of this demonstration, Land put wedge-shaped neutral density filters into the slide projectors so that the color of the light illuminating the quilt of papers would vary slowly across the quilt. Again, although the photometer readings vary significantly from one end of a patch to another, the audience sees the patch as having a constant color.

disregard information from their color constancy system. As a result, people can often report:

- the color a surface would have in white light (often called *surface color*);

- the color of the light arriving at the eye (a useful skill that allows artists to paint surfaces illuminated by colored lighting); and

- the color of the light falling on the surface.

The model of image color in Section 3.4 is

$$C(\boldsymbol{x}) = g_d(\boldsymbol{x})\boldsymbol{d}(\boldsymbol{x}) + g_s(\boldsymbol{x})\boldsymbol{s}(\boldsymbol{x}) + \boldsymbol{i}(\boldsymbol{x}).$$

We decided to ignore the interreflection term $\boldsymbol{i}(\boldsymbol{x})$. In principle, we could use the methods of Section 3.5.1 to generate new images without specularities. This brings us to the term $g_d(\boldsymbol{x})\boldsymbol{d}(\boldsymbol{x})$. Assume that $g_d(\boldsymbol{x})$ is a constant, so we are viewing a flat, frontal surface. The resulting term, $\boldsymbol{d}(\boldsymbol{x})$, models the world as a collage of flat, frontal, diffuse colored surfaces. Such worlds are sometimes called *Mondrian worlds*, after the painter. Notice that, under our assumptions, $\boldsymbol{d}(\boldsymbol{x})$ consists of a set of patches of fixed color. We assume that there is a single illuminant that has a constant color over the whole image. This term is a conglomeration of illuminant, receptor, and reflectance information. It is impossible to disentangle these completely in a realistic world. However, current algorithms can make quite usable estimates of surface color from image colors given a well-populated world of colored surfaces and a reasonable illuminant.

Recall from Section 3.4 that if a patch of perfectly diffuse surface with diffuse spectral reflectance $\rho(\lambda)$ is illuminated by a light whose spectrum is $E(\lambda)$, the spectrum of the reflected light is $\rho(\lambda)E(\lambda)$ (multiplied by some constant to do with surface orientation, which we have already decided to ignore). If a linear photoreceptor of the kth type sees this surface patch, its response is:

$$p_k = \int_\Lambda \sigma_k(\lambda)\rho(\lambda)E(\lambda)d\lambda,$$

where Λ is the range of all relevant wavelengths, and $\sigma_k(\lambda)$ is the sensitivity of the kth photoreceptor.

Finite-Dimensional Linear Models

This response is linear in the surface reflectance and linear in the illumination, which suggests using linear models for the families of possible surface reflectances and illuminants. A *finite-dimensional linear model* models surface spectral albedoes and illuminant spectral energy density as a weighted sum of a finite number of basis functions. We need not use the same bases for reflectances and for illuminants.

If a finite-dimensional linear model of surface reflectance is a reasonable description of the world, any surface reflectance can be written as

$$\rho(\lambda) = \sum_{j=1}^{n} r_j\phi_j(\lambda),$$

where the $\phi_j(\lambda)$ are the basis functions for the model of reflectance, and the r_j vary from surface to surface. Similarly, if a finite-dimensional linear model of the illuminant is a reasonable model, any illuminant can be written as

$$E(\lambda) = \sum_{i=1}^{m} e_i\psi_i(\lambda),$$

where the $\psi_i(\lambda)$ are the basis functions for the model of illumination.

When both models apply, the response of a receptor of the kth type is

$$
\begin{aligned}
p_k &= \int \sigma_k(\lambda)\left(\sum_{j=1}^{n} r_j\phi_j(\lambda)\right)\left(\sum_{i=1}^{m} e_i\psi_i(\lambda)\right)d\lambda \\
&= \sum_{i=1,j=1}^{m,n} e_i r_j \left(\int \sigma_k(\lambda)\phi_j(\lambda)\psi_i(\lambda)\right)d\lambda \\
&= \sum_{i=1,j=1}^{m,n} e_i r_j g_{ijk},
\end{aligned}
$$

where we expect that the

$$g_{ijk} = \int \sigma_k(\lambda)\phi_j(\lambda)\psi_i(\lambda)d\lambda$$

are known, as they are components of the world model (they can be learned from observations; see the exercises).

Inferring Surface Color

The finite-dimensional linear model describes the interaction between illumination color, surface color, and image color. To infer surface color from image color, we need some sort of assumption. There are several plausible cues that can be used.

Specular reflections at dielectric surfaces have uniform specular albedo. We could find the specularities with the methods of that section, then recover surface color using this information. At a specularity, we have

$$p_k = \int \sigma_k(\lambda) \sum_{i=1}^{m} e_i\psi_i(\lambda)d\lambda,$$

and so if we knew the spectral sensitivities of the sensor and the basis functions ψ_i, we could solve for e_i by solving a linear system. Now we know all e_i, and all p_k for each pixel. We can solve the linear system

$$p_k = \sum_{i=1,j=1}^{m,n} e_i r_j g_{ijk}$$

in the unknown r_j to recover reflectance coefficients.

Known average reflectance is another plausible cue. In this case, we assume that the spatial average of reflectance in all scenes is constant and known (e.g., we might assume that all scenes have a spatial average of reflectance that is dull gray). In the finite-dimensional basis for reflectance, we can write this average as

$$\sum_{j=1}^{n} \overline{r_j}\phi_j(\lambda).$$

Now if the average reflectance is constant, the average of the receptor responses must be constant too (if the imaging process is linear; see the discussion), and the average of the response of the kth receptor can be written as:

$$\overline{p_k} = \sum_{i=1,j=1}^{m,n} e_i g_{ijk}\overline{r_j}.$$

We know $\overline{p_k}$ and $\overline{r_j}$, and so have a linear system in the unknown light coefficients e_i. We solve this, and then recover reflectance coefficients at each pixel, as for the case of specularities. For reasonable choices of reflectors and dimension of light and surface basis, this linear system will have full rank.

The **gamut** of a color image is revealing. The gamut is the set of different colors that appears in the image. Generally, it is difficult to obtain strongly colored pixels under white light with current imaging systems. Furthermore, if the picture is taken under strongly colored light, that will tend to bias the gamut. One doesn't see bright green pixels in images taken under deep red light, for example. As a result, the image gamut is a source of information about the illumination. If an image gamut contains two pixel values—call them p_1 and p_2—then it must be possible to take an image *under the same illuminant* that contains the value $tp_1 + (1 - t)p_2$ for $0 \leq t \leq 1$ (because we could mix the colorants on the surfaces). This means that the illuminant information depends on the convex hull of the image gamut. There are now various methods to exploit these observations. There is usually more than one illuminant consistent with a given image gamut, and geometric methods can be used to identify the consistent illuminants. This set can be narrowed down using probabilistic methods (for example, images contain lots of different colors (Forsyth 1990)) or physical methods (for example, the main sources of illumination are the sun and the sky, well modelled as black bodies (Finlayson and Hordley 2000)).

3.6 NOTES

There are a number of important general resources on the use of color. We recommend Hardin and Maffi (1997), Lamb and Bourriau (1995), Lynch and Livingston (2001), Minnaert (1993), Trussell *et al.* (1997), Williamson and Cummins (1983). Wyszecki and Stiles (1982) contains an enormous amount of helpful information. Recent textbooks with an emphasis on color include Velho *et al.* (2008), Lee (2009), Reinhard *et al.* (2008), Gevers *et al.* (2011) and Burger and Burge (2009).

Trichromacy and Color Spaces

Until quite recently, there was no conclusive explanation of why trichromacy applied, although it was generally believed to be due to the presence of three different types of color receptor in the eye. Work on the genetics of photoreceptors can be interpreted as confirming this hunch (see Nathans *et al.* (1986*a*) and Nathans *et al.* (1986*b*)), although a full explanation is still far from clear because this work can also be interpreted as suggesting many individuals have more than three types of photoreceptor (Mollon 1995).

There is an astonishing number of color spaces and color appearance models available. The important issue is not in what coordinate system one measures color, but how one counts the difference, so color metrics may still bear some thought.

Color metrics are an old topic; usually, one fits a metric tensor to MacAdam ellipses. The difficulty with this approach is that a metric tensor carries the strong implication that you can measure differences over large ranges by integration, whereas it is very hard to see large-range color comparisons as meaningful. Another concern is that the weight observers place on a difference in a Maxwellian view and the semantic significance of a difference in image colors are two very different things.

Specularity Finding

The specularity finding method we describe is due to Shafer (1985), with improvements due to Klinker *et al.* (1987), (1990), and to Maxwell and Shafer (2000).

Specularities can also be detected because they are small and bright (Brelstaff and Blake 1988*a*), because they differ in color and motion from the background (Lee and Bajcsy 1992*a*, Lee and Bajcsy 1992*b*, Zheng and Murata 2000), or because they distort patterns (Del Pozo and Savarese 2007). Specularities are a prodigious nuisance in reconstruction, because specularities cause matching points in different images to have different colors; various motion-based strategies have been developed to remove them in these applications (Lin *et al.* 2002, Swaminathan *et al.* 2002, Criminisi *et al.* 2005).

Color Constancy

Land reported a variety of color vision experiments (Land (1959*a*), (1959*b*), (1959*c*), (1983)). Finite-dimensional linear models for spectral reflectances can be supported by an appeal to surface physics as spectral absorption lines are thickened by solid state effects. The main experimental justifications for finite-dimensional linear models of surface reflectance are measurements, by Cohen (1964), of the surface reflectance of a selection of standard reference surfaces known as *Munsell chips*, and measurements of a selection of natural objects by Krinov (1947). Cohen (1964) performed a principal axis decomposition of his data to obtain a set of basis functions, and Maloney (1984) fitted weighted sums of these functions to Krinov's date to get good fits with patterned deviations. The first three principal axes explained in each case a high percentage of the sample variance (near 99 %), and hence a linear combination of these functions fitted all the sampled functions rather well. More recently, Maloney (1986) fitted Cohen's (1964) basis vectors to a large set of data, including Krinov's (1947) data, and further data on the surface reflectances of Munsell chips, and concluded that the dimension of an accurate model of surface reflectance was on the order of five or six.

Finite-dimensional linear models are an important tool in color constancy. There is a large collection of algorithms that follow rather naturally from the approach. Some algorithms exploit the properties of the linear spaces involved (Maloney (1984); Maloney and Wandell (1986); Wandell (1987)). Illumination can be inferred from: reference objects (Abdellatif *et al.* 2000); specular reflections (Judd (Judd 1960) writing in 1960 about early German work in surface color perception refers to this as "a more usual view"; recent work includes (D'Zmura and Lennie 1986, Flock 1984, Klinker *et al.* 1987, Lee 1986)); the average color (Buchsbaum 1980, Gershon 1987, Gershon *et al.* 1986); and the gamut (Forsyth (1990), Barnard (2000), Finlayson and Hordley (1999), (2000)).

The structure of the family of maps associated with a change in illumination has been studied quite extensively. The first work is due to Von Kries (who didn't think about it quite the way we do). He assumed that color constancy was, in essence, the result of independent lightness calculations in each channel, meaning that one can rectify an image by scaling each channel independently. This practice is known as Von Kries' law. The law boils down to assuming that the family of maps consists of diagonal matrices. Von Kries' law has proved to be a remarkably good law (Finlayson *et al.* 1994*a*). Current best practice involves applying a linear transformation to the channels and then scaling the result using diagonal maps (Finlayson *et al.* (1994*a*), (1994*b*)).

Reference datasets are available for testing methods (Barnard *et al.* 2002*c*). Color constancy methods seem to work quite well in practice (Barnard *et al.* 2002*a*, Barnard *et al.* 2002*b*); whether this is good enough is debated (Funt *et al.* 1998, Hordley and Finlayson 2006). Probabilistic methods can be applied to color constancy (Freeman and Brainard 1997). Prior models on illumination are a significant cue (Kawakami *et al.* 2007).

There is surprisingly little work on color constancy that unifies a study of the spatial variation in illumination with solutions for surface color, which is why we were reduced to ignoring a number of terms in our color model. Ideally, one would work in shadows and surface orientation, too. Again, the whole thing looks like an inference problem to us, but a subtle one. The main papers on this extremely important topic are Barnard *et al.* (1997), Funt and Drew (1988). There is substantial room for research here, too.

Interreflections between colored surfaces lead to a phenomenon called *color bleeding*, where each surface reflects colored light onto the other. The phenomenon can be surprisingly large in practice. People seem to be quite good at ignoring it entirely, to the extent that most people don't realize that the phenomenon occurs at all. Discounting color bleeding probably uses spatial cues. Some skill is required to spot really compelling examples. The best known to the authors is occasionally seen in southern California, where there are many large hedges of white oleander by the roadside. White oleander has dark leaves and white flowers. Occasionally, in bright sunlight, one sees a hedge with yellow oleander flowers; a moment's thought attributes the color to the yellow service truck parked by the road reflecting yellow light onto the white flowers. One's ability to discount color bleeding effects seems to have been disrupted by the dark leaves of the plant breaking up the spatial pattern. Color bleeding contains cues to surface color that are quite difficult to disentangle (see Drew and Funt (1990), Funt and Drew (1993), and Funt *et al.* (1991) for studies).

It is possible to formulate and attack color constancy as an inference problem (Forsyth 1999, Freeman and Brainard 1997). The advantage of this approach is that, for given data, the algorithm could report a range of possible surface colors, with posterior weights.

PROBLEMS

3.1. Sit down with a friend and a packet of colored papers, and compare the color names that you use. You need a large packet of papers—one can very often get collections of colored swatches for paint, or for the Pantone color system very cheaply. The best names to try are basic color names—the terms *red*, *pink*, *orange*, *yellow*, *green*, *blue*, *purple*, *brown*, *white*, *gray* and *black*, which (with a small number of other terms) have remarkable canonical properties that apply widely across different languages (the papers in Hardin and Maffi (1997) give a good summary of current thought on this issue). You will find it surprisingly easy to disagree on which colors should be called blue and which green, for example.

3.2. In the CMY space, the three primary colors are cyan, magenta and yellow. CMY mixing is *subtractive*; recall we showed that mixing cyan and magenta by overprinting resulted in blue. What color is obtained by mixing cyan and yellow? What color is obtained by mixing magenta and yellow?

3.3. Linear color spaces are obtained by choosing primaries and then constructing color matching functions for those primaries. Show that there is a linear transformation that takes the coordinates of a color in one linear color space to those in another; the easiest way to do this is to write out the transformation in terms of the color matching functions.

3.4. Exercise 3 means that, in setting up a linear color space, it is possible to choose primaries arbitrarily, but there are constraints on the choice of color matching functions. Why? What are these constraints?

3.5. Two surfaces that have the same color under one light and different colors under another are often referred to as *metamers*. An *optimal color* is a spectral reflectance or radiance that has value 0 at some wavelengths and 1 at others. Although optimal colors don't occur in practice, they are a useful device (due to Ostwald) for explaining various effects.

    (a) Use optimal colors to explain how metamerism occurs.

    (b) Given a particular spectral albedo, show that there are an infinite number of metameric spectral albedoes.

    (c) Use optimal colors to construct an example of surfaces that look different under one light (say, red and green) and the same under another.

    (d) Use optimal colors to construct an example of surfaces that swop apparent color when the light is changed (i.e., surface one looks red and surface two looks green under light one, and surface one looks green and surface two looks red under light two).

3.6. You have to map the gamut for a printer to that of a monitor. There are colors in each gamut that do not appear in the other. Given a monitor color that can't be reproduced exactly, you could choose the printer color that is closest. Why is this a bad idea for reproducing images? Would it work for reproducing "business graphics" (bar charts, pie charts, and the like, which all consist of many differernt large blocks of a single color)?

3.7. Why do artificial light sources tend to produce colored light?

3.8. Read the book *Color Vision: From Genes to Perception*, by Karl R. Gegenfurtner, L. T. Sharpe, Cambridge University Press, 1995.

3.9. In section 3.5.3, we described the gamut as a possible cue to illuminant color. Write G for the convex hull of the gamut of the given image, W for the convex hull of the gamut of an image of many different surfaces under white light, and $\mathcal{M}_e$ for the map that takes an image seen under illuminant e to an image seen under white light.

    (a) Show the only illuminants we need to consider are those such that $\mathcal{M}_e(G) \in W$.

    (b) Show that, for the case of finite dimensional linear models, $\mathcal{M}_e$ depends linearly on e.

    (c) Show that, for the case of finite dimensional linear models, the set of $\mathcal{M}_e$ such that $\mathcal{M}_e(G) \in W$ is convex.

    (d) How would you represent this set?

PROGRAMMING EXERCISES

3.10. Spectra for illuminants and for surfaces are available on the web (try http://www.it.lut.fi/ip/research/color/database/database.html). Fit a finite-dimensional linear model to a set of illuminants and surface reflectances using principal components analysis, render the resulting models, and compare your rendering with an exact rendering. Where do you get the most significant errors? Why?

3.11. Print a colored image on a color inkjet printer using different papers and compare the result. It is particularly informative to (a) ensure that the driver knows what paper the printer will be printing on, and compare the variations in colors (which are ideally imperceptible), and (b) deceive the driver about what paper it is printing on (i.e., print on plain paper and tell the driver it is printing on photographic paper). Can you explain the variations you see? Why is photographic paper glossy?

3.12. Fitting a finite-dimensional linear model to illuminants and reflectances separately is somewhat ill-advised because there is no guarantee that the *interactions* will be represented well (they're not accounted for in the fitting error). It turns out that one can obtain g_{ijk} by a fitting process that sidesteps the use of basis functions. Implement this procedure (which is described in detail in Marimont and Wandell (1992)), and compare the results with those obtained from the previous assignment.

3.13. Build a color constancy algorithm that uses the assumption that the spatial average of reflectance is constant. Use finite-dimensional linear models. You can get values of g_{ijk} from your solution to the previous exercise.

3.14. We ignore color interreflections in our surface color model. Do an experiment to get some idea of the size of color shifts possible from color interreflections (which are astonishingly big). Humans seldom interpret color interreflections as surface color. Speculate as to why this might be the case, using the discussion of the lightness algorithm as a guide.

3.15. Build a specularity finder along the lines described in Section 3.5.1.

3.16. Build a shadow remover along the lines described in Section 3.5.2 (this is much easier than it sounds, and the results are usually rather good).

PART TWO

EARLY VISION: JUST ONE IMAGE

CHAPTER 4

Linear Filters

Pictures of zebras and of dalmatians have black and white pixels, and in about the same number, too. The differences between the two have to do with the characteristic appearance of small groups of pixels, rather than individual pixel values. In this chapter, we introduce methods for obtaining descriptions of the appearance of a small group of pixels.

Our main strategy is to use weighted sums of pixel values using different patterns of weights to find different image patterns. Despite its simplicity, this process is extremely useful. It allows us to smooth noise in images, and to find edges and other image patterns.

4.1 LINEAR FILTERS AND CONVOLUTION

Many important effects can be modeled with a simple model. Construct a new array, the same size as the image. Fill each location of this new array with a weighted sum of the pixel values from the locations surrounding the corresponding location in the image *using the same set of weights each time*. Different sets of weights could be used to represent different processes. One example is computing a local average taken over a fixed region. We could average all pixels within a $2k + 1 \times 2k + 1$ block of the pixel of interest. For an input image $\mathcal{F}$, this gives an output

$$\mathcal{R}_{ij} = \frac{1}{(2k+1)^2} \sum_{u=i-k}^{u=i+k} \sum_{v=j-k}^{v=j+k} \mathcal{F}_{uv}.$$

The weights in this example are simple (each pixel is weighted by the same constant), but we could use a more interesting set of weights. For example, we could use a set of weights that was large at the center and fell off sharply as the distance from the center increased to model the kind of smoothing that occurs in a defocused lens system.

Whatever the weights chosen, the output of this procedure is *shift invariant*—meaning that the value of the output depends on the pattern in an image neighborhood, rather than the position of the neighborhood—and *linear*—meaning that the output for the sum of two images is the same as the sum of the outputs obtained for the images separately. The procedure is known as **linear filtering**.

4.1.1 Convolution

We introduce some notation at this point. The pattern of weights used for a linear filter is usually referred to as the *kernel* of the filter. The process of applying the filter is usually referred to as *convolution*. There is a catch: For reasons that will appear later (Section 4.2.1), it is convenient to write the process in a non-obvious way. In particular, given a filter kernel $\mathcal{H}$, the convolution of the kernel with image

$\mathcal{F}$ is an image $\mathcal{R}$. The i, jth component of $\mathcal{R}$ is given by

$$R_{ij} = \sum_{u,v} H_{i-u,j-v} F_{u,v}.$$

This process defines convolution: we say that $\mathcal{H}$ has been convolved with $\mathcal{F}$ to yield $\mathcal{R}$. You should look closely at this expression; the "direction" of the dummy variable u (resp. v) has been reversed compared with correlation. This is important because if you forget that it is there, you compute the wrong answer. The reason for the reversal emerges from the derivation of Section 4.2.1. We carefully avoid inserting the range of the sum; in effect, we assume that the sum is over a large enough range of u and v that all nonzero values are taken into account. Furthermore, we assume that any values that haven't been specified are zero; this means that we can model the kernel as a small block of nonzero values in a sea of zeros. We use this common convention regularly in what follows.

Example: Smoothing by Averaging

Images typically have the property that the value of a pixel usually is similar to that of its neighbor. Assume that the image is affected by noise of a form where we can reasonably expect that this property is preserved. For example, there might be occasional dead pixels, or small random numbers with zero mean might have been added to the pixel values. It is natural to attempt to reduce the effects of this noise by replacing each pixel with a weighted average of its neighbors, a process often referred to as *smoothing* or *blurring*.

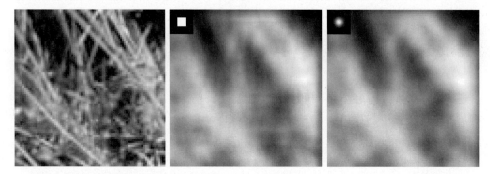

FIGURE 4.1: Although a uniform local average may seem to give a good blurring model, it generates effects not usually seen in defocusing a lens. The images above compare the effects of a uniform local average with weighted average. The image on the **left** shows a view of grass; in the **center**, the result of blurring this image using a uniform local model; and on the **right**, the result of blurring this image using a set of Gaussian weights. The degree of blurring in each case is about the same, but the uniform average produces a set of narrow vertical and horizontal bars—an effect often known as *ringing*. The small insets show the weights used to blur the image, themselves rendered as an image; bright points represent large values and dark points represent small values (in this example, the smallest values are zero).

Replacing each pixel with an unweighted average computed over some fixed region centered at the pixel is the same as convolution with a kernel that is a block of ones multiplied by a constant. You can (and should) establish this point by close attention to the range of the sum. This process is a poor model of blurring; its output does not look like that of a defocused camera (Figure 4.1). The reason is clear. Assume that we have an image in which every point but the center point is zero, and the center point is one. If we blur this image by forming an unweighted average at each point, the result looks like a small, bright box, but this is not what defocused cameras do. We want a blurring process that takes a small bright dot to a circularly symmetric region of blur, brighter at the center than at the edges and fading slowly to darkness. As Figure 4.1 suggests, a set of weights of this form produces a much more convincing defocus model.

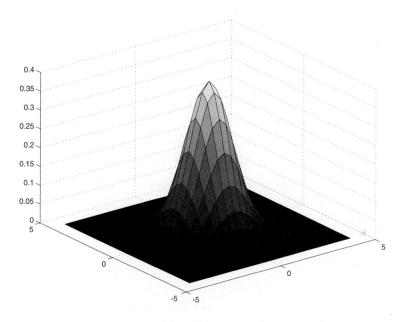

FIGURE 4.2: The symmetric Gaussian kernel in 2D. This view shows a kernel scaled so that its sum is equal to one; this scaling is quite often omitted. The kernel shown has $\sigma = 1$. Convolution with this kernel forms a weighted average that stresses the point at the center of the convolution window and incorporates little contribution from those at the boundary. Notice how the Gaussian is qualitatively similar to our description of the point spread function of image blur: it is circularly symmetric, has strongest response in the center, and dies away near the boundaries.

Example: Smoothing with a Gaussian

A good formal model for this fuzzy blob is the *symmetric Gaussian kernel*

$$G_\sigma(x, y) = \frac{1}{2\pi\sigma^2} \exp\left(-\frac{(x^2 + y^2)}{2\sigma^2}\right)$$

illustrated in Figure 4.2. σ is referred to as the *standard deviation* of the Gaussian (or its "sigma"!); the units are interpixel spaces, usually referred to as *pixels*. The constant term makes the integral over the whole plane equal to one and is often ignored in smoothing applications. The name comes from the fact that this kernel has the form of the probability density for a 2D normal (or Gaussian) random variable with a particular covariance.

This smoothing kernel forms a weighted average that weights pixels at its center much more strongly than at its boundaries. One can justify this approach qualitatively: Smoothing suppresses noise by enforcing the requirement that pixels should look like their neighbors. By downweighting distant neighbors in the average, we can ensure that the requirement that a pixel looks like its neighbors is less strongly imposed for distant neighbors. A qualitative analysis gives the following:

- If the standard deviation of the Gaussian is very small—say, smaller than one pixel—the smoothing will have little effect because the weights for all pixels off the center will be very small.

- For a larger standard deviation, the neighboring pixels will have larger weights in the weighted average, which in turn means that the average will be strongly biased toward a consensus of the neighbors. This will be a good estimate of a pixel's value, and the noise will largely disappear at the cost of some blurring.

- Finally, a kernel that has a large standard deviation will cause much of the image detail to disappear, along with the noise.

Figure 4.3 illustrates these phenomena. You should notice that Gaussian smoothing can be effective at suppressing noise.

In applications, a discrete smoothing kernel is obtained by constructing a $2k + 1 \times 2k + 1$ array whose i, jth value is

$$H_{ij} = \frac{1}{2\pi\sigma^2} \exp\left(-\frac{((i - k - 1)^2 + (j - k - 1)^2)}{2\sigma^2}\right).$$

Notice that some care must be exercised with σ. If σ is too small, then only one element of the array will have a nonzero value. If σ is large, then k must be large, too; otherwise, we are ignoring contributions from pixels that should contribute with substantial weight.

Example: Derivatives and Finite Differences

Image derivatives can be approximated using another example of a convolution process. Because

$$\frac{\partial f}{\partial x} = \lim_{\epsilon \to 0} \frac{f(x + \epsilon, y) - f(x, y)}{\epsilon},$$

we might estimate a partial derivative as a symmetric *finite difference*:

$$\frac{\partial h}{\partial x} \approx h_{i+1,j} - h_{i-1,j}.$$

This is the same as a convolution, where the convolution kernel is

$$\mathcal{H} = \left\{\begin{array}{ccc} 0 & 0 & 0 \\ 1 & 0 & -1 \\ 0 & 0 & 0 \end{array}\right\}.$$

σ=0.05   σ=0.1   σ=0.2

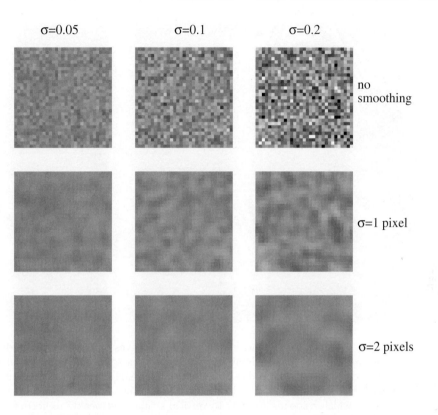

no smoothing

σ=1 pixel

σ=2 pixels

FIGURE 4.3: The **top row** shows images of a constant mid-gray level corrupted by additive Gaussian noise. In this noise model, each pixel has a zero-mean normal random variable added to it. The range of pixel values is from zero to one, so that the standard deviation of the noise in the first column is about 1/20 of full range. The **center row** shows the effect of smoothing the corresponding image in the top row with a Gaussian filter of σ one pixel. Notice the annoying overloading of notation here; there is Gaussian noise and Gaussian filters, and both have σ's. One uses context to keep these two straight, although this is not always as helpful as it could be, because Gaussian filters are particularly good at suppressing Gaussian noise. This is because the noise values at each pixel are independent, meaning that the expected value of their average is going to be the noise mean. The **bottom row** shows the effect of smoothing the corresponding image in the top row with a Gaussian filter of σ two pixels.

Notice that this kernel could be interpreted as a template: it gives a large positive response to an image configuration that is positive on one side and negative on the other, and a large negative response to the mirror image.

As Figure 4.4 suggests, finite differences give a most unsatisfactory estimate of the derivative. This is because finite differences respond strongly (i.e., have an output with large magnitude) at fast changes, and fast changes are characteristic of noise. Roughly, this is because image pixels tend to look like one another. For example, if we had bought a discount camera with some pixels that were stuck at either black or white, the output of the finite difference process would be large at those

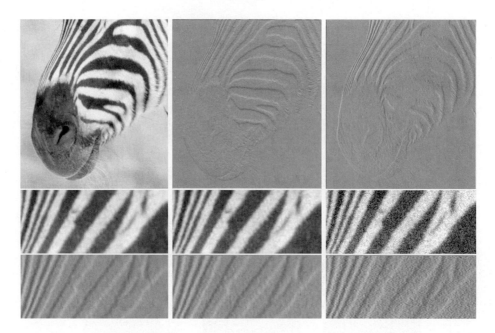

FIGURE 4.4: The **top row** shows estimates of derivatives obtained by finite differences. The image at the **left** shows a detail from a picture of a zebra. The **center** image shows the partial derivative in the y-direction—which responds strongly to horizontal stripes and weakly to vertical stripes—and the **right** image shows the partial derivative in the x-direction—which responds strongly to vertical stripes and weakly to horizontal stripes. However, finite differences respond strongly to noise. The image at **center left** shows a detail from a picture of a zebra; the next image in the row is obtained by adding a random number with zero mean and normal distribution ($\sigma = 0.03$; the darkest value in the image is 0, and the lightest 1) to each pixel; and the third image is obtained by adding a random number with zero mean and normal distribution ($\sigma = 0.09$) to each pixel. The **bottom row** shows the partial derivative in the x-direction of the image at the head of the row. Notice how strongly the differentiation process emphasizes image noise; the derivative figures look increasingly grainy. In the derivative figures, a mid-gray level is a zero value, a dark gray level is a negative value, and a light gray level is a positive value.

pixels because they are, in general, substantially different from their neighbors. All this suggests that some form of smoothing is appropriate before differentiation; the details appear in Section 5.1.

4.2 SHIFT INVARIANT LINEAR SYSTEMS

Convolution represents the effect of a large class of system. In particular, most imaging systems have, to a good approximation, three significant properties:

- **Superposition:** We expect that

$$R(f + g) = R(f) + R(g);$$

that is, the response to the sum of stimuli is the sum of the individual responses.

- **Scaling:** The response to a zero input is zero. Taken with superposition, we have that the response to a scaled stimulus is a scaled version of the response to the original stimulus; that is,

$$R(kf) = kR(f).$$

A device that exihibits superposition and scaling is *linear*.

- **Shift invariance:** In a *shift invariant* system, the response to a translated stimulus is just a translation of the response to the stimulus. This means that, for example, if a view of a small light aimed at the center of the camera is a small, bright blob, then if the light is moved to the periphery, we should see the same small, bright blob, only translated.

A device that is linear and shift invariant is known as a *shift invariant linear system*, or often just as a *system*.

The response of a shift invariant linear system to a stimulus is obtained by convolution. We demonstrate this first for systems that take discrete inputs—say, vectors or arrays—and produce discrete outputs. We then use this to describe the behavior of systems that operate on continuous functions of the line or the plane, and from this analysis we obtain some useful facts about convolution.

4.2.1   Discrete Convolution

In the 1D case, we have a shift invariant linear system that takes a vector and responds with a vector. This case is the easiest to handle because there are fewer indices to look after. The 2D case—a system that takes an array and responds with an array—follows easily. In each case, we assume that the input and output are infinite dimensional. This allows us to ignore some minor issues that arise at the boundaries of the input. We deal with these in Section 4.2.3.

Discrete Convolution in One Dimension

We have an input vector f. For convenience, we assume that the vector has infinite length and its elements are indexed by the integers (i.e., there is an element with index -1, say). The ith component of this vector is f_i. Now f is a weighted sum of basis elements. A convenient basis is a set of elements that have a one in a single component and zeros elsewhere. We write

$$e_0 = \ldots 0, 0, 0, 1, 0, 0, 0, \ldots$$

This is a data vector that has a 1 in the zeroth place, and zeros elsewhere. Define a shift operation, which takes a vector to a shifted version of that vector. In particular, the vector $\mathtt{Shift}(f, i)$ has, as its jth component, the $j - i$th component of f. For example, $\mathtt{Shift}(e_0, 1)$ has a zero in the first component. Now, we can write

$$f = \sum_i f_i \mathtt{Shift}(e_0, i).$$

We write the response of our system to a vector $\boldsymbol{f}$ as

$$R(\boldsymbol{f}).$$

Now, because the system is shift invariant, we have

$$R(\texttt{Shift}(\boldsymbol{f}, k)) = \texttt{Shift}(R(\boldsymbol{f}), k).$$

Furthermore, because it is linear, we have

$$R(k\boldsymbol{f}) = kR(\boldsymbol{f}).$$

This means that

$$
\begin{aligned}
R(\boldsymbol{f}) &= R\left(\sum_i f_i \texttt{Shift}(\boldsymbol{e}_0, i)\right) \\
&= \sum_i R(f_i \texttt{Shift}(\boldsymbol{e}_0, i)) \\
&= \sum_i f_i R(\texttt{Shift}(\boldsymbol{e}_0, i)) \\
&= \sum_i f_i \texttt{Shift}(R(\boldsymbol{e}_0), i)).
\end{aligned}
$$

This means that to obtain the system's response to any data vector, we need to know only its response to $\boldsymbol{e}_0$. This is usually called the system's *impulse response*. Assume that the impulse response can be written as $\boldsymbol{g}$. We have

$$R(\boldsymbol{f}) = \sum_i f_i \texttt{Shift}(\boldsymbol{g}, i) = \boldsymbol{g} * \boldsymbol{f}.$$

This defines an operation—the 1D, discrete version of convolution—which we write with a $*$.

   This is all very well, but it doesn't give us a particularly easy expression for the output. If we consider the jth element of $R(\boldsymbol{f})$, which we write as R_i, we must have

$$R_j = \sum_i g_{j-i} f_i,$$

which conforms to (and explains the origin of) the form used in Section 4.1.1.

   Discrete Convolution in Two Dimensions   We now use an array of values and write the i, jth element of the array $\mathcal{D}$ as D_{ij}. The appropriate analogy to an impulse response is the response to a stimulus that looks like

$$
\mathcal{E}_{00} =
\begin{matrix}
\cdots & \cdots & \cdots & \cdots & \cdots \\
\cdots & 0 & 0 & 0 & \cdots \\
\cdots & 0 & 1 & 0 & \cdots \\
\cdots & 0 & 0 & 0 & \cdots \\
\cdots & \cdots & \cdots & \cdots & \cdots
\end{matrix}
$$

If $\mathcal{G}$ is the response of the system to this stimulus, the same considerations as for 1D convolution yield a response to a stimulus $\mathcal{F}$, that is,

$$R_{ij} = \sum_{u,v} G_{i-u,j-v}F_{uv},$$

which we write as

$$\mathcal{R} = \mathcal{G} ** \mathcal{H}.$$

4.2.2   Continuous Convolution

There are shift invariant linear systems that produce a continuous response to a continuous input; for example, a camera lens takes a set of radiances and produces another set, and many lenses are approximately shift invariant. A brief study of these systems allows us to study the information lost by approximating a continuous function—the incoming radiance values across an image plane—by a discrete function—the value at each pixel.

The natural description is in terms of the system's response to a rather unnatural function, the δ-function, which is not a function in formal terms. We do the derivation first in one dimension to make the notation easier.

Convolution in One Dimension

We obtain an expression for the response of a continuous shift invariant linear system from our expression for a discrete system. We can take a discrete input and replace each value with a box straddling the value; this gives a continuous input function. We then make the boxes narrower and consider what happens in the limit.

Our system takes a function of one dimension and returns a function of one dimension. Again, we write the response of the system to some input $f(x)$ as $R(f)$; when we need to emphasize that f is a function, we write $R(f(x))$. The response is also a *function*; occasionally, when we need to emphasize this fact, we write $R(f)(u)$. We can express the linearity property in this notation by writing

$$R(kf) = kR(f)$$

(for k some constant) and the shift invariance property by introducing a $\texttt{Shift}$ operator, which takes functions to functions:

$$\texttt{Shift}(f, c) = f(u - c).$$

With this $\texttt{Shift}$ operator, we can write the shift invariance property as

$$R(\texttt{Shift}(f, c)) = \texttt{Shift}(R(f), c).$$

We define the *box* function as:

$$box_\epsilon(x) = \left\{ \begin{array}{ll} 0 & abs(x) > \frac{\epsilon}{2} \\ 1 & abs(x) < \frac{\epsilon}{2} \end{array} \right. .$$

The value of $box_\epsilon(\epsilon/2)$ does not matter for our purposes. The input function is $f(x)$. We construct an even grid of points x_i, where $x_{i+1} - x_i = \epsilon$. We now construct a vector $\boldsymbol{f}$ whose ith component (written f_i) is $f(x_i)$. This vector can be used to represent the function.

We obtain an approximate representation of f by $\sum_i f_i \text{Shift}(box_\epsilon, x_i)$. We apply this input to a shift invariant linear system; the response is a weighted sum of shifted responses to box functions. This means that

$$R\left(\sum_i f_i \text{Shift}(box_\epsilon, x_i)\right) = \sum_i R(f_i \text{Shift}(box_\epsilon, x_i))$$

$$= \sum_i f_i R(\text{Shift}(box_\epsilon, x_i))$$

$$= \sum_i f_i \text{Shift}(R(\frac{box_\epsilon}{\epsilon}\epsilon), x_i)$$

$$= \sum_i f_i \text{Shift}(R(\frac{box_\epsilon}{\epsilon}), x_i)\epsilon.$$

So far, everything has followed our derivation for discrete functions. We now have something that looks like an approximate integral if $\epsilon \to 0$.

We introduce a new device, called a δ-function, to deal with the term box_ϵ/ϵ. Define

$$d_\epsilon(x) = \frac{box_\epsilon(x)}{\epsilon}.$$

The δ-function is:

$$\delta(x) = \lim_{\epsilon \to 0} d_\epsilon(x).$$

We don't attempt to evaluate this limit, so we need not discuss the value of $\delta(0)$. One interesting feature of this function is that, for practical shift invariant linear systems, the response of the system to a δ-function exists and has *compact support* (i.e., is zero except on a finite number of intervals of finite length). For example, a good model of a δ-function in 2D is an extremely small, extremely bright light. If we make the light smaller and brighter while ensuring the total energy is constant, we expect to see a small but finite spot due to the defocus of the lens. The δ-function is the natural analogue for $\boldsymbol{e}_0$ in the continuous case.

This means that the expression for the response of the system,

$$\sum_i f_i \text{Shift}(R(\frac{box_\epsilon}{\epsilon}), x_i)\epsilon,$$

turns into an integral as ϵ limits to zero. We obtain

$$R(f) = \int \{R(\delta)(u - x')\} f(x')dx'$$

$$= \int g(u - x')f(x')dx',$$

where we have written $R(\delta)$—which is usually called the **impulse response** of the system—as g and have omitted the limits of the integral. These integrals could be from $-\infty$ to ∞, but more stringent limits could apply if g and h have compact support. This operation is called **convolution** (again), and we write the foregoing expression as

$$R(f) = (g * f).$$

Convolution is *commutative*, meaning

$$(g * h)(x) = (h * g)(x).$$

Convolution is *associative*, meaning that

$$(f * (g * h)) = ((f * g) * h).$$

This latter property means that we can find a single shift invariant linear system that behaves like the composition of two different systems. This will be useful when we discuss sampling.

Convolution in Two Dimensions

The derivation of convolution in two dimensions requires more notation. A box function is now given by $box_{\epsilon^2}(x, y) = box_\epsilon(x)box_\epsilon(y)$; we now have

$$d_\epsilon(x, y) = \frac{box_{\epsilon^2}(x, y)}{\epsilon^2}.$$

The δ-function is the limit of $d_\epsilon(x, y)$ function as $\epsilon \to 0$. Finally, there are more terms in the sum. All this activity results in the expression

$$R(h)(x, y) = \int \int g(x - x', y - y')h(x', y')dxdy$$
$$= (g * *h)(x, y),$$

where we have used two $*$s to indicate a two-dimensional convolution. Convolution in 2D is *commutative*, meaning that

$$(g * *h) = (h * *g),$$

and *associative*, meaning that

$$((f * *g) * *h) = (f * *(g * *h)).$$

A natural model for the impulse response of a two-dimensional system is to think of the pattern seen in a camera viewing a very small, distant light source (which subtends a very small viewing angle). In practical lenses, this view results in some form of fuzzy blob, justifying the name *point spread function*, which is often used for the impulse response of a 2D system. The point spread function of a linear system is often known as its *kernel*.

4.2.3   Edge Effects in Discrete Convolutions

In practical systems, we cannot have infinite arrays of data. This means that when we compute the convolution, we need to contend with the edges of the image; at the edges, there are pixel locations where computing the value of the convolved image requires image values that don't exist. There are a variety of strategies we can adopt:

- **Ignore these locations**, which means that we report only values for which every required image location exists. This has the advantage of probity, but the disadvantage that the output is smaller than the input. Repeated convolutions can cause the image to shrink quite drastically.

- **Pad the image with constant values**, which means that, as we look at output values closer to the edge of the image, the extent to which the output of the convolution depends on the image goes down. This is a convenient trick because we can ensure that the image doesn't shrink, but it has the disadvantage that it can create the appearance of substantial gradients near the boundary.

- **Pad the image in some other way**. For example, we might think of the image as a doubly periodic function so that if we have an $n \times m$ image, then column $m + 1$—required for the purposes of convolution—would be the same as column $m - 1$. This can create the appearance of substantial second derivative values near the boundary.

4.3   SPATIAL FREQUENCY AND FOURIER TRANSFORMS

We have used the trick of thinking of a signal $g(x, y)$ as a weighted sum of a large (or infinite) number of small (or infinitely small) box functions. This model emphasizes that a signal is an element of a vector space. The box functions form a convenient basis, and the weights are coefficients on this basis. We need a new technique to deal with two related problems so far left open:

- Although it is clear that a discrete image version cannot represent the full information in a signal, we have not yet indicated what is lost.

- It is clear that we cannot shrink an image simply by taking every kth pixel— this could turn a checkerboard image all white or all black—and we would like to know how to shrink an image safely.

All of these problems are related to the presence of fast changes in an image. For example, shrinking an image is most likely to miss fast effects because they could slip between samples; similarly, the derivative is large at fast changes.

These effects can be studied by *a change of basis*. We change the basis to be a set of sinusoids and represent the signal as an infinite weighted sum of an infinite number of sinusoids. This means that fast changes in the signal are obvious, because they correspond to large amounts of high-frequency sinusoids in the new basis.

FIGURE 4.5: The real component of Fourier basis elements shown as intensity images. The brightest point has value one, and the darkest point has value zero. The domain is $[-1, 1] \times [-1, 1]$, with the origin at the center of the image. On the **left**, $(u, v) = (0, 0.4)$; in the **center**, $(u, v) = (1, 2)$; and on the **right** $(u, v) = (10, -5)$. These are sinusoids of various frequencies and orientations described in the text.

4.3.1 Fourier Transforms

The change of basis is effected by a *Fourier transform*. We define the Fourier transform of a signal $g(x, y)$ to be

$$\mathcal{F}(g(x, y))(u, v) = \int\!\!\!\int\limits_{-\infty}^{\infty} g(x, y) e^{-i2\pi(ux+vy)} dx dy.$$

Assume that appropriate technical conditions are true to make this integral exist. It is sufficient for all moments of g to be finite; a variety of other possible conditions are available (Bracewell 1995). The process takes a complex valued function of x, y and returns a complex valued function of u, v (images are complex valued functions with zero imaginary component).

For the moment, fix u and v, and let us consider the meaning of the value of the transform at that point. The exponential can be rewritten

$$e^{-i2\pi(ux+vy)} = \cos(2\pi(ux + vy)) + i\sin(2\pi(ux + vy)).$$

These terms are sinusoids on the x, y plane, whose orientation and frequency are given by u, v. For example, consider the real term, which is constant when $ux + vy$ is constant (i.e., along a straight line in the x, y plane whose orientation is given by $\tan \theta = v/u$). The gradient of this term is perpendicular to lines where $ux + vy$ is constant, and the frequency of the sinusoid is $\sqrt{u^2 + v^2}$. These sinusoids are often referred to as *spatial frequency components*; a variety are illustrated in Figure 4.5.

The integral should be seen as a dot product. If we fix u and v, the value of the integral is the dot product between a sinusoid in x and y and the original function. This is a useful analogy because dot products measure the amount of one vector in the direction of another.

In the same way, the value of the transform at a particular u and v can be seen as measuring the amount of the sinusoid with given frequency and orientation in the signal. The transform takes a function of x and y to the function of u and v whose value at any particular (u, v) is the amount of that particular sinusoid in the original function. This view justifies the model of a Fourier transform as a change of basis.

Linearity
The Fourier transform is linear:

$$\mathcal{F}(g(x,y) + h(x,y)) = \mathcal{F}(g(x,y)) + \mathcal{F}(h(x,y))$$

and

$$\mathcal{F}(kg(x,y)) = k\mathcal{F}(g(x,y)).$$

The Inverse Fourier Transform   It is useful to recover a signal from its Fourier transform. This is another change of basis with the form

$$g(x,y) = \int\int_{-\infty}^{\infty} \mathcal{F}(g(x,y))(u,v) e^{i2\pi(ux+vy)} du dv.$$

Fourier Transform Pairs   Fourier transforms are known in closed form for a variety of useful cases; a large set of examples appears in Bracewell (1995). We list a few in Table 4.1 for reference. The last line of Table 4.1 contains the *convolution theorem*; convolution in the signal domain is the same as multiplication in the Fourier domain.

Phase and Magnitude   The Fourier transform consists of a real and a complex component:

$$\begin{aligned}
\mathcal{F}(g(x,y))(u,v) &= \int\int_{-\infty}^{\infty} g(x,y)\cos(2\pi(ux+vy))dxdy + \\
&\quad i\int\int_{-\infty}^{\infty} g(x,y)\sin(2\pi(ux+vy))dxdy \\
&= \Re(\mathcal{F}(g)) + i * \Im(\mathcal{F}(g)) \\
&= \mathcal{F}_R(g) + i * \mathcal{F}_I(g).
\end{aligned}$$

It is usually inconvenient to draw complex functions of the plane. One solution is to plot $\mathcal{F}_R(g)$ and $\mathcal{F}_I(g)$ separately; another is to consider the *magnitude* and *phase* of the complex functions, and to plot these instead. These are then called the *magnitude spectrum* and *phase spectrum*, respectively.

The value of the Fourier transform of a function at a particular u, v point depends on the whole function. This is obvious from the definition because the domain of the integral is the whole domain of the function. It leads to some subtle properties, however. First, a local change in the function (e.g., zeroing out a block of points) is going to lead to a change *at every point* in the Fourier transform. This means that the Fourier transform is quite difficult to use as a representation (e.g.,

TABLE 4.1: A variety of functions of two dimensions and their Fourier transforms. This table can be used in two directions (with appropriate substitutions for u, v and x, y) because the Fourier transform of the Fourier transform of a function is the function. Observant readers might suspect that the results on infinite sums of δ functions contradict the linearity of Fourier transforms. By careful inspection of limits, it is possible to show that they do not (see, for example, Bracewell (1995)). Observant readers also might have noted that an expression for $\mathcal{F}(\frac{\partial f}{\partial y})$ can be obtained by combining two lines of this table.

Function	Fourier transform
$g(x, y)$	$\int\int\limits_{-\infty}^{\infty} g(x, y)e^{-i2\pi(ux+vy)}dxdy$
$\int\int\limits_{-\infty}^{\infty} \mathcal{F}(g(x, y))(u, v)e^{i2\pi(ux+vy)}dudv$	$\mathcal{F}(g(x, y))(u, v)$
$\delta(x, y)$	1
$\frac{\partial f}{\partial x}(x, y)$	$u\mathcal{F}(f)(u, v)$
$0.5\delta(x + a, y) + 0.5\delta(x - a, y)$	$\cos 2\pi au$
$e^{-\pi(x^2+y^2)}$	$e^{-\pi(u^2+v^2)}$
$box_1(x, y)$	$\frac{\sin u}{u}\frac{\sin v}{v}$
$f(ax, by)$	$\frac{\mathcal{F}(f)(u/a, v/b)}{ab}$
$\sum_{i=-\infty}^{\infty} \sum_{j=-\infty}^{\infty} \delta(x - i, y - j)$	$\sum_{i=-\infty}^{\infty} \sum_{j=-\infty}^{\infty} \delta(u - i, v - j)$
$(f * *g)(x, y)$	$\mathcal{F}(f)\mathcal{F}(g)(u, v)$
$f(x - a, y - b)$	$e^{-i2\pi(au+bv)}\mathcal{F}(f)$
$f(x \cos\theta - y \sin\theta, x \sin\theta + y \cos\theta)$	$\mathcal{F}(f)(u \cos\theta - v \sin\theta, u \sin\theta + v \cos\theta)$

it might be very difficult to tell whether a pattern was present in an image just by looking at the Fourier transform). Second, the magnitude spectra of images tends to be similar. This appears to be a fact of nature, rather than something that can be proven axiomatically. As a result, the magnitude spectrum of an image is surprisingly uninformative (see Figure 4.6 for an example).

4.4 SAMPLING AND ALIASING

The crucial reason to discuss Fourier transforms is to get some insight into the difference between discrete and continuous images. In particular, it is clear that some information has been lost when we work on a discrete pixel grid, but what? A good, simple example comes from an image of a checkerboard, and is given in

FIGURE 4.6: The second image in each row shows the log of the magnitude spectrum for the first image in the row; the third image shows the phase spectrum scaled so that $-\pi$ is dark and π is light. The final images are obtained by swapping the magnitude spectra. Although this swap leads to substantial image noise, it doesn't substantially affect the interpretation of the image, suggesting that the phase spectrum is more important for perception than the magnitude spectrum.

Figure 4.7. The problem has to do with the number of samples relative to the function; we can formalize this rather precisely given a sufficiently powerful model.

4.4.1   Sampling

Passing from a continuous function—like the irradiance at the back of a camera system—to a collection of values on a discrete grid —like the pixel values reported by a camera—is referred to as *sampling*. We construct a model that allows us to obtain a precise notion of what is lost in sampling.

Sampling in One Dimension

Sampling in one dimension takes a function and returns a discrete set of values. The most important case involves sampling on a uniform discrete grid, and we assume that the samples are defined at integer points. This means we have a process that takes some function and returns a vector of values:

$$\texttt{sample}_{1D}(f(x)) = \boldsymbol{f}.$$

We model this sampling process by assuming that the elements of this vector are the values of the function $f(x)$ at the sample points and allowing negative indices to the vector (Figure 4.8). This means that the ith component of $\boldsymbol{f}$ is $f(x_i)$.

Sampling in Two Dimensions

FIGURE 4.7: The two checkerboards on the **top** illustrate a sampling procedure that appears to be successful (whether it is or not depends on some details that we will deal with later). The gray circles represent the samples; if there are sufficient samples, then the samples represent the detail in the underlying function. The sampling procedures shown on the **bottom** are unequivocally unsuccessful; the samples suggest that there are fewer checks than there are. This illustrates two important phenomena: first, successful sampling schemes sample data often enough; and second, unsuccessful sampling schemes cause high-frequency information to appear as lower-frequency information.

Sampling in 2D is very similar to sampling in 1D. Although sampling can occur on nonregular grids (the best example being the human retina), we proceed on the assumption that samples are drawn at points with integer coordinates. This yields a uniform rectangular grid, which is a good model of most cameras. Our sampled images are then rectangular arrays of finite size (all values outside the grid being zero).

In the formal model, we sample a function of two dimensions, instead of one, yielding an array (Figure 4.9). We allow this array to have negative indices in both dimensions, and can then write

$$\mathtt{sample}_{2D}(F(x, y)) = \mathcal{F},$$

where the i, jth element of the array $\mathcal{F}$ is $F(x_i, y_j) = F(i, j)$.

Samples are not always evenly spaced in practical systems. This is quite often

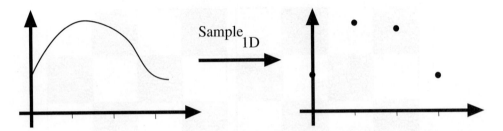

FIGURE 4.8: Sampling in 1D takes a function and returns a vector whose elements are values of that function at the sample points. For our purposes, it is enough that the sample points be integer values of the argument. We allow the vector to be infinite dimensional and have negative as well as positive indices.

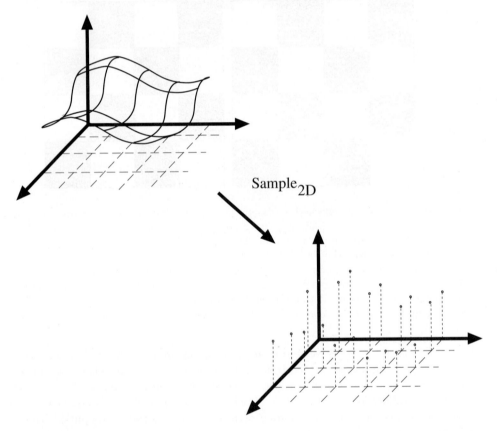

FIGURE 4.9: Sampling in 2D takes a function and returns an array; again, we allow the array to be infinite dimensional and to have negative as well as positive indices.

due to the pervasive effect of television; television screens have an aspect ratio of 4:3 (width:height). Cameras quite often accommodate this effect by spacing sample points slightly farther apart horizontally than vertically (in jargon, they have *non-square pixels*).

A Continuous Model of a Sampled Signal

We need a continuous model of a sampled signal. Generally, this model is used to evaluate integrals; in particular, taking a Fourier transform involves integrating the product of our model with a complex exponential. It is clear how this integral should behave: the value of the integral should be obtained by adding up values at each integer point. This means we cannot model a sampled signal as a function that is zero everywhere except at integer points (where it takes the value of the signal), because this model has a zero integral.

An appropriate continuous model of a sampled signal relies on an important property of the δ function:

$$
\begin{aligned}
\int_{-\infty}^{\infty} a\delta(x)f(x)dx &= a \lim_{\epsilon \to 0} \int_{-\infty}^{\infty} d(x;\epsilon)f(x)dx \\
&= a \lim_{\epsilon \to 0} \int_{-\infty}^{\infty} \frac{bar(x;\epsilon)}{\epsilon}(f(x))dx \\
&= a \lim_{\epsilon \to 0} \sum_{i=-\infty}^{\infty} \frac{bar(x;\epsilon)}{\epsilon}(f(i\epsilon)bar(x - i\epsilon;\epsilon))\epsilon \\
&= af(0).
\end{aligned}
$$

Here we have used the idea of an integral as the limit of a sum of small strips.

An appropriate continuous model of a sampled signal consists of a δ-function at each sample point weighted by the value of the sample at that point. We can obtain this model by multiplying the sampled signal by a set of δ-functions, one at each sample point. In one dimension, a function of this form is called a *comb function* (because that's what the graph looks like). In two dimensions, a function of this form is called a *bed-of-nails function* (for the same reason).

Working in 2D and assuming that the samples are at integer points, this procedure gets

$$
\begin{aligned}
\mathtt{sample}_{2D}(f) &= \sum_{i=-\infty}^{\infty} \sum_{j=-\infty}^{\infty} f(i,j)\delta(x - i, y - j) \\
&= f(x,y) \left\{ \sum_{i=-\infty}^{\infty} \sum_{j=-\infty}^{\infty} \delta(x - i, y - j) \right\}.
\end{aligned}
$$

This function is zero except at integer points (because the δ-function is zero except at integer points), and its integral is the sum of the function values at the integer points.

4.4.2   Aliasing

Sampling involves a loss of information. As this section shows, a signal sampled too slowly is misrepresented by the samples; high spatial frequency components of the original signal appear as low spatial frequency components in the sampled signal—an effect known as *aliasing*.

The Fourier Transform of a Sampled Signal

A sampled signal is given by a product of the original signal with a bed-of-nails function. By the convolution theorem, the Fourier transform of this product is the convolution of the Fourier transforms of the two functions. This means that the Fourier transform of a sampled signal is obtained by convolving the Fourier transform of the signal with another bed-of-nails function.

Now convolving a function with a shifted δ-function merely shifts the function (see exercises). This means that the Fourier transform of the sampled signal is the sum of a collection of shifted versions of the Fourier transforms of the signal, that is,

$$\mathcal{F}(\mathtt{sample}_{2D}(f(x,y))) = \mathcal{F}\left(f(x,y)\left\{\sum_{i=-\infty}^{\infty}\sum_{j=-\infty}^{\infty}\delta(x-i,y-j)\right\}\right)$$

$$= \mathcal{F}(f(x,y)) * *\mathcal{F}\left(\left\{\sum_{i=-\infty}^{\infty}\sum_{j=-\infty}^{\infty}\delta(x-i,y-j)\right\}\right)$$

$$= \sum_{i=-\infty}^{\infty}F(u-i,v-j),$$

where we have written the Fourier transform of $f(x,y)$ as $F(u,v)$.

If the support of these shifted versions of the Fourier transform of the signal does not intersect, we can easily reconstruct the signal from the sampled version. We take the sampled signal, Fourier transform it, and cut out one copy of the Fourier transform of the signal and Fourier transform this back (Figure 4.10).

However, if the support regions *do* overlap, we are not able to reconstruct the signal because we can't determine the Fourier transform of the signal in the regions of overlap, where different copies of the Fourier transform will add. This results in a characteristic effect, usually called *aliasing*, where high spatial frequencies appear to be low spatial frequencies (see Figure 4.12 and exercises). Our argument also yields *Nyquist's theorem*: the sampling frequency must be at least twice the highest frequency present for a signal to be reconstructed from a sampled version. By the same argument, if we happen to have a signal that has frequencies present only in the range $[2k-1\Omega, 2k+1\Omega]$, then we can represent that signal exactly if we sample at a frequency of at least 2Ω.

4.4.3 Smoothing and Resampling

Nyquist's theorem means it is dangerous to shrink an image by simply taking every kth pixel (as Figure 4.12 confirms). Instead, we need to filter the image so that spatial frequencies above the new sampling frequency are removed. We could do this exactly by multiplying the image Fourier transform by a scaled 2D bar function, which would act as a low-pass filter. Equivalently, we would convolve the image with a kernel of the form $(\sin x \sin y)/(xy)$. This is a difficult and expensive (a polite way of saying *impossible*) convolution because this function has infinite support.

The most interesting case occurs when we want to halve the width and height of the image. We assume that the sampled image has no aliasing (because if it

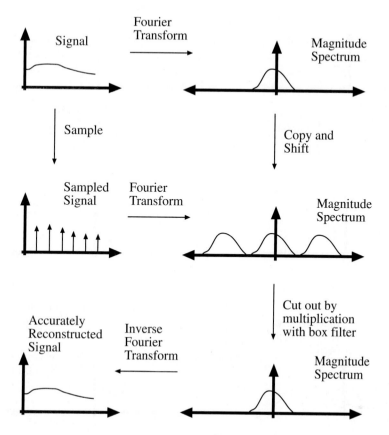

FIGURE 4.10: The Fourier transform of the sampled signal consists of a sum of copies of the Fourier transform of the original signal, shifted with respect to each other by the sampling frequency. Two possibilities occur. If the shifted copies do not intersect with each other (as in this case), the original signal can be reconstructed from the sampled signal (we just cut out one copy of the Fourier transform and inverse transform it). If they do intersect (as in Figure 4.11), the intersection region is added, and so we cannot obtain a separate copy of the Fourier transform, and the signal has aliased.

did, there would be nothing we could do about it anyway; once an image has been sampled, any aliasing that is going to occur has happened, and there's not much we can do about it without an image model). This means that the Fourier transform of the sampled image is going to consist of a set of copies of some Fourier transform, with centers shifted to integer points in u, v space.

If we resample this signal, the copies now have centers on the half-integer points in u, v space. This means that, to avoid aliasing, we need to apply a filter that strongly reduces the content of the original Fourier transform outside the range $|u| < 1/2$, $|v| < 1/2$. Of course, if we reduce the content of the signal *inside* this range, we might lose information, too. Now the Fourier transform of a Gaussian is a Gaussian, and Gaussians die away fairly quickly. Thus, if we were to convolve the image with a Gaussian—or multiply its Fourier transform by a Gaussian, which is

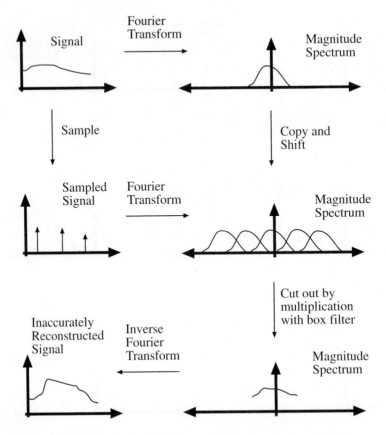

FIGURE 4.11: The Fourier transform of the sampled signal consists of a sum of copies of the Fourier transform of the original signal, shifted with respect to each other by the sampling frequency. Two possibilities occur. If the shifted copies do not intersect with each other (as in Figure 4.10), the original signal can be reconstructed from the sampled signal (we just cut out one copy of the Fourier transform and inverse transform it). If they do intersect (as in this figure), the intersection region is added, and so we cannot obtain a separate copy of the Fourier transform, and the signal has aliased. This also explains the tendency of high spatial frequencies to alias to lower spatial frequencies.

the same thing—we could achieve what we want.

The choice of Gaussian depends on the application. If σ is large, there is less aliasing (because the value of the kernel outside our range is very small), but information is lost because the kernel is not flat within our range; similarly, if σ is small, less information is lost within the range, but aliasing can be more substantial. Figures 4.13 and 4.14 illustrate the effects of different choices of σ.

We have been using a Gaussian as a low-pass filter because its response at high spatial frequencies is low and its response at low spatial frequencies is high. In fact, the Gaussian is not a particularly good low-pass filter. What one wants is a filter whose response is pretty close to constant for some range of low spatial frequencies—the pass band—and whose response is also pretty close to zero—for

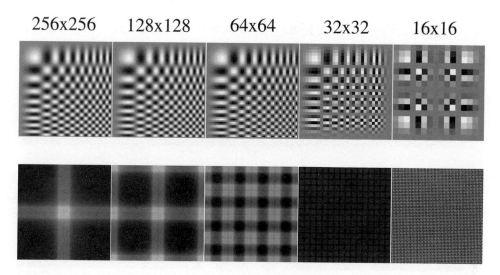

FIGURE 4.12: The **top row** shows sampled versions of an image of a grid obtained by
multiplying two sinusoids with linearly increasing frequency—one in x and one in y. The
other images in the series are obtained by resampling by factors of two without smoothing
(i.e., the next is a 128x128, then a 64x64, etc., all scaled to the same size). Note the
substantial aliasing; high spatial frequencies alias down to low spatial frequencies, and
the smallest image is an extremely poor representation of the large image. The **bottom
row** shows the magnitude of the Fourier transform of each image displayed as a log to
compress the intensity scale. The constant component is at the center. Notice that the
Fourier transform of a resampled image is obtained by scaling the Fourier transform of the
original image and then tiling the plane. Interference between copies of the original Fourier
transform means that we cannot recover its value at some points; this is the mechanism
underlying aliasing.

higher spatial frequencies—the stop band. It is possible to design low-pass filters
that are significantly better than Gaussians. The design process involves a detailed
compromise between criteria of ripple—how flat is the response in the pass band
and the stop band?—and roll-off—how quickly does the response fall to zero and
stay there? The basic steps for resampling an image are given in Algorithm 4.1.

Apply a low-pass filter to the original image
  (a Gaussian with a σ of between one
  and two pixels is usually an acceptable choice).
Create a new image whose dimensions on edge are half
  those of the old image
Set the value of the i, jth pixel of the new image to the value
  of the $2i, 2j$th pixel of the filtered image

Algorithm 4.1: Subsampling an Image by a Factor of Two.

256x256   128x128   64x64   32x32   16x16

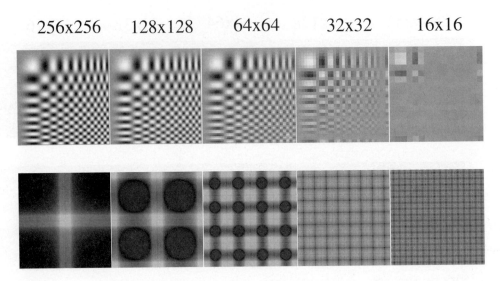

FIGURE 4.13: **Top:** Resampled versions of the image of Figure 4.12, again by factors of two, but this time each image is smoothed with a Gaussian of σ one pixel before resampling. This filter is a low-pass filter, and so suppresses high spatial frequency components, reducing aliasing. **Bottom:** The effect of the low-pass filter is easily seen in these log-magnitude images; the low-pass filter suppresses the high spatial frequency components so that components interfere less, to reduce aliasing.

256x256   128x128   64x64   32x32   16x16

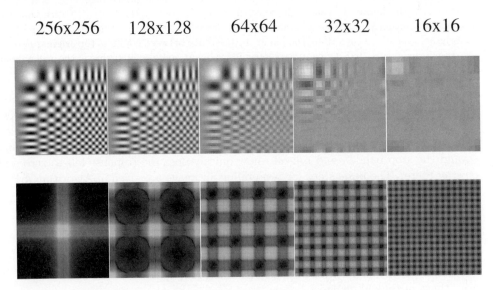

FIGURE 4.14: **Top:** Resampled versions of the image of Figure 4.12, again by factors of two, but this time each image is smoothed with a Gaussian of σ two pixels before resampling. This filter suppresses high spatial frequency components more aggressively than that of Figure 4.13. **Bottom:** The effect of the low-pass filter is easily seen in these log-magnitude images; the low-pass filter suppresses the high spatial frequency components so that components interfere less, to reduce aliasing.

4.5 FILTERS AS TEMPLATES

It turns out that filters offer a natural mechanism for finding simple patterns because filters respond most strongly to pattern elements that look like the filter. For example, smoothed derivative filters are intended to give a strong response at a point where the derivative is large. At these points, the kernel of the filter looks like the effect it is intended to detect. The x-derivative filters look like a vertical light blob next to a vertical dark blob (an arrangement where there is a large x-derivative), and so on.

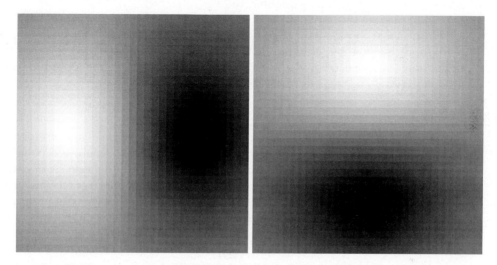

FIGURE 4.15: Filter kernels look like the effects they are intended to detect. On the **left**, a smoothed derivative of Gaussian filter that looks for large changes in the x-direction (such as a dark blob next to a light blob); on the **right**, a smoothed derivative of Gaussian filter that looks for large changes in the y-direction.

It is generally the case that filters intended to give a strong response to a pattern look like that pattern (Figure 4.15). This is a simple geometric result.

4.5.1 Convolution as a Dot Product

Recall from Section 4.1.1 that, for $\mathcal{G}$, the kernel of some linear filter, the response of this filter to an image $\mathcal{H}$ is given by

$$R_{ij} = \sum_{u,v} G_{i-u,j-v} H_{uv}.$$

Now consider the response of a filter at the point where i and j are zero. This is

$$R = \sum_{u,v} G_{-u,-v} H_{u,v}.$$

This response is obtained by associating image elements with filter kernel elements, multiplying the associated elements, and summing. We could scan the image into a vector and the filter kernel into another vector in such a way that associated elements are in the same component. By inserting zeros as needed, we can ensure that these two vectors have the same dimension. Once this is done, the process of multiplying associated elements and summing is precisely the same as taking a dot product.

This is a powerful analogy because this dot product, like any other, achieves its largest value when the vector representing the image is parallel to the vector representing the filter kernel. This means that a filter responds most strongly when it encounters an image pattern that looks like the filter. The response of a filter gets stronger as a region gets brighter, too.

Now consider the response of the image to a filter at some other point. Nothing significant about our model has changed. Again, we can scan the image into one vector and the filter kernel into another vector, such that associated elements lie in the same components. Again, the result of applying this filter is a dot product. There are two useful ways to think about this dot product.

4.5.2   Changing Basis

We can think of convolution as a dot product between the image and *a different vector* (because we have moved the filter kernel to lie over some other point in the image). The new vector is obtained by rearranging the old one so that the elements lie in the right components to make the sum work out. This means that, by convolving an image with a filter, we are representing the image on a new *basis* of the vector space of images—the basis given by the different shifted versions of the filter. The original basis elements were vectors with a zero in all slots except one. The new basis elements are shifted versions of a single pattern.

For many of the kernels discussed, we expect that this process will *lose* information—for the same reason that smoothing suppresses noise—so that the coefficients on this basis are redundant. This basis transformation is valuable in texture analysis. Typically, we choose a basis that consists of small, useful pattern components. Large values of the basis coefficients suggest that a pattern component is present, and texture can be represented by representing the relationships between these pattern components, usually with some form of probability model.

4.6   TECHNIQUE: NORMALIZED CORRELATION AND FINDING PATTERNS

We can think of convolution as comparing a filter with a patch of image centered at the point whose response we are looking at. In this view, the image neighborhood corresponding to the filter kernel is scanned into a vector that is compared with the filter kernel. By itself, this dot product is a poor way to find features because the value might be large simply because the image region is bright. By analogy with vectors, we are interested in the cosine of the angle between the filter vector and the image neighborhood vector; this suggests computing the root sum of squares of the relevant image region (the image elements that would lie under the filter kernel) and dividing the response by that value.

This yields a value that is large and positive when the image region looks like the filter kernel, and small and negative when the image region looks like a contrast-reversed version of the filter kernel. This value could be squared if contrast reversal doesn't matter. This is a cheap and effective method for finding patterns, often called *normalized correlation.*

4.6.1   Controlling the Television by Finding Hands by Normalized Correlation

It would be nice to have systems that could respond to human gestures. For example, you might wave at the light to turn the room lights on, point at the air conditioning to change the room temperature, or make an appropriate gesture at an annoying politician on television to change the channel. In typical consumer applications, there are quite strict limits to the amount of computation available, meaning that it is essential that the gesture recognition system be simple. However, such systems are usually quite limited in what they need to do, too.

Controlling the Television

Typically, a user interface is in some state—perhaps a menu is displayed—and then an event occurs—perhaps a button is pressed on a remote control. This event causes the interface to change state—a new menu item is highlighted, say—and the whole process continues. In some states, some events cause the system to perform some action, such as changing the channel. All this means that a state machine is a natural model for a user interface.

One way for vision to fit into this model is to provide events. This is good because there are generally few different kinds of event, and we know what kinds of event the system should care about in any particular state. As a result, the vision system needs to determine only whether either nothing or one of a small number of known kinds of event has occurred. It is quite often possible to build systems that meet these constraints.

A relatively small set of events is required to simulate a remote control; one needs events that look like button presses (e.g., to turn the television on or off), and events that look like pointer motion (e.g., to increase the volume; it is possible to do this with buttons, too). With these events, the television can be turned on, and an on-screen menu system can be navigated.

Finding Hands

Freeman *et al.* (1998) produced an interface where an open hand turns the television on. This can be robust because all the system needs to do is determine whether there is a hand in view. Furthermore, the user will cooperate by holding the hand up and open. Because the user is expected to be a fairly constant distance from the camera—so the size of the hand is roughly known, and there is no need to search over scales—and in front of the television, the image region that needs to be searched to determine whether there is a hand is quite small.

The hand is held up in a fairly standard configuration and orientation to turn the television set on, and it usually appears at about the same distance from the television (so we know what it looks like). This means that a normalized correlation score is sufficient to find the hand. Any points in the correlation image where the score is high enough correspond to hands. This approach can also be used to control volume and so on. To do so, we need some notion of where the hand is going—to one side turns the volume up, to the other turns it down—and this can be obtained by comparing the position in the previous frame with that in the current frame.

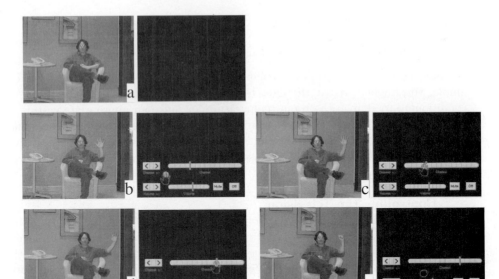

FIGURE 4.16: Examples of Freeman *et al.*'s system controlling a television set. Each state is illustrated with what the television sees on the **left** and what the user sees on the **right**. In **(a)**, the television is asleep, but a process is watching the user. An open hand causes the television to come on and show its user interface panel **(b)**. Focus on the panel tracks the movement of the user's open hand in **(c)**, and the user can change channels by using this tracking to move an icon on the screen in **(d)**. Finally, the user displays a closed hand in **(e)** to turn off the set. *This figure was originally published as Figure 12 of "Computer Vision for Interactive Computer Graphics," W. Freeman et al., IEEE Computer Graphics and Applications, 1998 © IEEE, 1998.*

The system displays an iconic representation of its interpretation of hand position so the user has some feedback as to what the system is doing (Figure 4.16). Notice that an attractive feature of this approach is that it could be self-calibrating. In this approach, when you install your television set, you sit in front of it and show it your hand a few times to allow it to get an estimate of the scale at which the hand appears.

4.7 TECHNIQUE: SCALE AND IMAGE PYRAMIDS

Images look quite different at different scales. For example, the zebra's muzzle in Figure 4.17 can be described in terms of individual hairs—which might be coded in terms of the response of oriented filters that operate at a scale of a small number of pixels—or in terms of the stripes on the zebra. In the case of the zebra, we would not want to apply large filters to find the stripes. This is because these filters are inclined to spurious precision—we don't wish to represent the disposition of each hair on the stripe—inconvenient to build, and slow to apply. A more practical approach than applying large filters is to apply smaller filters to smoothed and resampled versions of the image.

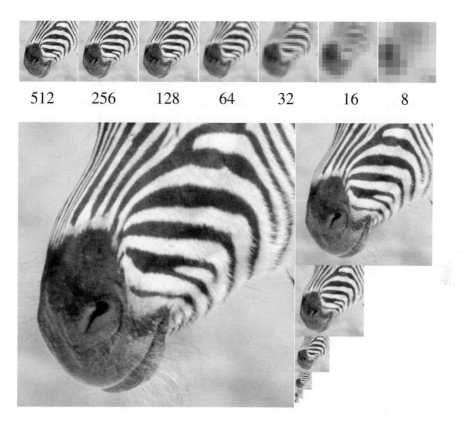

| 512 | 256 | 128 | 64 | 32 | 16 | 8 |

FIGURE 4.17: A Gaussian pyramid of images running from 512x512 to 8x8. On the top row, we have shown each image at the same size (so that some have bigger pixels than others), and the lower part of the figure shows the images to scale. Notice that if we convolve each image with a fixed-size filter, it responds to quite different phenomena. An 8x8 pixel block at the finest scale might contain a few hairs; at a coarser scale, it might contain an entire stripe; and at the coarsest scale, it contains the animal's muzzle.

4.7.1   The Gaussian Pyramid

An *image pyramid* is a collection of representations of an image. The name comes from a visual analogy. Typically, each layer of the pyramid is half the width and half the height of the previous layer; if we were to stack the layers on top of each other, a pyramid would result. In a *Gaussian pyramid*, each layer is smoothed by a symmetric Gaussian kernel and resampled to get the next layer (Figure 4.17). These pyramids are most convenient if the image dimensions are a power of two or a multiple of a power of two. The smallest image is the most heavily smoothed; the layers are often referred to as *coarse scale* versions of the image.

With a little notation, we can write simple expressions for the layers of a Gaussian pyramid. The operator $S^{\downarrow}$ downsamples an image; in particular, the j, kth element of $S^{\downarrow}(\mathcal{I})$ is the $2j$, $2k$th element of $\mathcal{I}$. The nth level of a pyramid $P(\mathcal{I})$

is denoted $P(\mathcal{I})_n$. With this notation, we have

$$P_{\text{Gaussian}}(\mathcal{I})_{n+1} = S^{\downarrow}(G_{\sigma} ** P_{\text{Gaussian}}(\mathcal{I})_n)$$
$$= (S^{\downarrow}G_{\sigma})P_{\text{Gaussian}}(\mathcal{I})_n)$$

(where we have written G_{σ} for the linear operator that takes an image to the convolution of that image with a Gaussian). The finest scale layer is the original image:

$$P_{\text{Gaussian}}(\mathcal{I})_1 = \mathcal{I}.$$

Set the finest scale layer to the image
For each layer, going from next to finest to coarsest
   Obtain this layer by smoothing the next finest
   layer with a Gaussian, and then subsampling it
end

Algorithm 4.2: Forming a Gaussian Pyramid.

4.7.2   Applications of Scaled Representations

Gaussian pyramids are useful because they make it possible to extract representations of different types of structure in an image. We give three applications here; in section 5.3.2, we describe another method that can be sped up using a Gaussian pyramid.

Search over Scale

Numerous objects can be represented as small image patterns. A standard example is a frontal view of a face. Typically, at low resolution, frontal views of faces have a quite distinctive pattern: the eyes form dark pools, under a dark bar (the eyebrows), separated by a lighter bar (specular reflections from the nose), and above a dark bar (the mouth). There are various methods for finding faces that exploit these properties (see Chapter 17.1.1). These methods all assume that the face lies in a small range of scales. All other faces are found by searching a pyramid. To find bigger faces, we look at coarser scale layers, and to find smaller faces we look at finer scale layers. This useful trick applies to many different kinds of feature, as we see in the chapters that follow.

Spatial Search

One application is spatial search, a common theme in computer vision. Typically, we have a point in one image and are trying to find a point in a second image that corresponds to it. This problem occurs in stereopsis—where the point has moved because the two images are obtained from different viewing positions—and in motion analysis—where the image point has moved, either because the camera moved or because it is on a moving object.

Searching for a match in the original pairs of images is inefficient because we might have to wade through a great deal of detail. A better approach, which is now pretty much universal, is to look for a match in a heavily smoothed and resampled image and then refine that match by looking at increasingly detailed versions of the image. For example, we might reduce 1024×1024 images down to 4×4 versions, match those, and then look at 8×8 versions (because we know a rough match, it is easy to refine it); we then look at 16×16 versions, and so on, all the way up to 1024×1024. This gives an extremely efficient search because a step of a single pixel in the 4×4 version is equivalent to a step of 256 pixels in the 1024×1024 version. This strategy is known as *coarse-to-fine matching*.

Feature Tracking

Most features found at coarse levels of smoothing are associated with large, high-contrast image events because for a feature to be marked at a coarse scale, a large pool of pixels need to agree that it is there. Typically, finding coarse-scale phenomena misestimates both the size and location of a feature. For example, a single pixel error in a coarse-scale image represents a multiple pixel error in a fine-scale image.

At fine scales, there are many features, some of which are associated with smaller, low-contrast events. One strategy for improving a set of features obtained at a fine scale is to track features across scales to a coarser scale and accept only the fine-scale features that have identifiable parents at a coarser scale. This strategy, known as *feature tracking* in principle, can suppress features resulting from textured regions (often referred to as noise) and features resulting from real noise.

4.8 NOTES

We don't claim to be exhaustive in our treatment of linear systems, but it wouldn't be possible to read the literature on filters in vision without a grasp of the ideas in this chapter. We have given a fairly straightforward account here; more details on these topics can be found in the excellent books by Bracewell (1995), (2000).

Real Imaging Systems versus Shift Invariant Linear Systems

Imaging systems are only approximately linear. Film is not linear—it does not respond to weak stimuli, and it saturates for bright stimuli—but one can usually get away with a linear model within a reasonable range. CCD cameras are linear within a working range. They give a small, but nonzero response to a zero input as a result of thermal noise (which is why astronomers cool their cameras) and they saturate for very bright stimuli. CCD cameras often contain electronics that transforms their output to make them behave more like film because consumers are used to film. Shift invariance is approximate as well because lenses tend to distort responses near the image boundary. Some lenses—fish-eye lenses are a good example—are not shift invariant.

Scale

There is a large body of work on scale space and scaled representations. The origins appear to lie with Witkin (1983) and the idea was developed by Koenderink and van Doorn (1986). Since then, a huge literature has sprung up (one might start with ter Haar Romeny *et al.* (1997) or Nielsen *et al.* (1999)). We have given only the briefest picture here because the analysis tends to be quite tricky. The usefulness of the techniques is currently hotly debated, too.

Image pyramids are useful. The next step from a Gaussian pyramid, which is a highly redundant, is the Laplacian pyramid, originally described by Burt and Adelson (1983). This is an efficient representation. Instead of storing each image level of a Gaussian pyramid, one stores the difference between the observed level of the Gaussian pyramid and that predicted by the upsampling the coarser scale level. Because coarse scale images are moderately good representations of finer scale images, this difference is small. As a result, there are numerous zeros in the pyramid, and it is a convenient image code.

Anisotropic Scaling

One important difficulty with scale space models is that the symmetric Gaussian smoothing process tends to blur out edges rather too aggressively for comfort. For example, if we have two trees near one another on a skyline, the large-scale blobs corresponding to each tree might start merging before all the small-scale blobs have finished. This suggests that we should smooth differently at edge points than at other points. For example, we might make an estimate of the magnitude and orientation of the gradient. For large gradients, we would then use an oriented smoothing operator that smoothed aggressively perpendicular to the gradient and little along the gradient; for small gradients, we might use a symmetric smoothing operator. This idea used to be known as *edge-preserving smoothing*.

In the modern, more formal version, due to Perona and Malik (1990*b*), we notice the scale space representation family is a solution to the *diffusion equation*

$$\frac{\partial \Phi}{\partial \sigma} = \frac{\partial^2 \Phi}{\partial x^2} + \frac{\partial^2 \Phi}{\partial y^2}$$
$$= \nabla^2 \Phi,$$

with the initial condition

$$\Phi(x, y, 0) = \mathcal{I}(x, y)$$

If this equation is modified to have the form

$$\frac{\partial \Phi}{\partial \sigma} = \nabla \cdot (c(x, y, \sigma) \nabla \Phi)$$
$$= c(x, y, \sigma) \nabla^2 \Phi + (\nabla c(x, y, \sigma)) \cdot (\nabla \Phi)$$

with the same initial condition, then if $c(x, y, \sigma) = 1$, we have the diffusion equation we started with, and if $c(x, y, \sigma) = 0$, there is no smoothing. We assume that c does not depend on σ. If we knew where the edges were in the image, we could construct a mask that consisted of regions where $c(x, y) = 1$, isolated by patches along the edges where $c(x, y) = 0$; in this case, a solution would smooth *inside* each separate region, but not over the edge. Although we do not know where the edges are—the exercise would be empty if we did—we can obtain reasonable choices of

$c(x, y)$ from the magnitude of the image gradient. If the gradient is large, then c should be small and vice versa. There is a substantial literature dealing with this approach; a good place to start is ter Haar Romeny (1994).

PROBLEMS

4.1. Show that forming the first-difference estimate of the derivative, which yields an operation of the form

$$\mathcal{R}_{ij} = \mathcal{F}_{i+1j} - \mathcal{F}_{ij}$$

is a convolution. What is the kernel of this convolution?

4.2. Write $\mathcal{E}_0$ for an image that consists of all zeros with a single one at the center. Show that convolving this image with the kernel

$$H_{ij} = \frac{1}{2\pi\sigma^2} \exp\left(-\frac{((i-k-1)^2 + (j-k-1)^2)}{2\sigma^2}\right)$$

(which is a discretised Gaussian) yields a circularly symmetric fuzzy blob.

4.3. Show that convolving an image with a discrete, separable 2D filter kernel is equivalent to convolving with two 1D filter kernels. Estimate the number of operations saved for an NxN image and a $2k + 1 \times 2k + 1$ kernel.

4.4. Why is representing the effect of a lens system with a convolution an approximation? In answering, you should consider how vignetting in a lens system affects its shift-invariance properties.

4.5. Show that convolving a function with a δ function simply reproduces the original function. Now show that convolving a function with a shifted δ function shifts the function.

4.6. We said that convolving the image with a kernel of the form $(\sin x \sin y)/(xy)$ is impossible because this function has infinite support. Why would it be impossible to Fourier transform the image, multiply the Fourier transform by a box function, and then inverse-Fourier transform the result? (Hint: Think support.)

4.7. Aliasing takes high spatial frequencies to low spatial frequencies. Explain why the following effects occur:

(a) In old cowboy films that show wagons moving, the wheel often seems to be stationary or moving in the wrong direction (i.e., the wagon moves from left to right, and the wheel seems to be turning counterclockwise).

(b) White shirts with thin, dark pinstripes often generate a shimmering array of colors on television.

(c) In ray-traced pictures, soft shadows generated by area sources look blocky.

PROGRAMMING EXERCISES

4.8. One way to obtain a Gaussian kernel is to convolve a constant kernel with itself many times. Compare this strategy with evaluating a Gaussian kernel.

(a) How many repeated convolutions do you need to get a reasonable approximation? (You need to establish what a reasonable approximation is; you might plot the quality of the approximation against the number of repeated convolutions).

(b) Are there any benefits that can be obtained like this? (Hint: Not every computer comes with an FPU.)

4.9. Write a program that produces a Gaussian pyramid from an image.

4.10. Write a program to double the edge length of an image (for example, your program should take an $n \times m$ image and produce a $2n \times 2m$ image). You should do this by doubling pixels, i.e. you replace each pixel by a 2×2 block of pixels with the same grey-level. Now evaluate the errors that your program makes by taking an image, smoothing and resampling it down to half-size, applying your program to return it to the original size, and comparing the result to the original image.

4.11. A sampled Gaussian kernel must alias because the kernel contains components at arbitrarily high spatial frequencies. Assume that the kernel is sampled on an infinite grid. As the standard deviation gets smaller, the aliased energy must increase. Plot the energy that aliases against the standard deviation of the Gaussian kernel in pixels. Now assume that the Gaussian kernel is given on a 7×7 grid. If the aliased energy must be of the same order of magnitude as the error due to truncating the Gaussian, what is the smallest standard deviation that can be expressed on this grid?

CHAPTER 5

Local Image Features

An object is separated from its background in an image by an *occluding contour*. Draw a path in the image that crosses such a contour. On one side, pixels lie on the object, and on the other, the background. Finding occluding contours is an important challenge, because the outline of an object—which is one cue to its shape—is formed by occluding contours. We can expect that, at occluding contours, there are often substantial changes in image brightness. There are other important causes of sharp changes in image brightness, including sharp changes in albedo, in surface orientation, or in illumination. Each can provide interesting information about the objects in the world. Occluding contours carry shape information; sharp changes in albedo carry texture information; sharp changes in surface orientation tell us about shape; and illumination changes might tell us where the sun is. All this means it is useful to find and reason about sharp changes in image intensity.

Sharp changes in brightness cause large image gradients. Section 5.1 describes methods to extract image gradients. One important use of gradients is to find *edges* or **edge points**, where the brightness changes particularly sharply (Section 5.2.1). The edge points produced tend to be sensitive to changes in contrast (i.e., the size of the difference in brightness across the edge), which can result from changes in lighting. Often, it is helpful to use the orientation of the gradient vector (Section 5.2.2), which does not depend on contrast. For example, at corners, the image gradient vector swings sharply in orientation.

Corners are important, because they are easy to match from image to image. At a corner, we expect to see strong image gradients that turn fast locally, and this cue yields a corner detector (Section 5.3). If we can describe a neighborhood around a corner, we can match descriptions across images. Such matching is an important basic subroutine in computer vision. Applications include: estimating a homography that will cause images to overlap (and so form a mosaic), Section 12.1.3; estimating the fundamental matrix, Section 7.1; reconstructing points in 3D from multiple views, Section 8.2.3; registering a 3D model with one or more images, Chapter 19. We must first find a natural size for a neighborhood around a corner, which we do by looking for the blob that best describes the local gray levels (Section 5.3.2). Once we have that neighborhood, there are two natural constructions that build representations of the orientation field in the neighborhood; the resulting features yield very well-behaved matchers (Section 5.4).

5.1 COMPUTING THE IMAGE GRADIENT

For an image $\mathcal{I}$, the gradient is

$$\nabla \mathcal{I} = (\frac{\partial \mathcal{I}}{\partial x}, \frac{\partial \mathcal{I}}{\partial y})^T,$$

which we could estimate by observing that

$$\frac{\partial \mathcal{I}}{\partial x} = \lim_{\delta x \to 0} \frac{\mathcal{I}(x + \delta x, y) - \mathcal{I}(x, y)}{\delta x} \approx \mathcal{I}_{i+1,j} - \mathcal{I}_{i,j}.$$

By the same argument, $\partial \mathcal{I} / \partial y \approx \mathcal{I}_{i,j+1} - \mathcal{I}_{i,j}$. These kinds of derivative estimates are known as *finite differences*. Image noise tends to result in pixels not looking like their neighbors, so that simple finite differences tend to give strong responses to noise. As a result, just taking one finite difference for x and one for y gives noisy gradient estimates. The way to deal with this problem is to smooth the image and then differentiate it (we could also smooth the derivative).

The most usual noise model is the *additive stationary Gaussian noise* model, where each pixel has added to it a value chosen independently from the same Gaussian probability distribution. This distribution almost always has zero mean. The standard deviation is a parameter of the model. The model is intended to describe thermal noise in cameras and is illustrated in Figure 5.1.

Smoothing works because, in general, any image gradient of significance to us has effects over a pool of pixels. For example, the contour of an object can result in a long chain of points where the image derivative is large. As another example, a corner typically involves many tens of pixels. If the noise at each pixel is independent and additive, then large image derivatives caused by noise are a local event. Smoothing the image before we differentiate will tend to suppress noise at the scale of individual pixels, because it will tend to make pixels look like their neighbors. However, gradients that are supported by evidence over multiple pixels will tend not to be smoothed out. This suggests differentiating a smoothed image (Figure 5.2).

5.1.1   Derivative of Gaussian Filters

Smoothing an image and then differentiating it is the same as convolving it with the derivative of a smoothing kernel. This fact is most easily seen by thinking about continuous convolution.

First, differentiation is linear and shift invariant. This means that there is some kernel—we dodge the question of what it looks like—that differentiates. That is, given a function $I(x, y)$,

$$\frac{\partial I}{\partial x} = K_{(\partial / \partial x)} * * I.$$

Now we want the derivative of a smoothed function. We write the convolution kernel for the smoothing as S. Recalling that convolution is associative, we have

$$(K_{(\partial / \partial x)} * * (S * * I)) = (K_{(\partial / \partial x)} * * S) * * I = (\frac{\partial S}{\partial x}) * * I.$$

This fact appears in its most commonly used form when the smoothing function is a Gaussian; we can then write

$$\frac{\partial (G_\sigma * * I)}{\partial x} = (\frac{\partial G_\sigma}{\partial x}) * * I,$$

that is, we need only convolve with the derivative of the Gaussian, rather than convolve and then differentiate. As discussed in Section 4.5, smoothed derivative

FIGURE 5.1: The **top row** shows three realizations of a stationary additive Gaussian noise process. We have added half the range of brightnesses to these images to show both negative and positive values of noise. From left to right, the noise has standard deviation 1/256, 4/256, and 16/256 of the full range of brightness, respectively. This corresponds roughly to bits zero, two, and five of a camera that has an output range of eight bits per pixel. The **lower row** shows this noise added to an image. In each case, values below zero or above the full range have been adjusted to zero or the maximum value accordingly.

filters look like the effects they are intended to detect. The x-derivative filters look like a vertical light blob next to a vertical dark blob (an arrangement where there is a large x-derivative), and so on (Figure 4.15). Smoothing results in much smaller noise responses from the derivative estimates (Figure 5.2).

The choice of σ used in estimating the derivative is often called the *scale* of the smoothing. Scale has a substantial effect on the response of a derivative filter. Assume we have a narrow bar on a constant background, rather like the zebra's whisker. Smoothing on a scale smaller than the width of the bar means that the filter responds on each side of the bar, and we are able to resolve the rising and falling edges of the bar. If the filter width is much greater, the bar is smoothed into the background and the bar generates little or no response (Figure 5.3).

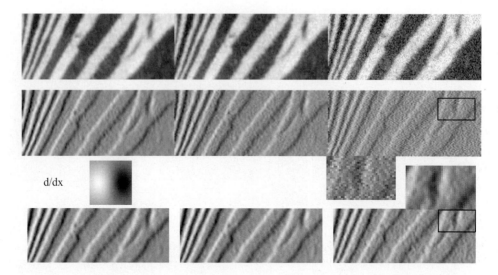

FIGURE 5.2: Derivative of Gaussian filters are less extroverted in their response to noise than finite difference filters. The image at **top left** shows a detail from a picture of a zebra; **top center** shows the same image corrupted by zero mean stationary additive Gaussian noise, with $\sigma = 0.03$ (pixel values range from 0 to 1). **Top right** shows the same image corrupted by zero mean stationary additive Gaussian noise, with $\sigma = 0.09$. The second row shows the finite difference in the x-direction of each image. These images are scaled so that zero is mid-gray, the most negative pixel is dark, and the most positive pixel is light; we used a different scaling for each image. Notice how the noise results in occasional strong derivatives, shown by a graininess in the derivative maps for the noisy images. The final row shows the partial derivative in the x-direction of each image, in each case estimated by a derivative of Gaussian filter with σ one pixel. Again, these images are scaled so that zero is mid-gray, the most negative pixel is dark, and the most positive pixel is light; we used a different scaling for each image. The images are smaller than the input image, because we used a 13×13 pixel discrete kernel. This means that the six rows (resp. columns) on the top and bottom of the image (resp. left and right) cannot be evaluated exactly, because for these rows the kernel covers some points outside the image; we have omitted these values. Notice how the smoothing helps reduce the impact of the noise; this is emphasized by the detail images (between the second and final row), which are doubled in size. The details show patches that correspond from the finite difference image and the smoothed derivative estimate. We show a derivative of Gaussian filter kernel, which (as we expect) looks like the structure it is supposed to find. This is not to scale (it'd be extremely small if it were).

5.2   REPRESENTING THE IMAGE GRADIENT

There are two important representations of the image gradient. The first is to compute edges, where there are very fast changes in brightness. These are usually seen as points where the magnitude of the gradient is extremal (Section 5.2.1). The second is to use gradient orientations, which are largely independent of illumination intensity (Section 5.7).

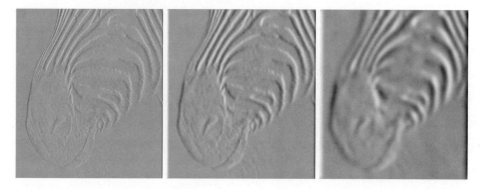

FIGURE 5.3: The scale (i.e., σ) of the Gaussian used in a derivative of Gaussian filter has significant effects on the results. The three images show estimates of the derivative in the x direction of an image of the head of a zebra obtained using a derivative of Gaussian filter with σ one pixel, three pixels, and seven pixels (**left** to **right**). Note how images at a finer scale show some hair, the animal's whiskers disappear at a medium scale, and the fine stripes at the top of the muzzle disappear at the coarser scale.

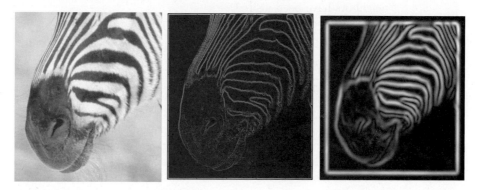

FIGURE 5.4: The gradient magnitude can be estimated by smoothing an image and then differentiating it. This is equivalent to convolving with the derivative of a smoothing kernel. The extent of the smoothing affects the gradient magnitude; in this figure, we show the gradient magnitude for the figure of a zebra at different scales. At the **center**, gradient magnitude estimated using the derivatives of a Gaussian with $\sigma = 1$ pixel; and on the **right**, gradient magnitude estimated using the derivatives of a Gaussian with $\sigma = 2$ pixel. Notice that large values of the gradient magnitude form thick trails.

5.2.1 Gradient-Based Edge Detectors

We think of sharp changes in image intensity as lying on curves in the image, which are known as *edges*; the curves are made up of *edge points*. Many effects can cause edges; worse, each effect that can cause an edge is not guaranteed to cause an edge. For example, an object may happen to be the same intensity as the background, and so the occluding contour will not result in an edge. This means that interpreting edge points can be very difficult. Nonetheless, they are worth finding.

In the most common method for finding edges, we start by computing an

Form an estimate of the image gradient
Compute the gradient magnitude
While there are points with high gradient
magnitude that have not been visited
   Find a start point that is a local maximum in the
      direction perpendicular to the gradient
      erasing points that have been checked
   While possible, expand a chain through
      the current point by:
          1) predicting a set of next points, using
              the direction perpendicular to the gradient
          2) finding which (if any) is a local maximum
            in the gradient direction
          3) testing if the gradient magnitude at the
            maximum is sufficiently large
          4) leaving a record that the point and
            neighbors have been visited
      record the next point, which becomes the current point
  end
end

Algorithm 5.1: Gradient-Based Edge Detection.

estimate of the gradient magnitude. The gradient magnitude is large along a thick trail in the image (Figure 5.4), but occluding contours are curves, so we must obtain a curve of the most distinctive points on this trail.

There is clearly no objective definition, and we can proceed by reasonable intuition. The gradient magnitude can be thought of as a chain of low hills. Marking local maxima would mark isolated points—the hilltops in the analogy. A better criterion is to slice the gradient magnitude along the gradient direction, which should be perpendicular to the edge, and mark the points along the slice where the magnitude is maximal. This would get a chain of points along the crown of the hills in our chain. Each point in the chain can be used to predict the location of the next point, which will be in a direction roughly at right angles to the gradient at the edge point (Figure 5.5). Forming these chains is called *nonmaximum suppression*. It is relatively straightforward to identify the location of these chains at a resolution finer than that of the pixel grid (Figure 5.5).

There are too many of these chains to come close to being a reasonable representation of object boundaries. In part, this is because we have marked maxima of the gradient magnitude without regard to how large these maxima are. It is more usual to apply a threshold test to ensure that the maxima are greater than some lower bound. This in turn leads to broken edge curves. The usual trick for dealing with this is to use *hysteresis*; we have two thresholds and refer to the *larger* when starting an edge chain and the *smaller* while following it. The trick often results in an improvement in edge outputs. These considerations yield Algorithm 5.1. Most

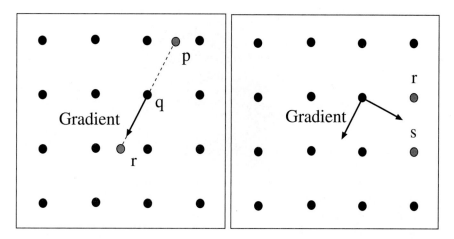

FIGURE 5.5: Nonmaximum suppression obtains points where the gradient magnitude is at a maximum *along the direction of the gradient*. The figure on the **left** shows how we reconstruct the gradient magnitude. The dots are the pixel grid. We are at pixel q, attempting to determine whether the gradient is at a maximum; the gradient direction through q does not pass through any convenient pixels in the forward or backward direction, so we must interpolate to obtain the values of the gradient magnitude at p and r. If the value at q is larger than both, q is an edge point. Typically, the magnitude values are reconstructed with a linear interpolate, which in this case would use the pixels to the left and right of p and r, respectively, to interpolate values at those points. On the **right**, we sketch how to find candidates for the next edge point given that q is an edge point; an appropriate search direction is perpendicular to the gradient, so that points s and t should be considered for the next edge point. Notice that, in principle, we don't need to restrict ourselves to pixel points on the image grid, because we know where the predicted position lies between s and t. Hence, we could again interpolate to obtain gradient values for points off the grid.

current edgefinders follow these lines.

5.2.2 Orientations

As the light gets brighter or darker (or as the camera aperture opens or closes), the image will get brighter or darker, which we can represent as a scaling of the image value. The image $\mathcal{I}$ will be replaced with $s\mathcal{I}$ for some value s. The magnitude of the gradient scales with the image, i.e., $\|\nabla\mathcal{I}\|$ will be replaced with $s\|\nabla\mathcal{I}\|$. This creates problems for edge detectors, because edge points may appear and disappear as the image gradient values go above and below thresholds with the scaling. One solution is to represent the *orientation* of image gradient, which is unaffected by scaling (Figure 5.7). The gradient orientation field depends on the smoothing scale at which the gradient was computed. Orientation fields can be quite characteristic of particular textures (Figure 5.9), and we will use this important property to come up with more complex features below.

FIGURE 5.6: Edge points marked on the pixel grid for the image shown on the **top**. The edge points on the **left** are obtained using a Gaussian smoothing filter at σ one pixel, and gradient magnitude has been tested against a high threshold to determine whether a point is an edge point. The edge points at the **center** are obtained using a Gaussian smoothing filter at σ four pixels, and gradient magnitude has been tested against a high threshold to determine whether a point is an edge point. The edge points on the **right** are obtained using a Gaussian smoothing filter at σ four pixels, and gradient magnitude has been tested against a low threshold to determine whether a point is an edge point. At a fine scale, fine detail at high contrast generates edge points, which disappear at the coarser scale. When the threshold is high, curves of edge points are often broken because the gradient magnitude dips below the threshold; for the low threshold, a variety of new edge points of dubious significance are introduced.

5.3   FINDING CORNERS AND BUILDING NEIGHBORHOODS

Points worth matching are corners, because a corner can be *localized*, which means we can tell where a corner is. This motivates the more general term *interest point* often used to describe a corner. In this view, corners are interesting because we can tell where they are. Place a small window over a patch of constant image value. If you translate the window in any direction, the image in the window will not change significantly. This means you cannot give a reliable estimate of the location of the window from its gray levels. Similarly, if you translate a window up and down an edge, the image in the window doesn't change, so you cannot estimate location along the edge (this observation used to be known as the *aperture problem*). But

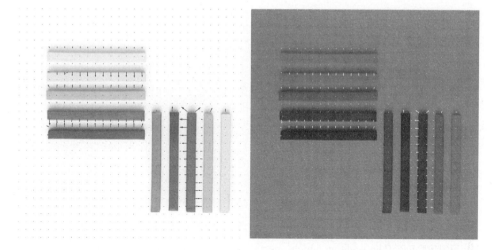

FIGURE 5.7: The magnitude of the image gradient changes when one increases or decreases the intensity. The orientation of the image gradient does not change; we have plotted every 10th orientation arrow, to make the figure easier to read. Note how the directions of the gradient arrows are fixed, whereas the size changes. *Philip Gatward © Dorling Kindersley, used with permission.*

with a corner, any movement of the window changes the image in the window (i.e., the patch of image around the corner is not *self-similar*), so you can estimate the location of the corner. Corners are not the only type of local image structure with this property (Section 5.3.2)

There are many ways of representing a neighborhood around an interesting corner. Methods vary depending on what might happen to the neighborhood. In what follows, we will assume that neighborhoods are only translated, rotated, and scaled (rather than, say, subjected to an affine or projective transformation), and so without loss of generality we can assume that the patches are circular. We must estimate the radius of this circle. There is technical machinery available for the neighborhoods that result from more complex transformations, but it is more intricate; see Section 5.6.

5.3.1 Finding Corners

One way to find corners is to find edges, and then walk the edges looking for a corner. This approach can work poorly, because edge detectors often fail at corners. At sharp corners or unfortunately oriented corners, gradient estimates are poor because the smoothing region covers the corner.

At a corner, we expect two important effects. First, there should be large gradients. Second, in a small neighborhood, the gradient orientation should swing sharply. We can identify corners by looking at variations in orientation within a

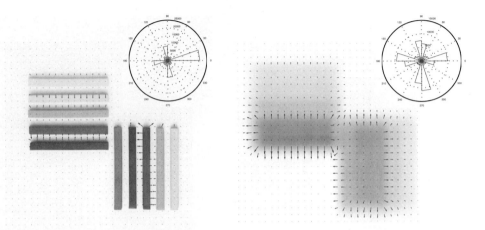

FIGURE 5.8: The scale at which one takes the gradient affects the orientation field. We show the overall trend of the orientation field by plotting a rose plot, where the size of a wedge represents the relative frequency of that range of orientations. **Left** shows an image of artists pastels at a fairly fine scale; here the edges are sharp, and so only a small set of orientations occurs. In the heavily smoothed version on the **right**, all edges are blurred and corners become smooth and blobby; as a result, more orientations appear in the rose plot. *Philip Gatward © Dorling Kindersley, used with permission.*

window. In particular, the matrix

$$
\mathcal{H} = \sum_{window} \left\{ (\nabla I)(\nabla I)^T \right\}
$$

$$
\approx \sum_{window} \left\{
\begin{array}{cc}
(\frac{\partial G_\sigma}{\partial x} **\mathcal{I})(\frac{\partial G_\sigma}{\partial x} **\mathcal{I}) & (\frac{\partial G_\sigma}{\partial x} **\mathcal{I})(\frac{\partial G_\sigma}{\partial y} **\mathcal{I}) \\
(\frac{\partial G_\sigma}{\partial x} **\mathcal{I})(\frac{\partial G_\sigma}{\partial y} **\mathcal{I}) & (\frac{\partial G_\sigma}{\partial y} **\mathcal{I})(\frac{\partial G_\sigma}{\partial y} **\mathcal{I})
\end{array}
\right\}
$$

gives a good idea of the behavior of the orientation in a window. In a window of constant gray level, both eigenvalues of this matrix are small because all the terms are small. In an edge window, we expect to see one large eigenvalue associated with gradients at the edge and one small eigenvalue because few gradients run in other directions. But in a corner window, both eigenvalues should be large.

The *Harris corner detector* looks for local maxima of

$$
\det(\mathcal{H}) - k(\frac{\text{trace}(\mathcal{H})}{2})^2
$$

where k is some constant (Harris and Stephens 1988); we used 0.5 for Figure 5.10. These local maxima are then tested against a threshold. This tests whether the product of the eigenvalues (which is $\det(\mathcal{H})$) is larger than the square of the average (which is $(\text{trace}(\mathcal{H})/2)^2$). Large, locally maximal values of this test function imply the eigenvalues are both big, which is what we want. Figure 5.10 illustrates corners found with the Harris detector. This detector is unaffected by translation and rotation (Figure 5.11).

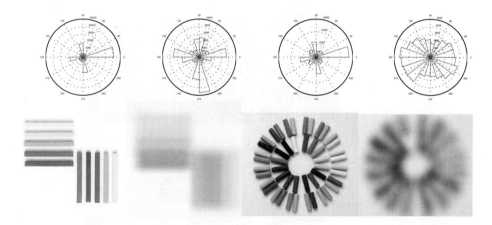

FIGURE 5.9: Different patterns have quite different orientation histograms. The **left** shows rose plots and images for a picture of artists pastels at two different scales; the **right** shows rose plots and images for a set of pastels arranged into a circular pattern. Notice how the pattern of orientations at a particular scale, and also the changes across scales, are quite different for these two very different patterns. *Philip Gatward © Dorling Kindersley, used with permission.*

5.3.2   Using Scale and Orientation to Build a Neighborhood

To turn a corner into an image neighborhood, we must estimate the radius of the circular patch (equivalently, its scale). The radius estimate should get larger proportionally when the image gets bigger. For example, in a 2x scaled version of the original image, our method should double its estimate of the patch radius. This property helps choose a method. We could center a blob of fixed appearance (say, dark on a light background) on the corner, and then choose the scale to be the radius of the best fitting blob. An efficient way to do this is to use a Laplacian of Gaussian filter.

The *Laplacian* of a function in 2D is defined as

$$(\nabla^2 f)(x, y) = \frac{\partial^2 f}{\partial x^2} + \frac{\partial^2 f}{\partial y^2}.$$

It is natural to smooth the image before applying a Laplacian. Notice that the Laplacian is a linear operator (if you're not sure about this, you should check), meaning that we could represent taking the Laplacian as convolving the image with some kernel (which we write as K_{∇^2}). Because convolution is associative, we have that

$$(K_{\nabla^2} * *(G_\sigma * *I)) = (K_{\nabla^2} * *G_\sigma) * *I = (\nabla^2 G_\sigma) * *I.$$

The reason this is important is that, just as for first derivatives, smoothing an image and then applying the Laplacian is the same as convolving the image with the Laplacian of the kernel used for smoothing. Figure 5.12 shows the resulting kernel for Gaussian smoothing; notice that this looks like a dark blob on a light background.

FIGURE 5.10: The response of the Harris corner detector visualized for two detail regions of an image of a box of colored pencils (**center**). **Top left**, a detail from the pencil points; **top center**, the response of the Harris corner detector, where more positive values are lighter. The **top right** shows these overlaid on the original image. To overlay this map, we added the images, so that areas where the overlap is notably dark come from places where the Harris statistic is negative (which means that one eigenvalue of $\mathcal{H}$ is large, the other small). Note that the detector is affected by contrast, so that, for example, the point of the mid-gray pencil at the top of this figure generates a very strong corner response, but the points of the darker pencils do not, because they have little contrast with the tray. For the darker pencils, the strong, contrasty corners occur where the lead of the pencil meets the wood. The **bottom** sequence shows corners for a detail of pencil ends. Notice that responses are quite local, and there are a relatively small number of very strong corners. *Steve Gorton © Dorling Kindersley, used with permission.*

Imagine applying a smoothed Laplacian operator to the image at the center of the patch. Write $\mathcal{I}$ for the image, ∇_σ^2 for the smoothed Laplacian operator with smoothing constant σ, $\uparrow_k \mathcal{I}$ for the the image with size scaled by k, (x_c, y_c) for the coordinates of the patch center, and (x_{kc}, y_{kc}) for the coordinates of the patch center in the scaled image. Assume that upscaling is perfect, and there are no effects resulting from the image grid. This is fair because effects will be small for the scales of interest for us. Then, we have

$$(\nabla_{k\sigma}^2 \uparrow_k \mathcal{I})(x_c, y_c) = (\nabla_\sigma^2 \mathcal{I})(x_{kc}, y_{kc})$$

(this is most easily demonstrated by reasoning about the image as a continuous function, the operator as a convolution, and then using the change of variables formula for integrals). Now choose a radius r for the circular patch centered at

FIGURE 5.11: The response of the Harris corner detector is unaffected by rotation and translation. The **top row** shows the response of the detector on a detail of the image on the **far left**. The **bottom row** shows the response of the detector on a corresponding detail from a rotated version of the image. For each row, we show the detail window (**left**); the response of the Harris corner detector, where more positive values are lighter (**center**); and the responses overlaid on the image (**right**). Notice that responses are quite local, and there are a relatively small number of very strong corners. To overlay this map, we added the images, so that areas where the overlap is notably dark come from places where the Harris statistic is negative (which means that one eigenvalue of $\mathcal{H}$ is large, the other small). The arm and hammer in the top row match those in the bottom row; notice how well the maps of Harris corner detector responses match, too. © *Dorling Kindersley, used with permission.*

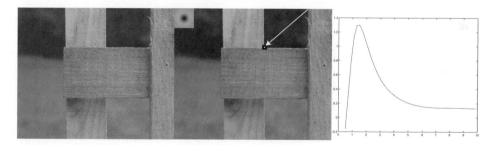

FIGURE 5.12: The scale of a neighborhood around a corner can be estimated by finding a local extremum, in *scale* of the response at that point to a smoothed Laplacian of Gaussian kernel. On the **left**, a detail of a piece of fencing. In the center, a corner identified by an arrow (which points to the corner, given by a white spot surrounded by a black ring). *Overlaid* on this image is a Laplacian of Gaussian kernel, in the **top right** corner; dark values are negative, mid gray is zero, and light values are positive. Notice that, using the reasoning of Section 4.5, this filter will give a strong positive response for a dark blob on a light background, and a strong negative response for a light blob on a dark background, so by searching for the strongest response at this point as a function of scale, we are looking for the size of the best-fitting blob. On the **right**, the response of a Laplacian of Gaussian *at the location of the corner*, as a function of the smoothing parameter (which is plotted in pixels). There is one extremal scale, at approximately 2 pixels. This means that there is one scale at which the image neighborhood looks most like a blob (some corners have more than one scale). © *Dorling Kindersley, used with permission.*

Assume a fixed scale parameter k
Apply a corner detector to the image $\mathcal{I}$
Initialize a list of patches
For each corner detected
   Write (x_c, y_c) for the location of the corner
   Compute the radius r for the patch at (x_c, y_c) as

$$r(x_c, y_c) = \underset{\sigma}{\operatorname{argmax}} \ \nabla^2_\sigma \mathcal{I}(x_c, y_c)$$

     by computing $\nabla^2_\sigma \mathcal{I}(x_c, y_c)$ for a variety of values of σ,
     interpolating these values, and maximizing
   Compute an orientation histogram $H(\theta)$ for gradient orientations within
     a radius kr of (x_c, y_c).
   Compute the orientation of the patch θ_p as

$$\theta_p = \underset{\theta}{\operatorname{argmax}} \ H(\theta). \text{ If there is more than}$$

     one theta that maximizes this histogram, make one copy of the
     patch for each.
   Attach (x_c, y_c, r, θ_p) to the list of patches for each copy

Algorithm 5.2: Obtaining Location, Radius and Orientation of Pattern Elements Using a Corner Detector.

(x_c, y_c), such that

$$r(x_c, y_c) = \underset{\sigma}{\operatorname{argmax}} \ \nabla^2_\sigma \mathcal{I}(x_c, y_c)$$

(Figure 5.12). If the image is scaled by k, then this value of r will be scaled by k too, which is the property we wanted. This procedure looks for the scale of the best approximating blob. Notice that a Gaussian pyramid could be helpful here; we could apply the same smoothed Laplacian operator to different levels of a pyramid to get estimates of the scale.

We can generalize this method, too, to detect interest points. Write $(\boldsymbol{x}, \sigma)$ for a triple consisting of a point and a scale around that point. We would like to detect such triples in a way that (a) when the image is translated, the triples translate, too and (b) when the image is scaled, the triples scale. This can be given a formal meaning. If $\mathcal{I}'(\boldsymbol{x}) = \mathcal{I}(\lambda\boldsymbol{x} + \boldsymbol{c})$ is a scaled and translated image, then for each point $(\boldsymbol{x}, \sigma)$ in the list of neighborhoods for $\mathcal{I}$, we want to have $(\lambda\boldsymbol{x} + \boldsymbol{c}, \lambda\sigma)$ in the list of neighborhoods for $\mathcal{I}'$. This property is referred to as *covariance* (although the term invariance is widely but incorrectly used).

We have already established that, at a particular point (given by our corner detector), we get a covariant scale estimate by choosing the local maximum *in scale* of the response of the Laplacian of Gaussian. We can build an interest point detector directly out of a Laplacian of Gaussian, by identifying local extrema *in position and scale* of the operator (if this looks slow to you, keep in mind that a Gaussian pyramid could speed up the process). Each such extremum is a triple $(\boldsymbol{x}, \sigma)$ with the properties we want. These points are different from the points

Assume a fixed scale parameter k
Find all locations and scales which are local extrema of
$\quad \nabla^2_\sigma \mathcal{I}(x, y)$ in location (x, y) and scale σ forming a list of triples (x_c, y_c, r)
For each such triple
$\quad$ Compute an orientation histogram $H(\theta)$ for gradient orientations within
$\quad\quad$ a radius kr of (x_c, y_c).
$\quad$ Compute the orientation of the patch θ_p as
$$\theta_p = \underset{\theta}{\operatorname{argmax}}\ H(\theta).\ \text{If there is more than one } \theta \text{ that}$$
$\quad$ maximizes this histogram, make one copy of the patch for each.
$\quad$ Attach (x_c, y_c, r, θ_p) to the list of patches for each copy

Algorithm 5.3: Obtaining Location, Radius, and Orientation of Pattern Elements Using the Laplacian of Gaussian.

obtained by using a corner detector and then estimating scale. Corner detectors respond to a corner structure at the point of interest; the Laplacian of Gaussian looks for structures that look like a circular blob of a particular scale centered at the point of interest. Corner detectors tend to produce neighborhoods where the estimate of the center is very accurate, but the scale estimate is poor. These are most useful in matching problems where we don't expect the scale to change much. Laplacian of Gaussian methods produce neighborhoods where the estimate of the center is less accurate, but the scale estimate is better. These are most useful in matching problems where large changes of scale might appear.

As we have seen, orientation histograms are a natural representation of image patches. However, we cannot represent orientations in image coordinates (for example, using the angle to the horizontal image axis), because the patch we are matching to might have been rotated. We need a reference orientation so all angles can be measured with respect to that reference. A natural reference orientation is the most common orientation in the patch. We compute a histogram of the gradient orientations in this patch, and find the largest peak. This peak is the reference orientation for the patch. If there are two or more peaks of the same magnitude, we make multiple copies of the patch, one at each peak orientation. The whole process is summarized in Algorithms 5.2 and 5.3. These estimates of patch neighborhoods are remarkably well behaved (Figure 5.13).

5.4 DESCRIBING NEIGHBORHOODS WITH SIFT AND HOG FEATURES

We know the center, radius, and orientation of a set of an image patch, and must now represent it. Orientations should provide a good representation. They are unaffected by changes in image brightness, and different textures tend to have different orientation fields. The pattern of orientations in different parts of the patch is likely to be quite distinctive. Our representation should be robust to small errors in the center, radius, or orientation of the patch, because we are unlikely to estimate these exactly right.

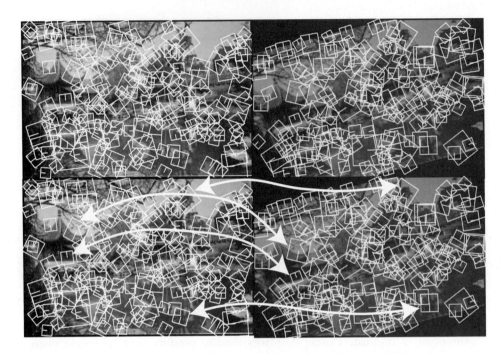

FIGURE 5.13: This figure shows local patches recovered using a method similar to that described in the text (the details of the corner detector were different). These patches are plotted as squares, rather than as circles. The location of the patch is the center of the square. The reference orientation of the patch is given by the line segment in the square, and the scale is the size of the square. The image on the **right** has been scaled, rotated, and translated to produce the image on the **left**. Notice that (a) most of the patches on the right have corresponding patches on the left and (b) the corresponding patches are translated, rotated, and scaled versions of the original patches. You can check this by looking at the grayscale version of the image. We have shown some of the many corresponding pairs of patches (**below**; the large white arrows). *This figure was originally published as Figure 1 of "Object recognition from local scale-invariant features" D.G. Lowe, Proc. IEEE ICCV, 1999 © IEEE 1999.*

You should think of these neighborhoods as being made up of pattern elements. In this case, the pattern elements will be orientations, but we will use this trick again for other kinds of pattern element. These elements move around somewhat inside the neighborhood (because we might not get the center right), but if most elements are there and are in about the right place, then the neighborhood has the right properties. We must build features that can make it obvious whether the pattern elements are present, and whether they are in about the right place, but are not affected by some rearrangement.

The most obvious approach is to represent the neighborhood with a histogram of the elements that appear there. This will tell us what is present, but it confuses too many patterns with one another. For example, all neighborhoods with vertical stripes will get mixed up, however wide the stripe. The natural approach is to take histograms locally, within subpatches of the neighborhood. This leads to a very

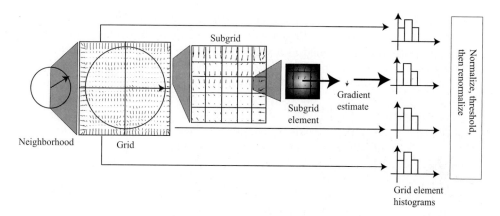

FIGURE 5.14: To construct a SIFT descriptor for a neighborhood, we place a grid over the rectified neighborhood. Each grid is divided into a subgrid, and a gradient estimate is computed at the center of each subgrid element. This gradient estimate is a weighted average of nearby gradients, with weights chosen so that gradients outside the subgrid cell contribute. The gradient estimates in each subgrid element are accumulated into an orientation histogram. Each gradient votes for its orientation, with a vote weighted by its magnitude and by its distance to the center of the neighborhood. The resulting orientation histograms are stacked to give a single feature vector. This is normalized to have unit norm; then terms in the normalized feature vector are thresholded, and the vector is normalized again.

important feature construction.

5.4.1 SIFT Features

We can now compute a representation that is not affected by translation, rotation, or scale. For each patch, we rectify the patch by translating the center to the origin, rotating so the orientation direction lies along (say) the x-axis, and scaling so the radius is one. Any representation we compute for this rectified patch will be invariant to translations, rotations, and scale. Although we do not need to rectify in practice—instead, we can work the rectification into each step of computing the description—it helps to think about computing descriptions for a rectified patch.

A *SIFT descriptor* (for Scale Invariant Feature Transform) is constructed out of image gradients, and uses both magnitude and orientation. The descriptor is normalized to suppress the effects of change in illumination intensity. The descriptor is a set of histograms of image gradients that are then normalized. These histograms expose general spatial trends in the image gradients in the patch but suppress detail. For example, if we estimate the center, scale, or orientation of the patch slightly wrong, then the rectified patch will shift slightly. As a result, simply recording the gradient at each point yields a representation that changes between instances of the patch. A histogram of gradients will be robust to these changes. Rather than histogramming the gradient at a set of sample points, we histogram local averages of image gradients; this helps avoid noise.

The standard SIFT descriptor is obtained by first dividing the rectified patch into an $n \times n$ grid. We then subdivide each grid element into an $m \times m$ subgrid of subcells. At the center of each subcell, we compute a gradient estimate. The gradient estimate is obtained as a weighted average of gradients around the center of the cell, weighting each by $(1 - d_x/s_x)(1 - d_y/s_y)/N$, where d_x (resp. d_y) is the x (resp. y) distance from the gradient to the center of the subcell, and s_x (resp. s_y) is the x (resp. y) spacing between the subcell centers. This means that gradients make contributions to more than one subcell, so that a small error in the location of the center of the patch leads to a small change in the descriptor.

We now use these gradient estimates to produce histograms. Each grid element has a q-cell orientation histogram. The magnitude of each gradient estimate is accumulated into the histogram cell corresponding to its orientation; the magnitude is weighted by a Gaussian in distance from the center of the patch, using a standard deviation of half the patch.

We concatenate each histogram into a vector of $n \times n \times q$ entries. If the image intensity were doubled, this vector's length would double (because the histogram entries are sums of gradient magnitudes). To avoid this effect, we normalize this vector to have unit length. Very large gradient magnitude estimates tend to be unstable (for example, they might result from a lucky arrangement of surfaces in 3D so that one faces the light directly and another points away from the light). This means that large entries in the normalized vector are untrustworthy. To avoid difficulties with large gradient magnitudes, each value in the normalized vector is thresholded with threshold t, and the resulting vector is renormalized. The whole process is summarized in Algorithm 5.4 and Figure 5.14. Standard parameter values are $n = 4$, $m = 4$, $q = 8$, and $t = 0.2$.

Given an image $\mathcal{I}$, and a patch with center (x_c, y_c),
   radius r, orientation θ, and parameters n, m, q, k and t.
For each element of the $n \times n$ grid centered at (x_c, y_c) with spacing kr
   Compute a weighted q element histogram of the averaged
      gradient samples at each point of the $m \times m$ subgrid,
      as in Algorithm 5.5.
Form an $n \times n \times q$ vector $\boldsymbol{v}$ by concatenating the histograms.
Compute $\boldsymbol{u} = \boldsymbol{v}/\sqrt{\boldsymbol{v} \cdot \boldsymbol{v}}$.
Form $\boldsymbol{w}$ whose i'th element w_i is $\min(u_i, t)$.
The descriptor is $\boldsymbol{d} = \boldsymbol{w}/\sqrt{\boldsymbol{w} \cdot \boldsymbol{w}}$.

Algorithm 5.4: Computing a SIFT Descriptor in a Patch Using Location, Orientation and Scale.

There is now extensive experimental evidence that image patches that match one another will have similar SIFT feature representations, and patches that do not will tend not to. SIFT features can be used to represent the local color pattern around a sample point, too. The natural procedure is to apply SIFT feature code to a color representation. For example, one could compute SIFT features for each of the hue, saturation, and value channels (HSV-SIFT; see Bosch *et al.* (2008)); for the opponent color channels (OpponentSIFT, which uses R-G and B-Y; see van de

Given a grid cell $\mathcal{G}$ for patch with center $\boldsymbol{c} = (x_c, y_c)$ and radius r

Create an orientation histogram
For each point $\boldsymbol{p}$ in an $m \times m$ subgrid spanning $\mathcal{G}$
    Compute a gradient estimate $\nabla \mathcal{I} \mid_{\boldsymbol{p}}$ estimate at $\boldsymbol{p}$
    as a weighted average of $\nabla \mathcal{I}$, using bilinear weights centered at $\boldsymbol{p}$.
    Add a vote with weight $\| \nabla \mathcal{I} \| \frac{1}{r\sqrt{2\pi}} \exp\left(-\frac{\|\boldsymbol{p}-\boldsymbol{c}\|^2}{r^2}\right)$
    to the orientation histogram cell for the orientation of $\nabla \mathcal{I}$.

Algorithm 5.5: Computing a Weighted q Element Histogram for a SIFT Feature.

FIGURE 5.15: The HOG features for each the two images shown here have been visualized by a version of the rose diagram of Figures 5.7–5.9. Here each of the cells in which the histogram is taken is plotted with a little rose in it; the direction plotted is at right angles to the gradient, so you should visualize the overlaid line segments as edge directions. Notice that in the textured regions the edge directions are fairly uniformly distributed, but strong contours (the gardener, the fence on the **left**; the vertical edges of the french windows on the **right**) are very clear. This figure was plotted using the toolbox of Dollár and Rabaud. *Left: © Dorling Kindersley, used with permission. Right: Geoff Brightling © Dorling Kindersley, used with permission.*

Sande *et al.* (2010)); for normalised opponent color channels (C-SIFT, which uses $(R - G)/(R + G + B)$ and $(B - Y)/(R + G + B)$; see Abdel Hakim and Farag (2006); Geusebroek *et al.* (2001); or Burghouts and Geusebroek (2009)); and for normalized color channels (rgSIFT, which uses $R/(R+G+B)$ and $G/(R+G+B)$; see van de Sande *et al.* (2010)). Each of these features will behave slightly differently when the light falling on an object changes, and each can be used in place of, or in addition to, SIFT features.

5.4.2 HOG Features

The *HOG feature* (for Histogram Of Gradient orientations) is an important variant of the SIFT feature. Again, we histogram gradient orientations in cells, but now adjust the process to try and identify high-contrast edges. We can recover contrast information by counting gradient orientations with weights that reflect how significant a gradient is compared to other gradients in the same cell. This means that, rather than normalize gradient contributions over the whole neighborhood, we normalize with respect to nearby gradients only. Normalization could occur on a grid of cells that is different from the orientation subgrid, too. A single gradient location might contribute to several different histograms, normalized in somewhat different ways; this means we will be relatively unlikely to miss boundaries that have low contrast.

Write $\|\nabla I_{\mathbf{x}}\|$ for the gradient magnitude at point $\mathbf{x}$ in the image. Write $\mathcal{C}$ for the cell whose histogram we wish to compute and $w_{\mathbf{x},\mathcal{C}}$ for the weight that we will use for the orientation at $\mathbf{x}$ for this cell. A natural choice of weight is

$$w_{\mathbf{x},\mathcal{C}} = \frac{\|\nabla I_{\mathbf{x}}\|}{\sum_{\mathbf{u}\in\mathcal{C}} \|\nabla I_{\mathbf{u}}\|}.$$

This compares the gradient magnitude to others in the cell, so that gradients that are large compared to their neighbors get a large weight. This normalization process means that HOG features are quite good at picking outline curves out of confusing backgrounds (Figure 5.15).

5.5 COMPUTING LOCAL FEATURES IN PRACTICE

We have sketched the most important feature constructions, but there is a huge range of variants. Performance is affected by quite detailed questions, such as the extent of smoothing when evaluating orientations. Space doesn't allow a detailed survey of these questions (though there's some material in Section 5.6), and the answers seem to change fairly frequently, too. This means we simply can't supply accurate recipes for building each of these features.

Fortunately, at time of writing, there are several software packages that provide good implementations of each of these feature types, and of other variations. Piotr Dollár and Vincent Rabaud publish a toolbox at `http://vision.ucsd.edu/~pdollar/toolbox/doc/index.html`; we used this to generate several figures. VLFeat is a comprehensive open-source package that provides SIFT features, vector quantization by a variety of methods, and a variety of other representations. At time of writing, it could be obtained from `http://www.vlfeat.org/`. SIFT features are patented (Lowe 2004), but David Lowe (the inventor) provides a reference object code implementation at `http://www.cs.ubc.ca/~lowe/keypoints/`. Navneet Dalal, one of the authors of the original HOG feature paper, provides an implementation at `http://www.navneetdalal.com/software/`. One variant of SIFT is PCA-SIFT, where one uses principal components to reduce the dimension of the SIFT representation (Ke and Sukthankar 2004). Yan Ke, one of the authors of the original PCA-SIFT paper, provides an implementation at `http://www.cs.cmu.edu/~yke/pcasift/`. Color descriptor code, which computes visual words based on various color SIFT features, is published by van de Sande *et al.* at `http://koen.me/research/colordescriptors/`.

5.6 NOTES

Edges

There is a huge edge detection literature. The earliest paper of which we are aware is Julez (1959) (yes, 1959!). Those wishing to be acquainted with the early literature in detail should start with a 1975 survey by Davis (1975); Herskovits and Binford (1970); Horn (1971); and Hueckel (1971), who models edges and then detects the model. There are many optimality criteria for edge detectors, and rather more "optimal" edge detectors. The key paper in this literature is by Canny (1986); significant variants are due to Deriche (1987) and to Spacek (1986). Faugeras' textbook contains a detailed and accessible exposition of the main issues Faugeras (1993). At the end of the day, most variants boil down to smoothing the image with something that looks a lot like a Gaussian before measuring the gradient. All edge detectors behave badly at corners; only the details vary.

Object boundaries are not the same as sharp changes in image values. There is a vast literature seeking to build boundary detectors; we can provide only some pointers. The reader could start with Bergholm (1987), Deriche (1990), Elder and Zucker (1998), Fleck (1992), Kube and Perona (1996), Olson (1998), Perona and Malik (1990*b*), or Torre and Poggio (1986). The best current boundary detector takes quite a lot of local information into account, and is described in Section 17.1.3.

The edges that our edge detectors respond to are sometimes called *step edges* because they consist of a sharp, "discontinuous" change in value that is sometimes modeled as a step. A variety of other forms of edge have been studied. The most commonly cited example is the *roof edge*, which consists of a rising segment meeting a falling segment, rather like some of the reflexes that can result from the effects of interreflections. Another example that also results from interreflections is a composite of a step and a roof. It is possible to find these phenomena by using essentially the same steps as outlined before (find an "optimal" filter, and do nonmaximum suppression on its outputs) (Canny 1986, Perona and Malik 1990*a*). In practice, this is seldom done. There appear to be two reasons. First, there is no comfortable basis in theory (or practice) for the models that are adopted. What particular composite edges are worth looking for? The easy answer—those for which optimal filters are reasonably easy to derive—is most unsatisfactory. Second, the semantics of roof edges and more complex composite edges is even vaguer than that of step edges. There is little notion of what one would *do* with roof edge once it had been found.

Corners, Neighborhoods, and Interest Points

The first corner detector we know of is due to Moravec (1980). Corner detectors are now very well studied (there is an excellent Wikipedia page that describes the various detectors and their relations at `http://en.wikipedia.org/wiki/Corner_detection`). The Harris and Stephens detector we described remains competitive. Important variants look at different eigenvalue criteria (Tomasi and Shi 1994); differential geometric criteria (Wang and Brady 1994); multiple scales (Lindeberg 1993); local self-similarity measures (Smith and Brady 1997, Trajkovic and Hedley 1998); and machine learning (Rosten *et al.* 2010).

For simplicity of exposition, we have elided corners and interest points (the other name under which corners are often studied). Interest points are usually thought of as a corner (or something like it) together with a neighborhood, covariant under some form of transformation. We like to see detecting the points and estimating their neighborhoods as distinct processes, though for strict covariance both the detector and the neighborhood estimator must be covariant. Various detectors are scale covariant (Mikolajczyk and Schmid 2002); affine covariant (Mikolajczyk and Schmid 2002); and illumination robust (Gevrekci and Gunturk 2009). The idea can be extended to spatio-temporal representations (Willems *et al.* 2008, Laptev 2005). There are now detailed experimental studies of the performance of interest point detectors (Schmid *et al.* 2000, Privitera and Stark 1998, Mikolajczyk *et al.* 2005).

Descriptors

The tricks to describing neighborhoods seem to be: describe a local texture pattern within a covariant neighborhood; work with orientations, because they're illumination invariant; and use histograms to suppress spatial detail, working with more detail at the center than at the boundary. These tricks appear in numerous papers in a variety of forms (e.g., Schmid and Mohr (1997); Belongie *et al.* (2001); Berg *et al.* (2005)), but SIFT and Hog features now dominate. Comparisons between local descriptors seem to support this dominance (Mikolajczyk and Schmid 2005).

PROBLEMS

5.1. Each pixel value in 500×500 pixel image $\mathcal{I}$ is an independent, normally distributed random variable with zero mean and standard deviation one. Estimate the number of pixels that, where the absolute value of the x derivative, estimated by forward differences (i.e., $|I_{i+1,j} - I_{i,j}|$, is greater than 3.

5.2. Each pixel value in 500×500 pixel image $\mathcal{I}$ is an independent, normally distributed random variable with zero mean and standard deviation one. $\mathcal{I}$ is convolved with the $2k + 1 \times 2k + 1$ kernel $\mathcal{G}$. What is the covariance of pixel values in the result? There are two ways to do this; on a case-by-case basis (e.g., at points that are greater than $2k+1$ apart in either the x or y direction, the values are clearly independent) or in one fell swoop. Don't worry about the pixel values at the boundary.

5.3. We have a camera that can produce output values that are integers in the range from 0 to 255. Its spatial resolution is 1024 by 768 pixels, and it produces 30 frames a second. We point it at a scene that, in the absence of noise, would produce the constant value 128. The output of the camera is subject to noise that we model as zero mean stationary additive Gaussian noise with a standard deviation of 1. How long must we wait before the noise model predicts that we should see a pixel with a negative value? (Hint: You may find it helpful to use logarithms to compute the answer as a straightforward evaluation of $\exp(-128^2/2)$ will yield 0; the trick is to get the large positive and large negative logarithms to cancel.)

5.4. Show that for a 2×2 matrix $\mathcal{H}$, with eigenvalues λ_1, λ_2
 (a) $\det \mathcal{H} = \lambda_1 \lambda_2$
 (b) $\text{trace} \mathcal{H} = \lambda_1 + \lambda_2$

PROGRAMMING EXERCISES

5.5. The Laplacian of a Gaussian looks similar to the difference between two Gaussians at different scales. Compare these two kernels for various values of the two scales. Which choices give a good approximation? How significant is the approximation error in edge finding using a zero-crossing approach?

5.6. Obtain an implementation of Canny's edge detector (you could try the vision home page; MATLAB also has an implementation in the image processing toolbox), and make a series of images indicating the effects of scale and contrast thresholds on the edges that are detected. How easy is it to set up the edge detector to mark only object boundaries? Can you think of applications where this would be easy?

5.7. It is quite easy to defeat hysteresis in edge detectors that implement it; essentially, one sets the lower and higher thresholds to have the same value. Use this trick to compare the behavior of an edge detector with and without hysteresis. There are a variety of issues to look at:

(a) What are you trying to do with the edge detector output? It is sometimes helpful to have linked chains of edge points. Does hysteresis help significantly here?

(b) Noise suppression: We often wish to force edge detectors to ignore some edge points and mark others. One diagnostic that an edge is useful is high contrast (it is by no means reliable). How reliably can you use hysteresis to suppress low-contrast edges without breaking high-contrast edges?

5.8. Build a Harris corner detector; for each corner, estimate scale and orientation as we have described. Now test how well your list of neighborhoods behaves under rotation, translation, and scale of the image. You do this by a simple exercise in matching. For each test image, prepare a rotated, translated, and scaled version of that image. Now you know where each neighborhood should appear in the new version of the image — check how often something of the right size and orientation appears in the right place. You should find that rotation and translation cause no significant problems, but large scale changes can be an issue.

C H A P T E R   6

Texture

Texture is a phenomenon that is widespread, easy to recognise, and hard to define. Typically, whether an effect is referred to as texture or not depends on the scale at which it is viewed. A leaf that occupies most of an image is an object, but the foliage of a tree is a texture. Views of large numbers of small objects are often best thought of as textures. Examples include grass, foliage, brush, pebbles, and hair. Many surfaces are marked with orderly patterns that look like large numbers of small objects. Examples include the spots of animals such as leopards or cheetahs; the stripes of animals such as tigers or zebras; the patterns on bark, wood, and skin. Textures tend to show *repetition*: (roughly!) the same local patch appears again and again, though it may be distorted by a viewing transformation.

Texture is important, because texture appears to be a very strong cue to object identity. Most modern object recognition programs are built around texture representation machinery of one form or another. This may be because texture is also a strong cue to *material properties*: what the material that makes up an object is like. For example, texture cues can be used to tell tree bark (which is moderately hard and rough) from bare metal (which is hard, smooth, and shiny). People seem to be able to predict some mechanical properties of materials from their appearance. For example, often you can distinguish somewhat viscous materials, like hand cream, from highly viscous materials, like cream cheese, by eye (Adelson 2001). Material properties are correlated to the identity of objects, but they are not the same thing. For example, although hammers are commonly made of metal, a plastic hammer, a metal hammer, and a wooden hammer are all still hammers.

There are three main kinds of texture representation. *Local texture representations* encode the texture very close to a point in an image. These representations can't be comprehensive, because they look at a small piece of the image. However, they are very useful in image segmentation, where we must break an image into large, useful components, usually called *regions* (the details of what makes a region useful are deferred to Chapter 9). One reasonable requirement is that points inside a region look similar to one another, and different from points outside the region, and segmentation algorithms need a description of the appearance close to the point to impose this requirement. Local texture representations are described in Section 6.1.

Other problems require a description of the texture within an image domain. We refer to such representations as *pooled texture representations*. For example, **texture recognition** is the problem of determining what texture is represented by a patch in an image. Here we have a domain (the patch) and we want a representation of the overall texture in the domain. Similarly, in **material recognition**, one must decide what material is represented by a patch in the image. Section 6.2 describes methods for building pooled texture representations.

Data-driven texture representations model a texture by a procedure that can

FIGURE 6.1: Although texture is difficult to define, it has some important and valuable properties. In this image, there are many repeated elements (some leaves form repeated "spots"; others, and branches, form "bars" at various scales; and so on). Our perception of the material is quite intimately related to the texture (what would the surface feel like if you ran your fingers over it? what is soggy? what is prickly? what is smooth?). Notice how much information you are getting about the type of plants, their shape, the shape of free space, and so on, from the textures. *Geoff Brightling © Dorling Kindersley, used with permission.*

generate a textured region from an example. These representations are not appropriate for segmentation or recognition applications, but are tremendously valuable for texture synthesis. In this problem, we must create regions of texture, for example, to fill holes in images (Section 6.3).

The texture on a surface can be a strong cue to its shape. If the texture is "the same" over the surface, then deformation of the texture from point to point can be a cue to the shape of the surface. For example, if we have a perspective view of an inclined plane with spots on it, the spots will be smaller closer to the horizon in the image. This can be used to recover the inclination of the plane. Similarly, on a curved surface, the foreshortening of texture elements gives some information about the local inclination of the surface. Recovering surface orientation or surface shape from an image texture is known as **shape from texture**; solutions to this

Fabric

Stone

FIGURE 6.2: Typically, different materials display different image textures. These are example images from a collection of 1,000 material images, described in by Sharan *et al.* (2009); there are 100 images in each of the ten categories, including the two categories shown here (fabric and stone). Notice how (a) the textures vary widely, even within a material category; and (b) different materials seem to display quite different textures. *This figure shows elements of a database collected by C. Liu, L. Sharan, E. Adelson, and R. Rosenholtz, and published at* http://people.csail.mit.edu/lavanya/research_sharan.html. *Figure by kind permission of the collectors.*

problem tend to use straightforward representations of texture together with strong constraints on the overall structure of the texture (Section 6.5).

6.1   LOCAL TEXTURE REPRESENTATIONS USING FILTERS

Image textures generally consist of repeated elements; an element is sometimes called a *texton*. For example, some of the fabric textures in Figure 6.2 consist of triangles of wool formed by the knit pattern. Similarly, some stone textures in that figure consist of numerous, near-circular, gray blobs. It is natural to represent a texture with some description of (a) what the textons are and (b) how they repeat. Notice that it is difficult to be precise about what a texton is, because if a large pattern repeats frequently, then so do its parts. This presents no major problems, because we do not need to extract textons accurately. Instead, what we need are representations that differ in ways that are easy to observe when two textures are significantly different. We can do this by assuming that all textons are made of

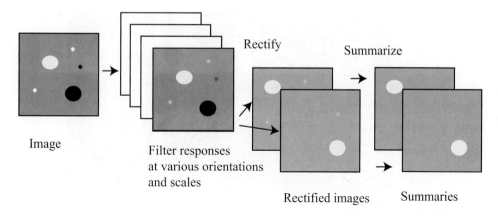

FIGURE 6.3: Local texture representations can be obtained by filtering an image with a set of filters at various scales, and then preparing a summary. Summaries ensure that, at a pixel, we have a representation of what texture appears near that pixel. The filters are typically spots and bars (see Figure 6.4). Filter outputs can be enhanced by rectifying them (so that positive and negative responses do not cancel), then computing a local summary of the rectified filter outputs. Rectifying by taking the absolute value means that we do not distinguish between light spots on a dark background and dark spots on a light background; the alternative, half-wave rectification (described in the text), preserves this distinction at the cost of a fuller representation. One can summarize either by smoothing (which will tend to suppress noise, as in the schematic example above) or by taking the maximum over a neighborhood. Compare this figure to Figure 6.7, which shows a representation for a real image.

generic subelements, such as spots and bars. We find subelements with filters, then represent each point in the image with a summary of the pattern of subelements nearby. This will work because the parts of a texton repeat in the same way that the texton does.

This suggests representing image textures in terms of the response of a collection of filters. Each filter is a detector for a subelement. The collection of different filters would represent subelements—spots and bars are usual—at a collection of scales (to identify bigger or smaller subelements). We can now represent each point in an image by the vector of filter outputs at that point. This vector gives a sense of how much the neighborhood around that point looks like each subelement at each scale (Figure 6.3).

6.1.1 Spots and Bars

But what filters should we use? There is no canonical answer. A variety of answers have been tried. By analogy with the human visual cortex, one could use some spot filters, some oriented edge filters, and some oriented bar filters at different orientations and scales (Figure 6.4). This seems like a natural choice, because these are in some sense "minimal" subelements. It would be hard to have subelements of patterns with less structure than a spot, and it would be hard to have oriented subelements with less structure than an edge.

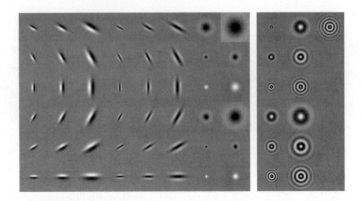

FIGURE 6.4: **Left** shows a set of 48 oriented filters used for expanding images into a series of responses for texture representation. Each filter is shown on its own scale, with zero represented by a mid-gray level, lighter values being positive, and darker values being negative. The left three columns represent edges at three scales and six orientations; the center three columns represent stripes; and the right two represent two classes of spots (with and without contrast at the boundary) at different scales. This is the set of filters used by Leung and Malik (2001). **Right** shows a set of orientation-independent filters, used by Schmid (2001), using the same representation (there are only 13 filters in this set, so there are five empty slots in the image). The orientation-independence property means that these filters look like complicated spots.

In some applications, we would like texture recognition performance to be unaffected if the texture sample is rotated. This is difficult to achieve with oriented filters, because one might need to sample the orientations very finely. An alternative to using oriented filters is to use filters that are orientation-independent, all of which must look like complicated spots (Figure 6.4).

6.1.2   From Filter Outputs to Texture Representation

Assume we have an image $\mathcal{I}$. A set of filter output maps (which would have the form $\mathcal{F}_i ** \mathcal{I}$ for different filters $\mathcal{F}_i$) is not, in itself, a representation of texture. The representation tells us what the window around a pixel looks like; but in a texture, what counts is not only what's at a pixel, but also what's nearby. For example, a field of yellow flowers may consist of many small yellow spots with some vertical green bars. What's important is not just the fact that a particular pixel looks a lot like a spot, but also that near the pixel there are no other spots, but some bars. This means the texture representation at a point should involve some kind of summary of nearby filter outputs, rather than just the filter outputs themselves.

The first step in building a reasonable summary is to notice that the summary must represent a neighborhood around a pixel that is rather bigger than the scale of the filter. To know whether the neighborhood around a pixel is "spotty," it is not enough to know that there is one strong spot in it; there should be many spots, each quite small compared to the size of the patch. However, it is important not to look at too large a neighborhood, or else the representation will not change much as we move across the image (because the neighborhoods overlap). The particular

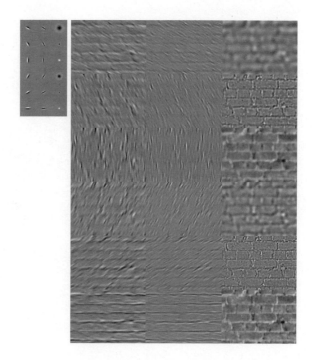

FIGURE 6.5: Filter responses for the oriented filters of Figure 6.4, applied to an image of a wall. At the **center**, we show the filters for reference (but not to scale, because they would be too small to resolve). The responses are laid out in the same way that the filters are (i.e., the response map on the top left corresponds to the filter on the top left, and so on). For reference, we show the image at the **left**. The image of the wall is small, so that the filters respond to structures that are relatively large; compare with Figure 6.6, which shows responses to a larger image of the wall, where the filters respond to smaller structures. These are filters of a fixed size, applied to a small version of the image, and so are equivalent to large-scale filters applied to the original version. Notice the strong response to the vertical and horizontal lines of mortar between the bricks, which are at about the scale of the bar filters. All response values are shown on the same intensity scale: lighter is positive, darker is negative, and mid-gray is zero.

arrangement of these spots within a neighborhood doesn't matter all that much, because the patch is small. This suggests that some form of average could give a fair description of what is going on; an alternative is to take the strongest response. We must process the responses before we summarize them. For example, a light spot filter will give a positive response to a light spot on a dark background, and a negative response to a dark spot on a light background. As a result, if we simply average filter responses over a patch, then a patch containing dark and light spots might record the same near-zero average as a patch containing no spots. This would be misleading.

We could compute the absolute value for each output map, to get $|\mathcal{F}_i * *\mathcal{I}|$. This does not distinguish between light spots on a dark background and dark spots on a light background. An alternative, which does preserve this distinction, is to report both $\max(0, \mathcal{F}_i * *\mathcal{I}(x,y))$ and $\max(0, -\mathcal{F}_i * *\mathcal{I}(x,y))$ (this is half-wave rectifi-

FIGURE 6.6: Filter responses for the oriented filters of Figure 6.4, applied to an image of a wall. At the **center**, we show the filters for reference (not to scale). The responses are laid out in the same way that the filters are (i.e., the response map on the top left corresponds to the filter on the top left, and so on). For reference, we show the image at the **left**. Although there is some response to the vertical and horizontal lines of mortar between the bricks, it is not as strong as the coarse scale (Figure 6.5); there are also quite strong responses to texture on individual bricks. All response values are shown on the same intensity scale: lighter is positive, darker is negative, and mid-gray is zero.

cation), which yields two maps per filter. We can now summarize the neighborhood around a pixel by computing a Gaussian weighted average (equivalently, convolving with a Gaussian). The scale of this Gaussian depends on the scale of the filter for the map; typically, it is around twice the scale of the filter.

6.1.3   Local Texture Representations in Practice

Several different sets of filters have been used for texture representation. The Visual Geometry Group at Oxford publishes code for different sets of filters, written by Manik Varma and by Jan-Mark Guesebroek, at `http://www.robots.ox.ac.uk/~vgg/research/texclass/filters.html`; this is part of an excellent web page on texture classification (`http://www.robots.ox.ac.uk/~vgg/research/texclass/index.html`). One important part of filtering an image with a large number of filters is doing so quickly; recent code for this purpose, by Jan-Mark Guesebroek, can be found at `http://www.science.uva.nl/research/publications/2003/GeusebroekTIP2003/`. Some sets of oriented filters allow fast, efficient representations and have good translation and rotation properties. One such set is

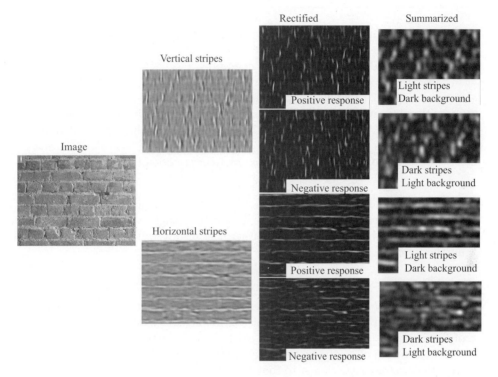

FIGURE 6.7: Filter-based texture representations look for pattern subelements such as oriented bars. The brick image on the **left** is filtered with an oriented bar filter (shown as a tiny inset on the top left of the image at full scale) to detect bars, yielding stripe responses (**center left**; negative is dark, positive is light, mid-gray is zero). These are rectified (here we use half-wave rectification) to yield response maps (**center right**; dark is zero, light is positive). In turn, these are summarized (here we smoothed over a neighborhood twice the filter width) to yield the texture representation on the **right**. In this, pixels that have strong vertical bars nearby are light, and others are dark; there is not much difference between the dark and light vertical structure for this image, but there is a real difference between dark and light horizontal structure.

the steerable pyramid of Simoncelli and Freeman (1995*a*). Code for these filters is available at http://www.cns.nyu.edu/~eero/steerpyr/.

6.2 POOLED TEXTURE REPRESENTATIONS BY DISCOVERING TEXTONS

A texture is a set of textons that repeat in some way. We could find these textons by looking for image patches that are common. An alternative is to find sets of texton subelements—that is, vectors of filter outputs—that are common (if textons are repeated, then so are their subelements). There are two important difficulties in finding image patches or vectors of filter outputs that commonly occur together. First, these representations of the image are continuous. We cannot simply count how many times a particular pattern occurs, because each vector is slightly different. Second, the representation is high dimensional in either case. A patch around a

Obtain a set of n filters representing subelements, at multiple scales
Apply each filter $\mathcal{F}_i$ to the image
For each filter response map $\mathcal{F}_i * *\mathcal{I}$, compute
    $\max(0, \mathcal{F}_i * *\mathcal{I}(x, y))$ and $\max(0, -\mathcal{F}_i * *\mathcal{I}(x, y))$
For each of the $2n$ rectified maps, compute local summaries
    either by convolving with a Gaussian of scale approximately twice the
    scale of the base filter, or by taking the maximum value over that radius.

Algorithm 6.1: Local Texture Representation Using Filters.

pixel might need hundreds of pixels to represent it well; similarly, hundreds of
different filters might be needed to represent the image at a pixel. This means we
cannot build a histogram directly, either, because it will have an unmanageable
number of cells.

6.2.1 Vector Quantization and Textons

Vector quantization is a strategy to deal with these difficulties. Vector quantization
is a way of representing vectors in a continuous space with numbers from a set
of fixed size. We first build a set of clusters out of a training set of vectors; this
set of clusters is often thought of as a dictionary. We now replace any new vector
with the cluster center closest to that vector. This strategy applies to vectors quite
generally, though we will use it for texture representation. Many different clusterers
can be used for vector quantization, but it is most common to use k-means or one
of its variants. For concreteness, we describe this algorithm in Section 6.2.2, but
the other clusterers of Chapter 9 would apply.

We can now represent a collection of vectors as a histogram of cluster centers.
This general recipe can be applied to texture representation by describing each
pixel in the domain with some vector, then vector quantizing and describing the
domain with the histogram of cluster centers. Natural vectors to use are: the local
summary representation described in Section 6.1; a vector of unprocessed filter
outputs, using filters appropriate for a local texture representation (Figure 6.9); or
even just a vector obtained by reshaping the pixels from a fixed-size patch around
the image pixel (Figure 6.10). In each case, we are building a representation in
terms of commonly repeated pattern elements.

6.2.2 K-means Clustering for Vector Quantization

We could use any clustering method to vector quantize (Chapter 9 describes a
number of different clustering methods in the context of segmentation). However,
by far the most common method used is *k-means* clustering. Assume we have a set
of data items that we wish to cluster. We now assume that we know how many
clusters there are in the data, which we write k. This is equivalent to fixing the
number of values we wish to quantize to. Each cluster is assumed to have a center;
we write the center of the ith cluster as c_i. The jth data item to be clustered
is described by a feature vector x_j. In our case, these items are vectors of filter

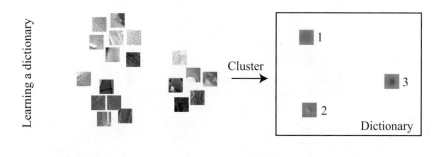

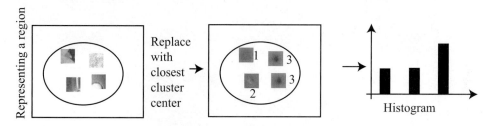

FIGURE 6.8: There are two steps to building a pooled texture representation for a texture in an image domain. First, one builds a dictionary representing the range of possible pattern elements, using a large number of texture patches. This is usually done in advance, using a training data set of some form. Second, one takes the patches inside the domain, vector quantizes them by identifying the number of the closest cluster center, then computes a histogram of the different cluster center numbers that occur within a region. This histogram might appear to contain no spatial information, but this is a misperception. Some frequent elements in the histogram are likely to be textons, but others describe common ways in which textons lie close to one another; this is a rough spatial cue. *This figure shows elements of a database collected by C. Liu, L. Sharan, E. Adelson, and R. Rosenholtz, and published at* `http://people.csail.mit.edu/lavanya/research_sharan.html`. *Figure by kind permission of the collectors.*

Build a dictionary:
    Collect many training example textures
    Construct the vectors $\boldsymbol{x}$ for relevant pixels; these could be
        a reshaping of a patch around the pixel, a vector of filter outputs
        computed at the pixel, or the representation of Section 6.1.
    Obtain k cluster centers $\boldsymbol{c}$ for these examples

Represent an image domain:
    For each relevant pixel i in the image
        Compute the vector representation $\boldsymbol{x}_i$ of that pixel
        Obtain j, the index of the cluster center $\boldsymbol{c}_j$ closest to that pixel
        Insert j into a histogram for that domain

Algorithm 6.2: Texture Representation Using Vector Quantization.

FIGURE 6.9: Pattern elements can be identified by vector quantizing vectors of filter outputs, using k-means. Here we show the top 50 pattern elements (or textons), obtained from all 1,000 images of the collection of material images described in Figure 6.2. These were filtered with the complete set of oriented filters from Figure 6.4. Each subimage here illustrates a cluster center. For each cluster center, we show the linear combination of filter kernels that would result in the set of filter responses represented by the cluster center. For some cluster centers, we show the 25 image patches in the training set whose filter representation is closest to the cluster center.   *This figure shows elements of a database collected by C. Liu, L. Sharan, E. Adelson, and R. Rosenholtz, and published at http: // people. csail. mit. edu/ lavanya/ research_ sharan. html . Figure by kind permission of the collectors.*

responses observed at image locations.

Because pattern elements repeat, and so are common, we can assume that most data items are close to the center of their cluster. This suggests that we cluster the data by minimizing the the objective function

$$\Phi(\text{clusters}, \text{data}) = \sum_{i \in \text{clusters}} \left\{ \sum_{j \in i\text{th cluster}} (\boldsymbol{x}_j - \boldsymbol{c}_i)^T (\boldsymbol{x}_j - \boldsymbol{c}_i) \right\}.$$

Notice that if we know the center for each cluster, it is easy to determine which cluster is the best choice for each point. Similarly, if the allocation of points to clusters is known, it is easy to compute the best center for each cluster. However, there are far too many possible allocations of points to clusters to search this space for a minimum. Instead, we define an algorithm that iterates through two activities:

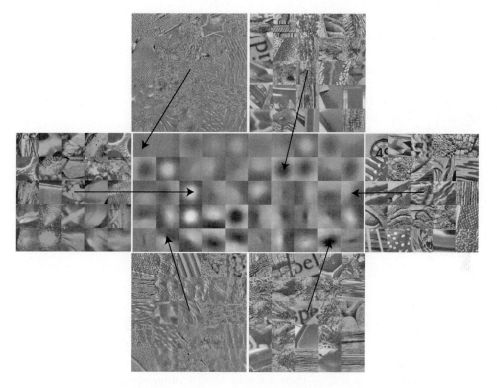

FIGURE 6.10: Pattern elements can also be identified by vector quantizing vectors obtained by reshaping an image window centered on each pixel. Here we show the top 50 pattern elements (or textons), obtained using this strategy from all 1,000 images of the collection of material images described in Figure 6.2. Each subimage here illustrates a cluster center. For some cluster centers, we show the closest 25 image patches. To measure distance, we first subtracted the average image intensity, and we weighted by a Gaussian to ensure that pixels close to the center of the patch were weighted higher than those far from the center. *This figure shows elements of a database collected by C. Liu, L. Sharan, E. Adelson, and R. Rosenholtz, and published at http://people.csail.mit.edu/lavanya/research_sharan.html. Figure by kind permission of the collectors.*

- Assume the cluster centers are known and, allocate each point to the closest cluster center.

- Assume the allocation is known, and choose a new set of cluster centers. Each center is the mean of the points allocated to that cluster.

We then choose a start point by randomly choosing cluster centers, and then iterate these stages alternately. This process eventually converges to a local minimum of the objective function (the value either goes down or is fixed at each step, and it is bounded below). It is not guaranteed to converge to the global minimum of the objective function, however. It is also not guaranteed to produce k clusters, unless we modify the allocation phase to ensure that each cluster has some nonzero number of points. This algorithm is usually referred to as *k-means* (summarized in

Algorithm 6.3). It is possible to search for an appropriate number of clusters by applying k-means for different values of k and comparing the results; we defer a discussion of this issue until Section 10.7.

Choose k data points to act as cluster centers
Until the cluster centers change very little
    Allocate each data point to cluster whose center is nearest.
    Now ensure that every cluster has at least
      one data point; one way to do this is by
      supplying empty clusters with a point chosen at random from
      points far from their cluster center.
    Replace the cluster centers with the mean of the elements
      in their clusters.
end

Algorithm 6.3: Clustering by K-Means.

6.3 SYNTHESIZING TEXTURES AND FILLING HOLES IN IMAGES

Many different kinds of user want to remove things from images or from video. Art directors might like to remove unattractive telephone wires; restorers might want to remove scratches or marks; there's a long history of government officials removing people with embarrassing politics from publicity pictures (see the fascinating pictures in King (1997)); and home users might wish to remove a relative they dislike from a family picture. All these users must then find something to put in place of the pixels that were removed. Ideally, a program would create regions of texture that fit in and look convincing, using either other parts of the original image, or other images.

There are other important applications for such a program. One is to produce large quantities of texture for digital artists to apply to object models. We know that good textures make models look more realistic (it's worth thinking about why this should be true). Tiling small texture images tends to work poorly, because it can be hard to obtain images that tile well. The borders have to line up properly, and even when they do, the resulting periodic structure can be annoying.

6.3.1 Synthesis by Sampling Local Models

As Efros and Leung (1999) point out, an example texture can serve as a probability model for texture synthesis (Figure 6.11). Assume for the moment that we know every pixel in the synthesized image, except one. To obtain a probability model for the value of that pixel, we could match a neighborhood of the pixel to the example image. Every matching neighborhood in the example image has a possible value for the pixel of interest. This collection of values is a conditional histogram for the pixel of interest. By drawing a sample uniformly and at random from this collection, we obtain the value that is consistent with the example image.

We must now take some form of neighborhood around the pixel of interest, compare it to neighborhoods in the example image, and select some of these to form a set of example values. The size and shape of this neighborhood is significant, because it codes the range over which pixels can affect one another's values directly (see Figure 6.12). Efros *et al.* use a square neighborhood, centered at the pixel of interest.

Choose a small square of pixels at random from the example image
Insert this square of values into the image to be synthesized
Until each location in the image to be synthesized has a value
   For each unsynthesized location on
      the boundary of the block of synthesized values
     Match the neighborhood of this location to the
       example image, ignoring unsynthesized
       locations in computing the matching score
     Choose a value for this location uniformly and at random
       from the set of values of the corresponding locations in the
       matching neighborhoods
   end
end

Algorithm 6.4: Non-parametric Texture Synthesis.

The neighborhoods we select will be similar to the image example in some sense. A good measure of similarity between two image neighborhoods can be measured by forming the *sum of squared differences* (or *ssd*) of corresponding pixel values. We assume that the missing pixel is at the center of the patch to be synthesized, which we write $\mathcal{S}$. We assume the patch is square, and adjust the indexes of the patch to run from $-n$ to n in each direction. The sum of squared differences between this patch and an image patch $\mathcal{P}$ of the same size is given by

$$\sum_{(i,j)\in\text{patch},(i,j)\neq(0,0)} (\mathcal{A}_{ij} - \mathcal{B}_{ij})^2.$$

The notation implies that because we don't know the value of the pixel to be synthesized (which is at $(0,0)$), we don't count it in the sum of squared differences. This similarity value is small when the neighborhoods are similar, and large when they are different (it is essentially the length of the difference vector). However, this measure places the same weight on pixels close to the unknown value as it does on distant pixels. Better results are usually obtained by weighting up nearby pixels and weighting down distant pixels. We can do so using Gaussian weights, yielding

$$\sum_{(i,j)\in\text{patch},(i,j)\neq(0,0)} (\mathcal{A}_{ij} - \mathcal{B}_{ij})^2 \exp\left(\frac{-(i^2 + j^2)}{2\sigma^2}\right).$$

Now we know how to obtain the value of a single missing pixel: choose uniformly and at random amongst the values of pixels in the example image whose neighborhoods match the neighborhood of our pixel. We cannot choose those matching

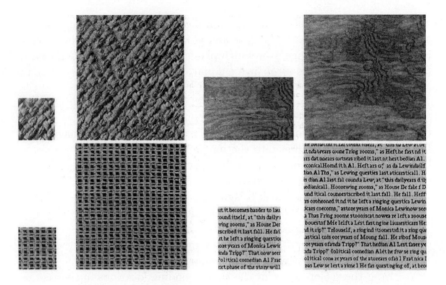

FIGURE 6.11: Efros and Leung (1999) synthesize textures by matching neighborhoods of the image being synthesized to the example image, and then choosing at random amongst the possible values reported by matching neighborhoods (Algorithm 6.4). This means that the algorithm can reproduce complex spatial structures, as these examples indicate. The small block on the **left** is the example texture; the algorithm synthesizes the block on the **right**. Note that the synthesized text looks like text: it appears to be constructed of words of varying lengths that are spaced like text, and each word looks as though it is composed of letters (though this illusion fails as one looks closely). *This figure was originally published as Figure 3 of "Texture Synthesis by Non-parametric Sampling," A. Efros and T.K. Leung, Proc. IEEE ICCV, 1999 © IEEE, 1999.*

neighborhoods by just setting a threshold on the similarity function, because we might not have any matches. A better strategy to find matching neighborhoods is to select all whose similarity value is less than $(1 + \epsilon)s_{min}$, where s_{min} is the similarity function of the closest neighborhood and ϵ is a parameter.

Generally, we need to synthesize more than just one pixel. Usually, the values of some pixels in the neighborhood of the pixel to be synthesized are not known; these pixels need to be synthesized too. One way to obtain a collection of examples for the pixel of interest is to count only the known values in computing the sum of squared differences, and scale the similarity to take into account the number of known pixels. Write $\mathcal{K}$ for the set of pixels around a point whose values are known, and $\sharp\mathcal{K}$ for the size of this set. We now have, for the similarity function,

$$\frac{1}{\sharp\mathcal{K}} \sum_{(i,j)\in\mathcal{K}} (\mathcal{A}_{ij} - \mathcal{B}_{ij})^2 \exp\left(\frac{-(i^2 + j^2)}{2\sigma^2}\right).$$

The synthesis process can be started by choosing a block of pixels at random from the example image, yielding Algorithm 6.4.

Filling in Patches

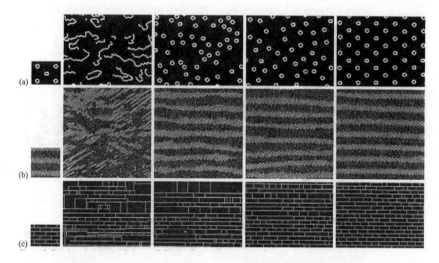

FIGURE 6.12: The size of the image neighborhood to be matched makes a significant difference in Algorithm 6.4. In the figure, the textures at the right are synthesized from the small blocks on the **left**, using neighborhoods that are increasingly large as one moves to the **right**. If very small neighborhoods are matched, then the algorithm cannot capture large-scale effects easily. For example, in the case of the spotty texture, if the neighborhood is too small to capture the spot structure (and so sees only pieces of curve), the algorithm synthesizes a texture consisting of curve segments. As the neighborhood gets larger, the algorithm can capture the spot structure, but not the even spacing. With very large neighborhoods, the spacing is captured as well. *This figure was originally published as Figure 2 of "Texture Synthesis by Non-parametric Sampling," A. Efros and T.K. Leung, Proc. IEEE ICCV, 1999 © IEEE, 1999.*

Synthesizing a large texture in terms of individual pixels will be unnecessarily slow. Because textures repeat, we expect that whole blocks of pixels also should repeat. This suggests synthesizing a texture in terms of image patches, rather than just pixels. Most of the mechanics of the procedure follow those for pixels: to synthesize a texture patch at a location, we find patches likely to fit (because they have pixels that match the boundary at that location), then choose uniformly and at random from among them. However, when we place down the new patch, we must deal with the fact that some (ideally, many) of its pixels overlap with pixels that have already been synthesized. This problem is typically solved by image segmentation methods, and we defer that discussion to Chapter 9.

6.3.2   Filling in Holes in Images

There are four approaches we can use to fill a hole in an image. **Matching methods** find another image patch that looks a lot like the boundary of the hole, place that patch over the hole, and blend the patch and the image together. The patch might well be found in the image (for example, Figure 6.13). If we have a very large set of images, we could find a patch by looking for another image that matches the image with a hole in it. Hays and Efros (2007) show this strategy can be extremely

FIGURE 6.13: If an image contains repeated structure, we have a good chance of finding examples to fill a hole by searching for patches that are compatible with its boundaries. **Top left:** An image with a hole in it (black pixels in a rough pedestrian shape). The pixels on the region outside the hole, but inside the boundary marked on the image, match pixels near the other curve, which represents a potentially good source of hole-filling pixels. **Top right:** The hole filled by placing the patch over the hole, then using a segmentation method (Chapter 9) to choose the right boundary between patch and image. This procedure can work for apparently unpromising images, such as the one on the **bottom left**, an image of the facade of a house, seen at a significant slant. This slant means that distant parts of the facade are severely foreshortened. However, if we rectify the facade using methods from Section 1.3, then there are matching patches. On the **bottom right**, the hole has been filled in using a patch from the rectified image, that is then slanted again. *This figure was originally published as Figures 3 and 6 of "Hole Filling through Photomontage," by M. Wilczkowiak, G. Brostow, B. Tordoff, and R. Cipolla, Proc. BMVC, 2005 and is reproduced by kind permission of the authors.*

successful. Blending is typically achieved using methods also used for image segmentation (Section 9.4.3 describes one method that can be used for blending).

As you would expect, matching methods work very well when a good match is available, and poorly otherwise. If the hole is in a region of relatively regular texture, then a good match should be easy to find. If the texture is less strongly structured, it might be hard to find a good match. In cases like this, it makes sense to try and synthesize the texture over the region of the hole, using the rest of the image as an example. Making such **texture synthesis methods** work well requires considerable care, because the order in which pixels are synthesized has a strong effect on the results. Texture synthesis tends to work better for patches when most of their neighbors are known, because the match is more constrained. As a result, one wants to synthesize patches at the boundary of the hole. It is also important to extend edges at the boundary of the hole into the interior (for

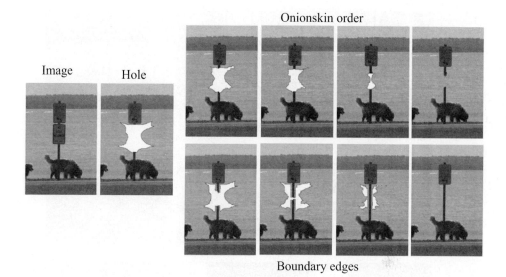

FIGURE 6.14: Texture synthesis methods can fill in holes accurately, but the order in which pixels are synthesized is important. In this figure, we wish to remove the sign, while preserving the signpost. Generally, we want to fill in pixels where most of the neighbors are known first. This yields better matching patches. One way to do so is to fill in from the boundary. However, if we simply work our way inwards (onionskin filling), long scale image structures tend to disappear. It is better to fill in patches close to edges first. *This figure was originally published as Figure 11 of "Region Filling and Object Removal by Exemplar-Based Image Inpainting," by A. Criminisi, P. Perez, and K. Toyama, IEEE Transactions on Image Processing, 2004 © IEEE, 2004.*

example, see Figure 6.14); in practice, this means that it is important to synthesize patches at edges on the boundary before one fills in other patches. It is possible to capture both requirements in a priority function ((Criminisi *et al.* 2004)), which specifies where to synthesize next.

If we choose an image patch at (i, j) as an example to fill in location (u, v) in the hole, then image patches near (i, j) are likely to be good for filling in points near (u, v). This observation is the core of **coherence methods**, which apply this constraint to texture synthesis. Finally, some holes in images are not really texture holes; for example, we might have a hole in a smoothly shaded region. Texture synthesis and matching methods tend to work poorly on such holes, because the intensity structure on the boundary is not that distinctive. As a result, we may find many matching patches, some of which have jarring interiors. **Variational methods** apply in these cases. Typically, we try to extend the level curves of the image into the hole in a smooth way. Modern hole-filling methods use a combination of these approaches, and can perform very well on quite demanding tasks (Figure 6.15).

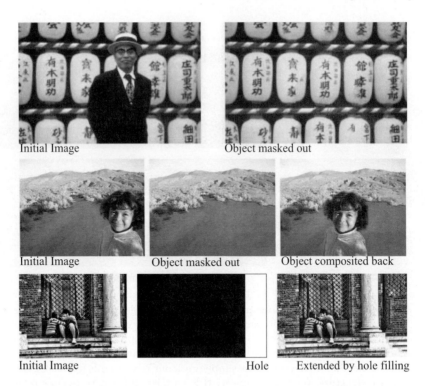

Initial Image   Object masked out

Initial Image   Object masked out   Object composited back

Initial Image   Hole   Extended by hole filling

FIGURE 6.15: Modern hole-filling methods get very good results using a combination of texture synthesis, coherence, and smoothing. Notice the complex, long-scale structure in the background texture for the example on the **top** row. The **center** row shows an example where a subject was removed from the image and replaced in a different place. Finally, the **bottom** row shows the use of hole-filling to resize an image. The white block in the center mask image is the "hole" (i.e., unknown pixels whose values are required to resize the image). This block is filled with a plausible texture. *This figure was originally published as Figures 9 and 15 of "A Comprehensive Framework for Image Inpainting," by A. Bugeau, M. Bertalmío, V. Caselles, and G. Sapiro, Proc. IEEE Transactions on Image Processing, 2010 © IEEE, 2010.*

6.4 IMAGE DENOISING

This section addresses the problem of reconstructing an image given the noisy observations gathered by a digital camera sensor. Today, with advances in sensor design, the signal is relatively clean for digital SLRs at low sensitivities, but it remains noisy for consumer-grade and mobile-phone cameras at high sensitivities (low-light and/or high-speed conditions). Adding to the demands of consumer and professional photography those of astronomy, biology, and medical imaging, it is thus clear that image restoration is still of acute and in fact growing importance. Working with noisy images recorded by digital cameras is difficult because different devices produce different kinds of noise, and introduce different types of artifacts and spatial correlations in the noise as a result of internal post-processing (demosaicking, white balance, etc.).

We have already seen that linear filters such as Gaussian kernels are effective at suppressing noise, but that the price to pay is a loss in image detail. We briefly discuss in this section three related approaches to image denoising that are much more effective. They rely on two properties of natural images: the prominence of *self-similarities*—that is, many small regions in the same picture often look the same—and the effectiveness of *sparse* linear models—that is, small image patches are typically well reconstructed as a linear combination of very few elements from a potentially large basis set, or *dictionary*.

6.4.1 Non-local Means

Efros and Leung (1999) have shown that the self-similarities inherent to natural images can be used effectively in texture synthesis tasks. Following this insight, Buades, Coll, and Morel (2005) have introduced the *non-local means* approach to image denoising, where the prominence of self-similarities is used as a prior on natural images. Concretely, let us consider a noisy image written as a column vector $\boldsymbol{y}$ in $\mathbb{R}^n$, and denote by $\boldsymbol{y}[i]$ the i-th pixel value and by $\boldsymbol{y}_i$ the patch of size m centered on this pixel and considered as an element of $\mathbb{R}^m$. Similar patches $\boldsymbol{y}_i$ and $\boldsymbol{y}_j$ should have similar values $\boldsymbol{y}[i]$ and $\boldsymbol{y}[j]$. This suggests estimating the denoised pixel $\boldsymbol{x}[i]$ as a weighted average (the so-called Nadaraya-Watson estimator) of all the other pixels in the image:

$$\boldsymbol{x}[i] = \sum_{j=1}^{n} \frac{G_h(\boldsymbol{y}_i - \boldsymbol{y}_j)}{\sum_{l=1}^{n} G_h(\boldsymbol{y}_i - \boldsymbol{y}_l)} \boldsymbol{y}[j], \qquad (6.1)$$

where G_h is a multi-dimensional Gaussian kernel of standard deviation h. The weights depend on appearance similarity instead of spatial proximity in the case of Gaussian smoothing, hence the name of non-local means. This simple approach gives excellent results in practice, and, although naive implementations are slow (all image pixels are used to denoise a single one), they can be sped up by using various heuristics (by considering only patches $\boldsymbol{y}_j$ in some fixed spatial neighborhood of $\boldsymbol{y}_i$, for example). The parameters h can be taken proportional to the standard deviation σ of the noise in practice; for example, $h = 12\sigma$ is used in the experiments of Buades, Coll and Morel (2005).

6.4.2 Block Matching 3D (BM3D)

Classical *shrinkage* is a very different method for denoising. It can be summarized as follows: Consider a signal $\boldsymbol{y}$ in $\mathbb{R}^m$ and some nonsingular $m \times m$ matrix $\mathcal{T}$. We associate with $\boldsymbol{y}$ its *code* $\boldsymbol{\alpha} = \mathcal{T}\boldsymbol{y}$ and the thresholded value $\boldsymbol{\alpha}_\varepsilon$, obtained by zeroing all coefficients α^i smaller than some $\varepsilon > 0$ in the *hard thresholding* case, or by setting

$$\alpha_\varepsilon^i = \text{sign}(\alpha^i)(|\alpha^i| - \varepsilon)_+,$$

in the *soft thresholding* one (here, x_+ is equal to x when $x > 0$, and to zero otherwise). The denoised signal is $\boldsymbol{x}_\varepsilon = \mathcal{T}^{-1}\boldsymbol{\alpha}_\varepsilon$, the idea being that noise shows up mostly in small coefficients in the transformed domain, which is of course true only for appropriate transformations. A classical example is *wavelet shrinkage* (Donoho and Johnstone 1995), where $\mathcal{T}$ is the orthogonal matrix representing the *discrete wavelet transform* (Mallat 1999), and the denoised signal is $\boldsymbol{x}_\varepsilon = \mathcal{T}^T \boldsymbol{\alpha}_\varepsilon$. In this case, a method for selecting ε for a given noise level is available, along with theoretical guarantees about the reconstructed signal.

By construction, the vector $\boldsymbol{x}_\varepsilon$ usually admits a *sparse* decomposition on the basis of $\mathbb{R}^m$ formed by the columns of $\mathcal{T}^T = \mathcal{T}^{-1}$—that is, only a few of the coefficients α_ε^i are nonzero. As further discussed in Chapter 22, sparse linear models are well suited to natural images, and Dabov *et al.* (2007) combine sparsity-inducing shrinkage with the use of self-similarities. They stack similar image patches into three-dimensional arrays (groups), then use shrinkage on the groups, coupled with transformations such as the (three-dimensional) *discrete cosine transform*, or *DCT*. Because the patches are similar, the decomposition of each group is expected to be quite sparse, and denoised patches $\boldsymbol{x}_\varepsilon$ are retrieved from the shrunken groups. The final value of a pixel is taken to be the average of the values $\boldsymbol{x}_\varepsilon$ at this point for all patches passing through it. In conjunction with a few simple heuristics, this simple idea has proven to be very effective, and it typically gives better results than regular non-local means.

6.4.3 Learned Sparse Coding

An alternative is to assume that the clean signal can be approximated by a sparse linear combination of elements from a (potentially large) set of vectors forming the k columns of a so-called *dictionary*, which may be *overcomplete* ($k > m$). Under this assumption, denoising a patch $\boldsymbol{y}$ in $\mathbb{R}^m$ with a dictionary $\mathcal{D}$ in $\mathbb{R}^{m \times k}$ composed of k elements amounts to solving the sparse decomposition problem

$$\min_{\boldsymbol{\alpha} \in \mathbb{R}^k} ||\boldsymbol{\alpha}||_1 \quad \text{s.t.} \quad ||\boldsymbol{y} - \mathcal{D}\boldsymbol{\alpha}||_2^2 \leq \varepsilon, \tag{6.2}$$

where $\mathcal{D}\boldsymbol{\alpha}$ is an estimate of the clean signal, and $||\boldsymbol{\alpha}||_1$ is the sparsity-inducing ℓ_1 norm formed by the sum of the absolute values of the coefficients of $\boldsymbol{\alpha}$. As shown in Chapter 22, the ℓ_1 regularization in Equation (6.2) leads to the convex *Lasso* (Tibshirani 1996) and *basis pursuit* (Chen *et al.* 1999) problems, for which efficient algorithms are available. As shown in Elad and Aharon (2006), ε can be chosen according to the standard deviation of the noise.

Various types of wavelets have been used as dictionaries for natural images. Elad and Aharon (2006) have proposed instead to *learn* a dictionary $\mathcal{D}$ adapted to the image at hand, and demonstrated that learned dictionaries lead to better empirical performance than off-the-shelf ones. For an image of size n, a dictionary in $\mathbb{R}^{m \times k}$ adapted to the n overlapping patches of size m (typically $m = 8 \times 8 \ll n$) associated with the image pixels, is learned by addressing the following optimization problem:

$$\min_{\mathcal{D} \in \mathcal{C}, \mathcal{A}} \sum_{i=1}^{n} ||\boldsymbol{\alpha}_i||_1 \quad \text{s.t.} \quad ||\boldsymbol{y}_i - \mathcal{D}\boldsymbol{\alpha}_i||_2^2 \leq \varepsilon, \tag{6.3}$$

where $\mathcal{C}$ is the set of matrices in $\mathbb{R}^{m \times k}$ with unit ℓ_2-norm columns, $\mathcal{A} = [\boldsymbol{\alpha}_1, \ldots, \boldsymbol{\alpha}_n]$ is a matrix in $\mathbb{R}^{k \times n}$, $\boldsymbol{y}_i$ is the i-th patch of the *noisy* image $\boldsymbol{y}$, $\boldsymbol{\alpha}_i$ is the corresponding code, and $\mathcal{D}\boldsymbol{\alpha}_i$ is the estimate of the denoised patch. Note that this procedure implicitly assumes that the patches are *independent* from each other, which is questionable because they overlap. However, this approximation makes the correspond-

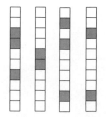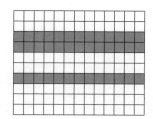

FIGURE 6.16: Sparsity vs. joint sparsity: Gray squares represents nonzero values in vectors (**left**) or matrix (**right**). *Reprinted from "Non-local Sparse Models for Image Restoration," by J. Mairal, F. Bach, J. Ponce, G. Sapiro, and A. Zisserman, Proc. International Conference on Computer Vision, (2009).* © *2009, IEEE.*

ing optimization tractable. Indeed, although dictionary learning is traditionally considered very costly, online algorithms such as the procedure described in Chapter 22 and Mairal, Bach, Ponce, and Sapiro (2010) make it possible to efficiently process millions of patches, allowing the use of large photographs and/or large image databases. In typical applications, the dictionary $\mathcal{D}$ is first learned on such a database, then refined on the image of interest itself using the same process.

Once the dictionary $\mathcal{D}$ and codes $\boldsymbol{\alpha}_i$ have been learned, every pixel admits m estimates (one per patch containing it), and its value can be computed by averaging these values.

Let us close this section by showing that self-similarities also can be exploited in this framework. Concretely, a joint sparsity pattern—that is, a common set of nonzero coefficients—can be imposed to a set of vectors $\boldsymbol{\alpha}_1, \ldots, \boldsymbol{\alpha}_l$ through a *grouped-sparsity regularizer* on the matrix $\mathcal{A} = [\boldsymbol{\alpha}_1, \ldots, \boldsymbol{\alpha}_l]$ in $\mathbb{R}^{k \times l}$ (Figure 6.16). This amounts to limiting the number of nonzero rows of $\mathcal{A}$, or replacing the ℓ_1 vector norm in Equation (6.3) by the $\ell_{1,2}$ matrix norm

$$||\mathcal{A}||_{1,2} = \sum_{i=1}^{k} ||\boldsymbol{\alpha}^i||_2, \tag{6.4}$$

where $\boldsymbol{\alpha}^i$ denotes the i-th row of $\mathcal{A}$.

Similar to the BM3D groups, we can define for each $\boldsymbol{y}_i$ the set S_i of patches similar to it, using for example a threshold on the inter-patch Euclidean distance. The dictionary learning problem can now be written as

$$\min_{(\mathcal{A}_i)_{i=1}^n, \mathcal{D} \in \mathcal{C}} \sum_{i=1}^{n} \frac{||\mathcal{A}_i||_{1,2}}{|S_i|} \quad \text{s.t.} \quad \forall i \sum_{j \in S_i} ||\boldsymbol{y}_j - \mathcal{D}\boldsymbol{\alpha}_{ij}||_2^2 \leq \varepsilon_i, \tag{6.5}$$

where $\mathcal{A}_i = [\boldsymbol{\alpha}_{ij}]_{j \in \S_i} \in \mathbb{R}^{k \times |S_i|}$, and an appropriate value of ε_i can be chosen as before. The normalization by $|S_i|$ gives equal weights for all groups. For a fixed dictionary, simultaneous sparse coding is convex and can be solved efficiently (Friedman 2001; Bach, Jenatton, Mairal, & Obozinski 2011). In turn, the dictionary can be learned using a simple and efficient modification of the algorithm presented in Chapter 22 and Mairal *et al.* (2010), and the final image is estimated by averaging the estimates of each pixel. In practice, this method gives better results than plain dictionary learning.

FIGURE 6.17: Denoising images artificially corrupted with additive Gaussian noise. **Left:** noisy images. **Right:** restored ones using LSSC. Note that the algorithm reproduces the original brick texture in the house image ($\sigma = 15$) and the hair texture for the man image ($\sigma = 50$), both hardly visible in the noisy images. *Reprinted from "Non-local Sparse Models for Image Restoration," by J. Mairal, F. Bach, J. Ponce, G. Sapiro, and A. Zisserman, Proc. International Conference on Computer Vision, (2009). © 2009, IEEE.*

6.4.4   Results

The three methods discussed in this section all give very good results, with a slight edge to BM3D and learned simultaneous sparse coding (or *LSSC*), according to the experiments of Dabov, Foi, Katkovnik, and Egiazarian (2007) and Mairal, Bach, Ponce, Sapiro, and Zisserman (2009), which use standard images with added Gaussian noise (Figure 6.17) for quantitative evaluation. Qualitative results on a photograph corrupted by real noise are shown in Figure 6.18. The image was taken by a Canon Powershot G9 digital camera at 1,600 ISO with a short time exposure. At this setting, pictures are typically quite noisy. This time, we compare the original JPEG output of the camera, and results from Adobe Camera Raw 5.0, the DxO Optics Pro 5.3 package for professional photographers, and LSSC.

FIGURE 6.18: From **left** to **right** and **top** to **bottom**: Camera JPEG output, Adobe Camera Raw, DxO Optics Pro, and LSSC. *Reprinted from "Non-local Sparse Models for Image Restoration," by J. Mairal, F. Bach, J. Ponce, G. Sapiro, and A. Zisserman, Proc. International Conference on Computer Vision, (2009).* © *2009, IEEE.*

6.5   SHAPE FROM TEXTURE

A patch of texture viewed frontally looks very different from the same patch viewed at a glancing angle because foreshortening causes the texture elements (and the gaps between them!) to shrink more in some directions than in others. This suggests that we can recover some shape information from texture, at the cost of supplying a texture model. This is a task at which humans excel (Figure 6.19). Remarkably, quite general texture models appear to supply enough information to infer shape.

6.5.1   Shape from Texture for Planes

If we know we are viewing a plane, shape from texture boils down to determining the configuration of the plane relative to the camera. Assume that we hypothesize a configuration; we can then project the image texture back onto that plane. If we have some model of the "uniformity" of the texture, then we can test that property for the backprojected texture. We now obtain the plane with the "best"

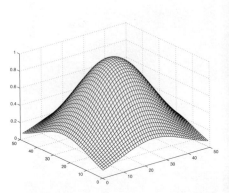 

FIGURE 6.19: Humans obtain information about the shape of surfaces in space from the appearance of the texture on the surface. The figure on the **left** shows one common use for this effect; away from the contour regions, our only source of information about the surface depicted is the distortion of the texture on the surface. On the **right**, the texture gives a clear sense of the orientation of the ground plane, how the plants stand out from the path, and how far away the building at the back is. *Geoff Brightling © Dorling Kindersley, used with permission.*

backprojected texture on it.

Assume that we are viewing a single textured plane in an orthographic camera. Because the camera is orthographic, there is no way to measure the depth to the plane. However, we can think about the orientation of the plane. Let us work in terms of the camera coordinate system. First, we need to know the angle between the normal of the textured plane and the viewing direction—sometimes called the *slant*—and second, the angle the projected normal makes in the camera coordinate system—sometimes called the *tilt* (Figure 6.20).

In an image of a plane, there is a *tilt direction*—the direction in the plane parallel to the projected normal.

An *isotropic* texture is one where the probability of encountering a texture element does not depend on the orientation of that element. This means that a probability model for an isotropic texture need not depend on the orientation of the coordinate system on the textured plane.

If we assume that the texture is isotropic, both slant and tilt can be read from the image. We could synthesize an orthographic view of a textured plane by first rotating the coordinate system by the tilt and then contracting along one coordinate direction by the cosine of the slant—call this process a **viewing transformation**. The easiest way to see this is to assume that the texture consists of a set of circles, scattered about the plane. In an orthographic view, these circles will project to ellipses, whose minor axes will give the tilt and whose aspect ratios will give the slant (see the exercises and Figure 6.20).

An orthographic view of an isotropic texture is *not* isotropic (unless the plane is parallel to the image plane). This is because the contraction in the slant direction interferes with the isotropy of the texture. Elements that point along the contracted

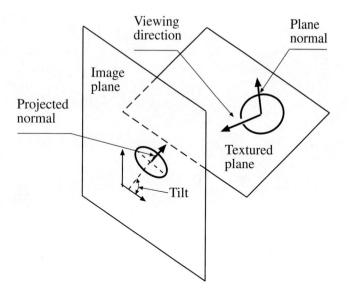

FIGURE 6.20: The orientation of a plane with respect to the camera plane can be given by the slant, which is the angle between the normal of the textured plane and the viewing direction, and the tilt, which is the angle the projected normal makes with the camera coordinate system. The figure illustrates the tilt, and shows a circle projecting to an ellipse. The direction of the minor axis of this image ellipse is the tilt, and the slant is revealed by the aspect ratio of the ellipse. However, the slant is ambiguous because the foreshortening is given by $\cos \sigma$, where σ is the slant angle. There will be two possible values of σ for each foreshortening, so two different slants yield the same ellipse (one is slanted forwards, the other backwards).

direction get shorter. Furthermore, elements that have a component along the contracted direction have that component shrunk. Now corresponding to a viewing transformation is an **inverse viewing transformation** (which turns an image plane texture into the object plane texture, given a slant and tilt). This yields a strategy for determining the orientation of the plane: find an inverse viewing transformation that turns the image texture into an isotropic texture, and recover the slant and tilt from that inverse viewing transformation.

There are various ways to find this viewing transformation. One natural strategy is to use the energy output of a set of oriented filters. This is the squared response, summed over the image. For an isotropic texture, we would expect the energy output to be the same for each orientation at any given scale, because the probability of encountering a pattern does not depend on its orientation. Thus, a measure of isotropy is the standard deviation of the energy output as a function of orientation. We could sum this measure over scales, perhaps weighting the measure by the total energy in the scale. The smaller the measure, the more isotropic the texture. We now find the inverse viewing transformation that makes the image looks most isotropic by this measure, using standard methods from optimization. The main difficulty with using an assumption of isotropy to recover the orientation of a plane is that there are very few isotropic textures in the world.

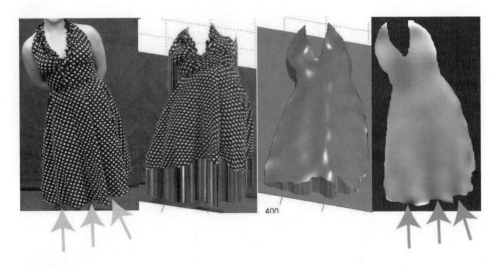

FIGURE 6.21: On the **left**, a textured surface, whose texture is a set of repeated elements, in this case, spots. **Center left**, a reconstruction of the surface, made using texture information alone. This reconstruction has been textured, which hides some of its imperfections. **Center right**, the same reconstruction, now rendered as a slightly glossy gray surface. Because texture elements are repeated, we can assume that if different elements have a significantly different brightness, this is because they experience different illumination. **Right** shows an estimate of the illumination on the surface obtained from this observation. Notice how folds in the dress (arrows) tend to be darker; this is because, for a surface element at the base of a fold, nearby cloth blocks a high percentage of the incident light. *This figure was originally published as Figure 4 of "Recovering Shape and Irradiance Maps from Rich Dense Texton Fields," by A. Lobay and D. Forsyth Proc. IEEE CVPR 2004 © IEEE, 2004.*

6.5.2   Shape from Texture for Curved Surfaces

Shape from texture is more complicated for curved surfaces, because there are more parameters to estimate. There are a variety of strategies, and there remains no consensus on what is best. If we assume that a texture consists of repeated small elements, then individual elements display no observable perspective effects (because they are small). Furthermore, curved surfaces often span fairly small ranges of depth, because if they curve fast enough, they must eventually turn away from the eye (if they don't, we might be able to model them as planes). All this suggests that we assume the surface is viewed in an orthographic camera.

Now consider a set of elements on a curved surface. Each element is an instance of a model element; you should think of the surface elements as copies of the model, which have been placed on the surface at different locations. Each is small, so we can model them as lying on the surface's tangent plane. Each element has different slant and tilt directions. This means that each *image instance* of the element is an instance of the model element, that has been rotated and translated to place it in the image, then scaled along the image slant direction. It turns out that, given sufficient image instances, we can infer both the model element and the surface normal at the element (up to a two-fold ambiguity; Figure 6.20) from this information (the proof will take us far out of our way; it is in Lobay and Forsyth (2006)). We must now fit a surface to this information. Doing so is complicated, because we need to resolve the ambiguity at each surface normal. This can be done by assuming that the surface is smooth (so that elements that lie near one another tend to share normal values), and by assuming we have some geometric constraints on the surface.

Interestingly, modeling a texture as a set of repeated elements reveals illumination information. If we can find multiple instances of an element on a surface, then the reason for their different image brightnesses is that they experience different illumination (typically, because they are at different angles to the incoming light). We can estimate surface irradiance directly from this information, even if the illumination field is complex (Figure 6.21).

6.6 NOTES

The idea that textures involve repetition of elements is fundamental, and appears in a wide variety of forms. Under some circumstances, one can try to infer the elements directly, as in Liu *et al.* (2004). Image compression can take advantage of the repetitions created by texture. If we have large, plane figures in view (say, the faces of buildings), then it can be advantageous to model viewing transformations to compress the image (because then the same element repeats more often). This means that, on occasion, image compression papers contain a shape from texture component (for example, Wang *et al.* (2008)).

Filters, Pyramids and Efficiency

If we are to represent texture with the output of a large range of filters at many scales and orientations, then we need to be efficient at filtering. This is a topic that has attracted much attention; the usual approach is to try and construct a tensor product basis that represents the available families of filters well. With an appropriate construction, we need to convolve the image with a small number of separable kernels, and can estimate the responses of many different filters by combining the results in different ways (hence the requirement that the basis be a tensor product). Significant papers include Freeman and Adelson (1991), Greenspan *et al.* (1994), Hel-Or and Teo (1996), Perona (1992), (1995), Simoncelli and Farid (1995), and Simoncelli and Freeman (1995*b*).

Pooled Texture Representations

The literature does not seem to draw the distinction between local and pooled texture representations explicitly. We think it is important, because quite different texture properties are being represented. There has been a fair amount of discussion of just what should be vector quantized to form these representations. Typically, one evaluates the goodness of a particular representation by its discriminative performance in a texture classification task; we discuss this topic in Chapter 16. Significant papers include Varma and Zisserman (2003), Varma and Zisserman (2005), Varma and Zisserman (2009), Leung and Malik (2001), Leung and Malik (1999), Leung and Malik (1996), Schmid (2001),

Texture Synthesis

Texture synthesis exhausted us long before we could exhaust it. Patch based texture synthesis is due to Efros and Freeman (2001); this paper hints at a form of conditional texture synthesis. Hertzmann *et al.* (2001) demonstrate that conditional texture synthesis can do the most amazing tricks. Vivek Kwatra and Li-Yi Wei organized an excellent course on texture synthesis at SIGGRAPH 2007; the notes are at `http://www.cs.unc.edu/~kwatra/SIG07_TextureSynthesis/index.htm`.

Denoising

Early work on image denoising relied on various smoothness assumptions—such as Gaussian smoothing, anisotropic filtering (Perona and Malik 1990c), total variation (Rudin *et al.* 2004), or image decompositions on fixed bases such as wavelets (Donoho & Johnstone 1995; Mallat 1999), for example. More recent approaches include non-local means filtering (Buades *et al.* 2005), which exploits image self-similarities, learned sparse models (Elad & Aharon 2006; Mairal *et al.* 2009), Gaussian scale mixtures (Portilla *et al.* 2003), fields of experts (Agarwal and Roth May 2002), and block matching with 3D filtering (BM3D) (Dabov *et al.* 2007). The idea of using self-similarities as a prior for natural images exploited by the non-local means approach of Buades *et al.* (2005) has in fact appeared in the literature in various guises and under different equivalent interpretations, e.g., kernel density estimation (Efros and Leung 1999), Nadaraya-Watson estimators (Buades *et al.* 2005), mean-shift iterations (Awate and Whitaker 2006), diffusion processes on graphs (Szlam *et al.* 2007), and long-range random fields (Li and Huttenlocher 2008). We have restricted our discussion of sparsity-inducing regularizers to the ℓ_1 norm here, but the ℓ_0 pseudo-norm, which counts the number of nonzero coefficients in the code associated with a noisy signal can be used as well. Chapter 22 discusses ℓ_0-regularized sparse coding and dictionary learning in some detail. Let us just note here that simultaneous sparse coding is also relevant in that case, the $\ell_{1,2}$ norm being replaced by the $\ell_{0,\infty}$ pseudo-norm, which directly counts the number of nonzero rows. See (Mairal *et al.* 2009) for details. An implementation of non-local means is available at: `http://www.ipol.im/pub/algo/bcm_non_local_means_denoising/`, and BM3D is available at `http://www.cs.tut.fi/~foi/GCF-BM3D/`. An implementation of LSSC is available at `http://www.di.ens.fr/~mairal/denoise_ICCV09.tar.gz`.

Shape from Texture

We have assumed that textures are albedo marks on smooth surfaces. This really isn't true, as van Ginneken *et al.* (1999) point out; an immense number of textures are caused by indentations on surfaces (the bark on a tree, for example, where the main texture effect seems to be dark shadows in the grooves of the bark), or by elements suspended in space (the leaves of a tree, say). Such textures still give us a sense of shape—for example, in Figure 6.1, one has a sense of the free space in the picture where one could move. The resulting changes in appearance as the illumination and view directions change are complicated (Dana *et al.* 1999, Lu *et al.* 1999, Lu *et al.* 1998, Pont and Koenderink 2002). We don't discuss this case because not much is known about how to proceed.

There is a long tradition of using marked point processes as texture models (explicitly in, for example (Ahuja and Schachter 1983a, Ahuja and Schachter 1983b, Blake and Marinos 1990, Schachter 1980, Schachter and Ahuja 1979) and implicitly in pretty much all existing literature). A **Poisson model** has the property that the expected number of elements in a domain is proportional to the area of the domain. The constant of proportionality is known as the model's **intensity**. A texture is **isotropic** if the choice of element rotation is uniform and random, and is **homogeneous** if the density from which texture elements are drawn is independent of position on the surface.

There are surprisingly few shape from texture methods. **Global methods** attempt to recover an entire surface model, using assumptions about the distribution of texture elements. Appropriate assumptions are isotropy (Witkin 1981) (the disadvantage of this method is that there are relatively few natural isotropic textures) or homogeneity (Aloimonos 1986, Blake and Marinos 1990).

Texture deformation can be exploited in global methods, with some assumptions about the element—see the methods in (Lee and Kuo 1998, Sakai and Finkel 1994, Stone and Isard 1995)). Alternatively, one observes that the per-element imaging transformations are going to affect the spatial frequency components on the surface; this means that if the texture has constrained spatial frequency properties, one may observe the orientation from the texture gradient (Bajcsy and Lieberman 1976, Krumm and Shafer 1990, Krumm and Shafer 1992, Sakai and Finkel 1994, Super and Bovik 1995).

Local methods recover some differential geometric parameters at a point on a surface (typically, normal and curvatures). This class of methods, which is due to Garding (1992), has been successfully demonstrated for a variety of surfaces by Malik and Rosenholtz (1997) and Rosenholtz and Malik (1997); a reformulation in terms of wavelets is due to Clerc and Mallat (1999). The methods have a crucial flaw; it is necessary either to know that texture element coordinate frames form a frame field that is locally parallel around the point in question, or to know the differential rotation of the frame field (see Garding (1995) for this point, which is emphasized by the choice of textures displayed in Rosenholtz and Malik (1997); the assumption is known as **texture stationarity**). For example, if one were to use these methods to recover the curvature of a doughnut dipped in chocolate sprinkles, it would be necessary to ensure that the sprinkles were all parallel on the surface (or that the field of angles from sprinkle to sprinkle was known).

One might construct a generative model, where object texture is modelled with a parametric random model, then choose a geometry and parameters that minimizes the difference between either a predicted image and the observed image (Choe and Kashyap 1991) or a predicted image density and the observed image density (Lee and Kuo 1998).

More recent local methods emphasize repetition. Forsyth (2001) infers shape from slant estimates only, establishing an analogy with shape from shading. Forsyth (2002) shows that element repetition is sufficient to get normal estimates up to an ambiguity, with a cleaner version in (Lobay and Forsyth 2006); Loh and Hartley (2005) give a method to reconstruct a surface in this case; and Lobay and Forsyth (2004) demonstrate that repetition of textons gives cues to illumination.

Applications for shape from texture have been largely absent, explaining its status as a minority interest. However, we believe that image-based rendering of clothing is an application with substantial promise. Cloth is difficult to model for a variety of reasons. It is much more resistant to stretch than to bend: this means that dynamical models result in stiff differential equations (for example, see (Terzopolous *et al.* 1987)) and that it buckles in fine scale, complex folds (for example, see (Bridson *et al.* 2002)). However, rendering cloth is an important technical problem, because people are interesting to look at and most people wear clothing. A natural strategy for rendering objects that are intrinsically difficult to model satisfactorily is to rearrange existing pictures of the objects to yield a rendering. In particular, one would wish to be able to retexture and reshade such images. Earlier work on motion capturing cloth used stereopsis, but faced difficulties with motion blur and calibration (Pritchard 2003, Pritchard and Heidrich 2003). More recent work prints a fine pattern on the cloth (White *et al.* 2007), or uses volume intersections (Bradley *et al.* 2008*b*). We believe that, in future, shape from texture methods might make it possible to avoid some of these problems.

PROBLEMS

6.1. Show that a circle appears as an ellipse in an orthographic view, that the minor axis of this ellipse is the tilt direction, and that the aspect ratio is the cosine of the slant angle.

6.2. We will study measuring the orientation of a plane in a perspective view, given that the texture consists of points laid down by a homogeneous Poisson point process. Recall that one way to generate points according to such a process is to sample the x and y coordinate of the point uniformly and at random. We assume that the points from our process lie within a unit square.

(a) Show that the probability that a point will land in a particular set is proportional to the area of that set.

(b) Assume we partition the area into disjoint sets. Show that the number of points in each set has a multinomial probability distribution.

We will now use these observations to recover the orientation of the plane. We partition the *image texture* into a collection of disjoint sets.

(c) Show that the area of each set, *backprojected onto the textured plane*, is a function of the orientation of the plane.

(d) Use this function to suggest a method for obtaining the plane's orientation.

PROGRAMMING EXERCISES

6.3. Texture synthesis: Implement the non-parametric texture synthesis algorithm of Algorithm 6.4. Use your implementation to study:

(a) the effect of window size on the synthesized texture;

(b) the effect of window shape on the synthesized texture; and

(c) the effect of the matching criterion on the synthesized texture (i.e., using a weighted sum of squares instead of a sum of squares, etc.).

PART THREE

EARLY VISION: MULTIPLE IMAGES

CHAPTER 7

Stereopsis

Fusing the pictures recorded by our two eyes and exploiting the difference (or *disparity*) between them allows us to gain a strong sense of depth. This chapter is concerned with the design and implementation of algorithms that mimic our ability to perform this task, known as *stereopsis*. Reliable computer programs for stereoscopic perception are of course invaluable in visual robot navigation (Figure 7.1), cartography, aerial reconnaissance, and close-range photogrammetry. They are also of great interest in tasks such as image segmentation for object recognition or the construction of three-dimensional scene models for computer graphics applications.

FIGURE 7.1: **Left:** The Stanford cart sports a single camera moving in discrete increments along a straight line and providing multiple snapshots of outdoor scenes. **Center:** The INRIA mobile robot uses three cameras to map its environment. **Right:** The NYU mobile robot uses two stereo cameras, each capable of delivering an image pair. As shown by these examples, although two eyes are sufficient for stereo fusion, mobile robots are sometimes equipped with three (or more) cameras. The bulk of this chapter is concerned with binocular perception but stereo algorithms using multiple cameras are discussed in Section 7.6. *Photos courtesy of Hans Moravec, Olivier Faugeras, and Yann LeCun.*

Stereo vision involves two processes: The *fusion* of features observed by two (or more) eyes and the *reconstruction* of their three-dimensional preimage. The latter is relatively simple: The preimage of matching points can (in principle) be found at the intersection of the rays passing through these points and the associated pupil centers (or pinholes; see Figure 7.2, left). Thus, when a single image feature is observed at any given time, stereo vision is easy. However, each picture typically consists of millions of pixels, with tens of thousands of image features such as edge elements, and some method must be devised to establish the correct correspondences and avoid erroneous depth measurements (Figure 7.2, right).

We start this chapter by examining in Section 7.1 the geometric *epipolar constraint* associated with a pair of cameras, which is a key to controlling the cost of the binocular fusion process. Next, we stay on the geometric side of things in Section 7.2 as we present a number of methods for binocular reconstruction. After

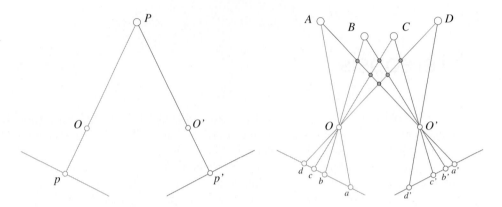

FIGURE 7.2: The binocular fusion problem: In the simple case of the diagram shown on the **left**, there is no ambiguity, and stereo reconstruction is a simple matter. In the more usual case shown on the **right**, any of the four points in the left picture may, *a priori*, match any of the four points in the right one. Only four of these correspondences are correct; the other ones yield the incorrect reconstructions shown as small gray discs.

a brief incursion into human stereopsis (Section 7.3), we switch with Section 7.4 to the presentation of several algorithms for binocular fusion that rely on the comparison of *local* brightness or edge patterns to establish correspondences. Section 7.5 shows that ordering and smoothness constraints among nearby pixels can be incorporated in the matching process. In this setting, stereo fusion is naturally cast as a combinatorial optimization problem, which can be solved by several efficient algorithms (Chapter 22). We conclude in Section 7.6 with a discussion of multi-camera stereo fusion (see also Chapter 19 for applications of multi-view stereopsis to image-based modeling and rendering).

Note: We assume throughout that all cameras have been carefully calibrated so their intrinsic and extrinsic parameters are precisely known relative to some fixed world coordinate system. The case of uncalibrated cameras is examined in the context of structure from motion in Chapter 8.

7.1   BINOCULAR CAMERA GEOMETRY AND THE EPIPOLAR CONSTRAINT

As noted in the introduction, it appears *a priori* that, given a stereo image pair, any pixel in the first (or *left*) image may match any pixel in the second (or *right*) one. As shown in this section, matching pairs of pixels are in fact restricted to lie on corresponding *epipolar lines* in the two pictures. This constraint plays a fundamental role in the stereo fusion process because it reduces the quest for image correspondences to a set of one-dimensional searches.

7.1.1   Epipolar Geometry

Consider the images p and p' of a point P observed by two cameras with optical centers O and O'. These five points all belong to the *epipolar plane* defined by the two intersecting rays OP and $O'P$ (Figure 7.3). In particular, the point p' lies on the line l' where this plane and the retina Π' of the second camera intersect.

The line l' is the *epipolar line* associated with the point p, and it passes through the point e' where the *baseline* joining the optical centers O and O' intersects Π'. Likewise, the point p lies on the epipolar line l associated with the point p', and this line passes through the intersection e of the baseline with the plane Π.

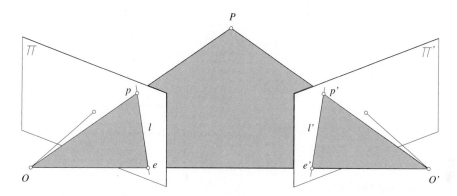

FIGURE 7.3: Epipolar geometry: The point P, the optical centers O and O' of the two cameras, and the two images p and p' of P all lie in the same plane. Here, as in the other figures of this chapter, cameras are represented by their pinholes and a *virtual* image plane located *in front* of the pinhole. This is to simplify the drawings; the geometric and algebraic arguments presented in the rest of this chapter hold just as well for *physical* image planes located *behind* the corresponding pinholes.

The points e and e' are called the *epipoles* of the two cameras. The *epipole* e' is the projection of the optical center O of the first camera in the image observed by the second camera, and vice versa. As noted before, if p and p' are images of the same point, then p' must lie on the epipolar line associated with p. This *epipolar constraint* plays a fundamental role in stereo vision and motion analysis.

In the setting studied in the rest of this chapter, where the cameras are internally and externally calibrated, the most difficult part of constructing an artifical stereo vision system is to find effective methods for establishing correspondences between the two images—that is, deciding which points in the second picture match the points in the first one. The epipolar constraint greatly limits the search for these correspondences. Indeed, since we assume that the rig is calibrated, the coordinates of the point p completely determine the ray joining O and p, and thus the associated epipolar plane $OO'p$ and epipolar line l'. The search for matches can be restricted to this line instead of the whole image (Figure 7.4). In the motion analysis setting studied in Chapter 8, each camera may be internally calibrated, but the rigid transformation separating the two camera coordinate systems is unknown. In this case, the epipolar geometry constrains the set of possible motions.

As shown next, it proves convenient to characterize the epipolar constraint in terms of the bilinear forms associated with two 3×3 *essential* and *fundamental* matrices.

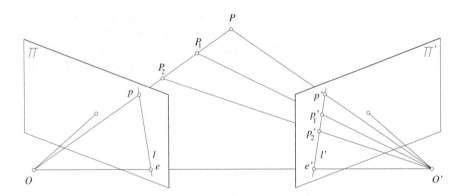

FIGURE 7.4: Epipolar constraint: Given a calibrated stereo rig, the set of possible matches for the point p is constrained to lie on the associated epipolar line l'.

7.1.2   The Essential Matrix

We assume in this section that the intrinsic parameters of each camera are known, and work in *normalized* image coordinates—that is, take $\boldsymbol{p} = \hat{\boldsymbol{p}}$. According to the epipolar constraint, the three vectors $\overrightarrow{Op}$, $\overrightarrow{O'p'}$, and $\overrightarrow{OO'}$ must be coplanar. Equivalently, one of them must lie in the plane spanned by the other two, or

$$\overrightarrow{Op} \cdot [\overrightarrow{OO'} \times \overrightarrow{O'p'}] = 0.$$

We can rewrite this coordinate-independent equation in the coordinate frame associated to the first camera as

$$\boldsymbol{p} \cdot [\boldsymbol{t} \times (\mathcal{R}\boldsymbol{p}')] = 0, \tag{7.1}$$

where $\boldsymbol{p}$ and $\boldsymbol{p}'$ denote the *homogeneous* normalized image coordinate vectors of p and p', $\boldsymbol{t}$ is the coordinate vector of the translation $\overrightarrow{OO'}$ separating the two coordinate systems, and $\mathcal{R}$ is the rotation matrix such that a free vector with coordinates $\boldsymbol{w}'$ in the second coordinate system has coordinates $\mathcal{R}\boldsymbol{w}'$ in the first one. In this case, the two projection matrices are given in the coordinate system attached to the first camera by $[\text{Id} \quad \boldsymbol{0}]$ and $[\mathcal{R}^T \quad -\mathcal{R}^T\boldsymbol{t}]$.

Equation (7.1) can finally be rewritten as

$$\boldsymbol{p}^T \mathcal{E} \boldsymbol{p}' = 0, \tag{7.2}$$

where $\mathcal{E} = [\boldsymbol{t}_\times]\mathcal{R}$, and $[\boldsymbol{a}_\times]$ denotes the skew-symmetric matrix such that $[\boldsymbol{a}_\times]\boldsymbol{x} = \boldsymbol{a} \times \boldsymbol{x}$ is the cross-product of the vectors $\boldsymbol{a}$ and $\boldsymbol{x}$. The matrix $\mathcal{E}$ is called the *essential matrix*, and it was first introduced by Longuet–Higgins (1981). Its nine coefficients are only defined up to scale, and they can be parameterized by the three degrees of freedom of the rotation matrix $\mathcal{R}$ and the two degrees of freedom defining the direction of the translation vector $\boldsymbol{t}$.

Note that $\boldsymbol{l} = \mathcal{E}\boldsymbol{p}'$ can be interpreted as the coordinate vector of the epipolar line l associated with the point p' in the first image. Indeed, Equation (7.2) can be written as $\boldsymbol{p} \cdot \boldsymbol{l} = 0$, expressing the fact that the point p lies on l. By symmetry, it is also clear that $l' = \mathcal{E}^T p$ is the coordinate vector representing the epipolar line l' associated with p in the second image. Essential matrices are singular because t is parallel to the coordinate vector e of the first epipole, so that $\mathcal{E}^T e = -\mathcal{R}^T[t_\times]e = 0$. Likewise, it is easy to show that e' is in the nullspace of $\mathcal{E}$. As shown by Huang and Faugeras (1989), essential matrices are in fact characterized by the fact that they are singular with two equal nonzero singular values (see the problems).

7.1.3   The Fundamental Matrix

The Longuet–Higgins relation holds in normalized image coordinates. In native image coordinates, we can write $p = \mathcal{K}\hat{p}$ and $p' = \mathcal{K}'\hat{p}'$, where $\mathcal{K}$ and $\mathcal{K}'$ are the 3×3 calibration matrices associated with the two cameras. The Longuet–Higgins relation holds for these vectors, and we obtain

$$p^T \mathcal{F} p' = 0, \qquad (7.3)$$

where the matrix $\mathcal{F} = \mathcal{K}^{-T}\mathcal{E}\mathcal{K}'^{-1}$, called the *fundamental matrix*, is not, in general, an essential matrix. It has again rank two, and the eigenvector of $\mathcal{F}$ (resp. $\mathcal{F}^T$) corresponding to its zero eigenvalue is as before the position e' (resp. e) of the epipole. Likewise, $l' = \mathcal{F}p'$ (resp. $l = \mathcal{F}^T p$) represents the epipolar line corresponding to the point p' (resp. p) in the first (resp. second) image.

The matrices $\mathcal{E}$ and $\mathcal{F}$ can readily be computed from the intrinsic and extrinsic parameters. Let us close this section by noting that Equations (7.2) and (7.3) also provide constraints on the entries of these matrices, *irrespective* of the 3D position of the observed points. In particular, this suggests that $\mathcal{E}$ and $\mathcal{F}$ can be computed from a sufficient number of image correspondences *without* the use of a calibration chart. We will come back to this issue in Chapter 8. For the time being, we will assume that the cameras are calibrated and that the epipolar geometry is known.

7.2   BINOCULAR RECONSTRUCTION

Given a calibrated stereo rig and two matching image points p and p', it is in principle straightforward to reconstruct the corresponding scene point by intersecting the two rays $R = Op$ and $R' = O'p'$ (Figure 7.2). However, the rays R and R' never actually intersect in practice, due to calibration and feature localization errors. In this context, various reasonable approaches to the reconstruction problem can be adopted. For example, consider the line segment perpendicular to R and R' that intersects both rays (Figure 7.5): its mid-point P is the closest point to the two rays and can be taken as the preimage of p and p'.

Alternatively, one can reconstruct a scene point using a purely algebraic approach: given the projection matrices $\mathcal{M}$ and $\mathcal{M}'$ and the matching points p and p', we can rewrite the constraints $Zp = \mathcal{M}P$ and $Z'p' = \mathcal{M}P$ as

$$\begin{cases} p \times \mathcal{M}P = 0 \\ p' \times \mathcal{M}'P = 0 \end{cases} \iff \begin{pmatrix} [p_\times]\mathcal{M} \\ [p'_\times]\mathcal{M}' \end{pmatrix} P = 0.$$

This is an overconstrained system of four independent linear equations in the homogeneous coordinates of P that is easily solved using the linear least-squares techniques introduced in Chapter 22. Unlike the previous approach, this reconstruction

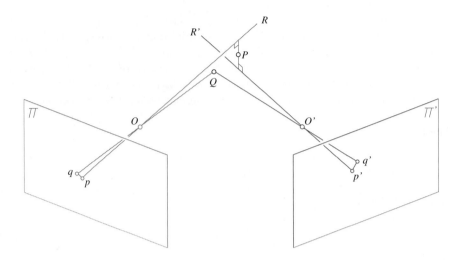

FIGURE 7.5: Triangulation in the presence of measurement errors. See text for details.

method does not have an obvious geometric interpretation, but generalizes readily to the case of three or more cameras, with each new picture simply adding two additional constraints.

Finally, one can reconstruct the scene point associated with p and p' as the point Q with images q and q' that minimizes $d^2(p, q) + d^2(p', q')$ (Figure 7.5). Unlike the two other methods presented in this section, this approach does not allow the closed-form computation of the reconstructed point, which must be estimated via nonlinear least-squares techniques such as those introduced in Chapter 22. The reconstruction obtained by either of the other two methods can be used as a reasonable guess to initialize the optimization process. This nonlinear approach also readily generalizes to the case of multiple images.

7.2.1   Image Rectification

The calculations associated with stereo algorithms are often considerably simplified when the images of interest have been *rectified*—that is, replaced by two equivalent pictures with a common image plane parallel to the baseline joining the two optical centers (Figure 7.6). The rectification process can be implemented by projecting the original pictures onto the new image plane. With an appropriate choice of coordinate system, the rectified epipolar lines are scanlines of the new images, and they are also parallel to the baseline. There are two degrees of freedom involved in the choice of the rectified image plane: (a) the distance between this plane and the baseline, which is essentially irrelevant because modifying it only changes the scale of the rectified pictures—an effect easily balanced by an inverse scaling of the image coordinate axes; and (b) the direction of the rectified plane normal in the plane perpendicular to the baseline. Natural choices include picking a plane parallel to the line where the two original retinas intersect and minimizing the distortion associated with the reprojection process.

In the case of rectified images, the informal notion of disparity introduced at

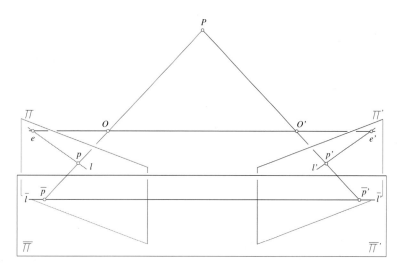

FIGURE 7.6: A rectified stereo pair: The two image planes Π and Π' are reprojected onto a common plane $\bar{\Pi} = \bar{\Pi}'$ parallel to the baseline. The epipolar lines l and l' associated with the points p and p' in the two pictures map onto a common scanline $\bar{l} = \bar{l}'$ also parallel to the baseline and passing through the reprojected points $\bar{p}$ and $\bar{p}'$. With modern computer graphics hardware and software, the rectified images are easily constructed by considering each input image as a polyhedral mesh and using texture mapping to render the projection of this mesh onto the plane $\bar{\Pi} = \bar{\Pi}'$.

the beginning of this chapter takes a concrete meaning: given two points p and p' located on the same scanline of the left and right images, with coordinates (x, y) and (x', y), the disparity is defined as the difference $d = x' - x$. We assume in the rest of this section that image coordinates are normalized—that is, as before, $\boldsymbol{p} = \hat{\boldsymbol{p}}$. As shown in the problems, if B denotes the distance between the optical centers, also called the baseline in this context, the depth of P in the (normalized) coordinate system attached to the first camera is $Z = -B/d$. In particular, the coordinate vector of the point P in the frame attached to the first camera is $\boldsymbol{P} = -(B/d)\boldsymbol{p}$, where $\boldsymbol{p} = (x, y, 1)^T$ is the vector of normalized image coordinates of p. This provides yet another reconstruction method for rectified stereo pairs.

7.3 HUMAN STEREOPSIS

Before moving on to algorithms for establishing binocular correspondences, let us pause for a moment to discuss the mechanisms underlying human stereopsis. First, it should be noted that, unlike the cameras rigidly attached to a passive stereo rig, the two eyes of a person can rotate in their sockets. At each instant, they *fixate* on a particular point in space (i.e., they rotate so that the corresponding images form in the centers of their foveas). Figure 7.7 illustrates a simplified, two-dimensional situation: if l and r denote the (counterclockwise) angles between the vertical planes of symmetry of two eyes and two rays passing through the same scene point, we define the corresponding disparity as $d = r - l$. It is an elementary exercise in trigonometry to show that $d = D - F$, where D denotes the angle between these

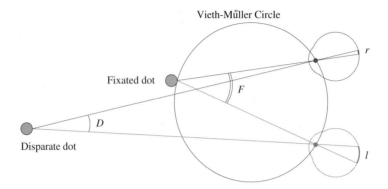

FIGURE 7.7: In this diagram, the close-by dot is fixated by the eyes, and it projects onto the center of their foveas with no disparity. The two images of the far dot deviate from this central position by different amounts, indicating a different depth.

rays, and F is the angle between the two rays passing through the fixated point. Points with zero disparity lie on the *Vieth–Müller circle* that passes through the fixated point and the optical centers of the eyes. Points lying inside this circle have a positive disparity, points lying outside it have, as in Figure 7.7, a negative disparity, and the locus of all points having a given disparity d forms, as d varies, the family of all circles passing through the two eyes' optical centers. This property is clearly sufficient to rank order dots that are near the fixation point according to their depth. However, it is also clear that the *vergence angles* between the vertical *median plane* of symmetry of the head and the two fixation rays must be known to reconstruct the absolute position of scene points.

The three-dimensional case is naturally more complicated, with the locus of zero-disparity points becoming a surface, the *horopter*, but the general conclusion is the same, and absolute positioning requires the vergence angles. There is some evidence that these angles cannot be measured accurately by our nervous system (Helmholtz 1909). However, *relative* depth, or rank ordering of points along the line of sight, can be judged quite accurately. For example, it is possible to decide which one of two targets near the horopter is closer to an observer for disparities of a few seconds of arc (*stereoacuity threshold*), which matches the minimum separation that can be measured with one eye (*monocular hyperacuity threshold*).

Concerning the construction of correspondences between the left and right images, Julesz (1960) asked the following question: Is the basic mechanism for binocular fusion a monocular process (where local brightness patterns [micropatterns] or higher organizations of points into objects [macropatterns] are identified *before* being fused), a binocular one (where the two images are combined into a single field where all further processing takes place), or a combination of both? To settle this matter, he introduced a new device, the *random dot stereogram*: a pair of synthetic images obtained by randomly spraying black dots on white objects, typically one (or several) small square plate(s) floating over a larger one (Figure 7.8). The results were striking. To quote Julesz: "When viewed monocularly, the images appear completely random. But when viewed stereoscopically, the image pair

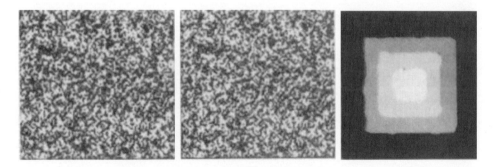

FIGURE 7.8: From **left** to **right**: the two pictures forming a random dot stereogram that depicts four planes at varying depth (a "wedding cake"), and the disparity map obtained by the Marr-Poggio (1976) algorithm. The layered structure of the scene is correctly recovered. *Reprinted from Vision: A Computational Investigation into the Human Representation and Processing of Visual Information, by David Marr, © 1982 by David Marr. Reprinted by permission of Henry Holt and Company, LLC.*

gives the impression of a square markedly in front of (or behind) the surround." The conclusion is clear: Human binocular fusion cannot be explained by peripheral processes directly associated with the physical retinas. Instead, it must involve the central nervous system and an imaginary *cyclopean retina* that combines the left and right image stimuli as a single unit.

Several *cooperative* models of human stereopsis—where near-by matches influence each other to avoid ambiguities and promote a global scene analysis—have been proposed, including Julesz's own *dipole* model (1960) and that of Marr and Poggio (1976). Although the latter has been implemented, allowing the reliable fusion of random dot stereograms (Figure 7.8), it fails on most natural images. In contrast, the algorithms proposed in the following sections do not attempt to model the human visual system, but they usually give good results on natural imagery.

7.4 LOCAL METHODS FOR BINOCULAR FUSION

We start here by introducing simple methods for stereo fusion that exploit purely local information, such as the similarity of brightness patterns near candidate matches, to establish correspondences.

7.4.1 Correlation

Correlation methods find pixel-wise image correspondences by comparing intensity profiles in the neighborhood of potential matches, and they are among the first techniques ever proposed to solve the binocular fusion problem (Kelly, McConnell & Mildenberger 1977; Gennery 1980). Concretely, let us consider a *rectified* stereo pair and a point (x, y) in the first image (Figure 7.9). We associate with the window of size $p = (2m + 1) \times (2n + 1)$ centered in (x, y) the vector $\boldsymbol{w}(x, y) \in \mathbb{R}^p$ obtained by scanning the window values one row at a time (the order is in fact irrelevant as long as it is fixed). Now, given a potential match $(x + d, y)$ in the second image, we can construct a second vector $\boldsymbol{w}'(x + d, y)$ and define the corresponding *normalized*

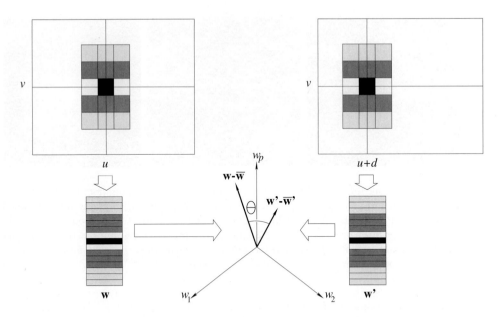

FIGURE 7.9: Correlation of two 3×5 windows along corresponding epipolar lines. The second window position is separated from the first one by an offset d. The two windows are encoded by vectors $\boldsymbol{w}$ and $\boldsymbol{w}'$ in $\mathbb{R}^{15}$, and the correlation function measures the cosine of the angle θ between the vectors $\boldsymbol{w} - \bar{\boldsymbol{w}}$ and $\boldsymbol{w}' - \bar{\boldsymbol{w}}'$ obtained by subtracting from the components of $\boldsymbol{w}$ and $\boldsymbol{w}'$ the average intensity in the corresponding windows.

correlation function as

$$C(d) = \frac{1}{||\boldsymbol{w} - \bar{\boldsymbol{w}}||} \frac{1}{||\boldsymbol{w}' - \bar{\boldsymbol{w}}'||} [(\boldsymbol{w} - \bar{\boldsymbol{w}}) \cdot (\boldsymbol{w}' - \bar{\boldsymbol{w}}')],$$

where the x, y, and d indexes have been omitted for the sake of conciseness and $\bar{\boldsymbol{a}}$ denotes the vector whose coordinates are all equal to the mean of the coordinates of $\boldsymbol{a}$.

The normalized correlation function C clearly ranges from -1 to $+1$. It reaches its maximum value when the image brightnesses of the two windows are related by an affine transformation $I' = \lambda I + \mu$ for some constants λ and μ with $\lambda > 0$ (see the problems). In other words, maxima of this function correspond to image patches separated by a constant offset and a positive scale factor, and stereo matches can be found by seeking the maximum of the C function over some predetermined range of disparities.[1]

At this point, let us make a few remarks about matching methods based on correlation. First, it is easily shown (see the problems) that maximizing the

---

[1] The invariance of C to affine transformations of the brightness function affords correlation-based matching techniques some degree of robustness in situations where the observed surface is not quite Lambertian or the two cameras have different gains or lenses with different f-numbers.

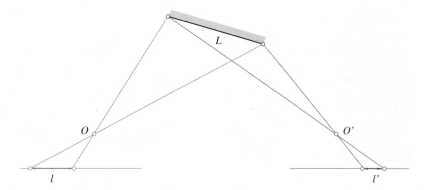

FIGURE 7.10: The foreshortening of an oblique plane is not the same for the left and right cameras: $l/L \neq l'/L$.

correlation function is equivalent to minimizing

$$| \frac{1}{||\boldsymbol{w} - \bar{\boldsymbol{w}}||}(\boldsymbol{w} - \bar{\boldsymbol{w}}) - \frac{1}{||\boldsymbol{w}' - \bar{\boldsymbol{w}}'||}(\boldsymbol{w}' - \bar{\boldsymbol{w}}')|^2,$$

or equivalently the sum of the squared differences between the pixel values of the two windows after they have been submitted to the corresponding normalization process. Second, although the calculation of the normalized correlation function at every pixel of an image for some range of disparities is computationally expensive, it can be implemented efficiently using recursive techniques (see problems). Third, other functions, such as the *sum of absolute difference* $\sum_{i=1}^{p} |w_i - w'_i|$, can be used to measure the discrepancy between two brightness patterns, and they may give better results in certain situations (Scharstein and Szeliski 2002). Finally, a major problem with correlation-based techniques for establishing stereo correspondences is that they implicitly assume that the observed surface is (locally) parallel to the two image planes, since the foreshortening of (oblique) surfaces depends on the position of the cameras observing them (Figure 7.10).

This suggests a two-pass algorithm where initial estimates of the disparity are used to warp the correlation windows to compensate for unequal amounts of foreshortening in the two pictures. For example, Devernay and Faugeras (1994) propose to define a warped window in the right image for each rectangle in the left one, using the disparity in the center of the rectangle and its derivatives. An optimization process is used to find the values of the disparity and its derivatives that maximize the correlation between the left rectangle and the right window, using interpolation to retrieve appropriate values in the right image. Figure 7.11 illustrates this approach with an example.

7.4.2 Multi-Scale Edge Matching

Slanted surfaces pose problems to correlation-based matchers. Other arguments against correlation can be found in Julesz (1960) and Marr (1982), suggesting that correspondences should be found at a variety of scales, with matches between (hopefully) physically significant image features such as edges preferred to matches be-

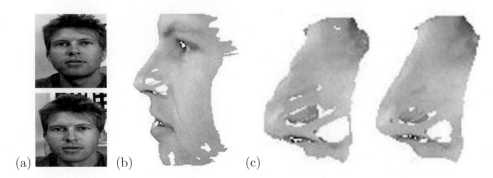

(a)   (b)   (c)

FIGURE 7.11: Correlation-based stereo matching: (a) a pair of stereo pictures; (b) a texture-mapped view of the reconstructed surface; (c) comparison of the regular (**left**) and refined (**right**) correlation methods in the nose region. The latter clearly gives better results. *Reprinted from "Computing Differential Properties of 3D Shapes from Stereopsis Without 3D Models," by F. Devernay and O.D. Faugeras, Proc. IEEE Conference on Computer Vision and Pattern Recognition, (1994). © 1994 IEEE.*

tween raw pixel intensities. These principles are implemented in Algorithm 7.1, which is due to Marr and Poggio (1979).

---

1. Convolve the two (rectified) images with $\nabla^2 G_\sigma$ filters of increasing standard deviations $\sigma_1 < \sigma_2 < \sigma_3 < \sigma_4$.

2. Find zero crossings of the Laplacian along horizontal scanlines of the filtered images.

3. For each filter scale σ, match zero crossings with the same parity and roughly equal orientations in a $[-w_\sigma, +w_\sigma]$ disparity range, with $w_\sigma = 2\sqrt{2}\sigma$.

4. Use the disparities found at larger scales to offset the images in the neighborhood of matches and cause unmatched regions at smaller scales to come into correspondence.

Algorithm 7.1: The Marr–Poggio (1979) Multi-Scale Binocular Fusion Algorithm.

Matching zero crossings at a single scale

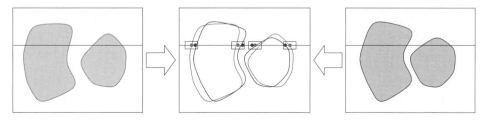

Matching zero crossings at multiple scales

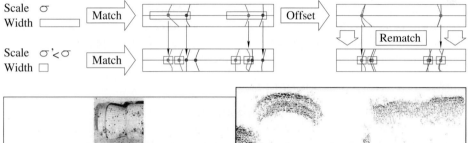

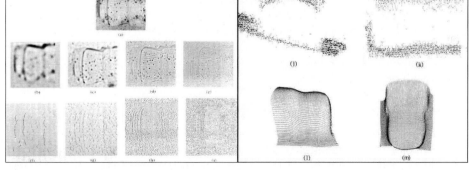

FIGURE 7.12: **Top:** Single-Scale matching. **Middle:** Multi-Scale matching. **Bottom:** Results. **Bottom left:** The input data (including one of the input pictures, the output of four $\nabla^2 G_\sigma$ filters, and the corresponding zero crossings). **Bottom right:** Two views of the disparity map constructed by the matching process and two views of the surface obtained by interpolating the reconstructed points. *Reprinted from Vision: A Computational Investigation into the Human Representation and Processing of Visual Information, by David Marr, © 1982 by David Marr. Reprinted by permission of Henry Holt and Company, LLC.*

Matches are sought at each scale in the $[-w_\sigma, w_\sigma]$ disparity range, where $w_\sigma = 2\sqrt{2}\sigma$ is the width of the central negative portion of the $\nabla^2 G_\sigma$ filter. This choice is motivated by psychophysical and statistical considerations. In particular, assuming that the convolved images are white Gaussian processes, Grimson (1981a) showed that the probability of a false match occurring in the $[-w_\sigma, +w_\sigma]$ disparity range of a given zero crossing is only 0.2 when the orientations of the matched features are within 30° of each other. A simple mechanism can be used to disambiguate the multiple potential matches that might still occur within the matching range. See Grimson (1981a) for details. Of course, limiting the search for matches to the $[-w_\sigma, +w_\sigma]$ range prevents the algorithm from matching *correct* pairs of zero crossings whose disparity falls outside this interval. Since w_σ is proportional to the scale σ at which matches are sought, eye movements (or equivalently image offsets) controlled by the disparities found at large scales must be used to bring large-disparity pairs of zero crossings within matchable range at a fine scale. This process occurs in Step 4 of Algorithm 7.1 and is illustrated by Figure 7.12 (top). Once matches have been found, the corresponding disparities can be stored in a buffer called the $2\frac{1}{2}$-*dimensional sketch* by Marr and Nishihara (1978). This algorithm has been implemented by Grimson (1981a), and extensively tested on random dot stereograms and natural images. An example appears in Figure 7.12 (bottom).

7.5 GLOBAL METHODS FOR BINOCULAR FUSION

The stereo fusion techniques presented in the previous section are purely local, in the sense that they match brightness or edge patterns around individual pixels, but ignore the constraints that may link nearby points. In contrast, we present in this section two *global* approaches to stereo fusion, that formulate this problem as the minimization of a single energy function incorporating *ordering* or *smoothness* constraints among adjacent pixels.

7.5.1   Ordering Constraints and Dynamic Programming

It is reasonable to assume that the order of matching image features along a pair of epipolar lines is the inverse of the order of the corresponding surface attributes along the curve where the epipolar plane intersects the observed object's boundary (Figure 7.13, left). This is the so-called *ordering constraint* introduced in the early 1980s (Baker & Binford 1981; Ohta & Kanade 1985). Interestingly enough, it might not be satisfied by real scenes, in particular when small solids occlude parts of larger ones (Figure 7.13, right) or more rarely, at least in robot vision, when transparent objects are involved. Despite these reservations, the ordering constraint remains a reasonable one, and it can be used to devise efficient algorithms relying on *dynamic programming* (Forney 1973; Aho, Hopcroft, & Ullman 1974) to establish stereo correspondences (see Figure 7.14 and Algorithm 7.2).

Specifically, let us assume that a number of feature points (say, edgels) have been found on corresponding epipolar lines. Our objective here is to match the intervals separating those points along the two intensity profiles (Figure 7.14, left). According to the ordering constraint, the order of the feature points must be the same, although the occasional interval in either image may be reduced to a single

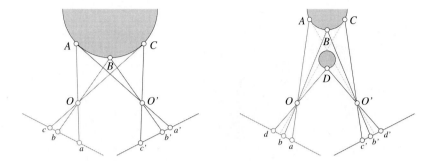

FIGURE 7.13: Ordering constraints. In the (usual) case shown in the **left** part of the diagram, the order of feature points along the two (oriented) epipolar lines is the same. In the case shown in the **right** part of the figure, a small object lies in front of a larger one. Some of the surface points are not visible in one of the images (e.g., A is not visible in the right image), and the order of the image points is not the same in the two pictures: b is on the right of d in the left image, but b' is on the left of d' in the right image.

point corresponding to missing correspondences associated with occlusion and/or noise.

This setting allows us to recast the matching problem as the optimization of a path's cost over a graph whose nodes correspond to pairs of left and right image features; and arcs represent matches between left and right intensity profile intervals bounded by the features of the corresponding nodes (Figure 7.14, right). The cost of an arc measures the discrepancy between the corresponding intervals (e.g., the squared difference of the mean intensity values). This optimization problem can be solved, exactly and efficiently, using dynamic programming (Algorithm 7.2). As given, this algorithm has a computational complexity of $O(mn)$, where m and n denote the number of edge points on the matched left and right scanlines, respectively.[2] Variants of this approach have been implemented by Baker and Binford (1981), who combine a coarse-to-fine intra-scanline search procedure with a cooperative process for enforcing inter-scanline consistency, and Ohta and Kanade (1985), who use dynamic programming for both intra- and inter-scanline optimization, the latter procedure being conducted in a three-dimensional search space. Figure 7.15 shows a sample result taken from Ohta and Kanade (1985).

7.5.2 Smoothness Constraints and Combinatorial Optimization over Graphs

Dynamic programming is a *combinatorial optimization* algorithm aimed at minimizing an error function (a path cost) over some discrete variables (correspondences between pairs of features). It was used in the previous section to incorporate ordering constraints in the matching process. We now present a different approach to stereo fusion that relies instead on smoothness constraints, and a different combinatorial optimization technique aimed at minimizing certain energy functions defined over graphs.

---

[2]Our version of the algorithm assumes that all edges are matched. To account for noise and edge-detection errors, it is reasonable to allow the matching algorithm to skip a bounded number of edges, but this does not change its asymptotic complexity (Ohta and Kanade 1985).

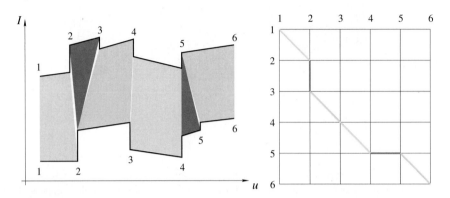

FIGURE 7.14: Dynamic programming and stereopsis: The **left** part of the figure shows two intensity profiles along matching epipolar lines. The polygons joining the two profiles indicate matches between successive intervals (some of the matched intervals may have zero length). The **right** part of the diagram represents the same information in graphical form: an arc (thick line segment) joins two nodes (i, i') and (j, j') when the intervals (i, j) and (i', j') of the intensity profiles match each other.

We assume the scanlines have m and n edge points, respectively (the endpoints of the scanlines are included for convenience). Two auxiliary functions are used: Inferior-Neighbors(k, l) returns the list of neighbors (i, j) of the node (k, l) such that $i \leq k$ and $j \leq l$, and Arc-Cost(i, j, k, l) evaluates and returns the cost of matching the intervals (i, k) and (j, l). For correctness, $C(1, 1)$ should be initialized with a value of zero.

% Loop over all nodes (k, l) in ascending order.
for $k = 1$ to m do
  for $l = 1$ to n do
    % Initialize optimal cost $C(k, l)$ and backward pointer $B(k, l)$.
    $C(k, l) \leftarrow +\infty; B(k, l) \leftarrow$ nil;
    % Loop over all inferior neighbors (i, j) of (k, l).
    for $(i, j) \in$ Inferior-Neighbors(k, l) do
      % Compute new path cost and update backward pointer if necessary.
      $d \leftarrow C(i, j) +$ Arc-Cost(i, j, k, l);
      if $d < C(k, l)$ then $C(k, l) \leftarrow d; B(k, l) \leftarrow (i, j)$ endif;
      endfor;
    endfor;
  endfor;
% Construct optimal path by following backward pointers from (m, n).
$P \leftarrow \{(m, n)\}; (i, j) \leftarrow (m, n)$;
while $B(i, j) \neq$ nil do $(i, j) \leftarrow B(i, j); P \leftarrow \{(i, j)\} \cup P$ endwhile.

Algorithm 7.2: A Dynamic-Programming Algorithm for Establishing Stereo Correspondences Between Two Corresponding Scanlines.

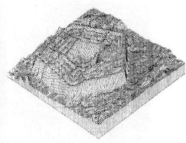

FIGURE 7.15: Two images of the Pentagon and an isometric plot of the disparity map computed by the dynamic-programming algorithm of Ohta and Kanade (1985). *Reprinted from "Stereo by Intra- and Inter-Scanline Search," by Y. Ohta and T. Kanade, IEEE Transactions on Pattern Analysis and Machine Intelligence, 7(2):139–154, (1985).* © *1985 IEEE.*

Let us assume as usual that the two input images have been rectified, and define a graph $\mathcal{G} = (\mathcal{V}, \mathcal{E})$ whose n nodes are the pixels of the first image and whose edges link pairs of adjacent pixels on the image grid (not necessarily on the same scanline). Given some allowed disparity range $\mathcal{D} = \{-K, \ldots, K\} \subset \mathbb{Z}$, we can define an energy function $E : \mathcal{D}^n \to \mathbb{R}$ by

$$E(\boldsymbol{d}) = \sum_{p \in \mathcal{V}} U_p(d_p) + \sum_{(p,q) \in \mathcal{E}} B_{pq}(d_p, d_q), \qquad (7.4)$$

where $\boldsymbol{d}$ is a vector of n integer disparities d_p associated with pixels p, $U_p(d_p)$ (*unary term*) measures the discrepancy between pixel p in the left image and pixel $p + d_p$ in the second one, and $B_{pq}(d_p, d_q)$ (*binary term*) measures the discrepancy between the pair of assignments $p \to p + d_p$ and $q \to q + d_q$.[3] The first of these terms records the similarity between p and $p + dp$. It may be, for example, the sum of squared differences $U_p(d_p) = \sum_{q \in \mathcal{N}(p)} [I(q) - I'(q + dp)]^2$, where $\mathcal{N}(p)$ is some neighborhood of p. The second one is used to *regularize* the optimization process, making sure that the disparity function is smooth enough. For example, a sensible choice may be $B_{pq}(d_p, d_q) = \gamma_{pq} |d_p - d_q|$ for some $\gamma_{pq} > 0$.

Under this model, binocular fusion can be formulated as the minimization of $E(\boldsymbol{d})$ with respect to $\boldsymbol{d}$ in $\mathcal{D}^n$. As discussed in Chapter 22 (Section 22.4), this is a particular instance of a general combinatorial optimization problem, related to maximum a posteriori (MAP) inference in first-order Markov random fields (Geman and Geman 1984), which is in general NP-hard but admits effective approximate and even exact algorithmic solutions under certain so-called *submodularity* assumptions. In particular, it can be shown (Ishikawa 2003; Schlesinger & Flach 2006; Darbon 2009) that when $B_{pq}(d_p, d_q) = \gamma_{pq} |d_p - d_q|$ for some $\gamma_{pq} > 0$ (*total-variation prior*) or, more generally, when $B_{pq} = g(d_p - d_q)$ for some convex real function $g : \mathbb{Z} \to \mathbb{R}$, minimizing $E(\boldsymbol{d})$ reduces to a submodular *quadratic pseudo-Boolean problem* that involves only binary variables and can be solved *exactly* in polynomial

---

[3]Here we abuse the notation and, if the images coordinates of pixel p are (u_p, v_p), denote by $p + d_p$ the pixel with coordinates $(u_p + d_p, v_p)$.

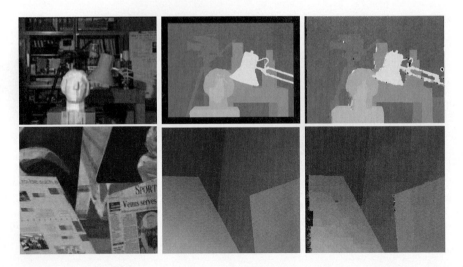

FIGURE 7.16: An application of alpha expansion to stereo fusion. The data used in this experiment is part of the benchmark described in Scharstein and Szeliski (2002), for which ground truth disparities are available. From **left** to **right**: Input image, ground truth disparities, and disparities recovered using alpha expansion. *Reprinted from "A Taxonomy and Evaluation of Dense Two-Frame Stereo Correspondence Algorithms," by D. Scharstein and R. Szeliski, International Journal of Computer Vision, 47(1/2/3):7–42, (2002).* © *2002 Springer.*

time by an efficient *min-cut/max-flow* algorithm (Ford & Fulkerson 1956; Goldberg & Tarjan 1988; Boykov & Kolmogorov 2004).

In practice, however, it may prove important to use binary terms that do not lead to submodular problems and thus cannot be solved in an exact manner. The Potts model, where $B_{pq}(d_p, d_q) = \gamma_{pq} \chi(d_p \neq d_q)$, the characteristic function χ is one if its argument is true and zero otherwise, and $\gamma_{pq} > 0$, is a typical example. Using it instead of, say, a total-variation prior to encourage the disparity function to be smooth, does not overpenalize the disparity discontinuities naturally associated with occlusion boundaries. In this setting, an *approximate* solution to the minimization of $E(\boldsymbol{d})$ over $\mathcal{D}^n$ can be found using *alpha expansion* (Boykov *et al.* 2001), an iterative procedure that also solves a min-cut/max-flow problem at each step, but makes weaker assumptions on the energy function it minimizes. Figure 7.16 shows the result of an experiment using this approach, taken from Scharstein and Szeliski (2002).

7.6   USING MORE CAMERAS

Adding a third camera eliminates (in large part) the ambiguity inherent in two-view point matching. In essence, the third image can be used to check hypothetical matches between the first two pictures (Figure 7.17): The three-dimensional point associated with such a match is first reconstructed and then reprojected into the third image. If no compatible point lies nearby, then the match must be wrong.

In most trinocular stereo algorithms, potential correspondences are hypothe-

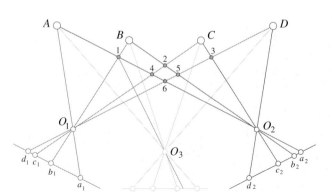

FIGURE 7.17: The small gray discs indicate the incorrect reconstructions associated with the left and right images of four points. The addition of a central camera removes the matching ambiguity: none of the corresponding rays intersects any of the six discs. Alternatively, matches between points in the first two images can be checked by reprojecting the corresponding three-dimensional point in the third image. For example, the match between b_1 and a_2 is obviously wrong because there is no feature point in the third image near the reprojection of the hypothetical reconstruction numbered 1 in the diagram.

sized using two of the images, then confirmed or rejected using the third one. In contrast, Okutami and Kanade (1993) have proposed to find matches simultaneously in three or more pictures. The basic idea is simple, but elegant: assuming that all the images have been rectified, the search for the correct disparities is replaced by a search for the correct depth, or rather its inverse. Of course, the inverse depth is proportional to the disparity for each camera, but the disparity varies from camera to camera, and the inverse depth can be used as a common search index. Picking the first image as a reference, Okutami and Kanade add the sums of squared differences associated with all other cameras into a global evaluation function E (as shown earlier, this is of course equivalent to adding the correlation functions associated with the images).

Figure 7.18 plots the value of E as a function of inverse depth for various subsets of 10 cameras observing a scene that contains a repetitive pattern (Figure 7.19). In that case, using only two or three cameras does not yield a single, well-defined minimum. However, adding more cameras provides a clear minimum corresponding to the correct match. Figure 7.19 shows a sequence of 10 rectified images and a plot of the surface reconstructed by the algorithm.

7.7 APPLICATION: ROBOT NAVIGATION

Applications of *wide-baseline* multi-view stereopsis to the construction of three-dimensional object and scene models are discussed in Chapter 19. Let us briefly discuss here an application of binocular stereo vision to navigation for the robot shown in Figure 7.1 (right). The system described in Hadsell *et al.* (2009) and Sermanet *et al.* (2009) uses two Point Grey Bumblebee stereo cameras, each capable of delivering a pair of 1024×768 color images at 15 frames per second, and runs a

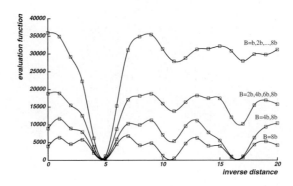

FIGURE 7.18: Combining multiple views: The sum of squared differences is plotted here as a function of the inverse depth for various numbers of input pictures. The data are taken from a scanline near the top of the images shown in Figure 7.19, whose intensity is nearly periodic. The diagram clearly shows that the minimum of the function becomes less and less ambiguous as more images are added. *Reprinted from "A Multiple-Baseline Stereo System," by M. Okutami and T. Kanade, IEEE Transactions on Pattern Analysis and Machine Intelligence, 15(4):353–363, (1993). © 1993 IEEE.*

separate binocular stereo process for each pair (Figure 7.20). The fusion algorithm itself is local, and uses the sum of absolute differences as a matching criterion, with additional heuristics to filter out outliers. The ground plane is then found by a voting procedure before obstacles are detected, based on the recovered point cloud distribution. The overall process runs at 5–10 160×120 frames per second, but its useful range is limited to 5 meters. A slower program (one 512×384 frame per second), combining stereo vision with *convolutional nets* used for classification, yields useful depth measurements for distances up to 12 meters, and detects obstacles up to 50 meters away. The overall system has been successfully used to drive the robot in field experiments with many outdoor settings, including parks and backyards, open fields, urban and suburban environments, military bases, sandy areas near beaches, forests with and without paths, etc. See (Hadsell *et al.* 2009; Sermanet *et al.* 2009) for details.

7.8   NOTES

The essential matrix as an algebraic form of the epipolar constraint was introduced in the computer vision community by Longuet-Higgins (1981), and its properties have been elucidated by Huang and Faugeras (1989). The fundamental matrix was introduced by Luong and Faugeras (1992, 1996). Just as a bilinear constraint holds for the image coordinates of two point matches, trilinear constraints hold among matching triples of points (Hartley 1997) and lines (Spetsakis & Aloimonos 1990; Weng, Huang & Ahuja 1992; Shashua 1995), and quadrilinear constraints also hold among matching quadruples of points (Faugeras and Mourrain 1995; Triggs 1995; Faugeras & Papadopoulo 1997). See the problems for some examples. Similar constraints have also been studied for decades in the photogrammetry domain (Slama *et al.* 1980).

The fact that disparity gives rise to stereopsis in human beings was first

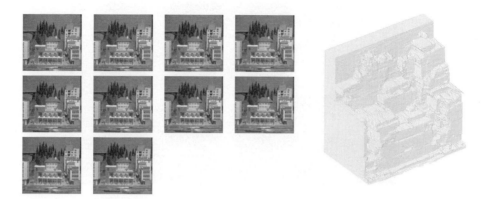

FIGURE 7.19: A series of 10 images and the corresponding reconstruction. The gridboard near the top of the images is the source for the nearly periodic brightness signal giving rise to ambiguities in Figure 7.18. *Reprinted from "A Multiple-Baseline Stereo System," by M. Okutami and T. Kanade, IEEE Transactions on Pattern Analysis and Machine Intelligence, 15(4):353–363, (1993).* © *1993 IEEE.*

demonstrated by Wheatstone's (1838) invention of the stereoscope. That disparity is sufficient for stereopsis without eye movements was demonstrated shortly afterward by Dove (1841) with illumination provided by an electric spark too brief for eye vergence to take place. Human stereopsis is further discussed in the classical book of Helmholtz (1909), an amazing read for anyone interested in the history of the field, as well as the books by Julesz (1960, 1971), Frisby (1980), and Marr (1982). Theories of human binocular perception not presented in this chapter for lack of space include Koenderink and Van Doorn (1976a), Pollard, Mayhew, and Frisby (1970), McKee, Levi, and Brown (1990), and Anderson and Nayakama (1994).

Excellent treatments of machine stereopsis can be found in the books of Grimson (1981b), Marr (1982), Horn (1986), and Faugeras (1993). Marr focuses on the computational aspects of human stereo vision, whereas Horn's account emphasizes the role of photogrammetry in artificial stereo systems. Grimson and Faugeras emphasize the geometric and algorithmic aspects of stereopsis. The constraints associated with stereo matching are discussed by Binford (1984). Early techniques for line matching in binocular stereo include Medioni and Nevatia (1984) and Ayache and Faugeras (1987). Algorithms for trinocular fusion include Milenkovic and Kanade (1985), Yachida, Kitamura, and Kimachi (1986), Ayache and Lustman (1987), and Robert and Faugeras (1991). Global approaches to dense stereo fusion based on combinatorial optimization and the underlying min-cut/max-flow algorithms include Ishikawa and Geiger (1998), Roy and Cox (1998), Boykov, Veksler, and Zabih (2001), and Kolgomorov and Zabih (2001). Variational approaches have also been used in this context, see Faugeras and Keriven (1998) for example.

All of the algorithms presented in this chapter (implicitly) assume that the images being fused are quite similar. This is equivalent to considering a *narrow baseline*. The *wide-baseline* case is treated in Chapter 19 in the context of image-based modeling and rendering. We have also limited our attention here to stereo rigs with

FIGURE 7.20: Robot navigation using the approach proposed in Hadsell *et al.* (2009) and Sermanet *et al.* (2009). The detected ground plane (lighter shade) and obstacles (darker one) are overlaid on one of the input images as well as a top view of the stereo reconstruction. Image courtesy of Yann LeCun.

fixed intrinsic and extrinsic parameters. *Active vision* is concerned with the construction of vision systems capable of dynamically modifying these parameters, e.g., changing camera zoom and vergence angles, and taking advantage of these capabilities in perceptual and robotic tasks (Aloimonos, Weiss & Bandyopadhyay 1987; Bajcsy 1988; Ahuja & Abbott 1993; Brunnström, Ekhlund, & Uhlin 1996).

Finally, let us mention the very useful resource assembled by D. Scharstein and R. Szeliski at `http://vision.middlebury.edu/stereo/`. One can find there benchmark data, an evaluation of various algorithms on this data, and code for many classical approaches to stereo fusion. See the web-site and Scharstein and Szeliski (2002) for details.

PROBLEMS

7.1. Show that one of the singular values of an essential matrix is 0 and the other two are equal. (Huang and Faugeras [1989] have shown that the converse is also true; that is, any 3×3 matrix with one singular value equal to 0 and the other two equal to each other is an essential matrix.)

Hint: The singular values of $\mathcal{E}$ are the eigenvalues of $\mathcal{E}\mathcal{E}^T$ (Chapter 22).

7.2. *Infinitesimal epipolar geometry.* Here we consider the case of *infinitesimal* camera displacements, and derive the instantaneous form of the Longuet–Higgins relation, Equation (7.2), which captures the epipolar geometry in the discrete case.

(a) We consider a moving camera with translational velocity $\boldsymbol{v}$ and rotational velocity $\boldsymbol{\omega}$. The matrix associated with the rotation whose axis is the unit vector $\boldsymbol{a}$ and whose angle is θ can be shown to be equal to

$$\mathcal{R} = e^{\theta[\boldsymbol{a}_\times]} \stackrel{\text{def}}{=} \sum_{i=0}^{+\infty} \frac{1}{i!}(\theta[\boldsymbol{a}_\times])^i.$$

Consider two frames separated by a small time interval δt, and denote by $\dot{\boldsymbol{p}} = (\dot{u}, \dot{v}, 0)^T$ the velocity of the point p, or *motion field*. Use this *expo-*

nential representation of rotation matrices to show that (to first order):

$$
\begin{cases}
\boldsymbol{t} = \delta t\,\boldsymbol{v}, \\
\mathcal{R} = \mathrm{Id} + \delta t\,[\boldsymbol{\omega}_\times], \\
\boldsymbol{p}' = \boldsymbol{p} + \delta t\,\dot{\boldsymbol{p}}.
\end{cases}
\tag{7.5}
$$

(b) Use this result to show that Equation (7.2) reduces to

$$
\boldsymbol{p}^T([\boldsymbol{v}_\times][\boldsymbol{\omega}_\times])\boldsymbol{p} - (\boldsymbol{p} \times \dot{\boldsymbol{p}}) \cdot \boldsymbol{v} = 0.
\tag{7.6}
$$

for infinitesimal motions.

7.3. *The focus of expansion.* Consider an infinitesimal translational motion ($\boldsymbol{\omega} = \boldsymbol{0}$). We define the *focus of expansion* (or *infinitesimal epipole*) as the point where the line passing through the optical center and parallel to the velocity vector $\boldsymbol{v}$ pierces the image plane. Use Equation (7.6) to show that the motion field points toward the focus expansion in this pure translational case.

7.4. How does one rectify a stereo pair of images?

7.5. Show that, in the case of a rectified pair of images, the depth of a point P in the normalized coordinate system attached to the first camera is $Z = -B/d$, where B is the baseline and d is the disparity.

7.6. Use the definition of disparity to characterize the accuracy of stereo reconstruction as a function of baseline and depth.

7.7. The epipolar constraint plays a fundamental role in stereo vision and motion analysis. How are the epipoles defined? Explain briefly how the epipoles of the two cameras are determined from correspondences.

7.8. How is dynamic programming used in stereopsis?

7.9. Show that the correlation function reaches its maximum value of 1 when the image brightnesses of the two windows are related by the affine transform $I' = \lambda I + \mu$ for some constants λ and μ with $\lambda > 0$.

7.10. Use the result of the previous exercise to describe situations where correlation-based matching should fail.

7.11. Recursive computation of the correlation function.
   (a) Show that $(\boldsymbol{w} - \bar{\boldsymbol{w}}) \cdot (\boldsymbol{w}' - \bar{\boldsymbol{w}}') = \boldsymbol{w} \cdot \boldsymbol{w}' - (2m + 1)(2n + 1)\bar{I}\bar{I}'$.
   (b) Show that the average intensity $\bar{I}$ can be computed recursively, and estimate the cost of the incremental computation.
   (c) Generalize the prior calculations to all elements involved in the construction of the correlation function, and estimate the overall cost of correlation over a pair of images.

7.12. Show how a first-order expansion of the disparity function for rectified images can be used to warp the window of the right image corresponding to a rectangular region of the left one. Show how to compute correlation in this case using interpolation to estimate right-image values at the locations corresponding to the centers of the left window's pixels.

7.13. *Trifocal and quadrifocal matching constraints.* We show in this exercise the existence of trilinear and quadrilinear constraints that must be satisfied by matching points in three or four images, and generalize the epipolar constraint to that case.
   (a) Suppose that we have four views of a point, with known intrinsic parameters and projection matrices $\mathcal{M}_i$ ($i = 1, 2, 3, 4$). Write an 8×4 homogeneous system of linear equations in the coordinate vector $\boldsymbol{P}$ in $\mathbb{R}^4$ of this point that must be satisfied by its projections into the four images.

Hint: Rewrite each projection equation as two linear equations in P, parameterized by the corresponding projection matrix and image coordinates.

(b) Use the fact that this homogeneous system of linear equations has P as a nontrivial solution to characterize matching constraints using two, three or four images.

Hint: Use determinants.

(c) Show that the conditions involving two images (say, the first and second one) reduces to the epipolar constraints of Equation (7.2) when we take $\mathcal{M}_1 = (\mathrm{Id} \quad \mathbf{0})$ and $\mathcal{M}_2 = (\mathcal{R}^T \quad -\mathcal{R}^T \mathbf{t})$.

(d) Show that the conditions involving three images are trilinear in the image coordinates and derive an explicit form for these conditions when $\mathcal{M}_1 = (\mathrm{Id} \quad \mathbf{0})$, $\mathcal{M}_2 = (\mathcal{R}_2^T \quad -\mathcal{R}_2^T \mathbf{t}_2)$, and $\mathcal{M}_3 = (\mathcal{R}_3^T \quad -\mathcal{R}_3^T \mathbf{t}_3)$.

(e) Show that the conditions involving four images are quadrilinear in the image coordinates.

(f) Can you imagine a method for deriving matching constraints involving more than four images?

7.14. Generalize the constructions of the previous problem to the uncalibrated case.

PROGRAMMING EXERCISES

7.15. Implement the rectification process.

7.16. Implement a correlation-based approach to stereopsis.

7.17. Implement a multi-scale approach to stereopsis.

7.18. Implement a dynamic-programming approach to stereopsis.

7.19. Implement a trinocular approach to stereopsis.

C H A P T E R   8

Structure from Motion

This chapter revisits the problem of estimating the three-dimensional shape of a scene from multiple pictures. In the context of stereopsis, the cameras used to acquire the input images are normally calibrated so their intrinsic parameters are known, and their extrinsic ones have been determined relative to some fixed world coordinate system. This greatly simplifies the reconstruction process and explains the emphasis put on binocular (or, more generally, multi-view) fusion in Chapter 7. We consider here a different setting where the cameras' positions and possibly their intrinsic parameters are *a priori* unknown and might change over time. This is typical of the *image-based modeling and rendering* applications discussed in Chapter 19, where images recorded by a handheld camcorder or multiple cameras scattered through a scene are used to capture its shape and render it under new viewing conditions. This is also relevant for active vision systems whose calibration parameters vary dynamically, and planetary robot probes for which these parameters may change due to the large accelerations at takeoff and landing. Recovering the cameras' positions is of course just as important as estimating the scene shape in the context of mobile robot navigation.

We assume in the rest of this chapter that the projections of n points have been matched across m pictures,[1] and focus instead on the purely geometric *structure-from-motion* (or *SFM* for short) problem of using this information to estimate both the three-dimensional positions of the points in some fixed coordinate system (the scene *structure*) and the projection matrices associated with the cameras observing them (or, equivalently, the apparant *motion* of the cameras relative to the points). Figure 8.1 shows a small dataset, consisting of 38 points matched in a six-image sequence of a toy house, courtesy of Françoise Veillon and Roger Mohr. Ground-truth data available for the 3D position of these points is used in the quantitative evaluation of most of the algorithms presented in the rest of this chapter.

We address in turn three instances of the structure-from-motion problem. We start in Section 8.1 with the case where the cameras are *internally calibrated*—that is, their intrinsic parameters are known, so it is possible to work in normalized image coordinates. We turn our attention to completely uncalibrated weak-perspective and perspective cameras in Sections 8.2 and 8.3.

8.1 INTERNALLY CALIBRATED PERSPECTIVE CAMERAS

Let us first consider m pinhole perspective cameras with known intrinsic parameters but unknown spatial configurations, observing a scene that consists of n fixed points P_j $(j = 1, \ldots, n)$. We work in normalized image coordinates, and assume that correspondences have been established between the m images, so the mn *homogeneous* coordinate vectors $\boldsymbol{p}_{ij} = \hat{\boldsymbol{p}}_{ij} = (x_{ij}, y_{ij}, 1)^T$ $(i = 1, \ldots, m)$ of the projections of the

---

[1]Methods for establishing such correspondences across both continuous image sequences and scattered views of a scene are discussed in Chapters 11 and 12.

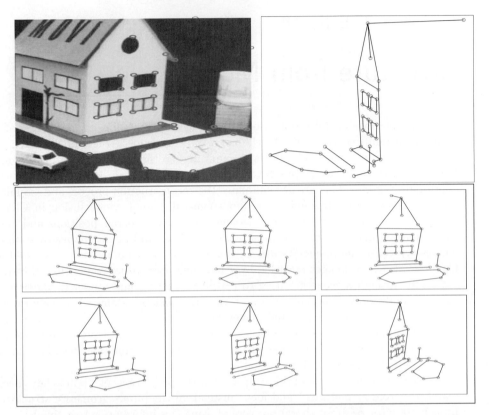

FIGURE 8.1: The house dataset. **Top left:** One frame in the sequence, with the matched points overlaid as small circles. **Top right:** A "wireframe" display of the corresponding ground-truth 3D points, observed from some arbitrary viewpoint, with line segments drawn between some of the points. **Bottom:** Wireframe views of the 38 data points matched in six images. The line segments shown in these pictures do not correspond to physical edges, and are never used in any computation. However, wireframe views are useful to visually compare various reconstructions of the scene's structure and epipolar geometry. Data and image courtesy of Françoise Veillon and Roger Mohr.

points P_j are known. Because the cameras are internally calibrated, we can write the corresponding perspective projection equations as

$$\boldsymbol{p}_{ij} = \frac{1}{Z_{ij}} \begin{pmatrix} \mathcal{R}_i & \boldsymbol{t}_i \end{pmatrix} \begin{pmatrix} \boldsymbol{P}_j \\ 1 \end{pmatrix}, \tag{8.1}$$

where $\mathcal{R}_i$ and $\boldsymbol{t}_i$ are respectively the rotation matrix and the translation vector representing the position and orientation of camera number i in some fixed coordinate system, $\boldsymbol{P}_j$ is the *nonhomogeneous* coordinate vector of the point P_j in that coordinate system, and Z_{ij} is the depth of that point relative to camera number i.

We define *Euclidean structure from motion* as the problem of estimating the n vectors $\boldsymbol{P}_j$, together with the m rotation matrices $\mathcal{R}_i$ and translation vectors $\boldsymbol{t}_i$, from the mn image correspondences $\boldsymbol{p}_{ij}$.[2]

8.1.1   Natural Ambiguity of the Problem

Before trying to solve this problem, let us first observe that its solution is, at best, defined up to a *rigid transformation ambiguity*. Indeed, given some arbitrary rotation matrix $\mathcal{R}$ and translation vector $\boldsymbol{t}$, we can rewrite Equation (8.1) as

$$\boldsymbol{p}_{ij} = \frac{1}{Z_{ij}} \left((\mathcal{R}_i \quad \boldsymbol{t}_i) \begin{pmatrix} \mathcal{R} & \boldsymbol{t} \\ \boldsymbol{0}^T & 1 \end{pmatrix} \right) \left(\begin{pmatrix} \mathcal{R}^T & -\mathcal{R}^T\boldsymbol{t} \\ \boldsymbol{0}^T & 1 \end{pmatrix} \begin{pmatrix} \boldsymbol{P}_j \\ 1 \end{pmatrix} \right) = \frac{1}{Z_{ij}} (\mathcal{R}'_i \quad \boldsymbol{t}'_i) \begin{pmatrix} \boldsymbol{P}'_j \\ 1 \end{pmatrix},$$

where $\mathcal{R}'_i = \mathcal{R}_i\mathcal{R}$, $\boldsymbol{t}'_i = \mathcal{R}_i\boldsymbol{t} + \boldsymbol{t}_i$, and $\boldsymbol{P}'_j = \mathcal{R}^T(\boldsymbol{P}_j - \boldsymbol{t})$. (Note that because $\mathcal{R}_i$ and $\mathcal{R}$ are rotations, so are $\mathcal{R}'_i$ and $\mathcal{R}^T$: as mentioned in Chapter 1, rotation matrices form a multiplicative group.)

This ambiguity simply stems from the fact that the structure and motion parameters consistent with image data can be expressed in different Euclidean frames, separated from each other by rigid transformations. Perhaps more surprisingly, it is in fact also impossible to recover the absolute scale of the observed scene, since we can rewrite Equation (8.1) as

$$\boldsymbol{p}_{ij} = \frac{1}{\lambda Z_{ij}} (\mathcal{R}_i \quad \lambda\boldsymbol{t}_i) \begin{pmatrix} \lambda\boldsymbol{P}_j \\ 1 \end{pmatrix} = \frac{1}{Z'_{ij}} (\mathcal{R}_i \quad \boldsymbol{t}'_i) \begin{pmatrix} \boldsymbol{P}'_j \\ 1 \end{pmatrix},$$

where λ is an arbitrary *positive* nonzero scalar (because the sign of the depth of a point lying in front of a camera must always be negative), $\boldsymbol{t}'_i = \lambda\boldsymbol{t}_i$, $\boldsymbol{P}'_j = \lambda\boldsymbol{P}_j$, and $Z'_{ij} = \lambda Z_{ij}$. Intuitively, this corresponds to a well-known property of perspective projection, already noted in Chapter 1: the apparent size of objects depends on their distance from the cameras observing them, and an object twice as large as another one will not appear any larger if it is twice as far.

The solution of the Euclidean SFM problem is thus defined only up to an arbitrary *similarity*—that is, a rigid transformation followed by an isotropic positive scaling. Like rotations, rigid transformations form a group under composition (and so do their 4×4 matrix representations under multiplication, of course). They map points onto points and lines onto lines, and preserve incidence relations—that is, the point where two lines (or, say, a line and a plane) intersect maps onto the intersection of their images, as well as angles, distances, and parallelism. Similarities form a group and include rigid transformations as a subgroup, sharing most of their properties, but not preserving distances. Instead, they preserve the ratio of distances measured along arbitrary directions. Because similarities form a group, it makes sense to talk about the *Euclidean shape* of a set of points as the equivalence class formed by all copies of these points related by these transformations (some authors use the term *metric shape*). See the problems at the end of this chapter.

In particular, Euclidean structure from motion can be thought of as the recovery of the Euclidean shape of the observed scene, along with the corresponding perspective projection matrices. Since Equation (8.1) provides $2mn$ constraints on

---

[2] As already noted in Chapter 1, the depths of the observed points relative to the cameras are *not* independent unknowns, because $Z_{ij} = \boldsymbol{r}_{i3} \cdot \boldsymbol{P}_j + t_{i3}$, where $\boldsymbol{r}_{i3}^T$ is the third row vector of the matrix $\mathcal{R}_i$, and t_{i3} is the third coordinate of the vector $\boldsymbol{t}_i$.

the $6m$ extrinsic parameters of the matrices $\mathcal{M}_i$ and the $3n$ parameters of the vectors $\boldsymbol{P}_j$, taking into account the ambiguity of this problem suggests that it admits a finite number of solutions as soon as $2mn \geq 6m + 3n - 7$. For $m = 2$, five point correspondences should thus be sufficient to determine (up to a similarity) a finite number of projection matrix pairs and the positions of all scene points.

In practice, $2mn$ is in general (much) greater than $6m + 3n - 7$, and Equation (8.1) does not admit an exact solution. Instead, an approximate solution can be found by minimizing the mean-squared error

$$E = \frac{1}{mn} \sum_{i,j} ||\boldsymbol{p}_{ij} - \frac{1}{Z_{ij}} (\mathcal{R}_i \quad \boldsymbol{t}_i) \binom{\boldsymbol{P}_j}{1}||^2 \tag{8.2}$$

with respect to the $6m + 3n - 7$ structure and motion parameters using the *nonlinear least squares* optimization techniques described in Chapter 22. The main problem with this approach is that these techniques require a reasonable initial guess to converge to something close to the global minimum of the error function they attempt to minimize. Reliable methods for finding such guesses are thus required.

8.1.2   Euclidean Structure and Motion from Two Images

We present in this section simple methods for computing the projection matrices associated with two cameras, which in turn allows the reconstruction of the associated scene points using triangulation. These techniques take as input the corresponding essential or fundamental matrices, so we first address the problem of estimating the epipolar geometry from point correspondences, a problem known as *weak calibration*.

Weak Calibration.   An essential matrix can be written as $\mathcal{E} = [\boldsymbol{t}_\times]\mathcal{R}$, and can thus be parameterized by two translation parameters ($\boldsymbol{t}$ is defined only up to scale) and three rotation angles. Each correspondence between points $\boldsymbol{p}$ and $\boldsymbol{p}'$ observed in two images provide one constraint $\boldsymbol{p}^T \mathcal{E} \boldsymbol{p}' = 0$ on these parameters, and thus one can expect that $\mathcal{E}$ can be estimated (perhaps up to some discrete ambiguity) from a minimum of five correspondences. Such five-point solutions to the weak calibration problem do exist (Nistér 2004), but they are too involved to be described here. We focus here on the simpler case where a redundant set of $n \geq 8$ point correspondences are available. When the internal camera parameters are *a priori* unknown, the output of weak calibration is an estimate of the fundamental matrix. On the other hand, when they are known and normalized image coordinates are used in the estimation process, additional constraints come into play, and an estimate of the essential matrix is obtained.

Let us start with the uncalibrated case. The epipolar constraint can be written as

$$\boldsymbol{p}^T \mathcal{F} \boldsymbol{p}' = [u, v, 1] \begin{pmatrix} F_{11} & F_{12} & F_{13} \\ F_{21} & F_{22} & F_{23} \\ F_{31} & F_{32} & F_{33} \end{pmatrix} \begin{pmatrix} u' \\ v' \\ 1 \end{pmatrix} = 0. \tag{8.3}$$

Given $n \geq 8$ point correspondences $p_j \leftrightarrow p'_j$ ($j = 1, \ldots, n$), we can rewrite the corresponding instances of Equation (8.3) as an $n \times 9$ system of homogeneous linear equations $\mathcal{U}\boldsymbol{f} = \boldsymbol{0}$ in the unknown entries of the fundamental matrix, where

$$
\mathcal{U} = \begin{pmatrix} x_1 x_1' & x_1 y_1' & x_1 & y_1 x_1' & y_1 y_1' & y_1 & x_1' & y_1' & 1 \\ x_2 x_2' & x_2 y_2' & x_2 & y_2 x_2' & y_2 y_2' & y_2 & x_2' & y_2' & 1 \\ \cdots & \cdots & \cdots & \cdots & \cdots & \cdots & \cdots & \cdots & \cdots \\ x_n x_n' & x_n y_n' & x_n & y_n x_n' & y_n y_n' & y_n & x_8' & y_n' & 1 \end{pmatrix} \quad \text{and} \quad \boldsymbol{f} = \begin{pmatrix} F_{11} \\ F_{12} \\ F_{13} \\ F_{21} \\ F_{22} \\ F_{23} \\ F_{31} \\ F_{32} \\ F_{33} \end{pmatrix}.
$$

Solving this equation in the least-squares sense amounts to minimizing

$$
E = \frac{1}{n}||\mathcal{U}\boldsymbol{f}||^2 = \frac{1}{n}\sum_{i=1}^{n}(\boldsymbol{p}_i^T \mathcal{F}\boldsymbol{p}_i')^2 \tag{8.4}
$$

with respect to the unknown entries of $\boldsymbol{f}$ (or equivalently of $\mathcal{F}$) under the constraint $||\boldsymbol{f}||^2 = 1$. As shown in Chapter 22, the solution is the eigenvector $\boldsymbol{f}$ associated with the smallest eigenvalue of $\mathcal{U}^T\mathcal{U}$.[3]

With exactly eight points, this method fails when the $n \times 9$ matrix $\mathcal{U}$ has a rank strictly smaller than eight. As shown in Faugeras (1993) and the problems, this happens only when the eight points and two optical centers lie on a quadric surface. Fortunately, this is quite unlikely because a quadric surface is completely determined by nine points, which means that there is generally no quadric that passes through these 10 points.

The least-squares error E defined by Equation (8.4) does not have an obvious geometric interpretation. Thus it may be preferable to minimize instead the mean-squared geometric distance between the image points and the corresponding epipolar lines—that is,

$$
\frac{1}{n}\sum_{i=1}^{n}[\mathrm{d}^2(\boldsymbol{p}_i, \mathcal{F}\boldsymbol{p}_i') + \mathrm{d}^2(\boldsymbol{p}_i', \mathcal{F}^T\boldsymbol{p}_i)],
$$

where $d(\boldsymbol{p}, \boldsymbol{l})$ denotes the (signed) Euclidean distance between the point $\boldsymbol{p}$ and the line $\boldsymbol{l}$, and $\mathcal{F}\boldsymbol{p}'$ and $\mathcal{F}^T\boldsymbol{p}$ are the epipolar lines associated with $\boldsymbol{p}'$ and $\boldsymbol{p}$. This is a nonlinear problem, but the minimization can be initialized with the result of the linear algorithm. This method, first proposed in Luong, Deriche, and Faugeras (Luong et al. 1993), gives much better results than the linear one.

Hartley (1995) has proposed instead to *normalize* the linear algorithm, observing that its poor performance is due, for the most part, to poor numerical conditioning.[4] He suggests translating and scaling the data so they are centered at

---

[3]We have ignored here the fact that $\mathcal{F}$ should be singular. When taking the nonlinear constraint $\mathrm{Det}(\mathcal{F}) = 0$ into account, it is in fact possible to compute $\mathcal{F}$ from seven correspondences (see problems).

[4]The columns of $\mathcal{U}$ have widely different scales for typical pictures where mean image coordinates might be, say, about 500 pixels. See the problems for an alternative to Hartley's method that also handles this issue.

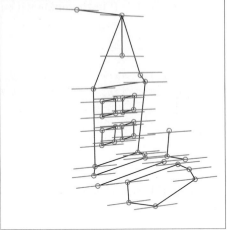

FIGURE 8.2: Weak-calibration experiment using two images of the house sequence and a linear least-squares implementation of weak calibration, together with Hartley's normalization. The mean distances between the points and the corresponding epipolar lines are 0.96 and 0.90 pixels for these two images. Without the normalization, they become 10.00 and 9.12 pixels.

the origin and the average distance to the origin is $\sqrt{2}$. In practice, this normalization dramatically improves the conditioning of the linear least-squares estimation process. Concretely, the algorithm is divided into four steps: First, transform the image coordinates using appropriate translation and scaling operators $\mathcal{T} : \boldsymbol{p}_i \to \tilde{\boldsymbol{p}}_i$ and $\mathcal{T}' : \boldsymbol{p}'_i \to \tilde{\boldsymbol{p}}'_i$. Second, use linear least squares to compute the matrix $\tilde{\mathcal{F}}$ minimizing

$$\frac{1}{n}\sum_{i=1}^{n}(\tilde{\boldsymbol{p}}_i^T \tilde{\mathcal{F}}\tilde{\boldsymbol{p}}'_i)^2.$$

Third, enforce the rank-2 constraint, as originally proposed by Tsai and Huang (1984) in the calibrated case: let $\tilde{\mathcal{F}} = \mathcal{U}\mathcal{W}\mathcal{V}^T$ be the singular value decomposition (or SVD) of $\tilde{\mathcal{F}}$, with $\mathcal{W} = \mathrm{diag}(r, s, t)$. As shown in Chapter 22, the rank-2 matrix $\bar{\mathcal{F}}$ minimizing the Frobenius norm of $\tilde{\mathcal{F}} - \bar{\mathcal{F}}$ is simply $\bar{\mathcal{F}} = \mathcal{U}\mathrm{diag}(r, s, 0)\mathcal{V}^T$. The last step of the algorithm sets $\mathcal{F} = \mathcal{T}^T\bar{\mathcal{F}}\mathcal{T}'$ as the final estimate of the fundamental matrix. Figure 8.2 shows the results of a weak-calibration experiment using this method with 38 point correspondences between two images of the toy house. The data points are shown in the figure as small discs, and the recovered epipolar lines are shown as short line segments.

As shown in Chapter 7, given the (internal) calibration matrices $\mathcal{K}$ and $\mathcal{K}'$ of two cameras and the corresponding essential matrix $\mathcal{E}$, the fundamental matrix can be written as $\mathcal{F} = \mathcal{K}^{-T}\mathcal{E}\mathcal{K}'^{-1}$. Conversely, given $\mathcal{F}$, $\mathcal{K}$, and $\mathcal{K}'$, we can compute an estimate of the essential matrix as $\mathcal{E} = \mathcal{K}^T\mathcal{F}\mathcal{K}'$. By construction, the matrix $\mathcal{E}$ has rank 2, but, due to numerical errors, its two nonzero singular values are, in general, not equal. The SVD once again proves useful in this setting: because it is impossible to recover the absolute scale of the vector $\boldsymbol{t}$ from image correspondences alone, we can take, without loss of generality, $\mathcal{E} = \mathcal{U} \operatorname{diag}(1, 1, 0)\mathcal{V}^T$, where $\mathcal{U}\mathcal{W}\mathcal{V}^T$ is this time the SVD of $\mathcal{K}^T \mathcal{F}\mathcal{K}'$.

From Essential Matrix to Camera Motion.   Let us assume from now on that the essential matrix $\mathcal{E}$ is known.   As shown in Chapter 7, given two internally calibrated cameras with projection matrices $(\operatorname{Id} \quad \mathbf{0})$ and $(\mathcal{R}^T \quad -\mathcal{R}^T t)$, the corresponding essential matrix is $\mathcal{E} = [t_\times]\mathcal{R}$. Specifying $\mathcal{R}$ and t—that is, the *camera motion* between the two views—obviously determines $\mathcal{E}$. We address in this section the inverse problem of recovering $\mathcal{R}$ and t from $\mathcal{E}$.

Because $\mathcal{E}^T = \mathcal{V} \operatorname{diag}(1, 1, 0)\mathcal{U}^T$, the nullspace of this matrix—that is, the set of all vectors v such that $\mathcal{E}^T v = \mathbf{0}$—is $\mathbb{R}u_3$, where u_3 is the third column of $\mathcal{U}$ and a unit vector. In turn, because $\mathcal{E}^T t = \mathbf{0}$, there are two possible solutions for t, defined up to *positive* scale factors, namely $t' = u_3$ and $t'' = -u_3$.

Let us now show that there are also two solutions for the rotational part of the essential matrix, namely

$$\mathcal{R}' = \mathcal{U}\mathcal{W}\mathcal{V}^T \quad \text{and} \quad \mathcal{R}'' = \mathcal{U}\mathcal{W}^T\mathcal{V}^T, \quad \text{where} \quad \mathcal{W} = \begin{pmatrix} 0 & -1 & 0 \\ 1 & 0 & 0 \\ 0 & 0 & 1 \end{pmatrix}.$$

First, let us observe that we can always assume that the orthogonal matrices $\mathcal{U}$ and $\mathcal{V}$ are rotation matrices: indeed, since the third singular value of $\mathcal{E}$ is zero, we can always replace the third column of either matrix by its opposite to make the corresponding determinant positive. The resulting decomposition of $\mathcal{E}$ is still a valid SVD. Since the matrices $\mathcal{U}$, $\mathcal{V}$, and $\mathcal{W}$ (and their transposes) are rotations, so are $\mathcal{R}'$ and $\mathcal{R}''$.

Now let u_1 and u_2 denote the first two columns of $\mathcal{U}$. Because $t' = u_3$ and U is a rotation matrix, we have $t' \times u_1 = u_2$ and $t' \times u_2 = -u_1$. In particular,

$$[t'_\times]\mathcal{R}' = \begin{pmatrix} u_2 & -u_1 & \mathbf{0} \end{pmatrix}\mathcal{W}\mathcal{V}^T = -\begin{pmatrix} u_1 & u_2 & \mathbf{0} \end{pmatrix}\mathcal{V}^T = -\mathcal{U}\operatorname{diag}(1, 1, 0)\mathcal{V}^T = -\mathcal{E}.$$

Likewise, it is easy to show that $[t'_\times]\mathcal{R}'' = \mathcal{E}$. Since $\mathcal{E}$ is defined only up to a (possibly negative) scale factor, both solutions are valid essential matrices. The same reasoning holds when t'' is used instead of t'. We therefore have four possible solutions for the camera motion. It is easy to show that only one of them places the reconstructed points in front of the two cameras (see problems). It is found by reconstructing one point and picking the solution that gives it negative depths relative to both cameras.

The Eight-Point Algorithm.   Putting weak calibration and motion estimation together, we obtain the "eight-point" algorithm for binocular motion estimation first proposed by Longuet-Higgins (1981) in the case where exactly eight point correspondences are available. The version shown in Algorithm 8.1 uses $n \geq 8$ correspondences and incorporates Hartley's normalization idea.

Figure 8.3 shows the result of an experiment involving two pictures in the house sequence from Figure 8.1. The left part of the diagram shows the reconstruction obtained by the algorithm and viewed from an arbitrary viewpoint. Its right part shows this reconstruction (solid lines) after it has been registered with the

1. **Estimate $\mathcal{F}$.**

   (a) Compute Hartley's normalization transformation $\mathcal{T}$ and $\mathcal{T}'$, and the corresponding points $\tilde{\boldsymbol{p}}_i$ and $\tilde{\boldsymbol{p}}_i'$.

   (b) Use homogeneous linear least squares to estimate the matrix $\tilde{\mathcal{F}}$ minimizing $\frac{1}{n}\sum_{i=1}^{n}(\tilde{\boldsymbol{p}}_i^T \tilde{\mathcal{F}} \tilde{\boldsymbol{p}}_i')^2$ under the constraint $||\tilde{\mathcal{F}}||_F^2 = 1$.

   (c) Compute the singular value decomposition $\mathcal{U}\mathrm{diag}(r, s, t)\mathcal{V}^T$ of $\tilde{\mathcal{F}}$, and set $\bar{\mathcal{F}} = \mathcal{U}\mathrm{diag}(r, s, 0)\mathcal{V}^T$.

   (d) Output the fundamental matrix $\mathcal{F} = \mathcal{T}^T \bar{\mathcal{F}} \mathcal{T}'$.

2. **Estimate $\mathcal{E}$.**

   (a) Compute the matrix $\tilde{\mathcal{E}} = \mathcal{K}^T \mathcal{F} \mathcal{K}'$.

   (b) Set $\mathcal{E} = \mathcal{U}\,\mathrm{diag}(1, 1, 0)\mathcal{V}^T$, where $\mathcal{U}\mathcal{W}\mathcal{V}^T$ is the singular value decomposition of the matrix $\tilde{\mathcal{E}}$.

3. **Compute $\mathcal{R}$ and t.**

   (a) Compute the rotation matrices $\mathcal{R}' = \mathcal{U}\mathcal{W}\mathcal{V}^T$ and $\mathcal{R}'' = \mathcal{U}\mathcal{W}^T\mathcal{V}^T$, and the translation vectors $\boldsymbol{t}' = \boldsymbol{u}_3$ and $\boldsymbol{t}'' = -\boldsymbol{u}_3$, where $\boldsymbol{u}_3$ is the third column of the matrix $\mathcal{U}$.

   (b) Output the combination of the rotation matrices $\mathcal{R}'$, $\mathcal{R}''$, and the translation vectors $\boldsymbol{t}'$, $\boldsymbol{t}''$ such that the reconstructed points lie in front of both cameras.

Algorithm 8.1: The Longuet-Higgins Eight-Point Algorithm for Euclidean Structure and Motion from Two Views.

ground-truth data (dashed lines) through a similarity transformation. Once registered, the mean Euclidean distance between the reconstructed and ground-truth 3D points is 0.87cm (the house is about 20cm high), or a mean relative error of 3.1% compared to the radius of a sphere bounding the points. The results of all algorithms presented in this section will be illustrated in the same format.

8.1.3 Euclidean Structure and Motion from Multiple Images

The binocular approach to Euclidean structure from motion described in the previous section does not readily generalize to multiple pictures. It is, however, a rather simple matter to stitch together the structure and motion estimates associated with different pairs of images: Consider the graph whose nodes correspond to image pairs and whose edges link two images that share at least three points. Let k and l denote the indices of two adjacent pictures in this graph, and let J_{kl} denote the set of indices of the points P_j observed in both images, with *homogeneous* coordinate vectors ${}^k P_j$ and ${}^l P_j$ in the corresponding camera frames. The 3×4 similarity transformation $\mathcal{S}_{kl}$ separating the coordinate systems associated

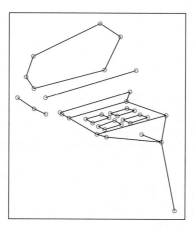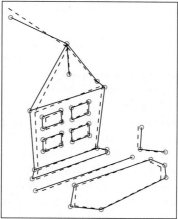

FIGURE 8.3: Euclidean reconstruction of the house from two views. The mean absolute and relative errors are respectively 0.87cm and 3.1%. See the text for details.

with these cameras can be estimated by minimizing

$$\frac{1}{n_{kl}} \sum_{j \in J_{kl}} ||^k P_j - \mathcal{S}_{kl}{}^l P_j||^2$$

with respect to the unknown rotation and translation parameters. Although this appears to be a nonlinear optimization problem, we will show in Chapter 14 that using *quaternions* to represent rotations reduces it to a simple eigenvalue problem when $|J_{kl}| \geq 3$.

Picking some arbitrary *base node* in the graph and applying this registration procedure to its neighbors, the neighbors' neighbors, etc., provides a simple method for estimating the projection matrices associated with all the nodes from the same connected component of the graph in the coordinate system of the base node. Once this is done, the position of every point observed by at least two cameras is easily triangulated. The camera projection matrices and the point positions can then be used as initial guesses for the nonlinear minimization of the error defined by Equation (8.2) (see Chapter 22 for how to solve this type of optimization problem). Note that this technique does not require all points to be visible in all images; a full reconstruction is possible as soon as the image graph is connected, and each point in the scene is visible in at least two images.

The reconstruction task becomes even easier when all points are visible in all images: Let us consider the $m-1$ image pairs $(1, k)$ with $k = 2, \ldots, m$. Applying the eight-point algorithm to any of these pairs yields a different reconstruction of the scene in the coordinate system associated with the first camera, with point positions $\boldsymbol{P}_{jk}$ $(j = 1, \ldots, n)$, and projection matrices $(\text{Id} \quad \mathbf{0})$ and $(\mathcal{R}_k^T \quad -\mathcal{R}_k^T \boldsymbol{t}_k)$. In the absence of measurement and numerical errors, the $m - 1$ reconstructions are scaled versions of each other (remember that the absolute scale cannot be recovered). In practice, it is a simple matter to (roughly) estimate the corresponding scale factors: defining $\lambda_k = ||\boldsymbol{P}_{12}||/||\boldsymbol{P}_{1k}||$, we can use $\boldsymbol{P}_{j2}$ $(j = 1, \ldots, n)$ and $(\mathcal{R}_k^T \quad -\lambda_k \mathcal{R}_k^T \boldsymbol{t}_k)$ $(k = 2, \ldots, m)$ as reasonable initial guesses for the scene structure and camera motion in the minimization of Equation (8.2). Note that this method is easily adapted to the case where at least eight points correspondences can be established between one (base) image and all other ones (these eight correspondences do not have to be the same from one picture to the next), and any two images have at least one point in common.

Figure 8.4 shows the results of an experiment using this method to recover the Euclidean structure of the toy house. The top-left part of the figure shows the reconstructions associated with the five corresponding image pairs, rescaled using the first triangulated point, as well as the track formed by the optical centers of the recovered cameras. The top-right part of the figure shows the recovered scene structure and camera positions after the nonlinear minimization of Equation (8.2). The bottom part of the figure shows the final reconstruction before and after alignment with the ground-truth 3D structure via a similarity transformation. Adding images clearly helps the quality of the reconstruction, with the reconstruction error dropping to 1.4% compared to 3.1% in the binocular case of Figure 8.3.

8.2   UNCALIBRATED WEAK-PERSPECTIVE CAMERAS

Let us now assume that the intrinsic parameters of the cameras are unknown. The cost to pay for this is an increased ambiguity in the reconstruction (from the class of similarity transformations to the larger classes of so-called *affine* and *projective* transformations; these will be defined shortly). However, using uncalibrated cameras has two distinct advantages: (1) This does not require a preliminary calibration stage for these parameters. Instead, the structure and motion estimation process is decomposed in two stages, where the "essential" (affine or projective) structure and motion parameters are first recovered using simple and robust algorithms, before additional constraints associated with known camera parameters are used to "upgrade" the reconstruction to a Euclidean one uniquely defined up to a similarity. (2) By "linearizing" the algebraic constraints associated with structure from motion, this approach affords simple and effective methods for handling multiple images in a uniform way.

We start in this section with the case of scenes whose relief is small compared with their overall depth relative to the cameras observing them, so perspective projection can be approximated by the simpler *weak-perspective* model of the imaging process. Concretely, according to Theorem 2 in Chapter 1, given n fixed points P_j $(j = 1, \ldots, n)$ observed by m affine cameras with unknown intrinsic and extrinsic parameters, and the corresponding mn *nonhomogeneous* coordinate vectors $\boldsymbol{p}_{ij}$ of their images, we can rewrite the corresponding weak-perspective projection equations as

$$\boldsymbol{p}_{ij} = \mathcal{M}_i \begin{pmatrix} \boldsymbol{P}_j \\ 1 \end{pmatrix} = \mathcal{A}_i \boldsymbol{P}_j + \boldsymbol{b}_i \quad \text{for} \quad i = 1, \ldots, m \quad \text{and} \quad j = 1, \ldots, n, \quad (8.5)$$

where $\mathcal{M}_i = \begin{pmatrix} \mathcal{A}_i & \boldsymbol{b}_i \end{pmatrix}$ is a general rank-2 2×4 matrix, and the vector $\boldsymbol{P}_j$ in $\mathbb{R}^3$ is the position of the point P_j in some fixed coordinate system. We define *affine structure from motion* as the problem of estimating the m matrices $\mathcal{M}_i$ and the n vectors $\boldsymbol{P}_j$ from the mn image correspondences $\boldsymbol{p}_{ij}$.

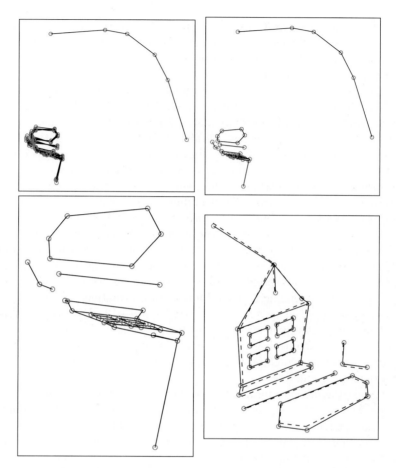

FIGURE 8.4: Euclidean structure and motion from multiple images. **Top:** Scene reconstruction and camera trajectory before (**left**) and after (**right**) nonlinear optimization. **Bottom:** The reconstructed house before (**left**) and after (**right**) alignment with the ground truth. The mean absolute and relative errors are respectively 0.38cm and 1.4%. See the text for details.

8.2.1   Natural Ambiguity of the Problem

In the Euclidean case, we have shown earlier that the 4×4 matrix associated with a rigid transformation (or a similarity) and its inverse can be inserted in the projection equations. Likewise, if $\mathcal{M}_i$ and $\boldsymbol{P}_j$ are solutions of Equation (8.5), so are $\mathcal{M}'_i$ and $\boldsymbol{P}'_j$, where

$$\mathcal{M}'_i = \mathcal{M}_i \mathcal{Q}, \quad \begin{pmatrix} \boldsymbol{P}'_j \\ 1 \end{pmatrix} = \mathcal{Q}^{-1} \begin{pmatrix} \boldsymbol{P}_j \\ 1 \end{pmatrix}, \tag{8.6}$$

and $\mathcal{Q}$ is an arbitrary *affine transformation* matrix; that is, it can be written as

$$\mathcal{Q} = \begin{pmatrix} \mathcal{C} & \boldsymbol{d} \\ \boldsymbol{0}^T & 1 \end{pmatrix} \quad \text{with} \quad \mathcal{Q}^{-1} = \begin{pmatrix} \mathcal{C}^{-1} & -\mathcal{C}^{-1}\boldsymbol{d} \\ \boldsymbol{0}^T & 1 \end{pmatrix}, \tag{8.7}$$

where $\mathcal{C}$ is a nonsingular 3×3 matrix and $\boldsymbol{d}$ is a vector in $\mathbb{R}^3$. It is easy to show that affine transformations are the most general class of 4×4 nonsingular matrices that preserve the relationship between coordinates expressed in Equation (8.6) for any point P_j (see the problems).

In particular, it follows that solutions to Equation (8.5) can *be defined only up to an affine transformation ambiguity.* Affine transformations form a group and include similarities as a subgroup. Like similarities, they map lines onto lines and planes onto planes, and preserve parallelism and incidence relationships. Unlike them, they do not preserve angles. They do, however, preserve the *ratio* of signed lengths along parallel lines, and they can be constructed by composing a rigid transformation, an anisotropic scaling with different scale factors along the three coordinate axes, and a shear. Clearly, affine transformations do not preserve shape in the Euclidean sense. Since they form a group, it is possible to talk about the *affine shape* of a set of points as the equivalence class formed by all the copies of these points separated from each other by some affine transformation. Affine SFM can thus be thought of as the problem of recovering the scene's affine shape, together with the corresponding affine projection matrices. Taking into account the 12 parameters defining a general affine transformation, we thus expect a finite number of solutions as soon as $2mn \geq 8m + 3n - 12$. For $m = 2$, this suggests that four point correspondences should be sufficient to determine (up to an affine transformation and possibly some discrete ambiguity) the two projection matrices and the three-dimensional positions of the scene points. This is confirmed formally in Sections 8.2.2 and 8.2.3.

When the intrinsic parameters of the cameras are known so the corresponding calibration matrices can be taken equal to the identity, the parameters of the projection matrices $\mathcal{M}_i = \begin{pmatrix} \mathcal{A}_i & \boldsymbol{b}_i \end{pmatrix}$ must obey additional constraints. For example, according to Equation (1.22) in Chapter 1, the matrix $\mathcal{A}_i$ associated with a (calibrated) weak-perspective camera is formed by the first two rows of a rotation matrix, scaled by the inverse of the depth of the corresponding reference point. As shown in Section 8.2.4, constraints such as these can be used to eliminate the affine ambiguity (or more precisely, to reduce it to a similarity ambiguity) when a sufficient number of images is available. This suggests decomposing the solution of the affine structure-from-motion problem into two steps: (a) first, use at least two views of the scene to reconstruct its three-dimensional affine shape and the corresponding projection matrices; then, (b) use additional views and the constraints associated with known camera calibration parameters to uniquely determine the rigid Euclidean structure of the scene. The first stage of this approach yields the essential part of the solution: the affine shape is a full-fledged three-dimensional representation of the scene, which can be used in its own right to synthesize new views of the scene, for example. The second step amounts to finding a *Euclidean upgrade* of the reconstruction—that is, to computing a single affine transformation that accounts for its rigidity and maps its affine shape onto a Euclidean one.

Using three or more images overconstrains the structure-from-motion problem and leads to more robust least-squares solutions. Accordingly, a significant portion of this section is devoted to the problem of recovering the affine shape of a scene from several (possibly many) pictures.

8.2.2 Affine Structure and Motion from Two Images

Let us start with the case where two affine images of the same scene are available. Introducing the affine equivalent of the epipolar constraint and exploiting the natural ambiguity of affine structure from motion will provide us with a very simple method for solving this problem.

Affine Epipolar Geometry. We consider two affine images and rewrite the corresponding projection equations

$$\begin{cases} \boldsymbol{p} = \mathcal{A}\boldsymbol{P} + \boldsymbol{b} \\ \boldsymbol{p}' = \mathcal{A}'\boldsymbol{P} + \boldsymbol{b}' \end{cases} \quad \text{as} \quad \begin{pmatrix} \mathcal{A} & \boldsymbol{p} - \boldsymbol{b} \\ \mathcal{A}' & \boldsymbol{p}' - \boldsymbol{b}' \end{pmatrix} \begin{pmatrix} \boldsymbol{P} \\ -1 \end{pmatrix} = \boldsymbol{0}.$$

A necessary and sufficient condition for these equations to admit a nontrivial solution is that

$$\mathrm{Det} \begin{pmatrix} \mathcal{A} & \boldsymbol{p} - \boldsymbol{b} \\ \mathcal{A}' & \boldsymbol{p}' - \boldsymbol{b}' \end{pmatrix} = 0,$$

or, equivalently,

$$\alpha x + \beta y + \alpha' x' + \beta' y' + \delta = 0, \tag{8.8}$$

where α, β, α', β', and δ are constants depending on $\mathcal{A}$, $\boldsymbol{b}$, $\mathcal{A}'$, and $\boldsymbol{b}'$. This is the *affine epipolar constraint*. Indeed, given a point p in the first image, the position of the matching point p' is constrained by Equation (8.8) to lie on the line l' defined by $\alpha' x' + \beta' y' + \gamma' = 0$, where $\gamma' = \alpha x + \beta y + \delta$ (Figure 8.5). Note that the epipolar lines associated with each image are parallel to each other. For example, moving p changes γ' or, equivalently, the distance from the origin to the epipolar line l', but does not modify the direction of l'.

The affine epipolar constraint can be rewritten in the familiar form

$$(x, y, 1)\mathcal{F} \begin{pmatrix} x' \\ y' \\ 1 \end{pmatrix} = 0, \quad \text{where} \quad \mathcal{F} = \begin{pmatrix} 0 & 0 & \alpha \\ 0 & 0 & \beta \\ \alpha' & \beta' & \delta \end{pmatrix} \tag{8.9}$$

is the *affine fundamental matrix*. This suggests that the affine epipolar geometry can be seen as the limit of the perspective one. Indeed, it can be shown that an affine picture is the limit of a sequence of images taken by a perspective camera that zooms in on the scene as it backs away from it. In turn, this leads to another derivation of Equation (8.9). See the problems for details.

Affine Weak Calibration. Given $n \geq 4$ point correspondences $p_j \leftrightarrow p_j'$ ($j = 1, \ldots, n$) between two images, we can rewrite the corresponding instances of Equation (8.8) as an $n \times 5$ system of homogeneous linear equations $\mathcal{U}\boldsymbol{f} = \boldsymbol{0}$ in the five unknown entries of the affine fundamental matrix where, this time:

$$\mathcal{U} = \begin{pmatrix} x_1 & y_1 & x_1' & y_1' & 1 \\ x_2 & y_2 & x_2' & y_2' & 1 \\ \cdots & \cdots & \cdots & \cdots & \cdots \\ x_n & y_n & x_n' & y_n' & 1 \end{pmatrix} \quad \text{and} \quad \boldsymbol{f} = \begin{pmatrix} \alpha \\ \beta \\ \alpha' \\ \beta' \\ \delta \end{pmatrix}.$$

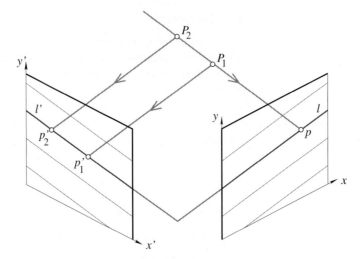

FIGURE 8.5: Affine epipolar geometry: Given two parallel-projection images, a point p in the right image and the two projection directions define an epipolar plane that intersects the left image along the epipolar line l'. As in the perspective case, any match p' for p is constrained to belong to this line. The same property holds for all other affine projection models.

As before, solving this equation in the least-squares sense amounts to computing the eigenvector f associated with the smallest eigenvalue of $\mathcal{U}^T\mathcal{U}$.

Figure 8.6 shows the results of a weak calibration experiment on two images in the house sequence. Weak perspective is a rather coarse approximation of the image formation process, and, as expected, errors are worse than in the perspective case (compare to Figure 8.2). Note that, as in that case, Hartley's normalization is essential for obtaining reasonable results.

From the Affine Fundamental Matrix to Camera Motion.   Let us now show that the projection matrices can be estimated from the epipolar constraint. The natural ambiguity of affine structure from motion allows us to simplify the calculations: according to Equations (8.6) and (8.7), if $\mathcal{M} = (\mathcal{A} \quad b)$ and $\mathcal{M}' = (\mathcal{A}' \quad b')$ are solutions of our problem, so are $\tilde{\mathcal{M}} = \mathcal{M}\mathcal{Q}$ and $\tilde{\mathcal{M}}' = \mathcal{M}'\mathcal{Q}$, where

$$\mathcal{Q} = \begin{pmatrix} \mathcal{C} & d \\ \mathbf{0}^T & 1 \end{pmatrix}$$

is an arbitrary affine transformation. The new projection matrices can be written as $\tilde{\mathcal{M}} = (\mathcal{A}\mathcal{C} \quad \mathcal{A}d + b)$ and $\tilde{\mathcal{M}}' = (\mathcal{A}'\mathcal{C} \quad \mathcal{A}'d + b')$. Note that, according to Equation (8.7), applying this transformation to the projection matrices amounts to applying the inverse transformation to every scene point P, whose position P is replaced by $\tilde{P} = \mathcal{C}^{-1}(P - d)$.

As shown in the problems at the end of this chapter, it is possible to choose

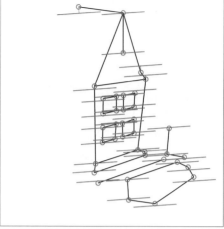

FIGURE 8.6: Affine weak-calibration experiment using two images of the house sequence and linear least squares, together with Hartley's normalization. The mean distances between the points and the corresponding epipolar lines are 3.24 and 3.15 pixels for these two images.

$\mathcal{C}$ and $\boldsymbol{d}$ so that the two projection matrices take the canonical forms:

$$\tilde{\mathcal{M}} = \begin{pmatrix} 1 & 0 & 0 & 0 \\ 0 & 1 & 0 & 0 \end{pmatrix} \quad \text{and} \quad \tilde{\mathcal{M}}' = \begin{pmatrix} 0 & 0 & 1 & 0 \\ a & b & c & d \end{pmatrix}, \tag{8.10}$$

which allows us to rewrite the epipolar constraint as

$$\text{Det} \begin{pmatrix} 1 & 0 & 0 & x \\ 0 & 1 & 0 & y \\ 0 & 0 & 1 & x' \\ a & b & c & y' - d \end{pmatrix} = -ax - by - cx' + y' - d = 0,$$

where the coefficients a, b, c, and d are related to the parameters α, β, α', β', and δ by $a : \alpha = b : \beta = c : \alpha' = -1 : \beta' = d : \delta$.

Once the coefficients a, b, c, and d have been estimated via linear least squares, the two projection matrices are known, and the position of any point can be estimated from its image coordinates by using once again linear least squares to solve the corresponding system of four equations,

$$\begin{pmatrix} 1 & 0 & 0 & x \\ 0 & 1 & 0 & y \\ 0 & 0 & 1 & x' \\ a & b & c & y' - d \end{pmatrix} \begin{pmatrix} \tilde{\boldsymbol{P}} \\ -1 \end{pmatrix} = 0, \tag{8.11}$$

for the three unknown coordinates of $\tilde{\boldsymbol{P}}$.

Note that, paradoxically perhaps, the first three equations in Equation (8.11) are in fact sufficient to solve for $\tilde{\boldsymbol{P}}$ as $(x, y, x')^T$ *without* estimating the coefficients

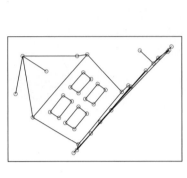
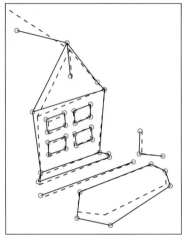

FIGURE 8.7: The affine reconstruction of the house from two views. **Left:** Affine reconstruction obtained by reducing the *second* row of $\mathcal{A}'$ to $(0, 0, 1)$. In this particular case, the computation is numerically much better behaved than when reducing the first row to the same form. **Right:** The reconstruction after affine registration with the ground-truth data. The mean Euclidean distance between the reconstructed and ground-truth points is 0.92cm, or a mean relative error of 3.2%.

a, b, c, and d, and *without* requiring a minimum number of matches. This is not as surprising as one might think. In the case of two calibrated orthographic cameras with perpendicular projection directions and parallel y axes, taking $X = x$, $Y = y$, and $Z = x'$ does yield the correct Euclidean reconstruction (have another look at Figure 8.5, assuming orthographic projection and imagining that the epipolar lines are parallel to the x and x' axes). In practice, of course, using all four equations might yield more accurate results. The proposed method reduces the first row of $\mathcal{A}'$ to $(0, 0, 1)$ via the affine transformation $\mathcal{Q}$. When the first row of the matrix $\mathcal{A}'$ (almost) lies in the plane spanned by the rows of $\mathcal{A}$, the matrix inversion involved in this process is numerically ill behaved, and it is preferable to apply instead the same reduction to the second row of $\mathcal{A}'$. When both matrices constructed in this fashion are singular, the two image planes are parallel and the scene structure cannot be recovered.

Figure 8.7 shows the 3D affine shape of the house recovered from two images. In this case, taking $X = x$, $Y = y$, and $Z = x'$ does not give very good results, due to numerical conditioning problems. However, it is striking that taking $X = x$, $Y = y$, and $Z = y'$ yields quite a reasonable reconstruction of the house, even if the mean relative error (3.2%) is slightly worse than that obtained by the eight-point algorithm (3.1%). (To be fair, note that the recovered shape is registered to the ground-truth one using an affine transformation in this case. With more degrees of freedom (12) than a similarity (7), it fits the data better, which biases the comparison a bit.)

8.2.3 Affine Structure and Motion from Multiple Images

The method presented in the previous section is aimed at recovering the affine scene structure and the corresponding projection matrices from a minimum number of images. We now address the problem of estimating the same information from a potentially large number of pictures.

As usual, it is convenient to simplify as much as possible all equations involved in our problem. Under affine projection, the image of the center of mass of a set of points is the center of mass of their images (see problems). When we let P_0 denote the center of mass of the n points $P_1, \ldots, P_n$, and let p_{i0} denote its projection into image number i, we have

$$\boldsymbol{p}_{i0} = \mathcal{A}_i \boldsymbol{P}_0 + \boldsymbol{b}_i, \quad \text{and thus} \quad \boldsymbol{p}_{ij} - \boldsymbol{p}_{i0} = \mathcal{A}_i(\boldsymbol{P}_j - \boldsymbol{P}_0).$$

Now, of course, we are free to pick P_0 as the origin of the world coordinate system, so $\boldsymbol{P}_0 = \boldsymbol{0}$. Because p_{i0} is "observable" as the center of mass of the points p_{ij}, we are also free to choose it as the origin of the coordinate system attached with image number i, so $\boldsymbol{p}_{i0} = 0$. This allows us to rewrite Equation (8.5) as

$$\boldsymbol{p}_{ij} = \mathcal{A}_i \boldsymbol{P}_j \quad \text{for} \quad i = 1, \ldots, m \quad \text{and} \quad j = 1, \ldots, n, \tag{8.12}$$

and reduce the affine ambiguity to a *linear* one.

The mn instances of Equation (8.12) can now be rewritten in matrix form as

$$\mathcal{D} = \mathcal{A}\mathcal{P}, \text{ where } \mathcal{D} = \begin{pmatrix} \boldsymbol{p}_{11} & \cdots & \boldsymbol{p}_{1n} \\ \cdots & \cdots & \cdots \\ \boldsymbol{p}_{m1} & \cdots & \boldsymbol{p}_{mn} \end{pmatrix}, \mathcal{A} = \begin{pmatrix} \mathcal{A}_1 \\ \vdots \\ \mathcal{A}_m \end{pmatrix}, \text{ and } \mathcal{P} = \begin{pmatrix} \boldsymbol{P}_1 & \cdots & \boldsymbol{P}_n \end{pmatrix}.$$

As the product of a $2m \times 3$ matrix and a $3 \times n$ matrix, the $2m \times 3n$ matrix $\mathcal{D}$ has, in general, rank 3. As shown by Tomasi and Kanade (1992), singular value decomposition provides a practical method for recovering both $\mathcal{A}$ and $\mathcal{P}$ from the (observed) data matrix $\mathcal{D}$. Indeed, if $\mathcal{U}\mathcal{W}\mathcal{V}^T$ is the SVD of the rank-3 matrix $\mathcal{D}$, only three of the singular values are nonzero, thus $\mathcal{D} = \mathcal{U}_3 \mathcal{W}_3 \mathcal{V}_3^T$, where $\mathcal{U}_3$ and $\mathcal{V}_3$ denote the $2m \times 3$ and $3 \times n$ matrices formed by the three leftmost columns of the matrices $\mathcal{U}$ and $\mathcal{V}$, and $\mathcal{W}_3$ is the 3×3 diagonal matrix formed by the corresponding nonzero singular values.

In the noiseless case where $\mathcal{D}$ is truly a rank-3 matrix, it is easy to exploit the inherent ambiguity of affine structure from motion to show that $\mathcal{A}_0 = \mathcal{U}_3 \sqrt{\mathcal{W}_3}$ and $\mathcal{P}_0 = \sqrt{\mathcal{W}_3} \mathcal{V}_3^T$ are representatives of the true (affine) camera motion and scene shape (see problems). In practice, due to image noise, errors in localization of feature points, and the mere fact that actual cameras are not affine, the equation $\mathcal{D} = \mathcal{A}\mathcal{P}$ does not hold exactly, and the matrix $\mathcal{D}$ has (in general) full rank. In this case, the best we can hope for is to minimize

$$E = \sum_{i,j} ||\boldsymbol{p}_{ij} - \mathcal{A}_i \boldsymbol{P}_j||^2 = \sum_j ||\boldsymbol{q}_j - \mathcal{A}\boldsymbol{P}_j||^2 = ||\mathcal{D} - \mathcal{A}\mathcal{P}||_F^2,$$

with respect to the matrices $\mathcal{A}_i$ $(i = 1, \ldots, m)$ and vectors $\boldsymbol{P}_j$ $(j = 1, \ldots, m)$ or, equivalently, with respect to the matrices $\mathcal{A}$ and $\mathcal{P}$. (Here $||\mathcal{A}||_F$ denotes, as in

Chapter 22, the Frobenius norm of the matrix $\mathcal{A}$—that is, the square root of the sum of the squared entries of that matrix.)

According to Theorem 6 in Chapter 22, the matrix $\mathcal{A}_0 \mathcal{P}_0$ is the closest rank-3 approximation to $\mathcal{D}$. Because the rank of $\mathcal{A}\mathcal{P}$ is 3 for any rank-3 $2m \times 3$ matrix $\mathcal{A}$ and rank-3 $3 \times n$ matrix $\mathcal{P}$, the minimum value of E is thus reached for $\mathcal{A} = \mathcal{A}_0$ and $\mathcal{P} = \mathcal{P}_0$, which confirms that $\mathcal{A}_0$ and $\mathcal{P}_0$ are the optimal estimates of the true camera motion and scene structure. This does not contradict the inherent ambiguity of affine structure from motion: all affinely equivalent solutions yield the same value for E, and we just as well could have taken $\mathcal{A} = \mathcal{A}_0 \mathcal{S}$ and $\mathcal{P} = \mathcal{S}^{-1}\mathcal{P}_0$ for any nonsingular 3×3 matrix $\mathcal{S}$. In particular, singular value decomposition provides a solution to the affine SFM problem, as illustrated by Algorithm 8.2.

---

1. Compute the singular value decomposition $\mathcal{D} = \mathcal{U}\mathcal{W}\mathcal{V}^T$.
2. Construct the matrices $\mathcal{U}_3$, $\mathcal{V}_3$, and $\mathcal{W}_3$ formed by the three leftmost columns of the matrices $\mathcal{U}$ and $\mathcal{V}$, and the corresponding 3×3 submatrix of $\mathcal{W}$.
3. Define
$$\mathcal{A}_0 = \mathcal{U}_3 \sqrt{\mathcal{W}_3} \quad \text{and} \quad \mathcal{P}_0 = \sqrt{\mathcal{W}_3}\mathcal{V}_3^T;$$
   the $2m \times 3$ matrix $\mathcal{A}_0$ is an estimate of the camera motion, and the $3 \times n$ matrix $\mathcal{P}_0$ is an estimate of the scene structure.

Algorithm 8.2: The Tomasi–Kanade Factorization Algorithm for Affine Shape from Motion.

Figure 8.8 shows the 3D (affine) shape of the house recovered from six images of 38 points of the house. The mean relative error of 2.8% is, as expected, smaller than the 3.2% obtained from two views only.

8.2.4   From Affine to Euclidean Shape

Let us now assume a weak-perspective model of the imaging process and (internally) calibrated cameras. Recall from Chapter 1 that a weak-perspective projection matrix can be written as

$$\mathcal{M} = \frac{1}{Z_r} \begin{pmatrix} k & s \\ 0 & 1 \end{pmatrix} \begin{pmatrix} \mathcal{R}_2 & \boldsymbol{t}_2 \end{pmatrix},$$

where Z_r is the depth of the reference point, k and s are aspect-ratio and skew parameters, $\mathcal{R}_2$ is the 2×3 matrix formed by the first two rows of a rotation matrix, and $\boldsymbol{t}_2$ is a vector in $\mathbb{R}^2$. When the camera is calibrated, we can use normalized image coordinates and take $k = s = 1$. The projection matrix becomes

$$\hat{\mathcal{M}} = \begin{pmatrix} \hat{\mathcal{A}} & \hat{\boldsymbol{b}} \end{pmatrix} = \frac{1}{Z_r} \begin{pmatrix} \mathcal{R}_2 & \boldsymbol{t}_2 \end{pmatrix}. \tag{8.13}$$

It follows from Equation (8.13) that the matrix $\hat{\mathcal{A}}$ is part of a (scaled) rotation matrix, with row vectors $\hat{\boldsymbol{a}}_1^T$ and $\hat{\boldsymbol{a}}_2^T$ that are orthogonal to each other and have the same norm. In other words, a (calibrated) weak-perspective camera is an affine

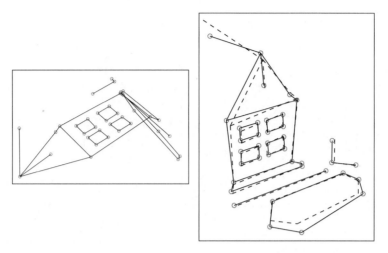

FIGURE 8.8: The affine reconstruction of the house from multiple views. **Left:** The original reconstruction. **Right:** An overlay of the reconstruction after it has been registered (via an affine transformation) with the ground truth data. The mean Euclidean distance between the reconstructed and ground-truth points is 0.77cm, or a mean relative error of 2.8%.

camera with the additional constraints

$$\hat{\boldsymbol{a}}_1 \cdot \hat{\boldsymbol{a}}_2 = 0 \quad \text{and} \quad ||\hat{\boldsymbol{a}}_1||^2 = ||\hat{\boldsymbol{a}}_2||^2. \tag{8.14}$$

Let us suppose that we have recovered the affine shape of a scene and the projection matrix $\mathcal{M}$ associated with each view. We already know that all solutions of the structure-from-motion problem are the same up to an affine ambiguity. In particular, the Euclidean coordinate vectors $\hat{\boldsymbol{P}}$ of scene points and the corresponding projection matrices $\hat{\mathcal{M}}$ must be related to their affine counterparts $\boldsymbol{P}$ and $\mathcal{M}$ by some affine transformation

$$\mathcal{Q} = \begin{pmatrix} \mathcal{C} & \boldsymbol{d} \\ \boldsymbol{0}^T & 1 \end{pmatrix}$$

such that $\hat{\mathcal{M}} = \mathcal{M}\mathcal{Q}$ and $\hat{\boldsymbol{P}} = \mathcal{C}^{-1}(\tilde{\boldsymbol{P}} - \boldsymbol{d})$. Such a transformation is called a *Euclidean upgrade* because it maps the affine shape of a scene onto its Euclidean one.

Let us now show how to compute such an upgrade when $m \geq 3$ weak-perspective images are available. Let $\mathcal{M}_i = (\mathcal{A}_i \quad \boldsymbol{b}_i)$ denote the corresponding projection matrices, estimated using the factorization method of Section 8.2.3, for example. If $\hat{\mathcal{M}}_i = \mathcal{M}_i \mathcal{Q}$, we can rewrite the weak-perspective constraints of Equation (8.14) as

$$\begin{cases} \hat{\boldsymbol{a}}_{i1} \cdot \hat{\boldsymbol{a}}_{i2} = 0, \\ ||\hat{\boldsymbol{a}}_{i1}||^2 = ||\hat{\boldsymbol{a}}_{i2}||^2, \end{cases} \Longleftrightarrow \begin{cases} \boldsymbol{a}_{i1}^T \mathcal{C}\mathcal{C}^T \boldsymbol{a}_{i2} = 0, \\ \boldsymbol{a}_{i1}^T \mathcal{C}\mathcal{C}^T \boldsymbol{a}_{i1} = \boldsymbol{a}_{i2}^T \mathcal{C}\mathcal{C}^T \boldsymbol{a}_{i2}, \end{cases} \quad \text{for} \quad i = 1, \dots, m, \tag{8.15}$$

where $\boldsymbol{a}_{i1}^T$ and $\boldsymbol{a}_{i2}^T$ denote the rows of the matrix $\mathcal{A}_i$. This overconstrained system of $3m$ quadratic equations in the coefficients of $\mathcal{C}$ can be solved via nonlinear least

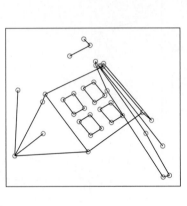
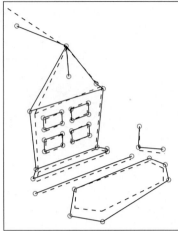

FIGURE 8.9: The Euclidean reconstruction of the house using a weak-perspective model. **Left:** The original reconstruction. **Right:** An overlay of the reconstruction after it has been registered (via a similarity transformation) with the ground-truth data. The mean Euclidean distance between the reconstructed and ground-truth points is 0.83cm, or a mean relative error of 3.0%. Note that the registration error is a bit larger than for the plain affine reconstruction shown in Figure 8.8. As before, this is not surprising, since an affine transformation has more "degrees of freedom" (12) than a similarity (7).

squares, but this requires some reasonable initial guess for these coefficients. An alternative is to consider Equation (8.15) as a set of *linear* constraints on the matrix $\mathcal{D} = \mathcal{C}\mathcal{C}^T$. The coefficients of $\mathcal{D}$ can be found in this case via linear least squares, and $\mathcal{C}$ can then be computed as $\sqrt{\mathcal{D}}$ using Cholesky decomposition. It should be noted that this requires that the recovered matrix $\mathcal{D}$ (or its opposite) be positive definite, which is not guaranteed in the presence of noise. Note also that the solution of Equation (8.15) is defined only up to an arbitrary rotation. To determine $\mathcal{Q}$ uniquely and simplify the calculations, it is possible to map $\mathcal{M}_1$ (and possibly $\mathcal{M}_2$) to canonical forms as before.

Figure 8.9 shows the weak-perspective upgrade associated with the Tomasi-Kanade affine reconstruction of the house shown in Figure 8.8. The mean relative error is 3.0% in this case.

8.3 UNCALIBRATED PERSPECTIVE CAMERAS

Let us come back to perspective projection, and assume again that the intrinsic parameters of the cameras are unknown. Given n fixed points P_j $(j = 1, \ldots, n)$ observed by m cameras and the corresponding mn *homogeneous* coordinate vectors $\boldsymbol{p}_{ij} = (x_{ij}, y_{ij}, 1)^T$ of their images, we write the corresponding perspective projection equations as

$$\begin{cases} x_{ij} = \dfrac{\boldsymbol{m}_{i1} \cdot \boldsymbol{P}_j}{\boldsymbol{m}_{i3} \cdot \boldsymbol{P}_j} \\ y_{ij} = \dfrac{\boldsymbol{m}_{i2} \cdot \boldsymbol{P}_j}{\boldsymbol{m}_{i3} \cdot \boldsymbol{P}_j} \end{cases} \quad \text{for} \quad i = 1, \ldots, m \quad \text{and} \quad j = 1, \ldots, n, \qquad (8.16)$$

where $\boldsymbol{m}_{i1}^T$, $\boldsymbol{m}_{i2}^T$, and $\boldsymbol{m}_{i3}^T$ denote the rows of the 3×4 projection matrix $\mathcal{M}_i$ associated with camera number i in some fixed coordinate system, and $\boldsymbol{P}_j$ denotes the *homogeneous* coordinate vector of the point P_j in that coordinate system.

According to Theorem 1 (Chapter 1), any 3×4 matrix $\mathcal{M} = (\mathcal{A} \quad \boldsymbol{b})$, where $\mathcal{A}$ is a nonsingular 3×3 matrix and $\boldsymbol{b}$ is an arbitrary vector in $\mathbb{R}^3$ can be interpreted as a perspective projection matrix; that is, it can be written as $\mathcal{M} = \rho \mathcal{K} (\mathcal{R} \quad \boldsymbol{t})$ for some nonzero real ρ, calibration matrix $\mathcal{K}$, 3×3 rotation matrix $\mathcal{R}$, and translation vector $\boldsymbol{t}$ in $\mathbb{R}^3$. We relax this condition a bit in this chapter, and define a *projective projection matrix* as an arbitrary rank-3 3×4 matrix. Clearly, perspective projection matrices are projective ones, but not all projective projection matrices are perspective ones. We will come back to the implications of this relaxation shortly. In the mean time, let us define *projective structure from motion* as the problem of estimating the m rank-3 matrices $\mathcal{M}_i$ and the n vectors $\boldsymbol{P}_j$ from the mn image correspondences $\boldsymbol{p}_{ij}$.

8.3.1   Natural Ambiguity of the Problem

When $\mathcal{M}_i$ and $\boldsymbol{P}_j$ are solutions of Equation (8.16), so are $\lambda_i \mathcal{M}_i$ and $\mu_j \boldsymbol{P}_j$ for any nonzero values of λ_i and μ_j. In particular, as already noted in Chapter 1, the matrices $\mathcal{M}_i$ satisfying Equation (8.16) are defined only up to scale, with 11 independent parameters, and so are the homogeneous coordinate vectors $\boldsymbol{P}_j$ in $\mathbb{R}^4$ (with only three independent parameters; when necessary, these can be reduced to the canonical form $(X_j, Y_j, Z_j, 1)^T$ as long as their fourth coordinate is not zero, which is the case in general). Like its affine cousin, projective SFM is subject to a deeper ambiguity that justifies its name: Let $\mathcal{Q}$ denote an arbitrary *projective transformation matrix* (or *homography*; the two terms are strictly equivalent)— that is, an arbitrary nonsingular 4×4 matrix. Postmultiplying $\mathcal{M}_i$ by $\mathcal{Q}$ does not change its rank, and it follows that, if $\mathcal{M}_i$ and $\boldsymbol{P}_j$ are solutions of the projective structure-from-motion problem, so are $\mathcal{M}_i' = \mathcal{M}_i \mathcal{Q}$ and $\boldsymbol{P}_j' = \mathcal{Q}^{-1} \boldsymbol{P}_j$.

Projective transformations form a group and include affine transformations as a subgroup. Like affine transformations, they map lines onto lines and planes onto planes, and preserve incidence relationships. Unlike these, however, they do not preserve parallelism, or the ratio of lengths along parallel lines, and thus do not preserve affine shape. They preserve instead the cross-ratio of four points along the same line (see problems). Because homographies form a group, it is again possible to talk about the *projective shape* of a set of points, and projective structure from motion can be thought of as the recovery of the observed scene's projective shape, along with the corresponding projection matrix parameters.

The matrix $\mathcal{Q}$ is defined only up to scale, with 15 free parameters, because multiplying it by a nonzero scalar simply amounts to applying inverse scalings to $\mathcal{M}_i$ and $\boldsymbol{P}_j$. Because Equation (8.16) provides $2mn$ constraints on the $11m$ parameters of the matrices $\mathcal{M}_i$ and the $3n$ parameters of the vectors $\boldsymbol{P}_j$, taking into account the natural ambiguity of structure from motion suggests that this problem admits a finite number of solutions as soon as $2mn \geq 11m + 3n - 15$. For $m = 2$, seven point correspondences should thus be sufficient to determine (up to a projective transformation and possibly a finite ambiguity) the two projection matrices and the position of any other point. This is confirmed in Sections 8.3.2 and 8.3.3.

Before proceeding, let us come back to the difference between (uncalibrated) perspective and projective structure from motion. A formal argument is beyond the scope of this book, but let us just note that a perspective projection matrix $\mathcal{M} = (\mathcal{A} \quad \boldsymbol{b})$ with $\det(\mathcal{A}) \neq 0$ is just the analytical representation in some Euclidean coordinate system of the geometric perspective projection operator which, given some pinhole O and retinal plane Π, associates with any point $P \neq O$ in $\mathbb{E}^3$ the point where the line joining P and O intersects Π. A projective projection matrix is just another representation for the same operator, expressed this time in a *projective coordinate system*, whose formal definition is once again beyond the scope of this book, but can be thought of intuitively as a warped frame in which the projective shape has its Euclidean coordinates.

Similar to the affine case, we will decompose in the rest of this section the solution to structure from motion into two steps: first, (a) use at least two views of the scene to reconstruct its three-dimensional projective shape and the corresponding projective projection matrices; then, (b) use additional views and the constraints associated with known camera calibration parameters to uniquely determine the Euclidean structure of the scene. The second step amounts to finding a Euclidean upgrade of the scene—that is, to computing a single projective transformation that maps its projective shape onto a Euclidean one.

8.3.2 Projective Structure and Motion from Two Images

Let us now assume that the fundamental matrix $\mathcal{F}$ associated with two pictures has been estimated from binocular correspondences. As in the affine case, the projection matrices can in fact be estimated from a parameterization of $\mathcal{F}$ that exploits the inherent ambiguity of projective SFM. In the projective setting, the scene structure and camera motion are defined only up to an arbitrary homography, and we can reduce the two matrices to canonical forms $\tilde{\mathcal{M}} = \mathcal{M}\mathcal{Q}$ and $\tilde{\mathcal{M}}' = \mathcal{M}'\mathcal{Q}$ by postmultiplying them by an appropriate 4×4 matrix $\mathcal{Q}$. (We must of course simultaneously premultiply the coordinate vector $\boldsymbol{P}$ of any point P by its inverse, yielding $\tilde{\boldsymbol{P}} = \mathcal{Q}^{-1}\boldsymbol{P}$.) This time, we take $\tilde{\mathcal{M}}'$ to be proportional to $(\mathrm{Id} \quad \boldsymbol{0})$ and leave $\tilde{\mathcal{M}}$ in the general form $(\mathcal{A} \quad \boldsymbol{b})$ (this determines 11 of $\mathcal{Q}$'s entries). Let us now derive a new expression for the fundamental matrix using the canonical form of $\tilde{\mathcal{M}}'$. If Z and Z' denote the depths of the point P relative to the two cameras, we can write the projection equations associated with the two cameras as $Z\boldsymbol{p} = (\mathcal{A} \quad \boldsymbol{b})\tilde{\boldsymbol{P}}$ and $Z'\boldsymbol{p}' = (\mathrm{Id} \quad \boldsymbol{0})\tilde{\boldsymbol{P}}$ or, equivalently,

$$Z\boldsymbol{p} = \mathcal{A}(\mathrm{Id} \quad \boldsymbol{0})\tilde{\boldsymbol{P}} + \boldsymbol{b} = Z'\mathcal{A}\boldsymbol{p}' + \boldsymbol{b}.$$

It follows that $Z\boldsymbol{b} \times \boldsymbol{p} = Z'\boldsymbol{b} \times \mathcal{A}\boldsymbol{p}'$, and forming the dot product of this expression with $\boldsymbol{p}$ finally yields

$$\boldsymbol{p}^T\mathcal{F}\boldsymbol{p}' = 0 \quad \text{where} \quad \mathcal{F} = [\boldsymbol{b}_\times]\mathcal{A}. \tag{8.17}$$

Note the similarity with the expression for the essential matrix derived in Chapter 7. In particular, we have $\mathcal{F}^T\boldsymbol{b} = 0$, so (as could have been expected) $\boldsymbol{b}$ is the homogeneous coordinate vector of the first epipole in the corresponding image coordinate system. This new parameterization of the matrix $\mathcal{F}$ provides a simple method for computing the projection matrix $\tilde{\mathcal{M}}$. First, note that because the overall scale of $\tilde{\mathcal{M}}$

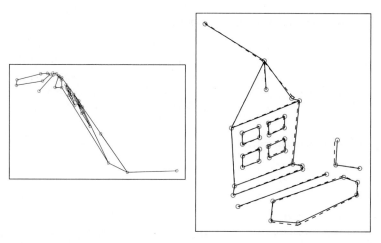

FIGURE 8.10: The projective reconstruction of the house from two views. **Left:** The original reconstruction. **Right:** An overlay of the reconstruction after it has been registered (via a projective transformation) with the ground-truth data. The mean Euclidean distance between the reconstructed and ground-truth points is 0.34cm, or a mean relative error of 1.2%.

is irrelevant, we can always take $||\boldsymbol{b}|| = 1$. This allows us to first compute $\boldsymbol{b}$ as the linear least-squares solution of $\mathcal{F}^T \boldsymbol{b} = 0$ with unit norm, and we pick $\mathcal{A}_0 = -[\boldsymbol{b}_\times]\mathcal{F}$ as the value of $\mathcal{A}$. It is easy to show that, for any vector $\boldsymbol{a}$, $[\boldsymbol{a}_\times]^2 = \boldsymbol{a}\boldsymbol{a}^T - ||\boldsymbol{a}||^2 \mathrm{Id}$, thus:

$$[\boldsymbol{b}_\times]\mathcal{A}_0 = -[\boldsymbol{b}_\times]^2\mathcal{F} = -\boldsymbol{b}\boldsymbol{b}^T\mathcal{F} + ||\boldsymbol{b}||^2\mathcal{F} = \mathcal{F},$$

since $\mathcal{F}^T\boldsymbol{b} = \boldsymbol{0}$ and $||\boldsymbol{b}||^2 = 1$. This shows that $\tilde{\mathcal{M}} = \begin{pmatrix} \mathcal{A}_0 & \boldsymbol{b} \end{pmatrix}$ is *a* solution of Equation (8.17).[5] As shown in the problems, there is in fact a four-parameter family of solutions whose general form is

$$\tilde{\mathcal{M}} = \begin{pmatrix} \mathcal{A} & \boldsymbol{b} \end{pmatrix} \quad \text{with} \quad \mathcal{A} = \lambda\mathcal{A}_0 + \begin{pmatrix} \mu\boldsymbol{b} & | & \nu\boldsymbol{b} & | & \tau\boldsymbol{b} \end{pmatrix}. \tag{8.18}$$

The four parameters correspond, as could have been expected, to the remaining degrees of freedom of the projective transformation $\mathcal{Q}$. Once the matrix $\tilde{\mathcal{M}}$ is known, we can compute the position of any point P by solving in the least-squares sense the nonhomogeneous linear system of equations in Z and Z' defined by $Z\boldsymbol{p} = Z'\mathcal{A}\boldsymbol{p}' + \boldsymbol{b}$.

Figure 8.10 shows the 3D (projective) shape of the house recovered from two images. The mean 3D reconstruction error is 0.34cm, for a relative error of 1.2%. (Homographies have more parameters [15] than affine transformations [12] or similarities [7]. They are thus expected to fit the data better, biasing a bit the evaluation in favor of the projective reconstruction.)

---

[5]The observant reader might have noticed that $\mathcal{A}_0$ is singular, so $\tilde{\mathcal{M}}$ does not satisfy the hypotheses of Theorem 1 in Chapter 1. This is not a problem in our setting, because $\tilde{\mathcal{M}}$ is easily shown to have rank 3.

8.3.3 Projective Structure and Motion from Multiple Images

We now present three approaches to projective structure from motion that use nonlinear optimization schemes to handle *all* input images in a uniform manner. They all require reasonable initial guesses for the matrices $\mathcal{M}_i$ and vectors $\boldsymbol{P}_j$ in Equation (8.16). Similar to the perspective case, these can be obtained from binocular reconstructions associated with pairs of images, for example.

Projective factorization.   Given m images of n points, we can rewrite Equation (8.16) as

$$\mathcal{D} = \mathcal{M}\mathcal{P}, \tag{8.19}$$

where

$$\mathcal{D} = \begin{pmatrix} Z_{11}\boldsymbol{p}_{11} & Z_{12}\boldsymbol{p}_{12} & \cdots & Z_{1n}\boldsymbol{p}_{1n} \\ Z_{21}\boldsymbol{p}_{21} & Z_{22}\boldsymbol{p}_{22} & \cdots & Z_{2n}\boldsymbol{p}_{2n} \\ \cdots & \cdots & \cdots & \cdots \\ Z_{m1}\boldsymbol{p}_{m1} & Z_{m2}\boldsymbol{p}_{m2} & \cdots & Z_{mn}\boldsymbol{p}_{mn} \end{pmatrix}, \; \mathcal{M} = \begin{pmatrix} \mathcal{M}_1 \\ \mathcal{M}_2 \\ \cdots \\ \mathcal{M}_m \end{pmatrix} \text{ and } \mathcal{P} = \begin{pmatrix} \boldsymbol{P}_1 & \boldsymbol{P}_2 & \cdots & \boldsymbol{P}_n \end{pmatrix},$$

and thus formulate projective structure from motion as the minimization of

$$E = \sum_{i,j} ||Z_{ij}\boldsymbol{p}_j - \mathcal{M}_i\boldsymbol{P}_j||^2 = ||\mathcal{D} - \mathcal{M}\mathcal{P}||_F^2 \tag{8.20}$$

with respect to the depths Z_{ij} and the entries of the matrices $\mathcal{M}$ and $\mathcal{P}$. When the depths Z_{ij} are known, we can compute $\mathcal{M}$ and $\mathcal{P}$ by using singular value decomposition to compute a rank-4 (as opposed to rank-3 in the affine case) factorization of $\mathcal{D}$. On the other hand, when $\mathcal{M}$ and $\mathcal{P}$ are known, we can read out the values of the depths Z_{ij} from Equation (8.19). This suggests an iterative scheme, alternating steps where one group of variables is estimated while the other one is kept constant. Note, however, that a trivial minimum of E corresponds to taking all variables Z_{ij}, $\mathcal{M}_i$, and $\boldsymbol{P}_j$ equal to zero. To avoid this, Sturm and Triggs (1996) propose renormalizing after each iteration the rows of the matrix $\mathcal{D}$, then its columns, so they have unit norm. Unfortunately, with this normalization, there is no guarantee that the error will decrease at each step or that the method will converge to some local minimum.

Bilinear projective SFM.   An alternative to this approach can be obtained by noting again that the variables Z_{ij} are *not* independent of $\mathcal{M}_i$ and $\boldsymbol{P}_j$, and trying to eliminate them to construct a nonredundant parameterization of projective SFM (Mahamud *et al.* 2001). Writing that the derivative of E with respect to Z_{ij} should be zero at an extremum of this function, a simple calculation shows that *at such a point* the value of E is given by:

$$E = \sum_{ij} ||\boldsymbol{p}_{ij} \times (\mathcal{M}_i\boldsymbol{P}_j)||^2, \tag{8.21}$$

where, without loss of generality, the vectors $\boldsymbol{p}_{ij}$ are supposed to have unit norm. Note that the depths Z_{ij} have been eliminated in the process.

It is thus possible to minimize E by alternating steps where the vectors $\boldsymbol{P}_j$ are kept constant (resp. estimated) while the matrices $\mathcal{M}_i$ are estimated (resp.

kept constant). Because the error term $\boldsymbol{p}_{ij} \times (\mathcal{M}_i \boldsymbol{P}_j)$ is bilinear in $\mathcal{M}_i$ and $\boldsymbol{P}_j$, the global optimum in $\mathcal{M}_i$ or $\boldsymbol{P}_j$ at each step of this algorithm can be obtained using linear least squares under the constraints $||\mathcal{M}_i||_F^2 = 1$ and $||\boldsymbol{P}_j||^2 = 1$ for $i = 1, \ldots, m$ and $j = 1, \ldots, n$. Note that this choice of constraints avoids the degenerate (global) minimum corresponding to $\mathcal{M}_i = 0$ and $\boldsymbol{P}_j = 0$. However, it does not necessarily avoid other degeneracies, corresponding, for example, to picking $\mathcal{M}_i = \mathcal{M}_0$ $(i = 1, \ldots, m)$ and $\boldsymbol{P}_j = \boldsymbol{P}_0$ $(j = 1, \ldots, n)$, where $\mathcal{M}_0$ is an arbitrary rank-3 3×4 matrix with unit Frobenius form and $\boldsymbol{P}_0$ is a unit vector in its nullspace (there are other trivial zeros corresponding to lower-rank values of $\mathcal{M}_0$ and families of vectors in their nullspaces).

It is possible to show that the error decreases at each iteration, and that the parameters converge to those of one of its critical points (Mahamud *et al.* 2001). As demonstrated experimentally by Hartley, however, the minimization process might be unstable, and after finding an acceptable solution in relatively few steps (say, 50 to 100), it might eventually switch to a degenerate zero minimum (typically after tens of thousands of iterations). It should therefore be stopped before that—for example, by monitoring the rate at which the error decreases, and stopping when it becomes small enough.

Bundle adjustment. As discussed in Mahamud *et al.* (2001), degeneracy problems may be unavoidable for any method attempting to minimize the error function defined by Equation (8.20). For example, the normalization mechanism used in Sturm and Triggs (1996) does not guarantee that *all* depth parameters Z_{ij} are nonzero. An alternative is to revert to the original formulation of projective SFM, and use nonlinear least squares to minimize directly

$$E = \frac{1}{mn} \sum_{i,j} \left[\left(x_{ij} - \frac{\boldsymbol{m}_{i1} \cdot \boldsymbol{P}_j}{\boldsymbol{m}_{i3} \cdot \boldsymbol{P}_j} \right)^2 + \left(y_{ij} - \frac{\boldsymbol{m}_{i2} \cdot \boldsymbol{P}_j}{\boldsymbol{m}_{i3} \cdot \boldsymbol{P}_j} \right)^2 \right]$$

with respect to the matrices $\mathcal{M}_i$ $(i = 1, \ldots, m)$ and vectors $\boldsymbol{P}_j$ $(j = 1, \ldots, n)$.

This is the method of *bundle adjustment*, whose name originates in the field of photogrammetry. It is not susceptible to degeneracies, and it combines all measurements to minimize a physically significant error measure—namely, the mean-squared error between the actual image point positions and those predicted using the estimated scene structure and camera motion. It also can take advantage of the variants of Newton's algorithm available for nonlinear least-squares problems (Chapter 1), which typically converge in fewer (although possibly more expensive) iterations than the alternation methods discussed so far. Figure 8.11 shows the projective reconstruction of the toy house obtained using this method after 15 iterations of the Levenberg-Marquardt implementation of nonlinear least squares, using the coordinates of the points reconstructed by affine factorization as initial guesses for the vectors $\boldsymbol{P}_j$ and the projections computed from these points as initial values for the matrices $\mathcal{M}_i$. The mean relative error is 0.2%.

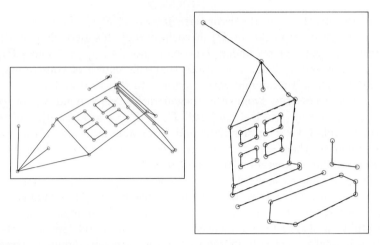

FIGURE 8.11: The projective reconstruction of the house from multiple views obtained using bundle adjustment. **Left:** The original reconstruction. **Right:** An overlay of the reconstruction after it has been registered (via a projective transformation) with the ground-truth data. The mean Euclidean distance between the reconstructed and ground-truth points is 0.07cm, or a mean relative error of 0.2%.

8.3.4   From Projective to Euclidean Shape

Although projective structure is useful by itself, in most cases it is the Euclidean structure of the scene that is the true object of interest. We saw in Section 8.1 that the best we can hope for is to estimate the Euclidean shape of the scene, defined up to an arbitrary similarity transformation.

Let us assume from now on that one of the techniques presented in Section 8.3.3 has been used to estimate the projection matrices $\mathcal{M}_i$ $(i = 1, \ldots, m)$ and the point positions $\boldsymbol{P}_j$ $(j = 1, \ldots, n)$ from m images of these points. We know that any other reconstruction, *and in particular a Euclidean one*, is separated from this one by a projective transformation. In other words, if $\hat{\mathcal{M}}_i$ and $\hat{\boldsymbol{P}}_j$ denote the Euclidean shape and the corresponding motion parameters, there must exist a 4×4 Euclidean upgrade matrix $\mathcal{Q}$ such that $\hat{\mathcal{M}}_i = \mathcal{M}_i \mathcal{Q}$ and $\hat{\boldsymbol{P}}_j = \mathcal{Q}^{-1} \boldsymbol{P}_j$. The rest of this section presents a method for computing $\mathcal{Q}$ and thus recovering the Euclidean shape and motion from the projective ones when (some of) the intrinsic parameters of the camera are known.

Let us first note that, since the individual matrices $\mathcal{M}_i$ are defined only up to scale, so are the matrices $\hat{\mathcal{M}}_i$ that can be written (in the most general case, where some of the intrinsic parameters are unknown) as

$$\hat{\mathcal{M}}_i = \rho_i \mathcal{K}_i (\mathcal{R}_i \quad \boldsymbol{t}_i),$$

where ρ_i accounts for the unknown scale of $\mathcal{M}_i$, and $\mathcal{K}_i$ is a calibration matrix as defined by Equation (1.14). In particular, if we write the Euclidean upgrade matrix as $\mathcal{Q} = (\mathcal{Q}_3 \quad \boldsymbol{q}_4)$, where $\mathcal{Q}_3$ is a 4×3 matrix and $\boldsymbol{q}_4$ is a vector in $\mathbb{R}^4$, we obtain immediately

$$\mathcal{M}_i \mathcal{Q}_3 = \rho_i \mathcal{K}_i \mathcal{R}_i. \tag{8.22}$$

When the intrinsic parameters of all cameras are known, so the matrices $\mathcal{K}_i$ can be taken equal to the identity, the 3×3 matrices $\mathcal{M}_i \mathcal{Q}_3$ are scaled rotation matrices. Writing that their rows $\boldsymbol{m}_{ij}^T$ ($j = 1, 2, 3$) are perpendicular to each other and have the same norm yields

$$\left\{ \begin{array}{l} \boldsymbol{m}_{i1}^T \mathcal{A} \boldsymbol{m}_{i2} = 0, \\ \boldsymbol{m}_{i2}^T \mathcal{A} \boldsymbol{m}_{i3} = 0, \\ \boldsymbol{m}_{i3}^T \mathcal{A} \boldsymbol{m}_{i1} = 0, \\ \boldsymbol{m}_{i1}^T \mathcal{A} \boldsymbol{m}_{i1} - \boldsymbol{m}_{i2}^T \mathcal{A} \boldsymbol{m}_{i2} = 0, \\ \boldsymbol{m}_{i2}^T \mathcal{A} \boldsymbol{m}_{i2} - \boldsymbol{m}_{i3}^T \mathcal{A} \boldsymbol{m}_{i3} = 0, \end{array} \right. \tag{8.23}$$

where $\mathcal{A} = \mathcal{Q}_3 \mathcal{Q}_3^T$. The upgrade matrix $\mathcal{Q}$ is of course defined only up to an arbitrary similarity. To determine it uniquely, we can assume that the world coordinate system and the first camera's frame coincide. Given m images, we obtain 12 linear equations and $5(m-1)$ quadratic ones in the coefficients of $\mathcal{Q}$. These equations can be solved using nonlinear least squares, which requires as usual a reasonable initial guess.

Alternatively, the constraints in Equation (8.23) are linear in the 10 coefficients of the symmetric matrix $\mathcal{A}$, allowing its estimation from at least two images via linear least squares. Note that $\mathcal{A}$ has rank 3—a constraint not enforced by our construction. To recover $\mathcal{Q}_3$, let us also note that, since $\mathcal{A}$ is symmetric, it can be diagonalized in an orthonormal basis as $\mathcal{A} = \mathcal{U}\mathcal{D}\mathcal{U}^T$, where $\mathcal{D}$ is the diagonal matrix formed by the eigenvalues of $\mathcal{A}$, and $\mathcal{U}$ is the orthogonal matrix formed by its eigenvectors. In the absence of noise, $\mathcal{A}$ is positive semidefinite with three positive and one zero eigenvalues, and $\mathcal{Q}_3$ can be computed as $\mathcal{U}_3\sqrt{\mathcal{D}_3}$, where $\mathcal{U}_3$ is the matrix formed by the columns of $\mathcal{U}$ associated with the positive eigenvalues of $\mathcal{A}$, and $\mathcal{D}_3$ is the corresponding submatrix of $\mathcal{D}$. Because of noise, however, $\mathcal{A}$ usually has maximal rank, and its smallest eigenvalue might even be negative. As shown in Ponce (2000), if we take this time $\mathcal{U}_3$ and $\mathcal{D}_3$ to be the submatrices of $\mathcal{U}$ and $\mathcal{D}$ associated with the three largest (positive) eigenvalues of $\mathcal{A}$, then $\mathcal{U}_3\mathcal{D}_3\mathcal{U}_3^T$ provides the best positive semidefinite rank-3 approximation of $\mathcal{A}$ in the sense of the Frobenius norm,[6] and we can take as before $\mathcal{Q}_3 = \mathcal{U}_3\sqrt{\mathcal{D}_3}$. At this point, the last column vector $\boldsymbol{q}_4$ of $\mathcal{Q}$ can be determined by (arbitrarily) picking the origin of the frame attached to the first camera as the origin of the world coordinate system.

Figure 8.12 shows the perspective upgrade associated with the projective reconstruction of the house obtained by bundle adjustment and shown in Figure 8.11, with a mean absolute error of 0.33cm and a relative error of 1.2%.

This method can be adapted easily to the case where only some of the intrinsic camera parameters are known. Using the fact that $\mathcal{R}_i$ is an orthogonal matrix allows us to write

$$\mathcal{M}_i \mathcal{A} \mathcal{M}_i^T = \rho_i^2 \mathcal{K}_i \mathcal{K}_i^T. \tag{8.24}$$

Thus, every image provides a set of constraints between the entries of $\mathcal{K}_i$ and $\mathcal{A}$. Assuming, for example, that the center of the image is known for each camera, we

---

[6]Note the similarity between this result and Theorem 6.

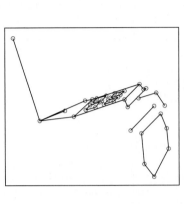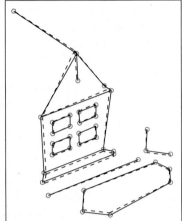

FIGURE 8.12: The Euclidean reconstruction of the house obtained by a Euclidean upgrade of the projective reconstruction obtained with bundle adjustment. **Left:** The original reconstruction. **Right:** An overlay of the reconstruction after it has been registered (via a similarity) with the ground-truth data. The mean Euclidean distance between the reconstructed and ground-truth points is 0.33cm, or a mean relative error of 1.2%. As before, the error has increased compared to the projective reconstruction because the similarity used for registration has fewer parameters than a homography.

can take $x_0 = y_0 = 0$ and write the square of the matrix $\mathcal{K}_i$ as

$$
\mathcal{K}_i \mathcal{K}_i^T = \begin{pmatrix} \alpha_i^2 \dfrac{1}{\sin^2 \theta_i} & -\alpha_i \beta_i \dfrac{\cos \theta_i}{\sin^2 \theta_i} & 0 \\[2ex] -\alpha_i \beta_i \dfrac{\cos \theta_i}{\sin^2 \theta_i} & \beta_i^2 \dfrac{1}{\sin^2 \theta_i} & 0 \\[2ex] 0 & 0 & 1 \end{pmatrix}.
$$

In particular, the part of Equation (8.24) corresponding to the zero entries of $\mathcal{K}_i \mathcal{K}_i^T$ provides two independent linear equations in the 10 coefficients of the 4×4 symmetric matrix $\mathcal{A}$:

$$
\begin{cases} \boldsymbol{m}_{i1}^T \mathcal{A} \boldsymbol{m}_{i3} = 0, \\ \boldsymbol{m}_{i2}^T \mathcal{A} \boldsymbol{m}_{i3} = 0. \end{cases}
$$

As might have been expected, these equations form a subset of those in Equation (8.23). With $m \geq 5$ images, the parameters can be estimated via linear least squares. Once $\mathcal{A}$ is known, $\mathcal{Q}$ can be estimated as before. Continuing to assume that $u_0 = v_0 = 0$, it is easy to add zero-skew and unit aspect-ratio constraints. For example, assuming zero skew ($\theta = \pi/2$) provides the additional constraint $\boldsymbol{m}_{i1}^T \mathcal{A} \boldsymbol{m}_{i2} = 0$.

8.4 NOTES

The interested reader is invited to consult the two excellent textbooks dedicated to structure from motion (Hartley & Zisserman 2000b; Faugeras, Luong, & Papadopoulo 2001) for details beyond the scope of this book. See also Ma, Soatto, and Sastry (2003*a*) and the first edition of this book. A deeper understanding of affine and projective SFM requires working knowledge of elementary affine and projective geometries. This is also beyond the scope of this book, but excellent textbooks are once again available for the interested reader—for example, (Snapper and Troyer 1989) for affine geometry, and Todd (1946), Coxeter (1974), Berger (1987), and Samuel (1988) for projective geometry.

The SFM problem was first studied in the calibrated orthographic setting by Ullman (1979). Longuet-Higgins (1981) then gave the first solution to the calibrated perspective case with the eight-point algorithm discussed in this chapter. A solution to the minimal five-point formulation of this problem can be found in Nistér (2004). The idea of stratifying SFM into a two-step problem where the affine or projective shape of a scene is recovered before additional constraints are brought into play to construct a Euclidean model is due to Koenderink and Van Doorn (1990) for the affine case, and to Faugeras (1995) for the projective one. In the affine case, the first solutions to this problem are due to Koenderink and Van Doorn (1990) and Tomasi and Kanade (1992). The initial, affine stage is valuable by itself: for example, it is the basis for the motion-based segmentation methods introduced by Gear (1998) and Costeira and Kanade (1998). The nonlinear least-squares method for computing the Euclidean upgrade matrix Q is due to Tomasi and Kanade (1992). The Cholesky approach to the same problem is due to Poelman and Kanade (1997); see Weinshall and Tomasi (1995) for another variant. Various extensions have been proposed recently, including the incremental recovery of structure and motion (Weinshall & Tomasi 1995; Morita & Kanade 1997).

The first solutions to projective SFM are due to Faugeras (1992) and Hartley *et al.* (1992). Other notable work in this area includes, for example, Mohr *et al.* (1992) and Shashua (1993). The two-view algorithm presented in this chapter is due to Hartley (1994*b*). The extension of factorization approaches to structure and motion recovery was first proposed by Sturm and Triggs (1996). The bilinear approach to projective SFM presented in Section 8.3.3 is an instance of a class of techniques called *resection-intersection* methods in photogrammetry (Triggs *et al.* 2000), which interleave steps where the camera parameters are estimated while the oberved point positions are kept fixed (*resection*) with steps where the point positions are estimated while the camera parameters are kept constant (*intersection*). This bilinear algorithm is due to Mahamud *et al.* (2001), and it is provably convergent to a critical point of its objective function. It should not, however, be run for too many iterations, because it usually falls in the basin of attraction of a degenerate solution after tens of thousands of steps. Algorithms for stitching together pairs, triples or quadruples of successive views can be found in Beardsley *et al.* (1997) and Pollefeys *et al.* (1999), for example.

Weak calibration is in fact an old problem: as mentioned by Faugeras (1993), the problem of calculating the epipoles and the epipolar transformations compatible with seven point correspondences was first posed by Chasles (1855) and solved by Hesse (1863). The problem of estimating the epipolar geometry from five point correspondences for internally calibrated cameras was solved by Kruppa (1913). An excellent modern account of Hesse's and Kruppa's techniques can be found in Faugeras and Maybank (1990), where the *absolute conic*, an imaginary conic section invariant through similarities, is used to derive two tangency constraints that make up for the missing point correspondences. These methods are of course mostly of theoretical interest because their reliance on a minimal number of correspondences limits their ability to deal with noise. The weak-calibration methods of Luong *et al.* (1993, 1996) and Hartley (1995) described in this chapter provide reliable and accurate alternatives.

The problem of computing Euclidean upgrades of projective reconstructions when some of the intrinsic parameters are known has been addressed by a number of authors (Heyden and Åström 1996; Triggs 1997; Pollefeys 1999). The matrix $\mathcal{A} = \mathcal{Q}_3 \mathcal{Q}_3^T$ introduced in Section 8.3.4 can be interpreted geometrically as the projective representation of the dual of the absolute conic, the *absolute dual quadric* (Triggs 1997). Like the absolute conic, this quadric surface is invariant through similarities, and the (dual) conic section associated with $\mathcal{K}_i \mathcal{K}_i^T$ is simply the projection of this quadric surface into the corresponding image. Self-calibration is the process of computing the intrinsic parameters of a camera from point correspondences with unknown Euclidean positions. Work in this area was pioneered by Faugeras and Maybank (1992) for cameras with fixed intrinsic parameters. A number of reliable self-calibration methods are now available (Hartley 1994a; Fitzgibbon and Zisserman 1998; Pollefeys *et al.* 1999), and they also can be used to upgrade projective reconstructions to Euclidean ones. The problem of computing Euclidean upgrades of projective reconstructions under minimal camera constraints such as zero skew is addressed in Heyden and Åström (1998, 1999), Pollefeys *et al.* (1999), Ponce *et al.* (2000, 2005), and Valdés *et al.* (2006).

PROBLEMS

8.1. We derive in this exercise a method for computing a minimal parameterization of the fundamental matrix and estimating the corresponding projection matrices.

(a) Show that two projection matrices $\mathcal{M}$ and $\mathcal{M}'$ can always be reduced to the following canonical forms by an appropriate projective transformation:

$$\tilde{\mathcal{M}} = \begin{pmatrix} 1 & 0 & 0 & 0 \\ 0 & 1 & 0 & 0 \\ 0 & 0 & 1 & 0 \end{pmatrix} \quad \text{and} \quad \tilde{\mathcal{M}}' = \begin{pmatrix} \boldsymbol{a}_1^T & b_1 \\ \boldsymbol{a}_2^T & b_2 \\ \boldsymbol{0}^T & 1 \end{pmatrix}.$$

Note: For simplicity, you can assume that all the matrices involved in your solution are nonsingular.

(b) Note that applying this transformation to the projection matrices amounts to applying the inverse transformation to every scene point P. Let us denote by $\tilde{\boldsymbol{P}} = (x, y, z)^T$ the position of the transformed point $\tilde{P}$ in the world coordinate system and by $\boldsymbol{p} = (u, v, 1)^T$ and $\boldsymbol{p}' = (u', v', 1)^T$ the homogeneous coordinate vectors of its images. Show that

$$(u' - b_1)(\boldsymbol{a}_2 \cdot \boldsymbol{p}) = (v' - b_2)(\boldsymbol{a}_1 \cdot \boldsymbol{p}).$$

(c) Derive from this equation an eight-parameter parameterization of the fundamental matrix, and use the fact that $\mathcal{F}$ is defined only up to a scale factor to construct a minimal seven-parameter parameterization.

(d) Use this parameterization to derive an algorithm for estimating $\mathcal{F}$ from at least seven point correspondences and for estimating the projective shape of the scene.

8.2. Show that all copies of a set of points in $\mathbb{E}^3$ that are related to each other by geometric transformations forming a group form an equivalence class.

8.3. Show that the parameter F_{33} can be easily estimated from the other entries of $\mathcal{F}$ during the minimization of E in Equation (8.4), resulting in an eigenvalue problem involving only eight parameters.

Hint: Write that $\partial E/\partial F_{33} = 0$ at a minimum of E.

8.4. Generalize this normalization to the estimation of the affine fundamental matrix.

8.5. Show that the eight-point algorithm fails to compute the fundamental matrix when the eight points and two optical centers lie on a quadric surface.

8.6. Show that only one of the four possible solutions for camera motion found by the binocular Euclidean SFM approach of Section 8.1 places the reconstructed points in front of the two cameras.

8.7. Show that affine transformations are the most general class of 4×4 nonsingular matrices that preserve the relationship between coordinates expressed in Equation (8.6) for any point P_j.

8.8. Show that the projection matrices associated with two affine cameras can always be reduced to the canonical forms of Equation (8.10) by an appropriate affine transformation.

8.9. Show that affine cameras (and the corresponding epipolar geometry) can be viewed as the limit of perspective images with increasing focal length receding away from the scene. Use this result to given an alternate derivation of Equation (8.9).

8.10. Show that, under affine projection, the image of the center of mass of a set of points is the center of mass of their images.

8.11. Define the ratio of three collinear points A, B, C as

$$R(A, B, C) = \frac{\overline{AB}}{\overline{BC}}$$

for some orientation of the line supporting the three points.

(a) Show that the area of any triangle PQR is

$$A(P, Q, R) = \frac{1}{2}PQ \times RH = \frac{1}{2}PQ \times PR\sin\theta,$$

where PQ denotes the distance between the two points P and Q, H is the projection of R onto the line passing through P and Q, and θ is the angle between the lines joining the point P to the points Q and R.

(b) Show that $R(A, B, C) = A(A, B, O)/A(B, C, O)$, where O is some point not lying on this line.

8.12. The cross-ratio of four collinear points A, B, C, and D is defined as

$$\{A, B; C, D\} = \frac{\overline{CA}}{\overline{CB}}\frac{\overline{DB}}{\overline{DA}}.$$

(a) Use the result of the previous problem to show that

$$\{A, B; C, D\} = \frac{\sin(a + b)\sin(b + c)}{\sin(a + b + c)\sin b},$$

where the angles a, b, and c are defined as below.

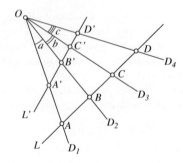

(b) Use this result to define the cross-ratio of four coplanar lines passing through the same point.

Hint: Consider the lines L and L' in the diagram.

8.13. Show that there exists a four-parameter family of solutions to the binocular projective SFM problem of Section 8.3.2, and that this family is given by Equation (8.18).

8.14. Show that the value of the error E defined by Equation (8.20) is given by Equation (8.21) at one of its extrema with respect to the variables Z_{ij}, assuming that the data vectors $\boldsymbol{p}_{ij}$ have unit norm.

PROGRAMMING EXERCISES

8.15. Implement the eight-point algorithm.

8.16. Implement the estimation of affine epipolar geometry from image correspondences and the estimation of scene structure from the corresponding projection matrices.

8.17. Implement the Tomasi–Kanade approach to affine shape from motion.

8.18. Implement the binocular projective SFM algorithm of Section 8.3.2.

8.19. Implement the bundle adjustment algorithm of Section 8.3.3.

8.20. Implement the Euclidean algorithm of Section 8.3.4 for cameras with known image center and zero skew.

PART FOUR

MID-LEVEL VISION

CHAPTER 9

Segmentation by Clustering

A crucial problem in mid-level vision involves coming up with image representations that are simultaneously compact and expressive. These representations must summarize information available from the first stages of visual processing, and pass them on. Summaries are necessary because early vision produces vast quantities of information. The richness of the available representation tends to overwhelm what is significant. Useful summaries could be computed from pixels or from groups of pixels—for example, by constructing groups of pixels that all have the same color or texture. They could also be computed from local pattern elements—for example, by collecting together edge points that seem to lie on a line or on a circle, or close to some complex geometric structure. The core idea is collecting together pixels or pattern elements into summary representations that emphasize important, interesting, or distinctive properties.

Obtaining such representation is known variously as *segmentation, grouping, perceptual organization,* or *fitting*. We use the term *segmentation* for a wide range of activities because, although techniques may differ, the motivation for all these activities is the same: obtain a compact representation of what is helpful in the image. It's hard to see that there could be a comprehensive theory of segmentation, not least because what is interesting and what is not depends on the application. There is certainly no comprehensive theory of segmentation at time of writing, and the term is used in different ways in different quarters.

FIGURE 9.1: As these images suggest, an important component of vision involves organizing image information into meaningful assemblies. The human vision system seems to do so rather well. In each of these three images, blobs are organized together to form textured surfaces that appear to bulge out of the page (you may feel that they are hemispheres). The blobs appear to be assembled "because they form surfaces," hardly a satisfactory explanation and one that begs difficult computational questions. Notice that saying that they are assembled because together they form the same texture also begs questions (how do we know?). In the case of the surface on the **left**, it might be quite difficult to write programs that can recognize a single coherent texture. This process of organization can be applied to many different kinds of input.

The details of what the summary representation should be depend on the task, but there are a number of quite general desirable features. First, there should be relatively few (that is, not more than later algorithms can cope with) components in the representation computed for typical pictures. Second, these components should be suggestive. It should be pretty obvious from these components whether the objects we are looking for are present, again for typical pictures.

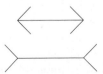

FIGURE 9.2: The famous Müller-Lyer illusion; the horizontal lines are in fact the same length, although that belonging to the lower figure looks longer. Clearly, this effect arises from some property of the relationships that form the whole (the *gestaltqualität*), rather than from properties of each separate segment.

There are two important threads in segmentation, which aren't wholly different. In the first, our summary is assembled purely locally, by clustering methods that focus on local relations between items. Here we are trying to assemble items that look like one another. This approach allows us, for example, to assemble together clumps of pixels that look similar; such clumps are commonly called *regions*. Generally, this approach uses clustering methods, and is the focus of this chapter. In the second approach, we assemble together items based on global relations—for example, all items that lie on a straight line. Figure 9.1 shows a collection of small groups of pixels. When one looks at this figure, these groups of pixels appear to belong together, most likely because taken together they suggest the presence of a surface. In this approach, we are interested in methods that can collect together tokens or pixels of groups of pixels that, when taken together, suggest the presence of a structure of some form. This approach emphasizes methods that can identify parametric models in pools of data; we describe such methods in Chapter 10.

9.1 HUMAN VISION: GROUPING AND GESTALT

A key feature of the human vision system is that context affects how things are perceived (e.g., see the illusion of Figure 9.2). This observation led the Gestalt school of psychologists to reject the study of responses to stimuli and to emphasize grouping as the key to understanding visual perception. To them, grouping meant the tendency of the visual system to assemble some components of a picture together and to perceive them together (this supplies a rather rough meaning to the word context used above). Grouping, for example, is what causes the Müller-Lyer illusion of Figure 9.2: the vision system assembles the components of the two arrows, and the horizontal lines look different from one another because they are peceived as components of a whole, rather than as lines. Furthermore, many grouping effects can't be disrupted by cognitive input; for example, you can't make the lines in Figure 9.2 look equal in length by deciding not to group the arrows.

A common experience of segmentation is the way that an image can resolve itself into a *figure*— typically, the significant, important object—and a *ground*—

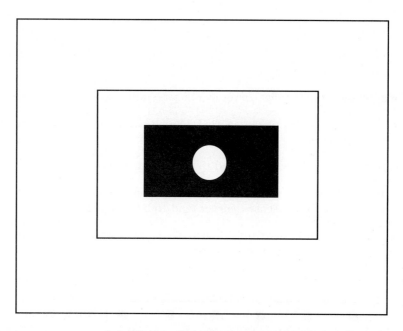

FIGURE 9.3: One view of segmentation is that it determines which component of the image forms the figure and which the ground. The figure illustrates one form of ambiguity that results from this view. The white circle can be seen as figure on the black rectangular ground, or as ground where the figure is a black rectangle with a circular hole in it and the ground is then a white square.

the background on which the figure lies. However, as Figure 9.3 illustrates, what is figure and what is ground can be profoundly ambiguous, meaning that a richer theory is required.

The Gestalt school used the notion of a *gestalt*—a whole or a group—and of its *gestaltqualität*—the set of internal relationships that makes it a whole (e.g., Figure 9.2) as central components in their ideas. Their work was characterized by attempts to write down a series of rules by which image elements would be associated together and interpreted as a group. There were also attempts to construct algorithms, which are of purely historical interest (see Gordon (1997) for an introductory account that places their work in a broad context).

The Gestalt psychologists identified a series of factors, which they felt predisposed a set of elements to be grouped. These factors are important because it is quite clear that the human vision system uses them in some way. Furthermore, it is reasonable to expect that they represent a set of preferences about when tokens belong together that lead to a useful intermediate representation.

There are a variety of factors, some of which postdate the main Gestalt movement:

- **Proximity:** Tokens that are nearby tend to be grouped.

- **Similarity:** Similar tokens tend to be grouped together.

- **Common fate:** Tokens that have coherent motion tend to be grouped together.

- **Common region:** Tokens that lie inside the same closed region tend to be grouped together.

- **Parallelism:** Parallel curves or tokens tend to be grouped together.

- **Closure:** Tokens or curves that tend to lead to closed curves tend to be grouped together.

- **Symmetry:** Curves that lead to symmetric groups are grouped together.

- **Continuity:** Tokens that lead to continuous—as in joining up nicely, rather than in the formal sense—curves tend to be grouped.

- **Familiar configuration:** Tokens that, when grouped, lead to a familiar object tend to be grouped together.

These laws are illustrated in Figures 9.4, 9.5, 9.7, and 9.1.

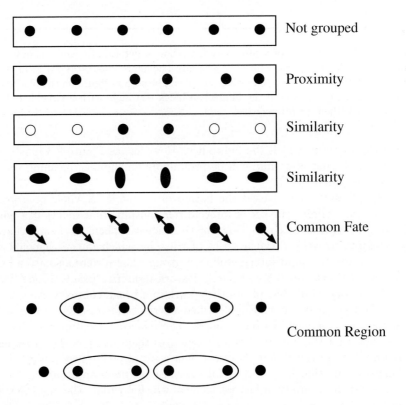

FIGURE 9.4: Examples of Gestalt factors that lead to grouping (which are described in greater detail in the text).

These rules can function fairly well as explanations, but they are insufficiently crisp to be regarded as forming an algorithm. The Gestalt psychologists had serious

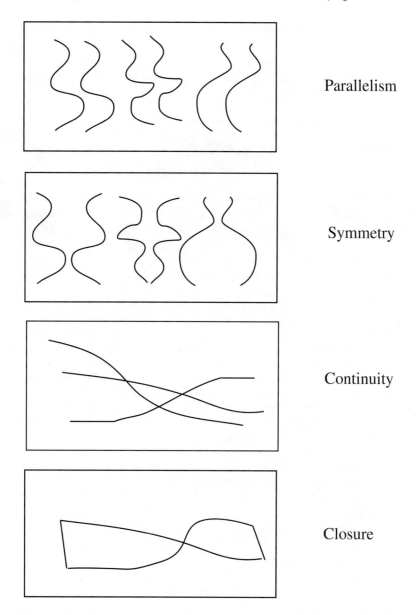

Parallelism

Symmetry

Continuity

Closure

FIGURE 9.5: Examples of Gestalt factors that lead to grouping (which are described in greater detail in the text).

difficulty with the details, such as when one rule applied and when another. It is difficult to supply a satisfactory algorithm for using these rules; the Gestalt movement attempted to use an extremality principle.

Familiar configuration is a particular problem. The key issue is to understand just *what* familiar configuration applies in a problem and how it is selected. For example, look at Figure 9.1. One might argue that the blobs are grouped because they yield a sphere. The difficulty with this view is explaining how this occurred—where did the hypothesis that a sphere is present come from? A search through all views of all objects is one explanation, but one must then explain how this search is organized. Do we check *every view* of *every* sphere with *every* pattern of spots? How can this be done efficiently?

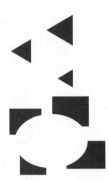

FIGURE 9.6: Occlusion appears to be an important cue in grouping. It may be possible to see the pattern on the **left** as a collection of digits; the pattern next to it is quite clearly some occluded digits. The black regions in each figure are the same. The important difference between the two figures seems to be that the superimposed gray regions supply evidence that the black regions are components of larger objects that are separated for a reason, rather than just scattered black regions. On the **right**, two figures consisting of tokens that suggest the presence of occluding objects whose boundaries don't contrast with much of the image. Notice that one has a clear impression of the position of the entire contour of the occluding figures. These contours are known as *illusory contours*.

The Gestalt rules do offer some insight because they explain what happens in various examples. These explanations seem to be sensible because they suggest that the rules help solve problems posed by visual effects that arise commonly in the real world—that is, they are *ecologically valid*. For example, continuity may represent a solution to problems posed by occlusion; sections of the contour of an occluded object could be joined up by continuity (see Figure 9.6).

This tendency to prefer interpretations that are explained by occlusion leads to interesting effects. One is the *illusory contour*, illustrated in Figure 9.6. Here a set of tokens suggests the presence of an object, most of whose contour has no contrast. The tokens appear to be grouped together because they provide a cue to the presence of an occluding object, which is so strongly suggested by these tokens that one could fill in the no-contrast regions of contour.

This ecological argument has some force because it is possible to interpret most grouping factors using it. Common fate can be seen as a consequence of the fact that components of objects tend to move together. Equally, symmetry is a useful grouping cue because there are a lot of real objects that have symmetric or close to symmetric contours. Essentially, the ecological argument says that tokens are grouped because doing so produces representations that are helpful for the visual world that people encounter. The ecological argument has an appealing, although vague, statistical flavor. From our perspective, Gestalt factors provide interesting

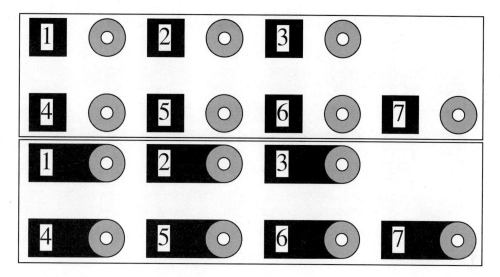

FIGURE 9.7: An example of grouping phenomena in real life. The buttons on an elevator in the computer science building at U.C. Berkeley used to be laid out as in the **top** figure. It was common to arrive at the wrong floor and discover that this was because you'd pressed the wrong button; the buttons are difficult to group unambiguously with the correct label, and it is easy to get the wrong grouping at a quick glance. A public-spirited individual filled in the gap between the numbers and the buttons, as in the **bottom** figure, and the confusion stopped because the proximity cue had been disambiguated.

hints, but should be seen as the *consequences* of a larger grouping process, rather than the process itself.

9.2   IMPORTANT APPLICATIONS

Simple segmentation algorithms are often useful in significant applications. Generally, simple algorithms work best when it is easy to tell what a useful decomposition is. Two important cases are *background subtraction*—where anything that doesn't look like a known background is interesting—and *shot boundary detection*—where substantial changes in a video are interesting.

More complex algorithms are required for two other very important applications. In *interactive segmentation*, a user guides a segmentation system to cut out an object from a picture. Finally, a major goal is to form image regions.

9.2.1   Background Subtraction

In many applications, objects appear on a largely stable background. The standard example is detecting parts on a conveyor belt. Another example is counting motor cars in an overhead view of a road; the road is pretty stable in appearance. Another, less obvious, example is in human-computer interaction. Quite commonly, a camera is fixed (say, on top of a monitor) and views a room. Pretty much anything in the view that doesn't look like the room is interesting.

In these kinds of applications, a useful segmentation can often be obtained by

FIGURE 9.8: The figure shows every fifth frame from a sequence of 120 frames of a child playing on a patterned sofa. The frames are used at an 80 x 60 resolution, for reasons we discuss in Figure 9.10. Notice that the child moves from one side of the frame to the other during the sequence.

FIGURE 9.9: Background subtraction results for the sequence of Figure 9.8 using 80 x 60 frames. We compare two methods of computing the background: (**a**) The average of all 120 frames. Notice that the child spent more time on one side of the sofa than the other, leading to the faint blur in the average there. (**b**) Pixels whose difference from the average exceeds a small threshold. (**c**) Those whose difference from the average exceeds a somewhat larger threshold. Notice that, in each case, there are some excess pixels and some missing pixels.

subtracting an estimate of the appearance of the background from the image and looking for large absolute values in the result. The main issue is obtaining a good estimate of the background. One method is simply to take a picture. This approach works rather poorly because the background typically changes slowly over time. For example, the road may get more shiny as it rains and less when the weather dries up; people may move books and furniture around in the room; and so on.

An alternative that usually works quite well is to estimate the value of background pixels using a **moving average**. In this approach, we estimate the value of

a   b   c

FIGURE 9.10: Registration can be a significant nuisance in background subtraction, particularly for textures. These figures show results for the sequence of Figure 9.8, using 160 x 120 frames. We compare two methods of computing the background: (**a**) The average of all 120 frames. Notice that the child spent more time on one side of the sofa than the other, leading to a faint blur in the average there. (**b**) Pixels whose difference from the average exceeds a small threshold. (**c**) Those whose difference from the average exceeds a somewhat larger threshold. Notice that the number of problem pixels—where the pattern on the sofa has been mistaken for the child—has markedly increased. This is because small movements can cause the high spatial frequency pattern on the sofa to be misaligned, leading to large differences.

Form a background estimate $\mathcal{B}^{(0)}$. At each frame $\mathcal{F}$
    Update the background estimate, typically by
        forming $\mathcal{B}^{(n+1)} = \dfrac{w_a \mathcal{F} + \sum_i w_i \mathcal{B}^{(n-i)}}{w_c}$
        for a choice of weights w_a, w_i and w_c.
    Subtract the background estimate from the
        frame, and report the value of each pixel where
        the magnitude of the difference is greater than some
        threshold.
end

Algorithm 9.1: Background Subtraction.

---

a particular background pixel as a weighted average of the previous values. Typically, pixels in the distant past should be weighted at zero, and the weights increase smoothly. Ideally, the moving average should track the changes in the background, meaning that if the weather changes quickly (or the book mover is frenetic), relatively few pixels should have nonzero weights, and if changes are slow, the number of past pixels with nonzero weights should increase. This yields Algorithm 9.1. For those who have read the filters chapter, this is a filter that smooths a function of time, and we would like it to suppress frequencies that are larger than the typical frequency of change in the background and pass those that are at or below that frequency. The approach can be quite successful, but needs to be used on quite coarse scale images as Figures 9.9 and 9.10 illustrate.

For each frame in an image sequence
    Compute a distance between this frame and the
      previous frame
   If the distance is larger than some threshold,
     classify the frame as a shot boundary.
end

Algorithm 9.2: Shot Boundary Detection Using Interframe Differences.

9.2.2 Shot Boundary Detection

Long sequences of video are composed of *shots*: much shorter subsequences that show largely the same objects. These shots are typically the product of the editing process. There is seldom any record of where the boundaries between shots fall. It is helpful to represent a video as a collection of shots; each shot can then be represented with a *key frame*. This representation can be used to search for videos or to encapsulate their content for a user to browse a video or a set of videos.

Finding the boundaries of these shots automatically—*shot boundary detection*—is an important practical application of simple segmentation algorithms. A shot boundary detection algorithm must find frames in the video that are significantly different from the previous frame. Our test of significance must take account of the fact that, within a given shot, both objects and the background can move around in the field of view. Typically, this test takes the form of a distance; if the distance is larger than a threshold, a shot boundary is declared (Algorithm 9.2).

There are a variety of standard techniques for computing a distance:

- **Frame differencing** algorithms take pixel-by-pixel differences between each two frames in a sequence and sum the squares of the differences. These algorithms are unpopular, because they are slow—there are many differences—and because they tend to find many shots when the camera is shaking.

- **Histogram-based** algorithms compute color histograms for each frame and compute a distance between the histograms. A difference in color histograms is a sensible measure to use because it is insensitive to the spatial arrangement of colors in the frame (e.g., small camera jitters will not affect the histogram).

- **Block comparison** algorithms compare frames by cutting them into a grid of boxes and comparing the boxes. This is to avoid the difficulty with color histograms, where a red object disappearing off-screen in the bottom-left corner is equivalent to a red object appearing on screen from the top edge. Typically, these block comparison algorithms compute an interframe distance that is a composite—taking the maximum is one natural strategy—of interblock distances, each computed using methods like those used for interframe distances.

- **Edge differencing** algorithms compute edge maps for each frame, and then compare these edge maps. Typically, the comparison is obtained by counting the number of potentially corresponding edges (nearby, similar orientation,

FIGURE 9.11: A user who wants to cut an object out of an image (**left**) could mark some foreground pixels and some background pixels (**center**), then use an interactive segmentation method to get the cut out components on the **right**. The method produces a model of foreground and background pixel appearance from the marked pixels, then uses this information to decide a figure ground segmentation. *This figure was originally published as Figure 9 of "Interactive Image Segmentation via Adaptive Weighted Distances," by Protiere and Sapiro, IEEE Transactions on Image Processing, 2007 © IEEE, 2007.*

etc.) in the next frame. If there are few potentially corresponding edges, there is a shot boundary. A distance can be obtained by transforming the number of corresponding edges.

These are relatively *ad hoc* methods, but are often sufficient to solve the problem at hand.

9.2.3 Interactive Segmentation

People very often want to cut objects out of images and move them into other images. There are lots of reasons to do this; we sketched some in Section 6.3, where we described methods to fill in the resulting hole in the source image. But to do this efficiently, we need good ways to select the object we want to cut out. It is too much work to have to paint the object's pixels, or its boundary on the image.

This is fairly clearly a segmentation problem, but a special one in which there are two segments, foreground and background. The foreground segment should be coherent, but the background segment might not be. Different ways to attack the problem are built around different types of interface. In an **intelligent scissors** interface, the user sketches a curve fairly close to the boundary of the object; this curve is then moved to the boundary using local information, typically image gradient cues. In a **painting** interface, the user paints some pixels with a foreground or background brush. These pixels are used to produce an appearance model of the foreground and of the background. In turn, these models are fed into a fast

FIGURE 9.12: In a grabcut interface for interactive segmentation, a user marks a box around the object of interest; foreground and background models are then inferred by a clustering method, and the object is segmented. If this segmentation isn't satisfactory, the user has the option of painting foreground and background strokes on pixels to help guide the model. *This figure was originally published as Figure 1 of "GrabCut Interactive Foreground Extraction using Iterated Graph Cuts" by C. Rother, V. Kolmogorov, and A. Blake, ACM Trans. on Graphics (ACM SIGGRAPH Proc), Vol. 23:3 © 2004, ACM, Inc.* `http://doi.acm.org/10.1145/1186562.1015720` *Reprinted by permission.*

graph-based segmenter (Section 9.4.3). Figure 9.11 illustrates the process. Finally, in a **grabcut** interface, the user draws a box around the object. This box yields an initial estimate of foreground and background pixels, and from this we get an initial segmentation, which yields foreground and background models, which yield an improved segmentation (Figure 9.12).

Quite often, pixels are neither pure background or pure foreground. For example, in a picture of a face, the pixels around the boundary of the hair are somewhat ambiguous; few pixels here contain only hair, or only background. Instead, because pixels average light coming in through the lens, most have a value that is a weighted average of hair and background. In this case, we could use interactive segmentations to prepare a *matte*, a mask of values in the range $[0 - 1]$. The matte is traditionally written as α, and our model of the ith pixel value is that it is $\alpha\boldsymbol{f} + (1 - \alpha)\boldsymbol{b}$, where $\boldsymbol{f}$ and $\boldsymbol{b}$ are foreground and background values (Figure 9.13). *Rotoscoping* is a process like matting, but applied to video; here one recovers a set of segments, one per frame, corresponding to a moving object. These segments could then be composited onto a new background, making it look as though the object is moving against the new background. Matting and rotoscoping methods are strongly related to segmentation methods, but involve slightly different representations. We give some pointers in the notes.

9.2.4 Forming Image Regions

One application of segmentation is to decompose an image into regions that have roughly coherent color and texture. Typically, the shape of these regions isn't particularly important, but the coherence is important. This process is quite widely studied—it is often referred to as the exclusive meaning of the term segmentation— and usually thought of as a first step in recognition. Regions are a valuable image representation in several applications. Regions can offer a route to compressing an image. Because each region has coherent appearance, we may be able to compress the image by describing the shape and appearance of the regions separately (as opposed to describing each pixel independently).

Regions can be used as the backbone of many other visual computations. For

FIGURE 9.13: Matting methods produce a real-valued mask (rather than a foreground-background mask) to try and compensate for effects in hair, at occluding boundaries, and so on, where some pixels consist of an average of foreground and background values. The matte is bright for foreground pixels and dark for background pixels; for some pixels in the hair, it is gray, meaning that when the foreground is transferred to a new image, these pixels should become a weighted sum of foreground and background. The gray value indicates the weight. *This figure was originally published as Figure 6 of "Spectral Matting," by A. Levin, A. Rav-Acha, and D. Lischinski, IEEE Transactions on Pattern Analysis and Machine Intelligence, 2008 © IEEE, 2008.*

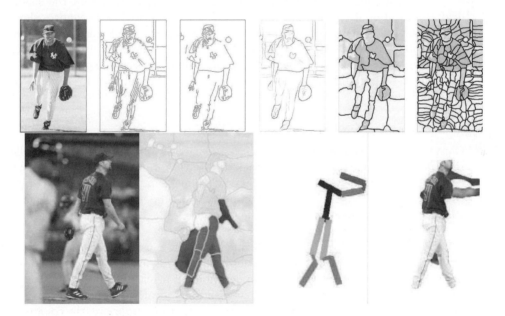

FIGURE 9.14: Superpixels often can expose structure in images that other representations conceal. Human body segments tend to appear as long, thin segments. In the **top** row, an image together with three different edge maps (the edge detector of Section 5.2.1, with two scales of smoothing, and the P_b of Section 17.1.3) and superpixels computed at two "scales" (in this case, the number of superpixels was constrained). Notice that the coarser superpixels tend to expose limb segments in a straightforward way. On the **bottom** row, another image, its superpixels, and two versions of the body layout inferred from the superpixel representation. *This figure was originally published as Figure 3 and part of Figure 10 of "Recovering human body configurations: Combining Segmentation and Recognition," by G. Mori, X. Ren, A. Efros, and J. Malik, Proc. IEEE CVPR, 2004 © IEEE, 2004.*

example, if we want to identify correspondences between two images—to compute optic flow or to register parts of the images, say—correspondences between regions might be the place to start. As a second example, if we want to label images with the names of the objects that are present, regions help us keep track of what has been labelled, because we can use them to tell which image pixels correspond to a particular label. As yet another example, regions could be matched to other regions within an image to find the kind of repetition that one sees in, for example, the windows on the facade of a building—not quite a texture, but still repetitious.

In some applications, regions need to be quite large and may have a complex shape. We might want regions to largely respect object boundaries (for example, if we are labelling objects in images). Most clustering methods can be adapted to produce segmenters that will construct regions like this.

In other applications, it is more useful to have small, compact regions. These are usually called *superpixels.* Superpixels are particularly useful when we need representation that is small compared to the pixel grid, but still very rich (such a representation is sometimes called an *oversegmentation*). One example application is in computing lightness (Section 2.2.3). If we wanted to represent the shading field, representing it on the pixel grid would be wasteful because it changes slowly; instead, we might have one shading value per superpixel, and smooth the result. Other applications are in recognition. For example, human arms and legs tend to be long and straight; we could try to find them by assembling superpixels to form suggestive groups. This seems to be easier than cutting up large regions (Figure 9.14).

9.3   IMAGE SEGMENTATION BY CLUSTERING PIXELS

Clustering is a process whereby a data set is replaced by **clusters**, which are collections of data points that belong together. It is natural to think of image segmentation as clustering; we would like to represent an image in terms of clusters of pixels that belong together. The specific criterion to be used depends on the application. Pixels may belong together because they have the same color, they have the same texture, they are nearby, and so on.

The general recipe for image segmentation by clustering is as follows. We represent each image pixel with a feature vector. This feature vector contains all measurements that may be relevant in describing a pixel. Natural feature vectors include: the intensity at the pixel; the intensity and location of the pixel; the color of the pixel, represented in whatever color space seems appropriate; the color of the pixel and its location; and the color of the pixel, its location, and a vector of filter outputs from a local texture represenation (compare to Section 6.1). We cluster these feature vectors. Every feature vector belongs to exactly one cluster, and so each cluster represents an image segment. We can obtain the image segment represented by a cluster by replacing the feature vector at each pixel with the number of that feature vector's cluster center. You should compare this procedure with vector quantization (Section 6.2.1), which is what it is. Notice that this description is extremely general; different feature vectors will lead to different kinds of image segment, as will different clusterers.

Whether a particular combination of feature vector and clusterer yields good performance depends on what one needs. It is possible to make some general statements, though. The general recipe doesn't guarantee that segments are connected, which may or may not matter. If one is segmenting images to compress them, then encoding the US flag as three segments (red, white and blue) might be a good choice; if one is segmenting to represent objects, this is probably a poor representation, because it regards all white stars as a single segment. If the feature vector contains a representation of the position of the pixel, the segments that result tend to be "blobby," because pixels that lie very far from the center of a segment will tend to belong to other clusters. This is one way to ensure that segments are connected. Representing color information tends to make segmenters better, because in this case it's hard to get easy images wrong (color doesn't seem to make hard images easier, though). For some applications, doing well at easy images is enough.

9.3.1   Basic Clustering Methods

There are two natural algorithms for clustering. In **divisive clustering**, the entire data set is regarded as a cluster, and then clusters are recursively split to yield a good clustering (Algorithm 9.4). In **agglomerative clustering**, each data item is regarded as a cluster, and clusters are recursively merged to yield a good clustering (Algorithm 9.3).

Make each point a separate cluster
Until the clustering is satisfactory
      Merge the two clusters with the
         smallest inter-cluster distance
end

Algorithm 9.3: Agglomerative Clustering or Clustering by Merging.

Construct a single cluster containing all points
Until the clustering is satisfactory
      Split the cluster that yields the two
         components with the largest inter-cluster distance
end

Algorithm 9.4: Divisive Clustering, or Clustering by Splitting.

There are two major issues in thinking about clustering:

- *What is a good inter-cluster distance?* Agglomerative clustering uses an inter-cluster distance to fuse nearby clusters; divisive clustering uses it to split insufficiently coherent clusters. Even if a natural distance between data points is available (which might not be the case for vision problems), there is no canonical inter-cluster distance. Generally, one chooses a distance that seems appropriate for the data set. For example, one might choose the distance be-

tween the closest elements as the inter-cluster distance, which tends to yield
extended clusters (statisticians call this method *single-link clustering*). Another natural choice is the maximum distance between an element of the first
cluster and one of the second, which tends to yield rounded clusters (statisticians call this method *complete-link clustering*). Finally, one could use an
average of distances between elements in the cluster, which also tends to yield
"rounded" clusters (statisticians call this method *group average clustering*).

- *How many clusters are there?* This is an intrinsically difficult task if there
  is no model for the process that generated the clusters. The algorithms we
  have described generate a hierarchy of clusters. Usually, this hierarchy is
  displayed to a user in the form of a *dendrogram*—a representation of the
  structure of the hierarchy of clusters that displays inter-cluster distances—
  and an appropriate choice of clusters is made from the dendrogram (see the
  example in Figure 9.15).

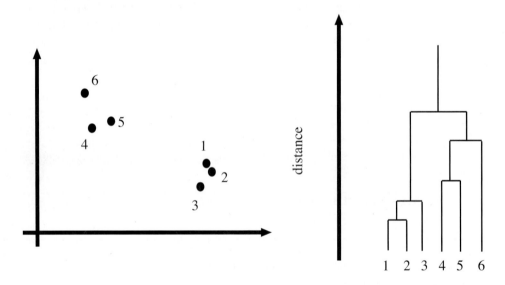

FIGURE 9.15: **Left**, a data set; **right**, a dendrogram obtained by agglomerative clustering
using single-link clustering. If one selects a particular value of distance, then a horizontal
line at that distance splits the dendrogram into clusters. This representation makes it
possible to guess how many clusters there are and to get some insight into how good the
clusters are.

The main difficulty in using either agglomerative or divisive clustering methods directly is that there are an awful lot of pixels in an image. There is no reasonable prospect of examining a dendrogram because the quantity of data means
that it will be too big. In practice, this means that the segmenters decide when
to stop splitting or merging by using a set of threshold tests. For example, an
agglomerative segmenter might stop merging when the distance between clusters
is sufficiently low or when the number of clusters reaches some value. A divisive
clusterer might stop splitting when the resulting clusters meet some similarity test.

FIGURE 9.16: Segmentation results from the watershed algorithm, applied to an image by Martin Brigdale. **Center:** watershed applied to the image intensity; notice some long superpixels. **Right:** watershed applied to image gradient magnitude; this tends to produce rounder superpixels. *Martin Brigdale © Dorling Kindersley, used with permission.*

It is straightforward to modify both divisive and agglomerative clusterers to ensure that regions are connected. Agglomerative clusterers need to merge only clusters with shared boundaries. It is more difficult to modify divisive clusterers, which need to ensure that the children of any split are connected. One way to do this is to split along spatial boundaries in the segment being split. It is usually impractical to look for the best split of a cluster (for a divisive method) or the best merge (for an agglomerative method). Divisive methods are usually modified by using some form of summary of a cluster to suggest a good split (for example, a histogram of pixel colors). Agglomerative methods also need to be modified, because the number of pixels means that one needs to be careful about the inter-cluster distance (the distance between cluster centers of gravity is often used). Finally, it can be useful to merge regions simply by scanning the image and merging all pairs whose distance falls below a threshold, rather than searching for the closest pair.

9.3.2 The Watershed Algorithm

An early segmentation algorithm that is still widely used is the *watershed* algorithm. Assume we wish to segment image $\mathcal{I}$. In this algorithm, we compute a map of the image gradient magnitude, $\|\nabla \mathcal{I}\|$. Zeros of this map are locally extreme intensity values; we take each as a seed for a segment, and give each seed a unique label. Now we assign pixels to seeds by a procedure that is, rather roughly, analogous to filling a height map with water (hence the name). Imagine starting at pixel (i, j); if we travel backward down the gradient of $\|\nabla \mathcal{I}\|$, we will hit a unique seed. Each pixel gets the label of the seed that is hit by this procedure.

You should recognize this description as a form of shortest path algorithm; it can also be seen as a form of agglomerative clusterer. We start with seed clusters, then agglomerate pixels to clusters when the path to the cluster is "downhill" from the pixel. This means that one can produce rather more efficient algorithms than the one we sketched, and there is a considerable literature of these algorithms. In this literature, authors tend to criticize the watershed algorithm for oversegmentation—that is, for producing "too many" segments. More recently, watershed algorithms are quite widely used because they produce tolerable superpixels, and are efficient. Good implementations of watershed algorithms are widely available; to produce Figure 9.16, we used the implementation in Matlab's Image processing toolbox. It is natural to use the gradient magnitude to drive a watershed transform, because this divides the image up into regions of relatively small gradient; however, one could also use the image intensity, in which case each region is the domain of attraction of an intensity minimum or maximum. Gradient watersheds tend to produce more useful superpixels (Figure 9.16).

9.3.3 Segmentation Using K-means

There is a strong resonance between image segmentation as we have described it, and vector quantization. In Chapter 6, we described vector quantization in the context of texture representation and introduced the k-means algorithm. K-means produces good image segments for some applications. Following the general recipe, we compute a feature vector representing each pixel, we apply k-means, and each pixel goes to the segment represented by the cluster center that claims its feature vector. The main consequence of using k-means is that we know how many segments there will be. For some applications, this is a good thing; for example, the segmentations of Figure 9.17 use five segments, and essentially represent a requantization of the image gray-levels (or colors, respectively) to five levels. This can be useful for some coding and compression applications.

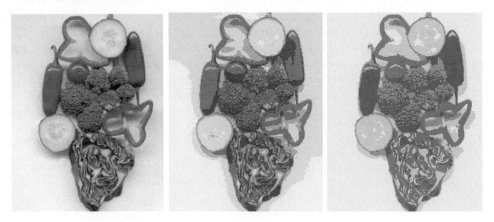

FIGURE 9.17: On the **left**, an image of mixed vegetables, which is segmented using k-means to produce the images at **center** and on the **right**. We have replaced each pixel with the mean value of its cluster; the result is somewhat like an adaptive requantization, as one would expect. In the center, a segmentation obtained using only the intensity information. At the right, a segmentation obtained using color information. Each segmentation assumes five clusters.

One difficulty with using this approach for segmenting images is that segments

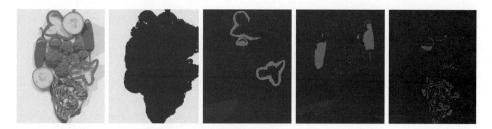

FIGURE 9.18: Here we show the image of vegetables segmented with k-means, assuming a set of 11 components. The **left** figure shows all segments shown together, with the mean value in place of the original image values. The other figures show four of the segments. Note that this approach leads to a set of segments that are not necessarily connected. For this image, some segments are actually quite closely associated with objects, but one segment may represent many objects (the peppers); others are largely meaningless. The absence of a texture measure creates serious difficulties, as the many different segments resulting from the slice of red cabbage indicate.

are not connected and can be very widely scattered (Figures 9.17 and 9.18). This effect can be reduced by using pixel coordinates as features—an approach that results in large regions being broken up (Figure 9.19).

FIGURE 9.19: Five of the segments obtained by segmenting the image of vegetables with a k-means segmenter that uses position as part of the feature vector describing a pixel, now using 20 segments rather than 11. Note that the large background regions that should be coherent have been broken up because points got too far from the center. The individual peppers are now better separated, but the red cabbage is still broken up because there is no texture measure.

9.3.4   Mean Shift: Finding Local Modes in Data

Clustering can be abstracted as a density estimation problem. We have a set of sample points in some feature space, which came from some underlying probability density. Comaniciu and Meer (2002) created an extremely important segmenter, using the mean shift algorithm, which thinks of clusters as local maxima (local modes) in this density. To do so, we need an approximate representation of the density. One way to build an approximation is to use *kernel smoothing*. Here we take a set of functions that look like "blobs" or "bumps," place one over each data point, and so produce a smooth function that is large when there are many data points close together and small when the data points are widely separated.

This is a quite general strategy that applies to many different bump functions. We will use a specific kernel smoother, writing

$$K(\boldsymbol{x}; h) = \frac{(2\pi)^{(-d/2)}}{h^d} \exp\left(-\frac{1}{2} \frac{\|\boldsymbol{x}\|^2}{h}\right)$$

for the bump function. We introduce a positive scale parameter h, which we can adjust to get the best representation. Then, our model of the density is

$$f(\boldsymbol{x}) = \left(\frac{1}{n}\right) \sum_{i=1}^{n} K\left(\boldsymbol{x}_i - \boldsymbol{x}; h\right)$$

(you should check that this is a density, i.e., that it is non-negative, and that its integral is one). We can estimate h by maximizing the average likelihood of held-out data. In this procedure, we repeat the following experiment numerous times: hold out one data point at random, fit a density model to the remaining data, and then compute the likelihood of the held-out data point as a function of h (perhaps by computing values at a set of different sample points in h). We average the likelihoods computed in this way, then use the h that maximizes that likelihood.

We can simplify notation by writing $k(u) = \exp\left(-\frac{1}{2}u\right)$ (this is called the *kernel profile*) and $C = \frac{(2\pi)^{(-d/2)}}{nh^d}$, so that

$$f(\boldsymbol{x}) = C \sum_{i=1}^{n} k\left(\left\|\frac{\boldsymbol{x} - \boldsymbol{x}_i}{h}\right\|^2\right) \tag{9.1}$$

Now write $g = \frac{d}{du} k(u)$. Starting from some point $\boldsymbol{x}_0$, we should like to find a nearby point that maximizes the density value. We will use this local maximum (local mode) as a cluster center. The mean shift procedure maximizes expressions of the form of Equation 9.1. We are seeking $\boldsymbol{y}$ such that the gradient ∇f vanishes at that point. We must require that

$$
\begin{aligned}
\nabla f(\boldsymbol{x})\, |_{\boldsymbol{x}=\boldsymbol{y}} \;&=\; 0 \\
&=\; C \sum_i \nabla k\!\left(\left\|\frac{\boldsymbol{x}_i - \boldsymbol{y}}{h}\right\|^2\right) \\
&=\; C\frac{2}{h} \sum_i [\boldsymbol{x}_i - \boldsymbol{y}] \left[g\!\left(\left\|\frac{\boldsymbol{x}_i - \boldsymbol{y}}{h}\right\|^2\right)\right] \\
&=\; C\frac{2}{h} \left[\frac{\sum_i \boldsymbol{x}_i g\!\left(\left\|\frac{\boldsymbol{x}_i - \boldsymbol{y}}{h}\right\|^2\right)}{\sum_i g\!\left(\left\|\frac{\boldsymbol{x}_i - \boldsymbol{y}}{h}\right\|^2\right)} - \boldsymbol{y}\right] \times \left[\sum_i g\!\left(\left\|\frac{\boldsymbol{x}_i - \boldsymbol{y}}{h}\right\|^2\right)\right].
\end{aligned}
$$

We expect that $\sum_i g(\|\frac{\boldsymbol{x}_i - \boldsymbol{y}}{h}\|^2)$ is nonzero, so that the maximum occurs when

$$\left[\frac{\sum_i \boldsymbol{x}_i g\!\left(\left\|\frac{\boldsymbol{x}_i - \boldsymbol{y}}{h}\right\|^2\right)}{\sum_i g\!\left(\left\|\frac{\boldsymbol{x}_i - \boldsymbol{y}}{h}\right\|^2\right)} - \boldsymbol{y}\right] = 0,$$

or equivalently, when

$$y = \frac{\sum_i x_i g(\|\frac{x_i - y}{h}\|^2)}{\sum_i g(\|\frac{x_i - y}{h}\|^2)}.$$

The mean shift procedure involves producing a series of estimates $y^{(j)}$ where

$$y^{(j+1)} = \frac{\sum_i x_i g(\|\frac{x_i - y^{(j)}}{h}\|^2)}{\sum_i g(\|\frac{x_i - y^{(j)}}{h}\|^2)}.$$

The procedure gets its name from the fact that we are shifting to a point which has the form of a weighted mean (see Algorithm 9.5).

Start with an estimate of the mode $y^{(0)}$ and a set of n data vectors x_i of dimension d, a scaling constant h, and g the derivative of the kernel profile

Until the update is tiny
    Form the new estimate
$$y^{(j+1)} = \frac{\sum_i x_i g(\|\frac{x_i - y^{(j)}}{h}\|^2)}{\sum_i g(\|\frac{x_i - y^{(j)}}{h}\|^2)}$$

Algorithm 9.5: Finding a Mode with Mean Shift.

9.3.5   Clustering and Segmentation with Mean Shift

Clustering with mean shift is, in principle, straightforward. We start the mean shift procedure at every data point, producing a mode for each data point. Because we are working with continuous variables, every one of these modes is different, but we expect the modes to be very tightly clustered. There should be a small set of actual modes, and each of these estimates is very close to one of them. These estimates are themselves useful, because they represent a form of filtering of the image. We could replace each pixel with its mode representation; this gives a significant smoothing of the image in a way that respects image boundaries (Figure 9.20). To cluster the data, we apply, say, an agglomerative clusterer to the mode estimates. Because we expect the modes to be very tightly clustered, group average distance is a good choice of distance, and we can stop clustering when this distance exceeds a small threshold. This will produce a set of small, tight clusters that are widely separated. We now map each data point to the cluster center corresponding to its mode (Algorithm 9.6).

This recipe can be applied nearly directly to image segmentation. We represent each pixel with a feature vector, then cluster the feature vectors; each cluster center represents a segment, and we replace each pixel with the number of its cluster center. Improved performance can be obtained by a representation that balances spatial and appearance features more explicitly. In particular, we represent the ith pixel with a feature vector x_i which has two components: x_i^s, which has dimension

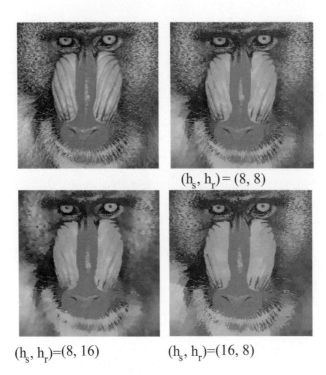

$(h_s, h_r) = (8, 8)$

$(h_s, h_r) = (8, 16)$ $(h_s, h_r) = (16, 8)$

FIGURE 9.20: An image (**top left**) and mean shift modes obtained with different clustering scales for space h_s and appearance h_r. If h_s is small, the method must produce clusters that are relatively small and compact spatially because the kernel function smoothes over a relatively small radius and so will allow many distinct modes. If h_r is small, the clusters are compact in appearance; this means that small h_s and large h_r will produce small, blobby clusters that could span a range of appearances, whereas large h_s and small h_r will tend toward spatially complex and extended clusters with a small range of appearances. Cluster boundaries will try harder to follow level curves of intensity. *This figure was originally published as Figure 5 of "Mean Shift: A Robust Approach Toward Feature Space Analysis," by D. Comaniciu and P. Meer, IEEE Transactions on Pattern Analysis and Machine Intelligence, 2002 © IEEE, 2002.*

For each data point $\boldsymbol{x}_i$
> Apply the mean shift procedure (Algorithm 9.5), starting with $\boldsymbol{y}^{(0)} = \boldsymbol{x}_i$
> Record the resulting mode as $\boldsymbol{y}_i$

Cluster the $\boldsymbol{y}_i$, which should form small tight clusters.
A good choice is an agglomerative clusterer with group average distance,
> stopping clustering when the group average distance exceeds a small threshold

The data point $\boldsymbol{x}_i$ belongs to the cluster that its mode $\boldsymbol{y}_i$ belongs to.

Algorithm 9.6: Mean Shift Clustering.

d_s and represents the location of the pixel and $\boldsymbol{x}_i^r$, which has dimension d_r and represents everything else. Now we use two kernels and two smoothing parameters in the density estimation procedure, writing

$$K(\boldsymbol{x}; h_s, h_r) = \left[\frac{(2\pi)^{(-d_s/2)}}{h_s^{d_s}} k\left(\frac{\boldsymbol{x}^s}{h_s}\right) \right] \left[\frac{(2\pi)^{(-d_r/2)}}{h_r^{d_r}} k\left(\frac{\boldsymbol{x}^r}{h_r}\right) \right].$$

This means that we can balance spatial and appearance clustering and require, for example, spatially tight clusters with a wide range of appearances, and so on. In this case, the mean shift update equation changes slightly (Exercises).

For each pixel, p_i, compute a feature vector $\boldsymbol{x}_i = (\boldsymbol{x}_i^s, \boldsymbol{x}_i^r)$ representing spatial and appearance components, respectively.

Choose h_s, h_r the spatial (resp. appearance) scale of the smoothing kernel.

Cluster the $\boldsymbol{x}_i$ using this data and mean shift clustering (Algorithm 9.6).

(Optional) Merge clusters with fewer than t_{min} pixels with a neighbor; the choice of neighbor is not significant, because the cluster is tiny.

The i'th pixel belongs to the segment corresponding to its cluster center (for example, one could label the cluster centers $1 \ldots r$, and then identify segments by computing a map of the labels corresponding to pixels).

Algorithm 9.7: Mean Shift Segmentation.

9.4   SEGMENTATION, CLUSTERING, AND GRAPHS

Clustering algorithms deal with similarity between data items. Some algorithms may summarize data items (for example, the cluster centers in the k-means algorithm), but the core issue is similarity between data items. It might not be useful to compare all pairs of data items; for example, there might be little real advantage in comparing very distant image pixels directly. All this rather naturally suggests a graph. Each data item would be a vertex. There would be a weighted edge between all pairs of data items that could usefully be compared. The process of clustering the data then becomes one of segmenting the graph into connected components.

9.4.1   Terminology and Facts for Graphs

We review terminology here very briefly, as it's quite easy to forget.

- A *graph* is a set of vertices V and edges E that connect various pairs of vertices. A graph can be written $G = \{V, E\}$. Each edge can be represented by a pair of vertices—that is, $E \subset V \times V$. Graphs are often drawn as a set of points with curves connecting the points.

- The *degree* of a vertex is the number of edges incident on that vertex.

FIGURE 9.21: Segmentations of images obtained using the mean shift algorithm. *This figure was originally published as Figure 10 of "Mean Shift: A Robust Approach Toward Feature Space Analysis," by D. Comaniciu and P. Meer, IEEE Transactions on Pattern Analysis and Machine Intelligence, 2002 © IEEE, 2002.*

- A *directed graph* is one in which edges (a, b) and (b, a) are distinct; such a graph is drawn with arrowheads indicating which direction is intended.

- An *undirected graph* is one in which no distinction is drawn between edges (a, b) and (b, a).

- A *weighted graph* is one in which a weight is associated with each edge.

- Two edges are *consecutive* if they have a vertex in common.

- A *path* is a sequence of consecutive edges.

- A *circuit* is a path which ends at the vertex at which it begins.

- A *self-loop* is an edge that has the same vertex at each end; self-loops don't occur in our applications.

- Two vertices are said to be *connected* when there is a sequence of edges starting at the one and ending at the other; if the graph is directed, then the arrows in this sequence must point the right way.

- A *connected graph* is one where every pair of vertices is connected.

- A *tree* is a connected graph with no circuits.

- Given a connected graph $G = \{V, E\}$, a *spanning tree* is a tree with vertices V and edges a subset of E. By our definition, trees are connected, so a spanning tree is connected.

- Every graph consists of a disjoint set of *connected components*—that is, $G = \{V_1 \cup V_2 \dots V_n, E_1 \cup E_2 \dots E_n\}$, where $\{V_i, E_i\}$ are all connected graphs and there is no edge in E that connects an element of V_i with one of V_j for $i \neq j$.

- A *forest* is a graph whose connected components are trees.

In a weighted graph, there are efficient algorithms for computing minimum weight spanning trees (see, for example, Jungnickel (1999) or Cormen *et al.* (2009)). Another very important problem that can be solved efficiently seeks to maximize flow in a directed graph. In particular, in a directed graph identify one vertex as a source s and another as a target t. Associate with each directed edge e a *capacity*, $c(e)$, which is a non-negative number. A *flow* is a non-negative value $f(e)$ associated with each edge with the following properties. First, $0 \leq f(e) \leq c(e)$. Second, at any vertex $v \in \{V - s - t\}$,

$$\sum_{e \text{ arriving at } v} f(e) - \sum_{e \text{ leaving from } v} f(e) = 0$$

(i.e., all flow arriving at a vertex leaves it; this is Kirchoff's law). The value of a flow is

$$\sum_{e \text{ arriving at } t} f(e).$$

There are efficient algorithms to maximize the flow in, for example, Ahuja *et al.* (1993) or Cormen *et al.* (2009). A dual problem is also interesting. Decompose the vertices into two disjoint sets $\mathcal{S}$ and $\mathcal{T}$, such that $s \in \mathcal{S}$ and $t \in \mathcal{T}$. This represents a *cut*. Consider $\mathcal{W} \in E$, the set of directed edges from $\mathcal{S}$ to $\mathcal{T}$. The value of the cut is

$$\sum_{e \in \mathcal{W}} c(e).$$

The value of the cut can again be minimized efficiently; algorithms appear in, for example, Ahuja *et al.* (1993), Jungnickel (1999), or Schrijver (2003).

9.4.2 Agglomerative Clustering with a Graph

Felzenszwalb and Huttenlocher (2004) showed how to use graph theoretic ideas to build a straightforward but very effective segmenter based around an agglomerative clusterer. Represent the image as a weighted graph. There are edges between any pair of pixels that are neighbors. Each edge has a weight that measures dissimilarity—i.e., weights are large if pixels are very different, and small if they are similar. The weights could come from a variety of pixel representations. For example, we could use the squared difference in intensity; we could represent the color at each pixel with a vector, and use the length of the difference vector; we could represent the texture at each pixel with a vector of filter outputs (after the

Start with a set of clusters $\mathcal{C}_i$, one cluster per pixel.
Sort the edges in order of non-decreasing edge weight, so that
$w(e_1) \geq w(e_2) \geq \ldots \geq w(e_r)$.

For $i = 1$ to r
    If the edge e_i lies inside a cluster
        do nothing
    Else
        One end is in cluster $\mathcal{C}_l$ and the other is in cluster $\mathcal{C}_m$
      If $diff(\mathcal{C}_l, \mathcal{C}_m) \leq MInt(\mathcal{C}_l, \mathcal{C}_m)$
          Merge $\mathcal{C}_l$ and $\mathcal{C}_m$ to produce a new set of clusters.

Report the remaining set of clusters.

Algorithm 9.8: Agglomerative Clustering with Graphs.

local texture representations of Section 6.1), then use the length of the difference vector; or we could use a weighted sum of all these distances.

We will start with every pixel forming a cluster, then merge clusters until there is no need to continue. To do this, we need some notion of the distance between two clusters. Each cluster is a component of the graph, formed from all the vertices (pixels) in the cluster, and all the edges that start and end inside the cluster. Then the difference between two components is the minimum weight edge connecting two components. Write $\mathcal{C}_1$, $\mathcal{C}_2$ for the two components, $\mathcal{E}$ for the edges, and $w(v_1, v_2)$ for the weight of the edge joining v_1 and v_2. Then, we have

$$\mathrm{diff}(\mathcal{C}_1, \mathcal{C}_2) = \min_{v_1 \in \mathcal{C}_1, v_2 \in \mathcal{C}_2, (v_1, v_2) \in \mathcal{E}} w(v1, v2).$$

It is also helpful to know how coherent a particular cluster is. This will help us stop clustering. We define the internal difference of a component to be the largest weight in the minimum spanning tree of the component. Write $M(\mathcal{C}) = \{V_{\mathcal{C}}, E_M\}$ for the minimum spanning tree of $\mathcal{C}$. Then, we have

$$\mathrm{int}(\mathcal{C}) = \max_{e \in M(\mathcal{C})} w(e).$$

We will start with a set of clusters (or segments) that consists of all the pixels, one cluster per pixel. We then merge clusters iteratively. We do so by sorting all edges in order of non-decreasing edge weight. For each edge, starting with the smallest, we consider the clusters at either end of the edge. If both ends of the edge lie in the same cluster, there is nothing to do. If there are distinct clusters at each end, then we could merge them. We do so when the edge weight is small compared to the internal difference of each of the clusters (this requires some care for small clusters; details below). We now proceed through all the edges, merging as necessary. The final segmentation is the set of clusters once the last edge has been visited (Algorithm 9.8).

FIGURE 9.22: Images segmented using Algorithm 9.8, shown next to segments. Figures obtained from `http://people.cs.uchicago.edu/~pff/segment/`, by kind permission of Pedro Felzenszwalb.

Comparing the edge weight to the internal difference of the clusters requires some care, because in small clusters the internal distance might be zero (if there is only one vertex), or implausibly small. To deal with this, Felzenszwalb and Huttenlocher (2004) define a function of two clusters, MInt, as

$$\mathrm{MInt}(\mathcal{C}_1, \mathcal{C}_2) = \min(\mathrm{int}(\mathcal{C}_1) + \tau(\mathcal{C}_1), \mathrm{int}(\mathcal{C}_2) + \tau(\mathcal{C}_2))$$

where $\tau(\mathcal{C})$ is a term that biases the internal difference upward for small clusters; Felzenszwalb and Huttenlocher (2004) use $\tau(\mathcal{C}) = k/ \mid \mathcal{C} \mid$, for k some constant parameter. This algorithm is notably fast and relatively accurate (Figure 9.22).

9.4.3 Divisive Clustering with a Graph

As we have seen (Section 9.2.3), it is extremely useful to separate an image into a foreground and background based on examples. Assume we have a map of pixels, one per image pixel, where each pixel in the map carries one of three labels: foreground, background or unknown (these maps are sometimes known as *trimaps*) depending on whether the corresponding image is in the foreground, background or is unknown. We should like to take the foreground and background pixels, build models from these, then label the unknown pixels with these models. There are two important constraints on the labels. First, a pixel that looks like the foreground examples should get a foreground label (similarly for background). Second, pixels should tend to have labels that are the same as their neighbors'.

Boykov and Jolly (2001) phrase this problem as energy minimization. Write $\mathcal{F}$ for the set of pixels with foreground labels, $\mathcal{B}$ for the set with background labels, and $\mathcal{U}$ for the unknown pixels. We associate a binary variable δ_i with the ith unknown pixel. We adopt the convention that $\delta_i = -1$ if the ith pixel is background, and $\delta_i = 1$ if the ith pixel is foreground. We will find a value for this binary variable that minimizes an energy function. The energy will have two types of term. The first type of term will encourage pixels similar to the foreground (resp. background) model to have foreground (resp. background) labels. The second will encourage pixels to have the same label as their neighbors.

Write $\boldsymbol{p}_i$ for a vector representing the ith pixel. The vector could contain intensity; intensity and color; intensity, color and texture; or other information. Write $d_f(\boldsymbol{p})$ for a function that compares the pixel vector $\boldsymbol{p}$ with the foreground model; this function is large when the pixel is not like the foreground, and small when it is like the foreground. Similarly, write $d_b(\boldsymbol{p})$ for a function that compares the pixel vector with the background. Write $\mathcal{N}(i)$ for the neighbors of pixel i. Write $B(\boldsymbol{p}_i, \boldsymbol{p}_j)$ for a non-negative, symmetric function that compares two pixels, which we will use as a cost for assigning neighboring pixels to different models. This could be as simple as a constant, which just encourages neighboring pixels to have the same label. More complicated B should be large for two pixels that are similar, and small for different pixels; in this case, we will encourage the label to change between pixels that look different.

Notice that $(\frac{1}{2})(1 - \delta_i\delta_j)$ has the value 1 when δ_i and δ_j are different, and 0 otherwise. Write $\mathcal{I}$ for the set of all pixels, $\mathcal{U}$ for the set of unknown pixels, $\mathcal{F}$ for the set of known foreground pixels, and $\mathcal{B}$ for the set of known background pixels. Now we can write an energy function

$$E^*(\delta) \;=\; \sum_{i \in \mathcal{I}} d_f(\boldsymbol{p}_i)\frac{1}{2}(1 + \delta_i) + d_b(\boldsymbol{p}_i)\frac{1}{2}(1 - \delta_i) +$$

$$\sum_{i \in \mathcal{I}} \sum_{j \in \mathcal{N}(i)} B(\boldsymbol{p}_i, \boldsymbol{p}_j)(\frac{1}{2})(1 - \delta_i\delta_j)$$

which we must minimize subject to $\delta_k = 1$ for $k \in \mathcal{F}$ and $\delta_k = 0$ for $k \in \mathcal{B}$. Notice that we can make this energy function small by labelling pixels that agree with the foreground model with $\delta = 1$, those that agree with the background model with $\delta = -1$, and ensuring that labels change at pixels that look different (i.e., where B is small). Minimizing this energy might be hard, because it is a combinatorial problem (δ_j can take only two values).

It turns out that minimizing E can be rephrased as minimizing a cut on a graph. The easiest way to see this is with a figure. Imagine a cut on the graph of Figure 9.23. In this graph, each pixel is represented by a vertex, the source vertex corresponds to the foreground label, and the target vertex corresponds to the background label. There is one edge connecting each pixel to the source and one connecting it to the target; we can cut the graph by cutting only one of these two edges, and if we cut both, the cut is not minimal. We can interpret a cut that cuts only one of these edges as a map from a pixel to foreground (resp. background) depending on whether the edge to the source (resp. target) remains uncut. Furthermore, the value of a cut that cuts only one of these two edges for each pixel is the same as the value of the energy function E for the corresponding labelling. As a result, we can minimize the energy function by computing the minimum cut. This is known to be polynomial (from the references in Section 9.4.1), but in fact

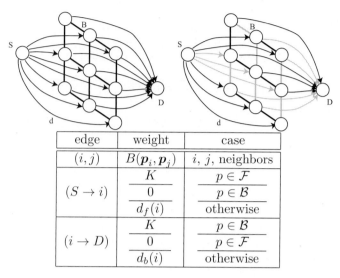

edge	weight	case
(i, j)	$B(\boldsymbol{p}_i, \boldsymbol{p}_j)$	i, j, neighbors
$(S \to i)$	K / 0 / $d_f(i)$	$p \in \mathcal{F}$ / $p \in \mathcal{B}$ / otherwise
$(i \to D)$	K / 0 / $d_b(i)$	$p \in \mathcal{B}$ / $p \in \mathcal{F}$ / otherwise

FIGURE 9.23: On the **left**, a graph derived from an image to set up foreground/background segmentation as a graph cut problem. We interpret pixels linked to the source (S) as foreground pixels, and pixels linked to the drain (D) as background pixels. Some pixels—whose labels are known—are linked to only one of the two, and to their neighbors. Link weights are given in the table. The links between neighbors have the same capacity in each direction, which is why they are drawn without a direction. On the **right**, a cut of that graph (edges that have been cut are grayed out). Notice that each pixel is linked to either the foreground or to the background, but not to both (because otherwise we would not have disconnected S and D) or to neither (because we could restore one of the two edges and get a cut with a better value). Furthermore, the sum of weights of cut edges is equal to the energy cost function. As a result, we can segment the image into foreground and background by solving for the minimum cost cut. With the weights shown in the table, the value of a cut on the graph is the same as the value of the energy function, as long as the cut does not cut both $(S \to i)$ and $(i \to D)$, and $K = 1 + \max_{\boldsymbol{p} \in \mathcal{I}} \sum_{\boldsymbol{q}:\{\boldsymbol{p},\boldsymbol{q}\} \in \mathcal{N}} B(\boldsymbol{p}, \boldsymbol{q})$. A minimum cut will not cut both, because a better cut will cut only one; this means that the energy function in the text can be minimized by cutting the graph.

specialized algorithms are now very fast at cutting graphs from images.

This procedure gives us one way to deal with the problem of Section 6.3.2. Here we had a hole in an image and a patch that matched the hole; but the patch typically is square, and the hole typically is not. Place the patch over the hole. For some pixels we know only one value (those inside the hole, and those outside the patch), but for others we know two values. For these, we would like to choose which pixel appears in the final image. Again, we have a combinatorial problem. Write δ_i for a variable that takes the value -1 if the ith pixel in the final image should come from the patch, and 1 otherwise. Write $\mathcal{U}$ for the pixels that could take either label, $\mathcal{P}$ for the pixels that can take values only from the patch, and $\mathcal{I}$ for the pixels that can take values only from the image. We do not have a foreground or background model. Generally, we would like pixels to have a δ that agrees with their neighbors. When two neighboring pixels have different δ values (i.e., at a point where we cut

Property	Affinity function	Notes
Distance	$\exp\left\{-\left((\boldsymbol{x}-\boldsymbol{y})^t(\boldsymbol{x}-\boldsymbol{y})/2\sigma_d^2\right)\right\}$	
Intensity	$\exp\left\{-\left((I(\boldsymbol{x})-I(\boldsymbol{y}))^t(I(\boldsymbol{x})-I(\boldsymbol{y}))/2\sigma_I^2\right)\right\}$	$I(\boldsymbol{x})$ is the intensity of the pixel at $\boldsymbol{x}$.
Color	$\exp\left\{-\left(\text{dist}(\boldsymbol{c}(\boldsymbol{x}),\boldsymbol{c}(\boldsymbol{y}))^2/2\sigma_c^2\right)\right\}$	$\boldsymbol{c}(\boldsymbol{x})$ is the color of the pixel at $\boldsymbol{x}$.
Texture	$\exp\left\{-\left((\boldsymbol{f}(\boldsymbol{x})-\boldsymbol{f}(\boldsymbol{y}))^t(\boldsymbol{f}(\boldsymbol{x})-\boldsymbol{f}(\boldsymbol{y}))/2\sigma_I^2\right)\right\}$	$\boldsymbol{f}(\boldsymbol{x})$ is a vector of filter outputs describing the pixel at $\boldsymbol{x}$ computed as in Section 6.1.

TABLE 9.1: Different affinity functions comparing pixels for a graph based segmenter. Notice that affinities can be combined. One attractive feature of the exponential form is that, say, location, intensity and texture affinities could be combined by multiplying them.

from patch to image), we would like the actual values of the pixels to be as similar as possible; this is to ensure that we blend at places where the image agrees with the patch. These criteria can be written into an energy function that can be minimized with graph cuts.

9.4.4 Normalized Cuts

Segmenting an image by min-cut usually does not work well without good foreground and background models. This is because one can get very good cut values by cutting off small groups of pixels. The cut does not balance the difference between segments with the coherence within segments. Shi and Malik (2000) suggest a *normalized cut*: cut the graph into two connected components such that the cost of the cut is a small fraction of the total affinity within each group.

To do this, we need a measure of affinity between pixels. We will model the image as a graph with one vertex at each pixel, and an edge from each pixel to all its neighbors. We must place a weight on each edge, which we will call the *affinity* between the pixels. The detailed form of the affinity measure depends on the problem at hand. The weight of an arc connecting similar nodes should be large, and the weight on an arc connecting different nodes should be small (in the last section, B was the cost of cutting an edge, and so was small when pixels were similar, and large when they were different). Table 9.1 gives some affinity functions in current use.

Recall that a normalized cut must cut the graph into two connected components such that the cost of the cut is a small fraction of the total affinity within each group. We can formalize this as decomposing a weighted graph V into two components A and B and scoring the decomposition with

$$\frac{cut(A,B)}{assoc(A,V)} + \frac{cut(A,B)}{assoc(B,V)}$$

(where $cut(A, B)$ is the sum of weights of all edges in V that have one end in A and the other in B, and $assoc(A, V)$ is the sum of weights of all edges that have one end in A). This score is small if the cut separates two components that have few edges of low weight between them and many internal edges of high weight. We would like to find the cut with the minimum value of this criterion, called a *normalized cut*. The criterion is successful in practice (Figure 9.24).

This problem is too difficult to solve in this form, because we would need to look at every graph cut. It is a combinatorial optimization problem, so we can't use continuity arguments to reason about how good a neighboring cut is given the value of a particular cut. Worse, it's an NP-complete problem, even for grid graphs. However, Shi and Malik (2000) give an approximation algorithm that generates a good cut.

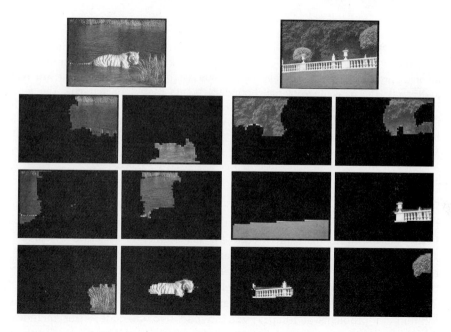

FIGURE 9.24: The images on top are segmented using the normalized cuts framework, described in the text, into the components shown. The affinity measures used involved intensity and texture, as in Table 9.1. The image of the swimming tiger yields one segment that is essentially tiger, one that is grass, and four components corresponding to the lake. Similarly, the railing shows as three reasonably coherent segments. Note the improvement over k-means segmentation obtained by having a texture measure. *This figure was originally published as Figure 2 of "Image and video segmentation: the normalized cut framework," by J. Shi, S. Belongie, T. Leung, and J. Malik, Proc. IEEE Int. Conf. Image Processing, 1998 © IEEE, 1998.*

9.5 IMAGE SEGMENTATION IN PRACTICE

Code is now available for many important image segmenters. The EDISON codes (from Rutgers' computer vision group, available at `http://coewww.rutgers.edu/`

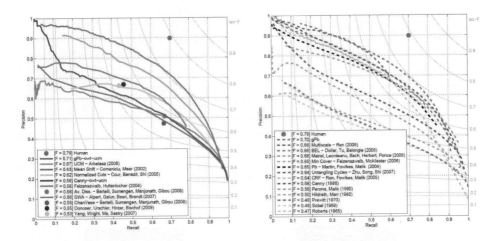

FIGURE 9.25: Segmenters and edge detectors can be evaluated by comparing the predicted boundaries to object boundaries that people mark on images. A natural comparison involves precision (the percentage of the marked boundary points that are real ones) and recall (the percentage of real boundary points that were marked); the F measure summarizes precision and recall into a single number $F = 2PR/(P + R)$. On the **left**, these measures for various segmenters; on the **right**, for various edge detectors. *This figure was originally published as Figures 1 and 2 of "Contour Detection and Hierarchical Image Segmentation" by P. Arbelaez, M. Maire, C. Fowlkes, and J. Malik, IEEE Transactions on Pattern Analysis and Machine Intelligence, 2011, © IEEE, 2011.*

`riul/research/robust.html`) implement mean shift image segmentation (Section 9.3.5). The same web page distributes a variety of other mean shift codes. Pedro Felzenszwalb distributes code for his segmenter (Section 9.4.2) at `http://people.cs.uchicago.edu/~pff/segment/`. Jianbo Shi distributes code for normalized cuts at `http://www.cis.upenn.edu/~jshi/software/`. Greg Mori distributes code for computing superpixels using normalized-cut algorithms at `http://www.cs.sfu.ca/~mori/research/superpixels/`. Yuri Boykov distributes code for min-cut problems at `http://vision.csd.uwo.ca/code/`; this includes codes for extremely large grids. Vladimir Kolmogorov distributes a min-cut code at `http://www.cs.ucl.ac.uk/staff/V.Kolmogorov/software.html`.

9.5.1 Evaluating Segmenters

Quantitative evaluation of segmenters is a somewhat vexed issue, because different methods have different goals. One reasonable goal is predicting object boundaries that people mark on images. This view yields a quantitative evaluation in terms of recall and precision for boundary points that people have marked on a test set. A natural comparison involves precision P (the percentage of the marked boundary points that are real ones, i.e., were marked by people) and recall R (the percentage of real boundary points that were marked); the F measure summarizes precision and recall into a single number, $F = 2PR/(P + R)$. In this framework, human performance can be evaluated by holding out a test person, comparing the test person's markup to all the rest, and then averaging performance statistics over held out test people. Modern segmenters can do quite well at this test, but not as well as people do (Figure 9.25).

The Berkeley Segmentation Data Set consists of 300 manually segmented images, and is distributed at `http://www.eecs.berkeley.edu/Research/Projects/CS/vision/bsds/`. This page also maintains up-to-date benchmarks on that dataset. A more recent version (BSDS-500) has 500 manually segmented images; see `http://www.eecs.berkeley.edu/Research/Projects/CS/vision/grouping/resources.html`. Again, there is a set of benchmarks on that dataset available. The Lotus Hill Institute provides a large dataset, free for academic use, at `http://www.imageparsing.com/`. Annotations are much richer than just region structure, and extend to a detailed semantic hierarchy of region relations.

9.6 NOTES

Segmentation is a difficult topic, and there are a huge variety of methods. Surveys of mainly historical interest are Riseman and Arbib (1977), Fu and Mui (1981), Haralick and Shapiro (1985), Nevatia (1986), and Pal and Pal (1993).

One reason is that it is typically quite hard to assess the performance of a segmenter at a level more useful than that of showing some examples. The original clustering segmenter is Ohlander *et al.* (1978). Clustering methods tend to be rather arbitrary—remember, this doesn't mean they're not useful—because there really isn't much theory available to predict what should be clustered and how. It is clear that what we should be doing is forming clusters that are helpful to a particular application, but this criterion hasn't been formalized in any useful way. In this chapter, we have attempted to give the big picture while ignoring detail, because a detailed record of what has been done would be unenlightening. Everyone should know about agglomerative clustering, divisive clustering, k-means, mean shift, and at least one graph-based clustering algorithm (your choice!), because these ideas are just so useful for so many applications; segmentation is just one application of clustering.

There is a large literature on the role of grouping in human visual perception. Standard Gestalt handbooks include Kanizsa (1979), and Koffka (1935). Subjective contours were first described by Kanizsa; there is a broad summary discussion in Kanizsa (1976). The authoritative book by Palmer (1999) gives a much broader picture than we can supply here. There is a great deal of information about the development of different theories of vision and the origins of Gestalt thinking in Gordon (1997). Some groups appear to be formed remarkably early in the visual process, a phenomenon known as *pop out* (Triesman 1982).

We believe the watershed is originally due to Digabel and Lantuéjoul (1978); see Vincent and Soille (1991). Fukunaga and Hostetler (1975) first described mean shift, but it was largely ignored until the work of Cheng (1995). It is now a mainstay of computer vision research; as we shall see in the following chapters, it has numerous applications.

A variety of graph theoretical clustering methods have been used in vision (see Sarkar and Boyer (1998), and Wu and Leahy (1993); there is a summary in Weiss (1999)).

Interactive segmentation became possible because of extremely fast min-cut algorithms that solve the relevant two-label Markov random field (see Vogler *et al.* (2000); Boykov and Jolly (2001); or Boykov and Funka Lea (2006)). There are now many important variants. Grabcut is due to Rother *et al.* (2004); Objcut uses prior information about object shapes to improve the cut (Kumar *et al.* 2010); and see also Duchenne *et al.* (2008). There are numerous matting methods, which Wang and Cohen (2007) survey in detail.

The normalized cuts formalism is due to Shi and Malik (1997) and (2000). Variants include applications to motion segmentation Shi and Malik (1998*a*) and methods for deducing similarity metrics from outputs Shi and Malik (1998*b*). There are numerous alternate criteria (e.g., Cox *et al.* (1996), Perona and Freeman (1998)).

There is a considerable early literature on the evaluation of segmentation. Useful references include: Zhang (1996*a*); Zhang (1997); Beauchemin and Thomson (1997); Zhang and Gerbrands (1994); Correia and Pereira (2003); Lei and Udupa (2003); Warfield *et al.* (2004); Paglieroni (2004); Cardoso and Corte Real (2005); Cardoso and Corte Real (2006); Cardoso *et al.* (2009); Carleer *et al.* (2005); and Crum *et al.* (2006). Evaluation is easier in the context of a specific task; papers dealing with assorted tasks include Yasnoff *et al.* (1977), Hartley *et al.* (1982), Zhang (1996*b*), and Ranade and Prewitt (1980). Martin *et al.* (2001) introduced the Berkeley segmentation dataset, which is now a standard for evaluation, but there are a variety of criteria one can use. Unnikrishnan *et al.* (2007) use the Rand index; Polak *et al.* (2009) use multiple object boundaries; Polak *et al.* (2009) give a detailed evaluation of four segmentation algorithms; Hanbury and Stottinger (2008) compare metrics; and Zhang *et al.* (2008) give a recent survey of evaluation methods. Good image segments are most likely internally coherent, but making that idea useful is hard (Bagon *et al.* 2008).

Since it is hard to get a segmentation right, Russell *et al.* (2006) suggest working with multiple segmentations and then choosing good pieces. This idea is now very influential. Multiple segmentations have been used to improve estimates of support (Malisiewicz and Efros 2007), and to drive recognition (Pantofaru *et al.* 2008) or (Malisiewicz and Efros 2008). One could organize the multiple segments into an inclusion hierarchy (Tacc and Ahuja 1997); the hierarchies yield object models (Todorovic and Ahuja 2008*b*), and can be matched (Todorovic and Ahuja 2008*a*).

We haven't discussed some aspects of perceptual organization in great detail mainly because our emphasis is on exposition rather than historical accuracy, and these methods follow from the unified view. For example, there is a long thread of literature on clustering image edge points or line segments into configurations that are unlikely to have arisen by accident. We cover some of these ideas in the following chapter, but also draw the readers attention to Amir and Lindenbaum (1996), Huttenlocher and Wayner (1992), Lowe (1985), Mohan and Nevatia (1992), Sarkar and Boyer (1993), and to Sarkar and Boyer (1994). In building user interfaces, it can (as we hinted before) be helpful to know what is perceptually salient (e.g., Saund and Moran (1995)).

PROBLEMS

9.1. The mean shift procedure for finding a mode of a function

$$f(\boldsymbol{x}) = C \sum_{i=1}^{n} k\left(\| \frac{\boldsymbol{x} - \boldsymbol{x}_i}{h} \|^2\right)$$

involves producing a series of estimates $\boldsymbol{y}^{(j)}$ where

$$\boldsymbol{y}^{(j+1)} = \frac{\sum_i \boldsymbol{x}_i g(\| \frac{\boldsymbol{x}_i - \boldsymbol{y}^{(j)}}{h} \|^2)}{\sum_i g(\| \frac{\boldsymbol{x}_i - \boldsymbol{y}^{(j)}}{h} \|^2)}.$$

Now assume we have a function

$$f(\boldsymbol{x}) = C \sum_{i=1}^{n} \left[\frac{(2\pi)^{(-d_s/2)}}{h_s^{d_s}} k\left(\frac{\boldsymbol{x}^s - \boldsymbol{x}_i^s}{h_s} \right) \right] \left[\frac{(2\pi)^{(-d_r/2)}}{h_r^{d_r}} k\left(\frac{\boldsymbol{x}^r - \boldsymbol{x}_i^r}{h_r} \right) \right].$$

What is the form of the mean shift estimate for this function?

PROGRAMMING EXERCISES

9.2. Implement a mean shift segmenter.

9.3. Implement a graph-based segmenter, after Section 9.4.2.

9.4. Implement a graph-based segmenter, after Section 9.4.3; for this, you should use one of the fast graph cut packages available on the Web.

9.5. Use your graph-based segmenter to build an interactive segmentation system.

CHAPTER 10

Grouping and Model Fitting

In the previous chapter, we collected together pixels that "looked like" one another, using various clustering methods and various ways of measuring similarity. This view could be applied to tokens (such as points, edge points, superpixels). It is an intrinsically local view.

An alternative, which emphasizes a more global view, is to collect together pixels, tokens, or whatever because they conform to some model. This approach appears rather similar to the clustering approach in intent, but the mechanisms and outcomes tend to be quite different. In the clustering approach, the results we produce can have local structure, but will not necessarily have a global structure. For example, if we try to assemble tokens into a line agglomeratively by testing whether the token to be added is close to the line formed by the previous two tokens, we might get a shape that is quite curved. We really need to check whether all tokens "agree" on the parameters of the line; local consistency is not enough.

These problems are rather difficult, and strategies to attack them for one kind of model tend to extend rather well to strategies for other kinds of model. In this chapter, we mainly concentrate on one core problem, which is simple enough to do in detail. We seek to find all the lines represented by a set of tokens. This problem is usually referred to as *fitting*, or sometimes as *grouping*. There are three important sub-problems here: If all the tokens agree on a model, what is the model? Which tokens contribute to a particular model, and which do not? And how many instances of the model are there?

10.1 THE HOUGH TRANSFORM

Assume we wish to fit a structure to a set of tokens (say, a line to a set of points). One way to cluster tokens that could lie on the same structure is to record all the structures on which each token lies and then look for structures that get many votes. This (quite general) technique is known as the *Hough transform*. To fit a structure with a Hough transform, we take each image token and determine all structures *that could pass through that token*. We make a record of this set—you should think of this as voting—and repeat the process for each token. We decide on what is present by looking at the votes. For example, if we are grouping points that lie on lines, we take each point and vote for all lines that could go through it; we now do this for each point. The line (or lines) that are present should make themselves obvious because they pass through many points and so have many votes.

10.1.1 Fitting Lines with the Hough Transform

A line is easily parametrized as a collection of points (x, y) such that

$$x \cos \theta + y \sin \theta + r = 0.$$

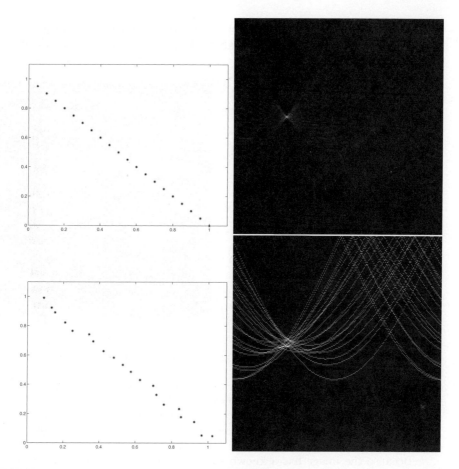

FIGURE 10.1: The Hough transform maps each point like token to a curve of possible lines (or other parametric curves) through that point. These figures illustrate the Hough transform for lines. The **left-hand column** shows points, and the **right-hand column** shows the corresponding accumulator arrays (the number of votes is indicated by the gray level, with a large number of votes being indicated by bright points). The **top** row shows what happens using a set of 20 points drawn from a line. On the **top right**, the accumulator array for the Hough transform of these points. Corresponding to each point is a curve of votes in the accumulator array; the largest set of votes is 20 (which corresponds to the brightest point). The horizontal variable in the accumulator array is θ, and the vertical variable is r; there are 200 steps in each direction, and r lies in the range $[0, 1.55]$. On the **bottom**, these points have been offset by a random vector, each element of which is uniform in the range $[0, 0.05]$. Note that this offsets the curves in the accumulator array shown next to the points and the maximum vote is now 6 (which corresponds to the brightest value in this image; this value would be difficult to see on the same scale as the top image).

Now any pair of (θ, r) represents a unique line, where $r \geq 0$ is the perpendicular distance from the line to the origin and $0 \leq \theta < 2\pi$. We call the set of pairs (θ, r) *line space*; the space can be visualized as a half-infinite cylinder. There is a family of lines that passes through any point token. In particular, the lines that lie on the curve *in line space* given by $r = -x_0 \cos\theta + y_0 \sin\theta$ all pass through the point token at (x_0, y_0).

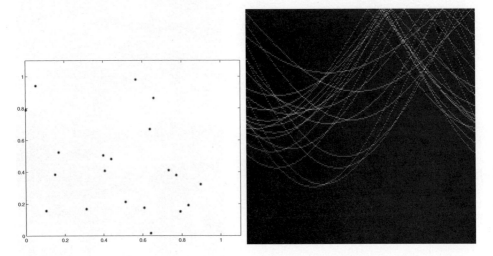

FIGURE 10.2: The Hough transform for a set of random points can lead to quite large sets of votes in the accumulator array. As in Figure 10.1, the **left-hand column** shows points, and the **right-hand column** shows the corresponding accumulator arrays (the number of votes is indicated by the gray level, with a large number of votes being indicated by bright points). In this case, the data points are noise points (both coordinates are uniform random numbers in the range $[0, 1]$); the accumulator array in this case contains many points of overlap, and the maximum vote is now 4 (compared with 6 in Figure 10.1).

Because the image has a known size, there is some R such that we are not interested in lines for $r > R$. These lines are too far away, from the origin for us to see them. This means that the lines we are interested in form a bounded subset of the plane, and we discretize this with some convenient grid. The grid elements can be thought of as buckets into which we place votes. This grid of buckets is referred to as the *accumulator array*. For each point token, we add a vote to the total formed for every grid element on the curve corresponding to the point token. If there are many point tokens that are collinear, we expect there to be many votes in the grid element corresponding to that line.

10.1.2   Using the Hough Transform

The Hough transform is an extremely general procedure. One could use the procedure described to fit, say, circles to points in the plane, or spheres or even ellipsoids to three-dimensional data. This works in principle, but in practice, the Hough transform as described is difficult to use, even for finding lines. There are several sources of difficulty.

- **Grid dimension:** The accumulator array for lines has dimension two, but for circles in the plane, it has dimension three (center location and radius); for axis-aligned ellipses in the plane it has dimension four; for general ellipses in the plane, five; for spheres in 3D, four; for axis-aligned ellipsoids in 3D, seven; and for general ellipsoids in 3D, 10. Even quite simple structures could result in high-dimensional accumulator arrays, which take unmanageable amounts of storage.

- **Quantization errors:** An appropriate grid size is difficult to pick. Too coarse a grid can lead to large values of the vote being obtained falsely because many quite different structures correspond to a single bucket. Too fine a grid can lead to structures not being found because votes resulting from tokens that are not exactly aligned end up in different buckets, and no bucket has a large vote (Figure 10.1).

- **Noise:** The attraction of the Hough transform is that it connects widely separated tokens that lie close to some structure. This is also a weakness because it is usually possible to find many quite good phantom structures in a large set of reasonably uniformly distributed tokens (Figure 10.2). This means that regions of texture can generate peaks in the voting array that are larger than those associated with the lines sought.

These difficulties can be avoided, to some extent, by recognizing the Hough transform as an attempt to find a mode in a distribution. The distribution is represented by the voting array, and some of the problems are created by the cells in that array. But to find a mode, we do not necessarily need to use an accumulator array; instead, we could apply mean shift. The algorithm of Section 9.3.4 can be applied directly. It can also be useful to ensure the minimum of irrelevant tokens by, for example, tuning the edge detector to smooth out texture, using lighting that ensures high-contrast edges, or using tokens with a more complex structure with edge points.

One natural application of the Hough transform is in object recognition. We defer the details to Section 18.4.2, but the general picture is as follows. Imagine an object is made out of known parts. These parts might move around a bit with respect to one another, but are substantial enough to be detected on their own. We can then expect each detected part to have an opinion about the location (and, perhaps, the state) of the object. This means we could detect objects by first detecting parts, then allowing each detected part to vote for location (and maybe state) of object instances, and finally using the Hough transform, most likely in mean shift form, to find instances on which many part detectors agree. This approach has been successfully applied in numerous forms (Maji and Malik 2009).

10.2 FITTING LINES AND PLANES

In many applications, objects are characterized by the presence of straight lines. For example, we might wish to build models of buildings using pictures of the buildings (as in the application in Chapter 19). This application uses polyhedral models of buildings, meaning that straight lines in the image are important. Similarly, many industrial parts have straight edges of one form or another; if we wish to recognize industrial parts in an image, straight lines could be helpful. In either case, a report of all straight lines in the image is an extremely useful segmentation. All this means that fitting a line to a set of plane tokens is extremely useful. Fitting planes to tokens in 3D is also useful, and our methods for fitting lines in the plane apply with little change.

10.2.1 Fitting a Single Line

We first assume that all the points that belong to a particular line are known, and the parameters of the line must be found. We adopt the notation

$$\overline{u} = \frac{\sum u_i}{k}$$

to simplify the presentation.

There is a simple strategy for fitting lines, known as *least squares*. This procedure has a long tradition (which is the only reason we describe it!), but has a substantial bias. Most readers will have seen this idea, but many will not be familiar with the problems that it leads to. For this approach, we represent a line as $y = ax + b$. At each data point, we have (x_i, y_i); we decide to choose the line that best predicts the measured y coordinate for each measured x coordinate. This means we want to choose the line that minimizes

$$\sum_i (y_i - ax_i - b)^2.$$

By differentiation, the line is given by the solution to the problem

$$\left(\begin{array}{c} \overline{y^2} \\ \overline{y} \end{array} \right) = \left(\begin{array}{cc} \overline{x^2} & \overline{x} \\ \overline{x} & 1 \end{array} \right) \left(\begin{array}{c} a \\ b \end{array} \right).$$

Although this is a standard linear solution to a classical problem, it's not much help in vision applications, because the model is an extremely poor one. The difficulty is that the measurement error is dependent on coordinate frame—we are counting vertical offsets from the line as errors, which means that near vertical lines lead to quite large values of the error and quite funny fits (Figure 10.3). In fact, the process is so dependent on coordinate frame that it doesn't represent vertical lines at all.

We could work with the actual distance between the point and the line (rather than the vertical distance). This leads to a problem known as *total least squares*. We can represent a line as the collection of points where $ax + by + c = 0$. Every line can be represented in this way, and we can think of a line as a triple of values (a, b, c). Notice that for $\lambda \neq 0$, the line given by $\lambda(a, b, c)$ is the same as the line represented by (a, b, c). In the exercises, you are asked to prove the simple, but extremely useful, result that the perpendicular distance from a point (u, v) to a line (a, b, c) is given by

$$\text{abs}(au + bv + c) \text{ if } a^2 + b^2 = 1.$$

In our experience, this fact is useful enough to be worth memorizing. To minimize the sum of perpendicular distances between points and lines, we need to minimize

$$\sum_i (ax_i + by_i + c)^2,$$

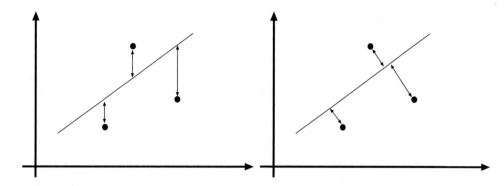

FIGURE 10.3: **Left:** Least squares finds the line that minimizes the sum of squared vertical distances between the line and the tokens (because it assumes that the error appears only in the y coordinate). This yields a (very slightly) simpler mathematical problem at the cost of a poor fit. **Right:** Total least-squares finds the line that minimizes the sum of squared perpendicular distances between tokens and the line; this means that, for example, we can fit near-vertical lines without difficulty.

subject to $a^2 + b^2 = 1$. Now using a Lagrange multiplier λ, we have a solution if

$$
\begin{pmatrix} \overline{x^2} & \overline{xy} & \overline{x} \\ \overline{xy} & \overline{y^2} & \overline{y} \\ \overline{x} & \overline{y} & 1 \end{pmatrix} \begin{pmatrix} a \\ b \\ c \end{pmatrix} = \lambda \begin{pmatrix} 2a \\ 2b \\ 0 \end{pmatrix}.
$$

This means that

$$
c = -a\overline{x} - b\overline{y},
$$

and we can substitute this back to get the eigenvalue problem

$$
\begin{pmatrix} \overline{x^2} - \overline{x}\,\overline{x} & \overline{xy} - \overline{x}\,\overline{y} \\ \overline{xy} - \overline{x}\,\overline{y} & \overline{y^2} - \overline{y}\,\overline{y} \end{pmatrix} \begin{pmatrix} a \\ b \end{pmatrix} = \mu \begin{pmatrix} a \\ b \end{pmatrix}.
$$

Because this is a 2D eigenvalue problem, two solutions up to scale can be obtained in closed form (for those who care, it's usually done numerically!). The scale is obtained from the constraint that $a^2 + b^2 = 1$. The two solutions to this problem are lines at right angles; one maximizes the sum of squared distances and the other minimizes it.

10.2.2 Fitting Planes

Fitting planes is very similar to fitting lines. We could represent a plane as $z = ux + vy + w$, then apply least squares. This will be biased, just like least squares line fitting, because it will not represent vertical planes well. Total least squares is a better strategy, just as in line fitting. We represent the plane as $ax + by + cz + d = 0$; then the distance from a point $x_i = (x_i, y_i, z_i)$ to the plane will be $(ax_i + by_i + cz_i + d)^2$ if $a^2 + b^2 + c^2 = 1$, and we can now use the analysis above with small changes.

10.2.3 Fitting Multiple Lines

Now assume we have a set of tokens (say, points), and we want to fit several lines to this set of tokens. This problem can be difficult because it can involve searching over a large combinatorial space. One approach is to notice that we seldom encounter isolated points; instead, in many problems, we are fitting lines to edge points. We can use the orientation of an edge point as a hint to the position of the next point on the line. If we are stuck with isolated points, then k-means can be applied.

Incremental line fitting algorithms take connected curves of edge points and fit lines to runs of points along the curve. Connected curves of edge points are fairly easily obtained from an edge detector whose output gives orientation (see exercises). An incremental fitter then starts at one end of a curve of edge points and walks along the curve, cutting off runs of pixels that fit a line well (the structure of the algorithm is shown in Algorithm 10.1). Incremental line fitting can work well, despite the lack of an underlying statistical model. One feature is that it reports groups of lines that form closed curves. This is attractive when the lines of interest can reasonably be expected to form a closed curve (e.g., in some object recognition applications) because it means that the algorithm reports natural groups without further fuss. When one uses this strategy, occlusion of an edge can lead to more than one line segment being fitted to the boundary. This difficulty can be addressed by postprocessing the lines to find pairs that (roughly) coincide, but the process is somewhat unattractive because it is hard to give a sensible criterion by which to decide when two lines do coincide.

Put all points on curve list, in order along the curve
Empty the line point list
Empty the line list
Until there are too few points on the curve
   Transfer first few points on the curve to the line point list
   Fit line to line point list
   While fitted line is good enough
     Transfer the next point on the curve
       to the line point list and refit the line
   end
   Transfer last point(s) back to curve
   Refit line
   Attach line to line list
end

Algorithm 10.1: Incremental Line Fitting.

Now assume that points carry no hints about which line they lie on (i.e., there is no color information or anything like it to help, and, crucially, the points are not linked). Furthermore, assume that we know how many lines there are. We can attempt to determine which point lies on which line using a modified version of k-means. In this case, the model is that there are k lines, each of which generates some subset of the data points. The best solution for lines and data points is obtained by minimizing

$$\sum_{l_i \in \text{lines}} \sum_{x_j \in \text{data due to } i\text{th line}} \text{dist}(l_i, x_j)^2$$

over both correspondences and lines. Again, there are too many correspondences to search this space.

It is easy to modify k-means to deal with this problem. The two phases are as follows:

- Allocate each point to the closest line.

- Fit the best line to the points allocated to each line.

This results in Algorithm 10.2. Convergence can be tested by looking at the size of the change in the lines, at whether labels have been flipped (probably the best test), or at the sum of perpendicular distances of points from their lines.

Hypothesize k lines (perhaps uniformly at random)
or
Hypothesize an assignment of lines to points
  and then fit lines using this assignment

Until convergence
  Allocate each point to the closest line
  Refit lines
end

Algorithm 10.2: K-means Line Fitting.

10.3   FITTING CURVED STRUCTURES

Curves in 2D are different from lines in 2D. For every token on the plane, there is a unique, single point on a line that is closest to it. This is not true for a curve. Because curves curve, there might be more than one point on the curve that looks locally as though it is closest to the token (Figure 10.4). This means it can be very hard to find the smallest distance between a point and a curve. Similar effects occur for surfaces in 3D. If one ignores this difficulty, fitting curves is similar to fitting lines. We minimize the sum of squared distances between the points and the curve as a function of the choice of curve.

Assume that the curve is implicit, and so has the form $\phi(x, y) = 0$. The vector from the closest point on the implicit curve to the data point is normal to the curve, so the closest point is given by finding all the (u, v) with the following properties:

1. (u, v) is a point on the curve, which means that $\phi(u, v) = 0$.
2. $s = (d_x, d_y) - (u, v)$ is normal to the curve.

FIGURE 10.4: There can be more than one point on a curve that looks locally as if it is closest to a token. This makes fitting curves to points very difficult. On the **left**, a curve and a token; dashed lines connect the token to the two points on the curve that, by a local test, could be closest. The local test checks that the dashed line and the tangent to the curve are at right angles. **Center** and **right**, we show copies of part of the curve; for each, the closest point on the segment to the token is different, because part of the curve is missing. As a result, we cannot perform a local test that guarantees that a point is closest. We must check all candidates.

Given all such s, the length of the shortest is the distance from the data point to the curve.

The second criterion requires a little work to determine the normal. The normal to an implicit curve is the direction in which we leave the curve fastest; along this direction, the value of ϕ must change fastest, too. This means that the normal at a point (u, v) is

$$\left(\frac{\partial \phi}{\partial x}, \frac{\partial \phi}{\partial y}\right),$$

evaluated at (u, v). If the tangent to the curve is $\boldsymbol{T}$, then we must have $\boldsymbol{T}.\boldsymbol{s} = 0$. Because we are working in 2D, we can determine the tangent from the normal, so that we must have

$$\psi(u, v; d_x, d_y) = \frac{\partial \phi}{\partial y}(u, v)\{d_x - u\} - \frac{\partial \phi}{\partial x}(u, v)\{d_y - v\} = 0$$

at the point (u, v). We now have two equations in two unknowns, and, *in principle* can solve them. However, this is very seldom as easy as it looks, because there might be many solutions. We expect d^2 in the case that ϕ is a polynomial of degree d, though some of them might be complex.

The situation is not improved by using a parametric curve. The coordinates of a point on a parametric curve are functions of a parameter, so if t is the parameter, the curve could be written as $(x(t), y(t))$. Assume we have a data point (d_x, d_y). The closest point on a parametric curve can be identified by its parameter value, which we shall write as τ. This point could lie at one or the other end of the curve. Otherwise, the vector from our data point to the closest point is normal to the curve. This means that $\boldsymbol{s}(\tau) = (d_x, d_y) - (x(\tau), y(\tau))$ is normal to the tangent vector, so that $\boldsymbol{s}(\tau).\boldsymbol{T} = 0$. The tangent vector is

$$\left(\frac{dx}{dt}(\tau), \frac{dy}{dt}(\tau)\right),$$

which means that τ must satisfy the equation

$$\frac{dx}{dt}(\tau)\left\{d_x - x(\tau)\right\} + \frac{dy}{dt}(\tau)\left\{d_y - y(\tau)\right\} = 0.$$

Now this is only one equation, rather than two, but the situation is not much better than that for parametric curves. It is almost always the case that $x(t)$ and $y(t)$ are polynomials because it is usually easier to do root finding for polynomials. At worst, $x(t)$ and $y(t)$ are ratios of polynomials because we can rearrange the left-hand side of our equation to come up with a polynomial in this case, too. However, we are still faced with a possibly large number of roots. The underlying problem is geometric: there may be many points on a curve that, locally, appear to be the closest point to a given data point. This is because the curve is not flat (Figure 10.4). There is no way to tell which is closest without checking each in turn. In some cases (for example, circles), one can duck around this problem. This difficulty applies to fitting curved surfaces to points in 3D as well.

There are two strategies for dealing with this quite general problem. One is to substitute some approximation for the distance between a point and a curve (or, in 3D, a point and a surface), which is sometimes effective. The other is to modify the representation of the curve or of the surface. For example, one might represent a curve with a set of samples, or with a set of line segments. Similarly, a surface might be represented with a set of samples, or a mesh. We could then use the methods of Chapter 12 to register these representations to the data, or even to deform them to fit the data.

10.4 ROBUSTNESS

All of the line fitting methods described involve squared error terms. This can lead to poor fits in practice because a single wildly inappropriate data point might give errors that dominate those due to many good data points; these errors could result in a substantial bias in the fitting process (Figure 10.5). This effect results from the squaring of the error. It is difficult to avoid such data points—usually called *outliers*—in practice.   Errors in collecting or transcribing data points is one important source of outliers. Another common source is a problem with the model. Perhaps some rare but important effect has been ignored or the magnitude of an effect has been badly underestimated. Finally, errors in correspondence are particularly prone to generating outliers. Practical vision problems usually involve outliers.

This problem can be resolved either by reducing the influence of distant points on the estimate (Section 10.4.1), or by identifying outlying points and ignoring them. There are two methods to identify outlying points. We could search for good points. A small set of good points will identify the thing we wish to fit; other good points will agree, and the points that disagree are bad points. This is the basis of an extremely important approach, described in Section 10.4.2. Alternatively, we could regard this as a problem with missing data, and use the EM algorithm described in Section 10.5.

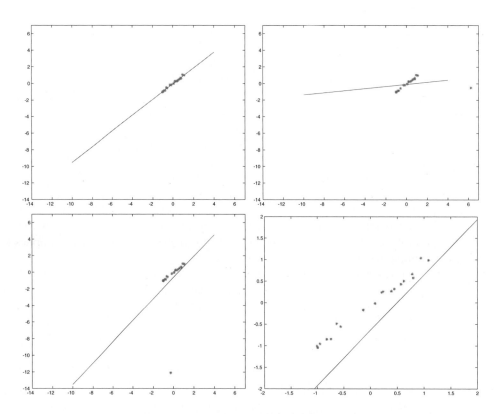

FIGURE 10.5: Line fitting with a squared error is extremely sensitive to outliers, both in x and y coordinates. We show an example using least squares. At the **top left**, a good least-squares fit of a line to a set of points. **Top right** shows the same set of points, but with the x coordinate of one point corrupted; this means that the point has been translated horizontally from where it should be. As a result, it contributes an enormous error term to the true line, and a better least-squares fit is obtained by making a significant change in the line's orientation. Although this makes the errors at most points larger, it reduces the very large error at the outlier. **Bottom left** shows the same set of points, but with the y coordinate of one point corrupted. In this particular case, the x intercept has changed. These three figures are on the same set of axes for comparison, but this choice of axes does not clearly show how bad the fit is for the third case. **Bottom right** shows a detail of this case, in which the line is clearly a bad fit.

10.4.1 M-Estimators

An *M-estimator* estimates parameters by replacing the squared error term with a term that is better behaved. This means we minimize an expression of the form

$$\sum_i \rho(r_i(\boldsymbol{x}_i, \theta); \sigma),$$

where θ are the parameters of the model being fitted (for example, in the case of the line, we might have the orientation and the y intercept), and $r_i(\boldsymbol{x}_i, \theta)$ is the residual error of the model on the ith data point. Using this notation, our least

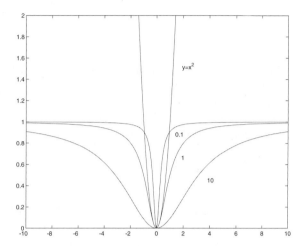

FIGURE 10.6: The function $\rho(x; \sigma) = x^2/(\sigma^2 + x^2)$, plotted for $\sigma^2 = 0.1$, 1, and 10, with a plot of $y = x^2$ for comparison. Replacing quadratic terms with ρ reduces the influence of outliers on a fit. A point that is several multiples of σ away from the fitted curve is going to have almost no effect on the coefficients of the fitted curve, because the value of ρ will be close to 1 and will change extremely slowly with the distance from the fitted curve.

squares and total least squares line-fitting errors—which differ only in the form of the residual error—both have $\rho(u; \sigma) = u^2$. The trick to M-estimators is to make $\rho(u; \sigma)$ look like u^2 for part of its range and then flattens out; we expect that $\rho(u; \sigma)$ increases monotonically, and is close to a constant value for large u. A common choice is

$$\rho(u; \sigma) = \frac{u^2}{\sigma^2 + u^2}.$$

The parameter σ controls the point at which the function flattens out, and we have plotted a variety of examples in Figure 10.6. There are many other M-estimators available. Typically, they are discussed in terms of their *influence function*, which is defined as

$$\frac{\partial \rho}{\partial \theta}.$$

This is natural because our minimization criterion yields

$$\sum_i \rho(r_i(\boldsymbol{x}_i, \theta); \sigma) \frac{\partial \rho}{\partial \theta} = 0$$

at the solution. For the kind of problems we consider, we would expect a good influence function to be antisymmetric— there is no difference between a slight overprediction and a slight underprediction—and to tail off with large values— because we want to limit the influence of the outliers.

There are two tricky issues with using M-estimators. First, the minimization problem is non-linear and must be solved iteratively. The standard difficulties apply: there might be more than one local minimum, the method might diverge, and the behavior of the method is likely to be quite dependent on the start point.

For $s = 1$ to $s = k$
   Draw a subset of r distinct points, chosen uniformly at random
   Fit to this set of points using least squares to obtain an initial
     set of parameters θ_s^0
   Estimate σ_s^0 using θ_s^0
   Until convergence (usually $|\theta_s^n - \theta_s^{n-1}|$ is small):
     Take a minimizing step using θ_s^{n-1}, σ_s^{n-1}
       to get θ_s^n
     Now compute σ_s^n
  end
end
Report the best fit of this set of k trials, using the median of the residuals
  as a criterion

Algorithm 10.3: Using an M-Estimator to Fit a Least Squares Model.

A common strategy for dealing with this problem is to draw a subsample of the dataset, fit to that subsample using least squares, and use this as a start point for the fitting process. We do this for a large number of different subsamples, enough to ensure that there is a high probability that there is at least one subsample that consists entirely of good data points (Algorithm 10.3).

Second, as Figures 10.7 and 10.8 indicate, the estimators require a sensible estimate of σ, which is often referred to as *scale*. Typically, the scale estimate is supplied at each iteration of the solution method; a popular estimate of scale is

$$\sigma^{(n)} = 1.4826 \; \text{median}_i \; |r_i^{(n)}(x_i; \theta^{(n-1)})| \; .$$

We summarize a general M-estimator in Algorithm 10.3.

10.4.2 RANSAC: Searching for Good Points

An alternative to modifying the cost function is to search the collection of data points for good points. This is quite easily done by an iterative process: First, we choose a small subset of points and fit to that subset, and then we see how many other points fit to the resulting object. We continue this process until we have a high probability of finding the structure we are looking for.

For example, assume that we are fitting a line to a dataset that consists of about 50% outliers. We can fit a line to only two points. If we draw pairs of points uniformly and at random, then about a quarter of these pairs will consist entirely of good data points. We can identify these good pairs by noticing that a large collection of other points lie close to the line fitted to such a pair. Of course, a better estimate of the line could then be obtained by fitting a line to the points that lie close to our current line.

Fischler and Bolles (1981) formalized this approach into an algorithm—search for a random sample that leads to a fit on which many of the data points agree. The algorithm is usually called *RANSAC*, for RANdom SAmple Consensus, and is

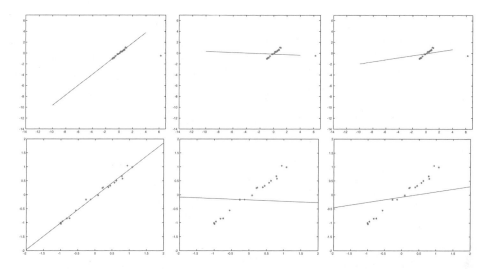

FIGURE 10.7: The **top row** shows lines fitted to the second dataset of Figure 10.5 using a weighting function that deemphasizes the contribution of distant points (the function ϕ of Figure 10.6). On the **left**, μ has about the right value; the contribution of the outlier has been down-weighted, and the fit is good. In the **center**, the value of μ is too small so that the fit is insensitive to the position of all the data points, meaning that its relationship to the data is obscure. On the **right**, the value of μ is too large, meaning that the outlier makes about the same contribution as it does in least squares. The **bottom row** shows closeups of the fitted line and the non-outlying data points for the same cases.

displayed in Algorithm 10.4. To make this algorithm practical, we need to choose three parameters.

The Number of Samples Required

Our samples consist of sets of points drawn uniformly and at random from the dataset. Each sample contains the minimum number of points required to fit the abstraction of interest. For example, if we wish to fit lines, we draw pairs of points; if we wish to fit circles, we draw triples of points, and so on. We assume that we need to draw n data points, and that w is the fraction of these points that are good (we need only a reasonable estimate of this number). Now the expected value of the number of draws k required to get one point is given by

$$
\begin{aligned}
\mathrm{E}[k] \quad = \quad & 1P(\text{one good sample in one draw}) + \\
& 2P(\text{one good sample in two draws}) + \ldots \\
= \quad & w^n + 2(1 - w^n)w^n + 3(1 - w^n)^2 w^n + \ldots \\
= \quad & w^{-n}
\end{aligned}
$$

(where the last step takes a little manipulation of algebraic series). We would like to be fairly confident that we have seen a good sample, so we wish to draw more than w^{-n} samples; a natural thing to do is to add a few standard deviations to this

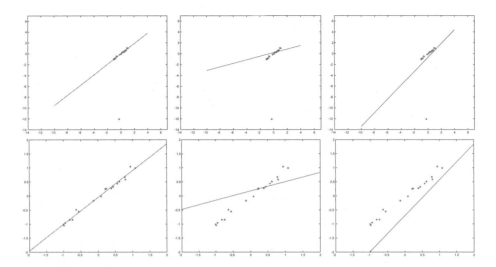

FIGURE 10.8: The **top row** shows lines fitted to the third dataset of Figure 10.5 using a weighting function that deemphasizes the contribution of distant points (the function ϕ of Figure 10.6). On the **left**, μ has about the right value; the contribution of the outlier has been down-weighted, and the fit is good. In the **center**, the value of μ is too small, so that the fit is insensitive to the position of all the data points, meaning that its relationship to the data is obscure. On the **right**, the value of μ is too large, meaning that the outlier makes about the same contribution as it does in least squares. The **bottom row** shows close ups of the fitted line and the non-outlying data points, for the same cases.

number. The standard deviation of k can be obtained as

$$SD(k) = \frac{\sqrt{1 - w^n}}{w^n}.$$

An alternative approach to this problem is to look at a number of samples that guarantees a low probability z of seeing only bad samples. In this case, we have

$$(1 - w^n)^k = z,$$

which means that

$$k = \frac{\log(z)}{\log(1 - w^n)}.$$

It is common to have to deal with data where w is unknown. However, each fitting attempt contains information about w. In particular, if n data points are required, then we can assume that the probability of a successful fit is w^n. If we observe a long sequence of fitting attempts, we can estimate w from this sequence. This suggests that we start with a relatively low estimate of w, generate a sequence of attempted fits, and then improve our estimate of w. If we have more fitting attempts than the new estimate of w predicts, the process can stop. The problem of updating the estimate of w reduces to estimating the probability that a coin comes up heads or tails given a sequence of fits.

Determine:
    n—the smallest number of points required (e.g., for lines, $n = 2$,
      for circles, $n = 3$)
    k—the number of iterations required
    t—the threshold used to identify a point that fits well
    d—the number of nearby points required
      to assert a model fits well
Until k iterations have occurred
    Draw a sample of n points from the data
      uniformly and at random
    Fit to that set of n points
    For each data point outside the sample
      Test the distance from the point to the structure
        against t; if the distance from the point to the structure
        is less than t, the point is close
    end
    If there are d or more points close to the structure
      then there is a good fit. Refit the structure using all
      these points. Add the result to a collection of good fits.
end
Use the best fit from this collection, using the
  fitting error as a criterion

Algorithm 10.4: RANSAC: Fitting Structures Using Random Sample Consensus.

Telling Whether a Point Is Close

We need to determine whether a point lies close to a line fitted to a sample. We do this by determining the distance between the point and the fitted line, and testing that distance against a threshold d; if the distance is below the threshold, the point lies close. In general, specifying this parameter is part of the modeling process. Obtaining a value for this parameter is relatively simple. We generally need only an order of magnitude estimate, and the same value applies to many different experiments. The parameter is often determined by trying a few values and seeing what happens; another approach is to look at a few characteristic datasets, fitting a line by eye, and estimating the average size of the deviations.

The Number of Points That Must Agree

Assume that we have fitted a line to some random sample of two data points, and we need to know whether that line is good. We do this by counting the number of points that lie within some distance of the line (the distance was determined in the previous section). In particular, assume that we know the probability that an outlier lies in this collection of points; write this probability as y. We would like to choose some number of points t such that the probability that all points near the line are outliers, y^t, is small (say, less than 0.05). Notice that $y \leq (1 - w)$ (because some outliers should be far from the line), so we could choose t such that $(1 - w)^t$

is small.

10.5   FITTING USING PROBABILISTIC MODELS

It is straightforward to build probabilistic models from the fitting procedures we have described. Doing so yields a new kind of model, and a new algorithm; both are extremely useful in practice. The key is to view our observed data as having been produced by a *generative model*. The generative model specifies how each data point was produced.

In the simplest case, line fitting with least squares, we can recover the same equations we worked with in Section 10.2.1 by using a natural generative model. Our model for producing data is that the x coordinate is uniformly distributed and the y coordinate is generated by (a) finding the point $ax_i + b$ on the line corresponding to the x coordinate and then (b) adding a zero mean normally distributed random variable. Now write $x \sim p$ to mean that x is a sample from the probability distribution p; write $U(R)$ for the uniform distribution over some range of values R; and write $N(\mu, \sigma^2)$ for the normal distribution with mean mu and variance σ^2. With our notation, we can write:

$$
\begin{aligned}
x_i &\sim U(R) \\
y_i &\sim N(ax_i + b, \sigma^2).
\end{aligned}
$$

We can estimate the unknown parameters of this model in a straightforward way. The important parameters are a and b (though knowing σ might be useful). The usual way to estimate parameters in a probabilistic model is to maximize the likelihood of the data, typically by working with the negative log-likelihood and minimizing that. In this case, the log-likelihood of the data is

$$
\begin{aligned}
\mathcal{L}(a, b, \sigma) &= \sum_{i \in \text{data}} \log P(x_i, y_i | a, b, \sigma) \\
&= \sum_{i \in \text{data}} \log P(y_i | x_i, a, b, \sigma) + \log P(x_i) \\
&= \sum_{i \in \text{data}} -\frac{(y_i - (ax_i + b))^2}{2\sigma^2} - \frac{1}{2} \log 2\pi\sigma^2 + K_b
\end{aligned}
$$

where K_b is a constant representing $\log P(x_i)$. Now, to minimize the negative log-likelihood as a function of a and b we could minimize $\sum_{i \in \text{data}} (y_i - (ax_i + b))^2$ as a function of a and b (which is what we did for least-squares line fitting in Section 10.2.1).

Now consider total least-squares line fitting. Again, we can recover the equations we worked with in Section 10.2.1 from a natural generative model. In this case, to generate a data point (x_i, y_i), we generate a point (u_i, v_i) uniformly at random along the line (or rather, along a finite length segment of the line likely to be of interest to us), then sample a distance ξ_i (where $\xi_i \sim N(0, \sigma^2)$, and move the point (u_i, v_i) perpendicular to the line by that distance. If the line is $ax + by + c = 0$ and if $a^2 + b^2 = 1$, we have that $(x_i, y_i) = (u_i, v_i) + \xi_i(a, b)$. We can write the log-likelihood of the data under this model as

$$
\begin{aligned}
\mathcal{L}(a,b,c,\sigma) &= \sum_{i \in \text{data}} \log P(x_i, y_i | a, b, c, \sigma) \\
&= \sum_{i \in \text{data}} \log P(\xi_i | \sigma) + \log P(u_i, v_i | a, b, c).
\end{aligned}
$$

But $P(u_i, v_i | a, b, c)$ is some constant, because this point is distributed uniformly along the line. Since ξ_i is the perpendicular distance from (x_i, y_i) to the line (which is $\|(ax_i + by_i + c)\|$ as long as $a^2 + b^2 = 1$), we must maximize

$$
\begin{aligned}
\sum_{i \in \text{data}} \log P(\xi_i | \sigma) &= \sum_{i \in \text{data}} -\frac{\xi_i^2}{2\sigma^2} - \frac{1}{2} \log 2\pi\sigma^2 \\
&= \sum_{i \in \text{data}} -\frac{(ax_i + by_i + c)^2}{2\sigma^2} - \frac{1}{2} \log 2\pi\sigma^2
\end{aligned}
$$

(again, subject to $a^2 + b^2 = 1$). For fixed (but perhaps unknown) σ this yields the problem we were working with in Section 10.2.1. So far, generative models have just reproduced what we know already, but a powerful trick makes them much more interesting.

10.5.1 Missing Data Problems

A number of important vision problems can be phrased as problems that happen to be missing useful elements of the data. For example, we can think of segmentation as the problem of determining from which of a number of sources a measurement came. This is a general view. More specifically, fitting a line to a set of tokens involves segmenting the tokens into outliers and inliers, then fitting the line to the inliers; segmenting an image into regions involves determining which source of color and texture pixels generated the image pixels; fitting a set of lines to a set of tokens involves determining which tokens lie on which line; and segmenting a motion sequence into moving regions involves allocating moving pixels to motion models. Each of these problems would be easy if we happened to possess some data that is currently missing (respectively, whether a point is an inlier or an outlier, which region a pixel comes from, which line a token comes from, and which motion model a pixel comes from).

A *missing data problem* is a statistical problem where some data is missing. There are two natural contexts in which missing data are important: In the first, some terms in a data vector are missing for some instances and present for others (perhaps someone responding to a survey was embarrassed by a question). In the second, which is far more common in our applications, an inference problem can be made much simpler by rewriting it using some variables whose values are unknown. Fortunately, there is an effective algorithm for dealing with missing data problems; in essence, we take an expectation over the missing data. We demonstrate this method and appropriate algorithms with two examples.

Example: Outliers and Line Fitting

We wish to fit a line to a set of tokens that are at $\boldsymbol{x}_i = (x_i, y_i)$. Some tokens might be outliers, but we do not know which ones are. This means we can model the process of generating a token as first, choosing whether it will come from the line or be an outlier, and then, choosing the token conditioned on the original choice. The first choice will be random, and we can write $P(\text{token comes from line}) = \pi$. We have already given two models of how a point could be generated from a line model. We model outliers as occuring uniformly and at random on the plane. This means that we can write the probability of generating a token as

$$
\begin{aligned}
P(\boldsymbol{x}_i | a, b, c, \pi) &= P(\boldsymbol{x}_i, \text{line} | a, b, c, \pi) + P(\boldsymbol{x}_i, \text{outlier} | a, b, c, \pi) \\
&= P(\boldsymbol{x}_i | \text{line}, a, b, c) P(\text{line}) + P(\boldsymbol{x}_i | \text{outlier}, a, b, c) P(\text{outlier}) \\
&= P(\boldsymbol{x}_i | \text{line}, a, b, c) \pi + P(\boldsymbol{x}_i | \text{outlier}, a, b, c)(1 - \pi).
\end{aligned}
$$

If we knew for every data item whether it came from the line or was an outlier, then fitting the line would be simple; we would ignore all the outliers, and apply the methods of Section 10.2.1 to the other points. Similarly, if we knew the line, then estimating which point is an outlier and which is not would be straightforward (the outliers are far from the line). The difficulty is that we do not; the key to resolving this difficulty is repeated re-estimation (Section 10.5.3), which provides a standard algorithm for this class of problem. Figure 10.9 shows typical results using the standard algorithm.

By a very small manipulation of the equations above (replace "line" with "background" and "outlier" with "foreground"), we can represent a background subtraction problem, too. We model the image in each frame of video as the same, multiplied by some constant to take account of automatic gain control, but with noise added. We model the noise as coming from some uniform source. Figures 10.10 and 10.11 show results, obtained with the standard algorithm for these problems (Section 10.5.3).

Example: Image Segmentation

At each pixel in an image, we compute a d-dimensional feature vector $\boldsymbol{x}$, which might contain position, color, and texture information. We believe the image contains g segments, and each pixel is produced by one of these segments. Thus, to produce a pixel, we choose an image segment and then generate the pixel from the model of that segment. We assume that the lth segment is chosen with probability π_l, and we model the density associated with the lth segment as a Gaussian, with known covariance Σ and unknown mean $\theta_l = (\boldsymbol{\mu}_l)$ that depends on the particular segment. We encapsulate these parameters into a parameter vector to get $\Theta = (\pi_1, \ldots, \pi_g, \theta_1, \ldots, \theta_g)$. This means that we can write the probability of generating a pixel vector $\boldsymbol{x}$ as

$$
p(\boldsymbol{x} | \Theta) = \sum_i p(\boldsymbol{x} | \theta_l) \pi_l.
$$

Fitting this model would be simple if we knew which segment produced which pixel, because then we could estimate the mean of each segment separately. Similarly, if we knew the means, we could estimate which segment produced the pixel. This is quite a general situation.

10.5.2   Mixture Models and Hidden Variables

Each of the previous examples are instances of a general form of model, known as a *mixture model*, where a data item is generated by first choosing a mixture component (the line or the outlier; which segment the pixel comes from), then generating the data item from that component. Call the parameters for the lth component θ_l, the probability of choosing the lth component π_l, and write $\Theta = (\pi_1, \ldots, \pi_l, \theta_1, \ldots, \theta_l)$. Then, we can write the probability of generating $\boldsymbol{x}$

$$p(\boldsymbol{x}|\Theta) = \sum_j p(\boldsymbol{x}|\theta_j)\pi_j.$$

This is a weighted sum, or *mixture*, of probability models; the π_l are usually called *mixing weights*. One can visualize this model as a density in the space of $\boldsymbol{x}$ that consists of a set of g "blobs" of probability, each of which is associated with a component of the model. We want to determine: (a) the parameters of each of these blobs, (b) the mixing weights, and usually (c) from which component each token came. The log-likelihood of the data for a general mixture model is

$$\mathcal{L}(\Theta) = \sum_{i \in \text{observations}} \log \left(\sum_{j=1}^{g} \pi_j p_j(\boldsymbol{x}_i|\theta_j) \right).$$

This function is hard to maximize, because of the sum inside the logarithm. Just like the last two examples, the problem would be simplified if we knew the mixture component from which each token came, because then we would estimate the components independently.

We now introduce a new set of variables. For each data item, we have a vector of indicator variables (one per component) that tells us from which component each data item came. We write δ_i for the vector associated with the ith data item, and δ_{ij} for the j'th component of δ_i. Then, we have

$$\delta_{ij} = \begin{cases} 1 & \text{if item } i \text{ came from component } j \\ 0 & \text{otherwise} \end{cases}.$$

and these variables are unknown. If we did know these variables, we could maximize the *complete data log-likelihood*,

$$\mathcal{L}_c(\Theta) = \sum_{i \in \text{observations}} \log P(\boldsymbol{x}_i, \delta_i|\Theta),$$

which would be quite easy to do (because it would boil down to estimating the components independently). We regard δ as part of our data that happens to be missing (which is why we call this the complete data log-likelihood). The form of $\mathcal{L}_c(\Theta)$ for mixture models is worth remembering because it involves a neat trick:

using the δ_{ij} to switch on and off terms. We have

$$
\begin{aligned}
\mathcal{L}_c(\Theta) &= \sum_{i \in \text{observations}} \log P(\boldsymbol{x}_i, \delta_i | \Theta) \\
&= \sum_{i \in \text{observations}} \log \prod_{j \in \text{components}} \left[p_j(\boldsymbol{x}_i | \theta_j) \pi_j \right]^{\delta_{ij}} \\
&= \sum_{i \in \text{observations}} \left(\sum_{j \in \text{components}} \left[(\log p_j(\boldsymbol{x}_i | \theta_j) \log \pi_j) \, \delta_{ij} \right] \right)
\end{aligned}
$$

(keeping in mind that the δ_{ij} are either one or zero, and that $\sum_j \delta_{ij} = 1$, equivalent to requiring that each data point comes from exactly one model).

10.5.3   The EM Algorithm for Mixture Models

For each of our examples, if we knew the missing data, we could estimate the parameters effectively. Similarly, if we knew the parameters, the missing data would follow. This suggests an iterative algorithm:

1. Obtain some estimate of the missing data using a guess at the parameters.
2. Form a maximum likelihood estimate of the free parameters using the estimate of the missing data.

We would iterate this procedure until (hopefully!) it converged. In the case of line fitting, the algorithm would look like this:

1. Obtain some estimate of which points lie on the line and which are off lines, using an estimate of the line.
2. Form a revised estimate of the line, using this information.

For image segmentation, this would look like the following:

1. Obtain some estimate of the component from which each pixel's feature vector came, using an estimate of the θ_l.
2. Update the θ_l and the mixing weights, using this estimate.

Although it would be nice if the procedures given for missing data converged, there is no particular reason to believe that they do. In fact, given appropriate choices in each stage, they do. This is most easily seen by showing that they are examples of a general algorithm—the *expectation-maximization* (EM) algorithm.

The key idea in EM is to obtain a set of working values for the missing data (and so for Θ) by substituting an expectation for each missing value. In particular, we fix the parameters at some value, and then compute the expected value of each δ_{ij}, given the value of $\boldsymbol{x}_i$ and the parameter values. We then plug the expected value of δ_{ij} into the complete data log-likelihood, which is much easier to work with, and obtain a value of the parameters by maximizing that. At this point, the expected values of δ_{ij} may have changed. We obtain an algorithm by alternating the expectation step with the maximization step and iterate until convergence. More formally, given $\Theta^{(s)}$, we form $\Theta^{(s+1)}$ by:

1. Computing an expected value for the *complete* data log-likelihood using the incomplete data and the current value of the parameters. That is, we compute

$$Q(\Theta; \Theta^{(s)}) = E_{\delta|\boldsymbol{x},\Theta^{(s)}} \mathcal{L}_c(\Theta).$$

Notice that this object is a *function* of Θ, obtained by taking an expectation of a function of Θ and δ; the expectation is with respect to $P(\delta|\boldsymbol{x}, \Theta^{(s)})$. This is referred to as the *E-step*.

2. Maximizing this object as a function of Θ. That is, we compute

$$\Theta^{(s+1)} = \arg\max_\Theta Q(\Theta; \Theta^{(s)}).$$

This is known as the *M-step*.

It can be shown that the incomplete data log-likelihood is increased at each step, meaning that the sequence $\boldsymbol{u}^s$ converges to a (local) maximum of the incomplete data log-likelihood (e.g., Dempster *et al.* (1977) or McLachlan and Krishnan (1996)). Of course, there is no guarantee that this algorithm converges to the *correct* local maximum, and finding the correct local maximum can be a mild nuisance.

EM is considerably easier than it looks for a mixture model. First, recall from Section 10.5.2 that the complete data log-likelihood for a mixture model is

$$\mathcal{L}_c(\Theta) = \sum_{i \in \text{observations}} \sum_{j \in \text{components}} [(\log p_j(\boldsymbol{x}_i|\theta_j) \log \pi_j) \delta_{ij}].$$

which is *linear* in δ. Because taking expectations is linear, $Q(\Theta; \Theta^{(s)})$ can be obtained from $\mathcal{L}_c(\Theta)$ by substituting the expected values of δ_{ij}. Now write

$$\alpha_{ij} = E_{\delta|\boldsymbol{x},\Theta^{(s)}}[\delta_{ij}]$$

(which is the expected value of δ_{ij}, taking the expectation using the posterior on δ given data and the current estimate of parameters $\Theta^{(s)}$); these are commonly called *soft weights*. We can now write

$$Q(\Theta; \Theta^{(s)}) = \sum_{i \in \text{observations}} \sum_{j \in \text{components}} [(\log p_j(\boldsymbol{x}_i|\theta_j) \log \pi_j) \alpha_{ij}].$$

Second, notice that the ith missing variable is conditionally independent of all others given the ith data point and the parameters of the model. If you find this confusing, think about the examples. In the case of line fitting, the only information you need to tell whether a particular point is an outlier is that point together with your estimate of the line; no other points have anything to say about it. Finally, notice that

$$
\begin{aligned}
\alpha_{ij} &= E_{\delta|\boldsymbol{x},\Theta^{(s)}}[\delta_{ij}] \\
&= E_{\delta_i|\boldsymbol{x}_i,\Theta^{(s)}}[\delta_{ij}] \\
&= 1 \cdot P(\delta_{ij} = 1|\boldsymbol{x}_i, \Theta^{(s)}) + 0 \cdot P(\delta_{ij} = 0|\boldsymbol{x}_i, \Theta^{(s)}) \\
&= P(\delta_{ij} = 1|\boldsymbol{x}_i, \Theta^{(s)}).
\end{aligned}
$$

Now we must compute

$$
\begin{aligned}
P(\delta_{ij} = 1 | \boldsymbol{x}_i, \Theta^{(s)}) &= \frac{P(\boldsymbol{x}_i, \delta_{ij} = 1 | \Theta^{(s)})}{P(\boldsymbol{x}_i | \Theta^{(s)})} \\
&= \frac{P(\boldsymbol{x}_i | \delta_{ij} = 1, \Theta^{(s)}) P(\delta_{ij} = 1 | \Theta^{(s)})}{P(\boldsymbol{x}_i | \Theta^{(s)})} \\
&= \frac{p_j(\boldsymbol{x}_i | \Theta^{(s)}) \pi_j}{\sum_l P(\boldsymbol{x}_i, \delta_{il} = 1 | \Theta^{(s)})} \\
&= \frac{p_j(\boldsymbol{x}_i | \Theta^{(s)}) \pi_j}{\sum_l p_l(\boldsymbol{x}_i | \Theta^{(s)}) \pi_l}
\end{aligned}
$$

because the numerator is the probability of getting a data point out of model j, and the denominator is the probability of getting that point at all. Our steps are then as follows.

The E-Step   For each i, j, compute the soft weights

$$
\alpha_{ij} = P(\delta_{ij} = 1 | \boldsymbol{x}_i, \Theta^{(s)}) = \frac{p_j(\boldsymbol{x}_i | \Theta^{(s)}) \pi_j}{\sum_l p_l(\boldsymbol{x}_i | \Theta^{(s)}) \pi_l}.
$$

Then, we have

$$
Q(\Theta; \Theta^{(s)}) = \sum_{i \in \text{observations}} \sum_{j \in \text{components}} \left[(\log p_l(\boldsymbol{x}_i | \theta_l) \log \pi_l) \, \alpha_{ij} \right].
$$

The M-Step   We must maximize

$$
Q(\Theta; \Theta^{(s)}) = \sum_{i \in \text{observations}} \sum_{j \in \text{components}} \left[(\log p_l(\boldsymbol{x}_i | \theta_l) \log \pi_l) \, \alpha_{ij} \right].
$$

as a function of Θ. Notice that this is equivalent to allocating each data point to the j'th model with weight α_{ij}, then maximizing the likelihood of each model separately. The process behaves as if each model accounts for some fraction of each data point, which is why these terms are called soft weights. This will become more apparent when you study the equations for the examples (see the exercises).

10.5.4 Difficulties with the EM Algorithm

EM is inclined to get stuck in local minima. These local minima typically are associated with combinatorial aspects of the problem being studied. In the example of fitting lines subject to outliers, the algorithm is, in essence, trying to decide whether a point is an outlier. Some incorrect labelings might be stable. For example, if there is only one outlier, the algorithm could find a line through that point and one other, and label all remaining points outliers (Figure 10.9).

One useful strategy is to notice that the final configuration of the algorithm is a deterministic function of its start point and use carefully chosen start points. One might start in many different (randomly chosen) configurations and sift through

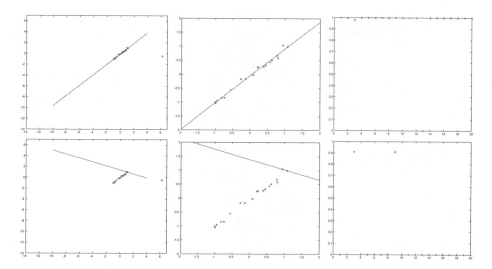

FIGURE 10.9: EM can be used to reject outliers. Here we demonstrate a line fit to the second dataset of Figure 10.5. The **top row** shows the correct local minimum, and the **bottom row** shows another local minimum. The **first column** shows the line superimposed on the data points using the same axes as Figure 10.5; the **second column** shows a detailed view of the line, indicating the region around the data points; and the **third column** shows a plot of the probability that a point comes from the line, rather than from the noise model, plotted against the index of the point. Notice that at the correct local minimum, all but one point is associated with the line, whereas at the incorrect local minimum, there are two points associated with the line and the others are allocated to noise.

the results looking for the best fit, rather like RANSAC. One might preprocess the data using something like a Hough transform to look for the best fit. Neither is guaranteed.

A second difficulty is that some points will have extremely small expected weights. This presents us with a numerical problem: it isn't clear what happens if we regard small weights as being equivalent to zero (this usually isn't a wise thing to do). In turn, we might need to adopt a numerical representation that allows us to add many very small numbers and come up with a nonzero result. This issue is rather outside the scope of this book, but you should not underestimate its nuisance value because we don't treat it in detail.

10.6 MOTION SEGMENTATION BY PARAMETER ESTIMATION

Consider two frames of a motion sequence produced by a moving camera. For a small movement, we will see relatively few new points, and lose relatively few points, so we can join each point in the first frame to its corresponding point on the second frame (which is overlaid) with an arrow. The head is at the point in the second frame, and, if the elapsed time is short, the field of arrows can be thought of as the instantaneous movement in the image. The arrows are known as the *optical flow*, a notion originally due to Gibson (1950). The structure of an optical

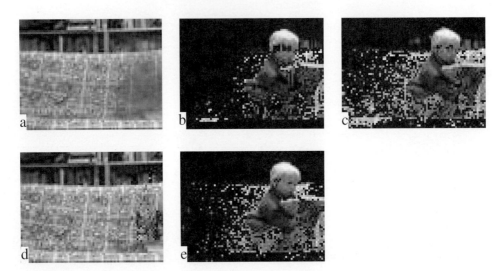

FIGURE 10.10: Background subtraction for the sequence of Figure 9.8, using EM. (a), (b), and (c) are from Figure 9.9, for comparison. (d) shows the estimated background and (e) shows the estimated foreground. Notice that, in each case, there are some excess pixels and some missing pixels.

FIGURE 10.11: Background subtraction for the sequence of Figure 9.8, using EM. (a), (b), and (c) are from Figure 9.10, for comparison. (d) shows the estimated background, and (e) shows the estimated foreground. Notice that the number of problem pixels—where the pattern on the sofa has been mistaken for the child—has markedly increased. This is because small movements can cause the high spatial frequency pattern on the sofa to be misaligned, leading to large differences.

flow field can be quite informative about a scene (Section 10.6.1), and quite simple parametric models of optical flow are often good representations (Section 10.6.2).

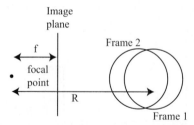 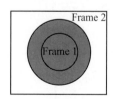 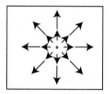

FIGURE 10.12: A sphere of radius R approaches a camera along the Z axis, at velocity V (side view on the **left**). The image is a circle, which grows as the sphere gets closer (**center**). The flow is radial, about a focus of expansion, and provides an estimate of the time to contact (**right**). This estimate works for other objects, too.

As a result, motion sequences often consist of large regions that have similar motion internally. In turn, this gives us a segmentation principle: we want to decompose a motion sequence into a set of moving layers, that compose to make the sequence (Section 10.6.3).

10.6.1 Optical Flow and Motion

Flow is particularly informative about relations between the viewer's motion, usually called *egomotion*, and the 3D scene. For example, when viewed from a moving car, distant objects have much slower *apparent motion* than close objects, so the rate of apparent motion can tell us something about distance. This means that the flow arrows on distant objects will be shorter than those on nearby objects. As another example, assume the egomotion is pure translation in some direction. Then the image point in that direction, which is known as the *focus of expansion*, will not move, and all the optical flow will be away from that point (Figure 10.12). This means that simply observing such a flow field tells us something about how we are moving. Further simple observations tell us how quickly we will hit something. Assume the camera points at the focus of expansion, and make the world move to the camera. A sphere of radius R whose center lies along the direction of motion and is at depth Z will produce a circular image region of radius $r = fR/Z$. If it moves down the Z axis with speed $V = dZ/dt$, the rate of growth of this region in the image will be $dr/dt = -fRV/Z^2$. This means that

$$\text{time to contact} = -\frac{Z}{V} = \frac{r}{\left(\frac{dr}{dt}\right)}.$$

The minus sign is because the sphere is moving down the Z axis, so Z is getting smaller and V is negative. The object doesn't need to be a sphere for this argument to work, and if the camera is spherical, we don't need to be looking in the direction we are traveling either. This means that an animal that is translating quickly can get an estimate of how long until it hits something very quickly and very easily.

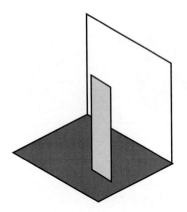 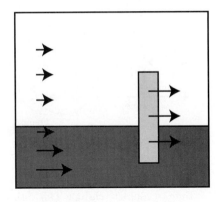

FIGURE 10.13: Optic flow fields can be used to structure or segment a scene. On the **left**, a very simple scene. Now imagine we view this scene with a camera whose image plane is parallel to the white rectangle, and that is moving left; we will see flow fields that look like the image on the **right**. The flow on the white rectangle is constant (because the plane is parallel to the direction of translation and the image plane) and small (it is distant); on the light gray rectangle, it is constant, but larger; and on the inclined plane, it is small at distant points and large at nearby points. With a parametric model of such flow fields, we could segment scenes like this, because different structures would correspond to different flow fields.

10.6.2 Flow Models

Quite simple parametric flow models can group together parts of a scene (Figure 10.13). It is helpful to build models that are linear in their parameters. Writing θ_i for the ith component of the parameter vector, $\boldsymbol{F}_i$ for the ith flow basis vector field, and $\boldsymbol{v}(\boldsymbol{x})$ for the flow vector at pixel $\boldsymbol{x}$, one has

$$\boldsymbol{v}(\boldsymbol{x}) = \sum_i \theta_i \boldsymbol{F}_i$$

In the *affine motion model*, we have

$$\boldsymbol{v}(\boldsymbol{x}) = \begin{pmatrix} 1 & x & y & 0 & 0 & 0 \\ 0 & 0 & 0 & 1 & x & y \end{pmatrix} \begin{pmatrix} \theta_1 \\ \theta_2 \\ \theta_3 \\ \theta_4 \\ \theta_5 \\ \theta_6 \end{pmatrix}.$$

If flows involve what are essentially 2D effects—this is particularly appropriate for lateral views of human limbs—a set of basis flows that encodes translation, rotation and some affine effects is probably sufficient. Write (x, y) for the components of $\boldsymbol{x}$.

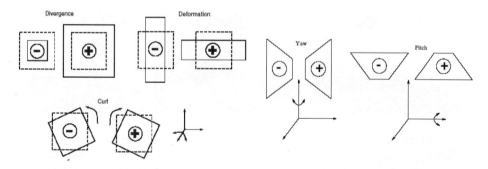

FIGURE 10.14: Typical flows generated by the model $(u(\boldsymbol{x}), v(\boldsymbol{x})^T = (\theta_1 + \theta_2 x + \theta_3 y + \theta_7 x^2 + \theta_8 xy, \theta_4 + \theta_5 x + \theta_6 y + \theta_y xy + \theta_8 y^2)$. Different values of the θ_i give different flows, and the model can generate flows typical of a 2D figure moving in 3D. **Divergence** occurs when the image is scaled; for example, $\theta = (0, 1, 0, 0, 0, 1, 0, 0)$. **Deformation** occurs when one direction shrinks and another grows (for example, rotation about an axis parallel to the view plane in an orthographic camera); for example, $\theta = (0, 1, 0, 0, 0, -1, 0, 0)$. **Curl** can result from in plane rotation; for example, $\theta = (0, 0, -1, 0, 1, 0, 0, 0)$. **Yaw** models rotation about a vertical axis in a perspective camera; for example $\theta = (0, 0, 0, 0, 0, 0, 1, 0)$. Finally, **pitch** models rotation about a horizontal axis in a perspective camera; for example $\theta = (0, 0, 0, 0, 0, 0, 0, 1)$. *This figure was originally published as Figure 2 of "Cardboard People: A Parameterized Model of Articulated Image Motion," S. Ju, M. Black, and Y. Yacoob, IEEE Int. Conf. Face and Gesture, 1996 © IEEE, 1996.*

One can obtain such flows using the simple model

$$
\boldsymbol{v}(\boldsymbol{x}) = \begin{pmatrix} 1 & x & y & 0 & 0 & 0 & x^2 & xy \\ 0 & 0 & 0 & 1 & x & y & xy & y^2 \end{pmatrix} \begin{pmatrix} \theta_1 \\ \theta_2 \\ \theta_3 \\ \theta_4 \\ \theta_5 \\ \theta_6 \\ \theta_7 \\ \theta_8 \end{pmatrix}.
$$

This model is linear in θ, and provides a reasonable encoding of flows resulting from 3D motions of a 2D rectangle (see Figure 10.14). Alternatively, we could obtain basis flows by a singular value decomposition of a pool of examples of the types of flow one would like to track, and try to find a set of basis flows that explains most of the variation (for examples, see Ju *et al.* (1996)).

10.6.3 Motion Segmentation with Layers

We now wish to segment a video sequence using a parametric flow model. Assume for the moment that there are just two frames in the sequence and that we know there are k segments (otherwise, we will need to use the methods of Section 10.7 to search over different numbers of segments). We will estimate a flow model for the two frames that is a mixture of k parametric flow models. The motion at each pixel in the first frame will come from this mixture, and will take the pixel to some

FIGURE 10.15: Frames 1, 15, and 30 of the MPEG flower garden sequence, which is often used to demonstrate motion segmentation algorithms. This sequence appears to be taken from a translating camera, with the tree much closer to the camera than the house and a flower garden on the ground plane. As a result, the tree appears to be translating quickly across the frame, and the house slowly; the plane generates an affine motion field. *This figure was originally published as Figure 6 from "Representing moving images with layers," by J. Wang and E.H. Adelson, IEEE Transactions on Image Processing, 1994, © IEEE, 1994.*

pixel in the second frame, which we expect will have the same brightness value. We could segment the first image (or the second; when we have the flow model, this doesn't really matter) by assigning each pixel to its flow model, so the pixels whose flow came from the first model would be in segment one, and so on. This model encapsulates a set of distinct, internally consistent motion fields, one per flow model. These might come from, say, a set of rigid objects at different depths and a moving camera (Figure 10.15). The separate motion fields are often referred to as *layers* and the model as a *layered motion* model.

Given a pair of images, we wish to determine (a) which motion field a pixel belongs to and (b) the parameter values for each field. All this should look a great deal like the first two examples, in that if we knew the first, the second would be easy, and if we knew the second, the first would be easy. This is again a missing data problem: the missing data is the motion field to which a pixel belongs, and the parameters are the parameters of each field and the mixing weights.

To work out the problem, we also need a probabilistic model of our observations. We assume that the intensity of a pixel in image two is obtained by taking the pixel in image one, moving it along the flow arrow for that pixel, and then adding a zero-mean Gaussian random variable with variance σ^2. Now assume that the pixel at (x, y) in the first image belongs to the lth motion field, with parameters θ_l. This means that this pixel has moved to $(x, y) + \boldsymbol{v}(x, y; \theta_l)$ in the second frame, and so that the intensity at these two pixels is the same, up to measurement noise. We write $I_1(x, y)$ for the image intensity of the first image at the x, yth pixel, and so on. The missing data is the motion field to which the pixel belongs. We can represent this by an indicator variable $V_{xy,j}$, where

$$V_{uv,j} = \left\{ \begin{array}{c} 1, \text{ if the } x, y\text{th pixel belongs to the } j\text{th motion field} \\ 0, \text{ otherwise} \end{array} \right\}.$$

The complete data log-likelihood becomes

$$L(V, \Theta) = -\sum_{xy,j} V_{xy,j} \frac{(I_1(x, y) - I_2(x + v_1(x, y; \theta_j), y + v_2(x, y; \theta_j)))^2}{2\sigma^2} + C,$$

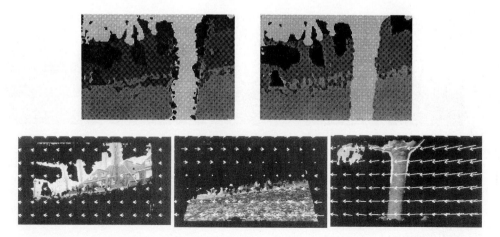

FIGURE 10.16: On the **top left**, a map indicating to which layer pixels in a frame of the flower garden sequence belong, obtained by clustering local estimates of image motion. Each gray level corresponds to a layer, and each layer is moving with a different affine motion model. This map can be refined by checking the extent to which the motion of pixel neighborhoods is consistent with neighborhoods in future and past frames, resulting in the map on the **top right**. Three of the layers and their motion models are shown on the **bottom**.   *This figure was originally published as Figures 11 and 12 from "Representing moving images with layers," by J. Wang and E.H. Adelson, IEEE Transactions on Image Processing, 1994, © IEEE, 1994.*

where $\Theta = (\theta_1, \ldots, \theta_k)$. Setting up the EM algorithm from here on is straightforward. As before, the crucial issue is determining

$$P\left\{V_{xy,j} = 1 | I_1, I_2, \Theta\right\}.$$

These probabilities are often represented as *support maps*—maps assigning a gray-level representing the maximum probability layer to each pixel (Figure 10.16).

Layered motion representations are useful for several reasons: First, they cluster together points moving "in the same way." Second, they expose motion boundaries. Finally, new sequences can be reconstructed from the layers in interesting ways (Figure 10.17).

10.7 MODEL SELECTION: WHICH MODEL IS THE BEST FIT?

To date, we have assumed that we knew how many components our model has. For example, we assumed that we were fitting a single line; in the image segmentation example, we assumed we knew the number of segments; for general mixture models, we assumed the number of components was known. Generally, this is not a safe assumption.

We could fit models with different numbers of components (such as lines, segments, and so on), and see which model fits best. This strategy fails, because the model with more components will *always* fit best. In the extreme case, a really good fit of lines to points involves passing one line through each pair of points. This representation will be a perfect fit to the data, but will be useless in almost every

FIGURE 10.17: One feature of representing motion in terms of layers is that one can reconstruct a motion sequence *without* some of the layers. In this example, the MPEG garden sequence has been reconstructed with the tree layer omitted. The figure on the **left** shows frame 1, that in the **center** shows frame 15, and that on the **right** shows frame 30. *This figure was originally published as Figure 13 from "Representing moving images with layers," by J. Wang and E.H. Adelson, IEEE Transactions on Image Processing, 1994,* © *IEEE, 1994.*

case. It will be useless because it is too complex to manipulate and because it will be very poor at predicting new data.

Another way to look at this point is as a trade off between bias and variance. The data points are a sample that comes from some underlying process, that we are trying to represent. Representing a lot of data points with, say, a single line is a biased representation, because it cannot represent all the complexity of the model that produced the dataset. Some information about the underlying process is inevitably lost. However, we can estimate the properties of the line used to represent the data points very accurately indeed with some care, so there is little variance in our estimate of the model that we do fit. Alternatively, if we were to represent the data points with a zigzag set of lines that joined them up, the representation would have no bias, but would be different for each new sample of data points from the same source. As a result, our estimate of the model we fit changes wildly from sample to sample; it is overwhelmed by variance.

We want a trade off. Fitting error gets smaller with the number of parameters, so we need to add a term to the fitting error that *increases* with the number of components. This penalty compensates for the decrease in fitting error (equivalently, negative log-likelihood) caused by the increasing number of parameters. Instead, we can choose from a variety of techniques, each of which uses a different discount corresponding to a different extremality principle and different approximate estimates of the criterion.

Another way to look at this point is that we wish to predict future samples from the model. Our dataset is a sample from a parametric model that is a member of a family of models. A proper choice of the parameters predicts future samples from the model—a *test set*—*as well as* the dataset (which is often called the *training set*). Unfortunately, these future samples are not available. Furthermore, the estimate of the model's parameters obtained using the dataset is likely to be biased because the parameters chosen ensure that the model is an optimal fit to the *training set*, rather than to the entire set of possible data. The effect is known as *selection bias*. The training set is a subset of the entire set of data that could have been drawn from the model; it represents the model exactly only if it is infinitely large. This is why the negative log-likelihood is a poor guide to the choice of model: the fit looks better because it is increasingly biased.

Now write the best choice of parameters as Θ^* and the log-likelihood of the fit to the dataset as $L(\boldsymbol{x}; \Theta^*)$, p for the number of free parameters, and N for the number of data items. We will compute a score from the log-likelihood and a penalty that discourages too many parameters. There are several possibilities for the score, but the procedure involves searching a space of models to find the one that optimizes this score (for example, we could increase the number of components).

AIC: An Information Criterion

Akaike proposed a penalty, widely called *AIC* (for "an information criterion," *not* "Akaike information criterion"), that leads to choosing the model with the minimum value of

$$-2L(\boldsymbol{x}; \Theta^*) + 2p.$$

There is a collection of statistical debate about the AIC. The first main point is that it lacks a term in the *number* of data points. This is suspicious because our estimate of the parameters of the real model should get better as the number of data points goes up. Second, there is a body of experience that the AIC tends to *overfit*—that is, to choose a model with too many parameters that fits the training set well but doesn't perform as well on test sets.

Bayesian Methods and Schwartz's BIC

For simplicity, let us write $\mathcal{D}$ for the data, $\mathcal{M}$ for the model, and θ for the parameters. Bayes' rule then yields:

$$
\begin{aligned}
P(\mathcal{M}|\mathcal{D}) &= \frac{P(\mathcal{D}|\mathcal{M})}{P}(\mathcal{M})P(\mathcal{D}) \\
&= \frac{\int P(\mathcal{D}|\mathcal{M}_i, \theta)P(\theta)d\theta P(\mathcal{M})}{P(\mathcal{D})}.
\end{aligned}
$$

Now we could choose the model for which the posterior is large. Computing this posterior can be difficult, but, by a series of approximations, we can obtain a criterion

$$-L(\mathcal{D}; \theta^*) + \frac{p}{2}\log N$$

(where N is the number of data items). Again, we choose the model that minimizes this score. This is called the *Bayes information criterion*, or BIC. Notice that this does have a term in the number of data items.

Description Length

Models can be selected by criteria not intrinsically statistical. After all, we are selecting the model, and we can say why we want to select it. A criterion that is somewhat natural is to choose the model that encodes the dataset most crisply. This *minimum description length* criterion chooses the model that allows the most efficient transmission of the dataset. To transmit the dataset, one codes and transmits the model parameters, and then codes and transmits the data given the model parameters. If the data fits the model poorly, then this latter term is large because one has to code a noise-like signal.

A derivation of the criterion used in practice is rather beyond our needs. The details appear in Rissanen (1983), (1987), and in Wallace and Freeman (1987); there are similar ideas rooted in information theory, due to Kolmogorov, and expounded in Cover and Thomas (1991). Surprisingly, the BIC emerges from this analysis, yielding

$$-L(\mathcal{D}; \theta^*) + \frac{p}{2} \log N.$$

Again, we choose the model that minimizes this score.

10.7.1 Model Selection Using Cross-Validation

The key difficulty in model selection is that we should be using a quantity we can't measure: the model's ability to predict data not in the training set. Given a sufficiently large training set, we could split the training set into two components, and use one to fit the model and the other the test the fit. This approach is known as *cross-validation*.

We can use cross-validation to determine the number of components in a model by splitting the dataset into training and test data, fitting a variety of different models to training data, and then choosing the model that performs best on the test data. To evaluate performance, we could look at log-likelihood on the test data. We expect this process to estimate the number of components because a model that has too many parameters will fit the training dataset well, but predict the test set badly.

Using a single choice of a split into two components introduces a different form of selection bias, and the safest thing to do is average the estimate over all such splits. This becomes unwieldy if the test set is large, because the number of splits is huge. The most usual version is *leave-one-out cross-validation*. In this approach, we fit a model to each set of $N-1$ of the training set, compute the error on the remaining data point, and sum these errors to obtain an estimate of the model error. The model that minimizes this estimate is then chosen.

10.8   NOTES

The origins of least squares fitting are opaque to us, though we believe that Gauss himself invented the method. Total least squares appears to be due to Deming (1943). There is a large literature on fitting curves or curved surfaces using least squares methods, or approximations (one could start with work on conics (Bookstein 1979, Fitzgibbon *et al.* 1999, Kanatani 2006, Kanatani 1994, Porrill 1990, Sampson 1982); more complicated problems in (Taubin 1991)).

The Hough Transform

The Hough transform is due to Hough (1962) (a note in Keith Price's wonderful bibliography remarks: "The most cited and least read reference"). There was a large literature on the Hough transform, which was seen as having theoretical significance; the interested might start with Ballard (1981), then Ballard (1984). The topic then began to seem dated, but was revived by mean shift methods and by the observation, due to Maji and Malik (2009), that not every token needed to have the same vote, and the weights could be learned. The idea that multiple pieces of an object could reinforce one another by voting on the location of the object is very old (see Ballard (1981); Ballard (1984)); the most important recent version is Bourdev *et al.* (2010).

RANSAC

RANSAC is a hugely important algorithm, very easy to implement and use, and very effective. The original paper (Fischler and Bolles 1981) is still worth reading. There are numerous variants, depending on what one knows about the data and the problem; see Torr and Davidson (2003) and Torr and Zisserman (2000) for a start.

EM and Missing Variable Models

EM was first formally described in the statistical literature by Dempster *et al.* (1977). A very good summary reference is McLachlan and Krishnan (1996), which describes numerous variants. For example, it isn't necessary to find the maximum of $Q(\boldsymbol{u}; \boldsymbol{u}^{(s)})$; all that is required is to obtain a better value. As another example, the expectation can be estimated using stochastic integration methods.

Missing variable models seem to crop up in all sorts of places. All the models we are aware of in computer vision arise from mixture models (and so have complete data log-likelihood that is linear in the missing variables), and so we have concentrated on this case. It is natural to use a missing variable model for segmentation (see, for example Belongie *et al.* (1998*a*); Feng and Perona (1998); Vasconcelos and Lippman (1997); Adelson and Weiss (1996); or Wells *et al.* (1996)). Various forms of layered motion now exist (see Dellaert *et al.* (2000); Wang and Adelson (1994); Adelson and Weiss (1996); Tao *et al.* (2000); and Weiss (1997)); one can also construct layers that lie at the same depth (see Brostow and Essa (1999); Torr *et al.* (1999*b*); or Baker *et al.* (1998)), or have some other common property. Other interesting cases include motions resulting from transparency, specularities, etc. (see Darrell and Simoncelli (1993); Black and Anandan (1996); Jepson and Black (1993); Hsu *et al.* (1994); or Szeliski *et al.* (2000)). The resulting representation can be used for quite efficient image based rendering (see Shade *et al.* (1998)).

EM is an extremely successful inference algorithm, but it isn't magical. The primary source of difficulty for the kinds of problem that we have described is local maxima. It is common for problems that have very large numbers of missing variables to have large numbers of local maxima. This could be dealt with by starting the optimization close to the right answer, which rather misses the point.

Model Selection

Model selection is a topic that hasn't received as much attention as it deserves. There is significant work in motion, the question being which camera model (orthographic, perspective, etc.) to apply (see Torr (1999); Torr (1997); Kinoshita and Lindenbaum (2000); or Maybank and Sturm (1999)). Similarly, there is work in segmentation of range data, where the question is to what set of parametric surfaces the data should be fitted (i.e., are there two planes or three, etc.) (Bubna and Stewart 2000). In reconstruction problems, one must sometimes decide whether a degenerate camera motion sequence is present (Torr *et al.* 1999*a*). The standard problem in segmentation is how many segments are present (see Raja *et al.* (1998); Belongie *et al.* (1998*a*); and Adelson and Weiss (1996)). If one is using models predictively, it is sometimes better to compute a weighted average over model predictions (real Bayesians don't do model selection) (Torr and Zisserman 1998, Ripley 1996). We have described only some of the available methods; one important omission is Kanatani's geometric information criterion (Kanatani 1998).

PROBLEMS

10.1. Prove the simple, but extremely useful, result that the perpendicular distance from a point (u, v) to a line (a, b, c) is given by abs$(au + bv + c)$ *if* $a^2 + b^2 = 1$.

10.2. Derive the eigenvalue problem

$$
\begin{pmatrix} \overline{x^2} - \overline{x}\,\overline{x} & \overline{xy} - \overline{x}\,\overline{y} \\ \overline{xy} - \overline{x}\,\overline{y} & \overline{y^2} - \overline{y}\,\overline{y} \end{pmatrix} \begin{pmatrix} a \\ b \end{pmatrix} = \mu \begin{pmatrix} a \\ b \end{pmatrix}
$$

from the generative model for total least squares. This is a simple exercise—maximum likelihood and a little manipulation will do it—but worth doing right and remembering. The technique is extremely useful.

10.3. How do we get a curve of edge points from an edge detector that returns orientation? Give a recursive algorithm.

10.4. An implicit curve is given by $\phi(x, y) = 0$. For this curve, we have the property that for every point (u, v), there is exactly one point (x_0, y_0) on the curve that satisfies the local equations for the close. Show that this curve is a line. (Hint: the normals at each point on the curve must be parallel).

10.5. A slightly more stable variation of incremental fitting cuts the first few pixels and the last few pixels from the line point list when fitting the line because these pixels might have come from a corner.

(a) Why would this lead to an improvement?

(b) How should one decide how many pixels to omit?

10.6. Assume we have a fixed camera with focal length f. Write the coordinates of world points in capital letters, and of image points in lowercase letters. Place the focal point of the camera at $(0, 0, 0)$, and the image plane at $Z = -f$. We have a plane object lying on the plane $Z = aX + b$, with $|a| > 0$, $|b| > 0$.

(a) What translations of this object give image motion fields that are exactly represented by an affine motion model?

(b) Under what circumstances does an affine motion model give a reasonable approximation to the image flow fields produced by translating this object?

10.7. Refer to Section 10.5.1 for notation for the line and outliers example. Write δ_i for an indicator variable for the ith example, where $\delta_i = 1$ if the example comes from the line and $\delta_i = 0$ otherwise. Assume that we wish to fit using total least squares. Assume we know σ, the standard deviation of the errors. Assume that the probability of an outlier is independent of its position. For this example, show that the complete data log-likelihood is

$$
\mathcal{L}_c(a, b, c, \pi) = \sum_i \left[-\frac{(ax_i + by_i + c)^2}{2\sigma^2} + \log \pi \right] \delta_i + [K + \log(1 - \pi)](1 - \delta_i) + L
$$

where K is a constant expressing the probability of obtaining an outlier and L does not depend on a, b, c, or π.

10.8. Refer to Section 10.5.1 and the previous example for notation for the line and outliers example. For this example, produce an expression for $\alpha_i = E_{\delta|\boldsymbol{x},\Theta^{(s)}}[\delta_i]$, where $\Theta = (a, b, c, \pi)$.

10.9. Refer to Section 10.5.1 for notation for the image segmentation example. Write δ_{ij} for an indicator variable for the ith example, where $\delta_{ij} = 1$ if the example comes from the j'th segment, and $\delta_{ij} = 0$ otherwise. Assume we know Σ, the covariance of the image segment probability distributions, and that this is the same per segment. For this example, show that the complete data log-likelihood is

$$\mathcal{L}_c(\pi_1, \ldots, \pi_g, \mu_1, \ldots, \mu_g) = \sum_{ij} \left[-\frac{(\boldsymbol{x}_i - \mu_j)^T \Sigma^{-1}(\boldsymbol{x}_i - \mu_j)}{2} + \log \pi_j \right] \delta_{ij} + L$$

where L does not depend on μ_j or π_j.

10.10. Refer to Section 10.5.1 for notation for the image segmentation example. For this example, produce an expression for $\alpha_{ij} = E_{\delta|\boldsymbol{x},\Theta^{(s)}}[\delta_{ij}]$, where $\Theta = (\pi_1, \ldots, \pi_g, \mu_1, \ldots, \mu_g)$.

10.11. Refer to Section 10.5.1 for notation for the line and outliers example. For this example, show that the updates produced in the M-step will be

$$\pi(s+1) = \frac{\sum_i \alpha_{ij}}{\sum_{i,j} \alpha_{ij}}$$

and

$$\mu_j^{(s+1)} = \frac{\sum_i \alpha_{ij}\boldsymbol{x}_i}{\sum_i \alpha_{ij}}$$

10.12. Refer to Section 10.5.1 for notation for the image segmentation example. For this example, show that the updates produced in the M-step will be

$$\pi_j^{(s+1)} = \frac{\sum_i \alpha_{ij}}{\sum_{i,j} \alpha_{ij}}$$

and

$$\mu_j^{(s+1)} = \frac{\sum_i \alpha_{ij}\boldsymbol{x}_i}{\sum_i \alpha_{ij}}$$

PROGRAMMING EXERCISES

10.13. Implement an incremental line fitter. Determine how significant a difference results from leaving out the first few pixels and the last few pixels from the line point list (put some care into building this; in our experience, it's a useful piece of software to have lying around).

10.14. Implement a Hough transform based line finder.

10.15. Count lines with an HT line finder. How well does it work?

10.16. Implement the algorithm for incremental line fitting.

10.17. Refer to Section 10.5.1 for notation for the image segmentation example. Use your expression for $\alpha_{ij} = E_{\delta|\boldsymbol{x},\Theta^{(s)}}[\delta_{ij}]$, where $\Theta = (\pi_1, \ldots, \pi_g, \mu_1, \ldots, \mu_g)$, to implement an EM algorithm to segment images. It is sufficient to use RGB color and location as a feature vector.

C H A P T E R 11

Tracking

Tracking is the problem of generating an inference about the motion of an object given a sequence of images. Generally, we will have some measurements that appear at each tick of a (notional) clock. These measurements could be the position of some image points, the position and moments of some image regions, or pretty much anything else. They are not guaranteed to be relevant, in the sense that some could come from the object of interest and some might come from other objects or from noise. We will have an encoding of the object's state and some model of how this state changes from tick to tick. We would like to infer the state of the world from the measurements and the model of dynamics.

Tracking problems are of great practical importance. There are very good reasons to want to, say, track aircraft using radar returns (good summary histories include Brown (2000); Buderi (1998); and Jones (1998); comprehensive reviews of technique in this context include Bar-Shalom and Li (2001); Blackman and Popoli (1999); and Gelb and of the Analytical Sciences Corporation (1974)). Other important applications include:

- **Motion Capture:** If we can track the 3D configuration of a moving person accurately, then we can make an accurate record of their motions. Once we have this record, we can use it to drive a rendering process; for example, we might control a cartoon character, thousands of virtual extras in a crowd scene, or a virtual stunt avatar. Furthermore, we could modify the motion record to obtain slightly different motions. This means that a single performer can produce sequences they wouldn't want to do in person.

- **Recognition from Motion:** The motion of objects is quite characteristic. We might be able to determine the identity of the object from its motion. We should be able to tell what it's doing.

- **Surveillance:** Knowing what the objects are doing can be very useful. For example, different kinds of trucks should move in different, fixed patterns in an airport; if they do not, then something is going wrong. Similarly, there are combinations of places and patterns of motions that should never occur (e.g., no truck should ever stop on an active runway). It could be helpful to have a computer system that can monitor activities and give a warning when it detects a problem case.

- **Targeting:** A significant fraction of the tracking literature is oriented toward (a) deciding what to shoot, and (b) hitting it. Typically, this literature describes tracking using radar or infrared signals (rather than vision), but the basic issues are the same: What do we infer about an object's future position from a sequence of measurements? Where should we aim?

Generally, we regard a moving object as having a *state*. This state—which might not be observed directly—encodes all the properties of the object we care to deal with, or need to encode its motion. For example, state might contain: position; position and velocity; position, velocity, and acceleration; position and appearance; and so on. This state changes at each tick of time, and we then get new measurements that depend on the new state. These measurements are referred to as *observations*. In many problems, the observations are measurements of state, perhaps incorporating some noise. For example, the state might be the position of the object, and we observe its position. In other problems, the observations are functions of state. For example, the state might be position and velocity, but we observe only position. In some tracking problems, we have a model of how the state changes with time. The information in this model is referred to as the object's *dynamics*. Tracking involves exploiting both observations and dynamics to infer state.

The most important property of visual tracking problems is that observations are usually hidden in a great deal of irrelevant information. For example, if we wish to track a face in a video frame, in most cases the face occupies fewer than a third of the pixels in the video frame. In almost every case, the pixels that do not lie on the face have nothing useful to offer about the state of the face. This means that we face significant problems identifying which observations are likely to be helpful. The main methods for doing so involve either building a detector (Section 11.1.1) or exploiting the tendency for objects to look the same over time, and to move coherently (Section 11.1.2 and Section 11.2). It is straightforward to balance dynamical predictions against measurements using probabilistic methods if the dynamical model is relatively straightforward, because the probability models are easy to represent (Section 11.3). Furthermore, dynamical predictions can be used to identify useful measurements (Section 11.4). Non-linear dynamical models can produce probability models that need to be represented with approximate methods (Section 11.5).

11.1 SIMPLE TRACKING STRATEGIES

There are two simple ways to track objects. In the first, *tracking by detection*, we have a strong model of the object, strong enough to identify it in each frame. We find it, link up the instances, and we have a track. Some additional machinery can compensate for weaker models in many cases, too (Section 11.1.1). In the second, *tracking by matching*, we have a model of how the object moves. We have a domain in the nth frame in which the object sits, and then use this model to search for a domain in the $n+1$th frame that matches it (Section 11.1.2). Tracking by matching strategies become more elaborate as the motion model and the matching model becomes more elaborate; we deal with the more elaborate strategies in Section 11.2.

11.1.1 Tracking by Detection

Assume that we will see only one object in each frame of video, that the state we wish to track is position in the image, and that we can build a reliable detector for the object we wish to track. In this case, tracking is straightforward: we report the location of the detector response in each frame of the video. This observation

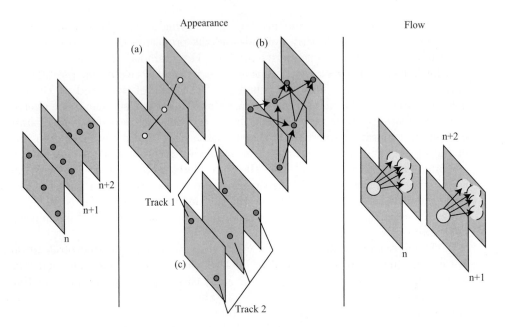

FIGURE 11.1: In tracking problems, we want to build space time paths followed by tokens—which might be objects, or regions, or interest points, or image windows—in an image sequence (**left**). There are two important sources of information; carefully used, they can resolve many tracking problems without further complexity. One is the appearance of the token being tracked. If there is only one token in each frame with a distinctive appearance, then we could detect it in each frame, then link the detector responses (**a**). Alternatively, if there is more than one instance per frame, a cost function together with weighted bipartite matching could be enough to build the track (**b**). If some instances drop out, we will need to link detector responses to abstract tracks (**c**); in the figure, track 1 has measurements for frames n and $n + 2$, but does not have a measurement for frame $n + 1$. Another important source of information is the motion of the token; if we have a manageable model of the flow, we could search for the flow that generates the best match in the next frame. We choose that match as the next location of the token, then iterate this procedure (**right**).

is a good source of simple and effective tracking strategies, because we can build good detectors for some objects. For example, consider tracking a red ball on a green background, where the detector might just look for red pixels. In other cases, we might need to use a more sophisticated detector; for example, we might wish to track a frontal face looking at a camera (detectors are discussed in detail in Chapter 17).

In most cases, we can't assume only one object, or a reliable detector. If objects can enter or leave the frame (or if the detector occasionally fails to detect something), then it isn't enough to just report the location of an object at each frame. We must account for the fact that some frames have too many (or too few) objects in them. To do this, we will have an abstraction called a **track**, which represents a timeline for a single object. Assume that we have tracked for a while and wish to deal with a new frame. We copy the tracks from the previous frame to this frame, and then allocate object detector responses to tracks. How we allocate depends on the application (we give some examples below). Each track will get at most one detector response, and each detector response will get at most one track. However, some tracks may not receive a detector response, and some detector responses may not be allocated a track. Finally, we deal with tracks that have no response and with responses that have no track. For every detector response that is not allocated to a track, we create a new track (because a new object might have appeared). For every track that has not received a response for several frames, we prune that track (because the object might have disappeared). Finally, we may postprocess the set of tracks to insert links where justified by the application. Algorithm 11.1 breaks out this approach.

The main issue in allocation is the cost model, which will vary from application to application. We need a charge for allocating detects to tracks. For slow-moving objects, this charge could be the image distance between the detect in the current frame and the detect allocated to the track in the previous frame. For objects with slowly changing appearance, the cost could be an appearance distance (e.g., a χ-squared distance between color histograms). How we use the distance again depends on the application. In cases where the detector is very reliable and the objects are few, well-spaced, and slow-moving, then a greedy algorithm (allocate the closest detect to each track) is sufficient. This algorithm might attach one detector response to two tracks; whether this is a problem or not depends on the application. The more general algorithm solves a bipartite matching problem. The tracks form one side of a bipartite graph, and the detector responses are the other side. Each side is augmented by NULL nodes, so that a track (or response) can go unmatched. The edges are weighted by matching costs, and we must solve a maximum weighted bipartite matching problem (Figure 11.1). We could solve this exactly with the Hungarian algorithm (see, for example, Cormen *et al.* (2009); Schrijver (2003); or Jungnickel (1999)); very often, however, the quite good approximation that a greedy algorithm will supply is sufficient. In some cases, we know where objects can appear and disappear, so that tracks can be created only for detects that occur in some region, and tracks can be reaped only if the last detect occurs in a disappear region.

Background subtraction is often a good enough detector in applications where the background is known and all trackable objects look different from the background. In such cases, it can be enough to apply background subtraction and regard the big blobs as detector responses. This strategy is simple, but can be very effective. One useful case occurs for people seen on a fixed background, such as a corridor or a parking lot. If the application doesn't require a detailed report of the body configuration, and if we expect people to be reasonably large in view, we can reason that large blobs produced by background subtraction are individual people. Although this method has weaknesses—for example, if people are still for a long time, they might disappear; it would require more work to split up the large blob of foreground pixels that occurs when two people are close together; and so on—many applications require only approximate reports of the traffic density, or alarms when a person appears in a particular view. The method is well suited to such cases.

This basic recipe for tracking by detection is worth remembering. In many

---

Notation:
Write $\mathbf{x}_k(i)$ for the k'th response of the detector in the ith frame
Write $t(k, i)$ for the k'th track in the ith frame
Write $*t(k, i)$ for the detector response attached to the k'th track in the ith frame
(Think C pointer notation)

Assumptions: We have a detector which is reasonably reliable.
We know some distance d such that $d(*t(k, i-1), *t(k, i))$ is always small.

First frame: Create a track for each detector response.

N'th frame:
Link tracks and detector responses by solving a bipartite matching problem.
Spawn a new track for each detector response not allocated to a track.
Reap any track that has not received a detector response for some number of frames.

Cleanup: We now have trajectories in space time. Link anywhere this is justified (perhaps by a more sophisticated dynamical or appearance model, derived from the candidates for linking).

Algorithm 11.1: Tracking by Detection.

---

situations, nothing more complex is required. The trick of creating tracks promiscuously and then pruning any track that has not received a measurement for some time is quite general and extremely effective.

11.1.2 Tracking Translations by Matching

Assume we have a television view of a soccer field with players running around. Each player might occupy a box about 10–30 pixels high, so it would be hard to determine where arms and legs are (Figure 11.2). The frame rate is 30Hz, and body parts don't move all that much (compared to the resolution) from frame to frame. In a case like this, we can assume that the domain translates. We can model a player's motion with two components. The first is the absolute motion of a box fixed around the player and the second is the player's movement relative to that box. To do so, we need to track the box, a process known as *image stabilization*. As another example of how useful image stabilization is, one might stabilize a box around an aerial view of a moving vehicle; now the box contains all visual information about the vehicle's identity.

In each example, the box translates. If we have a rectangle in frame n, we can search for the rectangle of the same size in frame $n + 1$ that is most like the original. We are looking for a box that looks a lot like the current box, so we can use the *sum-of-squared differences* (or *SSD*) of pixel values as a test for similarity. If we write $\mathcal{R}^{(n)}$ for the rectangle in the nth frame, $\mathcal{R}_{ij}^{(n)}$ for the i, jth pixel in the

FIGURE 11.2: A useful application of tracking is to stabilize an image box around a more interesting structure, in this case a football player in a television-resolution video. A frame from the video is shown on the **left**. Inset is a box around a player, zoomed to a higher resolution. Notice that the limbs of the player span a few pixels, are blurry, and are hard to resolve. A natural feature for inferring what the player is doing can be obtained by stabilizing the box around the player, then measuring the motion of the limbs with respect to the box. Players move relatively short distances between frames, and their body configuration changes a relatively small amount. This means the new box can be found by searching all nearby boxes of the same size to get the box whose pixels best match those of the original. On the **right**, a set of stabilized boxes; the strategy is enough to center the player in a box. *This figure was originally published as Figure 7 of "Recognizing Action at a Distance," A. Efros, A.C. Berg, G. Mori, and J. Malik, Proc. IEEE ICCV, 2003, © IEEE, 2003.*

rectangle in the nth image, then we choose $\mathcal{R}^{(n+1)}$ to minimize

$$\sum_{i,j} (\mathcal{R}_{ij}^{(n)} - \mathcal{R}_{ij}^{(n+1)})^2.$$

In many applications the distance the rectangle can move in an inter-frame interval is bounded because there are velocity constraints. If this distance is small enough, we could simply evaluate the sum of squared differences to every rectangle of the appropriate shape within that bound, or we might consider a search across scale for the matching rectangle (see Section 4.7 for more information).

Now write $\mathcal{P}_t$ for the indices of the patch in the tth frame and $I(\boldsymbol{x}, t)$ for the tth frame. Assume that the patch is at $\boldsymbol{x}_t$ in the tth frame and it translates to $\boldsymbol{x}_t + \boldsymbol{h}$ in the $t+1$th frame. Then we can determine $\boldsymbol{h}$ by minimizing

$$E(\boldsymbol{h}) = \sum_{\boldsymbol{u} \in \mathcal{P}_t} \left[I(\boldsymbol{u}, t) - I(\boldsymbol{u} + \boldsymbol{h}, t+1) \right]^2$$

as a function of $\boldsymbol{h}$. The minimum of the error occurs when

$$\nabla_h E(\boldsymbol{h}) = 0.$$

Now if $\boldsymbol{h}$ is small, we can write $I(\boldsymbol{u} + \boldsymbol{h}, t+1) \approx I(\boldsymbol{u}, t) + \boldsymbol{h}^T \nabla I$, where ∇I is the

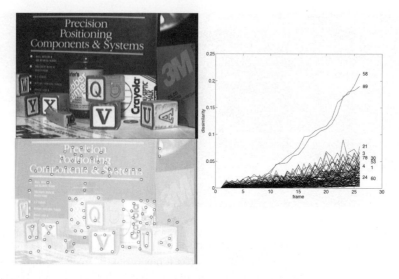

FIGURE 11.3: It is natural to track local neighborhoods, like those built in Section 5.3.2; however, for these neighborhoods to yield good tracks, they should pass a test of appearance complexity, shown in the text. This test checks that estimates of the translation of the neighborhood are stable. **Top left:** the first frame of an image sequence, with possible neighborhoods that pass this test shown on the **bottom left**. On the **right**, the sum-of-squared differences between the translated patch in frame n and the original in frame 1. Notice how this drifts up, meaning that the accumulated motion over many frames is *not* a translation; we need a better test to identify good tracks. *This figure was originally published as Figures 10, 11, 12 of "Good features to track," by J. Shi and C. Tomasi, Proc. IEEE CVPR 1994, © IEEE, 1994.*

image gradient. Substituting, and rearranging, we get

$$\left[\sum_{\boldsymbol{u}\in\mathcal{P}_t}(\nabla I)(\nabla I)^T\right]\boldsymbol{h}=\sum_{\boldsymbol{u}\in\mathcal{P}_t}\left[I(\boldsymbol{u},t)-I(\boldsymbol{u},t+1)\right]\nabla I,$$

which is a linear system we could solve directly for $\boldsymbol{h}$. The solution of this system will be unreliable if the smaller eigenvalue of the symmetric positive semidefinite matrix $\left[\sum_{\boldsymbol{u}\in\mathcal{P}_t}(\nabla I)(\nabla I)^T\right]$ is too small. This occurs when the image gradients in $\mathcal{P}$ are all small—so the patch is featureless—or all point in one direction—so that we cannot localize the patch along that flow direction. If the estimate of $\boldsymbol{h}$ is unreliable, we must end the track. As Shi and Tomasi (1994) point out, this means that we can test the smallest eigenvalue of this matrix to tell whether a local window is worth tracking.

11.1.3 Using Affine Transformations to Confirm a Match

Some patches are like the soccer player example in Figure 11.2: the patch just translates. For other patches, the movement from frame n to $n+1$ is quite like a translation, but when one compares frame 1 to frame $n+1$, a more complex model of deformation is required. This could occur because, for example, the surface

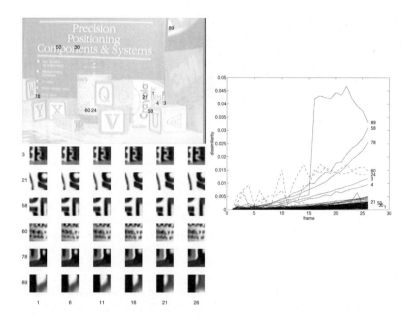

FIGURE 11.4: On the **top left**, the first frame of the sequence shown in Figure 11.3, with some neighborhoods overlaid. On the **bottom left**, the neighborhoods associated with these features (vertical) for different frames (horizontal). Notice how the pattern in the neighborhood deforms, perhaps because the object is rotating in 3D. This means that a translation model is good for the movement from frame n to frame $n + 1$, but does not explain the movement from frame 1 to frame $n + 1$. For this, we need to use an affine model. On the **right**, the value of the sum-of-squared differences between neighborhoods on a track in frame n and in frame 1, plotted against n. In this case, the neighborhood has been rectified by an affine transform, as in Section 11.1.3, before computing the SSD. Notice how some tracks are obviously good and others can be seen to have drifted. We could use this property to prune tracks. *This figure was originally published as Figures 13, 14, 15 of "Good features to track," by J. Shi and C. Tomasi, Proc. IEEE CVPR 1994, © IEEE, 1994.*

on which the patch lies is rotating in 3D. In cases such as this, we should use a translation model to build a track, and then prune tracks by checking the patch in frame $n + 1$ against frame 1. Because the image patch is small, an affine model is appropriate. The affine model means that the point $\boldsymbol{x}$ in frame 1 will become the point $\mathcal{M}\boldsymbol{x} + \boldsymbol{c}$ in frame t. To estimate $\mathcal{M}$ and $\boldsymbol{c}$, we will minimize

$$E(\mathcal{M}, \boldsymbol{c}) = \sum_{\boldsymbol{u} \in \mathcal{P}_1} \left[I(\boldsymbol{u}, 1) - I(\mathcal{M}\boldsymbol{u} + \boldsymbol{c}, t) \right]^2.$$

Notice that, because we are comparing the original patch in frame 1 with that in the current frame, the sum is over $\boldsymbol{u} \in \mathcal{P}_1$. Once we have $\mathcal{M}$ and $\boldsymbol{c}$, we can evaluate the SSD between the current patch and its original, and if this is below a threshold, the match is acceptable.

These two steps lead to a quite flexible mechanism. We can start tracks using an interest point operator, perhaps a corner detector. To build a tracker that can

FIGURE 11.5: Four frames from a sequence depicting football players, with superimposed domains. The object to be tracked is the blob on top of player 78 (at the center right in frame 30). We have masked off these blobs (**below**) to emphasize just how strongly the pixels move around in the domain. Notice the motion blur in the final frame. These blobs can be matched to one another, and this is done by comparing histograms (in this case, color histograms), which are less affected by deformation than individual pixel values. *This figure was originally published as Figure 1 of "Kernel-Based Object Tracking" by D. Comaniciu, V. Ramesh, and P. Meer, IEEE Transactions on Pattern Analysis and Machine Intelligence, 2003, © IEEE 2003.*

create and reap tracks as necessary, we find all interest points in frame 1. We then find the location of each of these in the next frame, and check whether the patch matches the original one. If so, it belongs to a track. If not, the track has ended. We now look for interest points or corners that don't belong to tracks and create new tracks there. Again, we advance tracks to the next frame, check each against their original patch, reap tracks whose patch doesn't match well enough, and create tracks at new interest points. In Section 11.4.1, we show how to link this procedure with a dynamical model built from a Kalman filter (Kalman filters are described in Section 11.3).

11.2   TRACKING USING MATCHING

Imagine tracking a face in a webcam. The face is not necessarily frontal, because computer users occasionally look away from their monitors, and so a detector will not work. But a face tends to be blobby, tends to have coherent appearance, and tends only to translate and rotate. As with the strategy of Section 11.1.2, we have a domain of interest in the nth image, $\mathcal{D}_n$, and we must search for a matching domain $\mathcal{D}_{n+1}$ in the $n + 1$st image, but our motion model is more complex.

There are two types of match we can work with. In *summary matching*, we match summary representations of the whole domain. We will represent a domain with a set of parameters; for example, we could work with circular domains of fixed radius, and represent the domain by the location of the center. We then compute a summary of the appearance within the circle $\mathcal{D}_n$ and find the best-matching circle $\mathcal{D}_{n+1}$ (Section 11.2.1). In *flow-based matching*, we search for a transformation of the pixels in the old domain that produces set of pixels that match well, and so a good new domain. This allows us to exploit strong motion models (Section 10.6.2).

Assume we have a sequence of N images; a domain $\mathcal{D}_1$,
in the first image represented by parameters
$\boldsymbol{y}_1$ (for a circular domain of fixed size, these would be the
location of the center; for a square, the center and edge length; and so on);
a kernel function k; a scale h; and a feature representation $\boldsymbol{f}$ of each pixel.

For $n \in [1, \ldots, N-1]$
    Obtain an initial estimate $\boldsymbol{y}_{n+1}^{(0)}$ of the next domain
        either from a Kalman filter, or using $\boldsymbol{y}_n$
    Iterate until convergence

$$\boldsymbol{y}_{n+1}^{(j+1)} = \frac{\sum_i w_i \boldsymbol{x}_i \, g\left(\left\|\frac{\boldsymbol{x}_i - \boldsymbol{y}^{(j)}}{h}\right\|^2\right)}{\sum_i w_i \, g\left(\left\|\frac{\boldsymbol{x}_i - \boldsymbol{y}^{(j)}}{h}\right\|^2\right)}$$

    where p_u, k, g are as given in the text

The track is the sequence of converged estimates $\boldsymbol{y}_1, \ldots, \boldsymbol{y}_N$.

Algorithm 11.2: Tracking with the Mean Shift Algorithm.

11.2.1 Matching Summary Representations

Look at the football player's uniform in Figure 9.3.4. From frame to frame, we see the player's back at different viewing angles. Individual pixels in one domain might have no corresponding pixels in the next. For example, the cloth may have folded slightly; as another example, there is motion blur in some frames. Nonetheless, the domain is largely white, with some yellow patches. This suggests that a summary representation of the domain might not change from frame to frame, even though the fine details do.

There is a quite general idea here. Write the domain of interest in frame n as $\mathcal{D}_n$. If we are tracking a deforming object, pixels in $\mathcal{D}_n$ might have no corresponding pixels in $\mathcal{D}_{n+1}$, or the motion of the pixels might be extremely complex, and so we should represent $\mathcal{D}_n$ with a well-behaved summary. If the patches deform, small-scale structures should be preserved, but the spatial layout of these structures might not be. Example small-scale structures include the colors of pixels, or the responses of oriented filters. A histogram representation of these structures is attractive because two histograms will be similar only when the two patches have similar numbers of similar structures in them, but the similarity is not disrupted by deformation.

We assume that we have a parametric domain, with parameters $\boldsymbol{y}$, so that $\boldsymbol{y}_n$ represents $\mathcal{D}_n$. For our treatment, we assume the domain is a circle of fixed radius whose center is at the pixel location $\boldsymbol{y}$, but the method can be reworked to apply to other kinds of domain. The **mean shift** procedure yields one way to find the $\mathcal{D}_{n+1}$ whose histogram is most like that of $\mathcal{D}_n$.

We assume that the features we are working with can be quantized so that the histogram can be represented as a vector of bin counts, and we write this vector as $\boldsymbol{p}(\boldsymbol{y})$; its uth component representing the count in the u'th bin is $p_u(\boldsymbol{y})$. We wish to find the $\boldsymbol{y}$ whose histogram is closest to that at $\boldsymbol{y}_n$. We are comparing two probability distributions, which we can do with the *Bhattacharyya coefficient*:

$$\rho(\boldsymbol{p}(\boldsymbol{y}), \boldsymbol{p}(\boldsymbol{y}_n)) = \sum_u \sqrt{p_u(\boldsymbol{y}) p_u(\boldsymbol{y}_n)}.$$

This will be one if the two distributions are the same and near zero if they are very different. To obtain a distance function, we can work with

$$d(\boldsymbol{p}(\boldsymbol{y}), \boldsymbol{p}(\boldsymbol{y}_n)) = \sqrt{1 - \rho(\boldsymbol{p}(\boldsymbol{y}), \boldsymbol{p}(\boldsymbol{y}_n))}.$$

We will obtain $\boldsymbol{y}_{n+1}$ by minimizing this distance. We will start this search at $\boldsymbol{y}_{n+1}^{(0)}$. We assume that $\boldsymbol{y}_{n+1}$ is close to $\boldsymbol{y}_{n+1}^{(0)}$, and as a result, $\boldsymbol{p}(\boldsymbol{y}_{n+1})$ is similar to $\boldsymbol{p}(\boldsymbol{y}_{n+1}^{(0)})$. In this case, a Taylor expansion of $\rho(\boldsymbol{p}(\boldsymbol{y}), \boldsymbol{p}(\boldsymbol{y}_n))$ about $\boldsymbol{p}(\boldsymbol{y}_{n+1}^{(0)})$ gives

$$\begin{aligned}
\rho(\boldsymbol{p}(\boldsymbol{y}), \boldsymbol{p}(\boldsymbol{y}_n)) &\approx \sum_u \sqrt{p_u(\boldsymbol{y}_{n+1}^{(0)}) p_u(\boldsymbol{y}_n)} + \\
&\quad \sum_u (p_u(\boldsymbol{y}) - p_u(\boldsymbol{y}_{n+1}^{(0)})) \left(\frac{1}{2} \sqrt{\frac{p_u(\boldsymbol{y}_n)}{p_u(\boldsymbol{y}_{n+1}^{(0)})}} \right) \\
&= \frac{1}{2} \sum_u \sqrt{p_u(\boldsymbol{y}_{n+1}^{(0)}) p_u(\boldsymbol{y}_n)} + \frac{1}{2} \sum_u p_u(\boldsymbol{y}) \sqrt{\frac{p_u(\boldsymbol{y}_n)}{p_u(\boldsymbol{y}_{n+1}^{(0)})}}.
\end{aligned}$$

This means that, to minimize the distance, we must maximize

$$\frac{1}{2} \sum_u p_u(\boldsymbol{y}) \sqrt{\frac{p_u(\boldsymbol{y}_n)}{p_u(\boldsymbol{y}_{n+1}^{(0)})}}. \tag{11.1}$$

Now we need a method to construct a histogram vector for the circle with center $\boldsymbol{y}$. We expect we are tracking a deforming object, so that pixels far away from the center of two matching circles may be quite different. To deal with this, we should allow pixels far away from the center to have a much smaller effect on the histogram than those close to the center. We can do this with a *kernel smoother*. Write the feature vector (for example, the color) for the pixel at location $\boldsymbol{x}_i$ in the circle as $\boldsymbol{f}_i^{(n)}$. This feature vector is d-dimensional. Write the histogram bin corresponding to $\boldsymbol{f}_i^{(n)}$ as $b(\boldsymbol{f}_i^{(n)})$. Each pixel votes into its bin in the histogram with a weight that decreases with $\|\boldsymbol{x}_i - \boldsymbol{y}\|$ according to a kernel profile k (compare Section 9.3.4). Using this approach, the fraction of total votes in bin u produced by all features is

$$p_u(\boldsymbol{y}) = C_h \sum_{i \in \mathcal{D}_n} k(\| \frac{\boldsymbol{x}_i - \boldsymbol{y}}{h} \|^2) \delta \left[b(\boldsymbol{f}_i - u) \right]. \tag{11.2}$$

where h is a scale, chosen by experiment, and C_h is a normalizing constant to ensure that the sum of histogram components is one. Substituting Equation 11.2

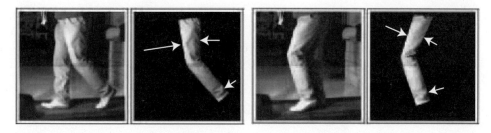

FIGURE 11.6: An important pragmatic difficulty with flow-based tracking is that appearance is not always fixed. The folds in loose clothing depend on body configuration, as these images of trousers indicate. The trousers were tracked using a flow-based tracker, but enforcing equality between pixel values will be difficult, as the patches indicated by the arrows suggest. The folds are geometrically small, but, because they produce cast shadows, have a disproportionate effect on image brightness. *This figure was originally published as Figure 4 of "Cardboard People: A Parameterized Model of Articulated Image Motion," by S. Ju, M. Black, and Y. Yacoob, IEEE Int. Conf. Face and Gesture, 1996 © IEEE, 1996.*

into Equation 11.1, we must maximize

$$f(\boldsymbol{y}) = \frac{C_h}{2} \sum_i w_i k(\|\frac{\boldsymbol{x}_i - \boldsymbol{y}}{h}\|^2), \tag{11.3}$$

where

$$w_i = \sum_u \delta\left[b(\boldsymbol{f}_i - u)\right] \sqrt{\frac{p_u(\boldsymbol{y}_n)}{p_u(\boldsymbol{y}_{n+1}^{(0)})}}.$$

We can use the mean shift procedure of Section 9.3.4 to maximize equation 11.3. Following the derivation there, the mean shift procedure involves producing a series of estimates $\boldsymbol{y}^{(j)}$ where

$$\boldsymbol{y}^{(j+1)} = \frac{\sum_i w_i \boldsymbol{x}_i g(\|\frac{\boldsymbol{x}_i - \boldsymbol{y}^{(j)}}{h}\|^2)}{\sum_i w_i g(\|\frac{\boldsymbol{x}_i - \boldsymbol{y}^{(j)}}{h}\|^2)}.$$

The procedure gets its name from the fact that we are shifting to a point that has the form of a weighted mean. The complete algorithm appears in Algorithm 11.2.

11.2.2 Tracking Using Flow

We can generalize the methods of Section 11.1.2 in a straightforward way. There we found the best matching translated version of an image domain. Instead, we could have a family of flow models, as in Section 10.6.1, and find the best matching domain resulting from a flow model. We write the image as a function of space and time as $\mathcal{I}(x, y, t)$, and scale and translate time so that each frame appears at an integer value of t.

We have a domain in the nth image, $\mathcal{D}_n$. We must find the domain in the $n + 1$th image that matches best under the flow model. We write $\rho(u, v)$ for a cost function that compares two pixel values u and v; this should be small when they match and large when they do not. We write $w(\boldsymbol{x})$ for a weighting of the cost function that depends on the location of the pixel. To find the new domain, we will find the best flow, and then allow our domain to follow that flow model. Finding the best flow involves minimizing

$$\sum_{\boldsymbol{x} \in \mathcal{D}_n} w(\boldsymbol{x}) \rho(\mathcal{I}(\boldsymbol{x}, n), \mathcal{I}(\boldsymbol{x} + \boldsymbol{v}(\boldsymbol{x}; \theta), n+1))$$

as a function of the flow parameters θ.

The cost function should not necessarily be the squared difference in pixel values. We might wish to compute a more complex description of each location (for example, a smoothed vector of filter outputs to encode local texture). Some pixels in the domain might be more reliable than others; for example, we might expect pixels near the boundary of the window to have more variation, and so we would weight them down compared to pixels near the center of the window. Robustness is another important issue. Outlier pixels, which are dramatically different from those predicted by the right transformation, could be caused by dead pixels in the camera, specularities, minor deformations on the object, and a variety of other effects. If we use a squared error metric, then such outlier pixels can have a disproportionate effect on the results. The usual solution is to adopt an M-estimator. A good choice of ρ is

$$\rho(u, v) = \frac{(u - v)^2}{(u - v)^2 + \sigma^2}$$

where σ is a parameter (there is greater detail on M-estimators in Section 10.4.1).

We now have the best value of θ, given by $\hat{\theta}$. The new domain is given by

$$\mathcal{D}_{n+1} = \left\{ \boldsymbol{u} \mid \boldsymbol{u} = \boldsymbol{x} + \boldsymbol{v}(\boldsymbol{x}; \hat{\theta}), \forall \boldsymbol{x} \in \mathcal{D}_n \right\}.$$

We can build domain models that simplify estimating $\mathcal{D}_{n+1}$; for example, if the domain is always a circle, then the flow must represent a translation, rotation, and scale, and we would allow the flow to act on the center, radius, and orientation of the circle.

Tracking can be started in a variety of ways. For a while, it was popular to start such trackers by hand, but this is now rightly frowned on in most cases. In some cases, objects always appear in a known region of the image, and in that case one can use a detector to tell whether an object has appeared. Once it has appeared, the flow model takes over.

The most important pragmatic difficulty with flow-based trackers is their tendency to drift. A detection-based tracker has a single appearance model for an object, encoded into the detector. This is applied to all frames. The danger is that this model might not properly account for changes in illumination, aspect, and so on, and as a result will fail to detect the object in some frames. In contrast, a flow-based tracker's model of the appearance of an object is based on what it looked like in the previous frame. This means that small errors in localization can accumulate. If the transformation estimated is slightly incorrect, then the new domain will be incorrect; but this means the new appearance model is incorrect, and might get worse. Section 11.1.3 showed how to prune tracks by testing against a model of appearance. If we have few tracks, we cannot just prune, but must correct the drift. This requires a fixed, global model of appearance, like those of Section 20.3.

Another important pragmatic difficulty is that an object's appearance is often not as fixed as one would like. Loose clothing is a particularly important problem here because it forms folds in different ways, depending on the body configuration. These folds are very minor geometric phenomena, but can cause significant changes in image brightness, because they shadow patches of surface. This means that there can be a strong, time-varying texture signal that appears on the body segments (Figure 11.6). Although this signal almost certainly contains some cues to configuration, they appear to be very difficult to exploit.

11.3 TRACKING LINEAR DYNAMICAL MODELS WITH KALMAN FILTERS

In Section 11.1.1, we described methods to match patches or object detector responses with tracks. This matching process is straightforward if we can be confident that the thing we are matching hasn't moved much: we search around the old location for the best match. To know where to search, we don't really need the object to be slow-moving. Instead, if it moves in a predictable way, the motion model can predict a search domain that might be far from the original location, but still reliable. Exploiting dynamical information effectively requires us to fuse information from observations with dynamical predictions. This is most easily done by building a probabilistic framework around the problem. The algorithmic goal is to maintain an accurate representation of the posterior on object state, given observations and a dynamical model.

We model the object as having some internal state; the state of the object at the ith frame is typically written as $\boldsymbol{X}_i$. The capital letter indicates that this is a random variable; when we want to talk about a particular value that this variable takes, we use small letters. The measurements obtained in the ith frame are values of a random variable $\boldsymbol{Y}_i$; we write $\boldsymbol{y}_i$ for the value of a measurement, and, on occasion, we write $\boldsymbol{Y}_i = \boldsymbol{y}_i$ for emphasis. In **tracking**, (sometimes called filtering or state estimation), we wish to determine some representation of $P(X_k|Y_0,\ldots,Y_k)$. In **smoothing** (sometimes called filtering), we wish to determine some representation of $P(X_k|Y_0,\ldots,Y_N)$ (i.e., we get to use "future" measurements to infer the state). These problems are massively simplified by two important assumptions.

- We assume measurements depend only on the hidden state, that is, that $P(Y_k|X_0,\ldots,X_N,Y_0,\ldots,Y_N) = P(Y_k|X_k)$.

- We assume that the probability density for a new state is a function only of the previous state; that is, $P(X_k|X_0,\ldots,X_{k-1}) = P(X_k|X_{k-1})$ or, equivalently, that X_i form a *Markov chain*.

We will use these assumptions to build a recursive formulation for tracking around three steps.

Prediction: We have seen $\boldsymbol{y}_0,\ldots,\boldsymbol{y}_{k-1}$. What state does this set of measurements predict for the ith frame? To solve this problem, we need to obtain a representation of $P(\boldsymbol{X}_i|\boldsymbol{Y}_0 = \boldsymbol{y}_0,\ldots,\boldsymbol{Y}_{k-1} = \boldsymbol{y}_{k-1})$. Straightforward manipulation of probability combined with the assumptions above yields that the *prior* or *predictive density*

$$P(X_k | \boldsymbol{Y}_0 = \boldsymbol{y}_0, \ldots, \boldsymbol{Y}_{k-1} = \boldsymbol{y}_{k-1}))$$

is equal to

$$\int P(X_k | X_{k-1}) P(X_{k-1} | Y_0, \ldots, Y_{k-1}) dX_{k-1}$$

Data association: Some of the measurements obtained from the ith frame may tell us about the object's state. Typically, we use $P(\boldsymbol{X}_i | \boldsymbol{Y}_0 = \boldsymbol{y}_0, \ldots, \boldsymbol{Y}_{i-1} = \boldsymbol{y}_{i-1})$ to identify these measurements. For example, we might use this predictive density to build a search location for the methods of Section 11.1.1.

Correction: Now that we have $\boldsymbol{y}_i$—the relevant measurements—we need to compute a representation of $P(\boldsymbol{X}_i | \boldsymbol{Y}_0 = \boldsymbol{y}_0, \ldots, \boldsymbol{Y}_i = \boldsymbol{y}_i)$. Straightforward manipulation of probability combined with the assumptions above yields that the *posterior*

$$P(X_k | \boldsymbol{Y}_0 = \boldsymbol{y}_0, \ldots, \boldsymbol{Y}_k = \boldsymbol{y}_k)$$

is given by

$$\frac{P(Y_k = \boldsymbol{y}_k | X_k) P(X_k | \boldsymbol{Y}_0 = \boldsymbol{y}_0, \ldots, \boldsymbol{Y}_k = \boldsymbol{y}_k)}{\int P(Y_k = \boldsymbol{y}_k | X_k) P(X_k | \boldsymbol{Y}_0 = \boldsymbol{y}_0, \ldots, \boldsymbol{Y}_k = \boldsymbol{y}_k) dX_k}.$$

Representing these probability distributions can be very difficult when the distributions have an arbitrary form. However, if the measurement models and the dynamical models are linear (in a sense to be described below), then all probability distributions will turn out to be Gaussian. In turn, this means that tracking and smoothing involve maintaining the values of the mean and covariance of the relevant densities (Section 11.3.2).

11.3.1 Linear Measurements and Linear Dynamics

We will use the simplest possible measurement model, where the measurement is obtained from the state by multiplying by some known matrix (which may depend on the frame), and then adding a normal random variable of zero mean and known covariance (which again may depend on the frame). We use the notation

$$\boldsymbol{x} \sim N(\boldsymbol{\mu}, \Sigma)$$

to mean that $\boldsymbol{x}$ is the value of a random variable with a normal probability distribution with mean $\boldsymbol{\mu}$ and covariance Σ. We write $\boldsymbol{x}_k$ for the state at step k. Our model is that $P(Y_k | X_k = \boldsymbol{x}_k)$ is a Gaussian with mean $\mathcal{B}_k \boldsymbol{x}_k$ and covariance Σ. Using the notation above, we can write our model of measurements as

$$\boldsymbol{y}_k \sim N(\mathcal{B}_k \boldsymbol{x}_k, \Sigma_k).$$

This model may seem limited, but is very powerful (it is the cornerstone of a huge control industry). We do not need to observe the whole of the state vector at any given time to infer it. For example, if we have enough measurements of the position of a moving point, we can deduce its velocity and its acceleration. This means that the matrix $\mathcal{B}_k$ does not need to have full rank (and in most practical cases, it doesn't).

In the simplest possible dynamical model, the state is advanced by multiplying it by some known matrix (which may depend on the frame) and then adding a normal random variable of zero mean and known covariance. Similarly, the measurement is obtained by multiplying the state by some matrix (which may depend on the frame) and then adding a normal random variable of zero mean and known covariance. We can write our dynamical model as

$$\boldsymbol{x}_i \sim N(\mathcal{D}_i \boldsymbol{x}_{i-1}; \Sigma_{d_i});$$

$$\boldsymbol{y}_i \sim N(\mathcal{M}_i \boldsymbol{x}_i; \Sigma_{m_i}).$$

Notice that the covariances could be different from frame to frame, as could the matrices. Although this model appears limited, it is in fact extremely powerful; we show how to model some common situations next.

Drifting Points   Let us assume that $\boldsymbol{x}$ encodes the position of a point. If $\boldsymbol{D}_i = Id$, then the point is moving under random walk; its new position is its old position plus some Gaussian noise term. This form of dynamics isn't obviously useful, because it appears that we are tracking stationary objects. It is quite commonly used for objects for which no better dynamic model is known; we assume that the random component is quite large and hope we can get away with it.

This model also illustrates aspects of the **measurement matrix** $\mathcal{M}$. The most important thing to keep in mind is that we don't need to measure every aspect of the state of the point at every step. For example, assume that the point is in 3D. Now, if $\mathcal{M}_{3k} = (0,0,1)$, $\mathcal{M}_{3k+1} = (0,1,0)$, and $\mathcal{M}_{3k+2} = (1,0,0)$, then at every third frame we measure, respectively, the z, y, or x position of the point. Notice that we can still expect to track the point, even though we measure only one component of its position at a given frame. If we have sufficient measurements, the state is **observable**, which means we can reconstruct it. We explore observability in the exercises.

Constant Velocity   Assume that the vector $\boldsymbol{p}$ gives the position and $\boldsymbol{v}$ the velocity of a point moving with constant velocity. In this case, $\boldsymbol{p}_i = \boldsymbol{p}_{i-1} + (\Delta t)\boldsymbol{v}_{i-1}$ and $\boldsymbol{v}_i = \boldsymbol{v}_{i-1}$. This means that we can stack the position and velocity into a single state vector, and our model applies (Figure 11.7). In particular,

$$\boldsymbol{x} = \left\{ \begin{array}{c} \boldsymbol{p} \\ \boldsymbol{v} \end{array} \right\}$$

and

$$\mathcal{D}_i = \left\{ \begin{array}{cc} Id & (\Delta t)Id \\ 0 & Id \end{array} \right\}.$$

Notice that, again, we don't have to observe the whole state vector to make a useful measurement. For example, in many cases, we would expect that

$$\mathcal{M}_i = \left\{ \begin{array}{cc} Id & 0 \end{array} \right\}$$

(i.e., that we see only the position of the point). Because we know that it's moving with constant velocity—that's the model—we expect that we could use these measurements to estimate the whole state vector rather well.

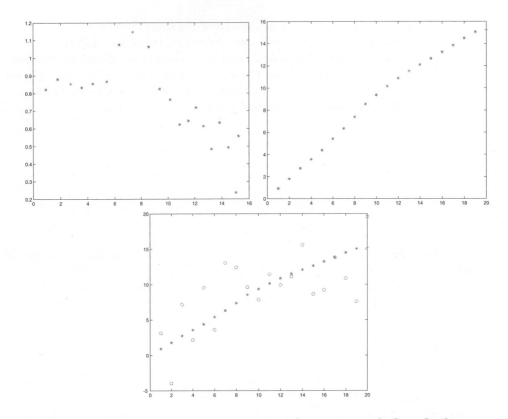

FIGURE 11.7: A constant velocity dynamic model for a point on the line. In this case, the state space is two dimensional, with one coordinate for position, one for velocity. The figure on the **top left** shows a plot of the state; each asterisk is a different state. Notice that the vertical axis (velocity) shows some small change compared with the horizontal axis. This small change is generated only by the random component of the model, so the velocity is constant up to a random change. The figure on the **top right** shows the first component of state (which is position) plotted against the time axis. Notice we have something that is moving with roughly constant velocity. The figure on the **bottom** overlays the measurements (the circles) on this plot. We are assuming that the measurements are of position only, and are quite poor; as we see, this doesn't significantly affect our ability to track.

Constant Acceleration   Assume that the vector p gives the position, vector v the velocity, and vector a the acceleration of a point moving with constant acceleration. In this case, $p_i = p_{i-1} + (\Delta t)v_{i-1}$, $v_i = v_{i-1} + (\Delta t)a_{i-1}$, and $a_i = a_{i-1}$. Again, we can stack the position, velocity, and acceleration into a single state vector, and our model applies (Figure 11.8). In particular,

$$x = \left\{ \begin{array}{c} p \\ v \\ a \end{array} \right\}$$

and

$$\mathcal{D}_i = \left\{ \begin{array}{ccc} Id & (\Delta t)Id & 0 \\ 0 & Id & (\Delta t)Id \\ 0 & 0 & Id \end{array} \right\}.$$

Notice that, again, we don't have to observe the whole state vector to make a useful measurement. For example, in many cases, we would expect that

$$\mathcal{M}_i = \left\{ \begin{array}{ccc} Id & 0 & 0 \end{array} \right\}$$

(i.e., that we see only the position of the point). Because we know that it's moving with constant acceleration—that's the model—we expect that we could use these measurements to estimate the whole state vector rather well.

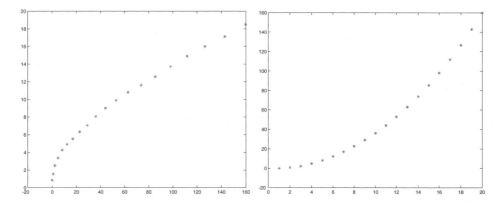

FIGURE 11.8: This figure illustrates a constant acceleration model for a point moving on the line. On the **left**, we show a plot of the first two components of state, with the position on the x-axis and the velocity on the y-axis. In this case, we expect the plot to look like (t^2, t), which it does. On the **right**, we show a plot of the position against time. Note that the point is moving away from its start position increasingly quickly.

Periodic Motion   Assume we have a point moving on a line with a periodic movement. Typically, its position p satisfies a differential equation such as

$$\frac{d^2p}{dt^2} = -p.$$

This can be turned into a first-order linear differential equation by writing the velocity as v and stacking position and velocity into a vector $\boldsymbol{u} = (p, v)$; we then have

$$\frac{d\boldsymbol{u}}{dt} = \left(\begin{array}{cc} 0 & 1 \\ -1 & 0 \end{array} \right) \boldsymbol{u} = \mathcal{S}\boldsymbol{u}.$$

Now assume we are integrating this equation with a forward Euler method, where the steplength is Δt; we have

$$
\begin{aligned}
\boldsymbol{u}_i &= \boldsymbol{u}_{i-1} + \Delta t \frac{d\boldsymbol{u}}{dt} \\
&= \boldsymbol{u}_{i-1} + \Delta t \mathcal{S} \boldsymbol{u}_{i-1} \\
&= \begin{pmatrix} 1 & \Delta t \\ -\Delta t & 1 \end{pmatrix} \boldsymbol{u}_{i-1}.
\end{aligned}
$$

We can either use this as a state equation or use a different integrator. If we use a different integrator, we might have some expression in $\boldsymbol{u}_{i-1}, \ldots, \boldsymbol{u}_{i-n}$, and we would need to stack $\boldsymbol{u}_{i-1}, \ldots, \boldsymbol{u}_{i-n}$ into a state vector and arrange the matrix appropriately (see exercises). This method works for points on the plane, in 3D, and so on (again, see exercises).

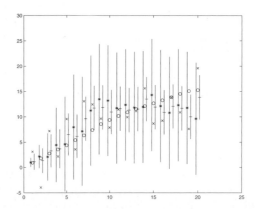

FIGURE 11.9: The Kalman filter for a point moving on the line under our model of constant velocity (compare with Figure 11.7). The state is plotted with open circles as a function of the step i. The *s give $\overline{\boldsymbol{x}}_i^-$, which is plotted slightly to the left of the state to indicate that the estimate is made before the measurement. The xs give the measurements, and the +s give $\overline{\boldsymbol{x}}_i^+$, which is plotted slightly to the right of the state. The vertical bars around the *s and the +s are three standard deviation bars, using the estimate of variance obtained before and after the measurement, respectively. When the measurement is noisy, the bars don't contract all that much when a measurement is obtained (compare with Figure 11.10).

11.3.2   The Kalman Filter

An important feature of linear dynamic models is that all the conditional probability distributions we need to deal with are normal distributions. In particular, $P(\boldsymbol{X}_i | \boldsymbol{y}_1, \ldots, \boldsymbol{y}_{i-1})$ is normal, as is $P(\boldsymbol{X}_i | \boldsymbol{y}_1, \ldots, \boldsymbol{y}_i)$. This means that they are relatively easy to represent; all we need to do is maintain representations of the mean and the covariance for the prediction and correction phase.

All this is much simplified when the emission model is linear, the dynamic model is linear, and all noise is Gaussian. In this case, all densities are normal, and the mean and covariance are sufficient to represent them. Both tracking and

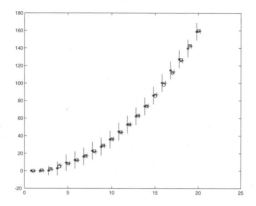

FIGURE 11.10: The Kalman filter for a point moving on the line under our model of constant acceleration (compare with Figure 11.8). The state is plotted with open circles as a function of the step i. The *s give $\overline{x}_i^-$, which is plotted slightly to the left of the state to indicate that the estimate is made before the measurement. The xs give the measurements, and the +s give $\overline{x}_i^+$, which is plotted slightly to the right of the state. The vertical bars around the *s and the +s are three standard deviation bars, using the estimate of variance obtained before and after the measurement, respectively. When the measurement is noisy, the bars don't contract all that much when a measurement is obtained.

filtering boil down to maintenance of these parameters. There is a simple set of update rules (given in Algorithm 11.3; notation below) known as the *Kalman filter*.

Notation: We write $X \sim N(\mu; \Sigma)$ to mean that X is a normal random variable with mean μ and covariance Σ. Both dynamics and emission are linear, so we can write

$$X_k \sim N(\mathcal{A}_k X_{k-1}; \Sigma_k^{(d)})$$

and

$$Y_k \sim N(\mathcal{B}_k X_k; \Sigma_k^{(m)}).$$

We will write $\overline{X}_i^-$ for the mean of $P(X_i|y_0, \ldots, y_{i-1})$ and $\overline{X}_i^+$ for the mean of $P(X_i|y_0, \ldots, y_i)$; the superscripts suggest that they represent our belief about X_i immediately before and immediately after the ith measurement arrives. Similarly, we will represent the standard deviation of $P(X_i|y_0, \ldots, y_{i-1})$ as Σ_i^- and of $P(X_i|y_0, \ldots, y_i)$ as Σ_i^+. In each case, we will assume that $P(X_{i-1}|y_0, \ldots, y_{i-1})$ is known, meaning that we know $\overline{X}_{i-1}^+$ and Σ_{i-1}^+.

11.3.3 Forward-backward Smoothing

It is important to notice that $P(\boldsymbol{X}_i|\boldsymbol{y}_0, \ldots, \boldsymbol{y}_i)$ is not the best available representation of $\boldsymbol{X}_i$; this is because it doesn't take into account the future behavior of the point. In particular, all the measurements *after* $\boldsymbol{y}_i$ could affect our representation of $\boldsymbol{X}_i$. This is because these future measurements might contradict the estimates obtained to date—perhaps the future movements of the point are more in agreement with a slightly different estimate of the position of the point. However, $P(\boldsymbol{X}_i|\boldsymbol{y}_0, \ldots, \boldsymbol{y}_i)$ *is* the best estimate available at step i.

Dynamic Model:

$$\boldsymbol{x}_i \quad \sim N(\mathcal{D}_i \boldsymbol{x}_{i-1}, \Sigma_{d_i})$$
$$\boldsymbol{y}_i \quad \sim N(\mathcal{M}_i \boldsymbol{x}_i, \Sigma_{m_i})$$

Start Assumptions: $\overline{\boldsymbol{x}}_0^-$ and Σ_0^- are known

Update Equations: Prediction

$$\overline{\boldsymbol{x}}_i^- \quad = \mathcal{D}_i \overline{\boldsymbol{x}}_{i-1}^+$$
$$\Sigma_i^- \quad = \Sigma_{d_i} + \mathcal{D}_i \sigma_{i-1}^+ \mathcal{D}_i$$

Update Equations: Correction

$$\mathcal{K}_i \quad = \Sigma_i^- \mathcal{M}_i^T \left[\mathcal{M}_i \Sigma_i^- \mathcal{M}_i^T + \Sigma_{m_i}\right]^{-1}$$
$$\overline{\boldsymbol{x}}_i^+ \quad = \overline{\boldsymbol{x}}_i^- + \mathcal{K}_i \left[\boldsymbol{y}_i - \mathcal{M}_i \overline{\boldsymbol{x}}_i^-\right]$$
$$\Sigma_i^+ \quad = \left[Id - \mathcal{K}_i \mathcal{M}_i\right] \Sigma_i^-$$

Algorithm 11.3: The Kalman Filter.

What we do with this observation depends on the circumstances. If our application requires an immediate estimate of position—perhaps we are tracking a car in the opposite lane—there isn't much we can do. If we are tracking off-line—perhaps for forensic purposes, we need the best estimate of what an object was doing given a videotape—then we can use all data points, and so we want to represent $P(\boldsymbol{X}_i|\boldsymbol{y}_0, \ldots, \boldsymbol{y}_N)$. A common alternative is that we need a rough estimate immediately, and can use an improved estimate that has been time-delayed by a number of steps. We want to represent $P(\boldsymbol{X}_i|\boldsymbol{y}_0, \ldots, \boldsymbol{y}_{i+k})$. We have to wait until time $i+k$ for this representation, but it should be an improvement on $P(\boldsymbol{X}_i|\boldsymbol{y}_0, \ldots, \boldsymbol{y}_i)$.

We can incorporate future measurements with a clever trick. We must combine $P(\boldsymbol{X}_i|\boldsymbol{y}_0, \ldots, \boldsymbol{y}_i)$—which we know how to obtain—with $P(\boldsymbol{X}_i|\boldsymbol{y}_{i+1}, \ldots, \boldsymbol{y}_N)$. We actually know how to obtain a representation of $P(\boldsymbol{X}_i|\boldsymbol{y}_{i+1}, \ldots, \boldsymbol{y}_N)$, too. We could simply run the Kalman filter *backward* in time, using *backward dynamics*, and take the predicted representation of $\boldsymbol{X}_i$ (we leave the details of relabeling the sequence, etc., to the exercises).

Now we have two representations of $\boldsymbol{X}_i$: one obtained by running a forward filter and incorporating all measurements up to $\boldsymbol{y}_i$; and one obtained by running a backward filter and incorporating all measurements after $\boldsymbol{y}_i$. We need to combine these representations. We can get the answer by noting that *this is like having another measurement*. In particular, we have a new measurement generated by $\boldsymbol{X}_i$—that is, the result of the backward filter—to combine with our estimate from

---

Forward filter: Obtain the mean and variance of $P(\boldsymbol{X}_i|\boldsymbol{y}_0,\ldots,\boldsymbol{y}_i)$ using the Kalman filter. These are $\overline{\boldsymbol{X}}_i^{f,+}$ and $\Sigma_i^{f,+}$.

Backward filter: Obtain the mean and variance of $P(\boldsymbol{X}_i|\boldsymbol{y}_{i+1},\ldots,\boldsymbol{y}_N)$ using the Kalman filter running backward in time. These are $\overline{\boldsymbol{X}}_i^{b,-}$ and $\Sigma_i^{b,-}$.

Combining forward and backward estimates: Regard the backward estimate as a new measurement for $\boldsymbol{X}_i$, and insert into the Kalman filter equations to obtain

$$\Sigma_i^* = \left[(\Sigma_i^{f,+})^{-1} + (\Sigma_i^{b,-})^{-1}\right]^{-1};$$

$$\overline{\boldsymbol{X}}_i^* = \Sigma_i^* \left[(\Sigma_i^{f,+})^{-1}\overline{\boldsymbol{X}}_i^{f,+} + (\Sigma_i^{b,-})^{-1}\overline{\boldsymbol{X}}_i^{b,-}\right].$$

Algorithm 11.4: Forward-Backward Smoothing.

the forward filter; this yields Algorithm 11.4. Forward-backward estimates can make a substantial difference, as Figure 11.11 illustrates.

Using smoothing requires some care about priors. In typical vision applications, we are tracking forward in time. This leads to an inconvenient asymmetry: we might have a good idea of where the object started, but only a poor one of where it stopped (i.e., we are likely to have a fair prior for $P(\boldsymbol{x}_0)$, but might have difficulty supplying a prior for $P(\boldsymbol{x}_N)$ for the forward-backward filter). One option is to use $P(\boldsymbol{x}_N|\boldsymbol{y}_0,\ldots,\boldsymbol{y}_N)$ as a prior. This is a dubious act, as this probability distribution does not in fact reflect our prior belief about $P(\boldsymbol{x}_N)$; we've used all the measurements to obtain it. Consequently, this distribution could understate our uncertainty in $\boldsymbol{x}_N$ and so lead to a forward-backward estimate that significantly underestimates the covariance for the later states. An alternative is to use the mean supplied by the forward filter but enlarge the covariance substantially; the consequences are a forward-backward estimate that overestimates the covariance for the later states.

Not all applications have this asymmetry. For example, if we are engaged in a forensic study of a videotape, we might be able to start both the forward tracker and the backward tracker by hand and provide a good estimate of the prior in each case. If this is possible, then we have a good deal more information that may be able to help choose correspondences, and so on; the forward tracker should finish rather close to where the backward tracker starts.

Although our formulation of forward-backward smoothing assumed that the backward filter started at the last data point, it is easy to start this filter a fixed number of steps ahead of the forward filter. If we do this, we obtain an estimate of state in real time (essentially immediately after the measurement) and an improved estimate some fixed numbers of measurements later. This is sometimes useful.

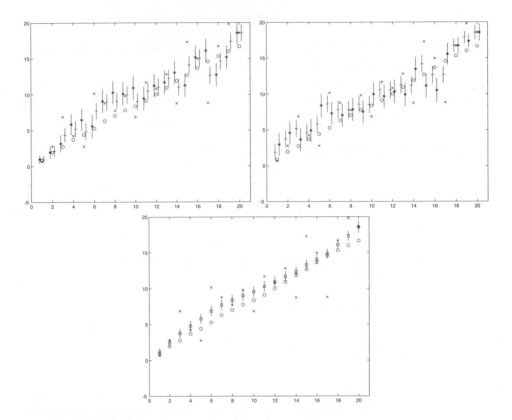

FIGURE 11.11: Forward-backward estimation for a dynamic model of a point moving on the line with constant velocity. We are plotting the position component of state against time. On the **top left**, we show the forward estimates, again using the convention that the state is shown with circles, the data is shown with an x, the prediction is shown with a *, and the corrected estimate is shown with a +; the bars give one standard deviation in the estimate. The predicted estimate is shown slightly behind the state, and the corrected estimate is shown slightly ahead of the state. You should notice that the measurements are noisy. On the **top right** we show the backward estimates. Now time is running backward (although we have plotted both curves on the same axis), so that the prediction is slightly ahead of the measurement and the corrected estimate is slightly behind. We have used the final corrected estimate of the forward filter as a prior. Again, the bars give one standard deviation in each variable. On the **bottom**, we show the combined forward-backward estimate. The squares give the estimates of state. Notice the significant improvement in the estimate.

Furthermore, it is an efficient way to obtain most of the improvement available from a backward filter if we can assume that the effect of the distant future on our estimate is relatively small compared with the effect of the immediate future. Notice that we need to be careful about priors for the backward filter here; we might take the forward estimate and enlarge its covariance somewhat.

11.4 DATA ASSOCIATION

Not all observations are informative. For example, if one wishes to track an aircraft—where state might involve pose, velocity and acceleration variables, and measurements might be radar returns giving distance and angle to the aircraft from several radar aerials—some of the radar returns measured might not come from the aircraft. Instead, they might be the result of noise, of other aircraft, of strips of foil dropped to confuse radar apparatus (*chaff* or *window*; see Jones (1998)), or of other sources. The problem of determining which observations are informative and which are not is known as *data association*. Data association is the dominant difficulty when tracking objects in video. This is because so few of the very many pixels in each frame lie on objects of interest. It can be spectacularly difficult to tell which pixels in an image come from an object of interest and which do not. The tracking methods of the first two sections focus on solving data association problems using familiar ideas of detection and of coherent appearance (Section 11.1.1). These methods can be linked to probabilistic representations, to exploit any dynamical information that happens to be available.

11.4.1 Linking Kalman Filters with Detection Methods

In Section 11.1.2, we took a patch in image n and looked for one in image $n+1$ that was "similar." To find a match, we assumed that the patch translated a relatively small distance from a known start point, and searched around that start point using an approximate method to find the best SSD match. In that section, we assumed that the start point was the patch's location in image n. It could, instead, be predicted by a Kalman filter. Similarly, in Section 11.2.1, we had a domain that was a circle of a fixed size in image n, and we searched around a start point for a matching domain in image $n+1$ using an approximate method to find the best matching histogram. Again, we assumed the start point was the circle's location in image n, but it could be predicted by a Kalman filter. We will describe the case of the circle in somewhat greater detail to illustrate how this works.

The circular domain was represented with a vector $\boldsymbol{y}$ giving the center of the circle. Our search needed a start point, which we wrote as $\boldsymbol{y}_0$. This start point could come from a dynamical model. In fact, assuming as we did in Section 11.2.1 that it was the configuration of domain in image n is a simple dynamical model where the object doesn't move. An alternative model might be better. For example, we might be observing an object in free fall in a plane parallel to the camera plane. In this case, the object might move a considerable distance between frames, but its location in image $n+1$ is quite easily predicted from earlier locations. To predict $\boldsymbol{y}_0$ with a Kalman filter, we choose a state vector representation, so that the configuration $\boldsymbol{y}$ is a linear function of the state vector. We apply the prediction step of the Kalman filter to obtain the predicted state vector, and compute $\boldsymbol{y}_0$ from that. We then search for $\boldsymbol{y}^{(n+1)}$, as in Section 11.2. The computed value is the observation for the Kalman filter, and we use this to obtain the revised estimate of the state vector.

As an example, the state vector is $\boldsymbol{x} = (\boldsymbol{y}, \dot{\boldsymbol{y}})^T$. The velocity drifts slightly, so the dynamical model is given by

$$\boldsymbol{x}_{n+1} = \mathcal{A}\boldsymbol{x}_n + \xi = \left(\begin{array}{cc} \mathcal{I} & \Delta t \mathcal{I} \\ 0 & \mathcal{I} \end{array} \right) \boldsymbol{x}_n + \xi_{n+1},$$

where $\xi_{n+1} \sim N(\mathbf{0}, \Sigma_d)$. The measurement model is given by

$$\boldsymbol{y}_n = \mathcal{B}\boldsymbol{x}_n = \left(\begin{array}{cc} \mathcal{I} & 0 \end{array}\right)\boldsymbol{x}_n + \eta_n,$$

where $\eta_n \sim N(\mathbf{0}, \Sigma_m)$. Now assume we have $\boldsymbol{x}_n^{(+)}$. We predict $\boldsymbol{x}_{n+1}^{(-)} = \mathcal{A}\boldsymbol{x}_n^{(+)}$, which gives a prediction $\boldsymbol{y}_0 = \mathcal{B}\boldsymbol{x}_{n+1}^{(-)}$. We start the search at this point, and obtain $\boldsymbol{y}^{(n+1)}$. This goes into the Kalman gain formula (Algorithm 11.3) to give $\boldsymbol{x}_{n+1}^{(+)}$. The advantage of doing this is that, if the object has a significant but fixed velocity, our search starts at the location predicted by this velocity model, and so is much more likely to find the match we want.

11.4.2   Key Methods of Data Association

The case of the Kalman filter applied to tracking by detection is an instance of a general strategy. In particular, we have an estimate of $P(X_n|Y_0, \ldots, Y_{n-1})$, and we know $P(Y_n|X_n)$. From this we can obtain an estimate of $P(Y_n|Y_0, \ldots Y_{n-1})$, which gives us hints as to where the measurement might be. These hints can be applied in a variety of ways.

One can use a *gate* and look only at measurements that lie in a domain where $P(Y_n|Y_0, \ldots, Y_{n-1})$ is big enough. This is a method with roots in radar tracking of missiles and airplanes, where one must deal with only a small number of returns compared with the number of pixels in an image. The idea has also been useful in visual tracking applications. For example, if we are tracking using an object detector, we would apply it only within the gate (or ignore detector responses outside the gate). This approach is quite commonly adopted within vision, and is useful.

One can use *nearest neighbors*. In the classical version, we have a small set of possible measurements, and we choose the measurement with the largest value of $P(Y_n|Y_0, \ldots, Y_{n-1})$. This has all the dangers of wishful thinking—we are deciding that a measurement is valid because it is consistent with our track—but is often useful in practice. Our example of using a Kalman filter to identify a start point for a search is a nearest neighbors strategy. Again, this approach is commonly adopted and is useful.

One can use *probabilistic data association*, where we construct a virtual observation from a weighted combination of measurements within a gate, weighted using (a) the predicted measurement and (b) the probability a detector has failed to detect. For example, if we are using tracking by detection, we could form a virtual observation as a weighted sum of detects that appear within a gate. This approach tends not to be used, however, perhaps because it is uncommon in practice to have a detector that is reliable enough to use like this but not good enough to support nearest neighbors.

11.5   PARTICLE FILTERING

The Kalman filter is the workhorse of estimation and can give useful results under many conditions. One doesn't need a guarantee of linearity to use a Kalman filter. If the logic of the application indicates that a linear model is reasonable, there is a good chance a Kalman filter will work. Nonlinear dynamics—or nonlinear measurement processes, or both—can create serious problems. The basic difficulty is that even quite innocuous looking setups can produce densities that are not normal, and are very difficult to represent and model. Quite small non-linearities in dynamics can cause probability to be concentrated in ways that are very difficult to represent. In particular, nonlinear dynamics are likely to produce densities with complicated sufficient statistics. There are cases where nonlinear dynamics does lead to densities that can be guaranteed to have finite-dimensional sufficient statistics (see Beneš (1981); Daum (1995b); or Daum (1995a)).

More generally, we expect it to be difficult to maintain a satisfactory representation of $P(\boldsymbol{x}_i | \boldsymbol{y}_0, \ldots, \boldsymbol{y}_i)$. This representation should handle multiple peaks in the distribution, and should be able to handle a high-dimensional state vector without difficulty. There is no completely satisfactory general solution to this problem (and there will never be). In this section, we discuss an approach that has been useful in many applications.

The richest source of multiple modes is data association problems. An easy example illustrates how nasty this problem can be. Assume we have a problem with linear dynamics and a linear measurement model. However, at each tick of the clock we receive more than one measurement, exactly one of which comes from the process being studied. We will continue to write the states as $\boldsymbol{X}_i$ and the measurements as $\boldsymbol{Y}_i$, but we now have δ_i, an indicator variable that tells which measurement comes from the process (and is unknown). $P(\boldsymbol{X}_N | \boldsymbol{Y}_{1..N}, \delta_{1..N})$ is clearly Gaussian. We want $P(\boldsymbol{X}_N | \boldsymbol{Y}_{1..N}) = \sum_{histories} P(\boldsymbol{X}_N | \boldsymbol{Y}_{1..N}, \delta_{1..N}) P(\delta_{1..N} | \boldsymbol{Y}_{1..N})$, which is clearly a mixture of Gaussians. The number of components is exponential in the number of frames—there is one component per possible history—meaning that $P(\boldsymbol{X}_N | \boldsymbol{Y}_{1..N})$ could have a very large number of modes.

11.5.1   Sampled Representations of Probability Distributions

A natural way to think about representations of probability distributions is to ask what a probability distribution is for. Computing a representation of probability distributions is not our primary objective; we wish to represent a probability distribution so that we can compute one or another expectation. For example, we might wish to compute the expected state of an object given some information, the variance in the state, the expected utility of shooting at an object, etc. Probability distributions are devices for computing expectations, thus our representation should be one that gives us a decent prospect of computing an expectation accurately. This means that there is a strong resonance between questions of representing probability distributions and questions of efficient numerical integration.

Monte Carlo Integration using Importance Sampling

Assume that we have a collection of N points $\boldsymbol{u}^i$, and a collection of weights w^i. These points are independent samples drawn from a probability distribution $S(\boldsymbol{U})$, which we call the **sampling distribution**; notice that we have broken with our usual convention of writing any probability distribution with a P. We assume that $S(\boldsymbol{U})$ has a probability density function $s(\boldsymbol{U})$.

The weights have the form $w^i = f(\boldsymbol{u}^i)/s(\boldsymbol{u}^i)$ for some function f. Now it is a fact that

$$\mathrm{E}\left[\frac{1}{N}\sum_i g(\boldsymbol{u}^i)w^i\right] = \int g(\boldsymbol{U})\frac{f(\boldsymbol{U})}{s(\boldsymbol{U})}s(\boldsymbol{U})d\boldsymbol{U}$$

$$= \int g(\boldsymbol{U})f(\boldsymbol{U})d\boldsymbol{U},$$

where the expectation is taken over the distribution on the collection of N independent samples from $S(\boldsymbol{U})$ (you can prove this fact using the weak law of large numbers). The variance of this estimate goes down as $1/N$, and is independent of the dimension of $\boldsymbol{U}$.

Representing Distributions Using Weighted Samples

Represent a probability distribution

$$p_f(\boldsymbol{X}) = \frac{f(\boldsymbol{X})}{\int f(\boldsymbol{U})d\boldsymbol{U}}$$

by a set of N weighted samples

$$\{(\boldsymbol{u}^i, w^i)\},$$

where $\boldsymbol{u}^i \sim s(\boldsymbol{u})$ and $w^i = f(\boldsymbol{u}^i)/s(\boldsymbol{u}^i)$.

Algorithm 11.5: Obtaining a Sampled Representation of a Probability Distribution.

We have a representation of a probability distribution

$$p_f(\boldsymbol{X}) = \frac{f(\boldsymbol{X})}{\int f(\boldsymbol{U})d\boldsymbol{U}}$$

by a set of weighted samples

$$\{(\boldsymbol{u}^i, w^i)\},$$

where $\boldsymbol{u}^i \sim s(\boldsymbol{u})$ and $w^i = f(\boldsymbol{u}^i)/s(\boldsymbol{u}^i)$. Then:

$$\int g(\boldsymbol{U})p_f(\boldsymbol{U})d\boldsymbol{U} \approx \frac{\sum_{i=1}^{N} g(\boldsymbol{u}^i)w^i}{\sum_{i=1}^{N} w^i}$$

Algorithm 11.6: Computing an Expectation Using a Set of Samples.

If we think about a distribution as a device for computing expectations—which are integrals—we can obtain a representation of a distribution from the integration method described above. This representation will consist of a set of weighted points. Assume that f is non-negative and that $\int f(\boldsymbol{U})d\boldsymbol{U}$ exists and is finite. Then

$$\frac{f(\boldsymbol{X})}{\int f(\boldsymbol{U})d\boldsymbol{U}}$$

is a probability density function representing the distribution of interest. We write this probability density function as $p_f(\boldsymbol{X})$.

Now we have a collection of N points $\boldsymbol{u}^i \sim S(\boldsymbol{U})$ and a collection of weights $w^i = f(\boldsymbol{u}^i)/s(\boldsymbol{u}^i)$. Using this notation, we have that

$$\mathrm{E}\left[\frac{1}{N}\sum_i w^i\right] = \int 1\frac{f(\boldsymbol{U})}{s(\boldsymbol{U})}s(\boldsymbol{U})d\boldsymbol{U}$$

$$= \int f(\boldsymbol{U})d\boldsymbol{U}.$$

Now this means that

$$\mathrm{E}_{p_f}[g] = \int g(\boldsymbol{U})p_f(\boldsymbol{U})d\boldsymbol{U}$$

$$= \frac{\int g(\boldsymbol{U})f(\boldsymbol{U})d\boldsymbol{U}}{\int f(\boldsymbol{U})d\boldsymbol{U}}$$

$$= \mathrm{E}\left[\frac{\sum_i g(\boldsymbol{u}_i)w_i}{\sum_i w_i}\right]$$

$$\approx \frac{\sum_i g(\boldsymbol{u}_i)w_i}{\sum_i w_i}$$

(where we have cancelled some Ns). This means that we can *in principle* represent a probability distribution by a set of weighted samples (Algorithm 11.5). There are some significant practical issues here, however. Before we explore these, we will discuss how to perform various computations with sampled representations. We have already shown how to compute an expectation (above, and in Algorithm 11.6). There are two other important activities for tracking: marginalization and turning a representation of a prior into a representation of a posterior.

Marginalizing a Sampled Representation

An attraction of sampled representations is that some computations are particularly easy. Marginalization is a good and useful example. Assume we have a sampled representation of $p_f(\boldsymbol{U}) = p_f((\boldsymbol{M}, \boldsymbol{M}))$. We write $\boldsymbol{U}$ as two components $(\boldsymbol{M}, \boldsymbol{N})$ so that we can marginalize with respect to one of them.

Now assume that the sampled representation consists of a set of samples, which we can write as

$$\left\{((\boldsymbol{m}^i, \boldsymbol{n}^i), w^i)\right\}.$$

In this representation, $(\boldsymbol{m}^i, \boldsymbol{n}^i) \sim s(\boldsymbol{M}, \boldsymbol{N})$ and $w^i = f((\boldsymbol{m}^i, \boldsymbol{n}^i))/s((\boldsymbol{m}^i, \boldsymbol{n}^i))$.

We want a representation of the marginal $p_f(\boldsymbol{M}) = \int p_f(\boldsymbol{M}, \boldsymbol{N})d\boldsymbol{N}$. We will use this marginal to estimate integrals, so we can derive the representation by thinking about integrals. In particular

$$\int g(\boldsymbol{M})p_f(\boldsymbol{M})d\boldsymbol{M} = \int g(\boldsymbol{M})\int p_f(\boldsymbol{M},\boldsymbol{N})d\boldsymbol{N}d\boldsymbol{M}$$

$$= \int\int g(\boldsymbol{M})p_f(\boldsymbol{M},\boldsymbol{N})d\boldsymbol{N}d\boldsymbol{M}$$

$$\approx \frac{\sum_{i=1}^{N}g(\boldsymbol{m}^i)w^i}{\sum_{i=1}^{N}w^i},$$

meaning that we can represent the marginal by dropping the $\boldsymbol{n}^i$ components of the sample (or ignoring them, which may be more efficient!).

Transforming a Prior into a Posterior

Appropriate manipulation of the weights of a sampled distribution yields representations of other distributions. A particularly interesting case is representing a posterior given some measurement. Recall that

$$p(\boldsymbol{U}|\boldsymbol{V}=v_0) = \frac{p(\boldsymbol{V}=v_0|\boldsymbol{U})p(\boldsymbol{U})}{\int p(\boldsymbol{V}=v_0|\boldsymbol{U})p(\boldsymbol{U})d\boldsymbol{U}}$$

$$= \frac{1}{K}p(\boldsymbol{V}=v_0|\boldsymbol{U}),p(\boldsymbol{U})$$

where v_0 is some measured value taken by the random variable $\boldsymbol{V}$.

Assume we have a sampled representation of $p(\boldsymbol{U})$, given by $\{(\boldsymbol{u}^i,w^i)\}$. We can evaluate K fairly easily:

$$K = \int p(\boldsymbol{V}=v_0|\boldsymbol{U})p(\boldsymbol{U})d\boldsymbol{U}$$

$$= \mathrm{E}\left[\frac{\sum_{i=1}^{N}p(\boldsymbol{V}=v_0|\boldsymbol{u}^i)w^i}{\sum_{i=1}^{N}w^i}\right]$$

$$\approx \frac{\sum_{i=1}^{N}p(\boldsymbol{V}=v_0|\boldsymbol{u}^i)w^i}{\sum_{i=1}^{N}w^i}.$$

Now let us consider the posterior

$$\int g(\boldsymbol{U})p(\boldsymbol{U}|\boldsymbol{V}=v_0)d\boldsymbol{U} = \frac{1}{K}\int g(\boldsymbol{U})p(\boldsymbol{V}=v_0|\boldsymbol{U})p(\boldsymbol{U})d\boldsymbol{U}$$

$$\approx \frac{1}{K}\frac{\sum_{i=1}^{N}g(\boldsymbol{u}^i)p(\boldsymbol{V}=v_0|\boldsymbol{u}^i)w^i}{\sum_{i=1}^{N}w^i}$$

$$\approx \frac{\sum_{i=1}^{N}g(\boldsymbol{u}^i)p(\boldsymbol{V}=v_0|\boldsymbol{u}^i)w^i}{\sum_{i=1}^{N}p(\boldsymbol{V}=v_0|\boldsymbol{u}^i)w^i}$$

(where we substituted the approximate expression for K in the last step). This means that, if we take $\{(\boldsymbol{u}^i,w^i)\}$ and replace the weights with

$$w'^i = p(\boldsymbol{V}=v_0|\boldsymbol{u}^i)w^i,$$

the result $\{(\boldsymbol{u}^i,w'^i)\}$ is a representation of the posterior.

Assume we have a representation of $p(\boldsymbol{U})$ as

$$\left\{(\boldsymbol{u}^i, w^i)\right\},$$

Assume we have an observation $\boldsymbol{V} = \boldsymbol{v}_0$, and a likelihood model $p(\boldsymbol{V}|\boldsymbol{U})$. The posterior, $p(\boldsymbol{U}|\boldsymbol{V} = \boldsymbol{v}_0)$ is represented by

$$\left\{(\boldsymbol{u}^i, w'^i)\right\},$$

where

$$w'^i = p(\boldsymbol{V} = \boldsymbol{v}_0|\boldsymbol{u}^i)w^i.$$

Algorithm 11.7: Obtaining a Sampled Representation of a Posterior from a Prior.

11.5.2 The Simplest Particle Filter

Assume that we have a sampled representation of $P(\boldsymbol{X}_{i-1}|\boldsymbol{y}_0, \ldots, \boldsymbol{y}_{i-1})$, and we need to obtain a representation of $P(\boldsymbol{X}_i|\boldsymbol{y}_0, \ldots, \boldsymbol{y}_i)$. We will follow the usual two steps of prediction and correction.

We can regard each sample as a possible state for the process at step $\boldsymbol{X}_{i-1}$. We are going to obtain our representation by first representing

$$P(\boldsymbol{X}_i, \boldsymbol{X}_{i-1}|\boldsymbol{y}_0, \ldots, \boldsymbol{y}_{i-1}),$$

and then marginalising out $\boldsymbol{X}_{i-1}$ (which we know how to do). The result is the prior for the next state, and because we know how to get posteriors from priors, we will obtain $P(\boldsymbol{X}_i|\boldsymbol{y}_0, \ldots, \boldsymbol{y}_i)$.

Prediction
Now,

$$p(\boldsymbol{X}_i, \boldsymbol{X}_{i-1}|\boldsymbol{y}_0, \ldots, \boldsymbol{y}_{i-1}) = p(\boldsymbol{X}_i|\boldsymbol{X}_{i-1})p(\boldsymbol{X}_{i-1}|\boldsymbol{y}_0, \ldots, \boldsymbol{y}_{i-1}).$$

Write our representation of $p(\boldsymbol{X}_{i-1}|\boldsymbol{y}_0, \ldots, \boldsymbol{y}_{i-1})$ as

$$\left\{(\boldsymbol{u}_{i-1}^k, w_{i-1}^k)\right\}$$

(the superscripts index the samples for a given step i, and the subscript gives the step).

Now for any given sample $\boldsymbol{u}_{i-1}^k$, we can obtain samples of $p(\boldsymbol{X}_i|\boldsymbol{X}_{i-1} = \boldsymbol{u}_{i-1}^k)$ fairly easily. This is because our dynamic model is

$$\boldsymbol{x}_i = \boldsymbol{f}(\boldsymbol{x}_{i-1}) + \xi_i,$$

where $\xi_i \sim N(0, \Sigma_{m_i})$. Thus, for any given sample $\boldsymbol{u}_{i-1}^k$, we can generate samples of $p(\boldsymbol{X}_i | \boldsymbol{X}_{i-1} = \boldsymbol{u}_{i-1}^k)$ as

$$\left\{ (f(\boldsymbol{u}_{i-1}^k) + \xi_i^l, 1) \right\},$$

where $\xi_i^l \sim N(0, \Sigma_{m_i})$. The index l indicates that we might generate several such samples for each $\boldsymbol{u}_{i-1}^k$.

We can now represent $p(\boldsymbol{X}_i, \boldsymbol{X}_{i-1} | \boldsymbol{y}_0, \dots, \boldsymbol{y}_{i-1})$ as

$$\left\{ ((f(\boldsymbol{u}_{i-1}^k) + \xi_i^l, \boldsymbol{u}_{i-1}^k), w_{i-1}^k) \right\}$$

(notice that there are *two* free indexes here, k and l; by this we mean that for each sample indexed by k, there might be several different elements of the set, indexed by l).

Because we can marginalize by dropping elements, the representation of

$$P(\boldsymbol{x}_i | \boldsymbol{y}_0, \dots, \boldsymbol{y}_{i-1})$$

is given by

$$\left\{ (f(\boldsymbol{u}_{i-1}^k) + \xi_i^l, w_{i-1}^k) \right\}$$

(we walk through a proof in the exercises). We will reindex this collection of samples—which may have more than N elements—and rewrite it as

$$\left\{ (\boldsymbol{u}_i^{k,-}, w_i^{k,-}) \right\},$$

assuming that there are M elements. Just as in our discussion of Kalman filters, the superscript "$-$" indicates that this is our representation of the ith state before a measurement has arrived. The superscript k gives the individual sample.

Correction   Correction is simple: we need to take the prediction, which acts as a prior, and turn it into a posterior. We do this by choosing an appropriate weight for each sample, following Algorithm 11.7. The weight is

$$p(\boldsymbol{Y}_i = \boldsymbol{y}_i | \boldsymbol{X}_i = \boldsymbol{s}_i^{k,-}) w_i^{k,-}$$

(you should confirm this by comparing it with Algorithm 11.7), and our representation of the posterior is

$$\left\{ (\boldsymbol{s}_i^{k,-}, p(\boldsymbol{Y}_i = \boldsymbol{y}_i | \boldsymbol{X}_i = \boldsymbol{s}_i^{k,-}) w_i^{k,-}) \right\}$$

11.5.3   The Tracking Algorithm

In principle, we now have most of a tracking algorithm. The only missing step is to explain where the samples of $p(\boldsymbol{X}_0)$ came from. The easiest thing to do here is to start with a diffuse prior of a special form that is easily sampled—a Gaussian with large covariance might do it—and give each of these samples a weight of 1. It is a good idea to implement this tracking algorithm to see how it works (see the exercises!); you will notice that it works poorly, even on the simplest problems (Figure 11.12 compares estimates from this algorithm to exact

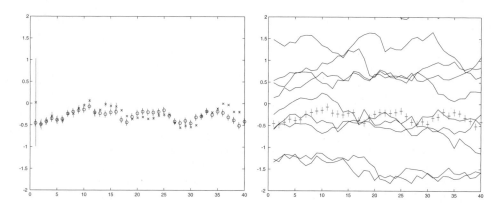

FIGURE 11.12: The simple particle filter behaves very poorly, as a result of a phenomenon called *sample impoverishment*, which is rather like quantization error. In this example, we have a point on the line drifting on the line (i.e., $x_i \sim N(x_{i-1}, \sigma^2)$). The measurements are corrupted by additive Gaussian noise. In this case, we can get an exact representation of the posterior using a Kalman filter. In the figure on the **left**, we compare a representation obtained exactly using a Kalman filter with one computed from simple particle filtering. We show the mean of the posterior as a point with a *one* standard deviation bar (previously we used three standard deviations, but that would make these figures difficult to interpret). The mean obtained using a Kalman filter is given as an x; the mean obtained using a particle filter is given as an o; and we have offset the standard deviation bars from one another to make the phenomenon clear. Notice that the mean is poor, but the standard deviation estimate is awful, and gets worse as the tracking proceeds. In particular, the standard deviation estimate woefully underestimates the standard deviation, which could mislead a user into thinking the tracker was working and producing good estimates, when in fact it is hopelessly confused. The figure on the **right** indicates what is going wrong. We plot the tracks of 10 particles, randomly selected from the 100 used. Note that relatively few particles ever lie within one standard deviation of the mean of the posterior; in turn, this means that our representation of $P(x_{i+1}|y_0, \dots, y_0)$ will tend to consist of many particles with very low weight and only one with a high weight. This means that the density is represented very poorly, and the error propagates.

expectations computed with a Kalman filter). The algorithm gives bad estimates because most samples represent no more than wasted computation. In jargon, the samples are called **particles**.

If you implement this algorithm, you will notice that weights get small very quickly; this isn't obviously a problem, because the mean value of the weights is cancelled in the division, so we could at each step divide the weights by their mean value. If you implement this step, you will notice that very quickly one weight becomes close to one and all others are extremely small. It is a fact that in the simple particle filter, the variance of the weights cannot decrease with i (meaning that, in general, it will increase and we will end up with one weight very much larger than all the others).

If the weights are small, our estimates of integrals are likely to be poor. In particular, a sample with a small weight is positioned at a point where $f(\boldsymbol{u})$ is much smaller than $p(\boldsymbol{u})$; in turn (unless we want to take an expectation of a function that is very large at this point), this sample is likely to contribute relatively little to the estimate of the integral.

Generally, the way to get accurate estimates of integrals is to have samples that lie where the integral is likely to be large; we certainly don't want to miss these points. We are unlikely to want to take expectations of functions that vary quickly, and so we would like our samples to lie where $f(\boldsymbol{u})$ is large. In turn, this means that a sample whose weight w is small represents a waste of resources; we'd rather replace it with another sample with a large weight. This means that the effective number of samples is decreasing; some samples make no significant contribution to the expectations we might compute, and should ideally be replaced (Figure 11.12 illustrates this important effect). In the following section, we describe ways of maintaining the set of particles that lead to effective and useful particle filters.

11.5.4 A Workable Particle Filter

Particles with very low weights are fairly easily dealt with; we will adjust the collection of particles to emphasize those that appear to be most helpful in representing the posterior. This will help us deal with another difficulty, too. In discussing the simple particle filter, we did not discuss how many samples there were at each stage. If, at the prediction stage, we drew several samples of $P(\boldsymbol{X}_i|\boldsymbol{X}_{i-1} = \boldsymbol{s}_{i-1}^{k,+})$ for each $\boldsymbol{s}_{i-1}^{k,+}$, the total pool of samples would grow as i got bigger. Ideally, we would have a constant number of particles N. All this suggests that we need a method to discard samples, ideally concentrating on discarding unhelpful samples. There are a number of popular strategies.

Resampling the Prior

At each step i, we have a representation of

$$P(\boldsymbol{X}_{i-1}|\boldsymbol{y}_0, \dots, \boldsymbol{y}_{i-1})$$

via weighted samples. This representation consists of N (possibly distinct) samples, each with an associated weight. Now, in a sampled representation, the frequency with which samples appear can be traded off against the weight with which they appear. For example, assume we have a sampled representation of $P(\boldsymbol{U})$ consisting of N pairs $(\boldsymbol{s}_k, w_k)$. Form a new set of samples consisting of a union of N_k copies of $(\boldsymbol{s}_k, 1)$ for each k. If

$$\frac{N_k}{\sum_k N_k} = w_k,$$

this new set of samples is also a representation of $P(\boldsymbol{U})$ (you should check this).

Furthermore, if we take a sampled representation of $P(\boldsymbol{U})$ using N samples, and draw N' elements from this set with replacement, uniformly and at random, the result will be a representation of $P(\boldsymbol{U})$, too (you should check this, too). This suggests that we could (a) expand the sample set and then (b) subsample it to get a new representation of $P(\boldsymbol{U})$. This representation will tend to contain multiple copies of samples that appeared with high weights in the original representation.

This procedure is equivalent to the rather simpler process of making N draws with replacement from the original set of samples, using the weights w_i as the probability of drawing a sample. Each sample in the new set would have weight

1; the new set would predominantly contain samples that appeared in the old set with large weights. This process of resampling might occur at every frame, or only when the variance of the weights is too high.

Initialization: Represent $P(\boldsymbol{X}_0)$ by a set of N samples

$$\left\{ (\boldsymbol{s}_0^{k,-}, w_0^{k,-}) \right\},$$

where

$$\boldsymbol{s}_0^{k,-} \sim P_s(\boldsymbol{S}) \text{ and } w_0^{k,-} = P(\boldsymbol{s}_0^{k,-})/P_s(\boldsymbol{S} = \boldsymbol{s}_0^{k,-}).$$

Ideally, $P(\boldsymbol{X}_0)$ has a simple form, and $\boldsymbol{s}_0^{k,-} \sim P(\boldsymbol{X}_0)$ and $w_0^{k,-} = 1$.

Prediction: Represent $P(\boldsymbol{X}_i|\boldsymbol{y}_0, \boldsymbol{y}_{i-1})$ by

$$\left\{ (\boldsymbol{s}_i^{k,-}, w_i^{k,-}) \right\},$$

where

$$\boldsymbol{s}_i^{k,-} = f(\boldsymbol{s}_{i-1}^{k,+}) + \xi_i^k \text{ and } w_i^{k,-} = w_{i-1}^{k,+} \text{ and } \xi_i^k \sim N(0, \Sigma_{d_i}).$$

Correction: Represent $P(\boldsymbol{X}_i|\boldsymbol{y}_0, \boldsymbol{y}_i)$ by

$$\left\{ (\boldsymbol{s}_i^{k,+}, w_i^{k,+}) \right\},$$

where

$$\boldsymbol{s}_i^{k,+} = \boldsymbol{s}_i^{k,-} \text{ and } w_i^{k,+} = P(\boldsymbol{Y}_i = \boldsymbol{y}_i | \boldsymbol{X}_i = \boldsymbol{s}_i^{k,-}) w_i^{k,-}.$$

Resampling: Normalize the weights so that $\sum_i w_i^{k,+} = 1$, and compute the variance of the normalized weights. If this variance exceeds some threshold, then construct a new set of samples by drawing, with replacement, N samples from the old set, using the weights as the probability that a sample will be drawn. The weight of each sample is now $1/N$.

Algorithm 11.8: A Practical Particle Filter Resamples the Posterior.

Resampling Predictions

A slightly different procedure is to generate several samples of $P(\boldsymbol{X}_i|\boldsymbol{X}_{i-1} = \boldsymbol{s}_{i-1}^{k,+})$ for each $\boldsymbol{s}_{i-1}^{k,+}$, make N draws, with replacement, from this set, using the weights w_i as the probability of drawing a sample, to get N particles. Again, this process will emphasize particles with larger weight over those with smaller weights.

The Consequences of Resampling

Figure 11.13 illustrates the improvements that can be obtained by resampling. Resampling is not a uniformly benign activity, however: it is possible—but

Initialization: Represent $P(\boldsymbol{X}_0)$ by a set of N samples

$$\left\{ (\boldsymbol{s}_0^{k,-}, w_0^{k,-}) \right\},$$

where

$$\boldsymbol{s}_0^{k,-} \sim P_s(\boldsymbol{S}) \text{ and } w_0^{k,-} = P(\boldsymbol{s}_0^{k,-})/P_s(\boldsymbol{S} = \boldsymbol{s}_0^{k,-}).$$

Ideally, $P(\boldsymbol{X}_0)$ has a simple form and $\boldsymbol{s}_0^{k,-} \sim P(\boldsymbol{X}_0)$ and $w_0^{k,-} = 1$.

Prediction: Represent $P(\boldsymbol{X}_i | \boldsymbol{y}_0, \boldsymbol{y}_{i-1})$ by

$$\left\{ (\boldsymbol{s}_i^{k,-}, w_i^{k,-}) \right\},$$

where

$$\boldsymbol{s}_i^{k,l,-} = f(\boldsymbol{s}_{i-1}^{k,+}) + \xi_i^l \text{ and } w_i^{k,l,-} = w_{i-1}^{k,+}$$

and

$$\xi_i^l \sim N(0, \Sigma_{d_i}).$$

and the free index l indicates that each $\boldsymbol{s}_{i-1}^{k,+}$ generates M different values of $\boldsymbol{s}_i^{k,l,-}$. This means that there are now MN particles.

Correction: We reindex the set of MN samples by k. Represent $P(\boldsymbol{X}_i | \boldsymbol{y}_0, \boldsymbol{y}_i)$ by

$$\left\{ (\boldsymbol{s}_i^{k,+}, w_i^{k,+}) \right\},$$

where

$$\boldsymbol{s}_i^{k,+} = \boldsymbol{s}_i^{k,-} \text{ and } w_i^{k,+} = P(\boldsymbol{Y}_i = \boldsymbol{y}_i | \boldsymbol{X}_i = \boldsymbol{s}_i^{k,-}) w_i^{k,-}.$$

Resampling: As in Algorithm 11.8.

Algorithm 11.9: An Alternative Practical Particle Filter.

unlikely—to lose important particles as a result of resampling, and resampling can be expensive computationally if there are many particles.

11.5.5   Ifs, Ands and Buts: Practical Issues in Building Particle Filters

Particle filters have been extremely successful in many practical applications in vision, but can produce some nasty surprises. One important issue has to do with the number of particles: the expected value of an integral estimated with a sampled representation is the true value of the integral, it may require a very large number of particles before the variance of the estimate is low enough to be acceptable. It is difficult to say how many particles will be required to produce usable estimates. In practice, this problem usually is solved by experiment.

Unfortunately, these experiments might be misleading. You can (and should!) think about a particle filter as a form of search; we have a series of estimates of state, which we update using the dynamic model, and then compare to the data;

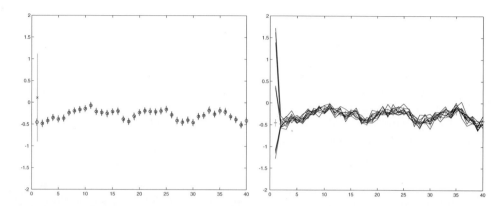

FIGURE 11.13: Resampling hugely improves the behavior of a particle filter. We now show a resampled particle filter tracking a point drifting on the line (i.e., $x_i \sim N(x_{i-1}, \sigma^2)$). The measurements are corrupted by additive Gaussian noise and are the same as for Figure 11.12. In the figure on the **left**, we compare an exact representation obtained using a Kalman filter with one computed from simple particle filtering. We show the mean of the posterior as a point with a one standard deviation bar. The mean obtained using a Kalman filter is given as an x; the mean obtained using a particle filter is given as an o and we have offset the standard deviation bars from one another so as to make the phenomenon clear. Notice that estimates of both mean and standard deviation obtained from the particle filter compare well with the exact values obtained from the Kalman filter. The figure on the **right** indicates where this improvement came from. We plot the tracks of 10 particles, randomly selected from the 100 used. Because we are now resampling the particles according to their weights, particles that tend to reflect the state rather well usually reappear in the resampled set. This means that many particles lie within one standard deviation of the mean of the posterior, and so the weights on the particles tend to have much smaller variance, meaning the representation is more efficient.

estimates that look as though they could have yielded the data are kept, and the others are discarded. The difficulty is that we might miss good hypotheses. This could occur when, for example, the likelihood function has many narrow peaks. We may end up with updated estimates of state that lie in some but not all of these peaks; this would result in good state hypotheses being missed. While this problem can occur in one dimension, it is particularly serious in high dimensions. This is because real likelihood functions can have many peaks, and these peaks are easy to miss in high dimensional spaces. It is extremely difficult to get good results from particle filters in spaces of dimension much greater than about 10.

The problem can be significant in low dimensions, too. Its significance depends, essentially, on how good a prediction of the likelihood we can make. This problem manifests itself in the best-known fashion when one uses a particle filter to track people. Because there tend to be many image regions that are long, roughly straight, and coherent, it is relatively easy to obtain many narrow peaks in the likelihood function. These correspond, essentially, to cases where the configuration for which the likelihood is being evaluated has a segment lying over one of these long, straight coherent image regions. Although there are several tricks for addressing this problem—all involve refining some form of search over the likelihood—there is no standard solution yet.

11.6 NOTES

There is an extensive and rich literature dealing with hard cases in visual tracking; typically, this literature emphasizes powerful and complex probabilistic machinery. What is sometimes missed is that careful use of detectors, models, and appearance reasoning can make hard cases easy. Generally, paying close attention to visual representation is a good way to attack a tracking problem.

The Kalman filter is an extremely useful trick. It is regularly rediscovered, and appears in different guises in different fields. Often dynamics that are not linear can be represented as linear dynamics well enough to fit a Kalman filter. We refer interested readers to Chui (1991), Gelb and of the Analytical Sciences Corporation (1974), and West and Harrison (1997).

We have not discussed the process of fitting a linear dynamic model. The matter is relatively straightforward *if* one knows the order of the model, a natural state space to use, and a reasonable measurement model. Otherwise, things get tricky. There is an entire field of control theory dedicated to the topic in this case known as *system identification*. We recommend, in the first instance, Ljung (1995).

If neither simple tricks nor a Kalman filter will work, you are in real trouble. Particle filters might help, but how helpful they are depends a lot on the details of the problem. We have been able to provide only a brief overview, and have deliberately phrased our discussion rather abstractly, to bring out the issues that are most problematic and to motivate a view of particle filters as convenient approximations. Particle filters have surfaced in a variety of forms in a variety of literatures. The statistics community, where they originated, knows them as particle filters (e.g. (Kitagawa 1987); see also the collection edited by Doucet *et al.* (2001)). In the AI community, the method is sometimes called survival of the fittest (Kanazawa *et al.* 1995). In the vision community, the method is sometimes known as condensation (see Isard and Blake (1996); Blake and Isard (1996); or Blake and Isard (1998)).

Particle filters have been the subject of a great deal of work in vision. Much of the work attempts to sidestep the difficulties with likelihood functions that we sketched in the particle filtering section (in particular, the annealing method of Deutscher *et al.* (2000) and the likelihood corrections of Sullivan *et al.* (1999)). Unfortunately, all uses of the particle filter have been relentlessly top-down, in the sense that one updates an estimate of state and then computes some comparison between an image and a rendering, which is asserted to be a likelihood. Although this strategy can represent an effective end-run around data association, it can also mean that we are committed to searching rather nasty likelihoods.

There is a strong analogy between particle filters and search. This can be used to give some insight into what they do and where they work well. For example, a high-dimensional likelihood function with many peaks presents serious problems to a particle filter. This is because there is no reason to believe that any of the particles each step advances will find a useful peak. This is certainly not an intrinsic property of the technique—which is just an algorithm—and is almost certainly a major strategic error.

Particle filters are an entirely general inference mechanism (meaning that they can be used to attack complex inference problems uniting high-level and low-level vision as in Isard and Blake (1998a) or (1998b)). This should be regarded as a sign that it can be very difficult to get them to work, because there are inference problems that are, essentially, intractable. One source of difficulties is the dimension of the state space. It is silly to believe that one can represent the covariance of a high-dimensional distribution with a small number of particles, unless the covariance is very strongly constrained. A particular problem is that it can be quite hard to tell when a particle filter is working. Obviously, if the tracker has lost track, there is a problem, but the fact that the tracker seems to be keeping track is not necessarily a guarantee that all is well. For example, the covariance estimates may be poor; we need to ask for how long the tracker will keep track; etc.

One way to simplify this problem is to use tightly parametrized motion models. This reduces the dimension of the state space in which we wish to track, but at the cost of not being able to track some objects *or* of being compelled to choose which model to use. This approach has been extremely successful in applications such as gesture recognition (Black and Jepson 1998); tracking moving people (Sidenbladh *et al.* 2000); and classifying body movements (Rittscher and Blake 1999). A tracker could track the state of its own platform, instead of tracking a moving object (Dellaert *et al.* 1999).

There are other methods for maintaining approximations of densities. One might, for example, use a mixture of Gaussians with a constant number of components. It is rather natural to do data association by averaging, which will result in the number of elements in the mixture going up at each step. One is then supposed to cluster the elements and cull some components.

PROBLEMS

11.1. We must maximize

$$f(\boldsymbol{y}) = \frac{C_h}{2} \sum_i w_i k(\| \frac{\boldsymbol{x}_i - \boldsymbol{y}}{h} \|^2) \tag{11.4}$$

(where k is a kernel profile) as a function of $\boldsymbol{y}$. Show that the iteration

$$\boldsymbol{y}^{(j+1)} = \frac{\sum_i w_i \boldsymbol{x}_i g(\| \frac{\boldsymbol{x}_i - \boldsymbol{y}^{(j)}}{h} \|^2)}{\sum_i w_i g(\| \frac{\boldsymbol{x}_i - \boldsymbol{y}^{(j)}}{h} \|^2)}.$$

has a stationary point when $\boldsymbol{y}^{(j)}$ is the location of the maximum (you can follow the form of the derivation in Section 9.3.4).

11.2. Assume we have a model $\boldsymbol{x}_i = \mathcal{D}_i \boldsymbol{x}_{i-1}$ and $y_i = \boldsymbol{M}_i^T \boldsymbol{x}_i$. Here the measurement y_i is a one-dimensional vector (i.e., a single number) for each i and $\boldsymbol{x}_i$ is a k-dimensional vector. We say model is *observable* if the state can be reconstructed from any sequence of k measurements.

(a) Show that this requirement is equivalent to the requirement that the matrix

$$\left[\boldsymbol{M}_i \mathcal{D}_i^T \boldsymbol{M}_{i+1} \mathcal{D}_i^T \mathcal{D}_{i+1}^T \boldsymbol{M}_{i+2} \dots \mathcal{D}_i^T \dots \mathcal{D}_{i+k-2}^T \boldsymbol{M}_{i+k-1} \right]$$

has full rank.

(b) The point drifting in 3D, where $\mathcal{M}_{3k} = (0,0,1)$, $\mathcal{M}_{3k+1} = (0,1,0)$, and $\mathcal{M}_{3k+2} = (1,0,0)$ is observable.

(c) A point moving with constant velocity in any dimension, with the observation matrix reporting position only, is observable.

(d) A point moving with constant acceleration in any dimension, with the observation matrix reporting position only, is observable.

11.3. A point on the line is moving under the drift dynamic model. In particular, we have $x_i \sim N(x_{i-1}, 1)$. It starts at $x_0 = 0$.

(a) What is its average velocity? (Remember, velocity is *signed*.)

(b) What is its average speed? (Remember, speed is *unsigned*.)

(c) (This one requires some thought.) Assume we have two nonintersecting intervals, one of length 1 and one of length 2; what is the limit of the ratio (average percentage of time spent in interval one)/ (average percentage of time spent in interval two) as the number of steps becomes infinite?

(d) You probably guessed the ratio in the previous question; now run a simulation and see how long it takes for this ratio to look like the right answer.

11.4. Assume that we have the dynamics

$$x_i \quad \sim \quad N(d_i x_{i-1}, \sigma_{d_i}^2);$$

$$y_i \quad \sim \quad N(m_i x_i, \sigma_{m_i}^2).$$

(a) $P(x_i|x_{i-1})$ is a normal density with mean $d_i x_{i-1}$ and variance $\sigma_{d_i}^2$. What is $P(x_{i-1}|x_i)$?

(b) Now show how we can obtain a representation of $P(\boldsymbol{x}_i|\boldsymbol{y}_{i+1}, \ldots, \boldsymbol{y}_N)$ using a Kalman filter.

PROGRAMMING EXERCISES

11.5. Implement a 2D Kalman filter tracker to track something in a simple video sequence. We suggest that you use a background subtraction process and track the foreground blob. The state space should probably involve the position of the blob, its velocity, its orientation—which you can get by computing the matrix of second moments—and its angular velocity.

11.6. If one has an estimate of the background, a Kalman filter can improve background subtraction by tracking illumination variations and camera gain changes. Implement a Kalman filter that does this. How substantial an improvement does this offer? Notice that a reasonable model of illumination variation has the background multiplied by a noise term that is near one; you can turn this into linear dynamics by taking logs.

PART FIVE

HIGH-LEVEL VISION

CHAPTER 12

Registration

Registration is the problem of finding a transformation that takes one dataset to another. In the most straightforward form of the problem, the two datasets have the same dimension (i.e., we are registering 3D data to 3D data or 2D data to 2D data), and the transformation is rotation, translation, and perhaps scale (Section 12.1). Good solutions to this problem are extremely useful. There are many cases where one wants to know the *pose*—the position and orientation in world coordinates—of a known object in a dataset of the same dimension of the object. For example, we might have an MRI image (which is a 3D dataset) of a patient's interior that we wish to superimpose on a view of the real patient to help guide a surgeon. In this case, we need to know the rotation, translation, and scale that will put one on top of the other. As another example, we might have a 2D image template of a building that we want to find in an overhead aerial image. Again, we need to know the rotation, translation, and scale that will put one on top of the other; we might also use a match quality score to tell whether we have found the right building. We can solve these problems using search, exploiting a property sometimes known as *pose consistency*. Pose consistency means that different groups of features on a rigid object will all report the same pose for the object. As a result, pretty much any search to register rigid objects should be simple, because we need to find only a small set of features to estimate the pose of the object, and we can then use all the others to confirm that pose.

An important variant of this problem treats registration under projection. In this case we see an image of a 3D object, and need to register the object to the image. Generally, this problem can be solved by the same search algorithms that register datasets of the same dimension, though some details need to be changed (Section 12.2). Here we are helped by a property sometimes known as *camera consistency*, which means that all the features in the image are viewed in the same camera. Camera consistency means that pretty much any search to register rigid objects to an image should be simple, too, because we need to find only a small set of features to estimate the pose of the object and the camera calibration, and we can then use all the others to confirm that pose.

The most complex registration problem treats objects that can deform. In this case, the family of transformations that could register the two datasets is large, and the search for a particular transformation is correspondingly more difficult (Section 12.3). Registering deformable objects is a core technology for medical image analysis, because human organs deform and because it is quite usual to image the same body component using different imaging modes.

12.1   REGISTERING RIGID OBJECTS

Imagine we have two point sets, $\mathcal{S} = \{\boldsymbol{x}_i\}$ a source set and $\mathcal{T} = \{\boldsymbol{y}_j\}$ a target set. The target set is a rotated, translated, and scaled version of the source set, and there might be some noise. We wish to compute the rotation, translation, and scale.

This problem can be formulated in a straightforward way, if we know which $\boldsymbol{x}_i$ corresponds to which $\boldsymbol{y}_j$. Write $c(i)$ for the index of the point in the target set corresponding to the ith source point. In that case, we could compute a least squares solution, minimizing

$$\sum_i \left[(s\mathcal{R}(\theta)\boldsymbol{x}_i + \boldsymbol{t}) - \boldsymbol{y}_{c(i)} \right]^2$$

for the scale s, the rotation $\mathcal{R}(\theta)$, and the translation $\boldsymbol{t}$. If the target isn't scaled, we can set $s = 1$. We could do this using a numerical optimization method, though in this case, a closed form solution is available. Horn (1987b) shows that the translation can be recovered from the centroids, and the rotation and scale from various moments of the point datasets. In fact, this paper shows that if we know that the target is a rotated, translated, and scaled version of the source, correspondences don't matter. This case is an important point of departure for registration problems, but it doesn't arise very often in practice.

More commonly, $\mathcal{S}$ is a set of points sampled from some geometric structure, and $\mathcal{T}$ is a set of points sampled from a rotated, translated, and scaled version of the same structure. For example, $\mathcal{S}$ might be a set of points on a geometrical model of an object, and $\mathcal{T}$ are points obtained from a stereo reconstruction or from a laser range finder. As another example, $\mathcal{S}$ and $\mathcal{T}$ might be points obtained from different 3D imaging datasets of anatomical structures with a feature detector. In each case, we are confident that $\mathcal{S}$ is like a rotated, translated, and scaled version of $\mathcal{T}$, but there might not be a point in $\mathcal{T}$ corresponding to any particular point in $\mathcal{S}$. Worse, the sampling procedure may mean that we can't estimate moments accurately, so Horn's algorithm doesn't apply. Worse still, one or another dataset may contain significant errors or outliers.

Now write
$$\mathcal{G}(s, \theta, \boldsymbol{t})\mathcal{S} = \{(s\mathcal{R}(\theta)\boldsymbol{x}_i + \boldsymbol{t}) \mid \boldsymbol{x}_i \in \mathcal{S}\}$$

for the data set obtained by rotating, translating, and scaling the source. At a solution to this problem, most points (all but the outliers) in $\mathcal{G}(s, \theta, \boldsymbol{t})\mathcal{S}$ should lie close to a point of $\mathcal{T}$, and this gives a correspondence between the two sets. We could search for the right transformation by estimating correspondences, then estimating a transformation given a correspondence, and repeating (Section 12.1.1). Alternatively, we could search for small groups that correspond, then use them to estimate the transformation (Section 12.1.2).

12.1.1   Iterated Closest Points

For the moment, assume we have no outliers. We expect that for any $\boldsymbol{y}_j \in \mathcal{T}$, there is some $\boldsymbol{z}_i \in \mathcal{G}$ that is closest. Furthermore, if we start with a plausible estimate of the transformation, the distance should not be too great. Notice that the index of this point depends on j, but also on the particular transformation $(s, \theta, \boldsymbol{t})$. Write the index of the closest such point $c(i, (s, \theta, \boldsymbol{t}))$. Assume we have an estimate of the transformation $(s, \theta, \boldsymbol{t})^{(n)}$. Then, we could refine this estimate by iterating: (a) transforming the points of $\mathcal{S}$; (b) for each, finding the closest point in $\mathcal{T}$; and (c) re-estimating the transformation with least squares. This yields an iterative algorithm, due to Besl and McKay (1992), known as the *iterated closest points* algorithm (which is described in greater detail in Section 14.3.2). It should be clear that the algorithm can converge to the right answer.

In practice, it usually does. Two points can help improve its behavior. First, the re-estimation procedure does not need to converge to make the algorithm useful. For example, rather than fully re-estimating the transformation, we could do a single step of gradient descent. This will improve the transformation slightly, and should change the corresponding closest points. Second, we do not need to incorporate all points in the minimization process. In particular, if the closest point is relatively far away, it might be better to omit it from the least squares for the next step. Doing so will help ensure the algorithm is robust.

You should regard this more as an algorithmic template than an algorithm; numerous features can be changed successfully. For example, it could be speeded up with care in data structures to keep track of the closest points. As another example, an alternative strategy to obtain robust behavior is to replace the squared error term with an M-estimator. In fact, this algorithm does not require that both $\mathcal{S}$ and $\mathcal{T}$ be point sets. For example, it is relatively straightforward to adapt to the case where $\mathcal{S}$ is a mesh and $\mathcal{T}$ is a point set (Besl and McKay 1992). Furthermore, there is good evidence that the objective function in $(s, \theta, \boldsymbol{t})$ that we are minimizing is quite well-behaved in practice. For example, even though it is not differentiable (because the closest point changes, leading to step changes in the derivative), second-order methods such as Newton's method or LBFGS actually behave rather well in practice (Fitzgibbon 2003).

12.1.2 Searching for Transformations via Correspondences

Iterated closest points repeatedly re-estimates a correspondence between source and target points, then uses it to estimate a transformation. As we have seen, this search might encounter numerous local minima. One alternative is to search the space of correspondences. This might seem unpromising, because there appear to be a lot of correspondences, but in the case of rigid objects a relatively small set of correspondences is enough to register the whole object. Another advantage of thinking about correspondences directly is that we can then work in terms of tokens, rather than points. For example, we might place line-segments, corners, or even point-like features such as blobs in correspondence; the type of the token can sometimes change details, but has little effect on the overall algorithmic approach.

Quite a small group of source tokens, placed in correspondence with target tokens, is enough to estimate a transformation. The size of the group depends somewhat on the transformation and on the tokens. We refer to a group of tokens from which a transformation could be computed as a *frame-bearing group* (sometimes frame group for short). Table 12.1 gives some examples of frame-bearing groups for the 2D to 2D case, and Table 12.2 gives some examples for the 3D to

Transformation	Frame-bearing groups
Rigid (Euclidean)	One point and one direction, or two points, or one line and one point
Rigid and scale	Two points, or one line and one point off the line
Affine	Three points, not co-linear

TABLE 12.1: Some frame-bearing groups for estimating transformations from 2D to 2D. Assume we have one such group in the source, another in the target, and a correspondence between the items in the group; then, we can estimate the transformation uniquely (see the exercises).

3D case. These are explored further in the exercises, too.

Now assume we have a frame-bearing group in the source and in the target. Then, if we have correspondences between the tokens, we could compute the relevant transformation to place the source on the target. There might be only one possible correspondence. For example, if the group is a line and a point, then we can only place the source line (point) in correspondence with the target line (point). But there might also be multiple possible correspondences; for example, the group might consist of three points, yielding six total possibilities.

If one of the groups or the correspondence is incorrect, then most of the source tokens will transform to locations well away from the target. But if they are correct, then many or most transformed source tokens should lie near target tokens. This means we can use RANSAC (Section 10.4.2), by repeatedly applying the following steps, then analyzing the results:

- Select a frame-bearing group for the target and for the source at random;

- Compute a correspondence between the source and target elements (if there is more than one, we could choose at random), and from this compute a transformation;

- Apply the transformation to the source data set, and compute a score comparing the transformed source to the target.

If we have done this sufficiently often, then we will very probably see at least one good correspondence between good groups, and we can identify this by looking at the scores of each probe. From this good correspondence, we can identify pairs of source and target points that match, and finally compute a transformation using least squares.

12.1.3 Application: Building Image Mosaics

One way to photograph a big, imposing object in detail is to take numerous small photographs, then patch them together. Back when it was usual to get photographs developed and printed, one way to do this was to overlay the pieces of paper on a corkboard, so that they joined up properly. This led to an *image mosaic*, a set of overlapping images. Image mosaics can now be built by registering digital images.

Transformation	Frame-bearing groups
Rigid (Euclidean)	Three points, or one line and one point off the line, or two intersecting lines
Rigid and scale	Three points, or one line and one point off the line, or two intersecting lines and a point off their plane.
Affine	Four points, no two co-planar

TABLE 12.2: Some frame-bearing groups for estimating transformations from 3D to 3D. Assume we have one such group in the source, another in the target, and a correspondence between the items in the group; then, we can estimate the transformation uniquely.

FIGURE 12.1: On the **left**, frames from a video taken by an aircraft overflying an airport. These frames are rectified to one another to form a mosaic on the **right**, which reveals (a) the overall structure of what was seen and (b) the flight path of the aircraft. *This figure was originally published as Figure 1 of "Video Indexing Based on Mosaic Representations," by M. Irani and P. Anandan, Proc. IEEE, v86 n5, 1998, © IEEE, 1998.*

One application is building larger images. There are several other important applications. For example, imagine we have image frames taken by, say, an orthographic camera attached to an aircraft; then, if we register the frames to one another, we see not only the pictures taken by the aircraft in a form that exposes all that it saw, but also a representation of the flight path, and so of what it could have seen (Figure 12.1). As another example, imagine we have a fixed camera, that collects video. By registering the frames with one another, we can make estimates of (a) the moving objects and (b) the background, and expose this information to viewers in a novel way (Figure 12.2). As yet another example, we could build either a *cylindrical panorama*, a set of pixel samples that mimic the image produced by a cylindrical camera, or even a *spherical panorama*, a set of pixel samples that mimic the image produced by a spherical camera. One feature of these panoramas is that it is easy to query them for a set of pixels that looks like a perspective image. In particular, it is easy to use these panoramas to imitate what one would see if a perspective camera were to rotate about its focal point.

Building mosaics is a useful application of registration. In the simplest case, we wish to register two images to one another. We do so by finding tokens, deciding which ones should match, and then choosing the transformation that minimizes

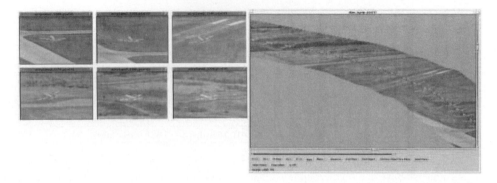

FIGURE 12.2: On the **left**, frames from a video of an aircraft in the air. These frames are rectified to one another to form a mosaic on the **right**, which reveals (a) the flight path of the aircraft in the video and (b) the flight path of the observer. Notice that mosaic reveals the speed with which the aircraft is moving (see how far apart each instance of the aircraft is in the mosaic; when they are far apart, it is moving quickly). *This figure was originally published as Figure 4 of "Video Indexing Based on Mosaic Representations," by M. Irani and P. Anandan, Proc. IEEE, v86 n5, 1998, © IEEE, 1998.*

the squared matching error. Brown and Lowe (2003) show one strategy for finding tokens; they find the interest points of Section 5.3, then compute SIFT features for the neighborhoods (as in Section 5.4.1), and then use approximate nearest neighbors methods to find matching pairs (as in Section 21.2.3). A small set of matches is sufficient to fit a transformation.

There are two types of transformation that are useful in this context. In the simplest case, the camera is an orthographic camera, and it translated. In turn, this means that image tokens translate, so we need only estimate a translation that places matching tokens on top of one another. In a more complex case, the camera is a perspective camera that rotates about its focal point. If we know nothing about the camera, the map between the relevant portions of $\mathcal{I}_1$ and $\mathcal{I}_2$ is a plane projective transformation, sometimes known as a *homography*. Knowing more about the camera and the circumstances might result in a more tightly constrained transformation.

In homogeneous coordinates, the transformation that takes the point $\boldsymbol{x}_1 = (x_1, y_1, 1)$ in $\mathcal{I}_1$ to its corresponding point in $\mathcal{I}_2$, $\boldsymbol{x}_2 = (x_2, y_2, 1)$, has the form of a generic 3×3 matrix with nonzero determinant. Write $\mathcal{H}$ for this matrix. We can estimate its elements using four corresponding points on the plane. Write $\boldsymbol{x}_1^{(i)} = (x_1^{(i)}, y_1^{(i)}, 1)$ for the ith point in $\mathcal{I}_1$, which corresponds to $\boldsymbol{x}_2^{(i)} = (x_2^{(i)}, y_2^{(i)}, 1)$. Now we have

$$\left(\begin{array}{c} x_2^{(i)} \\ y_2^{(i)} \end{array} \right) = \left(\begin{array}{c} \frac{h_{11}x_1^{(i)}+h_{12}y_1^{(i)}+h_{13}}{h_{31}x_1^{(i)}+h_{32}y_1^{(i)}+h_{33}} \\ \frac{h_{21}x_1^{(i)}+h_{22}y_1^{(i)}+h_{23}}{h_{31}x_1^{(i)}+h_{32}y_1^{(i)}+h_{33}} \end{array} \right),$$

so that if we cross-multiply and subtract, we get two homogeneous linear equations

FIGURE 12.3: An image of a mountain (**top left**) and local neighborhoods (**bottom left**) that match those in the second view of the mountain (**top center**; local neighborhoods are **bottom center**). These images may look as though they can be rectified by a translation, but in fact this works poorly. **Top right** shows a (manually chosen) translation that appears to work, with the left image superimposed on the center image. In fact, this isn't a particularly good registration, as one can see from the **bottom right**, where the center image is now on top. A homography is required for a good registration; compare Figure 12.4. *This figure was originally published as Figure 1 M. Brown and D. Lowe, "Recognizing Panoramas," Proc. ICCV 2003, © IEEE, 2003.*

in the unknown entries of the matrix for each pair of corresponding points, i.e.,

$$x_2^{(i)}(h_{31}x_1^{(i)} + h_{32}y_1^{(i)} + h_{33}) - (h_{11}x_1^{(i)} + h_{12}y_1^{(i)} + h_{13}) = 0$$
$$y_2^{(i)}(h_{31}x_1^{(i)} + h_{32}y_1^{(i)} + h_{33}) - (h_{21}x_1^{(i)} + h_{22}y_1^{(i)} + h_{23}) = 0.$$

This system admits a solution for $\mathcal{H}$ up to scale, which is all that is required (we are working in homogeneous coordinates). This is a good way to get an estimate of $\mathcal{H}$ for a small group of points, but might not lead to the most accurate solution when we have a large set of corresponding points. In this case, we should minimize as a function of $\mathcal{H}$

$$\sum_{i \in \text{points}} g\left((x_2^{(i)} - \frac{h_{11}x_1^{(i)} + h_{12}y_1^{(i)} + h_{13}}{h_{31}x_1^{(i)} + h_{32}y_1^{(i)} + h_{33}})^2 + (y_2^{(i)} - \frac{h_{21}x_1^{(i)} + h_{22}y_1^{(i)} + h_{23}}{h_{31}x_1^{(i)} + h_{32}y_1^{(i)} + h_{33}})^2\right)$$

where g could be the identity function, which is not a good idea if we have outliers, or is an M-estimator. This function is invariant to the scale of $\mathcal{H}$, so we need some form of normalization. We could normalize by setting one entry to one (not a good idea, as it biases the results), or by requiring that the Frobenius norm is one. Good software for estimating homographies is now available on the Web. Manolis Lourakis publishes a C/C++ library at `http://www.ics.forth.gr/~lourakis/homest/`; there is a set of MATLAB functions for multiple view geometry at `http://www.robots.ox.ac.uk/~vgg/hzbook/code/`, written by David Capel, Andrew Fitzgibbon, Peter Kovesi, Tomas Werner, Yoni Wexler, and Andrew Zisserman. Finally, OpenCV has homography estimation routines in it, too.

FIGURE 12.4: The two mountain images of Figure 12.3, now rectified with a homography. Notice how well all features line up; this transformation involves more than just rotation and translation, as you can see from the fact that the corner of the second image (which can be seen in the middle, near the top), is no longer a right angle. Notice also that intensity effects in the camera far field mean that the boundary where the two images overlap is unpleasantly obvious. *This figure was originally published as Figure 1 M. Brown and D. Lowe, "Recognizing Panoramas," Proc. ICCV 2003, © IEEE, 2003.*

Registering images into mosaics gets more interesting when there are more than two images. Imagine we have three images, $\mathcal{I}_1$, $\mathcal{I}_2$, and $\mathcal{I}_3$. We could register image one to image two, then image two to image three. But, if image three has some features that match to features in image one, this might not be wise. Write $\mathcal{T}_{2\to1}$ for the estimated transformation that takes image two into image one's frame (and so on). The problem is that $\mathcal{T}_{2\to1} \circ \mathcal{T}_{3\to2}$ might not be a good estimate of $\mathcal{T}_{3\to1}$ the transformation from image three's frame to image one's frame. The error might not be all that large in the case of just three images, but it can accumulate.

To deal with this accumulation, we need some method to estimate all registrations in one go, using all error terms. Doing so is often called *bundle adjustment*, by analogy with the relevant term in structure from motion (Section 8.3.3). A natural method is to choose a coordinate frame within which to work—for example, the frame of the first image—then search for a set of maps that take each other image into that frame and minimize the sum of squared errors between all matching pairs of points. For our example, write $\left(\boldsymbol{x}^{(i)}, \boldsymbol{x}^{(k)}\right)_j$ for the jth tuple consisting of a point $\boldsymbol{x}^{(i)}$ in image i that matches a point $\boldsymbol{x}^{(k)}$ in image k. We would estimate $\mathcal{T}_{2\to1}$ and

FIGURE 12.5: **Top**, 80 images registered automatically to one another to create a panoramic mosaic (which is what one would see if the camera had cylindrical film, and a 360° field of view). **Bottom**, the images feathered into one another to suppress the effects of intensity variation between different views of the same pixel. *This figure was originally published as Figure 3 M. Brown and D. Lowe, "Recognizing Panoramas," Proc. ICCV 2003, © IEEE, 2003.*

$\mathcal{T}_{3\to1}$ by minimizing

$$\sum_{j\in1,\ 2\ \text{matches}} g(\|\,\boldsymbol{x}_j^{(1)} - \mathcal{T}_{2\to1}\boldsymbol{x}_j^{(2)}\,\|^2)+$$

$$\sum_{j\in1,\ 3\ \text{matches}} g(\|\,\boldsymbol{x}_j^{(1)} - \mathcal{T}_{3\to1}\boldsymbol{x}_j^{(3)}\,\|^2)+$$

$$\sum_{j\in2,\ 3\ \text{matches}} g(\|\,\mathcal{T}_{2\to1}\boldsymbol{x}_j^{(2)} - \mathcal{T}_{3\to1}\boldsymbol{x}_j^{(3)}\,\|^2)$$

(where g might be the identity if there are no outliers, and an M-estimator otherwise), and then register with these transformations. Notice that, as the number of images goes up, this strategy will yield a large and nasty optimization problem that will most likely exhibit local minima, and so will need to be started with a good estimate of the transformations. Registering individual pairs of images can supply that start point. Once images have been registered to one another, we can come up with a single panorama by overlaying images, then carefully blending pixels to account for spatial variations in image brightness caused by the lens system (Figure 12.5).

12.2 MODEL-BASED VISION: REGISTERING RIGID OBJECTS WITH PROJECTION

We would now like to register rigid objects with images. Solutions to this problem can be extremely useful in practice, because they allow us to estimate the position, orientation, and scale of a known object in an image with respect to the camera, despite some uncertainty about which image features lie on the object. Such algorithms can be extremely useful in systems that must interact with the world. For example, if we wished to move an object into a particular position or grasp it, it could be really useful to know its configuration with respect to the camera. We use the same strategy for this problem that we used for registering 3D objects to 3D objects, that is, repeatedly: find a group; recover the transformation; apply this to the whole source; and score the similarity between the source and the target. At the end, we report the transformation with the best score. Furthermore, if the best available transformation score is good, then the object is there; if it is bad, then it isn't.

The source S now consists of tokens on some geometric structure, and T is the image (in one or another kind of camera) of another set of tokens on a rotated, translated, and scaled version of that structure. We would like to determine the rotation, translation, and scale applied. Usually this problem involves a significant number of outliers in T, which occur because we don't know which image features actually came from the object. Almost always the tokens are points or lines; for S, these are determined from a geometric model of the object, and for T, these come from edge points or fitting lines to edge points (we could use the machinery of Chapter 10 to get these lines). This case has two distinctive features. We might not be able to estimate all transform parameters (which typically won't matter all that much), and it can be quite difficult to come up with a satisfactory score of similarity between the source and the target.

There are numerous ways of estimating transform parameters. The details depend on whether we need to calibrate the camera, and on what camera model we impose. In the simplest case, assume we have an orthographic camera, calibrated up to unknown camera scale, looking down the z axis in the *camera* coordinate system. Then we cannot determine depth to the 3D object, because changing the depth does not change the image. We cannot determine the scale of the object separate from the scale of the camera, because by changing these two parameters together we can fix the image. For example, if we double the size of the object, and also halve the size of the camera units, then the image points will have the same coordinate values. However, this doesn't affect the reasoning behind the search processes described above. For example, if we build the right correspondence between source and target group, then visible source tokens should end up close to or on top of target tokens. This means that a RANSAC-style approach applies, as above. Similarly, if we represent the transformation parameters appropriately (we could set the camera scale arbitrarily to one), we could vote.

In the case of a single orthographic camera, calibrated up to unknown camera scale, correspondences between three points are enough to estimate rotation, the two observable components of translation, and scale (see the exercises, which also give other frame groups). In most applications, the range of depths across the object is small compared to the depth to the object. In turn, this means that a perspective camera can be approximated with the weak perspective approximation of Section 1.1.2. This is equivalent to a single orthographic camera, calibrated up to unknown camera scale. If the scale of the camera is known, then it is possible to recover depth to the object as well.

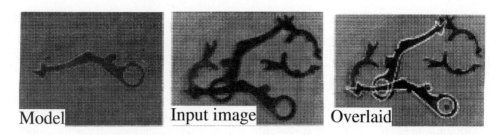

FIGURE 12.6: A plane object registered to an image. On the **left**, an image of an object; in the **center**, an image containing two instances of this object, along with some other stuff (the popular term is *clutter*). Feature points are detected, and then correspondences between groups—in this case, triples of points—are searched; each correspondence gives rise to an affine transformation from the model to the image. Satisfactory correspondences align many model edge points with image edge points, as in the figure on the **left**, which is why the method is sometimes called *alignment*. The images in this figure come from one of the earliest papers on the subject and are affected by the poor reproduction techniques of the time. *This figure was originally published as Figure 7 of "Object recognition using alignment," D.P. Huttenlocher and S. Ullman, Proc. IEEE ICCV, 1986. © IEEE, 1986.*

12.2.1 Verification: Comparing Transformed and Rendered Source to Target

The main difficulty with a RANSAC-style search for a transformation that registers a 3D object with an image is that, in practical cases, a good score is difficult to get. A strategy for computing a scoring function is straightforward, if we recall the term *render*, a general-purpose description for producing an image from models, encompassing everything from constructing line drawings to producing physically accurate shaded images. We take the estimated transformation, apply it to the object model, then render the transformed object model using our camera model. We now take the rendering, and compare it to the image. The difficulty lies in the form of the comparison (which will determine what we need to render).

We need a scoring function that can take into account all available image evidence. This could include tokens, which could be difficult to identify with certainty (such as corners or edge points) or such evidence as image texture. If we know all the lighting conditions under which the object is being viewed, we might even be able to use pixel intensity (this hardly ever happens in practice). Usually, all we know about the illumination is that it is bright enough that we can find some tokens, which is why we have a registration hypothesis to test. This means that comparisons should be robust to changes in illumination. By far the most important test in practice is to render the silhouette of the object and then compare it to edge points in an image.

A natural test is to overlay object silhouette edges on the image using the camera model, and then score the hypothesis by comparing these points with actual image edge points. The usual score is the fraction of the length of predicted silhouette edges that lie nearby actual image edge points. This is invariant to rotation and translation in the camera frame, which is a good thing, but changes with scale, which might not be a bad thing. It is usual to allow edge points to contribute to a verification score only if their orientation is similar to the orientation of the silhouette edge to which they are being compared. The principle here is that the more detailed the description of the edge point, the more likely one is to know whether it came from the object.

It is a bad idea to include invisible silhouette components in the score, so the rendering should be capable of removing hidden lines. The silhouette is used because edges internal to a silhouette may have low contrast under a bad choice of illumination. This means that their absence may be evidence about the illumination rather than the presence or absence of the object.

Edge proximity tests can be quite unreliable. Even orientation information doesn't really overcome these difficulties. When we project a set of model boundaries into an image, the *absence* of edges lying near these boundaries could well be a quite reliable sign that the model isn't there, but the *presence* of edges lying near the boundaries is *not* a particularly reliable sign that the object is there. For example, in textured regions, there are many edge points grouped together. This means that, in highly textured regions, it is possible to get high verification scores for almost any model at almost any pose (e.g., see Figure 12.7). Notice that counting similarity in edge orientation in the verification score hasn't made any difference here.

We can tune the edge detector to smooth texture heavily, in the hope that textured regions will disappear. This is a dodge, and a dangerous one, because it usually affects the contrast sensitivity so that the objects disappear, too. However, it can be made to work acceptably and is widely used.

12.3 REGISTERING DEFORMABLE OBJECTS

There are many applications that require registering deformable objects. For example, one might wish to register a neutral view of a face to a view displaying some emotion; in this case, the deformation of the face might reveal the emotion (Section 12.3.1). As another example, one might wish to register a medical image of an organ to another image of the same organ (Section 12.3.3). As yet another example, one might encode a family of shapes as one model shape and a family of deformations. Notoriously, D'Arcy Thompson argued that side views of different fish should be seen as deformations of one another (Thompson 1992).

Generally, we have registered objects by a search process that looks for a minimum of a cost function. This applies in rather a general way to deformable objects, but we usually cannot use RANSAC, because we cannot estimate the parameters with a subset of tokens. As a result, registration is usually much slower.

12.3.1 Deforming Texture with Active Appearance Models

An important case is matching face images to one another, despite deformations of the face, changes in head angle, and so on. In this case, the texture on the face is an important cue driving the match. Cootes *et al.* (2001) model the face as a plane mesh of triangles, as in Figure 12.8. Now assume that this mesh is placed over an image of a face. If we knew their configuration in a neutral frontal view of the face, we could generate the intensity field for that view. Call the original image $\mathcal{I}_o$. For the moment, we will assume there is just one triangle in the mesh.

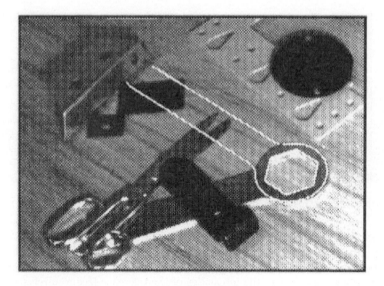

FIGURE 12.7: Edge orientation can be a deceptive cue for verification, as this figure illustrates. The edge points marked on the image come from a model of a spanner, recognized and verified with 52% of its outline points matching image edge points with corresponding orientations. Unfortunately, the image edge points come from the oriented texture on the table, not from an instance of the spanner. As the text suggests, this difficulty could be avoided with a much better description of the spanner's interior as untextured, which would be a poor match to the oriented texture of the table. *This figure was originally published as Figure 4 of "Efficient model library access by projectively invariant indexing functions," by C.A. Rothwell et al., Proc. IEEE CVPR, 1992, © IEEE, 1992.*

Each point on this triangle has a reference intensity value, which we can obtain by querying the image at that location on the triangle. Write $\boldsymbol{v}_1$, $\boldsymbol{v}_2$, $\boldsymbol{v}_3$ for the vertices of the triangle. We can represent interior points of the triangle using *barycentric coordinates*; with a point in the reference triangle given by (s,t) such that $0 \leq s \leq 1$, $0 \leq t \leq 1$ and $s + t \leq 1$, we associate the point

$$\boldsymbol{p}(s,t;\boldsymbol{v}) = s\boldsymbol{v}_1 + t\boldsymbol{v}_2 + (1 - s - t)\boldsymbol{v}_3$$

(which lies inside the triangle). The reference intensity value associated with the point (s,t) for the triangle $(\boldsymbol{v}_1, \boldsymbol{v}_2, \boldsymbol{v}_3)$ is $\mathcal{I}_o(\boldsymbol{p}(s,t;\boldsymbol{v}))$.

We can get the intensity field of the face in a neutral position by moving the reference points to neutral locations. This represents a deformation of both the geometry of the mesh and of the intensity field represented by the mesh. Assume in the neutral location the three triangle vertices $\boldsymbol{v}_i$ map to $\boldsymbol{w}_i$. Then, for a small triangle, we expect that the intensity field of the new triangle is a deformed version of the intensity field of the original triangle. Now the representation in terms of barycentric coordinates is useful; you can check that we expect

$$\mathcal{I}_n(\boldsymbol{p}(s,t;\boldsymbol{w})) = \mathcal{I}_o(\boldsymbol{p}(s,t;\boldsymbol{v}))$$

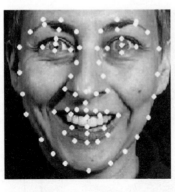 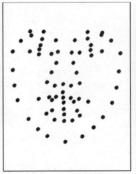 

Reference points   Relaxed points   Relaxed intensity

FIGURE 12.8: A set of reference points placed over a face, on the **left**. At the **center**, these points in a relaxed configuration. Now assume we have a reasonable triangulation of the original set of points. By placing those points in correspondence with the relaxed configuration, we can map the intensities of the reference face to a relaxed configuration (**right**). *This figure was originally published as Figure 1 of "Active Appearance Models," by T. Cootes, G. Edwards, and C. Taylor, IEEE Transactions on Pattern Analysis and Machine Intelligence, 2001, © IEEE, 2001.*

(i.e., that the (s, t) values naturally interpolate between the vertices of the triangle). We can then produce a neutral image of the face simply by moving the vertices to their neutral position (Figure 12.8).

There is nothing special about the neutral locations of the mesh vertices; we can generate an intensity field for any configuration of these vertices where triangles don't overlap. This means we can search for the location of a deformed triangle in a new image $\mathcal{I}_d$ by sampling (s, t) space at a set of points (s_j, t_j), and then minimizing

$$\sum_j g(\|\mathcal{I}_d(\boldsymbol{p}(s_j, t_j; \boldsymbol{w})) - \mathcal{I}_n(\boldsymbol{p}(s_j, t_j; \boldsymbol{v}))\|^2)$$

as a function of the vertices $\boldsymbol{w}_i$. Here, as before, if we do not expect outliers, then g is the identity, and if we do, it could be some M-estimator. If we expect that the illumination might change, then it makes sense to minimize

$$\sum_j g(\|a\mathcal{I}_d(\boldsymbol{p}(s_j, t_j; \boldsymbol{w})) + b - \mathcal{I}_n(\boldsymbol{p}(s_j, t_j; \boldsymbol{v}))\|^2)$$

as a function of the vertices $\boldsymbol{w}_i$ and of a, b.

When there is more than one triangle, the notation gets slightly more complicated. We write $\boldsymbol{v}^{(k)}$ and $\boldsymbol{w}^{(k)}$ for the vertices of the kth neutral and deformed triangles respectively. We do not expect the vertices to move independently. A variety of models are possible, but it is natural to try and make the model linear in some set of parameters. One reasonable model is obtained by writing $\mathcal{V} = [\boldsymbol{v}_1, \ldots, \boldsymbol{v}_n]$ (resp. $\mathcal{W} = [\boldsymbol{w}_1, \ldots, \boldsymbol{w}_n]$) for the $2 \times n$ matrices whose columns are the vertices of the neutral (resp. deformed) points. Now we have a set of r $2 \times n$ basis matrices $\mathcal{B}_l$,

FIGURE 12.9: Different face intensity masks generated by moving deformation parameters to different values. Each block shows the effect of a different parameter; the center of that block shows the parameter at the mean value (where the mean is taken over numerous example faces), and the left (resp. right) of the block shows the parameter at mean plus (resp. minus) three standard deviations. Note how a range of expressions is encoded by these parameter variations. *This figure was originally published as Figure 2 of "Active Appearance Models," by T. Cootes, G. Edwards, and C. Taylor, IEEE Transactions on Pattern Analysis and Machine Intelligence, 2001, © IEEE, 2001.*

a rotation matrix $\mathcal{R}$, a translation vector $\boldsymbol{t}$, and a set of parameters θ_l, and write

$$\mathcal{W} = \mathcal{R}(\mathcal{V} + \sum_l \mathcal{B}_l \theta_l) + \boldsymbol{t}$$

to get a model of the deformations that also incorporates rotation and translation of the neutral face.

The matrices $\mathcal{B}_l$ could be obtained by manually aligning a mesh with a deformed face, for example (Figure 12.9 shows some deformations encoded by one set of such matrices). The vertices $\boldsymbol{w}$ are a function of the parameters θ, and so we must minimize

$$\sum_{k \in \text{triangles}} \sum_j g(\| a\mathcal{I}_d(\boldsymbol{p}(s_j, t_j; \boldsymbol{w}^{(k)}(\theta))) + b - \mathcal{I}_n(\boldsymbol{p}(s_j, t_j; \boldsymbol{v}^{(k)})) \|^2)$$

as a function of $\mathcal{R}$, $\boldsymbol{t}$, θ_l, a, and b.

12.3.2 Active Appearance Models in Practice

We have shown several minimization problems for registering active appearance models. They are not easy minimization problems at all, though they can be solved (Figure 12.10). Numerous local minima are likely, and there are several important strategies that help minimize. First, it is helpful to have an estimate of rotation and translation before estimating the deformation. We expect that deformations are relatively small, and that major rotations and translations will be easy to estimate. It is natural to first produce a rotation and translation estimate, then fix that estimate (which is equivalent to working with a new $\mathcal{V}$ and a new set of $\mathcal{B}_l$) to estimate the deformations θ_l, and then finally polish all estimates simultaneously.

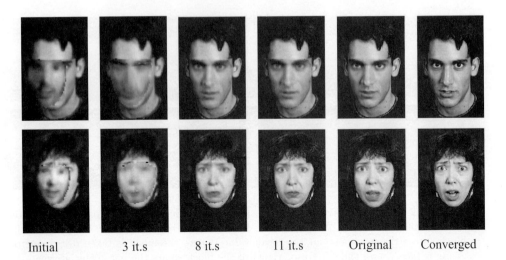

| Initial | 3 it.s | 8 it.s | 11 it.s | Original | Converged |

FIGURE 12.10: Active appearance models registered to face images. On the **left**, the initial configuration of the model (blurry blob over the face; original face is second from right). As the minimization process proceeds, the search improves the registration to produce, in the final converged state, the registration on the **right**. Once we have this registration, the location of the vertices of the mesh and the deformation parameters encode the shape of the face. *This figure was originally published as Figure 5 of "Active Appearance Models," by T. Cootes, G. Edwards, and C. Taylor, IEEE Transactions on Pattern Analysis and Machine Intelligence, 2001, © IEEE, 2001.*

Second, it is usually helpful to do all searches over scale. Using low-resolution neutral and deformed images creates an objective function that changes less dramatically with changes of parameters, which makes the search easier; this gives a good starting point for the search in a higher-resolution image. We could do this by starting with low-resolution neutral and deformed images, estimating rotation and translation, and then proceeding with increasingly high-resolution neutral and deformed images, starting the search for rotation and translation estimates at the point produced by the previous resolution. Once we have a rotation and translation estimate, we estimate deformation starting at the lowest resolution and working up, then polish rotation, translation, and deformation estimates starting at the lowest resolution and working up. Finally, the best results seem to come from using quite careful line searches (using either a gradient or the Newton direction).

The class of model we have described allows a rich range of variations. One could filter or otherwise process the neutral and deformed images, thereby changing the objective function in important ways (for example, emphasizing high spatial frequencies, or computing a vector of filter outputs to get a texture representation). The method can be applied to 3D models as well, with the only major change being the increased complexity of 3D mesh topologies. Different deformation models can be applied, and a wide range of search strategies have been used. Tim Cootes publishes a variety of software tools for building, displaying, and using active appearance models at http://personalpages.manchester.ac.uk/staff/timothy. f.cootes/software/am_tools_doc/index.html. There are also example datasets

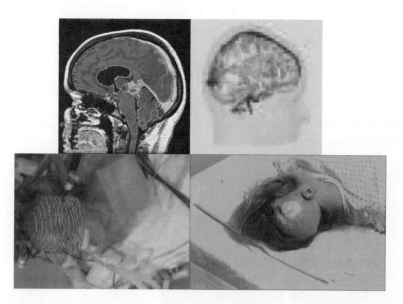

FIGURE 12.11: On the **top left**, a single slice of MRI data with an automatically acquired segmentation overlaid. The segmentation outlines the brain, vacuoles within the brain, and the tumor. MRI produces a sequence of slices, which yield a volume model; a view of a segmented volume model, with different colors showing different regions, is shown at the **top right**. Once this data is obtained, it is registered to a patient lying on a table. Registration is obtained using depth data measured by a laser ranger; the **bottom-left** figure shows a camera view of a patient with laser ranger data overlaid. By registering the segmented data to the patient on the operating table using this laser ranger data and the surface of the MRI data, we can display a processed version of the MRI imagery overlaid on the patient for the surgeon's information (**bottom right**). *Figures by kind permission of Eric Grimson; further information can be obtained from his web site,* http://www.ai.mit.edu/people/welg/welg.html.

and a beginner's guide on this page. Mikkel Stegmann publishes an open-source software package called AAM-API at http://www2.imm.dtu.dk/~aam/. Dirk-Jan Kroon has released an open-source set of MATLAB tools for active appearance models, available at the MATLAB file exchange.

12.3.3 Application: Registration in Medical Imaging Systems

In medical applications, it is usually known *what* is being looked at, but there is a crucial need for an accurate measurement of *where* it is. As a result, registration methods are a major component of medical applications of computer vision. Rigid registration methods are an important component of computer-supported surgery. For example, in brain surgery applications, surgeons are attempting to remove tumors while doing the minimum damage to a patient's faculties.

We show examples due to Grimson and colleagues. The general approach is to obtain images of the patient's brain, segment these images to show the tumor, and then display the images to the surgeon. The display is overlaid on pictures of the patient on the table, obtained using a camera near the surgeon's view, to cue the surgeon to the exact position of the tumor inside the patient. Various methods exist for attaching functional tags to the image of the brain —usually one stimulates a region of the brain and watches to see what happens — and this information can also be displayed to the surgeon so that the impact of any damage done can be minimized. The problem here is pure pose estimation; we need to know the pose of the brain image and the brain measurements with respect to the person on the table, so that the brain image can be superimposed on the patient in the surgeon's display (Figure 12.11).

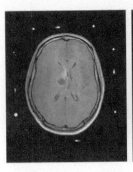 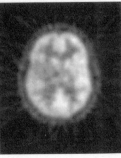 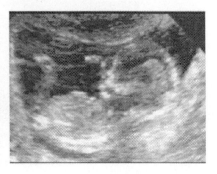

FIGURE 12.12: Images obtained with three different imaging modes. **Left**, an MR image of a brain, obtained with a patient wearing markers (the bright spots outside the skull). **Center**, a positron emission tomography (PET, a kind of NMI) image of the same brain. **Right**, a US image of a fetus in a womb. Notice how each modality shows different detail in different ways; there is high-resolution detail of the brain in the MR image. Compare this with the brain in the CT image of Figure 12.15, where the skull is much more visible. Notice the NM image is at low resolution, but in fact reflects function because regions that respond strongly have taken up some reagent. Finally, the US image has a significant noise component but shows details of soft tissue—you should be able to see a leg, the body, the head, and a hand of the fetus. *Part of this figure was originally published as Figure 10 of "Medical Image Registration using Mutual Information" by F. Maes, D. Vandermeulen and P. Suetens, Proc. IEEE, 2003 © IEEE, 2003.*

Deformable registration techniques are an extremely important, practical tool in medical imaging. Generally, one is trying to register one image of an organ to another image of the same organ. Organs are not rigid, and might deform during the imaging process. For example, some kinds of image take time to capture, and breathing motions might affect the organ. As another example, disease processes might cause the organ to change. Registering deformable structures is rich with important applications. If the images were two images of the same patient at different times, then the registered images might expose changes in the organ (Figure 12.13). If they were two images of different patients, then the registration might expose differences between individuals or disease processes. If one image were an *atlas*—an image labeled, perhaps by hand, with important structural information, such as the name of particular tissues—and the other an image of a patient, the registration could help label, and so segment, the patient image (Figure 12.14). In each of these applications, we expect that image pixel values in the source and target image have the same meaning, and much of the machinery described above applies directly.

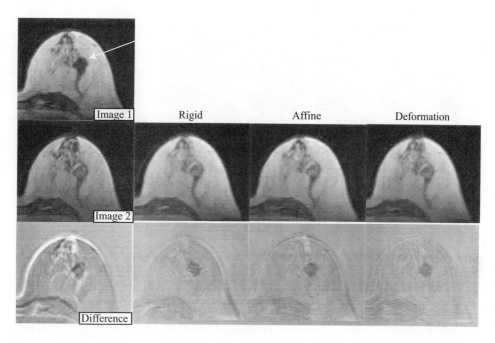

FIGURE 12.13: Registering images can expose changes in an organ. These are images of a breast, where a contrast medium is moving around (the dark material indicated by the arrow). Notice that in image 2, the contrast medium has moved. If these images are just superimposed and subtracted (**right** column), then structures in the difference image show that the breast moved between the images, too (notice the bright section on the edge; this means that the breast has shifted somewhat, which you can confirm by comparing the images). The other columns show registered (resp. difference) images under different models of motion. A rigid motion clearly improves the situation, as does an affine motion, but because breasts are deformable, a deformable registration gets a difference image that more clearly exposes the movement of the contrast medium. *This figure was originally published as Figures 6 and 7 of "Nonrigid registration using free-form deformation," by Ruekert et al., IEEE Trans. Medical Imaging, v18, n8, 1999 © IEEE, 1999.*

But a distinctive feature of medical imaging applications is the number of different ways in which images can be captured. It is desirable to be able to register two images captured using different imaging technologies. For example, if we have two images of the same patient captured using different technologies, then the registered images expose a much richer body of information about the underlying tissues than each separate image does (Figure 12.15).

There are a variety of imaging technologies available, including *magnetic resonance imaging* (MRI), which uses magnetic fields to measure the density of protons and is typically used for descriptions of organs and soft tissue; *computed tomography imaging* (CTI or CT), which measures the density of X-ray absorbtion and is typically used for descriptions of bones; *nuclear medical imaging* (NMI), which measures the density of various injected radioactive molecules and is typically used for functional imaging; and *ultra-sound imaging*, which measures variations in the speed of ultrasound propagation and is often used to obtain information about

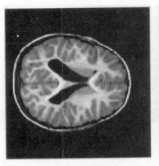  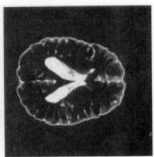

MR image   Segmentation using   Segmentation using
                        atlas registered with   atlas registered with
                        affine transformation   deformations

FIGURE 12.14: On the **left**, an image of a brain, showing enlarged ventricles (the dark butterfly-shaped blob in the middle). This is a volume of cerebro-spinal fluid, or CSF, inside the brain. It is desirable to segment the CSF, to measure the volume of the ventricles. One way to do this is to register this image to an atlas, a generic image of a brain that will be used to provide priors for the segmentation method. This brain will not be exactly the same in shape as the imaged brain. In the **center**, the CSF segmented by registering an atlas to the image using an affine transform; because the registration aligns the atlas to the brain relatively poorly, the segmentation shows poor detail. On the **right**, the same method applied to an atlas registered with a deformable model; notice the significant improvement in detail. *This figure was originally published as Figure 15 of "Medical Image Registration using Mutual Information," by F. Maes, D. Vandermeulen, and P. Suetens, Proc. IEEE, 2003 © IEEE, 2003.*

moving organs (Figure 12.12 illustrates these modes). All of these techniques can be used to obtain slices of data, which allow a 3D volume to be reconstructed.

Generally, a fair abstraction is that each of these imaging techniques produces a pixel (or in 3D, a voxel) intensity value that is largely determined by the type of the tissue inside that pixel (resp. voxel), with added noise. But the same type of tissue might produce quite different values at the same place (which is why we bother having different techniques in the first place; each tells us something quite different about the structure being imaged). This means that the registration techniques we have discussed to date don't apply directly, because they assume that matching pixels (resp. voxels) have the same intensity value. We could try to build a table recording the value that one technology will produce given the value that another one produces, but in practice this is difficult because the values are affected by the particular imaging setup.

This difficulty can be resolved by a clever trick. For the moment, assume we have an estimate of the registration between two modes. This estimated registration then yields an estimate of the joint probability of source and target pixel (or voxel) values. We get this by counting pairs of registered pixel values. Our model is that the pixel value is largely determined by the type of the underlying tissue. When the two images are correctly registered, each pixel in the source sees the same type of tissue as the corresponding pixel in the target. This means that, when the two

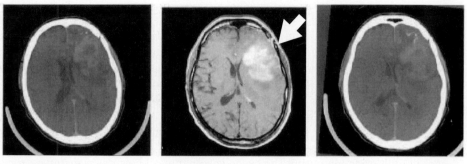

| CT image slice | MR image slice | Slice of registered volume |

FIGURE 12.15: On the **left**, a 2D slice of a 3D CT image of a brain. **Center**, a 2D slice of a 3D MR image of a brain. On the **right**, a slice through the registered volumes. Notice how some rotation was required to register the volumes. The two volume boundaries don't overlap exactly in the right image, and the line separating the hemispheres of the brain in the CT image needs to be rotated a few degrees to overlap the same line in the MR image. Some deformation may have been applied here, too. Notice also that each image emphasizes a different type of structure. In the CT image, the bone is clearly visible, but there isn't much contrast between different soft tissues. In the MR image, soft tissue detail is visible, and a lesion can be seen (arrow). This means that registering by lining up pixel values probably will work poorly, and this registration required the mutual information methods described in the text. By registering the two volumes, we have the most information about each voxel. *This figure was originally published as Figure 1 of "Medical Image Registration using Mutual Information," by F. Maes, D. Vandermeulen, and P. Suetens, Proc. IEEE, 2003 © IEEE, 2003.*

images are correctly registered, the joint probability of source and target values should be very highly concentrated. One way to measure this concentration is to compute the *mutual information* of this joint probability distribution.

Recall the mutual information

$$
\begin{aligned}
I(X;Y) &= \sum_x \sum_y p(x,y) \log \left(\frac{p(x,y)}{p(x)p(y)} \right) \\
&= H(X) - H(X|Y) \\
&= H(Y) - H(Y|X) \\
&= H(X) + H(Y) - H(X,Y)
\end{aligned}
$$

where $H(X) = -\sum_x p(x) \log p(x)$ is the *entropy* of the random variable X. You should think of this as the extent to which knowing the value of Y (resp. X) reveals the value of X (resp. Y). If the tissues were perfectly registered, then we expect to predict Y (the target pixel value) from X (the source pixel value) exactly; so the mutual information would then be high. This means in turn that we can register by maximizing the mutual information between deformed source and corresponding target pixel values. This strategy, originally due to Viola and III (1995) is now standard, and very effective (Figure 12.15).

12.4 NOTES

Registration is useful. Useful recent image registration surveys include Zitova and Flusser (2003); and Dawn *et al.* (2010). Registration algorithms were once used for object recognition—one registers a model to an image, then accepts the hypothesis based on a final score—but different algorithms now dominate in this area. We believe that future work will integrate what is known about registration with the statistical methods of Chapters 16 and 17.

A major difficulty in registration is computing the distance to the nearest point. *Chamfer matching* uses a representation of distance to the nearest point, cached on a grid; computing the cache is sometimes known as a *distance transformation*. Borgefors (1988) gives what we believe to be the first hierarchical search algorithm for registering objects using a distance transformation.

Model-Based Vision

The term alignment is due to Huttenlocher and Ullman (1990). It is a convenient term for a general class of algorithm that reasons about pose consistency. It is hard to determine who used the approach first, though it is quite likely Roberts (1965); other possibilities include Faugeras *et al.* (1984). A contemporary survey is Chin and Dyer (1986). The noise behavior of some alignment algorithms has been studied in detail (Grimson *et al.* 1992, Grimson *et al.* 1994, Grimson *et al.* 1990, Sarachik and Grimson 1993). As a result, alignment algorithms are widely used and there are numerous variants.

These algorithms fell away as object recognition methods because they have difficulty in the presence of rich textures, because they scale poorly with increasing numbers of models, and because they don't apply to objects that aren't rigid. Furthermore, although constrained search for a model that is present can be efficient, showing that a model is absent is expensive (Grimson 1992).

Pose clustering is due to Thompson and Mundy (1987). The analogy to the Hough transform means that the method can behave quite badly in the presence of noise (Grimson and Huttenlocher 1990).

Pose consistency can be used in a variety of forms. For example, recognition hypotheses yield estimates of camera intrinsic parameters. This means that if there are several objects in an image, all must give consistent estimates of camera intrinsic parameters (Forsyth *et al.* 1994).

Tokens could be more abstract than points and lines, and might be as complex as a stripey patch, an eye, or a nose (Ettinger 1988, Ullman 1996). Verification has been extremely poorly studied, (but see Grimson and Huttenlocher (1991)). Verification based on generic evidence—say, edge points—has the difficulty that we cannot tell which evidence should be counted. Similarly, if we use specific evidence—say, a particular camouflage pattern—we have problems with abstraction.

Deformable Models

Registering deformable models is a well-established problem with a long history. Jain *et al.* (1996) give an important early methods that applies to purely geometrical models. Matching algorithms naturally yield tracking algorithms, too (Zhong *et al.* 2000) There is a large range of active appearance models. Active shape models are a variant that encodes geometry, but not intensity, and active contour models, reviewed in Blake (1999), encode boundaries; a particularly important version became famous as a "snake" (Kass *et al.* 1988). We have chosen a model to expound for didactic, rather than historical, reasons. Good places to start in this literature are Cootes and Taylor (1992); Taylor *et al.* (1998); Cootes *et al.* (2001); and Cootes *et al.* (1994).

Medical Applications

This is not a topic on which we speak with any authority. Valuable surveys include: Ayache (1995); Duncan and Ayache (2000); Gerig *et al.* (1994); Pluim *et al.* (2003); Maintz and Viergever (1998); and Shams *et al.* (2010). The three main topics appear to be: **segmentation**, which is used to identify regions of (often 3D) images that correspond to particular organs; **registration**, which is used to construct correspondences between images of different modalities and between images and patients; and **analysis** of both morphology—how big is this? has it grown?—and function. McInerney and Terzopolous (1996) survey the use of deformable models. There are surveys of registration methods and issues in Lavallee (1996) and in Maintz and Viergever (1998), and a comparison between registration output and "ground truth" in West *et al.* (1997).

PROBLEMS

12.1. Show that one line and one point can be used as a frame-bearing group for 2D rigid transformations (i.e., rotations and translations in the plane). The easiest way to do this is to show that (a) the translation is determined by placing the source point over the target point; and (b) the rotation can then be determined by rotating to place the source line over the target line.

    (a) Does every such pair yield a rigid transformation? (Hint: think about the distance from the point to the line.)

    (b) Can the point lie on the line and still yield a unique rigid transformation? (Hint: does the line have symmetries?)

12.2. Explain how to get a high resolution photograph of a large object with a low resolution camera. Are there any limits to your strategy?

12.3. Show that three points can be used as a frame-bearing group for 3D rigid transformations (i.e., rotations and translations in the plane). Start by showing the translation is determined by placing a source point over a corresponding target point. Now the rotation follows in two steps: rotate to place a second source point over the corresponding target point, then rotate about the resulting axis to place the third source point over the third target point.

    (a) Does every such triple yield a rigid transformation? (Hint: think about the distances between the points.)

12.4. Use the methods of the previous exercise to establish that all the frame bearing-groups of Table 12.2 are, in fact, frame-bearing groups.

12.5. Check that a weak-perspective camera is equivalent to an orthographic camera, calibrated up to unknown scale.

12.6. Assume that we are viewing objects in an orthographic camera, calibrated up to unknown scale.

(a) Show that three points is a frame group.

(b) Show that a vertex-pair (two points, with a pair of directions leaving one of the points) is a frame group.

(c) Show that a line and a point is *not* a frame group.

(d) Explain why it is a good idea to have frame groups composed of different types of feature.

12.7. Give a brief explanation of how magnetic resonance imaging (MRI) and computed tomography imaging (CTI or CT) work, contrasting the two methods. How do they compare to ultrasound imaging?

PROGRAMMING EXERCISES

12.8. Build a robust iterated closest points matcher, and use it to match plane curves (for example, the edges of a letter to an instance of the letter; see Figure 1 of Fitzgibbon (2003)). You will find it helpful to read Fitzgibbon (2003), which shows that second-order methods can be used quite effectively, even though the objective function isn't differentiable.

12.9. Use one of the available sets of software to build an image mosaic of a large object.

12.10. Use one of the available sets of software for active appearance model matching to build an active appearance model of a face and then match it to a deformed face image.

CHAPTER 13

Smooth Surfaces and Their Outlines

Several chapters of this book have explored the *quantitative* relationship between simple geometric figures such as points, lines, and planes and the parameters of their image projections. In this one, we investigate instead the *qualitative* relationship between three-dimensional shapes and their pictures, focusing on the *outlines* of solids bounded by smooth surfaces. The outline, also named object *silhouette* or *image contour* in this chapter, is formed by intersecting the retina with a viewing cone (or cylinder in the case of orthographic projection) whose apex coincides with the pinhole and whose surface grazes the object along a surface curve called the *occluding contour*, or *rim* (Figure 13.1).

The image contour of a solid shape constrains it to lie within the associated viewing cone, but does not reveal the depth of its occluding contour. In the case of solids bounded by smooth surfaces, it provides additional information. In particular, the plane defined by the eye and the tangent to the image contour is tangent to the surface. Thus, the contour orientation determines the surface orientation along the occluding contour. In 1977, Marr argued that the silhouette does not, in general, tell us anything else about shape, claiming for example that the inflections of a snake's contour, that separate its convex parts from its concave ones (see the next section for a formal definition), in general have nothing to do with the intrinsic local surface shape, but correspond instead to the boundaries between far and near parts of the snake's body, the near regions appearing larger than the far ones due to perspective effects (Figure 13.2, left). Although intuitively plausible, this interpretation is incorrect. Indeed, as shown by Koenderink in a delightful 1984 article, the inflections of the contour are the projections of *parabolic* surface points that separate convex parts of the surface from saddle-shaped, or *hyperbolic* ones (Figure 13.2, right; we will prove a quantitative version of this result later in this chapter). Thus, they indeed always reveal something of the intrinsic shape of the observed object.

Koenderink's view is that of a physicist trying to understand and model the laws that govern the visual world, and it prevails in this chapter, where the accent is not on applications but on a theoretical understanding of what can, or cannot be said about the world by merely looking at it. The proper mathematical setting for this study is *differential geometry*, a field of mathematics whose primary aim is to model the shape of objects such as curves and surfaces *in the small*—that is, in the immediate vicinity of a point. This local analysis is particularly fruitful for understanding the relationship between solid shapes and their outlines. In particular, it can be shown that the occluding contour is in general a smooth curve, formed by *fold points* where the viewing ray is tangent to the surface and a discrete set of *cusp points* where the ray is tangent to the occluding contour as well. The image contour is piecewise smooth, and its only singularities are a discrete set of *cusps* formed by the projection of cusp points and *T-junctions* formed by the

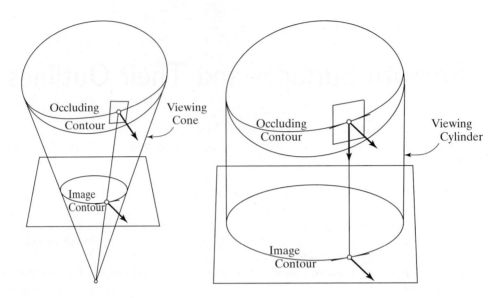

FIGURE 13.1: Occlusion boundaries of a smooth surface. The viewing cone associated with a perspective camera (**left**) degenerates into a viewing cylinder under orthographic projection (**right**). Most of the discussion in this chapter will focus on the orthographic case, but generalizes (rather) easily to the perspective one.

transversal superposition of pairs of fold points (Figure 13.3, top). The intuitive meaning of these exotic terms should be pretty clear: A fold is a point where the surface folds away from its viewer, and a contour cusps at a point where it suddenly decides to turn back, following a different path along the same tangent (this is for transparent objects only; contours of opaque objects terminate at cusps; see Figure 13.3, top). Likewise, two smooth pieces of contour cross at a T-junction (unless the object is opaque and one of the branches terminates at the junction). Figure 13.3 (bottom) shows these features in the outline of an opaque cup (left), or a transparent glass (right). At the bottom of the stem, two pieces of the contour form a T-junction (resp. cross) for the cup (resp. glass) before terminating (resp. cusping).[1] The outline in the middle of the figure is not physically possible.

Differential geometry can be used to characterize the static, or instantaneous, shape of solids' outlines, but it also dictates the manner in which the contour changes with viewpoint. This is captured by the *aspect graph*, a data structure first introduced by Koenderink and Van Doorn (1976*b*, 1979) under the name of *visual potential*. The aspect graph records all possible stable states of the contour, and all transitions, or *visual events*, between these states, and a remarkable fact of life is that there can be only a finite number of those. Visual events and aspect graphs are the last topic explored in this chapter. Let us start in the meantime by introducing the elementary notions of differential geometry that are necessary for

---

[1]The reader may have noticed that the contour junctions at the top of the stem and the top left and right sides of the cup/glass in Figure 13.3 (bottom) are neither cusps nor T-junctions. This is because the surface is not smooth there, and outlines of piecewise-smooth surfaces may exhibit more complex singularities, that are beyond the scope of this book.

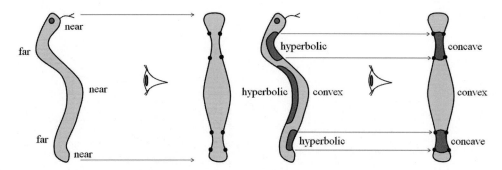

FIGURE 13.2: **Left:** A snake (far left) and, on its right, its outline as observed by a hypothetical eye. In Marr's interpretation, inflections, shown here as black dots, separate portions of the contour corresponding to near surface patches from far ones. **Right:** In Koenderink's (correct) interpretation, they separate convex parts of the contour corresponding to convex regions of the surface from concave ones corresponding to saddle-shaped (hyperbolic) portions of the surface. After Marr (1977) and Koenderink (1984).

understanding some of the geometric properties of our visual world.

13.1   ELEMENTS OF DIFFERENTIAL GEOMETRY

This section presents the rudiments of Euclidean differential geometry necessary to understand the local relationship between light rays and solid objects. We limit our discussion of surfaces to those bounding compact solids in $\mathbb{E}^3$. The topic of our discussion is of course technical, but we attempt to stay at a fairly informal level, emphasizing descriptive over analytical geometry. In particular, we refrain from picking a *global* coordinate system for $\mathbb{E}^3$, although *local* coordinate systems attached to a curve or surface in the vicinity of one of its points are used on several occasions. This is appropriate for the type of qualitative geometric reasoning that is the focus of this chapter. Analytical differential geometry is discussed in Chapter 14 in the (quantitative) context of range data analysis.

13.1.1   Curves

Let us start with the study of curves that lie in a plane. We examine a curve γ in the immediate vicinity of some point P and assume that γ does not intersect itself or, for that matter, terminate in P. If we draw a straight line L through P, it generally intersects γ in some other point Q, defining a *secant* of this curve (Figure 13.4). As Q moves closer to P, the secant L rotates about P and approaches a limit position T called the *tangent line* to γ in P.

By construction, the tangent T has more intimate contact with γ than any other line passing through P. Let us now draw a second line N through P and perpendicular to T and call it the *normal* to γ in P. Given an (arbitrary) choice for a unit *tangent vector* $\boldsymbol{t}$ along T, we can construct a right-handed coordinate frame whose origin is P and whose axes are $\boldsymbol{t}$ and a unit *normal vector* $\boldsymbol{n}$ along N. This *local* coordinate system is particularly well adapted to the study of the curve in the neighborhood of P: its axes divide the plane into four quadrants that can

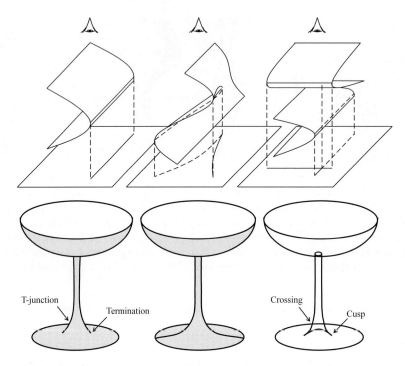

FIGURE 13.3: **Top:** A contour is made of three types of components, from left to right, folds, cusps, and T-junctions. The dashed part is not visible for an opaque surface. **Bottom:** An opaque cup and its outline are shown in the left panel of the diagram. A transparent glass with the same shape is shown in the right panel. The line drawing of the opaque cup in the middle panel is incorrect: the outline of the bottom part of the stem should not reach the sides of the base, but terminate on the way (or cusp, in the case of a transparent object). *The top part of this figure is reprinted from "Computing Exact Aspect Graphs of Curved Objects: Algebraic Surfaces," by S. Petitjean, J. Ponce, and D.J. Kriegman, International Journal of Computer Vision, 9(3):231–255, (1992). © 1992 Kluwer Academic Publishers.*

be numbered in counterclockwise order as shown in Figure 13.5, the first quadrant being chosen so it contains a particle traveling along the curve toward (and close to) the origin. In which quadrant will this particle end up just after passing P?

As shown by the figure, there are four possible answers to this question, and they characterize the shape of the curve near P. We say that P is *regular* when the moving point ends up in the second quadrant and *singular* otherwise. When the particle traverses the tangent and ends up in the third quadrant, P is called an *inflection* of the curve, and we say that P is a *cusp* of the *first* or *second kind* in the two remaining cases, respectively. This classification is independent of the orientation chosen for γ, and it turns out that almost all points of almost all curves are regular, with singularities occurring only at isolated points.

As noted before, the tangent to a curve γ in P is the closest linear approximation of γ passing through this point. In turn, constructing the closest *circular* approximation now allows us to define the *curvature* in P—another fundamental

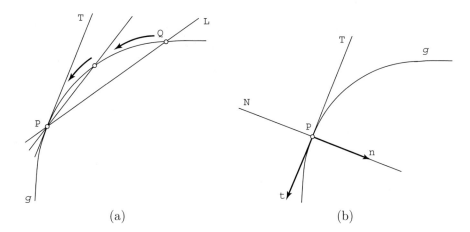

FIGURE 13.4: Tangents and normals: (a) definition of the tangent as the limit of secants, (b) the coordinate system defined by the (oriented) tangent and normal.

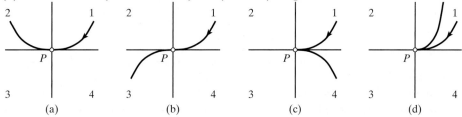

FIGURE 13.5: A classification of curve points: (a) a regular point, (b) an inflection, (c) a cusp of the first kind, (d) a cusp of the second kind. Note that the curve stays on the same side of the tangent at regular points.

characteristic of the curve shape. Consider a point P' as it approaches P along the curve, and let M denote the intersection of the normal lines N and N' in P and P' (Figure 13.6). As P' moves closer to P, M approaches a limit position C along the normal N, called the *center of curvature* of γ in P.

At the same time, if $\delta\theta$ denotes the (small) angle between the normals N and N' and δs denotes the length of the (short) curve arc joining P and P', the ratio $\delta\theta/\delta s$ also approaches a definite limit κ, called the *curvature* of the curve in P, as δs nears zero. It turns out that κ is just the inverse of the distance r between C and P (this follows easily from the fact that $\sin u \approx u$ for small angles; see problems). The circle centered in C with radius r is called the *circle of curvature* in P, and r is the *radius of curvature*.

A simple formula relates the tangent $\boldsymbol{t}$, the normal $\boldsymbol{n}$, and the curvature κ for planar curves parameterized by arc length: Let us assume that some basis has been chosen for $\mathbb{E}^3$ so we can identify this space with $\mathbb{R}^3$. Given some smooth parameterization $\boldsymbol{x} : U \to \mathbb{R}^3$ of the curve γ by its arc length in some neighborhood

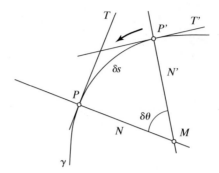

FIGURE 13.6: Definition of the center of curvature as the limit of the intersection of normal lines through neighbors of P.

$U \subset \mathbb{R}$ of one of its points, one can show that

$$\frac{d^2}{ds^2}\boldsymbol{x} = \frac{d}{ds}\boldsymbol{t} = \kappa\boldsymbol{n}. \tag{13.1}$$

It can also be shown that a circle drawn through P and two close-by points P' and P'' approaches the circle of curvature as P' and P'' move closer to P. This circle is indeed the closest circular approximation to γ passing through P. The curvature is zero at inflections, and the circle of curvature degenerates to a straight line (the tangent) there: inflections are the flattest points along a curve.

Let us now introduce a device that proves to be extremely important in the study of both curves and surfaces—the *Gauss map*. Let us pick an orientation for the curve γ and associate with every point P on γ the point Q on the unit circle where the tip of the associated normal vector meets the circle (Figure 13.7). This mapping from γ to the unit circle is the Gauss map associated with γ.[2]

Let us have another look at the limiting process used to define the curvature. As P' approaches P on the curve, the Gaussian image Q' of P' approaches the image Q of P. The (small) angle between N and N' is equal to the length of the arc joining Q and Q' on the unit circle. The curvature is therefore given by the limit of the ratio between the lengths of corresponding arcs of the Gaussian image and of the curve as both approach zero.

The Gauss map also provides an interpretation of the classification of curve points introduced earlier: Consider a particle traveling along a curve and the motion of its Gaussian image. The direction of traversal of γ stays the same at regular points and inflections, but reverses for both types of cusps (Figure 13.5). On the other hand, the direction of traversal of the Gaussian image stays the same at regular points and cusps of the first kind, but it reverses at inflections and cusps of the second kind (Figure 13.7). This indicates a double covering of the unit circle near these singularities: we say that the Gauss map *folds* at these points.

---

[2]The Gauss map could have been defined just as well by associating with each curve point the tip of its unit tangent on the unit circle. The two representations are equivalent in the case of planar curves. The situation will be different when we generalize the Gauss map to twisted curves and surfaces.

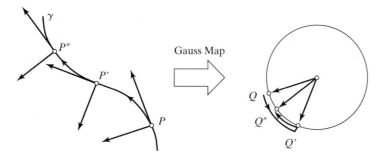

FIGURE 13.7: The Gaussian image of a plane curve. Observe how the direction of traversal of the Gaussian image reverses at the inflection P' of the curve. Also note that there are close-by points with parallel tangents/normals on either side of P'. The Gauss map folds at the corresponding point Q'.

A sign can be chosen for the curvature at every point of a plane curve γ by picking some orientation for this curve and deciding, say, that the curvature can (arbitrarily) be taken positive at a *convex point* where the center of curvature lies on the same side of γ as the tip of the oriented normal vector and negative at a *concave point* where these two points lie on opposite sides of γ. Thus, the curvature changes sign at inflections, and reversing the orientation of a curve also reverses the sign of its curvature.

Twisted space curves are more complicated animals than their planar counterparts. Although the tangent can be defined as before as a limit of secants, there is now an infinity of lines perpendicular to the tangent at a point P, forming a *normal plane* to the curve at this point. In general, a twisted curve does not lie in a plane in the vicinity of one of its points, but there exists a unique plane that lies closest to it. This is the *osculating plane*, defined as the limit of the plane containing the tangent line in P and some close-by curve point Q as the latter approaches P. The *principal normal* is the line where the normal and osculating planes intersect.

As in the planar case, the curvature of a twisted curve can be defined in a number of ways: as the inverse of the radius of the limit circle defined by three curve points as they approach each other (this circle of curvature lies in the osculating plane), as the limit ratio of the angle between the tangents at two close-by points and the distance separating these points as it approaches zero, and so on. Equation (13.1), which relates the derivative of the tangent to the curvature and the normal of a planar curve, still holds for twisted curves, but the vector n in this equation is the principal normal in this case. Likewise, the Gauss map concept can be extended to space curves, but this time the tips of the tangents and principal normals draw curves on a unit *sphere*. Note that it is not possible to give a meaningful sign to the curvature of a twisted curve. In general, such a curve does not have inflections, and its curvature can be taken to be positive everywhere.

13.1.2 Surfaces

Most of the discussion of the local characteristics of plane and twisted curves can be generalized in a simple manner to surfaces. Consider a point P on the surface

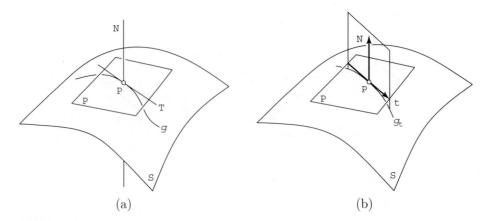

(a)   (b)

FIGURE 13.8: Tangent plane and normal sections. (a) The tangent plane Π and the associated normal line N at a point P of a surface; γ is a surface curve passing through P, and its tangent line T lies in Π. (b) The intersection of the surface S with the plane spanned by the normal vector $\boldsymbol{N}$ and the tangent vector $\boldsymbol{t}$ forms a normal section $\gamma_{\boldsymbol{t}}$ of S.

S and all the curves passing through P and lying on S. It can be shown that the tangents to these curves lie in the same plane Π, appropriately called the *tangent plane* in P (Figure 13.8a). The line N passing through P and perpendicular to Π is called the *normal line* to P in S, and the surface can be oriented (locally) picking a sense for a unit *normal vector* along N (unlike curves, surfaces admit a single normal but an infinity of tangents at every point). The surface bounding a solid admits a canonical orientation defined by letting the normal vectors locally point toward the outside of the solid.[3]

Intersecting a surface with the planes that contain the normal in P yields a one-parameter family of planar curves called *normal sections* (Figure 13.8b). These curves are, in general, regular in P or may exhibit an inflection there. The curvature of a normal section is called the *normal curvature* of the surface in the associated tangent direction. By convention, we choose a positive sign for the normal curvature when the normal section lies (locally) on the same side of the tangent plane as the inward-pointing surface normal and a negative sign when it lies on the other side. The normal curvature is, of course, zero when P is an inflection of the corresponding normal section.

With this convention, we can record the normal curvature as the sectioning plane rotates about the surface normal. It generally assumes its maximum value κ_1 in a definite direction of the tangent plane, and reaches its minimum value κ_2 in a second definite direction. These two directions are called the *principal directions* in P, and it can be shown that, unless the normal curvature is constant over all possible orientations, they are orthogonal to each other (see problems). The

---

[3]Of course, the reverse orientation, where, as Koenderink (1990, p. 137) puts it, "the normal vector points into the 'material' of the blob like the arrows in General Custer's hat," is just as valid. The main point is that either choice yields a coherent global orientation of the surface. Certain surfaces (e.g., Möbius strips) do not admit a global orientation, but they do not bound solids.

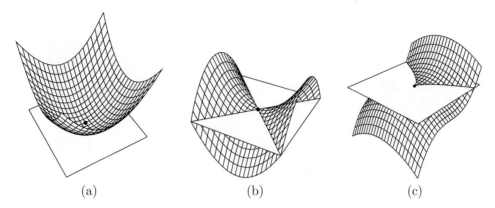

(a)   (b)   (c)

FIGURE 13.9: Local shape of a surface: (a) an elliptic point, (b) a hyperbolic point, and (c) a parabolic point (there are actually two distinct kinds of parabolic points; we come back to those in Section 13.3). *Reprinted from "On Computing Structural Changes in Evolving Surfaces and their Appearance," by S. Pae and J. Ponce, International Journal of Computer Vision, 43(2):113–131, (2001). © 2001 Kluwer Academic Publishers.*

principal curvatures κ_1 and κ_2 and the associated directions define the best local quadratic approximation of the surface. In particular, we can set up a coordinate system in P with x- and y-axes along the principal directions and z-axis along the outward-pointing normal; the surface can be described (up to second order) in this frame by the *paraboloid* $z = -1/2(\kappa_1 x^2 + \kappa_2 y^2)$.

The neighborhood of a surface point can locally take three different shapes depending on the sign of the principal curvatures (Figure 13.9). A point P where both curvatures have the same sign is said to be *elliptic*, and the surface in its vicinity is egg-shaped (Figure 13.9a). It does not cross its tangent plane, and looks like the outside shell of an egg (positive curvatures) or the inside of its broken shell (negative curvatures). We say that P is *convex* in the former case and *concave* in the latter one. When the principal curvatures have opposite signs, we have a *hyperbolic* point. The surface is locally saddle-shaped and crosses its tangent plane along two curves (Figure 13.9b). The corresponding normal sections have an inflection in P, and their tangents are called the *asymptotic directions* of the surface in P. They are bisected by the principal directions. The elliptic and hyperbolic points form patches on a surface. These areas are in general separated by curves formed by *parabolic* points where one of the principal curvatures vanishes. The corresponding principal direction is also an asymptotic direction, and the intersection of the surface and its tangent plane has (in general) a cusp in that direction (Figure 13.9c).

Naturally, we can define the Gaussian image of a surface by mapping every point onto the place where the associated unit normal pierces the unit sphere (that is sometimes referred to as the *Gauss sphere* in the sequel). In the case of plane curves, the Gauss map is one-to-one in the neighborhood of regular points, but the direction of traversal of the Gaussian image reverses in the vicinity of certain singularities. Likewise, it can be shown that the Gauss map is one-to-one in the neighborhood of elliptic or hyperbolic points. The orientation of a small, closed curve centered at an elliptic point is preserved by the Gauss map, but the orientation of a curve

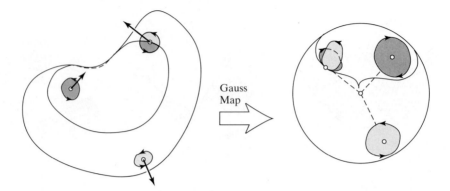

FIGURE 13.10: **Left:** A surface in the shape of a kidney bean. It is formed of a convex area, a hyperbolic region, and the parabolic curve separating them. **Right:** The corresponding Gaussian image. Darkly shaded areas indicate hyperbolic areas, and lightly shaded ones indicate elliptic ones. Note that the bean is not convex, but does not have any concavity. *Reprinted from "On Computing Structural Changes in Evolving Surfaces and their Appearance," by S. Pae and J. Ponce, International Journal of Computer Vision, 43(2):113–131, (2001). © 2001 Kluwer Academic Publishers.*

centered at a hyperbolic point is reversed (Figure 13.10).

The situation is a bit more complicated at a parabolic point. In this case, any small neighborhood contains points with parallel normals, indicating a double covering of the sphere near the parabolic point (Figure 13.10). We say that the Gaussian map *folds* along the parabolic curve. Note the similarity with inflections of planar curves.

Let us now consider a surface curve γ passing through P and parameterized by its arc length s in the neighborhood of P. Since the restriction of the surface normal to γ has constant (unit) length, its derivative with respect to s lies in the tangent plane in P. It is easy to show that the value of this derivative depends only on the unit tangent $\boldsymbol{t}$ to γ and not on γ itself. Thus, we can define a mapping $d\boldsymbol{N}$ that associates with each unit vector $\boldsymbol{t}$ in the tangent plane in P the corresponding derivative of the surface normal (Figure 13.11). Using the convention $d\boldsymbol{N}(\lambda\boldsymbol{t}) = \lambda d\boldsymbol{N}(\boldsymbol{t})$ when $\lambda \neq 1$, we can extend $d\boldsymbol{N}$ to a linear mapping defined over the whole tangent plane and called the *differential of the Gauss map* in P.

The *second fundamental form* in P is the bilinear form that associates with any two vectors $\boldsymbol{u}$ and $\boldsymbol{v}$ lying in the tangent plane the quantity

$$\mathrm{II}(\boldsymbol{u}, \boldsymbol{v}) \stackrel{\text{def}}{=} \boldsymbol{u} \cdot d\boldsymbol{N}(\boldsymbol{v}).$$

Because II can be shown to be symmetric—that is, $\mathrm{II}(\boldsymbol{u}, \boldsymbol{v}) = \mathrm{II}(\boldsymbol{v}, \boldsymbol{u})$—the mapping that associates with any tangent vector $\boldsymbol{u}$ the quantity $\mathrm{II}(\boldsymbol{u}, \boldsymbol{u})$ is a quadratic form. In turn, this quadratic form is intimately related to the curvature of the surface curves passing through P. Indeed, note that the tangent $\boldsymbol{t}$ to a surface curve is everywhere orthogonal to the surface normal $\boldsymbol{N}$. Differentiating the dot product of these two vectors with respect to the curve arc length yields

$$\kappa\boldsymbol{n} \cdot \boldsymbol{N} + \boldsymbol{t} \cdot d\boldsymbol{N}(\boldsymbol{t}) = 0,$$

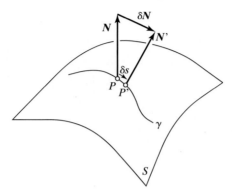

FIGURE 13.11: The directional derivative of the surface normal: if P and P' are nearby points on the curve γ, and N and N' denote the associated surface normals, with $\delta N = N' - N$, the derivative is defined as the limit of $\frac{1}{\delta s} \delta N$ as the length δs of the curve arc separating P and P' tends toward zero.

where n denotes the principal normal to the curve and κ denotes its curvature. This can be rewritten as

$$\mathrm{II}(t, t) = -\kappa \cos\phi, \qquad (13.2)$$

where ϕ is the angle between the surface and curve normals. For normal sections, we have $n = \mp N$, and it follows that the normal curvature in some direction t is

$$\kappa_t = \mathrm{II}(t, t),$$

where, as before, we use the convention that the normal curvature is positive when the principal normal to the curve and the surface normal point in opposite directions. In addition, Equation (13.2) shows that the curvature κ of a surface curve whose principal normal makes an angle ϕ with the surface normal is related to the normal curvature κ_t in the direction of its tangent t by $\kappa \cos\phi = -\kappa_t$. This is known as *Meusnier's theorem* (Figure 13.12).

It turns out that the principal directions are the eigenvectors of the linear map dN, and the principal curvatures are the associated eigenvalues. The determinant K of this map is called the Gaussian curvature, and it is equal to the product of the principal curvatures. Thus, the sign of the Gaussian curvature determines the local shape of the surface: a point is elliptic when $K > 0$, hyperbolic when $K < 0$, and parabolic when $K = 0$.

If δA is the area of a small patch centered in P on a surface S and $\delta A'$ is the area of the corresponding patch of the Gaussian image of S, it can also be shown that the Gaussian curvature is the limit of the (signed) ratio $\delta A'/\delta A$ as both areas approach zero (by convention, the ratio is chosen to be positive when the boundaries of both small patches have the same orientation and negative otherwise; see Figure 13.10). Note again the strong similarity with the corresponding concepts (Gaussian image and plain curvature) in the context of planar curves.

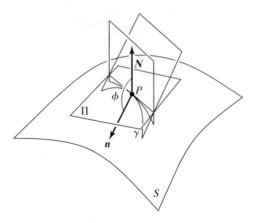

FIGURE 13.12: Meusnier's theorem.

13.2   CONTOUR GEOMETRY

Before studying the geometry of surface outlines, let us pause for a minute and examine the relationship between the local shape of a space curve Γ and that of its orthographic projection γ onto some plane Π (Figure 13.13). Let us denote by α the angle between the plane Π and the tangent t to Γ and by β the angle between Π and the osculating plane of Γ. These two angles completely define the local orientation of the curve relative to the image plane.

If κ denotes the curvature at some point on Γ and κ_a denotes its *apparent curvature* (i.e., the curvature of γ at the corresponding image point), it is easy to show analytically (see problems) that

$$\kappa_a = \kappa \frac{\cos \beta}{\cos^3 \alpha}. \tag{13.3}$$

In particular, when the viewing direction is in the osculating plane ($\cos \beta = 0$), the apparent curvature κ_a vanishes, and the image of the curve acquires an inflection. When, in addition, the viewing direction is tangent to the curve ($\cos \alpha = \cos \beta = 0$), κ_a is not well defined anymore and the projection acquires a cusp.

The theorem by Koenderink mentioned in the introduction relates in a similar fashion the local shape of the surface bounding a solid object to the shape of its image contour. We present in the rest of this section a few elementary properties of image contours before stating and proving this theorem formally.

13.2.1   The Occluding Contour and the Image Contour

As noted earlier, the image of a solid bounded by a smooth surface is itself bounded by an image curve, called the *contour*, *silhouette*, or *outline* of this solid. This curve is the intersection of the retina with a viewing cone whose apex coincides with the pinhole and whose surface grazes the object along a second curve, called the *occluding contour*, or *rim* (Figure 13.1, left). We assume orthographic projection in the rest of this section. In this case, the pinhole moves to infinity and the viewing cone becomes a cylinder whose generators are parallel to the (fixed) viewing

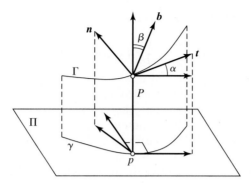

FIGURE 13.13: A space curve and its projection. The vector **b** is the *binormal* to Γ—that is, the normal to the osculating plane. The angle β between Π and the osculating plane is equal to the angle between the "vertical" viewing direction and **b**. Note that the tangent to γ is the projection of the tangent to Γ (e.g., think of the tangent as the velocity of a particle traveling along the curve). The normal to γ is *not*, in general, the projection of the normal **n** to Γ.

direction. The surface normal is constant along each one of these generators, and it is parallel to the image plane (Figure 13.1, right). The tangent plane at a point on the occluding contour projects onto the tangent to the image contour, and it follows that the normal to this contour is equal to the surface normal at the corresponding point of the occluding contour. It is important to note that the viewing direction **v** is *not*, in general, perpendicular to the occluding contour tangent **t** (as noted by Nalwa (1988), for example, the occluding contour of a tilted cylinder is parallel to its axis and not to the image plane). In fact, as shown in the next section, these two directions are *conjugate*—an extremely important property of the occluding contour.

More generally, the occluding contour is not (in general) planar. Shadows demonstrate this quite clearly: attached shadows are delineated by the occluding contours associated with the light sources, and cast shadows are bounded by the corresponding object outlines. Thus, we can see a "side view" of the occluding contour in this case, and observing the attached shadow boundaries of a person's face, for example, should convince the interested reader that these curves do not lie in a plane.

13.2.2   The Cusps and Inflections of the Image Contour

Two directions **u** and **v** in the tangent plane are said to be conjugate when $\mathrm{II}(\boldsymbol{u}, \boldsymbol{v}) = 0$. For example, the principal directions are conjugate because they are orthogonal eigenvectors of $d\boldsymbol{N}$, and asymptotic directions are self-conjugate.

It is easy to show that the tangent **t** to the occluding contour is always conjugate to the corresponding projection direction **v**. Indeed, **v** is tangent to the surface at every point of the occluding contour, and differentiating the identity $\boldsymbol{N} \cdot \boldsymbol{v} = 0$

with respect to the arc length of this curve yields

$$0 = \left(\frac{d}{ds}\mathbf{N}\right) \cdot \mathbf{v} = d\mathbf{N}(\mathbf{t}) \cdot \mathbf{v} = \mathrm{II}(\mathbf{t}, \mathbf{v}).$$

Let us now consider a hyperbolic point P_0 and project the surface onto a plane perpendicular to one of its asymptotic directions. Because asymptotic directions are self-conjugate, the occluding contour in P_0 must run along this direction. As shown by Equation (13.3), the curvature of the contour must be infinite in that case, and the contour acquires a cusp of the first kind.

We state in a moment a theorem by Koenderink (1984) that provides a quantitative relationship between the curvature of the image contour and the Gaussian curvature of the surface. In the meantime, we prove (informally) a weaker, but still remarkable result.

Theorem 3. Under orthographic projection, the inflections of the contour are images of parabolic points (Figure 13.14).

To see why this theorem holds, first note that, under orthographic projection, the surface normal at a point on the occluding contour is the same as the normal at the corresponding point of the image contour. Since the Gauss map folds at a parabolic point, the Gaussian image of the image contour must reverse direction at such a point. As shown earlier, the Gaussian image of a planar curve reverses at its inflections and cusps of the second kind. It is possible to show that the latter singularity does not occur for a general viewpoint, which proves the result.

In summary, the occluding contour is formed by points where the viewing direction $\mathbf{v}$ is tangent to the surface (the fold points mentioned in the introduction). Occasionally, it becomes tangent to $\mathbf{v}$ at a hyperbolic cusp point or crosses a parabolic line, and cusps (of the first kind) or inflections appear on the contour accordingly. Unlike the curves mentioned so far, the image contour may also cross itself (transversally) when two distinct branches of the occluding contour project onto the same image point, forming a T-junction (Figure 13.3). For general viewpoints, these are the only possibilities: there is no cusp of the second kind, nor any tangential self-intersection, for example. We come back to the study of exceptional viewpoints and the corresponding contour singularities in the next section.

13.2.3   Koenderink's Theorem

Let us now state the theorem by Koenderink (1984) that has already been mentioned several times. We assume as before orthographic projection, consider a point P on the occluding contour of a surface S, and denote by p its image on the contour.

Theorem 4. The Gaussian curvature K of S in P and the contour curvature κ_c in p are related by

$$K = \kappa_c \kappa_r,$$

where κ_r denotes the curvature of the *radial curve* formed by the intersection of S with the plane defined by the normal to S in P and the projection direction (Figure 13.15).

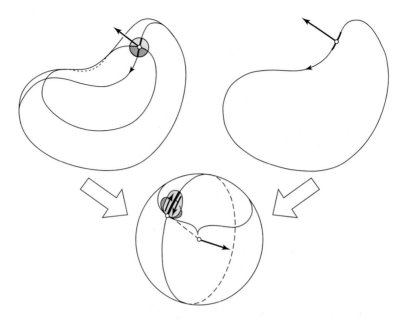

FIGURE 13.14: The inflections of the contour are images of parabolic points: The **top-left** side of this diagram shows the bean-shaped surface with an occluding contour overlaid, and its **top-right** side shows the corresponding image contour. As shown in the **bottom** part of the drawing, the Gauss map folds at the parabolic point, and so does its restriction to the great circle formed by the images of the occluding and image contours.

This remarkably simple relation has several important corollaries (starting with Theorem 3, of course): Note that the *radial curvature* κ_r remains positive (or zero) along the occluding contour because the projection ray locally lies inside the imaged object at any point where $\kappa_r < 0$. It follows that κ_c is positive when the Gaussian curvature is positive and negative otherwise. In particular, the theorem shows that convexities of the contour corresponds to elliptic points of the surface, whereas contour concavities correspond to hyperbolic points and contour inflections correspond to parabolic points.

Among elliptic surface points, it is clear that concave points never appear on the occluding contour of an opaque solid since their tangent plane lies (locally) completely inside this solid. Thus, convexities of the contour also correspond to convexities of the surface. Likewise, we saw earlier that the contour cusps when the viewing direction is an asymptotic direction at a hyperbolic point. In the case of an opaque object, this means that concave arcs of the contour may terminate at such a cusp, where a branch of the contour becomes occluded (on the other hand, a contour *cannot* terminate at a convex point!). Thus, we see that Koenderink's theorem strengthens and refines the earlier characterization of the geometric properties of image contours.

Let us now prove the theorem. It is related to a general property of conjugate directions: if $\kappa_{\boldsymbol{u}}$ and $\kappa_{\boldsymbol{v}}$ denote the normal curvatures in conjugate directions $\boldsymbol{u}$

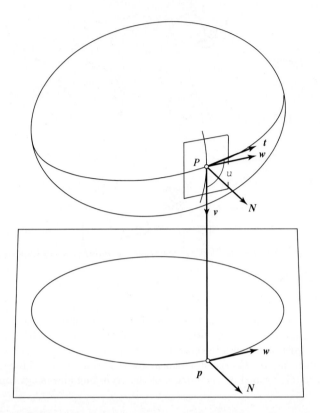

FIGURE 13.15: Occluding contour and image contour: the viewing direction v and the occluding contour tangent t are conjugate, and the radial curvature is always non-negative at a visible point of the contour for opaque solids.

and v, and K denotes the Gaussian curvature, then

$$K \sin^2 \theta = \kappa_u \kappa_v, \tag{13.4}$$

where θ is the angle between u and v. This relation is easy to prove by using the fact that the matrix associated with the second fundamental form is diagonal in the basis of the tangent plane formed by conjugate directions (see problems). It is obviously satisfied for principal directions ($\theta = \pi/2$) and asymptotic ones ($\theta = 0$).

In the context of Koenderink's theorem, we obtain

$$K \sin^2 \theta = \kappa_r \kappa_t,$$

where κ_t denotes the normal curvature of the surface along the occluding contour direction t (which is, of course, different from the actual curvature of the occluding contour). To complete the proof of the theorem, we use another general property of surfaces: the apparent curvature of any surface curve with tangent t is

$$\kappa_a = \frac{\kappa_t}{\cos^2 \alpha}, \tag{13.5}$$

where α denotes as before the angle between t and the image plane. As shown in the exercises, this property easily follows from Equation (13.3) and Meusnier's theorem.

In other words, the apparent curvature of any surface curve is obtained by dividing the associated normal curvature by the square of the cosine of the angle between its tangent and the image plane. Noting that κ_c is just the apparent curvature of the occluding contour now allows us to write

$$\kappa_c = \frac{\kappa_t}{\sin^2 \theta} \qquad (13.6)$$

because $\alpha = \theta - \pi/2$. Substituting Equation (13.6) into Equation (13.4) concludes the proof of the theorem.

13.3   VISUAL EVENTS: MORE DIFFERENTIAL GEOMETRY

Let us continue to assume orthographic projection, but consider this time a moving observer instead of a static one. Inflections, cusps, and T-junctions are stable features of the image contour that generally survive small eye movements: let us consider, for example, a contour inflection; as shown earlier in this chapter, it is the projection of a point where the occluding contour and a parabolic curve of the associated surface intersect (normally at a nonzero angle). Any small change in viewpoint deforms the occluding contour a bit, but the two curves still intersect transversally at a close-by point projecting onto a contour inflection.

It is natural to ask: what are the (peculiar) eye motions that make a stable contour feature appear or disappear? To answer this question, we take another look at the Gauss map and introduce the *asymptotic spherical map*, showing in the process that the boundaries of the images of a surface through these mappings determine the appearance and disappearance of inflections and cusps of its contour. This provides us with a characterization of *local visual events* (i.e., the changes in contour structure associated with the differential geometry of the surface at these boundaries). We also consider multiple contacts between visual rays and a surface. This leads us to the concept of *bitangent ray manifold*, and the characterization of its boundaries allows us to understand the genesis and annihilation of T-junctions and introduce the associated *multilocal visual events*. Together, the local and multilocal events capture the totality of the structural contour changes that determine the *aspect graph*, a data structure that records all qualitatively distinct appearances (different contour structures) an object may assume.

13.3.1   The Geometry of the Gauss Map

The Gauss map provides a natural setting for the study of the image contour and its inflections. Indeed, under orthographic projection, we saw in Section 13.2 that the occluding contour maps onto a great circle of the unit sphere, and that the intersections of this circle with the spherical image of the parabolic curves yield inflections of the contour. Therefore, it is clear that the contour gains (or loses) two inflections when a camera movement causes the corresponding great circle to cross the image of the parabolic curve (Figure 13.16).

A finer understanding of the creation of inflection pairs may be gained by

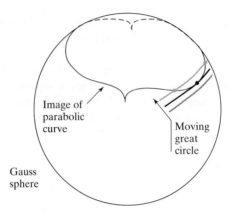

FIGURE 13.16: As the viewpoint changes, the great circle of the Gauss sphere associated with the (orthographic) occluding contour may become tangent to the spherical image of the parabolic curve. Afterward, the circle intersects this curve in two close-by points corresponding to two contour inflections.

taking a closer look at the geometry of the Gauss map. As shown in Section 13.1, the image of a surface on the Gauss sphere folds along the image of its parabolic curves. Figure 13.17 shows an example, with a single covering of the sphere on one side of the parabolic curve and a triple covering on the other side. The easiest way to think about the creation of such a fold is to grab (in your mind) a bit of the rubber skin of a deflated balloon, pinch it, and fold it over. As illustrated by the figure, this process generally introduces not only a fold of the spherical image, but two cusps as well (whose preimages are aptly named *cusps of Gauss* in differential geometry). Cusps and inflections of the image of the parabolic curve always come in pairs (two inflection pairs and one cusp pair here, but of course there may be no cusp or inflection at all). The inflections split the fold of the Gauss map into convex and concave parts, and their preimages are called *gutterpoints* (Figure 13.17).

What happens to the occluding contour as the associated great circle crosses the spherical image of the parabolic curve depends on *where* the crossing happens. As shown by Figure 13.17, there are several cases: When the crossing occurs along a convex fold of the Gauss map, an isolated point appears on the spherical image of the occluding contour before exploding into a small closed loop on the unit sphere (Figure 13.17, bottom right). In contrast, if the crossing occurs along a concave fold, two separate loops merge and then separate with a different connectivity (Figure 13.17, top right). These changes are, of course, reflected on the image contour in a way that is detailed in the next couple of sections.

The great circle associated with the occluding contour may also cross the image of the parabolic curve at a cusp. Unlike crossings that occur at regular fold points, this one is in general transversal and does not impose a tangency condition on the orientation of the great circle. There is no change in the topology of the intersection, but two inflections appear or disappear on the image contour. Finally, the great circle may cross the Gaussian image of a parabolic curve at one of its inflections. The change in topology in this case is too complicated to be described

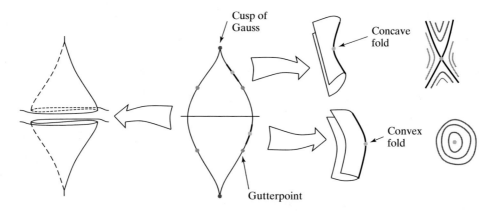

FIGURE 13.17: Folds and cusps of the Gauss map. The gutterpoints are the preimages of the inflections of the spherical image of the parabolic curve. To clarify the structure of the fold, it is drawn in the left and right sides of the figure as a surface folding in space. The changes in topology of the intersection between a great circle and the Gaussian image of the surface as the circle crosses the fold are illustrated in the far right portion of the figure. *Reprinted from "On Computing Structural Changes in Evolving Surfaces and their Appearance," by S. Pae and J. Ponce, International Journal of Computer Vision, 43(2):113–131, (2001). © 2001 Kluwer Academic Publishers.*

here. The good news is that there is only a finite number of viewpoints for which this situation can occur (since there is only a finite number of gutterpoints on a generic surface). In contrast, the other types of fold crossings occur for infinite one-parameter families of viewpoints: this is because the tangential crossings associated with convex or concave portions of the fold may occur anywhere along an extended curve arc drawn on the unit sphere, whereas the transversal crossings associated with cusps occur at isolated points, but for arbitrary orientations of the great circle. We identify the associated families of singular viewpoints in the next section.

13.3.2 Asymptotic Curves

We saw in Section 13.1 that ordinary hyperbolic points admit two distinct asymptotic tangents. More generally, the set of all asymptotic tangents on a hyperbolic patch can be divided neatly into two families such that each family admits a smooth field of integral curves, called *asymptotic curves*. Following Koenderink (1990), we give a color to each family and talk about the associated *red* and *blue* asymptotic curves. These curves cover only the hyperbolic part of a surface and must therefore be singular in the neighborhood of its parabolic boundary: indeed, a red asymptotic curve merges with a blue one at an ordinary parabolic point, forming a cusp and intersecting the parabolic curve at a nonzero angle (Figure 13.18a).[4]

Let us now study the behavior of the asymptotic curves under the Gauss map.

---

[4] The situation is different at cusps of Gauss, where the asymptotic curves meet the parabolic curve tangentially. This unusual behavior also occurs for planar parabolic curves of nongeneric objects (e.g., the two circular parabolic curves at the top and bottom of a torus lying on its side or, more generally, the parabolic lines of a solid of revolution that are associated with local extrema of the cross-section height along its axis).

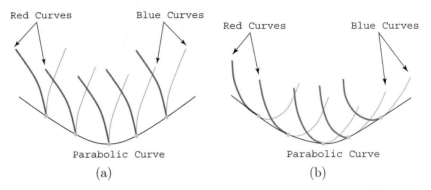

FIGURE 13.18: Contact of asymptotic and parabolic curves on (a) the surface, and (b) the Gauss sphere.

Remember from Section 13.1 that asymptotic directions are self-conjugate. This (literally) means that the derivative of the surface normal along an asymptotic curve is orthogonal to the tangent to this curve: the asymptotic curve and its spherical image have perpendicular tangents. On the other hand, all the directions of the tangent plane are conjugate to the asymptotic direction at a parabolic point, so the Gaussian image of *any* surface curve passing through a parabolic point is perpendicular to the corresponding asymptotic direction. In particular, the Gaussian image of a parabolic curve is the *envelope* of the images of the asymptotic curves intersecting it (i.e., it is tangent to these curves everywhere; see Figure 13.18b).

We can now characterize the viewpoints for which a pair of inflections appears (or disappears). Because the great circle associated with the occluding contour becomes tangent to the image of the parabolic curve on the Gauss sphere as they cross, the viewing direction normal to this great circle is along the corresponding asymptotic direction of the parabolic curve. A pair of inflections may of course also appear when the great circle crosses the image of a cusp of Gauss or, equivalently, when the line of sight crosses the tangent plane at such a point. As noted earlier, the topology of the image contour does not change in this case; it simply gains (or loses) an *undulation* (i.e., a small concave dent in one of its convex parts or a convex bump in one of its concave ones). The next section shows how the contour structure changes at the other types of singularities.

13.3.3 The Asymptotic Spherical Map

The Gauss map associates with every surface point the place where the tip of the corresponding normal pierces the unit sphere. We now define the *asymptotic spherical map*, which associates with every (hyperbolic) point the corresponding asymptotic directions. Let us make a few remarks before proceeding. First, there is really one asymptotic spherical image for each family of asymptotic curves, and the two images may or may not overlap on the sphere. Second, elliptic points obviously have no asymptotic spherical image at all, and the unit sphere may not be fully covered by the images of the hyperbolic points. However, it may also be fully covered, and, at least locally, it may be covered several times by members of

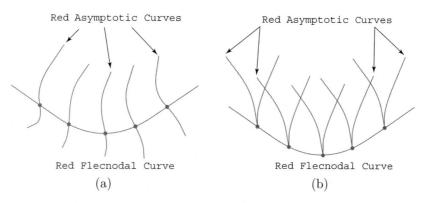

FIGURE 13.19: Contact of asymptotic and flecnodal curves on (a) the surface, and (b) the asymptotic spherical image.

a single family of asymptotic directions.

Because an image contour cusps when the line of sight is along an asymptotic direction, a cusp pair appears (or disappears) when the line of sight crosses a fold of the asymptotic spherical map (note the close analogy with contour inflections and folds of the Gauss map). As could be expected, the asymptotic spherical image of an asymptotic curve is singular at the fold boundary. There are again two possibilities (the image may join the boundary tangentially or cusp there), and they occur at two types of fold points: those associated with asymptotic directions along parabolic curves (because there is no asymptotic direction at all on their elliptic side), and those associated with asymptotic directions at *flecnodal points*. These points are inflections of the asymptotic curves' projections into their tangent plane (Figure 13.19a), and they form curves intersecting transversally the corresponding asymptotic curves. Like those, they come in two colors, depending on which asymptotic family has an inflection. The asymptotic spherical image of an asymptotic curve cusps at a flecnodal point (Figure 13.19b). It should also be noted that flecnodal curves intersect parabolic ones tangentially at cusps of Gauss.

It is clear that the contour structure changes when the line of sight crosses the parabolic or flecnodal boundaries of the asymptotic spherical image. Such a change is called a *visual event*, and the associated boundaries are called *visual event curves*. Before examining in more detail the various visual events, let us note a different but equivalent way of thinking of the associated boundaries. If we draw the singular asymptotic tangent line at each point along a parabolic or flecnodal surface, we obtain *ruled surfaces* swept by the tangents. A visual event occurs whenever the line of sight crosses one of these ruled surfaces, whose intersections with the sphere at infinity are exactly the visual event curves when this sphere is identified with the unit sphere. Thinking of contour evolution in terms of these ruled surfaces has the advantages of pointing toward a generalization of visual events to perspective projection (the view changes whenever the optical center crosses them) and allowing a clear visualization of the relationship between singular viewpoints and surface shape.

13.3.4   Local Visual Events

We are now in a position to understand how the contour structure changes at visual event boundaries. There are three *local* visual events that are completely characterized by the local differential surface geometry: *lip*, *beak-to-beak*, and *swallowtail*. Their colorful names are due to Thom (1972) and are related to the shape of the contour near the associated events.

Let us first examine the *lip* event, which occurs when the line of sight crosses the asymptotic spherical image of a convex parabolic point or, equivalently, the ruled surface defined by the associated asymptotic tangents (Figure 13.20, top). We have shown earlier that the intersection between the great circle associated with the occluding contour and the Gaussian image of the surface acquires a loop during the event (Figure 13.17, bottom right) with the creation of two inflections and two cusps on the contour. More precisely, there is no image contour before the event, with an isolated contour point appearing out of nowhere at the singularity before exploding into a closed contour loop consisting of a pair of branches meeting at two cusps (Figure 13.20, bottom). One of the branches is formed by the projection of both elliptic and hyperbolic points, with two inflections, whereas the other one is formed by the projection of hyperbolic points only. For opaque objects, one of the branches is always occluded by the object.

The *beak-to-beak* event occurs when the line of sight crosses the asymptotic spherical image of a concave parabolic point or, once again, the ruled surface defined by the associated asymptotic tangents (Figure 13.21, top). As shown earlier, the topology of the intersection between the great circle associated with the occluding contour and the Gaussian image of the surface changes during this event, with two loops merging and then splitting again with a different connectivity (Figure 13.17, top right). In the image, two distinct portions of the contour, each having a cusp and an inflection, meet at a point in the image. Before the event, each of the branches is divided by the associated cusp into a purely hyperbolic portion and a mixed elliptic-hyperbolic arc, one of which is always occluded. After the event, two contour cusps and two inflections disappear as the contour splits into two smooth arcs with a different connectivity. One of these is purely elliptic, whereas the other is purely hyperbolic, with one of the two always being occluded for opaque objects (Figure 13.21, bottom). The reverse transition is, of course, also possible, as for all other visual events.

Finally, the *swallowtail* event occurs when the eye crosses the surface ruled by the asymptotic tangents along a flecnodal curve of the same color. We know that two cusps appear (or disappear) in this event. As shown in Figure 13.22(a)–(b), the intersection of the surface and its tangent plane at a flecnodal point consists of two curves, one of which has an inflection. The corresponding asymptotic tangent is, of course, associated with the family of asymptotic curves having an inflection there, too. Unlike ordinary asymptotic rays (Figure 13.22c), which are blocked by the observed solid, this one grazes the solid's surface (Koenderink, 1990), causing a sharp V on the image contour at the singularity. The contour is smooth before the transition, but it acquires two cusps and a T-junction after it (Figure 13.22, bottom). All surface points involved in the event are hyperbolic. For opaque objects, one branch of the contour ends at the T-junction and the other one ends

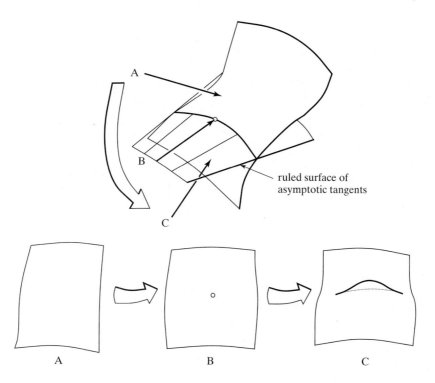

FIGURE 13.20: A lip event. The name is related to the shape of the contour on the right of the figure. Here, as in latter figures, the dashed part of the contour would be invisible due to occlusion for an opaque object. In this example, the two inflections are on the visible part of the contour, the hidden part being all hyperbolic, but the situation would be reversed by taking a viewpoint along the opposite direction. *Reprinted from "On Computing Structural Changes in Evolving Surfaces and their Appearance," by S. Pae and J. Ponce, International Journal of Computer Vision, 43(2):113–131, (2001). © 2001 Kluwer Academic Publishers.*

at a cusp.

13.3.5   The Bitangent Ray Manifold

Now remember from Section 13.1 that cusps and inflections are not the only kinds of stable contour features: T-junctions also occur over open sets of viewpoints. They form when two distinct pieces of the occluding contour project onto the same image location. The corresponding surface normals must be orthogonal to the *bitangent* line of sight joining the two points, but they are not (in general) parallel. That T-junctions are stable over small eye movements is intuitively clear: Consider a convex point P and its tangent plane (Figure 13.23, left). This plane intersects (in general) the surface along a closed (but possibly empty) curve, and there is an even number of points (P' and P'' in the figure) such that the rays drawn from P through these points are tangent to the curve. Each such tangency yields a bitangent ray and an associated T-junction. A small motion of the eye induces a small deformation of the intersection curve, but does not change (in general) the

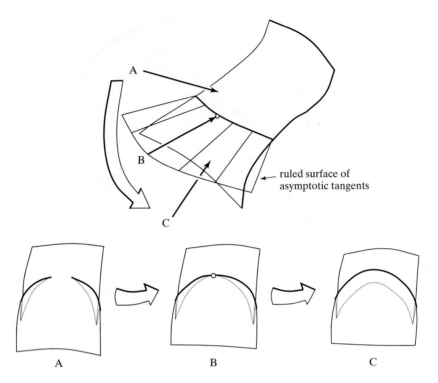

FIGURE 13.21: A beak-to-beak event (the name is related to the shape of the contour on the left of the figure). *Reprinted from "On Computing Structural Changes in Evolving Surfaces and their Appearance," by S. Pae and J. Ponce, International Journal of Computer Vision, 43(2):113–131, (2001). © 2001 Kluwer Academic Publishers.*

number of tangent points. Thus, T-junctions are indeed stable.

The bitangent rays form a two-dimensional *bitangent ray manifold*[5] in the four-dimensional space formed by all straight lines. Because bitangents map onto T-junctions in the projection process, it is clear that these contour features are created or destroyed at boundaries of the manifold. Because a T-junction appears or disappears during a swallowtail transition, it is also obvious that the singular asymptotic tangents along a flecnodal curve form one of these boundaries. What is not as clear is what the remaining boundaries are made of. This is the topic of the next section.

13.3.6   Multilocal Visual Events

A pair of T-junctions appear or disappear when the line of sight crosses the boundary of the bitangent ray manifold. The corresponding change in contour structure is called a *multilocal* visual event. This section shows that there are three types

---

[5]A manifold is a topological concept generalizing surfaces defined in Euclidean space to more abstract settings; its formal definition is omitted here. It is intuitively clear that the bitangent ray manifold is two-dimensional because there is a finite number of bitangent rays for each point of the (two-dimensional) surface being observed.

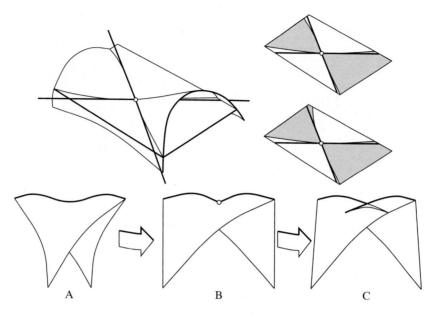

FIGURE 13.22: A swallowtail event. **Top:** Surface shape in the neighborhood of a flecnodal point (a), and comparison of the intersection of the associated solid and its tangent plane near such a point (b) and an ordinary hyperbolic point (c). **Bottom:** The event itself. *Reprinted from "On Computing Structural Changes in Evolving Surfaces and their Appearance," by S. Pae and J. Ponce, International Journal of Computer Vision, 43(2):113-131, (2001). © 2001 Kluwer Academic Publishers.*

of multilocal events—namely, the *tangent crossing, cusp crossing,* and *triple point,* besides the singularity associated with the crossing of a flecnodal curve that was mentioned in the previous section.

Let us first have a look at the *tangent crossing* event. An obvious boundary of the bitangent ray manifold is formed by the *limiting bitangents* (Figure 13.23, right), that occur when the curve formed by the intersection between the tangent plane at some point and the rest of the surface shrinks to a single point, and the plane becomes bitangent to the surface. The limiting bitangents sweep a ruled surface called the *limiting bitangent developable.* A tangent crossing occurs when the line of sight crosses this surface (Figure 13.24, top), with two separate pieces of contour becoming tangent to each other at the event before crossing transversally at two T-junctions (Figure 13.24, bottom). For opaque objects, either a previously hidden part of the contour becomes visible after the transition or, (as in the figure) another contour arc disappears due to occlusion.

The bitangent ray manifold is bounded by two more types of bitangents that touch the surface along a set of curves and sweep developable surfaces: the *asymptotic bitangents,* which intersect the surface along an asymptotic direction at one of their endpoints (Figure 13.25a), and the *tritangents,* which graze the surface in three distinct points (Figure 13.25b). The corresponding visual events occur when the line of sight crosses one of the associated developable surfaces, and they also

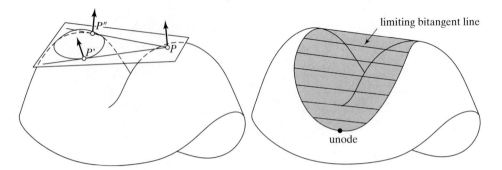

FIGURE 13.23: Bitangent rays. **Left:** The tangent plane to the surface in P intersects it along a closed curve with two bitangent rays PP' and PP'' grazing the surface along this curve. **Right:** The limiting bitangent developable surface ruled by the lines where a plane bitangent to a surface grazes it. Here the two curves where it touches the observed surface merge tangentially at a *unode*, a type of cusp of Gauss. *Reprinted from "Toward a Scale-Space Aspect Graph: Solids of Revolution," by S. Pae and J. Ponce, Proc. IEEE Conference on Computer Vision and Pattern Recognition, (1999). © 1999 IEEE.*

involve the appearance or disappearance of a pair of T-junctions: a *cusp crossing* occurs when a smooth piece of the image contour crosses another part of the contour at a cusp (or end point for an opaque object) of the latter (Figure 13.25c). Two T-junctions are created (or destroyed) in the process, only one of which is visible for opaque objects. A *triple point* is formed when three separate pieces of the contour momentarily join at nonzero angles (Figure 13.25d). For transparent objects, three T-junctions merge at the singularity before separating again. For opaque objects, a contour branch and two T-junctions disappear (or appear), while another T-junction appears (or disappears).

13.3.7 The Aspect Graph

Under orthographic projection, choosing a viewing direction determines the *aspect* of an object—that is, a graphical representation of its image contour, with nodes corresponding to T-junctions and cusps, and arcs to the smooth contour pieces between them. The range of possible viewpoints in this case is a *viewing sphere*, and it is partitioned by visual event boundaries into maximal cells where the aspect does not change. These cells, labeled by representative aspects, form the nodes of an *aspect graph*, with arcs attached to the visual event boundaries separating adjacent cells. The aspect graph was first introduced by Koenderink and Van Doorn (1976*b*, 1979) under the name of *visual potential*. Without entering into details that are outside the scope of this book, it is possible to determine the aspect graph of a solid bounded by a smooth polynomial surface by tracing the curves associated with visual events on this surface, and tracing the corresponding asymptotic directions and bitangents on the viewing sphere, thus revealing the corresponding cell structure.

Figure 13.26 (top) shows two line drawings of a squash-shaped solid whose surface is defined as the zero set of a polynomial density function. The two curves

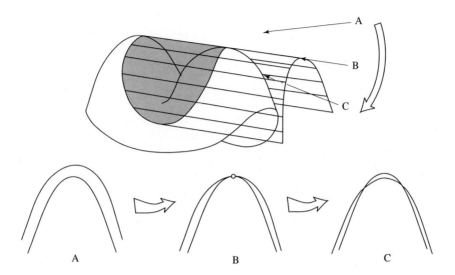

FIGURE 13.24: A tangent crossing event. The occlusion relationship between spatially distinct parts of the occluding contour changes when the viewpoint crosses the limiting bitangent developable surface in B. *Reprinted from "On Computing Structural Changes in Evolving Surfaces and their Appearance," by S. Pae and J. Ponce, International Journal of Computer Vision, 43(2):113–131, (2001). © 2001 Kluwer Academic Publishers.*

running roughly parallel to each other in Figure 13.26 (top left) are the parabolic curves of the squash, and they split its surface into two convex blobs separated by a saddle-shaped region. The self-intersecting curve also shown in the figure is the flecnodal curve. Figure 13.26 (top right) shows the limiting bitangent developable surface associated with the squash, whose rulings are the lines joining pairs of points on the squash surface that admit the same bitangent plane. The parabolic and flecnodal curves and the limiting bitangent developable have been found using curve tracing. There are no asymptotic bitangents or tritangents in this case. Figure 13.26 (bottom) shows the orthographic aspect graph of the opaque squash, computed using the cell-decomposition algorithm for algebraic surfaces of Petitjean, Ponce, and Kriegman (1992).

13.4 NOTES

As noted in the introduction, this chapter is dedicated to a mostly theoretical study of what can, or cannot be said of the world by visually observing it. In particular, we believe that the basic facts about image contours illustrated in Figures 13.2 and 13.3, and presented in Section 13.2 should be part of the common knowledge of all students of computer vision (the more advanced concepts related to visual events and presented in Section 13.3 are mostly intended for those with a deeper interest in geometry). Let us also note that the differential geometry of surfaces and their outlines has practical applications: for example, it plays a key part in recent algorithms for computing the *visual hull* of a solid bounded by a smooth surface (Lazebnik, Boyer, & Ponce 2001; Lazebnik, Furukawa, & Ponce 2007). We

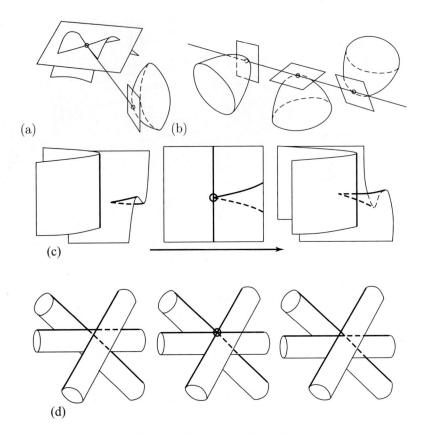

FIGURE 13.25: Multilocal events: (a) an asymptotic bitangent ray, (b) a tritangent ray, (c) a cusp crossing, and (d) a triple point. After Petitjean *et al.* (1992, Figure 6).

will come back to visual hulls in Chapter 19.

There are many excellent textbooks on differential geometry, including the accessible presentations found in do Carmo (1976) and Struik (1988). Our presentation is closer in spirit (if not in elegance) to the descriptive introduction to differential geometry found in Hilbert and Cohn-Vossen's (1952) wonderful book Geometry and the Imagination.

The theorem linking the local shape of a solid to that of its contour and proved in this chapter first appeared in Koenderink (1984). Our proof is different from the original one, but it is close in spirit to the proof given by Koenderink (1990) in his book Solid Shape (which, like Hilbert and Cohn-Vossen's book, should be required reading for anybody seriously interested in the geometric aspects of computer vision). Our choice here was motivated by our reluctance to use any formulas that require setting a particular coordinate system. Alternate proofs for various kinds of projection geometries can be found in Brady *et al.* (1985), Arbogast and Mohr (1991), Cipolla and Blake (1992), Vaillant and Faugeras (1992), and Boyer (1996).

The material of Section 13.3 is largely based on the work of Koenderink and

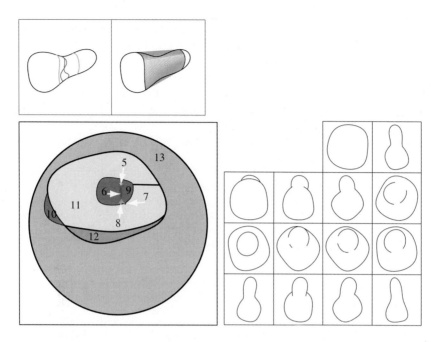

FIGURE 13.26: **Top:** A squash-shaped solid with the corresponding parabolic and flec-nodal curves (**left**) and limiting bitangent developable (**right**). **Bottom:** Its (opaque) orthographic aspect graph with (**left**) the view sphere cells and (**right**) the corresponding aspects. Note that only 9 of the 14 cells are visible on the hemisphere shown here, and that some of these (e.g., region 7) are quite small.

Van Doorn, including the seminal papers that introduced the idea of an aspect graph, albeit under a different name (Koenderink and Van Doorn 1976*b*, 1979), the article that presents in a very accessible manner the geometric foundations of this shape representation (Koenderink 1986), and, of course, the somewhat more demanding (but so rewarding for the patient student) book by Koenderink (1990). See also Platonova (1981), Kergosien (1981), and Callahan and Weiss (1985). Singularity and catastrophe theories are discussed in many books, including Whitney (1955), Arnol'd (1984), and Demazure (1989). See also Koenderink (1990) for a discussion of why chairs wobble and Thom (1972) for an in-depth discussion of this argument.

An algorithm for computing the aspect graph of a solid bounded by an algebraic surface can be found in Petitjean *et al.* (1992). It heavily relies on the ability to solve systems of polynomial equations, and in particular on the numerical *homotopy continuation* method proposed by Morgan (1987) for finding all the roots of a square system of multivariate polynomial equations. Symbolic methods such as multivariate resultants (Macaulay 1916; Collins 1971; Canny 1988; Manocha 1992) and cylindrical algebraic decomposition (Collins 1975; Arnon *et al.* 1984) are also available, and they have been used by Rieger (1987, 1990, 1992) in a different algorithm for constructing the aspect graph of an algebraic surface. It is probably fair to say that real-life applications of aspect graphs have been limited, to say the least. Yet, approximate aspect graphs of polyhedra have been successfully used in object localization tasks (Ikeuchi 1987; Ikeuchi and Kanade 1988). Variants include Chakravarty (1982) and Hebert and Kanade (1985).

PROBLEMS

13.1. What is (in general) the shape of the silhouette of a sphere observed by a perspective camera?

13.2. What is (in general) the shape of the silhouette of a sphere observed by an orthographic camera?

13.3. Prove that the curvature κ of a planar curve in a point P is the inverse of the radius of curvature r at this point.
Hint: Use the fact that $\sin u \approx u$ for small angles.

13.4. Given a fixed coordinate system, let us identify points of $\mathbb{E}^3$ with their coordinate vectors and consider a parametric curve $\boldsymbol{x} : I \subset \mathbb{R} \to \mathbb{R}^3$ not necessarily parameterized by arc length. Show that its curvature is given by

$$\kappa = \frac{||\boldsymbol{x}' \times \boldsymbol{x}''||}{||\boldsymbol{x}'||^3}, \tag{13.7}$$

where $\boldsymbol{x}'$ and $\boldsymbol{x}''$ denote, respectively, the first and second derivatives of $\boldsymbol{x}$ with respect to the parameter t defining it.
Hint: Reparameterize $\boldsymbol{x}$ by its arc length, and reflect the change of parameters in the differentiation.

13.5. Prove that, unless the normal curvature is constant over all possible directions, the principal directions are orthogonal to each other.

13.6. Let us denote by α the angle between the plane Π and the tangent to a curve Γ and by β the angle between the normal to Π and the binormal to Γ, and by κ the curvature at some point on Γ (Figure 13.13). Prove that if κ_a denotes the apparent curvature of the image of Γ at the corresponding point, then

$$\kappa_a = \kappa \frac{\cos \beta}{\cos^3 \alpha}.$$

(Note: This result can be found in Koenderink [1990, p. 191].)
Hint: Use the fact that $\boldsymbol{t} \times \boldsymbol{n} = \boldsymbol{b}$, and write the coordinates of the vectors $\boldsymbol{t}$, $\boldsymbol{n}$, and $\boldsymbol{b}$ in a coordinate system whose z-axis is orthogonal to the image plane, and use Equation (13.7) to compute κ_a.

13.7. Let $\kappa_{\boldsymbol{u}}$ and $\kappa_{\boldsymbol{v}}$ denote the normal curvatures in conjugate directions $\boldsymbol{u}$ and $\boldsymbol{v}$ at a point P, and let K denote the Gaussian curvature; prove that

$$K \sin^2 \theta = \kappa_{\boldsymbol{u}} \kappa_{\boldsymbol{v}},$$

where θ is the angle between the $\boldsymbol{u}$ and $\boldsymbol{v}$.
Hint: Relate the expressions obtained for the second fundamental form in the bases of the tangent plane respectively formed by the conjugate directions and the principal directions.

13.8. Show that the occluding contour is a smooth curve that does not intersect itself.
Hint: Use the Gauss map.

13.9. Show that the apparent curvature of any surface curve with tangent t is

$$\kappa_a = \frac{\kappa_t}{\cos^2 \alpha},$$

where α is the angle between the image plane and t.

Hint: Write the coordinates of the vectors t, n, and b in a coordinate system whose z-axis is orthogonal to the image plane, and use Equation (13.3) and Meusnier's theorem.

13.10. Is it possible for an object with a single parabolic curve (such as a banana) to have no cusp of Gauss at all? Why (or why not)?

13.11. Use an equation-counting argument to justify the fact that contact of order six or greater between lines and surfaces does not occur for generic surfaces.

Hint: Count the parameters that define contact.

13.12. We saw that an asymptotic curve and its spherical image have perpendicular tangents. Lines of curvature are the integral curves of the field of principal directions. Show that these curves and their Gaussian image have parallel tangents.

13.13. Use the fact that the Gaussian image of a parabolic curve is the envelope of the asymptotic curves intersecting it to give an alternate proof that a pair of cusps is created (or destroyed) in a lip or beak-to-beak event.

13.14. Draw the aspect graph of a torus and the corresponding visual events.

Hint: The parabolic curves of a torus are the two circles at its top and bottom when it lies on its side. The flecnodal lines are two parallel circles in the central hyperbolic part of the surface.

C H A P T E R   14

Range Data

This chapter discusses *range images* (or *depth maps*) that store, instead of brightness or color information, the depth at which the ray associated with each pixel first intersects the scene observed by a camera. In a sense, a range image is exactly the desired output of stereo, motion, or other shape-from vision modules. In this chapter, however, we will focus our attention on range images acquired by *active sensors* that project some sort of light pattern on the scene, using it to avoid the difficult and costly problem of establishing correspondences and construct dense and accurate depth pictures. After a brief review of range-sensing technology, this chapter will discuss image segmentation, multiple-image registration, three-dimensional model construction, and object recognition, focusing on the aspects of these problems that are specific to the range data domain. It will conclude with a presentation of the pose estimation algorithm behind Kinect, the technology for controlling video games with natural body motions introduced by Microsoft in 2010.

14.1 ACTIVE RANGE SENSORS

Triangulation-based range finders date back to the early seventies (Agin 1972; Shirai 1972). They function along the same principles as passive stereo vision systems, with one of the cameras being replaced by a source of controlled illumination (*structured light*) that avoids the correspondence problem mentioned in Chapter 7. For example, a laser and a pair of rotating mirrors may be used to sequentially scan a surface. In this case, as in conventional stereo, the position of the bright spot where the laser beam strikes the surface of interest is found as the intersection of the beam with the projection ray joining the spot to its image. Contrary to the stereo case, however, the laser spot normally can be identified without difficulty because it is in general much brighter than the other scene points (especially when a filter tuned to the laser wavelength is placed in front of the camera), altogether avoiding the correspondence problem. Alternatively, the laser beam can be transformed by a cylindrical lens into a plane of light (Figure 14.1). This simplifies the mechanical design of the range finder because it requires only one rotating mirror. More importantly, perhaps, it shortens the time required to acquire a range image because a laser stripe—the equivalent of a whole image column—can be acquired at each frame. It should be noted that this setup does not introduce matching ambiguities since the laser spot associated with an image pixel can be retrieved as the (unique) intersection of the corresponding projection ray with the plane of light.

Variants of these two techniques include using multiple cameras to improve measurement accuracy and exploiting (possibly time-coded) two-dimensional light patterns to improve data acquisition speed. The main drawbacks of the active triangulation technology are a relatively low acquisition speed, missing data at points where the laser spot is hidden from the camera by the object itself, and missing or erroneous data due to specularities. The latter difficulty is actually common to

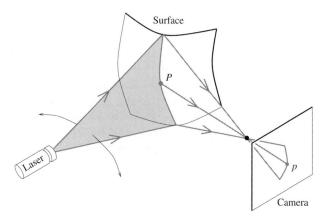

FIGURE 14.1: A range sensor using a plane of light to scan the surface of an object.

all active ranging techniques: a purely specular surface will not reflect any light in the direction of the camera unless it happens to lie in the corresponding mirror direction. Worse, the reflected beam may induce secondary reflections, giving false depth measurements. Additional difficulties include keeping the laser stripe in focus during the entire scanning procedure, and the loss of accuracy inherent in all triangulation techniques as depth increases (see the problems in Chapter 7; intuitively this is due to the fact that depth is inversely proportional to disparity). Several triangulation-based scanners are commercially available today. Figure 14.2 shows an example obtained using the Minolta VIVID range finder, which can acquire a 200×200 range image together with a registered 400×400 color image in 0.6s, within an operating range of 0.6 to 2.5m.

FIGURE 14.2: Range data captured by the Minolta VIVID scanner. As in several other figures in this chapter, the range image is displayed as a shaded mesh of $(x, y, z(x, y))$ points viewed in perspective. *Courtesy of D. Huber and M. Hebert.*

The second main approach to active ranging involves a signal transmitter, a receiver, and electronics for measuring the time of flight of the signal during its round trip from the range sensor to the surface of interest. Time-of-flight range finders are normally equipped with a scanning mechanism, and the transmitter and receiver are often coaxial, eliminating the problem of missing data common in triangulation approaches. There are three main classes of time-of-flight laser range sensors: *pulse time delay* technology directly measures the time of flight of a laser pulse; *AM phase-shift* range finders measure the phase difference between the beam emitted by an amplitude-modulated laser and the reflected beam, a quantity proportional to the time of flight; and finally, *FM beat* sensors measure the frequency shift (or *beat frequency*) between a frequency-modulated laser beam and its reflection, another quantity proportional to the round-trip flight time. Compared to triangulation-based systems, time-of-flight sensors have the advantage of offering a greater operating range (up to tens of meters), which is very valuable in outdoor robotic navigation tasks.

New technologies continue to emerge, including range sensors equipped with acoustico-optical scanning systems and capable of extremely high image acquisition rates, and range cameras that eliminate scanning altogether, using instead a large array of receivers to analyze a laser pulse covering the entire field of view. Two-dimensional light patterns are also making a very successful comeback with the emergence of the cheap, real-time Kinect sensor developed by Primesense, for example (Section 14.5).

14.2   RANGE DATA SEGMENTATION

This section adapts some of the edge detection and segmentation methods introduced in Chapters 5 and 9 to the specific case of range images. As will be shown in the rest of this section, the fact that surface geometry is readily available greatly simplifies the segmentation process, mainly because this provides objective, physically meaningful criteria for finding surface discontinuities and merging contiguous patches with a similar shape. But let us start by introducing some elementary notions of *analytical* differential geometry, which will turn out to form the basis for the approach to edge detection in range images discussed in this section.

14.2.1   Elements of Analytical Differential Geometry

Here we revisit the notions of differential geometry introduced in Chapter 13 in an analytical setting. Specifically, we will assume that $\mathbb{E}^3$ has been equipped with a fixed coordinate system and identify this space with $\mathbb{R}^3$ and each point with its coordinate vector, and consider a *parametric surface* defined as the smooth (i.e., indefinitely differentiable) mapping $\boldsymbol{x} : U \subset \mathbb{R}^2 \to \mathbb{R}^3$ that associates with any couple (u, v) in the open subset U of $\mathbb{R}^2$ the point $\boldsymbol{x}(u, v)$ in $\mathbb{R}^3$. To ensure that the tangent plane is well defined everywhere, we will assume that the partial derivatives $\boldsymbol{x}_u \overset{\text{def}}{=} \partial \boldsymbol{x}/\partial u$ and $\boldsymbol{x}_v \overset{\text{def}}{=} \partial \boldsymbol{x}/\partial v$ are linearly independent. Indeed, let $\boldsymbol{\alpha} : I \subset \mathbb{R} \to U$ denote a smooth planar curve, with $\boldsymbol{\alpha}(t) = (u(t), v(t))$, then $\boldsymbol{\beta} \overset{\text{def}}{=} \boldsymbol{x} \circ \boldsymbol{\alpha}$ is a parameterized space curve lying on the surface. According to the chain rule, a tangent vector to $\boldsymbol{\beta}$ at the point $\boldsymbol{\beta}(t)$ is $u'(t)\boldsymbol{x}_u + v'(t)\boldsymbol{x}_v$, and it follows that the plane tangent to the surface in $\boldsymbol{x}(u, v)$ is parallel to the vector plane spanned by the vectors $\boldsymbol{x}_u$ and $\boldsymbol{x}_v$. The (unit) surface normal is thus

$$\boldsymbol{N} = \frac{1}{||\boldsymbol{x}_u \times \boldsymbol{x}_v||}(\boldsymbol{x}_u \times \boldsymbol{x}_v).$$

Let us consider a vector $t = u' x_u + v' x_v$ in the tangent plane at the point x. It is easy to show that the second fundamental form is given by[1]

$$II(t, t) = t \cdot dN(t) = eu'^2 + 2fu'v' + gv'^2, \quad \text{where} \quad \begin{cases} e = -N \cdot x_{uu}, \\ f = -N \cdot x_{uv}, \\ g = -N \cdot x_{vv}. \end{cases}$$

Note that the vector t does not (in general) have unit norm. Let us define the *first fundamental form* as the bilinear form that associates with two vectors in the tangent plane their dot product, i.e., $I(u, v) \overset{\text{def}}{=} u \cdot v$. We can write

$$I(t, t) = ||t||^2 = Eu'^2 + 2Du'v' + Gv'^2, \quad \text{where} \quad \begin{cases} E = x_u \cdot x_u, \\ F = x_u \cdot x_v, \\ G = x_v \cdot x_v, \end{cases}$$

and it follows immediately that the normal curvature in the direction t is given by

$$\kappa_t = \frac{II(t, t)}{I(t, t)} = \frac{eu'^2 + 2fu'v' + gv'^2}{Eu'^2 + 2Du'v' + Gv'^2}.$$

Likewise, it is easily shown that the matrix associated with the differential of the Gauss map *in the basis* (x_u, x_v) of the tangent plane is

$$dN(t) = \begin{pmatrix} e & f \\ f & g \end{pmatrix} \begin{pmatrix} E & F \\ F & G \end{pmatrix}^{-1};$$

thus, since the Gaussian curvature is equal to the determinant of the operator dN, it is given by

$$K = \frac{eg - f^2}{EG - F^2}.$$

Asymptotic and principal directions are also easily found by using this parameterization: since an asymptotic direction verifies $II(t, t) = 0$, the corresponding values of u' and v' are the (homogeneous) solutions of $eu'^2 + 2fu'v' + gv'^2 = 0$. The principal directions, on the other hand, can be shown to verify

$$\begin{vmatrix} v'^2 & -u'v' & u'^2 \\ E & F & G \\ e & f & g \end{vmatrix} = 0. \tag{14.1}$$

Example 1. An important example of parametric surface is provided by *Monge patches*: consider the surface $x(u, v) = (u, v, h(u, v))$. In this case we have

$$\begin{cases} N = \dfrac{1}{(1 + h_u^2 + h_v^2)^{1/2}}(-h_u, -h_v, 1)^T, \\ E = 1 + h_u^2, F = h_u h_v, G = 1 + h_v^2, \\ e = -\dfrac{h_{uu}}{(1 + h_u^2 + h_v^2)^{1/2}}, f = -\dfrac{h_{uv}}{(1 + h_u^2 + h_v^2)^{1/2}}, g = -\dfrac{h_{vv}}{(1 + h_u^2 + h_v^2)^{1/2}}, \end{cases}$$

---

[1]This definition is in keeping with the orientation conventions defined in Chapter 13. The coefficients e, f, g are often defined with opposite signs (do Carmo 1976; Struik 1988).

and the Gaussian curvature has a simple form:

$$K = \frac{h_{uu}h_{vv} - h_{uv}^2}{(1 + h_u^2 + h_v^2)^2}.$$

Example 2. Another fundamental example is provided by the local parameterization of a surface in the coordinate system formed by its principal directions. This is of course a special case of a Monge patch. Writing that the origin of the coordinate system lies in the tangent plane immediately yields $h(0,0) = h_u(0,0) = h_v(0,0) = 0$. As expected, the normal is simply $\boldsymbol{N} = (0,0,1)^T$ at the origin, and the first fundamental form is the identity there. As shown in the problems, it follows easily from (14.1) that a necessary and sufficient condition for the coordinate curves of a parameterized surface to be principal directions is that $f = F = 0$ (this implies, for example, that the lines of curvature of a surface of revolution are its meridians and parallels). In our context we already know that $F = 0$ and this condition reduces to $h_{uv}(0,0) = 0$. The principal curvatures in this case are simply $\kappa_1 = e/E = -h_{uu}(0,0)$ and $\kappa_2 = g/G = -h_{vv}(0,0)$. In particular, we can write a Taylor expansion of the height function in the neighborhood of $(0,0)$ as

$$h(u,v) = h(0,0) + (u,v)\begin{pmatrix} h_u \\ h_v \end{pmatrix} + \frac{1}{2}(u,v)\begin{pmatrix} h_{uu} & h_{uv} \\ h_{uv} & h_{vv} \end{pmatrix}\begin{pmatrix} u \\ v \end{pmatrix} + \varepsilon(u^2 + v^2)^{3/2},$$

where the argument $(0,0)$ for the derivatives of h has been omitted for conciseness. This shows that the best second-order approximation to the surface in this neighborhood is the paraboloid defined by

$$h(u,v) = -\frac{1}{2}(\kappa_1 u^2 + \kappa_2 v^2),$$

i.e., the expression already encountered in Chapter 13.

14.2.2 Finding Step and Roof Edges in Range Images

This section presents a method for finding various types of edges in range images (Ponce and Brady 1987). This technique combines tools from analytical differential geometry and scale-space image analysis to detect and locate depth and orientation discontinuities in range data. Figure 14.3 shows a range image of a bottle of motor oil that will serve to illustrate the concepts introduced in this section.

The surface of the oil bottle can be modeled as a parametric surface $z(x,y)$ in the coordinate system attached to the sensor, and it presents two types of discontinuities: *steps*, where the actual depth is discontinuous, and *roofs*, where the depth is continuous but the orientation changes abruptly. As shown in the next section, it is possible to characterize the behavior of analytical models of step and roof edges under Gaussian smoothing and to show that they respectively give rise to parabolic points and extrema of the dominant principal curvature in the corresponding principal direction. This is the basis for the multi-scale edge detection scheme outlined in Algorithm 14.1.

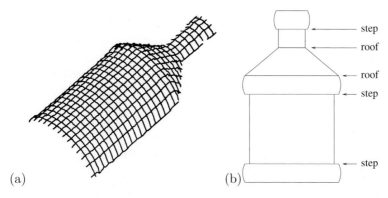

(a)   (b)

FIGURE 14.3: An oil bottle: (a) a range image of the bottle (the background has been thresholded away) and (b) a sketch of its depth and orientation discontinuities. This 128×128 picture was acquired using the INRIA range finder (Boissonnat and Germain 1981), with a depth accuracy of about 0.5mm.

---

1. Smooth the range image with Gaussian distributions at a set of scales σ_i ($i = 1, \ldots, 4$). Compute the principal directions and curvatures at each point of the smoothed images $z_{\sigma_i}(x, y)$.

2. Mark in each smoothed image $z_{\sigma_i}(x, y)$ the zero-crossings of the Gaussian curvature and the extrema of the dominant principal curvature in the corresponding principal direction.

3. Use the analytical step and roof models to match the features found across scales and output the points lying on these surface discontinuities.

Algorithm 14.1:   The Model-Based Edge-Detection Algorithm of Ponce and Brady (1987).

Edge models.   In the neighborhood of a discontinuity, the shape of a surface changes much faster in the direction of the discontinuity than in the orthogonal direction. Accordingly, we will assume in the rest of this section that the direction of the discontinuity is one of the principal directions, with the corresponding (dominant) principal curvature changing rapidly in this direction, while the other one remains roughly equal to zero. This will allow us to limit our attention to *cylindrical* models of surface discontinuities, i.e., models of the form $z(x, y) = h(x)$. These models are of course only intended to be valid in the neighborhood of an edge, with the direction of the $x - z$ plane being aligned with the corresponding dominant principal direction.

In particular, a step edge can be modeled by two sloped half-planes separated by a vertical gap, with normals in the $x - z$ plane. This model is cylindrical, and it is sufficient to study its univariate formulation (Figure 14.4, left), whose equation is

$$z = \begin{cases} k_1 x + c & \text{when} \quad x < 0, \\ k_2 x + c + h & \text{when} \quad x > 0. \end{cases} \tag{14.2}$$

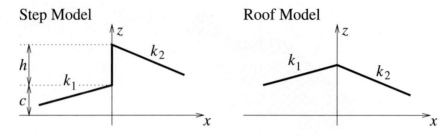

FIGURE 14.4: Edge models: a step consists of two half-planes separated by a distance h at the origin, and a roof consists of two half-planes meeting at the origin with different slopes.

In this expression, c and h are constants, with h measuring the size of the gap and k_1 and k_2 the slopes of the two half-planes. Introducing the new constants $k = (k_1 + k_2)/2$ and $\delta = k_2 - k_1$, it is easy to show (see problems) that convolving the z function with the second derivative of a Gaussian yields

$$z''_\sigma \stackrel{\text{def}}{=} \frac{\partial^2}{\partial \sigma^2} G_\sigma * z = \frac{1}{\sigma\sqrt{2\pi}} (\delta - \frac{hx}{\sigma^2}) \exp(-\frac{x^2}{2\sigma^2}). \tag{14.3}$$

As shown in the problems of Chapter 13, the curvature of a twisted parametric curve is $\kappa = ||\boldsymbol{x}' \times \boldsymbol{x}''||/||\boldsymbol{x}'||^3$. In the case of plane curves, the curvature can be given a meaningful sign, and this formula becomes $\kappa = (\boldsymbol{x}' \times \boldsymbol{x}'')/||\boldsymbol{x}'||^3$, where "$\times$" this time denotes the operator associating with two vectors in $\mathbb{R}^2$ the determinant of their coordinates. It follows that the corresponding curvature κ_σ vanishes in $x_\sigma = \sigma^2 \delta/h$. This point is at the origin only when $k_1 = k_2$, and its position is a quadratic function of σ otherwise. This suggests identifying step edges with zero-crossings of one of the principal curvatures (or equivalently of the Gaussian curvature), whose position changes with scale. To characterize qualitatively the behavior of these features as a function of σ, let us also note that because $z''_\sigma = 0$ in x_σ, we have

$$\frac{\kappa''_\sigma}{\kappa'_\sigma}(x_\sigma) = \frac{z''''_\sigma}{z''_\sigma}(x_\sigma) = -2\frac{\delta}{\sigma};$$

in other words, the ratio of the second and first derivatives of the curvature is independent of σ.

An analytical model for roof edges is obtained by taking $h = 0$ and $\delta \neq 0$ in the step model (Figure 14.4, right). In this case, it is easy to show (see problems) that

$$\kappa_\sigma = \frac{1}{\sigma\sqrt{2\pi}} \frac{\delta \exp(-\frac{x^2}{2\sigma^2})}{\left[1 + \left(k + \frac{\delta}{\sqrt{2\pi}} \int_0^{x/\sigma} \exp(-\frac{u^2}{2})du\right)^2\right]^{3/2}}. \tag{14.4}$$

It follows that, when $x_2 = \lambda x_1$ and $\sigma_2 = \lambda \sigma_1$, we must have $\kappa_{\sigma_2}(x_2) = \kappa_{\sigma_1}(x_1)/\lambda$. In turn, the maximum value of $|\kappa_\sigma|$ must be inversely proportional to

σ, and it is reached at a point whose distance from the origin is proportional to σ. This maximum tends toward infinity as σ tends toward zero, indicating that roofs can be found as local curvature extrema. In actual range images, these extrema should be sought in the direction of the dominant principal direction, in keeping with our assumptions about local shape changes in the vicinity of surface edges.

Computing the principal curvatures and directions. According to the models derived in the previous section, instances of step and roof edges can be found as zero crossings of the Gaussian curvature and extrema of the dominant principal curvature in the corresponding direction. Computing these differential quantities requires estimating the first and second partial derivatives of the depth function at each point of a range image. This can be done, as in Chapter 5, by convolving the images with the derivatives of a Gaussian distribution. However, range images are different from usual pictures. For example, the pixel values in a photograph are usually assumed to be piecewise constant in the neighborhood of step edges,[2] which is justified for Lambertian objects because the shape of a surface is, to first order, piecewise-constant near an edge, with a piecewise-planar intensity in that case. On the other hand, piecewise-constant (local) models of range images are of course unsatisfactory. Likewise, the maximum values of contrast along the significant edges of a photograph usually are assumed to have roughly the same magnitude. In range images, however, there are two different types of step edges: the large depth discontinuities that separate solid objects from each other and from their background, and the much smaller gaps that usually separate patches of the same surface. The edge detection scheme discussed in this section is aimed at the latter class of discontinuities. Blindly applying Gaussian smoothing across object boundaries will introduce radical shape changes that might overwhelm the surface details we are interested in (Figure 14.5, left and middle).

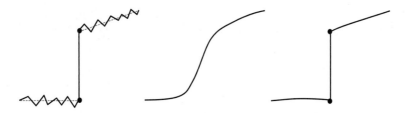

FIGURE 14.5: A schematic illustration of range data smoothing. **Left:** noisy range data near a (large) depth discontinuity. **Middle:** result of Gaussian smoothing. **Right:** smoothing using computational molecules removes the noise but preserves the essential shape features.

This suggests finding the major depth discontinuities first (thresholding will suffice in many cases), then somehow restricting the smoothing process to the surface patches enclosed by these boundaries. This can be achieved by convolving the range image with *computational molecules* (Terzopoulos 1984), i.e., linear templates

---

[2]This corresponds to taking $k_1 = k_2 = 0$ in the model given in the previous section; note that in that case, zero crossings do not move as scale changes.

that, added together, form a 3×3 averaging mask, e.g.,

$$
\begin{array}{|c|c|c|}
\hline
1 & & \\
\hline
& 2 & \\
\hline
& & 1 \\
\hline
\end{array}
+
\begin{array}{|c|c|c|}
\hline
2 & 4 & 2 \\
\hline
\end{array}
+
\begin{array}{|c|}
\hline
2 \\
\hline
4 \\
\hline
2 \\
\hline
\end{array}
+
\begin{array}{|c|c|c|}
\hline
& & 1 \\
\hline
& 2 & \\
\hline
1 & & \\
\hline
\end{array}
=
\begin{array}{|c|c|c|}
\hline
1 & 2 & 1 \\
\hline
2 & 12 & 2 \\
\hline
1 & 2 & 1 \\
\hline
\end{array}.
$$

Repeatedly convolving the image with the 3×3 mask (normalized so its weights add to one) yields, according to the central limit theorem, a very good approximation of Gaussian smoothing with a mask whose σ value is proportional to $\sqrt{n}$ after n iterations. To avoid smoothing across discontinuities, the molecules crossing these discontinuities are not used, while the remaining ones are once again normalized so the total sum of the weights is equal to one. The (idealized) effect is shown in Figure 14.5 (right).

After the surface has been smoothed, the derivatives of the height function can be computed via finite differences. The gradient of the height function is computed by convolving the smoothed image with the masks:

$$
\frac{\partial}{\partial x} = \frac{1}{6}
\begin{array}{|c|c|c|}
\hline
-1 & 0 & 1 \\
\hline
-1 & 0 & 1 \\
\hline
-1 & 0 & 1 \\
\hline
\end{array}
\quad \text{and} \quad
\frac{\partial}{\partial y} = \frac{1}{6}
\begin{array}{|c|c|c|}
\hline
1 & 1 & 1 \\
\hline
0 & 0 & 0 \\
\hline
-1 & -1 & -1 \\
\hline
\end{array},
$$

and the Hessian is computed by convolving the smoothed image with the masks

$$
\frac{\partial^2}{\partial x^2} = \frac{1}{3}
\begin{array}{|c|c|c|}
\hline
1 & -2 & 1 \\
\hline
1 & -2 & 1 \\
\hline
1 & -2 & 1 \\
\hline
\end{array},
\quad
\frac{\partial^2}{\partial x \partial y} = \frac{1}{4}
\begin{array}{|c|c|c|}
\hline
-1 & 0 & 1 \\
\hline
0 & 0 & 0 \\
\hline
1 & 0 & -1 \\
\hline
\end{array},
\quad \text{and} \quad
\frac{\partial^2}{\partial y^2} = \frac{1}{3}
\begin{array}{|c|c|c|}
\hline
1 & 1 & 1 \\
\hline
-2 & -2 & -2 \\
\hline
1 & 1 & 1 \\
\hline
\end{array}.
$$

Once the derivatives are known, the principal directions and curvatures are easily computed. In practice, using this method with 20 to 80 iterations of computational molecule smoothing gives satisfactory results for moderately noisy range images. For example, using 20 iterations on the oil bottle yields principal directions which are, as expected, aligned with the meridians and parallels of this surface of revolution.

Matching features across scales.   Given the principal curvatures and directions, parabolic points can be detected as (non-directional) zero-crossings of the Gaussian curvature, whereas local extrema of the dominant curvature along the corresponding principal direction can be found using the non-maximum suppression techniques discussed in Chapter 5. Although there may be a considerable amount of noise at fine resolutions (i.e., after a few iterations only), the situation improves as smoothing proceeds. Features due to noise can also be eliminated, at least in part, via thresholding of the zero-crossing slope for parabolic points, and of the curvature magnitude for extrema of principal curvatures. Nonetheless, experiments show that smoothing and thresholding are not sufficient to eliminate all irrelevant features. In particular, as illustrated by Figure 14.6 (left), curvature extrema parallel to the axis of the oil bottle show up more and more clearly as smoothing proceeds. These are due to the fact that points near the occluding boundary of the bottle do not get smoothed as much by the computational molecules as points closer to its center.

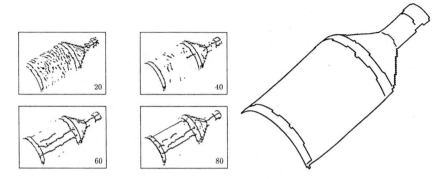

FIGURE 14.6: Finding step and roof edges on the oil bottle. **Left:** The features found after 20, 40, 60, and 80 smoothing iterations and thresholding. The thresholds have been chosen empirically to eliminate most false features while retaining those corresponding to true surface discontinuities. Still, artifacts such as the extrema of curvature parallel to the axis of the bottle subsist. **Right:** the output of model-based edge detection. The three step edges and two roof discontinuities of the oil bottle have been correctly identified. *Reprinted from "Towards a Surface Primal Sketch," by J. Ponce and J.M. Brady, in THREE-DIMENSIONAL MACHINE VISION, T. Kanade (ed.), pp. 195–240, Kluwer Academic Publishers, (1987). ©1987 Kluwer Academic Publishers.*

A multi-scale approach to edge detection solves this problem. Features are tracked from coarse to fine scales, with all features at a given scale not having an ancestor at a coarser one being eliminated. The evolution of the principal curvatures and their derivatives is also monitored. Surviving parabolic features such that the ratio $\kappa_\sigma''/\kappa_\sigma'$ remains (roughly) constant across scales are output as step edge points, whereas directional extrema of the dominant curvature such that $\sigma\kappa_\sigma$ remains (roughly) constant are output as roof points. Finally, because, for both our models, the distance between the true discontinuity and the corresponding zero-crossing or extremum increases with scale, the finest scale is used for edge localization. Figure 14.6 (right) shows the results of applying this strategy to the oil bottle.

14.2.3 Segmenting Range Images into Planar Regions

We saw in the last section that edge detection is implemented by quite different processes in photographs and depth maps. The situation is similar for image segmentation into regions. In particular, meaningful segmentation criteria are elusive in the intensity domain because pixel brightness is only a cue to physical properties such as shape or reflectance. In the range domain, however, geometric information is directly available, making it possible to use, say, the average distance between a set of surface points and the plane best fitting them as an effective segmentation criterion. The region-growing technique of Faugeras and Hebert (1986) is a good example of this approach. This algorithm iteratively merges planar patches by maintaining a graph whose nodes are the patches and whose arcs link adjacent patches. Each arc is assigned a cost corresponding to the average error between the points of the two patches and the plane best fitting these points. The best arc is always selected, and the corresponding patches are merged. Note that the remaining arcs associated with these patches must be deleted while new arcs linking the new patch to its neighbors are introduced. The situation is illustrated by Figure 14.7.

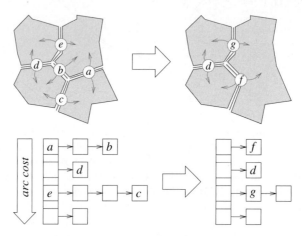

FIGURE 14.7: This diagram illustrates one iteration of the region-growing process during which the two patches incident to the minimum-cost arc labeled a are merged. The heap shown in the bottom part of the figure is updated as well: the arcs a, b, c, and e are deleted, and two new arcs f and g are created and inserted in the heap.

The graph structure is initialized by using a triangulation of the range data, and it is updated efficiently by maintaining a heap of active arcs. The triangulation can be constructed either directly from a range image (by splitting the quadrilaterals associated with the pixels along one of their diagonals) or from a global surface model constructed from multiple images, as described in the next section. The heap storing the active arcs can be represented, for example, by an array of buckets indexed by increasing costs, which supports fast insertion and deletion (Figure 14.7, bottom). Figure 14.8 shows an example, where the complex shape of an automobile part is approximated by 60 planar patches.

14.3   RANGE IMAGE REGISTRATION AND MODEL ACQUISITION

Geometric models of real objects are useful in manufacturing, e.g., for process and assembly planning or inspection. Closer to the theme of this book, they are also key components of many object recognition systems, and are more and more in demand in the entertainment industry, as synthetic pictures of real objects now routinely appear in feature films and video games (we will come back to this issue in much greater detail in Chapter 19). Range images are an excellent source of data for constructing accurate geometric models of real objects, but a single picture will, at best, show half of the surface of a given solid, and the construction of complete object models requires the integration of multiple range images. This section addresses the dual problems of registering multiple images in the same coordinate system and fusing the three-dimensional data provided by these pictures into a single integrated surface model. Before attacking these two problems, let

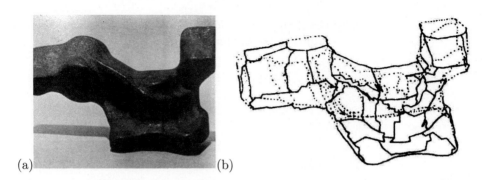

(a)   (b)

FIGURE 14.8: The Renault part: (a) photo of the part and (b) its model. *Reprinted from "The Representation, Recognition, and Locating of 3D Objects," by O.D. Faugeras and M. Hebert, International Journal of Robotics Research, 5(3):27–52, (1986). © 1986 Sage Publications. Reprinted by permission of Sage Publications.*

us introduce quaternions, which will provide us with linear methods for estimating rigid transformations from point and plane correspondences in both the registration context of this section and the recognition context of the next one. We will assume in the rest of this chapter that $\mathbb{E}^3$ has been equipped with a fixed coordinate system and identify this space with $\mathbb{R}^3$ and each point with its coordinate vector.

14.3.1   Quaternions

Quaternions were invented by Hamilton (1844). Like complex numbers in the plane, they can be used to represent rotations in space in a very convenient manner. A quaternion q is defined by its *real part*, a scalar a, and its *imaginary part*, a vector $\boldsymbol{\alpha}$ in $\mathbb{R}^3$, and it is usually denoted by $\mathsf{q} = a + \boldsymbol{\alpha}$. This is justified by the fact that real numbers can be identified with quaternions with a zero imaginary part, and vectors can be identified with quaternions with a zero real part, while addition between quaternions is defined by

$$(a + \boldsymbol{\alpha}) + (b + \boldsymbol{\beta}) \stackrel{\text{def}}{=} (a + b) + (\boldsymbol{\alpha} + \boldsymbol{\beta}).$$

The multiplication of a quaternion by a scalar is defined naturally by $\lambda(a + \boldsymbol{\alpha}) \stackrel{\text{def}}{=} \lambda a + \lambda \boldsymbol{\alpha}$, and these two operations give quaternions the structure of a four-dimensional vector space.

It is also possible to define a multiplication operation that associates with two quaternions the quaternion

$$(a + \boldsymbol{\alpha})(b + \boldsymbol{\beta}) \stackrel{\text{def}}{=} (ab - \boldsymbol{\alpha} \cdot \boldsymbol{\beta}) + (a\boldsymbol{\beta} + b\boldsymbol{\alpha} + \boldsymbol{\alpha} \times \boldsymbol{\beta}).$$

Quaternions, equipped with the operations of addition and multiplication as defined above, form a non-commutative field, whose zero and unit elements are respectively the scalars 0 and 1.

The *conjugate* of the quaternion $\mathsf{q} = a + \boldsymbol{\alpha}$ is the quaternion $\bar{\mathsf{q}} \stackrel{\text{def}}{=} a - \boldsymbol{\alpha}$ with opposite imaginary part. The squared norm of a quaternion is defined by

$$||\mathsf{q}||^2 \stackrel{\text{def}}{=} \mathsf{q}\bar{\mathsf{q}} = \bar{\mathsf{q}}\mathsf{q} = a^2 + ||\boldsymbol{\alpha}||^2,$$

and it is easily verified that $||\mathsf{qq}'|| = ||\mathsf{q}|| \, ||\mathsf{q}'||$ for any pair of quaternions q and q'.
Now, it can be shown that the quaternion

$$\mathsf{q} = \cos\frac{\theta}{2} + \sin\frac{\theta}{2}\boldsymbol{u}$$

represents the rotation $\mathcal{R}$ of angle θ about the *unit* vector $\boldsymbol{u}$ in the following sense:
if $\boldsymbol{\alpha}$ is some vector in $\mathbb{R}^3$, then

$$\mathcal{R}\boldsymbol{\alpha} = \mathsf{q}\boldsymbol{\alpha}\bar{\mathsf{q}}. \tag{14.5}$$

Note that $||\mathsf{q}|| = 1$ and that $-\mathsf{q}$ also represents the rotation $\mathcal{R}$. Reciprocally,
the rotation matrix $\mathcal{R}$ associated with a given unit quaternion $\mathsf{q} = a + \boldsymbol{\alpha}$ with
$\boldsymbol{\alpha} = (b, c, d)^T$ is

$$\mathcal{R} = \begin{pmatrix} a^2 + b^2 - c^2 - d^2 & 2(bc - ad) & 2(bd + ac) \\ 2(bc + ad) & a^2 - b^2 + c^2 - d^2 & 2(cd - ab) \\ 2(bd - ac) & 2(cd + ab) & a^2 - b^2 - c^2 + d^2 \end{pmatrix}, \tag{14.6}$$

a fact easily deduced from Equation (14.5). (Note that the four parameters a, b, c, d
are not independent since they satisfy the constraint $a^2 + b^2 + c^2 + d^2 = 1$.)
Finally, if q_1 and q_2 are unit quaternions, and $\mathcal{R}_1$ and $\mathcal{R}_2$ are the corresponding rotation matrices, the quaternions $\mathsf{q}_1\mathsf{q}_2$ and $-\mathsf{q}_1\mathsf{q}_2$ are both representations of
the rotation matrix $\mathcal{R}_1\mathcal{R}_2$.

14.3.2 Registering Range Images Using the Iterative Closest-Point Method

Besl and McKay (1992) have proposed an algorithm capable of registering two sets
of three-dimensional points, i.e., of computing the rigid transformation that maps
the first point set onto the second one. Their algorithm simply minimizes the average distance between the two point sets by iterating over the following steps: first
establish correspondences between scene and model features by matching every
scene point to the model point closest to it, then estimate the rigid transformation mapping the scene points onto their matches, and finally apply the computed
displacement to the scene. The iterations stop when the change in mean distance
between the matched points falls below some preset threshold. Pseudocode for this
iterated closest-point (or *ICP*) algorithm is given below.
It is easy to show that Algorithm 14.2 forces the error E to decrease monotonically with each iteration; indeed, the average error decreases during the registration
stage, and the individual errors decrease as well during the determination of the
closest point pairs. By itself, this does not guarantee convergence to a global (or
even local) minimum, and a reasonable guess for the rigid transformation sought by
the algorithm must be provided. A variety of methods are available for that purpose, including roughly sampling the set of all possible transformations, and using
the moments of both the scene and model point sets to estimate the transformation.

Finding the closest point pairs. At every iteration of the algorithm, finding
the closest point M in the model to a given (registered) scene point S takes (naively)
$O(n)$ time, where n is the number of model points. In fact, various algorithms can
be used to answer such a nearest-neighbor query in $\mathbb{R}^3$ in sublinear time at the cost

---

The auxiliary function Initialize-Registration uses some global registration method, based on moments, for example, to compute a rough initial estimate of the rigid transformation mapping the scene onto the model.

The function Return-Closest-Pairs returns the indices (i, j) of the points in the registered scene and the model such that point number j is the closest to point number i.

The function Update-Registration estimates the rigid transformation between selected pairs of points in the scene and the model.

The function Apply-Registration applies a rigid transformation to all the points in the scene.

Function ICP(Model, Scene);
begin
E' ← +∞;
(Rot, Trans) ← Initialize-Registration(Scene, Model);
repeat
  E ← E';
  Registered-Scene ← Apply-Registration(Scene, Rot, Trans);
  Pairs ← Return-Closest-Pairs(Registered-Scene, Model);
  (Rot, Trans, E') ← Update-Registration(Scene, Model, Pairs, Rot, Trans);
  until |E' − E| < τ;
return (Rot, Trans);
end.

Algorithm 14.2: The Iterative Closest-Point Algorithm of Besl and McKay (1992).

of additional preprocessing of the model, using *k-d trees* (Friedman *et al.* 1977), or more complex data structures. For example, the general randomized algorithm of Clarkson (1988) takes preprocessing time $O(n^{2+\varepsilon})$, where ε is an arbitrarily small positive number, and query time $O(\log n)$. The efficiency of repeated queries can also be improved by *caching* the results of previous computations. For example, Simon *et al.* (1994) store at each iteration of the ICP algorithm the k closest model points to each scene point (a typical value for k is 5). Since the incremental update of the rigid transformation normally is small, it is likely that the closest neighbor of a point after an iteration will be among its k closest neighbors from the previous one. It is in fact possible to determine efficiently and conclusively whether the closest point is in the cached set; see Simon, Hebert, and Kanade (1994) for details.

Estimating the rigid transformation. Under the rigid transformation defined by the rotation matrix $\mathcal{R}$ and the translation vector $\boldsymbol{t}$, a point $\boldsymbol{x}$ maps onto the point $\boldsymbol{x}' = \mathcal{R}\boldsymbol{x} + \boldsymbol{t}$. Thus, given n pairs of matching points $\boldsymbol{x}_i$ and $\boldsymbol{x}'_i$, with $i = 1, \ldots, n$, we seek the rotation matrix $\mathcal{R}$ and translation vector $\boldsymbol{t}$ minimizing the error

$$E = \sum_{i=1}^{n} ||\boldsymbol{x}'_i - \mathcal{R}\boldsymbol{x}_i - \boldsymbol{t}||^2.$$

Let us first note that the value of t minimizing E must satisfy

$$0 = \frac{\partial E}{\partial t} = -2 \sum_{i=1}^{n} (x_i' - \mathcal{R}x_i - t),$$

or

$$t = \bar{x}' - \mathcal{R}\bar{x}, \quad \text{where} \quad \bar{x} \stackrel{\text{def}}{=} \frac{1}{n} \sum_{i=1}^{n} x_i \quad \text{and} \quad \bar{x}' \stackrel{\text{def}}{=} \frac{1}{n} \sum_{i=1}^{n} x_i' \qquad (14.7)$$

denote respectively the centroids of the two sets of points x_i and x_i'.

Introducing the centered points $y_i = x_i - \bar{x}$ and $y_i' = x_i' - \bar{x}$ $(i = 1, \ldots, n)$ yields

$$E = \sum_{i=1}^{n} ||y_i' - \mathcal{R}y_i||^2.$$

Quaternions now can be used to minimize E as follows: let q denote the quaternion associated with the matrix $\mathcal{R}$. Using the fact that $||q||^2 = 1$ and the multiplicativity properties of the quaternion norm allows us to write

$$E = \sum_{i=1}^{n} ||y_i' - qy_i\bar{q}||^2 ||q||^2 = \sum_{i=1}^{n} ||y_i'q - qy_i||^2.$$

As shown in the problems, this allows us to rewrite the rotational error as $E = q^T \mathcal{B}q$, where $\mathcal{B} = \sum_{i=1}^{n} \mathcal{A}_i^T \mathcal{A}_i$, and

$$\mathcal{A}_i = \begin{pmatrix} 0 & y_i^T - y_i'^T \\ y_i' - y_i & [y_i + y_i']_\times \end{pmatrix}.$$

Note that the matrix $\mathcal{A}_i$ is antisymmetric with (in general) rank 3, but that the matrix $\mathcal{B}$ will have, in the presence of noise, rank 4. As shown in Chapter 22, minimizing E under the constraint $||q||^2 = 1$ is a (homogeneous) linear least-squares problem whose solution is the eigenvector of $\mathcal{B}$ associated with the smallest eigenvalue of this matrix. Once $\mathcal{R}$ is known, t is obtained from Equation (14.7).

Results. Figure 14.9 shows an example, where two range images of an African mask are matched by the algorithm. The average distance between matches is 0.59mm for this 9cm object.

14.3.3 Fusing Multiple Range Images

Given a set of registered range images of a solid object, it is possible to construct an integrated surface model of this object. In the approach proposed by Curless and Levoy (1996), this model is constructed as the zero set S of a volumetric density function $D : \mathbb{R}^3 \to \mathbb{R}$, i.e., as the set of points (x, y, z) such that $D(x, y, z) = 0$. Like any other level set of a continuous density function, S is by construction guaranteed to be a closed, "watertight" surface, although it may have several connected components (Figure 14.10).

The difficulty, of course, is to construct an appropriate density function from registered range measurements. Curless and Levoy embed the corresponding surface

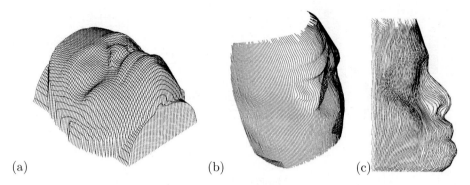

(a)   (b)   (c)

FIGURE 14.9: Registration results: (a) a range image serving as model for an African mask; (b) a (decimated) view of the model, serving as scene data; (c) a view of the two datasets after registration. *Reprinted from "A Method for Registration of 3D Shapes," by P.J. Besl and N.D. McKay, IEEE Transactions on Pattern Analysis and Machine Intelligence, 14(2):238–256, (1992). © 1992 IEEE.*

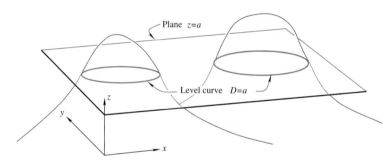

FIGURE 14.10: A 2D illustration of volumetric density functions and their level sets. In this case, the "volume" is of course the (x, y) plane, and the "surface" is a curve in this plane, with two connected components in the example shown here.

fragments into a cubic grid, and assign to each cell of this grid, or *voxel*, a weighted sum of the signed distances between its center and the closest point on the surface intersecting it (Figure 14.11, left). This averaged signed distance is the desired density function, and its zero set can be found using classical techniques, such as the *marching cubes* algorithm developed by Lorensen and Cline (1987) to extract isodensity surfaces from volumetric medical data.

Missing surface fragments corresponding to unobserved parts of the scene are handled by initially marking all voxels as *unseen*, or equivalently assigning them a depth equal to some large positive value (standing for $+\infty$), then assigning as before to all voxels close to the measured surface patches the corresponding signed distance, and finally carving out (i.e., marking as *empty*, or having a large negative depth standing for $-\infty$) the voxels that lie between the observed surface patches and the sensor (Figure 14.11, right).

Figure 14.12 shows an example of model built from multiple range images of a Buddha statuette acquired with a Cyberware 3030 MS optical triangulation

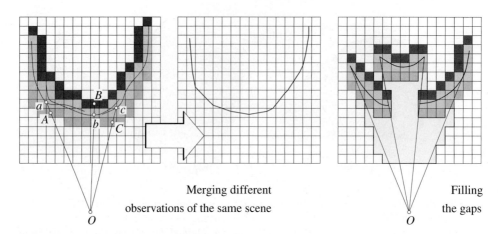

FIGURE 14.11: A 2D illustration of the Curless-Levoy method for fusing multiple range images. In the **left** part of the figure, three views observed by the same sensor located at the point O are merged by computing the zero set of a weighted average of the signed distances between voxel centers (e.g., points A, B, and C) and surface points (e.g., a, b, and c) along viewing rays. In general, distances to different sensors would be used instead. The light-gray area in the **right** part of the figure is the set of voxels marked as empty in the gap-filling part of the procedure.

scanner, as well as a physical model constructed from the geometric one via stereo-lithography (Curless and Levoy 1996).

14.4 OBJECT RECOGNITION

We now turn to actual object recognition from range images. The registration techniques introduced in the previous section will play a crucial role in the two algorithms discussed in this one.

14.4.1 Matching Piecewise-Planar Surfaces Using Interpretation Trees

The recognition algorithm proposed by Faugeras and Hebert (1986) is a recursive procedure exploiting rigidity constraints to efficiently search an interpretation tree for the path(s) corresponding to the best sequence(s) of matches. The basic procedure is given in pseudocode in Algorithm 14.3. To correctly handle occlusions (and the fact that, as noted earlier, a range finder will "see," at best, one half of the object facing it), at every stage of the search, the algorithm must consider the possibility that a model plane might not match any scene plane. This is done by always incorporating in the list of potential matches of a given plane a token "null" plane.

Selecting potential matches. The selection of potential matches for a given model plane is based on various criteria depending on the number of correspondences already established, with each new correspondence providing new geometric constraints and more stringent criteria. At the beginning of the search, we know only that a model plane with area A should be matched to scene planes with a com-

FIGURE 14.12: 3D Fax of a statuette of a Buddha. From left to right: photograph of the statuette; range image; integrated 3D model; model after hole filling; and physical model obtained via stereolithography. *Courtesy of Marc Levoy. Reprinted from "A Volumetric Method for Building Complex Models from Range Images," by B. Curless and M. Levoy, Proc. SIGGRAPH, (1996).* © *1996 ACM, Inc. http://doi.acm.org/10.1145/237170.237269 Reprinted by permission..*

patible area, i.e., in the range $[\alpha A, \beta A]$. Reasonable values for the two thresholds might be 0.5 and 1.1, which allows for some discrepancy between the unoccluded areas, and also affords a degree of occlusion up to 50%.

After the first correspondence has been established, it is still too early to try and estimate the rigid transformation mapping the model onto the scene, but it is clear that the angle between the normals to any matching planes should be (roughly) equal to the angle θ between the normals to the first pair of planes, say those that lie in the interval $[\theta - \varepsilon, \theta + \varepsilon]$. The normals to the corresponding planes lie in a band of the Gauss sphere, and they can be retrieved efficiently by discretizing this sphere and associating to each cell a bucket that stores the scene planes whose normal falls into it (Figure 14.13).

A second pairing is sufficient to completely determine the rotation separating the model from its instance in the scene: this is geometrically clear (and will be confirmed analytically in the next section) since a pair of matching vectors constrains the rotation axis to lie in the plane bisecting these vectors. Two pairs of matching planes determine the axis of rotation as the intersection of the corresponding bisecting planes, and the rotation angle is readily computed from either of the matches. Given the rotation and a third model plane, one can predict the orientation of the normal to its possible matches in the scene, which can be recovered efficiently using once again the discrete Gauss sphere mentioned before. After three pairings have been found, the translation can also be estimated and used to predict the distance between the origin and any scene plane matching a fourth scene plane. The same is true for any further pairing.

The recursive function Match returns the best set of matching plane pairs found by recursively visiting the interpretation tree. It is initially called with an empty list of pairs and null values for the rotation and translation arguments rot and trans. The auxiliary function Potential-Matches returns the subset of the planes in the scene that are compatible with the model plane Π and the current estimate of the rigid transformation mapping the model planes onto their scene matches (see text for details).
The auxiliary function Update-Registration-2 uses the matched plane pairs to update the current estimate of the rigid transformation.

```
Function Match(model, scene, pairs, rot, trans);
begin
bestpairs ← nil; bestscore ← 0;
for Π in model do
    for Π′ in Potential-Matches(scene, pairs, Π, rot, trans) do
        rot ← Update-Registration-2(pairs, Π, Π′, rot, trans);
        (score, newpairs) ← Match(model−Π, scene−Π′, pairs+(Π, Π′), rot, trans);
        if score>bestscore then bestscore ← score; bestpairs ← newpairs endif;
        endfor;
    endfor;
return bestpairs;
end.
```

Algorithm 14.3: The Plane-Matching Algorithm of Faugeras and Hebert (1986).

Estimating the rigid transformation. Let us consider a plane Π defined by the equation $\boldsymbol{n} \cdot \boldsymbol{x} - d = 0$ in some fixed coordinate system. Here, $\boldsymbol{n}$ denotes the unit normal to the plane and d its (signed) distance from the origin. Under the rigid transformation defined by the rotation matrix $\mathcal{R}$ and the translation vector $\boldsymbol{t}$, a point $\boldsymbol{x}$ maps onto the point $\boldsymbol{x}' = \mathcal{R}\boldsymbol{x} + \boldsymbol{t}$, and Π maps onto the plane Π' whose equation is $\boldsymbol{n}' \cdot \boldsymbol{x}' - d' = 0$, with

$$\begin{cases} \boldsymbol{n}' = \mathcal{R}\boldsymbol{n}, \\ d' = \boldsymbol{n}' \cdot \boldsymbol{t} + d. \end{cases}$$

Thus, estimating the rigid transformation that maps n planes Π_i onto the matching planes Π_i' $(i = 1, \ldots, n)$ amounts to finding the rotation matrix $\mathcal{R}$ that minimizes the error

$$E_r = \sum_{i=1}^{n} ||\boldsymbol{n}_i' - \mathcal{R}\boldsymbol{n}_i||^2$$

and the translation vector $\boldsymbol{t}$ that minimizes

$$E_t = \sum_{i=1}^{n} (d_i' - d_i - \boldsymbol{n}_i' \cdot \boldsymbol{t})^2.$$

The rotation $\mathcal{R}$ minimizing E_r can be computed, exactly as in Section 14.4.1, by using the quaternion representation of matrices and solving an eigenvector problem.

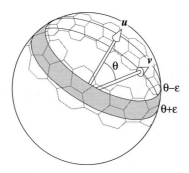

FIGURE 14.13: Finding all vectors $\boldsymbol{v}$ that make an angle in the $[\theta - \varepsilon, \theta + \varepsilon]$ range with a given vector $\boldsymbol{u}$. It should be noted that the unit sphere does not admit tesselations with an arbitrary level of detail by regular (spherical) polygons. The tesselation shown in the diagram is made of hexagons with unequal edge lengths. See, for example, (Horn 1986, Chap. 16) for a discussion of this problem and various tesselation schemes.

The translation vector $\boldsymbol{t}$ minimizing E_t is the solution of a (non-homogeneous) linear least-squares problem, whose solution can be found using the techniques presented in Chapter 22.

Results.   Figure 14.14 shows recognition results obtained using a bin of Renault parts such as the one shown in Figure 14.8. The range image of the bin has been segmented into planar patches using the technique presented in Section 14.2.3. The matching algorithm is run three times on the scene, with patches matched during each run removed from the scene before the next iteration. As shown by the figure, the three instances of the part present in the bin are correctly identified, and the accuracy of the pose estimation process is attested by the reprojection into the range image of the model in the computed pose.

14.4.2   Matching Free-Form Surfaces Using Spin Images

As demonstrated in Section 14.2.2, differential geometry provides a powerful language for describing the shape of a surface *locally*, i.e., in a small neighborhood of each one of its points. On the other hand, the region-growing algorithm discussed in Section 14.2.3 is aimed at constructing a *globally* consistent surface description in terms of planar patches. We introduce in this section a *semi-local* surface representation, the spin image of Johnson and Hebert (1998, 1999), that captures the shape of a surface in a relatively large neighborhood of each one of its points. As will be shown in the rest of this section, the spin image is invariant under rigid transformations, and it affords an efficient algorithm for pointwise surface matching, thus completely bypassing segmentation in the recognition process.

Spin image definition.   Let us assume as in Section 14.2.3 that the surface Σ of interest is given in the form of a triangular mesh. The (outward-pointing) surface normal at each vertex can be estimated by fitting a plane to this vertex and its neighbors, turning the triangulation into a net of *oriented points*. Given an oriented

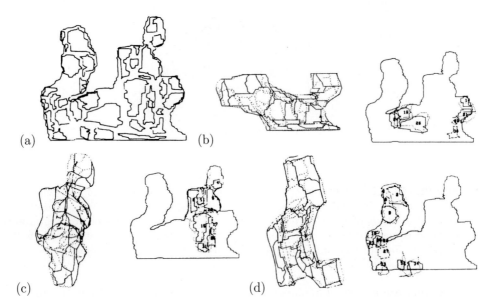

FIGURE 14.14: Recognition results: (a) a bin of parts, and (b)–(d) the three instances of the Renault part found in that bin. In each case, the model is shown both by itself in the position and orientation estimated by the algorithm, as well as superimposed (dotted lines) in this pose over the corresponding planes of the range image. *Reprinted from "The Representation, Recognition, and Locating of 3D Objects," by O.D. Faugeras and M. Hebert, International Journal of Robotics Research, 5(3):27–52, (1986). © 1986 Sage Publications. Reprinted by permission of Sage Publications.*

point P, the spin coordinates of any other point Q can now be defined as the (non-negative) distance α separating Q from the (oriented) normal line in P and the (signed) distance β from the tangent plane to Q (Figure 14.15). Accordingly, the *spin map* $s_P : \Sigma \to \mathbb{R}^2$ associated with P is defined for any point Q on Σ as

$$s_P(Q) \stackrel{\text{def}}{=} (\underbrace{||\overrightarrow{PQ} \times \boldsymbol{n}||}_{\alpha}, \underbrace{\overrightarrow{PQ} \cdot \boldsymbol{n}}_{\beta}).$$

As shown by Figure 14.15, this mapping is not injective. This is not surprising because the spin map provides only a partial specification of a cylindrical coordinate system: the third coordinate that would normally record the angle between some reference vector in the tangent plane and the projection of $\overrightarrow{PQ}$ into this plane is missing. The principal directions are obvious choices for such a reference vector, but focusing on the spin coordinates avoids their computation, a process that is susceptible to noise since it involves second derivatives and may be ambiguous for (almost) planar or spherical patches.

The *spin image* associated with an oriented point is a histogram of the α, β coordinates in a neighborhood of this point. Concretely, the α, β plane is divided into a rectangular array of $\delta\alpha \times \delta\beta$ bins that accumulate the total surface area spanned by points with α, β values in that range.[3] As shown in Carmichael, Hubert,

---

[3]The corresponding point sets may actually be divided into several connected components.

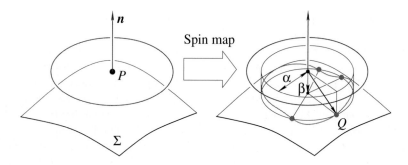

FIGURE 14.15: Definition of the spin map associated with a surface point P: the spin coordinates (α, β) of the point Q are respectively defined by the lengths of the projections of $\overrightarrow{PQ}$ onto the tangent plane and its surface normal. Note that there are three other points with the same (α, β) coordinates as Q in this example.

and Hebert (1999) and the problems, each triangle in the surface mesh maps onto a region of the α, β plane whose boundaries are hyperbola arcs. Its contribution to the spin image can thus be computed by assigning to each bin that this region traverses the area of the patch where the triangle intersects the annular region of $\mathbb{R}^3$ associated with the bin (Figure 14.16). The bins can be found efficiently using *scan conversion* (Foley *et al.* 1990), a process routinely used in computer graphics to find in optimal time the pixels traversed by a generalized polygon with straight or curved edges.

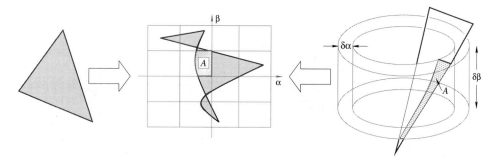

FIGURE 14.16: Spin image construction: the triangle shown in the left of the diagram maps onto a region with hyperbolic boundaries in the spin image; the value of each bin intersected by this region is incremented by the area of the portion of the triangle that intersects the annulus associated with the bin. After Carmichael *et al.* (1999, Figure 3).

Spin images are defined by several key parameters (Johnson and Hebert 1999). The first one is the support distance d that limits to a sphere of radius d centered in P the range of the *support points* used to construct the image. This sphere must be large enough to provide good descriptive power but small enough to support

For example, for small enough values of $\delta\alpha$ and $\delta\beta$, there are four connected components in the example shown in Figure 14.15, corresponding to small patches centered at the points having the same α, β coordinates as Q.

recognition in the presence of clutter and occlusion. In practice, an appropriate choice for d might be a tenth of the object's diameter; thus, as noted earlier, the spin image is indeed a semi-local description of the shape of a surface in an *extended* neighborhood of one of its points. Robustness to clutter can be improved by limiting the range of surface normals at the support points to a cone of half-angle θ centered in $\boldsymbol{n}$. As in the support distance case, choosing the right value for θ involves a trade-off between descriptive power and insensitivity to clutter; a value of 60° has empirically been shown to be satisfactory. The last parameter defining a spin image is its size (in pixels), or equivalently, given the support distance, its bin size (in meters), and it can be shown that an appropriate choice for the bin size is the average distance between mesh vertices in the model. Figure 14.17 shows the spin images associated with three oriented points on the surface of a rubber duck.

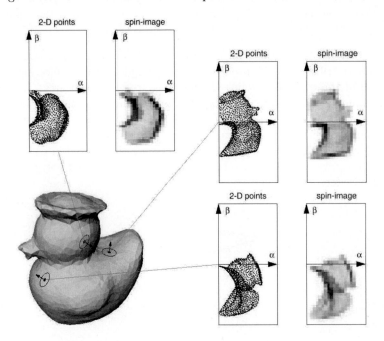

FIGURE 14.17: Three oriented points on the surface of a rubber duck and the corresponding spin images. The α, β coordinates of the mesh vertices are shown besides the actual spin images. *Reprinted from "Using Spin Images for Efficient Object Recognition in Cluttered 3D Scenes," by A.E. Johnson and M. Hebert, IEEE Transactions on Pattern Analysis and Machine Intelligence, 21(5):433–449, (1999). © 1999 IEEE.*

Matching spin images. One of the most important features of spin images is that they are (obviously) invariant under rigid transformations. Thus an image comparison technique such as correlation can in principle be used to match the spin images associated with oriented points in the scene and the object model. Things are not that simple, however: we already noted that the spin map is not injective; in general, it is not surjective either, and empty bins (or equivalently zero-valued pixels) may occur for values of α and β that do not correspond to physical surface points (see the blank areas in Figure 14.17, for example). Occlusion may cause the appearance of zero pixels in the scene image, whereas clutter may introduce irrelevant non-empty bins. It is therefore reasonable to restrict the comparison of two spin images to their common nonzero pixels. In this context, Johnson and Hebert (1998) have shown that

$$S(\boldsymbol{I}, \boldsymbol{J}) \stackrel{\text{def}}{=} [\text{Arctanh}(C(\boldsymbol{I}, \boldsymbol{J}))]^2 - \frac{3}{N - 3}$$

is an appropriate similarity measure for two spin images whose overlap regions contain N pixels and are represented by the vectors $\boldsymbol{I}$ and $\boldsymbol{J}$ of $\mathbb{R}^N$. In this formula, $C(\boldsymbol{I}, \boldsymbol{J})$ denotes the normalized correlation of the vectors $\boldsymbol{I}$ and $\boldsymbol{J}$, and Arctanh denotes the hyperbolic arc tangent function. Armed with this similarity measure, we can now outline a recognition algorithm that uses spin images to establish pointwise correspondences.

Off-line:

Compute the spin images associated with the oriented points of a surface model and store them into a table.

On-line:

1. Form correspondences between a set of spin images randomly selected in the scene and their best matches in the model table using the similarity measure S to rank-order the matches.
2. Filter and group correspondences using geometric consistency constraints, and compute the rigid transformations best aligning the matched scene and model features.
3. Verify the matches using the ICP algorithm.

Algorithm 14.4: Pointwise Matching of Free-Form Surfaces Using Spin Images, after Johnson and Hebert (1998, 1999).

The various stages of this algorithm are mostly straightforward. Let us note, however, that the filtering/grouping step relies on comparing the spin coordinates of model points relative to the other mesh vertices in their group with the spin coordinates of the corresponding scene points relative to their own group. Once consistent groups have been identified, an initial estimate of the rigid transformation aligning the scene and the model is computed from (oriented) point matches using the quaternion-based registration technique described in Section 14.3.2. Finally, consistent sets of correspondences are verified by iteratively spreading the matching process to their neighbors, updating along the way the rigid transformation that aligns the scene and the model.

Results. The matching algorithm presented in the previous section has been extensively tested in recognition tasks with cluttered indoor scenes that contain both industrial parts and various toys (Johnson & Hebert 1998, 1999). It has also been used in outdoor navigation/mapping tasks with very large datasets covering thousands of squared meters of terrain (Carmichael *et al.* 1999). Figure 14.18 shows sample recognition results in the toy domain.

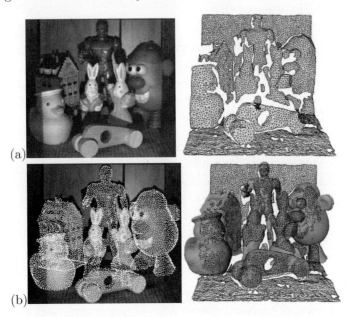

(a)

(b)

FIGURE 14.18: Spin-image recognition results: (a) a cluttered image of toys and the mesh constructed from the corresponding range image; (b) recognized objects overlaid on the original pictures. *Reprinted from "Using Spin Images for Efficient Object Recognition in Cluttered 3D Scenes," by A.E. Johnson and M. Hebert, IEEE Transactions on Pattern Analysis and Machine Intelligence, 21(5):433–449, (1999). © 1999 IEEE.*

14.5 KINECT

Kinect is a video game technology developed by Microsoft for its Xbox 360 platform that allows its users to control games using natural body motions. It has three main components: a sensor that delivers accurate depth maps and color images at frame rate, an effective algorithm for estimating the pose (joint positions) of the players in every frame, and a tracking algorithm using this information to smoothly recover the parameters (joint angles) of a 3D kinematic model (skeleton) over time. This section discusses the pose estimation algorithm used by Kinect (Shotton *et al.* 2011), which relies on *random forests* to classify individual pixels from a single range image into one of a few predefined body parts, then uses a voting/averaging procedure to compute these parts' locations (joint positions) in 3D.

Kinect is a success story for computer vision, with several million units shipped as of 2011. Before getting into the details of its presentation, it may be worth examining some key elements that might explain (at least in part, and marketing and user-interface issues aside) some of this success:

1. The sensor, developed by Primesense,[4] delivers at 30Hz a depth map with VGA resolution (480×640 pixels) and a registered RGB image with UXGA resolution (1200×1600 pixels). The corresponding *Light Coding*^{TM} technology uses a projected infrared pattern observed by a black-and-white camera and decoded on a dedicated chip. The two main features of this sensor is that it is *fast*, much faster than conventional range finders using mechanical scanning, and *cheap*—cheap enough, in fact, to ship as part of a mass-market video game package.

2. Range images are a lot easier to simulate realistically than ordinary photographs (no color, texture, or illumination variations). In turn, this means that it is easy to generate synthetic data for training accurate classifiers without overfitting.

3. Voting procedures are relatively robust to errors among individual voters. As shown later in this section, this explains that excellent pose estimation results can be achieved despite relatively large error rates (40%) at the individual pixel level.

4. Kinect's overall effectiveness and robustness are doubtless due in part to its tracking component, whose details are proprietary but, like any other approach to tracking (see Chapter 11), has temporal information at its disposal for smoothing the recovered skeleton parameters and recovering from joint detection errors.

One may also argue that depth map features are more robust, or invariant to viewpoint changes, than those found in photographs. This is certainly true to some extent (see the spin images of Section 14.4.2). On the other hand, one may also argue that, in the context of video games, where the viewpoint does not vary much, the key advantage of these images might be that they readily provide occlusion boundary/silhouette information. Indeed, it is relatively easy to separate objects from background in range images, and all the data processed by the approach to pose estimation presented in the rest of this section is presegmented by a separate and effective background subtraction module.

14.5.1 Features

For efficiency reasons, Kinect uses very simple features that are related to spin images, but without the corresponding tangent plane computations. Instead, they simply measure depth differences in the neighborhood of each pixel. Concretely, let us denote by $z(\boldsymbol{p})$ the depth at pixel $\boldsymbol{p}$ in some range image. Given image displacements $\boldsymbol{\lambda}$ and $\boldsymbol{\mu}$, a very simple scalar feature can be computed as

$$f_{\boldsymbol{\lambda},\boldsymbol{\mu}}(\boldsymbol{p}) = z\left[\boldsymbol{p} + \frac{1}{z(\boldsymbol{p})}\boldsymbol{\lambda}\right] - z\left[\boldsymbol{p} + \frac{1}{z(\boldsymbol{p})}\boldsymbol{\mu}\right].$$

In turn, given some allowed range of displacements, one can associate with each pixel $\boldsymbol{p}$ the feature vector $\boldsymbol{x}(\boldsymbol{p})$ whose components are the D values of $f_{\boldsymbol{\mu},\boldsymbol{\mu}}(\boldsymbol{p})$ for all distinct unordered pairs $(\boldsymbol{\lambda}, \boldsymbol{\mu})$ in that range.

---

[4]http://en.wikipedia.org/wiki/PrimeSense.

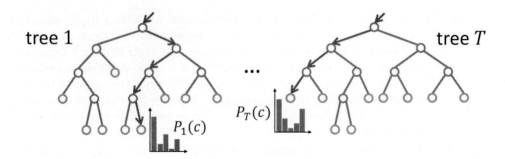

FIGURE 14.19: Random forests. See text for details. *Reprinted from "Real-Time Human Pose Recognition in Parts from Single Depth Images," by J. Shotton et al., Proc. IEEE Conference on Computer Vision and Pattern Recognition, (2011). © 2011 IEEE.*

As detailed in Section 14.5.3, these features are used to train an ensemble of simple *decision tree* classifiers, in the form of a *random forest*. After training, the feature x associated with each pixel of a new depth map is passed to every tree in the forest, where it is recursively redirected to the left or right descendants of the root according to simple binary tests until it reaches a leaf and is assigned some tree-dependent posterior probability of belonging to each body part (Figure 14.19). The overall class probability of the pixel is finally computed as an average of the tree probabilities. Before detailing this process, let us now present a bit more formally decision trees and random forests.

14.5.2   Technique: Decision Trees and Random Forests

Decision trees. Decision trees have long been used in machine learning and pattern recognition as efficient multi-label classifiers. Let us consider a classification problem with features $x = (x_1, \dots, x_D)^T$ in $\mathbb{R}^D$ and K different classes. A decision tree is a binary tree where every non-terminal node is associated with some coordinate x_d, with d in $\{1, \dots, D\}$, and a threshold τ. A feature vector x is assigned to the node's left child if $x_d < \tau$, and to its right child otherwise. This recursive process eventually assigns any feature to some leaf in the tree.

Decision trees split the feature space into hyper-rectangular regions associated with their leaves. Given some labeled training data

$$\mathcal{D} = \{(x_i, y_i),\ x_i \in \mathbb{R}^D\ y_i \in \{1, \dots, K\},\ i = 1, \dots, N\},$$

they also classify any unlabeled feature by taking a majority vote among the labeled examples in $\mathcal{D}$ that have reached the same leaf.

Given some fixed tree structure—say, a balanced tree with depth L—training a decision tree amounts to selecting the feature space coordinates and the thresholds associated with its non-leaf nodes. This can be achieved by maximizing at every node the *information gain* associated with the corresponding coordinate x_d and threshold τ.

Intuitively, a decision tree should split any labeled data into subsets that are as homogeneous as possible, and ideally, all data reaching a leaf should have the same label. This can be formalized using the concept of *cross-entropy*. If the number of points in $\mathcal{D}$ that belong to class k is N_k, its cross-entropy is defined as

$$E(\mathcal{D}) = -\sum_{k=1}^{K} p_k(\mathcal{D}) \log p_k(\mathcal{D}),$$

where $p_k(\mathcal{D}) = N_k/N$ is just the proportion of the points in class k. The cross-entropy reaches its maximum (positive) value of $\log K$ when the data is spread equally into all classes, and reaches its minimum value of zero when all the points belong to the same class. The goal is thus to decrease the cross-entropy as much as possible each time the data is split by a non-terminal node.

The information gain associated with some partition of the data $\mathcal{D}$ into left and right subsets $\mathcal{L}$ and $\mathcal{R}$ is the difference between the original cross-entropy and a weighted sum of the entropies associated with the partition, namely

$$G(\mathcal{D}, \mathcal{L}, \mathcal{R}) = E(\mathcal{D}) - \frac{|\mathcal{L}|}{|\mathcal{D}|} E(\mathcal{L}) - \frac{|\mathcal{R}|}{|\mathcal{D}|} E(\mathcal{R}).$$

Now, given some feature space coordinate x_d and threshold τ, let us define the corresponding left and right subsets of $\mathcal{D}$ as

$$\mathcal{L}_{d,\tau}(\mathcal{D}) = \{(\boldsymbol{x}, y) \in \mathcal{D}, \ x_d < \tau\} \quad \text{and} \quad \mathcal{R}_{d,\tau}(\mathcal{D}) = \{(\boldsymbol{x}, y) \in \mathcal{D}, \ x_d \geq \tau\}.$$

The information gain associated with d and τ can thus be defined as

$$G_{d,\tau}(\mathcal{D}) = G(\mathcal{D}, \mathcal{L}_{d,\tau}(\mathcal{D}), \mathcal{R}_{d,\tau}(\mathcal{D})),$$

and training a decision tree amounts to picking, for each of its non-terminal nodes, the values of d and τ that maximize $G_{d,\tau}$ for the corresponding subset of the labeled data. This procedure is described in Algorithm 14.5.

The arguments of the recursive procedure TrainDT for its first call are the tree root, 0, and the full dataset. Here, $Node.L$ and $Node.R$ respectively denote the left and right children of $Node$. The tree structure is assumed to be fixed, e.g., a balanced tree.

Procedure TrainDT($Node$,l,$\mathcal{D}$);

1. Find the pair (d, τ) maximizing $G_{d,\tau}(\mathcal{D})$;
2. If $l < L$ then

   (a) TrainDT($Node.L$,$\mathcal{L}_{d,\tau}(\mathcal{D})$,$l + 1$);
   (b) TrainDT($Node.R$,$\mathcal{R}_{d,\tau}(\mathcal{D})$,$l + 1$).

Algorithm 14.5: Training a Decision Tree.

For small feature space dimensions and labeled datasets, decision trees can be trained efficiently by exhaustively trying all splitting coordinates, and for each one of these, sorting all features. It is normally wise to grow a rather large decision tree, and then prune it to balance its size with classification accuracy and avoid overfitting (*CART* procedure; see Breiman, Friedman, Ohlsen, and Stone [1984] for details).

As noted earlier, a decision tree classifies a feature vector $\boldsymbol{x}$ by taking a majority vote among the labeled training examples that have reached the same leaf. Alternatively, it is also possible to estimate the posterior probability $P(k|\boldsymbol{x})$ that $\boldsymbol{x}$ belongs to class k as the proportion of labeled samples with class k associated with that leaf.

A typical choice for D^* is $\sqrt{D}$. Adapted from Hastie *et al.* (2009).

1. For $b = 1$ to B do

   (a) Draw a bootstrap sample $\mathcal{D}^*$ from $\mathcal{D}$.
   (b) Grow a decision tree $\mathcal{T}_b$ for $\mathcal{D}^*$ using TrainDT modified such that, at each recursive step, $D^* \leq D$ out of the original D coordinates are picked randomly as splitting candidates;

2. Output the trees $\{\mathcal{T}_b, \ b = 1, \ldots, B\}$.

Algorithm 14.6: Training a Random Forest.

Random forests. A simple method for improving the classification accuracy of decision trees is *bagging* (or *bootstrap aggregation*): Given a dataset $\mathcal{D}$ consisting of N points, a *bootstrap sample* $\mathcal{D}^*$ is formed by randomly drawing N points with replacement from $\mathcal{D}$ (the same point can be drawn several times, and some points present in $\mathcal{D}$ might not appear in $\mathcal{D}^*$). Bagging consists of constructing B bootstrap samples, growing a decision tree for each one of them, and using a majority vote among the trees for classification. This process can be shown to reduce the variance of the prediction when the errors associated with the individual trees are uncorrelated. *Random forests* improve upon bagging by randomly selecting a subset of the input variables at each recursive step of the training process (Algorithm 14.6). The intended effect is to reduce the correlation between the constructed trees, thus reducing the variance of their mean prediction. In practice, as shown in Hastie, Tibshirani, and Friedman (2009) for example, random forests typically do not require pruning, and are easier to train and tune than boosting techniques, with very similar performance for many problems.

After training, a new feature is classified using a majority vote among the trees in the forest. As before, it is also possible to estimate the posterior probability $P(k|\boldsymbol{x})$ that $\boldsymbol{x}$ belongs to class k as the mean of the corresponding probabilities for each tree.

14.5.3   Labeling Pixels

The objective is to construct a classifier that assigns to every pixel in a range image one out of a few body parts, such as a person's face, left arm, etc. There are 10

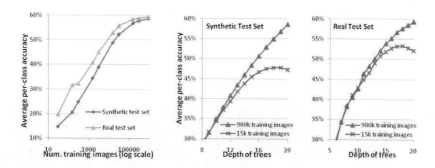

FIGURE 14.20: Effect of the number of (**left**) training images and (**center** and **right**) tree depth on classification accuracy on 5,000 synthetic depth images and 8,808 real hand-labeled ones. Figure courtesy of Jamie Shotton. *Reprinted from "Real-Time Human Pose Recognition in Parts from Single Depth Images," by J. Shotton et al., Proc. IEEE Conference on Computer Vision and Pattern Recognition, (2011). © 2011 IEEE.*

main body parts in Kinect (head, torso, two arms, two legs, two hands, and two feet), some of which are further divided into sub-parts, such as the upper/lower and left/right sides of a face, for a total of 31 parts. The classifier is trained as a random forest, using the features described in Section 14.5.1 and Algorithm 14.6, but replacing the bootstrap sample used for each tree by a random subset of the training data (2,000 random pixels from each one of hundreds of thousands of training images).

One of the main features of the training process is in fact this data: Its primary source is a set of several hundred *motion capture* sequences featuring actors engaged in typical video game activities such as driving, dancing, kicking, etc. After clustering close-by pictures and retaining one sample per cluster, a set of about 100K poses is obtained. The measured articulation parameters are transferred (*retargeted*) to 15 parametric mesh models of human beings with a variety of body shapes and sizes. Body parts defined manually in texture maps are also transferred to these models (Figure 14.21, top), which are then *skinned* by adding different types of clothing and hairstyle (Figure 14.21, center), and rendered from different viewpoints as both depth and label maps using classical computer graphics techniques (Figure 14.21, bottom).

Hundreds of thousands of labeled images can easily be created in this way. The experiments described in Shotton *et al.* (2011) typically use 2,000 pixels per image and per tree to train random forests made of three trees of depth 20, with 2,000 splitting coordinates and 50 thresholds per node. This takes about one day on a 1,000-core cluster for up to one million training images. Experiments with synthetic and real data show that increasing the size of the training sample improves the classification rate, and suggest that increasing tree depth also helps, at least for large datasets (Figure 14.20): The overfitting observed starting at depth 17 for small datasets of 15K images disappears for the largest datasets with 900K images. The best results are observed with 900K training images and trees of depth 20, with a pixelwise classification rate of about 60%.

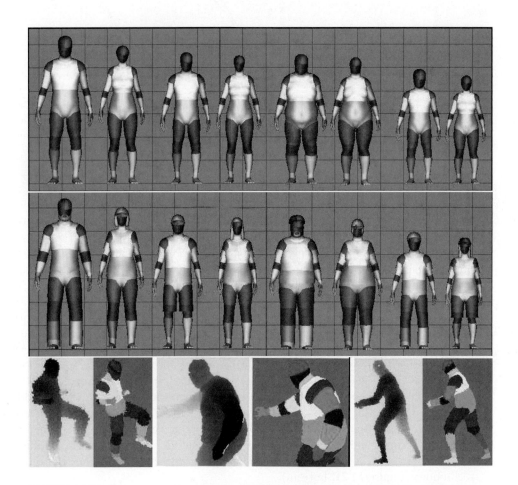

FIGURE 14.21: Data generation process with, from top to bottom: sample models generated by retargeting the motion capture data on meshes corresponding to different body types; models after skinning using different types of clothing and hairstyle; and rendered depth maps together with their labels. *Reprinted from "Real-Time Human Pose Recognition in Parts from Single Depth Images: Supplementary Material," by J. Shotton et al., Proc. IEEE Conference on Computer Vision and Pattern Recognition, (2011).* © *2011 IEEE.*

14.5.4 Computing Joint Positions

The classifier described in the previous section assigns to each pixel some body part, but this process does not directly provide the joint positions because there is no underlying kinematic model. Instead, the position of each body part k could (for example) be estimated as some weighted average of the positions of the 3D points corresponding to pixels labeled k, or using some voting scheme. To improve robustness, it is also possible to use mean shifts to estimate the mode of the following 3D density distribution:

$$f_k(\boldsymbol{X}) \propto \sum_{i=1}^{N} P(k|\boldsymbol{x}_i) A(\boldsymbol{p}_i) \exp[-\frac{1}{\sigma_k^2}||\boldsymbol{X} - \boldsymbol{X}_i||^2],$$

where "$\propto$" stands for "is proportional to," $\boldsymbol{X}_i$ denotes the position of the 3D point associated with pixel $\boldsymbol{p}_i$, and $A(\boldsymbol{p}_i)$ is the area in world units of a pixel at depth $z(\boldsymbol{p}_i)$, proportional to $z(\boldsymbol{p}_i)^2$, so as to make the contribution of each pixel invariant to the distance between the sensor and the user. Each mode of this distribution is assigned the weighted sum of the probability scores of all pixels reaching it during the mean shift optimization process, and the joint is considered to be detected when the confidence of the highest mode is above some threshold. Since modes tend to lie on the front surface of the body, the final joint estimate is obtained by pushing back the maximal mode by a learned depth amount.

Figure 14.22 shows several results obtained on real data. Quantitative results can be obtained by measuring the per-joint precision, measured by counting the proportion of proposals within 0.1m of the true joint positions in hand-labeled depth maps. Experiments using the same synthetic and real data as before shows that the average per-joint precision over all joints and all test images is 0.914 for the real data, and 0.731 for the synthetic one, which is much more challenging due to a great variability in pose and body shape. In realistic game scenarios, the precision of the recovered joint parameters is good enough to drive a tracking system that smoothly and very robustly recovers the parameters of a 3D kinematic model (skeleton) over time, which can in turn be used to effectively control a video game with natural body motions.

14.6 NOTES

Excellent surveys of active range finding techniques can be found in Jarvis (1983), Nitzan (1988), Besl (1989), and Hebert (2000). The model-based approach to edge detection presented in Section 14.2.2 is only one of the many techniques that have been proposed for segmenting range pictures using notions from differential geometry (Fan, Medioni, & Nevatia 1987; Besl & Jain 1988). An alternative to the computational molecules used to smooth a range image in that section is provided by anisotropic diffusion, where the amount of smoothing at each point depends on the value of the gradient (Perona and Malik 1990c). The method for segmenting surfaces into (almost) planar patches presented in Section 14.2.3 is easily extended to quadric patches (see Faugeras and Hebert [1986] and the problems). Extensions to higher-order surface primitives is more problematic, in part because surface fitting is more difficult in that case. There is a vast amount of literature on the

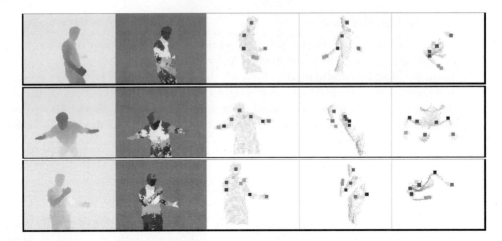

FIGURE 14.22: Sample results with, from left to right, the input depth map, the color-coded classification of pixel into body parts, and renderings of the recovered joint positions from three different viewpoints. *Reprinted from "Real-Time Human Pose Recognition in Parts from Single Depth Images: Supplementary Material," by J. Shotton et al., Proc. IEEE Conference on Computer Vision and Pattern Recognition, (2011). © 2011 IEEE.*

latter problem, using superquadrics (Pentland 1986; Bajcsy & Solina 1987; Gross & Boult 1988) and algebraic surfaces (Taubin, Cukierman, Sullivan, Ponce, & Kriegman 1994; Keren, Cooper, & Subrahmonia 1994; Sullivan, Sandford, & Ponce 1994) for example.

Different variants of the ICP algorithm presented in Section 14.3.2 and Besl and McKay (1992) have been developed over the years, including robust ones capable of handling missing data and/or outliers (Zhang 1994; Wheeler & Ikeuchi 1995), and they have been applied to a number of global registration problems (Shum, Ikeuchi, & Reddy 1995; Curless & Levoy 1996).

Alternatives to the Curless and Levoy (1996) approach to the fusion of multiple range images include the Delaunay triangulation algorithm of Boissonnat (1984), the zippered polygonal meshes of Turk and Levoy (1994), and the crust technique of Amenta *et al.* (1998). The quaternion-based approach to the estimation of rigid transformations described in this chapter was developed independently by Faugeras and Hebert (1986) and Horn (1987*a*). The recognition technique discussed in Section 14.4.1 is closely related to other algorithms using interpretation trees to control the combinatorial cost of feature matching in the two- and three-dimensional cases (Gaston & Lozano-Pérez 1984; Ayache & Faugeras 1986; Grimson & Lozano-Pérez 1987; Huttenlocher & Ullman 1987).

The spin images discussed in Section 14.4.2 have been used to establish pointwise correspondences between range images and surface models. Related approaches to this problem include the structural indexing method of Stein and Medioni (1992) and the point signatures proposed by Chua and Jarvis (1996). The original algorithm described in Section 14.4.2 has been extended in various directions: a scene can now be matched simultaneously to several models using principal component analysis (Johnson and Hebert 1999), and learning techniques are used to prune false matches in cluttered scenes (Carmichael *et al.* 1999).

Kinect's pose estimation algorithm is detailed in Shotton *et al.* (2011). Decision trees date back to the 1960s, and classical treatments can be found in (Breiman *et al.* 1984; Quinlan 1993). The bootstrap was introduced in Efron (1979), bagging was proposed in Breiman (1996), and random forests in (Amit & Geman 1997; Breiman 2001). See Hastie *et al.* (2009) for a synthesis of these techniques.

PROBLEMS

14.1. Use Equation (14.1) to show that a necessary and sufficient condition for the coordinate curves of a parameterized surface to be principal directions is that $f = F = 0$.

14.2. Show that the lines of curvature of a surface of revolution are its meridians and parallels.

14.3. Step model: compute $z_\sigma(x) = G_\sigma * z(x)$, where $z(x)$ is given by (14.2). Show that z_σ'' is given by Equation (14.3). Conclude that $\kappa_\sigma''/\kappa_\sigma' = -2\delta/h$ in the point x_σ where z_σ'' and κ_σ vanish.

14.4. Roof model: show that κ_σ is given by Equation (14.4).

14.5. The Rodrigues formula. Consider a rotation $\mathcal{R}$ of angle θ about the axis $\boldsymbol{u}$ (a unit vector). Show that $\mathcal{R}\boldsymbol{x} = \cos\theta\,\boldsymbol{x} + \sin\theta\,\boldsymbol{u} \times \boldsymbol{x} + (1 - \cos\theta)(\boldsymbol{u} \cdot \boldsymbol{x})\boldsymbol{u}$.
Hint: A rotation does not change the projection of a vector $\boldsymbol{x}$ onto the direction $\boldsymbol{u}$ of its axis and applies a planar rotation of angle θ to the projection of $\boldsymbol{x}$ into the plane orthogonal to $\boldsymbol{u}$.

14.6. Use the Rodrigues formula to show that the quaternion $\mathsf{q} = \cos\frac{\theta}{2} + \sin\frac{\theta}{2}\boldsymbol{u}$ represents the rotation $\mathcal{R}$ of angle θ about the unit vector $\boldsymbol{u}$ in the sense of Equation (14.5).

14.7. Show that the rotation matrix $\mathcal{R}$ associated with a given unit quaternion $\mathsf{q} = a + \boldsymbol{\alpha}$ with $\boldsymbol{\alpha} = (b, c, d)^T$ is given by Equation (14.6).

14.8. Show that the matrix $\mathcal{A}_i$ constructed in Section 14.3.2 is equal to

$$\mathcal{A}_i = \begin{pmatrix} 0 & \boldsymbol{y}_i^T - \boldsymbol{y}_i'^T \\ \boldsymbol{y}_i' - \boldsymbol{y}_i & [\boldsymbol{y}_i + \boldsymbol{y}_i']_\times \end{pmatrix}.$$

14.9. As mentioned earlier, the ICP method can be extended to various types of geometric models. We consider here the case of polyhedral models and piecewise parametric patches.
   (a) Sketch a method for computing the point Q in a polygon that is closest to some point P.
   (b) Sketch a method for computing the point Q in the parametric patch $\boldsymbol{x} : I \times J \to \mathbb{R}^3$ that is closest to some point P. Hint: use Newton iterations.

14.10. Develop a linear least-squares method for fitting a quadric surface to a set of points under the constraint that the quadratic form has unit Frobenius form.

14.11. Show that a surface triangle maps onto a patch with hyperbolic edges in α, β space.

PROGRAMMING EXERCISES

14.12. Implement the model-based edge-detection algorithm of Ponce and Brady.

14.13. Implement the region-growing approach to plane segmentation described in this chapter.

14.14. Implement an algorithm for computing the lines of curvature of a surface from its range image. Hint: use a curve-growing algorithm analogous to the region-growing algorithm for plane segmentation.

14.15. Implement the Besl-McKay ICP registration algorithm.

14.16. Marching squares in the plane: develop and implement an algorithm for finding the zero set of a planar density function. Hint: work out the possible ways a curve may intersect the edges of a pixel, and use linear interpolation along these edges to identify the zero set.

14.17. Implement the registration part of the Faugeras-Hebert algorithm.

C H A P T E R   15

Learning to Classify

A *classifier* is a procedure that accepts a set of features and produces a class label for them. There could be two, or many, classes, though it is usual to produce multi-class classifiers out of two-class classifiers. Classifiers are built by taking a set of labeled examples and using them to come up with a rule that assigns a label to any new example. In the general problem, we have a training dataset $(\mathbf{x}_i, y_i)$; each of the *feature vectors* $\boldsymbol{x}_i$ consists of measurements of the properties of different types of object, and the y_i are labels giving the type of the object that generated the example.

Classifiers are a crucial tool in high-level vision, because many problems can be abstracted in a form that looks like classification. In this chapter, we describe the basic ideas and methods of classification, abstracted away from any vision problem (Chapter 16 applies classifiers to vision problems). Section 15.1 describes basic notions. In Section 15.2, we describe different ways to build classifiers. Finally, Section 15.3 gives some important practical tricks.

15.1 CLASSIFICATION, ERROR, AND LOSS

You should think of a classifier as a rule, though it might not be implemented that way. We pass in a feature vector, and the rule returns a class label. We know the relative costs of mislabeling each class and must come up with a rule that can take any plausible $\boldsymbol{x}$ and assign a class to it, in such a way that the expected mislabeling cost is as small as possible, or at least tolerable. For most of this chapter, we will assume that there are two classes, labeled 1 and -1. Section 15.3.2 shows methods for building multi-class classifiers from two-class classifiers.

15.1.1 Using Loss to Determine Decisions

The choice of classification rule must depend on the cost of making a mistake. A two-class classifier can make two kinds of mistake. A *false positive* occurs when a negative example is classified positive; a *false negative* occurs when a positive example is classified negative. For example, pretend there is only one disease; then doctors would be classifiers, deciding whether a patient had it or not. If this disease is dangerous, but is safely and easily treated, then false negatives are expensive errors, but false positives are cheap. Similarly, if it is not dangerous, but the treatment is difficult and unpleasant, then false positives are expensive errors and false negatives are cheap.

Generally, we write outcomes as $(i \rightarrow j)$, meaning that an item of type i is classified as an item of type j. There are four outcomes for the two-class case. Each outcome has its own cost, which is known as a *loss*. Hence, we have a loss function that we write as $L(i \rightarrow j)$, meaning the loss incurred when an object of type i is classified as having type j. Since losses associated with correct classification should not affect the design of the classifier, $L(i \rightarrow i)$ must be zero, but the other losses could be any positive numbers.

The *risk function* of a particular classification strategy is the expected loss when using that strategy, as a function of the kind of item. The *total risk* is the total expected loss when using the classifier. The total risk depends on the strategy, but not on the examples. Write $p(-1 \rightarrow 1|\text{using } s)$ for the probability that class -1 is labeled class 1 (and so on). Then, if there were two classes, the total risk of using strategy s would be

$$R(s) = p(-1 \rightarrow 1|\text{using } s)L(-1 \rightarrow 1) + p(1 \rightarrow -1|\text{using } s)L(-1 \rightarrow 1).$$

The desirable strategy is one that minimizes this total risk.

A Two-class Classifier that Minimizes Total Risk

Assume that the classifier can choose between two classes and we have a known loss function. There is some boundary in the feature space, which we call the *decision boundary*, such that points on one side belong to class one and points on the other side to class two.

We can resort to a trick to determine where the decision boundary is. If the decision boundary is optimal, then *for points on the decision boundary*, either choice of class has the same expected loss; if this weren't so, we could obtain a better classifier by always choosing one class (and so moving the boundary). This means that, for measurements on the decision boundary, choosing label -1 yields the same expected loss as choosing label 1.

Now write $p(-1|\boldsymbol{x})$ for the posterior probability of label -1 given feature vector $\boldsymbol{x}$ (and so on). Although this might be very hard to know in practice, we can manipulate the abstraction and gain some insight. A choice of label $y = 1$ for a point $\boldsymbol{x}$ at the decision boundary yields an expected loss

$$p(-1|\boldsymbol{x})L(-1 \rightarrow 1) + p(1|\boldsymbol{x})L(1 \rightarrow 1) = p(-1|\boldsymbol{x})L(-1 \rightarrow 1),$$

and if we choose the other label, the expected loss is

$$p(1|\boldsymbol{x})L(1 \rightarrow -1),$$

and these two terms must be equal. This means our decision boundary consists of the points $\boldsymbol{x}$, where

$$p(-1|\boldsymbol{x})L(-1 \rightarrow 1) = p(1|\boldsymbol{x})L(1 \rightarrow -1).$$

At points off the boundary, we must choose the class with the *lowest* expected loss. Recall that if we choose label 1 for a point $\boldsymbol{x}$, the expected loss is

$$p(-1|\boldsymbol{x})L(-1 \rightarrow 1),$$

and so on. This means that we should choose label -1 if

$$p(-1|\boldsymbol{x})L(-1 \rightarrow 1) > p(1|\boldsymbol{x})L(1 \rightarrow -1)$$

and label 1 if the inequality is reversed. Notice it does not matter which label we choose at the decision boundary.

A Multi-class Classifier that Minimizes Total Risk

Analyzing expected loss gives a strategy for choosing from any number of classes. We allow the option of refusing to decide which class an object belongs to, which is useful in some problems. Refusing to decide costs d. Conveniently, if d is larger than any misclassification loss, we will never refuse to decide. This means our analysis covers the case when we are forced to decide. The same reasoning applies as above, but there are more boundaries to consider. The simplest case, which is widely dominant in vision, is when loss is *0-1 loss*; here the correct answer has zero loss, and any error costs one.

In this case, the best strategy, known as the *Bayes classifier*, is given in Algorithm 15.1. The total risk associated with this rule is known as the *Bayes risk*; this is the smallest possible risk that we can have using a classifier for this problem. It is usually rather difficult to know what the Bayes classifier—and hence the Bayes risk—is because the probabilities involved are not known exactly. In a few cases, it is possible to write the rule out explicitly. One way to tell the effectiveness of a technique for building classifiers is to study the behavior of the risk as the number of examples increases (e.g., one might want the risk to converge to the Bayes risk in probability if the number of examples is large). The Bayes risk is seldom zero, as Figure 15.1 illustrates.

For a loss function

$$L(i \rightarrow j) = \begin{cases} 1 & i \neq j \\ 0 & i = j \\ d & \text{no decision} \end{cases}$$

the best strategy is

- *if $p(k|\mathbf{x}) > p(i|\mathbf{x})$ for all i not equal to k, and if this probability is greater than $1 - d$, choose type k;*
- *if there are several classes $k_1 \ldots k_j$ for which $p(k_1|\mathbf{x}) = p(k_2|\mathbf{x}) = \ldots = p(k_j|\mathbf{x}) = p > p(i|\mathbf{x})$ for all i not in $k_1, \ldots k_j$, and if $p > 1-d$, choose uniformly and at random between $k_1, \ldots k_j$;*
- *if for all i we have $1 - d \geq q = p(k|\mathbf{x}) \geq p(i|\mathbf{x})$, refuse to decide.*

Algorithm 15.1: The Bayes Classifier.

15.1.2   Training Error, Test Error, and Overfitting

It can be quite difficult to know a good loss function, but one can usually come up with a plausible model. If we knew the posterior probabilities, building a classifier would be straightforward. Usually we don't, and must build a model from data. This model could be a model of the posterior probabilities, or an estimate of the decision boundaries. In either case, we have only the training data to build it with. *Training error* is the error a model makes on the training data set.

Generally, we will try to make this training error small. However, what we really want to minimize is the *test error*, the error the classifier makes on test data. We cannot minimize this error directly, because we don't know the test set (if we

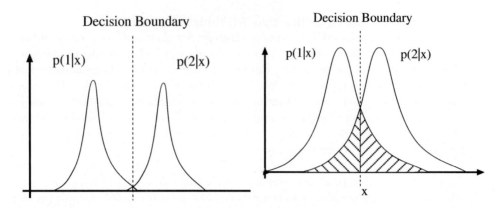

FIGURE 15.1: This figure shows typical elements of a two-class classification problem. We have plotted $p(\text{class}|x)$ as a function of the feature x. Assuming that $L(-1 \to 1) = L(1 \to -1)$, we have marked the classifier boundaries. In this case, the Bayes risk is the sum of the amount of the posterior for class one in the class two region and the amount of the posterior for class two in the class one region (the hatched area in the figures). For the case on the left, the classes are well separated, which means that the Bayes risk is small; for the case on the right, the Bayes risk is rather large.

did, special procedures in training apply Joachims (1999)). However, classifiers that have small training error might not have small test error. One example of this problem is the (silly) classifier that takes any data point and, if it is the same as a point in the training set, emits the class of that point and otherwise chooses randomly between the classes. This classifier has been learned from data, and has a zero error rate on the training dataset; it is likely to be unhelpful on any other dataset, however.

The phenomenon that causes test error to be worse than training error is sometimes called *overfitting* (other names include *selection bias*, because the training data has been selected and so isn't exactly like the test data, and *generalizing badly*, because the classifier fails to generalize). It occurs because the classifier has been trained to perform well *on the training dataset*. The training dataset is not the same as the test dataset. First, it is quite likely smaller. Second, it might be biased through a variety of accidents. This means that small training error may have to do with quirks of the training dataset that don't occur in other sets of examples. It is quite possible that, in this case, the test error will be larger than the training error. Generally, we expect classifiers to perform somewhat better on the training set than on the test set. Overfitting can result in a substantial difference between performance on the training set and performance on the test set. One consequence of overfitting is that classifiers should always be evaluated on test data. Doing this creates other problems, which we discuss in Section 15.1.4.

15.1.3   Regularization

The idea of *regularization* is to attach a penalty term to the training error to get a better estimate of the test error. This penalty term could take a variety of different forms, depending on the requirements of the application. Often, but not always, the penalty term looks like a norm of the classifier parameters.

Logistic regression is a classifier that gives a good, simple example of why regularization should be helpful. In logistic regression, we model the class-conditional densities by requiring that

$$\log \frac{p(1|\boldsymbol{x})}{p(-1|\boldsymbol{x})} = \boldsymbol{a}^T \boldsymbol{x}$$

where $\boldsymbol{a}$ is a vector of parameters. The decision boundary here will be a hyperplane passing through the origin of the feature space. Notice that we can turn this into a general hyperplane in the original feature space by extending each example's feature vector by attaching a 1 as the last component. This trick simplifies notation, which is why we adopt it here. It is straightforward to estimate $\boldsymbol{a}$ using maximum likelihood. Note that

$$p(1|\boldsymbol{x}) = \frac{\exp \boldsymbol{a}^T \boldsymbol{x}}{1 + \exp \boldsymbol{a}^T \boldsymbol{x}}$$

and

$$p(-1|\boldsymbol{x}) = \frac{1}{1 + \exp \boldsymbol{a}^T \boldsymbol{x}},$$

so that we can estimate the correct set of parameters $\hat{\boldsymbol{a}}$ by solving for the minimum of the negative log-likelihood, i.e.,

$$\hat{\boldsymbol{a}} = \begin{array}{c} \text{argmin} \\ \boldsymbol{a} \end{array} \left[-\sum_{i \in \text{examples}} (\frac{1 + y_i}{2}) \boldsymbol{a}^T \boldsymbol{x} - \log \left(1 + \boldsymbol{a}^T \boldsymbol{x} \right) \right].$$

It turns out that this problem is convex, and is easily solved by Newton's method (e.g., Hastie *et al.* (2009)).

In fact, when we use maximum likelihood, we are choosing a classifier boundary that minimizes a loss function, and this is a better way to think about the problem. For example i, we write $\gamma_i = \boldsymbol{a}^T \boldsymbol{x}_i$. Our classifier will be:

$$\text{choose} \begin{cases} 1 \text{ if } \gamma_i > 0 \\ -1 \text{ if } \gamma_i < 0 \\ \text{randomly if } \gamma_i = 0. \end{cases}$$

Now write the loss for the ith example

$$\begin{aligned} L(y_i, \gamma_i) &= -\left[\frac{1}{2}(1 + y_i)\gamma_i - \log \left(1 + \exp \gamma_i \right) \right] \\ &= \log \left(1 + \exp \left(-y_i \gamma_i \right) \right) \end{aligned}$$

(where the step follows from simple manipulations; see the exercises). This is plotted in Figure 15.2. This loss is sometimes known as the *logistic loss*. Notice that this loss very strongly penalizes a large positive γ_i if y_i is negative (and vice versa). However, there is no significant advantage to having a large positive γ_i if y_i is positive. This means that the significant components of the loss function will be due to examples that the classifier gets wrong, but also due to examples that have

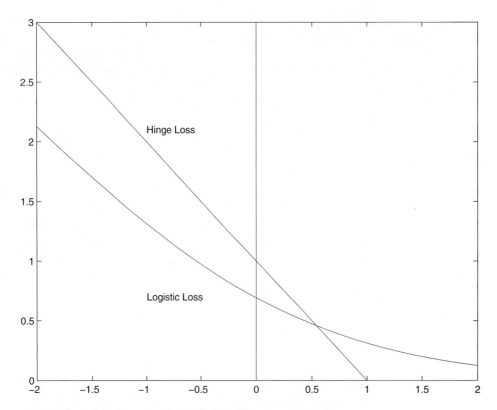

FIGURE 15.2: The logistic loss and the hinge loss, plotted for the case $y_i = 1$. In the case of the logistic loss, the horizontal variable is the $\gamma_i = \boldsymbol{a} \cdot \boldsymbol{x}_i$ of the text. In the case of the hinge loss, the horizontal variable is the $\boldsymbol{w} \cdot \boldsymbol{x}_i + b$ of the text. Notice that in each case, giving a strong negative response to this positive example causes a loss, that grows linearly as the magnitude of the response grows (if it grew faster, we might fear robustness problems). Notice also that giving an insufficiently positive response also causes a loss. The hinge loss isn't differentiable, and the logistic loss is.

γ_i near zero (i.e., the example is close to the decision boundary). Now the total risk of applying this classifier to our set of examples is

$$\sum_{i \in \text{examples}} -\left[\frac{1}{2}(1 + y_i)\gamma_i - \log\left(1 + \exp \gamma_i\right)\right],$$

and it is natural to minimize this risk as a function of $\boldsymbol{a}$ using Newton's method (see Hastie *et al.* (2009)). The Hessian will be

$$\mathcal{H} = \sum_{i \in \text{examples}} \frac{\exp \gamma_i}{(1 + \exp \gamma_i)^2} \boldsymbol{x}_i \boldsymbol{x}_i^T.$$

Notice that data points where γ_i has a large absolute value make little contribution to the Hessian—it is affected mainly by points where γ_i is small, that is, points near the boundary. For these points, the Hessian looks like a weighted covariance matrix. Now if we have features that are strongly correlated, we can expect that the Hessian is poorly conditioned, because the covariance matrix will have some small eigenvalues. These will be caused by the high covariance of the features. We would typically maximize using Newton's method, which involves updating an estimate $a^{(n)}$ by computing $a^{(n+1)} = a^{(n)} + \delta a$, where we get the step δa by solving $\mathcal{H}(\delta a) = -\nabla f$. When this linear system is very poorly conditioned, it means that a wide range of different $a^{(n+1)}$ have essentially the same value of loss. In turn, many choices of a will give about the same loss *on the training data*. The training data offers no reason to choose between these a.

However, a with very large norm may behave badly on future test data, because they will tend to produce large values of $a^T x$ for test data items x. In turn, these can produce large losses, particularly if the sign is wrong. This suggests that we should use a value of a that gives small training loss, and also has a small norm. In turn, this suggests we change the objective function by adding a term that discourages a with large norm. This term is referred to as a *regularizer*, because it tends to discourage solutions that are large (and so have possible high loss on future test data) but are not strongly supported by the training data. The objective function becomes

$$\text{Training Loss} + \text{Regularizer}$$

which is

$$\text{Training Loss} + \lambda \, (\text{Norm of } a)$$

which is

$$\sum_{i \in \text{examples}} \left(\frac{1}{2}(1 + y_i)\gamma_i - \log\left(1 + \exp\gamma_i\right) \right) + \lambda a^T a$$

where $\lambda > 0$ is a constant chosen for good performance. Too large a value of λ, and the classifier will behave poorly on training and test data; too small a value, and the classifier will behave poorly on test data.

Usually, the value of λ is set with a validation dataset. We train classifiers with different values of λ on a test dataset, then evaluate them on a validation set—data whose labels are known, but which is not used for training—and finally choose the λ that gets the best validation error.

Regularizing training loss using the norm is a general recipe, and can be applied to most of the classifiers we describe. For some classifiers, the reasons this approach works are more recondite than those sketched here, but the model here is informative. Norms other than L_2—that is, $\|x\|_2^2 = x^T x$—can be used successfully. The most commonly used alternative is L_1—that is, $\|x\|_1 = \sum_i |x_i|$—which leads to much more intricate minimization problems but strongly encourages zeros in the coefficients of the classifier, which is sometimes desirable.

15.1.4   Error Rate and Cross-Validation

There are a variety of methods to describe the performance of a classifier. Natural, straightforward choices are to report the *error rate*, the percentage of classification attempts on a test set that result in the wrong answer. This presents an important difficulty. We cannot estimate the error rate of the classifier using training data, because the classifier has been trained to do well on that data, which will mean our error rate estimate will be an underestimate. An alternative is to split some training data to form a validation set, then train the classifier on the rest of the data, and evaluate on the validation set. This has the difficulty that the classifier will not be the best estimate possible, because we have left out some training data when we trained it. This issue can become a significant nuisance when we are trying to tell which of a set of classifiers to use—did the classifier perform poorly on validation data because it is not suited to the problem representation or because it was trained on too little data?

We can resolve this problem with *cross-validation*, which involves repeatedly: splitting data into training and validation sets uniformly and at random, training a classifier on the training set, evaluating it on the validation set, and then averaging the error over all splits. This allows an estimate of the likely future performance of a classifier, at the expense of substantial computation.

Choose some class of subsets of the training set, for example, singletons.

For each element of that class, construct a classifier by omitting that element in training, and compute the classification errors (or risk) on the omitted subset.

Average these errors over the class of subsets to estimate the risk of using the classifier trained on the entire training dataset.

Algorithm 15.2: Cross-Validation

The most usual form of this algorithm involves omitting single items from the dataset and is known as *leave-one-out cross-validation*. Errors are usually estimated by simply averaging over the class, but more sophisticated estimates are available (see, e.g., Ripley (1996)). We do not justify this tool mathematically; however, it is worth noticing that leave-one-out cross-validation, in some sense, looks at the sensitivity of the classifier to a small change in the training set. If a classifier performs well under this test, then large subsets of the dataset look similar to one another, which suggests that a representation of the relevant probabilities derived from the dataset might be quite good.

For a multi-class classifier, it is often helpful to know which classes were misclassified. We can compute a *class-confusion matrix*, a table whose i, jth entry is the number of times an item of true class i was labeled j by the classifier (notice that this definition is not symmetric). If there are many classes, this matrix can be rendered as an image (Figure 15.3), where the intensity values correspond to counts; typically, larger values are lighter. Such images are quite easy to assess at a glance. One looks for a light diagonal (because the diagonal elements are the counts of correct classifications), for any row that seems dark (which means that there were few elements in that class), and for bright off-diagonal elements (which

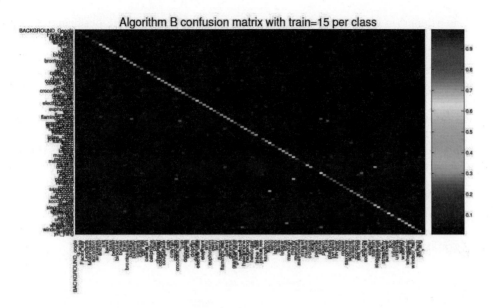

FIGURE 15.3: An example of a class confusion matrix from a recent image classification system, due to Zhang *et al.* (2006*a*). The vertical bar shows the mapping of color to number (warmer colors are larger numbers). Note the redness of the diagonal; this is good, because it means the diagonal values are large. There are spots of large off-diagonal values, and these are informative, too. For example, this system confuses: schooners and ketches (understandable); waterlily and lotus (again, understandable); and platypus and mayfly (which might suggest some feature engineering would be a good idea). *This figure was originally published as Figure 5 of "SVM-KNN: Discriminative Nearest Neighbor Classification for Visual Category Recognition," by H. Zhang, A. Berg, M. Maire, and J. Malik, Proc. IEEE CVPR, 2006, © IEEE, 2006.*

are high-frequency misclassifications).

15.1.5 Receiver Operating Curves

For a two-class classifier, we can make a more comprehensive report of the error behavior than just giving the error rate. In this case, the ratio of losses,

$$h = L(1 \rightarrow -1)/L(-1 \rightarrow 1+),$$

rather than the losses is what determines the decision. Because $p(1|\boldsymbol{x}) = 1 - P(-1|\boldsymbol{x})$, we can rearrange terms to indicate that we should choose label 1 if

$$p(1|\boldsymbol{x}) > \frac{1}{1+h}$$

and label -1 otherwise. In most two-class classification problems we do not know $p(1|\boldsymbol{x})$ and may not know h either. Nonetheless, we have a general recipe for building a classifier: build a model of $p(1|\boldsymbol{x})$ from data, and test that model against a threshold, which could range from zero to one. Plotting the behavior of the classifier as a function of this threshold tells us a great deal about the performance of the model. As we increase the threshold from zero to one, the classifier will classify more examples as class two. If we think of class two as the positive class, then, as the threshold goes up, we will detect more positive cases, and also incorrectly mark more negative examples as positive.

A *receiver operating characteristic curve*, or *ROC*, is a plot of the *detection rate* or *true positive rate* as a function of the *false positive rate* for a particular model as the threshold changes (Figure 15.4). An ideal model would detect all positive cases and produce no false positives, for any threshold value; in this case, the curve would be a single point. A model that has no information about whether an example is a positive or a negative will produce the line from $(0,0)$ to $(1,1)$. If the ROC lies below this line, then we can produce a better classifier by inverting the decision of the original classifier, so this line is the worst possible classifier. The detection rate never goes down as the false positive rate goes up, so the ROC is the graph of a non-decreasing function.

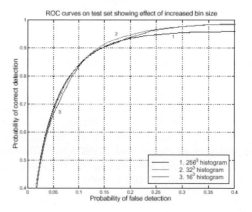

FIGURE 15.4: The receiver operating curve for a classifier, used to build a skin detector by Jones and Rehg. This curve plots the detection rate against the false-negative rate for a variety of values of the parameter θ. A perfect classifier has an ROC that, on these axes, is a horizontal line at 100% detection. There are three different versions of this classifier, depending on the detailed feature construction; each has a slightly different ROC. *This figure was originally published as Figure 7 of "Statistical color models with application to skin detection," by M.J. Jones and J. Rehg, Proc. IEEE CVPR, 1999 © IEEE, 1999.*

Models of a classification problem can be compared by comparing their ROC's. Alternatively, we can build a summary of the ROC. Most commonly used in computer vision is the area under the ROC (the *AUC*), which is 1 for a perfect classifier, and 0.5 for a classifier that has no information about the problem. The area under the ROC has the following interpretation: assume we select one positive example and one negative example uniformly at random, and display them to the classifier; the AUC is the probability that the classifier tells correctly which of these two is positive.

15.2 MAJOR CLASSIFICATION STRATEGIES

Usually, we do not know $p(1|\boldsymbol{x})$, or $p(1)$, or $p(\boldsymbol{x}|1)$ exactly, and we must determine a classifier from an example dataset. There are two rather general strategies:

- **Explicit probability models:** We can use the example data set to build a probability model (of either the likelihood or the posterior, depending on taste and circumstance). There is a wide variety of ways of doing this, some of which we see in the following sections.

- **Determining decision boundaries directly:** Quite bad probability models can produce good classifiers, as Figure 15.5 indicates. This is because the decision boundaries, rather than the details of the probability model, are what determine the performance of a classifier (the main role of the probability model in the Bayes classifier is to identify the decision boundaries). This suggests that we could ignore the probability model and attempt to construct good decision boundaries directly. This approach is often extremely successful; it is particularly attractive when there is no reasonable prospect of modeling the data source.

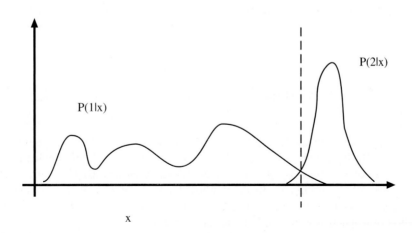

FIGURE 15.5: The figure shows posterior densities for two classes. The optimal decision boundary is shown as a dashed line. Notice that although a normal density may provide rather a poor fit *to the posteriors*, the quality of the classifier it provides depends only on *how well it predicts the position of the boundaries*. In this case, assuming that the posteriors are normal may provide a fairly good classifier because $P(2|x)$ looks normal, and the mean and covariance of $P(1|x)$ look as if they would predict the boundary in the right place.

15.2.1 Example: Using Mahalanobis Distance with Normal Class-Conditional Densities

Assume that $p(\boldsymbol{x}|k)$ for each class k are known to be normal. We can either assume that the priors are known or estimate the priors by counting the number of data items from each class. We can use the data items and the usual procedures to obtain the mean $\boldsymbol{\mu}_k$ and covariance Σ_k for each class. Now because $\log a > \log b$ implies

$a > b$, we can work with the logarithm of the posterior. This yields a classifier of the form in Algorithm 15.3.

Assume we have N classes, and the kth class contains N_k examples, of which the ith is written as $\boldsymbol{x}_{k,i}$.

For each class k, estimate the prior, the mean and standard deviation for that class-conditional density.

$$p(k) = \frac{N_k}{\sum_i N_i}$$

$$\boldsymbol{\mu}_k = \frac{1}{N_k} \sum_{i=1}^{N_k} \boldsymbol{x}_{k,i};$$

$$\Sigma_k = \frac{1}{N_k - 1} \sum_{i=1}^{N_k} (\boldsymbol{x}_{k,i} - \boldsymbol{\mu}_k)(\boldsymbol{x}_{k,i} - \boldsymbol{\mu}_k)^T;$$

To classify an example $\boldsymbol{x}$,

Choose the class k with the smallest value of $\delta(\mathbf{x}; \boldsymbol{\mu}_k, \Sigma_k)^2 - p(k)$

where

$$\delta(\mathbf{x}; \boldsymbol{\mu}_k, \Sigma_k) = \frac{1}{2} \left((\mathbf{x} - \boldsymbol{\mu}_k)^T \Sigma_k^{-1} (\mathbf{x} - \boldsymbol{\mu}_k) \right)^{(1/2)}.$$

Algorithm 15.3: Multi-class Classification Assuming Class-Conditional Densities are Normal

The term $\delta(\mathbf{x}; \boldsymbol{\mu}_k, \Sigma_k)$ in this algorithm is known as the *Mahalanobis distance* (e.g., see Ripley (1996)). The algorithm can be interpreted geometrically as saying that the correct class is the one whose mean is closest to the data item *taking into account the variance*. In particular, distance from a mean along a direction where there is little variance has a large weight, and distance from the mean along a direction where there is a large variance has little weight. This classifier can be simplified by assuming that each class has the same covariance (with the advantage that we have fewer parameters to estimate). In this case, because the term $\boldsymbol{x}^T \Sigma^{-1} \boldsymbol{x}$ is common to all expressions, the classifier actually involves comparing expressions that are *linear in $\boldsymbol{x}$*. If there are only two classes, the process boils down to determining whether a linear expression in $\mathbf{x}$ is greater than or less than zero (see the exercises).

15.2.2   Example: Class-Conditional Histograms and Naive Bayes

If we have enough labeled data, we could model the class-conditional densities with histograms. This really is practical only in low dimensions, but is sometimes useful. We obtain $p(\boldsymbol{x}|y = 1)$ by producing a histogram of the features of the positive examples, $p(\boldsymbol{x}|y = -1)$ from a histogram of the features of the negative examples, and $p(y = 1)$ by counting positive versus negative examples. Then,

$$p(y = 1|\boldsymbol{x}) = \frac{p(\boldsymbol{x}|y = 1)p(y = 1)}{p(\boldsymbol{x}|y = 1)p(y = 1) + p(\boldsymbol{x}|y = -1)(1 - p(y = 1))},$$

and we can plot an ROC.

Models like this become impractical in high dimensions because the number of boxes required goes up as a power of the dimension. We can dodge this phenomenon by assuming that features are independent conditioned on the class. Although this appears to be an aggressive oversimplification—it is known by the pejorative name *naive Bayes*—it is often very well-behaved, and is competitive for many problems. In particular, we assume that

$$p(\boldsymbol{x}|y = 1) = p([x_0, x_1, \ldots, x_n]|y = 1) = p(x_0|y = 1)p(x_1|y = 1)\ldots p(x_n|y = 1).$$

Now each of these conditional distributions is low-dimensional, and so easy to model (either a normal distribution or a histogram are good candidates).

15.2.3   Example: A Nonparametric Classifier Using Nearest Neighbors

It is reasonable to assume that example points near an unclassified point should indicate the class of that point. *Nearest neighbors* methods build classifiers using this heuristic. We could classify a point by using the class of the nearest example whose class is known, or use several example points and make them vote. It is reasonable to require that some minimum number of points vote for the class we choose.

A (k, l) nearest neighbor classifier finds the k example points closest to the point being considered, and classifies this point with the class that has the highest number of votes, as long as this class has more than l votes (otherwise, the point is classified as unknown). A $(k, 0)$-nearest neighbor classifier is usually known as a *k-nearest neighbor classifier*, and a $(1, 0)$-nearest neighbor classifier is usually known as a *nearest neighbor classifier*.

Nearest neighbor classifiers are known to be good, in the sense that the risk of using a nearest neighbor classifier with a sufficiently large number of examples lies within quite good bounds of the Bayes risk. As k grows, the difference between the Bayes risk and the risk of using a k-nearest neighbor classifier goes down as $1/\sqrt{k}$. In practice, one seldom uses more than three nearest neighbors. Furthermore, if the Bayes risk is zero, the expected risk of using a k-nearest neighbor classifier is also zero (see Devroye *et al.* (1996) for more detail on all these points). Finding the k nearest points for a particular query can be difficult, and Section 21.2.3 reviews this point.

A second difficulty in building such classifiers is the choice of distance. For features that are obviously of the same type, such as lengths, the usual metric may be good enough. But what if one feature is a length, one is a color, and one is an angle? One possibility is to use a covariance estimate to compute a Mahalanobis-like distance. It is almost always a good idea to scale each feature independently so that the variance of each feature is the same, or at least consistent; this prevents features with very large scales dominating those with very small scales.

Ensure that all feature vectors are appropriately scaled.
Given a feature vector $\boldsymbol{x}$

1. determine the k training examples that are nearest, $\boldsymbol{x}_1, \ldots, \boldsymbol{x}_k$;
2. determine the class c that has the largest number of representatives n in this set;
3. if $n > l$, classify $\boldsymbol{x}$ as c, otherwise refuse to classify it.

Algorithm 15.4: (k, l) Nearest Neighbor Classification

15.2.4 Example: The Linear Support Vector Machine

Assume we have a set of N example points $\boldsymbol{x}_i$ that belong to two classes, which we indicate by 1 and -1. These points come with their class labels, which we write as y_i; thus, our dataset can be written as

$$\{(\boldsymbol{x}_1, y_1), \ldots, (\boldsymbol{x}_N, y_N)\}.$$

We seek a rule that predicts the sign of y for any point $\boldsymbol{x}$; this rule is our classifier.

At this point, we distinguish between two cases: either the data is linearly separable or it isn't. The linearly separable case is much easier, and we deal with it first.

Support Vector Machines for Linearly Separable Datasets   In a linearly separable dataset, there is some choice of $\boldsymbol{w}$ and b (which represent a hyperplane) such that

$$y_i (\boldsymbol{w} \cdot \boldsymbol{x}_i + b) > 0$$

for every example point (notice the devious use of the sign of y_i). There is one of these expressions for each data point, and the set of expressions represents a set of constraints on the choice of $\boldsymbol{w}$ and b. These constraints express the constraint that all examples with a negative y_i should be on one side of the hyperplane and all with a positive y_i should be on the other side.

In fact, because the set of examples is finite, there is a family of separating hyperplanes. Each of these hyperplanes must separate the convex hull of one set of examples from the convex hull of the other set of examples. The most conservative choice of hyperplane is the one that is farthest from both hulls. This is obtained by joining the closest points on the two hulls, and constructing a hyperplane perpendicular to this line and through its midpoint. This hyperplane is as far as possible from each set, in the sense that it maximizes the minimum distance from example points to the hyperplane (Figure 15.6).

Now we can choose the scale of $\boldsymbol{w}$ and b because scaling the two together by a positive number doesn't affect the validity of the constraints $y_i(\boldsymbol{w} \cdot \boldsymbol{x}_i + b) > 0$. This means that we can choose $\boldsymbol{w}$ and b such that for every data point we have

$$y_i (\boldsymbol{w} \cdot \boldsymbol{x}_i + b) \geq 1$$

and such that equality is achieved on at least one point on each side of the hyperplane. Now assume that $\boldsymbol{x}_k$ achieves equality and $y_k = 1$, and $\boldsymbol{x}_l$ achieves equality

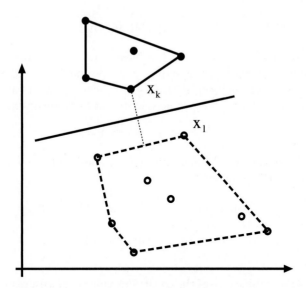

FIGURE 15.6: The hyperplane constructed by a support vector classifier for a plane dataset. The filled circles are data points corresponding to one class, and the empty circles are data points corresponding to the other. We have drawn in the convex hull of each dataset. The most conservative choice of hyperplane is one that maximizes the minimum distance from each hull to the hyperplane. A hyperplane with this property is obtained by constructing the shortest line segment between the hulls and then obtaining a hyperplane perpendicular to this line segment and through its midpoint. Only a subset of the data determines the hyperplane. Of particular interest are points on each convex hull that are associated with a minimum distance between the hulls. We use these points to find the hyperplane in the text.

and $y_l = -1$. This means that $\boldsymbol{x}_k$ is on one side of the hyperplane and $\boldsymbol{x}_l$ is on the other. Furthermore, the distance from $\boldsymbol{x}_l$ to the hyperplane is minimal (among the points on the same side as $\boldsymbol{x}_l$), as is the distance from $\boldsymbol{x}_k$ to the hyperplane. Notice that there might be several points with these properties.

This means that $\boldsymbol{w} \cdot (\boldsymbol{x}_1 - \boldsymbol{x}_2) = 2$, so that

$$dist(\boldsymbol{x}_k, \text{hyperplane}) + dist(\boldsymbol{x}_l, \text{hyperplane})$$

which is

$$(\frac{\boldsymbol{w}}{|\boldsymbol{w}|} \cdot \boldsymbol{x}_k + \frac{b}{|\boldsymbol{w}|}) - (\frac{\boldsymbol{w}}{|\boldsymbol{w}|} \cdot \boldsymbol{x}_1 + \frac{b}{|\boldsymbol{w}|}),$$

becomes

$$\frac{\boldsymbol{w}}{|\boldsymbol{w}|} \cdot (\boldsymbol{x}_1 - \boldsymbol{x}_2) = \frac{2}{|\boldsymbol{w}|}.$$

This means that maximizing the distance is the same as *minimizing* $(1/2)\boldsymbol{w} \cdot \boldsymbol{w}$. We now have the constrained minimization problem:

$$\text{minimize} \qquad (1/2)\boldsymbol{w} \cdot \boldsymbol{w}$$

$$\text{subject to} \qquad y_i\,(\boldsymbol{w} \cdot \boldsymbol{x}_i + b) \geq 1,$$

where there is one constraint for each data point.

Support Vector Machines for Non-separable Data

In many cases, a separating hyperplane does not exist. To allow for this case, we introduce a set of *slack variables*, $\xi_i \geq 0$, which represent the amount by which the constraint is violated. We can now write our new constraints as

$$y_i\,(\boldsymbol{w} \cdot \boldsymbol{x}_1 + b) \geq 1 - \xi_i,$$

and we modify the objective function to take account of the extent of the constraint violations to get the problem

$$\text{minimize} \qquad \tfrac{1}{2}\boldsymbol{w} \cdot \boldsymbol{w} + C \sum_{i=1}^{N} \xi_i$$

$$\text{subject to} \quad y_i\,(\boldsymbol{w} \cdot \boldsymbol{x}_1 + b) \geq 1 - \xi_i$$
$$\text{and} \qquad\qquad\qquad\qquad \xi_i \geq 0.$$

Here C gives the significance of the constraint violations with respect to the distance between the points and the hyperplane.

The Hinge Loss

Support vector machines fit into the recipe, given in Section 15.1.3, of minimizing regularized test loss. The *hinge loss* compares the known value at an example with the response of the SVM at that example. Write $y_i^{(k)}$ for the known value and $y_i^{(p)}$ for the response; then, the hinge loss for that example is

$$L_h(y_i^{(k)}, y_i^{(p)}) = \max(0, 1 - y_i^{(k)} y_i^{(p)}).$$

This loss is always non-negative (Figure 15.2). For the moment, assume $y_i^{(k)} = 1$; then, any prediction by the classifier with value greater than one will incur no loss, and any smaller prediction will incur a cost that is linear in the prediction value (Figure 15.2). This means that minimizing the loss will encourage the classifier to (a) make strong positive (or negative) predictions for positive (or negative) examples and (b) for examples it gets wrong, make the most positive (negative) prediction that it can.

Support vector machines minimize the regularized hinge loss. We can see this by rewriting the constraints, to get $\xi_i \geq 1 - y_i\,(\boldsymbol{w} \cdot \boldsymbol{x}_1 + b)$. Now ξ_i will take the smallest value that it can, and $\xi_i \geq 0$, so

$$\xi_i = \max\left(0, 1 - y_i\,(\boldsymbol{w} \cdot \boldsymbol{x}_1 + b)\right) = L_h(y_i, \boldsymbol{w} \cdot \boldsymbol{x}_i + b).$$

In turn, solving the SVM above is equivalent to solving the unconstrained problem

$$\text{minimize Loss} + \text{ Regularizer} = \sum_{i=1}^{N} L_h(y_i, \boldsymbol{w} \cdot \boldsymbol{x}_i + b) + \frac{1}{2C}\boldsymbol{w} \cdot \boldsymbol{w}.$$

Solving this problem requires care because it is not differentiable (the max term in the hinge loss is the problem). However, rewriting an SVM in this way is helpful, because it exposes what the SVM does.

15.2.5   Example: Kernel Machines

Using the notation of Section 15.2.4, we write a separable linear support vector machine as:

$$\text{minimize} \qquad \tfrac{1}{2}\boldsymbol{w}\cdot\boldsymbol{w}$$

$$\text{subject to} \qquad y_i\left(\boldsymbol{w}\cdot\boldsymbol{x}_1+b\right)\geq 1.$$

We can solve this problem by introducing Lagrange multipliers α_i to obtain the Lagrangian

$$(1/2)\boldsymbol{w}\cdot\boldsymbol{w}-\sum_{1}^{N}\alpha_i\left(y_i\left(\boldsymbol{w}\cdot\boldsymbol{x}_1+b\right)-1\right).$$

This Lagrangian needs to be minimized with respect to $\boldsymbol{w}$ and $\boldsymbol{b}$ and maximized with respect to α_i: these are the Karush-Kuhn-Tucker conditions, described in optimization textbooks (see, for example, Gill $et\ al.$ (1981)). A little manipulation leads to the requirements that

$$\sum_{1}^{N}\alpha_i y_i=0$$

and

$$\boldsymbol{w}=\sum_{1}^{N}\alpha_i y_i\boldsymbol{x}_i.$$

Now by substituting these expressions into the original problem and manipulating, we obtain the $dual\ problem$ given by

$$\text{maximize} \qquad \sum_{i}^{N}\alpha_i-\tfrac{1}{2}\sum_{i,j=1}^{N}\alpha_i(y_iy_j\boldsymbol{x}_i\cdot\boldsymbol{x}_j)\alpha_j$$

$$\text{subject to} \qquad\qquad\qquad \alpha_i\geq 0$$

$$\text{and} \qquad\qquad\qquad \sum_{i=1}^{N}\alpha_i y_i=0.$$

For many datasets, it is unlikely that a hyperplane will yield a good classifier. Instead, we want a decision boundary with a more complex geometry. One way to achieve this is to map the feature vector into some new space and look for a hyperplane in that new space. For example, if we had a plane dataset that we were convinced could be separated by plane conics, we might apply the map

$$(x,y)\rightarrow(x^2,xy,y^2,x,y)$$

to the dataset. A classifier boundary that is a hyperplane in this new feature space is a conic in the original feature space. In this form, this idea is not particularly useful, because we might need to map the data into a high-dimensional space (e.g., assume that we know the classifier boundary has degree two, and the data is 10 dimensional; we would need to map the data into a 65-dimensional space). Write the map as $\boldsymbol{x}'=\phi(\boldsymbol{x})$. Write out the dual optimization problem for the new points $\boldsymbol{x}_i'$; you will notice that the only form in which $\boldsymbol{x}_i'$ appears is in the terms

$$\boldsymbol{x}_i'\cdot\boldsymbol{x}_j',$$

which we could write as $\phi(\boldsymbol{x}_i) \cdot \phi(\boldsymbol{x}_j)$. Apart from always being positive, this term doesn't give us much information about ϕ. In particular, the map doesn't appear explicitly in the optimization problem. If we did solve the optimization problem, the final classifier would be

$$f(\boldsymbol{x}) = \text{sign}\left(\sum_1^N (\alpha_i y_i \boldsymbol{x}' \cdot \boldsymbol{x}_i' + b)\right)$$

$$= \text{sign}\left(\sum_1^N (\alpha_i y_i \phi(\boldsymbol{x}) \cdot \phi(\boldsymbol{x}_i) + b)\right).$$

Assume that we have a function $k(\boldsymbol{x}, \boldsymbol{y})$ that is positive for all pairs of $\boldsymbol{x}$, $\boldsymbol{y}$. This function is known as a *kernel*. It can be shown that, under various technical conditions of no interest to us, there is some ϕ such that $k(\boldsymbol{x}, \boldsymbol{y}) = \phi(\boldsymbol{x}) \cdot \phi(\boldsymbol{y})$. All this allows us to adopt a clever trick. Instead of constructing ϕ explicitly, we obtain some appropriate $k(\boldsymbol{x}, \boldsymbol{y})$ and use it in place of ϕ. In particular, the dual optimization problem becomes

maximize $\qquad \sum_i^N \alpha_i - \frac{1}{2} \sum_{i,j=1}^N \alpha_i (y_i y_j k(\boldsymbol{x}_i, \boldsymbol{x}_j)) \alpha_j$

subject to $\qquad\qquad\qquad\qquad\qquad\qquad \alpha_i \geq 0$

and $\qquad\qquad\qquad\qquad\qquad\qquad \sum_{i=1}^N \alpha_i y_i = 0,$

and the classifier becomes

$$f(\boldsymbol{x}) = \text{sign}\left(\sum_1^N (\alpha_i y_i k(\boldsymbol{x}, \boldsymbol{x}_i) + b)\right).$$

Of course, these equations assume that the dataset is separable in the new feature space represented by k. This might not be the case, in which case the problem becomes

maximize $\qquad \sum_i^N \alpha_i - \frac{1}{2} \sum_{i,j=1}^N \alpha_i (y_i y_j k(\boldsymbol{x}_i, \boldsymbol{x}_j)) \alpha_j$

subject to $\qquad\qquad\qquad\qquad\qquad\qquad C \geq \alpha_i \geq 0$

and $\qquad\qquad\qquad\qquad\qquad\qquad \sum_{i=1}^N \alpha_i y_i = 0,$

and the classifier becomes

$$f(\boldsymbol{x}) = \text{sign}\left(\sum_1^N (\alpha_i y_i k(\boldsymbol{x}, \boldsymbol{x}_i) + b)\right).$$

There are a variety of possible choices for $k(\boldsymbol{x}, \boldsymbol{y})$. The main issue is that it must be positive for all values of $\boldsymbol{x}$ and $\boldsymbol{y}$. An important kernel is the *Gaussian kernel*, where

$$k(\boldsymbol{x}, \boldsymbol{y}; \sigma) = \exp\left(\frac{-\|\boldsymbol{x} - \boldsymbol{y}\|^2}{2\sigma^2}\right)$$

and σ is a scale parameter, selected using (say) cross-validation. The Gaussian kernel can exploit any feature representation that can be coerced into the form of a vector. There are two other widely used and effective kernels: the **histogram intersection kernel** (Section 16.1.3) and the **pyramid kernel** (Section 16.1.4).

There is no evidence one kernel is always better than another, so we could use many kernels and weight them with respect to one another. For example, we could construct different Gaussian kernels with different scale parameters for color, texture, and shape features, and then use optimization techniques to weight the kernels relative to one another. This strategy applies to kernels of a much more complex form, too. The strategy is known as *multiple kernel learning*.

15.2.6 Example: Boosting and Adaboost

One strategy to get a better classifier is to combine multiple classifiers. A natural approach is as follows: train a classifier on some dataset; now train a new classifier, weight each example to push the new classifier to get examples right if the previous classifier got them wrong; repeat this a number of times. The final result is a weighted combination of the outputs of all these classifiers. This general process is called *boosting*. There are a variety of ways to choose the weights for the examples and the combination of classifiers. We introduce the notation $\mathbf{1}$ [condition] for a function that takes the value 1 when the condition is true and 0 otherwise.

Typically, one boosts classifiers that are not by themselves expected to be particularly effective; all that is required is a *weak learner*, which is capable of an error rate slightly better than a random choice. A particularly popular weak learner in vision is a *decision stump* (named by gross analogy with a truncated decision tree), where one tests a single feature against a threshold. It is straightforward to train a decision stump to produce a minimum weighted error on a training set of N examples. One checks each of the $N + 1$ possible thresholds, and takes the one with the smallest error (Algorithm 15.5). Usually, the feature to be tested is chosen uniformly at random, but a useful alternative is to compute a random projection of the feature vector.

Assuming a weak learner, Algorithm 15.6 gives *discrete Adaboost*, after Friedman *et al.* (1998). An alternative is RealAdaboost, given in Algorithm 15.7, after Schapire (2002).

In practice, boosting provides quite successful classifiers. Boosting can continue after the training error rate falls to zero, and the number of rounds of boosting usually is chosen with a validation set (one continues to boost until the error on the validation set rises).

15.3 PRACTICAL METHODS FOR BUILDING CLASSIFIERS

We have described several apparently very different classifiers here. But which classifier should one use for a particular application? Generally, this should be dealt with as a practical rather than a conceptual question: that is, one tries several, and uses the one that works best. With all that said, experience suggests that the first thing to try for most problems is a linear SVM (or logistic regression, which tends to be much the same thing). If that doesn't work, either a kernel SVM or a boosting method (according to taste) are next.

The Mahalanobis distance is appropriate for relatively few applications, because (a) the model usually doesn't apply and (b) it is hard to estimate the covari-

Given a set of N training examples $(\boldsymbol{x}_i, y_i)$, where $y_i \in \{1, -1\}$ and a set of weights, one per example, w_i such that $\sum_i w_i = 1$

1. Determine a variable to test.

   - Either choose a single feature index r uniformly and at random, and construct a new training set by projecting onto the rth feature to get $(u_i = \Pi_r(\boldsymbol{x}_i), y_i)$

   - Or choose a random unit vector $\boldsymbol{v}$ and construct a new training set $(u_i = \boldsymbol{v} \cdot \boldsymbol{x}_i, y_i)$

2. Sort the new training set so that $u_1 \leq u_2 \leq u_i \leq u_N$.

3. There are now at most $2(N+1)$ possible error values. For each of the thresholds $t_0 = u_1 - \epsilon, t_1 = (1/2)(u_1 + u_2), \ldots, t_i = (1/2)(u_i + u_{i+1}), \ldots, t_N = u_N + \epsilon$, there are two possible decision stumps:

$$\phi_1(u, t_k) = \begin{cases} 1 & \text{if } u > t_k \\ -1 & \text{otherwise} \end{cases}$$

   and

$$\phi_2(u, t_k) = \begin{cases} 1 & \text{if } u \leq t_k \\ -1 & \text{otherwise} \end{cases} .$$

   Each of these has an error value. Compute the error values $E_1(t_k) = \sum_i w_i \mathbf{1}[y_i \neq \phi_1(u_i, t_k)]$ and $E_2(t_k) = \sum_i w_i \mathbf{1}[y_i \neq \phi_2(u_i, t_k)] = 1 - E_1(t_k)$.

4. Choose the decision stump that has the smallest error value.

Algorithm 15.5: Training a Two-Class Decision Stump

ance matrices accurately when the feature vectors are high-dimensional, and there are some cases where it is useful. It can be a good thing to try for low-dimensional problems with lots of training data and multiple classes. Nearest neighbor strategies are always useful, and are consistently competitive with other approaches when there is lots of training data and one has some idea of appropriate relative scaling of the features. The main difficulty with nearest neighbors is actually finding the nearest neighbors of a query. Approximate methods are now very good, and are reviewed in Section 21.2.3. The attraction of these methods is that it is relatively easy to build multi-class classifiers, and to add new classes to a system of classifiers.

The loss function one uses is supposed to be dictated by the natural logic of the underlying problem. This is all very well, but in practice we often do not know what a good loss function is, particularly in multi-class cases. The 0-1 loss is almost universally used, but this loss can impose severe (and, worse, uninformative) penalties in multi-class cases. For example, is labeling a cat with the label "dog" really as bad as labeling it with the label "motorcycle"? The difficulty here is we do not have a good, ready-made loss function that encodes what we really want to do for some classification problems. We explore this point further in Section 16.2.4.

Given a set of N training examples $(\boldsymbol{x}_i, y_i)$, where $y_i \in \{1, -1\}$

1. Give the ith example the initial weight $w_i^{(0)} = 1/N$.
2. For each $m = 1, 2, \ldots, M$

   (a) Compute a weak learner $\phi_m(\boldsymbol{x})$ using the current set of weights on the training data.
   (b) Compute $E_m = \sum_i w_i^{(m-1)} \mathbf{1}[y_i \neq \phi_m(\boldsymbol{x}_i)]$, $c_m = \log((1 - E_m)/E_m)$.
   (c) Recompute the weights for each example using

   $$w_i^{(m)} = w_i^{(m-1)} \exp(c_m \mathbf{1}[y_i \neq \phi_m(\boldsymbol{x}_i)]).$$

3. The classifier is now sign $\left[\sum_{m=1}^{M} c_m \phi_m(\boldsymbol{x}) \right]$.

Algorithm 15.6: Discrete Adaboost

15.3.1   Manipulating Training Data to Improve Performance

Generally, more training data leads to a better classifier. However, training classifiers with large datasets can be difficult, and it can be hard to get enough training data. Typically, only a relatively small number of example items are really important in determining the behavior of a classifier (we see this phenomenon in greater detail in Section 15.2.4). The really important examples tend to be rare cases that are quite hard to discriminate. This is because these cases affect the position of the decision boundary most significantly. We need a large dataset to ensure that these cases are present.

There are two useful tricks that help. First, for many or most cases in computer vision, we can expand the set of training examples with quite simple tricks. For concreteness, imagine we are training a classifier to recognize pictures of kitchens. The first step is to collect many pictures of kitchens. But we aren't guaranteed that an image of a kitchen will appear at a fixed size, or at a fixed rotation, or with a fixed crop. Usually we would resize the images to a fixed size using a uniform scaling, cropping as necessary. However, we could vary the scaling slightly, vary the cropping slightly, or vary the rotation of the image slightly (Figure 15.7). This means that each picture of a kitchen can generate a large number of positive examples. It is usually less helpful to do this with negative examples, because it is usually easy to get a large number of negative examples. A second useful trick can avoid much redundant work. We train on a subset of the examples, run the resulting classifier on the rest of the examples, and then insert the false positives and false negatives into the training set to retrain the classifier. This is because the false positives and false negatives are the cases that give the most information about errors in the configuration of the decision boundaries. We may repeat this several times, and in the final stages, we may use the classifier to seek false positives. For example, we might collect pictures from the Web, classify them, and then look at the positives for errors. This strategy is sometimes called *bootstrapping* (the name

Given a set of N training examples $(\boldsymbol{x}_i, y_i)$, where $y_i \in \{1, -1\}$

1. Give the ith example the initial weight $w_i^{(0)} = 1/N$.

2. For each $m = 1, 2, \ldots, M$

    (a) Compute a weak learner $\phi_m(\boldsymbol{x})$ using the current set of weights on the training data.

    (b) Compute

$$\alpha_m^* = \operatorname*{argmin}_{\alpha} \sum_i w_i^{(m-1)} \exp\left(-\alpha y_i \phi_m(\boldsymbol{x}_i)\right).$$

    (c) Recompute the weights for each example using

$$u_i^{(m)} = w_i^{(m-1)} \exp(-\alpha^*_m y_i \phi_m(\boldsymbol{x}_i))$$

$$w_i^{(m)} = \frac{u_i^{(m)}}{\sum_i u_i^{(m)}}.$$

3. The classifier is now $\operatorname{sign}\left[\sum_{m=1}^{M} \alpha_m^* \phi_m(\boldsymbol{x})\right]$.

Algorithm 15.7: Real Adaboost

is potentially confusing because there is an unrelated statistical procedure known as bootstrapping; nonetheless, we're stuck with it at this point).

There is an extremely important variant of this approach called *hard negative mining*. This applies to situations where we have a moderate supply of positive examples, but an immense number of negative examples. Such situations occur commonly when we use classifiers to detect objects (Section 17.1). The general

    Original   Rescale and Crop   Rotate and Crop   Flip

FIGURE 15.7: A single positive example can be used to generate numerous positive examples by slight rescaling and cropping, small rotations and crops, or flipping. These transformations can be combined, too. For most applications, these positive examples are informative, because objects usually are not framed and scaled precisely in images. In effect, these examples inform the classifier that, for example, the stove could be slightly more or slightly less to the right of the image or even to the left. *Jake Fitzjones* © *Dorling Kindersley, used with permission.*

procedure is to test every image window to tell whether it contains, say, a face. There are a lot of image windows, and it is quite easy to obtain a lot of images that are certain not to contain a face. In this case we can't use all the negative examples in training, but we need to search for negative examples that are most likely to improve the classifier's performance. We can do so by selecting a set of negative examples, training with these, and then searching the rest of the negative examples to find ones that generate false positives—these are hard negatives. We can iterate the procedure of training and searching for hard negatives; typically, we expand the pool of negative examples at each iteration.

15.3.2 Building Multi-Class Classifiers Out of Binary Classifiers

There are two standard methods to build multi-class classifiers out of binary classifiers. In the *all-vs-all* approach, we train a binary classifier for each pair of classes. To classify an example, we present it to each of these classifiers. Each classifier decides which of two classes the example belongs to, then records a vote for that class. The example gets the class label with the most votes. This approach is simple, but scales very badly with the number of classes.

In the *one-vs-all* approach, we build a binary classifier for each class. This classifier must distinguish its class from all the other classes. We then take the class with the largest classifier score. One possible concern with this method is that training algorithms usually do not compel classifiers to be good at ranking examples. We train classifiers so that they give positive scores for positive examples, and negative scores for negative examples, but we do nothing explicit to ensure that a more positive score means the example is more like the positive class. Another important concern is that the classifier scores must be calibrated to one another, so that when one classifier gives a larger positive score than another, we can be sure that the first classifier is more certain than the second. Some classifiers, such as logistic regression, report posterior probabilities, which require no calibration. Others, such as the SVM, report numbers with no obvious semantics and need to be calibrated. The usual method to calibrate these numbers is an algorithm due to Platt (1999), which uses logistic regression to fit a simple probability model to SVM outputs. One-vs-all methods tend to be reliable and effective even when applied to uncalibrated classifier outputs, most likely because training algorithms do tend to encourage classifiers to rank examples correctly.

Neither strategy is particularly attractive when the number of classes is large, because the number of classifiers we must train scales poorly (linearly in one case, quadratically in the other) with the number of classes. If we were to allocate each class a distinct binary vector, we would need only $\log N$ bits in the vector for N classes. We could then train one classifier for each bit, and we should be able to classify into N classes with only $\log N$ classifiers. This strategy tends to founder on questions of which class should get which bit string, because this choice has significant effects on the ease of training the classifiers. Nonetheless, it gives an argument that suggests that we should not need as many as N classifiers to tell N classes apart. This question is becoming important because the number of object categories that modern methods can deal with is growing quickly. For example, one now sees methods that do 10,000-class classification for vision objects (Deng *et al.* 2010). The difference between training 10,000 SVMs and training 14 is very significant, and we can expect considerable research on this matter.

15.3.3 Solving for SVMS and Kernel Machines

We obtain a support vector machine by solving one of the constrained optimization problems given above. Although these problems are quadratic programs, it is not a good idea to simply dump them into a general-purpose optimization package, because they have quite special structure. One would usually use one of the many packages available on the web for SVMs.

There are two general threads in solving for SVMs. One can either solve the primal problems (the ones shown here), or write out the Lagrangian, eliminate the primal variables w and b, and solve the dual problem in the Lagrange multipliers. This dual problem has a large number of variables because there is one Lagrange multiplier for each active constraint. However, our original argument about convex hulls suggests that most of these must be zero at the solution. Equivalently, most constraints are not active, because relatively few points are enough to determine a separating hyperplane. Dual solvers typically exploit this property, and are built around an efficient search for nonzero Lagrange multipliers.

The alternative to solving the dual problem is to solve the primal problem. This approach is particularly useful when the dataset is very large, and is unlikely to be linearly separable. In this case, the objective function is an estimate of the loss incurred in applying the classifier, regularized by the norm of the hyperplane. For many applications, it is sufficient to get the error rate below a threshold (as opposed to exactly minimizing it). This means that the value of the objective function is a guide to when training can stop, as long as one trains in primal. Modern primal training algorithms visit single examples at random, updating the estimated classifier slightly on each visit. These algorithms can be very efficient for extremely large datasets.

LIBSVM (which can be found using Google, or at `http://www.csie.ntu.edu.tw/~cjlin/libsvm/`) is a dual solver that is now widely used; it searches for nonzero Lagrange multipliers using a clever procedure known as SMO (sequential minimal optimization). A good primal solver is PEGASOS; source code can be found using Google, or at `http://www.cs.huji.ac.il/~shais/code/index.html`.

SVMLight (Google, or `http://svmlight.joachims.org/`) is a comprehensive SVM package with numerous features. It can produce sophisticated estimates of the error rate, learn to rank as well as to classify, and copes with hundreds of thousands of examples. Andrea Vedaldi, Manik Varma, Varun Gulshan, and Andrew Zisserman publish code for a multiple kernel learning-based image classifier at `http://www.robots.ox.ac.uk/~vgg/software/MKL/`. Manik Varma publishes code for general multiple-kernel learning at `http://research.microsoft.com/en-us/um/people/manik/code/GMKL/download.html`, and for multiple-kernel learning using SMO at `http://research.microsoft.com/en-us/um/people/manik/code/SMO-MKL/download.html`. Peter Gehler and Sebastian Nowozin publish code for their recent multiple-kernel learning method at `http://www.vision.ee.ethz.ch/~pgehler/projects/iccv09/index.html`.

15.4 NOTES

We warn readers that a search over classifiers is not a particularly effective way to solve problems; instead, look to improved feature constructions. However, many application problems have special properties, and so there is an enormous number of different methods to build classifiers. We have described methods that reliably give good results. Classification is now a standard topic, with a variety of important textbooks. Accounts of most mainstream classifiers can be found in major recent texts. We recommend Bishop (2007), Hastie *et al.* (2009), Devroye *et al.* (1996), and MacKay (2003). An important theoretical account of when classification methods can be expected to work or to fail is in Vapnik (1998).

PROBLEMS

15.1. What are the advantages of using nearest neighbor classifiers?

15.2. Assume we have two classes, where $p(\boldsymbol{x}|k)$ is known to be normal. Assume that the loss is 0-1, and that the priors are the same for each class. Show that classifying the data using the Mahalanobis distance is equivalent to checking the sign of an expression that is *linear* in $\boldsymbol{x}$.

15.3. We wish to build a two-class classifier with logistic regression (see Section 15.1.3).

    (a) Show that the log-likelihood of the data is

$$\mathcal{L}(\boldsymbol{a}) = \sum_{i \in \text{examples}} (\frac{1 + y_i}{2})\boldsymbol{a}^T\boldsymbol{x} - \log\left(1 + \boldsymbol{a}^T\boldsymbol{x}\right).$$

    (b) Compute expressions for the gradient and Hessian of $-\mathcal{L}(\boldsymbol{a})$.

    (c) Show that either $-\mathcal{L}(\boldsymbol{a})$ is convex, or the feature vectors $\vec{x}_i$ lie on an affine subspace of the feature space.

15.4. Check that

$$
\begin{aligned}
L(y_i, \gamma_i) &= -\left[\frac{1}{2}(1 + y_i)\gamma_i - \log\left(1 + \exp\gamma_i\right)\right] \\
&= \log\left(1 + \exp\left(-y_i\gamma_i\right)\right).
\end{aligned}
$$

It is helpful to recall that $x - \log(1 + \exp(x)) = -\log(1 + \exp(-x))$, which you can prove by division.

15.5. Describe how to use Naive Bayes to build a multi-class classifier (without using one-vs-all or one-vs-one strategies).

15.6. Briefly describe the two methods to build multi-class classifiers out of binary classifiers. Now write N for the number of classes. Show that, *in principle*, $O(\log(N))$ classifiers are needed. How many classifiers does one-vs-one require? How many does one-vs-all require?

C H A P T E R   16

Classifying Images

Many modern computer vision problems can be solved by using a classifier. Here we will survey a set of applications where one passes a whole image into a classifier, and in the next chapter show an extremely important extension where one applies the classifier to windows in the image. The recipe is straightforward: one finds a labelled dataset, builds features, and then trains a classifier. Even better, there is a set of reliable feature building tricks that apply in many important cases. This recipe is so powerful and has proven so effective that it is worth a considerable effort to rephrase a problem into a form in which it applies; and whenever it does apply, it is essential to check how well it works before doing anything more elaborate.

Each application needs a set of features that can represent the image appearance usefully. Section 16.1 describes general tricks for building appearance features in the context of some particular applications. We then look at the general problem of image classification, where one takes a test image and must classify it into one of a set of categories (Section 16.2). There are two important threads in the current state of the art: Building methods that perform better on a fixed set of categories (Section 16.2.3); and building methods that apply to increasingly large numbers of categories (Section 16.2.4). Finally, Section 16.3 gives pointers to software and datasets that are useful for research in this area.

16.1 BUILDING GOOD IMAGE FEATURES

The core difficulty in applying our recipe is choosing good image features. Different feature constructions are good for different applications. The key is to build features that expose *between-class variation*, which is the tendency for classes to look different from one another, and suppress *within-class variation*, the tendency for instances within a class to look different. Some feature constructions seem to be quite good at this for many problems, but most problems have special properties.

16.1.1 Example Applications

Detecting explicit images: There are numerous reasons to try and detect images that depict nudity or sexual content. In some jurisdictions, possession or distribution of such pictures might be illegal. Many employers want to ensure that work computers are not used to collect or view such images; in fact, vendors of image filtering software have tried to persuade employers that they might face litigation if they don't do so. Advertisers want to be careful that their ads appear only next to images that will not distress their customers. Web search companies would like to allow users to avoid seeing images they find distressing.

It is difficult for jurists to be clear about what images are acceptable and what are not. In the United States, images that are not obscene have first amendment protections, but the test for whether an image is obscene is far too vague to be useful

FIGURE 16.1: Material is not the same as object category (the three cars on the **top** are each made of different materials), and is not the same as texture (the three checkered objects on the **bottom** are made of different materials). Knowing the material that makes up an object gives us a useful description, somewhat distinct from its identity and its texture. *This figure was originally published as Figures 2 and 3 of "Exploring Features in a Bayesian Framework for Material Recognition," by C. Liu, L. Sharan, E. Adelson, and R. Rosenholtz Proc. CVPR 2010, 2010 © IEEE, 2010.*

to the technical community (even the legal community finds it tricky; see histories in, for example, O'Brien (2010) or de Grazia (1993)). For most applications, it is enough to filter pictures that likely show nakedness or sexual content, and that could be done with a classifier. Much of the research on this topic is done at large industrial laboratories, behind a wall of secrecy. All published methods rely on finding skin in the image; some then reason about the layout of the skin. For us, there are two classification steps: we need classify pixels into skin and not-skin; and we need to classify images into explicit vs. not-explicit based on the layout of skin.

Material classification: Imagine we have an image window. What material (e.g., "wood," "glass," "rubber," and "leather") does the window cover? If we could answer this question, we could decide whether an image patch was cloth—and so might be part of a person, or of furniture—or grass, or trees, or sky. Generally, different materials produce different image textures, so natural features to use for this multiclass classification problem will be texture features. However, materials tend to have some surface relief (for example, the little pores on the surface of an orange; the bumps on stucco; the grooves in tree bark), and these generate quite complex shading behavior. Changes in the illumination direction can cause the shadows attached to the relief to change quite sharply, and so the overall texture changes. Furthermore, as Figure 16.1 illustrates, texture features might indicate the material an object is made of, but objects can have the same texture and be made of quite different materials.

Scene classification: Pictures of a bedroom, of a kitchen, or of a beach show different *scenes*. Scenes provide an important source of context to use in

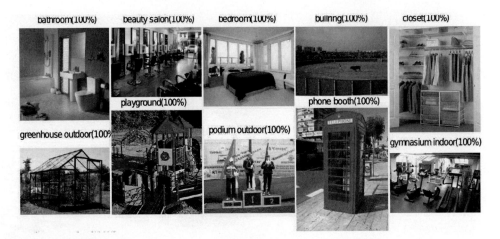

FIGURE 16.2: Some scenes are easily identified by humans. These are examples from the SUN dataset (Xiao *et al.* 2010) of scene categories that people identify accurately from images; the label above each image gives its scene type. *This figure was originally published as Figure 2 of "SUN database: Large-scale Scene Recognition from Abbey to Zoo," by J. Xiao, J. Hays, K. Ehinger, A. Oliva, and A. Torralba, Proc. IEEE CVPR 2010, © IEEE, 2010.*

interpreting images. You could reasonably expect to see a pillow, but not a toaster or a beachball, in a bedroom; a toaster, but not a pillow or a beachball, in a kitchen; or a beachball and perhaps a pillow, but not a toaster, on a beach. We should like to be able to tell what scene is depicted in an image. This is difficult, because scenes vary quite widely in appearance, and this variation has a strong spatial component. For example, the toaster could be in many different locations in the kitchen. In *scene classification*, one must identify the scene depicted in the image. Scene labels are more arbitrary than object labels, because there is no clear consensus on what the different labels should be. Some labels seem fairly clear and are easy to assign accurately (Figure 16.2), for example, "kitchen," "bedroom," and other names of rooms in a house. Other labels are uncertain: should one distinguish between "woodland paths" and "meadows", or just label them all "outdoors"? Humans seem to have a problem here, too (Figure 16.18). However, there are several scene datasets, each with its own set of labels, so methods can be compared and evaluated.

There are some important general points about these and most other applications, that can guide feature construction. Any representation should be robust to rotation, translation, or scaling of the image, because these transformations will not affect the label of the image (an explicit image is an explicit image, even when it is upside down). The driving observations behind the SIFT and HOG feature constructions are (a) **exact intensity values are not important**, because we might encounter versions of the image taken under brighter or darker illumination; and (b) **image curves are important**, because they might be object outlines. As we saw in Section 5.4, these observations justified working with gradient orientations and normalizing the resulting features in various ways. There are two more

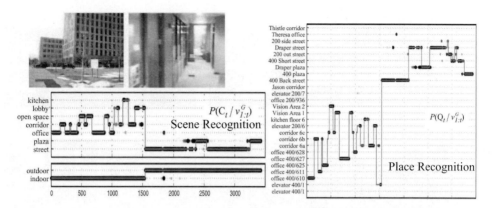

FIGURE 16.3: GIST features can be used to identify scenes, particularly the place where the image was taken. Torralba *et al.* (2003) demonstrated a vision system that moves through a known environment, and can tell where it is from what it sees using scene recognition ideas. Images (examples on the **top left**) are represented with GIST features. These are used to compute a posterior probability of place conditioned on observations and the place of the last image, which is shown on the **right**. The shaded blobs correspond to posterior probability, with darker blobs having higher probability. The thin line superimposed on the figure gives the correct answer; notice that almost all probability lies on the right answer. For places that are not known, the type of place can be estimated (**bottom left**); again, the shaded blobs give posterior probability, darker blobs having higher probability, and the thin line gives the right answer. *This figure was originally published as Figures 2 and 3 of "Context-based vision system for place and object recognition," by A. Torralba, K. Murphy, W.T. Freeman, and M.A. Rubin, Proc. IEEE ICCV 2003, © IEEE 2003.*

important observations. First, **image texture is important**, and is usually highly diagnostic. Although this isn't at all obvious, it turns out to be an essential part of building good features. This suggests looking at summary statistics of orientation (for example, horizontal stripes give lots of vertically oriented gradients, spotty regions should have uniformly distributed orientations, and so on). Second, **exact feature locations are not important**, because small changes in the layout of the image would not change its class. For example, moving the toaster on a shelf doesn't stop the kitchen from being a kitchen. We have seen a version of this issue before, at a finer spatial scale. The histogramming step in SIFT and HOG features tries to account for small shifts in the location of orientation components, local to a particular neighborhood, by summarizing that neighborhood. We will use similar summarization mechanisms to deal with larger scale shifts of larger structures.

16.1.2 Encoding Layout with GIST Features

One natural cue to the scene is the overall layout of a picture. If there are large, smooth regions on either side, many vertical straight lines, and relatively little sky visible, then you might be in an urban canyon; if there is a lot of sky visible, and rough brown stuff at the bottom of the picture, then you might be outdoors; and so on. There is a lot of evidence that people can make very fast, accurate

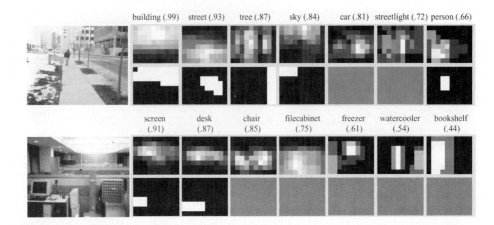

FIGURE 16.4: Scenes are important, because knowing the type of scene shown in an image gives us some information about the objects that are present. For example, street's are typically at the bottom center of street scenes. These maps show probabilities of object locations (**top row**, for each image) extracted from scene information for the image to the left; brighter values are higher probabilities. Compare these with the true support of the object (**bottom row**, for each image); notice that, while knowing the scene doesn't guarantee that an object is present, it does suggest where it is likely to be. This could be used to cue object detection processes. *This figure was originally published as Figure 10 of "Context-based vision system for place and object recognition," by A. Torralba, K. Murphy, W.T. Freeman, and M.A. Rubin, Proc. IEEE ICCV 2003, © IEEE 2003.*

judgments about pictures, which appear to be based on the overall layout of the picture (Henderson and Hollingworth 1999).

GIST features attempt to capture this layout. Oliva and Torralba (2001) constructed these features by reasoning about a set of perceptual dimensions that might encode the layout of a scene. The dimensions include whether the scene is natural or man-made; whether there is wide-open space or just a narrow enclosure; whether it is rugged or not. They then build features that tend to be good at predicting these dimensions. These features typically result from a spectral analysis of all or part of the scene. For example, images that show urban canyons have lots of strong vertical edges, which will mean high energy at high spatial frequencies at particular (vertical) phases; similarly, ruggedness will translate into strong energy at high spatial frequencies.

A natural feature will be comparable to the texture representations of Chapter 6, but summarized to represent the whole image. Oliva and Torralba apply a bank of oriented filters at a range of scales (eight orientations and four scales). They then average the magnitude of the filter output over a four by four grid of non-overlapping windows. The result is a $512 (= 4 \times 4 \times 8 \times 4)$ dimensional vector. This is then projected onto a set of principal components computed on a large dataset of natural images. The result is a set of features that (a) give a sense of the strength of texture activity at various scales and orientations in various blocks of the image and (b) tend to differ between natural scenes. These features are now

FIGURE 16.5: The original application of visual word representations was to search video sequences for particular patterns. On the **left**, a user has drawn a box around a pattern of interest in a frame of video; the **center** shows a close-up of the box. On the **right**, we see neighborhoods computed from this box. These neighborhoods are ellipses, rather than circles; this means that they are covariant under affine transforms. Equivalently, the neighborhood constructed for an affine transformed patch image will be the affine transform of the neighborhood constructed for the original patch (definition in Section 5.3.2). *This figure was originally published as Figure 11 of J. Sivic and A. Zisserman "Efficient Visual Search for Objects in Videos," Proc. IEEE, Vol. 96, No. 4, April 2008 © IEEE 2008.*

very widely used. There is strong evidence that they do encode scene layout (for example Oliva and Torralba (2007); Oliva and Torralba (2001); or Torralba *et al.* (2003)), and they are widely used in applications where scene context is likely to help performance.

16.1.3 Summarizing Images with Visual Words

Features that represent scenes should summarize. It is generally more important to know that something is present (the toaster in our example), than to know where it is. This suggests using a representation that has the form of a histogram. Such histograms are useful for other cases, too. Imagine we would like to classify images containing large, relatively isolated objects. The objects might deform, the viewpoint might move, and the image might have been rotated or scaled. Apart from these effects, we expect the object appearance to be fairly stable (that is, we're not trying to match a striped object with a spotted object). This means that the absolute location of structures in the image is probably not very informative, but the presence of these structures is very important. Again, this suggests a representation that is like a histogram. The big question is what to record in the histogram.

An extremely successful answer is to record characteristic local image patches. When we discussed texture, we called these textons (Section 6.2), but in recognition applications they tend to be called *visual words*. The construction follows the same lines. We detect interest points and build neighborhoods around them (Section 5.3). We then describe those neighborhoods with SIFT features (Section 5.4). We vector quantize these descriptions, then build a representation of the overall pattern of vector-quantized neighborhoods.

There are many plausible strategies to vector quantize SIFT descriptors. For concreteness, assume we obtain a large training set of SIFT descriptors from relevant images and cluster them with k-means. We now vector quantize a new SIFT

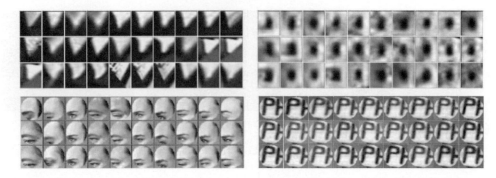

FIGURE 16.6: Visual words are obtained by vector quantizing neighborhoods like those shown in Figure 16.5. This figure shows 30 examples each of instances of four different visual words. Notice that the words represent a moderate-scale local structure in the image (an eye, one and a half letters, and so on). Typical vocabularies are now very large, which means that the instances of each separate word tend to look a lot like one another. *This figure was originally published as Figure 3 of "Efficient Visual Search for Objects in Videos," by J. Sivic and A. Zisserman, Proc. IEEE, Vol. 96, No. 4, April 2008 © IEEE 2008.*

descriptor by replacing it with the number of the closest cluster center. The resulting numbers are very like words (for example, you can count the number of times a particular type of interest point occurs in an image, and images with similar counts are likely to be similar). Sivic and Zisserman (2003), who pioneered the approach, call these numbers *visual words*. Perhaps the most important difference between visual words and the textons of Section 6.2.1 is that a visual word could describe a larger image domain than a texton might.

Although individual visual words should be somewhat noisy, the overall picture of local patches should be the same in comparable images (or regions). For example, Figure 16.7 is relatively typical of visual word representations. Not all the neighborhoods in the query were matched in each response. Noise could be caused by the neighborhood procedure not finding the correct neighborhood, or by the vector quantization sending the neighborhood to the wrong visual word. As a result, we need to summarize the set of visual words in a way that is robust to errors. In practice, histograms are an excellent summary. If most of the words in one image match most of the words in the other image, then the histograms should be similar. Furthermore, the histograms should not be significantly affected by change of image intensity, rotations, scaling, and deformations.

In the histogram representation, two images that are similar should have similar histograms, and two images that are different will have different histograms. This means that it is somewhat unnatural (and, in practice, not particularly effective) to simply apply a linear classifier to a histogram represented as a vector. We expect positive (resp. negative) examples to lie on a fairly complex structure in this feature space, and the classification procedure should compare test examples to multiple training examples. This means that kernel methods (Section 15.2.5) are particularly well adapted to histogram features. One can use the χ-*squared kernel*,

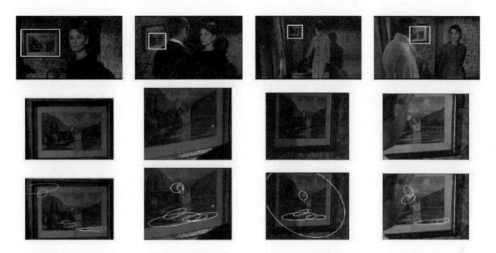

FIGURE 16.7: This figure shows results from the query of Figure 16.5, obtained by looking for image regions that have a set of visual words strongly similar to those found in the query region. The first row shows the whole frame from the video sequence; the second row shows a close-up of the box that is the result (indicated in the first row); and the third row shows the neighborhoods in that box that generated visual words that match those in the query. Notice that some, but not all, of the neighborhoods in the query were matched. *This figure was originally published as Figure 11 of J. Sivic and A. Zisserman "Efficient Visual Search for Objects in Videos," Proc. IEEE, Vol. 96, No. 4, April 2008 © IEEE 2008.*

where

$$K(\boldsymbol{h}, \boldsymbol{g}) = \frac{1}{2} \sum_i \frac{(h_i - g_i)^2}{h_i + g_i}$$

is the χ-square distance between the histograms. A widely adopted alternative is the *histogram intersection kernel*, where

$$K(\boldsymbol{h}, \boldsymbol{g}) = \sum_i \min(h_i, g_i)$$

which will be large if $\boldsymbol{h}$ and $\boldsymbol{g}$ have many boxes of similar weight, and small otherwise. You can see this as an estimate of the number of elements of the ith type that can be matched. Notice that this applies to normalized histograms, which means that if one image has many elements of the ith kind and the other has few, then not only will the ith term in the sum be small, but others must be small, too. The histogram intersection kernel can be evaluated very quickly, with appropriate tricks (Maji *et al.* 2008).

16.1.4 The Spatial Pyramid Kernel

Histograms of visual words are a very powerful representation, as we shall see in Section 16.2. However, they suppress all spatial information, which creates problems in scene recognition. Imagine we are building a kernel to compare scene images. We should like the kernel value to be large for similar scenes, and small for

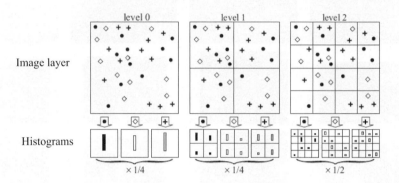

FIGURE 16.8: A simplified example of constructing a spatial pyramid kernel, with three levels. There are three feature types, too (circles, diamonds, and crosses). The image is subdivided into one-, four-, and sixteen-grid boxes. For each level, we compute a histogram of how many features occur in each box for each feature type. We then compare two images by constructing an approximate score of the matches from these histograms. *This figure was originally published as Figure 1 of "Beyond bags of features: Spatial pyramid matching for recognizing natural scene categories," by S. Lazebnik, C. Schmid, and J. Ponce, Proc. IEEE CVPR 2006, © IEEE 2006.*

different ones. We expect two images of the same scene to have many objects in common, but these objects will move around somewhat. For example, two kitchen pictures should have a high similarity score. Since the ceilings, windows, counters, and floors are at about the same height in different kitchens, we need a score that respects rough spatial structure. The score should not be affected by fine spatial details (for example, moving the toaster from the counter on the left to that on the right).

Lazebnik *et al.* (2006) show how to build an important variant of a histogram of visual words that yields a kernel that has a very effective rough encoding of spatial layout. If you think of each image as a pattern, made up of elements, which could be visual words, then two images should be similar if about the same elements were present in comparable places. In particular, if the elements of one image can be matched to elements of the same kind that lie nearby in another image, then the two images should have high similarity. We cannot compute similarity by matching elements exactly between two images, because there are too many elements and computing an exact matching would be too expensive.

A rough estimate of the number of elements that can be matched is easy to get. If there are $N_{i,1}$ elements of type i in image 1 and $N_{i,2}$ elements of type i in image 2, then $\min(N_{i,1}, N_{i,2})$ elements of type i could match. This is the reasoning underlying the histogram intersection kernel (Section 16.1.3). However, this is a relatively poor estimate of the number of matching elements, because some of these elements may have to match others that are very far away. We can get an improved estimate by breaking each image into four quarters, and applying the same reasoning to each quarter to come up with the score for matching that quarter

FIGURE 16.9: Measurements of similarity using a spatial pyramid kernel offer natural methods for scene classification, because similar scenes should have about the right features in about the right place. This figure shows results obtained by querying a set of scene images with the query shown on the **left**. On the **right**, images from a test collection ranked by the value of the similarity score, with the most similar image on the left. The responses on the first row are mainly wrong (the name of the room is below the image when the response is wrong), perhaps because the kitchen in the query image has an eccentric layout. Other responses are mostly right. *This figure was originally published as Figure 4 of "Beyond bags of features: Spatial pyramid matching for recognizing natural scene categories," by S. Lazebnik, C. Schmid, and J. Ponce, Proc. IEEE CVPR 2006, © IEEE 2006.*

to the corresponding quarter of the other image. We now have five estimates (one for the whole image, and one for each quarter) and must combine them. We do so using weights that depend on the size of the image partitions for which the estimates were computed. We could subdivide the quarters again to create even smaller boxes and weight the local estimates appropriately, but boxes that are too small are not terribly informative.

We can now give a formal expression for the similarity score between two images, which is the kernel value. For simplicity, assume the patterns we work with are all the same size. We wish to compare $\mathcal{I}$ and $\mathcal{J}$. To get an estimate of the number of features that would match, we break each image into a grid of squares. We will use several different grids, indexed by l (Figure 16.8). We write $H^l_{\mathcal{I},t}(i)$ for the number of features of type t in the ith box in grid l on image $\mathcal{I}$. We assume that elements in a particular box in a particular grid over $\mathcal{I}$ can match only to elements in the corresponding box and grid over $\mathcal{J}$. We also assume that all elements that can be matched within a box, are matched. This means that the number of elements of type t in box i in grid l that match is

$$\min(H^l_{\mathcal{I},t}(i), H^l_{\mathcal{J},t}(i)),$$

and the similarity between $\mathcal{I}$ and $\mathcal{J}$, as measured at grid level l, is

$$\sum_{i \in \text{grid boxes}} \min(H^l_{\mathcal{I},t}(i), H^l_{\mathcal{J},t}(i)).$$

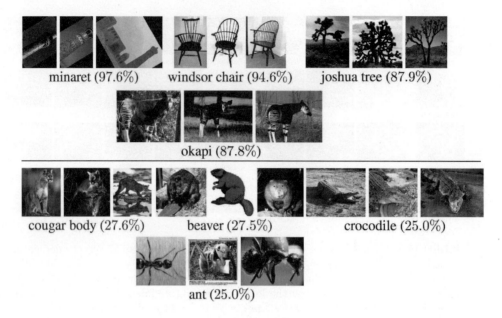

minaret (97.6%)   windsor chair (94.6%)   joshua tree (87.9%)

okapi (87.8%)

cougar body (27.6%)   beaver (27.5%)   crocodile (25.0%)

ant (25.0%)

FIGURE 16.10: The spatial pyramid kernel is capable of complex image classification tasks. Here we show some examples of categories from the Caltech 101 collection on which the method does well (**top row**) and poorly (**bottom row**). The number is the percentage of images of that class classified correctly. Caltech 101 is a set of images of 101 categories of objects; one must classify test images into this set of categories (Section 16.3.2). *This figure was originally published as Figure 5 of "Beyond bags of features: Spatial pyramid matching for recognizing natural scene categories," by S. Lazebnik, C. Schmid, and J. Ponce, Proc. IEEE CVPR 2006, © IEEE 2006.*

Each grid gives us an estimate of how well the features match, but generally we would like to place more weight on matches in fine grids and less weight on matches in coarse grids. We can do this by weighting matches by the inverse of the cell width at each level; write this weight as w_l. We will assume that matches between features of different types have the same weight, and obtain a total similarity score

$$\sum_{t\in\text{feature types}}\sum_{l\in\text{levels}}\sum_{i\in\text{grid boxes}} w_l \min(H^l_{\mathcal{I},t}(i), H^l_{\mathcal{I},t}(i)).$$

The resulting similarity estimates can be used either to rank image similarity (as in Figure 16.9), or as a kernel for a kernel-based classifier.

The spatial pyramid kernel does very well at classifying images by scene, and can outperform histogram intersection kernels on standard image classification tasks, even on datasets where the background on which objects appear varies very widely (Lazebnik *et al.* 2006). It can work well with very rich pools of features. In the work of Lazebnik *et al.* (2006), visual words are not constructed at interest points alone, but on a grid across the whole image; this means that there is a much richer—and much larger—set of visual words available to represent the image. It is notable that spatial pyramid kernels seem to represent relatively isolated objects or natural scenes well, but have trouble with textureless objects or objects that blend well into their backgrounds (Figure 16.10).

16.1.5 Dimension Reduction with Principal Components

Our constructions tend to produce high-dimensional feature vectors. This will tend to make it more difficult to estimate a classifier accurately, because it will tend to increase the variance of the estimate. It can be useful to reduce the dimension of a feature vector. We can do so by projecting onto a low-dimensional basis. One way to choose this basis is to insist that the new set of features should capture as much of the old set's variance as possible. As an extreme example, if the value of one feature can be predicted precisely from the value of the others, it is clearly redundant and can be dropped. By this argument, if we are going to drop a feature, the best one to drop is the one whose value is most accurately predicted by the others, that is, features that have relatively little variance.

In *principal component analysis*, the new features are linear functions of the old features. We take a set of data points and construct a lower dimensional linear subspace that best explains the variation of these data points from their mean. This method (also known as the Karhunen–Loéve transform) is a classical technique from statistical pattern recognition (see, for example Duda and Hart (1973), Oja (1983), or Fukunaga (1990)).

Assume we have a set of n feature vectors $\boldsymbol{x}_i$ $(i = 1, \ldots, n)$ in $\mathbb{R}^d$. The mean of this set of feature vectors is $\boldsymbol{\mu}$ (you should think of the mean as the center of gravity in this case), and their covariance is Σ (you can think of the variance as a matrix of second moments). We use the mean as an origin and study the offsets from the mean $(\boldsymbol{x}_i - \boldsymbol{\mu})$.

Our features are linear combinations of the original features; this means it is natural to consider the projection of these offsets onto various different directions. A unit vector $\boldsymbol{v}$ represents a direction in the original feature space; we can interpret this direction as a new feature $v(\boldsymbol{x})$. The value of u on the ith data point is given by $v(\boldsymbol{x}_i) = \boldsymbol{v}^T(\boldsymbol{x}_i - \boldsymbol{\mu})$. A good feature captures as much of the variance of the original dataset as possible. Notice that v has zero mean; then the variance of v is

$$\mathrm{var}(v) = \frac{1}{n-1} \sum_{i=1}^{n} v(\boldsymbol{x}_i) v(\boldsymbol{x}_i)^T$$

$$= \frac{1}{n} \sum_{i=1}^{n-1} \boldsymbol{v}^T(\boldsymbol{x}_i - \boldsymbol{\mu})(\boldsymbol{v}^T(\boldsymbol{x}_i - \boldsymbol{\mu}))^T$$

$$= \boldsymbol{v}^T \left\{ \sum_{i=1}^{n-1} (\boldsymbol{x}_i - \boldsymbol{\mu})(\boldsymbol{x}_i - \boldsymbol{\mu})^T \right\} \boldsymbol{v}$$

$$= \boldsymbol{v}^T \Sigma \boldsymbol{v}.$$

Now we should like to maximize $\boldsymbol{v}^T \Sigma \boldsymbol{v}$ subject to the constraint that $\boldsymbol{v}^T \boldsymbol{v} = 1$. This is an eigenvalue problem; the eigenvector of Σ corresponding to the largest eigenvalue is the solution. Now if we were to project the data onto a space *perpendicular* to this eigenvector, we would obtain a collection of $d - 1$ dimensional vectors. The highest variance feature for this collection would be the eigenvector of Σ with second largest eigenvalue, and so on.

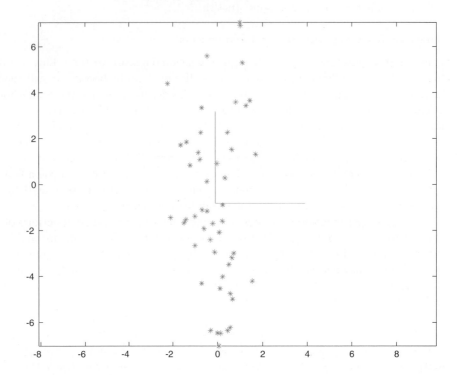

FIGURE 16.11: A dataset that is well represented by a principal component analysis. The axes represent the directions obtained using PCA; the vertical axis is the first principal component, and is the direction in which the variance is highest.

This means that the eigenvectors of Σ—which we write as $\boldsymbol{v}_1, \boldsymbol{v}_2, \ldots, \boldsymbol{v}_d$, where the order is given by the size of the eigenvalue and $\boldsymbol{v}_1$ has the largest eigenvalue—give a set of features with the following properties:

- They are independent (because the eigenvectors are orthogonal).

- Projection onto the basis $\{\boldsymbol{v}_1, \ldots, \boldsymbol{v}_k\}$ gives the k-dimensional set of linear features that preserves the most variance.

You should notice that, depending on the data source, principal components can give a good or a bad representation of a data set (see Figures 16.11, 16.12, and 16.13).

16.1.6   Dimension Reduction with Canonical Variates

Principal component analysis yields a set of linear features of a particular dimension that best represents the variance in a high-dimensional dataset. There is no guarantee that this set of features is good for *classification*. For example, Figure 16.13 shows a dataset where the first principal component would yield a bad classifier, and the second principal component would yield quite a good one, despite not capturing the variance of the dataset.

Assume we have a set of n feature vectors $\boldsymbol{x}_i$ $(i = 1, \ldots, n)$ in $\mathbb{R}^d$. Write

$$\boldsymbol{\mu} = \frac{1}{n} \sum_i \boldsymbol{x}_i$$

$$\Sigma = \frac{1}{n-1} \sum_i (\boldsymbol{x}_i - \boldsymbol{\mu})(\boldsymbol{x}_i - \boldsymbol{\mu})^T$$

The unit eigenvectors of Σ—which we write as $\boldsymbol{v}_1, \boldsymbol{v}_2, \ldots, \boldsymbol{v}_d$, where the order is given by the size of the eigenvalue and $\boldsymbol{v}_1$ has the largest eigenvalue—give a set of features with the following properties:

- They are independent.

- Projection onto the basis $\{\boldsymbol{v}_1, \ldots, \boldsymbol{v}_k\}$ gives the k-dimensional set of linear features that preserves the most variance.

Algorithm 16.1: Principal Components Analysis

Linear features that emphasize the distinction between classes are known as *canonical variates*. To construct canonical variates, assume that we have a set of data items $\boldsymbol{x}_i$, for $i \in \{1, \ldots, n\}$. We assume that there are p features (i.e., that the $\boldsymbol{x}_i$ are p-dimensional vectors). We have g different classes, and the jth class has mean $\boldsymbol{\mu}_j$. Write $\overline{\boldsymbol{\mu}}$ for the mean of the class means, that is,

$$\overline{\boldsymbol{\mu}} = \frac{1}{g} \sum_{j=1}^{g} \boldsymbol{\mu}_j.$$

Write

$$\mathcal{B} = \frac{1}{g-1} \sum_{j=1}^{g} (\boldsymbol{\mu}_j - \overline{\boldsymbol{\mu}})(\boldsymbol{\mu}_j - \overline{\boldsymbol{\mu}})^T.$$

Note that $\mathcal{B}$ gives the variance of the class means. In the simplest case, we assume that each class has the same covariance Σ, and that this has full rank. We would like to obtain a set of axes where the clusters of data points belonging to a particular class group together tightly, whereas the distinct classes are widely separated. This involves finding a set of features that maximizes the ratio of the separation (variance) between the class means to the variance within each class. The separation between the class means is typically referred to as the *between-class variance*, and the variance within a class is typically referred to as the *within-class variance*.

Now we are interested in linear functions of the features, so we concentrate on

$$v(\boldsymbol{x}) = \boldsymbol{v}^T \boldsymbol{x}.$$

We should like to maximize the ratio of the between-class variances to the within-class variances for $\boldsymbol{v}_1$.

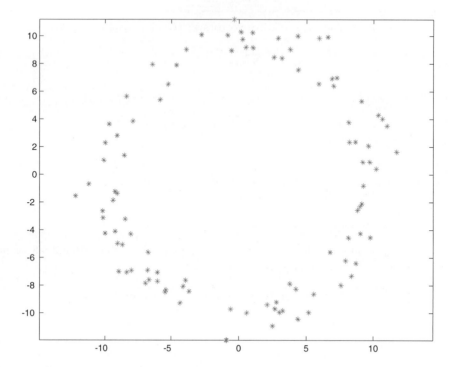

FIGURE 16.12: Not every dataset is well represented by PCA. The principal components of this dataset are relatively unstable, because the variance in each direction is the same for the source. This means that we may well report significantly different principal components for different datasets from this source. This is a secondary issue; the main difficulty is that projecting the dataset onto some axis suppresses the main feature, its circular structure.

Using the same argument as for principal components, we can achieve this by choosing v to maximize

$$\frac{v_1^T \mathcal{B} v_1}{v_1^T \Sigma v_1}.$$

This problem is the same as maximizing $v_1^T \mathcal{B} v_1$ subject to the constraint that $v_1^T \Sigma v_1 = 1$. In turn, a solution has the property that

$$\mathcal{B} v_1 + \lambda \Sigma v_1 = 0$$

for some constant λ. This is known as a *generalized eigenvalue problem*; if Σ has full rank, one solution is to find the eigenvector of $\Sigma^{-1} \mathcal{B}$ with largest eigenvalue. It is usually better to use specialized routines within the relevant numerical software environment, which can deal with the case Σ does not have full rank.

Now for each v_l, for $2 \leq l \leq p$, we would like to find features that extremize the criterion and are independent of the previous v_l. These are provided by the other eigenvectors of $\Sigma^{-1} \mathcal{B}$. The eigenvalues give the variance along the features (which are independent). By choosing the $m < p$ eigenvectors with the largest eigenvalues,

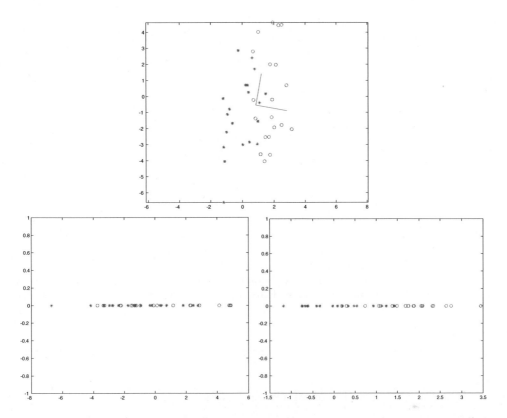

FIGURE 16.13: Principal component analysis doesn't take into account the fact that there may be more than one class of item in a dataset. This can lead to significant problems. For a classifier, we would like to obtain a set of features that reduces the number of features and makes the difference between classes most obvious. For the dataset on the **top**, one class is indicated by circles and the other by stars. PCA would suggest projection onto a vertical axis, which captures the variance in the dataset but cannot be used to discriminate between the classes, as we can see from the axes obtained by PCA, which are overlaid on the dataset. The **bottom row** shows the projections onto those axes. On the **bottom left**, we show the projection onto the first principal component, which has higher variance but separates the classes poorly, and on the **bottom right**, we show the projection onto the second principal component, which has significantly lower variance (look at the axes) and gives better separation.

we obtain a set of features that reduces the dimension of the feature space while best preserving the separation between classes. This doesn't guarantee the best error rate for a classifier on a reduced number of features, but it offers a good place to start by reducing the number of features while respecting the category structure. Details and examples appear in McLachlan and Krishnan (1996) and in Ripley (1996).

If the classes don't have the same covariance, it is still possible to construct canonical variates. In this case, we estimate a Σ as the covariance of all the offsets of each data item *from its own class mean* and proceed as before. Again, this is an

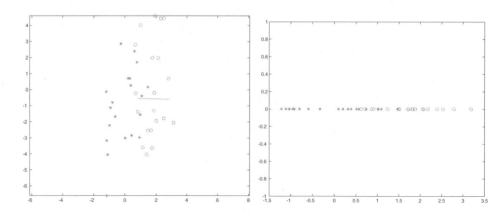

FIGURE 16.14: Canonical variates use the class of each data item as well as the features in estimating a good set of linear features. In particular, the approach constructs axes that separate different classes as well as possible. The dataset used in Figure 16.13 is shown on the **left**, with the axis given by the first canonical variate overlaid. On the **bottom right**, we show the projection onto that axis, where the classes are rather well separated.

approach without a guarantee of optimality, but one that can work quite well in practice.

16.1.7 Example Application: Identifying Explicit Images

All published explicit image classifiers start by detecting skin. Skin detection is an important problem in its own right. Skin detectors are very useful system components, because they can be used to focus searches. If one is searching for explicit images, then skin will likely be involved. But if one is looking for faces, skin is a good place to start, too (Section 17.1.1). If one is trying to interpret sign language, hands are important, and hands usually show skin (for example, systems in Buehler *et al.* (2009), Buehler *et al.* (2008), Farhadi and Forsyth (2006), Farhadi *et al.* (2007), and Bowden *et al.* (2004)). Skin detection is also a natural example of a very general recipe for detection: apply a classifier at each location likely to be of interest. For example, we can detect skin by (a) building a skin classifier, then (b) applying it to each pixel in an image independently. Formally, this involves (the clearly false) assumption that pixels are independent; in practice, pretending that pixels are independent is quite satisfactory for skin detection.

Skin is quite easy to identify by color. This does not depend on how dark the skin is. The color of human skin is caused by a combination of light reflected from the surface of the skin (which will have a white hue), from blood under the surface (which gives skin a red tinge), and from melanin under the surface (which absorbs light and darkens the apparent color). The intensity of light reflected from skin can vary quite a lot, because the intensity of illumination can change, specular reflection from oils and grease on the surface can be very bright, and skin with more melanin in it absorbs more light (and so looks darker under fixed illumination). But the hue and saturation of skin do not vary much; the hue will tend to be in the red-orange

Assume that we have a set of data items of g different classes. There are n_k items in each class, and a data item from the kth class is $\boldsymbol{x}_{k,i}$, for $i \in \{1, \ldots, n_k\}$. The jth class has mean $\boldsymbol{\mu}_j$. We assume that there are p features (i.e., that the $\boldsymbol{x}_i$ are p-dimensional vectors).

Write $\overline{\boldsymbol{\mu}}$ for the mean of the class means, that is,

$$\overline{\boldsymbol{\mu}} = \frac{1}{g} \sum_{j=1}^{g} \boldsymbol{\mu}_j,$$

Write

$$\mathcal{B} = \frac{1}{g-1} \sum_{j=1}^{g} (\boldsymbol{\mu}_j - \overline{\boldsymbol{\mu}})(\boldsymbol{\mu}_j - \overline{\boldsymbol{\mu}})^T.$$

Assume that each class has the same covariance Σ, which is either known or estimated as

$$\Sigma = \frac{1}{N-1} \sum_{c=1}^{g} \left\{ \sum_{i=1}^{n_c} (\boldsymbol{x}_{c,i} - \boldsymbol{\mu}_c)(\boldsymbol{x}_{c,i} - \boldsymbol{\mu}_c)^T \right\}.$$

The unit eigenvectors of $\Sigma^{-1}\mathcal{B}$, which we write as $\boldsymbol{v}_1, \boldsymbol{v}_2, \ldots, \boldsymbol{v}_d$, where the order is given by the size of the eigenvalue and $\boldsymbol{v}_1$ has the largest eigenvalue, give a set of features with the following property:

- Projection onto the basis $\{\boldsymbol{v}_1, \ldots, \boldsymbol{v}_k\}$ gives the k-dimensional set of linear features that best separates the class means.

Algorithm 16.2: Canonical Variates

range (blue or green skin look very unnatural), and the color will not be strongly saturated. This means that a large number of image pixels can be quite reliably rejected as non-skin pixels by inspecting their color alone.

The simplest learned skin detector, which is very effective, uses a class-conditional histogram classifier (as in Section 15.2.2), and is due to Jones and Rehg (Jones and Rehg 2002). Each pixel is classified as skin or not skin based on

Create an output image $\mathcal{O}$, and fill it with zeros.

For each pixel I_{ij} in the input (binary) image
    If I_{ij} is 1 and all neighbors are 1
        $O_{ij} = 1$
    End
End

Algorithm 16.3: Dilation

FIGURE 16.15: The figure shows a variety of images together with the output of the skin detector of Jones and Rehg applied to the image. Pixels marked black are skin pixels and white are background. Notice that this process is relatively effective and could certainly be used to focus attention on, say, faces and hands. *This figure was originally published as Figure 6 of "Statistical color models with application to skin detection," by M.J. Jones and J. Rehg, Proc. IEEE CVPR, 1999 © IEEE, 1999.*

its R, G, and B coordinates. The quantization of these color values seems not to affect the accuracy of the detector all that much; this should be read as experimental evidence that the range of skin colors is fairly tightly clustered. One important source of errors are specular reflections on skin, which tend to be bright and white. If the skin detector marks such pixels as positives, huge areas of some images will become false positives; but if it marks them as negatives, most faces will have missing chunks of skin around the nose and forehead. Pixels neighboring skin pixels are probably themselves skin pixels, and the same applies to non-skin pixels. We can exploit this with a simple trick. Regard the output of the skin detector as a binary image, with skin pixels labeled 1. We apply several steps of *erosion*, a binary image operator (Algorithm 16.3). This will tend to remove isolated skin pixels, and make holes in skin bigger. We then apply several steps of *dilation*, another binary image operator (Algorithm 16.4). This will tend to fill holes in the skin mask. More com-

Create an output image $\mathcal{O}$, and fill it with zeros.

For each pixel I_{ij} in the input (binary) image
    If any of its neighbors are 1
        $O_{ij} = 1$
    End
End

Algorithm 16.4: Erosion

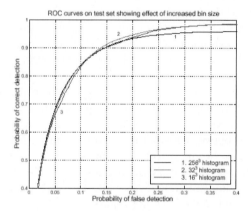

FIGURE 16.16: The receiver operating curve for the skin detector of Jones and Rehg. This plots the detection rate against the false-negative rate for a variety of values of the parameter θ. A perfect classifier has an ROC that, on these axes, is a horizontal line at 100% detection. Notice that the ROC varies slightly with the number of boxes in the histogram. *This figure was originally published as Figure 7 of "Statistical color models with application to skin detection," by M.J. Jones and J. Rehg, Proc. IEEE CVPR, 1999 © IEEE, 1999.*

plex skin detectors rely on the fact that skin has relatively little texture, so quite simple texture features can be discriminative (Forsyth and Fleck 1999). This skin detector suggests a recipe for detecting other things: search image windows using a detector. This recipe is immensely useful, and is explored in detail in Section 17.1.

Building an explicit image detector is now quite straightforward. We detect skin, then compute features from the skin regions, then pass these features to a classifier. All these methods work tolerably well on experimental datasets. Bosson *et al.* (2002) started the tradition of building simple region layout features from the skin regions. They use, among other features, number of skin regions, fractional area of the largest skin region, fraction of skin that is accounted for by a face (see Section 17.1.1 for face detection), and classify with a support vector machine. Forsyth and Fleck (1999) find groups of skin regions that appear to be body segments (arms, legs, etc.), then decide a naked person is present when a large enough group is found. Deselaers *et al.* (2008) use a histogram of visual words, followed by either an SVM or logistic regression. We know of no system that uses a spatial pyramid kernel for this problem, but expect that that would work rather well. Easy experiments—think of a phrase likely to produce alarming pictures, then search with the search filter turned on—with commercial image search programs suggest that these have low-false positive rates, though the false-negative rate is extremely hard to assess (and may not be known even to the manufacturers). Commercial methods may use text on pages and link topology information as well as image features to classify pictures, too.

16.1.8 Example Application: Classifying Materials

Leung and Malik (2001) show that a texton representation (see Section 6.2, and keep in mind the similarities between textons and visual words) can be used to classify materials. Assuming simple textures (where there is no relief, and so no illumination effect), they represent image patches with a vector of 48 filter responses evaluated at the center of the patch. Their textons are constructed by vector quantizing these vectors, using k-means. A single patch of texture is then represented by (a) computing the texton for each pixel in the patch, then (b) computing the overall histogram of these textons. Textures are classified by nearest neighbors, using the ξ-squared distance between histograms. Now assume that the texture is really a material. In this case, we need to have multiple images of the same patch to train, because the appearance of the patch changes widely. In their experiment, the test sample consisted of multiple images as well. The texton labels could be unreliable, because some accident of lighting might have caused a patch to look like some other patch. However, because we can record how textons change under the lighting changes, we have an estimate of what the right labels could be for each texton. To compare a test sample with a training example, we search the different available labellings of textons for the test sample, computing the ξ-squared distance between the resulting histograms and the training example's histogram. The distances will tend to be big when the two do not match, even though we can relabel textons to bring them closer. A variety of alternative constructions are available, varying mainly in how the textons are built. Varma and Zisserman (2005) show improved classification using a small set of rotationally invariant filters; in a later paper, they show even better classification results produced by vector quantizing small image patches (Varma and Zisserman 2009).

All this work uses images of isolated patches of material. When one is presented with an image of an object, Liu *et al.* (2010) show that determining its material remains very hard. They collected a new dataset of images of objects made of a single predominant material, then applied visual words and other methods to classify it. As Figure 16.17 shows, this problem remains extremely difficult.

16.1.9 Example Application: Classifying Scenes

The original scene classification method, due to Oliva and Torralba (2001), used k-nearest neighbors to classify scenes using GIST features. This classifies single images into one of eight classes. Torralba *et al.* (2003) then showed that GIST

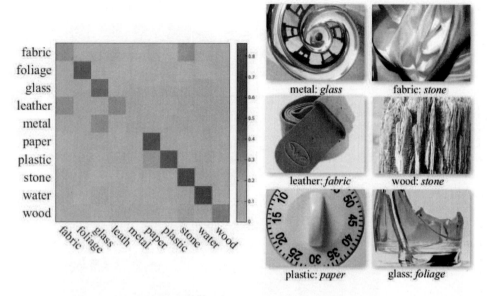

FIGURE 16.17: Liu *et al.* (2010) prepared a material classification dataset from flickr images, and used a combination of SIFT features and novel features to classify the materials. This is a difficult task, as the class confusion matrix on the **left** shows; for example, it is quite easy to mix up metal with most other materials, particularly glass. On the **right**, examples of misclassified images (the italic label is the incorrect prediction). *This figure was originally published as Figure 12 of "Exploring Features in a Bayesian Framework for Material Recognition," by C. Liu, L. Sharan, E. Adelson, and R. Rosenholtz Proc. CVPR 2010, 2010 © IEEE, 2010.*

features could be used to identify place, that is, where an image was taken, chosen from a fixed vocabulary of known places. For images taken in places that are not in the vocabulary, their system could describe the type of place, for example, "kitchen" or "lobby" (Figure 16.3). Their system assumed the camera was attached to a moving observer, but did not explicitly use motion cues; instead, their system uses a form of conditional random field so that prior probabilities of state transitions can affect the classification of an image (Torralba *et al.* 2003). A scene is a context in which some objects are likely to occur (for example, "toasters" are more common in "kitchens" than "outdoors"). Furthermore, some objects are more likely to occur in some locations in a scene ("toasters" are likely on "tables," but not on "floors"), so we expect that knowing the scene identity offers some cues to likely object location. This turns out to be the case, as Torralba *et al* demonstrate (Figure 16.4). As we have seen above, spatial pyramid kernels do well at scene classification, too.

Xiao *et al.* (2010) report scene classification results on a recent, very large, dataset (SUN; 397 categories with at least 100 images each; see Section 16.3.2). They compare a variety of methods, the best getting a recognition rate of approximately 38% (i.e., approximately 38% of classification attempts on test data are correct). As Figures 16.2 and 16.18 suggest, we might not expect a classification performance of 100%.

FIGURE 16.18: Not all scene categories are easily distinguished by humans. These are examples from the SUN dataset (Xiao *et al.* 2010). On the **top** of each column is an example of a difficult category; **below** are examples from three categories that are commonly confused with it by people. Such confusions might result from difficulties in knowing the category boundaries (which aren't canonical), or the terms (or categories) are unfamiliar, or because the images are ambiguous. *This figure was originally published as Figure 3 of "SUN database: Large-scale Scene Recognition from Abbey to Zoo," by J. Xiao, J. Hays, K. Ehinger, A. Oliva, and A. Torralba, Proc. IEEE CVPR 2010, © IEEE, 2010.*

16.2   CLASSIFYING IMAGES OF SINGLE OBJECTS

Many interesting images contain essentially a single object on a simple background. Some images, such as catalogue pictures, are composed this way. Others just happen to be this way. Images like this are important in image search, because searchers typically compose quite simple queries (e.g., "elephant" rather than "long shot showing mopani bush near a waterhole with an elephant in the bottom left and baboons frolicking") and so might not object to quite simple responses. Another reason that they're important is that it might be easier to learn models of object category from such images, rather than from general images. A core challenge in computer vision is to learn to classify such images.

A bewildering variety of features and classifiers has been tried on this problem; Section 16.2.1 makes some general remarks about approaches that seem successful. The classification process is rather naturally linked to image search, and so image search metrics are the usual way to evaluate classifiers (Section 16.2.2). Large-scale experimental work in image classification is difficult (one must collect and label images; and one must train and evaluate methods on very large datasets), and as a result there are unavoidable flaws in all experimental paradigms at present. However, trends suggest significant improvements in the understanding of image classification over the last decade. There are two general threads in current work. One can try to increase the accuracy of methods using a fixed set of classes (Section 16.2.3), and so gain some insight into feature constructions. Alternatively, one might try to handle very large numbers of classes (Section 16.2.4), and so gain some insight into what is discriminative in general.

16.2.1 Image Classification Strategies

The general strategy is to compute features, and then present feature vectors to a multi-class classifier. A very great variety of methods can be produced using this strategy, depending on what features and what classifier one uses. However, there are some general statements one can make. The features we described earlier predominate (which is why we described them). Methods typically use variants of HOG and SIFT features, combined with color features. Methods commonly use dictionaries of visual words, though there is great variation in the precise way these dictionaries are built. Spatial pyramid and pyramid match kernels seem to give very strong performance in representing images. A wide variety of classifiers are then applied to the resulting features; different reasonable choices of classifier give slightly different results, but no single classifier appears to have an overwhelming advantage.

Most research in this area is experimental in nature, and building datasets is a major topic. Fortunately, datasets are freely shared, and there is much competition to get the best performance on a particular dataset. Furthermore, much feature and classifier code is also freely shared. In turn, this means that it is usually relatively straightforward to try and reproduce cutting-edge experiments. Section 16.3 gives a detailed survey of datasets and code available as of the time of writing.

There are so many methods, each with slight advantages, that it is difficult to give a crisp statement of best practice. The first thing we would do when presented with a novel image classification problem would be to compute visual words for feature locations on an image grid. These visual words would be vector quantized with a large number of types (10^4 or 10^5, if enough data is available). We would then represent images with a histogram of the visual words and classify them using a histogram intersection kernel. If we were unhappy with the results, we would first vary the number of types of visual word, then apply a spatial pyramid kernel. After that, we would start searching through the different packages for feature computation described in Section 16.3.1, and perhaps search different types of classifier.

16.2.2 Evaluating Image Classification Systems

Image retrieval is related to image classification. In image retrieval, one queries a very large collection of images with a query—which could be keywords, or an image—and wishes to get matching images back (Chapter 21 surveys this area). If the query is a set of keywords and we expect keyword matches, then there must be some form of image classification engine operating in the background to attach keywords to images. For this reason, it is quite usual to use metrics from image retrieval to evaluate image classification methods.

Information retrieval systems take a query, and produce a response from a collection of data items. The most important case for our purposes is a system that takes a set of keywords and produces a set of images taken from a collection. These images are supposed to be relevant to the keyword query. Typically, two terms are used to describe the performance of information retrieval systems. The percentage of relevant items that are actually recovered is known as the *recall*. The percentage of recovered items that are actually relevant is known as the *precision*. It is natural to use these measures to evaluate an image classification system, because this system is attaching a label — which is rather like a keyword—to a set of test images.

It is tempting to believe that good systems should have high recall and high precision, but this is not the case. Instead, what is required for a system to be good depends on the application, as the following examples illustrate.

Patent searches: Patents can be invalidated by finding "prior art" (material that predates the patent and contains similar ideas). A lot of money can depend on the result of a prior art search. This means that it is usually much cheaper to pay someone to wade through irrelevant material than it is to miss relevant material, so very high recall is essential, even at the cost of low precision.

Web and email filtering: US companies worry that internal email containing sexually explicit pictures might create legal or public relations problems. One could have a program that searched email traffic for problem pictures and warned a manager if it found anything. Low recall is fine in an application like this; even if the program has only 10% recall, it will still be difficult to get more than a small number of pictures past it. High precision is very important, because people tend to ignore systems that generate large numbers of false alarms.

Looking for an illustration: There are various services that provide stock photographs or video footage to news organizations. These collections tend to have many photographs of celebrities; one would expect a good stock photo service to have many thousands of photographs of Nelson Mandela, for example. This means that a high recall search can be a serious nuisance, as no picture editor really wants to wade through thousands of pictures. Typically, staff at stock photo organizations use their expertise and interviews with customers to provide only a very small subset of relevant pictures.

There are a variety of ways of summarizing recall and precision data to make it more informative. *F-measures* are weighted harmonic means of precision and recall. Write P for precision and R for recall. The F_1-*measure* weights precision and recall evenly, and is given by

$$F_1 = 2\frac{PR}{P + R}.$$

The F_β-*measure* weights recall β times as strongly as recall, and is given by

$$F_\beta = (1 + \beta^2)\frac{PR}{\beta^2 P + R}.$$

Usually, it is possible to adjust the number of items that a system returns in re-

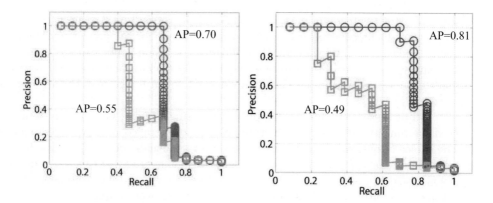

FIGURE 16.19: Plots of precision as a function of recall for six object queries. Notice how precision generally declines as recall goes up (the occasional jumps have to do with finding a small group of relevant images; such jumps would become arbitrarily narrow and disappear in the limit of an arbitrarily large dataset). Each query is made using the system sketched in Figure 16.5. Each graph shows a different query, for two different configurations of that system. On top of each graph, we have indicated the average precision for each of the configurations. Notice how the average precision is larger for systems where the precision is higher for each recall value. *This figure was originally published as Figure 9 of J. Sivic and A. Zisserman "Efficient Visual Search for Objects in Videos," Proc. IEEE, Vol. 96, No. 4, April 2008 © IEEE 2008.*

sponse to a query. As this pool gets bigger, the recall will go up (because we are recovering more items) and the precision will go down. This means we can plot precision against recall for a given query. Such a plot gives a fairly detailed picture of the system's behavior, and particular profiles are important for particular applications (Figure 16.19). For example, for web search applications, we would typically like high precision at low recall, and are not concerned about how quickly the precision dies off as the recall increases. This is because people typically don't look at more than one or two pages of query results before rephrasing their request. For patent search applications, on the other hand, the faster the precision dies off, the more stuff we might have to look at, so the rate at which precision falls off becomes important.

An important way to summarize a precision-recall curve is the *average precision*, which is computed for a ranking of the entire collection. This statistic averages the precision at which each new relevant document appears as we move down the list. Write rel(r) for the binary function that is one when the rth document is relevant, and otherwise zero; $P(r)$ for the precision of the first r documents in the ranked list; N for the number of documents in the collection; and N_r for the total number of relevant documents. Then, average precision is given by

$$A = \frac{1}{N_r} \sum_{r=1}^{N} (P(r)\mathrm{rel}(r))$$

Notice that average precision is highest (100%) when the top N_r documents are the relevant documents. Averaging over all the relevant documents means the statistic incorporates information about recall; if we were to average over the top 10 relevant documents, say, we would not know how poor the precision was for the lowest-ranked relevant document. The difficulty for vision applications is that many relevant documents will tend to be ranked low, and so average precision statistics tend to be low for image searches. This doesn't mean image searches are useless, however.

All of these statistics are computed for a single query, but most systems are used for multiple queries. Each statistic can be averaged over multiple queries. The choice of queries to incorporate in the average usually comes from application logic. *Mean average precision*, the average precision averaged over a set of queries, is widely used in object recognition circles. In this case, the set of possible queries is typically relatively small, and the average is taken over all queries.

16.2.3   Fixed Sets of Classes

The Pascal Challenge is a series of challenge problems set to the vision community by members of the Pascal network. From 2005–2010, the Pascal Challenge has included image classification problems. From 2007–2010, these problems involved 20 standard classes (including aeroplane, bicycle, car and person). Examples of these images can be found at `http://pascallin.ecs.soton.ac.uk/ challenges/VOC/voc2010/examples/index.html`. Table 16.1 shows average precisions obtained by the best method *per class* (meaning that the method that did best on aeroplanes might not be the same as the method that did best at bicycles) from 2007–2010. Note the tendency for results to improve, though there is by no means monotonic improvement. For these datasets, the question of selection bias does not arise, as a new dataset is published each year. As a result, it is likely that improvements probably do reflect improved features or improved classification methodologies. However, it is still difficult to conclude that methods that do well on this challenge are good, because the methods might be adapted to the set of categories. There are many methods that participate in this competition, and differences between methods are often a matter of quite fine detail. The main website (`http://pascallin.ecs.soton.ac.uk/challenges/VOC/`) is a rich mine of information, and has a telegraphic description of each method as well as some pointers to feature software.

Error rates are still fairly high, even with relatively small datasets. Some of this is most likely caused by problematic object labels. These result from the occasional use of obscure terms (for example, few people know the difference between a "yawl" and a "ketch" or what either is, but each is represented in the Caltech 101 dataset). Another difficulty is a natural and genuine confusion about what term applies to what instance. Another important source of error is that current methods cannot accurately estimate the spatial support of the object (respectively, background), and so image representations conflate the two somewhat. This is not necessarily harmful—for example, if objects are strongly correlated with their backgrounds, then the background is a cue to object identity—but can cause errors. Most likely, the main reason that error rates are high is that we still do not fully understand how to represent objects, and the features that we use do not encapsulate all that is important, nor do they suppress enough irrelevant information.

Category	2007	2008	2009	2010
aeroplane	0.775	0.811	0.881	0.933
bicycle	0.636	0.543	0.686	0.790
bird	0.561	0.616	0.681	0.716
boat	0.719	0.678	0.729	0.778
bottle	0.331	0.300	0.442	0.543
bus	0.606	0.521	0.795	0.859
car	0.780	0.595	0.725	0.804
cat	0.588	0.599	0.708	0.794
chair	0.535	0.489	0.595	0.645
cow	0.426	0.336	0.536	0.662
diningtable	0.549	0.408	0.575	0.629
dog	0.458	0.479	0.593	0.711
horse	0.775	0.673	0.731	0.820
motorbike	0.640	0.652	0.723	0.844
person	0.859	0.871	0.853	0.916
pottedplant	0.363	0.318	0.408	0.533
sheep	0.447	0.423	0.569	0.663
sofa	0.509	0.454	0.579	0.596
train	0.792	0.778	0.860	0.894
tvmonitor	0.532	0.647	0.686	0.772
# methods	2	5	4	6
# comp	17	18	48	32

TABLE 16.1: Average precision of the best classification method for each category for the Pascal image classification challenge by year (per category; the method that was best at "person" might not be best at "pottedplant"), summarized from `http://pascallin.ecs.soton.ac.uk/challenges/VOC/`. The **bottom** rows show the number of methods in each column and the total number of methods competing (so, for example, in 2007, only 2 of 17 total methods were best in category; each of the other 15 methods was beaten by something for each category). Notice that the average precision grows, but not necessarily monotonically (this is because the test set changes). Most categories now work rather well.

16.2.4 Large Numbers of Classes

The number of categories has grown quite quickly. A now little-used dataset had five classes in it; in turn, this was replaced with a now obsolete ten class dataset; a 101-class dataset; a 256-class dataset; and a 1,000-class dataset (details in Section 16.3.2). Figure 16.20 compares results of recent systems on Caltech 101 (the 101-class dataset described in Section 16.3.2) and on Caltech 256 (256-classes; Section 16.3.2). For these datasets, some care is required when one computes error statistics. Two statistics are natural. The first is the percent of classification attempts that are successful over all test examples. This measure is not widely used, for the following reason: imagine that one class is numerous, and easy to classify; then the error statistic will be dominated by this class, and improvements may just mean that one is getting better at classifying this class. However, for some applications, this might be the right thing. For example, if one is confident that the dataset represents the relative frequency of classes well, then this error rate is

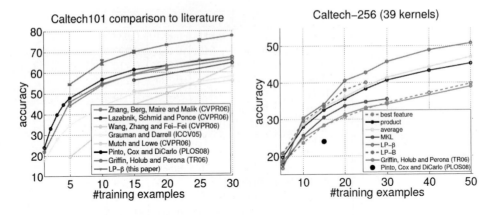

FIGURE 16.20: Graphs illustrating typical performance on Caltech 101 for single descriptor types (**left**) and on Caltech 256 for various types of descriptor (**right**; notice the vertical scale is different), plotted against the number of training examples. Although these figures are taken from a paper advocating nearest neighbor methods, they illustrate performance for a variety of methods. Notice that Caltech 101 results, while not perfect, are now quite strong; the cost of going to 256 categories is quite high. Methods compared are due to: Zhang *et al.* (2006*b*), Lazebnik *et al.* (2006), Wang *et al.* (2006), Grauman and Darrell (2005), Mutch and Lowe (2006), Griffin *et al.* (2007), and Pinto *et al.* (2008); the graph is from Gehler and Nowozin (2009), which describes multiple methods (anything without a named citation on the graph). *This figure was originally published as Figure 2 of "On Feature Combination for Multiclass Object Classification," by P. Gehler and S. Nowozin Proc. ICCV 2009, 2009 © IEEE 2009.*

a good estimate of the problems that will be encountered when using the classifier.

The other statistic that is natural is the average of per-class error rates. This weights down the impact of frequent classes in the test dataset; to do well at this error measure, one must do well at all classes, rather than at frequent classes. This statistic is now much more widely used, because there is little evidence that classes occur in datasets with the same frequency they occur in the world.

It is usual to report performance as the number of training examples goes up, because this gives an estimate of how well features (a) suppress within class variations and (b) expose between class variations. Notice how the performance of all methods seems to stop growing with the number of training examples (though it is hard to confirm what happens with very large numbers, as some categories have relatively few examples).

Generally, strong modern methods do somewhat better on Caltech 101 than on Caltech 256, and better on Caltech 256 than on datasets with more categories, though it is difficult to be sure why. One possibility is that classification becomes a lot harder when the number of categories grows, most likely because of feature effects. Deng *et al.* (2010) show that the performance of good modern methods declines as the number of categories increases, where the set of categories is selected at random from a very large set. This suggests that increasing the number of categories exposes problems in feature representations that might otherwise go unnoticed, because it increases the chances that two of the categories are quite similar (or at least look similar to the feature representation). As a result, performance tends to go down as the number of categories is increased. Another possibility is that Caltech 101 is a more familiar dataset, and so feature design practices have had more time to adapt to its vagaries. If this is the case, then methods that do well on this dataset are not necessarily good methods; instead, they are methods that have been found by the community to do well *on a particular dataset*, which is a form of selection bias. Yet another, equally disturbing possibility is that no current methods do well on large collections of categories because it is so hard to search for a method that does so. The pragmatics of dealing with large numbers of categories is very demanding. Simply training a single method may take CPU years and a variety of clever tricks; classifying a single image also could be very slow (Deng *et al.* 2010).

Working with large numbers of categories presents other problems, too. Not all errors have the same significance, and the semantic status of the categories is unclear (Section 18.1.3). For example, classifying a cat as a dog is probably not as offensive as classifying it as a motorcycle. This is a matter of loss functions. In practice, it is usual to use the so-called *0-1 loss*, where any classification error incurs a loss of one (equivalently, to count errors). This is almost certainly misleading, and is adopted mainly because it is demanding and because there is no consensus on an appropriate replacement. One possibility, advocated by (Deng *et al.* 2010), is to use semantic resources to shape a loss function. For example, Wordnet is a large collection of information about the semantic relations between classes (Fellbaum (1998); Miller *et al.* (1990)). Words are organized into a hierarchy. For example, "dog" (in the sense of an animal commonly encountered as a domestic pet) has child nodes (*hyponyms*), such as "puppy," and ancestors (*hypernyms*) "canid," "carnivore," and, eventually, "entity." A reasonable choice of loss function could be the hop distance in this tree between terms. In this case, "dog" and "cat" would be fairly close, because each has "carnivore" as a grandparent node, but "dog" and "motorcycle" are quite different, because their first common ancestor is many levels removed ("whole"). One difficulty with this approach is that some objects that are visually quite similar and appear in quite similar contexts might be very different in semantics (bird and aircraft, for example). Deng *et al.* (2010) advocate using the height above the correct label of the nearest ancestor, common between the correct and predicted label.

16.2.5   Flowers, Leaves, and Birds: Some Specialized Problems

Image classification techniques are valuable in all sorts of specialized domains. For example, there has been considerable recent progress in classifying flowers automatically from pictures. A natural system architecture is to query a collection of labeled flower images with a query image. If a short list of similar images contains the right flower, that might be sufficient, because geographic distribution cues might rule out all other flowers on the list. The problem is tricky because within-class variation could be high, as a result of pictures taken from different viewing directions, and between-class variation can be low (Figure 16.21). Nilsback and Zisserman (2010) describe a system for matching flower images that computes color, texture, and shape features, then learns a combination of distances in each feature that gives

Pansy   Fritillary   Tiger Lily

Dandelion - A   Colts' foot   Dandelion -B

FIGURE 16.21: Identifying a flower from an image is one useful specialized application for image classification techniques. This is a challenging problem. Although some flowers have quite distinctive features (for example, the colors and textures of the pansy, the fritillary, and the tiger lily), others are easy to confuse. Notice that dandelion-A (**bottom**) looks much more like the colts' foot than like dandelion-B. Here the within-class variation is high because of changes of aspect, and the between-class variation is small. *This figure was originally published as Figures 1 and 8 of "A Visual Vocabulary for Flower Classification," by M.E. Nilsback and A. Zisserman, Proc. IEEE CVPR 2006, © IEEE 2006.*

the best performance for this short list; the best results on this dataset to date are due to a complex multiple-kernel learning procedure (Gehler and Nowozin 2009).

Belhumeur *et al.* (2008) describe a system for automatic matching of leaf images to identify plants; they have released a dataset at `http://herbarium.cs.columbia.edu/data.php`. This work has recently resulted in an iPad app, named Leafsnap, that can identify trees from photographs of their leaves (see `http://leafsnap.com`).

Often, although one cannot exactly classify every image, one can reduce the load on human operators in important ways with computer vision methods. For example, Branson *et al.* (2010) describe methods to classify images of birds to species level that use humans in the loop, but can reduce the load on the human operator. Such methods are likely to lead to apps that will be used by the very large number of amateur birdwatchers.

16.3   IMAGE CLASSIFICATION IN PRACTICE

Numerous codes and datasets have been published for image classification; the next two sections give some pointers to materials available at the time of writing. Image classification is a subject in flux, so methods change quickly. However, one can still make some general statements. Section 16.3.3 summarizes the difficulties that result because datasets cannot be as rich as the world they represent, and Section 16.3.4 describes methods for collecting data relatively cheaply using crowdsourcing.

16.3.1 Codes for Image Features

Oliva and Torralba provide GIST feature code at `http://people.csail.mit.edu/torralba/code/spatialenvelope/`, together with a substantial dataset of outdoor scenes.

Color descriptor code, which computes visual words based on various color SIFT features, is published by van de Sande *et al* at `http://koen.me/research/colordescriptors/`.

The pyramid match kernel is an earlier variant of the spatial pyramid kernel described in Section 16.1.4; John Lee provides a library, `libpmk`, that supports this kernel at `http://people.csail.mit.edu/jjl/libpmk/`. There are a variety of extension libraries written for `libpmk`, including implementations of the pyramid kernel, at this URL.

Li Fei-Fei, Rob Fergus, and Antonio Torralba publish example codes for core object recognition methods at `http://people.csail.mit.edu/torralba/shortCourseRLOC/`. This URL is the online repository associated with their very successful short course on recognizing and learning object categories.

VLFeat is an open-source library that implements a variety of popular computer vision algorithms, initiated by Andrea Vedaldi and Brian Fulkerson; it can be found at `http://www.vlfeat.org`. VLFeat comes with a set of tutorials that show how to use the library, and there is example code showing how to use VLFeat to classify Caltech-101.

There is a repository of code links at `http://featurespace.org`.

At the time of writing, multiple-kernel learning methods produce the strongest results on standard problems, at the cost of quite substantial learning times. Section 15.3.3 gives pointers to codes for different multiple-kernel learning methods.

16.3.2 Image Classification Datasets

There is now a rich range of image classification datasets, covering several application topics. Object category datasets have images organized by category (e.g., one is distinguishing between "bird"s and "motorcycle"s, rather than between particular species of bird). Five classes (motorbikes, airplanes, faces, cars, spotted cats, together with background, which isn't really a class) were introduced by Fergus *et al.* (2003) in 2003; they are sometimes called Caltech-5. Caltech-101 has 101 classes, was introduced in Perona *et al.* (2004) and by Fei-Fei *et al.* (2006), and can be found at `http://www.vision.caltech.edu/Image_Datasets/Caltech101/`. This dataset is now quite well understood, but as Figure 16.20 suggests, it is not yet exhausted. Caltech-256 has 256 classes, was introduced by (Griffin *et al.* 2007), and can be found at `http://www.vision.caltech.edu/Image_Datasets/Caltech256/`. This dataset is still regarded as challenging.

LabelMe is an image annotation environment that has been used by many users to mark out and label objects in images; the result is a dataset that is changing and increasing in size as time goes on. LabelMe was introduced by Russell *et al.* (2008), and can be found at `http://labelme.csail.mit.edu/`.

The Graz-02 dataset contains difficult images of cars, bicycles, and people in natural scenes; it is originally due to Opelt *et al.* (2006), but has been recently reannotated Marszalek and Schmid (2007). The reannotated edition can be found

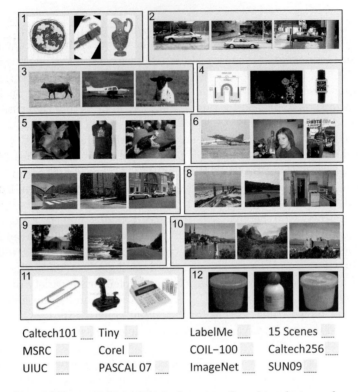

FIGURE 16.22: Torralba and Efros (2011) show one disturbing feature of modern classification datasets; that it is quite easy for skilled insiders to "name that dataset." Here we show a sample of images from current datasets (those not described in the text can be found by a search); you should try and match the image to the dataset. It is surprisingly easy to do. *This figure was originally published as Figures 1 of "Unbiased look at dataset bias," by A. Torralba and A. Efros, Proc. IEEE CVPR 2011, © IEEE 2011.*

at `http://lear.inrialpes.fr/people/marszalek/data/ig02/`.

Imagenet contains tens of millions of examples, organized according to the Wordnet hierarchy of nouns; currently, there are examples for approximately 17,000 nouns. Imagenet was originally described in Deng *et al.* (2009), and can be found at `http://www.image-net.org/`.

The Lotus Hill Research Institute publishes a dataset of images annoted in detail at `http://www.imageparsing.com`; the institute is also available to prepare datasets on a paid basis.

Each year since 2005 has seen a new Pascal image classification dataset; these are available at `http://pascallin.ecs.soton.ac.uk/challenges/VOC/`.

There are numerous specialist datasets. The Oxford visual geometry group publishes two flower datasets, one with 17 categories and one with 102 categories; each can be found at `http://www.robots.ox.ac.uk/~vgg/data/flowers/`. Other datasets include a "things" dataset, a "bottle" dataset, and a "camel" dataset, all from Oxford (`http://www.robots.ox.ac.uk/~vgg/data3.html`).

There is a bird dataset published by Caltech and UCSD jointly at `http:`

`//www.vision.caltech.edu/visipedia/CUB-200.html`.

Classifying materials has become a standard task, with a standard dataset. The Columbia-Utrecht (or CURET) material dataset can be found at `http://www.cs.columbia.edu/CAVE/software/curet/`; it contains image textures from over 60 different material samples observed with over 200 combinations of view and light direction. Details on the procedures used to obtain this dataset can be found in Dana *et al.* (1999). More recently, Liu *et al.* (2010) offer an alternative and very difficult material dataset of materials on real objects, which can be found at `http://people.csail.mit.edu/celiu/CVPR2010/FMD/`.

We are not aware of collections of explicit images published for use as research datasets, though such a dataset would be easy to collect.

There are several scene datasets now. The largest is the SUN dataset (from MIT; `http://groups.csail.mit.edu/vision/SUN/`; Xiao *et al.* (2010)) contains 130,519 images of 899 types of scene; 397 categories have at least 100 examples per category. There is a 15-category scene dataset used in the original spatial pyramid kernel work at `http://www-cvr.ai.uiuc.edu/ponce_grp/data/`.

It isn't possible (at least for us!) to list all currently available datasets. Repositories that contain datasets, and so are worth searching for a specialist dataset, include: the pilot European Image Processing Archive, currently at `http://peipa.essex.ac.uk/index.html`; Keith Price's comprehensive computer vision bibliography, whose root is `http://visionbib.com/index.php`, and with dataset pages at `http://datasets.visionbib.com/index.html`; the Featurespace dataset pages, at `http://www.featurespace.org/`; and the Oxford repository, at `http://www.robots.ox.ac.uk/~vgg/data.html`.

16.3.3 Dataset Bias

Datasets can suffer from *bias*, where properties of the dataset misrepresent properties of the real world. This is not due to mischief in the collecting process; it occurs because the dataset must be much smaller than the set of all images of an object. Some bias phenomena can be quite substantial. For example, Figure 16.22 shows that people can get quite good at telling which dataset a picture was taken from, as can computers (Figure 16.23, whose caption gives the right answers for Figure 16.22). As another example, Figure 16.24 shows the mean image of a set of Caltech 101 images. Clearly, in this case, each image in the dataset looks quite a lot like every other image in its class and not much like images in other classes. This doesn't mean that it is easy to get very strong recognition results; compare Figure 16.20. The best current strategies for avoiding bias are (a) to collect large datasets from a variety of different sources; (b) to evaluate datasets carefully using baseline methods before using them to evaluate complex methods; and (c) to try and quantify the effects of bias by evaluating on data collected using a different strategy than that used to collect the training data. Each is fairly crude. Improved procedures would be most valuable.

16.3.4 Crowdsourcing Dataset Collection

Recently, dataset builders have made extensive use of *crowdsourcing*, where one pays people to label data. One such service is Amazon's Mechanical Turk. Crowd-

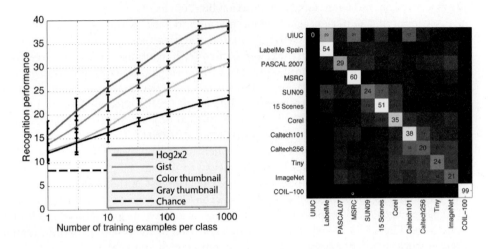

FIGURE 16.23: Computers do very well at "name that dataset." On the **left**, classification accuracy as a function of training size for some different features; notice that classifiers are really quite good at telling which dataset a picture came from. On the **right**, the class confusion matrix, which suggests that these datasets are well-separated. The answers to the question in Figure 16.22 are: (1) Caltech-101, (2) UIUC, (3) MSRC, (4) Tiny Images, (5) ImageNet, (6) PASCAL VOC, (7) LabelMe, (8) SUNS-09, (9) 15 Scenes, (10) Corel, (11) Caltech-256, (12) COIL-100. *This figure was originally published as Figure 2 of "Unbiased look at dataset bias," by A. Torralba and A. Efros, Proc. IEEE CVPR 2011,* © *IEEE 2011.*

sourcing services connect people on the Internet willing to do tasks for money with people who have tasks and money. Generally, one builds an interface to support the task (for example, your interface might display an image and some radio buttons to identify the class), then registers the task and a price. Workers then do the task, you pay the service, and they transmit money to the workers. Important issues here are quality control—are people doing what you want them to do?—and pricing—how much should you pay for a task? Quality control strategies include: prequalifying workers; sampling tasks and excluding workers who do the task poorly; and using another set of workers to evaluate the results of the first set. We are not aware of good principled pricing strategies right now. However, some guidelines can be helpful. Workers seem to move quickly from task to task, looking for ones that are congenial and well-paid. This means that all tasks seem to experience a rush of workers, which quickly tails off if the price is wrong. Paying more money always seems to help get tasks completed faster. There seems to be a pool of workers who are good at identifying overpaid tasks with poor quality control, but most workers are quite conscientious. Finally, interface design can have a huge impact on the final accuracy of labeled data. These ideas are now quite pervasive. Examples of recent datasets built with some input from Mechanical Turk include Deng *et al.* (2009), Endres *et al.* (2010), Parikh and Grauman (2011), and Xiao *et al.* (2010). Sorokin and Forsyth (2008) give a variety of strategies and methods to use the service. Vijayanarasimhan and Grauman (2011) supply good evidence that active

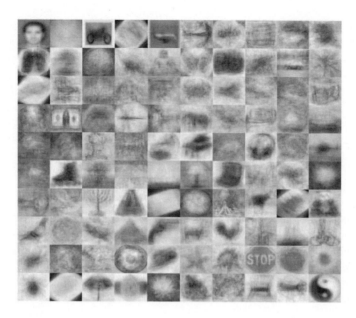

FIGURE 16.24: The average image for each of 100 categories from the Caltech 101 image classification dataset. Fairly obviously, these pictures consist of isolated objects, and the mean of each class is far away from the mean of other classes. This does not mean that these images are easy to classify (compare Figure 16.20); instead, it is an illustration of the fact that all datasets must contain statistical regularities that are not present in the world. *This figure created by A. Torralba, and used with his permission.*

learning can improve costs and quality; see also Vijayanarasimhan and Grauman (2009). Vondrick *et al.* (2010) show methods to balance human labor (which is expensive and slow, but more accurate) with automatic methods (which can propagate existing labels to expose what is already known, and can be fast and cheap) for video annotation. Crowdflower, which is a service that helps build APIs and organize crowdsourcing, can be found at `http://crowdflower.com/`.

16.4 NOTES

Generally, successful work in image classification involves constructing features that expose important properties of the classes to the classifier. The classifier itself can make some difference, but seems not to matter all that much. We have described the dominant feature constructions, but there is a particularly rich literature on feature constructions; there are pointers to this in the main text.

We suspect that the best methods for explicit image detection are not published now, but instead just used, because good methods appear to have real financial value. All follow the lines sketched out in our section, but using a range of different features and of classifiers. Experiments are now on a relatively large scale.

One application we like, but didn't review in this chapter, is sign language understanding. Here an automated method watches a signer, and tries to transcribe the sign language into text. Good start points to this very interesting literature include Starner *et al.* (1998), Buehler *et al.* (2009), Cooper and Bowden (2009), Farhadi *et al.* (2007), Erdem and Sclaroff (2002), Bowden *et al.* (2004), Buehler *et al.* (2008), and Kadir *et al.* (2004). Athitsos *et al.* (2008) describe a dataset.

Visual words are a representation of important local image patches. While the construction we described is fairly natural, it is not the only possible construction. It is not essential to describe only interest points; one could use a grid of sample points, perhaps as fine as every pixel. The description does not have to be in terms of SIFT features. For example, one might extend it by using some or all of the color sift features described briefly in Section 5.4.1. Many authors instead compute a vector of filter responses (section 6.1 for this as a texture representation; section 16.1.8 for applications to texture material classification). An important alternative is to work directly with small local image patches, say 5×5 pixels in size. The vocabulary of such visual words could be very big indeed, and special clustering techniques are required to vector quantize. In each case, however, the main recipe remains the same: decide on a way of identifying local patches (interest points, sampling, etc.); decide on a local patch representation; vector quantize this representation to form visual words; then represent the image or the region with a histogram of the important visual words.

PROGRAMMING EXERCISES

16.1. Build a classifier that classifies materials using the dataset of Liu *et al.* (2010). Compare the performance of your system using the main feature constructions described here (GIST features; visual words; spatial pyramid kernel). Investigate the effect of varying the feature construction; for example, is it helpful to use C-SIFT descriptors?

16.2. Build a classifier that classifies scenes using the dataset of Xiao *et al.* (2010). Compare the performance of your system using the main feature constructions described here (GIST features; visual words; spatial pyramid kernel). Investigate the effect of varying the feature construction; for example, is it helpful to use C-SIFT descriptors?

16.3. Search online for classification and feature construction codes, and replicate an image classification experiment on a standard dataset (we recommend a Caltech dataset or a PASCAL dataset; your instructor may have an opinion, too). Do you get exactly the same performance that the authors claim? Why?

C H A P T E R   17

Detecting Objects in Images

Chapter 16 described methods to classify images. When we assumed that the image contained a single, dominating object, these methods were capable of identifying that object. In this chapter, we describe methods that can detect objects. These methods all follow a surprisingly simple recipe—essentially, apply a classifier to subwindows of the image—which we describe with examples in Section 17.1. We then describe a more complex version of this recipe that applies to objects that can deform, or that have complex appearance (Section 17.2). Finally, we sketch the state of the art of object detection, giving pointers to available software and data (Section 17.3).

17.1   THE SLIDING WINDOW METHOD

Assume we are dealing with objects that have a relatively well-behaved appearance, and do not deform much. Then we can detect them with a very simple recipe. We build a dataset of labeled image windows of fixed size (say, $n \times m$). The examples labeled positive should contain large, centered instances of the object, and those labeled negative should not. We then train a classifier to tell these windows apart. We now pass every $n \times m$ window in the image to the classifier. Windows that the classifier labels positive contain the object, and those labeled negative do not. This is a search over location, which we could represent with the top left-hand corner of the window.

There are two subtleties to be careful about when applying this recipe. First, not all instances of an object will be the same size in the image. This means we need to search over scale as well. The easy way to do this is to prepare a Gaussian pyramid of the image (Section 4.7), and then search $n \times m$ windows in each layer of the pyramid. Searching an image whose edge lengths have been scaled by s for $n \times m$ windows is rather like searching the original image for $(sn) \times (sm)$ windows (the differences are in resolution, in ease of training, and in computation time).

The second subtlety is that some image windows overlap quite strongly. Each of a set of overlapping windows could contain all (or a substantial fraction of) the object. This means that each might be labeled positive by the classifier, meaning we would count the same object multiple times. This effect cannot be cured by passing to a bigger training set and producing a classifier that is so tightly tuned that it responds only when the object is exactly centered in the window. This is because it is hard to produce tightly tuned classifiers, and because we will never be able to place a window exactly around an object, so that a tightly tuned classifier will tend to behave badly. The usual strategy for managing this problem is *non-maximum suppression*. In this strategy, windows with a local maximum of the classifier response suppress nearby windows. We summarize the whole approach in Algorithm 17.1.

Train a classifier on $n \times m$ image windows. Positive examples contain the object and negative examples do not.
Choose a threshold t and steps Δx and Δy in the x and y directions

Construct an image pyramid.

For each level of the pyramid
    Apply the classifier to each $n \times m$ window, stepping by
    Δx and Δy, in this level to get a response strength c.
    If $c > t$
        Insert a pointer to the window into a ranked list $\mathcal{L}$, ranked by c.

For each window $\mathcal{W}$ in $\mathcal{L}$, starting with the strongest response
    Remove all windows $\mathcal{U} \neq \mathcal{W}$ that overlap $\mathcal{W}$ significantly,
        where the overlap is computed in the original image by expanding windows
        in coarser scales.

$\mathcal{L}$ is now the list of detected objects.

Algorithm 17.1: Sliding Window Detection.

The sliding window detection recipe is wholly generic and behaves very well in practice. Different applications require different choices of feature and sometimes benefit from different choices of feature. Notice that there is a subtle interaction between the size of the window, the steps Δx and Δy, and the classifier. For example, if we work with windows that tightly surround the object, then we might be able to use a classifier that is more tightly tuned, but we will have to use smaller steps and so look at more windows. If we use windows that are rather larger than the object, then we can look at fewer windows, but our ability to detect objects next to one another might be affected, as might our ability to localize the objects. Cross-validation is one way to make appropriate choices here. As a result, there is some variation in the appearance of the window caused by the fact our search is quantized in translation and scale; the training tricks in Section 15.3.1 are extremely useful for controlling this difficulty.

17.1.1 Face Detection

In frontal views at a fairly coarse scale, all faces look basically the same. There are bright regions on the forehead, the cheeks, and the nose, and dark regions around the eyes, the eyebrows, the base of the nose, and the mouth. This suggests approaching face finding as a search over all image windows of a fixed size for windows that look like a face. Larger or smaller faces can be found by searching coarser- or finer-scale images.

A face illuminated from the left looks different than a face illuminated from the right, which might create difficulties for the classifier. There are two options: we could use HOG features, as in Section 5.4; or we could correct the image window to reduce illumination effects. The pedestrian detector of Section 17.1.2 uses HOG features, so we will describe methods to correct image windows here.

Generally, illumination effects look enough like a linear ramp (one side is bright, the other side is dark, and there is a smooth transition between them) that we can simply fit a linear ramp to the intensity values and subtract that from the image window. Another way to do this would be to log-transform the image and then subtract a linear ramp fitted to the logs. This has the advantage that (using a rather rough model) illumination effects are additive in the log transform. There doesn't appear to be any evidence in the literature that the log transform makes much difference in practice. Another approach is to histogram equalize the window to ensure that its histogram is the same as that of a set of reference images (histogram equalization is described in Figure 17.1).

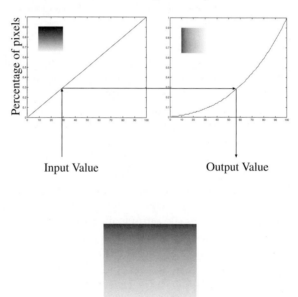

FIGURE 17.1: Histogram equalization uses cumulative histograms to map the gray levels of one image so that it has the same histogram as another image. The figure at the top shows two cumulative histograms with the relevant images inset in the graphs. To transform the left image so that it has the same histogram as the right image, we take a value from the left image, read off the percentage from the cumulative histogram of that image, and obtain a new value for that gray level from the inverse cumulative histogram of the right image. The image on the **left** is a linear ramp (it looks nonlinear because the relationship between brightness and lightness is not linear); the image on the **right** is a cube root ramp. The result—the linear ramp, with gray levels remapped so that it has the same histogram as the cube root ramp—is shown on the **bottom row**.

Once the windows have been corrected for illumination, we need to determine whether there is a face present. The orientation isn't known, and so we must either

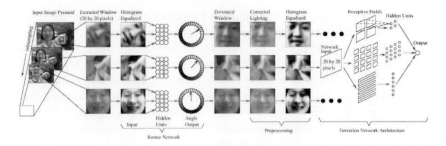

FIGURE 17.2: The architecture of Rowley, Baluja, and Kanade's system for finding faces. Image windows of a fixed size are corrected to a standard illumination using histogram equalization; they are then passed to a neural net that estimates the orientation of the window. The windows are reoriented and passed to a second net that determines whether a face is present. *This figure was originally published as Figure 2 from "Rotation invariant neural-network based face detection," H.A. Rowley, S. Baluja, and T. Kanade, Proc. IEEE CVPR, 1998, © IEEE, 1998.*

determine it or produce a classifier that is insensitive to orientation. A *neural net* is a procedure for parametric regression that produces an output that is a function of input and parameters. Neural nets are typically trained by gradient descent on an error function that compares computed output to labels for numerous labeled examples. Rowley *et al.* (1998*b*) produced a face finder that finds faces very successfully by first estimating the orientation of the window using one neural net then reorienting the window so that it is frontal, and then passing the frontal window onto another neural net (see Figure 17.2; the paper is a development of Rowley *et al.* (1996) and (1998*a*)). The orientation finder has 36 output units, each coding for a 10° range of orientations; the window is reoriented to the orientation given by the largest output. Examples of the output of this system are given in Figure 17.3.

There is now an extremely rich face detection literature based on the sliding window recipe. The most important variant is due to Viola and Jones (2001), who point out that a clever choice of classifier and of features results in an extremely fast system. The key is to use features that are easy to evaluate to reject most windows early. Viola and Jones (2001) use features that are composed of sums of the image within boxes; these sums are weighted by 1 or −1, then added together. This yields the form

$$\sum_k \delta_k B_k(\mathcal{I}),$$

where $\delta_i \in \{1, -1\}$ and

$$B_k(\mathcal{I}) = \sum_{i=u_1(k)}^{u_2(k)} \sum_{j=v_1(k)}^{v_2(k)} \mathcal{I}_{ij}.$$

Such features are extremely fast to evaluate with a device called an *integral image*. Write $\hat{\mathcal{I}}$ for the integral image formed from the image $\mathcal{I}$. Then

$$\hat{\mathcal{I}}_{ij} = \sum_{u=1}^{i} \sum_{v=1}^{j} \mathcal{I}_{uv}.$$

FIGURE 17.3: Typical responses for the Rowley, Baluja, and Kanade system for face finding; a mask icon is superimposed on each window that is determined to contain a face. The orientation of the face is indicated by the configuration of the eye holes in the mask. *This figure was originally published as Figure 7 from "Rotation invariant neural-network based face detection," H.A. Rowley, S. Baluja, and T. Kanade, Proc. IEEE CVPR, 1998, © IEEE, 1998.*

This means that any sum within a box can be evaluated with four queries to the integral image. It is easy to check that

$$\sum_{i=u_1}^{u_2} \sum_{j=v_1}^{v_2} \mathcal{I}_{ij} = \hat{\mathcal{I}}_{u_2 v_2} - \hat{\mathcal{I}}_{u_1 v_2} - \hat{\mathcal{I}}_{u_2 v_1} + \hat{\mathcal{I}}_{u_1 v_1},$$

which means that any of the features can be evaluated by a set of integral image queries. Now imagine we build a boosted classifier, using decision stumps based around these features. The resulting score will be a weighted sum of binary terms,

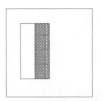

FIGURE 17.4: Face detection can be made extremely fast using features that are easy to evaluate, and that can reject most windows early. On the **left**, features can be built up out of sums of the image within boxes, weighted by 1 or −1. The drawings show two two-box features (some readers might spot a relationship to Haar wavelets). On the **right**, the features used for the first two tests (equivalently, the first two classifiers in the cascade) by Viola and Jones (2001). Notice how they check for the distinctive dark bar at the eyes with the lighter bar at the cheekbones, then the equally distinctive vertical specularity along the nose and forehead. *This figure was originally published as Figures 1 and 3 from "Rapid Object Detection using a Boosted Cascade of Simple Features," by P. Viola and M. Jones, Proc. IEEE CVPR 2001 © IEEE 2001.*

FIGURE 17.5: Examples of pedestrian windows from the INRIA pedestrian dataset, collected and published by Dalal and Triggs (2005). Notice the relatively strong and distinctive curve around the head and shoulders; the general "lollipop" shape, caused by the upper body being wider than the legs; the characteristic "scissors" appearance of separated legs; and the strong vertical boundaries around the sides. These seem to be the cues used by classifiers. *This figure was originally published as Figure 2 of "Histograms of Oriented Gradients for Human Detection," N. Dalal and W. Triggs, Proc. IEEE CVPR 2005, © IEEE, 2005.*

one for each feature. Now we can order the features by complexity of evaluation (for example, two box features will be much faster to evaluate than ten box features). For the simplest feature, we can then adjust the threshold of the weak learner such that there are few or no false negatives. Now any window that returns a feature value below that threshold can be rejected *without looking at the other features*; this means that many or most image windows can be rejected at the first test (Figure 17.4). If the window passes the first test, we can test the next feature with a threshold adjusted so it produces few or no false negatives *on the output of the first test*. Again, we expect to be able to reject many or most windows. We apply this strategy repeatedly to get an architecture of repeated classifiers referred to as a *cascade*. Classifiers in the cascade do not need to use only a single feature. Viola and Jones (2001) train the cascade by requiring that each stage meet or exceed targets for the reduction in false positives (which should be big) and the decrease

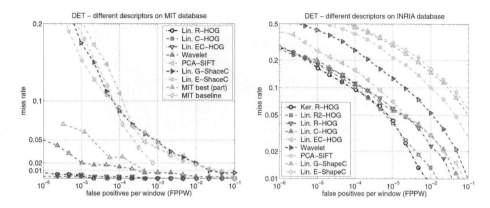

FIGURE 17.6: The performance of the pedestrian detector of Dalal and Triggs (2005), for various choices of features and two different datasets. On the **left**, results using the MIT pedestrian dataset, and on the **right**, results using the INRIA dataset. The results are reported as the miss rate (so smaller is better) against the false positive per window (FPPW) rate, and so evaluate the classifier rather than the system. Overall system performance will depend on how many windows are presented to the detector in an average image (details in the text; see Figure 17.8). Notice that different datasets result in quite different performance levels. The best performance on the INRIA dataset (which is quite obviously the harder dataset) is obtained with a kernel SVM (circles, Ker. R-HOG), but there is very little difference between this and a linear SVM (squares, Lin. R2-HOG). *This figure was originally published as Figure 3 of "Histograms of Oriented Gradients for Human Detection," N. Dalal and W. Triggs, Proc. IEEE CVPR 2005, © IEEE, 2005.*

in detection rate (which should be small); they add features to the stage until the targets are met.

Generally, frontal face detection is now a reliable part of vision systems (e.g., Section 21.4.4); usually other components of a system cause more problems than face detection does. It is much more difficult to detect faces in lateral views; there seem to be two major reasons. First, the profile of the face is quite important, and variable between subjects. This means that classifier windows must take an awkward shape, and some pixels in the window do not lie on the face and so contribute noise. Second, lateral views of faces seem to have a less constrained appearance than frontal views, so that classifiers must be more flexible to find them.

17.1.2   Detecting Humans

Being a pedestrian is dangerous, and even more so if one is intoxicated. Counting pedestrian deaths is hard, but reasonable estimates give nearly 900,000 pedestrians killed worldwide in 1990 (Jacobs and Aeron-Thomas 2000). If a car could tell whether it were heading for a pedestrian, it might be able to prevent an accident. As a result, there is much interest in building pedestrian detectors.

The sliding window recipe applies naturally to pedestrian detection because pedestrians tend to take characteristic configurations. Standing pedestrians look

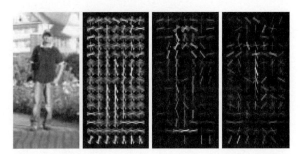

FIGURE 17.7: As Figure 17.6 indicates, a linear SVM works about as well as the best detector for a pedestrian detector. Linear SVMs can be used to visualize what aspects of the feature representation are distinctive. On the **left**, a typical pedestrian window, with the HOG features visualized on the **center left**, using the scheme of Figure 5.15. Each of the orientation buckets in each window is a feature, and so has a corresponding weight in the linear SVM. On the **center right**, the HOG features weighted by positive weights, then visualized (so that an important feature is light). Notice how the head and shoulders curve and the lollipop shape gets strong positive weights. On the **right**, the HOG features weighted by the absolute value of negative weights, which means a feature that strongly suggests a person is not present is light. Notice how a strong vertical line in the center of the window is deprecated (because it suggests the window is not centered on a person). *This figure was originally published as Figure 6 of "Histograms of Oriented Gradients for Human Detection," N. Dalal and W. Triggs, Proc. IEEE CVPR 2005, © IEEE, 2005.*

like lollipops (wider upper body and narrower legs), and walking pedestrians have a quite characteristic scissors appearance (Figure 17.5). Dalal and Triggs (2005) invented HOG features for this purpose, and used a linear SVM to classify windows, because it is as good as the best classifier, but simpler (Figure 17.6). Another advantage of a linear SVM is that one can get some insight into what features are distinctive (Figure 17.7).

Evaluating sliding window methods can be difficult. Dalal and Triggs (2005) advocate plotting the detection rate (percentage of true positives detected) against the false positives per window (FPPW). Figure 17.6 shows performance for various configurations of their system plotted on these axes. When evaluating these plots, it is important to keep in mind that they characterize the behavior of the *classifier*, rather than the whole system. This is attractive if you are interested in features and classifiers, but perhaps less so if you are interested in systems. A higher FPPW rate may be tolerable if you have to look at fewer windows, though looking at fewer windows might affect the detect rate. Dollar *et al.* (2009) have conducted a systematic evaluation of pedestrian detectors on a large dataset built for that purpose. As Figure 17.8 shows, the ranking of methods changes depending on whether one plots FPPW or false positive per image (FPPI); generally, we expect that FPPI is more predictive of performance in applications.

Our sliding window recipe has one important fault: it assumes that windows are independent. In pedestrian detection applications, windows aren't really independent, because pedestrians are all about the same size, have their feet on or close to the ground, and are usually seen outdoors, where the ground is a plane. If

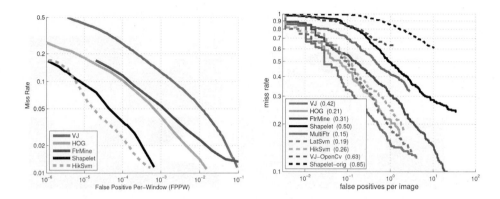

FIGURE 17.8: The FPPW statistic is useful for evaluating classifiers, but less so for evaluating systems. On the **left**, results on the INRIA pedestrian dataset for a variety of systems, plotted using miss rate against FPPW by Dollar *et al.* (2009). In this plot, curves that lie lower on the figure represent better performance (because they have a lower miss rate for a given FPPW rate). On the **right**, results plotted using miss rate against false positive per image (FPPI), a measure that takes into account the number of windows presented to the classifier. Again, curves that lie lower are better. Notice how different the ranking of the systems is.   *This figure was originally published as Figure 8 of "Pedestrian Detection: A Benchmark" P. Dollár, C. Wojek, B. Schiele, and P. Perona, Proc. IEEE CVPR 2009 © IEEE 2009.*

we knew the horizon of the ground plane and the height of the camera above that ground plane, then many windows could not be legitimate pedestrians. Windows whose base is above the horizon would be suspect because they would imply pedestrians in the air; windows whose base is closer to the horizon should be smaller (otherwise, we would be dealing with gigantic pedestrians). The height of the camera above the ground plane matters because in this problem there is an absolute scale, given by the average height of a pedestrian. Assume the horizon is in the center of the image. Then, for cameras that are higher above the ground plane, legitimate pedestrian windows get smaller more quickly as their base approaches the horizon. There are two strong sources of information about the horizon and the camera height. First, the textures of the ground, buildings, and sky are all different, and these can be used to make a rough decomposition of the image that suggests the horizon. Second, observing some reliable detection responses should give us clues to where the horizon lies, and how high the focal point is above the ground plane. Hoiem *et al.* (2008) show that these global geometric cues can be used to improve the behavior of pedestrian and car detectors (Figure 17.9; see also Hoiem *et al.* (2006)).

17.1.3   Detecting Boundaries

Edges are not the same as occluding contours, as we said in Chapter 5, because many effects—changes in albedo, shadow boundaries, fast changes in surface normal—can create edges. Rather than relying on the output of an edge detector, we could explicitly build an occluding contour detector, using the sliding window recipe. At

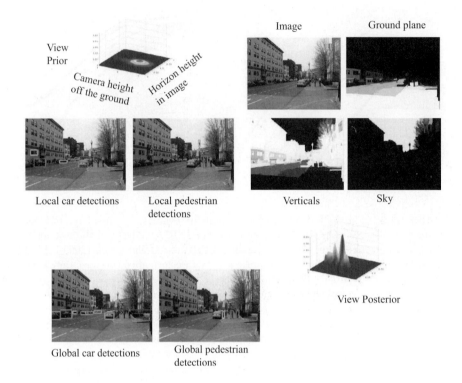

FIGURE 17.9: Hoiem *et al.* (2008) show geometric consistency can be used to improve detector performance. The main parameters are the height of the camera above the ground, and the positition of the image horizon. The texture of the ground plane, the sky, and vertical walls tend to be different, so that discriminative methods can classify pixels into these classes; with this information, combined with detector responses (**local detector results**), they obtain a significantly improved posterior estimate of the geometric parameters, and an improved detection rate for a given false positive rate (**global detector results**). *This figure was originally published as Figure 5 of "Putting Objects in Perspective," by D. Hoiem, A. Efros, and M. Hebert, Proc. IEEE CVPR 2006 © IEEE 2006.*

each window, we would look at a set of relevant features within the window, then use these to decide whether the pixel at the center of the window is an occluding contour or not. In practice, it is sometimes more useful to produce the posterior probability that each pixel lies on a boundary, at that pixel. Martin *et al.* (2004), who pioneered the method, call these maps the P_b, for **probability of boundary**.

For this problem, it makes sense to work with circular windows. Boundaries are oriented, so we will need to search over orientations. Each oriented window can be visualized as a circle cut in half by a line through the center. If this line is an object boundary, we expect substantial differences between the two sides, and so features will compare these sides. Martin *et al.* (2004) build features for a set of properties (raw image intensity, oriented energy, brightness gradient, color gradient, raw texture gradient, and localized texture gradient) by taking a histogram

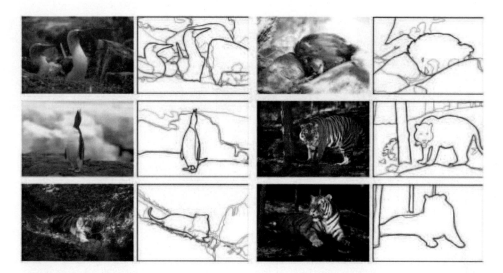

FIGURE 17.10: Object boundaries marked by human informants for some images from the Berkeley segmentation dataset, used by Martin *et al.* (2004) to train detectors that report the probability of boundary. Maps produced by many informants have been averaged, so that pixels are darker when many informants agree that they represent boundaries.

This figure was originally published as Figure 1 of "Learning to Detect Natural Image Boundaries Using Local Brightness, Color, and Texture Cues," by D.R. Martin, C.C. Fowlkes, and J. Malik, IEEE Transactions on Pattern Analysis and Machine Intelligence, 2004 © IEEE 2004.

representing that property for each side, then computing the χ^2 distance between the histograms. This means that each feature encodes the tendency of a particular property to look different on the two sides of the circle. This set of features is then supplied to logistic regression.

The boundary detector is trained using images whose boundaries have been marked by humans (Figure 17.10). Human annotators don't get boundaries perfectly right (or else they'd agree, which they certainly don't; see also Figure 17.12). This means that the training dataset might contain multiple copies of the same window with different annotations—some humans marked the point a boundary point, and others didn't. However, the set of windows is very large, so that such inconsistencies should be averaged out in training. The procedure we have described can be used to build two methods. One reports $P_b(x, y, \theta)$, that is, the probability the point is a boundary point as a function of position and orientation; the other reports $P_b(x, y) = \max_\theta P_b(x, y, \theta)$. The second is most widely used (Figure 17.11).

Testing requires some care, because reporting a boundary point close to, but not on, a boundary point marked by a human is not a failure. Martin *et al.* (2004) cope with this issue by building a weighted matching between the boundary points marked by a human and those predicted by the method. Weights depend on distance, with larger distances being more unfavorable. A predicted boundary point too far away from any human-marked point is a false positive. Similarly, if there are no boundary points predicted close enough to a human-marked point, then that

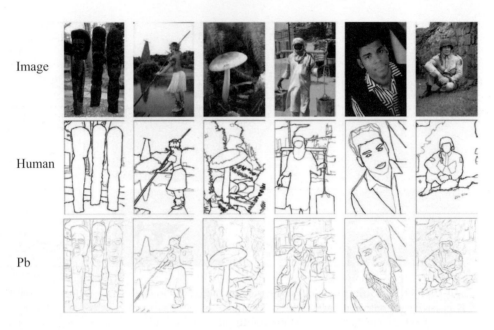

FIGURE 17.11: Some images from the dataset used by Martin *et al.* (2004). Boundaries predicted by humans (averaged over multiple informants; darker pixels represent boundary points on which more informants agree) compare well with boundaries predicted by the P_b method. Some P_b errors are unavoidable (see the detailed windows in Figure 17.13); the method has no-long scale information about the objects present in the image. *This figure was originally published as Figure 15 of "Learning to Detect Natural Image Boundaries Using Local Brightness, Color, and Texture Cues," by D.R. Martin, C.C. Fowlkes, and J. Malik, IEEE Transactions on Pattern Analysis and Machine Intelligence, 2004 © IEEE 2004.*

point counts as a false negative. We can then threshold the P_b map at some value, and compute recall and precision of the method; by varying the threshold, we get a recall-precision curve (Figure 17.12). Although this method doesn't perform as well as humans, who can use context and object identity cues (and so predict illusory contours, as in Figure 17.13), it significantly outperforms other methods for finding boundaries. P_b is now widely used as a feature, and implementations are available (Section 17.3.1). The most recent variant is globalP_b, which gets improved results by linking the P_b method to a segmenter, and so filling in pixels that are required to ensure that object boundaries are closed curves. You can see this as a method to force windows not to be independent. Precision-recall curves for this method appear in Figure 9.25, which should be compared with Figure 17.11.

17.2 DETECTING DEFORMABLE OBJECTS

The basic sliding window detection recipe is extremely powerful. It does assume (incorrectly) that windows are independent, but we have shown ways to manage the cost of that assumption. However, the recipe must fail when the classifier fails. There are two important effects that cause the classifier to fail: The object might

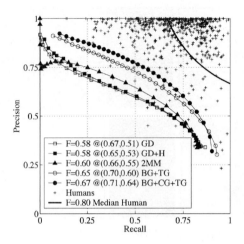

FIGURE 17.12: Martin *et al.* (2004) evaluate P_b (or probability of boundary) detectors by comparison to boundaries marked by humans. One plots the recall and precision of a set of boundaries for a given detector threshold by placing predicted points in correspondence with boundary points predicted by humans, weighting correspondences so that distant pairings are discouraged. Some predicted points are then unmatched, and so are false positives. Unmatched human boundary points give a count of false negatives. Varying the threshold gives a recall-precision curve. On this plot, the $+$ signs are human informants, who differ from one another in where they place boundary points. The median F measure for humans is 0.8, and the human curve is the $F = 0.8$ curve. Using different subsets of the feature set gives slightly different performance statistics; using all the features we have described gives the $BG + CG + TG$ curve. *This figure was originally published as Figure 3 of "Learning to Detect Natural Image Boundaries Using Local Brightness, Color, and Texture Cues," by D.R. Martin, C.C. Fowlkes, and J. Malik, IEEE Transactions on Pattern Analysis and Machine Intelligence, 2004 © IEEE 2004.*

change shape, usually referred to as *deformation*; and we might see the object from different views, usually referred to as *aspect*. Recent work has shown that these effects can be mitigated very significantly by natural changes to the classifier.

To deal with aspect, we could build more than one classifier for the same object. Each classifier responds to different views of that object. The response of this system of classifiers at a given window is obtained by taking the maximum of each of the separate classifier responses. The learning procedure will need to take this into account, to ensure that the classifiers are calibrated to one another. In particular, training the learning procedure will be considerably simplified if it knows *which* of the multiple classifiers should have the strongest response for each positive training example. We do not expect this information to be part of the training set, and so it forms a *latent variable*—a variable that simplifies modelling, but is itself unknown. We will have to estimate it during training.

This notion of a latent variable yields extremely powerful methods to deal with deformation, too. Deformation is a rather fluid concept at time of writing, because it must cover such varied effects as people moving their arms and legs around, the tendency of some motorcars to be longer than others, and the tendency of (say)

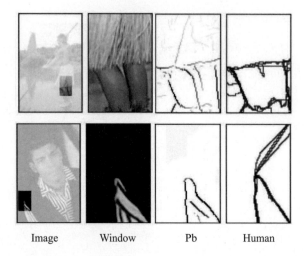

Image   Window   Pb   Human

FIGURE 17.13: Detailed local examination of P_b results can be informative. On the **top**, a texture boundary that is difficult to identify with conventional edge-detection techniques found by P_b. On the **bottom**, an illusory contour (a contour that must be present by the nature of the object viewed, but where no contrast exists to identify it) defeats the P_b method because it does not have global object derived features; people quite reliably mark this boundary. *This figure was originally published as Figure 17 of "Learning to Detect Natural Image Boundaries Using Local Brightness, Color, and Texture Cues," by D.R. Martin, C.C. Fowlkes, and J. Malik, IEEE Transactions on Pattern Analysis and Machine Intelligence, 2004 © IEEE 2004.*

amoebas or jellyfish to have little reliable shape at all. The most useful meaning of the term to date is the observation that many objects have patches that look like one another—the head of a person, or the bonnet of a motorcar—but can be found in somewhat different places in different instances of the whole object. For example, a station wagon and a sedan are like one another because each has doors, wheels, and headlights—reliable patches that look like one another—but pictures of station wagons might have headlights and wheels rather farther away from the doors than pictures of sedans will. This suggests modelling an object as a *root*— an approximate model that gives the overall location of the object— and a set of *parts*—object components that have quite reliable appearance, but might appear at somewhat different locations on the root for different instances. Parts are typically considerably smaller than roots. Each part has an appearance model and a natural location. Finding a window that looks a lot like the part close to that part's natural location with respect to the root yields evidence that the object is present.

We now build classifiers that use this model of an object, and apply them in our sliding window recipe. The overall score for a window will be the sum of several distinct scores. One compares the root to the window. Each part has its own separate score, consisting of an appearance term and a location term (Figure 17.14). The appearance term compares the appearance of the part to the image, and the location term penalizes the part if it lies too far away from its natural location. The appearance model for the root and for each part will be a linear function of HOG

Root   Parts   Offset costs

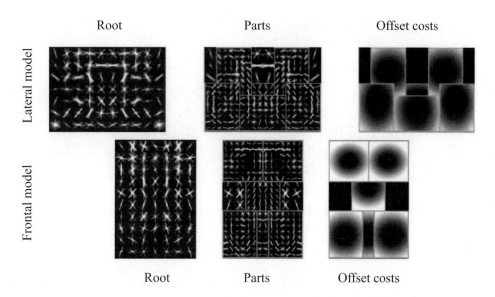

Root   Parts   Offset costs

FIGURE 17.14: A model for a bicycle, built using the scheme of Felzenszwalb *et al.* (2010*b*). There are two components, corresponding to a frontal and a lateral view. Each component has a root and six parts. The root and the part appearance models are visualized with the scheme of Figure 5.15. Notice how the root for each view corresponds to a rough layout, but (for example) the wheels in the lateral view or the handlebar in the frontal view are hard to spot. This is because bicycles will not be in exactly the same place, or at exactly the same orientation, in each window. The parts can compensate for that, and the part models show quite clear wheels and handlebars. The offset costs are registered to the parts, and smaller values are darker. For example, the wheels in the lateral view can move somewhat apart, but it becomes expensive to separate them by too much, or place them too close together. The score for a particular image window is the maximum of the component scores, which are described in the text. *This figure was originally published as Figure 2 of "Object Detection Using Discriminatively Trained Part-based Models," by P. Felzenszwalb, R. Girshick, D. McAllester, and D. Ramanan, IEEE Transactions on Pattern Analysis and Machine Intelligence, 2010 © IEEE 2010.*

features, so the resulting model will have strong analogies with a linear SVM—in fact, a linear SVM is a special case of the model we are building, in that it has a root but no parts.

We can now introduce some notation to describe a single component model. Each component has the same form, so there is no loss of generality in this; we are just suppressing some notation that keeps track of the component under discussion. The root model will consist of a set of linear weights, $\beta^{(r)}$, to be applied to the feature vector describing the root window (which is a HOG feature vector in all implementations we know of, but doesn't have to be). The ith part model will consist of a set of linear weights, $\beta^{(p_i)}$, to be applied to the feature vector describing the part window; a natural offset with respect to the root, $\boldsymbol{v}^{(p_i)} = (u^{(p_i)}, v^{(p_i)})$; and a set of distance weights $\boldsymbol{d}^{(p_i)} = (d_1^{(p_i)}, d_2^{(p_i)}, d_3^{(p_i)}, d_4^{(p_i)})$. Now write $\phi(x, y)$ for the feature vector describing the part window at location (x, y) with respect to the

FIGURE 17.15: Examples of bicycles detected using the model of Figure 17.14. The large boxes are bicycle instances; the smaller boxes inside are the locations of the detected parts. The wheelie is not detected by rotating the box, but because the parts are allowed to move within the box. *This figure was originally published as Figure 2 of "Object Detection Using Discriminatively Trained Part-based Models," by P. Felzenszwalb, R. Girshick, D. McAllester, and D. Ramanan, IEEE Transactions on Pattern Analysis and Machine Intelligence, 2010 © IEEE 2010.*

root coordinate system. Write $(dx, dy) = (u^{(p_i)}, v^{(p_i)}) - (x, y)$ for the offset from the part's ideal location in the root coordinate system. The score for the ith part at this location (x, y) with respect to the root is given by

$$
\begin{aligned}
\text{Part score at } (x, y) &= \text{Appearance score} - \text{Offset cost} \\
&= S^{(p_i)}(x, y; \beta^{(p_i)}, \boldsymbol{d}^{(p_i)}, \boldsymbol{v}^{(p_i)}) \\
&= \beta^{(p_i)} \cdot \phi(x, y) - (d_1^{(p_i)} dx + d_2^{(p_i)} dy + d_3^{(p_i)} dx^2 + d_4^{(p_i)} dy^2),
\end{aligned}
$$

and we define the score for the ith part to be the best score obtained over all possible offsets, that is

$$
\text{Part } i \text{ score} = \max_{(x, y)} S^{(p_i)}(x, y; \beta^{(p_i)}, \boldsymbol{d}^{(p_i)}, \boldsymbol{v}^{(p_i)}).
$$

Now the score for the object model at a particular root window is

$$
\text{Model score} = \text{Root appearance score} + \sum_i \text{Part } i \text{ score}.
$$

Assume we have an object model. This could consist of several components of the form described, one for each aspect. Then detection is straightforward: for each window, we compute the model score for each component, take the maximum over all components, and use this maximum in our sliding window recipe. To do so, we will need to deal with maximizing the score for each part as a function of (x, y). Blank search could do this, though Felzenszwalb *et al.* (2010*b*) and Felzenszwalb *et al.* (2010*a*) offer much better strategies.

Learning a model takes care. We must deal with two kinds of latent variable. First, we do not know which component should respond for each positive example;

negative examples are somewhat easier to deal with, because all components should have a negative score. Second, we do not know the locations of the parts in the training example. Notice that, if we knew the component and the part location for each example, training would boil down to training a linear SVM. However, we can apply a strategy of repeated re-estimation. We assume locations and components are known, and then compute part appearance and offset models for each component. Then, given part appearance and offset models for each component, we can estimate locations and components again.

One feature of our sliding window recipe becomes apparent here. Sliding window detectors must process immense numbers of image windows, most of which are negative. As a result, apparently small false positive rates can become a major problem. It is extremely important to train detection models with a very large dataset, to expose them to as many negative examples as possible. This takes care in the framework we have described, because enough negative examples may become overwhelming. One valuable strategy, introduced by Felzenszwalb *et al.* (2010*b*), is known as *hard negative mining*. As we train the classifier, we apply it to negative examples, looking for ones that get a strong response; these are cached, and used in the next round of training. If this is properly done, one can guarantee that the classifier has the same support vectors it would have if it had seen every negative example.

This method is now the standard, dominant detector. Most other successful detectors are variants on this recipe. Code for training and testing this method is available at `http://people.cs.uchicago.edu/~pff/latent/`. At time of writing, any novel object detection method needs to be compared to this method because there is a good chance it will outperform the novel method.

17.3   THE STATE OF THE ART OF OBJECT DETECTION

The main forum for competition between general object detection methods is now the Pascal challenge (compare Section 16.2.3), which has a detection challenge for the same set of objects used in the classification challenge. From 2007–2010, these problems involved 20 standard classes (including aeroplane, bicycle, car, and person). Bounding boxes for each instance of the relevant objects are available for training images.

Evaluation is by average precision, computed using an *overlap test*. Assume a detector predicts a bounding box $\mathcal{B}_p$; this prediction is taken as a true positive if it is the strongest prediction overlapping some marked-up box $\mathcal{B}_m$ *and* if

$$\frac{\text{area of } (\mathcal{B}_p \cap \mathcal{B}_m)}{\text{area of } (\mathcal{B}_p \cup \mathcal{B}_m)} > 0.5.$$

All other predictions overlapping that marked-up box are false positives. We now sort the predicted boxes by the strength of their prediction, and compute recall and precision, where relevant items are true positives. It is usual to summarize performance using average precision.

There are numerous reasonable critiques of this test. First, it is quite crude as to localization. For example, if the predicted and true boxes happen to have the same area, then the overlap area needs to be only about two-thirds of a box

Category	2007	2008	2009	2010
aeroplane	0.262	0.365	0.478	0.584
bicycle	0.409	0.420	0.468	0.553
bird	0.098	0.113	0.174	0.192
boat	0.094	0.114	0.158	0.210
bottle	0.214	0.282	0.285	0.351
bus	0.393	0.238	0.438	0.555
car	0.432	0.366	0.372	0.491
cat	0.240	0.213	0.340	0.477
chair	0.128	0.146	0.150	0.200
cow	0.140	0.177	0.228	0.315
diningtable	0.098	0.229	0.575	0.277
dog	0.162	0.149	0.251	0.372
horse	0.335	0.361	0.380	0.519
motorbike	0.375	0.403	0.437	0.563
person	0.221	0.420	0.415	0.475
pottedplant	0.120	0.126	0.132	0.130
sheep	0.175	0.194	0.251	0.378
sofa	0.147	0.173	0.280	0.330
train	0.334	0.296	0.463	0.503
tvmonitor	0.289	0.371	0.376	0.419
# methods	5	3	6	6
# comp	9	7	17	19

TABLE 17.1: Average precision of the best classification method for each category for the Pascal image classification challenge by year (per category; the method that was best at "person" might not be best at "pottedplant"), summarized from `http://pascallin.ecs.soton.ac.uk/challenges/VOC/`. On the bottom rows, the number of methods in each column and the total number of methods competing (so, for example, in 2007, only 2 of 17 total methods were best in category; each of the other 15 methods was beaten by something for each category). Notice that the average precision grows, but not necessarily monotonically (this is because the test set changes). Most categories now work moderately well.

to pass the test; this is a moderately big target, though in practice very hard to hit. Methods tend to perform very badly with tighter thresholds on the overlap. Second, detectors that chatter—i.e., produce multiple responses nearby—can be severely penalized, because one of these responses will count as a true positive, and each other response will count as a false positive. This can interact with the difficulty in getting accurate mark up for, say, crowds of people, so that detectors that appear to be performing quite well qualitatively perform poorly quantitatively. Third, a box is an extremely crude representation of the support of an object, so that predicting a box well might not actually be evidence of good detection. These critiques notwithstanding, at time of writing there is no better scoring mechanism that is available and widely used.

Table 17.1 shows average precisions obtained by the best method *per class* (meaning that the method that did best on aeroplanes might not be the same as the method that did best at bicycles) from 2007–2010. Some objects—pottedplants, chairs, birds—appear to be very difficult to detect, or perhaps they have such

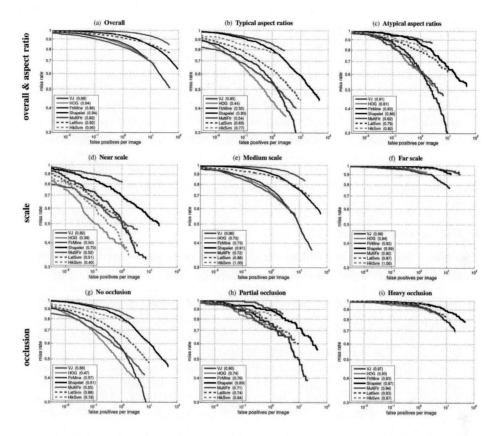

FIGURE 17.16: Performance of various pedestrian detectors for a test dataset (**top left**, labeled "overall") and for various special subsets of that test dataset, performed using the testbed of Dollar *et al.* (2009). Detectors that do well for some cases (for example, near-scale pedestrians) can do poorly for other cases (for example, medium-scale pedestrians). Some cases are hard for all detectors. *This figure was originally published as Figure 9 of "Pedestrian Detection: A Benchmark" P. Dollár, C. Wojek, B. Schiele, and P. Perona, Proc. IEEE CVPR 2009 © IEEE 2009.*

complex spatial support that using windows shaped like boxes is unwise. There is clear evidence of progress for most objects, though. Note the tendency for results to improve, though there is by no means monotonic improvement. For these datasets, the question of selection bias does not arise, as a new dataset is published each year. As a result, it is likely that improvements probably do reflect improved features or improved classification methodologies. However, it is still difficult to conclude that methods that do well on this challenge are good, because the methods might be adapted to the set of categories. There are many methods that participate in this competition, and differences between methods are often a matter of quite fine detail. The main website (http://pascallin.ecs.soton.ac.uk/challenges/VOC/) is a rich mine of information, and has a telegraphic description of each method as well as some pointers to software. Detection seems to be much harder than classification, as a comparison between Tables 16.1 and 17.1 shows.

There is evidence that some detection problems are quite subtle. Figure 17.16 shows a comparison of various pedestrian detector systems, applied to particular subsets of the test data by Dollar *et al.* (2009). In this figure, lower curves are better. Notice how all the systems studied behave better for pedestrians who are at a near scale, or are unoccluded, and suffer serious difficulties for far scale or heavily occluded pedestrians. Notice also how a change from a typical to an atypical aspect ratio of the pedestrian window—which is rough evidence the pedestrian is doing something other than standing or walking—seems to affect system performance quite strongly. Determining the relative frequency of these cases in the real world is hard (Section 16.3.3), so accurate predictions of the performance of deployed systems are extremely difficult to obtain.

17.3.1 Datasets and Resources

Pedestrian detection datasets: There are multiple pedestrian datasets. The INRIA pedestrian dataset, used in Dalal and Triggs (2005), is published by Dalal and Triggs at `http://pascal.inrialpes.fr/data/human/`. The MIT pedestrian dataset, introduced in Papageorgiou and Poggio (2000), is published at `http://cbcl.mit.edu/software-datasets/PedestrianData.html`.

There is a set of pointers to implementations of systems and to datasets at `http://www.pedestrian-detection.com/`.

Dollár, Wojek, Schiele, and Perona publish several very large pedestrian datasets (including the Caltech training dataset, test dataset, and Japan dataset) at `http://www.vision.caltech.edu/Image_Datasets/CaltechPedestrians/`, and describe them in Dollar *et al.* (2009). This location also contains pointers to other pedestrian datasets.

Ess, Leibe, Schindler, and van Gool publish a dataset of tracked humans—who are likely pedestrians—at `http://www.vision.ee.ethz.ch/~aess/dataset/`; this dataset is described in detail in Ess *et al.* (2009).

Overett, Petersson, Brewer, Andersson, and Pettersson publish the NICTA pedestrian dataset at `http://nicta.com.au/research/projects/AutoMap/computer_vision_datasets`; this dataset is described in detail in Overett *et al.* (2008).

Wojek, Walk, and Schiele publish a dataset of pedestrians in motion at `http://www.mis.tu-darmstadt.de/tud-brussels`; this dataset is described in detail in Wojek *et al.* (2009).

There are several datasets associated with Daimler Chrysler which can be found at `http://www.gavrila.net/Research/Pedestrian_Detection/Daimler_Pedestrian_Benchmarks/daimler_pedestrian_benchmarks.html`.

Enzweiler and Gavrila publish the Daimler pedestrian benchmark dataset at this URL and it described in detail in Enzweiler and Gavrila (2009). Munder and Gavrila publish the Daimler pedestrian classification dataset at this URL and it is described in detail in Munder and Gavrila (2006). Enzweiler, Eigenstetter, Schiele, and Gavrila publish the Daimler multi-cue occluded pedestrian detection benchmark dataset at this URL and it is described in Enzweiler *et al.* (2010).

The computer vision center at the Universitat Autònoma de Barcelona publishes several pedestrian datasets at `http://www.cvc.uab.es/adas/index.php?`

section=other_datasets. There is a dataset of virtual pedestrians at this URL, published by Marín, Vázquez, Gerónimo, and López; it is described in detail in Marin *et al.* (2010). Gerónimo, Sappa, López, and Ponsa publish a dataset of pedestrians captured around Barcelona at this URL; this dataset is described in detail in Gerónimo *et al.* (2007).

Maji, Berg, and Malik publish pedestrian detector code that uses pyramid HOG features and an intersection kernel SVM at `http://www.cs.berkeley.edu/ ~smaji/projects/ped-detector/`. The code is described in Maji *et al.* (2008).

Face detection codes and datasets: The number of face detection datasets is so great that we provide pointers to pages that collect datasets. These pages provide pointers to codes as well. There is a collection of 12 datasets, including several well-known face datasets, at `http://robotics.csie.ncku.edu.tw/ Databases/FaceDetect_PoseEstimate.htm`. Frischholz maintains a face detection home page, containing demonstrations, publications, datsets, and links, at `http: //www.facedetection.com/`; many more face datasets appear in the dataset component at `http://www.facedetection.com/facedetection/datasets.htm`. Grgic and Delac supply codes and datasets for face recognition at `http://face-rec. org/`. Some sample codes, and further datasets can be found at `http://vision. ai.uiuc.edu/mhyang/face-detection-survey.html`.

General object detection codes and datasets: All datasets from the PASCAL challenge are published at `http://pascallin.ecs.soton.ac.uk/chall enges/VOC/`, and described in detail by Everingham *et al.* (2010). Most of the strongest methods on this challenge are based on the detector we described in Section 17.2; code for training and testing this method is available at `http:// people.cs.uchicago.edu/~pff/latent/`.

Pb codes and data are published by Arbelaez, Maire, Fowlkes, and Malik at `http://www.eecs.berkeley.edu/Research/Projects/CS/vision/grouping/ resources.html`; there is a description in Arbelaez *et al.* (2011).

17.4   NOTES

The sliding window method is one of the mainstays of modern computer vision. This is marginally embarrassing, because it suggests that grouping and segmentation processes are so poor that it is better to just search all translations and scales to find what you want (see the critiques in Maji and Malik (2009), in Gu *et al.* (2009), and in Todorovic and Ahuja (2008*b*)). Early papers using the method include Schneiderman and Kanade (2000), Rowley *et al.* (1998*a*), Sung and Poggio (1998), and Osuna *et al.* (1997).

PROGRAMMING EXERCISES

17.1. Build a face detector using the sliding window method, HOG features, and a linear SVM. How significantly can you improve its performance by applying the trick of Figure 15.7 to your training data set?

17.2. Apply the code of `http://people.cs.uchicago.edu/~pff/latent/` to build a detector for the object of your choice. How well does it work? You should be able to improve performance significantly by building a large dataset of negatives. How helpful is iterative mining for examples?

CHAPTER 18

Topics in Object Recognition

Computer vision has come a very long way since its start in the 1960's. Some of this advance has to do with the astonishing drop in price of fast computers and imaging systems; a lot more has to do with an increased understanding of the component problems. The result is that right now there are many practical problems that can usefully be solved using techniques from computer vision. This is a triumph. However, there are core problems that are unsolved and very difficult to think about in a productive fashion. These core problems have to do with the representation and recognition of objects.

In Section 18.1, we discuss the considerable gap between what object recognition systems should do and what they do now. In following sections, we sketch some promising lines of research in feature representation that might help close this gap. Section 18.2 focuses on feature constructions; Section 18.3 discusses how geometric cues might help recognition; and Section 18.4 describes different ways of thinking about what a recognition system might report.

18.1 WHAT SHOULD OBJECT RECOGNITION DO?

How should one think about recognition in general? People can name many thousands of different kinds of object. This facility is not affected by superficial changes in individual objects—for example, disrupting the spot pattern on a cheetah, or changing the upholstery or the design of a chair. Furthermore, people need to see only very few examples of a new object to "get it," and be able to recognize other instances of this object at some later date.

It would be very useful to have computer programs that, even partially, shared these skills. People probably posess them because they have practical value (knowing what to eat, who owes you food, when to fight, when to flee, what is going to eat you, etc.). Section 18.1.1 sketches some desirable features that a computer object recognition system should have. No current strategy seems to meet these needs (Section 18.1.2). Object categories are an important, and poorly understood, idea in object recognition, which we describe in Section 18.1.3. Selection—choosing which objects to describe and which to ignore—is another poorly understood idea, which we discuss in Section 18.1.4.

18.1.1 What Should an Object Recognition System Do?

The ideal object recognition system would have several important properties. It should *recognize many different objects*. This is much more difficult than it sounds: to recognize very large numbers of objects, we need to know how to organize them into a data structure that is easily searched given image data. In particular, we need to know what measurements can be used to distinguish between objects as opposed to distinguishing between instances (one cat might be tabby, the other gray, but they are both cats).

An ideal system would *recognize objects seen against many different backgrounds*. Again, this appears to be very difficult. Ideally, an appropriate object representation would help by organizing the image into segments that might have come from an object category (without reference to a particular instance) and those that could not.

It would *recognize objects at an appropriate level of abstraction*. Humans can tell a chair is a chair even if they have not seen that particular chair before. They do not even need to have seen that model of chair before, either. Ideally, our programs would be able to recognize both leopards and cheetahs as spotted cats, before drawing a distinction. Precisely what is an appropriate level of abstraction is mysterious. The word "category" is widely used to denote a class of objects at the appropriate level of abstraction, though the term does not resolve the question of what that level of abstraction is. In such a class, some objects will differ from others in some ways, but categories are a useful way of thinking about generalizing object properties. One reason I may wish to recognize any chair as a chair is that I know I can sit on chairs.

It would *make useful inferences about the special properties of particular instances*. Assume, for example, that all chairs are instances of a single category (it is by no means obvious this is true). It would not be particularly helpful to simply name every chair a chair; we may need to know something about the special properties of this instance to sit in it. Is it large enough? Does it have a padded seat? Does it have arms? And so on. These considerations suggest that, within a given category, there are principled and important variations.

It would *produce useful responses to unfamiliar objects*. Humans often encounter objects that are, at least in detail, unfamiliar, and can usually cope with this unfamiliarity. Few people can name most species of mammal, for example, but most can tell whether an animal they cannot name is furry, is asleep, and so on. For the foreseeable future, computer vision systems will encounter unfamiliar objects regularly, and they cannot simply be ignored.

It would *produce responses that help achieve goals*. How we categorize an object that we see might reasonably depend on what we want to do. If I wish to sit, a large, flat rock might be a seat. If I wish to flatten something, the rock might be an anvil. It might also be a weapon, or a good place to make a fire. Furthermore, the same rock may occupy distinct categories (seat; good place to make a fire; anvil) at the same time. This is not true of all rocks, so this collection of possible uses cannot be obtained by inheritance.

It would *produce responses of useful complexity*. An object recognition system that named every object in an image might be very difficult to use, because most images have very many objects, most of which are not interesting. A picture of a room might well have a chair in it, a floor, and some cushions. But it might also contain a light fitting, which will have some associated screws; the chair might have nails in it; and so on. We are surrounded by immense numbers of objects, most of which should be ignored most of the time.

Current recognition strategies typically perform rather poorly when measured against these requirements. This is not because they are bad; the problem is just very difficult.

18.1.2   Current Strategies for Object Recognition

The dominant current object recognition strategy involves attaching a plausible set of features to a multiclass classifier, and then training the classifier with a set of examples for each class, as described in Chapters 15, 16 and 17. All such recognizers can be described, rather broadly, as template matchers (where the template and matching cost are implicit in the classifier). Their main virtue is that, unlike purely geometric approaches, they exploit the great discriminatory power of image texture information, and sometimes color information too. However, they normally require an additional segmentation step that separates the objects of interest from the image background (what Chapter 16's assumption that objects are prominent in images, and Chapter 17's moving window are all about). Such methods require that texture be discriminative, which isn't always the case. These methods may not be able to cope with complex shape variations, and they suppress internal structures within object categories. Finally, current versions of these methods assume that each instance belongs to just one category of objects.

An important alternative is to represent an object in terms of some spatial relations between some templates. Examples include the detection model of Section 17.2 and the human parsing method of Section 20.2. You should regard these methods in their current form as richer template matchers, and so they inherit the difficulties implicit in that class of method. Current versions of this approach can cope only with relatively limited sets of relations; they might not be able to cope with complex shape variation; and they suppress internal structures within object categories.

The third alternative uses the registration techniques of Chapter 12. One has a geometric model of an object, and then attempts to register it to the image; if the registration score is good enough, the object is present. If there are multiple types of object, then each has a geometric model, each model is registered, and the scores are used to decide what is present. Such methods cope very poorly with object classes that display complex geometric variations (like chairs, for example). They handle multiple objects poorly, and they cannot make useful statements about unfamiliar objects.

18.1.3   What Is Categorization?

A world in which every instance is distinct from every other instance presents serious practical difficulties. We would like to tell how objects behave, how they will react, how we can use them, and how other people will react to them. If each instance is distinct, we must discover answers to these and other questions independently for each instance. One way to generalize is to say that many instances can be grouped together because they share some properties. The shared properties that are used to collect instances are those for which we care to generalize; for example, all these instances are collected together because we can sit on them. We can refer to such groups as *categories*. Unfortunately, the word "category" is used in many different and somewhat contradictory senses in the literature. This is because it is genuinely hard to know which usage is most helpful.

One usage is the (very broad) sense we have given, of arbitrary but useful groupings of instances. Notice that in this usage, the same instance might appear in many different groupings (for example, a particular chair might simultaneously be a chair, a weapon, a source of discomfort, and a source of firewood). The groupings are made because they are useful. They depend on (a) what we are trying to do and (b) on our need to communicate with others. This means that it is helpful to have broad conventions about some groupings. For example, it is helpful when most instances that I call chairs are instances that you call chairs, too (it is too much to ask that we agree on all instances).

In the computer vision literature, the term is often used in a much more restrictive sense. The usual meaning is that each instance belongs to a single category (for example, this is a chair, and that is a table); that these categories are commonly accepted (for example, you and I agree that this is a chair and that is a table); and that they have some kind of canonical status. This usage probably should be deprecated, because the notion omits some important properties.

It seems to be the rule, rather than the exception, that *instances can belong to multiple categories*. This is most likely because *useful categorizations depend on circumstances*—i.e., different groupings of instances meet different needs. For example, if I need to sit down, one useful category is chairs; if I need a fire, things that burn is a useful category. Some chairs can be burned and others can't, so I cannot simply inherit one grouping from another. Experiments with cups and vases by Labov (1973) demonstrate that people do not necessarily agree on what category an instance belongs to. Some cups look quite like some vases. If one shows people a sequence of instances running from strongly cup-like to strongly vase-like, then they will label an intermediate instance a cup; if one shows the sequence in the other order, the same intermediate will be called a vase. This means that people can be persuaded to allocate the same instance to distinct, and apparently mutually exclusive, categories by context.

There are practical reasons to believe that instances can belong to multiple categories, too. Imagine we wish to build a dog detector. We obtain many pictures of dogs, and many pictures without dogs. During the hard-negative mining process, we are likely to find pictures of cats that look a lot like dogs. Our training process strongly encourages the classifier to produce negative responses to these, and positive responses to dogs that look a lot like cats. This is most likely a source of instability, because it will be hard to find reliable features to distinguish between them; as a result, the performance of the dog detector might depend quite strongly on which dog-like cats appear in the negative dataset. An alternative is to not use the most dog-like cats in training; we will get false positives, but we will also get a more reliable estimate of the detector. In particular, if we then build a cat detector (now not using the most cat-like dogs as negatives), we might be able to tell the ambiguous classes apart by looking at the relative, rather than absolute, responses of the detectors. At this point, we have three types of example: clear cats, clear dogs, and somewhat uncertain small, furry animals. This might result in a much better-performing detection system than insisting that there are clear category boundaries.

18.1.4   Selection: What Should Be Described?

The desired output of a recognition system remains puzzling, because most images are very rich in objects. In turn, this means that preparing a list of everything in the image is quite unmanageable. The fact that some objects might belong to more than one category makes this list even more unattractive. Instead, we need some principle by which objects—or image domains, perhaps—can be ignored as irrelevant. Objects might be irrelevant because they are too small to be worth mentioning; because they cannot affect the task at hand; because they are subsumed by visual phrase or scene representations; or perhaps for other reasons. There are some indications that people ignore—or at least, don't report—many or most objects in images.

For example, Rashtchian *et al.* (2010) produced a dataset by asking human labelers to produce five different sentences describing each of 5,000 images. What is remarkable about these descriptions is (a) how strongly the sentences agree and (b) how few of the objects present in the image are actually described. This suggests the presence of some mechanisms, most likely affected by what we are trying to do, that can select what is worth noticing in an image. Another dataset that suggests this was collected by Spain and Perona (2008), who asked people to produce short lists of what was present in an image; these lists are remarkably consistent.

All this suggests that it is fruitful to study what output a recognition system should produce. There is an apparently easy solution: an object recognition system should produce a representation of the world that is small enough but is detailed and accurate enough to be useful to the agent using it. To be less vague, we would need to study recognition in the context of a variety of concrete tasks, so that we could link the representations produced with the utility of the agent. This has not been done to date, because there have not been recognition methods that are accurate enough to make the question interesting. Recent methods are now good enough that this topic could be studied usefully, and we hope that significant advances will result.

18.2   FEATURE QUESTIONS

The feature constructions we have described in Chapters 5 and 16 are very powerful, and the underlying principles seem to have driven almost all of the advances in modern object recognition. Nonetheless, it is reasonable to hope that they can be improved. First, we could look for more effective versions of the current constructions (Section 18.2.1). Second, because current constructions largely describe image textures, we could look for other types of feature (Section 18.2.2).

18.2.1   Improving Current Image Features

Current feature constructions rest on two important ideas. First, features such as visual words try to encode the rich collection of image patches with a dictionary of examples. By doing so, they can suppress small differences in appearance between patches, and identify patches that are distinctive or discriminative. This is a general strategy, which is usually called *coding*. Second, SIFT features, HOG features, and histograms of visual words all summarize information over neighborhoods to suppress the effects of small translations, scale errors, and the like. This is a general strategy, which is usually called *pooling*. It is natural to try and produce sets of features by applying and generalizing these ideas systematically.

Coding allows us to think of image patches as pattern elements. Strongly different image patches are coded differently, so that the overall tendency of a texture in a domain can be represented by the statistics of the codes. We can generalize the original coding procedure that produced visual words in a straightforward way. Rather than encoding an image patch with a single dictionary entry, we allow the patch to be a linear combination of dictionary entries, but require that relatively few of these entries be used. We represent each image patch in a training set with a vector; this could be a vector of filter outputs, but it also could just involve reshaping the array. Write $\mathcal{I}_i$ for the ith such vector. We now seek a matrix $\mathcal{D}$ and a set of vectors z_i such that

$$\sum_{i \in \text{training set}} \| \mathcal{I}_i - \mathcal{D}z_i \|^2 + \lambda \, |z_i|_1$$

is minimized. We can think of $\mathcal{D}$ as the dictionary, because the 1-norm strongly encourages each z_i to have many zeros in it, and so each patch is encoded as a combination of a small number of dictionary entries. We expect such an encoding to be sparse, i.e., that there are few nonzero terms in each z_i. A new patch $\mathcal{I}_n$ can then be represented by finding the z_n that minimizes

$$\| \mathcal{I}_n - \mathcal{D}z_n \|^2 + \lambda \, |z_n|_1 \, .$$

This z_n will be sparse, too. Encoding test patches like this involves a complex minimization, but there are now methods to learn functions that take $\mathcal{I}_n$ and predict z_n relatively cheaply (see Ranzato *et al.* (2007); Kavukcuoglu *et al.* (2009)).

Coding can create problems. For example, if we code by vector quantization, two very similar image patches might get very different codes, because the cluster center closest to each is different. This could be a rich source of noise. One way to suppress this noise is to modify the coding process to take into account k of the nearest neighbors. For example, the patch might be represented as a linear combination of its k-nearest neighbors (see Yang *et al.* (2009*a*); Yang *et al.* (2010*b*)). We could then expect that similar patches get more similar codes.

Pooling allows us to represent spatial trends in pattern elements within a domain, without representing spatial information in too much detail. One example of pooling is building a histogram of visual words; here the pool is the histogram. This is often called *average pooling*. Alternative methods are to build a bit vector with a one for each word that occurs in the domain, however often it occurs, and a zero otherwise (called *max pooling*) or to produce a histogram with tf-idf or other weights. Pooling has several merits. First, pooling can suppress noise created in coding. For example, if we expect that two similar patches get different codes, then a histogram taken over many different patches should still be informative. Second, pooling can highlight overall distinctions between patterns—for example, spots and stripes should involve very different families of patches—while suppressing spatial detail. Finally, pooling can suppress the effects of small translations, rotations, and deformations of the domain in which the representation is computed.

However, pooling can also create problems. Pooling loses spatial information. There is a tension here: pooling over large domains might suppress noise more effectively, but it also suppresses more spatial information. Pooling over small domains produces representations with more spatial information at the cost of less noise suppression. Pyramid constructions, like that of Section 16.1.4, are most likely helpful because they manage this tension well.

A second difficulty is that averaging codes with quite different meanings might create uninformative vectors. This issue is particularly uncomfortable with a sparse coding representation. Two very different image patches might produce codes that have some nonzero components in common. Averaging these terms is unlikely to be helpful, and might suppress information. Instead, we might want to pool only over coherent domains in both the image and feature space. One way to do so uses *preclustering*. We build a k-means clustering of the feature space. Each of these cluster centers is associated with a bin, and we pool only the codes of features that (a) fall into the same bin and (b) are in some image-pooling domain. Proper uses of pooling and coding strategies are key to competitive performance on current test datasets. There is now a considerable body of experimental information dealing with the effects of different choices of coding and pooling schemes (pointers to sources in the notes).

18.2.2   Other Kinds of Image Feature

Modern image features strongly emphasize texture, both because it seems to be discriminative and because we know how to build quite good texture features. Other classes of feature remain more mysterious. Generally, we could expect that contour features, shape features, and shading features might have some information about the nature of an observed object, but little is known about how to exploit this information. We discuss some of the technical problems encountered in building shape features in Section 18.3, and the others here.

Some contours appear to be distinctive, at least to people. For example, one doesn't need much artistic competence to draw a curve that is highly suggestive of a body segment (try it). One doesn't even need to show all, or even most, of the outline of the segment to get an effect. Building image features that exploit contour remains complicated. It remains difficult to get whole contours reliably in images, meaning that one must cope with noise created by the contour detection process. This noise will tend to involve large sections of the contour going missing. Worse, there will be other image contours that are not relevant but are difficult to omit from representation. One strategy for representing contours is to try to register an example contour template to the image; by doing so, we can potentially pool information from multiple local curves in the image. The difficulty is that we might need many templates, and worse, many registration attempts for each.

HOG features try to deal with these difficulties by (a) dealing with local image orientations, so we never need to join up a whole contour; (b) using multiple different normalizations, so that contour components with weak contrast might still appear in the representation; and (c) pooling locally in small domains so that small registration errors are suppressed. The classifier must then resolve the question of what is distinctive contour information and what is mere texture. Figure 17.7

suggests that classifiers can do this to some extent, and so that HOG features do respond to contour. However, better methods for exposing contour information and suppressing texture information would be a significant advance. Such methods might require integrating improved segmenters (Chapter 9) with measures of contour such as P_b (Section 17.1.3).

Shading features remain largely mysterious, though there are some reasons to believe that shading patterns can be distinctive for some objects (see Haddon and Forsyth (1998c)). Current feature constructions suppress shading information at the earliest stages by computing orientations. Most likely, shading information is useful only at a relatively long image scale (i.e., the pattern of shading across a whole object might be quite helpful), and only relative to a domain (i.e., you need to know the support of the object in the image to compute this pattern of shading). Finding the domain of support of an object remains very difficult indeed.

18.3 GEOMETRIC QUESTIONS

The object recognition methods we have described primarily have involved statistical reasoning. We have shown some evidence that geometric reasoning improves these methods (Section 17.1.2). How much geometric reasoning should be applied in object recogntion, what it does, and where it applies, have become important open questions.

Geometric information could help object recognition by supplying a form of context for objects. Image appearance features for each of a set of objects sitting on a ground plane are correlated by the facts that (a) they sit on the same ground plane and (b) they are seen in the same camera. This is the core of the method of Section 17.1.2. There is some evidence that there are other possible cases. For example, several methods can now recover an approximate estimate of the shape of a room from a picture of that room. The method described in Figure 18.1 (due to Hedau *et al.* (2009)) models the room as a box, then uses vanishing points to estimate the rotation of that box, and estimated appearance features to estimate its translation and aspect ratio. Many alternative representations are available, from local surface normals to more complex polyhedral models (see Hoiem *et al.* (2005); Barinova *et al.* (2008); Delage *et al.* (2006); Lee *et al.* (2009); Nedovic *et al.* (2010); Saxena *et al.* (2008); Saxena *et al.* (2009)). One reason to know a model of the room is to estimate free space, as in Figure 18.1. Another is to improve furniture detection; for example, Hedau *et al.* (2010) show that beds can be detected more accurately if one knows the geometry of the room they are in. Yet another, due to Gupta *et al.* (2011), is to make estimates of the affordances of surfaces in the room—for example, where could a person sit? Where could one place objects? (see Figure 18.2.)

Another important role for geometry is in representing shape. There seem to be two important difficulties here. First, our methods for representing 2D shape do not work satisfactorily with our methods for identifying objects. Second, the apparent 2D shape of an object changes when one looks at it from different directions, an effect known as *aspect*.

There are two main approaches in the literature for representing image shape. In one approach, one decomposes the shape into a variety of primitive subshapes,

FIGURE 18.1: On the **top left**, an image of a cluttered room. Hedau *et al.* (2009) use vanishing points to estimate the rotation (i.e., the orientation of the edges) of the main "box" of the room, and then they estimate the translation (i.e., the location of corners) with a learned combination of features. In turn, this yields an estimate of the appearance of each face of the box, so that clutter can be discounted, resulting in an improved box estimate shown superimposed on the **top right** image. Once we have the "box" and the clutter maps (**bottom left**), we can estimate free space, shown as the voxels on the **bottom right**. *This figure was originally published as Figures 1 and 8 of "Recovering the spatial layout of cluttered rooms," by V. Hedau, D. Hoiem, and D.A. Forsyth, Proc. IEEE ICCV 2009 © 2009 IEEE.*

typically represented by their spines, and then works with the set of primitives. However, changing the image shape slightly can generate quite large changes in the shape representation. As a result, these methods currently seem to work only in quite special cases (you should see the pictorial structure model of Section 20.2.1 as one version of this class of model). The alternative is to represent potential shapes by a collection of templates, and then describe new shapes by registering them to the templates (using methods like those of Section 12.3). The problem here is that the registration process is slow, so it is difficult to use these methods to describe shapes for large-scale recognition.

These problems are made harder by the fact that the image shape of an object changes as one looks at an object from different directions. Representing this effect remains difficult. Chapter 13 describes a representation of the topological changes undergone by the image contour as the view moves; there has been no success in using this representation in practical applications. Savarese and Fei-Fei (2007) describe a less detailed representation where they decompose objects into a set of faces, each of which behaves simply, and then reason about which faces are in view and so about the object (see also Savarese and Fei-Fei (2008)). Alternatively,

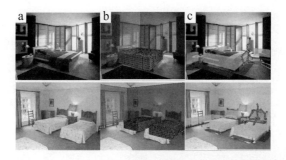

FIGURE 18.2: Estimates of room geometry can be used to produce very rich semantic representations. Gupta *et al.* (2011) describe a method to tag boxes and surfaces within a room with affordances—properties related to the potential for human action. The rooms in column (a) produce the geometric representation in column (b). In turn, places where a person could sit against a backrest are indicated in column (c); without a backrest in (d); lie down in (e); and different types of reachable domain are indicated in (f). *This figure was originally published as Figure 6 of "From 3D Scene Geometry to Human Workspace," by A. Gupta, S. Satkin, A. Efros, and M. Hebert, Proc. IEEE CVPR 2011 © 2011 IEEE.*

Farhadi *et al.* (2009*b*) describe feature constructions that suppress changes due to aspect, then build a specialized classifier that is largely aspect-independent. No current method can deal with a puzzling property of human recognition. People seem to be able to infer the aspectual properties of an object from a single view of that object; that is, they have a good estimate of what the new object will look like from a new view, from only one image, presumably based on their experience of other objects. Current methods require multiple views of the new object to build representations that are robust to aspect. One possible architecture for generalizing aspect behavior would be to have clusters of shapes that had similar behaviors; then, when we see a new object, we infer which cluster it belongs to and so determine how it will look for new views. The details of how one could do this remain obscure.

18.4 SEMANTIC QUESTIONS

Thinking about what the output of an object recognition system should be seems to be fruitful. In Section 18.1.4, we pointed out that a simple list of all objects is not plausible, because it mostly will be too long and too full of irrelevancies. Assume

FIGURE 18.3: One way to deal with unfamiliar objects is to produce a description in terms that are useful for describing familiar objects. These terms are commonly called attributes. The figure shows attributes predicted for the rectangular window in each image, using the method of Farhadi *et al.* (2009a), with the attributes listed below the image. Predictions that are incorrect have a large X next to them. Each window circumscribes an object of a category that is not present in data used to train the method. Notice that these descriptions are moderately useful, and sometimes very helpful. *This figure was originally published as Figure 5 of "Describing objects by their attributes," A. Farhadi, I. Endres, D. Hoiem, and D. Forsyth, Proc. IEEE CVPR 2009, © 2009 IEEE.*

we know how to choose what to report. We must still deal with making useful statements about unfamiliar objects (Section 18.4.1). Some objects might be made of parts, which themselves are somewhat like objects; for example, a "wheel" could be a part of a larger object, or an object itself. In Section 18.4.2, we discuss some recent thinking about parts. This opens the question of exactly what we should try to detect—parts, or objects, or groups of objects, or scenes—and we discuss this in Section 18.4.3.

18.4.1 Attributes and the Unfamiliar

We regularly encounter objects that are somewhat unfamiliar; we may know something about them without knowing their name. A strong source of examples is animals. It is quite usual to look at an animal species you haven't seen before and be able to make some inferences about its nature and behavior without knowing its name. This suggests that part of recognition is being able to make some useful statements about objects even when we cannot name them.

One way to do this is to describe objects by *attributes*, properties of the object that are useful to know and are discernible from images. Some attributes might refer to parts of the object. For example, it is useful to know when objects have heads, have wheels, and so on. Other attributes might refer to appearance (is it red, or stripey); to material (is it made of wood); or to shape (is it boxy). Farhadi

FIGURE 18.4: One advantage of describing objects (rather than just naming them) is that one can then identify special properties of objects whose name is known. On the **top row**, examples of objects identified by the system of (Farhadi *et al.* 2009*a*), where the instance in the image is special because it has an attribute that most examples of that object lack. Notice that this system has a limited notion of object semantics, and so does not know that birds never have extra leaves (the leaves must come from something else). On the **bottom row**, examples of objects, where the instance in the image is special because it lacks an attribute that most examples of that object have. Again, because the underlying semantics are quite simple, the method does not distinguish between birds that do not have tails, and birds whose tails just happen not to be visible. *This figure was originally published as Figures 6 and 7 of "Describing objects by their attributes," A. Farhadi, I. Endres, D. Hoiem, and D. Forsyth, Proc. IEEE CVPR 2009, © 2009 IEEE.*

et al. (2009*a*) describe one system for predicting attributes from images of objects. In their approach, a list of attributes is chosen, and then example data is marked up with these attributes. This is used to train classifiers that use appearance features and then the attributes of test images are predicted with these classifiers. Attributes can be predicted for images of objects that never appear in the training set (Figure 18.3). Because the attributes were chosen to be discriminative, they can be used to predict the name of the object present, if it is known. Furthermore, if an object is present and has unusual attributes, their system can tell (Figure 18.4). A wide range of attributes can be predicted with moderate accuracy (Figure 18.5). There are a variety of ways to predict attributes from pictures, as Lampert *et al.* (2008) point out. One is to identify the attributes independently and then perhaps the object from the attributes. Another is to identify the object first, then inherit the attributes. A third is to predict object and attributes simultaneously. If attributes are spatially localized, Farhadi *et al.* (2010*a*) show that one can make generalizations about objects that have never been seen before (Figure 18.6).

18.4.2   Parts, Poselets and Consistency

Some objects seem to be made of *parts*, structures that are shared across categories. These parts are often somewhat homologous in appearance and function. For example, cars, trucks, and buses have wheels and doors; people and animals have legs

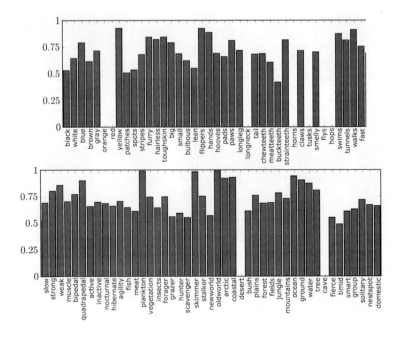

FIGURE 18.5: A wide range of attributes can be predicted with useful accuracy. The figure shows the AUC for a series of attributes, predicted using the methods of Lampert *et al.* (2008). Zeros correspond to cases where there was no test data for the test-training split used (because the split was on object images, rather than per attribute). With this accuracy, one could expect to produce a quite useful description of an unfamiliar object from the domain to which the attributes apply (animals). *This figure was originally published as Figure 6 of "Learning to detect unseen object classes by between-class attribute transfer," C. Lampert, H. Nickisch, and S. Harmeling, Proc. IEEE CVPR 2009, © 2009 IEEE.*

and heads; birds and bats have wings. In some contexts, it may be reasonable to think about parts as being objects themselves, though doing so opens some confusing and difficult issues. For example, should we think about a face as an object, or as an assembly of distinct objects (eyes, nose, and mouth)? It is difficult to tell how parts and objects are distinct. For example, a screw that holds a chair together could quite reasonably be a part of that chair, but in an appropriate context it is itself an object. The reason to put up with this confusion is that parts are useful. When a part is shared across many categories, it presents opportunities to tie models (i.e., one can learn only one wheel detector, rather than learning one for each wheeled vehicle) and to generalize (as in Figure 18.6).

One important use of the idea of parts occurs in *poselet* methods. A poselet is a local structure on an object that (a) has distinctive appearance and (b) can be used to infer some of the configuration of an object (e.g., translation; translation and rotation; translation, rotation, and scale; and so on; see Figure 18.7). Bourdev and Malik (2009) offer a clustering algorithm for choosing a set of poselets to represent an object category. Finding an object becomes quite straightforward. One

FIGURE 18.6: Most animals have heads, bodies, and legs; most vehicles are boxy and have wheels; watercraft are boxy, with a pointed bow. This means that, if we can identify these semantic parts and reason about their relationships, we could recognize an animal without ever having seen examples of that kind of animal, as Farhadi *et al.* (2010a) demonstrate. On the **top two rows**, examples showing animals, vehicles, and watercraft identified in images by their system, despite its never having seen that kind of animal, vehicle, or watercraft in training (though it did see the parts). They demonstrate that such a system can make rich reports about the familiar objects it encounters (**third row**); mistakes are shown on the **fourth row**. *This figure was originally published as Figure 7 of "Attribute-centric recognition for cross-category generalization," A. Farhadi, I. Endres, and D. Hoiem, Proc. IEEE CVPR 2010, © 2010 IEEE.*

FIGURE 18.7: Poselets are image patches of characteristic, relatively constrained appearance that suggest a restricted range of configurations. These are examples of image patches corresponding to four distinct poselets (associated with face, arms, whole body, and head) from Bourdev and Malik (2009). Notice how each could likely be found with current detectors in a relatively straightforward way. *This figure was originally published as Figure 1 of "Poselets: Body Part Detectors Trained Using 3D Human Pose Annotations," L. Bourdev and J. Malik, Proc. IEEE ICCV 2009, © 2009 IEEE.*

FIGURE 18.8: Bourdev and Malik (2009) show that poselets can be used to find, say, the torso of the body even though it might not be visible. Each detected poselet can cast a vote, whose value is determined discriminatively, for the location of the torso. The likely torso locations are then clustered, to identify groups of votes that agree. Finally, the strongest cluster gives a torso location, if it is strong enough. Notice how some of the marked torsos could not be identified by direct image information. *This figure was originally published as Figure 10 of "Poselets: Body Part Detectors Trained Using 3D Human Pose Annotations," L. Bourdev and J. Malik, Proc. IEEE ICCV 2009, © 2009 IEEE.*

builds a detector for each poselet (which is manageable, because the poselets are chosen to have a distinctive appearance). Each strong poselet response votes for the object configuration, and the object is either present or absent at that configuration depending on the strength of the vote (Figure 18.8). The great attraction of poselets is that they can pool discriminative, but local evidence over long spatial scales without having to segment the image accurately to compute pooling domains (compare Section 18.2). In Section 20.5.2, we describe an application of poselets that are chosen to be discriminative of human activities.

18.4.3 Chunks of Meaning: Parts, Poselets, Objects, Phrases, and Scenes

The detectors we described were focused on finding objects, but it is very hard to be crisp about what an object is. Some object categories are extremely difficult to detect, as Table 17.1 shows. Scenes are composites of objects that can be relatively straightforward to classify (Section 16.1.9). It seems reasonable to look for a notion that lies somewhere between an object and a scene. These are *visual phrases*, composites of objects that have relatively simple appearance, and so are relatively easy to detect. A good example is a person riding a bicycle; this turns out to be much easier to detect with current methods than a person (because there isn't much one can do on a bicycle), and somewhat easier to detect with current methods than a bicycle (because having a rider limits the possibilities for a bicycle, too). We expect that there are fewer training examples for composites, because they are more complicated. If they are also easier to detect, this does not matter. Recent experimental work by Farhadi and Sadeghi (2011) suggests that there are some

FIGURE 18.9: Visual phrases are composites of objects that are easier to detect than their components. Farhadi and Sadeghi (2011) demonstrate that some visual phrases exist and are useful. For example, it is much easier to detect a person drinking from a bottle than it is to detect a person, because a person drinking from a bottle has a more limited and more characteristic range of appearances. These figures show some examples of visual phrases, detected using the methods of Section 17.2. *This figure was originally published as Figure 1 of "Recognition using Visual Phrases," A. Farhadi and A. Sadeghi, Proc. IEEE CVPR 2011, © 2011 IEEE.*

visual phrases that are much easier to detect than their components (Figure 18.9). Notice that having a detector for a person on a horse doesn't mean we don't have a detector for a person and another for a horse. Usually we think of a person riding a horse as a composite of objects. The fact that some visual phrases are easy to detect suggests that we might sometimes want to think about (say) a person as a part of (say) a person riding a horse. This part is shared across many categories (person riding a bicycle; and so on) and, like wheels, is sometimes easier thought of as an object. To confuse things further, the person in turn might consist of parts or poselets.

Now assume we build a set of detectors, some for detecting objects and others for detecting visual phrases. We may have strong responses from different detectors (for example, detectors for a person on a horse, a person, and a horse). These responses are not necessarily mutually exclusive. Furthermore, crosstalk between detectors means that the *pattern* of detector responses might be quite revealing. We must look at the pattern of detector responses for a given image and draw conclusions about what is correct, a process Farhadi and Sadeghi (2011) call *decoding*.

Decoding can be phrased as a quite general problem: look at a pool of detector responses, and draw conclusions. By this definition, the poselet-based activity recognition method of Section 20.5.2 involves decoding. There are a variety of possible mechanisms for decoding. One could use a greedy algorithm (as in Desai

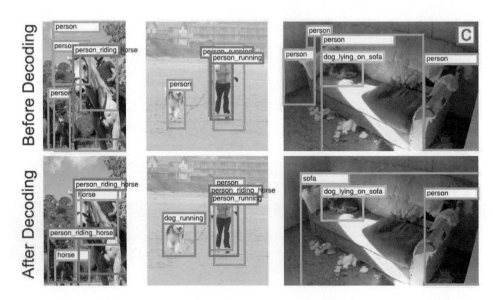

FIGURE 18.10: Detection systems that use visual phrases must be able to deal with ambiguous and possibly mutually exclusive detector responses. For example, when there is a person drinking from a bottle, there must also be a person and a bottle, and all three detectors might respond. Resolving what to report given a set of detector responses is called decoding by Farhadi and Sadeghi (2011). The **top row** shows some detector responses for each image before decoding (there are too many to show all; these are the stronger ones); the **bottom row** shows the detectors marked as correct by the decoding stage. This stage is able to use the local context of detector responses. For example, a strong response from a dog lying on sofa detector implies a sofa, and so the sofa can be believed; similarly, a believable sofa implies that many of the person detector responses are unlikely. Farhadi and Sadeghi (2011) demonstrate that decoding improves the performance of all detectors in the system, and that having visual phrase detectors and a decoding stage improves the performance of conventional object detectors, most likely by exposing contextual information that strengthens or reduces the plausibility of the detector response. *This figure was originally published as Figure 6 of "Recognition using Visual Phrases," A. Farhadi and A. Sadeghi, Proc. IEEE CVPR 2011, © 2011 IEEE.*

et al. (2009)); one could use a discriminative method to tell which detector responses one believes (as in Farhadi and Sadeghi (2011)); one could pool responses by voting on location (as in Bourdev and Malik (2009)); or one could look at all responses then draw a single conclusion (as in Maji *et al.* (2011)). Now if we admit poselets and part detectors, we might have detectors for parts, poselets, objects, visual phrases, and scenes. Furthermore, in an environment with multiple detectors, detector cross-talk becomes a significant potential source of information, so the decoding problem looks very rich. We believe that more detailed studies of decoding will be rewarding.

PART SIX

APPLICATIONS AND TOPICS

CHAPTER 19

Image-Based Modeling and Rendering

The entertainment industry touches hundreds of millions of people every day, and synthetic pictures of real scenes, often mixed with actual film footage, are now common place in computer games, sports broadcasting, TV advertising, and feature films. Using prerecorded images of a scene to create a visual model supporting the synthesis of novel images of this scene is what *image-based modeling and rendering* is all about, and the topic of this chapter (this model must capture both shape and color/texture information, but, as shown at the end of this chapter, it is not necessarily three-dimensional). We present three representative approaches to image-based modeling and rendering. The first one is purely geometric, and given an object's silhouettes recorded in a number of calibrated images, outputs an approximation of its shape in the form of a *visual hull* (Section 19.1). Realistic images can then be rendered by reprojecting the input images on the reconstructed surface, a form of *texture mapping*. The second approach mixes geometric and photometric constraints and generalizes the stereo fusion techniques introduced in Chapter 7 to the multi-view, wide-baseline setting where several (possibly many) views of a scene can be taken from very different viewpoints (Section 19.2). Finally, we discuss the *light field*, an approach to image-based modeling and rendering that entirely forsakes the construction of a three-dimensional object representation, and models instead the set of all pictures of a scene by the space formed by light rays equipped with the corresponding radiance values (Section 19.3).

19.1 VISUAL HULLS

We saw in Chapter 13 that the silhouette of an object constrains it to lie within a viewing cone to which it is tangent. When several images and the corresponding contours are available, it is rather natural to approximate the observed shape by the intersection of the corresponding cones, called its *visual hull* (Figure 19.1, top). This idea dates back to the mid-1970s (Baumgart 1974) and has been rediscovered several times since then. Of course, as they are constructed from silhouette information alone, visual hulls provide only an outer approximation of the solids they represent. In particular, they do not reveal surface concavities because these do not show up on the image contour. Nonetheless, given a sufficient number of images, visual hulls provide a reasonable approximation of the convex and saddle-shape parts of the observed surfaces (Figure 19.1, bottom), and over the years they have become a popular and effective tool for image-based modeling and rendering. We thus present in this section a simple algorithm for computing the visual hull from contours observed by n calibrated perspective cameras.

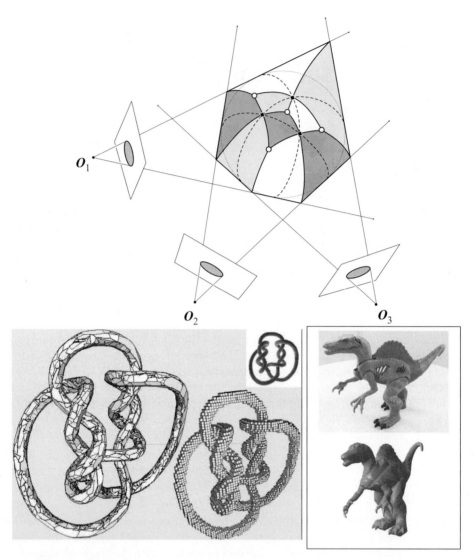

FIGURE 19.1: **Top:** Three cameras with pinholes O_1, O_2, and O_3 observe an egg-shaped object. The visual hull is the intersection of the three viewing cones. Its surface consists of three *cone strips*, indicated by three different shades of gray. **Bottom:** Examples of visual hulls. **Left:** A knotted solid is recovered from 42 synthetic views of the mesh, shown as a small insert. The leftmost visual hull is recovered as the intersection of poly-hedral viewing cones using the method of Franco and Boyer (2009), and the one on its right is simply obtained as the intersection of voxel-based viewing cones. **Right:** One of the 12 input images of a dinosaur figurine, and the corresponding visual hull model, obtained using the algorithm described in this section. *Top and bottom-right parts of the figure reprinted from "Projective Visual Hulls," by S. Lazebnik, Y. Furukawa, and J. Ponce, International Journal of Computer Vision, 74(2):137–165, (2007). © 2007 Springer. Bottom-left part of the figure reprinted from "Efficient polyhedral modeling from silhouettes," by J.-S. Franco and E. Boyer, IEEE Transactions on Pattern Analysis and Machine Intelligence, 31(3):414–427, (2009). © 2009 IEEE.*

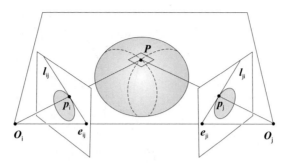

FIGURE 19.2: A frontier point. The epipolar plane is tangent to the surface in P, and the two occluding contours cross there. The corresponding epipolar lines l_{ij} and l_{ji} are tangent to the two image contours at the points p_i and p_j. *Reprinted from "Projective Visual Hulls," by S. Lazebnik, Y. Furukawa, and J. Ponce, International Journal of Computer Vision, 74(2):137–165, (2007). © 2007 Springer.*

19.1.1 Main Elements of the Visual Hull Model

As illustrated by Figure 19.1 (bottom), several algorithms are available for computing the visual hull, depending on the underlying object representation (e.g., a polyhedral mesh or a voxel-based volumetric model). This chapter focuses on solid objects bounded by smooth surfaces. The boundary of the visual hull is in this case a *generalized polyhedron*, whose faces are patches belonging to the boundaries of viewing cones, edges are segments of *intersection curves* between pairs of these patches, and vertices are points where three or four faces intersect each other (Figure 19.1, top). Equivalently, it can be described as the union of *cone strips* belonging to the surfaces of individual cones.

   In general, all vertices of a polyhedron (or generalized polyhedron, for that matter) are formed by the transversal intersection of three faces—that is, two faces meet at a nonzero angle along a line (or more generally, a curve), and the third one cuts that line at a nonzero angle to form a vertex. This is not the case for visual hulls, whose vertices come in two flavors: *Triple points* (the white discs in Figure 19.1, top) are ordinary vertices where the surfaces of three viewing cones intersect in a transversal manner, and the three corresponding intersection curves meet each other at nonzero angles. *Frontier points* (the black diamonds in the same figure) are more peculiar. They are vertices where the surfaces of two viewing cones intersect tangentially, two intersection curve branches cross each other, and the two occluding contours cross as well. They occur for most pairs of images because they are also the places where an epipolar plane is tangent to the surface, with both projection rays in that plane, and the corresponding epipolar lines are tangent to the two contours at the projections of these points (Figure 19.2).

   Before giving an explicit algorithm for constructing the visual hull, let us note that all the concepts introduced in the rest of this section are illustrated throughout using the toy example of Figure 19.3: The two outlines γ_i and γ_j shown in this diagram are intended as front and side views of a solid, rectified so the epipolar lines are horizontal. The first outline is egg-shaped, and the second one is U-shaped, the lower leg of the U giving rise to an isolated bump in the

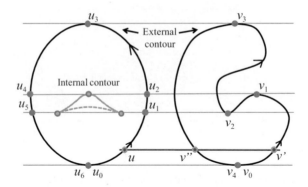

FIGURE 19.3: Two rectified views γ_i (**left**) and γ_j (**right**) of a solid. The epipolar lines associated with extremal points are shown as thin, horizontal straight lines. In the context of visual hull construction, the internal part of a contour, as shown in the left part of the diagram, typically is not observable, with the only available information coming from the silhouette and thus the external part of the contour. Once extremal point parameters—here, (u_0, v_0), (u_1, v_2), (u_2, v_1), (u_3, v_3), (u_4, v_1), and (u_5, v_2)— have been computed, and sorted in ascending u order, the intersection curve ϕ_{ij} can be identified by sampling the $[u_k, u_{k+1}]$ intervals at regular values, and marching from one sample to the next in these intervals, computing the corresponding values of v—here, v' and v''—by intersecting γ_j with the corresponding epipolar line. [Note that the parameter values u_0 and u_6 (resp. v_0 and v_4) are identified to emphasize the periodic nature of the contours' parameterization.]

left contour (the dashed lines correspond to hidden parts of the outline, following the conventions of Chapter 13). This bump lies inside the silhouette, and like all internal contour structures, it is ignored during visual hull construction. This is, in part, because, although it is relatively easy to find outer image boundaries in controlled situations (using background subtraction for example), it is difficult in practice to accurately delineate internal ones. But this is also because exploiting the corresponding geometric information is difficult, and, as far as we know, still an open problem. On the other hand, holes in the silhouette—as in the case of a torus, for example—do not pose any particular problem during the construction of visual hulls.

Without loss of generality, we will assume from now on that, as in Figure 19.3, the outlines γ_i and γ_j observed in two images I_i and I_j are parameterized by two variables u and v, and that I_i and I_j have been rectified so that matching epipolar lines are represented by the same horizontal line. Under this assumption, a necessary and sufficient condition for the visual rays associated with the parameters u and v on γ_i and γ_j to intersect is that the corresponging contour points be in epipolar correspondence—that is, lie on the same horizontal line. This constraint implicitly defines three different curves: The first one, ϕ_{ij}, is drawn in the (u, v) plane and characterizes matching pairs of these parameters. For each point on ϕ_{ij}, there exists a point $\boldsymbol{P}(u, v)$ on a second curve, δ_{ij}, drawn in $\mathbb{R}^3$ and where the two cone boundaries intersect. Finally, the depth $z(u, v)$ of $\boldsymbol{P}(u, v)$ relative to camera number i defines a third curve, ψ_{ij}, drawn in the (u, z) plane (Figure 19.4).[1]

---

[1]As shown in Chapter 7, $z(u, v)$ is a function of the horizontal disparity between the two

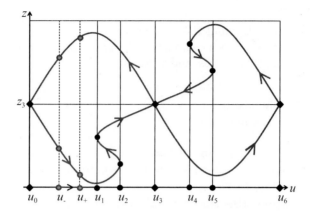

FIGURE 19.4: The intersection curve ψ_{ij} associated with the outlines of Figure 19.3 is traced here in the (u, z) plane. The parameter values u_1 and u_4 correspond to opening points, and the values u_2 and u_5 to closing ones. The parameter values $u_0 \equiv u_6$ and u_3 correspond to frontier points. Although the lower (first in ascending z order) and upper (second) branches of the curve in the interval $[u_0, u_1]$ are constructed from left to right by the curve-tracing algorithm, the orientation of the second branch is reversed during post-processing. The same is done for all branches with an even index so as to construct a consistent counterclockwise ordering of the edges and vertices of the curves.

The intersection curve of two viewing cones can be characterized by tracing any of these three curves, but it turns out to be most convenient to trace ψ_{ij}, from which the other two curves can readily be recovered. Visual rays project onto horizontal epipolar lines in the rectified image plane. They also correspond to vertical lines in the (u, z) plane. We will go back and forth between the two representations in the rest of this section, so the reader should always keep in mind that we talk about the outlines γ_i and γ_j in the rectified image plane when we refer to horizontal lines, and about the curve ψ_{ij} in the (u, z) plane when we refer to vertical ones.

Let us now present a simple algorithm for computing the visual hull (Algorithm 19.1): First, we construct the *skeleton* formed by its edges and vertices. We then "fill in" the interior of the cone strips. Because the vertices of the visual hull are frontier points and triple ones, computing the skeleton amounts to identifying frontier points (as well as other *extremal points* that will be defined in the next section) and tracing the intersection curve branches linking them for all pairs of images (Section 19.1.2), then clipping these curves against each other and computing the corresponding triple points (Section 19.1.3). The last major component of Algorithm 19.1 is the triangulation of the cone strips whose vertices and edges have been identified, as described in Section 19.1.4.

19.1.2   Tracing Intersection Curves

Tracing ψ_{ij} turns out to be easy for intervals of the u axis where any vertical line in the (u, z) plane intersects this curve a constant number of times. (As will be

corresponding contour points. It is indeed inversely proportional to the disparity in the rectified coordinate system attached to the camera.

The algorithm takes as input the image contours $\gamma_1, \ldots, \gamma_n$ extracted from n calibrated images, and outputs a combinatorial representation of the visual hull boundary in terms of its faces, edges, and vertices.

% Find the skeleton.

1. For $i = 1, \ldots, n$ do

(a) **Tracing (Section 19.1.2):** For $j = 1, \ldots, n$, $j \neq i$, identify the extremal points associated with the contours γ_i and γ_j and trace the intersection curve ψ_{ij}.

(b) **Clipping (Section 19.1.3):** For $j, k = 1, \ldots, n$, $j \neq i$, $k \neq i$, $j \neq k$, clip the intersection curves ψ_{ij} and ψ_{ik} against each other, and compute the corresponding triple points.

% Find the visual hull faces (Section 19.1.4).

2. For $i = 1, \ldots, n$ do

(a) Triangulate the ith cone strip.

Algorithm 19.1: Visual Hull Construction.

explained shortly, this is because it is easy to link successive samples on ψ_{ij} in this case.) These intervals are delimited by *extremal* points with a vertical tangent (Figure 19.4). This happens when γ_j is tangent to an epipolar line—in other words, it has a horizontal tangent (see the problems; intuitively, the slope of the disparity function is infinite there). In the usual case where γ_i is *not* also tangent to this horizontal line, there are two types of extremal points, *opening* and *closing* ones. When the epipolar lines are ordered in increasing u order, as in Figure 19.3, the former correspond to *minimal* tangencies where both branches of γ_j are (locally) above the horizontal tangent (e.g., (u_1, v_2) in Figure 19.3), and the latter to *maximal* ones where they are both below (e.g., (u_2, v_1) in the same figure). Both types of points can indeed be identified using this characteristic property. Equivalently, the two segments of ψ_{ij} incident to an opening (resp. closing) point are on its right (resp. left) in the (u, z) plane (Figure 19.4). When matching epipolar lines are tangent to *both* γ_i and γ_j, the points where they graze these curves (e.g., (u_0, v_0) and (u_3, v_3) in Figure 19.3) are the projections of frontier points where the occluding contours cross on the surface, with both projection rays in the tangent plane there (Figure 19.2). At the corresponding point of ψ_{ij}, two of this curve's branches have a transversal intersection (Figure 19.4).

In practice, extremal points are found by searching γ_j for horizontal tangents, and computing the intersections of the corresponding epipolar lines with γ_i. Their type is then easily assessed from its defining properties (minimal, maximal, or double tangency). Once the extremal points have been identified and sorted in ascending u order, it is a simple matter to trace ψ_{ij} by regularly sampling the intervals of the u axis delimited by the extremal points, and marching from one u sample to the next one in each interval, computing at every step the corresponding values of the parameter z for each branch of the intersection curve by intersecting γ_j with the corresponding horizontal line (Figure 19.3), and linking the corresponding (u, z) samples to those found at the previous iteration. This requires a consistent ordering of the samples during curve tracing, which is one of the main reasons for tracing ψ_{ij} instead of ϕ_{ij}: indeed, these points can be sorted in increasing z order, and each one can be assigned a *depth index* according to whether it is the first, second, ... point along the ray as seen from the optical center O_i. In particular, the number of intersections between an epipolar line and the contour γ_j remains constant for all values of u in the interior of the interval delimited by two consecutive extremal points, which greatly simplifies the tracing process (Algorithm 19.2).

The algorithm takes as input two contours γ_i and γ_j and outputs a graphical description of the curve ψ_{ij}. The parameter q controlling the number of samples per interval can be adapted easily to the interval size.

1. Compute the extremal points of the curve ψ_{ij}. If there are $K+1$ of them, sort them in increasing u order and denote by u_k $(k = 0, \ldots, K)$ the corresponding parameter values.
2. Compute the sample points of ψ_{ij} associated with $u_- = u_0$.
3. For $k = 1$ to K do

   (a) $\delta u \leftarrow (u_k - u_{k-1})/q$; $u_+ \leftarrow u_- + \delta u$.
   (b) For $p = 1$ to q do

      i. Compute the sample points corresponding to u_+.
      ii. Link these points with the points corresponding to u_- that have the same depth index.
      iii. $u_- \leftarrow u_+$; $u_+ \leftarrow u_+ + \delta u$.

4. Reverse the orientation of all back edges.
5. Return the oriented graph whose vertices consist of extremal points and edges are the polygonal chains linking them.

Algorithm 19.2: A Curve-Tracing Algorithm.

The main idea of this algorithm is to represent every curve branch on each interval $[u_{k-1}, u_k]$ by a polygonal chain, using the facts that the number of branches remains the same on that interval, and that the depth indices of successive sample points can be used to link them. Some care has to be taken at the endpoints of each interval, where u_- or u_+ corresponds to an extremal point. When $u_- = u_{k-1}$, there are two cases: when u_- corresponds to a frontier point or an opening one, this point must be duplicated in the corresponding list of intersections before linking; otherwise, u_- corresponds to a closing point, and it must be deleted from the list before linking. When $u_+ = u_k$, there are also two cases: when u_+ corresponds to

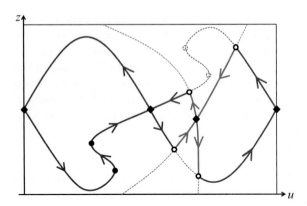

FIGURE 19.5: Clipping the intersection curves. The white discs represent triple points. The dashed parts of the two curves are clipped away.

a frontier point or a closing one, this point must be duplicated; otherwise, it is an opening point, and it must be deleted.[2]

With these conventions, there is always an even number of curve branches on each interval, and an even number of ordered pairs (u, z) associated with the parameters u_- and u_+ at each iteration of the tracing procedure. The "solid" parts of the strip that actually lie within the viewing cone associated with γ_j are delimited by the first (front, as seen from the camera) branch and the second (back) one, the third (front) and the fourth (back) ones, and so on. In particular, this ensures that the output of the curve-tracing algorithm is easily transformed by reversing the orientation of back edges into a graphical representation of the curve ψ_{ij}, with vertices corresponding to extremal points, and edges to polygonal branches between these points, oriented counterclockwise so the solid part of the strip always lies on the left of its boundary (Figure 19.4).[3]

19.1.3 Clipping Intersection Curves

Let us now move to the problem of computing the skeleton of the visual hull, and the key step of that procedure—that is, clipping the intersection curves traced in the previous section against the viewing cones associated with the remaining images (Figure 19.5). Let us consider a third image I_k and the intersection curve ψ_{ik} defined by I_i and I_k. The intersections of ψ_{ij} and ψ_{ik} are easily found by searching each curve for successive points that are on opposite sides of the other one, and using linear interpolation to locate the intersection points of the corresponding line segments. They are the projections of triple points, whose 3D position is easily obtained using linear least squares,[4] and they are inserted in the corresponding

---

[2]In this case the duplication or deletion is temporary, since the u_+ parameter will be reused as a u_- parameter at the next iteration.

[3]Holes in the silhouette of an object—when the camera faces a donut or a person with her hand on her hip, for example—are easily handled by maintaining consistent orientations for the different connected components of the contour.

[4]Triple points show up in the (u, z) plane as the intersection of *two* curves, ψ_{ij} and ψ_{ik}. One should, however, keep in mind that they also lie on the ψ_{jk}/ψ_{ji} and ψ_{ki}/ψ_{kj} intersections. They

curve branches. The part of each curve that must be dismissed because it lies outside the other one can then be identified by using orientation information. The connectivity information needed to complete the skeleton is also easily obtained from the different contours' orientation once the triple points have been found.

19.1.4 Triangulating Cone Strips

The complete boundary of the visual hull consists of *strips* lying on the surfaces of the original visual cones. The skeleton obtained at the end of the clipping stage gives a complete combinatorial representation of all the strip boundaries, consisting of vertices that correspond to extremal and triple points, and edges that represent the smooth intersection curve branches between them as polygonal chains. However, it does not provide an explicit description of the strip interiors. For this, we must *triangulate* the cone strips (Algorithm 19.3).

This takes as input a cone strip and outputs its triangulation.

1. Create the event list by sorting the parameter values of the endpoints of all edges on the boundary of the cone strip. Initialize the active list with all edges that contain some starting position u_0.

2. For each event u_k do

   % Fill in triangles from u_{k-1} to u_k.

   (a) For each pair (E, E') of adjacent edges in the active list such that E is a front edge and E' is a back edge, do

      i. Fill in triangles between E and E' in the interval $[u_{k-1}, u_k]$.

   % Update the active edge list.

   (b) If u_k is an event where a pair of edges start, then insert this pair of edges into the active list.

   (c) if u_k is an event where a pair of edges end, then delete this pairs of edges from the active list.

Algorithm 19.3: The Strip Triangulation Algorithm.

As in our curve tracing procedure, the triangulation is essentially performed as a line sweep of the (u, z) plane (Figure 19.6). The two key data structures maintained by the triangulation algorithm are an *event list* and an *active list*. The event list contains the u coordinates, sorted in increasing order, of the extremal and triple points, corresponding to the endpoints of all the strip edges. The active list, updated at each successive event value, is a list of edges that intersect the sweeping ray at its current location. If the ray passes the first endpoint of an edge, that edge is inserted into the active list, and if the ray passes the second endpoint of an edge already in the list, that edge is deleted. The edges in the active

---

are indeed points where *three* curve branches intersect on the visual hull's boundary.

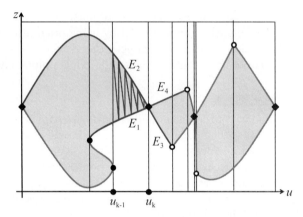

FIGURE 19.6: Triangulating a cone strip between two consecutive events u_{k-1} and u_k. The active edge list consists of edges E_1 and E_2 before the event, and of the edges E_3 and E_4 afterwards.

list are kept sorted according to their depth index along the sweeping ray, and successive pairs of edges bound pieces of the cone strip, or *cells*, in their interior. For example, in Figure 19.6, the interior of the strip is bounded between edge pairs (E_1, E_2), then (E_3, E_4). These cells are *monotone*, i.e., they intersect the sweeping ray along at most a single interval. They are triangulated using a simple linear-time algorithm for monotone polygons (O'Rourke 1998). In practice, a post-processing stage (remeshing) is added to turn the elongated triangles found by this procedure into more regular ones.

19.1.5   Results

The algorithm as presented implicitly assumes that there is always at least one pair of frontier points per pair of images to initiate curve tracing. This is true when the epipoles lie *outside* the object's outline, which is the most common case. On the other hand, there is no frontier point for a convex solid observed by two cameras with a baseline passing through its interior, so the two epipoles are inside the corresponding (convex) contours. In practice, this case is easily dealt with by creating a "fake" extremal point at some random u value.

It should also be noted that, because of the measurement errors unavoidable in real data, the epipolar match in I_i (resp. I_j) of an epipolar tangent to γ_j (resp. γ_i) can never be exactly tangent to the image contour: locally, it either intersects this curve twice, or not at all, turning frontier points into ordinary extremal points of the intersection curves (Figure 19.7, left), with the effect that the strip may become disconnected at these points (Figure 19.7, right). If the epipolar tangent to γ_j is a minimal or maximal one—that is, it does not intersect γ_i at any other point—the corresponding extremal point may be missed altogether. These degenerate extremal frontier points are handled using the same "fake extremal point" trick as before.

Figure 19.8 illustrates the different steps of the construction of the visual hull from nine photos of a gourd-shaped object. Its top part shows the epipolar tangencies found in two views of the gourd taken from (essentially) opposite sides,

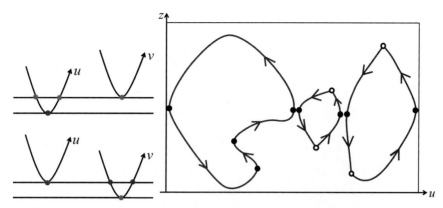

FIGURE 19.7: **Left:** A degenerate frontier point. We assume as before that the images have been rectified so that two matching epipolar lines are represented by the same horizontal line. In the top part of the diagram, the epipolar tangent associated with γ_j (locally) intersects γ_i in two separate points, and the epipolar tangent to γ_i completely misses γ_j (locally). The situation is reversed in the bottom part of the diagram. In both cases, the frontier point that would normally be detected by intersecting γ_i with the epipolar tangent at γ_j is turned into an ordinary extremal point. **Right:** This phenomenon results in disconnected strips.

and the corresponding curve ϕ_{ij} reconstructed after tracing ψ_{ij}. The central part of the diagram shows how the intersection curves associated with two views of a gourd are clipped against a third in its image plane, as well as the skeleton computed for that object. Finally, the bottom of the figure shows the nine strips recovered in the end. Note that the strips are not connected. This is due to the problem of "noisy" frontier points mentioned earlier. However, because the successive steps of the algorithm are geometrically consistent, so are the strips, and the surface of the visual hull is watertight.

Figure 19.1 shows the visual hull of a dinosaur figurine constructed from 12 images each of resolution $2,000 \times 1,500$. Figure 19.9 shows two more examples, with the visual hulls of a human skull and a Roman warrior action figure, computed from 4, 8, and 12 pictures with resolutions $1,900 \times 1,800$, and $3,500 \times 2,300$ pixels respectively. Note that the visual quality, although far from perfect, is already decent for eight views of these complex objects. Concavities, such as the eye cavities of the skull, are of course not recovered, but the overall shape is captured, in sufficient detail for many applications. This is further demonstrated by Figure 19.10, which shows texture-mapped visual hulls rendered by reprojecting the input images on the corresponding surface meshes. As could have been expected, the reprojected texture/color patterns hide much of the geometric imperfections of the underlying models, making them quite realistic.

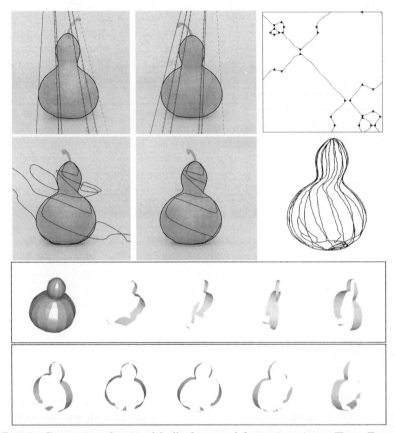

FIGURE 19.8: Computing the visual hull of a gourd from nine views. **Top:** From left to right, two images of the gourd, with tangential epipolar lines overlaid (the actual tangential epipolar lines are solid, and the epipolar lines matching frontier points in the other image are dashed), and the corresponding intersection curve traced in the (u, v) plane, with opening and closing points depicted by ◄ and ► symbols. **Center:** From left to right, the intersection curves associated with two views, reprojected into a third one; these curves after clipping; and the complete skeleton computed from nine views. **Bottom:** The visual hull of the gourd and its nine strips. *Reprinted from "Projective Visual Hulls," by S. Lazebnik, Y. Furukawa, and J. Ponce, International Journal of Computer Vision, 74(2):137–165, (2007). © 2007 Springer.*

FIGURE 19.9: Visual hull models. From **left** to **right**, the two rows show one input image, and the visual hulls computed from 4, 8, and 12 images respectively. *Reprinted from "Projective Visual Hulls," by S. Lazebnik, Y. Furukawa, and J. Ponce, International Journal of Computer Vision, 74(2):137–165, (2007). © 2007 Springer.*

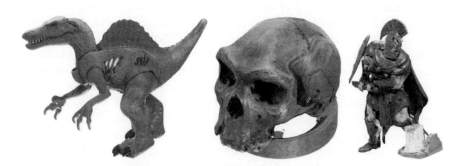

FIGURE 19.10: Texture-mapped visual hull examples. The three models have been constructed from 12 images. *Reprinted from "Projective Visual Hulls," by S. Lazebnik, Y. Furukawa, and J. Ponce, International Journal of Computer Vision, 74(2):137–165, (2007). © 2007 Springer.*

FIGURE 19.11: The carved visual hull approach to image-based modeling and rendering, illustrated using the dinosaur data from Figure 19.1 (bottom right). From **left** to **right**: the visual hull and the identified occluding contour segments (these may be difficult to see in this black and white rendering); the carved visual hull after graph cuts; and the final model after iterative refinement. Note that the undulations of the fin are recovered correctly, even though the variations in surface height there are well below 1mm for this object, about 20cm wide. *Reprinted from "Carved Visual Hulls for Image-Based Modeling," by Y. Furukawa and J. Ponce, International Journal of Computer Vision, 81(1):53–67, (2009a).* © *2009 Springer.*

19.1.6 Going Further: Carved Visual Hulls

The visual hull provides only an outer approximation of the observed solid, ignoring internal contours, hiding concavities, and perhaps more important forsaking all photometric information in favor of purely geometric constraints. We briefly discuss in this section a simple method for using photometric consistency (or *photoconsistency* for short in the rest of this chapter) constraints to refine this initial and rather coarse model while making sure that the corresponding geometric consistency (or *geoconsistency* for short) constraints are still respected.

The details of this technique are beyond the scope of this book. Let us just sketch its main ideas: First, only the points where the boundary of the visual hull of a solid touches its surface belong to the occluding contours associated with the images used to construct it (Figure 19.1, top). All others lie *outside* the solid. In particular, this means that the occluding contour points give rise to true stereo correspondences in the images in which they are visible, with consistent brightness and/or color patterns there. In other words, they are the only photoconsistent points in the cone strips. The occluding contour branches located within each strip can thus be found as polygonal paths with maximal photoconsistency using dynamic programming. With these fixed, the visual hull can now be *carved* to recover the surface main features, including its concavities. This can be achieved by deforming its surface inwards, creating a finite sequence of deeper and deeper layers, easily structured as a (three-dimensional) graph structure. By linking the top layer to a source node and the bottom one to a sink, it is then possible to find the surface with maximal photoconsistency separating these two nodes using graph cuts. This procedure yields the global optimum of the corresponding photoconsistency function, but recovers only a rough approximation of the observed shape because the layers considered are discrete. Fine surface details are finally revealed by (locally) optimizing a smooth energy function that incorporates both geo- and photoconsistency constraints. The overall process is illustrated in Figure 19.11.

FIGURE 19.12: Shaded and texture-mapped renderings of carved visual hulls, including some close-ups. *Reprinted from "Carved Visual Hulls for Image-Based Modeling," by Y. Furukawa and J. Ponce, International Journal of Computer Vision, 81(1):53–67, (2009a).* © *2009 Springer.*

Figure 19.12 shows some more 3D models obtained using this method. Note that some of the surface details are not recovered accurately. In some cases, this is simply due to the fact that the surface is not visible from any cameras; see for example the bottom part of the skull stand. In other cases, missing details correspond to failure modes of the algorithm: for example, the eye sockets of the skull are simply too deep to be carved away by graph cuts or local refinement. The person is a particularly challenging example, because of the extremely complicated folds of the cloth, and its high-frequency stripe patterns. Nonetheless, the algorithm performs rather well in general, correctly recovering minute details such as the fin undulations for the toy dinosaur, with corresponding height variations well below 1mm, or the bone junctions for the skull.

19.2 PATCH-BASED MULTI-VIEW STEREOPSIS

The approach to image-based modeling and rendering presented in the previous section is effective, but best suited for controlled situations where image silhouettes can be delineated accurately, through background subtraction for instance. For more general settings—for example, when using hand-held cameras in outdoor environments—it is tempting to revisit the stereopsis techniques presented in Chapter 7 in a context where thousands of images taken from very different viewpoints may be available. Two key ingredients of several of the techniques presented in that chapter are how they compare image brightness or color patterns in the neighborhood of potential matches, and how they enforce spatial consistency among pairs of these correspondences. As shown in Chapter 7, these are easily generalized to multiple images for *narrow-baseline* scenarios, where the cameras are close to each other, and can be assumed to share the same neighborhood structure—that is, if

FIGURE 19.13: The PMVS approach to image-based modeling and rendering, illustrated using 48 $1,800 \times 1,200$ images of a Roman soldier action figure. From **left** to **right**: A sample input image; detected features; reconstructed patches after the initial matching; and final patches after expansion and filtering. *Reprinted from "Accurate, Dense, and Robust Multi-View Stereopsis," by Y. Furukawa and J. Ponce, IEEE Transactions on Pattern Analysis and Machine Intelligence, 32(8):1362–1376, (2010).* © 2010 IEEE.

pixels are adjacent in some reference picture, so are their matches in the others. In the context of image-based modeling and rendering, the observed scene can in this case be reconstructed as a depth map, where the grid structure (or some triangulation) of the reference image provides a mesh whose vertices have coordinates in the form $(x, y, z(x, y))$, then can be rendered with classical computer graphics technology.

In the *wide-baseline* case, cameras may be positioned anywhere—all around an object, for example, or perhaps scattered over a large area. This case is much more challenging. Each image encodes part of the scene connectivity, but hides some of it as well, due in part to occlusion phenomena. Although various heuristics for stitching partial reconstructions obtained from a few views into a single mesh structure are available (see Chapter 14 for the case of range data), optimizing both the correspondences and the global mesh structure of the reconstructed points today remains, as far as we know, an open problem. This section thus abandons a full mesh model of the reconstructed scene in favor of small patches tangent to the surface, using the image topology as a proxy for their connectivity. This information is not used for rendering purposes, but instead to enforce spatial consistency and handle the visibility constraints (is some patch visible in the input images given other patch hypotheses?) that are crucial in wide-baseline stereopsis.

This technique, dubbed *PMVS* for *Patch-Based Multi-View Stereo* (Furukawa and Ponce 2010), has proven quite effective in practice. After an initial feature-matching step aimed at constructing a sparse set of *photoconsistent* patches, in the sense of the previous section—that is, patches whose projections in the images where they are visible have similar brightness or color patterns—it divides the input images into small square cells a few pixels across, and attempts to reconstruct a patch in each one of them, using the cell connectivity to propose new patches, and visibility constraints to filter out incorrect ones (Algorithm 19.4). The overall process is illustrated in Figure 19.13.

In practice, the expansion and filtering steps are iterated $K = 3$ times.

1. **Matching (Section 19.2.2):** Use feature matching to construct an initial set of patches, and optimize their parameters to make them maximally photoconsistent.

2. Repeat K times:

   (a) **Expansion (Section 19.2.3):** Iteratively construct new patches in empty spots near existing ones, using image connectivity and depth extrapolation to propose candidates, and optimizing their parameters as before to make them maximally photoconsistent.

   (b) **Filtering (Section 19.2.4):** Use again the image connectivity to remove patches identified as outliers because their depth is not consistent with a sufficient number of other nearby patches.

Algorithm 19.4: The PMVS Algorithm.

19.2.1   Main Elements of the PMVS Model

As in the previous section, we assume throughout that n cameras with known intrinsic and extrinsic parameters observe a static scene, and respectively denote by O_i and I_i $(i = 1, \ldots, n)$ the optical centers of these cameras and the images they have recorded of the scene. The main elements of the PMVS model of multi-view stereo fusion and scene reconstruction are small rectangular patches, intended to be tangent to the observed surfaces, and a few of these patches' key properties—namely, their geometry, which images they are visible in and whether they are photoconsistent with those, and some notion of connectivity inherited from image topology. Before detailing in Sections 19.2.2 to 19.2.4 the different stages of Algorithm 19.4, let us give concrete definitions for these properties.

Patch Geometry.   We associate with every rectangular patch p some reference image $\mathcal{R}(p)$. We will see in the following sections how to determine this picture but, intuitively, p should obviously be visible in $\mathcal{R}(p)$, and preferably nearly parallel to its retinal plane. As illustrated by Figure 19.14 (left), p is defined geometrically by its center $c(p)$; its unit normal $n(p)$, oriented towards the cameras observing it; its orientation about $n(p)$, chosen so one of the rectangle's edges is aligned with the rows of $\mathcal{R}(P)$; and its extent, chosen so its projection into $\mathcal{R}(p)$ fits within a square of size $\mu \times \mu$ pixels. As in the case of the correlation windows used in narrow-baseline stereopsis, this size is chosen to capture a sufficiently rich description of the local image pattern, yet remain small enough to be robust to occlusion. Taking $\mu = 5$ gives good results in practice.

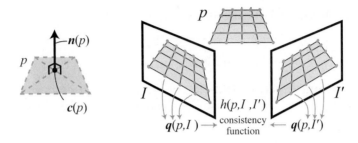

FIGURE 19.14: A patch p (**left**) and its projection into two images I and I' (**right**). The photoconsistency of p, I, and I' is measured by the normalized correlation between the sets $\boldsymbol{q}(p, I)$ and $\boldsymbol{q}(p, I')$ of interpolated pixel colors at the projections of the patch's grid points. *Reprinted from "Accurate, Dense, and Robust Multi-View Stereopsis," by Y. Furukawa and J. Ponce, IEEE Transactions on Pattern Analysis and Machine Intelligence, 32(8):1362–1376, (2010). © 2010 IEEE.*

Visibility. We say that a patch p is *potentially visible* in an image I_i when it lies in the field of view of the corresponding camera and faces it—that is, the angle between $\boldsymbol{n}(p)$ and the projection ray joining $\boldsymbol{c}(p)$ to O_i is below some threshold $\alpha < \pi/2$. Let us denote by $\mathcal{V}(p)$ the set of images where p is potentially visible. We also say that the patch p is *definitely visible* in an image I_i of $\mathcal{V}(p)$ when its center $\boldsymbol{c}(p)$ is the closest to O_i among all patches potentially visible in I_i.

Photoconsistency. In narrow-baseline stereo settings, photoconsistency is typically measured by the normalized correlation between fixed-sized image patches whose brightness or color patterns are naturally sampled on the corresponding image grids. As shown in Chapter 7, this might become problematic in the presence of foreshortening, which can be quite severe in wide-baselines scenarios. In this context, it is more natural to overlay a $\nu \times \nu$ grid on the rectangle associated with a patch p, and measure its photoconsistency with two images I and I' as the normalized cross-correlation $h(p, I, I')$ between (bilinearly) interpolated pixel values at the projections of the grid points in the two images (Figure 19.14, right). It is also natural to take $\mu = \nu$ because this ensures that cells on the patch grid roughly correspond to pixels in the reference image. The photoconsistency of a patch p with some image I in $\mathcal{V}(p)$ can now be defined as

$$g(p, I) = \frac{1}{|\mathcal{V}(p) \setminus I|} \sum_{I' \in \mathcal{V}(p) \setminus I} h(p, I, I'),$$

and we say that p is *photoconsistent* with I when $g(p, I)$ is above some threshold β. Note that the overall photoconsistency of a patch p can be measured as $f(p) = g(p, \mathcal{R}(p))$. This measure can be used to select potential matches between image features. More interestingly, it can also be used to refine the parameters of a patch p to make it maximally photoconsistent along the corresponding projection ray of $\mathcal{R}(p)$: in practice, the simplex method (Nelder and Mead 1965) is used to (locally) maximize $f(p)$ with respect to the two orientation parameters of $\boldsymbol{n}(p)$ and the depth

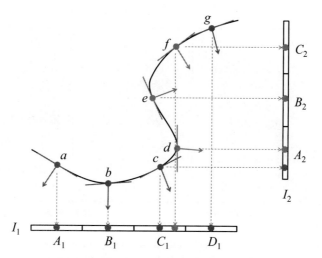

FIGURE 19.15: A toy 2D example with seven patches a to g and two orthographic input images I_1 and I_2. I_1 is divided into four cells, A_1 to D_1, and serves as the reference image for the patches a, b, c, g. I_2 is divided into three cells A_2, B_2, C_2 and serves as reference image for d, e, f. Here we have, for example, $\mathcal{C}_1(b) = B_1$ and $\mathcal{C}_2(e) = B_2$. Also note that, although the projections of the patches d and e into I_1 fall inside the cell C_1, these two patches don't belong to $\mathcal{P}(C_1) = \{c, f\}$ because the angles between their normals and the direction of projection into I_1 is larger than $\alpha = \pi/3$ (e actually faces away from I_1). Indeed, $\mathcal{V}(d) = \mathcal{V}(e) = \{I_2\}$. On the other hand, we have, for example, $\mathcal{V}(f) = \{I_1, I_2\}$. Although the patches c and f are potentially visible in I_1, only c can be said to be definitely visible in this image. Likewise, d is definitely visible in I_2, but c can only be ascertained to be potentially visible in that image.

of $\boldsymbol{c}(p)$ along the ray, but any other nonlinear optimization technique could be used instead.

Connectivity.   As noted earlier, the image topology can be used as a proxy for the connectivity of reconstructed surface patches. Concretely, one can overlay on each picture a regular grid of small square cells a few pixels across (potentially up to one cell per pixel, although 2×2 cells are used in all experiments presented in this chapter), and associate with any patch p and image I_i in $\mathcal{V}(p)$ the cell $\mathcal{C}_i(p)$ where it projects, and with any cell A_i of some image I_i the list $\mathcal{P}(A_i)$ of patches p such that I_i belongs to $\mathcal{V}(p)$ and $\mathcal{C}_i(p) = A_i$ (Figure 19.15). This allows us to define the *potential neighbors* of a patch p as the patches p' that belong to $\mathcal{P}(A'_i)$ for some image I_i and some cell A'_i adjacent to $\mathcal{C}_i(p)$. A potential neighbor p' of p is a *definite neighbor* of this patch when p and p' are consistent with a smooth surface—that is, on average, the center of each patch lies close enough to the plane of the other one, or

$$\frac{1}{2} \left(|[\boldsymbol{c}(p') - \boldsymbol{c}(p)] \cdot \boldsymbol{n}(p)| + |[\boldsymbol{c}(p) - \boldsymbol{c}(p')] \cdot \boldsymbol{n}(p')| \right) < \gamma$$

for some threshold γ.

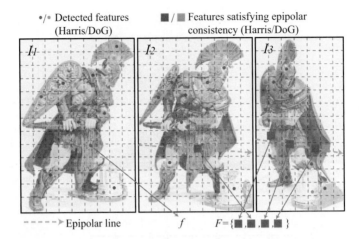

FIGURE 19.16: Feature-matching example showing the features f' in F satisfying the epipolar constraint in images I_2 and I_3 as they are matched to feature f in image I_1. (This is an illustration only, not showing actual detected features.) *Reprinted from "Accurate, Dense, and Robust Multi-View Stereopsis," by Y. Furukawa and J. Ponce, IEEE Transactions on Pattern Analysis and Machine Intelligence, 32(8):1362–1376, (2010). © 2010 IEEE.*

The heuristic nature of the definitions given in this section is obvious, and somewhat unsatisfactory, because they require hand-picking appropriate values for the parameters α, β, and γ. In practice, however, default values give satisfactory results for the vast majority of situations. In particular, Furukawa and Ponce (2010) always use a value of $\pi/3$ for α, and use values of $\beta = 0.4$ before patch refinement and $\beta = 0.7$ afterwards in the initial feature-matching stage of Algorithm 19.4, loosening (decreasing) these thresholds by a factor of 0.8 after each expansion/filtering iteration to gather more patches in challenging areas. Likewise, when deciding whether two patches p and p' are neighbors, γ is automatically set to the lateral distance between the preimages of the corresponding cell centers at the depth of the mid-point between $c(p)$ and $c(p')$.

19.2.2 Initial Feature Matching

In the first stage of Algorithm 19.4, Harris and DoG interest points are matched to construct an initial set of patches (Figure 19.16). The parameters of these patches are then optimized to make them maximally photoconsistent. Consider some input image I_i, and denote as before by O_i the optical center of the corresponding camera. For each feature f detected in I_i, we collect in the other images the set F of features f' of the same type (Harris or DoG) that lie within two pixels from the corresponding epipolar lines. Each pair (f, f') defines a 3D point and an initial patch hypothesis p centered at that point $c(p)$ with a normal $n(p)$ aligned with the corresponding projection ray. These hypotheses are examined one by one in increasing depth order from O_i until either one of them leads to the creation of a photoconsistent patch or their list is exhausted. This simple heuristic gives good results in practice for a modest computational cost. Given some initial patch hypothesis p with center $c(p)$ and normal $n(p)$, let us now define $\mathcal{R}(p) = I_i$. The extent and orientation of p are easily computed from these parameters, and $\mathcal{V}(p)$ is then determined using the threshold β. The optimization procedure described in the previous section can then be used to refine p's parameters and update $\mathcal{V}(p)$. When p is found to be visible in at least δ photographs (in practice, taking $\delta = 3$ yields good results), the patch generation procedure is deemed a success, and p is stored in the corresponding cells of the images in $\mathcal{V}(p)$. The overall procedure is given in Algorithm 19.5.

This outputs an initial list P of patch candidates.

$P \leftarrow \emptyset$.

For each image I_i with optical center O_i and for each feature f detected in I_i do

1. $F \leftarrow$ {Features satisfying the epipolar constraint}.
2. Sort F in increasing depth order from O_i.
3. For each feature f' in F do

    (a) Initialize a patch p by computing $c(p)$, $n(p)$, and $\mathcal{R}(p)$.
    (b) Initialize $\mathcal{V}(p)$ with $\beta = 0.4$.
    (c) Refine $c(p)$ and $n(p)$.
    (d) Update $\mathcal{V}(p)$ with $\beta = 0.7$.
    (e) If $|\mathcal{V}(p)| \geq \delta$, then

        i. Add p to $\mathcal{P}(\mathcal{C}_i(p))$.
        ii. Add p to P.

Algorithm 19.5: The Feature-Matching Algorithm of PMVS.

19.2.3 Expansion

Patch expansion is an iterative procedure that repeatedly tries to generate new patches in "empty" cells $\mathcal{E}(p)$ adjacent to the projections of existing patches p in the input images. The new patches are initialized by extrapolating the depth of the old ones, and their parameters are then optimized as before to make them maximally photoconsistent. Let us first define $\mathcal{D}(p)$ as the set of cells adjacent to $C_i(p)$ for all images I_i in $\mathcal{V}(p)$ (Figure 19.17). These are candidates for expansion, but some of them must be pruned because they are already consistent with p—that is, they contain one of its definite neighbors—or with I_i—that is, they contain a patch p' photoconsistent with this image. The latter case typically corresponds to occlusion boundaries, where the observed surface folds away from camera j between the patches p and p'. The set $\mathcal{E}(p)$ of empty cells adjacent to p thus consists of the elements of $\mathcal{D}(p)$ that are neither consistent with p nor with I_i (Figure 19.17).

For each image cell A_i in $\mathcal{E}(p)$, a depth extrapolation procedure is performed to generate a new patch p', initializing $c(p')$ as the point where the viewing ray

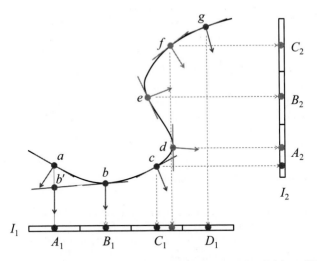

FIGURE 19.17: Candidate cells for expansion. In this example, $\mathcal{D}(c) = \{B_1, D_1, B_2\}$ and $\mathcal{D}(b) = \{A_1, C_1\}$. Assume that all patches except a have been constructed, that they are consistent with the two images, and that b and c are neighbors. In this case, $\mathcal{E}(c)$ is empty because b is a neighbor of c, thus B_1 must be eliminated, and g and e are respectively consistent with I_1 and I_2, thus D_1 and B_2 must be eliminated as well. On the other hand, $\mathcal{E}(b) = \{A_1\}$ because A_1 is (so far) empty. During the expansion procedure, the patch b' is generated in the unique cell A_1 of $\mathcal{E}(b)$, and it is then refined into the patch a.

passing through the center of A_i intersects the plane containing p. The parameters $\boldsymbol{n}(p'), \mathcal{R}(p')$, and $\mathcal{V}(p')$ are then initialized with the corresponding values for p, and $\mathcal{V}(p')$ is pruned using the threshold β to eliminate extraneous pictures. After this step, $\boldsymbol{c}(p')$ and $\boldsymbol{n}(p')$ are refined as before (Figure 19.17). After the optimization, we add to $\mathcal{V}(p')$ additional images where p is deemed definitely visible. A visibility test with a tighter threshold ($\beta = 0.7$) is then applied as before to filter out extraneous images. Finally, p' is accepted as a new patch when $\mathcal{V}(p')$ contains at least δ images, and $\mathcal{P}(\mathcal{C}_k(p'))$ is updated for all images I_k in $\mathcal{V}(p')$. The procedure is detailed in Algorithm 19.6.

19.2.4 Filtering

This stage of the algorithm again exploits image connectivity information to remove patches identified as outliers because their depth is not consistent with a sufficient number of other nearby patches. Three filters are used for this task. The first one is based on visibility consistency constraints: two patches p and p' are said to be inconsistent when they are not definite neighbors in the sense of Section 19.2.1, yet are stored in the same cell for one of the images (Figure 19.18). For each reconstructed patch p, if U denotes the set of patches inconsistent with p, p is discarded as an outlier when

$$|\mathcal{V}(p)|g(p) < \sum_{p' \in U} g(p').$$

It takes as input the candidate patches P from Algorithm 19.5 and outputs an expanded set of patches P'.

$P' \leftarrow P$.

While $P \neq \emptyset$ do

1. Pick and remove a patch p from P.

2. For each cell A_i in $\mathcal{E}(p)$ do

    (a) Create a new patch candidate p', with $\boldsymbol{c}(p')$ defined as the intersection of the plane containing p and the ray joining O_i to the center of A_i.

    (b) $\boldsymbol{n}(p') \leftarrow \boldsymbol{n}(p)$, $\mathcal{R}(p') \leftarrow \mathcal{R}(p)$, $\mathcal{V}(p') \leftarrow \mathcal{V}(p)$.

    (c) Update $\mathcal{V}(p')$ with $\beta = 0.4$.

    (d) Refine $\boldsymbol{c}(p')$ and $\boldsymbol{n}(p')$.

    (e) Add images where p' is definitely visible to $\mathcal{V}(p')$.

    (f) Update $\mathcal{V}(p')$ with $\beta = 0.7$.

    (g) If $|\mathcal{V}(p')| \geq \delta$ then

        i. Add p' to P and P'.

        ii. Add p' to $\mathcal{P}(\mathcal{C}_k(p'))$ for all I_k in $\mathcal{V}(p)$.

Algorithm 19.6: The Patch-Expansion Algorithm of PMVS.

Intuitively, when p is an outlier, both $g(p)$ and $|\mathcal{V}(p)|$ are expected to be small, and p is likely to be removed.

The second filter also enforces visibility constraints by simply rejecting all patches that are not definitely visible, in the sense of Section 19.2.1, in at least δ images. Finally, the third filter enforces a weak form of smoothness: For each patch p, we collect the patches lying in its own and adjacent cells in all images of $\mathcal{V}(p)$. If the proportion of patches that are neighbors of p in this set is lower than 25%, p is removed as an outlier.

19.2.5 Results

Figure 19.19 shows some results using four datasets, with 48 input images for the Roman soldier figurine, 16 for the dinosaur, 24 for the skull, and 4 for the face. Like the number of these photographs, their resolution varies with the dataset, from $1,800 \times 1,200$ pixels for the Roman soldier to 640×480 for the dinosaur. The top part of the figure shows one image per dataset, and its central part shows two views of each reconstructed model. Although the models might look like texture-mapped meshes, they are just—rather dense, to be sure—sets of floating patches, each rectangle being painted with the mean of the interpolated pixel values used to reconstruct it. Finally, the bottom part of the figure shows shaded views of meshes fitted to the patch models using the method presented in Furukawa and Ponce (2010). This procedure takes as input an outer approximation of the model, such as a visual hull of the observed scene if silhouette information is available, or

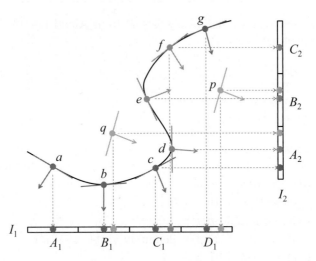

FIGURE 19.18: Filtering outliers. The patch p is rejected as an outlier by the first filter, granted that the photoconsistency scores of e and g are high enough because these two patches project into the same cells (respectively B_2 and D_1) and are inconsistent with p—that is, $U = \{e, g\}$. The patch q is eliminated by the second filter because it is not definitely visible in any image.

the convex hull of the reconstructed patches otherwise, and iteratively deforms the corresponding mesh to fit it to these patches under both smoothness and photo-consistency constraints. The reader is refered to Furukawa and Ponce (2010) for the details of this algorithm, which are beyond the scope of this book.

FIGURE 19.19: From **top** to **bottom**: Sample input images, reconstructed patches, and final mesh models. *Reprinted from "Accurate, Dense, and Robust Multi-View Stereopsis," by Y. Furukawa and J. Ponce, IEEE Transactions on Pattern Analysis and Machine Intelligence, 32(8):1362–1376, (2010). © 2010 IEEE.*

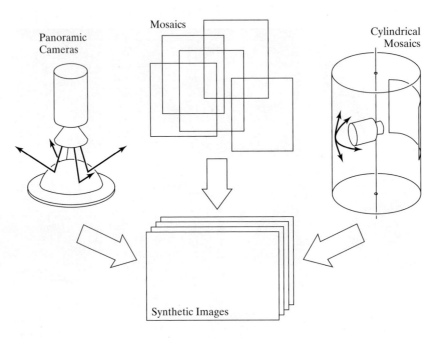

FIGURE 19.20: Constructing synthetic views of a scene from a fixed viewpoint.

19.3   THE LIGHT FIELD

This section discusses a totally different approach to image-based modeling and rendering, that entirely forsakes the construction of a three-dimensional object model, yet is capable of synthesizing realistic new views of scenes with arbitrarily complex geometries. To show that this is possible, let us consider, for example, a panoramic camera that optically records the radiance along rays passing through a single point and covering a full hemisphere (Peri and Nayar 1997). It is possible to create any image observed by a virtual camera whose pinhole is located at this point by mapping the original image rays onto virtual ones. This allows a user to arbitrarily pan and tilt the virtual camera and interactively explore his or her visual environment. Similar effects can be obtained by stitching together close-by images taken by a hand-held camcorder into a mosaic (see Shum and Szeliski [1998] and Figure 19.20, middle), or by combining the pictures taken by a camera panning (and possibly tilting) about its optical center into a cylindrical mosaic (see Chen [1995] and Figure 19.20, right).

These techniques have the drawback of limiting the viewer motions to pure rotations about the optical center of the camera. A more powerful approach can be devised by considering the *plenoptic function* (Adelson and Bergen 1991) that associates with each point in space the (wavelength-dependent) radiant energy along a ray passing through this point at a given time (Figure 19.21, left). The *light field* (Levoy and Hanrahan 1996) is a snapshot of the plenoptic function for light traveling in a vacuum in the absence of obstacles. This relaxes the dependence of the radiance on time and on the position of the point of interest along the corresponding ray (since radiance is constant along straight lines in a nonabsorbing medium) and

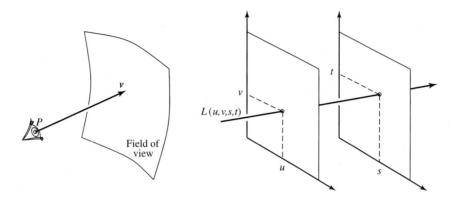

FIGURE 19.21: The plenoptic function and the light field. **Left:** The plenoptic function can be parameterized by the position P of the observer and the viewing direction $\boldsymbol{v}$. **Right:** The light field can be parameterized by the four parameters u, v, s, t defining a light slab. In practice, several light slabs are necessary to model a whole object and obtain full spherical coverage.

yields a representation of the plenoptic function by the radiance along the four-dimensional set of light rays. In the image-based rendering context, a convenient parameterization of these rays is the *light slab*, where each ray is specified by the coordinates of its intersections with two arbitrary planes (Figure 19.21, right).

The light slab is the basis for a two-stage approach to image-based rendering. During the learning stage, many views of a scene are used to create a discrete version of the slab that can be thought of as a four-dimensional lookup table. At synthesis time, a virtual camera is defined, and the corresponding view is interpolated from the lookup table. The quality of the synthesized images depends on the number of reference images. The closer the virtual view is to the reference images, the better the quality of the synthesized image. Note that constructing the light slab model of the light field does not require establishing correspondences between images. It should be noted that, unlike most methods for image-based rendering that rely on texture mapping and thus assume (implicitly) that the observed surfaces are Lambertian, light-field techniques can be used to render (under a fixed illumination) pictures of objects with *arbitrary* reflectance functions.

In practice, a sample of the light field is acquired by taking a large number of images and mapping pixel coordinates onto slab coordinates. Figure 19.22 illustrates the general case: the mapping between any pixel in the (x, y) image plane and the corresponding areas of the (u, v) and (s, t) plane defining a light slab is a planar projective transformation. Hardware- or software-based texture mapping can thus be used to populate the light field on a four-dimensional rectangular grid. In the experiments described in Levoy and Hanrahan (1996), light slabs are acquired in the simple setting of a camera mounted on a planar gantry and equipped with a pan-tilt head so it can rotate about its optical center and always point toward the center of the object of interest. In this context, all calculations can be simplified by taking the (u, v) plane to be the plane in which the camera's optical center is

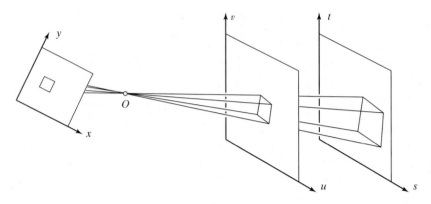

FIGURE 19.22: The acquisition of a light slab from images and the synthesis of new images from a light slab can be modeled via projective transformations between the (x, y) image plane and the (u, v) and (s, t) planes defining the slab.

constrained to remain.

At rendering time, the projective mapping between the (virtual) image plane and the two planes defining the light slab can once again be used to efficiently synthesize new images. Figure 19.23 shows sample pictures generated using the light-field approach. The top three image pairs were generated using synthetic pictures of various objects to populate the light field. The last pair of images was constructed by using the planar gantry mentioned earlier to acquire 2,048 256×256 images of a toy lion, grouped into four slabs consisting of 32×16 images each.

An important issue is the size of the light slab representation; for example, the raw input images of the lion take 402MB of disk space. There is, of course, much redundancy in these pictures, as in the case of successive frames in a motion sequence. A simple but effective two-level approach to image (de)compression is proposed in Levoy and Hanrahan (1996): the light slab is first decomposed into four-dimensional tiles of color values. These tiles are encoded using *vector quantization* (Gersho and Gray 1992), a lossy compression technique where the 48-dimensional vectors representing the RGB values at the 16 corners of the original tiles are replaced by a relatively small set of reproduction vectors, called *codewords*, that best approximate in the mean-squared-error sense the input vectors. The light slab is thus represented by a set of indexes in the *codebook* formed by all codewords. In the case of the lion, the codebook is relatively small (0.8MB) and the size of the set of indexes is 16.8MB. The second compression stage consists of applying the *gzip* implementation of *entropy coding* (Ziv and Lempel 1977) to the codebook and the indexes. The final size of the representation is only 3.4MB, corresponding to a compression rate of 118:1. At rendering time, entropy decoding is performed as the file is loaded in main memory. Dequantization is performed on demand during display, and it allows interactive refresh rates.

FIGURE 19.23: Images of three scenes synthesized with the light field approach. *Reprinted from "Light Field Rendering," by M. Levoy and P. Hanrahan, Proc. SIGGRAPH, (1996).* © *1996 ACM, Inc.* http://doi.acm.org/10.1145/10.1145/237170.237199 *Reprinted by permission.*

19.4   NOTES

Visual hulls date back to Baumgart's PhD thesis (1974), and their geometric properties have been studied in Laurentini (1995) and Petitjean (1998). Voxel- and octree-based volumetric methods for computing the visual hull include Martin and Aggarwal (1983) and Srivastava and Ahuja (1990); see also Kutulakos and Seitz (1999) for a related approach, called *space carving*, where empty voxels are iteratively removed using photoconsistency constraints. Visual hull algorithms based on polyhedral models include Baumgart (1974), Connolly and Stenstrom (1989), Niem and Buschmann (1994), Matusik, Buehler, Raskar, Gortler, and McMillan (2001), and, more recently, Franco and Boyer (2009). The problem of computing the visual hull of a solid bounded by a smooth surface is addressed in Lazebnik, Boyer, and Ponce (2001) and Lazebnik, Furukawa, and Ponce (2007). The algorithm described in Section 19.1 in the context of cameras with known intrinsic and extrinsic parameters actually also applies to weakly calibrated images. Not suprisingly, its output is defined only up to a projective transformation. Combining photometric information with the geometric constraints associated with visual hulls was first proposed in Sullivan and Ponce (1998). Variants of the carved visual hulls proposed in Furukawa and Ponce (2009a) and described in Section 19.1 include, for example, Hernandez Esteban and Schmitt (2004) and Sinha and Pollefeys (2005). The fact that a viewing cone is tangent to the surface observed by the corresponding camera, used in Furukawa and Ponce (2009a) to carve a visual hull, is also the basis for various methods that reconstruct a surface from a continuous sequence of outlines under known or unknown camera motions (Arbogast & Mohr 1991; Cipolla & Blake 1992; Vaillant & Faugeras 1992; Cipolla, Åström & Giblin 1995; Boyer & Berger 1996; Cheng, Fu & Zhang 1999; Joshi, Ahuja, & Ponce 1999).

Many different approaches to multi-view stereopsis have been developed over the past 10 years or so, and several of them, including the PMVS algorithm described in Section 19.2 and Furukawa and Ponce (2010), achieve a relative accuracy better than 1/200 (1mm for a 20cm wide object) on the low-resolution (640 × 480) images from the benchmark of Seitz, Curless, Scharstein and Szeliski (2006). Volumetric, voxel-based methods include Faugeras and Keriven (1998), Paris, Sillion, and Quan (2004), Pons, Keriven, and Faugeras (2005), Vogiatzis, Torr, and Cipolla (2005), Hornung and Kobelt (2006), Tran and Davis (2006), and Sinha, Mordohai, and Pollefeys (2007). They often use level sets of graph cuts techniques to obtain photoconsistent reconstructions, but must be provided with a bounding box containing the scene to construct the corresponding voxels. Other approaches to multi-view stereo iteratively deform polygonal surface meshes to minimize some energy function (Hernandez Esteban, & Schmitt 2004; Zaharescu, Boyer, & Horaud 2007; Hiep, Keriven, Labatut, & Pons 2009). This typically requires a good initialization, for example in the form of a visual hull. Several other algorithms reconstruct the scene by merging multiple depth maps (Goesele, Curless, & Seitz 2006; Strecha, Fransens, & van Gool 2006; Bradley, Boubekeur, & Heidrich 2008a). Finally, like the method presented in Section 19.2 and Furukawa and Ponce (2010), other approaches model objects by small surface patches (Lhuillier & Quan 2005; Habbecke & Kobbelt 2006), but require a separate algorithm (Kazhdan *et al.* 2006) to construct a mesh if one is desired.

Some of this technology is now widely available. For example, the PMVS software developed by Y. Furukawa is available at `http://grail.cs.washington.edu/software/pmvs/`. Multi-view stereo systems require the camera parameters as input, but fortunately structure-from-motion (SFM) software suites are now also available. For example, Bundler is an SFM/bundle adjustment package developed by N. Snavely as part of the Photo-Tourism project (Snavely *et al.* 2008), and it is available at `http://phototour.cs.washington.edu/bundler/`. PMVS and Bundler are also both integrated in CMVS (Furukawa *et al.* 2010), which is available at `http://grail.cs.washington.edu/software/cmvs/`. An alternative to the mesh-fitting procedure outlined at the end of Section 19.2 is Poisson surface reconstruction (Kazhdan *et al.* 2006), a method that is applicable to any collection of small oriented patches, and gives very good results in practice. Its implementation is also publicly available at `http://www.cs.jhu.edu/~misha/`.

A number of techniques have been developed for interactively exploring a user's visual environment from a fixed viewpoint, as we mentioned in Section 19.3. These include *QuickTime VR*, developed at Apple by S. Chen (1995), and algorithms that reconstruct pinhole perspective images from panoramic pictures acquired by special-purpose cameras (Peri and Nayar 1997). Similar effects can be obtained in a less controlled setting by stitching together close-by images taken with a handheld camcorder into a mosaic (Irani *et al.* 1996; Shum & Szeliski 1998; Brown & Lowe 2007). For images of distant terrains or cameras rotating about their optical center, the mosaic can be constructed by registering successive pictures via planar homographies. In this context, estimating the *optical flow* (i.e., the vector field of apparent image velocities at every image point, a notion that has, admittedly, largely been ignored in this book), may also prove important for fine registration and *deghosting* (Shum & Szeliski 1998). Variants of the light field approach discussed in Section 19.3 include McMillan and Bishop (1995) and Gortler *et al.* (1996).

Let us conclude by noting that in this chapter we have focused on the acquisition and rendering of static models of rigid objects observed in photographs. The dynamic case where nonrigid surfaces deform over time in video sequences is beyond the scope of this book, but of course at least as important, for example, in the movie industry. As of this printing, *Avatar* comes to mind in this context. The details of the technology used in this film are not publicly available, but it is likely that the level of realism achieved required some manual intervention by a team of animators. See, for example, Carceroni and Kutulakos (2002), Zhang, Snavely, Curless, and Seitz (2004), Vedula, Baker, and Kanade (2005), Hernandez Esteban, Vogiatzis, Brostow, Stenger, and Cipolla (2007), Pons, Keriven, and Faugeras (2007), White, Crane, and Forsyth (2007), and Furukawa and Ponce (2008, 2009b) for efforts to automate this *markerless motion capture* process in the academic community.

PROBLEMS

19.1. Using the rectified image setting of Section 19.1, show that the extremal points of the curve ψ_{ij} defined in that section correspond to epipolar tangents of γ_i.

19.2. Show the same result without assuming that the images have been rectified.

PROGRAMMING EXERCISES

19.3. Implement a voxel-based approach to visual hull construction.

19.4. Write a program for constructing a cylindrical mosaic from images taken from the same viewpoint (or rather close-by ones), and rendering new views seen from that vantage point.

C H A P T E R   20

Looking at People

Numerous applications of computer vision must deal with people. One reason is that people are a common theme of pictures and videos. Another is that many applications need some information about what people are doing. Many security systems require components that can tell whether people are in places they shouldn't be, or are doing things they shouldn't be doing. These are not only policing or military applications; for example, frail people might be able to live at home longer if they had a security system that could call for help when they had an accident. A system that could tell what people were doing could be useful in healthcare applications, too; for example, stroke patients seem to recover better when they keep up with daily activities, but this is difficult to do, and they benefit from being reminded to do things. There are tremendous applications in entertainment. Several consumer systems (e.g., Sony's Eyetoy and Eyetoy II, and Microsoft's Kinect) allow people to control computer games by moving their bodies. A long-term goal of much research in this area is building systems that can understand sign language, which requires watching the body movements of a signer.

There are several core problems. We discussed detecting people in Section 17.1.2. The other problems are best discussed in the context of models that can manage temporal and spatial relations, which we introduce in Section 20.1. We use these models to describe methods that determine how the body is laid out in the image (Section 20.2). In turn, these methods can be used to build trackers that can follow arms and legs (Section 20.3). Knowing the 2D layout of a body gives a surprising amount of information about the 3D configuration, though there are ambiguities (Section 20.4). Section 20.5 summarizes the very large field of activity recognition, and Section 20.6 gives a guide to the experimental datasets and code published as of time of writing.

20.1 HMM'S, DYNAMIC PROGRAMMING, AND TREE-STRUCTURED MODELS

We will need models that can represent time sequences with a fair amount of structure, and that are relatively easy to work with. Hidden Markov models (HMM's; Section 20.1.1) are a useful choice of probabilistic model, with straightforward procedures for inference (Section 20.1.2) and learning (Section 20.1.3). It turns out that inference methods appropriate to hidden Markov models apply to a broader class of model, which doesn't have to be probabilistic and isn't purely temporal. This class of model, which we call a tree-structured model (Section 20.1.4), is the mainstay of the parsing community.

20.1.1 Hidden Markov Models

A program that reads American Sign Language from a video sequence of someone signing must infer a state, internal to the user, for each sign. The program will infer state from measurements of hand position that are unlikely to be accurate, but will depend—hopefully quite strongly—on the state. The signs change state in a random (but quite orderly) fashion. In particular, some sequences of states occur very seldom (e.g., a sequence of letter signs for the sequence "wkwk" is extremely unlikely). This means that both the measurements *and* the relative probabilities of different sequences of signs can be used to determine what actually happened.

The elements of this kind of problem are:

- there is a sequence of random variables (in our example, the signs), each of which is conditionally independent of all others given its predecessor and

- each random variable generates a measurement (the measurements of hand position) whose probability distribution depends on the state.

Similar elements are to be found in examples such as interpreting the movement of dancers or of martial artists. An extremely useful formal model, known as a *hidden Markov model*, corresponds to these elements.

A sequence of random variables X_n is said to be a *Markov chain* if

$$P(\boldsymbol{X}_n = \boldsymbol{a} | \boldsymbol{X}_{n-1} = \boldsymbol{b}, \boldsymbol{X}_{n-2} = \boldsymbol{c}, \dots, \boldsymbol{X}_0 = \boldsymbol{x}) = P(\boldsymbol{X}_n = \boldsymbol{a} | \boldsymbol{X}_{n-1} = \boldsymbol{b})$$

and a *homogeneous Markov chain* if this probability does not depend on n. Markov chains can be thought of as sequences with very little memory; the new state depends on the previous state, but not on the whole history. It turns out that this property is surprisingly useful in modeling, both because many physical variables appear to have it and because it enables a variety of simple inference algorithms. There are very slightly different notations for Markov chains on discrete and continuous state spaces; we shall discuss only the discrete case.

Assume that we have a finite discrete state space. Write the elements of the space as s_i and assume that there are k elements. Assume that we have a sequence of random variables taking values in that state space that forms a homogeneous Markov chain. Now we write

$$P(X_n = s_j | X_{n-1} = s_i) = p_{ij},$$

and because the chain is independent of n, so is p_{ij}. We can write a matrix $\mathcal{P}$ with i, jth element p_{ij} which describes the behavior of the chain; this matrix is called the *state transition matrix*. Assume that X_0 has probability distribution $P(X_0 = s_i) = \pi_i$, and we will write $\boldsymbol{\pi}$ as a vector with ith element π_i. This means that

$$
\begin{aligned}
P(X_1 = s_j) &= \sum_{i=1}^{k} P(X_1 = s_j | X_0 = s_i) P(X_0 = s_i) \\
&= \sum_{i=1}^{k} P(X_1 = s_j | X_0 = s_i) \pi_i \\
&= \sum_{i=1}^{k} p_{ij} \pi_i.
\end{aligned}
$$

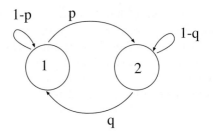

FIGURE 20.1: A simple, two-state Markov chain. In this chain, the probability of going from state one to state two is p; from state one to state one is $1 - p$; etc. Its stationary distribution is $(q/(p+q), p/(p+q))$. This makes sense; for example, if p is very small and q is close to one, the chain will spend nearly all its time in state one. Notice that, if p and q are both very small, the chain will stay in one state for a long time, and then flip to the other state, where it will stay for a long time.

and so the probability distribution for the state of X_1 is given by $\mathcal{P}^T \boldsymbol{\pi}$. By a similar argument, the probability distribution for the state of X_n is given by $(\mathcal{P}^T)^n \boldsymbol{\pi}$. For all Markov chains, there is at least one distribution $\boldsymbol{\pi}^s$ such that $\boldsymbol{\pi}^s = \mathcal{P}^T \boldsymbol{\pi}^s$; this is known as the *stationary distribution*. Markov chains allow quite simple and informative pictures. We can draw a weighted, directed graph with a node for each state and the weight on each edge, indicating the probability of a state transition (Figure 20.1).

If we observe the random variable X_n, then inference is easy—we know what state the chain is in. This is a poor observation model, however. A much better model is to say that, for each element of the sequence, we observe *another* random variable, whose probability distribution depends on the state of the chain. That is, we observe some Y_n, where the probability distribution is some $P(Y_n | X_n = s_i) = q_i(Y_n)$. We can arrange these elements into a matrix $\mathcal{Q}$. Specifying a hidden Markov model requires providing the state transition process, the relationship between state and the probability distribution on Y_n, and the initial distribution on states, i.e., the model is given by $(\mathcal{P}, \mathcal{Q}, \boldsymbol{\pi})$. We will assume that the state space has k elements.

We will assume that we are dealing with a hidden Markov model on a discrete state space; this simplifies computation considerably, usually at no particular cost. There are two important problems:

- **Inference:** We need to determine what underlying set of states gave rise to our observations. This will make it possible to, for example, infer what the dancer is doing or the signer is saying.

- **Fitting:** We need to choose a hidden Markov model that represents a sequence of past observations well.

Each has an efficient, standard solution.

20.1.2 Inference for an HMM

Assume that we have a series of N measurements $\boldsymbol{Y}_i$ that we believe to be the output of a hidden Markov model. We can set up these measurements in a structure

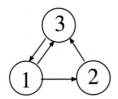

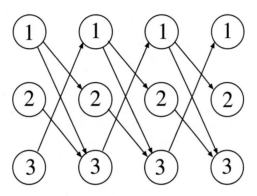

FIGURE 20.2: At the **top**, a simple state transition model. Each outgoing edge has some probability, though the topology of the model forces two of these probabilities to be 1. Below, the trellis corresponding to that model. Notice that each path through the trellis corresponds to a legal sequence of states, for a sequence of four measurements. We weight the arcs with the log of the transition probabilities, and the nodes with the log of the emission probabilities; weights are not shown here, to reduce the complexity of the drawing.

called a *trellis*. This is a weighted, directed graph consisting of N copies of the state space, which we arrange in columns. There is a column corresponding to each measurement. We weight the node representing the case that state $\boldsymbol{X}_j = s_k$ in the column corresponding to $\boldsymbol{Y}_j$ with $\log q_k(\boldsymbol{Y}_j)$.

We join up the elements from column to column as follows. Consider the column corresponding the $\boldsymbol{Y}_j$; we join the element in this column representing state $\boldsymbol{X}_j = s_k$ to the element in the column corresponding to $\boldsymbol{Y}_{j+1}$ representing state $\vec{X}_{j+1} = s_l$ if p_{kl} is nonzero. This arc represents the fact that there is a possible transition between these states. This arc is weighted with $\log p_{kl}$. Figure 20.2 shows a trellis constructed from an HMM.

The trellis has the following interesting property: each (directed) path through the trellis represents a legal sequence of states. Now because each node of the trellis is weighted with the log of the emission probability and each arc is weighted with the log of the transition probability, the joint probability of a sequence of states with the measurements can be obtained by identifying the path corresponding to this sequence, and summing the weights (of arcs and nodes) along the path. This yields an extremely effective algorithm for finding the best path, known as either *dynamic programming* or the *Viterbi algorithm*.

We start at the *final* column of the tellis. We know the log-likelihood of a one-state path, ending at each node, as this is just the weight of that node. Now consider a two-state path, which will start at the second last column of the trellis. We can easily obtain the best path leaving each node in this column. Consider a node: we know the weight of each arc leaving the node and the weight of the node at the far end of the arc, so we can choose the path segment with the largest value of the sum; this arc is the best we can do leaving that node. Now, for each node, we add the weight at the node to the value of the best path segment leaving that node (i.e., the arc weight plus the weight of the node at the far end). This sum is the best value obtainable on reaching that node—which we'll call the *node value*.

Now, because we know the best value obtainable on reaching each node in the second-last column, we can figure out the best value obtainable on reaching each node in the third-last column. At each node in the third-last column, we have a choice of arcs, each reaching a node whose value we know. We choose the arc with the largest value of (arc weight plus node value), then add this value to the weight at the starting node in the third last column, and this yields the value of the starting node. We can repeat this process, until we have a value for each of the nodes in the first column; the largest value is the maximum likelihood.

We can also get the path with the maximum likelihood value. When we compute the value of a node, we erase all but the best arc leaving that node. Once we reach the first column, we simply follow the path from the node with the best value. Figure 20.3 illustrates this extremely simple and very powerful algorithm.

We can write all this out more formally. For inference, we have a series of observations $\{Y_0, Y_1, \ldots, Y_n\}$, and we would like to obtain the sequence of $n + 1$ states $\boldsymbol{S} = \{S_0, S_1, \ldots, S_n\}$ that maximizes

$$P(\boldsymbol{S}|\{Y_0, Y_1, \ldots, Y_n\}, (\mathcal{P}, \mathcal{Q}, \boldsymbol{\pi})),$$

which is the same as maximizing the joint distribution

$$P(\boldsymbol{S}, \{Y_0, Y_1, \ldots, Y_n\}|(\mathcal{P}, \mathcal{Q}, \boldsymbol{\pi})).$$

There is a standard algorithm for this purpose, the *Viterbi algorithm*. We seek an $n + 1$ element path through the states (from S_0 to S_n). There are k^{n+1} such paths, because we could choose from each state for every element of the path (assuming that there are no zeros in $\mathcal{P}$; in most cases, there are certainly $O(k^{n+1})$ paths). We can't look at every path, but in fact we don't have to. The approach is as follows: assume that, for each possible state s_l, we know the value of the joint for the best n-step path that ends in $S_{n-1} = s_l$; then, the path that maximizes the joint for an $n + 1$ step path must consist of one of these paths, combined with another step. All we have to do is find the missing step.

We can approach finding the path with the maximum value of the joint as an induction problem. Assume that, for each value j of S_{n-1}, we know the value of the joint for the best path that ends in $S_{n-1} = j$, which we write as

$$\delta_{n-1}(j) = \max_{S_0, S_1, \ldots, S_{n-2}} P(\{S_0, S_1, \ldots, S_{n-1} = j\}, \{Y_0, Y_1, \ldots, Y_{n-1}\}|(\mathcal{P}, \mathcal{Q}, \boldsymbol{\pi})).$$

This algorithm yields the path through an HMM that maximizes the joint, and the value of the joint at this path. Here δ and ψ are convenient bookkeeping variables (as in the text); p^* is the maximum value of the joint; and q_t^* is the tth state in the optimal path.

1. **Initialization:**

$$
\begin{aligned}
\delta_1(j) &= \pi_j q_j(Y_1) \quad 1 \leq j \leq N \\
\psi_1(j) &= 0
\end{aligned}
$$

2. **Recursion:**

$$
\begin{aligned}
\delta_n(j) &= \left(\max_i \delta_{n-1}(i) P_{ij} \right) q_j(Y_n) \\
\psi_n(j) &= \arg\max \left(\delta_{n-1}(i) P_{ij} \right)
\end{aligned}
$$

3. **Termination:**

$$
\begin{aligned}
p^* &= \max_i \left(\delta_N(i) \right) \\
q_N^* &= \arg\max_i \left(\delta_N(i) \right)
\end{aligned}
$$

4. **Path backtracking:**

$$
q_t^* = \psi_{t+1}(q_{t+1}^*)
$$

Algorithm 20.1: The Viterbi Algorithm

We fit a model to a data sequence $\boldsymbol{Y}$ is achieved by a version of EM. We assume a model $(\mathcal{P}, \mathcal{Q}, \boldsymbol{\pi})_i$, and then compute the coefficients of a new model; this iteration is guaranteed to converge to a local maximum of $P(\boldsymbol{Y}|(\mathcal{P}, \mathcal{Q}, \boldsymbol{\pi}))$.

Until $(\mathcal{P}, \mathcal{Q}, \boldsymbol{\pi})_{i+1}$ is the same as $(\mathcal{P}, \mathcal{Q}, \boldsymbol{\pi})_i$
   compute the forward variables α and β
   using the procedures of algorithms 20.3 and 20.4

   compute $\xi_t(i,j) = \dfrac{\alpha_t(i) p_{ij} q_j(Y_{t+1}) \beta_{t+1}(j)}{\sum_{i=1}^{N} \sum_{j=1}^{N} \alpha_t(i) p_{ij} q_j(Y_{t+1}) \beta_{t+1}(j)}$

   compute the updated parameters using the procedures of Algorithm 20.5

   These values are the elements of $(\mathcal{P}, \mathcal{Q}, \boldsymbol{\pi})_{i+1}$
end

Algorithm 20.2: Fitting Hidden Markov Models with EM

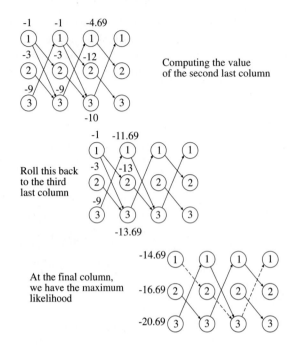

FIGURE 20.3: It is a simple matter to find the best path through the trellis of Figure 20.2 (or any other trellis, for that matter!). We assume that each 1 node has log-probability -1, each 2 node has log-probability -3, and each 3 node has log-probability -9. We also assume that the probabilities of leaving a node are uniform (check our numbers!). Now the value of each node in the second-last column is the value of the node plus the best value to be obtained by leaving that node. This is easily computed. The algorithm involves computing the value of each node in the second-last column; then of each node in the third-last column, etc., as described in the text. Once we get to the start of the trellis, the largest weight is the maximum of the log-likelihood; because we erased all but the best path segments, we have the best path, too (indicated by a dashed line).

Now we have that

$$\delta_n(j) = \left(\max_i \delta_{n-1}(i) P_{ij} \right) q_j(Y_n).$$

We need not only the maximum *value*, but also the path that gave rise to this value. We define another variable

$$\psi_n(j) = \arg\max \left(\delta_{n-1}(i) P_{ij} \right)$$

(i.e., the best path that ends in $S_n = j$). This gives us an inductive algorithm for getting the best path.

The reasoning is as follows: I know the best path to each state for the $n - 1$th measurement; for each state for the nth measurement, I can look backward and choose the best state for the $n - 1$th measurement; but I know the best path from there, so I have the best path to each state for the nth measurements. We have put everything together in Algorithm 20.1.

$$\alpha_0(j) \;=\; \pi_j q_j(Y_0)$$

$$\alpha_{t+1}(j) \;=\; \left[\sum_{l=1}^{k} \alpha_t(l) p_{lj}\right] q_j(Y_{t+1}) \qquad 1 \le t \le n-1$$

Algorithm 20.3: Computing the Forward Variable for Fitting an HMM

$$\beta_N(j) \;=\; 1$$

$$\beta_t(j) \;=\; \left[\sum_{l=1}^{k} p_{jl} q_l(Y_{t+1})\right] \beta_{t+1}(j) \qquad 1 \le t \le k-1$$

Algorithm 20.4: Computing the Backward Variable for Fitting an HMM

20.1.3 Fitting an HMM with EM

We have a dataset Y for which we believe a hidden Markov model is an appropriate model, but which hidden Markov model should we use? We wish to choose a model that best represents a set of data. To do this, we will use a version of the Expectation-Maximization algorithm of Section 10.5.3. In this algorithm, we assume that we have an HMM, $(\mathcal{P}, \mathcal{Q}, \boldsymbol{\pi})$; we now want to use this model and our dataset to estimate a new set of values for these parameters. We now estimate $(\overline{\mathcal{P}}, \overline{\mathcal{Q}}, \overline{\boldsymbol{\pi}})$ using a procedure that is given below. There will be two possibilities (a fact that we won't prove). Either $P(Y|(\overline{\mathcal{P}}, \overline{\mathcal{Q}}, \overline{\boldsymbol{\pi}})) > P(Y|(\mathcal{P}, \mathcal{Q}, \boldsymbol{\pi}))$, or $(\overline{\mathcal{P}}, \overline{\mathcal{Q}}, \overline{\boldsymbol{\pi}}) = (\mathcal{P}, \mathcal{Q}, \boldsymbol{\pi})$.

The updated values of the model parameters will have the form:

$$\overline{\pi}_i \;=\; \text{expected frequency of being in state } s_i \text{ at time 1}$$

$$\overline{p_{ij}} \;=\; \frac{\text{expected number of transitions from } s_i \text{ to } s_j}{\text{expected number of transitions from state } s_i}$$

$$\overline{q_j(k)} \;=\; \frac{\text{expected number of times in } s_j \text{ and observing } Y = y_k}{\text{expected number of times in state } s_j}$$

We need to be able to evaluate these expressions. In particular, we need to be able to determine

$$P(X_t = s_i, X_{t+1} = s_j | Y, (\mathcal{P}, \mathcal{Q}, \boldsymbol{\pi})),$$

$$
\overline{\pi_i} \;=\; \text{expected frequency of being in state } s_i \text{ at time 1}
$$

$$
=\; \sum_{j=1}^{N} \xi_1(i,j)
$$

$$
\overline{p_{ij}} \;=\; \frac{\text{expected number of transitions from } s_i \text{ to } s_j}{\text{expected number of transitions from state } s_i}
$$

$$
=\; \frac{\sum_{t=1}^{T} \xi_t(i,j)}{\sum_{t=1}^{T} \sum_{j=1}^{N} \xi_t(i,j)}
$$

$$
\overline{q_i(k)} \;=\; \frac{\text{expected number of times in } s_i \text{ and observing } Y = y_k}{\text{expected number of times in state } s_i}
$$

$$
=\; \frac{\sum_{t=1}^{T} \sum_{j=1}^{N} \xi_t(i,j)\delta(Y_t, y_k)}{\sum_{t=1}^{T} \sum_{j=1}^{N} \xi_t(i,j)}
$$

here $\delta(u,v)$ is one if its arguments are equal and zero otherwise.

Algorithm 20.5: Updating Parameters for Fitting an HMM

which we shall write as $\xi_t(i,j)$. If we know $\xi_t(i,j)$, we have

$$
\text{expected number of transitions from } s_i \text{ to } s_j \;=\; \sum_{t=1}^{T} \xi_t(i,j)
$$

$$
\text{expected number of transitions from } s_i \;=\; \sum_{t=1}^{T} \sum_{j=1}^{N} \xi_t(i,j)
$$

$$
\text{expected number of times in } s_i \;=\; \sum_{t=1}^{T} \sum_{j=1}^{N} \xi_t(i,j)
$$

$$
\text{expected frequency of being in } s_i \text{ at time 1} \;=\; \sum_{j=1}^{N} \xi_1(i,j)
$$

$$
\text{expected number of times in } s_i \text{ and observing } Y = y_k \;=\; \sum_{t=1}^{T} \sum_{j=1}^{N} \xi_t(i,j)\delta(Y_t, y_k)
$$

where $\delta(u,v)$ is one if its arguments are equal and zero otherwise.

To evaluate $\xi_t(i,j)$, we need two intermediate variables: a *forward variable* and a *backward variable*.

The forward variable is $\alpha_n(j) = P(Y_0, Y_1, \ldots, Y_n, X_n = s_j | (\mathcal{P}, \mathcal{Q}, \boldsymbol{\pi}))$.

The backward variable is $\beta_t(j) = P(\{Y_{t+1}, Y_{t+2}, \ldots, Y_n\} | X_t = s_j, (\mathcal{P}, \mathcal{Q}, \boldsymbol{\pi}))$.

If we assume that we know the values of these variables, we have that

$$
\begin{aligned}
\xi_t(i,j) &= P(X_t = s_i, X_{t+1} = s_j | \boldsymbol{Y}, (\mathcal{P}, \mathcal{Q}, \boldsymbol{\pi})) \\
&= \frac{P(\boldsymbol{Y}, X_t = s_i, X_{t+1} = s_j | (\mathcal{P}, \mathcal{Q}, \boldsymbol{\pi}))}{P(\boldsymbol{Y} | (\mathcal{P}, \mathcal{Q}, \boldsymbol{\pi}))} \\
&= \frac{\left\{ \begin{array}{l} P(Y_0, Y_1, \ldots, Y_t, X_t = s_i | (\mathcal{P}, \mathcal{Q}, \boldsymbol{\pi})) \\ \times P(Y_{t+1} | X_{t+1} = s_j, (\mathcal{P}, \mathcal{Q}, \boldsymbol{\pi})) \\ \times P(X_{t+1} = s_j | X_t = s_i, (\mathcal{P}, \mathcal{Q}, \boldsymbol{\pi})) \\ \times P(Y_{t+2}, \ldots, Y_N | X_{t+1} = s_j, (\mathcal{P}, \mathcal{Q}, \boldsymbol{\pi})) \end{array} \right\}}{P(\boldsymbol{Y} | (\mathcal{P}, \mathcal{Q}, \boldsymbol{\pi}))} \\
&= \frac{\alpha_t(i) p_{ij} q_j(Y_{t+1}) \beta_{t+1}(j)}{P(\boldsymbol{Y} | (\mathcal{P}, \mathcal{Q}, \boldsymbol{\pi}))} \\
&= \frac{\alpha_t(i) p_{ij} q_j(Y_{t+1}) \beta_{t+1}(j)}{\sum_{i=1}^{N} \sum_{j=1}^{N} \alpha_t(i) p_{ij} q_j(Y_{t+1}) \beta_{t+1}(j)}.
\end{aligned}
$$

Both the forward and backward variables can be evaluated by induction. We get $\alpha_n(j)$, by observing that:

$$
\begin{aligned}
\alpha_0(j) &= P(Y_0, X_0 = s_j | (\mathcal{P}, \mathcal{Q}, \boldsymbol{\pi})) \\
&= \pi_j q_j(Y_0)
\end{aligned}
$$

$$
\begin{aligned}
\alpha_{t+1}(j) &= P(Y_0, Y_1, \ldots, Y_{t+1}, X_{t+1} = s_j | (\mathcal{P}, \mathcal{Q}, \boldsymbol{\pi})) \\
&= P(Y_0, Y_1, \ldots, Y_t, X_{t+1} = s_j | (\mathcal{P}, \mathcal{Q}, \boldsymbol{\pi})) P(Y_{t+1} | X_{t+1} = s_j) \\
&= \sum_{l=1}^{k} [P(Y_0, Y_1, \ldots, Y_t, X_t = s_l, X_{t+1} = s_j | (\mathcal{P}, \mathcal{Q}, \boldsymbol{\pi})) P(Y_{t+1} | X_{t+1} = s_j)] \\
&= \left(\sum_{l=1}^{k} \left[\begin{array}{l} P(Y_0, Y_1, \ldots, Y_t, X_t = s_l | (\mathcal{P}, \mathcal{Q}, \boldsymbol{\pi})) \\ \times P(X_{t+1} = s_j | X_t = s_l) \end{array} \right] P(Y_{t+1} | X_{t+1} = s_j) \right) \\
&= \left[\sum_{l=1}^{k} \alpha_t(l) p_{lj} \right] q_j(Y_{t+1}) \qquad 1 \le t \le n - 1.
\end{aligned}
$$

This backward variable can also be obtained by induction as:

$$
\begin{aligned}
\beta_N(j) &= P(\text{no further output}|X_n = s_j, (\mathcal{P}, \mathcal{Q}, \boldsymbol{\pi})) \\
&= 1
\end{aligned}
$$

$$
\begin{aligned}
\beta_t(j) &= P(\{Y_{t+1}, Y_{t+2}, \dots, Y_n\}|X_t = s_j, (\mathcal{P}, \mathcal{Q}, \boldsymbol{\pi})) \\
&= \sum_{l=1}^{k} [P(\{Y_{t+1}, Y_{t+2}, \dots, Y_n\}, X_t = s_l|X_{t+1} = s_j, (\mathcal{P}, \mathcal{Q}, \boldsymbol{\pi}))] \\
&= \left(\begin{array}{l} \left[\sum_{l=1}^{k} P(X_t = s_l, Y_{t+1}|X_{t+1} = s_j)\right] \\ \times P(\{Y_{t+2}, \dots, Y_n\}|X_{t+1} = s_j, (\mathcal{P}, \mathcal{Q}, \boldsymbol{\pi})) \end{array} \right) \\
&= \left[\sum_{l=1}^{k} p_{jl} q_l(Y_{t+1})\right] \beta_{t+1}(j) \qquad 1 \le t \le k - 1.
\end{aligned}
$$

As a result, we have a simple fitting algorithm, collected in Algorithm 20.2.

20.1.4 Tree-Structured Energy Models

A major attraction of hidden Markov models is the relative simplicity of inference and learning. This is a consequence of the combinatorial structure of the model; in fact, our algorithms apply to somewhat richer combinatorial structures, and to models that are not intrinsically probabilistic. We now consider a situation where we will choose values for a set discrete variables, traditionally written X_i for $i = 1, \dots, n$, to maximize the value of an objective function $f(X_1, \dots, X_n)$. This objective function is a sum of *unary terms* (i.e., functions that take one argument), which we write $u_j(X_i)$, and *binary terms* (i.e., functions that take two arguments), which we write $b_k(X_i, X_j)$. This is a relatively general model of parts and relations. There is one score (which would be the u_k) associated with each part (which would be the X_i) and another associated with some of the relations (i.e., the b_k). For example, in the case of the HMM, the variables would be the hidden states, the unary terms would be the logs of emission probabilities, and binary terms would be the logs of transition probabilities. It is natural to think of the unary terms as nodes in a graph, and the binary terms as edges. However, it is not required to think of the unary or binary terms as log probabilities; instead, you could think of them as negative energies (because we are maximizing), or you could minimize, and think of them as energies or costs. For this kind of model, maximization is straightforward if the graph we have described is a forest.

HMM's are a special case, because the graph in that case is a chain. We will redescribe inference for an HMM in this more general setting, because it will then follow easily that the method applies to a forest. We can write the objective function as

$$
f_{\text{chain}}(X_1, \dots, X_n) = \sum_{i=1}^{i=n} u_i(X_i) + \sum_{i=1}^{i=n-1} b_i(X_i, X_i + 1)
$$

and we wish to maximize this function (you should check that the terms match terms in the expression for the joint for an HMM; a strategically placed logarithm will help). Now we define a new function, the *cost-to-go function*, with a recursive definition. Write

$$f_{\text{cost-to-go}}^{(n-1)}(X_{n-1}) = \max_{X_n} b_{n-1}(X_{n-1}, X_n) + u_n(X_n),$$

and notice that we have

$$\operatorname*{argmax}_{X_1, \ldots, X_n} f_{\text{chain}}(X_1, \ldots, X_n)$$

is equal to

$$\operatorname*{argmax}_{X_1, \ldots, X_{n-1}} \left(f_{\text{chain}}(X_1, \ldots, X_{n-1}) + f_{\text{cost-to-go}}^{(n-1)}(X_{n-1}) \right),$$

which means that we can eliminate the nth variable from the optimization by replacing the term $b_{n-1}(X_{n-1}, X_n) + u_n(X_n)$ with a function of X_{n-1}. This function is obtained by maximizing this term with respect to X_n. Equivalently, assume we must choose a value for X_{n-1}. The cost-to-go function tells us the value of $b_{n-1}(X_{n-1}, X_n) + u_n(X_n)$ obtained by making the best choice of X_n conditioned on our choice of X_{n-1}. Because any other choice would not lead to a maximum, if we know the cost-to-go function at X_{n-1}, we can now compute the best choice of X_{n-1} conditioned on our choice of X_{n-2}. This yields that

$$\max_{X_{n-1}, X_n} \left[b_{n-2}(X_{n-2}, X_{n-1}) + u_{n-1}(X_n - 1) + b_{n-1}(X_{n-1}, X_n) + u_n(X_n) \right]$$

is equal to

$$\max_{X_{n-1}} \left[b_{n-2}(X_{n-2}, X_{n-1}) + u_{n-1}(X_n - 1) + \left(\max_{X_n} b_{n-1}(X_{n-1}, X_n) + u_n(X_n) \right) \right].$$

But all this can go on recursively, yielding

$$f_{\text{cost-to-go}}^{(k)}(X_k) = \max_{X_{k+1}} b_k(X_k, X_{k+1}) + u_k(X_k) + f_{\text{cost-to-go}}^{(k+1)}(X_{k+1}).$$

We can expand this to describe our use of the trellis in Section 20.1.2. Notice that

$$\operatorname*{argmax}_{X_1, \ldots, X_n} f_{\text{chain}}(X_1, \ldots, X_n)$$

is equal to

$$\operatorname*{argmax}_{X_1, \ldots, X_{n-1}} \left(f_{\text{chain}}(X_1, \ldots, X_{n-1}) + f_{\text{cost-to-go}}^{(n-1)}(X_{n-1}) \right)$$

which is equal to

$$\operatorname*{argmax}_{X_1, \ldots, X_{n-2}} \left(f_{\text{chain}}(X_1, \ldots, X_{n-2}) + f_{\text{cost-to-go}}^{(n-2)}(X_{n-2}) \right),$$

and we can apply the recursive definition of the cost-to-go function to get

$$\underset{X_1,\ldots,X_n}{\mathrm{argmax}} \; f_{\mathrm{chain}}(X_1,\ldots,X_n) = \underset{X_1}{\mathrm{argmax}} \; \left(f_{\mathrm{chain}}(X_1) + f^1_{\mathrm{cost\text{-}to\text{-}go}}(X_1) \right),$$

which yields an extremely powerful maximization strategy. We start at X_n, and construct $f^{(n-1)}_{\mathrm{cost\text{-}to\text{-}go}}(X_{n-1})$. We can represent this function as a table, giving the value of the cost-to-go function for each possible value of X_{n-1}. We build a second table giving the optimum X_n for each possible value of X_{n-1}. From this, we can build $f^{(n-2)}_{\mathrm{cost\text{-}to\text{-}go}}(X_{n-2})$, again as a table, and also the best X_{n-1} as a function of X_{n-2}, again as a table, and so on. Now we arrive at X_1. We obtain the solution for X_1 by choosing the X_1 that yields the best value of $\left(f_{\mathrm{chain}}(X_1) + f^2_{\mathrm{cost\text{-}to\text{-}go}}(X_2) \right)$. But from this solution, we can obtain the solution for X_2 by looking in the table that gives the best X_2 as a function of X_1; and so on. It should be clear that this process yields a solution in polynomial time; in the exercises, you will show that, if each X_i can take one of k values, then the time is $O(nK^2)$.

This strategy will work for a model with the structure of a forest. The proof is an easy induction. If the forest has no edges (i.e., consists entirely of nodes), then it is obvious that a simple strategy applies (choose the best value for each X_i independently). This is clearly polynomial. Now assume that the algorithm yields a result in polynomial time for a forest with e edges, and show that it works for a forest with $e + 1$ edges. There are two cases. The new edge could link two existing trees, in which case we could re-order the trees so the nodes that are linked are roots, construct a cost-to-go function for each root, and then choose the best pair of states for these roots from the cost-to-go functions. Otherwise, one tree had a new edge added, joining the tree to an isolated node. In this case, we reorder the tree so that this new node is the root and build a cost-to-go function from the leaves to the root. The fact that the algorithm works is a combinatorial insight, but many kinds of model have a tree structure. Models of this form are particularly important in cases of tracking and of parsing.

20.2   PARSING PEOPLE IN IMAGES

A *human parser* must produce some report of the configuration of the body in an image window. A human parse offers cues to what the person is doing, by reporting where the arms, legs, and so on are. Applications could include building a user interface that can respond to someone's gestures or building a medical support system that can tell, by watching video, whether a physically frail person is safe at home or has sustained an injury and needs care. Tracking people is a particularly useful technology (we'll discuss its applications below), and currently the most reliable technologies for human tracking involve a combination of detection and parsing.

20.2.1   Parsing with Pictorial Structure Models

Parsing can be attacked by maximizing a tree-structured model. For example, we could discretize the set of possible segments in an image by quantizing segment orientation to a fixed set of values, and quantizing the top-left corner of the segment to the pixel grid. We set up one variable per body segment, where the value of the variable identifies which image segment corresponds to that body segment (you can think of these variables as segment pointers). This set of variables can be scored by evaluating (a) the extent to which the body segment looks like the corresponding image and (b) the extent to which segments are consistent with each other. The set of pointers that maximizes this objective function is the parse. We now use a tree-structured model to ensure the maximization component is tractable.

A *pictorial structure model* is a tree structured model, where unary terms compare parts to image observations, and binary terms evaluate relative configuration. Such models are particularly well adapted to parsing people. Assume we know the appearance of each of a set of limb segments that model a person (Figure 20.4). This means that we can build a set of unary functions that compare the image segment that X_i points to with the corresponding model segment. Because we are maximizing, larger values mean a more compatible appearance. We also obtain a set of pairwise relations for a tree-structured subset of this model. It seems natural to use the tree indicated in Figure 20.4. These terms evaluate the relative location of the image segment endpoints, and perhaps the angles between the image segments (there are numerous useful variants, as we shall see). For example, there might be a term checking that the outer end of the thigh is close to the upper end of the shin, and that the angle between the two is acceptable. Again, larger values mean that the two image segments pointed to by the variables are compatible with the relevant labels.

Models of this form can be used to find people in images in a fairly straightforward manner, and are the core technology of parsing. Felzenszwalb and Huttenlocher (2000) assume that segments have known color patterns—typically, a mixture of skin color and blue—and then compare the actual image color with these patterns for the unary terms; the binary terms ensure endpoints are close and angles are appropriate. This leads to a fairly satisfactory matcher (Figure 20.4), with the proviso that the person's clothing should be known in advance. It should look natural to extend the appearance model to score similarities in texture as well as in color, but this has not proven successful to date, most likely because folds in clothing generate strong texture noise effects.

A persistent nuisance with tree-structured models as we have described them is that the best parse typically will place the left leg (resp. arm) on top of the right leg (resp. arm). This is because configuration cues are usually not strong enough to force the legs (resp. arms) apart in the image, and one of the two image legs (resp. arms) will look more like the model than the other does. It is difficult to change the model to avoid this problem; inserting a term that forces the arms apart will create inference difficulties. Instead, there is a simple trick that helps. We regard the energy as the log of a probability distribution, and draw a large pool of samples from this probability distribution. Each sample is a parse, and samples with high energy will appear more commonly. We then search this pool of samples for a parse where the legs and arms do not overlap, a relatively easy test.

The process of drawing a sample is straightforward. Our tree-structured model yields a probability model $P(X_1, \ldots, X_n)$. We can use the reasoning of Section 20.1.3 to compute marginals (look at the α and β terms). Now compute the marginal $P(X_1)$, and draw a sample from that distribution to get, say, $X_1 = r$.

FIGURE 20.4: On the **left**, a tree-structured model of a person. Each segment is colored with the image color expected within this segment. The model attempts to find a configuration of these 11 body segments (nine limb segments, face, and hair) that (a) matches these colors and (b) is configured like a person. This can be done with dynamic programming, as described in the text. The other three frames show matches obtained using the method. *This figure was originally published as Figure 4 of "Efficient Matching of Pictorial Structures," by P. Felzenszwalb and D.P. Huttenlocher, Proc. IEEE CVPR 2000, © 2000, IEEE.*

We then draw a sample from $P(X_2|X_1 = r) = P(X_1 = r, X_2)/\sum_{X_2} P(X_1 = r, X_2)$, and so on.

20.2.2 Estimating the Appearance of Clothing

One crucial difficulty with the pictorial structure model, as we have described it, is that we need to know the appearance of the body segments. We could avoid this difficulty by changing the segment appearance models. Body segments are extended, and we expect some contrast at either side, so the segment appearance model could just require that there be strong edges on either side of the segment. It turns out that this model works poorly, because there tend to be numerous such segments in the image.

However, as Ramanan (2006) points out, this model can be used to start a

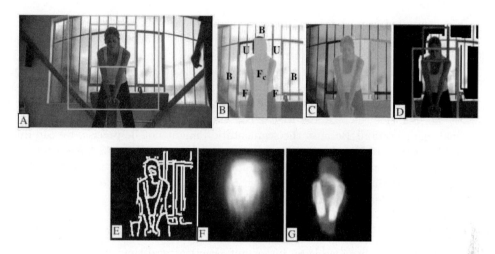

FIGURE 20.5: The human parser of Ramanan (2006) is a search of all spatial layouts in the image to find one that is consistent with the constraints we know on appearance. Ferrari *et al.* (2008) show that reducing the search space improves the results. First, one finds upper bodies, and builds a box around those detections using constraints on the body size (**A**). Outside this box is background, and some pixels inside this box are, too. In **B**, body constraints mean that pixels labeled F_c and F are very likely foreground, U are unknown, and B are very likely background. One then builds color models for foreground and background using this information, then uses an interactive segmenter to segment, requiring that F_c pixels be foreground, to get **C**. The result is a much reduced search domain for the human parser, which starts using an edge map **D**, to get an initial parse **E**, and, after iterating, produces **F**. *This figure was originally published as Figure 2 of "Progressive search space reduction for human pose estimation," by V. Ferrari, M. Marín-Jiménez, and A. Zisserman, Proc. IEEE CVPR 2008, © IEEE 2003.*

process that first estimates appearance, then parses, then re-estimates appearance, and so on. We start by assuming that segments have edges on their boundaries. We use this model to generate multiple estimates of configuration, using the procedure for sampling in Section 20.2.1. In turn, we can use these estimates to build a map of the posterior probability a pixel is, for example, a head pixel, by rendering the head segment for each of the sampled estimates of configuration and then summing the images. In turn, this means we have a set of weighted head/non-head pixels, which can be used to build a discriminative appearance model for the head. From this and other such discriminative appearance models, we can re-estimate the configuration (and then re-estimate appearance, and so on). The technical details are beyond the scope of this chapter, but the procedure can produce simultaneous estimates of parses and appearance models for complex images.

If the person covers a relatively small percentage of the image pixels, then this strategy will work poorly because there is a strong chance the initial estimate of configuration might be completely wrong, and then re-estimation is unlikely to help. Ferrari *et al.* (2008) show improved parses obtained by pruning the search domain using appearance information. They first detect the figure's upper body, and then use that information to derive a set of bounds. Everything outside a large box computed from the torso cannot be on the body (because the arms have fixed length, and so on). Similarly, a smaller box can be guaranteed to line on the body, because we have found the upper body. We can now use an interactive segmentation method (Section 20.2.1) to segment an estimate of the person from the background. The background color model can be estimated from pixels outside the box, and some inside the box; the foreground color model can be estimated from some of the pixels inside the box; and we can constrain some pixels to be foreground in the final segmentation. Because the segmentation might not be precise, we can dilate it (Algorithm 16.3) to get a somewhat larger domain. We now have a relatively small search domain and a very rough initial estimate of configuration to start the iterative re-estimation process. Further constraints are available if we are working with a motion sequence; these are explored in Section 20.3.

20.3 TRACKING PEOPLE

Tracking people in video is an important practical problem. If we could tell how people behave inside and outside buildings, it might be possible to design more effective buildings. If we could reliably report the location of arms, legs, torso, and head in video sequences, we could build much-improved game interfaces and surveillance systems.

20.3.1 Why Human Tracking Is Hard

Any tracking system, for any target, must balance two kinds of evidence to produce tracks. The first kind is direct measurements of state. In the extreme case, if we can detect perfectly, building tracking systems isn't that demanding. The second kind is predictable dynamics, which allows a system to pool evidence over multiple frames and produce good state estimates even when measurements are poor.

Tracking people is difficult, because detecting people is difficult and because human motion can be quite unpredictable. Detection is hard because many effects cause people to look different from window to window. There is a range of body shapes and sizes. Changes in body configuration and in viewpoint can produce dramatic changes in appearance. The appearance of clothing also can vary widely. At time of writing, no published method can find clothed people wearing unknown clothing in arbitrary configurations in complex scenes reliably (but see Section 17.1.2). The main cues to help overcome these difficulties are the fairly strong constraints on the layout of the body, and the relatively restricted appearance of a range of human body parts and configurations.

Motion cues present more subtle difficulties. If the people we are observing are engaged in known activities, their motions might be quite predictable. But the body can accelerate very quickly—think of the degree of motion blur in sports videos as an example—and the body parts that can engage in the most unpredictable motions tend also to be the ones that are hardest to detect. Forearms turn out to be difficult to track (small and fast moving), hands are even harder, and we are not aware of finger trackers that behave reliably for the full range of (potentially very fast-changing) finger motions.

Even so, motion is almost certainly a useful cue for detecting people or segments. Motion also can contribute by predicting plausible locations for detections in the next frame, through some form of filtering procedure. Although body configurations change quickly from frame to frame, appearance changes very slowly, particularly if one is careful about illumination. This is because people tend not to change clothes from frame to frame. Generally, building a good person tracker seems to involve paying close attention to image appearance and data association, rather than to dynamical models or probabilistic inference. As a result, recent methods strongly emphasize various tracking by detection ideas, and the main kinds of distinction between methods are the same as those for detection.

There is a rich range of options for representing the body when we track, and a range of levels of detail are useful. Representing a person as a single point is sometimes useful; for example, such representations are enough to tell where and when people gather in a public space, or during a fire drill. Alternatives include: representing the head and torso; representing the head, torso, and arms; representing head, torso, arms, and legs; and so on, down to the fingers. Tracking becomes increasingly difficult as the number of degrees of freedom goes up, and we are not aware of any successful attempts to track the body from torso to fingers (they are a lot smaller than torsos, which introduces other problems). Most procedures for tracking single point representations use the methods of Chapter 11 directly, typically combining background subtraction with some form of blob appearance tracker.

We focus on trackers that try to represent the body with fairly detailed kinematic models, because such trackers use procedures specialized for tracking people. The state of the body could be represented in 3D or in 2D. If there are many cameras, a 3D state representation is natural, and multicamera tracking of people against constrained backgrounds now works rather well (see the notes). The flavor of this subject is more like reconstruction than like detection or recognition, and it doesn't fit very well into general pattern of single camera tracking. In many important cases—for example, an interface to a computer game—there will be only one camera. If we require a representation of the body in three dimensions, then we could use a 3D representation of state, perhaps joint locations in 3D, or a set of body segments in 3D modeled as surfaces. Alternatively, we could track the body using a 2D state representation, and then "lift" it to produce a 3D track. Relations between the 2D figure and the 3D track are complicated and might be ambiguous. The heart of the question is the number of possible 3D configurations that could explain a single image, and this depends quite a lot on what we observe in the image.

Generally, we favor tracking using a 2D representation then lifting the track to 3D, and we will discuss only this strategy in any detail. This is mainly a question of clarity. Methods for tracking using 3D state representations must deal with data association and with lifting ambiguity simultaneously, and this leads to complexity. In contrast, tracking in 2D is a data association problem alone, and lifting the track is a problem of ambiguity alone. Another advantage to working in 2D first, then lifting, is that the lifting process can use image evidence on longer timescales without having any significant effect on the complexity of the tracking algorithm. We will return to this argument in Section 20.4.

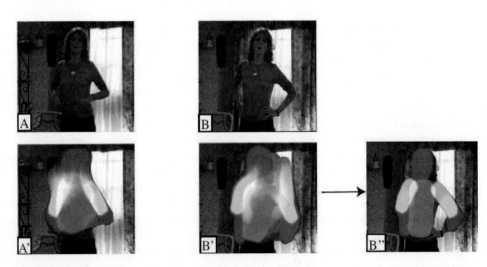

FIGURE 20.6: Human body segments do not change appearance much over time, so using multiple frames can yield a better appearance model and so a better parse. **A** shows a frame, and **A'** shows its parse, derived by the method of Ferrari *et al.* (2008), described in Section 20.2.2 and Figure 20.5. In this case, the parse has relatively low entropy, and we have a fairly accurate model of where everything is. The frame in **B** is more difficult, and a single frame method produces the parse of **B'**, which has relatively high entropy. By requiring that appearance be coherent over time, and that segments not move much from frame to frame, we can obtain the tighter parse of **B"**. *This figure was originally published as Figure 6 of "Progressive search space reduction for human pose estimation," by V. Ferrari, M. Marín-Jiménez, and A. Zisserman, Proc. IEEE CVPR 2008,* © *IEEE 2003.*

20.3.2   Kinematic Tracking by Appearance

In Section 20.3.2, we described methods to identify an appearance model for a person from a single image. Generally, the strategy was to find a small but plausible spatial domain in the image, then iterate configuration estimation and appearance estimation in that domain. In a motion sequence, we can build a much better appearance model by exploiting the fact that body segment appearance doesn't change over time. Furthermore, the sampling time of the video is relatively fast compared to body movement, which means we know roughly which search domain in the $n+1$th frame corresponds to which in the nth frame. This means that we can strengthen the appearance model by using multiple frames to estimate appearance. We can improve configuration estimates both by using the improved appearance model, and by exploiting the fact that segments move relatively slowly. Ferarri *et al.* show significant improvements in practice for upper body models estimated using these two constraints (Figure 20.6).

There is an alternative method to obtain an appearance model. It turns out that people adopt a lateral walking configuration rather often, meaning that if we have a long enough sequence (minutes are usually enough), we will detect this configuration somewhere. Once we have detected it, we can read off an appearance model because we know where the arms, legs, torso, and head are. The pictorial structure model can detect lateral walking configurations without knowing the color or texture of body segments. We set up ϕ to score whether there are image edges close to the edges of the segment rectangles, and use strong angular constraints in ψ to detect only the lateral walking configuration. The resulting detector can be tuned to have a very low false positive rate, though it will then have a low detect rate, too. Now we run this lateral walking detector over every frame in the sequence. Because the detector has a low false positive rate, we know when it responds that we have found a real person; and because we have localized the torso, arms, legs, and head, we know what these segments look like.

We can now build a discriminative appearance model for arms, legs, etc., and use this in a new pictorial structure model to detect each instance of the person. We take example pixels from each detected segment and from its background, and use, say, logistic regression to build a classifier that gives a one at segment pixels and a zero otherwise. Applying these to the images yields a set of segment maps, and the ϕ for each segment scores how many ones appear inside the image rectangle on the relevant segment map. We can now pass over the video again, using a pictorial structure with weak constraints to detect instances of this person.

20.3.3 Kinematic Human Tracking Using Templates

Some human motions—walking, jumping, dancing—are highly repetitive, and the relatively free structure of a fully deformable model is not necessary to track them. If we are confident that we will be dealing with such motions, then we could benefit by using more restrictive models of spatial layout. For example, if we are tracking only walking people in lateral views, then there are relatively few configurations that we will see, and so our estimate of layout should be better. There is another advantage to doing this: we can identify body configurations that are wholly out of line with what we expect, and report unusual behavior.

Toyama and Blake (2002) encode image likelihoods using a mixture built out of templates, which they call *exemplars* (see also Toyama and Blake (2001)). Assume we have a single template, which could be a curve, or an edge map, or some such. These templates may be subject to the action of some (perhaps local) group, for example, translations, rotations, scale, or deformations. We model the likelihood of an image patch given a template and its deformation with an exponential distribution on distance between the image patch and the deformed template (one could regard this as a simplified maximum entropy model; we are not aware of successful attempts to add complexity at this point). The normalizing constant is estimated with Laplace's method. Multiple templates can be used to encode the important possible appearances of the foreground object. State is now (a) the template and (b) the deformation parameters, and the likelihood can be evaluated conditioned on state as above.

We can think of this method as a collection of template matchers linked over time with a dynamical model (Figure 20.8). The templates, and the dynamical model, are learned from training sequences. Because we are modeling the foreground, the training sequences can be chosen so that their background is simple, so that responses from (say) edge, curve, and related detectors all originate on the moving person. Choosing templates now becomes a matter of clustering. Once

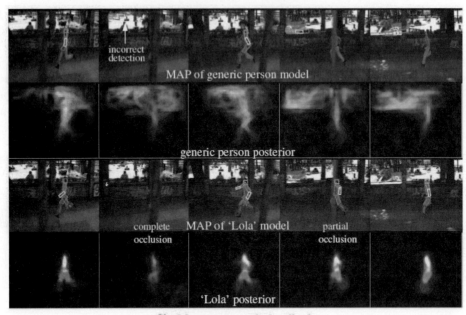

% of frames correctly localized			
Model	Torso	Arm	Leg
Generic	31.4	13.0	22.2
'Lola'	98.1	94.3	100

FIGURE 20.7:   Ramanan (2005) shows that tracking people is easier with an instance-specific model as opposed to a generic model. The **top two rows** show detections of a pictorial structure where parts are modeled with edge templates. The figure shows both the MAP pose—as boxes—and a visualization of the entire posterior obtained by overlaying translucent, lightly colored samples (so major peaks in the posterior give strong coloring). Note that the generic edge model is confused by the texture in the background, as evident by the bumpy posterior map. The **bottom two rows** show results using a model specialized to the subject of the sequence, using methods described above (part appearances are learned from a stylized detection). This model does a much better job of data association; it eliminates most of the background pixels. The table quantifies this phenomenon by recording the percentage of frames where limbs are accurately localized. Clearly, the specialized model does a much better job. *Figure reprinted from D. Ramanan's UC Berkeley PhD thesis, "Tracking People and Recognizing their Activities," 2005,* © *2005 D. Ramanan.*

templates have been chosen, a dynamical model is estimated by counting.

What makes the resulting method attractive is that it relies on *foreground enhancement*—the template groups together image components that, taken together, imply a person is present. The main difficulty with the method is that many templates might be needed to cover all views of a moving person. Furthermore, inferring state might be quite difficult.

FIGURE 20.8: Toyama and Blake (2001) show that human motion can be tracked by matching templates then linking the templates over time. The templates encode possible body configuration, and are allowed to deform to account for camera variations. This representation has the advantage that a template can pool otherwise possibly unreliable edge evidence; tracking uses a particle filter (Section 11.5). The figure shows frames from two motion sequences, with the best matching template superimposed (ignore the horizontal line structure in the frames; this is just interlacing effects in the video). On the **left** of the bar, frames from a test sequence showing a person who also appears in the training sequences (i.e., it's the same actor, but not the same frames). Templates generalize across individuals well; the **right** shows frames from a test sequence featuring an actor who does not appear in the training sequences. *This figure was originally published as Figures 1 and 4 of "Probabilistic Tracking in a Metric Space," by K. Toyama and A. Blake, Proc. IEEE ICCV 2001, © IEEE, 2001.*

20.4 3D FROM 2D: LIFTING

Surprisingly, the 2D configuration of a person in an image allows reconstructing that person's 3D configuration, from some straightforward geometric reasoning. There are two kinds of reconstruction. An *absolute reconstruction* reconstructs the configuration of the body with respect to a global world coordinate system. A *relative reconstruction* yields the configuration of body segments with respect to some *root coordinate system*. The root coordinate system is carried with the body, with its origin typically in the torso.

Absolute reconstruction is difficult, even with motion information, because each separate frame is missing a translation in depth, and motion information is not usually enough to recover this. Absolute reconstruction with a moving camera is particularly tricky, because one would need good camera egomotion estimates to produce such a reconstruction (we are not aware of any such reconstructions in the literature at the time of writing). Relative reconstruction is enough for most purposes. For example, absolute reconstruction doesn't seem to be necessary to label activities.

Reconstructions appear to be ambiguous, but might not be. There are methods for avoiding ambiguity that exploit appearance details (Section 20.4.2). Furthermore, there may be disambiguating information in motion (Section 20.4.3).

20.4.1 Reconstruction in an Orthographic View

People in pictures typically are far from the camera compared to the range of depths they span (the body is quite flat), and so a scaled orthographic camera model is usually appropriate. One case where it fails is a person pointing toward

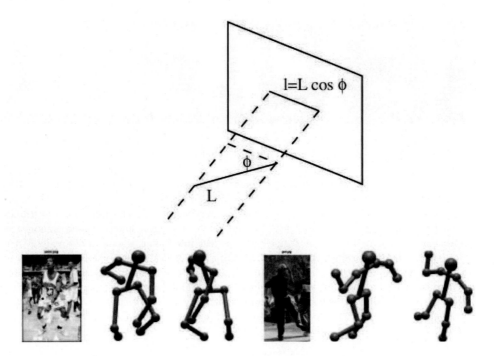

FIGURE 20.9:   An orthographic view of a segment of known length L will have length $sL \cos \phi$, where ϕ is the angle of inclination of the segment to the camera and s is the camera scale linking meters to pixels (which is one in the figure above). In turn, this means that if we know the length of the body segment and can guess the camera scale, we can estimate $\cos \phi$ and so know the angle of inclination to the frame up to a twofold ambiguity. This method is effective; **below** we show two 3D reconstructions obtained by Taylor (2000), for single orthographic views of human figures. The image appears **left**, with joint vertices on the body identified by hand (the user also identifies which vertex on each segment is closer to the camera). **Center** shows a rendered reconstruction in the viewing camera, and **right** shows a rendering from a different view direction. *This figure was originally published as Figures 1 and 4 of "Reconstruction of articulated objects from point correspondences in a single uncalibrated image," by C.J. Taylor, Proc. IEEE CVPR, 2000 © 2000 IEEE.*

the camera; if the hand is quite close, compared with the length of the arm there may be distinct perspective effects over the hand and arm and in extreme cases the hand can occlude much of the body.

Regard each body segment as a cylinder and assume we know its length. If we know the camera scale, and can mark each end of the body segment, then we know the cosine of the angle between the image plane and the axis of the segment, which means we have the segment in 3D up to a twofold ambiguity and translation in depth (Figure 20.9 gives examples). We can reconstruct each separate segment and obtain an ambiguity of translation in depth (which is important and often forgotten) and a two fold ambiguity at each segment. We can now reconstruct the body by obtaining a reconstruction for each segment, and joining them up. Each segment has a single missing degree of freedom (depth), but the segments must join up, meaning that we have a discrete set of ambiguities. Depending on circumstances, one might work with from 9 to 11 body segments (the head is often omitted; the torso can reasonably be modeled with several segments), yielding from 512 to 2,048 possible reconstructions. These ambiguities persist for perspective images; examples appear in Figure 20.10.

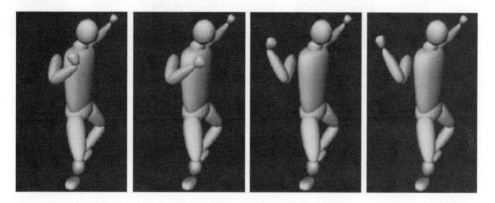

FIGURE 20.10:   Ambiguous reconstructions of a 3D figure, all consistent with a single view, from Sminchisescu and Triggs (2003). The ambiguities are most easily visualized by an argument about scaled orthographic cameras, given in the text, but persist for perspective views as these authors show. Note that the cocked wrist in the leftmost figure violates kinematic constraints; no person with an undamaged wrist can take this configuration. *This figure was originally published as Figure 2 of "Kinematic jump processes for monocular 3D human tracking," by C. Sminchisescu and W. Triggs, Proc. IEEE CVPR, 2003 © 2003 IEEE.*

In this very simple model of the body, 3D reconstruction from a single image is ambiguous. However, the model oversimplifies in some important ways, and the true extent of ambiguity in this case is quite uncertain. One important oversimplification is that we assume that all 3D configurations are available. In practice, there are many constraints on the available joint rotations (for example, your elbow will move through about 70°), so some of the ambiguous configurations might not be consistent with the kinematics of the body. Unfortunately, there is clear evidence that there are multiple kinematically acceptable reconstructions consistent with a single image (Figure 20.10). It is not known whether there are multiple acceptable reconstructions associated with most images, or with only a few images.

20.4.2   Exploiting Appearance for Unambiguous Reconstructions

Mori and Malik (2005) deal with discrete ambiguities by matching (see also Mori *et al.* (2002)). They have a set of example images with joint positions marked. The outline of the body in each example is sampled, and each sample point is encoded with a *shape context* (an encoding that represents local image structure at high resolution and longer scale image structure at a lower resolution). Keypoints are marked in the examples by hand, and this marking includes a representation of which end of the body segment is closer to the camera. The outline of the body is identified in a test image (Mori and Malik use an edge detector; a cluttered back-

    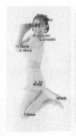 

FIGURE 20.11: Mori *et al.* (2002) deal with discrete ambiguities by matching test image outlines to exemplars, which have keypoints marked. The keypoint markup includes which end of the segment is closer to the view. The images on the **left** show example test images, with keypoints established by the matching strategy superimposed. The resulting reconstruction appears on the **right**. See also Mori and Malik (2005). *This figure was originally published as Figures 6 and 7 of "Estimating Human Body Configurations using Shape Context Matching," by G. Mori and J. Malik, IEEE Workshop on Models versus Exemplars in Computer Vision 2001 © IEEE, 2001.*

ground might present issues here), and sample points on the outline are matched to sample points in examples. A global matching procedure then identifies appropriate exemplars for each body segment and an appropriate 2D configuration. The body is represented as a set of segments, allowing (a) kinematic deformations in 2D and (b) different body segments in the test image to be matched to segments in different training images. The best matching example keypoint can be extracted from the matching procedure, and an estimate of the position of that keypoint in the test image is obtained from a least-squares fit transformation that aligns a number of sample points around that keypoint. The result is a markup of the test image with labeled joint positions and with which end of the segment is closest to the camera. A 3D reconstruction follows, as above (Figure 20.11 gives some examples).

An alternative is to regress the joint angles against an image of the body. The simplest regression method is to match the input to its nearest neighbor in a large training set then output the value associated with that nearest neighbor. Shakhnarovich *et al.* (2003) built a data set of 3D configurations and rendered frames, obtained using POSER (a program that renders human figures, from Creative Labs). They show error rates on held out data for a variety of regression methods applied to the pool of neighbors obtained using parameter-sensitive hashing. Generally, performance improves with more neighbors, with using a linear locally weighted regression (where one builds a linear regression model out of a pool of nearest neighbors), and when the method is robust. The best is a robust, linear, locally weighted regression. Their method produces estimates of joint angles with root mean square errors of approximately $20°$ for a 13 degree of freedom upper body model; a version of this approach can produce full 3D shape estimates (Grauman *et al.* 2004).

FIGURE 20.12: The 3D configuration of the body can be reconstructed using a form of nonparametric regression. Shakhnarovich *et al.* (2003) match the input frame (**top row**) to a large selection of labeled frames. The nearest neighbors are shown in the **center row**; these give a fair reconstruction in most cases, but can be improved by finding multiple nearest neighbors and building a robust linear regression (**bottom row**). *This figure was originally published as Figure 5 of "Fast Pose Estimation with Parameter-Sensitive Hashing," by G. Shakhnarovich, P. Viola, and T. Darrell, Proc. CVPR 2003, 2003.* © *IEEE, 2003.*

20.4.3 Exploiting Motion for Unambiguous Reconstructions

In many applications there is a video sequence of a moving person. In such cases, it does not make sense to infer the 3D structure for each frame. It is a reliable rule of thumb from the animation community that most body motions are quite slow compared to reasonable video frame rates. Evidence includes, for example, the relative ease with which motion capture sequences can be compressed with minimal loss (Arikan 2006). This means that reconstructed body configurations for each frame will not be independent, so that future (or past) frames may disambiguate the current reconstruction.

Howe (2004) incorporates dynamical information into the distance cost, by matching entire 3D motion paths to 2D image tracks. For each frame of a motion sequence, we render every motion capture frame in our collection using a discretized grid containing every possible camera and every possible root coordinate system. Now we must construct a sequence of 3D motion reconstructions that (a) joins up well and (b) looks like the tracked frames. This is an optimization problem. We build a transition cost for going from each triple of (motion capture frame, camera, root coordinate system) to every other such triple. This cost should penalize excessively large body segment and camera velocities. We compute a match cost comparing the rendered frame with the tracked frame. Write F_i for the ith frame in tracked sequence, S for a reconstruction of that sequence, and (L_i, C_i, R_i) for the reconstruction frame and camera corresponding to F_i. The cost function for a reconstruction is then

$$\text{cost}(S) = \sum_{i \in S} \left[\begin{array}{c} \text{transition cost}((L_i, C_i, R_i) \rightarrow (L_{i+1}, C_{i+1}, R_{i+1})) \\ + \text{match cost}((L_i, C_i, R_i) \rightarrow F_i) \end{array} \right],$$

and in principle we can minimize this cost with dynamic programming. In practice, this would be very difficult to do, because there are a very large number of triples (L_i, C_i, R_i), but some of this complexity is quite easily reduced. For example, the number of cameras that could apply is quite small, and we can estimate the image plane location of the root with elementary methods from the track. If the motion capture data set is very large, we may be able to prune the frames, or avoid searching any triple where the match cost exceeds a threshold (Howe 2004).

We can extend the method described to take accelerations and higher-order dynamics into account by matching short *snippets* (short runs of frames centered about a given frame) of motion capture to short snippets of video. To do this, we need to assume that the root moves relatively slowly with respect to the camera, so that using a single camera and root configuration for each snippet is acceptable.

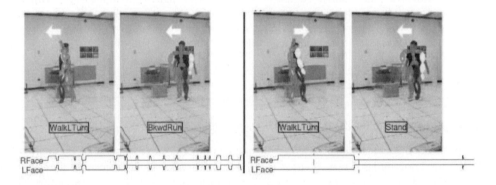

FIGURE 20.13:   **Left frames** are taken from a walking sequence, matched to motion capture data ((Ramanan and Forsyth 2003)). Matches are independent from frame to frame. Note that the lateral view of the body (**far left**) is ambiguous, and can be reconstructed inaccurately. This ambiguity does not persist, because the camera cannot move freely from frame to frame. **Right frames** show reconstructions obtained using dynamic programming to enforce a model of camera cost. The correct reconstruction usually is available, because the person does not stay in an ambiguous configuration. The frames are taken from a time sequence, and the graphs **below** show an automatically computed annotation sequence—facing left versus facing right—as a function of time. Note that the case on the **left** shows an essentially random choice of direction when the ambiguity is present (the person appears to flip from facing left to facing right regularly). This is because the free rotation of the camera means the ambiguity appears on a per-frame basis. For the case on the **right**, the smoothing created by charging for fast camera rotations means that the labels seldom change (and are, in fact, correct). *Figure reprinted from D. Ramanan's UC Berkeley PhD thesis, "Tracking People and Recognizing their Activities," 2005,* © *2005 D. Ramanan.*

Some ambiguities seem to have a long-term character. For example, it remains very difficult to tell whether the left leg or the right leg is leading in a lateral view of a walking figure. This is because very little in the image changes between these cases; there is little contrast between the trouser legs, so that it is hard to tell whether the left thigh occludes the right, or vice versa. Ambiguities like these might be resolvable by propagating disambiguating evidence over long time scales. For example, if one does not have a face detector, then it can be very difficult to tell which way a person is facing in a lateral standing view. However, if the person walks off (and if one assumes that the camera does not move fast), they reveal the direction in which they are facing, and this information can be propagated.

20.5 ACTIVITY RECOGNITION

Activity recognition methods try to label single images or video with a representation of the activity depicted. This representation is usually, but not always, a name. Activity recognition methods can use motion capture data (measurements of 3D body configuration), as well as visual data. Motion capture data is usually collected for purposes of human animation, and we discuss some relevant points from the animation literature in Section 20.5.1. A natural method to recognize activity is to parse the body and then match the parse to labeled data (Section 20.5.2). Alternatively, one can build appearance features and then classify (Section 20.5.3). An important difficulty suggested by the animation literature is that human actions seem to compose; this means that any label vocabulary might be too small to use, because motions can be cut up and rearranged. Some methods model this process explicitly (Section 20.5.4).

20.5.1 Background: Human Motion Data

Motion capture refers to special arrangements made to measure the configuration of a human body with (relatively) non-invasive processes. More recent systems involve optical markers. One can use either *passive markers* (for example, make people wear tight-fitting black clothing with small white spots on them) or *active markers* (for example, flashing infrared lights attached to the body). A collection of cameras views some open space within which people wearing markers move around. The 3D configuration of the markers is reconstructed for each individual; this is then cleaned up (to remove bad matches, etc.; see below) and mapped to an appropriate *skeleton*—a kinematic tree of joints of known properties and modeled as points separated by segments of fixed, known lengths, that *approximates* the kinematics of the human body. The configuration of the skeleton can be specified either in terms of its *joint angles*, or in terms of the position in 3D of the segment endpoints (*joint positions*). Data represented using one skeleton cannot necessarily be transferred to a different skeleton reliably. Motion capture is a complex and sophisticated technology; typical modern motion capture setups require a substantial quantity of skilled input to produce data. **Reviews** of available techniques in motion capture appear in, for example Bodenheimer *et al.* (1997); Gleicher (2000); Liverman (2004); Menache (1999); Moeslund (1999); or Silaghi *et al.* (1998).

An important practical problem is *footskate*, where the feet of a rendered motion appear to slide on the ground plane. In the vast majority of actual motions, the feet of the actor stay fixed when they are in contact with the floor (there are exceptions such as skating or various sliding movements). This property is quite

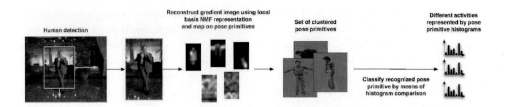

FIGURE 20.14: Many activities involve quite characteristic body poses. Thurau and Hlavac (2008) show that a simple and effective representation of composite activities can be built by finding these distinctive poses, then reporting a histogram. To provide some temporal information, the histogram contains n-grams of poses (i.e., sequences of n poses), rather than single poses. This representation performs well on established activity classification datasets, but also produces sensible reports when faced with novel activities. *This figure was originally published as Figure 4 of "Action Recognition from a Distributed Representation of Pose and Appearance," by C. Thurau and V. Hlavac Proc. IEEE CVPR 2008, © IEEE, 2008.*

| phoning | running | walking | ridinghorse |

FIGURE 20.15: In many activities, some parts of the body have highly characteristic appearance. Maji *et al.* (2011) show that one can classify activities using a vocabulary of action specific poselets, local patches that (a) look like body parts and (b) convey discriminative information about the action. This figure shows some such poselets; notice, for example, how the head takes a characteristic tilt when one is phoning; how the legs take a characteristic scissor shape when one is walking; and how riding a horse requires a distinctive configuration of torso and arms. *This figure was originally published as Figure 10 of "Action Recognition from a Distributed Representation of Pose and Appearance," by S. Maji, L. Bourdev, and J. Malik, Proc. CVPR 2011, © IEEE, 2011.*

sensitive to measurement problems, which tend to result in reconstructions where some point quite close to, but not on, the bottom of the foot is stationary with respect to the ground. The result is that the reconstructed foot appears to slide on the ground (and sometimes penetrates it). The effect can be both noticeable and offensive visually.

Although human motion is complex, it does seem to be a composite of smaller pieces of motion. For example, when people walk, they repeat roughly the same motion again and again. Many everyday motions are stereotyped. Think of reaching for a kitchen knife, chopping onions, climbing stairs, dressing, and so on. There is a fair body of practical evidence that motions are composites (or at least, that it is useful to pretend that they are). The simplest mechanism is *temporal composition*, where motions are strung together in time to produce a new, more complex motion. For example, a subject might walk into a room, halt, look around, walk to a chair,

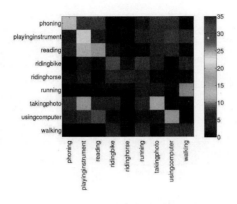 

FIGURE 20.16: Activities can be classified using a vector of poselet activations, which gives the strength of support for the presence of each poselet (those of Figure 20.15 and others like them). On the **left**, a class-confusion matrix for this process applied to a set of nine activities from the Pascal activity challenge; on the **right**, misclassified examples from Maji *et al.* (2011). *This figure was originally published as Figures 12 and 13 of "Action Recognition from a Distributed Representation of Pose and Appearance," by S. Maji, L. Bourdev, and J. Malik, Proc. IEEE CVPR 2011, © IEEE, 2011.*

and then sit down.

The use of motion capture data by, for example, the computer game industry reflects this belief. Typically, motions are created for a game by writing and capturing a script of motions, using a set of "complete" motions that start and end at one of a few *rest positions*. The motions can be thought of as building blocks that can be joined if one ends and the next starts at the same rest position. The choice of which block is joined to the end of the last block can be made by a game engine. Motions captured for a particular title are then usually discarded, as reuse presents both economic and legal difficulties.

These blocks of motion can be thought of as *motion primitives*. There would be important advantages to knowing a large dictionary of motion primitives that can encode many motions well. Such a dictionary could be used to compress motion data. It could be used to produce long time-scale statistics about how motions are constructed, by representing motions with the dictionary and then looking for important co-occurrences. For example, we know that people can walk backward and sometimes do; but if you want to move to a point a long way behind you, you will turn around and walk forwards toward the point. As another example, it is quite uncommon to reach in a direction you haven't looked in recently. Long time-scale activities can be seen as a sequence of motion primitives assembled according to a model. Building a dictionary of motion primitives seems to require iterative re-estimation. One uses an existing dictionary (equivalently, a set of clustered motions) to segment a set of motion sequences, and then uses that segmentation to re-estimate the dictionary. Estimating motion primitives well remains difficult.

A practical representation that is currently more successful involves a more fluid encoding of possible transitions between motions, usually known as a *motion*

(a) cricket defensive shot   (b) cricket defensive shot   (c) tennis forehand   (d) tennis serve

FIGURE 20.17: The objects that occur near people can strongly suggest their pose, and the activities they are engaged in; similarly, pose information suggests the activity and what objects might be nearby; and activity information suggests pose and nearby objects, too. Yao and Li (2010) show that estimating all three jointly, using a graphical model, produces better results for each task. For each activity shown in this figure, there are four results. The **upper left** shows object detection (for a cricket bat and tennis racket respectively) using their joint method, and the **upper right** shows a parse of the body using their joint method. The **lower left** shows detections using a scanning window method, and the **lower right** shows a parse recovered with a state-of-the-art method. Notice the improvements resulting from joint estimation. *This figure was originally published as Figure 9 of "Modeling Mutual Context of Object and Human Pose in Human-Object Interaction Activities," by B. Yao and L. Fei-Fei, Proc. IEEE CVPR 2010, © IEEE, 2010.*

graph. The details vary from author to author, but the simplest model regards every frame of motion as a node and inserts a directed edge from a frame to any frame that could succeed it. *Computed edges* identify transitions that could have been observed, but are not in the current dataset. Computed edges can be inserted by matching; if two frames are sufficiently similar, their futures (or pasts) could be interchanged. Frames can be matched using point locations and velocities. Once the graph is built, there are numerous methods for searching it to produce a motion that meets a demand, typically specified by a set of constraints. Experience has shown that any path in a motion graph that does not involve too many computed edges does look very much like a human motion. For our purposes, what is important about motion graphs is that they work fairly well. This is strong evidence that human motions compose over time.

Motions can be constructed by using different building blocks for different parts of the body. For example, it is possible to walk while scratching your head with one hand, and the arm motion involved in scratching your head with your left hand is basically a reflected version of the arm motion involved in scratching your head with your right hand. We refer to this idea as *composition across the body.* Such composite motions could be produced from motion capture data by cutting a limb off one sequence and attaching it to another sequence. Many such transplants are successful, but some apparently innocuous transplants generate motions that are extremely bad (Ikemoto and Forsyth 2004). It is difficult to be precise about the source of difficulty, but at least one kind of problem appears to result from

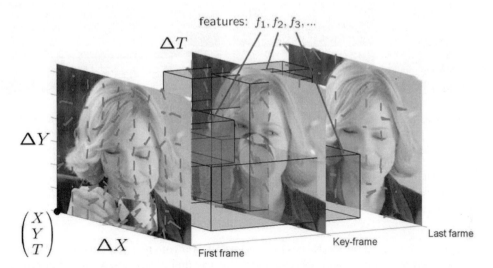

FIGURE 20.18: The feature constructions described in Chapters 5 and 16 can be extended to produce features for motion sequences. There are two steps: first, we consider optic flow vectors (as in Section 10.6.1) as well as gradient vectors; second, we can build histograms that are essentially spatial (the set of buckets covering the X and Y directions here), or essentially temporal (the buckets extending in the T directions here). *This figure was originally published as Figure 3 of "Retrieving Actions in Movies," Y. Laptev and P. Perez, Proc. IEEE ICCV 2007, © IEEE, 2007.*

passive reactions. For example, assume the actor punches his left arm in the air very hard; then there is typically a small transient wiggle in the right arm. If one transplants the right arm to another sequence where there is no such punch, the resulting sequence often looks very bad, with the right arm apparently the culprit. One might speculate that humans can identify movements that both don't look as though they have been commanded by a normal central nervous system and can't be explained as a passive phenomenon.

20.5.2   Body Configuration and Activity Recognition

It seems natural to recover the body from frames of video, and then use this information to classify activities. There are two important difficulties. First, parsing and tracking are genuinely difficult problems, as we have seen, and noise incurred in parsing might overwhelm any signal. Second, it isn't clear what features we would compute.

One possible feature emphasizes some poses that might appear in a sequence. There is now a lot of direct (as well as merely suggestive) evidence that there are highly distinctive poses associated with most of the activities in current activity recognition datasets. This suggests finding these poses, and then representing the sequence with a summary of the distinctive poses that are there. For example, one might match poses to a vocabulary of distinctive poses, or vector quantize the poses, then build a histogram. A plain histogram omits any sequencing information,

FIGURE 20.19: Laptev and Perez (2007) show that complex activities can be detected with a classifier applied to spatio-temporal features constructed as in Figure 20.18. Here we show the top 10 responses for drinking, ranked by the strength of their response. The lighter boxes are true positives, and the darker boxes are false positives. The detector is relatively accurate for such a complex activity. *This figure was originally published as Figure 8 of "Retrieving Actions in Movies," Y. Laptev and P. Perez, Proc. IEEE ICCV 2007, © IEEE, 2007.*

and this tends to be worth having because it is a rough representation of motion. An n-gram of poses is a sequence of n vector quantized poses, and Thurau and Hlavac (2008) obtain good results by building a histogram of these n-grams, and then classifying (Figure 20.14).

An alternative to matching the whole pose is to find body components, and then reason about the pool of available parts; this is a version of the poselet method (Section 18.4.2). Maji *et al.* (2011) build poselets that are individually discriminative, using a variant of the poselet clustering procedure of Bourdev and Malik (2009) sketched in that section (Figure 20.15). Now, rather than trying to link up the poselets or localize the individual, they build a feature that reports the activation of each of these poselets. This feature is then used to classify, and is effective (Figure 20.16). We do not need to pass from the poselets to a parse, because we are unlikely to find a pool of poselets that (a) agree on an activity and (b) are close together but are not, in fact, joined up.

There is a rich and complex relationship between activity, body configuration, and nearby objects. Knowing one or two of these three pieces of information strongly constrains the unknowns. Yao and Li (2010) build a model that links all three, then use this to estimate objects and configuration and activity. Coupling these three properties results in significantly improved estimates (Figure 20.17). At the time of writing, such methods had been applied only to static images, but we expect methods that work on motion sequences to appear soon.

20.5.3 Recognizing Human Activities with Appearance Features

We can find faces with classifiers because all faces look similar to each other, and largely different from reasonable backgrounds. For many activities, this general idea applies too. For example, consider drinking in a frontal view; we expect to see a face, a hand, and perhaps a mug in front of the face, and a set of motions around the mouth as the hand comes up to the face. This information should be characteristic, and it turns out that it is.

Feature construction methods mirror those described in Chapters 5 and 16, but with the added complexity of building features that represent motion. One

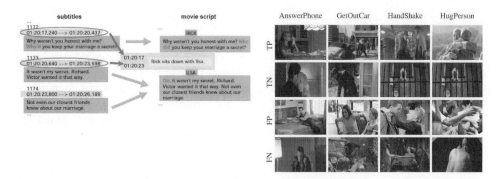

FIGURE 20.20: Laptev *et al.* (2008) learn discriminative models of actions by obtaining film scripts, where actions will be named, and then aligning subtitles in the film with the script (**left**) to get windows of film where an action is very likely to occur. With enough examples, they can learn a classifier despite the odd mislabeled example. This classifier can then be used to spot actions of considerable complexity. On the **right**, some examples of true positives (TP), true negatives (TN), false positives (FP), and false negatives (FN) for some complex actions detected with this method. *This figure was originally published as Figure 10 of "Learning realistic human actions from movies," by I. Laptev, M. Marszalek, C. Schmid, and B. Rozenfeld, Proc. IEEE CVPR 2008, © IEEE, 2008.*

natural procedure is to find spatio-temporal interest points, build spatio-temporal neighborhoods around them, in those regions compute a spatio-temporal analog of a SIFT feature, vector quantize these into spatio-temporal analogs of visual words, and then proceed as before with a histogram of those visual words. Another is to generalize the HOG feature to have spatio-temporal support. Neither procedure is complicated.

The main alternatives to deal with in generalization are as follows. We could either generalize image gradients to space-time gradients (i.e., look at $\frac{\partial \mathcal{I}}{\partial x}$, $\frac{\partial \mathcal{I}}{\partial y}$, and $\frac{\partial \mathcal{I}}{\partial t}$, yielding two image orientations), or work with optical flow vectors and image gradient vectors separately. Our histograms could be primarily spatial (i.e., the buckets extend across individual frames), primarily temporal (i.e., the buckets are in a small section of a frame, extending over time), or spatio-temporal (Figure 20.18). Laptev and Perez (2007) favor boosting methods, because each weak learner can use a relatively local histogram of a particular type, and the question of which type is most informative can be avoided.

The recipe of generalizing local neighborhood features and then classifying, has been extremely successful for surprisingly complex activities (Figures 20.19 and 20.20). Laptev *et al.* (2008) show that successful recognizers for complex activities can be trained by aligning film scripts to video (using subtitles, and speech), then cutting out blocks of video corresponding to an activity named in the script. Although not every training example found in this way is correct, enough are to produce good recognizers (Figure 20.20).

20.5.4   Recognizing Human Activities with Compositional Models

The evidence that human activities are composites seems very strong. If activities are truly composite, then the number of activity labels could be very large indeed. For example, if motions are composed across time and across the body, we could have an activity where both legs walk, left arm walks, and right arm reaches, followed by both legs walking and both arms reaching, followed by . . . and so on. It should be clear that very significant complexity could result. This creates disturbing problems for purely discriminative methods. We might not have a set of labels that is big enough to represent all this complexity. Some of the complexity may be irrelevant, in the sense that representing or observing it does not affect our task performance. For example, if you want to find only standing people, then there isn't any particular reason to represent all the things that people are inclined to do while they walk.

If we did have a sufficient set of labels, n-gram pose histograms (Section 20.5.2) look like a plausible representation. They have the attractive property of suppressing temporal details while preserving some information about sequencing. An alternative is to have an explicit model of how local labels might be composed. For example, Ikizler and Forsyth (2008) build local models of how body quarters move for each of a set of basic labels. These models are strung together to build a large HMM (Figure 20.21), where local models carry labels (for example, some states represent a leg walking). They then use this HMM to query a set of activity videos for activities that have never been seen, but are represented by a finite-state automaton linking arm and leg labels in time. It turns out to be easy to evaluate the posterior that a sequence was generated by a finite state automaton (FSA), and they rank sequences by this posterior.

Explicit representations of composition are attractive, because they allow us to have a label space that has very high complexity but is still relatively easy to represent. One difficulty is that current methods force one to parse the body, because it is essential to know where to cut when composing. As a result, they are susceptible to parsing problems. Parsing methods are getting a lot better at the time of writing, and we can expect this difficulty to be overcome in the not-too-distant future. Another difficulty is that it is hard to know what makes a good set of basic labels.

20.6   RESOURCES

Ferrari, Eichner, Marín-Jiménez, and Zisserman publish the Buffy stickman dataset at `http://www.robots.ox.ac.uk/~vgg/data/stickmen/index.html`.

Ferrari, Eichner, Marín-Jiménez, and Zisserman publish a dataset of labeled pose classes (i.e., hands on hips, standing), taken from the fifth season of *"Buffy the Vampire Slayer"*, at `http://www.robots.ox.ac.uk/~vgg/data/buffy_pose_classes/index.html`.

Patron-Perez, Marszalek, Zisserman, and Reid publish a dataset of 300 video clips showing 4 interactions (handshakes, and so on), at `http://www.robots.ox.ac.uk/~vgg/data/tv_human_interactions/index.html`.

Buehler, Everingham, and Zisserman publish a dataset of frames of human signers, labeled with segmentation masks for arm and hand, at `http://www.robots.`

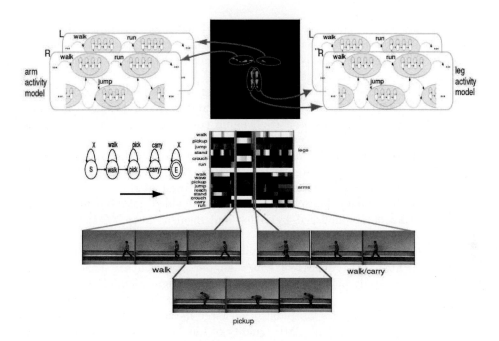

FIGURE 20.21: Ikizler and Forsyth (2007) build composite models of action by joining up short hidden Markov models that encode the behavior of arms (resp. legs) for particular activities (for example, walk; jump; run). Two states can be joined up if the 3D configurations and velocities are similar. The resulting model is very large, but does not require much parameter learning (**top**). A path through this model produces a sequence of labels for arms (resp. legs). A motion can now be represented either by the posterior weights of states in the HMM trellis (**bottom**); notice how this trellis suggests segmenting the sequence into three blocks. Alternatively, one could evaluate the posterior that the trellis represents a finite-state-automaton. This figure shows an FSA for walking, then picking up, then carrying. The representation allows for one FSA for the arms and another for the legs. *This figure was originally published as Figure 3 of "Searching Video for Complex Activities with Finite State Models," by N. Ikizler and D.A. Forsyth, Proc. IEEE CVPR 2007, © IEEE, 2007.*

ox.ac.uk/~vgg/data/sign_language/index.html.

Gorelick, Blank, Shechtman, Irani, and Basri publish a dataset of labeled activities, usually called the Weizmann dataset, at http://www.wisdom.weizmann.ac.il/~vision/SpaceTimeActions.html.

Ikizler-Cinbis publishes datasets for learning actions from the Web, for searching for complex composite actions, and for recognizing actions from still images at http://web.cs.hacettepe.edu.tr/~nazli/research.html.

Yuan, Liu, and Wu publish the MSR action dataset of 16 video sequences depicting 63 actions by 10 subjects at http://research.microsoft.com/en-us/um/people/zliu/actionrecorsrc/default.htm.

Laptev and Caputo publish a widely used dataset (the KTH dataset) of video of six types of actions in four different scenarios at http://www.nada.kth.se/cvap/actions/.

Shah and others publish several large datasets of human activity, including the UCF 50 dataset (50 action categories, using video taken from YouTube), an infrared dataset, a sports action dataset, and an aerial action dataset at `http://server.cs.ucf.edu/~vision/data.html`.

Niebles, Chen, and Fei-Fei publish a dataset of 16 classes of Olympic sports activity with 50 example videos per class at `http://vision.stanford.edu`.

The VIRAT dataset is a challenging collection of surveillance video data, available at `http://www.viratdata.org/`.

Laptev publishes several human action datasets, including data collected from movies aligned with their scripts (see Figures 20.19 and 20.20), at `http://www.irisa.fr/vista/Equipe/People/Laptev/download.html`.

The HumanEva dataset is a collection of video data synchronized to motion capture data, published by Black and Sigal at `http://vision.cs.brown.edu/humaneva/`.

PPMI is a dataset of people playing musical instruments, released by Yao and Fei-Fei at `http://ai.stanford.edu/~bangpeng/ppmi.html`. This dataset makes it possible to study interactions between body configuration, objects, and activity labels.

The CMU graphics lab publishes a large motion capture database at `http://mocap.cs.cmu.edu`. The CMU Quality of Life lab publishes a collection of data recorded in several different forms, covering people preparing food in a kitchen, at `http://kitchen.cs.cmu.edu/`.

The IXMAS dataset, collected by Weinland, shows a range of human actions collected from five different viewing directions; it can be found at `http://4drepository.inrialpes.fr/public/datasets`, together with several other motion datasets.

20.7 NOTES

Applying computer vision methods to pictures or video of people seems to be developing as a topic of its own; Moeslund *et al.* (2011) is a good synthesis of this topic. Faces are one crucial subtopic. We have described face detection in Chapter 17. We refer readers to Li and Jain (2005) for face recognition. There is a review of tracking methods, detection methods, and animation topics in Forsyth *et al.* (2006). Parsing has become an immensely active topic recently. We suggest Sapp *et al.* (2010), Tran and Forsyth (2007), Tran and Forsyth (2010), Yang and Ramanan (2011), and Wang *et al.* (2011) as good start points for reading.

C H A P T E R   21

Image Search and Retrieval

Very large collections of digital pictures seem to spring up quite easily. Many appear on the Web in various forms, including picture sharing websites, news websites, museum websites, and websites that sell pictures or access to pictures. Collections of family photographs and home videos, which can get quite big, are not necessarily on the Web but are still important. We would like to be able to search and to organize these collections. Searching for images raises some very difficult problems. For example, assume you had a perfect object recognition system; how would you describe the picture you wanted? As Armitage and Enser (1997), Enser (1995) and Enser (1993) show, using human indexers and language doesn't seem to work even close to perfectly. Computer programs are nowhere near as effective as people are at describing images, meaning that search tools can be quite erratic in practice.

Tools for interacting with collections of documents are now quite sophisticated. One important interaction is *search*, where one describes what one wants, and then gets a set of documents back. The other is *browsing*, where one looks through a set of documents to see what is interesting. To search, one needs to be able to judge the relevance of a document to a query and to rank the documents that have been retrieved. To browse, one needs to be able to organize the documents to be browsed in a way that makes sense.

The key questions for visual materials are the same as for documents. We need to be able to score relevance to a query, to rank items that have been retrieved, and to organize items in a useful way.

In Section 21.1, we describe various applications, user needs, and metrics. Section 21.2 describes basic technologies of information retrieval, which are used to search for text documents. Using vector quantization, we can obtain image features that can be treated like words, and Section 21.3 shows how to apply information retrieval ideas to these features. Section 21.4 introduces the alternative strategy of trying to attach words to images, then using these words as a search feature. Finally, Section 21.5 summarizes the current state of this approach.

21.1 THE APPLICATION CONTEXT

An image retrieval system takes some representation of the images that are being searched for, and returns some pictures. Assume that we can build one—what would we use it for? This is important, because the systems we can build will find images that are "similar" to the query, and different applications often involve quite different notions of how images are similar. An important part of the problem here is that users have quite a wide range of needs, and tend to use image retrieval systems in quite different ways.

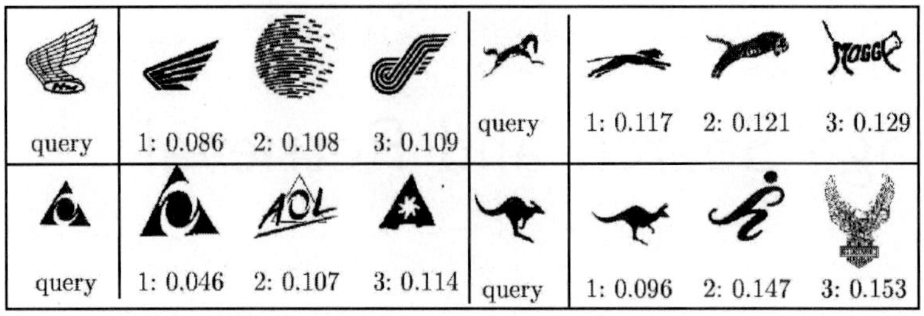

FIGURE 21.1: A trademark identifies a brand; customers should find it unique and special. This means that, when one registers a trademark, it is a good idea to know what other similar trademarks exist. The appropriate notion of similarity is a near duplicate. Here we show results from Belongie *et al.* (2002), who used a shape-based similarity system to identify trademarks in a collection of 300 that were similar to a query. The figure shown below each response is a distance (i.e., smaller is more similar). *This figure was originally published as Figure 12 of "Shape matching and object recognition using shape contexts," by S. Belongie, J. Malik, and J. Puzicha, IEEE Transactions on Pattern Analysis and Machine Intelligence, 2002,* © *IEEE, 2002.*

21.1.1 Applications

We have organized sample applications of image search systems under different notions of image similarity. For some applications, one wants images that look very similar to a query image. For others, one wants images that meet some semantic description; for example, they contain a "hammer," or are not offensive. For yet other applications, one would like to expose trends or structure in a collection to a user, where this structure is defined by a form of similarity that might be difficult to define explicitly. This is rather a rough organization, and there are many applications where one wants more than one of these types of similarity.

Finding Near Duplicates

There are several important applications of *near duplicate detection*, where one looks for pictures that look very similar to a query picture, possibly ignoring changes in size, resolution, and orientation, some cropping, compression noise and similar effects. A *trademark* needs to be unique, and a user who is trying to register a trademark can search for other similar trademarks that are already registered (e.g., Eakins *et al.* (1998); Jain and Vailaya (1998); Kato *et al.* (1988); and Kato and Fujimura (1990)). Near duplicate detection can be used to protect *copyright*. For example, at the time of writing, the owner of rights to a picture could register it with an organization called BayTSP, which then searches for stolen copies of the picture on the Web. Alternatively, if you are trying to get people to use images (as in a viral marketing campaign), you could tell how successful you are by looking for near-exact matches. If you keep a large enough library of pictures on your computer, you could be able to save space by detecting and removing duplicate images.

Semantic Searches

Other applications require more complex search criteria. For example, a *stock photo library* is a commercial library that survives by selling the rights to use particular images. Users contact the library and ask for pictures of, say, "the smoking of kippers," and the library finds the picture and sells rights to the user. How users of these libraries behave has been studied in some detail (somebody really did query for "the smoking of kippers"; see Enser (1993)).

An automatic method for conducting such searches will need quite a deep understanding of the query and of the images in the collection. *Internet image search* shows one can build useful image searches without using deep object recognition methods (it is a safe bet that commercial service providers don't understand object recognition much better than the published literature). These systems seem to be useful, though it is hard to know how much or to whom.

More narrow applications are also important. One is *identifying distressing images* (which usually, but not always, depict nudity or sexual behavior). There are many reasons to do this. Businesses might want to discourage employees from viewing this material on company time. Some governments would like to prevent their citizens from viewing this material on the Internet. Businesses that sell space on web pages to advertisers are motivated to check that the space they sell is not next to something that will worry the advertiser.

Trends and Browsing

In *data mining*, one uses simple statistical analyses on large datasets to spot trends. Such fishing expeditions can suggest genuinely useful or novel hypotheses that can be checked by domain experts. Good methods for exposing the contents of images to data mining methods would find many applications. For example, we might data mine satellite imagery of the earth to answer questions like: how far does urban sprawl extend?; what acreage is under crops?; how large will the maize crop be?; how much rainforest is left?; and so on (see Smith (1996)). Similarly, we might data mine medical imagery to try and find visual cues to long-term treatment outcomes.

21.1.2 User Needs

Retrieval systems can be difficult to evaluate, because we need to know what is relevant to a query. This is a question on which competent human informants can differ. The difficulty is particularly true in the case of images. Users of image search systems seem to judge relevance using both whether the image is about the search criterion, and what the image looks like (Choi and Rasmussen 2002, Boyce 1982). What a picture is about might bear an obscure relationship to what the picture looks like. For example, a picture of an airplane taking off might mean "General Pinochet leaving on the Chilean Airforce jet at RAF Waddington, Lincolnshire, today" (an example due to Enser (2000)). However, assuming we can make these judgments, we use recall and precision measures, as in Section 16.2.2.

A more important assessment is whether the system does something that users want. One way to assess this is to look at deployed systems. Google's image search and Bing's image search have made enough people happy that they have survived. Even if the companies knew how well these systems work (which they probably don't; could one really mark up a big enough set of images with enough right answers to get a sensible recall estimate?), the information would be commercially sensitive. One problem is that keywords seem like a fairly weak device for dealing with image queries, because it is hard to be precise. For example, if you want to get a picture of a kitchen scene, lit from the right, with some fish on a cutting board on the table in the center of the room, what do you do? Another problem is that it is hard to associate images with keywords accurately. One great strength of commercial systems is that they give quick responses, so you can try several different approaches; this may be what makes them useful.

Another way to determine what users want is to study how they use analogous resources, for example, stock photo services. Up until recently, getting a photo from a stock photo service involved a discussion with a professional picture librarian. Researchers have studied query logs for these services to draw conclusions about what users are seeking. It is useful to divide queries into a rich system of types (details in Section 21.1.3). People use a range of tactics to find what they want, and very often find browsing important (details in Section 21.1.4).

21.1.3   Types of Image Query

Most researchers divide image queries into different types. Although there are several systems, most are based on the work of Shatford (1986), itself drawing from work by Panofsky (1962). These are interesting to us because different users seem to make different types of query, and because many types of query are currently quite inaccessible to modern systems. Shatford sorted different types of meaning that people attach to images into a table (shown in Table 21.1, after Armitage and Enser (1997)). There are a variety of simpler systems, usually a simplification of this table. Enser and Mcgregor (1992) use four classes, unique objects (instances; for example, Winston Churchill); unique objects with refiners (for example, Winston Churchill in 1920); non-unique objects (categories; for example, a rhinoceros); and non-unique objects with refiners (modified categories; for example, a rhinoceros coated in mud). Users usually can tell quite accurately how their query should be categorized in this taxonomy (Chen 2001). Hung (2005) divides queries into specific (an instance of a category, for example, the neighbor's tortoiseshell cat), general (elements of a category, for example, a cat), and subjective (emotional or abstract content, for example, catness).

Notice that these taxonomies are more refined than those current in the vision literature. Although we can regard specific queries or unique object queries as being like near duplicate matching (or, for that matter, instance recognition), there is little work on refiners for unique objects. Similarly, general or non-unique object queries are like semantic matching (or category recognition), but again there is little known about refiners. Finally, types of match that are important to people (for example, subjective queries; much iconography and all iconology) remain mysterious to computer vision systems.

Users of stock photo libraries seem to formulate quite precise queries, mainly for unique objects, and interact with the photo librarian to refine the search (Enser and Mcgregor 1992). Users of home collections—where all the photographs are their own—like to have these pictures chronologically organized and like to see browsing screens with many small thumbnails (Rodden and Wood 2003). These users seem

	Iconography (instances)	Pre-Iconography (categories)	Iconology (abstractions)
Who?	Named person or thing (Winston Churchill)	Type of person or thing (Prime Ministers)	Mythical or fictitious being (Plantagenet Palliser)
What?	Named event or action (Battle of Waterloo)	Kind of event or action (Battle)	Emotion or abstraction (Conflict)
Where?	Named place (Urbana-Champaign)	Kind of place (Small town)	Symbolized place (Utopia)
When?	Specific time, date or period (9/11)	Season, time of day (Fall afternoon)	Abstraction symbolized by time (A Dance to the Music of Time)

TABLE 21.1: Different types of query, according to Armitage and Enser (1997)

not to want to annotate their pictures, perhaps because when the pictures are new they see no need, and later they either can't remember what annotations apply or don't bother to annotate. Users of large online collections are more willing to search for non-unique objects, or for categories (see Jörgensen (1998); Jörgensen and Jörgensen (2005); or Hollinka *et al.* (2004)), perhaps because it is easy to change or refine their search and to browse. Analysis of search logs can be complicated by internet users who search aggressively for sexual materials but relatively few terms seem to have high frequencies (Goodrum and Spink 2001).

21.1.4   What Users Do with Image Collections

People seem to use a range of tactics to find what they want. Online users have a wider range of tactics available to them than users interacting with a librarian; they can change search engine, look for surrogate sites that hold small, relevant picture collections, browse, and so on. Image professionals studied by Jörgenson often retried their query with some modifications (Jörgensen and Jörgensen 2005). These modifications appeared to be experimental, rather than the result of some clear strategy. There are detailed studies of how people change search tactics (Hung 2005). The most important points for us are that: (a) people do change their search tactics often, meaning a responsive interface is important; and (b) browsing is a very important tactic.

Browsing is consistently important in all studies. Frost *et al.* (2000) study the behavior of users of a collection of art images. In this work, users could engage in keyword search or browse, and users who did not know much about the collection very much preferred to browse the collection, whereas users who knew the collection preferred to search. Similarly, McDonald and Tait (2003) find users who know what they want sketch or navigate, but users who don't, browse. Markkula and Sormunen (2000) study users of a newspaper photo archive, who typically search with a small number of keywords and then browse the results. For the image professionals studied by Jörgensen and Jörgensen (2005), a search that resulted in a download typically involved a browsing step, and a useful browsing interface seemed to be important in the process of selecting an image to use. Browsing behavior is affected by how images are arranged. If images are laid out randomly, users select the image they want quickly, but if the images are laid out according to similarity in appearance, then users take longer to select the image they want, but tend to be happier with the result (Rodden *et al.* 2001).

21.2   BASIC TECHNOLOGIES FROM INFORMATION RETRIEVAL

Some techniques and ideas from text information retrieval are widely appropriated in vision. Typical text information retrieval systems expect a set of query words. They use these to query some form of index, producing a list of putative matches. From this list they chose documents with a large enough similarity measure between document and query. These are ranked by a measure of significance, and returned.

21.2.1   Word Counts

Much of text information retrieval is shaped by the fact that a few words are common, but most words are rare. The most common words—typically including "the," "and," "but," "it"—are sometimes called *stop words* and are ignored because almost every document contains many of them. Other words tend to be rare, which means that their frequencies can be quite distinctive. Quite often, it is enough to know whether the word is there or not. For example, documents containing the words "stereo," "fundamental," "trifocal," and "match" are likely to be about 3D reconstruction; documents containing "chrysoprase," "incarnadine," "cinnabarine," and "importunate" are lists of 11 letter words ending in "e" (many such lists exist, for crossword puzzle users; you can check this using Google).

Indexing Documents

It is straightforward to build a table representing the documents in which each word occurs, because very few words occur in many documents, so the table is sparse. Write N_w for the number of words and N_d for the number of documents. We could represent the table as an array of lists. There is one list for each word, and the list entries are the documents that contain that word. This object is referred to as an *inverted index*, and can be used to find all documents that contain a logical combination of some set of words. For example, to find all documents that contain any one of a set of words, we would: take each word in the query, look up all documents containing that word in the inverted index, and take the union of the resulting sets of documents. Similarly, we could find documents containing all of the words by taking an intersection, and so on. Such logical queries usually are not sufficient, because the result set might be either very large or too small, and because we have no notion of which elements of the result set are more important. We need a more refined notion of similarity between documents, and between a document and a query.

Similarity from Word Counts

One measure of similarity for two documents is to compare word frequencies.

Assume we have a fixed set of terms that we will work with. We represent each document by a vector c, with one entry for each term. These entries are zero when the term is absent, and contain some measure of the word frequency when the word is present. This measure might be as simple as a one if the word appears at least once in the document, or might be a count of the number of words. Write c_1, c_2 for two such vectors; the *cosine similarity* between the documents they represent is

$$\frac{c_1 \cdot c_2}{\|c_1\|\|c_2\|}.$$

Two documents that both use an uncommon word are most likely more similar than two documents that both use a common word. We can account for this effect by weighting word counts. The most usual way to do this is called *tf-idf weighting* (for "term frequency-inverse document frequency"). Terms that should have most weight appear often in the particular document we are looking at, but seldom in all documents. Write N_d for the total number of documents and N_t for the number of documents that contain the particular term we are interested in. Then, the inverse document frequency can be estimated as $N_d/(1 + N_t)$ (where we add one to avoid dividing by zero). Write $n_t(j)$ for the number of times the term appears in document j and $n_w(j)$ for the total number of words that appear in that document. Then, the tf-idf weight for term t in document j is

$$\left(\frac{n_t(j)}{n_w(j)}\right) / \log\left(\frac{N_d}{(1 + N_t)}\right).$$

We divide by the log of the inverse document frequency because we do not want very uncommon words to have excessive weight. Inserting this tf-idf weight into the count vectors above will get a cosine similarity that weights uncommon words that are shared more highly than common words that are shared.

21.2.2   Smoothing Word Counts

Our measurement of similarity will not work well on most real document collections, even if we weight by tf-idf. This is because words tend to be rare, so that most pairs of documents share only quite common words, and so most pairs of documents will have quite small cosine similarity. The real difficulty here is that zero word counts can be underestimates. For example, a document that uses the words "elephant," "tusk," and "pachyderm" should have some affinity for "trunk." If that word does not appear in the document, it is an accident of counting. This means that to measure similarity, we would do well to smooth the word counts.

We can do so by looking at how all terms are distributed across all documents. An alternative representation of the information in an inverted index is as an N_w by N_d table $\mathcal{D}$, where each cell contains an entry if the relevant word is not in the relevant document and a zero otherwise. Entries could be one if the word occurs, or a count of the number of times the word occurs, or the tf-idf weight for the term in the document. In any case, this table is extremely sparse, so it can be stored and manipulated efficiently. A column of the table is a representation of the words in a document, and the cosine similarity between columns is our original measure of similarity between documents.

Zeros in $\mathcal{D}$ might be the result of counting accidents, as above. We would like a version of this table that smooths word counts. There are likely to be many documents for any particular topic in the collection, so the smoothed version of the table should have many columns that are similar. This means it will be significantly rank-deficient. We compute a singular value decomposition of $\mathcal{D}$ as $\mathcal{D} = \mathcal{U}\Sigma\mathcal{V}^T$. Write $\mathcal{U}_k$ for the matrix consisting of the first k columns of $\mathcal{U}$, $\mathcal{V}_k$ for the matrix consisting of the first k columns of $\mathcal{V}$, Σ_k for Σ with all but the k largest singular values set to be zero, and write $\hat{\mathcal{D}} = \mathcal{U}_k\Sigma_k\mathcal{V}_k^T$.

Now consider the ith column of $\mathcal{D}$, which we write as $\boldsymbol{d}_i$. The corresponding column $\hat{\boldsymbol{d}}_i$ of $\hat{\mathcal{D}}$ lies in the span of $\mathcal{U}_k$. The word counts are smoothed by forcing them to lie in this span. For example, assume that there are many documents discussing elephants, and only one uses the word "pachyderm." The count vectors for each of these documents could be represented by a single column, but error will be minimized if there is a small count for "pachyderm" in each. Because of this smoothing effect, cosine distances between documents represented by columns of $\hat{\mathcal{D}}$ are a much more reliable guide to similarity.

To compute cosine similarity between an old document and a new document with count vector $\boldsymbol{q}$, we project the new document's count vector onto the columns of $\mathcal{U}_k$ to obtain $\hat{\boldsymbol{q}} = \mathcal{U}_k\mathcal{U}_k^T\boldsymbol{q}$. We can then take the inner product of $\hat{\boldsymbol{q}}$ and $\hat{\boldsymbol{d}}_i$. A complete table of inner products (cosine distances) between documents is given by

$$\hat{\mathcal{D}}^T\hat{\mathcal{D}} = (\mathcal{V}_k\Sigma_k)(\Sigma_k\mathcal{V}^T) = (\Sigma_k\mathcal{V}_k^T)^T(\Sigma_k\mathcal{V}^T),$$

so that we can think of the columns of $\Sigma_k\mathcal{V}^T$ as points in a k-dimensional "concept space" that represents the inner products exactly. One could, for example, cluster documents in this space rather than the original count space, and expect a better clustering. Computing the SVD of $\mathcal{D}$ is known as *latent semantic analysis*; using the concept space for indexing is known as *latent semantic indexing*.

$\hat{\mathcal{D}}$ is useful in other ways, too. There is a rough tendency of words that have similar meaning to appear near similar words in similar documents, an idea known as *distributional semantics*. This means that cosine similarity between *rows* of $\hat{\mathcal{D}}$ is an estimate of the similarity of meaning of two terms, because it counts the extent to which they co-occur. Furthermore, $\hat{\mathcal{D}}$ can be used as an inverted index. If we use it in this way, we are not guaranteed that every document recovered contains all the words we used in the query; instead, it might contain very similar words. This is usually a good thing. The columns of $\mathcal{U}$ are sometimes called *topics* and can be thought of as model word frequency vectors; the coordinates of a column in the semantic space show the weights with which topics should be mixed to obtain the document.

21.2.3   Approximate Nearest Neighbors and Hashing

Smoothing word counts may mean that the term-document table is no longer sparse, and indexing will not be an efficient way to find documents with high similarity. Instead, we can notice relations between the cosine similarity and the inner product. In particular, for two documents with fixed length count vectors $\mathbf{c}_1$ and $\mathbf{c}_2$, a large value of cosine similarity implies a small value of $\|\mathbf{c}_1 - \mathbf{c}_2\|^2$.

This leads us to a general, and difficult, problem. We need to find the members of a set of high dimensional vectors that are close or closest to some query vector. A linear search through the dataset is fine for a small set of data items, but we will operate at scales where we need something more efficient. The main trick to obtaining a good approximate solution is to carve the space into cells, then look at items that lie in cells near the query vector; there are two methods that are worth discussing in detail here.

Locality Sensitive Hashing

In *locality sensitive hashing*, we build a set of hash tables containing the data items, using different hashing functions for each table. For a query item, we recover whatever is in each hash table at the location corresponding to the hash code computed for the query item. We search this set, keeping any data items from this set that are sufficiently close to the query. There are many choices of hash function; the most widely used in vision is *random projection*. Write v for a vector, representing either a query or a data item. We now obtain a single bit of a hash code by choosing a random vector r and then computing $sign(v \cdot r)$. Computing a k-bit hash code involves choosing k such random vectors, then computing one bit for each. There is a set of k such random vectors associated with each hash table. Geometrically, choosing an r corresponds to choosing a hyperplane in the data space, and the hashing bit corresponds to which side of the hyperplane v lies on. A k-bit hash code identifies a cell in an arrangement of k hyperplanes in which v lies. k will be small compared to the dimension, and so we are cutting the space into 2^k cells. This means that there will be relatively few data items that lie in the same cell as a query. Some nearby data items may not lie in the same cell, because they could be on the other side of a hyperplane, but these items should lie in the same cell in another hash table.

All these assertions can be made precise, resulting in a guarantee that: (a) a data item that is almost as close as the nearest neighbor will be found with high probability; and (b) all data items closer to the query than some threshold will be found with high probability, whereas data items that are significantly more distant will be found with low probability. Straightforward geometric intuition suggests that this approach will work best when the data items have zero mean, which is easy to arrange. Notice that using n k-bit hash tables is not the same as using one nk-bit hash table. In the first case, the list of points returned from a particular query is a union of the lists returned from each of the n hash tables. This means that points that are near the query but just happen to lie outside the query's cell for one hash table, have a good chance of being found in another hash table. In the second case, the list we must handle is much shorter (because there are more cells), but there is a better chance of missing nearby points. The choice of n and k will depend on dimension and on the nature of the probabilistic guarantee one wants. There are a variety of other possible choices of hash function. Details of other choices, and precise statements of the relevant guarantees, can be found in (Indyk and Motwani 1998).

KD-Trees for Approximate Nearest Neighbors

Random projection methods build a cell structure that is independent of the distribution of the data. This means trouble if data is heavily concentrated in some

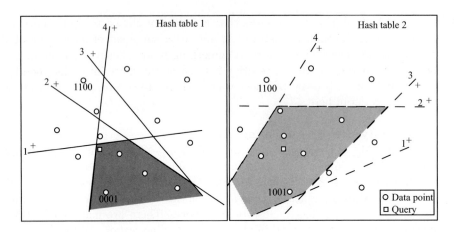

FIGURE 21.2: In locality sensitive hashing using a random projection hash function, the hash function is equivalent to a hyperplane in the data space. Items that lie on one side of the hyperplane corresponding to the nth bit have that bit set to one; otherwise, it is zero. These hyperplanes cut the space of data into a set of cells. All the data items in a cell get a binary hash code (shown for two points in each figure; we have marked the order of the bits by labeling the hyperplanes, and the +s show which side of the hyperplane gets a one). To query, we find all data items in the same hash table entry as the query (the filled polygons in the figure), and then find the closest. However, the nearest neighbor might not be in this cell (for example, the case on the **left**). To reduce the probability of error from this cause, we use more than one hash table and search the union of the sets of points lying in the query cell. In the case illustrated, the nearest neighbor of the query lies in the query cell for the second hash table, on the **right**. The hash tables reduce the set of points we need to search, with high probability of finding a point that is almost as close as the nearest neighbor.

regions, because queries that land in a heavily populated cell of the hash table will need to search a long list. An alternative method is to use a *k-d tree* to build the cell structure. A k-d tree is built by recursively splitting cells. The root will be the whole space. To generate the children of a cell, select one dimension d, perhaps at random, and select some threshold value t_d. Write the dth component of v as v_d. Now all data items in a cell with $v_d \leq t_d$ are placed in the left child, and all others in the right. We now apply this splitting procedure recursively to the root, until the children are sufficiently small. If we choose the threshold value appropriately (for example, the median of the data in the cell), we can ensure that cells are small in dense components of the space and large in sparse components.

The nearest neighbor to a query can then be found by walking the tree to find the cell containing the query point. We then check any data items in that cell. Write the distance from the query to the closest as d_c. We now backtrack, investigating cells that could contain points closer than d_c and updating d_c when we find a better point. We can prune any branch of the tree that represents a

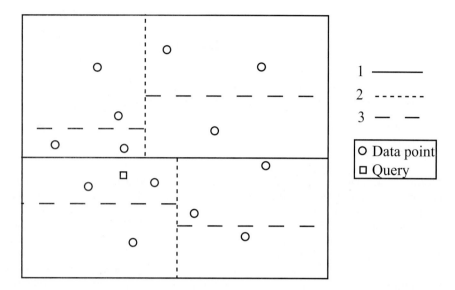

FIGURE 21.3: A k-d tree is built by recursively splitting cells along dimensions. The order in which cells are split for this tree is shown by the dashes on the lines. The nearest neighbor for the query point is found by (a) finding the closest item in the query point's cell, then (b) backtracking, and looking at cells that could contain closer items. Notice that in this example one will need to go right up to the root of the tree and down the other side to find the nearest neighbor. In high dimensions, this backtracking becomes intractable, but if an approximate nearest neighbor is sufficient, the amount of backtracking can be controlled successfully.

volume that is further from the query than d_c. This procedure works well for low dimensions, but becomes unattractive in high dimensions because we will need to explore too many cells (the number of neighbors of a cell goes up exponentially with dimension).

This difficulty can be avoided if an approximate nearest neighbor is sufficient. In the *best bin first* approach, we look at a fixed number N_c of cells, then report the best point found so far. Promising cells will tend to have some points that are close to the query, and we define the distance between a cell and the query to be the shortest distance from the query to any point on the cell's boundary. Whenever we investigate the child of a cell, we insert the other child into a priority queue, ordered by distance to the query. Once we have checked a cell, we retrieve the next cell from the priority queue. We do this until we have looked at N_c cells. We will look mainly at cells that are close to the query, and so the point we report is a good approximate nearest neighbor.

Good performance of a particular method depends somewhat on the dataset. For most applications, the choice of method can be made offline using the dataset, or a subset of it. Muja and Lowe (2009) describe a software package that can choose an approximate nearest neighbors method that is fastest for a particular dataset. Generally, they find that using multiple randomized k-d trees is usually the best; at the time of writing, software could be found at http://www.cs.ubc.ca/~mariusm/

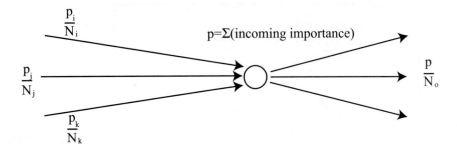

FIGURE 21.4: The structure of the Web offers cues to what is important and what is not; important documents have many links coming in from other important documents. We model this process by associating an importance p_i with the ith node. The importance at any particular node is the sum of incoming contributions. Each node shares its importance equally across the outgoing links. In turn, we obtain an eigenvalue equation that is too big to solve. However, we can estimate importance by simulating a random walk through the directed graph. This random walk chooses an outgoing edge with uniform probability then proceeds along that edge; it will spend more time at more important documents.

`index.php/FLANN/FLANN.`

21.2.4 Ranking Documents

These measures can tell how similar terms or documents are to one another and how similar a document is to a query, but they do not tell us anything about how important a document is. In very large collections, documents that may be very similar to a query might not be very interesting. Web search engines must choose which documents appear first in response to a query. The procedure used now seems to be very complex, and is influenced by potential revenues from advertising and so on, but is based on an important simple insight: the structure of the Web itself offers cues to what is important and what is not. This is because Web documents have oriented links between them, and important documents will tend to have links pointing to them. Write the importance of the jth document as p_j. We assume that: (a) if many important documents point to j, then it must be important; (b) importance is additive; and (c) each document shares its importance evenly over outgoing links. This means that, if we write $N(k)$ for the number of outgoing links in a document, we can write

$$p_j = \sum_{k \to j} \frac{p_k}{N(k)}$$

(where the sum is over all documents with links pointing to j).

Equivalently, we can write a matrix $\mathcal{A}$ that is an N_d by N_d table recording all links. If there is no link from the kth document to the jth document, then the j, kth element of this matrix, a_{jk}, is zero; otherwise, we have $a_{jk} = 1/N(k)$. We write $\boldsymbol{p}$ whose jth component is the importance of the jth document. Then we have

$$\boldsymbol{p} = \mathcal{A}\boldsymbol{p}.$$

In practice, $\mathcal{A}$ is far too big to write out explicitly. Instead, we can estimate importance using a random walk. Notice that, for mild conditions on $\mathcal{A}$, the vector defined by $\boldsymbol{p} = \mathcal{A}\boldsymbol{p}$ is the stationary distribution of a random walk whose state transition matrix is $\mathcal{A}$. This justifies estimating importance by a random walk that starts at some randomly chosen document, then chooses outgoing links uniformly and at random. Because we do not know whether the Web has only one connect component, it is a good idea to modify this random walk slightly. At each node, we allow the walk to have a small constant probability of transitioning to any other document (rather than just documents that are linked to the current one). If we let this walk go on for many state transitions, then documents will appear with a probability corresponding to their importance. Equivalently, if we leave a note each time the random walk visits a document, the number of notes left at each document is approximately proportional to the importance of the document. The importance reported by this algorithm is known as *Pagerank* (after its inventor, Larry Page). The Pagerank algorithm seems to have been at the core of Google's early success, and may still be part of its operations.

21.3   IMAGES AS DOCUMENTS

In *near duplicate detection* we have a query image and want to find a near duplicate in a very large collection. The core problem here is to come up with a quick procedure to reduce the main dataset to a small set of pictures that are very likely to be near duplicates, and that is very likely to contain all the near duplicates. The small set can then be checked in detail with a slow algorithm. We need a representation that is efficient enough to scale well, but informative enough to be accurate. Visual words (Section 16.1.3) are a natural choice.

The advantage of the word analogy is we can adopt standard strategies of information retrieval, and all the machinery of Section 21.2 applies. Visual words that are very common are analogous to stop words, and so can be ignored. We can use inverted indexes to find logical combinations of visual words. We can represent an image with a count vector of its visual words. This vector could be unweighted, or weighted with TF-IDF. We can represent the similarity of two images by the cosine similarity of these vectors. We can smooth count vectors. And we can find near duplicates by finding images that have a large cosine similarity, using either approximate nearest neighbors or an inverted index. Sivic and Zisserman (2003), who first made this observation, applied this strategy to search for near duplicates of user-identified objects in video (Figure 16.5), but it applies to near duplicate image detection.

The visual word analogy makes other information retrieval ideas useable for images. For example, in *query expansion*, we take the first set of responses to a query, then query with those, and then merge the responses from those queries. This could help overcome noise issues by finding things that are missed by the original query but look very similar to it. However, it could make the results worse, by finding things that look a lot like errors in the response to the original query. Chum *et al.* (2007) show that, as long as the expanded query is carefully checked with a verification procedure, query expansion can give significant improvements in results.

One way in which images differ from documents is that relations between local interest points in images are a great deal richer than relations between words. Straightforward analogies with information retrieval based on visual words can't exploit this observation, so two images that have a high cosine similarity could have similar sets of visual words in a different spatial arrangement. However, we could build a quite efficient system by first retrieving images that have high cosine similarity to a query and then checking the results for spatial consistency with the query. This is efficient because we can't make two different sets of visual words look more similar by moving the words around in an image, so two images with high cosine similarity will have many matching visual words. We just need to check that the matched pairs are consistent with each other. We could check that each match has nearby good matches. For example, Sivic and Zisserman find the 15 visual words closest in the image to each good match; any of those 15 that also matches a visual word in the query gets to cast a vote for similarity, and images are ranked by the total number of votes. This is a rough form of spatial consistency because nearby words that match might not actually be in the right place, but it is effective.

21.3.1 Matching Without Quantization

A problem with visual words is that some of the details that are suppressed by vector quantization might be important. Jegou *et al.* (2010) show that this difficulty can be evaded by computing several different vector quantizations. In effect, one builds multiple systems using different k-means clusterings; each reports a ranked list of similar near-duplicates; and one combines these lists by giving each image its median rank. Another strategy is to use an extremely large vocabulary. It is difficult to use a large vocabulary with k-means because vector quantizing a local descriptor requires finding the closest cluster center, which will require a linear search across the cluster centers. An alternative is to use hierarchical k-means. Here we cluster to k centers using k-means, then cluster each cluster with k-means again; we can repeat this recursively. The result is a tree, where finding the closest leaf involves repeatedly finding the closest of k cluster centers. Nister and Stewenius (2006) use this approach to produce a very large vocabulary. They have built what is now a standard dataset, with near duplicates marked to allow easy evaluation (at http://www.vis.uky.edu/~stewe/ukbench/ as of time of writing).

An alternative to vector quantization is to search for all interest points that match a query. Ke *et al.* (2004) use LSH to find images that have many interest points that match interest points in the query image, then check that the matching interest points support the idea that there is an affine transform from the query image to the returned images. Ke *et al.* use PCA-SIFT, rather than SIFT, to describe interest points, and find similar interest points using locality sensitive hashing. From this list, they extract the names of images that have many matching interest points. For each of these images, they use RANSAC to search for an affine transformation consistent with the (now relatively short) list of potentially matching interest points. If they find such a transformation with a fixed number of inliers, they regard the image as a near duplicate. The required number of inliers is a parameter; too small a value will mean false positives and too large a value will mean false negatives.

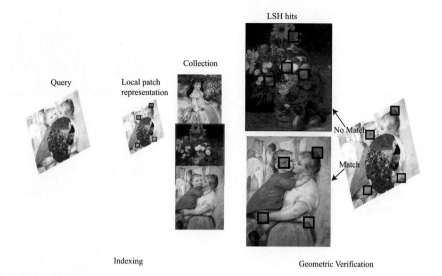

FIGURE 21.5: An alternative to using visual words is to apply locality sensitive hashing to representations of local windows and then verify matches geometrically. Ke *et al.* (2004)'s system takes a query image, computes representations of windows around image points (they use PCA-SIFT; other representations would work), and then uses LSH to identify all images which contain interest points within some distance of any interest point in the query image. They then post-process this list, using RANSAC to search for an affine transformation consistent with the potentially matching interest points; if there are sufficient inliers for the transformation that is found, then the image is a near duplicate. *This figure kindly generated by Rahul Sukthankar, and used with his permission.*

Numerous variants on these general recipes are possible. In the case of copyright enforcement, for example, the true near duplicates will be rotated, scaled, and cropped versions of the original. Once we have a small set of potential duplicates with matched interest points, we can estimate the transformation from the point matches (as Ke *et al.* (2004) do, above), then transform the query image and compare to the duplicate with, for example, a sum of squares difference on the intensity. If most overlapping pixels have similar intensity, then there is a near duplicate.

21.3.2 Ranking Image Search Results

Reranking the results of an image search is usually an essential part of presenting them to a user. This is because large image collections are often "clumpy." If there is one, say, side view of the Eiffel tower, there will be many similar views; worse, there is very likely to be another clump of images of the Eiffel tower from above. Typically, images from similar view directions will have similar relevance to a query. This means that it is not helpful to present the user with images ranked by relevance, because then the user will see several pages of side views followed by several pages of top views, and so on. Instead, we must rerank the search results in a way that gives a fair representation of all the kinds of results.

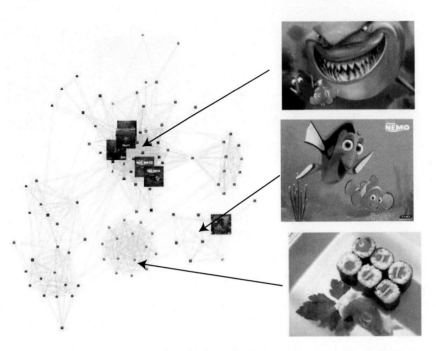

FIGURE 21.6: Jing and Baluja (2008) use a version of pagerank to rerank the results of an image query. The graph shows results for a query for "Nemo"; notice there are several tightly linked clumps of images, representing themes. Edges are built using a strategy comparable to locality sensitive hashing. If an interest point in one image hashes to the same location as an interest point in another image, then there is an edge between those images; the number of such interest points gives the weight of the edge. Jing and Baluja then use pagerank to identify important images. Pagerank will produce representatives from strong clusters, like the inset images. Simply looking for images with high degree will overemphasize pictures that appear repeatedly, for example, the strong cluster of Nemo sushi images near the bottom of the figure. *This figure was originally published as Figures 2 and 9 of "VisualRank: Applying PageRank to Large-Scale Image Search," by Y. Jing and S. Baluja, IEEE Transactions on Pattern Analysis and Machine Intelligence, 2008, © IEEE, 2008.*

The main question in reranking is which images should appear high in the final ranking. The criterion should be relatively fast to implement, because we expect to be dealing with many pools of result images. It should visit all the clumps of images, and should emphasize bigger ones more strongly than small ones, but not to the extent that small ones are missed completely.

Jing and Baluja (2008) do this with a variant of pagerank. For some k, the top k query results are arranged into a graph. We will apply the pagerank random walk, with restart, to this graph. We can then get the final ranked set of images by occasionally (perhaps after a fixed number of steps of the random walk) reporting an image when we visit its node. We expect this approach to work well, because pagerank is good at identifying strongly linked nodes. It can be implemented very quickly and efficiently. The trick is that we do not need to build the graph at any time. All we need to know at a given node is which other nodes are connected to it, and with what weights. Jing and Baluja obtain this information from a set of hash tables. Before the random walk is started, a single pass through all the query results computes local features at a set of interest points for each image. These local features are hashed into a collection of hash tables, each using a different hashing function. To take a step of the random walk, we must find all images connected to the current image. We do so by querying the hash tables with each local feature in the current image; any collision that occurs in enough hash tables corresponds to a link. The number of local features that collide with local features in another image gives the weight of the link to that image. This is reasonable, because images that share many local features are likely to be more similar than images that share few.

21.3.3 Browsing and Layout

We have developed an analogy between images and text documents, but like all analogies, it is only good as far as it goes. One failure of the analogy, as we have seen briefly, is that spatial relations between points in images tend to be more complex than those between words in documents. Another is that it is natural to lay out documents in a ranked order list (perhaps with a little extra structure to highlight adverts or sponsored results), but images might be laid out in much more complex ways. Supporting browsing with complex layouts doesn't seem to work well for documents, but might for images, because it is easier to interpret an image at a glance. Such layouts are interesting, because they can support browsing.

Browsing is tricky to define, but there seem to be four important components: a browser sees a display of a broad range of options; selects one; examines it; then either acquires it or rejects it (Bates 2007). This means that browsing tools should:

- allow a user to get a sense of the totality of a collection, perhaps by displaying a representation of clusters of images where similar clusters might be close together; big clusters might be large; and so on;

- provide some form of interaction that makes it possible to select, possibly at different levels of detail (perhaps one wants to see a particular image, or the elements of a particular cluster);

- display what has been selected, which could be an image or a group of images, in some detail;

- and allow a user to move on, perhaps by making it possible to see and to move through the collection in different "directions" or by displaying subsets of images that are "similar."

Browsing and search tools naturally complement one another. A user could first browse the collection, and then frame a search. Having searched, the user might then choose to browse items "near" to any hits returned by the search tool, and so on.

21.3.4 Laying Out Images for Browsing

Generally, browsing systems involve a user interface built on top of a set of image clusters. Constructing a good user interface for a browsing system is tricky. Desirable features include: responsiveness (so the user can move around without getting frustrated); fluid navigation (so that minor puzzles created by errors in the image clustering are easily resolved); and a sensible spatial metaphor, so that it is natural to know where to go next as one moves around the collection. We can achieve these goals by computing meaningful distances between images or image clusters and then laying out those images in a way that reflects the distances.

We can compute inter-image distances by taking histograms (for some reason, color histograms were particularly popular; now one would use a histogram of visual words), then using χ-squared or similar distances between histograms. The method shown in Figure 21.7 uses an alternative, the earthmovers distance, which is a measure of similarity between vector quantized sets, each represented using different collections of visual words (Rubner *et al.* 2000).

The general problem of finding embeddings for points in some dimension so that the distances are similar to a given table of distances is known as *multidimensional scaling*. Assume we have n points we wish to embed in an r-dimensional space. Write $\mathcal{D}^2$ for a table of *squared* distances between points, with d_{ij}^2 the squared distance between point i and point j. Notice that if $\mathcal{D}^2$ is a table of distances, it will be symmetric. Write the embedding for point i as $\boldsymbol{x}_i$. Because translation does not change the distances between points, we can choose the origin, and we will place it at the mean of the points, so that $\frac{1}{n}\sum_i \boldsymbol{x}_i = \boldsymbol{0}$. Write $\boldsymbol{1}$ for the n-dimensional vector containing all ones, and $\mathcal{I}$ for the identity matrix. By noticing that $d_{ij}^2 = \|\boldsymbol{x}_i - \boldsymbol{x}_j\|^2 = \boldsymbol{x}_i \cdot \boldsymbol{x}_i - 2\boldsymbol{x}_i \cdot \boldsymbol{x}_j + \boldsymbol{x}_j \cdot \boldsymbol{x}_j$, we can show that

$$\mathcal{M} = -\frac{1}{2}\left[\mathcal{I} - \frac{1}{n}\boldsymbol{1}\boldsymbol{1}^T\right]\mathcal{D}^2\left[\mathcal{I} - \frac{1}{n}\boldsymbol{1}\boldsymbol{1}^T\right]$$

has i, jth entry $\boldsymbol{x}_i \cdot \boldsymbol{x}_j$. This means that, to estimate the embedding, we must obtain a matrix $\mathcal{X}$ whose columns are the embedded points, so that $\mathcal{M}$ is "close" to $\mathcal{X}^T\mathcal{X}$. A variety of notions of "closeness" might be appropriate; the easiest to use is least squares. In this case, we can apply a singular value decomposition to $\mathcal{M}$ to get $\mathcal{M} = \mathcal{U}\Sigma\mathcal{U}^T$. We form $\mathcal{G} = \Sigma^{1/2}\mathcal{U}^T$, and the first r rows of $\mathcal{G}$ are the $\mathcal{X}$ we require.

We can use multidimensional scaling (MDS) to lay out sets of images using an inter-image distance, as in Figure 21.7 (which uses the earthmovers' distance, applied to a color and texture representation). This figure illustrates one form of selection of level of detail, where the user can select a subset of images in a neighborhood, and have this subset laid out with MDS. We expect the relative position of the images to change, because we expect the subset to have a different distribution of distances between images. When the set of images is large, another approach is to cluster them and then represent each cluster center with an image (perhaps the image closest to the cluster center). We then build a squared distance matrix out of inter-cluster distances, and again use MDS to lay out the cluster centers, placing a thumbnail for the representative image at its most appropriate location. We can then display finer-scale detail by allowing the user to select a

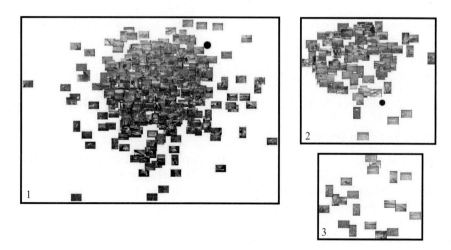

FIGURE 21.7: Multidimensional scaling allows us to compute locations on a screen that are consistent with inter-image distances, and so lay out images in a suggestive way. Frame 1 shows 500 images, the response to a query for a desert landscape. Multidimensional scaling has been used to compute locations for the thumbnails. Notice how strongly different images are far apart (this image distance places strong weight on global color distances, and the purple images are to the left of this frame, while more yellow images are to the right). The user then clicks on the black dot (near top right of the frame), and the 100 images closest to that point are selected; a new multidimensional scaling is computed for this subset of images, and they are laid out to give frame 2. The layout changes because the statistics of distances have changed. Again, the user clicks on the black dot (lower center of the frame), to select a subset of 20 images; again, a new scaling is computed for this subset, and they are laid out to give frame 3. *This figure was originally published as Figure 4 of "A Metric for Distributions with Applications to Image Databases," by Y. Rubner, C. Tomasi, and L. Guibas, Proc. IEEE ICCV 1998, © IEEE, 1998.*

cluster center, then see all the elements of the cluster.

21.4 PREDICTING ANNOTATIONS FOR PICTURES

Appearance-based searches for images seem to be useful only in quite special applications. In most cases, people appear to want to search for images using more general criteria, like what objects are present, or what the people depicted are doing (Jörgensen 1998). These searches are most easily specified with words. Relatively few pictures come with keywords directly attached to them. Many pictures have words nearby, and a fair strategy is to treat some of these words as keywords (Section 21.4.1). More interesting to us is the possibility of learning to predict good annotating words from image features. We could do so by predicting words from the whole image (Section 21.4.2). Words tend to be correlated to one another, and prediction methods that take this into account tend to perform better (Section 21.4.3). Linking names in a caption to faces in an image is an important special case (Section 21.4.4), which suggests a general strategy of thinking about correspondences between image regions and words (Section 21.4.5).

Image annotation is important for two reasons: first, there are useful practical applications in image search; and second, it emphasizes a question that is crucial for object recognition—what should we say about a picture? The main distinction between methods is how they deal with the fact that image annotations tend to be quite strongly correlated. Some methods model correlations explicitly, and others allow words to be conditionally independent given image structures, and allow the correlation between image structures to encode the correlation between words.

21.4.1 Annotations from Nearby Words

The name of the image might yield words. A picture called `mydog.jpg` likely shows a dog, but it is hard to tell what might be in `13789.jpg`. If the image appears on a web page, then it is most likely in an `IMG` tag. The standard for these tags requires an `alt` attribute, which is the text that should appear when the image can't be displayed. Words that appear in this attribute could also be used as keywords. Unfortunately, HTML does not have a single standard way of captioning images, but a text matcher could identify some of the many methods used to display images with captions. If a caption is found, words that appear in the caption might be used as keywords. Finally, one could use words that render on the web page near to the image. One could also cluster any or all of these sources of words to try to suppress noise, and attach cluster tags rather than keywords to images. Notice that some kinds of web page might be more fruitful for this kind of analysis than others. For example, a catalog might contain a lot of images whose identity is quite obvious.

If you experiment informally with commercial image search engines, you will notice that most pictures returned for simple one-word object queries are pictures in which a single object is dominant. This underlines an important point. The images that we are dealing with in Internet search applications may not be at all like the images that appear at the back of your eye. There are quite strong relationships between object recognition and image search, but they're not the same problem. Apart from this very important point, these pictures are there either because people want such pictures (and so the search results are biased to place them at the top), or because search engines are biased toward finding them (because they look in places where such pictures are prominent and easily obtained).

21.4.2 Annotations from the Whole Image

The simplest way to attach words to pictures is to use a classifier to predict one word for the whole picture (methods described in Chapter 16). The vocabulary might need to be quite big, and the approach might not work well for images that don't contain a dominant object. A more attractive approach is to try to predict more than one word. A simple and natural way to try and do this is to annotate each image with a binary code. This code is the length of the vocabulary. Each bit in the code corresponds to a word in the vocabulary, and there is a one if the word is present and a zero if it is absent. We then find the set of codes that actually appear (a set that will be much smaller than the set that could appear. Typical vocabularies might run to 400 words or more, and the number of possible codes is then 2^{400}). We treat each code that actually appears as a word, and build a multi-class classifier. This sounds easy, but is wholly impractical, because there

Predicted keywords	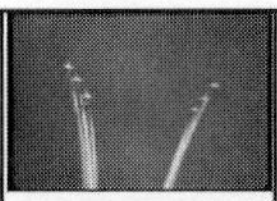 sky, jet, plane, smoke, formation	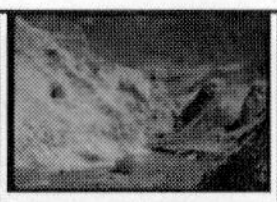 grass, rocks, sand, valley, canyon	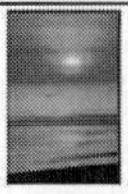 sun, water, sea, waves, birds	 water, tree, grass, deer, white-tailed	 bear, snow, wood, deer, white-tailed
Human annotation	sky, jet, plane, smoke	rocks, sand, valley, canyon	sun, water, clouds, birds	tree, forest, deer, white-tailed	tree, snow, wood, fox

FIGURE 21.8: A comparison of words predicted by human annotators and by the method of Makadia *et al.* (2008) for images from the Corel5K dataset. *This figure was originally published as Figure 4 of "A New Baseline for Image Annotation," by A. Makadia, V. Pavlovic, and S. Kumar, Proc. European Conference on Computer Vision. Springer Lecture Notes in Computer Science, Volume 5304, 2008 © Springer, 2008.*

will be very few examples for each code. By failing to pool data, we are wasting examples. For example, our strategy would treat an image labeled with "sheep," "field," "sky," and "sun" as completely different from an image labeled "sheep," "field," and "sky," which is absurd.

So we must treat words individually; but words tend to be correlated, and we should exploit this correlation in our prediction methods. Straightforward methods are extremely strong. Makadia *et al.* (2008) describe a method based around k-nearest neighbors, which performs as well as, or better than, more complex methods in the literature (see also Makadia *et al.* (2010)). They use color and texture features in a straightforward labeling algorithm (Algorithm 21.1). They compare their method to a number of more complicated methods. It is highly competitive (see Table 21.2 for comparative performance information).

To predict n tags:
  obtain the k-nearest neighbors of the query image
  sort the tags of the closest image in order of frequency, then report the first n
  If the closest image has fewer than n tags:
    rank tags associated with the other $k - 1$ neighbors according to:
      (a) their cooccurrence with the tags already chosen and
      (b) their frequency in the k-nearest neighbor set.
  The remaining tags are the best in this ranked set.

Algorithm 21.1: Nearest Neighbor Tagging.

Some of the tags on the nearest neighbor might be much rarer than the tags on the second nearest neighbor. To account for this, we can modify the tagging algorithm to account for both similarity between nearby neighbors and tag frequency. One plausible strategy is due to Kang *et al.* (2006). For a given query image, they build a confidence measure associating each tag with that image. Larger values of the measure associate the tag to the image more strongly. To do so, they require a ranking of the tags in importance; this ranking is given by a vector of values, one per tag. Write α_j for the ranking value of the jth tag; $\boldsymbol{x}_i$ for the feature vector of the ith training example image, and $\boldsymbol{x}_t$ for the feature vector of the test image; $K(\cdot, \cdot)$ for a kernel comparing images; $\Omega(\cdot, \cdot)$ for a kernel comparing *sets* of tags; and $z_{t,k}$ for the confidence with which the kth tag is associated with the test image. We must compute $z_{t,k}$. Kang *et al.* use a submodular function argument to derive an algorithm for concave Ω, though in their examples they use

$$\Omega(\mathcal{S}, \mathcal{S}') = \begin{cases} 0 & \text{if } \mathcal{S} \cap \mathcal{S}' \neq \emptyset \\ 1 & \text{otherwise} \end{cases}.$$

Their method is a straightforward greedy algorithm, which appears in Algorithm 21.2. Once we have the confidence for each tag for a test image, we can choose the tags to report with a variety of strategies (top k; top k if all confidences exceed a threshold; all whose confidence exceeds a threshold; and so on). This method works well (see Table 21.2).

Using the notation of the text

For $k = 1, \ldots, m$:
    Let $\mathcal{T}_k = \{1, 2, \ldots, k\}$
    $f(\mathcal{T}_k) = \sum_{i=1}^n K(\boldsymbol{x}_i, \boldsymbol{x}_t) \Omega(\mathcal{S}_i, \mathcal{T}_k)$
    $z_{t,k} = f(\mathcal{T}_k) - f(\mathcal{T}_{k-1})$

Algorithm 21.2: Greedy Labeling Using Kernel Similarity Comparisons.

21.4.3 Predicting Correlated Words with Classifiers

When word annotations are heavily correlated, we could predict some words based on image evidence, and then predict others using the original set of word predictions. A more efficient method is to train the classifiers so that their predictions are coupled. For example, we will train a set of linear support vector machines, one per word. Write N for the number of training images; T for the size of the tag vocabulary; m for the number of features; $\boldsymbol{x}_i$ for the feature vector of the ith training image; $\mathcal{X}$ for the $m \times N$ matrix $(\boldsymbol{x}_1, \ldots, \boldsymbol{x}_N)$; $\boldsymbol{t}_i$ for the tag vector of the ith image (this is a 0-1 vector whose length is the vocabulary size, with a 0 value if the tag corresponding to that slot is absent and a 1 if it is present); and $\mathcal{T}$ for the $T \times N$ matrix $(\boldsymbol{t}_1, \ldots, \boldsymbol{t}_N)$. Training a set of linear SVMs to predict each word independently involves choosing a $T \times m$ matrix $\mathcal{C}$ to minimize some loss $\mathcal{L}$ that compares $\mathcal{T}$ to the predictions $sign(\mathcal{CX})$. If we chose to use the hinge loss, then the result is a set of independent linear SVMs.

    Loeff and Farhadi (2008) suggest that these independent linear SVMs can be coupled by penalizing the rank of $\mathcal{C}$. Assume for the moment that $\mathcal{C}$ does have low rank; then it can be factored as $\mathcal{GF}$, where the inner dimension is small. Then $\mathcal{CX} = \mathcal{GFX}$. The term $\mathcal{FX}$ represents a reduced dimension feature space

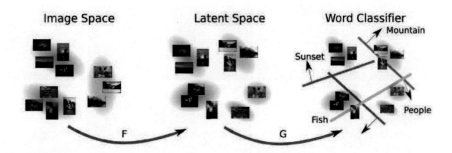

FIGURE 21.9: One way to build correlated linear classifiers is to learn a matrix of linear classifiers $\mathcal{C}$ while penalizing the rank of $\mathcal{C}$. A low rank solution factors into two terms as $\mathcal{C} = \mathcal{G}\mathcal{F}$. The term $\mathcal{F}$ maps image features to a reduced dimensional space of linear features, and $\mathcal{G}$ maps these features to words. The word predictors must be correlated, because the number of rows of $\mathcal{G}$ is greater than the dimension of the reduced dimensional feature space. *This figure was originally published as Figure 1 of "Scene Discovery by Matrix Factorization," by N. Loeff and A. Farhadi, Proc. European Conference on Computer Vision. Springer Lecture Notes in Computer Science, Volume 5304, 2008 © Springer, 2008.*

(it is a linear map of the original feature space to a lower dimensional feature space; Figure 21.9). Similarly, $\mathcal{G}$ is a set of linear classifiers, one per row. But these classifiers have been coupled to one another (because there are fewer linearly independent rows of $\mathcal{G}$ than there are classifiers, see Figure 21.9).

Penalizing rank can be tricky numerically. One useful measure of the rank is the *Ky-Fan norm*, which is the sum of the absolute values of the singular values of the matrix. An alternative definition is

$$\lambda \,|! \,|\mathcal{C}\|_{kf} = \inf_{\mathcal{U},\mathcal{V}|\mathcal{U}\mathcal{V}=\mathcal{C}} (\|\mathcal{U}\|^2 + \|\mathcal{V}\|^2).$$

Loeff and Farhadi learn by minimizing

$$\mathcal{L}(\mathcal{T}, \mathcal{C}\mathcal{X}) + \lambda \,|! \,|\mathcal{C}\|_{kf}$$

as a function of the matrix of classifiers $\mathcal{C}$, and they offer several algorithms to minimize this objective function; the algorithm can be kernelized (Loeff *et al.* 2009). These correlated word predictors are close to, or at, the state of the art for word prediction (see Table 21.2). Results in this table support the idea that correlation is important only rather loosely; there is no clear advantage for methods that correlate word predictions. To some extent, this is an effect of the evaluation scheme. Image annotators very often omit good annotations (see the examples in Figure 21.10), and we do not have methods that can score word predictions that are accurate and useful but not predicted by annotators. Qualitative results do suggest that explicitly representing word correlation is helpful (Figure 21.10).

21.4.4   Names and Faces

Rather than predict all tags from the whole image, we could cut the image into pieces (which might or might not overlap), then predict the tags from the pieces.

FIGURE 21.10: Word predictions for examples from the Corel 5K dataset, using the method of Loeff and Farhadi (2008). Blue words are correct predictions; red words are predictions that do not appear in the annotation of the image; and green words are annotations that were not predicted. Notice that the extra (red) words are strongly correlated to those that are correctly predicted, and are often good annotations. Image annotators often leave out the obvious—sky is present in the center image of the top row—and current scoring methods do not account for this phenomenon well. *his figure was originally published as Figure 5 of "Scene Discovery by Matrix Factorization," by N. Loeff and A. Farhadi, Proc. European Conference on Computer Vision. Springer Lecture Notes in Computer Science, Volume 5304, 2008 © Springer, 2008.*

This will increase the chance that that individual tag predictors could be trained independently. For example, it is unlikely that names in news captions are independent (in 2010, the name "Elin Nordegren" was very likely to co-occur with "Tiger Woods"). But this doesn't mean we need to couple name predictors when we train them; instead, we could find each individual face in the image and then predict names independently for the individual faces. This assumes that the major reason that the names are correlated is that the faces tend to appear together in the images.

Linking faces in pictures with names and captions is a useful special case because news images are mainly about people, and captions very often give names. It is also a valuable example for developing methods to apply to other areas because it illustrates how correspondence between tags and image components can be exploited. Berg *et al.* (2004) describe a method to take a large dataset of captioned images, and produce a set of face images with the correct names attached. In their dataset, not every face in the picture is named in the caption, and not every name in the caption has a face in the picture (see the example in Figure 21.11). The first step is to detect names in captions using an open source named entity recognizer (Cunningham *et al.* 2002). The next is to detect (Mikolajczyk n.d.), rectify, and represent faces using standard appearance representations. We construct the feature vector so that Euclidean distance in feature vector space is a reasonable metric. We can now represent the captioned images as a set of data items that

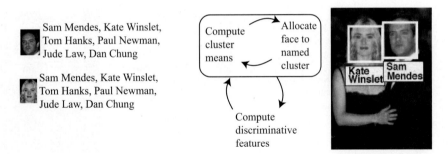

FIGURE 21.11: Berg *et al.* (2004) take a collection of captioned news images and link the faces in each image to names in the caption They preprocess the images by detecting faces, then rectifying them and computing a feature representation of the rectified face. They detect proper names in captions using an open source named entity recognizer (Cunningham *et al.* 2002). The result is a set of data items that consist of (a) a face representation and (b) a list of names that could be associated with that face. *Part of this figure was originally published as Figure 2 of "Names and Faces in the News," by T. Berg, A. Berg, J. Edwards, M. Maire, R. White, Y-W. Teh, E. Learned-Miller and D. Forsyth, Proc. IEEE CVPR 2004, © IEEE 2004.*

consist of a feature representation of a face, and a list of names that could go to that face (notice that some captioned images will produce several data items, as in Figure 21.11).

We must now associate names with faces (Figure 21.12). This can be seen as a form of k-means clustering. We represent each name with a cluster of possible appearance vectors, represented by the cluster mean. Assume we have an initial appearance model for each name; for each data item, we now allocate the face to the closest name in its list of possible names. Typically, these lists are relatively short, so we need only tell which item in a short list the face belongs to. We now re-estimate the appearance models, and repeat until labels do not change. At this point, we can re-estimate the feature space using the labels associated with the face images, then re-estimate the labeling. A natural variant is to allocate a face only when the closest name is closer than some threshold distance. The procedure can be started by allocating faces to the names in their list at random, or by exploiting cases where there is just one face and just one name. This strategy is crude, but works quite well, because it exploits two important features of the problem. First, on the whole, multiple instances of one individual's face should look more like one another than like another individual's face. Second, allocating one of a short list of names to a face is a lot easier than recognizing a face.

21.4.5 Generating Tags with Segments

The most attractive feature of these names-and-faces models is that by reasoning about correspondence between pieces of image (in the models above, faces) and tags, we can learn models for tags independently. The fact that some tags co-occur strongly with others is caused by some pieces of image co-occuring strongly with others, so it doesn't need to be accounted for by the model. There is now a

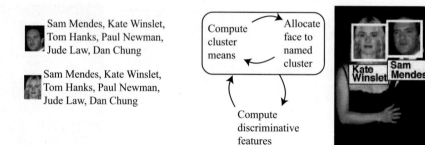

FIGURE 21.12: We associate faces with names by a process of repeated clustering. Each name in the dataset is associated with a cluster of appearance vectors, represented by a mean. Each face is then allocated to the closest name *in that face's list of names.* We now re-estimate the cluster means, and then reallocate faces to clusters. Once this process has converged, we can re-estimate the feature space using linear discriminants (Section 16.1.6), then repeat the labeling process. The result is a correspondence between image faces and names (**right**). *Part of this figure was originally published as Figure 2 of "Names and Faces in the News," by T. Berg, A. Berg, J. Edwards, M. Maire, R. White, Y-W. Teh, E. Learned-Miller and D. Forsyth, Proc. IEEE CVPR 2004, © IEEE 2004.*

huge variety of such models for tagging images with words. Generally, they can be divided into two classes: in one class, we reason explicitly about correspondence, as in the names and faces examples; in the other, the correspondence information is hidden implicitly in the model.

Explicit correspondence models follow the lines of the names and faces example. Duygulu *et al.* (2002) describe a model to which many other models have been compared. The image is segmented, and a feature descriptor incorporating size, location, color, and texture information is computed for each sufficiently large image segment. These descriptors are vector quantized using k-means. This means each tagged training image can be thought of as a bag that contains a set of vector quantized image descriptors and a set of words. There are many such bags, and we think of each bag as a set of samples from some process. This process generates image segments and then some image segments generate words probabilistically. This problem is analogous to one that occurs in the discipline of machine translation. Imagine we wish to build a dictionary giving the French word that corresponds to each English word. We could take the proceedings of the Canadian Parliament as a dataset. These proceedings conveniently appear in both French and English, and what a particular parliamentarian said in English (resp. French) is carefully translated into French (resp. English). This means we can easily build a rough paragraph-level correspondence. Corresponding pairs of paragraphs are bags of French words generated by (known) English words; what we don't know is which English word produced which French word. The vision problem is analogous if we replace English words with vector quantized image segments, and French words with words (Figure 21.13).

Brown *et al.* (1990) give a series of natural models and corresponding algorithms for this problem. The simplest model that applies is known as model 2 (there are five in total; the more complex models deal with the tendency of some

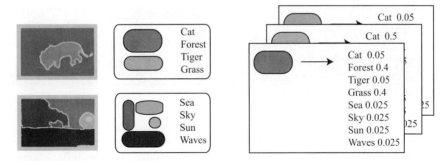

FIGURE 21.13: Duygulu *et al.* (2002) generate annotations for images by segmenting the image (**left**) and then allowing each sufficiently large segment to generate a tag. Segments generate tags using a lexicon (**right**), a table of conditional probabilities for each tag given a segment. They learn this lexicon by abstracting each annotated image as a bag of segments and tags (**center**). If we had a large number of such bags, and knew which tag corresponded to which segment, then building the lexicon just involves counting; similarly, if we knew the lexicon, we could estimate which tag corresponded to which segment in each bag. This suggests using an EM method to estimate the lexicon. *This figure was originally published as Figure 1 of "Object Recognition as Machine Translation: Learning a lexicon for a fixed image vocabulary," by P. Duygulu, K. Barnard, N. deFreitas, and D. Forsyth, Proc. European Conference on Computer Vision. Springer Lecture Notes in Computer Science, Volume 2353, 2002 © Springer, 2002.*

languages to be wordier than others, or to have specific word orders, and do not apply). We assume that each word is generated by a single blob, and associate a (hidden) correspondence variable with each bag. We can then estimate $p(w|b)$, the conditional probability that a word type is generated by a blob type (analogous to a dictionary), using EM.

Once we have a lexicon, we can tag each sufficiently large region with its highest probability word; or do so, but refuse to tag regions where the predicted word has too low a probability; or tag only the k regions that predict words with the highest probability; or do so, but check probabilities against a threshold. This method as it stands is now obsolete as an image tagger, but is widely used as a comparison point because it is natural, quite easily beaten, and associated with an easily available dataset (the Corel5K dataset described in Section 21.5.1).

The cost of reasoning explicitly about correspondence between individual regions and individual words is that such models ignore larger image context. An alternative is to build a form of generative model that explains the bag of segments and words without reasoning about which segment produced which word. An example of such an implicit correspondence model is the cross-media relevance model of Jeon *et al.* (2003). We approximate words as conditionally independent given an image, which means we need to build a model of the probability of a single word conditioned on an image, $P(w|I)$. We approximate this as $P(w|b_1, \ldots, b_n)$, and must now model this probability. We will do so by modelling the joint probability $P(w, b_1, \ldots, b_n)$. We assume a stochastic relationship between the blobs and the image; and we assume that, conditioned on the image, the blobs and the words are

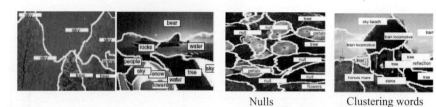

Nulls   Clustering words

FIGURE 21.14: The basic correspondence method we described in the text can produce reasonable results for some image tags (**left**), but tends to perform better with tags that describe "stuff" rather than tags that describe "things" (**center left**). Some of this is because the method has very weak shape representations, and cannot fuse regions. However, it is extremely flexible. Improved word predictions can be obtained by refusing to predict words for regions where the conditional probability of the most likely word is too low (**center right**, "null" predictions), and by fusing words that are predicted by similar image regions (**right**, "train" and "locomotive"). *This figure was originally published as Figures 8, 10, and 11 of "Object Recognition as Machine Translation: Learning a lexicon for a fixed image vocabulary," by P. Duygulu, K. Barnard, N. deFreitas, and D. Forsyth, Proc. European Conference on Computer Vision. Springer Lecture Notes in Computer Science, Volume 2353, 2002 © Springer, 2002.*

independent. If we write $\mathcal{T}$ for the training set, we have

$$
\begin{aligned}
P(w, b_1, \ldots, b_n) &= \sum_{j \in \mathcal{T}} P(J)P(w, b_1, \ldots, b_n | J) \\
&= \sum_{j \in \mathcal{T}} P(J)P(w|J) \prod_{j=1}^{\#w} P(b_j | J),
\end{aligned}
$$

and these component probabilities can be estimated by counting and smoothing. Jeon *et al.* assume that $P(J)$ is uniform over the training images. Now write $c(w, J)$ for the number of times the word w appears as a tag for image J and $c_w(J)$ for the total number of words tagging J. Then we could estimate

$$
P(w|J) = (1 - \alpha)\frac{c(w, J)}{c_w(J)} + \alpha \frac{c(w, \mathcal{T})}{c_w(\mathcal{T})}
$$

(where we have smoothed the estimate so that all words have some small probability of being attached to J). Notice that this is a form of non-parametric topic model. Words and blobs are not independent in the model as a result of the sum over training images, but there is no explicit tying of words to blobs. This model is simple and produces quite good results. As a model, it is now obsolete, but it is a good example of a very large family of models.

21.5 THE STATE OF THE ART OF WORD PREDICTION

Word prediction is now an established problem that operates somewhat independently from object recognition. It is quite straightforward to start research because good standard datasets are available (Section 21.5.1), and methods are quite easy to compare quantitatively because there is at least a rough consensus on appropriate evaluation methodologies (Section 21.5.2). Finally, there are numerous good open questions (Section 21.5.3), which are worth engaging with because the search application is so compelling.

21.5.1   Resources

Most of the code that would be used for systems described in this chapter is feature code (Section 16.3.1) or classifier code (Section 15.3.3). Code for approximate nearest neighbors that can tell whether k-d trees or locality sensitive hashing works better on a particular dataset, and can tune the chosen method, is published by Marius Muja at `http://www.cs.ubc.ca/~mariusm/index.php/FLANN/FLANN`.

The Corel5K dataset contains 5,000 images collected from a larger set of stock photos, split into 4,500 training and 500 test examples. Each image has 3.5 keywords on average, from a dictionary of 260 words that appear in both the training and the test set. The dataset was popularized by Duygulu *et al.* (2002). As of the time of writing, an archive of features and tags for this dataset can be found at `http://lear.inrialpes.fr/people/guillaumin/data.php`.

The IAPRTC-12 dataset contains 20,000 images, accompanied by free text captions. Tags are then extracted from the text by various parsing methods. As of the time of writing, the dataset can be obtained from `http://imageclef.org/photodata`. Various groups publish the features and tags they use for this dataset. See `http://lear.inrialpes.fr/people/guillaumin/data.php`, or `http://www.cis.upenn.edu/~makadia/annotation/`.

The ESP dataset consists of 21,844 images collected using a collaborative image labeling task (von Ahn and Dabbish 2004); two players assign labels to an image without communicating, and labels they agree on are accepted. Images can be reassigned, and then only new labels are accepted (see `http://www.espgame.org`). This means that the pool of labels for an image grows, with easy labels being assigned first.

MirFlickr is a dataset of a million Flickr images, licensed under creative commons and released with concrete visual tags associated (see `http://press.liacs.nl/mirflickr/`).

21.5.2   Comparing Methods

Generally, methods can be compared using recall, precision, and F_1 measure on appropriate datasets. Table 21.2 gives a comparison of methods applied to Corel5K using these measures. The performance statistics are taken from the literature. Some variations between experiments mean that comparisons are rough and ready: CorrLDA predicts a smaller dictionary than the other methods; PicSOM predicts only five annotations; and the F_1 measure for Submodular is taken by eye from the graph of figure 3 in (Kang *et al.* 2006), in the method's most favorable configuration. Table 21.2 suggests that (a) performance has improved over time, though the nearest neighbor method of Section 21.4.2 is simultaneously the simplest and the best performing method; and (b) that accounting for correlations between labels helps, but isn't decisive (for example, neither Submodular nor CorrPred decisively beats JEC). This suggests there is still much to be learned about the image annotation problem.

Method	P	R	F_1	Ref
Co-occ	0.03	0.02	0.02	(Mori *et al.* 1999)
Trans	0.06	0.04	0.05	(Duygulu *et al.* 2002)
CMRM	0.10	0.09	0.10	(Jeon *et al.* 2003)
TSIS	0.10	0.09	0.10	(Celebi 30 Nov. - 1 Dec. 2005)
MaxEnt	0.09	0.12	0.10	(Jeon and Manmatha 2004)
CRM	0.16	0.19	0.17	(Lavrenko *et al.* 2003)
CT-3×3	0.18	0.21	0.19	(Yavlinsky *et al.* 2005)
CRM-rect	0.22	0.23	0.23	(Feng *et al.* 2004)
InfNet	0.17	0.24	0.23	(Metzler and Manmatha 2004)
MBRM	0.24	0.25	0.25	(Feng *et al.* 2004)
MixHier	0.23	0.29	0.26	(Carneiro and Vasconcelos 2005)
CorrLDA[1]	0.06	0.09	0.072	(Blei and Jordan 2002)
JEC	0.27	0.32	0.29	(Makadia *et al.* 2010)
JEC[2]	0.32	0.40	0.36	(Makadia *et al.* 2010)
Submodular	-	-	0.26	(Kang *et al.* 2006)
CorrPred	0.27	0.27	0.27	(Loeff and Farhadi 2008)
CorrPredKernel	0.29	0.29	0.29	(Loeff and Farhadi 2008)
PicSOM[3]	0.35	0.35	0.35	(Viitaniemi and Laaksonen 2007)

TABLE 21.2:   Comparison of the performance of various word annotation prediction methods by precision, recall, and F1-measure, on the Corel 5K dataset. The methods described in the text are: *Trans*, which is the translation model of Section 21.4.5; *CMRM*, which is the cross-media relevance model of Section 21.4.5; *CorrPred*, which is the correlated classifier method of Section 21.4.3; *JEC*, which is the nearest neighbor method of Section 21.4.2; and *Submodular*, which is the submodular optimization method of Section 21.4.2. Other performance figures are given for information, and details of the models appear in the papers cited.

21.5.3   Open Problems

One important open problem is *selection*. Assume we wish to produce a textual representation of an image—what should it contain? It is unlikely that a list of all objects present is useful or helpful. For most pictures, such a list would be much too long and dominated by extraneous detail; preparing it would involve dealing with issues like whether the nut used to hold the chairleg to the chair is a separate object, or just a part of the chair. Several phenomena seem to affect selection; some objects are interesting by their nature and tend to get mentioned if they occur in an image. Spain and Perona (2008) give a probabilistic model that can often predict such mentions. Other objects are interesting because of where they occur in the image, or how big they are in the image. Yet other objects are interesting because they have unusual properties (say, a glass cat or a car without wheels), and identifying this remains difficult. Some objects are depicted in unusual circumstances (for example, a car that is upsidedown). This means that context cues might help tell what is worth mentioning. Choi *et al.* (2010) show a variety of contextual cues that can be computed and identify an object as unusual for context.

Without spatial relations

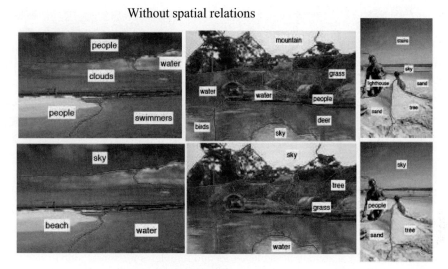

With spatial relations

FIGURE 21.15: Gupta and Davis (2008) show that image labeling can be improved by representing spatial relations between regions, and taking these relations into account when labeling. The top row shows labelings predicted using the method of (Duygulu *et al.* 2002), which considers only individual regions when labeling; the bottom row shows predictions made by their method. Notice that, for example, the "lighthouse" and the "steps" in the image on the right are overruled by the other patches and given better labels by the context. *This figure was originally published as Figure 7 of "Beyond nouns; exploiting prepositions and comparative adjectives for learning visual classifiers," by A. Gupta and L. Davis, Proc. European Conference on Computer Vision. Springer Lecture Notes in Computer Science, Volume 5302, 2008 © Springer, 2002.*

Modifiers, such as adjectives or adjectival phrases, present interesting possibilities to advance learning. Yanai and Barnard (2005) demonstrated that it was possible to learn local image features corresponding to color words (e.g., "pink") without knowing what parts of the image the annotation referred to (Yanai and Barnard 2005). This raises the interesting possibility that possessing phrases can help learning: for example, it is easier to learn from "pink cadillac" than from "cadillac," because the "pink" helps tell where the "cadillac" is in the image. Small improvements have been demonstrated using this approach (Wang and Forsyth 2009). A discipline in linguistics, known as *pragmatics*, studies the things that people choose to say; one guideline is that people mention things that are unusual or important. This suggests that, for example, there is no particular value in mentioning that a sheep is white or a meadow is green. This means that we face two problems: first, we must determine what modifiers apply to a particular object, and second, we must determine whether that modifier is worth mentioning. Farhadi *et al.* (2009*a*) have demonstrated a method that can identify instances of objects that either have unusual attributes, or lack usual ones. This method may be capable of predicting what modifiers are worth mentioning.

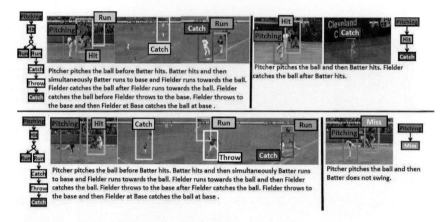

FIGURE 21.16: In structured video, we can predict narratives by exploiting the structure of what can happen. This figure shows examples from the work of Gupta *et al.* (2009), who show that by searching possible actors and templates for sports videos, one can come up with matches that are accurate enough to build a reasonable narrative from templates. *This figure was originally published as Figure 7 of "Understanding Videos, Constructing Plots Learning a Visually Grounded Storyline Model from Annotated Videos," by A. Gupta, P. Srinivasan, J. Shi, and L.S. Davis, Proc. IEEE CVPR 2009, © IEEE 2009.*

Another way to obtain richer descriptions of images is to use spatial **relations** between objects. Heitz and Koller (2008) improve the performance of object detectors by identifying patches of *stuff*—materials such as grass, tarmac, sky and so on, where the shape of the region has little to offer in identifying what it is— that lie nearby. They train a probabilistic graphical model to enhance the detector response when appropriate materials lie in appropriate places (and weaken the response when they don't); the result is a small improvement in detector performance. Gupta and Davis (2008) use images labeled with relational phrases (e.g., "bear in water") to learn to label regions with noun tags together with models of spatial relations. Relational cues could improve learning by disambiguating correspondence quite strongly; for example, if one has a good model of "grass" and of the spatial relation "on," then "sheep on the grass" offers strong cues as to which region is "sheep." Experiments suggest that both of these effects are significant and helpful; the paper shows significant improvements in region labeling (Figure 21.15).

The natural goal of all this generalization is to produce **sentences** from images. Even short sentences can represent a great deal of information in a compact form. To produce a sentence, we would need to select what is worth mentioning; we would need to decide what was happening, what was doing it, and to what it was being done; and we would need to know what modifiers to attach where. In some kinds of video (for example, of a sport), the narrative structure of what is likely to happen is quite stylized, and so quite good sentences can be produced (Figure 21.16). Gupta *et al.* (2009) have shown this means that we can search for sets of actors that fit a template of an action, then report that action in quite a rich sentence form. Yao *et al.* (2010) have been able to link image parsing strategies to text generation strategies to generate informative sentences about video. For

	(transportation, move, track)	A man stands next to a train on a cloudy day
	(bike, ride, track)	A backpacker stands beside a green train
	(transportation, move, road)	This is a picture of a man standing next to a green train
	(pet, sleep, ground)	There are two men standing on a rocky beach, smiling at the camera.
	(bike, ride, road)	This is a person laying down in the grass next to their bike in front of a strange white building.
	(display, place, table)	This is a lot of technology.
	(furniture, place, furniture)	Somebody's screensaver of a pumpkin
	(furniture, place, furniture)	A black laptop is connected to a black Dell monitor
	(bottle, place, table)	This is a dual monitor setup
	(furniture, place, home)	Old school Computer monitor with way to many stickers on it

FIGURE 21.17: Farhadi *et al.* (2010*b*) link sentences to pictures by first computing an affinity with an intermediate representation, then using this to compute a score for a sentence-image pair; the sentence that produces the best score is the annotation. On the **left**, two example images; in the **center**, the top five intermediate representations, given as triples of (actor, scene, action); on the **right**, the top five sentences for each image. Notice how sentence details tend to be inaccurate, but the general thrust of the sentence is often right. *This figure was originally published as Figure 3 of "Every picture tells a story: Generating sentences from images," by A. Farhadi, M. Hejrati, M.A. Sadeghi, P. Young, C. Rastchian, J. Hockenmaier, and D. Forsyth, Proc. European Conference on Computer Vision. Springer Lecture Notes in Computer Science, Volume 6314, 2010* © *Springer, 2009.*

static images, the problem remains very difficult; Farhadi *et al.* (2010*b*) describe one method to link static images to sentences, using an intermediate representation to manage difficulties created by the fact that we have no detector for most of the words encountered (Figure 21.17).

21.6 NOTES

There are many datasets of images with associated words. Examples include: collections of museum material (Barnard *et al.* 2001*b*); the Corel collection of images, described in (Barnard and Forsyth 2001, Duygulu *et al.* 2002, Chen and Wang 2004), and numerous other papers; any video with sound or closed captioning (Satoh and Kanade 1997, Satoh *et al.* 1999, Wang *et al.* 2000); images collected from the Web with their enclosing web pages (Berg and Forsyth 2006); or captioned news images (Berg *et al.* 2004). It is a remarkable fact that, in these collections, pictures and their associated annotations are complementary. The literature is very extensive, and we can mention only the most relevant papers here. For a more complete review, we refer readers to (Datta *et al.* 2005), which has 120 references. There are three natural activities: One might wish to cluster images; to search for images using keywords; or to attach keywords to new images. Typically, models intended for one purpose can produce results for others.

Search: Belongie *et al.* (1998*b*) demonstrate examples of joint image-keyword searches. Joshi *et al.* (2004) show that one can identify pictures that illustrate a story by searching annotated images for those with relevant keywords, then ranking the pool of images based on similarity of appearance. **Clustering:** Barnard and Forsyth (2001) cluster Corel images and their keywords jointly to produce a browsable representation; the clustering method is due to Hofmann and Puzicha (1998). Barnard *et al.* (2001*b*) show that this form of clustering can produce a useful, browsable representation of a large collection of annotated art in digital form.

Attaching keywords to images: Clustering methods can typically be used to predict keywords from images, and accuracy at keyword prediction is used as one test of such methods (see also Barnard *et al.* (2003*b*)). There are two prediction tasks: predicting words associated with an image (*auto-annotation*) and predicting words associated with particular image structures (which is a form of object recognition). Maron and Ratan (1998) attach keywords to images using *multiple-instance learning*. Multiple-instance learning is a general strategy to build classifiers from "bags" of labeled examples. Typically, one knows only that a bag contains or does not contain a positive example, but not which example is positive. Methods attempt to find small regions in the feature space that appear in all positive bags and no negative bags; one can visualize these methods either as a form of smoothing (Maron and Lozano-Pérez 1998, Zhang and Goldman 2001), with an SVM (Andrews *et al.* 2003, Tao *et al.* 2004), or using geometric reasoning (Dietterich *et al.* 1997). Comparisons between methods appear in (Ray and Craven 2005). Chen and Wang describe a variant multiple-instance learning method, and use it to predict keywords from regions (Chen and Wang 2004). Blei and Jordan use a variant of latent Dirichlet allocation to predict words corresponding to particular image regions in an auto-annotation task (Blei and Jordan 2003). Barnard *et al.* (2003*a*) demonstrate and compare a wide variety of methods to predict keywords, including several strategies for reasoning about correspondence directly. Li and Wang (2003) used 2-dimensional multi-resolution hidden markov models on categorized images to train models representing a set of concepts. They then used these concepts for automatic linguistic indexing of pictures. Jeon *et al.* (2003) demonstrate annotation and retrieval with a cross-media relevance model. Lavrenko *et al.* (2003) used continuous space relevance models to predict the probability of generating a word given image regions for automatic image annotation and retrieval.

Other activities: Relations between text and images appear to be deep and complex. Barnard and Johnson (2005) show one can disambiguate the senses of annotating words using image information. Berg and Forsyth (2006) Berg and Forsyth show that one can find images of complex categories ("monkey"; "penguin") by searching for images with distinctive words nearby and containing distinctive image structures. Yanai and Barnard (2005) use region entropy to identify words that have straightforwardly observed visual properties ("pink" as opposed to "affectionate"). All this work has tended to emphasize general image constructs (such as regions), but one might instead use detectors and link the detector responses with words. Faces are of particular interest.

PART SEVEN

BACKGROUND MATERIAL

C H A P T E R   22

Optimization Techniques

Many computer vision tasks can be modeled as solving some optimization problem—that is, the minimization or maximization of some real *energy* function, often averaged over some data points, with respect to some parameters of interest. For example, camera calibration, structure from motion, or pose estimation are naturally cast as the minimization of some mean squared error function over data points. Such *least-squares* problems come in two flavors: *linear* ones when the error function is linear in its parameters and the energy is a quadratic form; and *nonlinear* ones for general smooth error functions. In the former case, the exact optimum can be found using numerical tools for computing the eigenvalues and eigenvectors of a matrix, its pseudoinverse, or its singular value decomposition (Section 22.1). In the latter one, an approximate solution is usually found using some iterative variant of Newton's method, without guarantee of reaching a global optimum (Section 22.2).

Recent work in image processing and computer vision has shown that state-of-the-art results in problems ranging from image denoising to object categorization can be obtained by modeling the underlying data as sparse linear combinations of basis vectors taken from a potentially large *dictionary*. We present in Section 22.3 a brief introduction to this approach to data modeling, and to the optimization techniques underlying it. In particular, we show how to compute the sparse decomposition of a signal on a given dictionary (*sparse coding*) and how to learn the dictionary to adapt it to specific data and to tasks such as classification and regression.

Some computer vision tasks are more naturally modeled by energy functions depending on a discrete set of parameters than smooth functions of real variables, leading to *combinatorial optimization* problems. For example, stereo fusion and, more generally, matching problems are naturally cast this way, with the parameters of interest being integer pixel disparities or the indices of matching pairs of points, for example. As shown in Section 22.4, these optimization problems are, in general, NP-hard, but under certain regularity conditions (*submodularity*), they are amenable to efficient algorithms based on polynomial *min-cuts* algorithms, which in some cases can be shown to provide an exact solution to the original optimization problem.

22.1 LINEAR LEAST-SQUARES METHODS

Let us consider a system of p linear equations in q unknowns:

$$\begin{cases} a_{11}x_1 + a_{12}x_2 + \ldots + a_{1q}x_q = y_1 \\ a_{21}x_1 + a_{22}x_2 + \ldots + a_{2q}x_q = y_2 \\ \ldots \\ a_{p1}x_1 + a_{p2}x_2 + \ldots + a_{pq}x_q = y_p \end{cases}, \tag{22.1}$$

which can be rewritten as $\mathcal{A}\boldsymbol{x} = \boldsymbol{b}$, where $\mathcal{A}$ is a $p \times q$ real matrix, and $\boldsymbol{x}$ and $\boldsymbol{b}$ are vectors in $\mathbb{R}^q$ and $\mathbb{R}^p$ respectively, defined by

$$
\mathcal{A} = \begin{pmatrix} a_{11} & a_{12} & \ldots & a_{1q} \\ a_{21} & a_{22} & \ldots & a_{2q} \\ \ldots & \ldots & \ldots & \ldots \\ a_{p1} & a_{p2} & \ldots & a_{pq} \end{pmatrix}, \quad \boldsymbol{x} = \begin{pmatrix} x_1 \\ x_2 \\ \ldots \\ x_q \end{pmatrix} \quad \text{and} \quad \boldsymbol{y} = \begin{pmatrix} y_1 \\ y_2 \\ \ldots \\ y_p \end{pmatrix}.
$$

We know from elementary linear algebra that (in general)

- when $p < q$, the set of solutions to Equation (22.1) forms a $(q-p)$-dimensional vector subspace of $\mathbb{R}^q$;

- when $p = q$, there is a unique solution;

- when $p > q$, there is no solution.

This statement is true when the maximum number of independent rows or columns of $\mathcal{A}$ (its *rank*) is maximal—that is, equal to $\min(p, q)$ (this is what we mean by *in general*). When the rank is smaller than $\min(p, q)$, the existence of solutions to Equation (22.1) depends on the value of $\boldsymbol{y}$ and whether it belongs to the subspace of $\mathbb{R}^p$ spanned by the columns of $\mathcal{A}$ (its *range*).

22.1.1   Normal Equations and the Pseudoinverse

Let us now focus on the overconstrained case $p > q$ and assume that $\mathcal{A}$ has maximal rank q. Because there is no exact solution in this case, we content ourselves with finding the vector $\boldsymbol{x}$ that minimizes the error measure

$$
E(\boldsymbol{x}) \stackrel{\text{def}}{=} \sum_{i=1}^{p} (a_{i1}x_1 + \ldots + a_{iq}x_q - y_i)^2 = \|\mathcal{A}\boldsymbol{x} - \boldsymbol{y}\|^2,
$$

where $\|\boldsymbol{y}\|$ denotes the Euclidean norm of the vector $\boldsymbol{y}$.

This is a *linear least-squares* problem, whose name stems from the facts that E is proportional to the mean-squared error associated with the equations and that each term before squaring is linear in the parameters of interest.

Now, we can write $E = \boldsymbol{e} \cdot \boldsymbol{e}$, where $\boldsymbol{e} \stackrel{\text{def}}{=} \mathcal{A}\boldsymbol{x} - \boldsymbol{y}$. To find the vector $\boldsymbol{x}$ minimizing $E(\boldsymbol{x})$, we write that the derivatives of this error measure with respect to the coordinates x_i $(i = 1, \ldots, q)$ of $\boldsymbol{x}$ must be zero—that is,

$$
\frac{\partial E}{\partial x_i} = 2\frac{\partial \boldsymbol{e}}{\partial x_i} \cdot \boldsymbol{e} = 0 \quad \text{for} \quad i = 1, \ldots, q.
$$

But if the columns of $\mathcal{A}$ are the vectors $\boldsymbol{c}_j = (a_{1j}, \ldots, a_{mj})^T$ $(j = 1, \ldots, q)$, we have

$$
\frac{\partial \boldsymbol{e}}{\partial x_i} = \frac{\partial}{\partial x_i}\left[\begin{pmatrix} \boldsymbol{c}_1 & \ldots & \boldsymbol{c}_q \end{pmatrix}\begin{pmatrix} x_1 \\ \ldots \\ x_q \end{pmatrix} - \boldsymbol{y}\right] = \frac{\partial}{\partial x_i}(x_1\boldsymbol{c}_1 + \ldots + x_q\boldsymbol{c}_q - \boldsymbol{y}) = \boldsymbol{c}_i.
$$

In particular, writing that $\partial E / \partial x_i = 0$ implies that $\mathbf{c}_i^T (\mathcal{A}\mathbf{x} - \mathbf{y}) = 0$, and stacking the constraints associated with the q coordinates of $\mathbf{x}$ yields the *normal equations* associated with our least-squares problem—that is,

$$\mathbf{0} = \begin{pmatrix} \mathbf{c}_1^T \\ \dots \\ \mathbf{c}_q^T \end{pmatrix} (\mathcal{A}\mathbf{x} - \mathbf{y}) = \mathcal{A}^T (\mathcal{A}\mathbf{x} - \mathbf{y}) \iff \mathcal{A}^T \mathcal{A}\mathbf{x} = \mathcal{A}^T \mathbf{y}. \qquad (22.2)$$

When $\mathcal{A}$ has maximal rank q, the matrix $\mathcal{A}^T \mathcal{A}$ is easily shown to be invertible, and the solution of Equation (22.2) is

$$\mathbf{x} = \mathcal{A}^\dagger \mathbf{y} \quad \text{with} \quad \mathcal{A}^\dagger \stackrel{\text{def}}{=} [(\mathcal{A}^T \mathcal{A})^{-1} \mathcal{A}^T]. \qquad (22.3)$$

The $q \times q$ matrix $\mathcal{A}^\dagger$ is called the *pseudoinverse* of $\mathcal{A}$. It coincides with $\mathcal{A}^{-1}$ when the matrix $\mathcal{A}$ is square and nonsingular. Linear least-squares problems can be solved without explicitly computing the pseudoinverse, using, for example, QR decomposition or singular value decomposition (as described in Section 22.1.5), which might have a better numerical behavior.

22.1.2 Homogeneous Systems and Eigenvalue Problems

Let us now consider a variant of our original problem, where we have again a system of p linear equations in q unknowns, but the vector $\mathbf{y}$ is zero:

$$\begin{cases} a_{11}x_1 + a_{12}x_2 + \dots + a_{1q}x_q = 0 \\ a_{21}x_1 + a_{22}x_2 + \dots + a_{2q}x_q = 0 \\ \dots \\ a_{p1}x_1 + a_{p2}x_2 + \dots + a_{pq}x_q = 0 \end{cases} \iff \mathcal{A}\mathbf{x} = \mathbf{0}. \qquad (22.4)$$

This is a *homogeneous* system of equations in $\mathbf{x}$—that is, if $\mathbf{x}$ is a solution, so is $\lambda \mathbf{x}$ for any $\lambda \neq 0$. When $p = q$ and the matrix $\mathcal{A}$ is nonsingular, Equation (22.4) admits as a unique solution $\mathbf{x} = \mathbf{0}$. Conversely, when $p \geq q$, nontrivial (nonzero) solutions may exist only when $\mathcal{A}$ is singular with rank strictly smaller than q. In this context, minimizing $E(\mathbf{x}) = ||\mathcal{A}\mathbf{x}||^2$ makes sense only when some additional constraint is imposed on $\mathbf{x}$ because the value $\mathbf{x} = \mathbf{0}$ yields the zero global minimum of E. By homogeneity, we have $E(\lambda \mathbf{x}) = \lambda^2 E(\mathbf{x})$, and it is reasonable to choose the constraint $||\mathbf{x}||^2 = 1$, which avoids the trivial solution and forces the uniqueness of the result.

The error $E(\mathbf{x})$ can be rewritten as $||\mathcal{A}\mathbf{x}||^2 = \mathbf{x}^T (\mathcal{A}^T \mathcal{A})\mathbf{x}$. The $q \times q$ matrix $\mathcal{A}^T \mathcal{A}$ is by construction symmetric positive semidefinite—that is, its eigenvalues are all positive or zero, and it can be diagonalized in an orthonormal basis of eigenvectors $\mathbf{e}_i$ $(i = 1, \dots, q)$ associated with the eigenvalues $\lambda_1 \geq \dots \geq \lambda_q \geq 0$ sorted in decreasing order. Thus we can write any unit vector as $\mathbf{x} = \mu_1 \mathbf{e}_1 + \dots + \mu_q \mathbf{e}_q$ with $\mu_1^2 + \dots + \mu_q^2 = 1$. In particular,

$$\begin{aligned} E(\mathbf{x}) - E(\mathbf{e}_q) &= \mathbf{x}^T (\mathcal{A}^T \mathcal{A})\mathbf{x} - \mathbf{e}_q^T (\mathcal{A}^T \mathcal{A})\mathbf{e}_q = \lambda_1 \mu_1^2 + \dots + \lambda_q \mu_q^2 - \lambda_q \\ &\geq \lambda_q (\mu_1^2 + \dots + \mu_q^2 - 1) = 0. \end{aligned}$$

It follows that:

The unit vector x minimizing $E(x) = ||Ax||^2$ is the eigenvector e_q associated with the minimum eigenvalue λ_q of $A^T A$, and the corresponding minimum value of E is λ_q.

Various methods are available for computing the eigenvectors and eigenvalues of a symmetric matrix, including Jacobi transformations and reduction to tridiagonal form followed by QR decomposition. Singular value decomposition also can be used to compute the eigenvectors and eigenvalues without actually constructing the matrix $A^T A$.

22.1.3 Generalized Eigenvalues Problems

Before illustrating the use of homogeneous linear least-squares techniques with an example, let us pause for a minute to consider the slightly more general problem of minimizing $||Ax||^2$ under the constraint $||Bx||^2 = 1$, where B is an $r \times q$ matrix (this reduces to homogeneous linear least squares when $B = \text{Id}$). A vector x and a scalar λ such that

$$A^T Ax = \lambda B^T Bx$$

are called a *generalized eigenvector* and the corresponding *generalized eigenvalue* of the $q \times q$ symmetric matrices $A^T A$ and $B^T B$. It turns out that the solution of the constrained optimization problem is precisely the generalized eigenvector associated with the minimum generalized eigenvalue (which in this case is guaranteed to be positive or zero by construction). As before, effective methods for computing the generalized eigenvectors and eigenvalues of a pair of symmetric matrices are available.

22.1.4 An Example: Fitting a Line to Points in a Plane

Consider n points p_i $(i = 1, \ldots, n)$ in a plane, with coordinates (x_i, y_i) in some fixed coordinate system (Figure 22.1). What is the straight line that best fits these points? To answer this question, we must first quantify how well a line δ fits a set of points or, equivalently, define some error function E measuring the discrepancy between this line and the points. The best-fitting line can then be found by minimizing E.

A reasonable choice for the error function is the mean-squared distance between the points and the line (Figure 22.1). The equation of a line with unit normal $n = (a, b)^T$ lying at a distance d from the origin is $ax + by = d$, and the perpendicular distance between a point with coordinates $(x, y)^T$ and this line is $|ax + by - d|$. We can therefore use

$$E(a, b, d) = \sum_{i=1}^{n} (ax_i + by_i - d)^2 \qquad (22.5)$$

as our error measure, and the line-fitting problem reduces to the minimization of E with respect to a, b, and d under the constraint $a^2 + b^2 = 1$.[1]

---

[1] One could also formulate the line-fitting problem as the minimization of Equation (22.5) with respect to a, b, and d under the constraint that $a^2 + b^2 + d^2 = 1$ (d cannot be interpreted as a distance in this case, but this is not important). This formulation "works" too, but has the disadvantage that the associated A matrix has one column consisting only of ones, with a scale potentially very different from the other two. This may lead to some numerical difficulties, and the solution proposed in the main text should *always* be used instead for this type of problems.

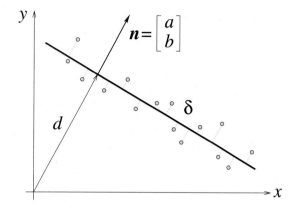

FIGURE 22.1: The line that best fits n points in the plane can be defined as the line δ that minimizes the mean-squared perpendicular distance to these points (the mean-squared length of the short parallel line segments joining δ to the points).

Differentiating E with respect to d shows that, at a minimum of this function, we must have $0 = \partial E/\partial d = -2\sum_{i=1}^{n}(ax_i + by_i - d)$, thus

$$d = a\bar{x} + b\bar{y}, \quad \text{where} \quad \bar{x} = \frac{1}{n}\sum_{i=1}^{n}x_i \quad \text{and} \quad \bar{y} = \frac{1}{n}\sum_{i=1}^{n}y_i, \qquad (22.6)$$

and the two scalars $\bar{x}$ and $\bar{y}$ are simply the coordinates of the center of mass of the input points. Substituting this expression for d in the definition of E yields

$$E = \sum_{i=1}^{n}[a(x_i - \bar{x}) + b(y_i - \bar{y})]^2 = ||\mathcal{A}\boldsymbol{n}||^2 \quad \text{where} \quad \mathcal{A} = \begin{pmatrix} x_1 - \bar{x} & y_1 - \bar{y} \\ \dots & \dots \\ x_n - \bar{x} & y_n - \bar{y} \end{pmatrix},$$

and our original problem finally reduces to minimizing $||\mathcal{A}\boldsymbol{n}||^2$ with respect to $\boldsymbol{n}$ under the constraint $||\boldsymbol{n}||^2 = 1$. We recognize a homogeneous linear least-squares problem, whose solution is the unit eigenvector associated with the minimum eigenvalue of the 2×2 matrix $\mathcal{A}^T\mathcal{A}$. Once a and b have been computed, the value of d is immediately obtained from Equation (22.6). Note that $\mathcal{A}^T\mathcal{A}$ is easily shown to be equal to

$$\begin{pmatrix} \sum_{i=1}^{n}x_i^2 - n\bar{x}^2 & \sum_{i=1}^{n}x_iy_i - n\bar{x}\bar{y} \\ \sum_{i=1}^{n}x_iy_i - n\bar{x}\bar{y} & \sum_{i=1}^{n}y_i^2 - n\bar{y}^2 \end{pmatrix},$$

that is, the matrix of second moments of inertia of the points p_i. In fact, the line best fitting these points in the sense defined in this section is simply their axis of least inertia as defined in elementary mechanics.

22.1.5 Singular Value Decomposition

It turns out that both homogeneous and non-homogeneous linear least-squares problems can be solved *without* computing the matrix $\mathcal{A}^T\mathcal{A}$: *any* real $p \times q$ matrix

$\mathcal{A}$, with $p \geq q$, can be written as

$$\mathcal{A} = \mathcal{U} \mathcal{W} \mathcal{V}^T,$$

where

- $\mathcal{U}$ is a $p \times q$ column-orthogonal matrix—that is, $\mathcal{U}^T \mathcal{U} = \mathrm{Id}_p$;

- $\mathcal{W}$ is a diagonal matrix whose diagonal entries w_i $(i = 1, \ldots, q)$ are the singular values of $\mathcal{A}$ with $w_1 \geq w_2 \geq \ldots \geq w_q \geq 0$;

- and $\mathcal{V}$ is a $q \times q$ orthogonal matrix—that is, $\mathcal{V}^T \mathcal{V} = \mathcal{V} \mathcal{V}^T = \mathrm{Id}_q$.

This is the *singular value decomposition (SVD)* of the matrix $\mathcal{A}$, and it can be computed using the algorithm described in Wilkinson and Reich (1971).

The SVD of a matrix $\mathcal{A}$ can be used to solve non-homogeneous linear least-squares problems *without* computing $\mathcal{A}^T \mathcal{A}$. Indeed, the pseudoinverse associated with the normal equations defined in Section 22.1.1 can be rewritten as

$$\mathcal{A}^\dagger = (\mathcal{A}^T \mathcal{A})^{-1} \mathcal{A}^T = [(\mathcal{V} \mathcal{W}^T \mathcal{U}^T)(\mathcal{U} \mathcal{W} \mathcal{V}^T)]^{-1} (\mathcal{V} \mathcal{W}^T \mathcal{U}^T) = \mathcal{V} \mathcal{W}^{-1} \mathcal{U}^T,$$

because $\mathcal{U}$ is column-orthogonal and $\mathcal{V}$ is orthogonal.

As shown by the following theorem, the singular value decomposition of a matrix is related to the eigenvalues and eigenvectors of its square.

Theorem 5. The singular values of the matrix $\mathcal{A}$ are the square roots of the eigenvalues of the matrix $\mathcal{A}^T \mathcal{A}$, and the columns of the matrix $\mathcal{V}$ are the corresponding eigenvectors.

This theorem can be used to solve overconstrained homogeneous linear equations as defined in the previous section without explicitly computing the corresponding matrix $\mathcal{A}^T \mathcal{A}$. The solution is simply the column vector of the matrix $\mathcal{V}$ in the singular value decomposition of $\mathcal{A}$ that is associated with the smallest singular value.

This result can easily be shown directly without resorting to Theorem 5. Indeed, let us denote by $\boldsymbol{e}_1, \ldots, \boldsymbol{e}_q$ the columns of the matrix $\mathcal{V}$. As before, we can decompose any unit vector $\boldsymbol{x}$ on the basis formed by these vectors as

$$\boldsymbol{x} = \mu_1 \boldsymbol{e}_1 + \ldots + \mu_q \boldsymbol{e}_q = \mathcal{V} \boldsymbol{\mu}$$

with $||\boldsymbol{\mu}||^2 = \mu_1^2 + \ldots + \mu_q^2 = 1$. In particular,

$$E(\boldsymbol{x}) = \boldsymbol{x}^T (\mathcal{A}^T \mathcal{A}) \boldsymbol{x} = (\boldsymbol{\mu}^T \mathcal{V}^T)(\mathcal{V} \mathcal{W}^T \mathcal{U}^T)(\mathcal{U} \mathcal{W} \mathcal{V}^T)(\mathcal{V} \boldsymbol{\mu}) = \boldsymbol{\mu}^T \mathcal{W}^T \mathcal{W} \boldsymbol{\mu} = \sum_{i=1}^{q} w_i^2 \mu_i^2$$

because $\mathcal{U}$ is column-orthogonal, and $\mathcal{V}$ is orthogonal. It follows that

$$E(\boldsymbol{x}) - E(\boldsymbol{e}_q) = w_1^2 \mu_1^2 + \ldots + w_q^2 \mu_q^2 - w_q^2 \geq w_q^2 (\mu_1^2 + \ldots + \mu_q^2 - 1) = 0$$

since the singular values are sorted in decreasing order.

The SVD of a matrix can also be used to characterize matrices that are rank-deficient. Suppose that $\mathcal{A}$ has rank $r < q$. Then the matrices $\mathcal{U}$, $\mathcal{W}$, and $\mathcal{V}$ can be written as

$$\mathcal{U} = \begin{array}{|c|c|} \hline \mathcal{U}_r & \mathcal{U}_{q-r} \\ \hline \end{array}, \quad \mathcal{W} = \begin{array}{|c|c|} \hline \mathcal{W}_r & 0 \\ \hline 0 & 0 \\ \hline \end{array}, \quad \text{and} \quad \mathcal{V}^T = \begin{array}{|c|} \hline \mathcal{V}_r^T \\ \hline \mathcal{V}_{q-r}^T \\ \hline \end{array},$$

and

- the columns of $\mathcal{U}_r$ form an orthonormal basis of the range of $\mathcal{A}$

- and the columns of $\mathcal{V}_{q-r}$ for a basis of the space spanned by the solutions of $A\boldsymbol{x} = 0$ (the *null space* of this matrix).

The $p \times r$ and $q \times r$ matrices $\mathcal{U}_r$ and $\mathcal{V}_r$ are both column-orthogonal, and we of course have $\mathcal{A} = \mathcal{U}_r \mathcal{W}_r \mathcal{V}_r^T$.

The following theorem shows that singular value decomposition also provides a valuable *approximation* procedure. There, $\mathcal{U}_r$ and $\mathcal{V}_r$ denote as before the matrices formed by the r leftmost columns of the matrices $\mathcal{U}$ and $\mathcal{V}$, and $\mathcal{W}_r$ is the $r \times r$ diagonal matrix formed by the r largest singular values. This time, however, $\mathcal{A}$ might have maximal rank q, and the remaining singular values might be nonzero.

Theorem 6. When $\mathcal{A}$ has a rank greater than r, $\mathcal{U}_r \mathcal{W}_r \mathcal{V}_r^T$ is the best possible rank-r approximation of $\mathcal{A}$ in the sense of the Frobenius norm.[2]

This theorem plays a fundamental role in the factorization approach to structure from motion presented in Chapter 8.

22.2   NONLINEAR LEAST-SQUARES METHODS

Let us now consider a general system of p equations in q unknowns:

$$\begin{cases} f_1(x_1, x_2, \ldots, x_q) = 0 \\ f_2(x_1, x_2, \ldots, x_q) = 0 \\ \ldots \\ f_p(x_1, x_2, \ldots, x_q) = 0 \end{cases} \iff \boldsymbol{f}(\boldsymbol{x}) = \boldsymbol{0}. \tag{22.7}$$

Here, $\boldsymbol{f} : \mathbb{R}^q \to \mathbb{R}^p$ is a twice differentiable function with components $f_i : \mathbb{R}^q \to \mathbb{R}$, $i = 1, \ldots, p$. In general,

- when $p < q$, the solutions form a $(q-p)$-dimensional *subset* of $\mathbb{R}^q$;

- when $p = q$, there is a *finite set* of solutions;

- when $p > q$, there is no solution.

Let us emphasize the main differences with the linear case: In general, the dimension of the solution set is still $q - p$ in the underconstrained case, but this set does not form a vector space anymore. Its structure depends on the nature of the functions f_i. Likewise, in the case $p = q$, usually there is a finite number of solutions instead of a unique one.

---

[2] The Frobenius norm of a matrix is the square root of the sum of the squares of its entries.

There is no general method for finding all the solutions of Equation (22.7) when $p = q$ or for finding the global minimum of the least-squares error

$$E(\boldsymbol{x}) \stackrel{\text{def}}{=} ||\boldsymbol{f}(\boldsymbol{x})||^2 = \sum_{i=1}^{p} f_i^2(\boldsymbol{x})$$

when $p > q$. Instead, we present next a number of iterative methods that linearize the problem in hope of finding at least one suitable solution. They all rely on a first-order Taylor expansion of the functions f_i in the neighborhood of a point $\boldsymbol{x}$:

$$f_i(\boldsymbol{x}+\delta\boldsymbol{x}) = f_i(\boldsymbol{x}) + \delta x_1 \frac{\partial f_i}{\partial x_1}(\boldsymbol{x}) + \ldots + \delta x_q \frac{\partial f_i}{\partial x_q}(\boldsymbol{x}) + O(||\delta\boldsymbol{x}||^2) \approx f_i(\boldsymbol{x}) + \nabla f_i(\boldsymbol{x}) \cdot \delta\boldsymbol{x}.$$

Here, $\nabla f_i(\boldsymbol{x}) = (\partial f_i/\partial x_1, \ldots, \partial f_i/\partial x_q)^T$ is the *gradient* of f_i at the point $\boldsymbol{x}$, and we have neglected the second-order term $O(||\delta\boldsymbol{x}||^2)$. It follows immediately that

$$\boldsymbol{f}(\boldsymbol{x} + \delta\boldsymbol{x}) \approx \boldsymbol{f}(\boldsymbol{x}) + \mathcal{J}_{\boldsymbol{f}}(\boldsymbol{x})\delta\boldsymbol{x}, \tag{22.8}$$

where $\mathcal{J}_{\boldsymbol{f}}(\boldsymbol{x})$ is the *Jacobian* of $\boldsymbol{f}$—that is, the $p \times q$ matrix

$$\mathcal{J}_{\boldsymbol{f}}(\boldsymbol{x}) \stackrel{\text{def}}{=} \begin{pmatrix} \nabla f_1^T(\boldsymbol{x}) \\ \ldots \\ \nabla f_p^T(\boldsymbol{x}) \end{pmatrix} = \begin{pmatrix} \dfrac{\partial f_1}{\partial x_1}(\boldsymbol{x}) & \cdots & \dfrac{\partial f_1}{\partial x_q}(\boldsymbol{x}) \\ \ldots & \ldots & \ldots \\ \dfrac{\partial f_p}{\partial x_1}(\boldsymbol{x}) & \cdots & \dfrac{\partial f_p}{\partial x_q}(\boldsymbol{x}) \end{pmatrix}.$$

22.2.1   Newton's Method: Square Systems of Nonlinear Equations.

As mentioned earlier, Equation (22.7) admits (in general) a finite number of solutions when $p = q$. Although there is no general method for finding all of these solutions when $\boldsymbol{f}$ is arbitrary, Equation (22.8) can be used as the basis for a simple iterative algorithm for finding one of these solutions: given some current estimate $\boldsymbol{x}$ of the solution, the idea is to compute a perturbation $\delta\boldsymbol{x}$ of this estimate such that $\boldsymbol{f}(\boldsymbol{x} + \delta\boldsymbol{x}) \approx \boldsymbol{0}$, or, according to Equation (22.8),

$$\mathcal{J}_{\boldsymbol{f}}(\boldsymbol{x})\delta\boldsymbol{x} = -\boldsymbol{f}(\boldsymbol{x}).$$

When the Jacobian is nonsingular, $\delta\boldsymbol{x}$ is easily found as the solution of this $q \times q$ system of linear equations, and the process is repeated until convergence.

Newton's method converges rapidly once close to a solution: It has a *quadratic convergence rate*, that is, the error at step $k+1$ is proportional to the square of the error at step k. When started far from a solution, Newton's method as presented here might be unreliable. Various strategies can be used to improve its robustness, but their discussion is beyond the scope of this book.

22.2.2   Newton's Method: Overconstrained Systems of Nonlinear Equations

When p is greater than q, we seek a local minimum of the least-squares error E (there is no guarantee in general to reach its global minimum). Newton's method can be adapted to this case by noting that such a minimum is a zero of the error's gradient. More precisely, we introduce $\boldsymbol{F}(\boldsymbol{x}) = \frac{1}{2}\nabla E(\boldsymbol{x})$ and use Newton's method to find the desired minimum as a solution of the $q \times q$ system of nonlinear equations $\boldsymbol{F}(\boldsymbol{x}) = \boldsymbol{0}$. Differentiating E shows that

$$\boldsymbol{F}(\boldsymbol{x}) = \mathcal{J}_{\boldsymbol{f}}^T(\boldsymbol{x})\boldsymbol{f}(\boldsymbol{x}), \tag{22.9}$$

and differentiating this expression shows in turn that the Jacobian of $\boldsymbol{F}$ is

$$\mathcal{J}_{\boldsymbol{F}}(\boldsymbol{x}) = \mathcal{J}_{\boldsymbol{f}}^T(\boldsymbol{x})\mathcal{J}_{\boldsymbol{f}}(\boldsymbol{x}) + \sum_{i=1}^{p} f_i(\boldsymbol{x})\mathcal{H}_{f_i}(\boldsymbol{x}). \tag{22.10}$$

In this equation, $\mathcal{H}_{f_i}(\boldsymbol{x})$ denotes the *Hessian* of f_i—that is, the $q \times q$ matrix of second derivatives

$$\mathcal{H}_{f_i}(\boldsymbol{x}) \stackrel{\text{def}}{=} \begin{pmatrix} \dfrac{\partial^2 f_i}{\partial x_1^2}(\boldsymbol{x}) & \cdots & \dfrac{\partial^2 f_i}{\partial x_1 x_q}(\boldsymbol{x}) \\ \cdots & \cdots & \cdots \\ \dfrac{\partial^2 f_i}{\partial x_1 x_q}(\boldsymbol{x}) & \cdots & \dfrac{\partial^2 f_i}{\partial x_q^2}(\boldsymbol{x}) \end{pmatrix}.$$

The term $\delta\boldsymbol{x}$ in Newton's method satisfies $\mathcal{J}_{\boldsymbol{F}}(\boldsymbol{x})\delta\boldsymbol{x} = -\boldsymbol{F}(\boldsymbol{x})$. Equivalently, combining Equations (22.9) and (22.10) shows that $\delta\boldsymbol{x}$ is the solution of

$$[\mathcal{J}_{\boldsymbol{f}}^T(\boldsymbol{x})\mathcal{J}_{\boldsymbol{f}}(\boldsymbol{x}) + \sum_{i=1}^{p} f_i(\boldsymbol{x})\mathcal{H}_{f_i}(\boldsymbol{x})]\delta\boldsymbol{x} = -\mathcal{J}_{\boldsymbol{f}}^T(\boldsymbol{x})\boldsymbol{f}(\boldsymbol{x}). \tag{22.11}$$

22.2.3 The Gauss–Newton and Levenberg–Marquardt Algorithms

Newton's method requires computing the Hessians of the functions f_i, which may be difficult and/or expensive. We discuss here two other approaches to nonlinear least-squares that do not involve the Hessians. Let us first consider the Gauss–Newton algorithm: In this approach, we use again a first-order Taylor expansion of $\boldsymbol{f}$ to minimize E, but this time we seek the value of $\delta\boldsymbol{x}$ that minimizes $E(\boldsymbol{x} + \delta\boldsymbol{x})$ for a given value of $\boldsymbol{x}$. Substituting Equation (22.8) into Equation (22.7) yields

$$E(\boldsymbol{x} + \delta\boldsymbol{x}) = ||\boldsymbol{f}(\boldsymbol{x} + \delta\boldsymbol{x})||^2 \approx ||\boldsymbol{f}(\boldsymbol{x}) + \mathcal{J}_{\boldsymbol{f}}(\boldsymbol{x})\delta\boldsymbol{x}||^2.$$

At this point, we are back in the linear least-squares setting, and the adjustment $\delta\boldsymbol{x}$ can be computed as the solution of $\mathcal{J}_{\boldsymbol{f}}^\dagger(\boldsymbol{x})\delta\boldsymbol{x} = -\boldsymbol{f}(\boldsymbol{x})$ or, equivalently, according to the definition of the pseudoinverse,

$$\mathcal{J}_{\boldsymbol{f}}^T(\boldsymbol{x})\mathcal{J}_{\boldsymbol{f}}(\boldsymbol{x})\delta\boldsymbol{x} = -\mathcal{J}_{\boldsymbol{f}}^T(\boldsymbol{x})\boldsymbol{f}(\boldsymbol{x}). \tag{22.12}$$

Comparing Equations. (22.11) and (22.12), we see that the Gauss–Newton algorithm can be thought of as an approximation of Newton's method where the term involving the Hessians $\mathcal{H}_{f_i}$ has been neglected. This is justified when the values of the functions f_i at a solution (the *residuals*) are small because the matrices

$\mathcal{H}_{f_i}$ are multiplied by these residuals in Equation (22.11). In this case, the performance of the Gauss–Newton algorithm is comparable to that of Newton's method, with (nearly) quadratic convergence close to a solution. When the residuals at the solution are too large, however, it might converge slowly or not at all.

When Equation (22.12) is replaced by

$$[\mathcal{J}_{f}^{T}(\boldsymbol{x})\mathcal{J}_{f}(\boldsymbol{x}) + \mu\mathrm{Id}]\delta\boldsymbol{x} = -\mathcal{J}_{f}^{T}(\boldsymbol{x})\boldsymbol{f}(\boldsymbol{x}), \tag{22.13}$$

where the parameter μ is allowed to vary at each iteration, we obtain the Levenberg–Marquardt algorithm, popular in computer vision circles. This is another variant of Newton's method where the term involving the Hessians is this time approximated by a multiple of the identity matrix. The Levenberg–Marquardt algorithm has convergence properties comparable to its Gauss–Newton cousin, but it is more robust: for example, unlike the Gauss–Newton algorithm, it can be used when the Jacobian $\mathcal{J}_{f}$ does not have maximal rank and its pseudoinverse does not exist.

22.3 SPARSE CODING AND DICTIONARY LEARNING

Linear models representing data vectors as sparse combinations of dictionary elements are widely used in computer vision, machine learning, neuroscience, signal processing, and statistics. This section gives an informal introduction to this approach to data modeling, and briefly discusses modern optimization techniques for computing the sparse decomposition of a vector given a predefined dictionary, a process known as *sparse coding* (Section 22.3.1), and for learning the dictionary to adapt it to specific data (Section 22.3.2). In both cases, the objective function minimized can be thought of as a constrained version of a least-squares error, with the aim of reconstructing the data as well as possible given the sparsity constraints. We conclude in Section 22.3.3 by showing that sparse models can also be used for tasks such as classification and regression, and presenting a formulation of dictionary learning adapted to this *supervised* setting.

22.3.1 Sparse Coding

Consider a vector $\boldsymbol{x}$ in $\mathbb{R}^m$ and a *dictionary* $\mathcal{D}$ in $\mathbb{R}^{m \times k}$, whose columns are called *atoms*. (In the image processing or computer vision domain, $\boldsymbol{x}$ may be a small image patch, and $\mathcal{D}$ may be composed of wavelets [Mallat 1999], for example.) We define *sparse coding* as

$$\min_{\boldsymbol{\alpha} \in \mathbb{R}^k} ||\boldsymbol{x} - \mathcal{D}\boldsymbol{\alpha}||^2 + \lambda||\boldsymbol{\alpha}||_p \tag{22.14}$$

where λ is some positive parameter, and $||\boldsymbol{\alpha}||_p$ is the ℓ_p (pseudo) norm of $\boldsymbol{\alpha}$.[3] Note that *overcomplete dictionaries* with $k > m$ are allowed in this setting because the *regularization term* in $||\boldsymbol{\alpha}||_p$ lifts the ambiguity associated with the corresponding undetermined linear system, and we denote by $\boldsymbol{\alpha}^{\star}(\boldsymbol{x}, \mathcal{D})$ the solution of Equation (22.14), assuming it is unique. When $p = 0$, the regularization term associated with the ℓ_0 pseudo norm counts the nonzero coefficients of the vector $\boldsymbol{\alpha}^{\star}(\boldsymbol{x}, \mathcal{D})$,

---

[3]The ℓ_p norm of a vector $\boldsymbol{x}$ in $\mathbb{R}^m$ is defined, for $p \geq 1$, by $||\boldsymbol{x}||_p = (\sum_{i=1}^{m} |\boldsymbol{x}[i]|^p)^{1/p}$. Following tradition, we denote by $||\boldsymbol{x}||_0$ the number of nonzero elements of the vector $\boldsymbol{x}$. This ℓ_0 sparsity measure is not a true norm.

and naturally encourages it to be sparse. When $p = 1$, the regularization term associated with the ℓ_1 (true) norm is known to yield a sparse solution of Equation (22.14), but there is no direct analytic link between the value of $||\boldsymbol{\alpha}^\star(\boldsymbol{x}, \mathcal{D})||_1$ and its effective sparsity.

The scalar λ controls the trade-off between the least-squares error term and the ℓ_p regularizer. It can also be used as a *Lagrange multiplier* to impose constraints on the optimization process: indeed, given two positive thresholds T' and T'', the problem defined by Equation (22.14) is equivalent to

$$\min_{\boldsymbol{\alpha} \in \mathbb{R}^k} ||\boldsymbol{x} - \mathcal{D}\boldsymbol{\alpha}||^2 \quad \text{such that} \quad ||\boldsymbol{\alpha}||_p \leq T' \tag{22.15}$$

for some value of λ, and to

$$\min_{\boldsymbol{\alpha} \in \mathbb{R}^k} ||\boldsymbol{\alpha}||_p \quad \text{such that} \quad ||\boldsymbol{x} - \mathcal{D}\boldsymbol{\alpha}||^2 \leq T'' \tag{22.16}$$

for some other value of this parameter. Again, there is no analytical link between these values of λ and the values of T' and T''.

When $p = 1$, the problem defined by Equation (22.14) or, equivalently, by Equations (22.15)–(22.16), is also known as *basis pursuit* (Chen *et al.* 1999), or the *Lasso* (Tibshirani 1996). It is convex, and efficient algorithms, such as *LARS*—for *least-angle regression* (Efron *et al.* 2004), are available for solving it. When $p = 0$, solving Equation (22.14) is NP-hard, and one must rely on greedy (but efficient) algorithms such as *forward selection* (Weisberg 1980), also known as *orthogonal matching pursuit* (Mallat and Zhang 1993), to find an approximate solution.

22.3.2   Dictionary Learning

Using a *learned* dictionary adapted to the data instead of a predefined one has recently led to state-of-the-art results in numerous signal processing tasks, such as image denoising, texture synthesis, and audio processing, as well as computer vision ones, such as image classification, showing that sparse learned models are well adapted to a wide range of natural signals. Classical techniques for learning the dictionary (Olshausen & Field 1997; Engan, Aase, & Husoy 1999; Lewicki & Sejnowski 2000; Aharon, Elad, & Bruckstein 2006) consider a finite training set of signals $\mathcal{X} = [\boldsymbol{x}_1, \ldots, \boldsymbol{x}_n]$ in $\mathbb{R}^{m \times n}$, and minimize the *empirical cost function*

$$f_n(\mathcal{D}) = \frac{1}{n} \sum_{i=1}^{n} l(\boldsymbol{x}_i, \mathcal{D}), \quad \text{where} \quad l(\boldsymbol{x}, \mathcal{D}) = \min_{\boldsymbol{\alpha} \in \mathbb{R}^k} \frac{1}{2} ||\boldsymbol{x} - \mathcal{D}\boldsymbol{\alpha}||_2^2 + \lambda ||\boldsymbol{\alpha}||_1, \tag{22.17}$$

with respect to $\mathcal{D}$. The number of samples n is usually large, and the signal dimension m is usually comparatively small, for example, $m = 100$ for 10×10 image patches, and $n \geq 100,000$ for typical image processing applications. In general, we also have $k \ll n$ (e.g., $k = 200$ for $n = 100,000$), but each signal only uses a few elements of $\mathcal{D}$ in its representation, say 10 for instance.

To prevent the Frobenius norm of $\mathcal{D}$ from being arbitrarily large, which would lead to arbitrarily small vectors $\boldsymbol{\alpha}_i = \boldsymbol{\alpha}^\star(\boldsymbol{x}_i, \mathcal{D})$, it is common to constrain its columns $\boldsymbol{d}_1, \ldots, \boldsymbol{d}_k$ to have an ℓ_2-norm less than or equal to one. We will call $\mathcal{C}$ the convex set of matrices verifying this constraint:

$$\mathcal{C} = \{\mathcal{D} \in \mathbb{R}^{m \times k} \text{ s.t. } \forall j = 1, \ldots, k, \ \ ||\boldsymbol{d}_j||^2 \leq 1\}. \tag{22.18}$$

Note that the problem of minimizing the empirical cost $f_n(\mathcal{D})$ is not convex with respect to $\mathcal{D}$. It can be rewritten as a joint optimization problem with respect to the dictionary $\mathcal{D}$ and the matrix $\mathcal{A} = [\boldsymbol{\alpha}_1, \ldots, \boldsymbol{\alpha}_n]$ in $\mathbb{R}^{k \times n}$ formed by the coefficients of the sparse decompositions:

$$\min_{\mathcal{D} \in \mathcal{C}, \mathcal{A} \in \mathbb{R}^{k \times n}} \sum_{i=1}^{n} \left(\frac{1}{2} \|\boldsymbol{x}_i - \mathcal{D}\boldsymbol{\alpha}_i\|_2^2 + \lambda \|\boldsymbol{\alpha}_i\|_1 \right), \tag{22.19}$$

or equivalently as the matrix factorization problem

$$\min_{\mathcal{D} \in \mathcal{C}, \mathcal{A} \in \mathbb{R}^{k \times n}} \frac{1}{2} \|\mathcal{X} - \mathcal{D}\mathcal{A}\|_F^2 + \lambda \|\mathcal{A}\|_{1,1}, \tag{22.20}$$

where $\|\mathcal{A}\|_{1,1}$ denotes the ℓ_1 norm of the matrix $\mathcal{A}$—that is, the sum of the magnitudes of its coefficients.

The problem defined by Equations (22.19)–(22.20) is not jointly convex in $\mathcal{D}$ and $\mathcal{A}$, but it is convex in each of these variables separately. This suggests alternating between the two variables, minimizing the empirical cost with respect to one while keeping the other fixed, as proposed by Engan *et al.* (1999) and Aharon *et al.* (2006), for example.

As pointed out by Bottou and Bousquet (2007), however, the empirical cost $f_n(\mathcal{D})$ is only a substitute for the *expected cost*

$$f(\mathcal{D}) = \mathbb{E}_{\boldsymbol{x}}[l(\boldsymbol{x}, \mathcal{D})] = \lim_{n \to \infty} f_n(\mathcal{D}) \quad \text{almost surely,} \tag{22.21}$$

where the expectation (which is supposed finite) is taken relative to the probability distribution $p(\boldsymbol{x})$ of the data. Of course, $p(\boldsymbol{x})$ is unknown, but this suggests that, given a finite training set, one should not spend too much effort on accurately minimizing the empirical cost, because it is only an approximation of the expected one. An "inaccurate" solution may indeed have the same or better expected cost than a "well-optimized" one. Bottou and Bousquet (2007) further show that stochastic gradient algorithms, whose convergence rate is very poor in conventional optimization terms, may in fact in certain settings be shown, both theoretically and empirically, to be faster in reaching a solution with low expected cost than second-order, Newton-like, batch methods.

Olshausen and Field (1997) learn a dictionary using stochastic gradient descent. Mairal *et al.* (2010) have proposed recently a different online algorithm that exploits the specific structure of the dictionary learning problem to efficiently solve it by sequentially minimizing a quadratic local surrogate of the expected cost. Concretely, assuming that the training set is composed of i.i.d. samples of a distribution $p(\boldsymbol{x})$, its inner loop draws one element $\boldsymbol{x}_t$ at a time, as in stochastic gradient descent, and alternates classical sparse coding steps using the LARS algorithm to compute the decomposition $\boldsymbol{\alpha}_t = \boldsymbol{\alpha}^\star(\boldsymbol{x}_t, \mathcal{D}_{t-1})$ of $\boldsymbol{x}_t$ over the dictionary $\mathcal{D}_{t-1}$ obtained at the previous iteration, with dictionary update steps where the new dictionary $\mathcal{D}_t$ is computed by minimizing over $\mathcal{C}$ the function

$$\hat{f}_t(\mathcal{D}) = \frac{1}{t} \sum_{i=1}^{t} \left(\frac{1}{2} \|\boldsymbol{x}_i - \mathcal{D}\boldsymbol{\alpha}_i\|_2^2 + \lambda \|\boldsymbol{\alpha}_i\|_1 \right), \tag{22.22}$$

and the vectors $\boldsymbol{\alpha}_i$ for $i < t$ have been computed during the previous steps of the algorithm. It can be shown that, under mild conditions, this simple procedure converges almost surely to an optimum of $f(\mathcal{D})$. In addition, its computational cost is lower than classical batch algorithms, with low memory consumption, and it scales up gracefully to large data sets with millions of training samples (Mairal *et al.* 2010).

22.3.3   Supervised Dictionary Learning

Suppose now that we are interested in predicting a variable $\boldsymbol{y}$ in $\mathcal{Y}$ from the observation $\boldsymbol{x}$, where $\mathcal{Y}$ is either a finite set of labels in the case of classification, or $\mathbb{R}^q$ for some integer q in the case of regression. The simplest formulation consists of learning a linear model for predicting the variable $\boldsymbol{y}$ using $\boldsymbol{\alpha}^\star(\boldsymbol{x}, \mathcal{D})$ as feature vector. More generally, and without restricting ourselves to a linear model, one can learn model parameters $\mathcal{W}$ by solving an optimization problem of the form

$$\min_{\mathcal{D} \in \mathcal{C}, \mathcal{W} \in \mathcal{V}} f(\mathcal{D}, \mathcal{W}) + \frac{\nu}{2} ||\mathcal{W}||_F^2, \tag{22.23}$$

where $\mathcal{C}$ is the set of constraints defined in Equation (22.18), $\mathcal{V}$ is a convex subset of $\mathbb{R}^d$ for some integer d, ν is a regularization parameter, and f has the form

$$f(\mathcal{D}, \mathcal{W}) = \mathbb{E}_{(\boldsymbol{y}, \boldsymbol{x})}[l(\boldsymbol{y}, \mathcal{W}, \boldsymbol{\alpha}^\star(\boldsymbol{x}, \mathcal{D}))], \tag{22.24}$$

where $l : \mathcal{Y} \times \mathcal{V} \times \mathbb{R}^k \to \mathbb{R}$ is a convex loss function. The expectation is taken with respect to the unknown probability distribution p of the data $(\boldsymbol{y}, \boldsymbol{x})$. Depending on the setting (classification or regression), different choices for l are possible, for example the square loss, the logistic one, or the hinge loss from support vector machines, potentially combined with some kernel (Raina *et al.* 2007). For example, using the square loss and a linear model for binary classification amounts to taking $l(\boldsymbol{y}, \mathcal{W}, \boldsymbol{\alpha}) = (y - \mathcal{W} \cdot \boldsymbol{\alpha})^2$ with $\boldsymbol{y}$ in $\{-1, +1\}$.

The main difficulty with the optimization of the function f defined by Equation (22.24) is that $\boldsymbol{\alpha}^\star(\boldsymbol{x}, \mathcal{D})$ is not differentiable with respect to $\mathcal{D}$. This suggesting replacing the original formulation of sparse coding by a slightly different one, the *elastic net* (Zou and Hastie 2005), defined by

$$\boldsymbol{\alpha}^\star(\boldsymbol{x}, \mathcal{D}) = \arg\min_{\boldsymbol{\alpha} \in \mathbb{R}^p} \frac{1}{2} ||\boldsymbol{x} - \mathcal{D}\boldsymbol{\alpha}||_2^2 + \lambda_1 ||\boldsymbol{\alpha}||_1 + \frac{\lambda_2}{2} ||\boldsymbol{\alpha}||_2^2. \tag{22.25}$$

The solution of this problem is always unique and well defined for $\lambda_2 > 0$, and although it is not smooth either, Mairal *et al.* (2011) show that, in that case, the function f is in fact differentiable, and that its gradient can be computed in closed form in the form of an expectation (the main idea is that the places where $\boldsymbol{\alpha}^\star$ is not differentiable are negligible in the expectation from Equation [22.24]). Stochastic descent methods are typically well suited to this kind of problems, and a projected first-order stochastic gradient algorithm (Kushner and Yin 2003) gives good results in practice.

22.4   MIN-CUT/MAX-FLOW PROBLEMS AND COMBINATORIAL OPTIMIZATION

So far we have considered smooth optimization problems. We now turn to *combinatorial optimization*, where the parameters of interest are integers. We focus

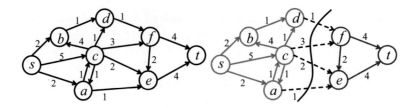

FIGURE 22.2: A graph (**left**) and its minimum cut (**right**), consisting of the dashed edges, with a value of 7. Here, $S = \{s, a, b, c, d\}$ and $T = \{e, f, t\}$.

on two such problems: the partition of a directed graph with non-negative weights into two components S and T such that the sum of the weights of arcs originating in S and terminating in T is minimal (*min-cut problem*); and the minimization of a quadratic function of n binary variables (*quadratic pseudo-Boolean function*). It turns out that the former problem can be solved in polynomial time by several efficient algorithms, although the latter one can be reduced to a min-cut problem— and thus also can be solved in polynomial time—when the function verifies certain regularity properties (*submodularity*), and is NP hard otherwise. We conclude by considering the more general case of functions of n integer variables defined over some finite interval that can be written as a sum of unary and binary terms in these variables, and show that their minimization can also be reduced to a min-cut problem when they are submodular.

22.4.1   Min-Cut Problems

Consider a *directed* graph, or *network*, $\mathcal{G} = (\mathcal{V}, \mathcal{E})$ with vertices $\mathcal{V}$ and edges $\mathcal{E}$; two *terminal* nodes s and t respectively called the *source* and *sink*; and n non-terminal nodes, say, $v_1, \ldots, v_n$. Let us define a *cut* of $\mathcal{G}$ as a partition of its nodes into disjoint subsets S and T such that s is in S and t is in T, and the corresponding *cut set* $C(S, T)$ as the set of edges (v, w) such that v belongs to S and w belongs to T (Figure 22.2). Given some non-negative cost (or *capacity*) function $c : \mathcal{V} \times \mathcal{V} \to \mathbb{R}^+$ such that $c(v, w) = 0$ when there is no edge between the vertices v and w, we define the cost of the cut (S, T) as

$$\sum_{(v,w) \in C(S,T)} c(v, w).$$

It turns out that a cut with minimal cost (*min-cut problem*) is equivalent to solving a linear programming problem.

Given the capacity function c, a *flow* is a non-negative function $f : V \times V \to \mathbb{R}^+$ such that

$$\begin{cases} \forall (v, w) \in V \times V, \ f(v, w) \leq c(v, w), \\ \forall (v, w) \in V \times V, \ f(v, w) = -f(w, v), \\ \forall v \in V \backslash \{s, t\}, \ \sum_{u \in V} f(u, v) = 0. \end{cases}$$

The first of these three constraints states that the flow through an edge cannot exceed its capacity, and the second and third constraints express a conservation law: except for source and sink nodes, the sum of the flows entering a node is equal to the sum of the flows leaving it. The value of the flow f is defined as

$$|f| = \sum_{v \in V} f(s, v).$$

It can be shown that computing a maximal flow (*max-flow problem*) also amounts to solving a linear program, and that the max-flow and min-cut values of a given network are the same (Ford and Fulkerson 1956, minimal cut theorem). Contrary to the case of general linear programming problems, efficient polynomial algorithms for solving the max-flow problem, and thus the min-cut problem too, are available (Ford & Fulkerson 1956; Goldberg & Tarjan 1988; Boykov & Kolgomorov 2004).[4]

22.4.2   Quadratic Pseudo-Boolean Functions

Let us now consider the class of energy functions $E : \{0,1\}^n \to \mathbb{R}$ that can be written as a sum of unary and binary terms in a vector $\boldsymbol{x} = (x_1, \ldots, x_n)^T$ of n binary variables—that is,

$$E(\boldsymbol{x}) = \sum_{i=1}^n E_i(x_i) + \sum_{1 \leq i < j \leq n} E_{ij}(x_i, x_j). \tag{22.26}$$

Note that any function that can be written as a sum of unary terms associated with the nodes of some finite oriented graph $\mathcal{G}$ and binary terms associated with its edges can be written this way. Without loss of generality, the nodes of $\mathcal{G}$ can be identified with integers between 1 and n, and its edges can be identified with the ordered pairs (p, q) such that $1 \leq p < q \leq n$. This is done by assigning a zero cost to edges not present in the original graph, and replacing the two terms associated to reverse edges by their sum.

We show in the rest of this section that, under certain regularity conditions, minimizing functions with the form defined by Equation (22.26) reduces to a min-cut problem.

Let us first note that it is always possible to write any energy function depending on a single binary variable as an affine function of this variable:

$$E_i(x_i) = \mu_i x_i + \nu_i, \quad \text{where} \quad \mu_i = E_i(1) - E_i(0) \quad \text{and} \quad \nu_i = E_i(0). \tag{22.27}$$

Likewise, it is possible to write any energy function depending on two different binary variables as the sum of a constant and a quadratic function in these two variables. Indeed, it is easy to check that the following identity holds for any value of the binary variables x_i and x_j:

$$E_{ij}(x_i, x_j) = \beta_{ij} x_i x_j + \gamma_{ij} x_i + \gamma_{ji} x_j + \delta_{ij}, \tag{22.28}$$

where

$$\begin{cases} \beta_{ij} = E_{ij}(0,0) + E_{ij}(1,1) - E_{ij}(0,1) - E_{ij}(1,0), \\ \gamma_{ij} = E_{ij}(1,0) - E_{ij}(0,0), \\ \gamma_{ji} = E_{ij}(0,1) - E_{ij}(0,0), \\ \delta_{ij} = E_{ij}(0,0). \end{cases}$$

---

[4] Although the simplex method for linear programming is in the worst case exponential in the number of variables, polynomial *interior-point* algorithms do exist (Boyd and Vandenberghe 2004), but they are designed for generic linear programming problems, and not as efficient in general as dedicated min-cit/max-flow solutions.

It follows immediately from Equations (22.27) and (22.28) that $E(\boldsymbol{x})$ can always be rewritten, *up to some additive constant*, as

$$E(\boldsymbol{x}) = \sum_{i=1}^{n} \alpha_i x_i + \sum_{1 \leq i < j \leq n} \beta_{ij} x_i x_j, \quad \text{where } \alpha_i = \mu_i + \sum_{j \neq i} \gamma_{ij}, \tag{22.29}$$

which is a quadratic function of the binary variables $x_1, \ldots, x_n$—that is, a *quadratic pseudo-Boolean function*.

For any binary variable x, let us define $\bar{x} = 1 - x$. The energy function in Equation (22.29) can also be rewritten, *up to a (different) additive constant*, as

$$E(\boldsymbol{x}) = \sum_{i \in P} \rho_i x_i - \sum_{i \in N} \rho_i \bar{x}_i - \sum_{1 \leq i < j \leq n} \beta_{ij} x_i \bar{x}_j, \quad \text{where} \quad \begin{cases} \rho_i = \alpha_i + \sum_{j > i} \beta_{ij}, \\ P = \{i | \rho_i > 0\}, \\ N = \{i | \rho_i \leq 0\}. \end{cases} \tag{22.30}$$

Note that all the coefficients of the unary terms in Equation (22.30) are non-negative.

When the coefficients β_{ij} are negative, the minimization of energy functions of the form shown in Equation (22.29), or equivalently, Equation (22.30), is equivalent to a min-cut problem, and thus amenable to efficient computational solutions. To show this, let us follow the construction of Boros and Hammer (2002), and consider a graph $\mathcal{G} = (\mathcal{V}, \mathcal{E})$ with $n + 2$ vertices $\mathcal{V}$, including source and sink nodes s and t, the remaining vertices being identified with the n binary variables. The arcs of the graph correspond to the various terms in Equation (22.30):

$$\mathcal{E} = \{(s, x_i; -\rho_i) | i \in N\} \cup \{(x_i, t; \rho_i) | i \in P\} \cup \{(x_i, x_j; -\beta_{ij}) | 1 \leq i < j \leq n\},$$

where $(x, y; c)$ denotes the arc linking nodes x and y with capacity c. Each value of the binary vector $\boldsymbol{x}$ can be identified with the cut $(S_{\boldsymbol{x}}, T_{\boldsymbol{x}})$ of G such that $S_{\boldsymbol{x}}$ consists of s and the nodes x_i such that $x_i = 1$, and $T_{\boldsymbol{x}}$ consists of t and the nodes x_i such that $x_i = 0$. It is easy to check that the cost of the cut $(S_{\boldsymbol{x}}, T_{\boldsymbol{x}})$ is equal to the value of $E(\boldsymbol{x})$. Thus, *when $\beta_{ij} \leq 0$ for all ordered pairs (i, j) such that $1 \leq i < j \leq n$*, which ensures that all the network capacities are non-negative, minimizing $E(\boldsymbol{x})$ amounts to solving a min-cut problem, which can be done *exactly* in polynomial time.

The regularity condition $\beta_{ij} \leq 0$ is a special case of *submodularity*, a condition on general *set functions* (real functions defined on the power set of some finite set) that guarantees that they can be minimized in polynomial time (Boros and Hammer 2002). On the other hand, minimizing an arbitrary quadratic pseudo-Boolean function that is not submodular is NP-hard.

Note that Equation (22.29) can be rewritten as

$$E(\boldsymbol{x}) = \sum_{i=1}^{n} \left(\alpha_i + \frac{1}{2} \sum_{j \neq i} \beta_{ij} \right) x_i - \frac{1}{2} \sum_{1 \leq i < j \leq n} \beta_{ij} (x_i - x_j)^2 \tag{22.31}$$

by using the fact that for any binary variable x_i, $x_i = x_i^2$. In particular, it follows from our discussion that the energy functions of the form in Equation (22.26) that can be optimized efficiently are exactly those for which the binary terms are *attractive*—that is, the weights $-1/2\beta_{ij}$ of the terms $(x_i - x_j)^2$ are positive.

22.4.3 Generalization to Integer Variables

We consider in this section a generalization of the problem considered so far. Now the energy $E : \mathcal{K}^n \to \mathbb{R}$ is a function of a vector $\boldsymbol{x} = (x_1, \ldots, x_n)^T$ of n integer variables within some fixed range $\mathcal{K} = \{0, \ldots, K\}$ instead of binary ones; however, the energy can still be written as a sum of unary and binary terms

$$E(\boldsymbol{x}) = \sum_{i=1}^{n} E_i(x_i) + \sum_{1 \leq i < j \leq n} E_{ij}(x_i, x_j). \tag{22.32}$$

Reduction to a Quadratic Pseudo-Boolean Optimization Problem
It turns out that the integer problem defined by Equation (22.32) can *always* be reduced to a quadratic pseudo-Boolean one, and thus solved using a min-cut/max-flow algorithm when certain submodularity conditions are satisfied. We follow the reduction proposed by Darbon (2009) in this section; see Ishikawa (2003) and Schlesinger and Flach (2006) for related approaches.

Given some integer variable x, let us define the characteristic function of its lower level-set for some value k in $\mathcal{K}$ as

$$x^k = 0 \quad \text{if} \quad x \leq k \quad \text{and} \quad 1 \quad \text{otherwise},$$

and note that (a) it satisfies the monotony property $x^k \leq x^l$ for all $k \geq l$ in $\mathcal{K}$, and (b) $x = \max\{k \in \mathcal{K}, x^k = 0\}$. In particular, it can be shown that any family of K binary functions satisfying the first of these properties defines an integer value in $\mathcal{K}$, which can be recovered using the second one.

A simple calculation shows that any energy function depending on a single integer variable with values in $\mathcal{K}$ can be rewritten as

$$E_i(x_i) = \left[\sum_{k=0}^{K-1} \mu_i^k x_i^k \right] + \nu_i, \text{ where } \mu_i^k = E_i(k+1) - E_i(k) \text{ and } \nu_i = E_i(0). \tag{22.33}$$

Likewise, any energy function depending on two variables with values in $\mathcal{K}$ can be rewritten as

$$E_{ij}(x_i, x_j) = \left[\sum_{k,l=0}^{K-1} \beta_{ij}^{kl} x_i^k x_j^l \right] + \left[\sum_{k=0}^{K-1} \gamma_{ij}^k x_i^k + \gamma_{ji}^k x_j^k \right] + \delta_{ij}, \tag{22.34}$$

where

$$\begin{cases} \beta_{ij}^{kl} = E_{ij}(k, l) + E_{ij}(k+1, l+1) - E_{ij}(k, l+1) - E_{ij}(k+1, l), \\ \gamma_{ij}^k = E_{ij}(k+1, 0) - E_{ij}(k, 0), \\ \gamma_{ji}^k = E_{ij}(0, k+1) - E_{ij}(0, k), \\ \delta_{ij} = E_{ij}(0, 0). \end{cases} \tag{22.35}$$

It follows immediately from Equations (22.33) and (22.34) that $E(\boldsymbol{x})$ always can be rewritten, *up to some additive constant*, as

$$E(\boldsymbol{x}) = \sum_{i=1}^{n} \sum_{k=0}^{K-1} \alpha_i^k x_i^k + \sum_{1 \leq i < j \leq n} \sum_{k,l=0}^{K-1} \beta_{ij}^{kl} x_i^k x_j^l, \text{ where } \alpha_i^k = \mu_i^k + \sum_{j \neq i} \gamma_{ij}^k, \tag{22.36}$$

which is a quadratic function of the integer variables x_i^k, with i in $\{1, \ldots, n\}$ and k in $\mathcal{K}$.

Note the strong similarity of this expression with that obtained in the binary case (Equation [22.29]). Assuming that E is submodular—that is, all the parameters β_{ij}^{kl} are nonpositive—E obviously can be minimized exactly using a min-cut/max-flow algorithm.

Note, however, that the monotony condition must be enforced for the corresponding binary variables values to define an integer value in $\mathcal{K}$. This is easily achieved by minimizing instead

$$E'(\boldsymbol{x}) = E(\boldsymbol{x}) + \sum_{i=1}^{n} \sum_{k=0}^{K-1} T(x_i^{k+1} - x_i^k), \quad \text{where } T(r) = 0 \text{ if } r \leq 0 \text{ and } +\infty \text{ otherwise.}$$

Adding this penalty term forces all solutions with finite cost to be monotone. On the other hand, any monotone solution will have zero penalty, and thus minimizing $E'(\boldsymbol{x})$ yields a labeling also minimizing $E(\boldsymbol{x})$.

Alpha Expansion   The reduction of an integer combinatorial optimization problem to a binary one which we have just discussed is attractive because it allows for an efficient procedure[5] that yields the global optimum of the objective function.

However, the submodularity condition $\beta_{ij}^{kl} \leq 0$ that is associated with Equation (22.35) may be too restrictive for certain applications. Functions E_{ij} that can be written as $E_{ij}(x_i, x_j) = g(x_i - x_j)$, where $g : \mathbb{Z} \to \mathbb{R}$ is convex, do satisfy this condition (Darbon 2009). A classical example of such a function in the image processing domain is total variation, where $E_{ij}(x_i, x_j) = \gamma_{ij}|x_i - x_j|$, and $\gamma_{ij} > 0$. On the other hand, *discontinuity preserving* binary terms, such as the Potts model $E_{ij}(x_i, x_j) = \gamma_{ij}\chi(x_i \neq x_j)$ (where the characteristic function χ is one if its argument is true and zero otherwise, and $\gamma_{ij} > 0$), do not obey the submodularity conditions of Eq (22.35). Handling such terms may be important in practice; for example, one might not want to overpenalize changes in disparity in stereo fusion tasks because this function is discontinuous at occlusion boundaries, thus preferring a Potts penalty term to a total variation one to encourage disparity smoothness. This is one of the motivations for using alternate optimization approaches, such as the *alpha expansion* procedure of Boykov *et al.* (2001), that make weaker assumptions on the energy functions they minimize. The price to pay is that they do not give, in general, a global optimum of these functions.

Alpha expansion is an iterative algorithm, where, at each iteration, an arbitrary number of integer variables x_i are allowed to change their value to some α in $\mathcal{K}$, and the change in $\boldsymbol{x}$ minimizing E among these *alpha expansion* moves is retained. A full iteration of the algorithm examines all possible values of α in some arbitrary order, and the algorithm iterates until no further improvement of the energy value is obtained (Algorithm 22.1).

The key step of this algorithm is the minimization of $E(\boldsymbol{x}')$. It can be rewritten as an energy minimization over a vector $\boldsymbol{y}$ of n *binary* variables y_i as follows: Let

---

[5]One should keep in mind, however, that the number of binary variables in the reduced problem is $n(K+1)$ instead of n for the original problem, which prevents scaling up this method to problems with large numbers of variables *and* integer values.

---

1. Initialize $\boldsymbol{x}$ randomly.

2. Repeat

   (a) For each α in $\mathcal{K}$ do

       i. Find the value $\boldsymbol{x}'$ minimizing $E(\boldsymbol{x}')$ among integer variables within one α expansion of $\boldsymbol{x}$.

       ii. If $E(\boldsymbol{x}') < E(\boldsymbol{x})$ then $\boldsymbol{x} \leftarrow \boldsymbol{x}'$; Done$\leftarrow$ false else Done$\leftarrow$true.

   (b) until Done.

3. Return $\boldsymbol{x}$.

Algorithm 22.1: The Alpha Expansion Algorithm of Boykov *et al.* (2001).

us define

$$E'(\boldsymbol{y}) = \sum_{i=1}^{n} E_i(x_i'(y_i)) + \sum_{1 \leq i < j \leq n} E_{ij}(x_i'(y_i), x_j'(y_j)), \qquad (22.37)$$

where $x_i'(y_i) = x_i$ when $y_i = 0$ and $x_i'(y_i) = \alpha$ when $y_i = 1$. Minimizing $E(\boldsymbol{x}')$ with respect to the variables $\boldsymbol{x}'$ within one α expansion of $\boldsymbol{x}$ is clearly equivalent to minimizing $E'(\boldsymbol{y})$ with respect to $\boldsymbol{y}$, which amounts to solving a quadratic pseudo-Boolean optimization problem with the submodularity condition

$$E_{ij}(x_i, x_j) + E_{ij}(\alpha, \alpha) \leq E_{ij}(x_i, \alpha) + E_{ij}(\alpha, x_j), \qquad (22.38)$$

which must be satisfied for all pairs (i, j) such that $1 \leq i < j \leq n$ and for all α in $\mathcal{K}$. This is clearly the case, for example, when the functions E_{ij} are distances, for which $E_{ij}(\alpha, \alpha) = 0$ and the triangular inequality $E_{ij}(x_i, x_j) \leq E_{ij}(x_i, \alpha) + E_{ij}(\alpha, x_j)$ is satisfied. This is also the case for the Potts model discussed earlier.

    In general, the submodularity condition of Equation (22.38) is weaker than the corresponding condition $\beta_{ij}^{kl} \leq 0$ associated with Equation (22.35) in the previous section. Alpha expansion can thus be applied to a wider variety of problems. Each of its iterations is also cheaper because the number n of binary variables is equal to the number of integer ones, and not to $n(K+1)$ in Darbon's reduction. As already mentioned, however, the price to pay is that alpha expansion returns only a local minimum of the corresponding objective function.

Ordering Issues   Any combinatorial optimization problem where one must minimize the function $E(\boldsymbol{x})$ defined by Equation (22.32) over some finite *but not necessarily integer, or ordered,* set of labels can be reduced to an integer optimization problem by picking some arbitrary order for the labels. One should keep in mind, however, that this *makes sense only* when a natural ordering can be imposed on the labels. This is the case, for example, in stereo fusion with rectified images, where the labels are horizontal disparities, but not in a general graph-matching scenario. Otherwise, an exponential number of orderings must *a priori* be considered, which in general is computationally intractable, and whatever optimization method is used, picking a particular ordering might lead to a suboptimal solution. In the case of alpha expansion, the order for the α values can be chosen randomly at each iteration, for example.

22.5   NOTES

General optimization techniques for smooth functions of their parameters are discussed in Luenberger (1984), Bertsekas (1995), and Heath (2002), for example. An excellent survey and discussion of least-squares methods in the structure-from-motion context of Chapter 8 can be found in Triggs *et al.* (2000). The output of least-squares methods admits a statistical interpretation in maximum-likelihood terms when the coordinates of the data points are modeled as random variables obeying a normal distribution. This intepretation is discussed in Chapter 10.

The introduction to sparse coding and dictionary learning presented in Section 22.3 is largely based on Mairal *et al.* (2010, 2011). Various types of wavelets have been used as dictionaries for natural images (Mallat 1999). The convex basis pursuit and Lasso problems are defined in (Chen *et al.* 1999; Tibshirani 1996). A number of recent methods for solving this type of problems are based on coordinate descent with soft thresholding (Fu 1998; Friedman, Hastie, Hölfling, & Tibshirani 2001; Wu & Lange 2008). The LARS algorithm of Efron *et al.* (2004) provides an efficient alternative when the columns of the dictionary are highly correlated, which is often the case for learned dictionaries in image processing and computer vision applications. The ℓ_0 sparse coding problem is NP-hard, and greedy algorithms for finding an approximate solution can be found in Weisberg (1980) and Mallat and Zhang (1993). Building on ideas proposed in Olshausen and Field (1997) to model neuronal responses in the V1 area of the brain, Elad and Aharon (2006) have proposed to learn a dictionary $\mathcal{D}$ adapted to the image at hand instead of using a predefined one, and demonstrated that learned dictionaries lead to better empirical performance than off-the-shelf ones. Many other applications of learned dictionaries have been proposed for tasks ranging from image denoising (Elad & Aharon 2006; Mairal *et al.* 2009), texture synthesis (Peyre 2008), and audio processing (Grosse, Raina, Kwong, & Ng 2007; Zibulevsky & Pearlmutter 2001), to image classification (Raina *et al.* 2007; Mairal *et al.* 2008; Bradley & Bagnell 2009). The supervised formulation presented in Section 22.3 is especially relevant for the latter tasks because it allows for discriminative dictionary learning (Yang, Yu, Gong, & Huang 2009*b*; Boureau, Bach, LeCun, & Ponce 2009; Yang, Yu, & Huang 2010*a*; Mairal *et al.* 2011).

Classical treatments of min-cut/max-flow problems and algorithms include Ford and Fulkerson (1956) and Goldberg and Tarjan (1988) for example. The reduction of a submodular pseudo-Boolean optimization problem to a min-cut one described in this chapter is due to Boros and Hammer (2002). The reduction of an integer optimization problem to a binary one also presented in this chapter is due to Darbon (2009). See Ishikawa (2003) and Schlesinger and Flach (2006) for related approaches. The iterative alpha expansion algorithm is described in Boykov, Veksler, and Zabih (2001), that also proposes an alternative $\alpha - \beta$ technique for solving the same problem.

In the computer vision domain, min-cut/max-flow algorithms are often known under the nickname of *graph-cuts* algorithms. They have been popularized in large part by Boykov *et al.* (2001), Boykov and Kolgomorov (2004), and Kolgomorov and Zabih (2004), although they were used in earlier work, such as Greig, Porteous & Seheult (1989), Roy and Cox (1998), and Ishikawa and Geiger (1998), for example. Our presentation of combinatorial optimization does not assume or require any probabilistic model. It is worth noting, however, that the energy functions discussed in Section 22.4 (Equations [22.26,22.32]) also arise in the context of probabilistic first-order Markov random fields, popularized in computer vision by Geman and Geman (1984), who proposed to use *simulated annealing* to solve the corresponding labeling problem.

Finally, let us close this chapter by noting that implementations of the various algorithms discussed in this chapter are widely available. For example, freely available libraries such as LAPACK (see `http://www.netlib.org/lapack/`) and MINPACK (see `http://www.netlib.org/minpack/`) offer a wide variety of functions for linear and nonlinear least-squares, singular value decomposition, and (generalized) eigenvalue problems. MATLAB implements similar functionalities. SPAMS, an extensive open-source library for sparse coding and dictionary learning, developed by J. Mairal, and implementing Mairal *et al.* (2010), is available at `http://www.di.ens.fr/willow/SPAMS/`. Freely available code for solving min-cut/max-flow and multi-label optimization problems, developed by Y. Boykov, A. Delong, V. Kolmogorov, and O. Veksler, and implementing (Boykov *et al.* 2001; Boykov & Kolmogorov 2004) can be found at `http://vision.csd.uwo.ca/code/`.

Bibliography

Abdel Hakim, A. and Farag, A. (2006), Csift: A sift descriptor with color invariant characteristics, *in* 'IEEE Conf. on Computer Vision and Pattern Recognition (CVPR)', pp. II: 1978–1983.

Abdellatif, M., Tanaka, Y., Gofuku, A. and Nagai, I. (2000), 'Color constancy using the inter-reflection from a reference nose', *International Journal of Computer Vision* **39**(3), 171–194.

Adelson, E. (2001), On seeing stuff: the perception of materials by humans and machines, *in* 'Proc. SPIE', Vol. 4299: Human Vision and Electronic Imaging VI, pp. 1–12.

Adelson, E. and Bergen, J. (1991), The plenoptic function and the elements of early vision, *in* M. Landy and J. Movshon, eds, 'Computational Models of Visual Processing', MIT Press, Cambridge, MA.

Adelson, E. and Weiss, Y. (1996), A unified mixture framework for motion segmentation: Incorporating spatial coherence and estimating the number of models, *in* 'IEEE Conf. on Computer Vision and Pattern Recognition (CVPR)', pp. 321–326.

Agarwal, S. and Roth, D. (May 2002), 'Learning a Sparse Representation for Object Detection', *Proceedings of ECCV'02*.

Agin, G. (1972), Representation and description of curved objects, PhD thesis, Stanford University, Stanford, CA.

Aharon, M., Elad, M. and Bruckstein, A. M. (2006), 'The K-SVD: An algorithm for designing of overcomplete dictionaries for sparse representations', **54**(11), 4311–4322.

Aho, A., Hopcroft, J. and Ullman, J. (1974), *The design and analysis of computer algorithms*, Addison-Wesley.

Ahuja, N. and Abbott, A. (1993), 'Active stereo: Integrating disparity, vergence, focus, aperture, and calibration for surface estimation', *IEEE Trans. Pattern Analysis and Machine Intelligence* **15**(10), 1007–1029.

Ahuja, N. and Schachter, B. (1983a), 'Image models', *ACM Computing Surveys* **15**(1), 83–84.

Ahuja, N. and Schachter, B. (1983b), *Pattern Models*, Wiley.

Ahuja, R., Magnanti, T. and Orlin, J. (1993), *Network Flows: Theory, Algorithms and Applications*, Prentice-Hall.

Aloimonos, Y. (1986), Detection of surface orientation from texture. i. the case of planes., *in* 'IEEE Conf. on Computer Vision and Pattern Recognition (CVPR)', pp. 584–593.

Aloimonos, Y. (1990), 'Perspective approximations', *Image and Vision Computing* **8**(3), 177–192.

Aloimonos, Y., Weiss, I. and Bandyopadhyay, A. (1987), 'Active vision', *International Journal of Computer Vision* **1**(4), 333–356.

Amenta, N., Bern, M. and Kamvysselis, M. (1998), 'A new voronoi-based surface reconstruction algorithm', *ACM Transactions on Graphics: Proc. SIGGRAPH 1998* pp. 415–421.

Amir, A. and Lindenbaum, M. (1996), Quantitative analysis of grouping processes, *in* 'Proc. European Conference on Computer Vision (ECCV)', pp. I:371–384.

Amit, Y. and Geman, D. (1997), 'Shape quantization and recognition with randomized trees', *Neural Computation* **9**, 1545–1588.

Anderson, B. and Nayakama, K. (1994), 'Toward a general theory of stereopsis — binocular matching, occluding contours, and fusion', *Psychological Review* **101**(3), 414–445.

Andrews, S., Tsochantaridis, I. and Hofmann, T. (2003), Support vector machines for multiple-instance learning, *in* 'Proc. NIPS 15', MIT Press, pp. 561–568.

Arbelaez, P., Maire, M., Fowlkes, C. and Malik, J. (2011), 'Contour detection and hierarchical image segmentation', *IEEE Trans. Pattern Analysis and Machine Intelligence* **33**(5), 898–916.

Arbogast, E. and Mohr, R. (1991), '3D structure inference from image sequences', *Journal of Pattern Recognition and Artificial Intelligence*.

Arikan, O. (2006), 'Compression of motion capture databases', *ACM Transactions on Graphics: Proc. SIGGRAPH 2006*.

Armitage, L. and Enser, P. (1997), 'Analysis of user need in image archives', *Journal of Information Science* **23**(4), 287–299.

Arnol'd, V. (1984), *Catastrophe Theory*, Springer-Verlag, Heidelberg.

Arnon, D., Collins, G. and McCallum, S. (1984), 'Cylindrical algebraic decomposition I and II', *SIAM J. Comput.* **13**(4), 865–889.

Athitsos, V., Neidle, C., Sclaroff, S., Nash, J., Stefan, A., Yuan, Q. and Thangali, A. (2008), The American Sign Language lexicon video dataset, *in* 'IEEE Workshop on Computer Vision and Pattern Recognition for Human Communicative Behavior Analysis', pp. 1–8.

Awate, S. and Whitaker, R. (2006), 'Unsupervised, information-theoretic, adaptive image filtering for image restoration', *IEEE Trans. Pattern Analysis and Machine Intelligence* pp. 364–376.

Ayache, N. (1995), 'Medical computer vision, virtual-reality and robotics', *Image and Vision Computing* **13**(4), 295–313.

Ayache, N. and Faugeras, O. (1986), 'Hyper: a new approach for the recognition and positioning of two-dimensional objects', *IEEE Trans. Pattern Analysis and Machine Intelligence* **8**(1), 44–54.

Ayache, N. and Faugeras, O. (1987), Building, registrating, and fusing noisy visual maps, *in* 'Proc. Int. Conf. on Computer Vision (ICCV)', pp. 73–82.

Ayache, N. and Lustman, F. (1987), Fast and reliable passive trinocular stereovision, *in* 'Proc. Int. Conf. on Computer Vision (ICCV)', pp. 422–427.

Bach, F., Jenatton, R., Mairal, J. and Obozinski, G. (2011), Convex optimization with sparsity-inducing norms, *in* S. Sra, S. Nowozin and S. Wright, eds, 'Optimization for Machine Learning', MIT Press.

Bagon, S., Boiman, O. and Irani, M. (2008), What is a good image segment? a unified approach to segment extraction, *in* 'Proc. European Conference on Computer Vision (ECCV)', pp. IV: 30–44.

Bajcsy, R. (1988), 'Active perception', *Proceedings of the IEEE* **76**(8), 996–1005.

Bajcsy, R. and Lieberman, L. (1976), 'Texture gradient as a depth cue', *Computer Graphics Image Processing* **5**(1), 52–67.

Bajcsy, R. and Solina, F. (1987), Three-dimensional object representation revisited, *in* 'Proc. Int. Conf. on Computer Vision (ICCV)', London, U.K., pp. 231–240.

Baker, H. and Binford, T. (1981), Depth from edge- and intensity-based stereo, *in* 'Int. Joint Conf. Artificial Intelligence', pp. 631–636.

Baker, S., Szeliski, R. and Anandan, P. (1998), A layered approach to stereo reconstruction, *in* 'IEEE Conf. on Computer Vision and Pattern Recognition (CVPR)', pp. 434–441.

Ballard, D. (1981), 'Generalizing the Hough transform to detect arbitrary shapes', *Pattern Recognition* **13**(2), 111–122.

Ballard, D. (1984), 'Parameter nets', *Artificial Intelligence* **22**(3), 235–267.

Bar-Shalom, Y. and Li, X.-R. (2001), *Estimation with Applications to Tracking and Navigation*, John Wiley & Sons, Inc., New York, NY, USA.

Barinova, O., Konushin, V., Yakubenko, A., Lee, K., Lim, H. and Konushin, A. (2008), Fast automatic single-view 3-d reconstruction of urban scenes, *in* 'Proc. European Conference on Computer Vision (ECCV)', pp. II: 100–113.

Barnard, K. (2000), Improvements to gamut mapping colour constancy algorithms, *in* 'Proc. European Conference on Computer Vision (ECCV)', pp. 390–402.

Barnard, K. and Forsyth, D. (2001), Learning the semantics of words and pictures, *in* 'Proc. Int. Conf. on Computer Vision (ICCV)', pp. 408–15.

Barnard, K. and Johnson, M. (2005), 'Word sense disambiguation with pictures', *Artif. Intell.* **167**(1-2), 13–30.

Barnard, K., Cardei, V. and Funt, B. (2002*a*), 'A comparison of computational color constancy algorithms-part i: Methodology and experiments with synthesized data', *IEEE Trans. Image Processing* **11**(9), 972–984.

Barnard, K., Ciurea, F. and Funt, B. (2001*a*), 'Sensor sharpening for computational color constancy', *Journal of the Optical Society of America* **18**(11), 2728–2743.

Barnard, K., Duygulu, P. and Forsyth, D. (2001*b*), Clustering art, *in* 'IEEE Conf. on Computer Vision and Pattern Recognition (CVPR)', pp. II:434–441.

Barnard, K., Duygulu, P., de Freitas, N., Forsyth, D., Blei, D. and Jordan, M. I. (2003*a*), 'Matching words and pictures', *Journal of Machine Learning Research* **3**, 1107–1135.

Barnard, K., Duygulu, P., Guru, R., Gabbur, P., and Forsyth, D. (2003*b*), The effects of segmentation and feature choice in a translation model of object recognition, *in* 'Proceedings of Computer Vision and Pattern Recognition (CVPR)'.

Barnard, K., Finlayson, G. and Funt, B. (1997), 'Color constancy for scenes with varying illumination', *Computer Vision and Image Understanding* **65**(2), 311–321.

Barnard, K., Martin, L., Coath, A. and Funt, B. (2002*b*), 'A comparison of computational color constancy algorithms-part ii: Experiments with image data', *IEEE Trans. Image Processing* **11**(9), 985–996.

Barnard, K., Martin, L., Funt, B. and Coath, A. (2002*c*), 'A data set for colour research', *Color Research and Applications* **27**, 147–151.

Basri, R. and Jacobs, D. W. (2003), 'Lambertian reflectance and linear subspaces', *IEEE Trans. Pattern Analysis and Machine Intelligence* **25**(2), 218–233.

Bates, M. (2007), 'What is browsing really? A model drawing from behavioural science research', *Information Research*.

Baumgart, B. (1974), Geometric modeling for computer vision, Technical Report AIM-249, Stanford University. Ph.D. Thesis. Department of Computer Science.

Beardsley, P., Zisserman, A. and Murray, D. (1997), 'Sequential updating of projective and affine structure from motion', *International Journal of Computer Vision* **23**(3), 235–259.

Beauchemin, M. and Thomson, K. (1997), 'The evaluation of segmentation results and the overlapping area matrix', *International Journal of Remote Sensing* **18**(18), 3895–3899.

Beckmann, P. and Spizzichino, A. (1987), *Scattering of Electromagnetic Waves from Rough Surfaces*, Artech House.

Belhumeur, P. and Kriegman, D. (1998), 'What is the set of images of an object under all possible illumination conditions?', *International Journal of Computer Vision* **28**(3), 245–260.

Belhumeur, P., Chen, D., Feiner, S., Jacobs, D., Kress, W., Ling, H., Lopez, I., Ramamoorthi, R., Sheorey, S., White, S. and Zhang, L. (2008), Searching the world's herbaria: A system for visual identification of plant species, *in* 'Proc. European Conference on Computer Vision (ECCV)', pp. IV: 116–129.

Belongie, S., Carson, C., Greenspan, H. and Malik, J. (1998*a*), Color- and texture-based image segmentation using the expectation-maximization algorithm and its application to content-based image retrieval, *in* 'Proc. Int. Conf. on Computer Vision (ICCV)', pp. 675–682.

Belongie, S., Carson, C., Greenspan, H. and Malik, J. (1998*b*), Color and texture-based image segmentation using EM and its applications to content based image retrieval, *in* 'Proc. Int. Conf. on Computer Vision (ICCV)'.

Belongie, S., Malik, J. and Puzicha, J. (2001), Matching shapes, *in* 'Proc. Int. Conf. on Computer Vision (ICCV)', pp. I: 454–461.

Belongie, S., Malik, J. and Puzicha, J. (2002), 'Shape matching and object recognition using shape contexts', *IEEE Trans. Pattern Analysis and Machine Intelligence* **24**(4), 509–522.

Beneš, V. (1981), 'Exact finite-dimensional filters with certain diffusion non-linear drift', *Stochastics* **5**, 65–92.

Berg, A., Berg, T. and Malik, J. (2005), Shape matching and object recognition using low distortion correspondences, *in* 'IEEE Conf. on Computer Vision and Pattern Recognition (CVPR)', pp. I: 26–33.

Berg, T. and Forsyth, D. (2006), Animals on the web, *in* 'IEEE Conf. on Computer Vision and Pattern Recognition (CVPR)', Vol. 2, pp. 1463–1470.

Berg, T., Berg, A., Edwards, J., Maire, M., White, R., Teh, Y., Learned Miller, E. and Forsyth, D. (2004), Names and faces in the news, *in* 'IEEE Conf. on Computer Vision and Pattern Recognition (CVPR)', pp. II: 848–854.

Berger, M. (1987), *Geometry*, Springer-Verlag.

Bergholm, F. (1987), 'Edge focusing', *IEEE Trans. Pattern Analysis and Machine Intelligence* **9**(6), 726–741.

Berns, R. (2000), *Billmeyer and Saltzman's Principles of Color Technology*, Wiley-Interscience.

Bertsekas, D. (1995), *Nonlinear programming*, Athena Scientific, Belmont, MA.

Besl, P. (1989), 'Active optical range imaging sensors', *Machine vision and applications* **1**, 127–152.

Besl, P. and Jain, R. (1988), 'Segmentation through variable-order surface fitting', *IEEE Trans. Pattern Analysis and Machine Intelligence* **10**(2), 167–192.

Besl, P. and McKay, N. (1992), 'A method for registration of 3D shapes', *IEEE Trans. Pattern Analysis and Machine Intelligence* **14**(2), 239–256.

Binford, T. (1984), Stereo vision: complexity and constraints, *in* 'Int. Symp. on Robotics Research', MIT Press, pp. 475–487.

Bishop, C. M. (2007), *Pattern Recognition and Machine Learning*, Springer.

Black, M. and Anandan, P. (1996), 'The robust estimation of multiple motions: Parametric and piecewise-smooth flow-fields', *Computer Vision and Image Understanding* **63**(1), 75–104.

Black, M. and Jepson, A. (1998), A probabilistic framework for matching temporal trajectories: CONDENSATION-based recognition of gestures and expressions, *in* 'Proc. European Conference on Computer Vision (ECCV)', pp. 909–924.

Blackman, S. and Popoli, R. (1999), *Design and Analysis of Modern Tracking Systems*, Artech House.

Blake, A. (1985), 'Boundary conditions for lightness computation in mondrian world', *CVGIP: Image Understanding* **32**(3), 314–327.

Blake, A. (1999), *Introduction to Active Contours and Visual Dynamics*, Online Book.

Blake, A. and Isard, M. (1996), The condensation algorithm - conditional density propagation and applications to visual tracking, *in* M. Mozer, M. Jordan and T. Petsche, eds, 'Advances in neural information processing systems 9'.

Blake, A. and Isard, M. (1998), 'Condensation - conditional density propagation for visual tracking', *International Journal of Computer Vision* **29**(1), 5–28.

Blake, A. and Marinos, C. (1990), 'Shape from texture: estimation, isotropy and moments', *Artificial Intelligence* **45**(3), 323–80.

Blake, A., Kohli, P. and Rother, C., eds (2011), *Markov Random Fields for Vision and Image Processing*, MIT Press.

Blei, D. M. and Jordan, M. I. (2002), Modeling annotated data, Technical Report CSD-02-1202, University of California Computer Science Division.

Blei, D. M. and Jordan, M. I. (2003), Modeling annotated data, *in* 'SIGIR '03: Proceedings of the 26th annual international ACM SIGIR conference on Research and development in informaion retrieval', ACM Press, New York, NY, USA, pp. 127–134.

Bodenheimer, B., Rose, C., Rosenthal, S. and Pella, J. (1997), The process of motion capture: Dealing with the data, *in* 'Computer Animation and Simulation '97. Proceedings of the Eurographics Workshop'.

Boissonnat, J.-D. (1984), 'Geometric structures for three-dimensional shape representation', *ACM Transaction on Computer Graphics* **3**(4), 266–286.

Boissonnat, J.-D. and Germain, F. (1981), A new approach to the problem of acquiring randomly-oriented workpieces from a bin, *in* 'Int. Joint Conf. Artificial Intelligence', Vancouver, Canada.

Bookstein, F. (1979), 'Fitting conic sections to scattered data', *Computer Graphics Image Processing* **9**(1), 56–71.

Borgefors, G. (1988), 'Hierarchical chamfer matching: A parametric edge matching algorithm', *IEEE Trans. Pattern Analysis and Machine Intelligence* **10**(6), 849–865.

Boros, E. and Hammer, P. (2002), 'Pseudo-boolean optimization', *Discrete applied mathematics* **123**(1-3), 155–225.

Bosch, A., Zisserman, A. and Munoz, X. (2008), 'Scene classification using a hybrid generative/discriminative approach', *IEEE Trans. Pattern Analysis and Machine Intelligence* **30**(4), 712–727.

Bosson, A., Cawley, G., Chan, Y. and Harvey, R. (2002), Non-retrieval: Blocking pornographic images, *in* 'Int. Conf. Image Video Retrieval', pp. 50–59.

Bottou, L. and Bousquet, O. (2007), The tradeoffs of large scale learning, *in* 'Advances in Neural Information Processing'.

Bourdev, L. and Malik, J. (2009), Poselets: Body part detectors trained using 3d human pose annotations, *in* 'Proc. Int. Conf. on Computer Vision (ICCV)', pp. 1365–1372.

Bourdev, L., Maji, S., Brox, T. and Malik, J. (2010), Detecting people using mutually consistent poselet activations, *in* 'Proc. European Conference on Computer Vision (ECCV)'.

Boureau, Y.-L., Bach, F., LeCun, Y. and Ponce, J. (2009), Learning mid-level features for recognition, *in* 'IEEE Conf. on Computer Vision and Pattern Recognition (CVPR)'.

Bowden, R., Windridge, D., Kadir, T., Zisserman, A. and Brady, M. (2004), A linguistic feature vector for the visual interpretation of sign language, *in* 'Proc. European Conference on Computer Vision (ECCV)', pp. Vol I: 390–401.

Boyce, B. (1982), 'Beyond topicality: a two stage view of relevance and the retrieval process', *Information Processing and Management* **18**, 105–109.

Boyd, S. and Vandenberghe, L. (2004), *Convex optimization*, Cambridge University Press.

Boyer, E. (1996), Object Models from Contour Sequences, *in* 'Proceedings of Fourth European Conference on Computer Vision, Cambridge, (England)', pp. 109–118. Lecture Notes in Computer Science, volume 1065.

Boyer, E. and Berger, M.-O. (1996), '3d surface reconstruction using occluding contours', *International Journal of Computer Vision*.

Boykov, Y. and Funka Lea, G. (2006), 'Graph cuts and efficient n-d image segmentation', *International Journal of Computer Vision* **70**(2), 109–131.

Boykov, Y. and Jolly, M. (2001), Interactive graph cuts for optimal boundary and region segmentation of objects in n-d images, *in* 'Proc. Int. Conf. on Computer Vision (ICCV)', pp. I: 105–112.

Boykov, Y. and Kolmogorov, V. (2004), 'An experimental comparison of min-cut/max-flow algorithms for energy minimization in computer vision', *IEEE Trans. Pattern Analysis and Machine Intelligence* **26**(9), 1124–1137.

Boykov, Y., Veksler, O. and Zabih, R. (2001), 'Fast approximate energy minimization via graph cuts', *IEEE Trans. Pattern Analysis and Machine Intelligence* **23**(11), 1222–1239.

Bracewell, R. (1995), *Two-Dimensional Imaging*, Prentice Hall.

Bracewell, R. (2000), *The Fourier Transform and its Applications, 3ed*, McGraw-Hill.

Bradley, D., Boubekeur, T. and Heidrich, W. (2008*a*), Accurate multi-view reconstruction using robust binocular stereo and surface meshing, *in* 'IEEE Conf. on Computer Vision and Pattern Recognition (CVPR)'.

Bradley, D. M. and Bagnell, J. A. (2009), Differentiable sparse coding, *in* 'Advances in Neural Information Processing', Vol. 21, pp. 113–120.

Bradley, D., Popa, T., Sheffer, A., Heidrich, W. and Boubekeur, T. (2008*b*), 'Markerless garment capture', *ACM Trans. Graph. (SIGGRAPH Proceedings)*.

Bradski, G. and Kaehler, A. (2008), *Learning OpenCV: Computer Vision with the OpenCV Library*, O'Reilly.

Brady, J., Ponce, J., Yuille, A. and Asada, H. (1985), 'Describing surfaces', *CVGIP: Image Understanding* **32**(1), 1–28.

Brainard, D. and Wandell, B. (1986), 'Analysis of the retinex theory of color vision', *Journal of the Optical Society of America* **3**, 1651–1661.

Branson, S., Wah, C., Babenko, B., Schroff, F., Welinder, P., Perona, P. and Belongie, S. (2010), Visual recognition with humans in the loop, *in* 'Proc. European Conference on Computer Vision (ECCV)'.

Breiman, L. (1996), 'Bagging predictors', *Machine Learning* **26**, 123–140.

Breiman, L. (2001), 'Random forests', *Machine Learning* **45**, 5–32.

Breiman, L., Friedman, J., Ohlsen, R. and Stone, C. (1984), *Classification and regression trees*, Wadsworth, NY.

Brelstaff, G. and Blake, A. (1987), 'Computing lightness', *Pattern Recognition Letters* **5**, 129–138.

Brelstaff, G. and Blake, A. (1988*a*), Detecting specular reflection using lambertian constraints, *in* 'Proc. Int. Conf. on Computer Vision (ICCV)', pp. 297–302.

Brelstaff, G. and Blake, A. (1988*b*), Detecting specular reflections using lambertian constraints, *in* 'Proc. Int. Conf. on Computer Vision (ICCV)'.

Bridson, R., Fedkiw, R. and Anderson, J. (2002), 'Robust treatment of collisions, contact and friction for cloth animation', *ACM Transactions on Graphics (SIGGRAPH Proceedings)* pp. 594–603.

Brostow, G. and Essa, I. (1999), Motion based decompositing of video, *in* 'Proc. Int. Conf. on Computer Vision (ICCV)', pp. 8–13.

Brostow, G., Hernández, C., Vogiatzis, G., Stenger, B. and Cipolla, R. (2011), 'Video normals from colored lights', *IEEE Trans. Pattern Analysis and Machine Intelligence*.

Brown, L. (2000), *A Radar History of World War II: Technical and Military Imperatives*, Institute of Physics Press.

Brown, M. and Lowe, D. (2003), Recognising panoramas, *in* 'Proc. Int. Conf. on Computer Vision (ICCV)', pp. 1218–1225.

Brown, M. and Lowe, D. (2007), 'Automatic panoramic image stitching using invariant features', *International Journal of Computer Vision* **74**(1), 59–73.

Brown, P. F., Cocke, J., Pietra, S. A. D., Pietra, V. J. D., Jelinek, F., Lafferty, J. D., Mercer, R. L. and Roossin, P. S. (1990), 'A statistical approach to machine translation', *Computational Linguistics* **16**(2), 79–85.

Brunnström, K., Ekhlund, J.-O. and Uhlin, T. (1996), 'Active fixation for scene exploration', *International Journal of Computer Vision* **17**(2), 137–162.

Buades, A., Coll, B. and Morel, J. (2005), A non-local algorithm for image denoising, *in* 'IEEE Conf. on Computer Vision and Pattern Recognition (CVPR)'.

Bubna, K. and Stewart, C. (2000), 'Model selection techniques and merging rules for range data segmentation algorithms', *Computer Vision and Image Understanding* **80**(2), 215–245.

Buchsbaum, G. (1980), 'A spatial processor model for object colour perception', *J. Franklin Inst.* **310**, 1–26.

Buderi, R. (1998), *The Invention that Changed the World*, Touchstone Press. reprint.

Buehler, P., Everingham, M., Huttenlocher, D. and Zisserman, A. (2008), Long term arm and hand tracking for continuous sign language tv broadcasts, *in* 'British Machine Vision Conference (BMVC)'.

Buehler, P., Zisserman, A. and Everingham, M. (2009), Learning sign language by watching tv (using weakly aligned subtitles), *in* 'IEEE Conf. on Computer Vision and Pattern Recognition (CVPR)', pp. 2961–2968.

Burger, W. and Burge, M. J. (2009), *Principles of Digital Image Processing: Fundamental Techniques*, Springer.

Burghouts, G. and Geusebroek, J. (2009), 'Performance evaluation of local colour invariants', *Computer Vision and Image Understanding* **113**(1), 48–62.

Burt, P. and Adelson, E. (1983), 'The Laplacian pyramid as a compact image code', *IEEE Trans. Communication* pp. 532–540.

Callahan, J. and Weiss, R. (1985), A model for describing surface shape, *in* 'IEEE Conf. on Computer Vision and Pattern Recognition (CVPR)', San Francisco, CA, pp. 240–245.

Canny, J. (1986), 'A computational approach to edge detection', *IEEE Trans. Pattern Analysis and Machine Intelligence* **8**(6), 679–698.

Canny, J. (1988), *The Complexity of Robot Motion Planning*, MIT Press.

Carceroni, R. and Kutulakos, K. (2002), 'Multi-view scene capture by surfel sampling: From video streams to non-rigid 3D motion, shape and reflectance', *International Journal of Computer Vision* **49**(2-3), 175–214.

Cardoso, J. and Corte Real, L. (2005), 'Toward a generic evaluation of image segmentation', *IEEE Trans. Image Processing* **14**(11), 1773–1782.

Cardoso, J. and Corte Real, L. (2006), 'A measure for mutual refinements of image segmentations', *IEEE Trans. Image Processing* **15**(8), 2358–2363.

Cardoso, J., Carvalho, P., Teixeira, L. and Corte Real, L. (2009), 'Partition-distance methods for assessing spatial segmentations of images and videos', *Computer Vision and Image Understanding* **113**(7), 811–823.

Carleer, A., Debeir, O. and Wolff, E. (2005), 'Assessment of very high spatial resolution satellite image segmentations', *Photogrammetric Engineering and Remote Sensing* **71**(11), 1285–1294.

Carmichael, O., Huber, D. and Hebert, M. (1999), Large data sets and confusing scenes in 3-D surface matching and recognition, *in* 'Second International Conference on 3-D Digital Imaging and Modeling (3DIM'99)', pp. 358–367.

Carneiro, G. and Vasconcelos, N. (2005), Formulating semantic image annotation as a supervised learning problem, *in* 'CVPR '05: Proceedings of the 2005 IEEE Computer Society Conference on Computer Vision and Pattern Recognition (CVPR'05) - Volume 2', pp. 163–168.

Celebi, E.; Alpkocak, A. (30 Nov. - 1 Dec. 2005), 'Combining textual and visual clusters for semantic image retrieval and auto-annotation', *Integration of Knowledge, Semantics and Digital Media Technology, 2005. EWIMT 2005. The 2nd European Workshop on the (Ref. No. 2005/11099)* pp. 219–225.

Chakravarty, I. (1982), The use of characteristic views as a basis for recognition of three-dimensional objects, Image Processing Laboratory IPL-TR-034, Rensselaer Polytechnic Institute.

Chasles, M. (1855), 'Question no. 296', *Nouv. Ann. Math.*

Chen, E. (1995), QuickTime VR - an image-based approach to virtual environment navigation, *in* 'Proc. of SIGGRAPH '95'.

Chen, H., Belhumeur, P. and Jacobs, D. (2000), In search of illumination invariants, *in* 'IEEE Conf. on Computer Vision and Pattern Recognition (CVPR)', pp. I:254–261.

Chen, H.-L. (2001), 'An analysis of image queries in the field of art history', *J. Am. Soc. Information Science and Technology* **52**(3), 260–273.

Chen, S., Donoho, D. and Saunders, M. (1999), 'Atomic decomposition by basis pursuit', *SIAM Journal on Scientific Computing* **20**, 33–61.

Chen, Y. and Wang, J. Z. (2004), 'Image categorization by learning and reasoning with regions', *J. Mach. Learn. Res.* **5**, 913–939.

Cheng, C.-H., Fu, A. W. and Zhang, Y. (1999), Entropy-based subspace clustering for mining numerical data, *in* 'Proc. 1999 Int. Conf. Knowledge Discovery and Data Mining (KDD'99)', San Diego, CA, pp. 84–93.

Cheng, Y. (1995), 'Mean shift, mode seeking, and clustering', *IEEE Trans. Pattern Analysis and Machine Intelligence* **17**(8), 790–799.

Chin, R. and Dyer, C. (1986), 'Model-based recognition in robot vision', *ACM Computing Surveys* **18**(1), 67–108.

Choe, Y. and Kashyap, R. (1991), '3-D shape from a shaded textural surface image', *IEEE Trans. Pattern Analysis and Machine Intelligence* **13**(9), 907–919.

Choi, M., Lim, J., Torralba, A. and Willsky, A. (2010), Exploiting hierarchical context on a large database of object categories, *in* 'IEEE Conf. on Computer Vision and Pattern Recognition (CVPR)', pp. 129–136.

Choi, Y. and Rasmussen, E. (2002), 'Users' relevance criteria in image retrieval in American history', *Information Processing and Management* **38**, 695–726.

Chua, C. and Jarvis, R. (1996), 'Point signatures: a new representation for 3D object recognition', *International Journal of Computer Vision* **25**(1), 63–85.

Chui, C. (1991), *Kalman Filtering: With Real-Time Applications*, Springer-Verlag.

Chum, O., Philbin, J., Sivic, J., Isard, M. and Zisserman, A. (2007), Total recall: Automatic query expansion with a generative feature model for object retrieval, *in* 'Proc. Int. Conf. on Computer Vision (ICCV)', pp. 1–8.

Cipolla, R. and Blake, A. (1992), 'Surface shape from the deformation of the apparent contour', *International Journal of Computer Vision* **9**(2), 83–112.

Cipolla, R., Astrom, K. and Giblin, P. (1995), Motion from the frontier of curved surfaces, *in* 'Proc. Int. Conf. on Computer Vision (ICCV)', Boston, MA, pp. 269–275.

Clarkson, K. (1988), 'A randomized algorithm for closest-point queries', *SIAM J. Computing* **17**, 830–847.

Clerc, M. and Mallat, S. (1999), Shape from texture through deformations, *in* 'Proc. Int. Conf. on Computer Vision (ICCV)', pp. 405–410.

Cohen, J. (1964), 'Dependency of the spectral reflectance curves of the munsell color chips', *Psychon. Sci.* **1**, 369–370.

Cohen, M. and Wallace, J. (1993), *Radiosity and realistic image synthesis*, Academic Press.

Collins, G. (1971), 'The calculation of multivariate polynomial resultants', *Journal of the ACM* **18**(4), 515–522.

Collins, G. (1975), *Quantifier Elimination for Real Closed Fields by Cylindrical Algebraic Decomposition*, Vol. 33 of *Lecture Notes in Computer Science*, Springer-Verlag, New York.

Comaniciu, D. and Meer, P. (2002), 'Mean shift: A robust approach toward feature space analysis', *IEEE Trans. Pattern Analysis and Machine Intelligence* **24**(5), 603–619.

Connolly, C. and Stenstrom, J. (1989), 3D scene reconstruction from multiple intensity images, *in* 'Proc. IEEE Workshop on Interpretation of 3D Scenes', Austin, TX, pp. 124–130.

Cook, R. and Torrance, K. (1987), A reflectance model for computer graphics, *in* 'ARPA Image Understanding Workshop', pp. 1–19.

Cooper, H. and Bowden, R. (2009), Learning signs from subtitles: A weakly supervised approach to sign language recognition, *in* 'IEEE Conf. on Computer Vision and Pattern Recognition (CVPR)', pp. 2568–2574.

Cootes, T. and Taylor, C. (1992), Active shape models: Smart snakes, *in* 'British Machine Vision Conference (BMVC)', pp. 267–275.

Cootes, T., Edwards, G. and Taylor, C. (2001), 'Active appearance models', *IEEE Trans. Pattern Analysis and Machine Intelligence* **23**(6), 681–685.

Cootes, T., Hill, A., Taylor, C. and Haslam, J. (1994), 'Use of active shape models for locating structure in medical images', *Image and Vision Computing* **12**(6), 355–365.

Cormen, T., Leiserson, C. and Rivest, R. (2009), *Introduction to Algorithms*, MIT Press.

Correia, P. and Pereira, F. (2003), 'Objective evaluation of video segmentation quality', *IEEE Trans. Image Processing* **12**(2), 186–200.

Costeira, J. and Kanade, T. (1998), 'A multi-body factorization method for motion analysis', *International Journal of Computer Vision* **29**(3), 159–180.

Cover, T. and Thomas, J. (1991), *Elements of Information Theory*, Wiley-Interscience.

Cox, I., Zhong, Y. and Rao, S. (1996), Ratio regions: A technique for image segmentation, *in* 'Proceedings, International Conference on Pattern Recognition', pp. 557–564.

Coxeter, H. (1974), *Projective Geometry*, Springer-Verlag. Second Edition.

Criminisi, A., Kang, S., Swaminathan, R., Szeliski, R. and Anandan, P. (2005), 'Extracting layers and analyzing their specular properties using epipolar-plane-image analysis', *Computer Vision and Image Understanding* **97**(1), 51–85.

Criminisi, A., Perez, P. and Toyama, K. (2004), 'Region filling and object removal by exemplar-based image inpainting', *IEEE Trans. Image Processing* **13**(9), 1200–1212.

Crum, W., Camara, O. and Hill, D. (2006), 'Generalized overlap measures for evaluation and validation in medical image analysis', *IEEE Trans. Medical Imaging* **25**(11), 1451–1461.

Cunningham, H., Maynard, D., Bontcheva, K. and Tablan, V. (2002), Gate: A framework and graphical development environment for robust nlp tools and applications, *in* '40th Anniversary Meeting of the Association for Computational Linguistics'.

Curless, B. and Levoy, M. (1996), A volumetric method for building complex models from range images, *in* 'ACM Trans. Graphics (SIGGRAPH Proceeding)', New Orleans, LA.

Cyganek, B. and Siebert, P. (2009), *An Introduction to 3D Computer Vision Techniques and Algorithms*, Wiley.

Dabov, K., Foi, A., Katkovnik, V. and Egiazarian, K. (2007), 'Image denoising by sparse 3-d transform-domain collaborative filtering', **16**(8), 2080–2095.

Dalal, N. and Triggs, B. (2005), Histograms of oriented gradients for human detection, *in* 'IEEE Conf. on Computer Vision and Pattern Recognition (CVPR)', pp. I: 886–893.

Dana, K., van Ginneken, B., Nayar, S. and Koenderink, J. (1999), 'Reflectance and texture of real-world surfaces', *ACM Transactions on Graphics* **18**(1), 1–34.

Darbon, J. (2009), 'Global optimization for first-order markov random fields with submodular priors', *Discrete Applied Mathematics* **157**(16), 3412–3423.

Darrell, T. and Simoncelli, E. (1993), 'Nulling' filters and the separation of transparent motions, *in* 'IEEE Conf. on Computer Vision and Pattern Recognition (CVPR)', pp. 738–739.

Datta, R., Li, J. and Wang, J. Z. (2005), Content-based image retrieval: approaches and trends of the new age, *in* 'MIR '05: Proceedings of the 7th ACM SIGMM international workshop on Multimedia information retrieval', ACM Press, New York, NY, USA, pp. 253–262.

Daum, F. (1995*a*), Beyond kalman filters: practical design of nonlinear filters, *in* 'Proc. SPIE', Vol. 2561, pp. 252–262.

Daum, F. (1995*b*), 'Exact finite dimensional nonlinear filters', *IEEE. Trans. Automatic Control* **31**, 616–622.

Davies, E. (2005), *Machine Vision, Third Edition: Theory, Algorithms, Practicalities: 3E*, Morgan Kauffmann.

Davis, L. (1975), 'A survey of edge detection techniques', *Computer Graphics Image Processing* **4**(3), 248–270.

Dawn, S., Saxena, V. and Sharma, B. (2010), Remote sensing image registration techniques: A survey, *in* 'Proc. Int. Conf. Image and Signal Processing', pp. 103–112.

de Grazia, E. (1993), *Girls lean back everywhere: The Law of Obscenity and the Assault on Genius*, Vintage.

Debevec, P. and Malik, J. (1997), Recovering high dynamic range radiance maps from photographs, *in* 'SIGGraph-97', pp. 369–378.

Del Pozo, A. and Savarese, S. (2007), Detecting specular surfaces on natural images, *in* 'IEEE Conf. on Computer Vision and Pattern Recognition (CVPR)', pp. 1–8.

Delage, E., Lee, H. and Ng, A. (2006), A dynamic Bayesian network model for autonomous 3d reconstruction from a single indoor image, *in* 'IEEE Conf. on Computer Vision and Pattern Recognition (CVPR)', pp. II: 2418–2428.

Dellaert, F., Burgard, W., Fox, D. and Thrun, S. (1999), Using the condensation algorithm for robust, vision-based mobile robot localization, *in* 'IEEE Conf. on Computer Vision and Pattern Recognition (CVPR)', pp. II:588–594.

Dellaert, F., Seitz, S., Thorpe, C. and Thrun, S. (2000), Structure from motion without correspondence, *in* 'IEEE Conf. on Computer Vision and Pattern Recognition (CVPR)', pp. II:557–564.

Demazure, M. (1989), *Catastrophes et Bifurcations*, Editions Ellipses.

Deming, W. (1943), *Statistical Adjustment of Data*, Wiley.

Dempster, A., Laird, N. and Rubin, D. (1977), 'Maximum likelihood from incomplete data via the EM algorithm', *Journal of the Royal Statistical Society* **39 (Series B)**, 1–38.

Deng, J., Berg, A., Li, K. and Fei-Fei, L. (2010), What does classifiying more than 10,000 image categories tell us?, *in* 'Proc. European Conference on Computer Vision (ECCV)'.

Deng, J., Dong, W., Socher, R., Li, L.-J., Li, K. and Fei-Fei, L. (2009), ImageNet: A Large-Scale Hierarchical Image Database, *in* 'CVPR09'.

Deriche, R. (1987), 'Using Canny's criteria to derive a recursively implemented optimal edge detector', *International Journal of Computer Vision* **1**(2), 167–187.

Deriche, R. (1990), 'Fast algorithms for low-level vision', *IEEE Trans. Pattern Analysis and Machine Intelligence* **12**(1), 78–87.

Desai, C., Ramanan, D. and Fowlkes, C. (2009), Discriminative models for multi-class object layout, *in* 'Proc. Int. Conf. on Computer Vision (ICCV)', pp. 229–236.

Deselaers, T., Pimenidis, L. and Ney, H. (2008), Bag-of-visual-words models for adult image classification and filtering, *in* 'Proceedings IAPR International Conference on Pattern Recognition', pp. 1–4.

Deutscher, J., Blake, A. and Reid, I. (2000), Articulated body motion capture by annealed particle filtering, *in* 'IEEE Conf. on Computer Vision and Pattern Recognition (CVPR)', pp. II:126–133.

Devernay, F. and Faugeras, O. (1994), Computing differential properties of 3D shapes from stereopsis without 3D models, *in* 'IEEE Conf. on Computer Vision and Pattern Recognition (CVPR)', Seattle, WA, pp. 208–213.

Devroye, L., Gyorfi, L. and Lugosi, G. (1996), *A Probabilistic Theory of Pattern Recognition*, Springer Verlag.

Devy, M., Garric, V. and Orteu, J. (1997), Camera calibration from multiple views of a 2D object using a global non-linear minimization method, *in* 'IEEE/RSJ International Conference on Intelligent Robots and Systems', Grenoble, France, pp. 1583–1589.

Dickinson, S., Leonardis, A., Schiele, B. and Tarr, M., eds (2009), *Object Categorization: Computer and Human Vision Perspectives*, Cambridge.

Dietterich, T. G., Lathrop, R. H. and Lozano-Pérez, T. (1997), 'Solving the multiple instance problem with axis-parallel rectangles', *Artif. Intell.* **89**(1-2), 31–71.

Digabel, H. and Lantuéjoul, C. (1978), Iterative algorithms, *in* J. Chermant, ed., 'Proc. 2nd European Symp. Quant. Analysis of Microstructures in Material Science, Biology and Medicine, 1977', Riederer Verlag, pp. 85–99.

do Carmo, M. (1976), *Differential Geometry of Curves and Surfaces*, Prentice-Hall, Englewood Cliffs, NJ.

Dollar, P., Wojek, C., Schiele, B. and Perona, P. (2009), Pedestrian detection: A benchmark, *in* 'IEEE Conf. on Computer Vision and Pattern Recognition (CVPR)', pp. 304–311.

Donoho, D. and Johnstone, I. (1995), 'Adapting to unknown smoothness via wavelet shrinkage', *Journal of the American Statistical Association* **90**(432), 1200–1224.

Doucet, A., Freitas, N. D. and Gordon, N. (2001), *Sequential Monte Carlo Methods in Practice*, Springer-Verlag.

Dove, H. (1841), 'Über Stereoskopie', *Annals Phys. Series 2* **110**, 494–498.

Drew, M. and Funt, B. (1990), Calculating surface reflectance using a single-bounce model of mutual reflection, *in* 'Proc. Int. Conf. on Computer Vision (ICCV)', pp. 393–399.

Duchenne, O., Audibert, J.-Y., Keriven, R., Ponce, J. and Segonne, F. (2008), Segmentation by transduction, *in* 'IEEE Conf. on Computer Vision and Pattern Recognition (CVPR)'.

Duda, R. and Hart, P. (1973), *Pattern Classification and Scene Analysis*, John Wiley & Sons.

Duncan, J. and Ayache, N. (2000), 'Medical image analysis: Progress over two decades and the challenges ahead', *IEEE Trans. Pattern Analysis and Machine Intelligence* **22**(1), 85–106.

Durou, J.-D., Falcone, M. and Sagona, M. (2008*a*), 'Numerical methods for shape-from-shading: A new survey with benchmarks', *Comput. Vis. Image Underst.* **109**(1), 22–43.

Durou, J., Falcone, M. and Sagona, M. (2008*b*), 'Numerical methods for shape-from-shading: A new survey with benchmarks', *Computer Vision and Image Understanding* **109**(1), 22–43.

Duygulu, P., Barnard, K., de Freitas, N. and Forsyth, D. (2002), Object recognition as machine translation, *in* 'Proc. European Conference on Computer Vision (ECCV)'.

D'Zmura, M. and Lennie, P. (1986), 'Mechanisms of colour constancy', *Journal of the Optical Society of America* **3**, 1662–1672.

Eakins, J., Boardman, J. and Graham, M. (1998), 'Similarity retrieval of trademark images', *IEEE Multimedia* **5**(2), 53–63.

Efron, B. (1979), 'Bootstrap methods: another look at the jacknife', *Annals of Statistics* **7**, 1–26.

Efron, B., Hastie, T., Johnstone, I. and Tibshirani, R. (2004), 'Least angle regression', *Ann. Statist.* **32**(2), 407–499.

Efros, A. and Freeman, W. (2001), 'Image quilting for texture synthesis and transfer', *ACM Trans. Graphics (SIGGRAPH Proceeding)* pp. 341–346.

Efros, A. and Leung, T. (1999), Texture synthesis by non-parametric sampling, *in* 'Proc. Int. Conf. on Computer Vision (ICCV)', pp. 1033–1038.

Elad, M. and Aharon, M. (2006), 'Image denoising via sparse and redundant representations over learned dictionaries', **54**(12), 3736–3745.

Elder, J. and Zucker, S. (1998), 'Local scale control for edge detection and blur estimation', *IEEE Trans. Pattern Analysis and Machine Intelligence* **20**(7), 699–716.

Endres, I., Farhadi, A., Hoiem, D. and Forsyth, D. (2010), The benefits and challenges of collecting richer object annotations, *in* 'Proc. IEEE Workshop on Advancing Computer Vision with Humans in the Loop', pp. 1–8.

Engan, K., Aase, S. O. and Husoy, J. H. (1999), Frame based signal compression using method of optimal directions (MOD), *in* 'Proc. of the IEEE Intern. Symposium Circuits Syst.', Vol. 4.

Enser, P. (1993), 'Query analysis in a visual information retrieval context', *J. Document and Text Management* **1**(1), 25–52.

Enser, P. (1995), 'Pictorial information retrieval', *Journal of Documentation* **51**(2), 126–170.

Enser, P. (2000), 'Visual image retrieval: seeking the alliance of concept-based and content-based paradigms', *J. Information Science*.

Enser, P. and Mcgregor, C. (1992), Analysis of visual information retrieval queries, Technical report, British Library R+D Report 6104.

Enzweiler, M. and Gavrila, D. (2009), 'Monocular pedestrian detection: Survey and experiments', *IEEE Trans. Pattern Analysis and Machine Intelligence* **31**(12), 2179–2195.

Enzweiler, M., Eigenstetter, A., Schiele, B. and Gavrila, D. (2010), Multi-cue pedestrian classification with partial occlusion handling, *in* 'IEEE Conf. on Computer Vision and Pattern Recognition (CVPR)', pp. 990–997.

Erdem, U. and Sclaroff, S. (2002), Automatic detection of relevant head gestures in American sign language communication, *in* 'Proceedings IAPR International Conference on Pattern Recognition', pp. I: 460–463.

Ess, A., Leibe, B., Schindler, K. and Van Gool, L. (2009), 'Robust multiperson tracking from a mobile platform', *IEEE Trans. Pattern Analysis and Machine Intelligence* **31**(10), 1831–1846.

Esteban, C. H., Vogiatzis, G., Brostow, G., Stenger, B. and Cipolla, R. (2007), Non-rigid photometric stereo with colored lights, *in* 'Proc. Int. Conf. on Computer Vision (ICCV)'.

Ettinger, G. (1988), Large hierarchical object recognition using libraries of parameterized model sub-parts, *in* 'IEEE Conf. on Computer Vision and Pattern Recognition (CVPR)', pp. 32–41.

Everingham, M., Van Gool, L., Williams, C. K. I., Winn, J. and Zisserman, A. (2010), 'The pascal visual object classes (voc) challenge', *International Journal of Computer Vision* **88**(2), 303–338.

Faig, W. (1975), 'Calibration of close-range photogrammetry systems: mathematical formulation', *Photogrammetric Engineering and Remote Sensing* **41**(12), 1479–1486.

Fairchild, M. (1998), *Color Appearance Models*, Addison-Wesley.

Fan, T., Médioni, G. and Nevatia, R. (1987), 'Segmented descriptions of 3D surfaces', **3**(6), 527–538.

Farenzena, M. and Fusiello, A. (2007), Recovering intrinsic images using an illumination invariant image, *in* 'IEEE Int. Conf. Image Processing'.

Farhadi, A. and Forsyth, D. (2006), Aligning asl for statistical translation using a discriminative word model, *in* 'IEEE Conf. on Computer Vision and Pattern Recognition (CVPR)', pp. II: 1471–1476.

Farhadi, A. and Sadeghi, A. (2011), Recognition using visual phrases, *in* 'IEEE Conf. on Computer Vision and Pattern Recognition (CVPR)'.

Farhadi, A., Endres, I. and Hoiem, D. (2010*a*), Attribute-centric recognition for cross-category generalization, *in* 'IEEE Conf. on Computer Vision and Pattern Recognition (CVPR)', pp. 2352–2359.

Farhadi, A., Endres, I., Hoiem, D. and Forsyth, D. (2009*a*), Describing objects by their attributes, *in* 'IEEE Conf. on Computer Vision and Pattern Recognition (CVPR)', pp. 1778–1785.

Farhadi, A., Forsyth, D. and White, R. (2007), Transfer learning in sign language, *in* 'IEEE Conf. on Computer Vision and Pattern Recognition (CVPR)', pp. 1–8.

Farhadi, A., Hejrati, M., Sadeghi, A., Young, P., Rashtchian, C., Hockenmaier, J. and Forsyth, D. (2010*b*), Every picture tells a story: Generating sentences for images, *in* 'Proc. European Conference on Computer Vision (ECCV)'.

Farhadi, A., Tabrizi, M., Endres, I. and Forsyth, D. (2009*b*), A latent model of discriminative aspect, *in* 'Proc. Int. Conf. on Computer Vision (ICCV)', pp. 948–955.

Faugeras, O. (1992), What can be seen in three dimensions with an uncalibrated stereo rig?, *in* G. Sandini, ed., 'Proc. European Conference on Computer Vision (ECCV)', Vol. 588 of *Lecture Notes in Computer Science*, Springer-Verlag, Santa Margherita, Italy, pp. 563–578.

Faugeras, O. (1993), *Three-Dimensional Computer Vision*, MIT Press.

Faugeras, O. (1995), 'Stratification of 3D vision: projective, affine and metric representations', **12**(3), 465–484.

Faugeras, O. and Hebert, M. (1986), 'The representation, recognition, and locating of 3-D objects', *International Journal of Robotics Research* **5**(3), 27–52.

Faugeras, O. and Keriven, R. (1998), 'Variational principles, surface evolution, PDE's, level set methods and the stereo problem', *IEEE Trans. Im. Proc.* **7**(3), 336–344.

Faugeras, O. and Maybank, S. (1990), 'Motion from point matches: multiplicity of solutions', *International Journal of Computer Vision* **4**(3), 225–246.

Faugeras, O. and Mourrain, B. (1995), On the geometry and algebra of the point and line correspondences between n images, Technical Report 2665, INRIA Sophia-Antipolis.

Faugeras, O. and Papadopoulo, T. (1997), Grassman-Caylay algebra for modeling systems of cameras and the algebraic equations of the manifold of trifocal tensors, Technical Report 3225, INRIA Sophia-Antipolis.

Faugeras, O., Hebert, M., Pauchon, E. and Ponce, J. (1984), Object representation, identification, and positioning from range data, *in* 'Robotics Research: The First International Symposium', MIT Press, pp. 425–446.

Faugeras, O., Luong, Q.-T. and Papadopoulo, T. (2001), *The Geometry of Multiple Images*, MIT Press.

Fei-Fei, L., Fergus, R. and Perona, P. (2006), 'One-shot learning of object categories', *IEEE Trans. Pattern Analysis and Machine Intelligence* **28**(4), 594–611.

Fellbaum, C., ed. (1998), *WordNet: An Electronic Lexical Database*, MIT Press. with a preface by George Miller.

Felzenszwalb, P. and Huttenlocher, D. (2000), Efficient matching of pictorial structures, *in* 'IEEE Conf. on Computer Vision and Pattern Recognition (CVPR)', pp. II:66–73.

Felzenszwalb, P. and Huttenlocher, D. (2004), 'Efficient graph-based image segmentation', *International Journal of Computer Vision* **59**(2), 167–181.

Felzenszwalb, P., Girshick, R. and McAllester, D. (2010*a*), Cascade object detection with deformable part models, *in* 'IEEE Conf. on Computer Vision and Pattern Recognition (CVPR)', pp. 2241–2248.

Felzenszwalb, P., Girshick, R., McAllester, D. and Ramanan, D. (2010*b*), 'Object detection with discriminatively trained part-based models', *IEEE Trans. Pattern Analysis and Machine Intelligence* **32**(9), 1627–1645.

Feng, S. L., Manmatha, R. and Lavrenko, V. (2004), Multiple bernoulli relevance models for image and video annotation, *in* 'IEEE Conf. on Computer Vision and Pattern Recognition (CVPR)', Vol. 02, pp. 1002–1009.

Feng, X. and Perona, P. (1998), Scene segmentation from 3D motion, *in* 'IEEE Conf. on Computer Vision and Pattern Recognition (CVPR)', pp. 225–231.

Fergus, R., Perona, P. and Zisserman, A. (2003), Object class recognition by unsupervised scale-invariant learning, *in* 'IEEE Conf. on Computer Vision and Pattern Recognition (CVPR)', pp. II: 264–271.

Ferrari, V., Marin Jimenez, M. and Zisserman, A. (2008), Progressive search space reduction for human pose estimation, *in* 'IEEE Conf. on Computer Vision and Pattern Recognition (CVPR)', pp. 1–8.

Finlayson, G. (1996), 'Colour in perspective', *IEEE Trans. Pattern Analysis and Machine Intelligence* **18**, 1034–1038.

Finlayson, G. and Hordley, S. (1999), 'Selection for gamut mapping colour constancy', *Image and Vision Computing* **17**(8), 597–604.

Finlayson, G. and Hordley, S. (2000), 'Improving gamut mapping color constancy', *IEEE Trans. Image Processing* **9**(10), 1774–1783.

Finlayson, G., Drew, M. and Funt, B. (1994*a*), 'Color constancy: Generalized diagonal transforms suffice', *Journal of the Optical Society of America* **11**(11), 3011–3019.

Finlayson, G., Drew, M. and Funt, B. (1994*b*), 'Spectral sharpening: Sensor transformations for improved color constancy', *Journal of the Optical Society of America* **11**(5), 1553–1563.

Fischler, M. and Bolles, R. (1981), 'Random sample consensus: A paradigm for model fitting with applications to image analysis and automated cartography', *Communications of the ACM* **24**(6), 381–395.

Fitzgibbon, A. (2003), 'Robust registration of 2d and 3d point sets', *Image and Vision Computing* **21**(12-13), 1145–1153.

Fitzgibbon, A. and Zisserman, A. (1998), Automatic 3D model acquisition and generation of new images from video sequences, *in* 'European Signal Processing Conference', Rhodes, Greece, pp. 311–326.

Fitzgibbon, A., Pilu, M. and Fisher, R. (1999), 'Direct least square fitting of ellipses', *IEEE Trans. Pattern Analysis and Machine Intelligence* **21**(5), 476–480.

Fleck, M. (1992), 'Multiple widths yield reliable finite differences', *IEEE Trans. Pattern Analysis and Machine Intelligence* **14**(4), 412–429.

Flock, H. (1984), 'Illumination: inferred or observed?', *Perception and Psychophysics*.

Foley, J., van Dam, A., Feiner, S. and Hughes, J. (1990), *Computer Graphics: Principle and Practice*, Addison-Wesley. Second edition.

Ford, L. and Fulkerson, D. (1956), 'Maximal flow through a network', *Canadian Journal of Mathematics* **8**, 399–404.

Forney, G. (1973), 'The Viterbi algorithm', *Proceedings of the IEEE*.

Forsyth, D. (1990), 'A novel algorithm for color constancy', *International Journal of Computer Vision* **5**(1), 5–36.

Forsyth, D. (1999), Sampling, resampling and colour constancy, *in* 'IEEE Conf. on Computer Vision and Pattern Recognition (CVPR)', pp. I:300–305.

Forsyth, D. (2001), Shape from texture and integrability, *in* 'Proc. Int. Conf. on Computer Vision (ICCV)', pp. II: 447–452.

Forsyth, D. (2002), Shape from texture without boundaries, *in* 'Proc. European Conference on Computer Vision (ECCV)', p. III: 225 ff.

Forsyth, D. and Fleck, M. (1999), 'Automatic detection of human nudes', *International Journal of Computer Vision* **32**(1), 63–77.

Forsyth, D. and Zisserman, A. (1989), Mutual illumination, *in* 'IEEE Conf. on Computer Vision and Pattern Recognition (CVPR)', pp. 466–473.

Forsyth, D. and Zisserman, A. (1990), 'Shape from shading in the light of mutual illumination', *Image and Vision Computing* **8**, 42–29.

Forsyth, D. and Zisserman, A. (1991), 'Reflections on shading', *IEEE Trans. Pattern Analysis and Machine Intelligence* **13**(7), 671–679.

Forsyth, D., Arikan, O., Ikemoto, L., O'Brien, J. and Ramanan, D. (2006), 'Computational aspects of human motion i: tracking and animation', *Foundations and Trends in Computer Graphics and Vision* **1**(2/3), 1–255.

Forsyth, D., Mundy, J., Zisserman, A. and Rothwell, C. (1994), Using global consistency to recognise euclidean objects with an uncalibrated camera, *in* 'IEEE Conf. on Computer Vision and Pattern Recognition (CVPR)', pp. 502–507.

Franco, J.-S. and Boyer, E. (2009), 'Efficient polyhedral modeling from silhouettes', *IEEE Trans. Pattern Analysis and Machine Intelligence* **31**(3), 414–427.

Freeman, W. and Adelson, E. (1991), 'The design and use of steerable filters', *IEEE Trans. Pattern Analysis and Machine Intelligence* **13**(9), 891–906.

Freeman, W. and Brainard, D. (1997), 'Bayesian color constancy', *Journal of the Optical Society of America* **14**(7), 1393–1411.

Freeman, W., Anderson, D. and et al., P. B. (1998), 'Computer vision for interactive computer graphics', *Computer Graphics and Applications* pp. 42–53.

Freeman, W., Pasztor, E. and Carmichael, O. (2000), 'Learning low-level vision', *International Journal of Computer Vision* **40**(1), 25–47.

Friedman, J. H. (2001), 'Greedy function approximation: A gradient boosting machine', *Ann. Statist.* **29**(5), 1189–1232.

Friedman, J. H., Bentley, J. L. and Finkel, R. A. (1977), 'An algorithm for finding best matches in logarithmic expected time', *ACM Transactions on Math Software* **3**, 209–226.

Friedman, J., Hastie, T. and Tibshirani, R. (1998), 'Additive logistic regression: a statistical view of boosting', *Annals of Statistics* **28**, 2000.

Frisby, J. (1980), *Seeing: Illusion, Brain and Mind*, Oxford University Press.

Frost, C. O., Taylor, B., Noakes, A., Markel, S., Torres, D. and Drabenstott, K. M. (2000), 'Browse and search patterns in a digital image database', *Information retrieval* **1**, 287–313.

Fu, K. and Mui, J. (1981), 'A survey of image segmentation', *Pattern Recognition* **13**(1), 3–16.

Fu, W. (1998), 'Penalized Regressions: The Bridge Versus the Lasso', *Journal of computational and graphical statistics* **7**, 397–416.

Fukunaga, K. (1990), *Introduction to Statistical Pattern Recognition*, Academic Press.

Fukunaga, K. and Hostetler, L. (1975), 'The estimation of the gradient of a density function, with applications in pattern recognition', *IEEE Trans. Information Theory* **21**(1), 32–40.

Funt, B. and Drew, M. (1988), Color constancy computation in near-mondrian scenes using a finite dimensional linear model, *in* 'IEEE Conf. on Computer Vision and Pattern Recognition (CVPR)', pp. 544–549.

Funt, B. and Drew, M. (1993), 'Color space analysis of mutual illumination', *IEEE Trans. Pattern Analysis and Machine Intelligence* **15**(12), 1319–1326.

Funt, B., Barnard, K. and Martin, L. (1998), Is machine colour constancy good enough?, *in* 'Proc. European Conference on Computer Vision (ECCV)', p. I: 445.

Funt, B., Drew, M. and Brockington, M. (1992), Recovering shading from color images, *in* 'Proc. European Conference on Computer Vision (ECCV)'.

Funt, B., Drew, M. and Ho, J. (1991), 'Color constancy from mutual reflection', *International Journal of Computer Vision* **6**(1), 5–24.

Furukawa, Y. and Ponce, J. (2008), Dense 3D motion capture from synchronized video streams, *in* 'IEEE Conf. on Computer Vision and Pattern Recognition (CVPR)'.

Furukawa, Y. and Ponce, J. (2009*a*), 'Carved visual hulls for image-based modeling', *International Journal of Computer Vision* **81**(1), 53–67.

Furukawa, Y. and Ponce, J. (2009*b*), Dense 3D motion capture for human faces, *in* 'IEEE Conf. on Computer Vision and Pattern Recognition (CVPR)'.

Furukawa, Y. and Ponce, J. (2010), 'Accurate, dense, and robust multiview stereopsis', *IEEE Trans. Pattern Analysis and Machine Intelligence* **32**(8), 1362–1376.

Furukawa, Y., Curless, B., Seitz, S. and Szeliski, R. (2010), Towards internet-scale multiview stereo, *in* 'IEEE Conf. on Computer Vision and Pattern Recognition (CVPR)'.

Garcia-Bermejo, J., Diaz Pernas, F. and Coronado, J. (1996), An approach for determining bidirectional reflectance parameters from range and brightness data, *in* 'IEEE Int. Conf. Image Processing', p. 16A2.

Garding, J. (1992), Shape from texture for smooth curved surfaces, *in* 'Proc. European Conference on Computer Vision (ECCV)', pp. 630–638.

Garding, J. (1995), Surface orientation and curvature from differential texture distortion, *in* 'Proc. Int. Conf. on Computer Vision (ICCV)', pp. 733–739.

Gaston, P. and Lozano-Pérez, T. (1984), 'Tactile recognition and localization using object models: The case of polyhedra in the plane', *IEEE Trans. Pattern Analysis and Machine Intelligence.*

Gear, C. (1998), 'Multibody grouping in moving objects', *International Journal of Computer Vision* **29**(2), 133–150.

Gehler, P. and Nowozin, S. (2009), On feature combination for multiclass object classification, *in* 'Proc. Int. Conf. on Computer Vision (ICCV)', pp. 221–228.

Gelb, A. and of the Analytical Sciences Corporation, S. (1974), *Applied Optimal Estimation*, MIT Press.

Geman, S. and Geman, D. (1984), 'Stochastic relaxation, gibbs distribution , and the Bayesian restoration of images', *IEEE Trans. Pattern Anal. Machine Intell.*

Gennery, D. (1980), Modelling the environment of an exploring vehicle by means of stereo vision, PhD thesis, Stanford University, Stanford, CA.

Georghiades, A. S., Belhumeur, P. N. and Kriegman, D. J. (2001), 'From few to many: Illumination cone models for face recognition under variable lighting and pose', *IEEE Trans. Pattern Analysis and Machine Intelligence* **23**(6), 643–660.

Gerig, G., Pun, T. and Ratib, O. (1994), 'Image analysis and computer vision in medicine', *Computerized Medical Imaging and Graphics* **18**(2), 85–96.

Gerónimo, D., Sappa, A., López, A. and Ponsa, D. (2007), Adaptive image sampling and windows classification for on-board pedestrian detection, *in* 'International Conference on Computer Vision Systems'.

Gersho, A. and Gray, R. (1992), *Vector quantization and signal compression*, Kluwer Academic Publishers.

Gershon, R. (1987), The Use of Color in Computational Vision, PhD thesis, University of Toronto.

Gershon, R., Jepson, A. and Tsotsos, J. (1986), 'Ambient illumination and the determination of material changes', *J. Opt. Soc. America* **A-3**(10), 1700–1707.

Geusebroek, J., van den Boomgaard, R., Smeulders, A. and Geerts, H. (2001), 'Color invariance', *IEEE Trans. Pattern Analysis and Machine Intelligence* **23**(12), 1338–1350.

Gevers, T., Gijsenij, A., van de Weijer, J. and Geusebroek, J.-M. (2011), *Color in Computer Vision: Fundamentals and Applications*, Wiley.

Gevrekci, M. and Gunturk, B. (2009), 'Illumination robust interest point detection', *Computer Vision and Image Understanding* **113**(4), 565–571.

Gibson, J. (1950), *The perception of the visual world*, Houghton-Mifflin.

Gilchrist, A., Kossyfidis, C., Bonato, F., Agostini, T., Cataliotti, J., Li, X., Spehar, B., Annan, V. and Economou, E. (1999), 'An anchoring theory of lightness perception', *Psychological Review* **106**(4), 795–834.

Gill, P., Murray, W. and Wright, M. (1981), *Practical Optimization*, Academic Press.

Gleicher, M. (2000), 'Animation from observation: Motion capture and motion editing', *SIGGRAPH Comput. Graph.* **33**(4), 51–54.

Goesele, M., Curless, B. and Seitz, S. M. (2006), Multi-view stereo revisited, *in* 'IEEE Conf. on Computer Vision and Pattern Recognition (CVPR)', pp. 2402–2409.

Goldberg, A. and Tarjan, R. (1988), 'A new approach to the maximum-flow problem', **35**(4), 921–940.

Goodrum, A. and Spink, A. (2001), 'Image searching on the excite web search engine', *Information Processing and Management* **37**, 295–311.

Gordon, I. (1997), *Theories of Visual Perception*, John Wiley & Son.

Gortler, S., Grzeszczuk, R., Szeliski, R. and Cohen, M. (1996), The lumigraph, *in* 'SIGGRAPH', New Orleans, LA, pp. 43–54.

Grauman, K. and Darrell, T. (2005), The pyramid match kernel: Discriminative classification with sets of image features, *in* 'Proc. Int. Conf. on Computer Vision (ICCV)', pp. II: 1458–1465.

Grauman, K., Shakhnarovich, G. and Darrell, T. (2004), Virtual visual hulls: Example-based 3d shape inference from silhouettes, *in* 'SMVP04', pp. 26–37.

Greenspan, H., Belongie, S., Perona, P., Goodman, R., Rakshit, S. and Anderson, C. (1994), Overcomplete steerable pyramid filters and rotation invariance, *in* 'IEEE Conf. on Computer Vision and Pattern Recognition (CVPR)', pp. 222–228.

Greig, D., Porteous, B. and Seheult, A. (1989), 'Exact maximum a posteriori estimation from binary images', *Journal of the Royal Statistical Society* **51**(2), 271–279.

Griffin, G., Holub, A. and Perona, P. (2007), Caltech-256 object category dataset, Technical Report 7694, California Institute of Technology.

Grimson, W. (1981*a*), 'A computer implementation of a theory of human stereo vision', *Philosophical Transactions of the Royal Society of London* pp. 217–253.

Grimson, W. (1981*b*), *From images to surfaces*, MIT Press.

Grimson, W. (1992), 'The cost of choosing the wrong model in object recognition by constrained search', *International Journal of Computer Vision* **7**(3), 195–210.

Grimson, W. and Huttenlocher, D. (1990), 'On the sensitivity of the Hough transform for object recognition', *IEEE Trans. Pattern Analysis and Machine Intelligence* **12**(3), 255–274.

Grimson, W. and Huttenlocher, D. (1991), 'On the verification of hypothesized matches in model-based recognition', *IEEE Trans. Pattern Analysis and Machine Intelligence* **13**(12), 1201–1213.

Grimson, W. and Lozano-Pérez, T. (1987), 'Localizing overlapping parts by searching the interpretation tree', *IEEE Trans. Pattern Analysis and Machine Intelligence* **9**(4), 469–482.

Grimson, W., Huttenlocher, D. and Alter, T. (1992), Recognizing 3D objects from 2D images: An error analysis, *in* 'IEEE Conf. on Computer Vision and Pattern Recognition (CVPR)', pp. 316–321.

Grimson, W., Huttenlocher, D. and Jacobs, D. (1994), 'A study of affine matching with bounded sensor error', *International Journal of Computer Vision* **13**(1), 7–32.

Grimson, W., Lozano-Perez, T. and Huttenlocher, D. (1990), *Object Recognition by Computer: The Role of Geometric Constraints*, MIT Press.

Gross, A. and Boult, T. (1988), Error of fit measures for recovering parametric solids, *in* 'Proc. Int. Conf. on Computer Vision (ICCV)', Tampa, FL, pp. 690–694.

Grossberg, M. and Nayar, S. (2002), What can be known about the radiometric response from images?, *in* 'Proc. European Conference on Computer Vision (ECCV)', p. IV: 189 ff.

Grosse, R., Johnson, M. K., Adelson, E. H. and Freeman, W. T. (2009), Ground truth dataset and baseline evaluations for intrinsic image algorithms, *in* 'Proc. Int. Conf. on Computer Vision (ICCV)'.

Grosse, R., Raina, R., Kwong, H. and Ng, A. Y. (2007), Shift-invariant sparse coding for audio classification, *in* 'Proceedings of the Twenty-third Conference on Uncertainty in Artificial Intelligence'.

Gu, C., Lim, J., Arbelaez, P. and Malik, J. (2009), Recognition using regions, *in* 'IEEE Conf. on Computer Vision and Pattern Recognition (CVPR)', pp. 1030–1037.

Gupta, A. and Davis, L. (2008), Beyond nouns: Exploiting prepositions and comparative adjectives for learning visual classifiers, *in* 'Proc. European Conference on Computer Vision (ECCV)', pp. I: 16–29.

Gupta, A., Satkin, S., Efros, A. A. and Hebert, M. (2011), From 3d scene geometry to human workspace, *in* 'IEEE Conf. on Computer Vision and Pattern Recognition (CVPR)'.

Gupta, A., Srinivasan, P., Shi, J. and Davis, L. (2009), Understanding videos, constructing plots learning a visually grounded storyline model from annotated videos, *in* 'IEEE Conf. on Computer Vision and Pattern Recognition (CVPR)', pp. 2012–2019.

Habbecke, M. and Kobbelt, L. (2006), Iterative multi-view plane fitting, *in* '11th Fall Workshop on VISION, MODELING, AND VISUALIZATION'.

Haddon, J. and Forsyth, D. (1997), Shading primitives, *in* 'Proc. Int. Conf. on Computer Vision (ICCV)'.

Haddon, J. and Forsyth, D. (1998*a*), Shading primitives: Finding folds and shallow grooves, *in* 'Proc. Int. Conf. on Computer Vision (ICCV)', pp. 236–241.

Haddon, J. and Forsyth, D. (1998*b*), Shape descriptions from shading primitives, *in* 'Proc. European Conference on Computer Vision (ECCV)'.

Haddon, J. and Forsyth, D. (1998*c*), Shape representations from shading primitives, *in* 'Proc. European Conference on Computer Vision (ECCV)', p. II: 415.

Hadsell, R., Sermanet, P., Scoffier, M., Erkan, A., Kavackuoglu, K., Muller, U. and LeCun, Y. (2009), 'Learning long-range vision for autonomous off-road driving', *Journal of Field Robotics* **26**(2), 120–144.

Hamilton, W. (1844), 'On a new species of imaginary quantities connected with a theory of quaternions', *Transactions of the Royal Irish Academy* **2**, 424–434.

Han, F. and Zhu, S.-C. (2005), Cloth representation by shape from shading with shading primitives, *in* 'IEEE Conf. on Computer Vision and Pattern Recognition (CVPR)', Vol. 1, pp. 1203–1210.

Han, F. and Zhu, S.-C. (2007), 'A two-level generative model for cloth representation and shape from shading', *IEEE Trans. Pattern Analysis and Machine Intelligence* **29**(7), 1230–1243.

Hanbury, A. and Stottinger, J. (2008), On segmentation evaluation metrics and region counts, *in* 'Proceedings IAPR International Conference on Pattern Recognition', pp. 1–4.

Haralick, R. and Shapiro, L. (1985), 'Image segmentation techniques', *CVGIP: Image Understanding* **29**(1), 100–132.

Haralick, R. and Shapiro, L. (1992), *Computer and robot vision*, Addison Wesley.

Hardin, C. and Maffi, L. (1997), *Color Categories in thought and lanuage*, Cambridge University Press.

Harris, C. and Stephens, M. (1988), A combined corner and edge detector, *in* 'Proc. Alvey Vision Conference', pp. 147–152.

Hartley, R. (1994*a*), An algorithm for self calibration from several views, *in* 'IEEE Conf. on Computer Vision and Pattern Recognition (CVPR)', Seattle, WA, pp. 908–912.

Hartley, R. (1994*b*), 'Projective reconstruction and invariants from multiple images', *IEEE Trans. Pattern Analysis and Machine Intelligence* **16**(10), 1036–1041.

Hartley, R. (1995), In defence of the 8-point algorithm, *in* 'Proc. Int. Conf. on Computer Vision (ICCV)', Boston, MA, pp. 1064–1070.

Hartley, R. (1997), 'Lines and points in three views and the trifocal tensor', *International Journal of Computer Vision* **22**(2), 125–140.

Hartley, R. and Zisserman, A. (2000*a*), *Multiple View Geometry in Computer Vision*, Cambridge University Press.

Hartley, R. and Zisserman, A. (2000*b*), *Multiple view geometry in computer vision*, Cambridge University Press.

Hartley, R., Gupta, R. and Chang, T. (1992), Stereo from uncalibrated cameras, *in* 'IEEE Conf. on Computer Vision and Pattern Recognition (CVPR)', Champaign, IL, pp. 761–764.

Hartley, R., Wang, C., Kitchen, L. and Rosenfeld, A. (1982), 'Segmentation of FLIR images: A comparative study', *IEEE Trans. Systems, Man and Cybernetics* **12**(4), 553–566.

Hastie, T., Tibshirani, R. and Friedman, J. (2009), *The Elements of Statistical Learning: Data Mining, Inference and Prediction Second Edition*, Springer Verlag.

Hays, J. and Efros, A. (2007), 'Scene completion using millions of photographs', *ACM Trans. Graph. (SIGGRAPH Proceedings)*.

Healey, G. and Binford, T. (1986), Local shape from specularity, Computer Science STAN-CS-86-1139, Stanford University.

Heath, M. (2002), *Scientific Computing: An Introductory Survey*, McGraw-Hill. Second edition.

Hebert, M. (2000), Active and passive range sensing for robotics, *in* 'Int. Conf. on Robotics and Automation', San Francisco, CA.

Hebert, M. and Kanade, T. (1985), The 3D profile method for object recognition, *in* 'IEEE Conf. on Computer Vision and Pattern Recognition (CVPR)', San Francisco, CA, pp. 458–463.

Hecht, E. (1987), *Optics*, Addison-Wesley.

Hedau, V., Hoiem, D. and Forsyth, D. (2009), Recovering the spatial layout of cluttered rooms, *in* 'Proc. Int. Conf. on Computer Vision (ICCV)', pp. 1849–1856.

Hedau, V., Hoiem, D. and Forsyth, D. (2010), Thinking inside the box: Using appearance models and context based on room geometry, *in* 'Proc. European Conference on Computer Vision (ECCV)'.

Heikkilä, J. (2000), 'Geometric camera calibration using circular control points', *IEEE Trans. Pattern Analysis and Machine Intelligence* **22**(10), 1066–1077.

Heitz, G. and Koller, D. (2008), Learning spatial context: Using stuff to find things, *in* 'Proc. European Conference on Computer Vision (ECCV)', pp. I: 30–43.

Hel-Or, Y. and Teo, P. (1996), Canonical decomposition of steerable functions, *in* 'IEEE Conf. on Computer Vision and Pattern Recognition (CVPR)', pp. 809–816.

Helmholtz, H. (1909), *Physiological optics*, Dover. 1962 edition of the English translation of the 1909 German original, first published by the Optical Society of America in 1924.

Helson, H. (1934), 'Some factors and implications of colour constancy', *Journal of the Optical Society of America* **48**, 555–567.

Helson, H. (1938*a*), Fundamental problems in color vision, i, *in* 'Journal of Experimental Psychology', Vol. 23.

Helson, H. (1938*b*), Fundamental problems in color vision, ii, *in* 'Journal of Experimental Psychology', Vol. 26.

Henderson, J. and Hollingworth, A. (1999), 'High-level scene perception', *Annual Review of Psychology* **50**(1), 243–271.

Hernandez, C., Vogiatzis, G. and Cipolla, R. (2008), Shadows in three-source photometric stereo, *in* 'Proc. European Conference on Computer Vision (ECCV)', pp. I: 290–303.

Hernández Esteban, C. and Schmitt, F. (2004), 'Silhouette and stereo fusion for 3D object modeling', *Computer Vision and Image Understanding* **96**(3), 367–392.

Herskovits, A. and Binford, T. (1970), On boundary detection, Technical report, MIT AI Lab.

Hertzmann, A., Jacobs, C., Oliver, N., Curless, B. and Salesin, D. (2001), 'Image analogies', *ACM Trans. Graph. (SIGGRAPH Proceedings)* pp. 327–340.

Hesse, O. (1863), 'Die cubische Gleichung, von welcher die Lösung des Problems der Homographie von M. Chasles abhängt', *J. Reine Angew. Math.* **62**, 188–192.

Heyden, A. and Åström, K. (1996), Euclidean reconstruction from constant intrinsic parameters, *in* 'International Conference on Pattern Recognition', pp. 339–343.

Heyden, A. and Åström, K. (1998), Minimal conditions on intrinsic parameters for Euclidean reconstruction, *in* 'Asian Conference on Computer Vision', Hong Kong.

Heyden, A. and Åström, K. (1999), Flexible calibration: minimal cases for auto-calibration, *in* 'Proc. Int. Conf. on Computer Vision (ICCV)', Kerkyra, Greece, pp. 350–355.

Hiep, V., Keriven, R., Labatut, P. and Pons, J.-P. (2009), Toward high-resolution large-scale multi-view stereo, *in* 'IEEE Conf. on Computer Vision and Pattern Recognition (CVPR)'.

Hilbert, D. and Cohn-Vossen, S. (1952), *Geometry and the Imagination*, Chelsea, New York.

Hofmann, T. and Puzicha, J. (1998), Statistical models for co-occurrence data, A.I. Memo 1635, Massachusetts Institute of Technology.

Hoiem, D., Efros, A. A. and Hebert, M. (2005), 'Automatic photo pop-up', *ACM Trans. Graph. - SIGGRAPH Proceedings*.

Hoiem, D., Efros, A. and Hebert, M. (2006), Putting objects in perspective, *in* 'IEEE Conf. on Computer Vision and Pattern Recognition (CVPR)', pp. II: 2137–2144.

Hoiem, D., Efros, A. and Hebert, M. (2008), 'Putting objects in perspective', *International Journal of Computer Vision* **80**(1), 3–15.

Hollinka, L., Schreiber, A., Wieling, B. and Worring, M. (2004), 'Classification of user image descriptions', *Int. J. Human-Computer Studies* **61**, 601–626.

Hordley, S. and Finlayson, G. (2006), 'Reevaluation of color constancy algorithm performance', *Journal of the Optical Society of America* **23**(5), 1008–1020.

Horn, B. (1970*a*), Shape from Shading: a Method for Obtaining the Shape of a Smooth Opaque Object from One View, PhD thesis, MIT Department of Electrical Engineering.

Horn, B. (1970*b*), Shape from shading: A method for obtaining the shape of a smooth opaque object from one view, Technical report, MIT AI Lab.

Horn, B. (1971), The Binford-Horn line finder, Technical report, MIT AI Lab.

Horn, B. (1974), 'Determining lightness from an image', *Computer Graphics Image Processing* **3**(1), 277–299.

Horn, B. (1975), Obtaining shape from shading information, *in* 'The Psychology of Computer Vision', McGraw-Hill, pp. 115–155.

Horn, B. (1977), 'Understanding image intensities', *Artificial Intelligence* **8**(2), 201–231.

Horn, B. (1986), *Robot Vision*, MIT Press, Cambridge,Mass.

Horn, B. (1987a), 'Closed-form solution of absolute orientation using unit quaternions', **4**(4), 629–642.

Horn, B. (1987b), 'Closed form solutions of absolute orientation using orthonormal matrices', *Journal of the Optical Society of America* **5**(7), 1127–1135.

Horn, B. (1990), 'Height and gradient from shading', *International Journal of Computer Vision* **5**(1), 37–76.

Horn, B. and Brooks, M. (1989), *Shape from Shading*, MIT Press.

Horn, B., Woodham, R. and Silver, W. (1978), Determining shape and reflectance using multiple images, Technical report, MIT AI Lab.

Hornung, A. and Kobbelt, L. (2006), Hierarchical volumetric multi-view stereo reconstruction of manifold surfaces based on dual graph embedding, *in* 'IEEE Conf. on Computer Vision and Pattern Recognition (CVPR)'.

Hough, P. (1962), Method and means for recognizing complex patterns, *in* 'US Patent'.

Howe, N. (2004), Silhouette lookup for automatic pose tracking, *in* 'IEEE Workshop on Articulated and Non-Rigid Motion', p. 15.

Hsu, S., Anandan, P. and Peleg, S. (1994), Accurate computation of optical flow by using layered motion representations, *in* 'Proceedings IAPR International Conference on Pattern Recognition', pp. A:743–746.

Huang, T. and Faugeras, O. (1989), 'Some properties of the E-matrix in two-view motion estimation', *IEEE Trans. Pattern Analysis and Machine Intelligence* **11**(12), 1310–1312.

Hueckel, M. (1971), 'An operator which locates edges in digitized pictures', *Journal of the ACM* **18**(1), 113–125.

Hung, T.-Y. (2005), 'Search moves and tactics for image retrieval in the field of journalism: A pilot study', *Journal of Educational Media & Library Sciences* **42**(3), 329–346.

Hurvich, L. and Jameson, D. (1957), 'An opponent process theory of color vision', *Psych. Review* **64**(6), 384–404.

Huttenlocher, D. and Ullman, S. (1987), Object recognition using alignment, *in* 'Proc. Int. Conf. on Computer Vision (ICCV)', London, U.K., pp. 102–111.

Huttenlocher, D. and Ullman, S. (1990), 'Recognizing solid objects by alignment with an image', *International Journal of Computer Vision* **5**(2), 195–212.

Huttenlocher, D. and Wayner, P. (1992), 'Finding convex edge groupings in an image', *International Journal of Computer Vision* **8**(1), 7–27.

Ikemoto, L. and Forsyth, D. (2004), Enriching a motion collection by transplanting limbs, *in* 'Proc. Symposium on Computer Animation'.

Ikeuchi, K. (1987), Precompiling a geometrical model into an interpretation tree for object recognition in bin-picking tasks, *in* 'Image Understanding Workshop', Los Angeles, CA, pp. 321–339.

Ikeuchi, K. and Kanade, T. (1988), 'Automatic generation of object recognition programs', *Proceedings of the IEEE* **76**(8), 1016–35.

Ikizler, N. and Forsyth, D. (2007), Searching video for complex activities with finite state models, *in* 'IEEE Conf. on Computer Vision and Pattern Recognition (CVPR)', pp. 1–8.

Ikizler, N. and Forsyth, D. (2008), 'Searching for complex human activities with no visual examples', *International Journal of Computer Vision* **80**(3), 337–357.

Indyk, P. and Motwani, R. (1998), Approximate nearest neighbors: towards removing the curse of dimensionality, *in* 'STOC: Proceedings of the thirtieth annual ACM symposium on Theory of computing'.

Irani, M., Anandan, P., Bergen, J., Kumar, R. and Hsu, S. (1996), 'Mosaic representations of video sequences and their applications', *Signal Processing: Image Communication.*

Isard, M. and Blake, A. (1996), Contour tracking by stochastic propagation of conditional density, *in* 'Proc. European Conference on Computer Vision (ECCV)', pp. I:343–356.

Isard, M. and Blake, A. (1998a), ICONDENSATION: Unifying low-level and high-level tracking in a stochastic framework, *in* 'Proc. European Conference on Computer Vision (ECCV)', pp. 893–908.

Isard, M. and Blake, A. (1998b), A mixed-state condensation tracker with automatic model-switching, *in* 'Proc. Int. Conf. on Computer Vision (ICCV)', pp. 107–112.

Ishikawa, H. (2003), 'Exact optimization for markov random fields with convex priors', *IEEE Trans. Pattern Analysis and Machine Intelligence* **25**(10), 1333–1336.

Ishikawa, H. and Geiger, D. (1998), Occlusions, discontinuities, and epipolar lines in stereo, *in* 'Proc. European Conference on Computer Vision (ECCV)', pp. 232–248.

Jacobs, D., Belhumeur, P. and Basri, R. (1998), Comparing images under variable illumination, *in* 'IEEE Conf. on Computer Vision and Pattern Recognition (CVPR)', pp. 610–617.

Jacobs, G. (1981), *Comparative Color Vision*, Academic Press, New York.

Jacobs, G. and Aeron-Thomas, A. (2000), A review of global road accident fatalities, *in* 'Paper commissioned by the Department for International Development (United Kingdom) for the Global Road Safety Partnership.'.

Jain, A. and Vailaya, A. (1998), 'Shape-based retrieval: a case study with trademark image databases', *Pattern Recognition* **31**(9), 1369–1390.

Jain, A., Zhong, Y. and Lakshmanan, S. (1996), 'Object matching using deformable templates', *IEEE Trans. Pattern Analysis and Machine Intelligence* **18**(3), 267–278.

Jarvis, R. (1983), 'A perspective on range finding techniques in computer vision', *IEEE Trans. Pattern Analysis and Machine Intelligence* **5**(2), 122–139.

Jegou, H., Schmid, C., Harzallah, H. and Verbeek, J. (2010), 'Accurate image search using the contextual dissimilarity measure', *IEEE Trans. Pattern Analysis and Machine Intelligence* **32**(1), 2–11.

Jeon, J. and Manmatha, R. (2004), Using maximum entropy for automatic image annotation, *in* 'Proceedings of international conference on image and video rettrieval', pp. 24–32.

Jeon, J., Lavrenko, V. and Manmatha, R. (2003), Automatic image annotation and retrieval using cross-media relevance models, *in* 'SIGIR '03: Proceedings of the 26th annual international ACM SIGIR conference on Research and development in informaion retrieval', pp. 119–126.

Jepson, A. and Black, M. (1993), Mixture models for optical flow computation, *in* 'IEEE Conf. on Computer Vision and Pattern Recognition (CVPR)', pp. 760–761.

Jing, Y. and Baluja, S. (2008), 'Visualrank: Applying pagerank to large-scale image search', *IEEE Trans. Pattern Analysis and Machine Intelligence* **30**(11), 1877–1890.

Joachims, T. (1999), Transductive inference for text classification using support vector machines, *in* 'International Conference on Machine Learning (ICML)', Bled, Slowenien, pp. 200–209.

Johnson, A. and Hebert, M. (1998), 'Surface matching for object recognition in complex three-dimensional scenes', *Image and Vision Computing* **16**, 635–651.

Johnson, A. and Hebert, M. (1999), 'Using spin images for efficient object recognition in cluttered 3D scenes', *IEEE Trans. Pattern Analysis and Machine Intelligence* **21**(5), 433–449.

Jones, M. and Rehg, J. (2002), 'Statistical color models with application to skin detection', *International Journal of Computer Vision* **46**(1), 81–96.

Jones, R. V. (1998), *Most Secret War*, Wordsworth Military Library. reprint.

Jörgensen, C. (1998), 'Attributes of images in describing tasks', *Information Processing & Management* **34**, 161–174.

Joshi, D., Wang, J. Z. and Li, J. (2004), The story picturing engine: finding elite images to illustrate a story using mutual reinforcement, *in* 'MIR '04: Proceedings of the 6th ACM SIGMM international workshop on Multimedia information retrieval', ACM Press, New York, NY, USA, pp. 119–126.

Joshi, T., Ahuja, N. and Ponce, J. (1999), 'Structure and motion estimation from dynamic silhouettes under perspective projection', *International Journal of Computer Vision* **31**(1), 31–50.

Jörgensen, C. and Jörgensen, P. (2005), 'Image querying by image professionals', *J. Am. Soc. Information Science and Technology* **56**(12), 1346–1359.

Ju, S. X., Black, M. J. and Yacoob, Y. (1996), Cardboard people: A parameterized model of articulated image motion, *in* 'Proc. Int. Conference on Face and Gesture', pp. 561–567.

Judd, D. (1940), 'Hue, saturation and lightness of surface colors with chromatic illumination', *Journal of the Optical Society of America* **30**(1), 2–32.

Judd, D. (1960), 'Appraisal of Land's work on two-primary color projections', *Journal of the Optical Society of America* **50**(3), 254–268.

Julesz, B. (1960), 'Binocular depth perception of computer-generated patterns', *The Bell-System Technical Journal* **39**(5), 1125–1162.

Julesz, B. (1971), *Foundations of Cyclopean Perception*, The University of Chicago Press, London.

Julez, B. (1959), 'A method of coding tv signals based on edge detection', *Bell System Tech. J.* **38**(4), 1001–1020.

Jungnickel, D. (1999), *Graphs, Networks and Algorithms*, Springer.

Kadir, T., Bowden, R., Ong, E. and Zisserman, A. (2004), Minimal training, large lexicon, unconstrained sign language recognition, *in* 'British Machine Vision Conference (BMVC)'.

Kanatani, K. (1994), 'Statistical bias of conic fitting and renormalization', *IEEE Trans. Pattern Analysis and Machine Intelligence* **16**(3), 320–326.

Kanatani, K. (1998), 'Geometric information criterion for model selection', *International Journal of Computer Vision* **26**(3), 171–189.

Kanatani, K. (2006), 'Ellipse fitting with hyperaccuracy', *Transactions Institute Elec. Info. and Comm. Eng.* **E89-D**(10), 2653–2660.

Kanazawa, K., Koller, D. and Russell, S. (1995), Stochastic simulation algorithms for dynamic probabilistic networks, *in* 'Proceedings of the Eleventh Conference on Uncertainty in Artificial Intelligence', Morgan Kaufmann, Montreal, Canada.

Kang, F., Jin, R. and Sukthankar, R. (2006), Correlated label propagation with application to multi-label learning, *in* 'IEEE Conf. on Computer Vision and Pattern Recognition (CVPR)', pp. II: 1719–1726.

Kanizsa, G. (1976), 'Subjective contours', *Scientific American*.

Kanizsa, G. (1979), *Organization in Vision: Essays on Gestalt Perception*, Praeger.

Kass, M., Witkin, A. and Terzopoulos, D. (1988), 'Snakes: Active contour models', *International Journal of Computer Vision* **1**(4), 321–331.

Kato, T. and Fujimura, K. (1990), 'Trademark: Multimedia image database system with intelligent human interface', *Systems and Computers in Japan* **21**(11), 33–45.

Kato, T., Shimogaki, H., Mizutori, T. and Fujimura, K. (1988), Trademark: Multimedia database with abstracted representation on knowledge base, *in* 'Proc. Second Int. Symp. on Interoperable Information Systems', pp. 245–252.

Kavukcuoglu, K., Ranzato, M., Fergus, R. and LeCun, Y. (2009), Learning invariant features through topographic filter maps, *in* 'IEEE Conf. on Computer Vision and Pattern Recognition (CVPR)'.

Kawakami, R., Takamatsu, J. and Ikeuchi, K. (2007), 'Color constancy from blackbody illumination', *Journal of the Optical Society of America* **24**(7), 1886–1893.

Kazhdan, M., Bolitho, M. and Hoppe, H. (2006), Poisson surface reconstruction, *in* 'Symposium on Geometry Processing', pp. 61–70.

Ke, Y. and Sukthankar, R. (2004), Pca-sift: a more distinctive representation for local image descriptors, *in* 'IEEE Conf. on Computer Vision and Pattern Recognition (CVPR)', pp. II: 506–513.

Ke, Y., Sukthankar, R., Huston, L., Ke, Y. and Sukthankar, R. (2004), Efficient near-duplicate detection and sub-image retrieval, *in* 'In ACM Multimedia', pp. 869–876.

Kelly, R., McConnell, P. and Mildenberger, S. (1977), 'The Gestalt photomapping system', *Photogrammetric Engineering and Remote Sensing* **43**(11), 1407–1417.

Keren, D., Cooper, D. and Subrahmonia, J. (1994), 'Describing complicated objects by implicit polynomials', *IEEE Trans. Pattern Analysis and Machine Intelligence* **16**(1), 38–53.

Kergosien, Y. (1981), 'La famille des projections orthogonales d'une surface et ses singularités', *C.R. Acad. Sc. Paris* **292**, 929–932.

King, D. (1997), *The Commissar Vanishes: The Falsification of Photographs and Art in Stalin's Russia*, Metropolitan books.

Kinoshita, K. and Lindenbaum, M. (2000), Camera model selection based on geometric AIC, *in* 'IEEE Conf. on Computer Vision and Pattern Recognition (CVPR)', pp. II:514–519.

Kitagawa, G. (1987), 'Non-gaussian state space modelling of non-stationary time series with discussion', *J. Am. Stat. Assoc.* **82**, 1032–1063.

Klinker, G., Shafer, S. and Kanade, T. (1987), Using a colour reflection model to separate highlights from object colour, *in* 'Proc. Int. Conf. on Computer Vision (ICCV)'.

Klinker, G., Shafer, S. and Kanade, T. (1990), 'A physical approach to color image understanding', *International Journal of Computer Vision* **4**(1. January 1990), 7–38.

Koenderink, J. (1984), 'What does the occluding contour tell us about solid shape?', *Perception* **13**, 321–330.

Koenderink, J. (1986), An internal representation for solid shape based on the topological properties of the apparent contour, *in* W. Richards and S. Ullman, eds, 'Image Understanding: 1985-86', Ablex Publishing Corp., Norwood, NJ, chapter 9, pp. 257–285.

Koenderink, J. (1990), *Solid Shape*, MIT Press, Cambridge, MA.

Koenderink, J. and Doorn, A. V. (1983), 'Geometrical modes as a method to treat diffuse interreflections in radiometry', *J. Opt. Soc. Am.* **73**(6), 843–850.

Koenderink, J. and Van Doorn, A. (1976*a*), 'Geometry of binocular vision and a model for stereopsis', *Biological Cybernetics* **21**, 29–35.

Koenderink, J. and Van Doorn, A. (1976*b*), 'The singularities of the visual mapping', *Biological Cybernetics* **24**, 51–59.

Koenderink, J. and Van Doorn, A. (1979), 'The internal representation of solid shape with respect to vision', *Biological Cybernetics* **32**, 211–216.

Koenderink, J. and van Doorn, A. (1983), 'Geometrical modes as a general method to treat diffuse interreflections in radiometry', *Journal of the Optical Society of America* **73**(6), 843–850.

Koenderink, J. and van Doorn, A. (1986), 'Dynamic shape', *Biological Cybernetics* **53**, 383–396.

Koenderink, J. and Van Doorn, A. (1990), 'Affine structure from motion', **8**, 377–385.

Koenderink, J., van Doorn, A., Dana, K. and Nayar, S. (1999), 'Bidirectional reflection distribution function of thoroughly pitted surfaces', *International Journal of Computer Vision* **31**(2/3), 129–144.

Koffka, K. (1935), *Principles of Gestalt Psychology*, Harcourt Brace.

Kolmogorov, V. and Zabih, R. (2001), Computing visual correspondences with occlusions using graph cuts, *in* 'Proc. Int. Conf. on Computer Vision (ICCV)', Vol. B, pp. 508–515.

Kolmogorov, V. and Zabih, R. (2004), 'What energy functions can be minimized via graph cuts', *IEEE Trans. Pattern Analysis and Machine Intelligence* **26**(2), 147–159.

Krinov, E. (1947), Spectral reflectance properties of natural formations, Technical report, National Research Council of Canada, Technical Translation: TT-439.

Krumm, J. and Shafer, S. (1990), Local spatial frequence analysis for computer vision, *in* 'Proc. Int. Conf. on Computer Vision (ICCV)', pp. 354–358.

Krumm, J. and Shafer, S. (1992), Shape from periodic texture using the spectorgram, *in* 'IEEE Conf. on Computer Vision and Pattern Recognition (CVPR)', pp. 284–289.

Kruppa, E. (1913), 'Zur Ermittung eines Objektes aus zwei Perspektiven mit innerer Orientierung', *Sitz.-Ber. Akad. Wiss., Wien, Math. Naturw. Kl., Abt. IIa.* **122**, 1939–1948.

Kube, P. and Perona, P. (1996), 'Scale-space properties of quadratic feature-detectors', *IEEE Trans. Pattern Analysis and Machine Intelligence* **18**(10), 987–999.

Kumar, M., Torr, P. and Zisserman, A. (2010), 'Objcut: Efficient segmentation using top-down and bottom-up cues', *IEEE Trans. Pattern Analysis and Machine Intelligence* **32**(3), 530–545.

Kushner, H. and Yin, G. (2003), *Stochastic Approximation and Recursive Algorithms and Applications*, Springer.

Kutulakos, K. and Seitz, S. (1999), A theory of shape by space carving, *in* 'Proc. Int. Conf. on Computer Vision (ICCV)', Corfu, Greece, pp. 307–314.

Labov, W. (1973), The boundaries of words and their meanings, *in* 'New Ways of Analyzing Variation in English', Georgetown University Press, pp. 340–373.

Lamb, T. and Bourriau, J., eds (1995), *Colour Art and Science*, Cambridge University Press.

Lampert, C., Blaschko, M. and Hofmann, T. (2008), Beyond sliding windows: Object localization by efficient subwindow search, *in* 'IEEE Conf. on Computer Vision and Pattern Recognition (CVPR)', pp. 1–8.

Land, E. (1959*a*), 'Color vision and the natural image: Part i', *Proceedings National Academy Science USA* **45**(1), 115–129.

Land, E. (1959*b*), 'Color vision and the natural image: Part ii', *Proceedings National Academy Science USA* **45**(4), 636–644.

Land, E. (1959*c*), 'Experiments in color vision', *Scientific American* **200**, 84–89.

Land, E. (1983), 'Color vision and the natural image', *Proceedings National Academy Science USA* **80**, 5163–5169.

Land, E. and McCann, J. (1971), 'Lightness and retinex theory', *Journal of the Optical Society of America* **61**(1), 1–11.

Laptev, I. (2005), 'On space-time interest points', *International Journal of Computer Vision* **64**(2-3), 107–123.

Laptev, I. and Perez, P. (2007), Retrieving actions in movies, *in* 'Proc. Int. Conf. on Computer Vision (ICCV)', pp. 1–8.

Laptev, I., Marszalek, M., Schmid, C. and Rozenfeld, B. (2008), Learning realistic human actions from movies, *in* 'IEEE Conf. on Computer Vision and Pattern Recognition (CVPR)', pp. 1–8.

Laurentini, A. (1995), 'How far 3D shapes can be understood from 2D silhouettes', *IEEE Trans. Pattern Analysis and Machine Intelligence* **17**(2), 188–194.

Lavallee, S. (1996), Registration for computer integrated surgery: Methodology and state of the art, *in* R. Taylor, S. Lavallee, G. Burdea and R. Mosges, eds, 'Computer Integrated Surgery', MIT Press.

Lavest, J.-M., Viala, M. and Dhome, M. (1998), Do we really need an accurate calibration pattern to achieve a reliable camera calibration?, *in* 'Proc. European Conference on Computer Vision (ECCV)', Vol. 1, pp. 158–174.

Lavrenko, V., Manmatha, R. and Jeon, J. (2003), A model for learning the semantics of pictures, *in* 'Neural Information Processing Systems'.

Lazebnik, S., Boyer, E. and Ponce, J. (2001), On computing exact visual hulls of solids bounded by smooth surfaces, *in* 'IEEE Conf. on Computer Vision and Pattern Recognition (CVPR)', pp. 156–161.

Lazebnik, S., Furukawa, Y. and Ponce, J. (2007), 'Projective visual hulls', *International Journal of Computer Vision* **74**(2), 137–165.

Lazebnik, S., Schmid, C. and Ponce, J. (2006), Beyond bags of features: Spatial pyramid matching for recognizing natural scene categories, *in* 'IEEE Conf. on Computer Vision and Pattern Recognition (CVPR)', pp. II: 2169–2178.

Lee, D., Hebert, M. and Kanade, T. (2009), Geometric reasoning for single image structure recovery, *in* 'IEEE Conf. on Computer Vision and Pattern Recognition (CVPR)', pp. 2136–2143.

Lee, H. (1986), 'Method for computing the scene-illuminant chromaticity from specular highlights', *J. Opt. Soc. Am.-A* **3**, 1694–1699.

Lee, H.-C. (2009), *Introduction to Color Imaging Science*, Cambridge.

Lee, K. and Kuo, C. (1998), Direct shape from texture using a parametric surface model and an adaptive filtering technique, *in* 'IEEE Conf. on Computer Vision and Pattern Recognition (CVPR)', pp. 402–407.

Lee, S. and Bajcsy, R. (1992*a*), Detection of specularity using colour and multiple views, *in* 'Proc. European Conference on Computer Vision (ECCV)', pp. 99–114.

Lee, S. and Bajcsy, R. (1992*b*), 'Detection of specularity using colour and multiple views', *Image and Vision Computing* **10**, 643–653.

Lei, T. and Udupa, J. (2003), 'Performance evaluation of finite normal mixture model-based image segmentation techniques', *IEEE Trans. Image Processing* **12**(10), 1153–1169.

Leung, T. and Malik, J. (1996), Detecting, localizing and grouping repeated scene elements from an image, *in* 'Proc. European Conference on Computer Vision (ECCV)', pp. I:546–555.

Leung, T. and Malik, J. (1999), Recognizing surfaces using three-dimensional textons, *in* 'Proc. Int. Conf. on Computer Vision (ICCV)', pp. 1010–1017.

Leung, T. and Malik, J. (2001), 'Representing and recognizing the visual appearance of materials using three-dimensional textons', *International Journal of Computer Vision* **43**(1), 29–44.

Levoy, M. and Hanrahan, P. (1996), 'Light field rendering', *ACM Trans. Graphics (SIGGRAPH Proceeding)* pp. 31–42.

Lewicki, M. and Sejnowski, T. (2000), 'Learning Overcomplete Representations', *Neural Computation* **12**(2), 337–365.

Lhuillier, M. and Quan, L. (2005), 'A quasi-dense approach to surface reconstruction from uncalibrated images', *IEEE Trans. Pattern Analysis and Machine Intelligence* **27**(3), 418–433.

Li, J. and Wang, J. Z. (2003), 'Automatic linguistic indexing of pictures by a statistical modeling approach', *IEEE Trans. on Pattern Analysis and Machine Intelligence*.

Li, S. and Jain, A. (2005), *A Handbook of face recognition*, Springer.

Li, Y. and Huttenlocher, D. P. (2008), Sparse long-range random field and its application to image denoising, *in* 'Proc. European Conference on Computer Vision (ECCV)'.

Lin, S., Gu, J., Yamazaki, S. and Shum, H. (2004), Radiometric calibration from a single image, *in* 'IEEE Conf. on Computer Vision and Pattern Recognition (CVPR)', pp. II: 938–945.

Lin, S., Li, Y., Kang, S., Tong, X. and Shum, H. (2002), Diffuse-specular separation and depth recovery from image sequences, *in* 'Proc. European Conference on Computer Vision (ECCV)', p. III: 210 ff.

Lindeberg, T. (1993), *Scale-Space Theory in Computer Vision*, Kluwer.

Liu, C., Sharan, L., Adelson, E. and Rosenholtz, R. (2010), Exploring features in a Bayesian framework for material recognition, *in* 'IEEE Conf. on Computer Vision and Pattern Recognition (CVPR)', pp. 239–246.

Liu, Y., Collins, R. and Tsin, Y. (2004), 'A computational model for periodic pattern perception based on frieze and wallpaper groups', *IEEE Trans. Pattern Analysis and Machine Intelligence* **26**(3), 354–371.

Liverman, M. (2004), *The Animator's Motion Capture Guide : Organizing, Managing,Editing*, Charles River Media.

Ljung, L. (1995), System identification, *in* W. S. Levine, ed., 'The Control Handbook', CRC Press, in cooperation with IEEE Press.

Lobay, A. and Forsyth, D. (2004), Recovering shape and irradiance maps from rich dense texton fields, *in* 'IEEE Conf. on Computer Vision and Pattern Recognition (CVPR)', pp. I: 400–406.

Lobay, A. and Forsyth, D. (2006), 'Shape from texture without boundaries', *International Journal of Computer Vision* **67**(1), 71–91.

Loeff, N. and Farhadi, A. (2008), Scene discovery by matrix factorization, *in* 'Proc. European Conference on Computer Vision (ECCV)', pp. IV: 451–464.

Loeff, N., Farhadi, A., Endres, I. and Forsyth, D. (2009), Unlabeled data improves word prediction, *in* 'Proc. Int. Conf. on Computer Vision (ICCV)', pp. 956–962.

Loh, A. and Hartley, R. (2005), Shape from non-homogeneous, non-stationary, anisotropic, perspective texture, *in* 'British Machine Vision Conference (BMVC)'.

Longuet-Higgins, H. (1981), 'A computer algorithm for reconstructing a scene from two projections', *Nature* **293**, 133–135.

Lorensen, W. and Cline, H. (1987), 'Marching cubes: a high resolution 3D surface construction algorithm', *Computer Graphics* **21**, 163–169.

Lowe, D. (1985), *Perceptual Organization and Visual Recognition*, Kluwer.

Lowe, D. (2004), 'Method and apparatus for identifying scale invariant features in an image and use of same for locating an object in an image', *U.S. Patent 6,711,293*.

Lu, R., Koenderink, J. and Kappers, A. (1998), 'Optical properties (bidirectional reflection distribution functions) of velvet', *Applied Optics* **37**(25), 5974–5984.

Lu, R., Koenderink, J. and Kappers, A. (1999), Specularities on surfaces with tangential hairs or grooves, *in* 'ICCV', pp. 2–7.

Luenberger, D. (1984), *Linear and nonlinear programming*, Addison-Wesley. Second edition.

Luong, Q.-T. (1992), Matrice fondamentale et calibration visuelle sur l'environnement: vers une plus grande autonomie des systèmes robotiques, PhD thesis, University of Paris XI, Orsay, France.

Luong, Q.-T. and Faugeras, O. (1996), 'The fundamental matrix: theory, algorithms, and stability analysis', *International Journal of Computer Vision* **17**(1), 43–76.

Luong, Q.-T., Deriche, R., Faugeras, O. and Papadopoulo, T. (1993), On determining the fundamental matrix: analysis of different methods and experimental results, Technical Report 1894, INRIA Sophia-Antipolis.

Lynch, D. and Livingston, W. (2001), *Color and Light in Nature*, Cambridge University Press.

Ma, Y., Soatto, S., Kosecka, J. and Sastry, S. (2003*a*), *An invitation to 3D vision – From images to geometric models*, Springer-Verlag.

Ma, Y., Soatto, S., Kosecka, J. and Sastry, S. S. (2003*b*), *An Invitation to 3-D Vision*, Springer Verlag.

MacAdam, D. (1942), 'Visual sensitivities to small color differences in daylight', *Journal of the Optical Society of America* **32**, 247.

Macaulay, F. (1916), *The Algebraic Theory of Modular Systems*, Cambridge University Press.

MacKay, D. J. (2003), *Information Theory, Inference and Learning Algorithms*, Cambridge University Press.

Mahamud, S., Hebert, M., Omori, Y. and Ponce, J. (2001), Provably-convergent iterative methods for projective structure from motion, *in* 'IEEE Conf. on Computer Vision and Pattern Recognition (CVPR)', pp. 1018–1025.

Maintz, J. and Viergever, M. (1998), 'A survey of medical image registration', *Medical Image Analysis* **2**(1), 1–16.

Mairal, J., Bach, F. and Ponce, J. (2011), 'Task-driven dictionary learning', *IEEE Trans. Pattern Analysis and Machine Intelligence*. Accepted for publication, preprint ArXiv:1009.5358.

Mairal, J., Bach, F., Ponce, J. and Sapiro, G. (2010), 'Online learning for matrix factorization and sparse coding', **11**, 19–60.

Mairal, J., Bach, F., Ponce, J., Sapiro, G. and Zisserman, A. (2008), Discriminative learned dictionaries for local image analysis, *in* 'IEEE Conf. on Computer Vision and Pattern Recognition (CVPR)', Anchorage, USA.

Mairal, J., Bach, F., Ponce, J., Sapiro, G. and Zisserman, A. (2009), Non-local sparse models for image restoration, *in* 'Proc. Int. Conf. on Computer Vision (ICCV)'.

Maji, S. and Malik, J. (2009), Object detection using a max-margin Hough transform, *in* 'IEEE Conf. on Computer Vision and Pattern Recognition (CVPR)', pp. 1038–1045.

Maji, S., Berg, A. and Malik, J. (2008), Classification using intersection kernel support vector machines is efficient, *in* 'IEEE Conf. on Computer Vision and Pattern Recognition (CVPR)', pp. 1–8.

Maji, S., Bourdev, L. and Malik, J. (2011), Action recognition from a distributed representation of pose and appearance, *in* 'IEEE Conf. on Computer Vision and Pattern Recognition (CVPR)'.

Makadia, A., Pavlovic, V. and Kumar, S. (2008), A new baseline for image annotation, *in* 'Proc. European Conference on Computer Vision (ECCV)', pp. III: 316–329.

Makadia, A., Pavlovic, V. and Kumar, S. (2010), 'Baselines for image annotation', *International Journal of Computer Vision* **90**(1), 88–105.

Malik, J. and Rosenholtz, R. (1997), 'Computing local surface orientation and shape from texture for curved surfaces', *International Journal of Computer Vision* pp. 149–168.

Malisiewicz, T. and Efros, A. (2007), Improving spatial support for objects via multiple segmentations, *in* 'British Machine Vision Conference (BMVC)'.

Malisiewicz, T. and Efros, A. (2008), Recognition by association via learning per-exemplar distances, *in* 'IEEE Conf. on Computer Vision and Pattern Recognition (CVPR)', pp. 1–8.

Mallat, S. (1999), *A Wavelet Tour of Signal Processing, Second Edition*, Academic Press, New York.

Mallat, S. and Zhang, Z. (1993), 'Matching pursuit in a time-frequency dictionary', **41**(12), 3397–3415.

Maloney, L. (1984), Computational Approaches to Color Vision, PhD thesis, Stanford University.

Maloney, L. (1986), 'Evaluation of linear models of surface spectral reflectance with small numbers of parameters', *Journal of the Optical Society of America* **3**(10), 1673–1683.

Maloney, L. and Wandell, B. (1986), 'Color constancy: A method for recovering surface spectral reflectance', *Journal of the Optical Society of America* **3**, 29–33.

Manocha, D. (1992), Algebraic and Numeric Techniques for Modeling and Robotics, PhD thesis, Computer Science Division, Univ. of California at Berkeley.

Marimont, D. and Wandell, B. (1992), 'Linear models of surface and illuminant spectra', *J. Opt. Soc. Am.-A* **9**, 1905–1913.

Marin, J., Vazquez, D., Geronimo, D. and Lopez, A. (2010), Learning appearance in virtual scenarios for pedestrian detection, *in* 'IEEE Conf. on Computer Vision and Pattern Recognition (CVPR)', pp. 137–144.

Markkula, M. and Sormunen, E. (2000), 'End-user searching challenges indexing practices in the digital newspaper photo archive', *Information retrieval* **1**, 259–285.

Maron, O. and Lozano-Pérez, T. (1998), A framework for multiple-instance learning, *in* 'NIPS '97: Proceedings of the 1997 conference on Advances in neural information processing systems 10', MIT Press, Cambridge, MA, USA, pp. 570–576.

Maron, O. and Ratan, A. (1998), Multiple-instance learning for natural scene classification, *in* 'The Fifteenth International Conference on Machine Learning'.

Marr, D. (1977), 'Analysis of occluding contour', *Proc. Royal Society, London* **B-197**, 441–475.

Marr, D. (1982), *Vision*, Freeman, San Francisco.

Marr, D. and Nishihara, K. (1978), 'Representation and recognition of the spatial organization of three-dimensional shapes', *Proc. Royal Society, London* **B-200**, 269–294.

Marr, D. and Poggio, T. (1976), 'Cooperative computation of stereo disparity', *Science* **194**, 283–287.

Marr, D. and Poggio, T. (1979), 'A computational theory of human stereo vision', *Proceedings of the Royal Society of London* **B 204**, 301–328.

Marszalek, M. and Schmid, C. (2007), Accurate object localization with shape masks, *in* 'IEEE Conf. on Computer Vision and Pattern Recognition (CVPR)', pp. 1–8.

Martin, D., Fowlkes, C. and Malik, J. (2004), 'Learning to detect natural image boundaries using local brightness, color, and texture cues', *IEEE Trans. Pattern Analysis and Machine Intelligence* **26**(5), 530–549.

Martin, D., Fowlkes, C., Tal, D. and Malik, J. (2001), A database of human segmented natural images and its application to evaluating segmentation algorithms and measuring ecological statistics, *in* 'Proc. 8th Int'l Conf. Computer Vision', Vol. 2, pp. 416–423.

Martin, W. and Aggarwal, J. (1983), 'Volumetric description of objects from multiple views', *IEEE Trans. Pattern Analysis and Machine Intelligence* **5**(2), 150–158.

Matusik, W., Buehler, C., Raskar, R., Gortler, S. and McMillan, L. (2001), Image-based visual hulls, *in* 'ACM Trans. Graphics (SIGGRAPH Proceeding)'.

Maxwell, B. and Shafer, S. (2000), 'Segmentation and interpretation of multicolored objects with highlights', *Computer Vision and Image Understanding* **77**(1), 1–24.

Maybank, S. and Faugeras, O. (1992), 'A theory of self-calibration of a moving camera', *International Journal of Computer Vision* **8**(2), 123–151.

Maybank, S. and Sturm, P. (1999), MDL, collineations and the fundamental matrix, *in* 'British Machine Vision Conference (BMVC)'.

McDonald, S. and Tait, J. (2003), Search strategies in content-based image retrieval, *in* 'Proc. ACM SIGIR Conference on Research and Development in Information Retrieval'.

McInerney, T. and Terzopolous, D. (1996), 'Deformable models in medical image analysis: a survey', *Medical Image Analysis* **1**(2), 91–108.

McKee, S., Levi, D. and Brown, S. (1990), 'The imprecision of stereopsis', *Vision Research* **30**(11), 1763–1779.

McLachlan, G. and Krishnan, T. (1996), *The EM Algorithm and Extensions*, John Wiley and Sons.

McMillan, L. and Bishop, G. (1995), Plenoptic modeling: an image-based rendering approach, *in* 'SIGGRAPH', Los Angeles, CA, pp. 39–46.

Medioni, G. and Nevatia, R. (1984), 'Matching images using linear features', *IEEE Trans. Pattern Analysis and Machine Intelligence* **6**(6), 675–685.

Menache, A. (1999), *Understanding Motion Capture for Computer Animation and Video Games*, Morgan-Kaufmann.

Metzler, D. and Manmatha, R. (2004), An inference network approach to image retrieval, *in* 'CIVR', pp. 42–50.

Mikolajczyk, K. (n.d.), Face detector, Technical report, INRIA Rhone-Alpes. Ph.D report.

Mikolajczyk, K. and Schmid, C. (2002), An affine invariant interest point detector, *in* 'Proc. European Conference on Computer Vision (ECCV)', p. I: 128 ff.

Mikolajczyk, K. and Schmid, C. (2005), 'A performance evaluation of local descriptors', *IEEE Trans. Pattern Analysis and Machine Intelligence* **27**(10), 1615–1630.

Mikolajczyk, K., Tuytelaars, T., Schmid, C., Zisserman, A., Matas, J., Schaffalitzky, F., Kadir, T. and Van Gool, L. (2005), 'A comparison of affine region detectors', *International Journal of Computer Vision* **65**(1-2), 43–72.

Milenkovic, V. and Kanade, T. (1985), Trinocular vision using photometric and edge orientation constraints, *in* 'Image Understanding Workshop', pp. 163–175.

Miller, G. A., Beckwith, R., Fellbaum, C., Gross, D. and Miller, K. J. (1990), 'Introduction to wordnet: an on-line lexical database', *International Journal of Lexicography* **3**(4), 235 – 244.

Minnaert, M. (1993), *Light and Color in the Outdoors*, Springer Verlag. Translator: L. Seymour.

Mitsunaga, T. and Nayar, S. (1999), Radiometric self calibration, *in* 'IEEE Conf. on Computer Vision and Pattern Recognition (CVPR)', pp. I: 374–380.

Moeslund, T. (1999), Summaries of 107 computer vision-based human motion capture papers, Technical Report LLA 99-01, University of Aalborg.

Moeslund, T., Hilton, A. and Sigal, L. (2011), *Visual Analysis of Humans*, Springer.

Mohan, R. and Nevatia, R. (1992), 'Perceptual organization for scene segmentation and description', *IEEE Trans. Pattern Analysis and Machine Intelligence* **14**(6), 616–635.

Mohr, R., Morin, L. and Grosso, E. (1992), Relative positioning with uncalibrated cameras, *in* J. Mundy and A. Zisserman, eds, 'Geometric Invariance in Computer Vision', MIT Press, Cambridge, Mass., pp. 440–460.

Mollon, J. (1982), 'Color vision', *Ann. Rev. Psychol.* **33**, 41–85.

Mollon, J. (1995), Seeing colour, *in* T. Lamb and J. Bourriau, eds, 'Colour Art and Science', Cambridge University Press.

Moravec, H. (1980), Obstacle avoidance and navigation in the real world by a seeing robot rover, *in* 'Tech. Report CMU Robotics Institute'.

Morgan, A. (1987), *Solving Polynomial Systems using Continuation for Engineering and Scientific Problems*, Prentice Hall, Englewood Cliffs, NJ.

Mori, G., and Malik, J. (2002), Estimating human body configurations using shape context matching, *in* 'European Conference on Computer Vision LNCS 2352', Vol. 3, pp. 666–680.

Mori, G. and Malik, J. (2005), 'Recovering 3d human body configurations using shape contexts', *IEEE Transactions on Pattern Analysis and Machine Intelligence*.

Mori, Y., Takahashi, H. and Oka, R. (1999), Image-to-word transformation based on dividing and vector quantizing images with words, *in* 'Proceedings of the First International Workshop on Multimedia Intelligent Storage and Retrieval Management'.

Morita, T. and Kanade, T. (1997), 'A sequential factorization method for recovering shape and motion from image sequences', *IEEE Trans. Pattern Analysis and Machine Intelligence*.

Muja, M. and Lowe, D. G. (2009), Fast approximate nearest neighbors with automatic algorithm configuration, *in* 'International Conference on Computer Vision Theory and Application VISSAPP'09)', INSTICC Press, pp. 331–340.

Mukawa, N. (1990), Estimation of shape, reflection coefficients and illuminant direction from image sequences, *in* 'Proc. Int. Conf. on Computer Vision (ICCV)', pp. 507–512.

Munder, S. and Gavrila, D. (2006), 'An experimental study on pedestrian classification', *IEEE Trans. Pattern Analysis and Machine Intelligence* **28**(11), 1863–1868.

Mutch, J. and Lowe, D. (2006), Multiclass object recognition with sparse, localized features, *in* 'IEEE Conf. on Computer Vision and Pattern Recognition (CVPR)', pp. I: 11–18.

Nalwa, V. (1988), 'Line-drawing interpretation: A mathematical framework', *International Journal of Computer Vision* **2**, 103–124.

Nathans, J., Piantanida, T., Eddy, R., Shows, T. and Hogness, D. (1986*a*), 'Molecular genetics of inherited variation in human color vision', *Science* **232**, 203–210.

Nathans, J., Thomas, D. and Hogness, D. (1986*b*), 'Molecular genetics of human color vision: The genes encoding blue, green, and red pigments', *Science* **232**, 193–203.

Navy, U. (1969), *Basic Optics and Optical Instruments*, Dover. Prepared by the Bureau of Naval Personnel.

Nayar, S. and Oren, M. (1993), Diffuse reflectance from rough surfaces, *in* 'IEEE Conf. on Computer Vision and Pattern Recognition (CVPR)', pp. 763–764.

Nayar, S. and Oren, M. (1995), 'Visual appearance of matte surfaces', *Science* **267**(5201), 1153–1156.

Nayar, S., Ikeuchi, K. and Kanade, T. (1990), 'Determining shape and reflectance of hybrid surfaces by photometric sampling', *IEEE Trans. Robotics and Automation* **6**(4), 418–431.

Nayar, S., Ikeuchi, K. and Kanade, T. (1991*a*), 'Shape from interreflections', *International Journal of Computer Vision* **6**(3), 173–195.

Nayar, S., Ikeuchi, K. and Kanade, T. (1991*b*), 'Shape from interreflections', *International Journal of Computer Vision* **6**(3), 173–195.

Nayar, S., Ikeuchi, K. and Kanade, T. (1991*c*), 'Surface reflection: Physical and geometrical perspectives', *IEEE Trans. Pattern Analysis and Machine Intelligence* **13**(7), 611–634.

Nedovic, V., Smeulders, A., Redert, A. and Geusebroek, J. (2010), 'Stages as models of scene geometry', *IEEE Trans. Pattern Analysis and Machine Intelligence* **32**(9), 1673–1687.

Nelder, J. and Mead, R. (1965), 'A simplex method for function minimization', *Computer Journal* **7**, 308–313.

Nevatia, R. (1986), Image segmentation, *in* K. Fu and T. Young, eds, 'Handbook of Pattern Recognition and Image Processing', Academic Press, pp. 215–231.

Nielsen, M., Johansen, P., Olsen, O. F. and Weickert, J., eds (1999), *Scale-Space Theory in Computer Vision*, Vol. 1682, Springer Verlag LNCS.

Niem, W. and Buschmann, R. (1994), Automatic modelling of 3D natural objects from multiple views, *in* 'European Workshop on Combined Real and Synthetic Image Processing for Broadcast and Video Production', Hamburg, Germany.

Nilsback, M. and Zisserman, A. (2010), 'Delving deeper into the whorl of flower segmentation', *Image and Vision Computing* **28**(6), 1049–1062.

Nistér, D. (2004), 'An efficient solution to the five-point relative pose problem', *IEEE Trans. Pattern Analysis and Machine Intelligence* **26**(6), 756–770.

Nister, D. and Stewenius, H. (2006), Scalable recognition with a vocabulary tree, *in* 'IEEE Conf. on Computer Vision and Pattern Recognition (CVPR)', pp. II: 2161–2168.

Nitzan, D. (1988), 'Three-dimensional vision structure for robot applications', *IEEE Trans. Pattern Analysis and Machine Intelligence* **10**(3), 291–309.

O'Brien, D. (2010), *Congress Shall Make No Law: The First Amendment, Unprotected Expression, and the U.S. Supreme Court*, Rowman & Littlefield.

Ohlander, R., Price, K. and Reddy, R. (1978), 'Picture segmentation by a recursive region splitting method', *Computer Graphics Image Processing* **8**, 313–333.

Ohta, Y. and Kanade, T. (1985), 'Stereo by intra- and inter-scanline search', *IEEE Trans. Pattern Analysis and Machine Intelligence* **7**(2), 139–154.

Ohta, Y., Maenobu, K. and Sakai, T. (1981), Obtaining surface orientation from texels under perspective projection, *in* 'Int. Joint Conf. Artificial Intelligence', pp. 746–751.

Oja, E. (1983), *Subspace methods of pattern recognition*, Research Study Press.

Okutami, M. and Kanade, T. (1993), 'A multiple-baseline stereo system', *IEEE Trans. Pattern Analysis and Machine Intelligence* **15**(4), 353–363.

Oliva, A. and Torralba, A. (2001), 'Modeling the shape of the scene: A holistic representation of the spatial envelope', *International Journal of Computer Vision* **42**(3), 145–175.

Oliva, A. and Torralba, A. (2007), 'The role of context in object recognition', *Trends in Cognitive Sciences* **11**(12), 520 – 527.

Olshausen, B. A. and Field, D. J. (1997), 'Sparse coding with an overcomplete basis set: A strategy employed by v1?', *Vision Research* **37**, 3311–3325.

Olson, C. (1998), Variable-scale smoothing and edge detection guided by stereoscopy, *in* 'IEEE Conf. on Computer Vision and Pattern Recognition (CVPR)', pp. 80–85.

Opelt, A., Pinz, A., Fussenegger, M. and Auer, P. (2006), 'Generic object recognition with boosting', *IEEE Trans. Pattern Analysis and Machine Intelligence* **28**(3), 416–431.

Oren, M. and Nayar, S. (1995), 'Generalization of the lambertian model and implications for machine vision', *International Journal of Computer Vision* **14**(3), 227–251.

O'Rourke, J. (1998), *Computational Geometry in C*, 2 edn, Cambridge University Press, Cambridge.

Osuna, E., Freund, R. and Girosi, F. (1997), Training support vector machines: An application to face detection, *in* 'IEEE Conf. on Computer Vision and Pattern Recognition (CVPR)', pp. 130–136.

Overett, G., Petersson, L., Brewer, N., Andersson, L. and Pettersson, N. (2008), A new pedestrian dataset for supervised learning, *in* 'IEEE Intelligent Vehicles Symposium'.

Pae, S. and Ponce, J. (1999), Toward a scale-space aspect graph: Solids of revolution, *in* 'IEEE Conf. on Computer Vision and Pattern Recognition (CVPR)', Vol. II, Fort Collins, CO, pp. 196–201.

Pae, S. and Ponce, J. (2001), 'On computing structural changes in evolving surfaces and their appearance', *International Journal of Computer Vision* **43**(2), 113–131.

Paglieroni, D. (2004), 'Design considerations for image segmentation quality assessment measures', *Pattern Recognition* **37**(8), 1607–1617.

Pal, N. and Pal, S. (1993), 'A review on image segmentation techniques', *Pattern Recognition* **26**(9), 1277–1294.

Palmer, S. (1999), *Vision Science : Photons to Phenomenology*, MIT Press.

Panofsky, E. (1962), *Studies in Iconology: Humanistic Themes in the Art of the Renaissance*, Harper & Row.

Pantofaru, C., Schmid, C. and Hebert, M. (2008), Object recognition by integrating multiple image segmentations, *in* 'Proc. European Conference on Computer Vision (ECCV)', pp. III: 481–494.

Papageorgiou, C. and Poggio, T. (2000), 'A trainable system for object detection', *International Journal of Computer Vision* **38**(1), 15–33.

Paragios, N., Chen, Y. and Faugeras, O., eds (2010), *Handbook of Mathematical Models in Computer Vision*, Springer.

Parikh, D. and Grauman, K. (2011), Interactively building a discriminative vocabulary of nameable attributes, *in* 'IEEE Conf. on Computer Vision and Pattern Recognition (CVPR)'.

Paris, S., Sillion, F. and Quan, L. (2004), A surface reconstruction method using global graph cut optimization, *in* 'Proc. Asian Conf. on Computer Vision (ACCV)'.

Parker, J. (2010), *Algorithms for Image Processing and Computer Vision*, Wiley.

Pentland, A. (1986), 'Perceptual organization and the representation of natural form', **28**, 293–331.

Peri, V. and Nayar, S. (1997), Generation of perspective and panoramic video from omnidirectional video, *in* 'Image Understanding Workshop', New Orleans, LA.

Perona, P. (1992), Steerable-scalable kernels for edge detection and junction analysis, *in* 'Proc. European Conference on Computer Vision (ECCV)', pp. 3–18.

Perona, P. (1995), 'Deformable kernels for early vision', *IEEE Trans. Pattern Analysis and Machine Intelligence* **17**(5), 488–499.

Perona, P. and Freeman, W. (1998), A factorization approach to grouping, *in* 'Proc. European Conference on Computer Vision (ECCV)', pp. 655–670.

Perona, P. and Malik, J. (1990*a*), Detecting and localizing edges composed of steps, peaks and roofs, *in* 'Proc. Int. Conf. on Computer Vision (ICCV)', pp. 52–57.

Perona, P. and Malik, J. (1990*b*), 'Scale space and edge detection using anisotropic diffusion', *IEEE Trans. Pattern Analysis and Machine Intelligence* **12**(7), 629–639.

Perona, P. and Malik, J. (1990*c*), 'Scale-space and edge detection using anisotropic diffusion', *IEEE Trans. Pattern Analysis and Machine Intelligence* **12**(7), 629–639.

Perona, P., Fergus, R. and Li, F. (2004), Learning generative visual models from few training examples: An incremental Bayesian approach tested on 101 object categories, *in* 'Proc. IEEE Workshop on Generative Model Based Vision', p. 178.

Petitjean, S. (1998), 'A computational geometric approach to visual hulls', *International Journal of Computational Geometry and Applications* **8**(4), 406–436.

Petitjean, S., Ponce, J. and Kriegman, D. (1992), 'Computing exact aspect graphs of curved objects: Algebraic surfaces', *International Journal of Computer Vision* **9**(3), 231–255.

Petrov, A. (1987), Light color and shape, *in* E. Velikhov, ed., 'Cognitive processes and their simulation', pp. 350–358. In Russian.

Petrov, A. (1991), Color and Grassman-Cayley coordinates of shape, *in* 'SPIE-Int. Soc. Opt. Eng. Proceedings of SPIE - the International Society for Optical Engineering', Vol. 1453, pp. 342–352.

Peyre, G. (2008), 'Sparse modeling of textures', *Journal of Mathematical Imaging and Vision*.

Pinto, N., Cox, D. and DiCarlo, J. (2008), 'Why is real-world visual object recognition hard?'.

Platonova, O. (1981), 'Singularities of the mutual disposition of a surface and a line', *Russian Mathematical Surveys* **36**(1), 248–249.

Platt, J. C. (1999), Probabilistic outputs for support vector machines and comparisons to regularized likelihood methods, *in* 'ADVANCES IN LARGE MARGIN CLASSIFIERS', MIT Press, pp. 61–74.

Pluim, J., Maintz, J. and Viergever, M. (2003), 'Mutual-information-based registration of medical images: a survey', *IEEE Trans. Medical Imaging* **22**(8), 986–1004.

Poelman, C. and Kanade, T. (1997), 'A paraperspective factorization method for shape and motion recovery', *IEEE Trans. Pattern Analysis and Machine Intelligence* **19**(3), 206–218.

Polak, M., Zhang, H. and Pi, M. (2009), 'An evaluation metric for image segmentation of multiple objects', *Image and Vision Computing* **27**(8), 1223–1227.

Pollard, S., Mayhew, J. and Frisby, J. (1970), 'A stereo correspondence algorithm using a disparity gradient limit', *Perception* **14**, 449–470.

Pollefeys, M. (1999), Self-calibration and metric 3D reconstruction from uncalibrated image sequences, PhD thesis, Katholieke Universiteit Leuven.

Pollefeys, M., Koch, R. and Van Gool, L. (1999), 'Self-calibration and metric reconstruction in spite of varying and unknown internal camera parameters', *International Journal of Computer Vision* **32**(1), 7–26.

Ponce, J. (2000), Metric upgrade of a projective reconstruction under the rectangular pixel assumption, *in* '3D Structure from Images — SMILE 2000', Dublin, Ireland, pp. 52–67.

Ponce, J. and Brady, J. (1987), Toward a surface primal sketch, *in* T. Kanade, ed., 'Three-dimensional machine vision', Kluwer Publishers, pp. 195–240.

Ponce, J., Papadopoulo, T., Teillaud, M. and Triggs, B. (2005), The absolute quadratic complex and its application to camera self calibration, *in* 'IEEE Conf. on Computer Vision and Pattern Recognition (CVPR)', Vol. I, pp. 780–787.

Pons, J.-P., Keriven, R. and Faugeras, O. (2005), Modelling dynamic scenes by registering multi-view image sequences, *in* 'IEEE Conf. on Computer Vision and Pattern Recognition (CVPR)', Vol. 2, pp. 822–827.

Pons, J.-P., Keriven, R. and Faugeras, O. (2007), 'Multi-view stereo reconstruction and scene flow estimation with a global image-based matching score', *International Journal of Computer Vision* **72**(2), 179–193.

Pont, S. and Koenderink, J. (2002), Bidirectional texture contrast function, *in* 'Proc. European Conference on Computer Vision (ECCV)', pp. 808–823.

Porrill, J. (1990), 'Fitting ellipses and predicting confidence envelopes using a bias corrected kalman filter', *Image and Vision Computing* **8**(1), 37–41.

Portilla, J., Strela, V., Wainwright, M. and Simoncelli, E. (2003), 'Image denoising using scale mixtures of Gaussians in the wavelet domain', **12**(11), 1338–1351.

Prados, E. and Faugeras, O. (2005*a*), 'A generic and provably convergent shape-from-shading method for orthographic and pinhole cameras', *International Journal of Computer Vision* **65**(1-2), 97–125.

Prados, E. and Faugeras, O. (2005*b*), Shape from shading: A well-posed problem?, *in* 'IEEE Conf. on Computer Vision and Pattern Recognition (CVPR)'.

Pritchard, D. (2003), Cloth parameters and motion capture, Master's thesis, University of British Columbia.

Pritchard, D. and Heidrich, W. (2003), 'Cloth motion capture', *Computer Graphics Forum (Eurographics 2003)* **22**(3), 263–271.

Privitera, C. and Stark, L. (1998), 'Evaluating image processing algorithms that predict regions of interest', *Pattern Recognition Letters* **19**(11), 1037–1043.

Quinlan, R. (1993), *C4.5: Programs for Machine Learning*, Morgan Kaufmann, San Mateo.

Radke, R. (2012), *Computer Vision for Visual Effects*, Cambridge.

Raina, R., Battle, A., Lee, H., Packer, B. and Ng, A. Y. (2007), Self-taught learning: transfer learning from unlabeled data, *in* 'Int. Conf. Machine Learning'.

Raja, Y., McKenna, S. and Gong, S. (1998), Colour model selection and adaptation in dynamic scenes, *in* 'Proc. European Conference on Computer Vision (ECCV)', pp. 460–474.

Ramamoorthi, R. and Hanrahan, P. (2001), A signal-processing framework for inverse rendering, *in* 'Proceedings of SIGGRAPH', pp. 117–128.

Ramanan, D. (2005), Tracking People and Recognizing their Activities, PhD thesis, U.C. Berkeley.

Ramanan, D. (2006), Learning to parse images of articulated objects, *in* 'Proc. NIPS'.

Ramanan, D. and Forsyth, D. (2003), Automatic annotation of everyday movements, *in* 'Advances in Neural Information Processing'.

Ranade, S. and Prewitt, J. (1980), A comparison of some segmentation algorithms for cytology, *in* 'Proceedings IAPR International Conference on Pattern Recognition', pp. 561–564.

Ranzato, M., Poultney, C., Chopra, S. and LeCun, Y. (2007), Efficient learning of sparse representations with an energy-based model, *in* 'Advances in Neural Information Processing'.

Rashtchian, C., Young, P., Hodosh, M. and Hockenmaier, J. (2010), Collecting image annotations using Amazons mechanical turk, *in* 'NAACL HLT 2010 Workshop on Creating Speech and Language Data with Amazons Mechanical Turk'.

Ray, S. and Craven, M. (2005), Supervised versus multiple instance learning: an empirical comparison, *in* 'ICML '05: Proceedings of the 22nd international conference on Machine learning', ACM Press, New York, NY, USA, pp. 697–704.

Reinhard, E., Khan, E. A., Akyüz, A. O. and Johnson, G. (2008), *Color Imaging: Fundamentals and Applications*, AK Peters.

Rieger, J. (1987), 'On the classification of views of piecewise-smooth objects', *Image and Vision Computing* **5**, 91–97.

Rieger, J. (1990), 'The geometry of view space of opaque objects bounded by smooth surfaces', **44**(1-2), 1–40.

Rieger, J. (1992), 'Global bifurcations sets and stable projections of non-singular algebraic surfaces', *International Journal of Computer Vision* **7**(3), 171–194.

Ripley, B. (1996), *Pattern Recognition and Neural Networks*, Cambridge University Press.

Riseman, E. and Arbib, M. (1977), 'Computational techniques in the visual segmentation of static scenes', *Computer Graphics Image Processing* **6**(3), 221–276.

Rissanen, J. (1983), 'A universal prior for integers and estimation by minimum description length', *Annals of Statistics* **11**, 416–431.

Rissanen, J. (1987), 'Stochastic complexity (with discussion)', *J. Roy. Stat. Soc. Series B* **49**, 223–239.

Rittscher, J. and Blake, A. (1999), Classification of human body motion, *in* 'Proc. Int. Conf. on Computer Vision (ICCV)', pp. 634–639.

Robert, L. and Faugeras, O. (1991), Curve-based stereo: figural continuity and curvature, *in* 'IEEE Conf. on Computer Vision and Pattern Recognition (CVPR)', Maui, Hawaii, pp. 57–62.

Roberts, L. (1965), Machine perception of 3-D solids, *in* J. Tippet, ed., 'Optical and Electro-Optical Information Processing', MIT Press, pp. 159–197.

Rodden, K. and Wood, K. (2003), How do people manage their digital photographs?, *in* 'Proc. SIGCHI conference on Human factors in computing systems (CHI)'.

Rodden, K., Basalaj, W., Sinclair, D. and Wood, K. (2001), Does organisation by similarity assist image browsing?, *in* 'Proc. SIGCHI conference on Human factors in computing systems (CHI)'.

Romeiro, F., Vasilyev, Y. and Zickler, T. (2008), Passive reflectometry, *in* 'Proc. European Conference on Computer Vision (ECCV)'.

Rosenholtz, R. and Malik, J. (1997), 'Surface orientation from texture: isotropy or homogeneity (or both)?', *Vision Research* **37**(16), 2283–2293.

Rosten, E., Porter, R. and Drummond, T. (2010), 'Faster and better: A machine learning approach to corner detection', *IEEE Trans. Pattern Analysis and Machine Intelligence* **32**(1), 105–119.

Rother, C., Kolmogorov, V. and Blake, A. (2004), '"grabcut": interactive foreground extraction using iterated graph cuts', *ACM Trans. Graph.*

Rowley, H., Baluja, S. and Kanade, T. (1996), Neural network-based face detection, *in* 'IEEE Conf. on Computer Vision and Pattern Recognition (CVPR)', pp. 203–208.

Rowley, H., Baluja, S. and Kanade, T. (1998*a*), 'Neural network-based face detection', *IEEE Trans. Pattern Analysis and Machine Intelligence* **20**(1), 23–38.

Rowley, H., Baluja, S. and Kanade, T. (1998*b*), Rotation invariant neural network-based face detection, *in* 'IEEE Conf. on Computer Vision and Pattern Recognition (CVPR)', pp. 38–44.

Roy, S. and Cox, I. (1998), A maximum-flow formulation of the n-camera stereo correspondence problem, *in* 'Proc. Int. Conf. on Computer Vision (ICCV)', pp. 492–499.

Rubner, Y., Tomasi, C. and Guibas, L. (2000), 'The earth mover's distance as a metric for image retrieval', *International Journal of Computer Vision* **40**(2), 99–121.

Rudin, C., Schapire, R. E. and Daubechies, I. (2004), Boosting based on a smooth margin., *in* 'COLT'.

Russell, B., Freeman, W., Efros, A., Sivic, J. and Zisserman, A. (2006), Using multiple segmentations to discover objects and their extent in image collections, *in* 'IEEE Conf. on Computer Vision and Pattern Recognition (CVPR)', pp. II: 1605–1614.

Russell, B., Torralba, A., Murphy, K. and Freeman, W. (2008), 'Labelme: A database and web-based tool for image annotation', *International Journal of Computer Vision* **77**(1-3), 157–173.

Sakai, K. and Finkel, L. (1994), A shape-from-texture algorithm based on the human visual psychophysics, *in* 'IEEE Conf. on Computer Vision and Pattern Recognition (CVPR)', pp. 527–532.

Sampson, P. (1982), 'Fitting conic sections to 'very scattered' data: An iterarive refinement of the bookstein algorithm', *Computer Graphics Image Processing* **18**(1), 97–108.

Samuel, P. (1988), *Projective Geometry*, Springer-Verlag. English translation of "Géométrie Projective", Presses Universitaires de France, 1986.

Sapp, B., Jordan, C. and Taskar, B. (2010), Adaptive pose priors for pictorial structures, *in* 'IEEE Conf. on Computer Vision and Pattern Recognition (CVPR)', pp. 422–429.

Sarachik, K. and Grimson, W. (1993), Gaussian error models for object recognition, *in* 'IEEE Conf. on Computer Vision and Pattern Recognition (CVPR)', pp. 400–406.

Sarkar, S. and Boyer, K. (1993), 'Integration, inference, and management of spatial information using Bayesian networks: Perceptual organization', *IEEE Trans. Pattern Analysis and Machine Intelligence* **15**(3), 256–274.

Sarkar, S. and Boyer, K. (1994), *Computing Perceptual Organization in Computer Vision*, World Scientific.

Sarkar, S. and Boyer, K. (1998), 'Quantitative measures of change based on feature organization: Eigenvalues and eigenvectors', *Computer Vision and Image Understanding* **71**(1), 110–136.

Satoh, S. and Kanade, T. (1997), Name-it: Association of face and name in video, *in* 'CVPR '97: Proceedings of the 1997 Conference on Computer Vision and Pattern Recognition (CVPR '97)', IEEE Computer Society, Washington, DC, USA, p. 368.

Satoh, S., Nakamura, Y. and Kanade, T. (1999), 'Name-it: naming and detecting faces in news videos', *IEEE Multimedia* **6**(1), 22–35.

Saund, E. and Moran, T. (1995), Perceptual organization in an interactive sketch editing application, *in* 'Proc. Int. Conf. on Computer Vision (ICCV)', pp. 597–604.

Savarese, S. and Fei-Fei, L. (2007), 3d generic object categorization, localization and pose estimation, *in* 'Proc. Int. Conf. on Computer Vision (ICCV)', pp. 1–8.

Savarese, S. and Fei-Fei, L. (2008), View synthesis for recognizing unseen poses of object classes, *in* 'Proc. European Conference on Computer Vision (ECCV)', pp. III: 602–615.

Saxena, A., Chung, S. and Ng, A. (2008), '3-d depth reconstruction from a single still image', *International Journal of Computer Vision* **76**(1), 53–69.

Saxena, A., Sun, M. and Ng, A. (2009), 'Make3d: Learning 3d scene structure from a single still image', *IEEE Trans. Pattern Analysis and Machine Intelligence* **31**(5), 824–840.

Schachter, B. (1980), 'Model-based texture measures', *IEEE Trans. Pattern Analysis and Machine Intelligence* **2**(2), 169–171.

Schachter, B. and Ahuja, N. (1979), 'Random pattern generation processes', *Computer Graphics Image Processing* **10**(1), 95–114.

Schapire, R. E. (2002), The boosting approach to machine learning an overview, *in* 'Deductive Database Workshops'.

Scharstein, D. and Szeliski, R. (2002), 'A taxonomy and evaluation of dense two-frame stereo correspondence algorithms', *International Journal of Computer Vision* **47**(1-3), 7–42.

Schlesinger, D. and Flach, B. (2006), Transforming an arbitrary minsum problem into a binary one, Technical Report TUD-FI06-01, Dresden University of Technology.

Schmid, C. (2001), Constructing models for content-based image retrieval, *in* 'IEEE Conf. on Computer Vision and Pattern Recognition (CVPR)', pp. II:39–45.

Schmid, C. and Mohr, R. (1997), 'Local grayvalue invariants for image retrieval', *IEEE Trans. Pattern Analysis and Machine Intelligence* **19**(5), 530–535.

Schmid, C., Mohr, R. and Bauckhage, C. (2000), 'Evaluation of interest point detectors', *International Journal of Computer Vision* **37**(2), 151–172.

Schneiderman, H. and Kanade, T. (2000), A statistical method for 3d object detection applied to faces and cars, *in* 'CVPR00', pp. I: 746–751.

Schrijver, A. (2003), *Combinatorial Optimization*, Springer. 3 Vols.

Seitz, S. M., Curless, B., Diebel, J., Scharstein, D. and Szeliski, R. (2006), A comparison and evaluation of multi-view stereo reconstruction algorithms, *in* 'IEEE Conf. on Computer Vision and Pattern Recognition (CVPR)'.

Sermanet, P., Hadsell, R., Scoffier, M., Grimes, M., Ben, J., Erkan, A., Crudele, C. and LeCun, Y. (2009), 'A multi-range architecture for collision-free off-road robot navigation', *Journal of Field Robotics* **26**(1), 58–87.

Shade, J., Gortler, S., Li-wei, H. and Szeliski, R. (1998), Layered depth images, *in* 'SIGGRAPH 98', pp. 231–242.

Shafer, S. (1985), 'Using color to separate reflection components', *Color Res. App.* **10**(4), 210–218.

Shakhnarovich, G., Viola, P. and Darrell, T. (2003), Fast pose estimation with parameter-sensitive hashing, *in* 'Proc. Int. Conf. on Computer Vision (ICCV)', pp. 750–757.

Shams, R., Sadeghi, P., Kennedy, R. and Hartley, R. (2010), 'A survey of medical image registration on multicore and the gpu', *IEEE Signal Processing Magazine* **27**(2), 50–60.

Sharan, L., Rosenholtz, R. and Adelson, E. (2009), 'Material perception: What can you see in a brief glance?', *Journal of Vision*.

Shashua, A. (1993), Projective depth: a geometric invariant for 3D reconstruction from two perspective/orthographic views and for visual recognition, *in* 'Proc. Int. Conf. on Computer Vision (ICCV)', Berlin, Germany, pp. 583–590.

Shashua, A. (1995), 'Algebraic functions for recognition', *IEEE Trans. Pattern Analysis and Machine Intelligence* **17**(8), 779–789.

Shatford, S. (1986), 'Analyzing the subject of a picture: A theoretical approach', *Cataloging & Classification Quarterly* **6**(3), 39–62.

Shi, J. and Malik, J. (1997), Normalized cuts and image segmentation, *in* 'IEEE Conf. on Computer Vision and Pattern Recognition (CVPR)', pp. 731–737.

Shi, J. and Malik, J. (1998a), Motion segmentation and tracking using normalized cuts, *in* 'Proc. Int. Conf. on Computer Vision (ICCV)', pp. 1154–1160.

Shi, J. and Malik, J. (1998b), Self-inducing relational distance and its application to image segmentation, *in* 'Proc. European Conference on Computer Vision (ECCV)', pp. 528–43.

Shi, J. and Malik, J. (2000), 'Normalized cuts and image segmentation', *IEEE Trans. Pattern Analysis and Machine Intelligence* **22**(8), 888–905.

Shi, J. and Tomasi, C. (1994), Good features to track, *in* 'IEEE Conf. Computer Vision and Pattern Recognition'.

Shirai, Y. (1972), 'Recognition of polyhedrons with a range finder', *Pattern Recognition* **4**, 243–250.

Shotton, J., Fitzgibbon, A., Cook, M., Sharp, T., Finocchio, M., Moore, R., Kipman, A. and Blake, A. (2011), Real-time human pose recognitiom in parts from single depth images, *in* 'IEEE Conf. on Computer Vision and Pattern Recognition (CVPR)'.

Shum, H. and Szeliski, R. (1998), Construction and refinement of panoramic mosaics with global and local alignment, *in* 'Proc. Int. Conf. on Computer Vision (ICCV)', Bombay, India, pp. 953–958.

Shum, H., Ikeuchi, K. and Reddy, R. (1995), 'Principal component analysis with missing data and its application to polyhedral object modeling', *IEEE Trans. Pattern Analysis and Machine Intelligence* **17**(9), 854–867.

Sidenbladh, H., Black, M. and Fleet, D. (2000), Stochastic tracking of 3d human figures using 2d image motion, *in* 'Proc. European Conference on Computer Vision (ECCV)'.

Silaghi, M.-C., Plänkers, R., Boulic, R., Fua, P. and Thalmann, D. (1998), Local and global skeleton fitting techniques for optical motion capture, *in* 'Modelling and Motion Capture Techniques for Virtual Environments', pp. 26–40. Proceedings of CAPTECH '98.

Sillion, F. (1994), *Radiosity and Global Illumination*, Morgan-Kauffman.

Simon, D., Hebert, M. and Kanade, T. (1994), Real-time 3D pose estimation using a high-speed range sensor, *in* 'Int. Conf. on Robotics and Automation', San Diego, CA, pp. 2235–2241.

Simoncelli, E. and Farid, H. (1995), Steerable wedge filters, *in* 'Proc. Int. Conf. on Computer Vision (ICCV)', pp. 189–194.

Simoncelli, E. and Freeman, W. (1995*a*), The steerable pyramid: A flexible architecture for multi-scale derivative computation, *in* 'Proc. Int. Conf. on Computer Vision (ICCV)', pp. III: 444–447.

Simoncelli, E. and Freeman, W. (1995*b*), The steerable pyramid: A flexible architecture for multi-scale derivative computation, *in* 'IEEE Int. Conf. Image Processing', pp. 444–7.

Sinha, S. and Pollefeys, M. (2005), Multi-view reconstruction using photo-consistency and exact silhouette constraints: A maximum-flow formulation, *in* 'Proc. Int. Conf. on Computer Vision (ICCV)'.

Sinha, S., Mordohai, P. and Pollefeys, M. (2007), Multi-view stereo via graph cuts on the dual of an adaptive tetrahedral mesh, *in* 'Proc. Int. Conf. on Computer Vision (ICCV)'.

Sivic, J. and Zisserman, A. (2003), Video Google: A text retrieval approach to object matching in videos, *in* 'Proc. Int. Conf. on Computer Vision (ICCV)', pp. 1470–1477.

Slama, C., Theurer, C. and Henriksen, S., eds (1980), *Manual of photogrammetry*, American Society of Photogrammetry. Fourth edition.

Sminchisescu, C. and Triggs, B. (2003), Kinematic jump processes for monocular 3d human tracking, *in* 'IEEE Conf. on Computer Vision and Pattern Recognition (CVPR)', pp. I: 69–76.

Smith, S. and Brady, J. (1997), 'Susan: A new approach to low-level image-processing', *International Journal of Computer Vision* **23**(1), 45–78.

Smith, T. (1996), 'A digital library for geographically referenced materials', *Computer* **29**(5), 54–60.

Snapper, E. and Troyer, R. (1989), *Metric Affine Geometry*, Dover Publications Inc. Reprinted from Academic Press, 1971.

Snavely, N., Seitz, S. and Szeliski, R. (2008), 'Modeling the world from internet photo collections', *International Journal of Computer Vision* **80**(2), 189–210.

Sorokin, A. and Forsyth, D. (2008), Utility data annotation with amazon mechanical turk, *in* 'Proc. IEEE Workshop on Internet Vision', pp. 1–8.

Spacek, L. (1986), 'Edge detection and motion detection', *Image and Vision Computing* **4**(1), 43–56.

Spain, M. and Perona, P. (2008), Some objects are more equal than others: Measuring and predicting importance, *in* 'Proc. European Conference on Computer Vision (ECCV)', pp. I: 523–536.

Spetsakis, M. and Aloimonos, Y. (1990), 'Structure from motion using line correspondences', *International Journal of Computer Vision* **4**(3), 171–183.

Srivastava, S. and Ahuja, N. (1990), 'Octree generation from object silhouettes in perspective views', *CVGIP: Image Understanding* **49**(1), 68–84.

Starner, T., Weaver, J. and Pentland, A. (1998), 'Real-time American sign language recognition using desk and wearable computer based video', *IEEE Trans. Pattern Analysis and Machine Intelligence* **20**(12), 1371–1375.

Steger, C., Ulrich, M. and Wiedemann, C. (2008), *Machine Vision Algorithms and Applications*, Wiley.

Stein, F. and Medioni, G. (1992), 'Structural indexing: efficient 3D object recognition', *IEEE Trans. Pattern Analysis and Machine Intelligence*.

Stone, J. and Isard, S. (1995), 'Adaptive scale filtering: A general-method for obtaining shape from texture', *IEEE Trans. Pattern Analysis and Machine Intelligence* **17**(7), 713–718.

Strecha, C., Fransens, R. and Gool, L. V. (2006), Combined depth and outlier estimation in multi-view stereo, *in* 'IEEE Conf. on Computer Vision and Pattern Recognition (CVPR)', pp. 2394–2401.

Struik, D. (1988), *Lectures on classical differential geometry*, Dover. Reprint of the second edition (1961) of the work first published by Addison-Wesley in 1950.

Sturm, P. and Triggs, B. (1996), A factorization-based algorithm for multi-image projective structure and motion, *in* 'Proc. European Conference on Computer Vision (ECCV)', pp. 709–720.

Sullivan, J., Blake, A., Isard, M. and MacCormick, J. (1999), Object localization by Bayesian correlation, *in* 'Proc. Int. Conf. on Computer Vision (ICCV)', pp. 1068–1075.

Sullivan, S. and Ponce, J. (1998), 'Automatic model construction, pose estimation, and object recognition from photographs using triangular splines', *IEEE Trans. Pattern Analysis and Machine Intelligence* **20**(10), 1091–1096.

Sullivan, S., Sandford, L. and Ponce, J. (1994), 'Using geometric distance fits for 3D object modelling and recognition', *IEEE Trans. Pattern Analysis and Machine Intelligence* **16**(12), 1183–1196.

Sung, K.-K. and Poggio, T. (1998), 'Example-based learning for view-based human face detection', *IEEE Trans. Pattern Analysis and Machine Intelligence* **20**, 39–51.

Super, B. and Bovik, A. (1995), 'Shape from texture using local spectral moments', *IEEE Trans. Pattern Analysis and Machine Intelligence* **17**(4), 333–343.

Swaminathan, R., Kang, S., Szeliski, R., Criminisi, A. and Nayar, S. (2002), On the motion and appearance of specularities in image sequences, *in* 'Proc. European Conference on Computer Vision (ECCV)', p. I: 508 ff.

Szeliski, R. (2010), *Computer Vision: Algorithms and Applications*, Springer.

Szeliski, R., Avidan, S. and Anandan, P. (2000), Layer extraction from multiple images containing reflections and transparency, *in* 'IEEE Conf. on Computer Vision and Pattern Recognition (CVPR)', pp. I:246–253.

Szlam, A., Maggioni, M. and Coifman, R. (2007), 'Regularization on graphs with function-adapted diffusion processes'.

Tacc, M. and Ahuja, N. (1997), 'Multiscale image segmentation by integrated edge and region detection', *IEEE Trans. Image Processing* **6**(5), 642–655.

Tagare, H. and de Figueiredo, R. (1992), 'Simultaneous estimation of shape and reflectance map from photometric stereo', *CVGIP: Image Understanding* **55**(3), 275–286.

Tagare, H. and de Figueiredo, R. (1993), 'A framework for the construction of reflectance maps for machine vision', *CVGIP: Image Understanding* **57**(3), 265–282.

Tankus, A., Sochen, N. and Yeshurun, Y. (2005), 'Shape-from-shading under perspective projection', *Int. J. Comput. Vision* **63**(1), 21–43.

Tao, H., Sawhney, H. and Kumar, R. (2000), Dynamic layer representation with applications to tracking, *in* 'IEEE Conf. on Computer Vision and Pattern Recognition (CVPR)', pp. II:134–141.

Tao, Q., Scott, S., Vinodchandran, N. V. and Osugi, T. T. (2004), Svm-based generalized multiple-instance learning via approximate box counting, *in* 'ICML '04: Proceedings of the twenty-first international conference on Machine learning', ACM Press, New York, NY, USA, p. 101.

Tappen, M., Freeman, W. and Adelson, E. (2006*a*), Estimating intrinsic component images using non-linear regression, *in* 'IEEE Conf. on Computer Vision and Pattern Recognition (CVPR)'.

Tappen, M., Freeman, W. and Adelson, E. (2006*b*), 'Recovering intrinsic images from a single image', *IEEE Trans. Pattern Analysis and Machine Intelligence.*

Taubin, G. (1991), 'Estimation of planar curves, surfaces, and nonplanar space curves defined by implicit equations with applications to edge and range image segmentation', *IEEE Trans. Pattern Analysis and Machine Intelligence* **13**(11), 1115–1138.

Taubin, G., Cukierman, F., Sullivan, S., Ponce, J. and Kriegman, D. (1994), 'Parameterized families of polynomials for bounded algebraic and surface curve fitting', *IEEE Trans. Pattern Analysis and Machine Intelligence* **16**(3), 287–303.

Taylor, C. (2000), Reconstruction of articulated objects from point correspondences in a single uncalibrated image, *in* 'IEEE Conf. on Computer Vision and Pattern Recognition (CVPR)', pp. 677–84.

Taylor, C., Edwards, G. and Cootes, T. (1998), Active appearance models, *in* 'Proc. European Conference on Computer Vision (ECCV)', p. II: 484.

ter Haar Romeny, B. (1994), Geometry-driven diffusion in computer vision, *in* 'Geometry Driven Diffusion in Computer Vision', Kluwer Academic Press.

ter Haar Romeny, B., Florack, L. M., Koenderink, J. J. and Viergever, M. A., eds (1997), *Scale-Space Theory in Computer Vision*, Vol. 1252, Springer Verlag LNCS.

Terzopolous, D., Platt, J., Barr, A. and Fleischer, K. (1987), 'Elastically deformable models', *Computer Graphics (SIGGRAPH 87 Proceedings)* pp. 205–214.

Terzopoulos, D. (1984), Multiresolution Computation of Visible-Surface Representations, PhD thesis, Massachusetts Institute of Technology, Cambridge, MA.

Thom, R. (1972), *Structural Stability and Morphogenesis*, Benjamin, New-York.

Thompson, D. (1992), *On growth and form*, Dover. Complete version of original 1917 edition; there is also a CUP edition in 1961.

Thompson, D. and Mundy, J. (1987), Three dimensional model matching from an unconstrained viewpoint, *in* 'International Conference on Robotics and Automation', pp. 208–220.

Thompson, M., Eller, R., Radlinski, W. and Speert, J., eds (1966), *Manual of Photogrammetry*, American Society of Photogrammetry. Third Edition.

Thurau, C. and Hlavac, V. (2008), Pose primitive based human action recognition in videos or still images, *in* 'IEEE Conf. on Computer Vision and Pattern Recognition (CVPR)', pp. 1–8.

Tibshirani, R. (1996), 'Regression shrinkage and selection via the lasso', *J. Royal. Statist. Soc B.* **58**(1), 267–288.

Todd, J. (1946), *Projective and Analytical Geometry*, Pitman Publishing Corporation, New York – Chicago.

Todorovic, S. and Ahuja, N. (2008*a*), 'Region-based hierarchical image matching', *International Journal of Computer Vision* **78**(1), 47–66.

Todorovic, S. and Ahuja, N. (2008*b*), 'Unsupervised category modeling, recognition, and segmentation in images', *IEEE Trans. Pattern Analysis and Machine Intelligence* **30**(12), 2158–2174.

Tomasi, C. and Kanade, T. (1992), 'Shape and motion from image streams under orthography: a factorization method', *International Journal of Computer Vision* **9**(2), 137–154.

Tomasi, C. and Shi, J. (1994), Good features to track, *in* 'IEEE Conf. on Computer Vision and Pattern Recognition (CVPR)', pp. 593–600.

Torr, P. (1997), An assessment of information criteria for motion model selection, *in* 'IEEE Conf. on Computer Vision and Pattern Recognition (CVPR)', pp. 47–52.

Torr, P. (1999), Model selection for two view geometry: a review, *in* D. Forsyth, J. Mundy, V. diGesu and R. Cipolla, eds, 'Shape, Contour and Grouping in Computer Vision', Springer-Verlag, pp. 277–301.

Torr, P. and Davidson, C. (2003), 'Impsac: Synthesis of importance sampling and random sample consensus', *IEEE Trans. Pattern Analysis and Machine Intelligence* **25**(3), 354–364.

Torr, P. and Zisserman, A. (1998), Concerning Bayesian motion segmentation, model averaging, matching and the trifocal tensor, *in* 'Proc. European Conference on Computer Vision (ECCV)', pp. 511–27.

Torr, P. and Zisserman, A. (2000), 'Mlesac: A new robust estimator with application to estimating image geometry', *Computer Vision and Image Understanding* **78**(1), 138–156.

Torr, P., Fitzgibbon, A. and Zisserman, A. (1999*a*), 'The problem of degeneracy in structure and motion recovery from uncalibrated image sequences', *International Journal of Computer Vision* **32**(1), 27–44.

Torr, P., Szeliski, R. and Anandan, P. (1999*b*), An integrated Bayesian approach to layer extraction from image sequences, *in* 'Proc. Int. Conf. on Computer Vision (ICCV)', pp. 983–990.

Torralba, A. and Efros, A. (2011), Unbiased look at dataset bias, *in* 'IEEE Conf. on Computer Vision and Pattern Recognition (CVPR)'.

Torralba, A., Murphy, K., Freeman, W. and Rubin, M. (2003), Context-based vision system for place and object recognition, *in* 'Proc. Int. Conf. on Computer Vision (ICCV)', pp. 273–280.

Torrance, K. and Sparrow, E. (1967), 'Theory for off-specular reflection from roughened surfaces', *Journal of the Optical Society of America* **57**, 1105–1114.

Torre, V. and Poggio, T. (1986), 'On edge detection', *IEEE Trans. Pattern Analysis and Machine Intelligence* **8**(2), 147–163.

Toyama, K. and Blake, A. (2001), Probabilistic tracking in a metric space, *in* 'Proc. Int. Conf. on Computer Vision (ICCV)', pp. II: 50–57.

Toyama, K. and Blake, A. (2002), 'Probabilistic tracking with exemplars in a metric space', *International Journal of Computer Vision* **48**(1), 9–19.

Trajkovic, M. and Hedley, M. (1998), 'Fast corner detection', *Image and Vision Computing* **16**(2), 75–87.

Tran, D. and Forsyth, D. (2007), Configuration estimates improve pedestrian finding, *in* 'Advances in Neural Information Processing'.

Tran, D. and Forsyth, D. (2010), Improved human parsing with a full relational model, *in* 'Proc. European Conference on Computer Vision (ECCV)'.

Tran, S. and Davis, L. (2006), 3d surface reconstruction using graph cuts with surface constraints, *in* 'Proc. European Conference on Computer Vision (ECCV)'.

Triesman, A. (1982), 'Perceptual grouping and attention in visual search for features and objects', *Journal of Experimental Psychology: Human Perception and Performance* **8**(2), 194–214.

Triggs, B. (1995), Matching constraints and the joint image, *in* 'Proc. Int. Conf. on Computer Vision (ICCV)', Boston, MA, pp. 338–343.

Triggs, B., McLauchlan, P., Hartley, R. and Fitzgibbon, A. (2000), Bundle adjustment - a modern synthesis, *in* B. Triggs, A. Zisserman and R. Szeliski, eds, 'Vision Algorithms: Theory and Practice', Springer-Verlag, pp. 298–372. Lecture Notes in Computer Science 1883.

Triggs, W. (1997), Auto-calibration and the absolute quadric, *in* 'IEEE Conf. on Computer Vision and Pattern Recognition (CVPR)', San Juan, Puerto Rico, pp. 609–614.

Trussell, H., Allebach, J., Fairchild, M., Funt, B. and Wong, P. (1997), 'Special issue: Digital color imaging', *IEEE Trans. Image Processing* **6**(7), 897–900.

Tsai, R. (1987), 'A versatile camera calibration technique for high-accuracy 3D machine vision metrology using off-the-shelf TV cameras', **RA-3**(4), 323–344.

Tsai, R. and Huang, T. (1984), 'Uniqueness and estimation of 3D motion parameters of rigid bodies with curved surfaces', *IEEE Trans. Pattern Analysis and Machine Intelligence* **6**, 13–27.

Turk, G. and Levoy, M. (1994), 'Zippered polygon meshes from range images', *ACM Trans. Graphics (SIGGRAPH Proceeding)* pp. 311–318.

Ullman, S. (1979), *The Interpretation of Visual Motion*, The MIT Press, Cambridge, MA.

Ullman, S. (1996), *High-Level Vision: Object Recognition and Visual Cognition*, MIT Press.

Unnikrishnan, R., Pantofaru, C. and Hebert, M. (2007), 'Toward objective evaluation of image segmentation algorithms', *IEEE Trans. Pattern Analysis and Machine Intelligence* **29**(6), 929–944.

Vaillant, R. and Faugeras, O. (1992), 'Using extremal boundaries for 3D object modeling', *IEEE Trans. Pattern Analysis and Machine Intelligence* **14**(2), 157–173.

Valdés, A., Ronda, J. and Gallego, G. (2006), 'The absolute line quadric and camera autocalibration', *International Journal of Computer Vision* **66**(3), 283–303.

van de Sande, K., Gevers, T. and Snoek, C. (2010), 'Evaluating color descriptors for object and scene recognition', *IEEE Trans. Pattern Analysis and Machine Intelligence* **32**(9), 1582–1596.

van Ginneken, B., Koenderink, J. and Dana, K. (1999), 'Texture histograms as a function of irradiation and viewing direction', *International Journal of Computer Vision* **31**(2/3), 169–184.

Vapnik, V. N. (1998), *Statistical Learning Theory*, John Wiley & Sons.

Varma, M. and Zisserman, A. (2003), Texture classification: are filter banks necessary?, *in* 'IEEE Conf. on Computer Vision and Pattern Recognition (CVPR)', pp. II: 691–698.

Varma, M. and Zisserman, A. (2005), 'A statistical approach to texture classification from single images', *International Journal of Computer Vision* **62**(1-2), 61–81.

Varma, M. and Zisserman, A. (2009), 'A statistical approach to material classification using image patch exemplars', *IEEE Trans. Pattern Analysis and Machine Intelligence* **31**(11), 2032–2047.

Vasconcelos, N. and Lippman, A. (1997), Empirical Bayesian em based motion segmentation, *in* 'IEEE Conf. on Computer Vision and Pattern Recognition (CVPR)', pp. 527–532.

Vedula, S., Baker, S. and Kanade, T. (2005), 'Image-based spatiotemporal modeling and view interpolation of dynamic events', *ACM Transactions on Graphics* **24**(2), 240–261.

Velho, L., Frery, A. C., Gomes, J. and Levy, S. (2008), *Image Processing for Computer Graphics and Vision*, Springer.

Viitaniemi, V. and Laaksonen, J. (2007), 'Evaluating the performance in automatic image annotation: Example case by adaptive fusion of global image features', *Image Commun.* **22**(6), 557–568.

Vijayanarasimhan, S. and Grauman, K. (2009), What's it going to cost you?: Predicting effort vs. informativeness for multi-label image annotations, *in* 'IEEE Conf. on Computer Vision and Pattern Recognition (CVPR)', pp. 2262–2269.

Vijayanarasimhan, S. and Grauman, K. (2011), 'Cost-sensitive active visual category learning', *International Journal of Computer Vision* **91**, 24–44.

Vincent, L. and Soille, P. (1991), 'Watersheds in digital spaces: An efficient algorithm based on immersion simulations', *IEEE Trans. Pattern Analysis and Machine Intelligence* **13**(6), 583–598.

Viola, P. A. and III, W. W. (1995), Alignment by maximization of mutual information, *in* 'International Journal of Computer Vision', pp. 16–23.

Viola, P. and Jones, M. (2001), Rapid object detection using a boosted cascade of simple features, *in* 'IEEE Conf. on Computer Vision and Pattern Recognition (CVPR)', pp. I:511–518.

Vogiatzis, G., Torr, P. H. and Cipolla, R. (2005), Multi-view stereo via volumetric graph-cuts, *in* 'IEEE Conf. on Computer Vision and Pattern Recognition (CVPR)'.

Vogler, C., Sun, H. and Metaxas, D. (2000), A framework for motion recognition with applications to American sign language and gait recognition, *in* 'IEEE Workshop on Human Motion'.

von Ahn, L. and Dabbish, L. (2004), Labeling images with a computer game, *in* 'Proceedings of the SIGCHI conference on Human factors in computing systems'.

Vondrick, C., Ramanan, D. and Patterson, D. (2010), Efficiently scaling up video annotation with crowdsourced marketplaces, *in* 'Proc. European Conference on Computer Vision (ECCV)'.

Wallace, C. and Freeman, P. (1987), 'Estimation and inference by compact encoding (with discussion)', *J. Roy. Stat. Soc. Series B* **49**, 240–265.

Wandell, B. (1987), 'The synthesis and analysis of color images', *IEEE Trans. Pattern Analysis and Machine Intelligence* **9**(1), 2–13.

Wandell, B. (1995), *Foundations of Vision*, Sinauer Associates, Inc., Sunderland, MA.

Wang, G. and Forsyth, D. (2009), Joint learning of visual attributes, object classes and visual saliency, *in* 'Proc. Int. Conf. on Computer Vision (ICCV)', pp. 537–544.

Wang, G., Zhang, Y. and Fei-Fei, L. (2006), Using dependent regions for object categorization in a generative framework, *in* 'IEEE Conf. on Computer Vision and Pattern Recognition (CVPR)', pp. II: 1597–1604.

Wang, H. and Brady, M. (1994), A practical solution to corner detection, *in* 'IEEE Int. Conf. Image Processing', pp. I: 919–923.

Wang, H., Wexler, Y., Ofek, E. and Hoppe, H. (2008), 'Factoring repeated content within and among images', *ACM Trans. Graph. (SIGGRAPH Proceedings)* **27**, 14:1–14:10.

Wang, J. and Adelson, E. (1994), 'Representing moving images with layers', *IEEE Trans. Image Processing* **3**(5), 625–638.

Wang, J. and Cohen, M. F. (2007), *Image and Video Matting: A Survey*, Foundations and Trends in Computer Graphics and Vision, Now.

Wang, Y., Liu, Z. and Huang, J.-C. (2000), 'Multimedia content analysis-using both audio and visual clues', *Signal Processing Magazine* **17**(6), 12–36.

Wang, Y., Tran, D. and Liao, Z. (2011), Learning hierarchical poselets for human parsing, *in* 'IEEE Conf. on Computer Vision and Pattern Recognition (CVPR)'.

Warfield, S., Zou, K. and Wells, W. (2004), 'Simultaneous truth and performance level estimation (staple): An algorithm for the validation of image segmentation', *IEEE Trans. Medical Imaging* **23**(7), 903–921.

Weinshall, D. and Tomasi, C. (1995), 'Linear and incremental acquisition of invariant shape models from image sequences', *IEEE Trans. Pattern Analysis and Machine Intelligence*.

Weisberg, S. (1980), *Applied Linear Regression*, Wiley, New York.

Weiss, Y. (1997), Smoothness in layers: Motion segmentation using nonparametric mixture estimation, *in* 'IEEE Conf. on Computer Vision and Pattern Recognition (CVPR)', pp. 520–526.

Weiss, Y. (1999), Segmentation using eigenvectors: A unifying view, *in* 'Proc. Int. Conf. on Computer Vision (ICCV)', pp. 975–982.

Weiss, Y. (2001), Deriving intrinsic images from image sequences, *in* 'Proc. Int. Conf. on Computer Vision (ICCV)'.

Wells, W., Grimson, W., Kikinis, R. and Jolesz, F. (1996), 'Adaptive segmentation of mri data.', *IEEE Transactions on Medical Imaging* **15**(4), 429–442.

Weng, J., Huang, T. and Ahuja, N. (1992), 'Motion and structure from line correspondences: closed-form solution, uniqueness, and optimization', *IEEE Trans. Pattern Analysis and Machine Intelligence* **14**(3), 318–336.

West, J., Fitzpatrick, M., Wang, M., Dawant, B., Maurer, C.R., J., Kessler, R., Maciunas, R., Barillot, C., Lemoine, D., Collignon, A., Maes, F., Suetens, P., Vandermeulen, D., van den Elsen, P., Napel, S., Sumanaweera, T., Harkness, B., Hemler, P., Hill, D., Hawkes, D., Studholme, C., Antoine Maintz, J., Viergever, M., Malandain, G., Pennec, X., Noz, M., Maguire, G.Q., J., Pollack, M., Pelizzari, C., Robb, R., Hanson, D. and Woods, R. (1997), 'Comparison and evaluation of retrospective intermodality registration techniques', *J. Computer Assisted Tomography* **21**(4), 554–566.

West, M. and Harrison, J. (1997), *Bayesian Forecasting and Dynamic Models*, Springer Verlag.

Wheatstone, C. (1838), 'On some remarkable, and hitherto unobserved, phenomena of binocular vision', *Philosophical Transactions of the Royal Society. (London)* **128**, 371–394.

Wheeler, M. and Ikeuchi, K. (1995), 'Probabilistic hypothesis generation and robust localization for object recognition', *IEEE Trans. Pattern Analysis and Machine Intelligence* **17**(3), 252–265.

White, R. and Forsyth, D. (2006), Combining cues: Shape from shading and texture, *in* 'IEEE Conf. on Computer Vision and Pattern Recognition (CVPR)', pp. II: 1809–1816.

White, R., Crane, K. and Forsyth, D. (2007), 'Capturing and animating occluded cloth', *ACM Trans. Graph. (SIGGRAPH Proceedings)*.

Whitney, H. (1955), 'On singularities of mappings of Euclidean spaces. I. Mappings of the plane into the plane', *Annals of Mathematics* **62**(3), 374–410.

Wilkinson, J. and Reinsch, C. (1971), *Linear Algebra - Vol. II of Handbook for Automatic Computation*, Springer-Verlag, New York. Chapter I.10 by G.H. Golub and C. Reinsch.

Willems, G., Tuytelaars, T. and Van Gool, L. (2008), An efficient dense and scale-invariant spatio-temporal interest point detector, *in* 'Proc. European Conference on Computer Vision (ECCV)', pp. II: 650–663.

Williamson, S. and Cummins, H. (1983), *Light and Color in Nature and Art*, John Wiley and Sons.

Witkin, A. (1981), 'Recovering surface shape and orientation from texture', *Artificial Intelligence* **17**, 17–45.

Witkin, A. (1983), Scale-space filtering, *in* 'International Joint Conference on Artificial Intelligence', pp. 1019–1022.

Wojek, C., Walk, S. and Schiele, B. (2009), Multi-cue onboard pedestrian detection, *in* 'IEEE Conf. on Computer Vision and Pattern Recognition (CVPR)', pp. 794–801.

Wolff, L., Nayar, S. and Oren, M. (1998), 'Improved diffuse reflection models for computer vision', *International Journal of Computer Vision* **30**(1), 55–71.

Woodham, R. (1979), Analyzing curved surfaces using reflectance map techniques, *in* 'Artificial Intelligence: An MIT Perspective', MIT Press, pp. 161–182.

Woodham, R. (1980), 'Photometric method for determining surface orientation from multiple images', *Optical Engineering* **19**(1), 139–144.

Woodham, R. (1989), Determining surface curvature with photometric stereo, *in* 'International Conference on Robotics and Automation', pp. 36–42.

Woodham, R. (1994), 'Gradient and curvature from the photometric-stereo method, including local confidence estimation', *Journal of the Optical Society of America* **11**(11), 3050–3068.

Woodham, R., Iwahori, Y. and Barman, R. (1991), Photometric stereo: Lambertian reflectance and light sources with unknown direction and strength, *in* 'Univ. of BC'.

Wu, T. and Lange, K. (2008), 'Coordinate descent algorithms for lasso penalized regression', *Annals of Applied Statistics* **2**(1), 224–244.

Wu, Z. and Leahy, R. (1993), 'An optimal graph theoretic approach to data clustering: Theory and its application to image segmentation', *IEEE Trans. Pattern Analysis and Machine Intelligence* **15**(11), 1101–1113.

Wyszecki, G. and Stiles, W. (1982), *Color Science: Concepts and Methods, Quantitative Data and Formulas*, Wiley.

Xiao, J., Hays, J., Ehinger, K., Oliva, A. and Torralba, A. (2010), Sun database: Large-scale scene recognition from abbey to zoo, *in* 'IEEE Conf. on Computer Vision and Pattern Recognition (CVPR)', pp. 3485–3492.

Yachida, M., Kitamura, Y. and Kimachi, M. (1986), Trinocular vision: new approach for correspondence problem, *in* 'Proceedings IAPR International Conference on Pattern Recognition', pp. 1041–1044.

Yanai, K. and Barnard, K. (2005), Image region entropy: a measure of "visualness" of web images associated with one concept, *in* 'MULTIMEDIA '05: Proceedings of the 13th annual ACM international conference on Multimedia', ACM Press, New York, NY, USA, pp. 419–422.

Yang, J., Yu, K. and Huang, T. (2010*a*), Efficient highly over-complete sparse coding using a mixture model, *in* 'Proc. European Conference on Computer Vision (ECCV)'.

Yang, J., Yu, K. and Huang, T. (2010*b*), Supervised translation-invariant sparse coding, *in* 'IEEE Conf. on Computer Vision and Pattern Recognition (CVPR)', pp. 3517–3524.

Yang, J., Yu, K., Gong, Y. and Huang, T. (2009*a*), Linear spatial pyramid matching using sparse coding for image classification, *in* 'IEEE Conf. on Computer Vision and Pattern Recognition (CVPR)', pp. 1794–1801.

Yang, J., Yu, K., Gong, Y. and Huang, T. (2009*b*), Linear spatial pyramid matching using sparse coding for image classification, *in* 'IEEE Conf. on Computer Vision and Pattern Recognition (CVPR)'.

Yang, Y. and Ramanan, D. (2011), Articulated pose estimation using flexible mixtures of parts, *in* 'IEEE Conf. on Computer Vision and Pattern Recognition (CVPR)'.

Yao, B. and Li, F. (2010), Modeling mutual context of object and human pose in human-object interaction activities, *in* 'IEEE Conf. on Computer Vision and Pattern Recognition (CVPR)', pp. 17–24.

Yao, B., Yang, X., Lin, L., Lee, M. and Zhu, S. (2010), 'I2t: Image parsing to text description', *Proceedings of IEEE* **98**(8), 1485–1508.

Yasnoff, W., Mui, W. and Bacus, J. (1977), 'Error measures in scene segmentation', *Pattern Recognition* **9**(4), 217–231.

Yavlinsky, A., Schofield, E. and Rger, S. (2005), Automated image annotation using global features and robust nonparametric density estimation, *in* 'Automated image annotation using global features and robust nonparametric density estimation', pp. 507–517.

Yu, Y., Debevec, P., Malik, J. and Hawkins, T. (1999), Inverse global illumination: Recovering reflectance models of real scenes from photographs from, *in* A. Rockwood, ed., 'Siggraph99, Annual Conference Series', Addison Wesley Longman, Los Angeles, pp. 215–224.

Zaharescu, A., Boyer, E. and Horaud, R. (2007), Transformesh : A topology-adaptive mesh-based approach to surface evolution., *in* Y. Yagi, S. B. Kang, I.-S. Kweon and H. Zha, eds, 'ACCV (2)', Vol. 4844 of *Lecture Notes in Computer Science*, Springer, pp. 166–175.

Zhang, H., Berg, A., Maire, M. and Malik, J. (2006*a*), Svm-knn: Discriminative nearest neighbor classification for visual category recognition, *in* 'IEEE Conf. on Computer Vision and Pattern Recognition (CVPR)', pp. II: 2126–2136.

Zhang, H., Fritts, J. and Goldman, S. (2008), 'Image segmentation evaluation: A survey of unsupervised methods', *Computer Vision and Image Understanding* **110**(2), 260–280.

Zhang, K., Kwok, J. and Tang, M. (2006*b*), Accelerated convergence using dynamic mean shift, *in* 'Proc. European Conference on Computer Vision (ECCV)', pp. II: 257–268.

Zhang, L., Curless, B. and Seitz, S. M. (2002), Rapid shape acquisition using color structured light and multi-pass dynamic programming, *in* 'Proc. Symposium on 3D Data Processing Visualization and Transmission (3DPVT)'.

Zhang, L., Snavely, N., Curless, B. and Seitz, S. M. (2004), 'Spacetime faces: high resolution capture for modeling and animation', *ACM Transactions on Graphics* **23**(3), 548–558.

Zhang, Q. and Goldman, S. (2001), Em-dd: An improved multiple-instance learning technique, *in* 'Proc NIPS', pp. 1073–1080.

Zhang, R., Tsai, P., Cryer, J. and Shah, M. (1999), 'Shape from shading: A survey', *IEEE Trans. Pattern Analysis and Machine Intelligence* **21**(8), 690–706.

Zhang, Y. (1996*a*), 'A survey on evaluation methods for image segmentation', *Pattern Recognition* **29**(8), 1335–1346.

Zhang, Y. (1996*b*), 'A survey on evaluation methods for image segmentation', *Pattern Recognition* **29**(8), 1335–1346.

Zhang, Y. (1997), 'Evaluation and comparison of different segmentation algorithms', *Pattern Recognition Letters* **18**(10), 963–974.

Zhang, Y. and Gerbrands, J. (1994), 'Objective and quantitative segmentation evaluation and comparison', *Signal Processing* **39**(1-2), 43–54.

Zhang, Z. (1994), 'Iterative point matching for registration of free-form curves and surfaces', *International Journal of Computer Vision* **13**(2), pages 119–152.

Zhang, Z. (2000), 'A flexible new technique for camera calibration', *IEEE Trans. Pattern Analysis and Machine Intelligence* **22**(11), 1330–1334.

Zheng, J. and Murata, A. (2000), 'Acquiring a complete 3d model from specular motion under the illumination of circular-shaped light sources', *IEEE Trans. Pattern Analysis and Machine Intelligence* **22**(8), 913–920.

Zhong, Y., Jain, A. and Dubuisson Jolly, M. (2000), 'Object tracking using deformable templates', *IEEE Trans. Pattern Analysis and Machine Intelligence* **22**(5), 544–549.

Zibulevsky, M. and Pearlmutter, B. (2001), 'Blind source separation by sparse decomposition in a signal dictionary', *Neural Computation* **13**(4), 863–882.

Zitova, B. and Flusser, J. (2003), 'Image registration methods: A survey', *Image and Vision Computing* **21**(11), 977–1000.

Ziv, J. and Lempel, A. (1977), 'A universal algorithm for sequential data compression', *IEEE Transactions on Information Theory* **IT-23**, 337–343.

Zou, H. and Hastie, T. (2005), 'Regularization and variable selection via the elastic net', *Journal of the Royal Statistical Society Series B* **67**(2), 301–320.

Index

List of Algorithms